FROM APOLOGY TO UTOPIA

This book presents a critical view of international law as an argumentative practice that aims to 'depoliticise' international relations. Drawing from a wide range of materials, Koskenniemi demonstrates how this effort fails as international law becomes vulnerable to the contrasting criticisms of being either an irrelevant moralist Utopia or a manipulable façade for State interests. He examines the conflicts and paradoxes inherent in the main strands of international law – sources, sovereignty, 'custom' and 'world order' – and shows how legal discourse about such subjects can be described in terms of a small number of argumentative rules.

From Apology to Utopia was originally published in English in Finland in 1989, and though it quickly became a classic, it has been out of print for some years. Cambridge University Press is proud to reissue this seminal text, together with a substantial, freshly written Epilogue in which the author both responds to critics of the original work, and reflects on the effect and significance of his 'deconstructive' approach today.

MARTTI KOSKENNIEMI is Professor of International Law at the University of Helsinki and Global Professor of Law at New York University. He is also a member of the International Law Commission. His other publications include *The Gentle Civilizer of Nations: The Rise and Fall of International Law 1870–1960*.

FROM APOLOGY TO UTOPIA

The Structure of International Legal Argument

Reissue with a new Epilogue

MARTTI KOSKENNIEMI

CAMBRIDGE
UNIVERSITY PRESS

CAMBRIDGE UNIVERSITY PRESS
Cambridge, New York, Melbourne, Madrid, Cape Town, Singapore, São Paulo, Delhi

Cambridge University Press
The Edinburgh Building, Cambridge CB2 8RU, UK

Published in the United States of America by Cambridge University Press, New York

www.cambridge.org
Information on this title: www.cambridge.org/9780521838061

Originally published in English as *From Apology to Utopia: The Structure of International Legal Argument* by the Finnish Lawyers' Publishing Company 1989 and © Martti Koskenniemi

Re-issued with Epilogue by Cambridge University Press 2005

© Martti Koskenniemi 2005

First published by Cambridge University Press 2005
Reprinted 2007

A catalogue record for this publication is available from the British Library

ISBN 978-0-521-83806-1 hardback
ISBN 978-0-521-54696-6 paperback

Transferred to digital printing 2009

All games have morals; and the game of Snakes and Ladders captures, as no other activity can hope to do, the eternal truth that for every ladder you climb, a snake is waiting just around the corner; and for every snake, a ladder will compensate. But it's more than that; no mere carrot-and-stick affair; because implicit in the game is the unchanging twoness of things, the duality of up against down, good against evil; the solid rationality of ladders balances the occult sinuosities of the serpent; in the opposition of staircase and cobra we can see, metaphorically, all conceivable oppositions, Alpha against Omega, father against mother; here is the war of Mary and Musa, and the polarities of knees and nose . . . but I found . . . that the game lacked one crucial dimension, that of ambiguity – because, as events are about to show, it is also possible to slither down a ladder and climb to triumph on the venom of a snake.

Salman Rushdie, *Midnight's Children* (Picador, London, 1981), p. 141

For T & L & A

CONTENTS

PREFACE TO THE REISSUE

This book was first published at a moment of enthusiasm about the spread of international cooperation and the rule of law in the world. Its central thesis – namely that international law reproduces the paradoxes and ambivalences of a liberal theory of politics – may have seemed awkward at a time when liberalism was just about to gain a knock-out victory over its alternatives. Little is left today of that enthusiasm. International institutions, multilateral diplomacy and indeed international law are widely seen to have failed to cope with the most pressing international problems. Instead, "liberalism" is now often associated with the expansion of a private, market-driven "globalization" or the spread of a rhetoric of "freedom" that instrumentalizes law for the advancement of particular values or interests. Examined from the outside, international law appears sidelined by the informal structures of private governance while, from the inside, its functional differentiation ("fragmentation") has raised the question of whether any unifying centre remains in public international law that would still seem worthy of professional or ideological commitment.

And yet, the supple fabric of liberalism accounts for the persistent attraction of liberal themes. The virtues of sovereignty remain as palpable as its vices. The ideal of a consensually based legal order between equal and self-determining collectivities has retained its political appeal despite the theoretical, doctrinal and practical problems with the ideas of consent, self-determination and inter-state equality. It now seems to me that the concepts and structures of international law, elaborated in this book, are not something that political actors may choose to apply or ignore at will. They are the *condition of possibility* for the existence of something like a sphere of the "international" as one for asserting and contesting political power, making and challenging claims of right and legitimacy that may be analysed as claims about legal justice. If international law did not exist, political actors would need to invent it.

To be sure, the political effects and meaning of international law remain ambivalent. While the way international law is spoken, and thus applied, reflects the profoundly inequitable constellation of power today, it also offers avenues of resistance and experimentation. It may be used to support and to challenge hegemony. Though it often empowers the "wrong" people and justifies the "bad" decision, this is by no means necessarily the case. In any case, suggestions to "do away" with international law seem to me both naive and ideological. They are naive because every aspect of the international world is always already "legalized", that is, amenable for description and analysis by reference to legal concepts and categories. As Hans Kelsen and Hersch Lauterpacht once argued, there is no "outside-of-law". If, as this book argues, every law is a "politics", it is likewise true that every politics can become known, and effective, only as "law", including above all a law that liberates some actors to decide in accordance with their preferences. The question is never whether or not to go by law but by *which law* or *whose law*. Which is why the assumption that there might be a sphere of "pure" non-law (of politics, economics, strategy, etc.) is ideological: with every political decision-maker, there comes a legal advisor, an expert in the language whose grammar is sketched in the following pages and whose assignment it is to enable the retreat of the decision-maker from the existential *Angst* of the decision to the comforting structures of the law. The challenge for us, legal experts, is to provide the right advice.

As my students know all too well, this book has been long out of print. I am therefore deeply grateful to Professor James Crawford and to Cambridge University Press for suggesting that it be reissued with only minor corrections of typographical errors and that I should write a substantial epilogue to reflect upon critiques and developments in the intervening years. The debts I have incurred during the years are too many to mention here. The original acknowledgements cover the most important ground: David, Tiina and my family continue to be the key participants in this venture. Colleagues and students in Helsinki, New York University, Geneva, Paris and other places have taught me many new things. I thank them all. The conversation continues.

Helsinki, 6 May 2005

ACKNOWLEDGEMENTS

Writing this book was made possible by a three-year grant from the Academy of Finland during 1985–1987 and a corresponding leave of absence given by my employer, the Ministry for Foreign Affairs of Finland. Within the latter, the continuous support for my academic pursuits given by my superiors Eero Kekomäki, Director for Legal Affairs and Holger Rotkirch, Director for Administrative Affairs, has been invaluable. My colleagues at the section for public international law have without complaint carried the additional work entailed by my academic folly. During the years – a much longer time than the grant – several academic and professional friends and colleagues have discussed with me many of the issues which I raise in this book. Unscrupulously, I have disturbed diplomats, judges of the International Court of Justice, professors of international law, legal theory and philosophy with my problems. I thank them, too.

The most important intellectual support has come from professor David Kennedy, Harvard Law School. His unorthodox work – which is frequently referred to in the course of the book – contains what can only be regarded as the most significant contribution to international legal scholarship by a contemporary lawyer. I am grateful for his numerous comments on my earlier work and for his unfailing encouragement. Whatever merit this book may have is due to my having been able to acquaint myself with him and his work.

Several people have provided technical help. The personnel of the Library of Parliament in Helsinki gave invaluable professional assistance during my three-year stay with them. Tiina Astola read the successive drafts and her comments on form and substance are reflected throughout. My two research assistants, Tuula Svinhufvud and Jaana Törrönen-Nwoko checked the notes and collected the bibliography efficiently and with care. Director of Publication, Anna-Liisa Laurila was instrumental in having publication arranged with Lakimiesliiton Kustannus. Kari Takamaa from the Library of the Law Faculty in Helsinki gave me access to books which would otherwise have been difficult to get hold of. Several institutions provided financial support. These included Suomen kulttuurirahaston Varsinais-Suomen rahasto, Turun yliopistosäätiö and Oskar Öflunds stiftelse.

Helsinki, 18 September 1988

ABBREVIATIONS

AFDI	Annuaire français de droit international
AJIL	American Journal of International Law
Am.U.J.Int'l L. & Pol'y	American University Journal of International Law and Policy
Arch. de philo. du droit	Archives de philosophie du droit
Arch.VR	Archiv des Völkerrechts
ARSP	Archiv für Rechts- und Sozialphilosophie
Buffalo L.R.	Buffalo Law Review
BYIL	British Year Book of International Law
Calif. L.R.	California Law Review
Can.YIL	Canadian Yearbook of International Law
Cardozo L.R.	Cardozo Law Review
CLP	Current Legal Problems
Columbia J. of Transnat'l Law	Columbia Journal of Transnational Law
CSCE	Conference on Security and Co-operation in Europe
ECHR	European Court of Human Rights
EJIL	European Journal of International Law
FYBIL	Finnish Yearbook of International Law
GYIL	German Yearbook of International Law
Harv.ILJ	Harvard International Law Journal
Harvard L.R.	Harvard Law Review
ICJ	International Court of Justice
ICLQ	International and Comparative Law Quarterly
IIL	Institute of International Law
IJIL	Indian Journal of International Law
ILA	International Law Association
ILC	International Law Commission
ILM	International Legal Materials

ILR	International Law Reports
Int'l Org.	International Organization
Iran-US CT	Iran-United States Claims Tribunal
JFT	Tidskrift utgiven av Juridiska Föreningen i Finland
JIR	Jahrbuch für Internationales Recht
KOIG	Kansainoikeus – Ius Gentium
LJIL	Leiden Journal of International Law
LM	Lakimies
Neth.YBIL	Netherlands Yearbook of International Law
NTIR	Nordisk Tidsskrift for International Ret
NtvIR	Nederlands Tijdschrift voor Internationaal Recht
OAS	Organization of American States
Oxford JLS	Oxford Journal of Legal Studies
ÖZöRV	Österreichische Zeitschrift für öffentliches Recht und Völkerrecht
PCIJ	Permanent Court of International Justice
RBDI	Revue belge de droit international public
RCADI	Recueil des Cours de l'Academie de Droit International
RDI	Revue de droit international
Reports	Reports of Judgements, Advisory Opinions and Orders of the International Court of Justice
Res.	Resolution
Rev.Int.Stud.	Review of International Studies
RGDIP	Revue générale de droit international public
RITD	Revue internationale de théorie du droit
Procès-verbaux PCIJ	Advisory Committee of Jurists, Procès-verbaux of the Proceedings of the Committee, 16 June – 21 July with Annexes
SC	Security Council
Schw.JB	Schweizerisches Jahrbuch für internationales Recht
Stanford L.R.	Stanford Law Review
UNCLOS	United Nations Conference (Convention) on the Law of the Sea

UNGA	United Nations General Assembly
UNRIAA	United Nations Reports of International Arbitral Awards
Yale L.J.	Yale Law Journal
YILC	Yearbook of the International Law Commission
ZaöRV	Zeitschrift für ausländisches öffentliches Recht und Völkerrecht

Introduction

I

This is not only a book in international law. It is also an exercise in social theory and in political philosophy. One of the principal theses of the book is that it is neither useful nor ultimately possible to work with international law in abstraction from descriptive theories about the character of social life among States and normative views about the principles of justice which should govern international conduct. Indeed, many international lawyers have recognized that this is so. They have stressed the need to elaborate more fully on the social determinants of State conduct. And they have emphasized the law's instrumental role in fulfilling normative ideals of "world order". But they have had difficulty to integrate their descriptive and normative commitments into analytical studies about the content of the law. Typically, reflection on the "political foundations" of international law has been undertaken in the introductory or "methodological" sections of standard treatises. These have had only marginal – if any – consequence on the doctrinal elaborations of different areas of international law. Lawyers seem to have despaired over seeing their specific methodology and subject-matter vanish altogether if popular calls for sociological or political analyses are taken seriously. Ultimately, they believe, there is room for a specifically "legal" discourse between the sociological and the political – a law "properly so called", as Austin put it – and that this is the sphere in which lawyers must move if they wish to maintain their professional identity as something other than social or moral theorists.

Discussion on "theory" about international law has become a marginalized occupation. This has not always been so. During the "early" period writers such as Vitoria, Suarez or Grotius engaged in an argument about international law in which the concrete and the abstract, description and prescription were not distinguished from each other. Indeed, the fact that these aspects of discourse were so closely interwoven gives early writing its distinct flavour, its sense of being "other" than the more methodological, or "professional" styles of later scholarship. The standard of scholarship developed by post-enlightenment lawyers includes the methodological *dictum* of separating "theory" from "doctrine". Not that this would automatically undermine theory. But it directs scholars to maintain distance between what they say about world order or international justice and what they come up with as expositions of "valid" legal rules and principles.

But this distinction contains a potential for distortion. For once the analytical task of exposing valid norms is separated from reflection about the sociological or normative environment of those norms, the lawyer easily finds himself confined to work within the former if he wishes to retain his professional identity. Beyond "doctrine", there seems to exist no space for a specifically juristic discourse. The distinction theory/doctrine has come to denote just that conceptual differentiation which grounds the specificity of the legal enterprise. Once that distinction is made, the "proper sphere of jurisprudence" seems to have been exhaustively defined. Engaging in "theory" the lawyer seems to engage himself, on his *own* assumptions, with something other than law.

By itself, the distinction between "theory" and "doctrine" need not be particularly worrying. It is only when the former is experienced as non-legal, indeterminate and incompatible with our collective experience of international life that the move to modern pragmatism becomes understandable. Post-enlightenment lawyers have been concerned about "theory". They have discussed at length such issues as the "basis of obligation", the meaning of "sovereignty", the character of social life among States ("community/society"), for example. What has seemed puzzling, however, has been the pervasive character of the disagreements encountered within those topics. Theoretical discourse has repeatedly ended up in a series of opposing positions without finding a way to decide between or overcome them. "Naturalism" is constantly opposed with "positivism", "idealism" is opposed with "realism", "rules" with "processes" and so on. Whichever "theoretical" position one has attempted to establish, it has seemed both vulnerable to valid criticisms from a contrasting position and without determining consequence on how one should undertake one's doctrinal tasks. Typically, regardless of one's methodological premises, the doctrinal exposition one has come up with has seemed practically indistinguishable from the exposition of one's "theoretical" adversary. This has made theory itself seem suspect. The endless and seemingly inconsequential character of theoretical discourse has forced modern lawyers to make a virtue out of a necessity and turn towards an unreflective pragmatism, with the implicit assumption that the problems of theory are non-problems and that the sociological and normative issues of world order can be best treated by closely sticking to one's doctrinal task of analysing valid law.

The modern international lawyer has assumed that frustration about theory can be overcome by becoming doctrinal, or technical. But it is doubtful whether this strategy has worked out very well. For the lawyer is constantly faced with two disappointing experiences. In the first place, the doctrinal outcomes often seem irrelevant. In the practice of States and international organizations these are every day overridden by informal, political practices, agreements and understandings. If they are not overridden, this seems to be more a matter of compliance being politically useful than a result of the "legal" character of the outcomes or the methods whereby they were received. To explain that despite this experience, international law is in some sense "relevant" will, however, demand a "theoretical" discussion about how to disentangle law from other aspects of social life among States. And this would seem to involve precisely the sort of conceptual analysis from which will emerge the indeterminate classic controversies about the "nature" of law. In the second place, most doctrinal outcomes remain controversial. Anyone with some experience in doctrinal argument will soon develop a feeling of *déjà-vu* towards that argument. In crucial doctrinal areas, treaties, customary law, general principles, *jus cogens* and so on conflicting views are constantly presented as "correct" normative outcomes. Each general principle seems capable of being opposed with an equally valid counter-principle. Moreover, these conflicting views and principles are very familiar and attempts to overcome the conflicts they entail seem to require returning to "theory" which, however, merely reproduces the conflicts at a higher level of abstraction. There is this dilemma: In order to avoid the problems of theory, the lawyer has retreated into doctrine. But doctrine constantly reproduces problems which seem capable of resolution only if one takes a theoretical position. And this will both threaten the lawyer's identity (for "theory" did not seem capable of discussion in any specifically juristic way) and reproduce the indeterminate discussion which to avoid the retreat to doctrine was made.

Now, when one starts to deal with an international legal problem, say a dispute about the rights of States, one very soon enters certain controlling assumptions which seem to demand solution before the problem can even be approached in some determinate way and a legal

solution be suggested. Do these rights exist simply by virtue of statehood?
Do they emerge from some higher normative code? Or are they merely
legislative constructions? Conventional scholarship associates such
assumptions alternatively with naturalism, positivism, idealism, realism
and so on. But I shall suggest that such labels are not at all useful for
attaining clarity on problems which have bothered modern international lawyers. They have to be disentangled. And this will entail
going beyond what is usually considered a boundary between international law and social theory, on the one hand, and international law
and political philosophy (or moral theory) on the other. One needs to
explicate the assumptions about the present character of social life
among States and on the desirable forms of such life which make it
seem that one's doctrinal outcomes are justified even as they remain
controversial. This does not mean that lawyers should become social
theorists or political visionaries. But it does mean that without a better
grasp of social theory and political principles lawyers will continue to be
trapped in the prison-house of irrelevance. They will continue to have
one foot in crude pragmatism and the other in indeterminate theorizing
without understanding the relations between the two and why taking
a position in either will immediately seem vulnerable to apparently
justifiable criticisms.

II

Most of this book is devoted to disentanglement, that is, to an exposition
and critical discussion of the assumptions which control modern discourse about international law. This will involve establishing a position
beyond the standard dichotomy of "theory"/"doctrine". The argument
is that in each theory there is a specific conception of normative doctrine
involved and each normative doctrine necessarily assumes a theory. To
see theory and doctrine united in this way I shall contend that all
international legal discourse presents a unified structure of argument.
Moreover, I shall argue that this structure reveals a particular conception about the relationship between social description and political
prescription.

In a sense, the whole of international legal "talk" is an extended effort
to solve certain problems created by a particular way of understanding
the relationship between description and prescription, facts and norms
in international life. My argument is that the persisting disputes within
the realms of theory and doctrine result from the fact that these disputes

bear a close relationship to controversial topics encountered beyond specifically "legal" disourses. The ideas of statehood, authority, legitimacy, obligation, consent, and so on which stand at the heart of international law are also hotly debated issues of social and political theory. In each of these realms the problems turn on the justifiability of assumptions about what the character of the present social world is and how it should be changed. It would be futile to assume that the assumptions which characterize modern social and political discourse are different, or separable from those which control legal discourse on these same matters. I have chosen to group those assumptions together under the label of *the liberal theory of politics*.

I have not met an international lawyer who would have said: "Look, here is my liberal theory of politics. The international law which I teach is based on that theory". (Though quite a few legal or political theorists have said it.) And yet, I know of no modern international lawyer who would not have accepted some central tenet in it. Obviously, this is not a matter of conscious political choice. I don't think it is a matter of choice at all – apart from the sense that one can, presumably, in some sense "choose" whether or not one wishes to become an international lawyer. The case appears that if one tries to engage in the sort of debate about international legality which international lawyers undertake, then one is bound to accept an international legal liberalism. Self-determination, independence, consent and, most notably, the idea of the Rule of Law, are all liberal themes. They create distinctly liberal problems: How to guarantee that States are not coerced by law imposed "from above"? How to maintain the objectivity of law-application? How to delimit off a "private" realm of sovereignty or domestic jurisdiction while allowing international action to enforce collective preferences or human rights? How to guarantee State "freedom" while providing the conditions for international "order"? These are all distinctly liberal problems, whose connection to domestic issues concerning the legitimation of social order against individual freedom appear evident.

It is difficult to understand "liberalism" as materially controlling because it does not accept for itself the status of a grand political theory. It claims to be unpolitical and is even hostile to politics. It claims to provide simply a framework *within* which substantive political choices can be made. But, as I shall attempt to show, it controls normative argument within international law in a manner which creates ultimately unacceptable material consequences for international life. This is not evident as it does this in a negative fashion, by ultimately being unable to coherently justify or criticize instances of State practice. Its claimed objectivity and formality hide from sight its controlling character. But while it cannot, on its *own* assumptions, consistently hold to its objective-formal character, it will have to resort to material principles which it will leave unjustified.

III

The approach followed here is one of "regressive analysis". I shall attempt to investigate discourse about international law by arguing back to the existence of certain conditions without which this discourse could not possess the kind of self-evidence for professional lawyers which it has. In other words, I shall argue, as it were, "backwards" from explicit arguments to their "deep-structure", the assumptions within which the problems which modern lawyers face, either in theory or in doctrine, are constituted.

The approach could also be labelled "deconstructive". By this contentious term I intend to refer less to certain metaphysical doctrines than a method, a general outlook towards analysing intellectual operations through which the social world appears to us in the way it does.[1] I shall,

---

[1] By "deconstruction" I refer to a certain intellectual current which originated in France during the late 1960s as a criticism of attempts to apply insights originally produced within structural linguistics to philosophy, literary criticism, social and cultural theory and psychoanalysis. Though its identity lies in this criticism, it shares many insights produced by structuralism, most notable of these being their hostility to thinking of human experience as something produced by an "essence" or "nature" residing outside experience itself. Their difference lies in that while structuralism attempted to explicate the internal laws whereby experience reproduces itself, deconstruction does away with such laws, stressing the unbounded, imaginative character of experience. For useful and accessible structuralist reading, see e.g. *Saussure* (Course); *Barthes* (Elements); *idem* (Mythologies); *Lévi-Strauss* (Structural); *idem* (Savage Mind). For good introductions, see *Kurzweil* (Age of Structuralism); *Culler* (Structuralist Poetics); *Robey* (ed: Structuralism); *Piaget* (Structuralism); *Wahl* (Philosophic). To the extent that my aim is to explicate the "grammar" or routine discourse, I have profited more from these than from standard deconstructive works.

Basic, if somewhat less accessible, readings in deconstructive philosophy include *Derrida* (Of Grammatology); *idem* (Writing and Difference); *idem* (Positions). Helpful introductions are e.g. *Spivak* (Translator's Preface to Derrida: Of Grammatology); *Culler supra* pp. 241–265; *idem* (On Deconstruction) esp. p. 85 *et seq*; *Norris* (Deconstruction); *Harland* (Superstructuralism). Critical surveys are included in *Dews* (Logics); *Rose* (Nihilism); *Merquior* (Prague to Paris).

For structural-semiotic analyses in law, see *Arnaud* (Essai); *idem* XIII Arch. de philo. du droit 1968 pp. 283–301; *idem* (Vorstudien) pp. 263–343. See also *Jackson* (Semiotics); *idem* XXVII Arch. de philo. du droit 1982 pp. 147–160; *Carzo-Jackson* (Semiotics). These I have not,

for the most part, defer the more "radical" consequences which such an outlook might produce in order to remain as close as possible to the style and *problématique* which international lawyers will recognize as theirs. Such an approach may be briefly characterized by reference to its holistic, formalistic and critical aspects.

The *holistic* aspect of my approach relates to my effort to go beyond specific doctrines about the content of international law. I shall discuss the realms of theory and doctrine as a unified whole, both exemplifying a similar structure of argumentative oppositions and revealing the same constitutive assumptions. I shall view all legal argument in both theory and doctrine as a movement between a limited set of available argumentative positions and try to make explicit:

1. what these positions are,
2. which intellectual operations lead into them, and
3. what it is that one needs to assume in order to believe that such positions and operations are justified.[2]

This can be clarified by first associating the method with that used in structural linguistics.

Linguistics makes the distinction between individual, historical speech-acts and the system of differences within which the meaning of speech-acts is constituted. The level of speech-acts (or *paroles*, to use Saussurean terminology) is merely the surface appearance of language (*langue*) which is the socially constituted code in which *paroles* receive meaning. Structural linguistics explains meaning-generation by linking individual *paroles* to

---

however, found particularly helpful. See my review in 84 LM 1986 pp. 1142–1147. More useful is the critical essay by *Heller* 36 Stanford L.R. 1984 pp. 127–198.

Deconstructive readings of legal texts have been used in particular within the group of American scholars associated with the Critical Legal Studies. For a good example of such reading, see *Dalton* 94 Yale L.J. 1985 pp. 999–1114. See also *Balkin* 96 Yale L.J. 1987 pp. 743–785.

[2] The work of (the early) Michel Foucault is perhaps most evidently relevant to the undertaking of such an enterprise. See *Foucault* (Archaeology), noting that the aim of what he dubs "archaeology" is the making explicit of historical *aprioris*, consisting of "the group of rules that characterize a discursive practice", p. 127. "Archaeology" seeks to make explicit "the law of what can be said", p. 129. This will be the "archive" – the "general system of the formation and transformation of statements" within a discursive formation, p. 130 and generally pp. 135–195. See also *idem* (Power/Knowledge) in which he develops this into "genealogy" – a "form of history which can account for the constitution of knowledges, discourses, domains of objects etc. without having to make a reference to a subject…", pp. 117, 85 and generally 78–108 and further *infra* ch. 2 n. 6. A useful introduction is, for example, *Sheridan* (Foucault) pp. 46–110.

the determining *langue*. Each individual speech-act is understood as a transformation of some code in the underlying language. The aim is to make that code apparent. I shall treat international law in a similar way. For me, express international legal arguments, doctrines and "schools" are a kind of *parole* which refers back to an underlying set of assumptions, capable of being explicated as the *langue* or "deep-structure"[3] of the law.[4]

In other words, the aim is to study particular legal arguments by attempting to see what links them together or keeps them separate and, in particular, what makes arguments within theory and doctrine constantly enter into oppositions which seem unresolvable on the argument's own premises. What is relevant is not so much what arguments happen to be chosen at some particular time or in some particular dispute but what *rules* govern the production of arguments and the linking of arguments together in such a familiar and a conventionally acceptable way and why it is that no definite resolution of standard problems has been attained.

I shall make much use of conceptual oppositions in this work. This strategy relates to a certain vision about the meaning of (legal) concepts. In structural linguistics, the meaning (signified, *signifié*) of an expression (signifier, *signifiant*) is established by a network of binary oppositions between it and all the other surrounding expressions in the underlying language. Meaning is not (as we commonsensically assume it to be) present in the expression itself. (The meaning of "tree" can also be attained by the French expression "arbre".) In a sense, expressions are

---

[3] I have put "deep-structure" within inverted commas as it will become apparent that it is ultimately impossible to find such "essence" for international law into which all arguments, norms, positions, theories etc. could be reduced. See *infra* ch. 8. For me, "deep-structure" refers to a set of assumptions which, when explicated, most lawyers would probably recognize as very basic to the identity of their "legal" profession.

[4] See generally *Saussure* (Course). For useful commentary, see *Culler* (Saussure). For structuralism's linguistic basis and application in literary criticism, analysis of signs and in anthropology, see *Culler* (Structuralist Poetics) pp. 3–31; *idem* (Robey: Structuralism) pp. 20–35; *Barthes* (Elements) p. 81 *et seq*; *Lévi-Strauss* (Structural) pp. 31–51, 67–80. See also generally the introductions *supra* n. 1. In Chomskyan linguistics, the *langue/parole* distinction appears in the opposition of competence/perfomance. See *Chomsky* (Selected Readings) pp. 7–17 and comment in *Lyons* (Chomsky) p. 38. This is extended into literary analysis by *Culler* (Structuralist Poetics) pp. 9, 113–130. For useful criticism of the implicit tendency towards reductionism – pure psychologism or vulgar economism – in this scheme, see *Glucksmann* (Structuralist) pp. 68–69, 88–93; *Seung* (Structuralism) pp. 17–20. See also *Heller* 36 Stanford L.R. 1984 pp. 147–151, 156–183 and *infra* ch. 8.1.2.–8.1.3.

like holes in a net. Each is empty in itself and has identity only through the strings which separate it from the neighbouring holes. The sense of an expression is not determined "from the inside" but by the *formal* differences which separate it, make it different from other expressions in that *langue*. Meaning is *relational*. Knowing a language – understanding the meaning of words – is to be capable of operating these differentiations.[5]

A deconstructive study applies this view of meaning in the discursive field it studies. It sees each discursive topic (e.g. "basis of obligation", "sovereignty", "nature of international law") to be constituted by a conceptual opposition (e.g. "naturalism"/"positivism", "idealism"/"realism", "rules"/"processes"). The opposition is what the topic (*problématique*) is about. The participants in the discourse proceed by attempting to establish the priority of one or the other of the opposing terms. The existence of disagreement, however, shows that this has not been successful. At that point, deconstructive criticism intervenes to show that disagreement persists because it is impossible to prioritize one term over the other.[6] For although the participants believe that the terms are fundamentally opposing (that is, that their meanings are non-identical), they turn out to depend on

---

[5] On the concept of the "sign" in its dual character as signifier-signified, see *Saussure* (Course) pp. 65–67. For the "arbitrary character of the sign" (i.e. of the relation signifier-signified), see *ibid*. pp. 67–70. On the extension of these principles in semiotics, see *Barthes* (Elements) pp. 101–120. For further descriptions of the structuralist view of the production of meaning by language, see e.g. *Lyons* (Robey: Structuralism) pp. 7–9; *Culler* (Structuralist Poetics) pp. 10–11 and with reference to law, *Heller* 36 Stanford L.R. 1984 pp. 141–144; *Sumner* (Reading) pp. 104–106.

[6] *Balkin* 96 Yale L.J. 1987 has usefully summarized the strategy of "deconstructing hierarchies". It involves: 1) the identification of two terms in an oppositional hierarchy, 2) showing that each defers to the other; 3) showing that each is fundamentally dependent on the other, pp. 746–751. In *Derrida* (Of Grammatology), the argument is that the underprivileged conceptual opposite – "that dangerous supplement" – will, under analysis, always show itself as the dominating one, p. 141 *et seq*. Thus he argues famously that Western philosophy has opposed speech to writing and has prioritized the former (because it is more "immediate", closer to the ideas which we aim to communicate thereby) but that, when analysed, speech becomes possible only by assuming writing (as the neutral, self-sufficient system of disseminating meanings) to be prior to it, p. 10 *et seq, passim*. In *Foucault* (Power/Knowledge) a parallel argument attains critical force: for now the bringing into surface of the supplementary – the "local, disqualified, illegitimate knowledges" (p. 83) – will make history appear as a production of "apparatuses" or "régimes" of truth (including scientific truth) with a "circular relation with systems of power which produce and maintain (them, MK)", p. 133. The usefulness of such a strategy in law is evident. (Indeed, *ibid*. contains useful hints towards that direction, pp. 93–96, 146–165.) Within the American Critical Legal Studies movement it has been used to demonstrate law's

each other. This will make the *problématique* appear as a false dilemma; the opposing positions turn out to be the same.

I believe this to be a fruitful way of understanding international legal argument as well.[7] I shall derive the sense of particular doctrines, arguments, positions or rules exhaustively from the way in which they *differentiate* themselves from other, competing doctrines, arguments etc. This involves envisaging that legal argument proceeds by establishing a *system of conceptual differentiations* and using it in order to justify whatever doctrine, position or rule (i.e. whatever argument) one needs to justify. And I shall then attempt to show that the fact that discourse stops at points of familiar disagreement follows from its inability to uphold these differentiations consistently. We cannot make a preference between alternative arguments because they are not alternative at all; they rely on the correctness of each other.

Such a deconstructive study of legal argument (I make no claim for this to be *the* deconstructive approach; indeed, I recognize that many "deconstructivists" would not accept it[8]) is not restricted to a description, or taxonomy, of legal doctrines, arguments, positions or

---

dependence on incoherent assumptions about the character of social life and political value. For a review of these criticisms, see *Kelman* (Guide) pp. 15–113.

[7] This type of argument is used in *Kennedy* (Structures) ("deconstructing" international legal argument about the sources, procedures and the substance of the law). My discussion has been very much influenced by this work which I regard as the most significant piece of contemporary international legal scholarship. See also *idem* 23 GYIL 1980 (a "methodological" argument) pp. 353–391. I have received the theme apology/utopia from this article, p. 389. See further *idem* 27 Harv.ILJ 1986 (on the early history of international law) pp. 1–90; *idem* 2 Am.U.J.Int'l L.& Pol'y 1987 (the chapter on legal sources from the book *supra*) pp. 1–96; *idem* 8 Cardozo L.R. 1987 (tracing the assumptions of the legal argument which started, in early 20th Century, to regard institutional architecture as the way to world order) pp. 841–988. See also *infra* ch. 5 n. 9 and e.g. *Bederman* 82 AJIL 1988 pp. 29–40.

[8] They would not accept it because the attempt to find a centre, or a "deep-structure" to common discourse may be taken to involve another "metaphysics of presence", akin to that which *Derrida* (See the works *supra* n. 1) detected in structural linguistics. It seems to involve a groundless belief in the explicated structure as a transcendental signifier – a foundational concept whose meaning would not be established by further reference to some ulterior concept, or structure, but by reference to itself. Yet, this is not what I am trying to argue. As will become evident in chapter 8, though I believe that the *routine* of legal argument does have a reasonably evident centre of assumptions and a very limited range of operations to draw consequences from them, this is only a historically contingent phenomenon which does not provide such overriding force as to be capable to squeeze all argument within itself. The weakness of the argumentative structure constantly compels lawyers to move beyond its conventional centre. *Gordon* 36 Stanford L.R. 1984 points out, usefully: "What the structure determines, is not any particular set of

rules or what we think of as the body of legal knowledge. It attempts to reach further, to a description of the controlling legal *langue*, the *conditions of what can acceptably be said within it*, or what it is possible to think or believe in it.[9] It does not attempt to make new interpretations about the law but to explain how the making of interpretations in the first place is possible.[10] In other words, it seeks to make explicit the legal "grammar" which controls the production of particular arguments within discourse and which counts for the lawyer's specific legal "competence".[11]

Such an approach does not aim to be a simply intellectual exercise. For it stresses the legal argument's *social* character, the way in which it constrains those who work within it. For it sees the legal *langue*, the system of conceptual differentiations as *prior* to any individual normative statements. At the *parole* level, human agents appear as conscious builders of the world. At the *langue* level they work within the possibilities offered by a historically given code which the actors are routinely unable to transgress.

Analogously, I shall argue that express arguments and doctrines about international law are only a contingent surface of a socially shared manner of envisaging international relations. A deconstruction of international legal argument will then inevitably relate that argument to that historically conditioned "code" – or "conceptual scheme". As it makes explicit that hidden code bears a *critical potential*.[12] For it is clear that this cannot be a code which is somehow "inherent" in the contexts in which we use it. It has neither descended from heaven to determine what we can see in international life, nor emerged as an aprioristic construction of an autonomous individual. Men, as Max Horkheimer points out, are the product of history and "the way they see and hear is inseparable from the social life-process".[13]

social consequences but the categories of thought and discourse wherein political conflict will be carried out", p. 118.

[9] See further *Foucault* (Archaeology). Compare *Lévi-Strauss* (Structural) pp. 33–36 *et seq*, 55–65 and *passim*.

[10] Here lies its similarity to structural analyses in literary theory. See, in particular, *Culler* (Structuralist Poetics) pp. 25–28, 113–130; *idem* (Pursuit of Signs) pp. 6–17 and *passim*; *idem* (Robey: Structuralism) p. 33.

[11] Yet, by "competence" I do not mean a Chomskyan biologico-genetic structure (the "essence" of law) but a historically relative projection of what it is to be a lawyer. This is discussed further in the Epilogue, pp. 566–573 *infra*.

[12] Whether this type of deconstructive outlook may consistently claim to possess critical potential will be discussed *infra* ch. 8.2–8.3.

[13] *Horkheimer* (Critical) p. 200.

Now, whether we associate the way in which we speak about international law with a "form of life" in the manner of recent analytic philosophy or with the "prejudice" or unreflective pre-understanding of the speaking subject, the point is that the concepts and categories with which we orient ourselves in the world are internalized in a process of *socialization*. We don't choose to use the concepts of international law when we enter international legal discourse. Rather, we must take a pre-existing language, a pre-existing system of interpreting the world and move within it if we wish to be heard and understood. In this sense, language precedes thought: We do not say that peoples have a right to self-determination because we think so. Rather, we come to think so because that is what we say.[14]

In regard to doctrine, socialization functions through the inherited conceptual framework. This mediates not only a vocabulary, but a pre-theoretical world-view, including a *problématique* and an interest of knowledge,[15] and pushes the scholar within the confines of what Thomas Kuhn has instructed us to call "normal science".[16] But even a legislator's will is conceptually constrained: when States adopt a norm they must use the available legal-linguistic conventions which thus become constitutive of what the States can subjectively "intend". Claude Lévi-Strauss makes the point about language in general:

> ... language continues to mold discourse beyond the consciousness of the individual, imposing on his thought conceptual schemes which are taken as objective categories.[17]

The same is true about the language of international law. It conveys to us a certain interpretation of the social reality to which it is addressed, under the veil of objectivity, or naturalness. Deconstruction seeks to bring out the conventional character of this interpretation and its dependence on certain contestable assumptions. It becomes critical as it shows that legal argument cannot produce the kinds of objective resolutions it claims to produce – indeed, the production of which it assumes for its principal justification. Thus it opens up a possibility for alternative descriptive – and simultaneously normative – characterizations of the world in which States live.

---

[14] See *infra* ch. 8.1.3.

[15] The relationship between Critical Theory's notion of "interest of knowledge" and the structuralist notion of *problématique* is usefully discussed by *Glucksmann* (Structuralist) pp. 2–8.

[16] *Kuhn* (Structure). See also *infra* ch. 8 n. 5.   [17] *Lévi-Strauss* (Structural) p. 217.

By providing an "insider's view" to legal discourse, such an approach might produce a therapeutic effect on lawyers frustrated with their inability to cope with the indeterminacy of theory and the irrelevance of doctrine. It will indicate that legal discourse cannot permanently solve the lawyer's problems for him. The line drawn in the midst of the universe of normative statements which has separated "subjective" politics from "objective" law will appear without foundation. By thus "politicizing" law (but equally "legalizing" politics) an analysis of its structure might point a way towards an alternative way of understanding the relationship between law and its neighbouring discourses, social description and political prescription.

To those who think that such an approach has little to do with the sort of style lawyers are supposed to argue their views it may be replied that this type of deconstruction seeks only to do what most traditional science has always attempted: to provide a parsimonious theory which can be used to explain a wide range of apparently different types of phenomena under explicated regularities. By explicating the laws (the "grammar") which govern the system's self-regulation – production of arguments – a grip can be had on law which is at least competitive in scientific rigour (if that is a positive value) with the prevalent routine of interpretative intuitionism.

Moreover, this is also a "pure law" approach in that it relies on the self-regulating nature of legal argument. Any study of separate social, historical or psychological "factors" is excluded from it. Rather, it understands discourse to be the means towards reaching society, history and psychology.

I shall not use the very technical conceptual apparatus of structuralism, semiotics or deconstructive philosophy. I have here situated my approach in the broad framework of those fields only to highlight its holistic, formalistic and critical character. I am aware of the objections directed at the "positivistic" character of such an approach, its implicit claim to "found" yet another method of attaining objective knowledge and its difficulty to explain why its own perspective could be independent from or preferable to the conceptual systems it studies. But I think that such deconstruction can still be usefully carried out, in particular for the following three reasons:

1. It incorporates a perspective which is external to the opposition between theory and doctrine and thus escapes the difficulties involved in adopting either one;
2. Its perspective is also external to the all-pervading opposition between social description and political prescription. By treating all

arguments, whether about social "facts" or political "ideas" in a
formal way, as merely parts of an argumentative structure, it will
remain untouched by the way discourse itself constantly opposes
"facts" to "ideas";

3. By linking express legal arguments to the underlying code of the
   liberal theory of politics, it will explain familiar theoretical and
   doctrinal disputes as simply consequences of a contingent but very
   popular way of thinking about international life and thus point
   beyond the problems created by that way of thinking. It explains
   what happens in legal argument when it starts to seem weak and
   indeterminate and opens up a possibility to develop alternative ways
   of arguing about international lawfulness which lead beyond the dead
   ends which standard argument constantly faces. Most importantly, it
   makes it possible for the lawyer to see his particular social identity
   and practical tasks in a new light.

IV

Public international law contains a wide range of more or less loosely
connected themes. Any attempt to look at it as a whole will necessarily
entail privileging some of those themes and downplaying the importance of others. For example, it might be possible to look at the whole of
the law as an annex to a theory about the just war. Or it might be possible
to describe the law from the perspective of the theory of sovereignty. Or
the law might be thought of as only so many ways to facilitate inter-
individual cooperation on a global scale. I have chosen to present the law
as most lawyers would present it, following closely the divisions of
modern textbooks. I shall look at it as the classical law of peace, concerned with the relations of sovereign States *vis-à-vis* each other.

To some extent, this oversimplifies what international law is about. It
also contains a wide repository of themes relating to war, human rights
and international organization. An alternative account of the law might
well see these – or perhaps some other – areas of the law as crucial and
what I termed the classical law of peace only as a way to deal with them.
Nevertheless, I feel justified in delimiting those three themes outside this
book for two reasons. First, most conventional understandings clearly
treat them as supplementary to the main body, or derivative from it
and I am interested in this conventional, mainstream understanding
of the law. Second, there is a tension between those three themes and
the rest of the law. Although the modern textbook tradition succeeds in

underprivileging the former, the development of any of them individually will conflict with crucial assumptions in the classical law of peace. An in-depth treatment of the law of war or of human rights will immediately lead into a discussion of the just war or fundamental rights. These are precisely the sort of discussions which the body of the law tries to refer away from itself. Though I am convinced of the importance of justice at war and individual rights, I shall set these issues aside as they so obviously conflict with the mainstream understanding of what is significant in international law.

I have excluded the theme of international integration for partly similar reasons. Though it is a significant theme, it, too, is usually treated as a "new development", existing somewhat uncomfortably with the classical law of inter-sovereign relations. Whatever the challenges it poses to the classical law, most lawyers have clearly not seen it as such an anomaly in their system as to occasion the need for a "paradigm-change". I shall not pursue the question whether they have succeeded in integrating it in the body of inter-sovereign law. I shall assume that they have and shall not discuss the possible tension between the two.

V

A word needs to be said about my use of footnotes. They are not intended to act as authoritative support. The internal argument of the book hopes to stand by itself, not by the authority of somebody mentioned in a footnote. There are two types of footnotes. A first set of footnotes merely guides the reader to a place where some conventional argument, or a tension within a conventional argument is clearly visible. These footnotes serve as illustrations. A second set of footnotes refers the reader to lawyers, philosophers, social and political theorists who have made or discussed an argument such as that in the text and whose discussion has influenced my internal argument or contains an interesting development thereof which I have been unable to pursue here. I am, of course, responsible for the way I have understood them (though I may not always have understood in the way they would have preferred). But I claim no responsibility for whatever else they might have said or left unsaid.

1

Objectivity in international law: conventional dilemmas

Things, says Hegel, exist in and through the boundaries which delimit them from other things. This applies also to such an abstract thing as international law. Any determination of what might count as "international law" involves a delimitation of that "thing" towards neighbouring intellectual territories, in particular theories about the character of international life (descriptions of political behaviour) and the normative principles of international politics. In this first chapter I shall discuss the attempt to give identity to international law as a specific realm of thought and action through the assumption that it can be delimited from the fields of descriptive and normative politics in some determinate way. Two intellectual operations go to establish these boundaries. International law is kept distinct from descriptions of the international political order by assuming that it tells people what to do and does not just describe what they have been doing. It is delimited against principles of international politics by assuming it to be less dependent on subjective beliefs about what the order among States should be like. These two delimitations establish what lawyers commonly assume to be the "objectivity" of international law. Inasmuch as international law has an identity, it must differ from descriptive and normative politics in the two senses outlined.

My argument is that these intellectual operations do not leave room for any specifically legal discourse. The two distinctions have not been – and, as I shall argue, cannot be – simultaneously maintained. Lawyers' law is constantly lapsing either into what seems like factual description or political prescription. What emerges is a way of speaking about international life in which each argument seems constantly vulnerable to justifiable counter-arguments produced by the two constitutive delimitations themselves. The argument which seeks to give identity to international law by referring to its greater objectivity (in the two senses outlined) has been a failure. No identifiable intellectual realm has emerged between historiography and politics.

1.1 The identity of international law: the requirements of normativity and concreteness

To prevent international law from losing its independence *vis-à-vis* international politics the legal mind fights a battle on two fronts. On the one hand, it attempts to ensure the *normativity* of the law by creating distance between it and State behaviour, will and interest. On the other hand, it attempts to ensure the law's *concreteness* by distancing it from a natural morality.

A law which would lack distance from State behaviour, will or interest would amount to a non-normative apology, a mere sociological description. A law which would base itself on principles which are unrelated to State behaviour, will or interest would seem utopian, incapable of demonstrating its own content in any reliable way. To show that an international law exists, with some degree of reality, the modern lawyer needs to show that the law is simultaneously normative and concrete – that it binds a State regardless of that State's behaviour, will or interest but that its content can nevertheless be verified by reference to actual State behaviour, will or interest.

It is not difficult to see that law is continuously in danger of lapsing into an apology for politics. Critics of any prevailing law regularly accuse it of having done just this. This is natural because just like politics, law is understood to exist for the pursuit of social goals and there is constant disagreement about the correct goals. The same is true of international law. Like international politics, it is assumed to emerge from the subjective, politically motivated State wills or interests. Law-creation is a matter of subjective, political choice.[1] But while law emerges from politics and

---

[1] The modern international lawyer moves within what I shall be calling a "social conception of law". Under it, law is seen as *determined* by its social environment, conceptualized alternatively in terms of State interests, political will or behaviour. But despite standard scholarship's constant reiteration of this perspective, few lawyers have taken the trouble to look onto the assumed process of determination – presumably because there exists no specifically juristic way of doing this. Nevertheless, some lawyers have outlined a sociology for international law or discussed its "political foundations" in some depth. Standard works include *Huber* (Grundlagen) (a balanced, mostly historical treatment of the emergence of the present coordination law and the tendencies moving it to a more *gesellschaftlich* organization); *Kaplan-Katzenbach* (Foundations) (a basic functionalistic analysis); *Stone* 89 RCADI 1956/I (a rather sceptical account of the possibilities of and, in particular, difficulties confronting sociological analyses in international law) pp. 65–175; *Gould-Barkun* (Social Sciences) (a "methodological" book, urging the lawyer to use the idiolect of social sciences); *Henkin* (How) (tracing the interconnections between international standards and national policy); *de Lacharrière* (Politique) (discussing the use of international legal argument to support foreign policy positions). Though many textbooks contain a brief discussion of the "sociological perspective in international law"

diplomacy, it is assumed to remain separable from them. It is assumed to be binding regardless of the interests or opinions of the State against which it is invoked. If such separation were not maintained, then we could only concede the critic's point and admit the law's political nature.

On the other hand, law cannot be completely independent from behaviour, will or interest. If it were, we would be at a loss about where to find or how to justify it. If law had no relation to power and political fact, it would be a form of natural morality, a closed normative code which would pre-exist the opinions or interests of individual States. An early scholarship did assume the existence of such a code. For it, the law existed autonomously as divine will or natural purpose and effectively determined what States should will or have a legitimate interest in. But modern scholarship lacks the faith needed to sustain such a code. For it, law is an artificial creation, based on the concrete behaviour, will and interest of States. Attempts to argue on the basis of a natural code are seen as camouflaged attempts to impose the speaker's subjective, political opinions on others.

This dual aspect of the law – its normative/concrete character – may be illustrated by reference to a standard argument such as that contained in Oscar Schachter's 1982 Hague Academy lectures. On the one hand, law needs to be argued in a concrete way. It is not a theory about a pre-existing, natural morality. It is based on politics and:

> ... involves the pursuit of social ends through the exercise of legitimate power ... (I)n this sense it is an aspect of the broader political process.[2]

(*Schwarzenberger-Brown* (Manual) pp. 7–12); the "origin and foundations of the international community" (*Cassese* (Divided) p. 9 *et seq*; *Mosler* (International Society) pp. 1–28; the law's "fundamental structures" (*Reuter* (Droit international public) pp. 13–33); the "factors" contributing to the emergence of international law (*Rousseau* (Droit international public I) pp. 16–24); or the relations of "law and politics" (*Levi* (Contemporary) pp. 16–17) and so on, these discussions do not usually proceed beyond giving metaphorical expression to the principle of social determination. Their point, presumably, is to give writing a more "realistic" tone than that in the other fashionable style which proceeds from a "definition of international law" or a discussion of its legal sources. Some lawyers, having wished to dissociate themselves from prevailing "formalism", have, however, expanded the scope of their sociological descriptions. A good example is *Falk* (Status) pp. 3 *et seq*, 60–83. At this end of the spectrum, the "policy approach" lawyers have self-consciously integrated sociological discussions *within* the normative analyses in a highly structured method and idiosyncratic language. For basic works, see *McDougal-Feliciano* (Minimum World Public Order); *McDougal-Lasswell-Chen* (Human Rights); *McDougal-Lasswell-Miller* (Interpretation). For discussion, see *infra*, ch. 3.3.3.

[2] *Schachter* 178 RCADI 82/V p. 24. He continues: the law is "... a product of political and social forces ... it is dependent on behavior and ... it is an instrument to meet changing needs and values," p. 26.

But though international law is an instrument of political purposes, this cannot exhaust its meaning: "we cannot reduce it into politics without eliminating it as law". It is essential that its rules are normative:

> ... that is, the rules must be accepted as a means of independent control that effectively limits the conduct of the entities subject to law.[3]

Or:

> To put the matter simply, we could not consider that a State ... is free to disregard the law because it conflicts with the policies of that State.[4]

The concreteness of international law manifests itself in its responsiveness to changing State behaviour, will and interests. This is sometimes called the political, instrumental or "process" aspect of the law.[5] In standard textbooks it is often discussed under the topic of the "functions" of international law.[6] The requirement of normativity follows from it. Law is unable to fulfil any functions unless it has a degree of autonomy from particular State behaviour,

---

[3] *Ibid.* p. 25.   [4] *Ibid.* p. 26.

[5] This "process" aspect has been emphasized by lawyers dissatisfied with the "formalism" implicit in a concentration on "rules". See *infra* ch. 3.3.3.

[6] The "functions" of international law can alternatively be envisaged in terms of some communitarian morality (a conception of common interests, for example) or in terms of State interests and purposes. The point of much discussion on functions is to explain these as compatible so as to avoid becoming vulnerable to the objections about utopianism and apologism. This is regularly achieved by envisaging the functions in a *formal* manner. Thus, *Gould-Barkun* (Social Sciences) identify the functions of communication, integration, adaptation and value-preservation while avoiding discussion on what kinds of values it is that should be "communicated", "integrated" etc. pp. 136–159. *Coplin* (Functions) does the same by postulating the primary function of "preservation of order" while "order" is conceptualized simply as an aggregate of States' preferred values, pp. 4–7, *passim*. *Friedmann* (Changing) stresses the twin functions of providing for stability and change while the content (what should be changed and what preserved) seems to be left beyond the functions of law, into political (or naturalist) determination, pp. 58–59 and *passim, de Lacharrière* (Politique) identifies the formal functions of determination and justification of State conduct, communication of intentions and international organization, pp. 204–213. See further *Bleckmann* (Grundprobleme) pp. 163–165; *Menzel-Ipsen* (Völkerrecht) (identifying, alongside the formal function of peace-preservation, the material function of enhancement of the "fundamentals of human existence" – without, however, discussing what these might be) pp. 18–21. *Schwarzenberger-Brown* (Manual) stress the functions of regulating reciprocal interests and coordinating common efforts, pp. 9–10. *Nardin* (Law, Morality) makes the point explicit. He criticizes attempts to identify material purposes for the law. For him, a relevant international law can only have the procedural function of organizing horizontal inter-State cooperation, pp. 3–5 and *passim*. By keeping law formal, it seems possible to avoid associating it with some given, natural values or the (conflicting) values held by individual States.

will and interests.[7] It must be normative in the sense of being capable of impartial ascertainment and application:

> ... a question as to the applicability of a rule ... should be capable of determination by an impartial judge (even if hypothetical) on the basis of legal standards that are valid and applicable independently of the purposes of the judge, of the parties or any other particular State.[8]

This duality is hardly a novelty.[9] It is expressed in the standard dichotomy of legislation/adjudication as well as those of process/rule, "progressive development"/"codification", for example. The law is both an instrument of policy and a momentary system of binding standards.[10] As Michel Virally points out, the former encapsulates the legislator's point of view while the latter manifests that of the user's or the law-applier's. Though the law emerges from politics, it also constitutes "un système normatif complet, autonome et autoregulé".[11]

Scholarship, too, needs to integrate a concrete and a normative aspect in itself. If the former were lacking, then it would need to assume the existence of a natural morality which is independent from State behaviour, will or interest. By lacking connection with practice, such scholarship would seem unable to demonstrate its norms in a tangible fashion. It would seem *utopian*. If the latter were lacking, then scholarship would lack critical distance from State behaviour, will or interest. It would remain unable to oppose to States standards which they refuse to accept at the moment of application and seem *apologist*. Therefore, modern

---

[7] "If rules were totally responsive to behaviour, they would serve no regulative function". *Gould-Barkun* (Social Sciences) p. 183; *Hoffmann* (Deutsch-Hoffmann: Relevance) p. 35. The law's resistance to change is also the basis of its social function. See further *Kegley* (Onuf: Lawmaking) pp. 206–207.

[8] *Schachter* 178 RCADI 1982/V p. 58. Or, as *Ehrlich* 105 RCADI 1962/1, points out in a classic study: "International law today is positive law, and by that is meant that its rules can be determined by means of objective criteria." p. 177. See also *Reuter* (Droit international public) pp. 35–36. For standard discussion on objectivity in international law and the threat of national bias to it, see *von Münch* 9 Arch.VR 1961–2 pp. 1 *et seq* 12–24. *Schwarzenberger* (Cheng: International Law) puts the point adroitly: "If international law is to be more than positive morality (Austin), ideology or propaganda, it must be capable of verification, or, more accurately, falsification (Popper)." p. 55.

[9] See e.g. *Huber* (Grundlagen) pp. 9–14. *Kelsen* (Principles), already, recognizes this in deriving the law's validity from a dynamic and a static principle – the former relating to the processes whereby law establishes competences, the latter relating to the ascertainment of existing law's content, pp. 557–559. See further *Weil* 77 AJIL 1983 p. 413.

[10] See e.g. *Henkin* (How) pp. 88–98.

[11] *Virally* 183 RCADI 1983/V pp. 26–27 and generally, pp. 25–35.

lawyers argue that legal study must focus on law as an interplay of (normative) rules and (concrete) processes.[12]

Richard Falk's argument summarizes this task. Having first identified the "extreme" positions of Kelsen and McDougal, Falk proceeds to criticize the former precisely of his inability to give regard to the political context of law. Kelsen's scholarship is portrayed as utopian. On the other hand, McDougal's sociological approach ends up in "encouraging excercises of national self-judgement" and thus seems apologist. The task of an adequate scholarship is to establish:

> ... an intermediate position, one that maintains the distinctiveness of the legal order while managing to be responsive to the extralegal setting of politics, history and morality.[13]

In other words, only by integrating both normativity and concreteness scholarship avoids the twin dangers of apologism and utopianism.

At a deeper level, this structure of argument expresses the *liberal theory of politics*. This is a theory which identifies itself on two assumptions. *First*, it assumes that legal standards emerge from the legal subjects themselves. There is no natural normative order. Such order is artificial and justifiable only if it can be linked to the concrete wills and interests of individuals. *Second*, it assumes that once created, social order will become binding on these same individuals. They cannot invoke their subjective opinions to escape its constraining force. If they could, then

---

[12] *Fawcett* (Law and Power) pp. 38–47.

[13] *Falk* (Falk-Black: Future) pp. 34–35. See also *idem* (Status) pp. 41–49; *idem* (Deutsch-Hoffmann: Relevance) pp. 178–189. The same reconciliatory mood persists in all the essays of that collection. See especially *Hoffmann* (*ibid.*) p. 65; *Fried* (*ibid.*) p. 124 *et seq.* Falk's reconciliatory rhetorics has become exceedingly popular among modern lawyers. See e.g. *Detter-Delupis* (Concept) (law as "rule" and "process") pp. 16–17; *Sheikh* (Behavior) pp. 5–6. *Henkin* (How) makes the plea for the political scientist – concerned with subjective behaviour – and the lawyer – concerned with the ascertainment of the law – to work "together", pp. 1–7. To the same effect, see *De Visscher* 86 RCADI 1954/II pp. 550–552; *Sur* (L'interprétation) (an extended discussion of the relations of law and politics and an attempt to reach a "synthesis" between normativist and realist positivism) pp. 15–61; *Menzel-Ipsen* (Völkerrecht) pp. 14–17; *Cassese* (Divided) thinks that what is needed is to combine "rigorous method of the positivist and 'normativist' schools" with an enquiry into the historical dimension of international law and the political and ideological motivations behind it in an "interdisciplinary" way, p. 2. The need to reconcile the two approaches, history and politics on the one hand and law on the other, has been a persistent modern theme. See also *Brierly* (Basis of Obligation) pp. 129–130, 132.

the point and purpose of their initial, order-creating will and interest would be frustrated.

Setting up a system of social control is a political task. It entails the establishment of organs authorized with law-applying and law-enforcement powers. This creates the danger that these powers are used in order to further the subjective interests of the law-appliers or law-enforcers in a way not warranted by the original authorization. To curb this threat, legal rules must be neutral and uniformly applicable and their content must be capable of verification. Thus, the two assumptions of the liberal theory of politics are indissociable from each other.[14] Concreteness at the level of rule-creation presumes normativity at the level of rule-ascertainment.

The way in which the legal mind distinguishes between international law, politics and natural morality assumes the correctness of the two assumptions behind the liberal theory of politics. Since Vattel, lawyers argue about "States-as-individuals" which pre-exist the law among them and which are bound by the law which they themselves have created. Thus, the "domestic analogy" which, while often expressly adopted, is necessarily entailed by the modern system of international law.[15]

True, there is an initial difficulty in applying this analogy. States have not established general law-applying or law-enforcement organs. To a large degree, they have reserved the function of law-ascertainment to themselves. This creates a danger to the distinction, so carefully made

[14] For this standard argument leading into making the distinction between law-making and law-applying, see *Rousseau* (Social Contract) Bk II, ch. 6; Bk III, ch. 17 (pp. 80–83, 145–146). See also *Hayek* (Road to Serfdom) pp. 54–65. An explicit, full-scale liberal argument is applied to international law by *Nardin* (Law, Morality). He argues that international law cannot be a system of furthering material purposes as there is too much variety on what such purposes might be – in other words, as they are "subjective". This leads him into thinking of the law's objectivity in terms of its *procedural* nature. Being not concerned with "purposes" it works so as to establish coordinating procedures through which different political purposes can be pursued, pp. 3–24, 187 *et seq* 308–324. In other words, the law works so as to guarantee the maximal freedom for States to pursue their (subjective) politics while it intervenes only so as to prevent conflict. These arguments can also be usefully found in the programmatic article by *Weil* 77 AJIL 1983 pp. 413 *et seq*, 420–421 (emphasizing the indissociability of voluntarism and the idea of neutrality and the need to distinguish the *lex ferenda* and *lex lata* aspects of law from each other).

[15] The analysis is explicit in *Rousseau* (Social Contract) Bk I, ch. 7 (p. 63). The connection between the domestic analogy and liberal-capitalist ideas about statehood (associating territory with property) is usefully discussed by *Carty* (Decay) pp. 8–11, 43–60 *et seq.* See further, *infra* ch. 2.1.2.

and so important to law's identity, between legislation and administration (adjudication). Therefore, doctrines about the *dédoublement fonctionnel* explain that States can and do distinguish between their subjective, political opinions and the law.[16] They argue that there is no *necessary* reason why the "is" and the "ought" could not be held separate and that the occasions where States have confused the two are either "hard cases" (that is, situations where reasonable men disagree) or *mala fide* applications of the law. Certainly States themselves continue to argue about international law in a way which assumes that they do not feel that they are putting forward "merely" political opinions.[17]

Whether States do keep the two separate is a question of fact. While it may affect how we think the legal character of international law is manifested in practice, it bears no consequence to the more fundamental issue of whether it is possible in principle to maintain the liberal doctrine of politics and the identity of international law that goes with it.

My focus in this study will be on the assumption that there is a distinct discourse called "international law" which is situated somewhere between politics and natural morality (justice) without being either. I shall concentrate, in particular, on the view that these distinctions can be maintained through seeing international law as objective in comparison to the subjectivity involved in politics and theories of justice. My argument will be that the separation of the creation and ascertainment of legal rules cannot be consistently maintained. Their fusion into each other threatens the law's concreteness and its normativity and makes ultimately doubtful whether any meaningful distinction between international law, politics and morality can be made.

1.2   Proving the objectivity of international law

Two criticisms have been advanced to deny the "legal" character of international law. One group of critics has accused international law of being too political in the sense of being too dependent on State policy.

---

[16] See *Scelle* (Festschrift Wehberg) pp. 324 *et seq*; *idem* 46 RCADI 1933/IV p. 358; *Strupp* 47 RCADI 1934/1 (basing his theory of international obligation on the important distinction between what States *willed* to be law and what they now *believe* to be so) p. 302. In a system which distinguishes subjectivity from objectivity and which assumes that law-creation is a matter of will, while law-ascertainment is not, such an argument – even if the *pactum tacitum* theory might seem old-fashioned – is a necessary premise.

[17] See also *Nardin's* (Law, Morality) argument to the effect that the "decentralization" of international law has *not* led into an abandonment of objectivism, p. 177 *et seq*.

Another group has argued that the law is too political because founded on speculative utopias. Both view international law as too ineffective to be taken seriously in the construction of world order. The standard point about the non-existence of specific legislative machineries, compulsory adjudication and enforcement incorporates both criticisms. From one perspective, this criticism highlights the infinite flexibility of international law (apologism), from another perspective, such criticism attacks the "moralistic" nature of the law (utopianism).

But mainstream scholarship remains unmoved by such criticisms. It points out that even if much of international law is in one sense or other "political", its core, namely the practice of dispute-settlement has independence from political ideologies and positions. It is *objective* in a way that politics is not. This means, it is explained, that the law is capable of providing justifiable solutions to normative problems (1.2.1). In order to be justifiable, such solutions must come about in a legally determined way, independently of political considerations (1.2.2). Nevertheless, it occurs frequently that "hard cases" appear in which the problem-solver needs to use his discretion. The ensuing uncertainty poses a *prima facie* threat to the objectivity of problem-solution. It is dealt with by the doctrine of "relative indeterminacy" (1.2.3). This doctrine, however, is ultimately unable to explain why indeterminacy would be restricted only to marginal cases and what basis there is to distinguish discretion from evaluation, that is, political choice.

This chapter will have to cover some ground which is very familiar to legal theorists but which has not been much discussed by international lawyers. The point is to provide a full description of the possibilities of legal argument within the liberal doctrine of politics. My purpose is to demonstrate that the practical problems which international lawyers face cannot be solved by standard legal theory because that theory incorporates the same problems in itself. This will serve as an introduction to my main argument, according to which the problems of practice and theory share a similar structure and are related to the contradictory character of more fundamental aspects of legal consciousness (1.3).

1.2.1 A preliminary point: international law as problem-solution

International law exists, it is assumed, to fulfil a social function. The argument is not an end in itself. We engage in it because we think that it helps us to solve problems, that it tells us what to do. The point of law is that it keeps in check our own subjectivities while providing justification for solving social problems. The demands for concreteness and normativity are embedded in such a description of the law's function. Concreteness relates to the verifiability of law, normativity to our duty to exclude everything that is not contained in verified rules from the justification we give for our solution. Together they count for the law's *objectivity*.

Now, legal objectivity is surely a discredited notion. It seems associated with outdated views about the automatic character of law-application and of the logic of legal deduction. In particular, traditional emphasis on objectivity has tended to overlook the fact that norms may be both hard to find and difficult to apply and that the problem-solvers have to use controversial principles and thumb-rules in order to decide cases.[18] But the realist criticisms which have stressed the political or "façade legitimation" character of legal problem-solution have, it is retorted, both failed to explain the "internal aspect" of legal rules and confused the contexts of discovery and justification of solutions. The theory of the "internal aspect" points out that rule-appliers experience rules as binding and that this experience cannot be counted for in other ways than by assuming that they do not coalesce with their political preferences.[19] The theory of justification stresses that how problem-solvers in fact (as a psychological process) arrive at their solutions is less important than whether they are able to justify those solutions by reference to legal rules.[20]

Objectivity, then, is related to the *justification* of solutions. The law's identity *vis-à-vis* politics concerns its capability to provide such justifications. Though justification has nothing automatic about it, it is assumed still to be rational in a way that will salvage the minimal conditions of objectivity. From this perspective, law appears as an autonomous repository of normative standards which, when invoked, will make the decision seem justified in law, whether or not we agree on its political appropriateness.[21]

We use law in order to justify a decison in situations which are envisaged as normative problems. Such problems seem to be of two kinds: problems of content and problems of application. The former relate to the

---

[18] For one analysis of what would be required for a legal system to be "objective" in such "automatic" way, see *Singer* 94 Yale L. J. 1984 pp. 14–19. For one attempt at downgrading the expectation of objectivity while preserving the view that law is at least minimally controlling, see *Schroeder* Nomos XXVIII pp. 112–118.

[19] For this criticism, see *Hart* (Concept) p. 55 *et seq*, 135, 143.

[20] See e.g. *Wasserström* (Judicial Decision) pp. 25–31; *MacCormick* (Reasoning) pp. 16–18 and *passim*; *Aarnio* (Point of View) pp. 97–98, 151–155 *et seq*. For problems in the discovery/justification scheme, see *Golding* Nomos XXVIII pp. 124–140.

[21] For as *Kelsen* 84 RCADI 1953/III notes, law can be autonomous only inasmuch as it regulates its own creation, p. 119. This is simply another way of putting the need for a

establishment of the meaning of norms *in abstracto*. If such norms are conventional, then the starting-point is an individual norm-formulation. If they are customary, then the starting-point is a factual behaviour. In both cases the end-result is a *meaning*. "What is the scope and content of the freedom of the High Seas?" is a problem of content. Its solution seems to depend partly on an interpretation of textual, partly of behavioural data. "All States are entitled to participate in uses of the High Seas" is a possible solution to a problem of content. Problems of application are concerned with the legal qualification of facts, i.e. the establishment of the meaning of norms *in concreto*. Starting-point in them is a factual state of affairs (e.g. exploitation of seabed minerals by the vessels of State A) and the end-result its subsumption under a rule (e.g. a rule such as "the principle of 'common heritage' prevents unilateral mining of seabed minerals"). There are no "pure" problems of content or of application. Each problem-solving situation involves a determination of the meaning of a norm.[22] In other words, the law's objectivity, in the sense outlined above, is dependent on the justifiability of the interpretations we make – of the meanings we produce.

However, some lawyers would disagree with adopting such a perspective. They argue that dispute-solution is only one marginal function of international law and that to concentrate on it is to assume a too "formalistic" or "judicial" approach. They point out that international law also works in more informal ways as a means for communicating shared values, creating expectations about future behaviour and structuring decision-contexts and that these are its main functions.[23]

But all such "functions" are parasitic upon the capacity of the law to provide determinate outcomes to normative problems. If the law lacked

---

legal doctrine of "sources". On the importance of the principle that "sources" give a full account of what standards count as "law", see *Thirlway* (Customary Law) pp. 37–39. The social conception of law, however, broadens sources doctrine so as to make it virtually meaningless. Under it, it suffices that there are some social rules of recognition which specify "the feature or features possession of which by a suggested rule is taken as conclusive indication that there is a (legal, MK) rule", *Hart* (Concept) p. 92.

[22] See *Koskenniemi*, XVIII Oikeustiede-Jurisprudentia 1985 p. 129 and notes therein. The same point is made by *De Visscher* (Problèmes) observing the unity of law and law-interpretation, pp. 27–31. See also *Jackson* (Semiotics) making the distinction between "questions of meaning" and "questions of interpretation", corresponding broadly to the distinction in the text, pp. 276–282.

[23] See e.g. *Merrills* (Anatomy) p. 11; *Coplin* (Functions) pp. 168–195; *Gould-Barkun* (Social Sciences) pp. 126–175; *Venkata Raman* (Reisman-Weston: Toward) pp. 365 et seq, 371–373. The point is to direct the study of law to encompass any "process of authoritative decision". See e.g. *McDougal-Lasswell-Reisman* (Falk-Black: Future I) pp. 81–94 and *infra* ch. 3.3.3.

determinate content, then it would be singularly useless in communicating any ideas, expectations or procedures.[24]

Other lawyers disagree because they use the term "law" in a way which blurs its connection with problem-solution. They equate it with factual behaviour or states of consciousness. Such uses, however, lose the law's normative character. In law we are not concerned with descriptions of physical or mental states but with normative statements about admissible and inadmissible behaviour. In as much as law has the function of guiding problem-solution (that is, in as much as it has a controlling social function) it must be envisaged as a set of directives, standards, rules etc. which have "binding force" in that they claim to determine a preference between competing solutions (rival meanings).[25]

Law, then, claims to justify solutions to normative problems. This calls for two specifications.

In the first place, a normative *problem* is present only if at least two *prima facie* plausible different solutions are available. Each solution involves, in this sense, ascertaining a preference between two solutions. In as much as legal arguments are objective, we must assume that this choice is justifiable by law and cannot be simply a matter of subjective preference. Secondly, normative problems emerge at all levels of discourse. A diplomat is concerned to know which rules he should take account of when conducting his business. A foreign office lawyer contemplates the constraints his colleagues in the operative section should bear in mind when proceeding with a relevant decision.[26] An international tribunal has

---

[24] *Hoffmann* (Deutsch-Hoffmann: Relevance) notes that whatever functions international law might have, those depend on its primary role to *restrain* behaviour, pp. 36–37. Similarly *Schachter* 178 RCADI 1982/V pp. 58–60.

[25] "Realist" schools of jurisprudence have wanted to associate law with "facts" of behaviour or psychology. See, for example, *Ross* (On Law and Justice) pp. 29 *et seq*, 44, 73–74; *Olivecrona* (Rättsordningen) *passim*. Critics have, however, observed that these approaches fail to explain the *internal aspect* of rules, the way in which law is experienced as external and binding. See *supra* n. 19 and *Jørgensen* (Values) p. 151 *et seq*; *Aarnio* (On Legal Reasoning) p. 343 *et seq*. For this point in international law, see *Le Fur* 46 RCADI 1935/IV (against the attempt to equate the law with sociological "facts") pp. 88–94, (against the effort to equate it with "psychology") pp. 145–146; *Allott* XLV BYIL 1971 pp. 127–128; *Guggenheim* (Lipsky: Law and Politics) p. 27.

[26] It is popularly assumed that legal considerations play little part in foreign affairs decision-making. Understandably, the experience of legal advisers tends to be the contrary. See generally e.g. the essays collected in *Merillat* (Legal Advisers), in particular pp. 15–25. See also *Vallat* (International Law and the Practitioner); *Sinclair* (Cheng: Teaching) pp. 123–134; *de Lacharrière* (Politique).

to determine and apply the law in respect of the States before it. And a scholar may wish to solve an abstract problem concerning, for example, the correct interpretation of the UN Charter.[27] In all such contexts the person faced with the problem turns to the law in order to seek justification for a legal solution and consequent action. For him, law is a kind of reservoir of directives for problem-solution. His is a "user's" point of view. This is what unifies what are usually thought of as separate realms of doctrine and practice. Both are assumed to be controlled by an objective rationality, not present in discourse about, say, legislation or literary criticism.

From this it does not, of course, follow that legal guidance, once ascertained, would be automatically followed. Other factors apart from law affect the solution of normative problems. But the crux is that we believe, and hold important, that it is at least possible to discover one or several "legal" solutions at the exclusion of other, legally inadmissible ones. The choice one is faced with is not free, but is constrained by law.

1.2.2   Objectivity and the practice of legal problem-solution

1.2.2.1   The basic position: objectivity and the judicial function

The basic position about the objectivity of international law is clearest within the doctrines of the judicial function. Their identity as distinct doctrines depends on the way they explain the law-ascertainment job as more objective than the legislative one.[28]

The classic separation of justiciable from non-justiciable disputes is one manner of upholding this distinction. In late 19th and early 20th century doctrines it was largely assumed that the prevalence of subjective State interests in some disputes rendered them incapable of legal settlement or that trying to find a general rule with which to solve them was pointless as the subjective interests would in any case overrule any attempt at legal solution.[29] It has, however, been impossible to make a

---

[27] See also *Raestad* (Philosophic) pp. 11–12.

[28] *Rosenne* (Law and Practice) expresses this by listing different third-party settlement strategies on a scale "from the extreme of politicization – negotiation – to the extreme of depoliticization – judicial settlement", p. 9. Similarly, *Scelle* 46 RCADI 1933/IV distinguishes between the judicial and other functions of settlement by the view that "le juge doit prendre des décisions *objectives*, sans jamais tenir compte de la situation personnelle des plaideurs", pp. 507–512.

[29] See the review and critical discussion by *Lauterpacht* (Function) pp. 19–20, 51 *et seq*, 139 *et seq*, 245 *et seq*.

clear distinction between these two types of disputes. The importance of an interest seems a matter which can be ascertained only by the State itself, that is to say, in a subjective manner. But letting the State itself decide whether a matter was justiciable or not gave it an absolute veto on judicial settlement which seemed to conflict with the latter's very character. It was an apologist doctrine.[30] On the other hand, making the distinction by reference to an objective rule would have required the presence of a constraining hierarchy of interests. But how could such a hierarchy be justified against a State which did not accept it? How could one State's subjective evaluation of its interest be overridden in favour of another State's or a judicial body's evaluation thereof? Assuming a hierarchy of interests seemed to assume the existence of a natural morality in the form of a theory of objective interests. It was a utopian doctrine. Consequently, the distinction between the two types of disputes has been largely abandoned.

In a manifest *petitio principii* modern doctrines delimit the scope of the judicial function by enquiring whether there exists law which is applicable to the matter at hand. And it is assumed that such law may exist regardless of whether the matter touches on important State interests. According to Article 38 (1) of the Statute of the International Court of Justice the function of the Court "is to decide in accordance with international law such disputes which are submitted to it". The provision is assumed to be applicable in contentious cases as well as in the "more political" advisory proceedings.[31] The message of the provision is clear: whatever the character of the dispute in political terms, the Court shall decide by law, not by reference to its subjective preferences or other "extralegal" dicta. The provision repeats the liberal distinction between legislation and adjudication. The acting subject is the law, not the Court. The subjective will of the legislator is carried out only if law-ascertainment is objective. Or, as Shabtai Rosenne puts it, while the function of the

---

[30] *Ibid.* pp. 163–165, 183–194, 353–357; *Elkind* (Non-Appearance) (pointing out the dependence of justiciability on what States *will* to be justiciable) pp. 187–203.

[31] The ICJ, for example, has frequently discussed the "legal" character of the question posed to it and sometimes reformulated that question so as to reveal its legal aspect. See e.g. ICJ: *Admission* Case, Reports 1948 p. 61; *Competence of the General Assembly* Case, Reports 1950 (the "abstract" character of the question) pp. 6–7; *Certain Expenses* Case, Reports 1962 pp. 155–156; *Namibia* Case, Reports 1971 p. 27 (§ 40); *Western Sahara* Case, Reports 1975 (the "factual" and "historical" character of the problem) pp. 18–21 (§§ 15–22); *Interpretation of the Agreement between the WHO and Egypt* Case, Reports 1980 pp. 88–89 (§ 35). See also the review by *Keith* (Advisory) pp. 224–226.

existence of the judicial function is political, the *performance* of that function is not.[32]

International lawyers take a more restricted view on the extent of subjective discretion in adjudication than their municipal colleagues.[33] More than the latter, they emphasize the law's consensual basis with which a wide discretionary power would conflict. Article 38(2) of the ICJ Statute indicates that the Court can resort to subjective evaluation only if the parties have so agreed. If they have, then the law's basis in State will – as commentators have pointed out[34] – remains unviolated.

The ICJ itself has frequently pointed out the objective-legal character of its function. In case legal standards have been lacking, the Court has refused to resort to subjective evaluation.

In the *Haya de la Torre* Case (1951), the Court observed that the diplomatic asylum granted to a person in the Colombian Embassy in Peru must be brought to an end. However, Colombia had no legal duty to surrender the person to Peruvian officials. On the other hand, the latter had no obligation to guarantee safe exit from Peruvian territory. The Court noted the deadlock but was unable to solve it in the absence of a determining rule. It was unable to give:

> ... any practical advice as to the various courses of action which might be followed with a view to terminating the asylum, since by doing it, it would depart from its judicial function.[35]

In the *South West Africa* Case (1966) the Court had occasion to express the same view in a number of passages. It was argued by the Applicants (Ethiopia and Liberia) *inter alia*, that "humanitarian considerations" were, by themselves, sufficent to generate their *locus standi* regarding the fulfilment or non-fulfilment by South Africa of its mandate in South

---

[32] *Rosenne* (Law and Practice) p. 4. Commentators stress that the function of several Articles in the Statute is to guarantee the independence of the judges. See e.g. *Carreau* (Droit international) p. 565.

[33] *Bleckmann* (Grundprobleme) p. 35. Thus international lawyers tend to emphasize the centrality of sources doctrine and constantly stress that judges must not "create" the law but only "apply" it. See e.g. *Ehrlich* 105 RCADI 1962/1 p. 254; *Degan* (L'interprétation) p. 161. See also the argument by *Fitzmaurice*, sep. op. ECHR: *Golder* Case, Ser. A 18, pp. 51–52. Also Soviet lawyers advocate maximum restraint from international judges – a position attributed by *McWhinney* (Festschrift Mosler) to their strict consensualism, pp. 569–570.

[34] *Kelsen* (Principles) p. 440; *Ehrlich* 105 RCADI 1962/1 p. 254; *Lauterpacht* (Function) pp. 313–329.

[35] ICJ: *Haya de la Torre* Case, Reports 1951 p. 83.

West Africa.[36] The Court made the subjective/objective distinction. It argued first that:

> Law exists, it is said, to serve a social need.[37]

In other words, law was based on politics. But, as it went on to say, even if all States:

> ... are interested – have an interest – in such (humanitarian, MK) matters ... the existence of an "interest" does not of itself entail that this interest is specifically juridical in character.[38]
>
> In order to generate legal rights and obligations, it must be given juridical expression and be clothed in legal form.[39]

An interest or humanitarian consideration is political and may "constitute the inspirational basis for rules of law" but in order to become applicable rules, they must become "objectified", separated from their immediate political basis by a formal legislative act, such as inclusion in a treaty.[40]

The Court's view appeared also in connection with the Applicants' "necessity argument" according to which each Member of the League had to have *locus standi* regarding the enforcement of the mandate because otherwise there would have existed no way in which the mandatory power could be compelled to fulfil its obligations.[41] But the Court held that no such system was included in the Covenant or the Mandate. Whether there were political reasons for giving the applicants *locus standi* was one thing. But the Court could not do so if it found that applicable law did not provide this:

> ... the Court is not a legislative body. Its duty is to apply the law as it finds it, not to make it.[42]

Although law serves a social need, it does not coalesce with such need. A need is not objective. It cannot be separated from what States at each moment hold as such. By contrast, law must have independence from momentary State views. If a need has not received objective affirmation

---

[36] See ICJ: *South West Africa* Case, Reports 1966 pp. 34–35 (§§ 49–54).
[37] *Ibid.* p. 34 (§ 49).   [38] *Ibid.* p. 34 (§ 50).   [39] *Ibid.* p. 34 (§ 51).
[40] *Ibid.* pp. 34 (§ 50), 34–35 (§ 52). For a strong, principled statement to the same effect, see *Fitzmaurice*, sep.op. ECHR: *Belgian Police* Case, Ser. A 19, pp. 33–34.
[41] ICJ: *South West Africa* Case, Reports 1966 p. 44 (§ 80) *et seq.*
[42] *Ibid.* p. 48 (§ 89). See also *ibid.* (§ 91). The Court observed that would it base its decision on humanitarian considerations "... it is not a legal service that would be rendered". *Ibid.* p. 34 (§ 49).

in law, a court cannot give effect to it. This view was affirmed by the Court
in the *Fisheries Jurisdiction* Cases (1974). Here the Court considered the
effect of the then on-going III UN Conference on the Law of the Sea on
the parties' rights and obligations. It pointed out that it:

> ... as a court of law, cannot render judgement *sub legis ferendae*, or
> anticipate the law before the legislator has laid it down.[43]

The Court's view in these cases may be summarized in four tenets: 1) the
legal system is based on political processes; 2) it is, however, autonomous from political views; 3) the court's function is to ascertain the
content of the legal system and apply it and 4) if legal standards are
lacking, then the claim must be dismissed. No discretion seems allowed.
Legal systems are absolutely determinate. If the Court cannot reach
decision, this is not due to any indeterminacy in law. It is because no
legal standards exist.[44]

Practical reasons support such a strict conception of determinacy.
There is enough distrust among States on international tribunals and
third-party settlement as it is. Wide powers of discretion would decrease
the predictability of judgements and invoke fear that judgements could
be contrary to important State interests.[45] Doctrines emphasizing the
creative nature of legal problem-solution seem opposed to the goal of a
legal world-order.[46] Recently, in the *Gulf of Maine* Case (1984) the
Chamber of the Court reaffirmed the need to reject subjective evaluation. The different socio-economic factors invoked by the parties:

> ... may require an examination of valid considerations of political or
> economic character.[47]

---

[43] ICJ: *Fisheries Jurisdiction* Case, Reports 1974 p. 24 (§ 53). That the Court did make
reference to the "new accepted trends" at the III UN Conference on the Law of the Sea in
the *Tunisia–Libya Continental Shelf Case*, Reports 1982, constitutes no departure from
this principle. Recourse to such "trends" was based on the *compromis* and thus seemed
to involve only giving effect to Party wills, pp. 23, 38 (§§ 4, 24).

[44] For similarly restrictive views, see e.g. PCIJ: *Competence of the ILO* Case, Ser. B 13
(exclusion of political and social factors) p. 23 and *Free Zones* Case, Ser. A/B. 46
(economic interests beyond the Court's competence) p. 162.

[45] On these points, see e.g. *Lauterpacht* (Development) pp. 75–77; *Castberg* 138 RCADI
1973/1 pp. 18–19.

[46] *D'Amato* (Onuf: Lawmaking) notes that what States wish to hear is what the law is and
not the subjective views of the judges of what would be good, p. 98 *et seq.* Among the few
international lawyers advocating a "free law method", see *Tanaka*, diss. op. ICJ: *South
West Africa* Case, Reports 1966 pp. 276, 278.

[47] ICJ: *Gulf of Maine* Case, Reports 1984 p. 278 (§ 59).

This was inadmissible:

> The Chamber is bound by its Statute, and required by the Parties, not to take
> a decision *ex aequo or bono*, but to achieve a result on the basis of law.[48]

But, of course, such ideas of automatic application of the law are difficult
to sustain. The very jurisprudence of the ICJ testifies to the controversial
character of its activity. Only five of the 51 judgements and one out of the
18 advisory opinions have been unanimous.[49] Many decisions have been
accompanied by several and often strongly worded dissenting opinions.[50]
In many recent cases of default or non-execution the relevant objections
have been formulated in legal terms. While it would be incorrect to say
that default or non-execution arises from differing interpretations of the
law, in many cases they do receive support from a feeling that the minority
opinion – or the opinion foreseeably to be left in the minority – is in some
respects a plausible legal opinion.[51] For example, legal opinion remains
sharply divided on the correctness of the majority judgement in the *South
West Africa* or the *Nuclear Tests* (1974) Cases, with respectable lawyers
arguing on both sides.[52]

---

[48] *Ibid.*

[49] For reviews, see *Hussain* (Opinions) pp. 39–69; *Sur* (L'interprétation) pp. 327–329. For
this enumeration of the cases, see ICJ Yearbook 1985–86, pp. 3–6.

[50] See e.g. *Jessup*, diss. op. ICJ: *South West Africa* Case Reports 1966 p. 325; *Guerrero,
McNair, Hsu Mo, Read*, joint diss. op. ICJ: *Reservations* Case, Reports 1951 p. 42. See
also generally *Hussain* (Opinions) pp. 49–54; *Prott* (Culture) pp. 81, 185–187.

[51] The question of the impartiality of the judges – much discussed by international lawyers –
is a relatively minor aspect of the problem. However impartial judges might be, if the
law remains ambiguous, their views about it do not possess automatic authority as
against what many States believe that law "really" is. The point is *not*, as many appear to
think, that law-breaking States refuse to go to the Court because that will make manifest
the illegal character of their policy. States refuse to go there because they will feel that
the Court does not share their legitimate views about the content of the law. The
question of the impartiality and authority of the ICJ is discussed in most essays in
Gross (Future I-II). Sobering views are presented e.g. by *Rovine* (*ibid.*) pp. 313–326;
Fitzmaurice (*ibid.*) pp. 461 *et seq*, 465–470, though they, too, regard non-recourse more
a matter of selfish interest of statesmen than a genuine feeling that the Court's law will
not be the same as "ours". *Anand* (*ibid.*) has probably a point in saying that "... the real
dilemma of the court is the dilemma of international law", p. 10 – although, I would
add, the dilemma relates more to the law's indeterminate character than its support for
an "old law of domination".

[52] For criticisms of the "conservatism" of the Court in the former case, see e.g. *Tanaka*,
diss. op. ICJ: *South West Africa* Case, Reports 1966 pp. 277–278; *Jessup*, diss. op. *ibid.*,
p. 439; *Friedmann*, 6 Columbia J. of Transnat'l Law 1967, p. 4 *et seq*; *McWhinney* (World
Court) pp. 17–19; *Gross* (Gross: Future) pp. 34–35; *Weissberg* (*ibid.*) pp. 140–141. For a
review, see *Hussain* (Opinions) pp. 172–181.

Hence, modern doctrines increasingly recognize that there is a range of discretion which is left to courts even in relatively clear cases:

> Judicial legislation, so long as it does not assume the form of deliberate disregard of the existing law, is a phenomenon both healthy and unavoidable.[53]

In other words, subjective discretion is necessary. But the identity of the judicial function is respected as such discretion must take place within "the existing law". Although there may be *relative* indeterminacy, it neither prevents the ascertainment of what the limits of existing law are nor staying within those limits in decision.

The reasons and forms of such relative indeterminacy will be discussed in the next section. Suffice it here to point out that many modern lawyers have argued for an "active" use of discretion by the ICJ.[54] To some extent the Court itself may, since the much criticized South West Africa judgement, have integrated some of the concerns about its "conservatism". Increasing use of purposive arguments or equity may be seen as indications thereof.[55]

---

[53] *Lauterpacht* (Development) pp. 155–223; *idem* (Function) esp. pp. 102–103, 270–347; *idem* (Symbolae Verzijl) pp. 210–220. See also *Brierly* (Basis of Obligation) p. 98; *Schwarzenberger* (International Law I) pointing out the "relative" nature of the distinction between law-finding and law-creation, p. 10.

[54] Judge *Alvarez* being the typical example of a modern lawyer stressing the need to use the Court actively for the purpose of social change. In the *Admission* Case, Reports 1947 he argued: "I hold that in this connexion the Court has a free hand to allow scope to the new spirit which is evolving in contact with the new conditions of international life: there must be a renewal of international law corresponding to the renewal of this life", pp. 47–48. See also *Hussain* (Opinions) pp. 93–96 and *infra* ch. 3.3.4. Similarly: *Ammoun*, sep. op. ICJ: *Namibia* Case, Reports 1971 p. 72 *et seq* and *idem*, *Western Sahara* Case, Reports 1975 (against the use of the "obsolete" *terra nullius* concept) pp. 85–87. Some Western writers, too, have aligned themelves with these views. See, in particular, *McWhinney* (World Court) pp. 17–23, 157–169 and *idem* (Festschrift Mosler) pp. 571–579.

[55] Thus, it is generally held that the Court used an ideological argument to guarantee the effectiveness of the League Mandates system in the *Status of South West Africa* Case, Reports 1950 p. 133 and in the *Namibia* Case, Reports 1971 pp. 30–32 (§§ 51–54) and to outline its "implied powers" doctrine in the *Reparation for Injuries* Case, Reports 1949 pp. 178–179. *Schwarzenberger* 10 CLP 1957, for example, reads the early cases as exemplifying a "wide" use of discretion, p. 294. The Court's very wide use of "equity" has been present since the *Anglo-Norwegian Fisheries* Case, Reports 1951 in which the solution seemed to follow from a "balancing of interests" test, p. 133. The *North Sea Continental Shelf* Cases, Reports 1969 then canonized equity as the overriding principle of maritime delimitation, pp. 46–47 (§ 85). On this development, see further *infra* ch. 4.5, 6.5.

But there is no consensus on the extent of permissible discretion. Commentators have not failed to point out the dangers inherent in increasing recourse to arguments which seem to express the Court's own subjective preferences. The use of equity – albeit *infra legem*[56] – by the Court has been criticized as threatening the very identity of the judicial process.[57] But, of course, the Court has never attempted to assume an openly legislative role. Discretion has been understood to take place "within the existing law".[58]

It may seem surprising, then, that international lawyers have had little to offer as practical advice on how to use discretion than general statements about the need to accommodate the concerns of stability and change. The courts should, in some way:

> ... steer a middle course between being over-conservative and ultra-progressive.[59]

Such generally formulated calls for "balancing" are, however, unlikely to help an international lawyer who feels that he is not receiving enough guidance to

---

[56] For the classic statement about equity *infra legem*, see ICJ: *North Sea Continental Shelf Cases*, Reports 1969 p. 48 (§ 88).

[57] British academic circles tended to agree with Judge *McNair*'s criticism of the "arbitrariness" of the Court's decision in the Anglo-Norwegian case which seemed to depart from the well-established rule concerning base-lines and especially the closing lines of bays at the time and gave too much emphasis to economic interests, diss. op. *Anglo-Norwegian Fisheries Case*, Reports 1951, p. 169. See *Waldock* XXVIII BYIL 1951 pp. 114, 131–137, 148, 167; *Fitzmaurice* XXXI BYIL 1954 pp. 412–414. Later, Judge *Gros* has established himself as the main critic of the Court's subjective-political use of equity. See e.g. sep. op. ICJ: *Nuclear Tests* Case, Reports 1974, p. 297; *idem* ICJ: *Tunisia–Libya Continental Shelf* Case, Reports 1982 pp. 147–156 (§§ 9–24). See further nn. 118, 121 *infra*.

[58] The discussion about "old" and "new" international law has been without consequence to the idea of the law's determinacy. No reformist movement within international law has preached for a law of more (or less) determinacy.

[59] *Fitzmaurice* (Essays McNair) p. 26. Likewise, see *Anand* (Gross: Future) p. 12; *Gross* (*ibid.*) p. 82; *Prott* (Culture) pp. 84–96; *Tanaka*, diss. op. ICJ: *South West Africa* Case, Reports 1966 p. 277. There is no consensus on how the balance should be attained. Moreover, lawyers are unable to establish fixed positions. Characteristically, position is taken to counter a deviating substantive view: emphasis on restraint is needed to counter another's view as "anarchistic"; stress on innovation enables to criticize an opponents' view as "conservative". For the former, see e.g. *Schwarzenberger* (International Law I) pp. 65–66; *Wolfke* (Custom) pp. 74–75. For the latter, see e.g. *Sørensen* (Sources) pp. 24–26. As the positions are relative to substantive views, it is impossible to class any of these lawyers permanently into "activists" or "conservatives". They may be (and typically are) activists in some, conservatives in other respects.

justify a decision from the unambiguous norms available.[60] The problem is how to use discretion so as not to violate the limits of "existing law"?

1.2.2.2   The revised position: the doctrine of "relative indeterminacy"

Neither the lawyer's common-sense intuition nor contemporary doctrine view the relation between law and legal decision as logical or otherwise "automatic" reduction. Criticizing such a vision – even if someone were to hold it, which is doubtful – would amount to flogging a dead horse. H. L. A. Hart summarizes conventional wisdom as follows:

> In every legal system a large and important field is left open for the exercise of discretion by Courts and other officials in rendering initially vague standards determinate, in resolving the incertainties of statutes, or in developing and qualifying rules only broadly communicated by the authoritative standards.[61]

Conventional doctrine understands legal rationality as a form of *practical rationality* which is not binding in any absolute sense but whose force lies in its persuasiveness, in the justificatory strength of the chain of arguments which leads to a solution. A determined solution to it is a *justified* solution, a solution which reasonable men can agree to be a correct legal solution whatever they might otherwise think of it.[62] The determining force of law is, under such a conception, always contextual. Determinacy depends on the acceptance of the chain of justifications by the relevant reference-group. In international law, that reference-group might be thought of as the "invisible college of international lawyers", for example.[63]

---

[60] *Schachter* (Festschrift Mosler) p. 816. *Charney* 78 AJIL 1984 has suggested to replace the intuitionalist style of arguing from equity by the ICJ in recent maritime delimitations by a more "rigorous" factor analysis of what goes to achieve an acceptable balance, pp. 596–606. Likewise, *Herman* 33 ICLQ 1984 pp. 853–858. While such analysis helps to identify relevant factors it, of course, fails to explain why this evaluation – on which everything depends – should be a non-subjective process (capable of being undertaken without reference to some (political) theory of distributive justice).

[61] *Hart* (Concept) p. 132.

[62] During the 1960s and 70s, legal theory started to associate itself with a theory of rhetorics, or argument, stressing the justificatory aspects of legal decision. Influential works include *Perelman-Olbrechts-Tyteca* (Traité); *Viehweg* (Topik). See also *Aarnio* (On Legal Reasoning); *idem* (Point of View) pp. 159–182. It is relatively rare to see such theory applied in international law. See, however, *Prott* (Culture) p. 119 *et seq* and *Kratochwil* (Falk-Kratochwil-Mendlowitz: International Law) studying international law as a "rhetorical device" and making express reference to the classics of legal argument theory, pp. 640–645 and *idem* 69 ARSP 1983 pp. 40–44.

[63] The term is borrowed from *Schachter*. For a discussion of what might constitute the appropriate "audience" for the purposes of treating international law within argument theory, see *Prott* (Culture) pp. 134–137, 152 *et seq*. For an early version of this approach

But there is a significant ambiguity here. In many cases what is actually (subjectively) accepted by the reference-group is unclear. Checking proposed solutions against such acceptance becomes impossible. Therefore, legal theorists, in particular, have moved on to speak of an "objectified" acceptance, of what *can be* rationally accepted.[64] The problem with this approach is how to justify the adopted standard of rationality itself. I will come back to the problem of justifying the conditions of "rational" consensus. Suffice it here to note the problem and that whatever the determinacy of the legal argument is taken to mean, it cannot mean any automatic, transcendental correctness of the argument. There are at least four well-known reasons for this.[65]

First, it is generally recognized that different types of legal standards have different degrees of justifying power. At least two types of standards with different degrees of determining force are commonly distinguished:

1. "Rules" which guide the solution of normative problems in that if they are applicable, they must be applied and their application exhaustively solves the case;[66]
2. "Principles", any single one of which does not determine the solution exhaustively (indeed, they may also conflict) but brings out arguments in favour or one solution or another. They work together in clusters so that a solution applying them and assigning their different "weights" can be said to arise as a "vector sum" which determines the solution.[67]

in international law, see *Spiropoulos* (Théorie) (arguing that all legal concepts are "subjective constructions" and that the only "objective principle" which restrains political choice is doctrinal mainstream's "dominant opinion") pp. x–xiii, 8–24 and *passim*. See also *Schachter* (Schwebel: Effectiveness) pp. 19–20 *et seq*. For a perceptive criticism, see *Le Fur* 54 RCADI 1935/IV pp. 45 *et seq*, 58–71 (pointing out the difficulty in Spiropoulos' argument – applicable to any consensualism: if the law is always constructed on the majority's opinion, then he himself lacks basis to criticize that opinion).

[64] See *Aarnio* (Oikeussäännösten) pp. 54–59, 167 *et seq*.
[65] For a more exhaustive listing, see *Marshall* (Miller-Siedentop: Nature) pp. 192–194. See also *Koskenniemi* XVII Oikeustiede-Jurisprudentia 1984 pp. 148–152.
[66] There is an abundance of writing of what should be properly called legal "rules". For the standard view according to which "rules" are either power-conferring or duty-imposing and that their validity requires neither being accompanied with sanction nor necessary connection with morality, see *Hart* (Concept) pp. 8–12, 27–32, 38–41, 97 *et seq*.
[67] For this characterization, see *Dworkin* (Taking) pp. 22–31. A typical case of two principles pointing at different directions and demanding evaluative solution in order to reach decision is the conflict between the principle of self-determination and that of territorial integrity within the law of decolonization. For a discussion, see *infra* ch. 7.3.

Although the determining force of principles seems weaker than that of rules, this does not mean that a legal solution applying principles would be wholly indeterminate. Indeed quite the contrary case has been made.[68] In any case, even if the ascertainment of the "relative weights" of different principles would involve a degree of subjective discretion, such discretion could be seen to take place "within existing law" which restricts the choice of principles to be used.

Secondly, to use Hart's well-known metaphor, linguistic expressions have in addition to their core of well-established meaning a penumbra of uncertainty. International normative language is loaded with expressions which are indeterminate in this sense. Words such as "aggression", "self-defence", "war", "intervention" or "combatant", to name only few within one central area of law, are notoriously ambiguous and require reflective interpretation before applicable in practice.[69] In addition, many legal expressions do not have the straightforward formulation of a rule or a principle. Some standards are general, others detailed; some express policies or goals, others lay down powers, duties or rights; some use prescriptive, others descriptive language and so on.

For a review of the very extensive recent discussion of legal principles in international law and legal theory, see *Koskenniemi* XVIII Oikeustiede-Jurisprudentia 1985 pp. 117–163. The discussion has been prompted, in particular, by the views of *Dworkin*, for whom legal principles *override* any legislative policies in their function of rationalizing the rights legal subjects have *against* the State. But this is not the only way to characterize a "principle". At least the following uses of the term in international law may be distinguished: 1) Standards of "second-order justification", i.e. norms which dictate the choice of applicable rules; 2) political standards at the background of rules; 3) non-normative abstractions from individual rules; 4) procedural standards of fairness; 5) natural law standards; 6) particularly important rules; 7) rules at a high hierarchical level; 8) rules common to all or most legal systems; 9) standards structuring the hierarchy of norms; 10) standards inherent in the judicial process. For sources not listed in my above-mentioned article, see also *Kennedy* 89 Harvard L.R. 1976 pp. 1687–1689; *Schachter* 178 RCADI 1982/V applying the Dworkinian conception, pp. 43, 75–82; *Castberg* 138 RCADI 1973/1 pp. 7–9; *Mosler* 36 ZaöRV 1976 distinguishing between natural, international, generally characterizing (structural) and logical principles, pp. 43–46; *Strebel* 36 ZaöRV 1976 adopting the "classical" view of principles as those accepted in municipal legal systems, pp. 338–343; *Blondel* (Mélanges Guggenheim) distinguishing between principles derived from the idea of law, those recognized by States and those inferred from the nature of an institution, pp. 211–234. See also ICJ: *Gulf of Maine* Case, Reports 1984, pp. 288–290 (§ 79) (distinguishing between principles and rules of maritime delimitation).

[68] See *infra* at notes 128–135.

[69] See *De Visscher* (Problèmes) p. 14; *Salmon* 175 RCADI 1982/II pp. 277–285; *Bleckmann* 36 ZaöRV 1976 (discussing the strategies for making "concrete" abstractly formulated norms) pp. 383–394; *Lauterpacht* (International Law I) pp. 25–27.

Various reasons of legal policy support the adoption of one or the other type of language.[70] In normative problem-solution, however, each of such expressions must be translated into normative language, that is language claiming to provide a justification for one or another solution. This translation is by no means "automatic". What, for instance, is the normative sense of the "common heritage of mankind", "sovereignty" or "immunity"? The concrete meaning given to such terms in particular disputes is clearly less a matter of application than "construction".[71]

A third problem is constituted by the frequent use of evaluative terminology in legal language. Expressions such as "undue delay" or "inhuman or degrading treatment" in the International Covenant on Civil and Political Rights are obvious examples. "Equity" or "equitable principle" are similar. The element of indeterminacy embedded in such expressions is highlighted whenever such terms need to be inter-culturally construed.[72]

A fourth case of relative indeterminacy is that the will of States does not – indeed cannot – provide solutions to all normative problems. As Merrills writes, one of the most important consequences of the decentralized nature of international lawmaking is that on many matters "there will simply be insufficient agreement among States".[73] Sometimes, as in the case of new technology, States have simply not even had the time to establish any standards. At other times, lack of agreement among States may have led to States leaving the matter unregulated quite consciously.[74] In such cases

---

[70] See generally *Kennedy* 89 Harvard L. R. 1976 pp. 1687–1713. For those strategies in international law-making, see *de Lacharrière* (Politique) pp. 63–103.

[71] See *Stone's* (Conflict) discussion of the descriptive-prescriptive meaning of "aggression", pp. 105–106 and *Henkin's* (How) discussion of the normative effects of the characterization of South Vietnam's status during the Vietnam war, pp. 306–308. See also *Gould-Barkun* (Social Sciences) p. 58.

[72] See further *Salmon* 175 RCADI 1982/II pp. 175–177. The matter seems particularly acute in respect of human rights language. In the *Wrongful Imprisonment for Fraud* Case, 14 July 1971, 72 ILR 1987, for example, the supreme court of the FRG observed that such expressions are frequently drafted in general terms so as to allow their compatibility with differing national practices. Their sense could not, therefore, be fixed to a single municipal concept, p. 311. For a comparison of the construction of UN supported human rights norms in traditional and modernist Islam, see *Abu-Sahlieh* 89 RGDIP 1985 pp. 625–718. For a general discussion of the effects of intercultural differences of meaning in legal language, see *Bozeman* (Multicultural) *passim*.

[73] *Merrills* (Anatomy) p. 5. See also *Lauterpacht* (Function) pp. 71–79; *Brierly* (Basis of Obligation) pp. 97–98.

[74] *Hart* (Concept) points out that many situations of application cannot be exhaustively provided for in the norm. In such cases, indeterminacy works as a deliberate legislative strategy, p. 127. *Jackson* (Semiotics) speaks of "motivated indeterminacy", pp. 163–166.

the normative materials are by definition incapable of providing determinate justification.[75]

The recognition of penumbral meanings and the need for interpretation poses a *prima facie* threat to the assumption that international law is
distinguished from politics by being more objective than this.
The doctrine of *relative indeterminacy*[76] seeks to explain how it is
possible not to abandon the important insight that the solution of
normative problems is not an automatic process and yet preserve the
law's identity *vis-à-vis* politics on the grounds that it is objectively
constraining.

According to this doctrine, the law's indeterminacy is only a marginal phenomenon, an incidental disturbance in the otherwise determining flow of legal information.[77] It is usually discussed under the
doctrine of "gaps", or *lacunae* in law.[78] The assumption is that the law

International lawyers frequently point out that international legal texts result from
formal compromises and include formulations which are wide enough to contain
contradictory political ideas, such as territorial integrity/self-determination, non-use
of force/self-defence etc. See e.g. *de Lacharrière* (Politique) pp. 89–109; *De Visscher*
(Theory) pp. 256–257 and e.g. *Mouton* (Mélanges Chaumont) pointing out the use of
this strategy in the application of the European Convention on Human Rights
pp. 412–416; *Bernhardt* 36 ZaöRV 1976 discussing it by reference to the 1970 UN
Friendly Relations Declaration, p. 54; *Stone* (Conflict) relating it to the definition of
aggression, p. 224 *et seq.* For further examples, see *Simma* (Macdonald-Johnston:
Structure and Process) pp. 491–492.

[75] For example, in the *Gulf of Maine* Case, the Chamber of the ICJ found that the
applicable law provided only some "basic legal principles" without specifying how
they should be adapted to particular cases. The Chamber found that: ". . . in the current
state of the law governing relations between them (the parties, MK) are not bound,
under a rule of treaty-law or other rule, to apply certain criteria or to use certain
particular methods for the establishment of a single maritime boundary . . ." It added,
enigmatically: "Consequently, the Chamber also is not so bound." Reports 1984 p. 312
(§ 155). And it went on to outline a set of "equitable criteria" and "practical methods"
for the delimitation, to compare these with the criteria and methods suggested by the
parties in order to arrive at an overall "equitable result". *Ibid.* pp. 312–344 (§§ 156–242).

[76] The term "relative indeterminacy" is used by *Hart* (Concept) to denote cases where
semantically wide expressions leave a margin of discretion. Discretion is "relative"
because its limits are assumed to be set by law, p. 128.

[77] For the argument that indeterminacy in international law is no greater than in national
law, see *Moore* (Falk-Kratochwil-Mendlowitz: International Law) p. 55; *Nardin* (Law,
Morality) pp. 179–186, 193–194.

[78] The doctrine of "gaps" is premised on the focal idea of the law as a complete system.
Inasmuch as uncertainty (gaps) arise, two ways seem open to salvage the idea of
completeness: A judge may note that the gap is only "spurious" (i.e. results from an
evaluative preference) in which case he may simply note that the law provides no
remedy – and thus dismiss the case by a legal standard. Or he may be referred to the
use of constructive principles which provide a substantive legal decision. For a strong

remains determinate when no gaps exist as well as to the extent that reasoning *within* the gap areas can be contained within some residual form of legal rationality (such as procedural presumptions, for example). If this cannot be guaranteed, then it must be assumed that the inevitable subjectivism in gap areas can at least be limited by some determinate rules or principles. In other words, conventional doctrine assumes a distinction between "normal" and "hard" cases. The former are those in which the justificatory chain of arguments is experienced (or could rationally be experienced) as persuasive by international lawyers. The latter are those in which reasonable lawyers are left to disagree. Even in these, however, it is assumed that the law does determine the broad outlines of the set of alternative solutions.

To safeguard the overall determinacy of legal argument in hard cases lawyers have developed specific "second order" methods for ensuring that their effect on the controlling force of legal argument remains marginal. Recourse is had to rules of interpretation, thumb-rules and procedural presumptions. Although such rules are sometimes treated as if they provided a fully determined solution, it is clearly more common to consider them as pragmatic directives which on the whole would seem to give the most satisfactory solution.[79] But there is much disagreement on the role and application of these methods. These disagreements reflect the twin concerns of modern lawyers: Their use should not be such as to allow States complete freedom (apologism). But they should neither lead into solutions which are not responsive to the social context (utopianism).

1.2.3 Objectivity in hard cases: the forms of modern doctrine

There exist two views about justification in hard cases. According to a *weak view*, only the broad outlines of the decision are then legally determined, or justified. Within a range of discretion, the problem-solver makes a subjective choice. According to a *strong view*, the "balancing" or evaluation involved in hard cases is ultimately controlled by

preference for the latter, see *Lauterpacht* (Symbolae Verzijl) pp. 196–221. For a conflicting view according to which there might sometimes be a duty on the judge to declare *non liquet*, see *Siorat* (lacunes) pp. 186–190. For a criticism of the idea of material completeness, see also *Stone* XXXV BYIL 1959 p. 124 *et seq*. See further *Fitzmaurice* (Mélanges Reuter) pp. 103–112.

[79] *Schwarzenberger-Brown* (Manual), for instance, regard interpretation a "balancing process", p. 133. See generally also *Sur* (L'interprétation) pp. 48–54, 65 *et seq* and *infra* ch. 5.2.

law. Both views assume that the law has an objective aspect which separates it from politics. In the weak view, objectivity is related only to determining the range of discretion while the strong view extends objectivity even to areas in which it first looked as if the problem-solver had discretion. Modern lawyers commonly adopt the weak view. I shall argue, however, that the strong version is the more plausible one and that even the adherents to the weak version must ultimately adopt it in order to make a distinction between legal and political argument.

The *weak version* readily accepts the existence of gaps in law. There is no one correct solution. There are two variations of this view in regard to what judges should do when faced with such gaps:

1. It is sometimes suggested that if a solution cannot be reached through law-application, then it is the lawyer's duty to say this and reject proposing any solution. In judicial practice this would mean the recognition of a *non liquet* and dismissing the case;
2. It is also sometimes suggested that in such a case the judge should use his best judgement and solve the case in some subjectively satisfactory manner by using political, economic or other extralegal criteria. In judicial practice this would seem to signify the right of a court to "legislate" for the parties.

The former variant may be associated with the doctrine making the distinction between legal and political disputes.[80] It shares a rigid concept of justification: law either determines the solution exhaustively or then not at all. The views expressed by the ICJ in the *South West Africa* Case come close to this version.[81]

---

[80] *Supra* at notes 29–30. The doctrine may take two different forms. It may mean 1) that some disputes are by nature or common recognition legal and some political so that norms governing the former cannot be transposed to the latter, or 2) that though there are no technical obstacles to applying legal standards in some disputes, their application only serves to aggravate them. Obviously, it is only the former view which encapsulates point 1 in the text and inasmuch as the latter concern needs to be taken account of it must be reformulated so as to appear in the same form (by including the beneficial nature of judicial settlement as a necessary *legal* condition for making a decision). See further *Jenks* (Prospects) p. 16; *Gamble-Fischer (Court)* pp. 19–20; *Lauterpacht* (Function) pp. 139–201; *Brierly* (Basis of Obligation) pp. 96–97, 100–103. See also *Lachs*, sep. op. ICJ: US *Military and Paramilitary Activities* Case, Reports 1986 pp. 166–170.

[81] The arguments by judges *Spender* and *Fitzmaurice* in the earlier phase of the case are likewise illustrative. They held that the Applicants' arguments had been "no more than motives or reasons for saying that it is politically desirable that the Applicants should be

But it is generally held that an international court is not allowed to rule *non liquet*.[82] There are no reported cases in which a court would have dismissed a case on grounds of non-existence of law. They have always been able to construct some legal – even if procedural – standard on which a decision one way or another has become possible.[83] But basically the first variant of the weak version fails because it shares a simplistic view of law-application in "normal" cases. It rests on the assumption that controversial cases are only few and easily distinguishable from non-controversial ones. This, however, is doubtful. In the first place, there is no reason to exclude the possibility that *any* legal expression may be affected by one or another of the reasons for indeterminacy listed above.[84] Secondly, and more importantly, however, any international dispute becomes a hard case by the simple fact that disputing States are *always* able to make a *prima facie* justification of their action by referring to their sovereign liberty. In such cases the decision-maker is compelled to make an interpretation of the extent of that liberty or to privilege one sovereign over another in a manner which necessitates the construction of a hierachy of values for evaluating sovereign action. The construction of such hierarchy, however, is necessarily a hard case in a system which excludes the presence of a natural morality from the perspective of which liberties could be evaluated.

allowed to invoke Article 7 (of the mandate, MK)". These, they held, "cannot have any bearing on the legal issues involved, and these must be our sole concern". *South West Africa* Case, joint diss. op. Reports 1962 p. 515. As the Court, four years later, took its final position, it seemed to adopt this view.

[82] For a discussion, see *Koskenniemi* XVII Oikeustiede-Jurisprudentia 1984 pp. 130–131 and notes therein; *Castberg* 43 RCADI 1933/I p. 342. The Court's position in the *Eastern Carelia* Case in which it observed that it could not deal with the request without departing from its judicial function was rather less a *non liquet* stand than an inference from its jurisdictionary rules, PCIJ Ser. B 5. pp. 27–28. See also *Fitzmaurice* (Mélanges Rousseau) p. 93; *Brierly* (Law of Nations) pp. 363–365; *Corbett* (Law and Society) p. 79.

[83] Sometimes, like in the *Serbian Loans* Case (1929) Ser. A 20, the construction whereby *non liquet* is avoided can be quite striking. Here, the PCIJ observed that there existed no rules of international law concerning the form of payment of certain Serbian loans to French bond-holders. Noting that Article 36(1) of the Statute compels it to reach a decision when the case is referred to it by a special agreement, the Court settled the matter by recourse to Serbian municipal law, p. 41. Whether in such and other cases in which procedural means are used because international law seems to remain silent we still wish to speak of the law's "completeness", is largely a matter of taste. Inasmuch as we see the procedural safeguards as expressions of a material principle (the principle of sovereignty, for example) then such form of speech is more legitimate than if we wish to detach procedural law from its substantive assumptions. See also *Fitzmaurice* (Mélanges Rousseau) (preferring to discard the idea of completeness) pp. 103–112.

[84] See *MacCormick* (Reasoning) pp. 195–228; *Goodrich* 3 Legal Studies 1983 pp. 164–166.

The second variant of the weak version admits that lawyers have discretion in hard cases. Having discretion does not, however, deviate from the *overall* determinacy of the legal system. This variant looks upon discretion as a legally allocated and controlled authority to use subjective evaluation in some limits. By thus combining the legal and the political this version fits well with the concern to avoid utopianism and apologism. Legal decision is understood to be only broadly determined by norms while the details of the decision are left for a contextual-political evaluation.[85]

The weak version must make an absolute distinction between law and discretion. Any such distinction, however, seems constantly threatened by the common experience that what once seemed like routine applications of the law have become or can be portrayed as increasingly problematic.[86] While, for example, the meaning of the "High Seas" used to be a relatively clear one, the introduction of the exclusive economic zone (EEZ) as well as other zones of special jurisdiction has made it increasingly uncertain. The same is true of the general prohibition of the use of force which is rendered ambiguous by the legitimacy accorded to self-defence and forcible struggle for national self-determination.[87]

To curb this threat, the weak version should incorporate within itself a rule about the limits of discretion. Moreover, it must assume a *strong* view as to the content of this rule. If the law/discretion distinction is to hold, it must be established by a rule which itself does not allow discretion. In this respect, the weak version is only a strong version in disguise and problems confronting the latter are equally applicable to it.

In the following I shall discuss *four* versions of the *strong view* common to which is the view that hard cases are merely cases of *primae*

---

[85] This is the standard version. See e.g. *Hart* (Concept) pp. 127–132 and *Lyons* (Ethics) pp. 90–92. For international lawyers emphasizing the need for international courts to "legislate" in gap-situations, see *Brierly* 58 RCADI 1936/IV p. 73. See also *Guggenheim* (Lipsky: Law and Politics) pp. 16–18. This view is alo implicit in *Weil* 77 AJIL 1983, arguing against the tendency of "blurring the normativity threshold" and that law is either "hard" or then no law at all, p. 413 *et seq*. For further characterization of this view, see *Dworkin* (Taking) p. 33; *idem* (Empire) pp. 115–117.

[86] See also *Henkin* (How) pointing out that most international cases do not admit of "easy" solutions and that the effectiveness of decisions rests significantly on the authority of the institution in which it has been made, pp. 328–329.

[87] Western States opposed the Soviet initiative for drafting a treaty on the non-use of force at the UN as any new formulation of that norm might have made the normativity of the prevailing standard doubtful. See UN Doc. A/33/41 (1978) pp. 8–9 (§§ 26, 28).

impressionis difficulty of finding the correct rule or principle to solve the case.

The first (formalistic) variant of the strong view in fact amounts to an objection to the above analysis. According to this view, indeterminacy does not signify the absence of an applicable norm as any legal system is always *formally complete*. Kelsen points out:

> That neither conventional nor customary international law is applicable to a concrete case is logically not possible ... If there is no norm of conventional or customary international law imposing upon the state (or another subject of international law) the obligation to behave in a certain way, the subject is under international law legally free to behave as it pleases; and by a decision to this effect existing international law is applied to the case.[88]

This view – which echoes the famous dictum of the PCIJ in the *Lotus* Case – argues that a legal system contains a residual principle which provides for the freedom of the State unless determinate rules exist to restrict it. The law is formally complete as a legal problem may always be solved by recourse to this residual rule.

It is difficult to sustain such formalism because it seems either based on utopian premises or lapses into simple apologism.[89] In the first place, it is based on a *naturalistic* principle which prefers State freedom to competing values such as, for example, international order or distributive justice. It encapsulates a morality which seems unjustifiable in any objective way. Kelsen himself admits that the choice between a State-centred and an international community-centred systematics is a *political* choice.[90] As such, it is inadmissible under the strong version. But formalism seems inadmissible also because apologist. Any rule-application is capable of being understood as an attempt to delimit the disputing States' freedoms. To say that "freedom" should be given preference fails singularly to indicate which State's freedom is meant. This version fails because it is devoid of criteria for preferring between

---

[88] *Kelsen* (Principles) pp. 438–439. Similarly *Guggenheim* (Traité I) p. 264; *Anzilotti* (Cours I) pp. 116–119. This, obviously, restates the principle of the law's formal completeness.

[89] For standard criticisms, see e.g. *Bruns* 1 ZaöRV 1929 pp. 25–40; *Reuter* (Droit international public) pp. 49–50; *Salmon* (Perelman: Problème) pp. 315–317; *Mosler* 36 ZaöRV 1976 pp. 40–41; *De Visscher* (Theory) pp. 65–67; *Bleckmann* (Grundprobleme) pp. 24–25.

[90] *Kelsen* 14 RCADI 1926/IV pp. 321–326; *idem* 19 ZaöRV 1958 pp. 244–246.

conflicting freedoms.[91] The construction of a solution entails inevitably looking beyond mere "freedom" into some material criteria of making the preference or determining the limits.[92] How to integrate such material criteria into the overall image of an objective law is a central problem for the strong view about determinacy.

The second variant of the strong version argues that certain material standards are inherent in any legal system and that if indeterminacy arises, they become applicable. They may be based on the immutability of human nature, the inherent quality of the legal process,[93] some hidden presuppositions of legal language,[94] exacting concerns of human dignity or existence[95] or a constitutional principle of *Gemeinschaftsgebundenheit*, for example.[96] It is these norms of substantive justice or juristic inevitability which judges must turn to if positive rules seem lacking.[97]

The ICJ has used arguments from natural justice in, for example, the *Corfu Channel* Case (1949) to condemn Albania's inaction in respect of warning foreign vessels about the presence of a minefield in its waters,[98] in the *Reservations to the Genocide Convention* Case (1951) to interpret a multilateral convention[99] and in the *Barcelona Traction* Case (1970) to

---

[91] *See infra.* ch. 4.5.   [92] See e.g. *Corbett* (Law and Society) p. 78.
[93] Principles of procedural justice are usually left unargued because held to be self-evident. See, however, e.g. *Brandt v. Attorney-General of Guayana*, 8 March 1971, 71 ILR 1986 (*audi alteram partem* regarded as "essential requirement of natural justice") pp. 465, 470–474.
[94] For the view that legal language expresses a basic moral consensus, see *Walzer* (Just War) pp. 12–16. See also *Nardin* (Law, Morality) pp. 246–248.
[95] See *infra* ch. 3.3.3.
[96] Modern arguments about natural law usually infer the "inherent" (or "structural") postulates from the law's assumed social necessity. This is the core of *Verdross'* doctrine of the (implicit) *Völkerrechtsverfassung* (Die Einheit) pp. 126–135 and *passim*. See also *Bernhardt* 36 ZaöRV 1976 p. 71; *D'Amato* (Onuf: Lawmaking) p. 90 *et seq.* See also *Hart*'s formulation of the minimal content of a (structural) natural law (Essays) pp. 79–82; *idem* (Concept) pp. 189–195.
[97] In classical and modern international law – in contrast to early doctrine – naturalistic arguments are commonly assumed to be applicable only in this secondary sense. See *Spiropoulos* (Théorie) pp. 111–113. For historical reviews, see e.g. *Scott* (Spanish) pp. 103–111; *Kosters* (Fondements) pp. 158–181. *Truyol y Serra* (Doctrines) pp. 67–104 notes that modern natural law doctrines agree "qu'il doit les traduire et les développer sous forme de droit positif", p. 69.
[98] ICJ: *Corfu Channel* Case, Reports 1949 ("elementary considerations of humanity") p. 22.
[99] ICJ: *Reservations* Case, Reports 1951 p. 23.

characterize what it called *erga omnes* obligations.[100] Such arguments have also appeared frequently in the judges' individual opinions.[101]

The problem with such arguments is not only that the Court has left open their nature or how to justify them. The difficulty is that they assume the existence of a natural justice and are vulnerable to the objection about utopianism.[102] In the first place, there is no degree of consensus among States about what such "natural" values or goals or the nature of the international community might be.[103] Secondly, even if we possessed knowledge about the nature of man or of the international community it would seem to involve a "naturalistic fallacy" to argue that we could derive material norms from it.[104] Thirdly, recourse to values, goals or other moralities seems only to increase law's indeterminacy as their formulation is wide and the more concrete they become, the less they seem to reflect historical experience.[105] Finally, the acceptance of a set of natural norms conflicts with the liberal theory of legislation. It assumes that States enter a pre-existing normative world. If natural norms existed, the point of legislation by formally neutral and universally applicable rules would be lost. Such norms would seem justifiable

---

[100] ICJ: *Barcelona Traction* Case, Reports 1970 p. 32 (§§ 33–34).

[101] See e.g. *Alvarez*, diss. op. ICJ: *Effect of Awards of Compensation* Case, Reports 1954 pp. 72–75 (for the interdependence argument as the basis for naturalistic construction). Similarly, see *Ammoun*, diss. op. ICJ: *Namibia* Case, Reports 1971 pp. 71–75. See also *Tanaka*, diss. op. ICJ: *South West Africa* Case, Reports 1966 p. 248 *et seq* and *Jessup*, diss. op. *ibid.*, p. 323 *et seq.*

[102] For the conventional criticism according to which naturalism "confuses" law with (indemonstrable) politics, see e.g. *Sur* (L'interprétation) pp. 25–32; *Bleckmann* (Grundprobleme) p. 263. See also *Strupp* 47 RCADI 1934/1 pp. 340–345. For a strongly worded criticism of the ambiguity and political manipulability of natural law, see *Verzijl* (I), pp. 391–393.

[103] For this standard point, see e.g. *Hall* (International Law) pp. 2–4; *Kelsen* (Principles) p. 443; *Friedmann* (Changing) pp. 77–79. It is of course true that for a naturalist, the validity of natural law is in no way dependent on general consensus or acceptance. To this extent, the standard criticism misses the point. See e.g. *Strauss* (Natural) pp. 9–34; *Verdross-Koeck* (Macdonald-Johnston: Structure and Process) pp. 41–42; *Finnis* (Natural Law) pp. 24–25, 29–33. The force of the criticism, however, relates to naturalistic epistemology, its incapability to show the law's content in other reliable ways than by appealing to self-evidence or to what *has been* subjectively accepted. The former strategy, however, seems utopian as it assumes a kind of agreement about self-evidence which may not exist. The latter strategy, again, tends to make naturalism indistinguishable from positivism.

[104] See e.g. *Gardies* (Essai) pp. 15–32.

[105] *Brierly* (Law of Nations) (arguing that this ambiguity results in "anarchy" as it allows each State to pose its own view as the norm) p. 22.

only in an instrumental way, as clarifiers of what the pre-existing code requires.

A third, purposive variant of the strong view does not share the (utopian) assumption of a natural justice. It argues that in the absence of other criteria, the decision must give effect either to some legislative purposes or to some conception of general utility, or equity. In its interpretation of the League of Nations' mandates system and the UN Charter, for example, the ICJ has stressed purposive points about "effectiveness".[106] In territorial disputes, it has emphasized the purposive idea of "stability and finality" of frontiers.[107] Human rights instruments, in particular, have been applied so as to stress their object and purpose.[108]

In its doctrinal formulation, this view objects to the conventional vision of legal decision-making as rule-application. Positive law is always indeterminate and contains only fragmented trends of past decision. The decision-maker's is always a choice between solutions each of which may, with some ingenuity, be justified by such trends. To make an enlightened choice he must balance the relevant interests at issue in light of overriding community goals.[109] Past trends – rules – may be relevant but only to the extent that they support these goals.

This variant attempts to preserve the law's concrete basis by linking the statement's naturalism inferred from an objective morality to community acceptance. To avoid apologism, it assumes, however, that the relevant purpose does not need *actual acceptance* by each State at the moment of application but that it has an autonomous, binding force.

A first problem with the purposive strategy is that to seem acceptable the inferred "purpose" must be formulated in very general terms. This makes it appear sometimes in the form of a "general principle of law accepted by civilized States", as referred to in Article 38(1)c of the ICJ Statute.[110] Inasmuch as these are not natural principles, they seem

---

[106] See e.g. ICJ: *Reparation for Injuries Case*, Reports 1949 p. 182; *Namibia Case*, Reports 1971 pp. 31–33 (§§ 53–57).

[107] See e.g. ICJ: *Temple Case*, Reports 1962 p. 34; *Rann of Kutch* Arbitration, XVII UNRIAA pp. 569–570.

[108] See e.g. ECHR: *Wemhoff* Case, Ser. A 7 p. 23 (§ 8); *König* Case, Ser. A 27 p. 30 (§ 88) and *ibid.* Matscher, sep.op., pp. 45–46. See further *infra* ch. 6 n. 262. On the object and purpose test, see also *infra* ch. 5.5.2.

[109] See e.g. McDougal-Reisman (Macdonald-Johnston: Structure and Process) pp. 121–129; Higgins (Reisman-Weston: Toward) pp. 79 *et seq*, 83–89.

[110] The reference to "general principles" was included in the Statute of the PCIJ in order to avoid *non liquet* situations. See e.g. Hudson (Cour Permanente) pp. 193, 618–620; *idem* Harvard Legal Essays 1934 pp. 136–137; Sørensen (Sources) pp. 123–126 *et seq*. See also

justifiable only as a kind of international policy whose ultimate validity lies in its (hypothesized) acceptance. Because of the relative difficulty to argue about such principles in a tangible fashion, their use by the ICJ has been marginal and restricted to invoking procedural standards of fairness or self-evidence.[111]

It is clearly more common for the purposive view to express itself in a generalized call for equity. This appears in the practice of reconciling important interests of a State or a part of its population so as to arrive at the most efficient interest-fulfilment for all. The standard examples are the *Anglo-Norwegian Fisheries* Case (1951), in which the interests of Norwegian fishermen were held a determining consideration[112] and the *Fisheries Jurisdiction* Cases (1974) where the Court's discussion focused on achieving a balance between British and German "historic" interests and Icelandic "preferential" interests.[113]

Natural resources law seems completely dominated by purposive considerations. In the *North Sea Continental Shelf* Cases (1969) the Court explained that continental shelf law required that delimitation be undertaken by "equitable principles".[114] In the *Tunisia–Libya Continental Shelf* Case (1982) equity was stretched to become the very goal of maritime delimitation:

> The result of the application of equitable principles must be equitable . . .
> The equitableness of a principle must be assessed in the light of its usefulness of arriving at an equitable result.[115]

Lauterpacht (Function) pp. 83–84, 85 *et seq*, 115–118 and generally *Koskenniemi*, XVIII Oikeustiede-Jurisprudentia 1985 p. 117 *et seq* and notes therein. See also *infra* ch. 6.2.

[111] For some procedural principles invoked by the Court, see e.g. *Administrative Tribunal of UNESCO* Case Reports 1956 p. 85; *IMCO Maritime Safety Committee* Case, Reports 1960 p. 153; *Northern Cameroons* Case, Reports 1963 p. 29. See also generally *Münch* 31 ZaöRV 1971 p. 712 *et seq*. Though the court has failed to make *express* references to its Statute, many of its arguments disclose a reference to something which is neither treaty nor custom. I have elsewhere treated such arguments as involving references to general principles. *Koskenniemi* XVIII Oikeustiede-Jurisprudentia 1985 p. 123. Cases outside the ICJ in which illustrative reference to general principles has been made include *B.P. v. Libyan Arab Republic* (1 August 1974), 53 ILR 1979 pp. 328–329; Iran-US Claims Tribunal: *Oil Field of Texas Inc. v. Iran* (7–8 December 1982), 69 ILR 1986 p. 581. For the use of general principles to interpret a treaty, see ECHR: *Golder* Case, Ser. A 18 p. 17 (§ 35).

[112] ICJ: *Anglo-Norwegian Fisheries* Case, Reports 1951 p. 133. See also *Grisbadarna* Case, XI UNRIAA p. 161.

[113] ICJ: *Fisheries Jurisdiction* Case, Reports 1974 pp. 22–30 (§§ 50–69).

[114] See ICJ: *North Sea Continental Shelf* Cases, Reports 1969 pp. 46–47 (§ 85).

[115] ICJ: *Tunisia–Libya Continental Shelf* Case, Reports 1982 p. 59 (§ 70).

Similarly, in the *Gulf of Maine* Case (1984), a Chamber of the Court observed the indeterminacy of the law applicable to the delimitation of a single maritime boundary. The Parties were bound by neither "general" nor "special" law between them.[116] Everybody, however, agreed on the "fundamental norm", worded by the Chamber as follows:

> ... delimitation must be based on the application of equitable criteria and the use of practical methods capable of ensuring an equitable result.[117]

There is a significant ambiguity in the Court's use of equity.[118] For it may be taken to express a wish to arrive at the most "just" solution for all the parties concerned. Such an idea of equity would be based on a substantive theory of justice. But if it were assumed that this theory be "objective" so as to provide determinate legal justification, it would fail to respect the principle of subjective value and coerce States by a norm which would not reflect their wills or interests (subjectively understood). If it did not assume the objectivity of this theory, it would lack justification for using it. In the North Sea Cases, the Court took pains to demonstrate that the equity it had in mind did not coalesce with allocating "just and equitable shares" – a doctrine expounded by the Federal Republic of Germany. This was, the Court noted, a "matter of abstract justice" with which the Court could not concern itself.[119] Therefore, I have assumed that the Court's equity is in fact a purposive strategy which aims at giving effect to the concrete wills and interests of all parties concerned in the form of a cost-benefit analysis aiming at the most efficient (and in this sense the most acceptable) solution.

---

[116] ICJ: *Gulf of Maine* Case, Reports 1984 pp. 303, 312 (§§ 124, 126, 155).

[117] *Ibid.* p. 300 (§ 113). For the Parties' near-identical formulations, see *ibid.* p. 295 (§ 99).

[118] For a criticism of the "arbitrary" character of the Court's use of equity, see *Gros*, diss. op. ICJ: *Tunisia–Libya Continental Shelf* Case, Reports 1982 pp. 151–156, *Oda*, diss. op. *ibid.* p. 157, *Evensen*, diss. op. *ibid.* p. 296. For the "factors" held relevant by the Court, see *North Sea Continental Shelf* Cases, Reports 1969 pp. 50–52, 54 (§§ 95–98, 101D); *Tunisia–Libya Continental Shelf* Case, Reports 1982 pp. 60–75 (§§ 72–107). The Court's identification and evaluation of the factors is particularly illustrative in the *Gulf of Maine* Case, Reports 1984 pp. 273–278, 326–328 (§§ 44–59, 192–196). For criticism, see *Gros*, diss. op. *ibid.* pp. 378–380 (§§ 30–32) *et seq.*

[119] See ICJ: *North Sea Continental Shelf* Cases, Reports 1969 pp. 20–22, 48 (§§ 15–20, 88). See also ICJ: *Tunisia–Libya Continental Shelf* Case, Reports 1982 p. 60 (§ 71). For the doctrine of *infra legem* equity generally, see e.g. *Akehurst* 25 ICLQ 1976 p. 801; *Bardonnet* (Mélanges Reuter) pp. 38–39; *Reuter* 8 RBDI 1980–81 p. 178; *Cheng* 8 CLP 1955 pp. 210–211; *De Visscher* (Theory) pp. 366, 120. For a discussion, see further *Koskenniemi* XVII Oikeustiede-Jurisprudentia 1984 pp. 137–142.

But there are three important problems in any such construction. In the first place, if the idea of objective justice is excluded, how can the relevant legislative purpose be discerned? This would require the existence of a rule establishing a hierarchy between the various individual policies involved in law-making. But no such rule exists apart from the formal rule which arose as the direct result of the legislative activity, often an expression of several different purposes. If this rule is indeterminate, there seems to exist no way of objectively ascertaining the overriding policy-consideration which prompted the rule itself. Besides, even if a hierarchy of legislative purposes could be ascertained, such hierarchy could hardly be opposed to a State which does not share it. For in such case we should accept that some subjective policies may override other subjective policies *outside* the scope of agreed rules. This would conflict with the equality of States and the assumed subjective character of value. To apply "goals and values" against a non-accepting State will ultimately assume the correctness of the *objectivist* view about morality – in this case a morality about the constraining force of majority will or general interest. Such objectivism, however, will remain vulnerable to the standard criticisms against naturalism.[120]

Secondly, if abstract purposes – expressed in the search for contextual equitableness – are determining, it is hard to see why formal rules would be needed at all. Problem-solution would become a matter of seeking political compromises. But the point of having rules is precisely to *avoid* going back to the political purposes which motivated them. The purposive strategy will ultimately undermine the Rule of Law.[121] Under it, legal rules have only instrumental value. Recourse to them is justified only so long as they remain instrumentally useful in enhancing the original purpose. At best law would count only as a presumption about equity. But it would lack independent normative force. It is easy

---

[120] As *Levine* (Liberal Democracy) points out, it is not possible to defend a theory of general, objective utility or "public interest" which would go beyond what Rousseau termed "the will of all" on the voluntaristic, liberal premises. At best, such a theory would work simply as a hypothesis about voting behaviour, pp. 65–67. The point is that there is no justification to argue that something is in the State's interests against the State's conflicting view. See further, *infra* ch. 5.1.1.

[121] *Guggenheim* (Lipsky: Law and Politics) points out that it leads into a "negation of the existence of general norms", pp. 25–27. The same point is made by *Gros*, diss. op. ICJ: *Tunisia–Libya Continental Shelf* Case, Reports 1982 p. 153; *idem* (Festschrift Mosler) (noting that the tendency to make equitable compromises threatens the Court's judicial function) pp. 351–358. See also *Oda*, diss. op. *Libya–Malta Continental Shelf* Case, Reports 1985 p. 125 *et seq.* Similarly, *Allott* XLV BYIL 1971 p. 127 *et seq.*

to see that this solution is either utopian (that is, workable only under the assumption that there is an "objective equity" or that States agree about their preferences) or apologist (because it justifies deviance if only this is explained in terms of some conception of equitableness).[122]

Thirdly, the purposive strategy fails to provide protection for rights. As it looks for *general* equity it will allow the overriding of particular sovereignties in case this would provide the greatest overall net benefit. The individuality of the State, its sovereignty, specific cultural character or the individual needs and interests of its population find no protection under it. Clearly, the point of sovereignty is precisely to guarantee a State a sphere of freedom which cannot be overridden even by a general cost-benefit calculation or community opinion about equity.[123] Following John Rawls we should rather think of equity in terms of "fairness" than general utility in order to safeguard the rights of individual States.[124] But this will again lead into embarrassing questions about how to justify our conception of "fairness" so as to avoid the objections voiced against naturalism.

A fourth and final version of the strong view attacks the problem of indeterminacy from another end. Instead of having recourse to an objective natural law or a policy, based on the subjective acceptance by the international community it emphasizes the constructive aspects of legal decision and the autonomous and systemic character of legal concepts.

For Lauterpacht, the legal system controls effectively all the outcomes of legal decision-making. There is a positive duty on the judge (lawyer) to

---

[122] *Bentham* (Fragment) himself points out that under this view, individuals: ". . . should obey . . . so long as the probable mischiefs of obedience are less than the probable mischiefs of resistance . . . it is their duty to obey just as long as it is in their interest and no longer . . ." ch. I, Sect. 43 (pp. 160–161). Many liberal political theorists and lawyers have pointed out that utilitarianism provides no coherent theory of obligation. See e.g. *Simmons* (Moral Principles) pp. 45–54; *Lyons* (Ethics) pp. 122–124; *Dworkin* (Empire) (noting that under utilitarianism any reference to "law" in decision-making serves only to give a false image of neutrality to purposive calculations) pp. 152–155. Non-liberal theorists have noted that the movement to purposive justification in Western-Liberal States will *conflict with* the liberal foundations of that society. Going beyond a formal rule of law undermines and ultimately conflicts with the liberal principles of subjective value and consent. See *Unger* (Knowledge) pp. 92–100; *idem* (Modern Society) pp. 192–233; *Lenoble-Ost* (Droit, Mythe) pp. 146–149.

[123] This point is expressly made by *Gros* against the practice of equitable delimitation, diss. op. ICJ: *Tunisia–Libya Continental Shelf Case*, Reports 1982 p. 153. That utilitarianism fails to provide protection for individual rights (as well as for equality) is the standard argument for rejecting it. See e.g. *Lyons* (Ethics) pp. 124–127; *Dworkin* (Empire) pp. 151–175.

[124] See *Rawls* (Theory) pp. 26–33, *passim*.

decide the cases brought to him, to determine the parties' rights and duties.[125] But exclusionary residual rules – such as the presumption of the freedom of the State – cannot suffice. Contrary to Kelsen, Lauterpacht does not postulate *formal* but *material* completeness of the law, constructed by the lawyer as he proceeds to solve the case. But this construction is neither arbitrary nor based on abstract principles of justice or derivations from the nature of the thing. It is more than an effort to ascertain community consensus or the actual background purposes. For Lauterpacht, legal problem-solution seeks to ensure the unity, consistency and effectiveness of international law as a whole.[126] By using analogy and abstracting general principles from individual rules the lawyer will be able to perceive the law as a coherent, meaningful whole which "is originally and ultimately not so much a body of legal rules as a body of legal principles".[127] These principles express the law's autonomous, systemic "coherence" which ultimately justifies the solution of hard cases.

Ronald Dworkin has recently taken up this thesis. Even in hard cases there is always a legally determined answer. Dworkin's view is based on the liberal principle according to which:

... political officials must make only such political decisions as they can justify within a political theory that also justifies the other political decisions they propose to make.[128]

---

[125] *Lauterpacht* (Symbolae Verzijl) pp. 196–221; *idem* (Function) pp. 60–65. For a criticism, see *Stone* XXXV BYIL 1959 pp. 124–161; *Reuter* (Droit international public) pp. 50–52.

[126] See *Lauterpacht* (Function) pp. 85–88, 100–104 and his discussion of the *Savarkar, Lotus, George W. Cook* and *Behring Fur Seals* Cases, pp. 88–100. To the same effect, see *Bruns* 1 ZaöRV 1929 pp. 29–31.

[127] *Lauterpacht* (Function) p. 102. See also *idem* (Symbolae Verzijl) p. 205. Much of *Lauterpacht*'s work stresses the importance of legal principles in the construction of the solution in a hard case. See *idem* (Private Law) *passim; idem* (Development) pp. 158–172; See similarly (and with express reference to Lauterpacht), *Castberg* 43 RCADI 1933/I pp. 342–367. Similarly, *Sørensen* 101 RCADI 1960/III p. 16. More recently, the same point has been taken up by *Bleckmann* (Aufgabe) arguing that the international lawyer's gap-filling task consists in applying the normative "structures" which can be abstracted from non-controversial individual rules, pp. 50–57; *idem* 9 Rechtstheorie 1978 pp. 151–159; *idem* (Grundprobleme) pp. 199–209. He stresses the function of doctrine in the organization of materials under "Völkerrechtsordnung, Völkerrechtsgemeinschaft, Rechtsinstitutionen und Strukturen der VR" which enable to see law in them. See *idem* (Funktionen) pp. 21–78 (for an extended review of the constructive tasks of doctrine).

[128] *Dworkin* (Taking) p. 87. On the political "duty to be coherent", see further *idem* (Empire) pp. 177–190, 225 *et seq.*

In other words, lawyers have a political responsibility to justify their decisions so that they appear coherent with the decision-making activity (by legislators as well as judges) within the legal system as a whole.[129] If no rule seems applicable, the lawyer must proceed on the basis of a theory of what this continuum of decisions requires. He must use his *background theory* about what it is that links legal activity into a coherent whole of protecting values and, especially, rights.[130] He must construct a theory which *justifies* different rules and practices under some principle.[131] On the basis of such a theory the lawyer can – and must – reach determinate decision. Dworkin is not saying that each lawyer has or should have actually formulated such a theory but rather that any lawyer has, through professional education and experience internalized a view which allows him to perceive legal activity as a meaningful whole and himself as a meaningful agent.[132] This internalized view forms the lawyer's background theory. It justifies the totality of the legal order and the individual practices appearing therein by construing the legal order as an autonomous whole of normative principles.[133]

These principles are neither purely objective (utopian) nor purely subjective (apologist) in the way that the former two variations of the strong view seemed to assume. They are independent from material

---

[129] The metaphors "chain of law" or law as a "chain novel" are illustrative, see *idem* (Empire) pp. 228–238.

[130] The point here is not to discover the goals and purposes actually held by legislators. They are impersonal constructions based on a social theory. See *Dworkin* (Taking) pp. 105–130; *idem* (Empire) pp. 59–69 (for a general criticism of intentionist theories of interpretation) and 114–150. For a recent view according to which the "fundamental principles of international law" should be understood as such constructions, see *Cassese* (Divided) pp. 126–128.

[131] Many modern lawyers have adopted this constructivist stand. See also *Simmonds* (Decline) pp. 23–27 and *passim*, and *MacCormick* (Reasoning) pp. 106–108, 119 *et seq*, 152 *et seq*. See also *Aarnio*'s strong emphasis on the "systematization" task of legal dogmatics and the use of developed systems and general concepts as justifying instruments in legal argument, (Denkweisen) pp. 50 *et seq*, 68–70, 76–77 and *passim*.

[132] The example *Dworkin* gives is that of a trained chess referee who knows the rules of chess and the way players expect these rules to be applied and interpreted. The referee has an idea of the "spirit" of the game, a "theory of chess" which allows him to judge if, for example, a player has engaged in prohibited disturbance of the other's game, (Taking) pp. 101–105.

[133] See further *Koskenniemi* XVIII Oikeustiede-Jurisprudentia 1985 pp. 136–142. For a recent attempt to construct a normative theory of *international* politics on the Dworkinian coherence-view, see *Frost* (Towards) pp. 102 *et seq* and 120–128 (for a listing of a set of "cohering" norms) and 161–180 (for the attempt to reconcile individual rights and State sovereignty in a "constitutive theory of individuality" which for Frost is the best theory justifying both).

justice as well as actual purposes of community members. They are sustained by the legal system's systemic coherence, as perceived by the judge through his background theory.[134]

The fact that reasonable men may disagree does not, according to Dworkin, disprove the idea of a justified solution. It merely shows that they have differing background theories. This does not compel the acceptance of all of such theories as equally valid. They do explain the legal order more or less adequately and are thus more or less correct. Different forms of indeterminacy are only *prima facie* difficulties. They can – and must – be overcome by making a decision which in the best possible way coheres with the legal system as a whole.[135]

According to this view, there exists a "coherent" principle or solution which can be grasped by anyone who only understands the legal system's internal value-coherence correctly. But why should we believe in the existence of such a solution? Can we really dismiss existing disagreements among lawyers or the public in general simply by postulating the existence of "one right answer"? Are we ready to accept the consequence that a majority of doctrines can be treated as simply incorrect because they do not reflect the legal system's coherence in the way that we assume correct?[136] As Hart asks, what purpose is served:

> ... by insisting that if a brother judge arrives after the same conscientious process at a different conclusion there is a unique right answer which would show which of the two judges, if either, is right, though this answer is laid up in a jurist's heaven and no one can demonstrate what it is?[137]

---

[134] *Simmonds* (Decline) pp. 23–24, 26–27.

[135] "... propositions of law are true if they figure in or follow from the principles of justice, fairness or procedural due process that provide the best constructive interpretation of the community's legal practice", *Dworkin* (Empire) p. 225.

[136] *Unger* (Critical) pp. 9–10, 89. The point is that for any legal problem, principles and counter-principles may be produced which serve to make *any* solution possible. Recapitulating this critical insight, *Yablon* 96 Yale L. J. 1987 concludes that it will, ultimately, "cast doubt on the ability of contemporary legal scholarship to explain the laws in much the same way that an earlier generation rejected explanations based on logical deductions from rules", p. 623.

[137] *Hart* (Essays) pp. 139–140, 156–158. See also his criticisms of Pound and Llewellyn on the same point, *ibid.* pp. 133–136. For similar criticism, see e.g. *MacCormick* (Legal Right) pp. 138–139. See also *Aarnio* (Oikeussäännösten) pp. 155–157. *Dworkin* seems to have conceded the critics' point by observing that he was not at all assuming that "coherence" could be validated in the same way as, for example, propositions in natural sciences. He points out, only, that the way in which we discuss normative propositions, and interpretations in particular, is meaningful only on the assumption

In other words, the constructivist view seems vulnerable precisely to the same criticisms which led modern lawyers to reject a pure naturalism: it seems ultimately utopian.

It may be suggested to avoid this *impasse* by laying stress on the determining quality of the unity of the legal profession within which background theories are validated.[138] This would take constructivism close to views emphasizing the audience- or paradigm-dependent aspects of legal argument. But it is quite uncertain whether the reference group of international lawyers, for example, possesses the kind of agreement about background values which this suggestion assumes. The unity of this group is constituted, not by reference to any substantive agreement about values but by its use of legal language the indeterminacy of which was the argument's starting-point. The implausibility of this suggestion derives from its circularity. If indeterminacy expresses itself precisely by the existence of disagreement among lawyers, it is hardly possible to invoke any consensus within that group as a validator of the "most coherent" solution.[139]

None of the four strong versions has been able to explain how decision-making in hard cases would be ultimately covered with justifying legal rules.

Let me summarize and somewhat expand the argument in this section. There existed a weak and a strong version of the attempt to explain why legal decision-making in hard cases is ultimately objective and thus distinguishable from pure politics. The difficulty with the weak version was that it either led into pure subjectivism, and thus destroyed the law/politics distinction or it had to hold a strong view on

---

that some views *are* better (i.e. more "coherent") than other views. (Empire) pp. 76–86, 266–271. But of course, this does not eliminate the more basic dilemma referred to in the text – that is, the problem that if two persons *disagree*, there is no external perspective from which their correctness could be ascertained. And if there is no such perspective, that is, if there is no way to evaluate the correctness of a conception without basing this evaluation on some already existing position on the issue, then there really is no basis to distinguish the choice of the background theory from political choice.

[138] *Dworkin* (Empire) himself tends towards that direction in his account of the pre-interpretative acceptance of a focal concept of law by lawyers which allows them to form a paradigm and work as an interpretative community, pp. 87–94 *et seq.*

[139] The difficulty with theories which seek normative validity from (actual) consensus is, partly, that they fail to indicate a solution when there is no consensus or when consensus is challenged by some material arguments and, partly, that they cannot distinguish between authentic consensus and consensus induced by force or (ideological) error.

the rule containing the limits of discretion. It was only a strong version in disguise.

The problem with the strong version of determinacy was how to count for the objectivity of the second-order solution. While classical legal positivists argued that lawyers have no business to discuss norms which are external to legislated "rules" or, if they discuss them, that such discussion is bound to remain uncontrolled by law, modern lawyers have attempted to envisage discussions about values, interests, purposes or principles as somehow controllable. Lawyers have, as Lauterpacht and Dworkin have argued, a political duty to solve normative problems in a manner justifiable under some general, neutral and objectively ascertainable rule or principle. Inferences from non-written principles, purposive calculations or from an abstract "coherence" remain, however, problematic. Nobody seems to feel sure about what would constitute a persuasive argument in respect of them. Insofar as the Kelsenian residual rule was rejected (and there was good reason to reject it) each of the three remaining variants (the naturalist, the purposive and the constructivist) attempted systemic closure by looking beyond rules to values, policies, goals, principles etc. But they seemed vulnerable to the objection of being political because either apologist or utopian. If concreteness was emphasized, then normativity was lost. If normativity was stressed, then the arguments lacked concreteness.

This dual structure of the discourse was reflected initially in the opposition between naturalist and purposive justifications. Purposive theories attempted to overcome the difficulties in naturalism by linking justification to what States had "accepted" as relevant purposes. In case of dispute about what it was that had been accepted, however, the purposive conception had to create distance between actual acceptance and the purpose in order to provide a solution. But how could it oppose its own interpretation of what was accepted to a State which did not share it? To the latter, such attempt seemed simply like imposing somebody else's values on it. Either the purposive solution rested on a naturalistic theory or it reflected other States' values. The former alternative looked utopian, the latter apologist.

Constructivism avoided this difficulty only provisionally. For in order to justify the constructed background theory ("coherence") and the solution based on it, it would ultimately have to invoke a utopian (e.g. the "nature of law", the "nature" of the interests or values at stake etc.) or an apologist (acceptance of the interests or values) justification. It remained hostage to a similar dilemma as that expressed in the

opposition between naturalism and purposive theories. Peter Goodrich
has well summarized the dilemma of conventional theory:

> On the one hand, it necessarily admits that values, and so also substantive
> questions of meaning, intrude upon and play a role in the history and
> realization of the legal order. On the other hand, the methodological
> exigencies of a unified legal science virtually preclude the possibility of
> any rational examination of the actual manner in which such values and
> meanings affect the realization of the system and so also, in a substantive
> sense, constitute that system.[140]

1.3   The structure of international legal argument: the dynamics of contradiction

The previous section ended in a dilemma. To sustain the distinction
between international law and politics doctrine assumed the former to
be more objective than the latter. It assumed that legal norms could be
both *concrete* and *normative*. The requirement of concreteness related to
the need to verify the law's content not against some political principles
but by reference to the concrete behaviour, will and interest of States.
The requirement of normativity related to the capacity of the law to be
opposable to State policy. But these requirements tended to overrule
each other. A doctrine with much concreteness seemed to lose its
normative nature and end up in descriptive apology. A truly normative
doctrine created a gap between itself and State practice in a manner
which made doubtful the objectivity of the method of verifying its
norms. It ended up in undemonstrable utopias.

In this section I shall outline the structure of international legal
argument which follows from its attempt to contain conflicting ideas.
I shall identify two mutually exclusive patterns of justifying norms
within contemporary doctrine (1.3.1) and then point out in an abstract
and initial way how the dynamics of legal argument follows from the
inability of doctrine to prefer either pattern. It is forced into constant
movement between them (1.3.2). Finally, I shall clarify the distinction I
shall make between the "structure" of international legal argument and
its material outcomes (1.3.3).

---

[140] *Goodrich* 3 Legal Studies 1983 p. 256.

1.3.1   The descending and ascending patterns of justification

There are two ways of arguing about order and obligation in international affairs. One argument traces them down to justice, common interests, progress, nature of the world community or other similar ideas to which it is common that they are anterior, or superior, to State behaviour, will or interest. They are taken as a given normative code which precedes the State and effectively dictates how a State is allowed to behave, what it may will and what its legitimate interests can be. Another argument bases order and obligation on State behaviour, will or interest. It takes as given the existence of States and attempts to construct a normative order on the basis of the "factual" State behaviour, will and interest. Following Walter Ullmann, I shall call these the *"descending" and "ascending" patterns of justification.*[141]

The two patterns – or sets of arguments – are both exhaustive and mutually exclusive. A point about world order or obligation can either be "descending" or "ascending" and is unable to be both at the same time. The former is premised on the assumption that a normative code *overrides* individual State behaviour, will or interest. As a legal method, it works so as to produce conclusions about State obligations from this code. The latter is premised on the assumption that State behaviour, will and interest are determining of the law. If State practice, will and interest point in some direction, the law must point in that direction, too. This view starts from the given existence of State behaviour, will and interest and attempts to produce a normative code from them. Either the normative code is superior to the State or the State is superior to the code. A middle position seems excluded.

---

[141] *Ullmann* (Law and Politics) pp. 30–31. It is easy to see that the opposition between the descending and the ascending bears a relationship to the more familiar dichotomy of deductivism/inductivism. I have preferred to use the less familiar terminology for two reasons. In the first place, the deductivism/inductivism dichotomy connotes, if not strictly logical, at least distinctly "scientific" ways of arguing. The descending/ascending distinction, however, is more a matter of literary style. This manifests the second, more important difference that while it is relatively easy to distinguish inductive and deductive arguments from each other, this is not so in respect of the descending and ascending patterns. It is precisely because we are unable to keep "statehood" and the "international community" fully separate that the two patterns emerge into each other. We can conceptualize "community" only by taking the point of view of the "State" while "statehood" seems thinkable only if one adopts a communitarian perspective. See ch. 7.1. *infra.*

It should not be difficult to recognize the normative/concrete opposition in these two argumentative patterns. The descending pattern privileges normativity over concreteness while the ascending pattern does
the reverse. Under the descending pattern, law becomes effectively
constraining. Justification is not received from mere factual power but
from normative "ideas" called rules. Under the ascending pattern, the
justifiability of rules is derived from the facts of State behaviour, will or
interest. The patterns oppose each other as they regard each other too
subjective. From the ascending perspective, the descending model falls
into subjectivism as it cannot demonstrate the content of its aprioristic
norms in a reliable manner (i.e. it is vulnerable to the objection of
utopianism).[142] From the descending perspective, the ascending model
seems subjective as it privileges State will or interest over objectively
binding norms (i.e. it is vulnerable to the charge of apologism).[143]

Consequently, international legal discourse cannot fully accept either
of the justificatory patterns.It works so as to make them seem compatible. The result, however, is an incoherent argument which constantly
shifts between the opposing positions while remaining open to challenge
from the opposite argument. This provides the dynamics for international legal argument.

1.3.2   Indeterminacy as contradiction

Raymond Aron expresses the common experience that international
legal argument is somehow contradictory:

> La permanence des contradictions, les objections valables contre
> n'importe quelle théorie, prise en elle-même ou dans sa portée politique,
> s'expliquent, me semble-t-il, par le caractère ambigu et, d'une certaine
> manière contradictoire du droit international et de "société internatio-
> nale" dont il est l'expression.[144]

Legal problem-solution is premised on the idea that it can produce
determinate results. Of course, it is recognized frequently that in a
situation X the norm N was applied although the norm N^1 was applied
in a previous, but similar case.[145] Thus "humanitarian considerations"

---

[142] This is typically the content of positivist criticisms of naturalism.
[143] This is typically the point of naturalist criticisms of positivism.
[144] *Aron* (Paix et Guerre) pp. 707 and generally 704–712.
[145] This is evident in the most various areas of the law. In her survey of arbitral practice
regarding awarding of damages, for example, *Gray* (Remedies) points out that nearly

were considered relevant in the *Corfu Channel* (1949) and the *US Military and Paramilitary Activities* (1986) Cases but dismissed in the *South West Africa* Case (1966). Economic factors were determining in the *Anglo-Norwegian Fisheries* (1951) and *Fisheries Jurisdiction* (1974) Cases but were held irrelevant in the *Tunisia–Libya Continental Shelf* (1982) and the *Gulf of Maine* (1984) Cases.[146] And so on. Reasons for such variations are, however, sought from extrasystemic factors, semantic uncertainty, change in law, incompetence of judges, political preference, or variations in the legal-philosophical outlook of judges (their adherence to positivism or naturalism) for example. Or it may be explained that in fact X was not similar to the earlier case although it *prima facie* seemed so.[147]

It is also commonly recognized that the openness of legal language causes contradiction in argument. One man's "aggression" is another's "self-defence". It is pointed out that although most countries use the available legal vocabulary, the meanings they attach to central expressions such as "equality", "humane treatment" or even "State" vary to a great extent. It has even been argued that the sense of words such as "law" and "State" in European, African, Arabic, Chinese and Indian cultures differs to the extent that even the possibility of mutual understanding seems excluded.[148]

---

any possible principle of compensation may be supported by arbitral precedent, pp. 5 *et seq*, 45–46.

[146] See ICJ: *Corfu Channel* Case, Reports 1949 p. 22; *US Military and Paramilitary Activities* Case, Reports 1986 pp. 113–114 (§ 49); *South West Africa* Case, Reports 1966 p. 34 (§ 49); *Anglo-Norwegian Fisheries* Case, Reports 1951 p. 133; *Fisheries Jurisdiction* Cases, Reports 1974 p. 30 (§ 70); *Tunisia–Libya Continental Shelf Case*, Reports 1982 pp. 77–78 (§ 107); *Gulf of Maine* Case, Reports 1984 p. 278 (§ 59).

[147] See also *Floum* 24 Harv.ILJ 1983 p. 279. The contradictory ways that precedents can be distinguished so as to support what anybody needs to support is a recurring theme in critical writing. See e.g. *Kairys* (Kairys: Politics) pp. 12–17. On the manipulability of the international legal system, see also *Onuf* (Onuf: Lawmaking) pp. 77–78, 80–81 and generally *de Lacharrière* (Politique) *passim*, and e.g., pp. 96–101 (on contradictory principles), 182–187 (on inconsistent justification). See further *Chaumont* (Essays Lachs) (noting the pressure of contradictory ideas in central concepts of international law) pp. 55–64.

[148] *Bozeman* (Multicultural) points out that: "... unless it can be known what meanings the terms "order" and "law" might carry in each of the states currently composing the world society, it will be impossible to understand any of the local governments on their own merits, to structure relations between different governments, or even to assess the factors that might make, or not make, for a reliable world order", p. 18. She points out that the very concept of "law" is a Western product, based on ideas about individualism and progress, pp. 34–49. In many other societies – such as Black Africa – law plays only a marginal role in social organization. *Ibid.* pp. 140–160, 85–120. Similarly,

Nevertheless, legal thought locates such problems as taking place in the *fringe areas* of the law or emerging from different cultural, linguistic or other backgrounds. The assumption remains that if only everybody "spoke the same language" the indeterminacies would be cleared.[149] Whatever uncertainty there might be about some particular application or interpretation of the law, the legal system itself is coherent, or at least it is possible, by the use of consistent principles, to make it appear so.[150] If only subjective backgrounds and interpretation would be excluded, then full determinacy would follow.

But my argument is not the fairly truistic one that different people tend to mean different things even when they use the same language. My point is that even if semantic or evaluative indeterminacies were cleared, the international legal system as a whole would still remain indeterminate. It would still lack the capacity of providing coherent justification. For indeterminacy follows as a structural property of the international legal language itself. It is not an externally introduced distortion. The legal system itself is, as another critic has put it:

> ... indeterminate at its core, in its inception, not just its applications. This indeterminacy exists because legal rules derive from structures of thought, the collective constructs of many minds, that are fundamentally contradictory.[151]

principles applicable in Moslim or Hindu cultures are far removed from Western ideas of international law, *ibid*. pp. 81–82, 125–132. Thus, she argues, even if non-Western cultures have assimilated a Western legal vocabulary, this has not been accompanied with the acceptance of common meanings. See also *ibid*. pp. 70–97 and *passim*, and *idem* Grotiana 1980, p. 65 *et seq*. The same point is made also by *Stone* (Visions) pp. 4–6; *Gould-Barkun* (Social Sciences) p. 148.

[149] For *Bleckmann* (Funktionen), it is precisely the task of legal doctrine to construct a metalanguage which will guarantee the completeness of the legal system, p. 21 *et seq, passim*.

[150] For a critical discussion of the way in which international doctrine has attempted to explain international law as a "complete system" through its use of the domestic analogy, see *Carty* (Decay) p. 13 *et seq, passim*. His argument is that States exist in a "state of nature" with only scattered rules here and there to govern their conduct. On the immensely influential fiction that law itself is rational and coherent, see generally *Lenoble-Ost* (Droit, Mythe) pointing out that the very purpose of legal reasoning is to ensure – through the use of logic, symmetry, hierarchy and order as well as the stylistic devices of harmony and elegance – the law's internal coherence, pp. 150–160, 175–186, 248–251.

[151] *Gordon* 36 Stanford L. R. 1984 p. 114. The strategy of "revealing" contradictions within legal argument and tracing them back to more fundamental distortions in our ways to conceptualize human nature and social life is a common theme of recent critical writing. Among the most influential is *Kennedy* 28 Buffalo L. R 1979 p. 205 *et seq*.

International legal discourse is incoherent as it incorporates *contradictory assumptions* about what it is to argue objectively about norms. This gives rise to conflicting legal arguments and the inability to prefer any of them.

On the one hand, we assume that the law's objectivity lies in its normativity, its capability to constrain even those who do not wish to be constrained by it. The law is external to State behaviour, will or interest. If the law were unable to constrain States in this fashion, it would be pointless. So, we adopt the descending pattern to justify our norms.

But a purely descending argument is vulnerable to the objections we have voiced against pure naturalism. For if law bears no relation to what States have accepted, it must be assumed to exist as a natural morality, an objective theory of justice. This conflicts with the principle of subjective value. But we cannot simply start assuming that values are, after all, non-subjective without this engendering consequences which themselves seem unacceptable. For if values are non-subjective, then we lose the justification behind the Rule of Law.[152] Legal rules would be justifiable only as instruments of natural justice, clarifiers of what objective morality requires in some specific context. We would have no basis to argue something as law merely because States have so willed or behaved or because it is in their interests.

Another possibility would be to assume that though the law is based on its subjective acceptance, we do not need every State's acceptance at any given time. This would seem to preserve the descending character of our justification while making it possible to identify law without having to assume that values are objective. It may simply be general consent that counts. But this position violates sovereign equality. It is important to notice that sovereign equality is not just another norm which may, if necessary, be overruled by other considerations. Sovereign equality is a

(identifying the opposition between individualism/altruism as the "fundamental contradiction"). See further e.g. *Heller* 36 Stanford L. R. 1984 p. 173; *Michelmas* Nomos XXVIII pp. 73–82 and, in particular, *Unger* (Knowledge) p. 13 *et seq*. For a review of this strategy in recent critical writing, see *Hunt* 6 Oxford JLS 1986 pp. 20–28. For a defence according to which there is no contradiction, only complexity, see *Johnson* 36 Stanford L. R. 1984 pp. 252–257; *Dworkin* (Empire) pp. 273–274. The strategy of revealing contradiction has been fruitfully used in a study of international legal discourse by *Kennedy* 23 GYIL 1980 (sovereign authority/community membership as the controlling contradiction which is transformed into the different opposing doctrines at other levels of argument), pp. 361–362 *et seq*.

[152] See generally *Unger* (Knowledge) pp. 67 *et seq*, 92–93.

consequence of the view which holds that values are subjective. If values are subjective, then there is no (objective) justification to make a difference or to overrule sovereign choice. Any such attempt will immediately appear as unjustified coercion.

Therefore, we need an ascending justification, a link to the subjective acceptance of the State against which we apply the law. This seems the only way to guarantee that the law we apply is objective in the sense of being concrete, that is, unrelated to a material theory of justice. Only an ascending argument can give expression to the principles of the subjectivity of value, freedom of the State, sovereign equality and the Rule of Law. But the point is, of course, that if it is subjective acceptance which counts, then we lose the law's normativity. If we need the State's acceptance, then we cannot apply the law on a non-accepting State.

Thus, *we cannot consistently prefer either set of arguments.* Adopting a descending pattern will seem political and subjective either because it assumes the existence of a natural morality or because it creates an arbitrary distinction between States. An ascending pattern will seem political and subjective because it cannot constrain at all. It simply accepts as law whatever the State will choose to regard as such at any moment. Both must be included in order to make law seem objective, that is, normative and concrete and, as such, something other than politics.

The standard strategy of reconciliation is recourse to *tacit consent.*[153] That is, we assume that though the law can be justified only by subjective acceptance, no *present* acceptance is needed for its application. The norm is binding because the State had agreed by means of conduct, an anterior statement, during the *travaux préparatoires*, or the like. This seems to preserve the law's concreteness while maintaining its normative force. But this reconciliation is a failure. Much of the substance of this study goes to show why it is so. Suffice it here to point out, briefly, that acceptance *cannot* be invoked against a State denying it without assuming either 1) that the law-applier "can know better" what the State has agreed to or 2) that there is some non-acceptance-related criterion whereby we can judge whether acceptance is present or not. Both points involve assuming an objective theory of justice; the former under the guise of "objective interests", the latter by reference to a naturalistic theory of good faith, reasonableness, or the like. Both are vulnerable to the objection about utopianism.

---

[153] See further, *infra* ch. 5.1.2.

Reconciliation is impossible. This results from the way both sets of arguments are based on the assumption that they overrule each other. Moreover, this is their *only* distinct sense. The point of making a descending argument is that it can override subjective acceptance. To make an ascending argument is to assume that subjective acceptance can overrule any alternative justification. The arguments are meaningful only in mutual exclusion. Therefore, each attempted reconciliation can be ultimately made to reveal itself as simply self-contradicting or in fact preferring the ascending or descending argument and unacceptable as such.[154]

The dynamics of international legal argument is provided by the contradiction between the ascending and descending patterns of argument and the inability to prefer either. Reconciliatory doctrines will reveal themselves as either incoherent or making a silent preference. In both cases, they remain vulnerable to criticisms from an alternative perspective. But this perspective, once forced to defend itself, will fare no better. Consequently, doctrine is forced to maintain itself *in constant movement from emphasizing concreteness to emphasizing normativity and vice-versa* without being able to establish itself permanently in either position.

Different doctrinal and practical disputes turn out as transformations of this contradiction. Any doctrine, argument or position can be criticized because either utopian or apologist. The more it tries to escape from one, the deeper it sinks into the other. This will explain why familiar disputes keep recurring without there seeming to exist any way of disposing of them permanently. Law is contrasted to discretion, "positivism" to "naturalism", consent to justice, sovereignty to community, autonomy to organization and so on.

The result is a curiously incoherent doctrine which is *ad hoc* and survives only because it is such. It retreats into general statements about the need to "combine" concreteness and normativity, realism and idealism which bear no consequence to its normative conclusions. It then advances in an *ad hoc* manner, emphasizing the contextuality of each solution – undermining thus its own emphasis on the general and impartial character of its system. Reflection on "theory" or doctrine's own assumptions is excluded because of the frustration it creates and the inability to do anything about it. The doctrine's own contradictions force it into an impoverished and unreflective pragmatism. On the one

---

[154] My argument on this point is strongly influenced by *Kennedy* (Structures).

hand, the "idealist" illusion is preserved that law can and does play a role in the organization of social life among States. On the other, the "realist" criticisms have been accepted and the law is seen as distinctly secondary to power and politics. Modern doctrine, as Philip Allott has shown, uses a mixture of positivistic and naturalistic, consensualistic and non-consensualistic, teleological, practical, political, logical and factual arguments in happy confusion, unaware of its internal contradictions.[155] The style survives because we recognize in it the liberal doctrine of politics within which we have been accustomed to pressing our political arguments.

The contradictions outlined in an abstract way give theoretical expression to the common feeling that international law is somehow "weak" or manipulable. One rule or argument seems to justify mutually opposing solutions. The same solutions are regularly justified by reference to contradictory arguments or rules. This feeling is ultimately explained by the *contradictory nature of the liberal doctrine of politics.*[156] In situations of uncertainty (hard cases) we are thrown back into having to argue both what the law's content is and why we consider it binding on the State. To avoid utopianism, we must establish the law's content so that it corresponds to concrete State practice, will and interest. But to avoid apologism, we must argue that it binds the State regardless of its behaviour, will or interest. Neither concreteness nor normativity can be consistently preferred. To seem coherent, individual

---

[155] *Allott* XLV BYIL 1971 pp. 100–105, 113. He links the "hotchpotch" character of standard writing in international law (drawing on the examples of Hall and Gidel) to: "an underlying structure of thought and argument which is more literary than scientific and more businesslike than concerned", p. 79. This he traces back to the "British tradition" of political and academic argument which expects a great deal of cooperative spirit, good faith and, above all, a common framework of recognition ("conceptual scheme") in the reader, pp. 95–98. Allott's analysis is delightful and intelligent and has a great deal of persuasive force. It sheds light on the way standard international legal discourse is much more structured by stylistic convention than by material content. Here also lies its intuitive acceptability. But my attempt here is to proceed deliberately in "bad faith" – to ask the imprudent "why?" and "what then?" in order to get behind this stylistic consensus into the controlling assumptions.

[156] See generally *Unger* (Knowledge) pp. 63–103. Liberalism's internal contradictions have frequently been the subject of analysis. Among the most useful is that by *Levine* (Liberal Democracy), arguing that liberal political theory contains two separate strands: 1) the postulate of individual freedom and 2) a programme for collective decision. The strands are contradictory. Any political decision infringes individual freedom as liberalism cannot consistently define "freedom" otherwise than as absence of (collective) constraint. For a review of the two strands, see pp. 16–32 and *passim*. See also *Macpherson* (Democratic) pp. 24–38 *et seq.* Much of the present work is inspired by such "internal" criticisms.

doctrines, arguments or positions will have to appear as if they laid stress on one or the other. But they will then remain open to challenge by valid legal argument from the opposing perspective. The weakness of international legal argument appears as its incapability to provide a coherent, convincing justification for solving a normative problem. The choice of solution is dependent on an ultimately arbitrary choice to stop the criticisms at one point instead of another.

In other words, my argument is that international law is singularly useless as a means for justifying or criticizing international behaviour.[157] Because it is based on contradictory premises it remains both over- and underlegitimizing: it is overlegitimizing as it can be ultimately invoked to justify any behaviour (apologism), it is underlegitimizing because incapable of providing a convincing argument on the legitimacy of any practices (utopianism).

1.3.3 The structure of international legal argument

One possible conclusion from an acceptance of these criticisms would be to think of legal decision-making as wholly irrational. If legal argument is understood capable of rendering any justification needed, then we seem to have renounced altogether the view of law as a structured discourse. But such conclusion would seem strongly counter-intuitive. It would fail to address the fact that legal arguments do tend to form patterns and that there is a limited set of arguments which can acceptably be invoked to justify a solution. Only certain arguments are acceptable while others are not.[158]

Legal concepts and categories do have a degree of autonomy which cannot be explained simply by reducing them to apologies for class interests or ideologies. To understand the law we need to count for this autonomy, the persisting intuition that legal argument somehow follows a logic which is external to lawyers' preferences or those of their social group.

Now, I have suggested that international legal argument does have an internal logic, a structure which is expressed in the opposition of the

---

[157] *Fishkin* Nomos XXVIII has made the argument that as it cannot uphold its own vision of objectivity, liberalism faces a legitimation crisis, pp. 207–231. See also *MacIntyre* (After Virtue) pp. 244–255.

[158] The patterned character of legal argument is also stressed by *Allot* XLV BYIL 1971 pp. 102–105.

descending and ascending patterns. This, I maintain, will explain the intuitive feeling that there is an autonomous legal reasoning, that legal argument is not simply an arbitrary aggregation of preferred solutions. However, this is not to say that such patterns would be normative. In the first place, they could simply give expression to a predictable interplay of such factors as ideologies, political opinions, the judges' role-perceptions, professional habits etc.[159] Secondly, and more importantly, they could also manifest a Court's attempt to *avoid material solution which would prefer either concreteness or normativity*.

Let me state the following hypothesis: The argumentative patterns which can be extracted from the practice of the ICJ, for example, do not provide material justification for solutions to legal problems. The argumentative structure is there only to avoid openly political rhetoric. But alone, it leads nowhere but into the *constant opposition, dissociation and association of points about concreteness and normativity* of the law. There is no end to this, however. The discursive structure is only a form of making arguments. It is not one for arriving at conclusions. In order to be defensible, each argument (doctrine, position etc.) will have to appear as both concrete and normative. But as concreteness and normativity are conflicting notions, it is possible for anyone wishing to challenge the argument to interpret it so as to be coherent and manifest only either one or the other. This will allow the critic immediately to

---

[159] It has been argued by an influential member of the Court that the judges' professional backgrounds bear an important effect on their behaviour at the Court. See *Fitzmaurice* (Gross: Future) pp. 467–469. The political election procedure is said to strengthen the effect of these "extralegal" factors, See e.g. *McWhinney* (Festschrift Mosler) pp. 571–572; *Prott* (Culture) pp. 32–33. On the much-belaboured point about the judges' opinions seldom differing from those of their home State see e.g. *Suh* 63 AJIL 1969 p. 224 *et seq*; *Schachter* (Festschrift Mosler) pp. 817–819; *idem* 178 RCADI 1982/ V, pp. 69–75; *Rosas* 108 JFT 1972 pp. 237–270.The argument that the deviations in the practice of the ICJ result from the Court sometimes adopting a positivist, sometimes a naturalist outlook and following certain opinion-leaders in this has been made by *Hussain* (Opinions) *passim*, and p. 73 *et seq*. To me, his analysis grossly simplifies both naturalism and positivism and fails to see why they are both indeterminate as such. The cases he cites to support a positivist outlook (*Fisheries Jurisdiction, Hostages* and *Aegean Sea Continental Shelf* Cases) may equally well be explained from a naturalistic perspective precisely because the two outlooks need to rely on each other. See *infra* ch. 5. Nothing material follows from adopting a "positivistic" or a "naturalist" argument. Moreover, his analysis seems to give too much weight to individual judges' views. This is not to say that opinion-leaders would not exist. See *Prott* (Culture) esp. pp. 45–52. Their views, however, cannot be credited with more consistency than the ideas which they profess to represent. Cultural and ideological backgrounds work in more subtle ways.

come up with a point about its ultimately apologetic or utopian character. Here lies the dynamics of international legal argument.

I have distinguished between the *formal structure* and the *material outcomes* of international legal argument. I shall argue that the structure or form of the international legal argument is indeed determinate in that it follows certain recurring patterns – a constant dissociation and association of arguments about normativity and concreteness and an attempt to avoid material solution. To this extent, international law has a structure. Not all arguments can be succesful within it. This explains why familiar doctrinal disputes keep re-emerging and why legal arguments within courts, diplomatic discussions and scholarly treatises are constantly patterned into familiar relations of association and opposition. "Positivism", "sovereignty" and "consent" do belong together in a stylistically recognizable manner. So do "natural law", "community" and "purpose". This is so even if neither of such sets of concepts suggests anything by way of solving any normative problems.

I shall argue, then, that law is incapable of providing convincing justifications to the solution of normative problems. Each proposed solution will remain vulnerable to criticisms which are justified by the system itself. Morover, depending on which of the system's two contradictory demands one is led to emphasize, different – indeed contradictory – solutions can be made to seem equally acceptable.

No coherent normative practice arises from the assumptions on which we identify international law. However, neither the demand for concreteness nor the requirement of normativity can be rejected without at the same time rejecting the idea that law is different from politics by being more "objective" than this. My suggestion will not be to develop a "more determinate" system of legal argument. Quite the contrary, I believe that lawyers should admit that if they wish to achieve justifications, they have to take a stand on political issues without assuming that there exists a privileged rationality which solves such issues for them. Before any meaningful attempt at reform may be attempted, however, the idea of legal objectivity – and with it the conventional distinction between law, politics and morality (justice) needs to be rethought.

1.4 Outline of the book

In the bulk of this work I shall attack the idea that international law provides a non-political way of dealing with international disputes. I shall do this by illustrating the functioning of the contradiction between the ascending and descending arguments about international law in different doctrinal spheres. In each, legal argument will appear structured by the way *lawyers try to maintain and defend their position* by making *other* positions seem subjective and political because either apologetic or utopian. However, each position is ultimately capable of being so classified and thus vulnerable to the corresponding objections. A position which establishes itself by criticizing alternative positions as utopian will *by that very movement* reveal itself as vulnerable to the objection of being apologist. And *vice-versa*.

I shall first clarify the assumptions behind this argumentative structure by linking it more closely to the liberal doctrine of politics. This takes place within an explication of doctrinal history as a continuing construction of strategies for reconciling the ascending and descending arguments (chapter 2). Thereafter, I shall operate a synchronic cut into present-day doctrine by outlining four possible strategies for dealing with the ensuing tensions (chapter 3). After these initial chapters I shall describe the functioning of the contradiction within the doctrines of sovereignty (chapter 4), sources (chapter 5) and custom (chapter 6). I shall link the doctrinal controversies in these areas with the way in which doctrine portrays the conditions of world order and its own project (chapter 7). A final section will expand the criticism into the field of method and outline a vision for an alternative way to look at problems concerning the international normative establishment (chapter 8).

Doctrinal history: the liberal doctrine of politics and its effect on international law

In order to grasp the structuring effect of the descending and ascending patterns of arguing about international order and obligation I shall relate them to the liberal doctrine of politics which emerged between the 16th and 18th centuries as an attempt to escape the anarchical conclusions to which loss of faith in an overriding theologico-moral world order otherwise seemed to lead. The demand for intellectual autonomy which started out as an epistemological break with scholasticism in natural sciences and philosophy led quite logically into a demand *for political* liberty.[1] And full political liberty seemed incompatible with society.

The fundamental problem of the liberal vision is how to cope with what seem like mutually opposing demands for individual freedom and social order. The liberal attempt to tackle with this conflict is by means of reconciliation, or paradox: to preserve freedom, order must be created to restrict it.[2] There is, in other words, an ascending, individualistic argument: social order is ultimately legitimate only insofar as it provides for individual freedom. And there is the descending, communitarian argument: individual freedom can be preserved only if there is a normatively compelling social order. This reconciliation rests on the Rule of Law: a legitimate social order is one which is objective, one that consists of formally neutral and objectively ascertainable rules, created in a process of popular legislation. The more the order is neutral and ascertainable (that is, the more it is normative and concrete) the better the freedoms (as mediated through legislation) can be guaranteed.

---

[1] On this "spill-over" effect of the epistemological break, epitomized in the work of Descartes, Newton and Locke, into politics, see especially *Spragens* (Irony) pp. 55–90 and *passim*.

[2] Or, as *Kielmansegg* (Volkssouveränität) puts it: "Herrschaft vom Ideal der Herrschaftslosigkeit zu legitimieren", p. 231.

If objectivity showed itself an illusion, this reconciliation, and the justification of liberalism, would collapse.[3]

In this chapter I shall discuss the emergence of an international legal *épistème* which is structured by the (liberal) effort to explain freedom and order as compatible notions. I shall begin with a general character-ization of liberalism and how it applies in international relations (2.1). Then I shall outline a non-liberal doctrine of international law as it was present in early Christian writers (2.2). To counter the problems inher-ent in the early doctrines a body of "classical" scholarship emerged in mid-18th century. This was structured by the attempt to integrate a descending and an ascending argument into itself and thus to escape the twin dangers of utopianism and apologism. I shall pay particular atten-tion to 19th century "professional" doctrines against which modern international law constituted itself. My argument is that modernism created its own identity by adopting one-sided interpretations of the professionals. Once the modernist interpretations are set aside, it will become possible to see present-day discourse as only so many variations of the classical-professional theme of reconciliation (2.3).

In discussing the transition from early to classical doctrine my con-cern is less historical than structural. I shall not look for the causes for the emergence of the classical doctrine in any political, economic or other "factual" developments. My intention is to operate vertical cuts into these two structures of thought so as to demonstrate what was taken as given and what was held as problematic within them.[4] I shall attempt to expose their rules of formation, the conceptual structure which explains the outcomes and specific doctrines adopted. I shall not only

---

[3] Quite a few political theorists have discussed this basic tension within liberalism. My discussion is especially influenced by *Unger* (Knowledge), in particular pp. 6–12, 29–144; *MacIntyre* (After Virtue) esp. pp. 6–108, 244–255; *Levine* (Liberal Democracy) *passim*; *Macpherson* (Possessive) *passim*, and *Spragens* (Irony) *passim*. For an identification of the tensions within the liberal-capitalist society's systems of economy, rationality and motivation and their contribution to a "legitimation crisis" in such society, see *Habermas* (Legitimation) esp. p. 33 *et seq*; *Taylor* (Philosophy) pp. 248–288.

[4] For such study of early scholarship, see *Kennedy* 27 Harv.ILJ 1986 pp. 1 *et seq*, 12–13. The distinction between history (diachrony) and structure (synchrony) is basic in structu-ralist thought, *de Saussure's* (Course) project was explicitly directed against earlier, exclusively diachronical linguistic studies. These, he held, were unable to explain the process of signification, p. 79 *et seq*. *Lévi-Strauss* (Structural), too, insisted upon the distinction between history and anthropology, understanding his own work in the latter field as having to do with culture's signifying, relational aspects, pp. 1–27. For a general discussion of this opposition and the presuppositions it involves, see *Heller* 36 Stanford L. R. 1984 pp. 133–155.

describe particular arguments but try to reconstruct them in their inter-relations, in what made the aguments seem coherent in the eyes of the contemporaries. This is not to say that I would consider early and classical writing in complete isolation from each other. On the contrary, I shall contend that the classical *problématique* can be understood only if we understand how classicism arose as an attempt to overcome the internal tensions of early doctrines.[5]

Nor is my concern biographical. I shall not try to find out in which respect a classical writer may belong to the early school or *vice-versa* or occupy a majority or minority position within them. The point is to attempt to understand the system and each position within it, as it were, "from the inside" without immediately accepting the interpretations or classifications of later lawyers – to construct each doctrine in its *best possible terms* to see why contemporaries could participate in it and see it as coherent and meaningful.[6]

---

[5] The "bracketing" of history in structural analyses has frequently been criticized, espe-cially by the political left, as involving conceptualism and positivism and disregarding historical "context". But the criticism really misses the target as the point is not to do away with diachrony altogether, only to have regard to the distinctiveness in each and thus *avoid* the reductionism inherent in sacrificing one for the other. See also *Arnaud* Arch. de philo. du droit 1968 pp. 273, 285–293. It is important to realize that the opposition early/classical-modern international law is not intended as a causal-historical explanation but as one giving a synchronic focus on a restricted totality of legal materials.

[6] As pointed out above (Introduction, n. 2), such method bears a relationship to what *Foucault* has dubbed "archaeology". See, in particular (Archaeology) p. 135 *et seq.* It differs from regular "history of ideas" in three respects: First, it does not treat its objects ("discursive formations") as manifestations of something else – history, politics, sociol-ogy, "tradition", authorial intent etc. It treats them as autonomous subjects, capable of being studied in themselves, in their "system of dispersion" which constitutes their being, pp. 31–39, 138–139. Second, such study "brackets" history as chronology, succes-sion of events or ideas, a "stream of consciousness". For it, a "period" is not a temporal but a discursive principle. It may unite discursive units widely separated in time as well as contemporaneous with each other. It "suspends the theme that succession is an absolute: a primary indissociable sequence to which discourse is subjected by the laws of its finitude", p. 169. Thirdly, and most importantly, it does not "try to restore what has been thought, wished, aimed at, experienced, desired by men in the very moment at which they expressed it in discourse", p. 139. It seeks not to describe what people have thought or felt but "to define the positions and functions that the subject could occupy in the diversity of discourse", p. 200. It describes discourse as a code for combining and dissociating ideas, not as a means for communicating them. It contains no claim to represent what somebody has thought "correctly" – not even what people in general may have thought. It is concerned with the principles which make thought possible. Indeed "nothing would be more false than to see in the analysis of discursive formations an attempt at totalitarian periodization, whereby from a certain moment and certain time everyone would think in the same way", p. 148.

2.1   The emergence and structure of the liberal doctrine of politics

The idea that social order should be based on the subjective consent of individuals is the most fundamental claim of the liberal tradition. Behind it stands the great epistemological break:[7] where know-ledge about ideas and facts had formerly related to these ideas and facts themselves and meaning had been discoverable in their name, knowledge now became a social product and meanings external to the ideas or things to which they belonged.[8] The ensuing uncertainty could only be disposed of by establishing a knowledge-producing pro-cess in a meaning-generative (name-giving) consensus in the State.[9] This enabled understanding political power as creative, not merely declaratory. Instead of an objective, pre-existing order, liberal con-sciousness created a projected order, constantly relative to its place of projection, the State.

A number of assumptions were entailed: a liberal psychology stressed the essential separateness of individuals from each other[10] and

---

Nevertheless, there are important differences. One relates to my use of the "funda-mental contradiction" as a unifying principle, or theme in discourse. (Compare *ibid.* pp. 149–156.) Though my analysis seeks description, it is not the kind of disinterested description implied by "archaeology". For the object is a political discourse which cannot but be affected by the analysis of its internal tensions. The description of the functioning of the contradiction entails also an internal criticism of the discourse (a criticism based on its own, not on externally introduced principles). In the tension which provides the unity of the discourse lies also the potential – if not for undoing the contradiction – for extending the discourse, developing it so as to achieve alternative legitimating principles. Second, while archaeology seeks to study and compare a wide range of discursive practices, I have had to limit myself mainly to scholarly discourse (compare *ibid.* pp. 157, 160–165). Undoubtedly, analysis of diplomatic discourse, or administrative organization relating to foreign affairs would have provided a more powerful statement of the laws governing international legal discourse. For obvious reasons of time and space, this has not been possible. Yet, even the idiosyncratic totality of scholarly discourse may provide at least an opening towards a comprehension of the peculiarity of diplomatic and administrative practices, too, at least inasmuch as they are legitimized by reliance on the liberal doctrine of politics.

[7]   There are, of course, many definitions of liberalism. They make usually some reference to the ideas individual autonomy, voluntarism, personal liberty, capacity of choice, human diversity and individualism. For one sympathetic characterization, see e.g. *Salvadori* (Liberal Democracy) pp. 17–35, 50–51.

[8]   Of the mass of literature on this subject, see e.g. *Spragens* (Irony) pp. 18–49 and *passim*.

[9]   See also *Navari* (Donelan: Reason) pp. 102–112.

[10] On liberalism's "atomistic individualism" (a view which denies social determination of individuality) see e.g. *Pateman* (Political Obligation) pp. 24–36, 134 *et seq*; *Levine* (Liberal Democracy) pp. 45–48, 74–75, 83–90; *Unger* (Knowledge) pp. 81–83; *Taylor* (Philosophy) pp. 187–210.

a liberal morality stressed the arbitrariness of value[11] and assumed that there existed harmony between freedom and reason: Out of the separate decisions of individuals would emerge a social order which necessarily reflected the separate ends and interests of each individual in the best possible way and which everybody therefore had good reason to agree with.[12]

In the liberal vision, there is no natural, objective social order which would pre-exist the human being's entry into it. Therefore, it is constantly in need of legitimation. The legitimation doctrine of popular sovereignty is two-sided: On the one hand, it stresses each individual's personal freedom to decide on his political preference. On the other hand, once these preferences are ascertained, the political order is sovereign to carry them out to the exclusion of deviating preferences – once legitimate, its decisions can no longer be protested against. In other words, political order is normatively constraining because it is based on the concrete wills and interests of individuals.

"Liberalism", like any other political doctrine, has meaning only insofar as it differs from other doctrines. Its identity rests, in this sense, on the distinction which it created between itself and what went before it. To understand liberalism, we must focus on the mechanism whereby this distinction was made.

---

[11] *On* the principle of "arbitrary value" in liberal theory generally, see U*nger* (Knowledge) pp. 76–81 *et seq*; *MacIntyre* (After Virtue) pp. 6–35. For the origins of this political irrationalism in early liberals' frustrated efforts to create a moral science which could attain the same kind of certainty as had been attained in natural sciences, see *Spragens* (Irony) pp. 196–255. On the moral objectivism of early liberals and the tension this created with their voluntarism, see *Shapiro* (Evolution) pp. 42–47 (Hobbes), 105–106 (Locke); *MacIntyre* (After Virtue) pp. 229–231 (Hume). See also generally *MacIntyre* (Whose Justice?) pp. 281 *et seq*, 326–348.

[12] This is perhaps best reflected in the idea of the "invisible hand" but liberals have generally extended the application of this idea (that the maximization of each individual's self-interest would be best for general interest) beyond economic theory to morality (in particular, utilitarianism) as well. Inasmuch as rational political behaviour is thought in terms of each individual having the legitimacy of pursuing his own needs, interests or values, it is difficult to see what other theory apart from the "invisible hand" liberalism could use to provide a programme for government without entering into contradiction with itself. On liberalism's difficulty to provide a coherent theory of human action, see *Levine* (Liberal Democracy) pp. 71–89. See also *Unger*'s (Knowledge) discussion of the effect of the separation of instrumental and practical rationality (moralities of reason and desire) on personality in general, pp. 55–59 and *passim*.

2.1.1   The structure of liberalism

For medieval thought, "order" was a natural state of affairs, existing by the force of creation and discoverable in the natural arrangement of things and men through faith or *recta ratio*. If doubt arose, it could always be dismissed by appeal to the Church's or the Emperor's authority.[13] Behind this authority stood the Christian idea of a *civitas maxima* which both legitimized and constitutionalized it.[14] Different institutions exercised powers in a system of mutual control, each submitted to legitimation proceeding "downwards" from the highest commands of divine law. Political order participated in the general arrangement of things in nature as well as in society, not yet differentiated from each other. It was visible in the hierarchical systems of loyalty between levels of society, accompanied by oaths of allegiance the network of which was sanctioned by Christian ideas of justice.[15]

The political organization of the State had not freed itself from the structures of civil society. The liberal distinction between the private and the public was singularly absent.[16] Consequently, the opposition which we now perceive between freedom and order is irrelevant, non-existent in medieval thought: Society was not seen as a system of antithetical, juxtaposed individuals. Order was a system in which all participated – neither for their own nor for the order's sake but for the achievement of moral or divine purpose. Medieval consciousness united the pursuits of individual and society. There was no individual freedom, no private realm which would have independent legitimacy as against the world at large. If there was freedom, it was allocated from above and retrievable at

---

[13] On the Pope's supreme authority to interpret divine and natural law, see e.g. *Schiffer* (Legal Community) pp. 15–29.

[14] To scholastic thought, the idea of a monarch's absolute power was alien. For example, Charlemagne's authority was understood to be delimited not only by divine and natural law but also by custom. See *Carlyle* (I) esp. pp. 210–292; *Ullmann* (Law and Politics) pp. 57–59; *Lessnoff* (Social Contract) pp. 15–17. On medieval "constitutionalism" (especially between 10th and 13th centuries), see *Carlyle* (III) pp. 30–74; *Hinsley* (Sovereignty) pp. 21–29. On the egalitarianism inherent in the medieval discourse about the State, see *Cassirer* (Myth) pp. 98–105. For a discussion of why the idea of the monarch's absolute authority *could* be received in Byzantic and Islamic theory and why it could not emerge in the political conditions of Europe in the Middle Ages, see *Hinsley* (Sovereignty) pp. 45–69. For early attempts at formulating absolutist theories in Europe, see *von der Heydte* (Geburtstunde) pp. 59–81.

[15] See e.g. *Carlyle* (III) p. 19 *et seq*; *Dennert* (Ursprung) pp. 8–11.

[16] See e.g. *Hinsley* (Sovereignty) pp. 15–22.

any time. It was not a personal "right" but rather a competence or an authorization to do what was necessary.[17]

The dissolution of the Pope's and the Emperor's authority was accompanied by a metamorphosis of the feudal community into the State where something like a *suprema potestas* was projected on the national monarch. Theories of secular legislation and political sovereignty emerged in the 13th century[18] and soon these were expressed in diverging demands for political authority which created tension between the estates and the King and threatened medieval constitutionalism.[19] Finally, through the individualistic ideas of the Renaissance and the Reformation a new consciousness was sown. What had been thought of as matters of faith were now seen as superstition. What had been presented as immutable, objective order now appeared – not least in the writings of Machiavelli – as subjective rationalizations of power politics.[20]

---

[17] On the development of the medieval idea of having a "ius", based on Roman law, into the liberal conception of personal "right", see e.g. *Tuck* (Natural Rights Theories) p. 7 *et seq*; *Villey* (Droit) pp. 43–54, 94–154.

[18] Central to medieval doctrine was the view that "all law was basically legal custom and that legislation had only the function of classifying and elucidating that customary law", *Friedrich* (History) p. 43. "Custom", however, must be understood to include Roman and canon law as well. For all these it was common that their authority was derived ultimately from God. See *Ullmann* (Law and Politics) pp. 31–50, *passim*. See further *Carlyle* (III) pp. 45–46. For discussion of the first theories of political sovereignty and secular legislation, see e.g. *Hinsley* (Sovereignty) pp. 69–70; *van Kleffens* 82 RCADI 1953/I pp. 27–39; *Dennert* (Ursprung) pp. 13–14; *Sauer* (Souveränität) pp. 16–20; *Scott* (Law) pp. 343–345; *Suontausta* (Souveraineté) pp. 5–6; *Wildhaber* (Macdonald-Johnston: Structure and Process) pp. 425–426; *von der Heydte* (Geburtstunde) traces the emergence of the idea of the sovereign State at the turn of the 13th and 14th centuries, pp. 41–43.

[19] Nevertheless, the monarch's authority rested divided with the estates and local power-centres in a system of consultation and mutual obligation. In 15th and 16th century France, for example, the King was still unable to change the law without the Parliament's consent and was subject to judicial scrutiny in his affairs. See *Franklin* (Bodin) pp. 1–22; *de Jouvenel* (Sovereignty) pp. 169–185, 1989–196; *Unger* (Modern Society) pp. 158–166; *Dennert* (Ursprung) pp. 16–20.

[20] On the attempt by catholic and protestant thinkers to avoid the consequence of secular absolutism, see *Dennert* (Ursprung) pp. 22–55. The last official document containing the idea of a *res publica Christiania* seems to have been the Treaty of Utrecht (1714) – characteristically also the first document to contain the idea of a balance of power. See *Keens-Soper* (Donelan: Reason) p. 27. For a review of the change from collectivism into individualism and the emergence of the idea of law based on consent in post-renaissance thought, see *Arnaud* (Vorstudien) pp. 288–294.

The collapse of belief in a natural, pre-existing normative code brought with it violent struggle and civil war. If order could not claim external justification, why remain obedient?

Events like the Saint Bartholomew Night massacre in 1572 seemed to convince writers such as Jean Bodin (1530–1596) of the need to provide a new justification for social order.[21] This could no longer rely on transcendental purpose. True, Bodin acknowledged moral ends and natural sociability. Contrary to the Thomistic tradition, however, he received political justification from neither. His political authority – sovereignty – arose from a logical argument: in a community, there could be only one place of supreme authority. As it was supreme, it could not be shared nor divided. If such was lacking, chaos and civil war would ensue.[22] The State's and the sovereign's legitimacy lay in their capacity to provide general security and well-being.[23] A residual divine/ natural law existed to restrict the sovereign's power.[24] But this could not be invoked by citizens.[25] Social order and individual security demanded that the sovereign be accountable only to God. The argument is ascending in that its starting-point lies in the individual's need of security.

There is not much indication that Bodin would have been seriously concerned with the effect of this view on inter-sovereign relations. If social order could be justified only by reference to the sovereign's power to prevent civil war, how could order between sovereigns at all be justified? Bodin did suggest there to exist a kind of *jus fetiale* between sovereigns. In case of outrages against natural law foreign sovereigns

---

[21] For Bodin's intellectual background and the relation of "Six Livres de la République" to his earlier work, see *Franklin* (Bodin) pp. 35–36, 41–53; *Brierly* (Law of Nations) pp. 8–11; *Gardot* 50 RCADI 1934/IV, pp. 558–579.

[22] *Bodin* (Six Livres) L. I, ch. VIII; L. I, ch. IX (pp. 162, 168). See also *Franklin* (Bodin) pp. 23, 50–51, 54–69.

[23] *Midgley* (Natural Law) pp. 111–113.

[24] See *Bodin* (Six Livres) e.g. L. I, ch. VIII (p. 129). See also *Gardot* 50 RCADI 1934/IV, pp. 581–601; *Brierly* (Basis of Obligation) p. 21. As *Friedrich* (History) observes, his conception of *puissance souveraine* already hints at laws being based on sovereign will rather than imposed on the sovereign externally. In any case, it tends to provide the sovereign with the uncontested capacity to interpret divine and natural law, pp. 58–59; *Gardot* 50 RCADI1934/IV p. 612. The same point is stressed by *Scott* (Law I), observing that Bodin ultimately thinks that the views and acts of the Prince are the correct manifestations of divine or natural law, pp. 335–336, 338–339.

[25] This, of course, is simply a consequence of the definition of the sovereign. *Franklin* (Bodin) pp. 70–93; *van Kleffens* 82 RCADI 1953/I pp. 54–56; *Verzijl* (I) p. 258; *Verdross* (Einheit) pp. 14–15.

could resort to enforcement action.[26] These are still medieval, descending arguments. Bodin was unable – or uninterested – in constructing an inter-sovereign law from the sovereigns' need for security and even less from their assumed initial liberty.

The decisive break from medieval argument took place through Thomas Hobbes (1588–1679) who, like Bodin, had lived through a civil war and for whom legitimacy had to be related to the sovereign's power to protect individuals. While his conclusions differed from those of his followers, the structure of his argument is liberal. It proceeds, in seemingly impeccable logic, from the non-existence of a constraining natural law to an (ascending) justification of order by reference to individual ends, associated with a (descending) construction of these ends in terms of an overriding need for security.[27]

For Hobbes, social order cannot be legitimized by reference to transcendental normative ideas. Such ideas are mere projections of individuals' passions and desires. What previous thinkers had regarded as an objective natural law was a set of subjective preferences under the disguise of (false) generalizability.[28] For Hobbes:

---

[26] *Franklin* (Bodin) pp. 82–83; *Hinsley* (Sovereignty) pp. 181–182; *Ruddy* (Enlightenment) pp. 14–15; *Gardot* 50 RCADI 1934/IV pp. 599, 677–679. For Bodin, then, no such "international law" existed which would have had authority independently of natural/divine law. See also *Scott* (Law I) pp. 338–339.

[27] At play in Hobbes' system is a logic under which different sections of knowledge are linked together in a unified science. Hobbes was a great admirer of the advances in natural sciences and believed that knowledge in the moral sciences could be attained by an "analytic-synthetic" method of making inferences from causes to effects. See *Hobbes* (Leviathan) Part II (pp. 85–221). On the holistic and scientistic nature of Hobbes' work generally, see *Goldsmith* (Science of Politics) *passim*, and esp. pp. 1–14, 228–242; *Pateman* (Political Obligation) pp. 37–38. In this belief of creating a truly "scientific" human science he was not alone. See *supra* n. 8.

[28] "For one calleth wisdom what another calleth fear, and one cruelty what another justice; and prodigality what another magnanimity ... etc. And therefrom such names can never be grounds for any ratiocination." *Hobbes* (Leviathan) ch. 4 (pp. 109–110). In other words, Hobbes is a nominalist – for him, "order", too, is not something inherent in but projected on things. For discussion of the scientism behind Hobbes' scepticism, see also *Strauss* (Natural Right) pp. 174–176 and *supra* n. 8. This scepticism leads quite naturally into making a distinction between "law" and "rights" and privileging the latter to the former. See *Shapiro* (Evolution) pp. 60–61. The individual becomes the reference-point of political discourse. *Villey* observes the ascending character of Hobbes' discourse in comparison to that of Grotius: "L'ordre de Hobbes me parait inverse. Chez lui, c'est le droit subjectif dont sont déduits l'ordre juridique et le système des lois juridiques, ce n'est pas la loi qui est première". Arch. de philo. du droit 1968 pp. 220–224, 228. Thus, as *Strauss* points out, the Hobbesian system is "liberal" despite its anti-democratic character, (Natural Right) p. 182. Similarly, *Pateman* (Political

> Good and evil are not objective or unchanging qualities of things but the subjective description of the apparently beneficial or harmful effects of things.[29]

All that natural law indicates is the right of self-preservation and the "right of doing any thing which, in (the human being's, MK) own judgement, and Reason, hee shall conceive to be the aptest means thereunto".[30] In addition, natural law tells what acts are causally related to the achievement of particular objects of desire, for example peace or war. But they do not dictate the choice between the two.[31]

From the absence of a controlling natural law it follows logically that individuals are both *free* and *equal* in a very special sense. There is no standard on which their subjective preferences or their individual worths could be evaluated.[32]

But how can social constraint against free and equal individuals at all be legitimized? The answer seems simple. It can only be legitimized by reference to individual ends. But individual ends differ, indeed conflict. In the absence of overriding principles civil war seems a constant threat. This is the consequence which Hobbes set himself out to avoid. To understand how he avoids it, it is necessary to understand how a binding, normative principle is received by him from apparently non-normative premises. This will also explain the peculiarly non-political character of the liberal argument.

The Hobbesian argument is based on two assumptions, causal and psychological. For Hobbes, human psychology is a kind of automated machine in which passion and desire determine all action and goal-setting.[33] In social life they are transformed into lust for power. The

Obligation) pp. 37, 54–55. Indeed, liberalism and democracy do not necessarily entail each other but may easily come to conflict. See e.g. *Macpherson's* (Life and Times) discussion of the different kinds of social and economic order associable with it, p. 23 *et seq.* See also *Spragens* (Irony) pp. 76–90.

[29] *Goldsmith* (Science of Politics) p. 85. See also generally *idem* pp. 93–128.
[30] *Hobbes* (Leviathan) ch. 14 (p. 189).
[31] *Ibid.* (pp. 189–191). This conception of natural law bears a direct connection with Hobbes' scientist wish to speak of laws only in terms of demonstrable, causal hypotheses and to avoid moral speculation. Such natural laws may be used to impose social organization in that they show the destructiveness of unlimited pursuit for self-interest. See *Strauss* (Natural Right) pp. 169, 179–180; *Pateman* (Political Obligation) pp. 45–49.
[32] See e.g. *Hobbes* (Leviathan) ch. 20 (p. 253), ch. 21 (p. 268). See also *Pateman* (Political Obligation) p. 40.
[33] *Hobbes* (Leviathan) ch. 7 (pp. 118–130). The term "automated machine" is borrowed from *Macpherson* (Possessive) pp. 31–32 and generally pp. 29–46. On Hobbes' mechanistic construction of human nature, see also *Goldsmith* (Science of Politics) pp. 48–83.

human being's appetite is unlimited unlike the goods he has lust for. Hence his natural desire to destroy or submit others – a state of permanent war and disorder.[34]

In the absence of a natural order, the only way to prevent war and to free individuals from constant fear is the institution of a sovereign as a "Mortall God" to whom everybody should be unconditionally subjected. Social order follows then from the simple causal fact that the sovereign has the power to curb the community's internal disruptive tension.[35]

Hobbes' point is that the existence of the sovereign is in the individuals' *self-interest*. The duty to obey the sovereign derives from the sovereign's capacity to protect individuals from each other. The sovereign makes it possible for them to pursue their subjective ends but prevents them from self-destruction. Though there are several ways to establish a sovereign, each of them is, in this sense, consensual, or self-assumed. Hobbes is able to interpret simple submission (even submission before a foreign conqueror) as consent because of his causal-psychological assumption: living under a sovereign is in all circumstances more in a person's self-interest than living in permanent war or fear of war.[36]

It follows that political legitimation loses its *political* character and becomes simply causal.[37] The sovereign need only refer to his overriding physical power, his ability to prevent the *bellum omnium* to justify himself and, moreover, to relate that justification to individuals' ends.

---

[34] *Hobbes* (Leviathan) ch. 13 (pp. 183–189). For discussions of the Hobbesian conception of the precariousness of life in the state of nature, that is, where human psychology can reign unhindered, see e.g. *Goldsmith* (Science of Politics) pp. 84–128; *Pateman* (Political Obligation) pp. 38–45; *Friedrich* (History) pp. 85–87. *Macpherson* (Possessive) points out that the state of nature is a *logical* hypothesis, drawn from Hobbes' perception of his contemporaries, not a historical assumption, pp. 19–26, see also generally pp. 17–46. It works as a discursive principle of coherence. The rest of the discourse seems coherent and justified only if the Hobbesian characterization of the natural state is assumed correct. Only then can life under a Leviathan seem an advance from a previous condition.

[35] *Hobbes* (Leviathan) ch. 17 (pp. 223–228). Hobbes defines the sovereign by his possession of overriding power. If a person held the outward manifestations of sovereignty but lacked the means for controlling the State, he would not be a sovereign. "Order" is indissociable from factual "authority". See also *Onuf* 73 AJIL 1979 p. 245.

[36] *Hobbes* (Leviathan) ch. 17 (pp. 228, 230). For the very wide concept of consent in Hobbes, see also *Pateman* (Political Obligation) pp. 43–46; *Macpherson* (Possessive) pp. 20–21; *Raphael* (Problems) pp. 63–65.

[37] See *Dennert* (Ursprung) pp. 95–100.

The State is no longer the Aristotelian *polis* but a Machiavellian instrument of authority. Politics in the sense of a normative theory of common good is rejected as subjective speculation.[38] Practical reason is transformed from a study of ends into a study of the instrumentalities of power – a descriptive *techne*.[39] Exercise of political power becomes a legal-technical instead of ethico-political matter.

Hobbes moves within an ascending-descending argument. Social order is justified by reference to individual ends, not some pre-existing normative code. The existence of free and equal but separate and egoistic individuals is the ascending argument's starting-point.[40] But this does not mean that each individual's particular wishes should be respected. This would be impossible. So, Hobbes assumes that the "real" ends and interests of individuals coalesce with the existence of a constraining social order and that what these are can be scientifically proved. This argument is received from a psychological assumption and an overriding causality principle. It allows the legitimation of social order in an ascending, even consensual, manner. But it also makes possible the (descending) ascertainment and application of constraint against individual dissenters under *a theory of objective interests*. The ascending argument legitimizes social order by reference to individual ends; the descending (and curiously non-political) argument allows overriding particular individual ends.[41]

Hobbes' sovereign is, by definition, absolutist. The legitimacy of his rule is based on physical power over his subjects. No constitutional

---

[38] This view is constantly restated in liberal writing. Thus *Bentham* (Political Fallacies): "It is by hopes and fears that the ends of actions are determined; all reason does is to find and determine the means." p. 213.

[39] See generally *Habermas* (Theory and Practice) pp. 41–61. *Wildhaber* (Macdonald-Johnston: Structure and Process) traces such instrumentalism back to Bodin, p. 428 while *von der Heydte* (Geburtstunde) finds it present already in Occam and Averroes, pp. 112–117, 179–190. For the transformation from (early) deductivism to (liberal) instrumentalism in legal thought, see *Simmonds* (Decline) pp. 48–60.

[40] On the atomistic individualism, entailed by this manner of looking at the social world, see *supra* n. 10. See further *Shapiro* (Evolution) pp. 284–294 *and passim*, and *Siedentop* (Miller-Siedentop: Political) (noting that the liberal idea of the State projects people as autonomous individuals whose social relations are characterized by their equal submission to it) pp. 57–72.

[41] *Shapiro* (Evolution) points out that Hobbes' concept of science – in particular his assumption that though ends are individual they are not *arbitrary* and that their formulation follows a logic which can be scientifically demonstrated – makes it possible for him to combine a "subjective theory of rights" with a "theory of objective interests", pp. 43–48, 74–75.

restraints on this power could exist. It seemed doubtful for later liberals whether life under such a sovereign was really preferable to, or fundamentally different from the *bellum omnium*. Hobbes' implicit theory of objective interests (that *any* society is better than the state of nature) was challenged as an absolutist apology. But how to retain the idea that social order needed a sovereign whose job it was to prevent individuals from destroying each other while restricting the sovereign's power so that it could not become itself a threat to individuals? Two troublesome modifications were added to the Hobbesian doctrine:

1. increased emphasis on consent;
2. reliance on fundamental human rights or a given distinction between a private and a public sphere.

We have seen that Hobbes was able to use a very wide conception of tacit consent which became indistinguishable from a theory of objective interests. This made it possible for him to make private rights and absolutism co-exist. Locke and Rousseau attempted to give more reality to the former, consensual strand. For them, consent is not only an initial authorization but also a continuing constraint on power.[42] But the argument's structure is preserved, even strengthened: a purely descending vision of natural law is opposed with an ascending-descending argument. The legitimacy of social order rests on its responsiveness to individuals' choices and interests (the ascending point). While Hobbes receives this argument from natural causality and psychology, united in his theory of objective interests, later liberals receive it from a doctrine about fundamental human rights or a given distinction between the "private" and the "public" spheres (the descending point). This allows envisaging limits on sovereign power. It is not enough for sovereignty to be consensually based. It must also in its day-to-day functioning respect individual liberty, envisaged either as "right" or a "private sphere". Otherwise, as J. S. Mill pointed out, social order was continuously in danger of lapsing into a "tyranny of the majority".[43]

The liberal cannot satisfy himself with a purely ascending or a purely descending argument. The former would re-create the danger of civil war – it would lack any binding principle. Hence Locke's problematic

---

[42] See *Rousseau* (Social Contract) Bk I, ch. 6 (p. 60); *Locke* (Two Treatises), Second Treatise, ch. XI (pp. 183–190).

[43] *Mill* (On Liberty) ch. III (p. 120 *et seq*).

distinction between liberty and licence, and Rousseau's argument about "forcing men to be free".[44] Not everybody's will must at every point be respected. There is an implicit theory about what it is that is rational to will. This theory, however, is curiously only implicit. Making it explicit would tend to lose the difference between liberalism and natural ends – oriented medievalism. The only legitimate social arrangement is one which provides for both: it must be ascending in that it is legitimized ultimately by reference to individual ends. It must be descending in that it contains a theory whereby some people's subjective ends can be overruled.

Now, the fundamental rights theory and the distinction between the private and the public spheres not only make liberal theory possible. They also provide threats to it.

The purpose of the fundamental rights theory is to guarantee liberty within social order. If no such rights existed, then the legislature could at any point violate individual freedom in its effort towards utility-maximization. To undertake its task, the fundamental rights doctrine must provide an objective and exhaustive definition of what count as such rights, a definition having priority over any subjective views to the contrary.[45] Rights cannot simply be a matter of legislation because this would lose their "fundamental" character; their task is precisely to restrict legislation. The problem is that there is no agreement on what

---

[44] It has frequently been pointed out that Locke had difficulty to reconcile his theological variant of natural law and his moral cognitivism with his voluntarism. See *Locke* (Two Treatises) ch. XI s. 135 (pp. 184–186). For commentary, see e.g. *Shapiro* (Evolution) p. 102 *et seq*; *Dunn* (Rethinking) pp. 21–33. *Rousseau*, likewise, thinks that liberty is not arbitrary licence, such as that which human beings have in the state of nature. In the social contract, liberty becomes virtually synonymous with social virtue and social virtue is something beyond liberty itself; it is an antecedent moral code which individuals must learn. Learning it will be their "liberty", (Social Contract) Bk II, ch. 6 (p. 83). See also *ibid.* Bk II, ch. 8 (pp. 88–89) and ch. 12 (pp. 99–100). Rousseau also emphasizes the importance of morality and regards autocracy as the best form of government. Bk III ch. 5 (pp. 114–116) and especially Bk IV, ch. 1–2 (pp. 149–154) in which he distinguishes between the (normative) general will and the (non-normative) will of all. See also *Cranston* (Introduction to Rousseau: Social Contract) pp. 40–43.

[45] All the liberals held that there existed limits to what an individual could effectively consent. Consent to being reduced to slavery, for example, was ineffectual because it conflicted with (the non-consensually valid) liberty. *Hobbes* (Leviathan) ch. 14 (p. 192); *Locke* (Two Treatises) Second Treatise, ch. 4 (pp. 127–128); *Rousseau* (Social Contract) Bk I ch. 4 (p. 54). Many have pointed out the difficulty to justify the "paternalist" (purely descending) constraint which fundamental rights provide within the presuppositions about arbitrary value in liberal theory. See e.g. *Salvadori* (Liberal Theory) pp. 42–43; *Habermas* (Theory and Practice) pp. 92–94; *Shapiro* (Evolution) pp. 102–118.

such rights are nor what hierarchy they stand in. The argument from fundamental rights is vulnerable to the same criticism which liberalism directed at other material natural law doctrines.[46] If we assume the existence of a set of objective (descending) fundamental rights, then we have moved beyond liberalism. If we deny their existence, we cannot achieve the reconciliation between freedom and social order. The former is constantly in danger of being devoured by the latter.[47]

Liberalism hides this consequence by keeping its rights theory purely formal – that is, by linking it to an unsubstantiated view of "liberty".[48] This is where it differs from the natural law of medieval theory. Liberalism is no grand political theory.[49] It provides no material legitimation for social practices, no programme to the Government, no ends or values to be pursued beyond the general and formal aim of maximizing liberty. It liberates citizens to look after their subjective interests, while the market-place is left to determine whatever is socially valuable, in economic and in political terms.[50] It maintains the distinction between (material but subjective) morality and (formal but objective) law.[51] But it is precisely by its being formal that it ultimately fails. For if liberalism does not indicate any material rights as fundamental, then it cannot provide the constraint for government for which it was made. The tension between general good and individual right is established in the heart of liberal theory.[52]

Other liberals have attempted to achieve the reconciliation by assuming an essential distinction between the "private" and the "public" spheres ("self-regarding" and "other-regarding" actions).[53] It transforms the subjective/objective distinction and is isomorphous to the differentiations between morality/law, freedom/right, desire/reason and legislation/adjudication. In each dichotomy, the left side expresses the

---

[46] *Simmons* (Moral Principles) pp. 66–68.   [47] *Levine* (Liberal Democracy) pp. 121–138.

[48] From a naturalist perspective, such as *Strauss'* (Natural Right), such rights are no true natural rights at all, pp. 220–226.

[49] *Levine* (Liberal Democracy) p. 14. In a sense, liberalism contains an implicit claim of not being a political theory at all but merely an objective, neutral structure *within* which different political theories may compete for influence.

[50] See *Macpherson* (Possessive) pp. 1–4 *et seq; Strauss* (Natural Right) p. 234 *et seq.*

[51] See also *Habermas* (Theory and Practice) pp. 82–86 *et seq.*

[52] On this tension, see e.g. *Hart* (Essays) pp. 198–222; *Lyons* (Ethics) pp. 124–129. See also *supra* ch. 1.

[53] ". . . there is a sphere of action in which society, as distinguished from the individual, has, if any, only an indirect interest: comprehending that portion of a person's life and conduct which affects only himself . . ." *Mill* (On Liberty) Introduction (p. 71).

postulate of subjective freedom while the right has to do with unfreedom and social constraint.[54] In the private sphere, everybody is entitled to pursue happiness according to one's own (private) value-system and desire. In the public sphere, the Government may interfere as provided by objective law.

But it is easy to see that this construction faces the same dilemmas as the fundamental rights doctrine. To be workable, it must contain a non-arbitrary, substantive theory about how to delimit the private and public spheres.[55] A private sphere determined as such only by legislation is insufficient. For the function of the distinction is precisely to delimit the scope of legislation. But ideas about this matter are historically contingent; there seems little essential in them. Take, for instance, J. S. Mill's attempt to achieve the delimitation through the "harm principle". According to him:

> ... the only purpose for which power can be rightfully exercised over any member of a civilized community, against his will, is to prevent harm to others.[56]

This solution could, in principle, undertake the task of delimitation if what counts as "harm" could be determined in some non-arbitrary way.[57] But this is not possible without entering into contradiction with liberalism's consensual strand. This is easiest to see if we think of harm as violation of interest. There are two ways of determining what acts count as violations of individuals' interests. On an objective argument, some interests are possessed by individuals even when they do not acknowledge them. This was Hobbes' point and was tacitly recognized by Locke and Rousseau as well. But accepting that people can be constrained by the argument that something is "in their interests" requires that we possess a theory of natural, or objective interests, distinguishable from what people want. But a theory of objective interests is a theory of the "natural good" and as such inadmissible under liberalism. For

---

[54] For critical discussion, see e.g. *Singer* 94 Yale L. J. 1984 pp. 40–45; *Unger* (Knowledge) pp. 38–41 ("reason/desire"), 67–69 ("rule/value"), 88–100 (adjudication/legislation).

[55] See generally *Unger* (Knowledge) pp. 72–76; *Levine* (Liberal Democracy) pp. 101–103 *et seq.*

[56] *Mill* (On Liberty) Introduction, p. 68.

[57] For an extended attempt (in the field of criminal law), see *Feinberg* (Harm). Many critics have pointed out the threat to orthodox liberalism posed by the relativity of the notion of "harm". See e.g. *O'Hagan* (End of Law) pp. 108–111; *MacCormick* (Legal Right) pp. 28–30.

liberalism, "interest" can only be the same as "want".[58] But if harm is anything that directs itself against what people want, then there is no determinate concept of harm at all. Quite the contrary, people often want other people to behave in ways in which they do not behave. If the continuing (private) behaviour of some people could count as "harm" (because it directs itself against somebody's wants) then we would ultimately violate the *ratio* of the harm principle itself, namely the purpose of establishing and protecting people's private spheres.[59]

In other words, liberalism contains two *separate* strands which continuously threaten each other. The ascending strand legitimizes political order by reference to individual ends. The existence of natural values is denied. Individuals can be constrained only to prevent "harm to others". But any constraint seems a violation of individual freedom as what counts as "harm" can only be subjectively determined. The descending strand fares no better. It assumes that a set of fundamental rights or a natural distinction between private and public spheres exist to guarantee that liberty is not violated. But this blocks any collective action as the content of those freedoms (either as "rights" or a "private sphere") can be justifiably established only by reference to individuals' views thereof. Collective action becomes possible only by an utilitarian interpretation of the descending argument.[60] But utility conflicts with rights. The system is held together only by the Mandevillian assumption that self-interested behaviour will ultimately be for the greatest benefit of all. To think the system as coherent, or workable, this is what one *has to assume*.

---

[58] See *Levine* (Liberal Democracy) pp. 24, 49, 65–66, 113–114; *Unger* (Knowledge) pp. 67–68. The problem with a definition of interests which does not differentiate between interests and wants is that it makes political discussion about the justice in patterns of want-formation impossible. See e.g. *Lukes* (Power) (arguing for a "three-dimensional view" of power which includes also power to make someone want something which is not in his/her *real interests) et seq.* See also *Benton* (Graham: Contemporary Political Philosophy) pp. 9 *et seq*, 23–33. The dilemma is this: if interests are unrelated to actual wants, the danger of illegitimate coercion will arise; if interests are identified with wants, then we lack a perspective from which to make inter-personal comparisons to decide disputes. See further *Fishkin* (Tyranny) pp. 18–25.

[59] See *Levine* (Liberal Democracy) pp. 105–120. For criticisms of the "private/public spheres" distinction which point out the modern irony in the increased need for governmental intervention to uphold liberal institutions, see *Pateman* (Political Obligation) pp. 129–133, 164 *et seq*. See further *Habermas* (Legitimation Crisis) p. 33 *et seq*; *Unger* (Knowledge) pp. 97–99, 174–188; *idem* (Modern Society) p. 192 *et seq*.

[60] *Mill*'s justification of liberty, too, was dressed in terms of a utilitarian argument. See (On Liberty) ch. II–ch. III and comment by *Levine* (Liberal Democracy) pp. 74–75.

Finally, a word needs to be said about the difficulties in the Rule of Law. According to liberalism, social order is based on the individuals' need of it. Unless they join together, their desires will be thwarted. But their desires will be thwarted also within society unless they can be sure that Government is exercised independently of the desires of those who have been vested with governmental power. It must be exercised in accordance with the Rule of Law, that is, by reference to neutral and objectively verifiable rules.[61] Hence the production of written codes of law with the attempt to create complete and logically organized wholes, accessible to verification by judges and the consequent emphasis on the autonomy of the judicial function. Morals and politics are subjective and, therefore, have no place in the administration of liberal society.[62] If legal rules are lacking, then the liberal metaprinciple of freedom is to be adhered to.[63] But this creates difficulties for: 1) rules are ambiguous and 2) freedoms clash against each other.

In the first chapter, I argued that liberal legal theory has no convincing argument about the objectivity of rule-ascertainment. Interpretation of rules and behaviour rests controversial. Recourse to the metaprinciple of freedom (expressed also in the "harm principle") provides, however, no relief as any solution can, under it, be seen as an illegitimate interference. A metarule would be needed which would allow the ranking of conflicting freedoms (or conflicting interpretations of "harm"). To do this, it should be independent of the idea of "freedom" itself and, moreover, capable of *overruling* subjective interpretations of freedom. But it would thereby institute itself as a natural morality against which the liberal argument legitimized itself.[64]

---

[61] "A free people obeys but it does not serve; it has magistrates but not masters; it obeys nothing but the laws, and thanks to the force of laws, it does not obey men." *Rousseau* (Pléiade, vol. 3, ss. 841–2) quoted by *Cranston* (Introduction to Social Contract) p. 32.

[62] For the institution of the "cult of legality" to organize the "paix bourgeoise", see *Arnaud* (Vorstudien) pp. 294–300. For the role of legal texts to which authority was attributed in a professional-technical – and above all, "objective" – way in the legitimation of the emergent bourgeois order in the 19th century, see also *Goodrich* (Reading) p. 21 *et seq*; *Lenoble-Ost* (Droit, Mythe) (pointing out that a theory of subjective legislation and objective law is forced to accept the myth of the rational legislator) pp. 75 *et seq*, 253–269. See also *Mensch* (Kairys: Politics) (noting that as law was thought to be a matter of rights the judicial function was defined as boundary determination which needed to be objective in order not to violate the rights) p. 24.

[63] For a recent defence of this view, see *Nozick* (Anarchy) pp. 149–182.

[64] Many have pointed out that if there are competing interpretations about the extent of rights, liberal theory really cannot justify privileging one over another without going beyond itself – that is, without assuming the correctness of a metatheory about rights. See *Unger* (Knowledge) pp. 92–94, 97–103; *Kennedy* 21 Harv.ILJ 1980 pp. 302–304.

Modern liberalism has moved on to argue about values or goals behind legislation against which norms could be interpreted and conflicting freedoms (or interpretations of "harm") could be weighed. But to pursue this line liberalism should ultimately contain an external criterion for the scaling of values, independent from the formal Rule of Law. Such scaling is required even at the stage of isolating legislative purposes. In other words, the success of liberal law-ascertainment would require the existence of objective standards allowing the disposal of insecurity in cases of *prima facie* indeterminacy. Assuming that values or goals are objective in the sense that they provide a scaling of subjective liberties entails, however, assumptions which liberalism cannot coherently accept.[65] There is this dilemma: if liberalism preserves its radical scepticism about values, then it cannot ground a coherent problem-solving practice – if it makes reference to the objective nature of some values it will undermine liberty.

2.1.2 Liberalism and international law

What basis is there to claim that the problems discussed in the preceding section have relevance to, or are even somehow responsible for the structure of international legal argument? To be sure, none of the classic liberal theorists showed any particular interest towards international relations or international law. On the other hand, most of them felt that they had to say something about this matter, too. And they did this by adopting the "domestic analogy" – assuming that the principles which they regarded as valid in inter-individual relations could, on the whole, be applied in inter-State relations as well.[66] In a similar fashion modern liberals – Hart, Rawls – too, consider themselves capable of discussing international relations as a mere annex to their overall theory – though it

---

[65] *Unger* (Knowledge) pp. 94–103; *Midgley* (Natural Law) pp. 328–329 and generally pp. 276–327.

[66] For the domestic analogy in liberal theorists, see e.g. *Rousseau* (Social Contract) Bk I, ch. 7 (p. 63) and *Locke* (Two Treatises) Second Treatise, sect. 183 (p. 211). For a comment on the origins of the analogy, see *Brewin* (Mayall: Community) pp. 35–36; *Vinogradoff* (Types) pp. 55–57; *Dickinson* (Equality) pp. 29–31, 49–50, 73, 97–98, 111–113; *Raphael* (Problems) pp. 157–164; *Kosters* (Fondements) (for a review of the analogy in 19th century doctrine) pp. 158 *et seq*, 169–172. See also *Gidel* 10 RCADI 1925/V pp. 554–560. For further useful analysis, see *Walzer* (Just War) pp. 58–63; *Beitz* (Political Theory) p. 74 *et seq*. A link between the analogy and liberalism is expressly made by *Carty* (Decay) p. 88. See also *Weil* 77 AJIL 1983 p. 419.

is not evident why liberals should be entitled to treat such collective
entities as States as simply so many individuals.

For Bodin there existed a residually controlling natural law among
States. For Hobbes there can be none. When he speaks of international
law as a part of natural law he means that it is a means for sovereigns to
attain the objects they desire. The initial analogy is made: States are like
human beings in the state of nature, constantly threatening each other.[67]
The idea of a set of rules binding on a sovereign was irreconcilable with
the definition of the sovereign.[68] But this seems to make nonsense of any
idea of international order. To conceive of order among States you had
to assume either that the initial hypothesis was simply wrong – there was
no natural hostility among States – or that some rules were necessary to
prevent an all-out war. Both ideas were endorsed by later liberals.

Pufendorf and Locke agree with Hobbes; States are amongst each
other in a state of nature.[69] But this does not mean that they would be
engaged in a *bellum omnium*. There exists a natural law which is not
merely instrumentalistic. The problem is how to justify it without falling
back upon the kind of assumptions which had characterized scholastic
doctrine and which, it was assumed, had revealed themselves as
subjective beliefs, not demonstrable by reason. Liberal natural law has
a twofold normative character: On the one hand, it sets States-as-
individuals in a position of "equality, freedom and independence" towards
each other.[70] This follows from the absence of a pre-existing material

---

[67] *Hobbes* (Leviathan) ch. 13 (pp. 187–188).

[68] See *supra* n. 35. See also *Lauterpacht's* 62 RCADI 1937/IV discussion of Spinoza's
construction of international law, pp. 116–118; *idem* VIII BYIL 1927 pp. 89–107.

[69] Both of them argue that the natural state is not simply one of war and thus seem initially
to differ from Hobbes. See *Locke* (Two Treatises) Second Treatise, ch. II sect. 14, ch. VIII
sect. 95, ch. XVI sect. 183 (pp. 124, 164, 211) and ch. III sect. 19 (p. 126). For Locke's
conception of international law generally, see especially *Cox* (Locke on Peace and War)
pointing out the essential similarity of Locke's system with that of Hobbes, despite the
former's communitarian rhetorics, pp. 1 *et seq*, 136–163, 184–195. *Pufendorf* (De Jure
Naturae) takes explicitly issue with Hobbes. For him, natural law orders man to join
society. The rest of its precepts follow as corollaries from this, Bk II, ch. II sect. 3
(pp. 158–159), ch. III sect. 15 (pp. 207–210). Similarly *idem* (De Officio Hominis) Bk I,
ch. III, sect. 8, 9 (p. 19).

[70] *Locke* (Two Treatises) Second Treatise, sect. 4, 95 (pp. 118, 164). For commentary, see
Cox (Locke on Peace and War) pp. 147–151. *Pufendorf* (De Jure Naturae) traces the
origin of society in a natural state of perfect freedom and equality, Bk II ch. II sect 3;
Bk III ch. II (pp. 158, 330–345). He associates this with the situation between nations
and expressly points out that States exist in a natural condition of freedom and equality
vis-à-vis each other, Bk VII ch. II, sect.13 (p. 983); Bk II, ch. III, sect.10 (p. 197). For

morality. On the other hand, it directs States to coordinate their actions in order to avoid the dangers which would accompany life in an unregulated condition.[71] This construction *avoids* falling back into a scholastic natural law as it is purified of material content and simply liberates the State by laying down its primary right (or, sometimes, duty) *of self-preservation*. Each State has the right (and maybe the duty) to do whatever is needed to this effect.[72] The law simply accepts that States are equal and free in the absence of a constraining material code.

Now, anarchy is avoided by the assumption of the "invisible hand". Following one's self-interest will also enhance the general interest. Conversely, self-interest is best enhanced in cooperation. To be sure, States do not always perceive this so clearly. They are tempted by short-term gains. Therefore, specific laws are needed. Though they are binding, they bind in the interests of States themselves. Hume's argument is illustrative: It is self-interest, ultimately, which grounds the binding force of precepts of justice.[73] I must keep my promises because

commentary on Pufendorf's significance to the liberal doctrine of equality of States, see e.g. *Nussbaum* (History) pp. 149–150; *Dickinson* (Equality) pp. 75 *et seq*, 82.

[71] *Locke* (Two Treatises) observes that the enjoyment of natural rights (especially property) in the natural state is "very uncertain and constantly exposed to the invasion of others". Second Treatise, ch. IX sect. 123 (p. 179). It follows, therefore, that the "great and chief end" of men joining in political community is the "preservation of their property", *ibid.* sect. 124 (p. 180). *Pufendorf* (De Jure Naturae), too, points out that man's weakness "made it necessary that he should not live without law". Bk II ch. I sect. 8 (pp. 152–153). The natural peace is "but a weak and untrustworthy thing". Bk II ch. II sect. 12 (p. 176). He, too, grounds Government, not on any transcendental purpose but on the need to protect men's security and wealth. See e.g. *ibid.* Bk VII, ch. I; ch. II, sect 5 (pp. 949–966, 971–973). For commentary on Pufendorf's non-naturalistic (ascending) justification of government (and property), see *Stein* (Evolution) pp. 5–7.

[72] *Locke* (Two Treatises) speaks repeatedly of self-preservation as a "fundamental law of Nature", Second Treatise, ch. III sect. 16 (p. 125). It also overrides any duty towards others. See esp. *ibid.* ch. IX sect. 128, 129 (p. 181). *Cox* (Locke on Peace and War) points out that this principle "permeates the whole of his political teaching ... In short, the 'law' of Nature turns out to be first and foremost concerned with the 'right' of self-preservation and only secondarily or derivatively with a 'duty' to others or a transcendent order", pp. 84–85.

[73] Hume's is a utilitarian justification. "Natural" obligations of justice are those which dictate what is necessary for subsistence and self-preservation. This explains the binding force of conventional legal arrangements. ". . . 'tis only from the selfishness and confin'd generosity of men, along with the scanty provision nature has made for his wants, that justice derives its origin". *Hume* (A Treatise) Bk III sect. II (pp. 536–552). Hume, like Hobbes, is an objectivist in disguise. He assumes that justice may stem from a factual principle of causality: following rules is obligatory because this is in everyone's self-interest. See also generally the discussion in *MacIntyre* (Self-Images) pp. 113–122.

otherwise I shall not be trusted. And it is in my self-interest that I shall be trusted.[74] The argument is ascending-descending. Order is justified by an ascending point about freedom and self-interest. It is maintained through a descending postulate about the ultimate equivalence between particular and general interest.

Later liberals extend this vision into international relations. Sometimes, like in Bentham's "Principles of International Law", the constraining principle is received from the assumption of a "common and equal utility of nations" which is best enforced through enlightened public opinion.[75] Kant's "Perpetual Peace" contains the same idea: the constraining principle is expressed in the moral imperative which lets each State have as much freedom as is compatible with the equal freedom of all other States – an early formulation of Mill's "harm principle". This is possible on two conditions: one, the State itself must become a liberal, republican State and States in general should join in a Federation which both guarantees their inviolability and avoids the natural state of war and enmity.[76]

---

[74] *Hume* (A Treatise) Bk III sect. V (pp. 568–577). In his discussion of the law of nations, Hume assumes that the principles of justice between States arise from equivalent considerations: "the same *natural* obligation of interest takes place among independent kingdoms, and gives rise to the same *morality* ..." However, he believes that the natural obligation of justice – that is, the instrumental value of inter-State arrangements for human subsistence – among States is less than between individuals, *ibid.* sect. XI (p. 619).

[75] *Bentham* (Works II) pp. 537–560. The domestic analogy is explicit. Bentham asks what principles should guide an international lawyer and concludes that these are the same principles which should direct national legislation, pp. 537–540. The overriding principle is general utility, or "the most extensive welfare of all nations on the earth", p. 538. This should also override national interest – though not the primary principle of self-preservation – if only the evil to it is lesser than the net benefit. Bentham assumes that such altruism will be possible if only people are enlightened about foreign affairs – hence his concern with abolishing diplomatic secrecy, pp. 554–560.

[76] *Kant* (Zum ewigen Frieden) pp. 5–18 (introduction to the principle of freedom and moral responsibility) and *ibid.* ch. II (pp. 24–36) (for the organization of eternal peace). The latter starts with the Hobbesian analogy: "Völker, als Staaten, können wie einzelne Menschen beurteilt werden", in particular as regards their hostility in the natural state and the need to preserve maximal freedom within social organization, pp. 28–33. In a general way, Kant assumes peace to be a problem of rational, enlightened choice. A democratic society will develop a "hospitable" mentality among peoples – war becomes an anathema. This idea is shared by much professional discourse. It was assumed that if everyone will have the possibility of thinking out his mind in an uncoerced manner, peace will ensue. This way of thinking of conflict as "error" is evident e.g. in the belief in the ultimately constraining character of (enlightened) public opinion in democratic States. For this point, see e.g. *Root* 2 AJIL 1908 pp. 452–457.

Modern liberals have likewise extended their domestic systems into international relations. Rawls argues that inter-state justice can be based on a hypothetical contract between States. The principles which States would choose in such situation – behind a "veil of ignorance" of their own and others' particular interests, capabilities, wants etc. – would be, he says, "familiar" and would essentially seek to guarantee equality and independence.[77] Hart takes issue with both the "deniers" of international law and those who base its binding force on the existence of sanctions. Neither position is correct. Like in domestic law, international law's validity is simply a matter of the acceptance (by conduct) by States of its rules.[78]

In a sense, the structuring power of liberal ideas in international law is evident already at the terminological level. International order exists to protect the freedom and to enhance the purposes of individual States. To prevent international order from encroaching on State freedom (sovereignty), recourse is had variably to a doctrine of "fundamental rights", a principle of non-interference or a delimitation between matters of (private) domestic jurisdiction and (public) international concern. The Friendly Relations Declaration passed by the UN General Assembly in 1970 is a declaration of liberalism writ large: It constructs international order from (private) State ends; it guarantees each State the right to choose its value-system and to pursue its own ideas of the good to the extent that no harm is caused to other States.[79]

It is clear that sovereign equality, characterized sometimes as the "fundamental premise on which all international relations rest"[80] is a

---

[77] *Rawls* (Theory) pp. 378–379. See also *infra* ch. 5 n. 45. His discussion of international relations is, however, confined to a short introduction into the issue of conscientious objection. For a criticism of the minimal interest in international justice in Rawls, see *Barry* (Liberal Theory) pp. 130–133. For an intelligent elaboration of Rawls' view in international theory of resource distribution see *Beitz* (Political Theory) p. 129 *et seq.*

[78] *Hart* (Concept) (holding international law sufficiently analogous to municipal law, despite its lack of one "rule of recognition". The validity of its rules derive from their being each individually regarded as binding) pp. 226–231.

[79] UNGA Res. 2625 (XXV) 24 October 1970. The Declaration preaches tolerance and pluralism and restates the liberal principles of self-determination, non-intervention, sovereign equality and sovereign cooperation. Two concerns emerge: to delineate a "private" realm for each State and to conceptualize the "public" realm of international life in a pluralistic, coordinating way.

[80] *Cassese* (Divided) p. 130. See also *Brownlie* (Principles) (characterizing sovereign equality as the "basic constitutional doctrine of international law") p. 287 and generally *Touret* 77 RGDIP 1973 (regarding sovereign equality the *Grundnorm* of international law) pp. 172 *et seq*, 183–184.

liberal premise. Or rather, it is not a premise but a consequence of the more fundamental assumption about the non-existence of a pre-existing hierarchy of values.[81] One need not assume more than the absence of a materially constraining natural law in order to conclude that everybody has the sovereign right to decide about his values and that in this respect all are equal. The three ideas – denial of natural law, independence, equality – all presume each other. If one were to show itself untenable, the other two would lose their foundation.

The order which was instituted between sovereigns in the Peace of Westphalia (1648) marks the transition from a Christian view of the world as an objective hierarchy of normative meaning to a historically relative consensus. This was manifested in three ways: It was recognized that even the possible existence of universal values was not a sufficient *casus belli*; secondly, the formal equality of the European sovereigns guaranteed the legitimacy of the internal policies of these same sovereigns; thirdly, the arrangement proceduralized inter-sovereign relations and allowed national interest as legitimate reason of war if only proper formalities were followed.[82] At Westphalia, the sovereigns made a social contract. This involved accepting an ascending and a descending argument about international legitimacy: order was to emerge from the sovereigns themselves and the right of sovereigns to constitute an order of their liking was assumed as "inherent".

[81] The link between the denial of a material natural law and the principles of independence and equality is usefully expressed in *Strupp* 47 RCADI 1934/I pp. 333 *et seq*, 499, 508–509. See also *Gidel* 10 RCADI 1925/V (for equality as a necessary consequence of the absence of a superior code) pp. 546–549, *passim*.

[82] It is customary to date modern international law back to the conclusion of the thirty years war. For standard analyses of the "Westphalia system" of sovereign equality, religious agnosticism and balance of power, see *Westlake* (chapters) pp. 54–59; *Hobza* 5 RCADI 1924/IV (for an express discussion of the links between liberal ideas, the peace of Westphalia and international law) pp. 377–379; *Nussbaum* (History) pp. 115–118; *Gross* 42 AJIL 1948, pp. 20–41. See also *Nardin* (Law, Morality) pp. 57–58; *Mayall* (Donelan: Reason) pp. 139–141; *Cassese* (Divided) pp. 34–38 *et seq*. In his preface to de Martens' "Précis", *Ch. Vergé* summarizes the classical understanding as follows: "... tel fut le principe de l'équilibre européen qui ne se fonde plus ni sur l'identité de croyance, ni sur l'identité de loi, mais sur la solidarité des intérêts, sur la besoin commun de sécurité." (*De Martens* (Précis du Droit International) p. xiii). For a (rather non-analytic) discussion of the effect of reformation thought on international law (with particular reference to the ideas of sovereignty and independence), see *Boegner* 6 RCADI 1925/1 p. 248 *et seq*.

2.2 Early scholarship

I have chosen to call "early scholarship" that discourse which shares the pre-liberal assumption of an objective, universally binding code which pre-exists the human being but is graspable by him through faith or *recta ratio*.[83] This initial assumption entails that the controlling dichotomy faith/sin cannot be problematized within early discourse itself. It will provide the "deep-structural" principle against which early writing can be understood as coherent. It need not concern itself with reconciling the demands of freedom and order or balancing the freedoms of two or more sovereigns. It can simply define these as compatible. The problem of indeterminacy of legal rules is located at the realm of faith and solved by recourse to authority. Only when the sense of disparity between the normative outcomes and the perceived reality became too great, faith could be questioned and a transition to classical discourse could take place.

Among the first features to catch a modern reader's eye in the work of Vitoria (1480–1546) or Grotius (1583–1645) is their assertive tone.[84] Both use a wide variety of authorities, theological and secular, and the latter also haphazardly chosen historical events without discussing their relative authoritativeness. Rather, their authority is taken for granted and no need is experienced to justify the method. So strong is Vitoria's faith in Christian doctrine, for example, that he is able to argue that if there is doubt about the right course of action one's decision should be based on authority rather than on one's reason. Reliance on authority is complete excuse even when the result will show itself erroneous. Moreover: reliance on reason instead of authority would be a sin even if the result were correct.[85]

At the outset it would seem that there is complete difference between Vitoria and Grotius in this respect.[86] For the latter, it is reason which

---

[83] The early doctrine of international law developed, in particular, within the Catholic church from the 13th century onwards. Its sources were originally Canon law and its sanctions religious. See *Ehrlich* 105 RCADI 1962/I pp. 179–224; *Nussbaum* (History) pp. 17–60; *Brierly* (Law of Nations) pp. 2–5.

[84] For commentary, see especially *Kennedy* 27 Harv.ILJ 1986 pp. 5–7. My reading of the early scholars is much influenced by this article.

[85] *Vitoria* (De Indis) sect. I (pp. 116–117). *Cassirer* (*Myth*) (noting that scholasticism holds reason secondary to revelation and revelation identical with opinions in works of Christian authority) pp. 106–115.

[86] For *Vitoria*, the task of demonstrating the content of law was a religious task. For example, his work on the status of American Indians begins as a gloss on St Matthew (De Indis) sect. I (p. 116). Both *Vitoria* (De Indis) sect. I (pp. 119–120) and *Suarez*

emerges as the all-powerful authority: natural law would exist even on the assumption – *per impossibile* – that there were no God.[87] But they portray a similar argumentative structure. All norms, and all legitimate authority is derived from the same source. Whether or not some putative norm is authoritative or an action in accordance with the law are matters which are not decided by recourse to independent legislative authority but by looking at the standard's content; whether or not it correctly reproduces the demands of faith or reason.

Now, "faith" and "reason" are not fundamentally different categories in the early lawyers' argument. Both direct themselves towards grasping a pre-existing normative order in its authenticity – that is, as manifested in unquestioned authority, be this that of recognized theologians or of "better times and better peoples".[88] If language, too, is a part of the world's natural, normative arrangement, then what was said about things and actions by writers or States of authority represented things and actions in their intrinsic quality.[89] This explains their confidence in citing anything that was written as a representative of the normative order. As correct language, that is correct knowledge, was possessed by those to whom the normative order was revealed by faith or reason, it was only natural that what these men had said or done also represented the normative order in its authenticity. It was not that it illustrated the content of that order, it was its very embodiment.[90]

(De Legibus) Preface (pp. 13–14) emphasize the theological character of their writing. See also *Grotius'* discussion of sources in De Jure belli, Prolegomena, §§ 37 *et seq*, 48–51 (pp. 22 *et seq*, 26–28) in which he combines religious and secular authority while leaving the question of their relative precedence open.

[87] *Grotius* (De Jure belli) Prolegomena, § 11 (p. 13). But, of course, he does hold that God exists and repeatedly points out that the law's ultimate source is divine will. Nevertheless, standard interpretation has it that Grotius did cut the ties which related natural law with God. For a Catholic criticism, see *Midgley* (Natural Law) pp. 137–167.

[88] *Grotius* (De Jure belli) was careful to avoid the implication that international law would emerge with present state practice – indeed, he justifies his law precisely as a criticism of the practice which he had perceived around him, Prolegomena *passim*, and § 46 (p. 26). His constant reference to the practice of the Greeks and the Romans is taken by *von Bulmerincq* (Systematik) to make his positive law non-positive, pp. 16–19. A similar method is followed by *Ayala* (De Jure), noting expressly that references to Roman practice are made not because of the intrinsically normative character of that practice but because it was *evidence* of the content of natural law, ch. I (pp. 3–6).

[89] See generally *Foucault* (Order of Things) pp. 34–44.

[90] *Grotius* (De Jure belli) frequently points out that natural law is to be found in the work of men or States to which God had revealed the intrinsic "quality of moral baseness or moral necessity" of actions, Bk I, ch. I, Sect. X (pp. 38–39).

Whether argument refers to God or nature is immaterial to the argument's structure. The faith which links normative conclusions to God and the reason which links them to nature act in a similar fashion. Both assume that obligation is something transcendental and discoverable in immediate reflection or deduction from first principles. In fact, keeping the two apart seems both difficult and, for the conclusions reached, irrelevant. In one way or another, natural law becomes derivation of divine law while the content of the latter makes itself known in the former. Both take argumentative positions in contrast to non-normative, arbitrary will.

Inasmuch as "will" has a normative role to play, it, too, acts in a similar fashion. St Thomas Aquinas (1224/5–1274) explains that man's nature is an indivisible unity of faith, intellect and will within which exists, as innate, the knowledge of natural law.[91] The human being's natural inclination is to act in accordance with the pre-existing normative code of God/nature.[92] The task of intellect is to inform individuals to will correctly and the proper role of will is to will in accordance with intellect. But if faith, intellect and right will are not distinct but merely aspects of the same, innate capacity to know the good, then there can be but one overriding normative code towards which faith, reason and will all direct themselves. Consequently, early writers have no basis on which to make a distinction between two kinds of arguments, "moral" and "legal". A fortiori, the idea that natural law is an objectified camouflage of will is completely alien to such construction. The basis of social order is natural law and the human being's natural inclination to act in accordance with it. Politics is not an attempt to fulfil subjective desires. It aims at the common good which can be identified with the natural ends of human existence.[93]

It follows, then, that the sovereign's authority is not so conceived as to establish a boundary between international and municipal law, either.[94] Vitoria and Grotius experience no difficulty to discuss inter-sovereign

---

[91] See Midgley (Natural Law) pp. 9–15, 18.

[92] In Grotius (De Jure belli), of course, man's innate capacity to know the good is indistinguishable from his essentially social nature, Prolegomena §§ 6–8 (pp. 11–12).

[93] See Midgley (Natural Law) pp. 17–22.

[94] Quite consistently, early scholars assume that men are united by an objective normative code derived from God. See Vitoria (De Indis) sect. I (pp. 120–122); Suarez (De Legibus) Bk II, ch. XIX, sect 9. (pp. 348–349); Grotius (De Jure belli) Prolegomena §16 (p. 15); Bk I, ch. I, sect. X (pp. 38–39) and passim. For this point generally, see Kennedy 27 Harv.ILJ 1986 pp. 15–21 (Vitoria), 40–50 (Suarez), 78–84 (Grotius), 62–65 (Gentili).

relations, relations between the sovereign and his subjects or even family relations by reference to the same or interdependent rules.[95] The Prince's will has no independent authority following from the "inside" of his postulated freedom, no "reserved domain" which would emerge in contrast or conflict to the normative order. His authority is delegated competence, constantly controlled by the normative order.[96] The Prince is an agent of the normative order. As States exist for the attainment of the common good (defined by God/nature)[97] there can exist no sovereign capacity to impose a will which would conflict with the good.

This does not mean that early lawyers would regard all law as "divine" or "natural". On the contrary, elaborate distinctions are made between divine, natural, human and international law.[98] But the point is that though the *content* of the law is not always revealed in divine order or natural reason, its *authority* goes always back to these.[99] The distinctions relate only to the way in which the order manifests itself. A *consensus gentium*, or custom, may be evidence of rules (just as it may be evidence

---

[95] Much has been made by later lawyers of the apparently unitary, communitarian character of the early scholars' law. It is, in particular, emphasized that the *ius gentium* of Vitoria or Grotius is not so much international as inter-individual law, applicable on a universal scale. See e.g. *Remec* (Position) pp. 26–27; *Kosters* (Fondements) pp. 32–33; *Corbett* (Law and Society) pp. 53–54; *Schiffer* (Legal Community) pp. 30–48; *Landheer* Grotiana 1981 pp. 19–27; *Pound* (Philosophy) pp. 76–78; *Lauterpacht* XXIII BYIL 1946 pp. 26–30.

[96] *Suarez* (De Legibus) points out that only a "right and virtuous rule" can emerge as "law", Bk I, ch. I, sect. 6; ch. IX (pp. 24, 106–108, 113, 128). Even such a "moderate" naturalist as *Gentili* (De Jure) holds that "nothing is to be regarded as just (meaning legally allowed, MK) which cannot be desired honorably, without shame, with modesty and with reverence", p. 10. On the limits of the delegation of legislative authority, see also *Midgley* (Natural Law) pp. 356–358. For a review of the idea of sovereign authority as competence allocated and defined by the normative order, see *Verdross* (Einheit) pp. 18–24. See further *infra* ch. 4.

[97] See *Suarez* (De Legibus) Bk I, ch. VII (pp. 90–101).

[98] See, in particular, *Suarez* (De Legibus) Bk I, ch. III, sect. 5–21 (pp. 39–50). For commentary, see *Scott* (Spanish Origins) pp. 90–102; *Trelles* 43 RCADI 1933/I pp. 441–462; *Corbett* (Law and Society) pp. 21–35; *Kennedy* 27 Harv.ILJ 1986 pp. 40–45; *Walker* (History) pp. 152–155. For corresponding distinctions and their hierarchical relations in Thomistic doctrine, see *Midgley* (Natural Law) pp. 2–22, 28–38.

[99] *Grotius* (De Jure belli) Prolegomena, Bk I, ch. XII, sect. 1 (pp. 14–15, 42); *Suarez* (De Legibus) Preface; Bk II, ch. IX, sect 12; BK III, ch. I (pp. 14; 229–230; 362–391). For commentary, see *Verdross* (Verfassung) pp. 25–28; *Hinsley* (Sovereignty) pp. 187–192. *Lorimer* (Droit) points out that Grotius is frequently misunderstood here, pp. 46–50. For the distinction between the ruler (or law) and his (its) authority in Christian doctrine, see *Ullmann* (Law and Politics) pp. 35–36; *Finnis* (Natural Law) pp. 43–44; *Simmonds* (Decline) p. 53.

of God's existence) but it has no independent binding authority. It is not law simply by being a consensus.[100] Later lawyers sometimes overemphasize the importance of these distinctions. Divine, natural, human and international law are only types, or aspects, of the same immanent order. The possibility of conflict is defined away: all law stems from the same source. By definition, then, human law cannot enter into conflict with natural law because if it entered, it would not be "law". *Ius gentium* is proper law, not contract, and therefore not binding simply because willed.

The unity of law and morality is the unity of reason (or revelation) and right will. For Grotius, natural law may be discovered by *a priori* reasoning as well as *a posteriori* evidence.[101] Its deduction from first principles is just as "objective" as drawing inferences about it from sovereign behaviour. This is natural as the sovereign is merely an agent of the normative order.[102]

The unitarian character of early doctrine is visible in its discussion of war. What later lawyers termed the law of peace is only an annex to the just war doctrine.[103] The former has to do with the rights and duties the violation of which constitutes *casus belli*. Early doctrine attempts merely to enlighten Princes about the conditions of just war, the just war being the overriding principle which ensures the unity of the order and structures doctrinal discussion.[104] As we shall see, it was precisely the difficulties with this doctrine which ultimately collapsed the convincing nature of early scholarship as a whole.

The just war doctrine also illustrates the non-existence of the liberal distinction between matters of private morality and public duty. The conditions of just war in St Thomas as well as in Suarez (1548–1617)

---

[100] *Midgley* (Natural Law) pp. 83–87.

[101] *Grotius* (De Jure belli) Bk I, ch. XII, sect. 1 (p. 42).

[102] *Midgley* (Natural Law) argues that there is a (rebuttable) presumption that the Prince's conduct is in accordance with natural (divine) law, pp. 120–121, 228–229. But it is probably more correct to say that there is a *definition* to this effect. If the Prince *violates* natural/divine law, he is not really acting in his (public) capacity as a Prince, see *infra* p. 80.

[103] This is the principal thesis of the impressive study by *Haggenmacher* (Grotius et la Doctrine de la Guerre Juste). According to him, only later imagination could see in Grotius' work the outline for a (modern) international law. On its own terms, the work is simply an exploration of the *iustitia belli*, pp. 615–621. Similarly, *Corbett* (Law and Society) p. 19; *von Bulmerincq* (Systematik) pp. 20–24.

[104] This was often explicitly stated by early lawyers themselves. See e.g. *Grotius* (De Jure belli) Dedication (pp. 3–9); *Ayala* (De Jure) Dedicatory letter pp. i–vi.

include not only external behaviour but also right state of mind. Even if war were outwardly just – that is, waged by legitimate authority for just cause – it would still be objectively unjust if waged with hatred in the Prince's heart.[105] As war is an instrument of the law and not of private vengeance it was necessary to wage it with an impartial mind.

Situations where liberal doctrine would envisage a conflict between private morality and public duty are defined away by seeing duties which conflict with faith as non-duties. Discussing conscientious objection, Vitoria holds, first, that there exists a duty of subjects to follow the Prince to war. This duty extends to cases where there is doubt about the war's justness.[106] But if the subject is convinced of the war's unjustness he ought not to serve in it.[107] The threat that this poses to the order is dealt with by the strong view that subjects in general should not decide this matter themselves but leave it to the Prince's counsellors, assumed to be Christian elders.[108] But if such conviction is genuine – a matter to be decided by the Church's decision as to what is needed to show faith or heresy – it overrides legal obligation, makes such obligation non-existent. This is not an argument for freedom of belief. The unbeliever's private convictions do not ground for him any right.[109] Only genuine Christian faith – even if erroneous in its qualification of a particular fact – can and must override otherwise existing obligation.[110]

Early discourse proceeds by a series of differentiations and definitions which aim at securing that the faith/sin distinction can remain the operative principle. When later lawyers focus on the conflicts which arise from the juxtaposition of *per se* legitimate sovereigns or from the *per se* legitimacy of the sovereign and the demands of the legal order, early scholarship remains unaware of such conflicts. They are simply defined away by the manner in which early lawyers see as crucial the question of the justness of sovereign authority and elaborate on the conditions of such justness with the unquestioned assumption that once correct definitions are reached no conflicts between the Princes or their freedoms and the demands of the legal order can arise. Take first the strategy of excluding conflicts between the freedom of two sovereigns. This is visible in Vitoria's treatment of Spanish rights in America. The

[105] See *Walker* (History) p. 211; *Midgley* (Natural Law) pp. 43–55.
[106] *Vitoria* (De Indis) Second relectio, sect. 31 (pp. 176–177).
[107] *Ibid.* sect. 22 (p. 173). Similarly *Suarez* (De Triplici) sect. VI (pp. 832–833).
[108] *Vitoria* (De Indis) Second relectio, sect. 25 (p. 174).   [109] *Ibid.* sect. 26 (p. 174).
[110] See also *Grotius* (De Jure belli) Bk II, ch. XXVI (p. 587 *et seq*) and comment in *Midgley* (Natural Law) pp. 120–131.

potential conflict between Indian and Spanish sovereignty is defined away by defining the sovereignties as coterminous with each other.[111] Vitoria's discussion is an elaborate exposition of how God had given possession to Indians and what conditions the Spanish must fulfil in order to gain possession rightfully. God had given territory to Indians and thereby established their legitimate authority.[112] Any human attempt to interfere with it is invalid *ab initio*. Claims of the Pope and the Emperor are rejected.[113] It is significant how his treatment of the case differs from that of a modern lawyer's. There are no elaborate definitions of "statehood" – an effort only meaningful if we regard that an abstract category such as "State" is relevant *per se* to infer what rights people have.[114] For Vitoria, "statehood" is no starting-point for normative deductions. It can become such only after legal concepts receive autonomy and legitimacy within a neutral and universally applicable system of such concepts. For Vitoria, the problem was which rights God had given to Indians and to the Spanish.[115] There was no assumption that these rights would be symmetrical or depend upon some formal status vested in the Spanish and the Indians respectively. The asymmetrical nature of sovereign rights is demonstrated also in Suarez' discussion of intervention. If an infidel Prince prevents his population from being converted into Christianity, any Christian sovereign may intervene. But an infidel Prince may not intervene if the Christian sovereign does not allow his subjects to be converted into heretics. Proof of this is that to prevent Christ's law from being accepted does irreparable harm while prevention of other law's acceptance does not.[116]

---

[111] See the commentary in *Kennedy* 27 Harv.ILJ 1986 pp. 24–31.

[112] *Vitoria* (De Indis) sect. I (pp. 116 *et seq*, 120–128). For a similar argument, see *Ayala* (De Jure) ch. II §§ 28–29 (pp. 20–21).

[113] *Vitoria* (De Indis) sect. II (pp. 129–139).

[114] In this respect *Scott* (Spanish origins) misleadingly suggests that Vitoria's argument intended to prove that the Indians lived in a "State", p. 25. Vitoria's as well as Suarez' discussion of statehood relates solely to the identification of lawful Princes and makes exclusive reference to European entities. *Vitoria* (De Indis) Second relectio (p. 169); *Suarez* (De Triplici) Sect. II (p. 808). See also *Crawford* (Creation of States) pp. 5–7; *Midgley* (Natural Law) p. 62.

[115] He states, simply, that the conflict must be solved through "what natural reason has established among all nations", *Vitoria* (De Indis) sect. III (pp. 150–160).

[116] *Suarez* (De Triplici) sect. V (pp. 826–827). See also *Vitoria* (De Indis) on the question of killing for sacrificial purposes or prohibiting of Christian proselytizing, sect. III (p. 159).

Take, then, the strategy whereby conflicts between the normative order and sovereign authority are defined away. As pointed out earlier, the Prince's sovereignty (his "freedom") is defined and controlled by the normative order. The definition works both ways: the normative order is *already present* in the sovereign's public behaviour. As the microcosm is a manifestation of the macrocosm,[117] so also the sovereign's individual actions manifest the content of the normative order in its authenticity.[118] In this, early scholars agree. Sovereign behaviour is significant because it is evidence of the law's content.

But this creates a problem: what to do if the sovereign's acts are *manifestly* contrary to divine or natural law? This can be dealt with by insisting on the definition of sovereign authority as always consistent with the law. A sovereign transgressing the limits of law would not be a sovereign at all – he would be a person acting in a private capacity or worse, a tyrant.[119] To be a sovereign was to act in accordance with the law.

For example, the sole just cause of war was a wrong done.[120] Such wrong was an objective breach of the law, unrelated to any idea of subjective right.[121] The justness of war was unrelated to its defensive or offensive character.[122] If an objective wrong had been committed, then it was the sovereign's task to punish for it. But if a sovereign would start a war – offensive of defensive – without a just cause, he would thereby renounce his sovereign status.[123]

It is easy to see that such construction faces the danger of being hopelessly idealistic in a world where many sovereigns had committed

---

[117] *Foucault* (Order of Things) pp. 25–42.

[118] Sometimes, as in *Ayala* (De Jure) the very extreme consequence is drawn that disobedience is always a sin "and the disobedient can be called an infidel", ch. II § 23 (p. 16).

[119] *Suarez* (Defensio) ch. IV (p. 705). This does not, however, ground an automatic right of resistance – such right being a function of the gravity of the breach, *ibid.* (pp. 706–725, 854–855). See also *De Visscher* (Theory) p. 13.

[120] See *Vitoria* (De Indis) Second relectio, sect. 13–20 (pp. 170–179); *Suarez* (De Triplici) sect. IV (pp. 816–817), sect. VI (pp. 828–831); *Grotius* (De Jure belli) Bk II, ch. I, sect. II (p. 171).

[121] See e.g. *Grotius* (De Jure belli) Bk II, ch. XX, sect. XL (pp. 504–506) and generally *Midgley* (Natural Law) pp. 43–45, 160–163.

[122] *Vitoria* (De Indis) Second relectio (pp. 166–167). *Grotius* (De Jure belli) is, however, closer to the classical position. He makes the point that only defensive war is just – though he admits that "defence" may sometimes require striking first, Bk II, ch. I and esp. sect. V (pp. 169–185).

[123] In *Grotius* (De Jure belli) the unlawful war has the status of private conflict, Bk I, ch. III, sect. I (p. 91).

outrages against clear natural law rules and still continued to remain formally sovereigns. How to cope with this? Early lawyers admitted that it was sometimes difficult to find out what the law said in particular cases. It was emphasized that the sovereigns should study the legitimacy of their actions carefully. But there might still remain doubt as to the right course of action.[124] This applied also to the problem whether a war was just. Therefore, even a sovereign who had committed a breach – for example, started an unjust war – could be *excused* if he only had conscientiously studied the problem before taking action.[125] By thus applying the metarule of faith early lawyers attempted to explain the fact that many sovereigns continued to exist as such even when they had started an unjust war. It could always be presumed that they had started it in good faith – believing that they had just cause.

The same strategy can be illustrated by reference to the problem of whether a war can be just on both sides. For early lawyers, war is no "power-conflict" between legitimate sovereigns but a public procedure against a wrong-doer. The relation of the combatants is that between the judge and the accused.[126] There is no conflict between sovereignties and no symmetry between their positions. A war cannot be objectively just on both sides. If the sovereign erred in making his judgement he may, however, be excused.[127] This does not affect the intrinsic quality of the war as a public procedure. But it absolves the sovereign who had no right cause and explains how he can continue to remain sovereign thereafter.

The obvious weakness in such construction is that excusability could hardly be claimed if the war was manifestly unjust. Significantly, the Spanish theologians do not discuss this matter. For them, military victory or even survival of the manifestly unjust sovereign is unthinkable. Received titles remain illegitimate if gained in an unjust manner and remain provisional until final justice is done.

For Grotius, however, this is unsatisfactory. And so he takes a significant leap towards abandoning the early discourse altogether. In

---

[124] *Vitoria* (De Indis) Second relectio, sect. 21–27 (pp. 173–175); *Suarez* (De Triplici) sect. VI (pp. 828–830); *Grotius* (De Jure belli) Bk II, ch. XXIII (pp. 557–565).

[125] *Vitoria* (De Indis) Second relectio, sect. 58–59 (pp. 186–187) makes this dependent on the gravity of the offence.

[126] *Vitoria* (De Indis) Second relectio, sect. 19, 60 (pp. 172, 187); *Suarez* (De Triplici) sect. VI (pp. 828–830); *Grotius* (De Jure belli) Bk II, ch. XX, sect. XXXVII *et seq.* (p. 502). On the aspect of war as public enforcement, see also *Scott* (Spanish Origins) pp. 43–59, 81–88; *Trelles* 43 RCADI 1933/I pp. 487–531; *Schiffer* (Legal Community) pp. 32–35.

[127] *Vitoria* (De Indis) Second relectio, sect. 32 (p. 177); *Suarez* (De Triplici) sect VI (pp. 828–830); *Grotius* (De Jure belli) Bk II, ch. XXIII (pp. 565–566).

the first place, he allows war for private vengeance in some cases. The right to punish becomes an individual, subjective right.[128] Secondly, and more significantly, Grotius (and Ayala) start to worry about the explanation of laws of war if only one sovereign has a just cause. Grotius now makes the distinction between just war and the formally legal war, the latter being defined by the mere fact that it is conducted by sovereign authority. All wars between sovereigns can be called formally legal and the laws of war are equally applicable in respect of both belligerents in them.[129]

True, Grotius assumes that by their consciences the belligerents remain constrained by the normative order, conserving the dichotomy just/unjust war.[130] But this does not affect the formally legal character of both sovereigns' acts.[131] Hence, also unjust war may produce titles which are legal in the sense that the wronged sovereign's claim remains non-enforceable. Grotius attempts to justify the distinction between non-enforceable (natural) law and formally legal acts by contending that unless the belligerents are treated equally and the question of the justice of the war is set aside, more chaos and suffering will arise – especially as there is no central authority to decide the matter.[132] As natural law generally seeks to avoid chaos and suffering, Grotius assumes, it can include within itself also this construction. The "lesser evil postulate" of natural law allows the incorporation of the formally legal war within it. This construction – which also legitimizes neutrality on the part of third States[133] – remains, however, fragile and demonstrates that Grotius is well on the way to perceiving war as a conflict between formally equal sovereigns and acknowledging – although he did not do this – the need to "balance" the freedoms of sovereigns.

[128] *Grotius* (De Jure belli) Bk I, ch. III, sect. II–III (pp. 92–96) and *ibid.* Bk II, ch. XX, sect. III (pp. 472–475) and sect. XL (pp. 504–506).

[129] *Grotius* (De Jure belli) Bk III, ch. IV (p. 641 *et seq*). See also *Ayala* (De Jure) ch. II, sect. 34 (pp. 222–223) and *Zouche* (Iuris) pp. 32, 112.

[130] *Grotius* (De Jure belli) Bk III, ch. IV, sect. VI (pp. 641–644).

[131] For critical commentary, see *Remec* (Position) pp. 109–113; *Midgley* (Natural Law) pp. 160–163; *Corbett* (Law and Society) p. 211; *del Vecchio* (Humanité) pp. 192–194. See also *Lauterpacht* XXIII BYIL 1946, pp. 5–7.

[132] *Grotius* (De Jure belli) Bk II, ch. XXIII, sect. II (p. 558); Bk III, ch. IV, sect. IV (p. 644).

[133] In a war pursued against a wrong-doer, obviously, neutrality is inconceivable. Grotius is hesitant to go all the way, however. At one point, he assumes that neutral duties persist against all belligerents. In a later passage, he defines neutrality so as to contain the duty only not to aid the wrong-doer. In doubtful cases, however, symmetry seems required. *Grotius* (De Jure belli) Bk III, ch. I, sect. V (pp. 601–605), Bk III, ch. XVII, sect. III (pp. 786–787).

The manner in which early lawyers avoid overlaps or conflicts between a sovereign's freedom and the normative order is perfectly consistent. Any actual conflicts immediately signal injustice. Once it is found what the normative order requires the conflict is solved. The focus of early scholars is not on reconciling, or balancing, freedom and order. These are assumed *a priori* to be consistent and the issue is only to define what is just and what unjust. Once that problem is solved, whatever there is left for sovereign freedom is defined in a correct manner. Such essential distinctions as Prince/tyrant or just/unjust war are relevant only if we assume as given and unproblematic the distinctions between faith and sin, reason and unreason. It is impossible to understand, let alone be convinced by, the early lawyers' argument without these dichotomies. They are no rhetorical attempts to escape the problem of freedom so crucial to later scholars. They are a necessary consequence of a view which assumes that the world is united in its pursuit for the good and whatever is good is found in either revelation or reason. This unity related together human beings, not such abstract entities as States or peoples which, insofar as recognized, were only instruments for a common purpose.

The objection by later lawyers according to which such reasoning is question-begging because everyone has his own idea of the good is meaningful only if we think that values are subjective. This, of course, early lawyers did not think. The faculty of distinguishing objectively between the good and the evil was inherent in human beings. The charge of dogmatism is unfounded inasmuch as early lawyers did admit that it was sometimes difficult to say what was just and what not. Differing views were admitted to exist. But the correct view was assumed to exist, too, and there seemed little reason to think that anyone would know it better than the highest authorities.

This argument could hold only so far as there was no important doubt about the human capacity to know the good. As normative outcomes became increasingly varied, belief in them was shattered.[134] What presented itself as objectivity was increasingly seen as subjectivity. As faith in a singular concept of the just was dissolved, the latent conflict between

---

[134] *De Visscher* (Theory) notes: "... the difficulty ... to reconcile the Christian conception of the unity of the human race with the historical fact of the distribution of power among sovereign States", p. 13. But it is probably not so much this mere fact which was threatening as the kind of *use* of the power which was difficult to reconcile with Christian ethics.

sovereign freedoms or sovereignty and the normative order surfaced. To argue – as Grotius did – that in case of doubt about the justness of war it was best to set the whole question aside is to open the door for admitting that both belligerents may be equally correct in their perception of justice – the conclusion drawn by Gentili.[135] In such case, the primacy of the normative order is wiped away and discourse must start, instead, from the sovereign's assumed subjective authority.

2.3 Classical scholarship

Classicism arose, Midgley writes, from:

> ... almost a methodological doubt about the capacity of any human being, whether ruler or ruled, to judge rightly those matters of fact and law which determine the objective justice or injustice of State policies.[136]

Classicism constructed itself through the distance it made between itself and early writing. Reliance on faith was now understood as utopianism or, worse, dressing subjective opinions in the guise of objective truths.[137] In its self-consciousness and concern for concreteness and method classical writing claimed for itself the objectivity which it denied from early writers.[138] By focusing on the facts of State behaviour, on history and power instead of moral or religious generalities, it seemed possible to delineate a scientific legal study. The task which classical legal doctrine assumed was, in other words, to justify normative order in a concrete fashion: by building it on the equal right of independence and sovereignty – liberty – of each State.[139]

---

[135] *Gentili* (De Jure) Bk I, ch. VI (pp. 31–32).   [136] *Midgley* (Natural Law) p. 189.

[137] "... religion and politics have the same purpose among men; it is simply that at the birth of nations, the one serves as the instrument of the other". *Rousseau* (Social Contract) Bk II, ch. 7 (p. 88).

[138] Indeed, even early classical laywers, whether those usually called "naturalists" or "positivists", feel they have to emphasize the "scientific" character of their enterprise. Among the former, *Wolff* (Ius Gentium) does this by attempting to base international law on a mathematical model. See also commentary in *Nippold* (Introduction to Wolff: Ius Gentium) p. xxvii *et seq*; *Nussbaum* (History) pp. 150–156 (a highly critical view), pp. 175–179.

[139] As in the domestic context, appeal was made to the fundamental rights construction also internationally. Just as this threatened liberal consciousness from the inside (see *supra*, n. 45), it also threatened international legitimacy in a similar fashion. For the argument could now be advanced – and was, in due course, advanced by the moderns – that the fundamental rights were merely another "metaphysical juristic hypothesis". *Corbett* (Law and Society) p. 17. See also *infra* ch. 3 n. 5.

In principle, it is possible to imagine the history of international legal writing as a continuous flow of transformations, or movements, from a descending position to an ascending one and *vice-versa*.[140] The question of the position will normally remain latent. It will emerge only when doctrinal outcomes start to seem unacceptably controversial. This will produce a potential for "paradigm-change" which takes place by isolating a set of assumptions behind "normal science" and projecting them as either apologist (that is, too concrete) or utopian (that is, too abstract).[141] The criticism will contain the seeds of a new perspective which allows the solution of problems inherent or otherwise unresolved in the old position. But from this will emerge different problems which may receive unsatisfactory answers. The perspective needs to be changed again. And so on.

It is important not to associate this model with any clear-cut temporal boundaries or conventional doctrinal differentiations (such as naturalism/positivism, normativism/policy-science approach). I have pointed out, and shall argue, that each doctrine and position needs an ascending and a descending strand within itself. None of the conventional "paradigms" are "essentially" ascending or descending. They are only made to seem so by interpretation, projection from an opposing standpoint. This brings out the interminable character of the process: any controversial solution will immediately allow the criticism that the doctrine which produced it is either utopian or apologist. It is not that solutions seem controversial because they have not been argued well enough. It is because solutions seem controversial that the arguments advanced to support them come to look inadequate.

Classicism projected early doctrines as unacceptable because subjective – that is, either utopian or apologist. Early writing seems utopian because it cannot demonstrate the correctness of its norms. It seems apologist because these norms will bend in any way to suit the Prince.

---

[140] See also *Kennedy* 27 Harv.ILJ 1986 noting the opposition between early and classical positions and the apparent inevitability of modern eclecticism pp. 10–11.

[141] I use the popular vocabulary contained in *Kuhn* (Structure) without thereby implying that Kuhn's analysis – which was originally restricted to natural sciences – could be applied in any automatic fashion in reflecting upon change and development in legal science. For reflection on this point, see e.g. *Aarnio* (Oikeussäännösten) pp. 27–30.

Nevertheless, as will become evident, I *do* think that what I have called "position" or "perspective" is essentially prior to individual perception and analysis or the arguments by individual lawyers in particular (doctrinal or practical) issues. In this sense, the inherited conceptual framework and the assumptions which it contains are responsible, and provide an explanation, for the dynamics of legal-scientific discourse.

Rousseau's criticism of Grotius is well known. Behind a naturalist rhetoric the latter simply offers fact as proof of right:

> It is possible to imagine a more logical method, but not one more favourable to tyrants.[142]

Mainstream classicism does not simply adopt an ascending argument to counter the utopian character of early writing or a descending one to counter its apologism. It is best understood as a process of reconciliation, a constant shifting of perspectives from an ascending to a descending one and *vice versa*. The former is used to guarantee the law's concreteness, the latter to secure its binding force. The identity of classicism, on its own terms, against early writing depends on the incorporation of both perspectives. My discussion of it will, therefore, pay particular attention to its strategies of reconciliation. This will serve to suggest that modern doctrines simply continue within the classical *problématique*.

2.3.1   Early classicists: Vattel

Despite its methodological scepticism, classicism does not deny the existence of divine or natural law. It merely doubts their applicability in concrete social circumstances. Divine and natural law exist in such abstract manner and so distant from everyday life that it is both difficult to know their content and apply them in practice. Rousseau, for example, points out that all justice comes from God. But God's law is made for a perfect society and lacks sanction. As such, it will only benefit the wicked who have no reason to follow it. Therefore, a concrete, human law is needed.[143]

In a similar fashion, early classicists do recognize the existence of an overriding, pre-existing normative system of divine and/or natural law. But they assume this law to be of very general nature. Its function is exhausted in the way it liberates States to create a society of their liking among themselves.

Christian Wolff (1679–1754) attempts to present international law in a scientific form. For him, States are by nature free and equal and their relations are based on natural law. On two points he explicitly

---

[142] *Rousseau* (Social Contract), Bk I, ch. 2 (p. 51). See also the argument in Bk I, ch. 3 (pp. 52–53).
[143] *Ibid.* Bk II, ch. 6 (pp. 80–81).

foreshadows the classical argument. First, for Wolff, natural law is restricted to only few very general maxims. Most important of these is the duty of the State to preserve and perfect itself.[144] Natural duties towards other States are secondary.[145] Self-preservation is the metaprinciple epitomized in the primacy of individual State will against material order and organization.[146] Wolff's natural law is a Hobbesian instrument of the "self". It does not lay down any goals external to the self's pursuits.

The more interesting argument in Wolff, however, relates to the manner in which he attempts a reconciliation between a given natural law and a law which emerges from international reality. He makes a difference between "pure" natural law and the natural law applicable to States. The latter ("voluntary law") consists of interpretations or "deductions" from the former.[147] For, Wolff explains, on the one hand:

> ... nations in their relations with each other use no other law than that which is established by nature.[148]

But the law of nature was originally applicable between individuals and cannot, therefore, be applied between States in its purity. Thus:

> ... the law of nations does not remain the same in all respects as the law of nature ...[149]

This seems like contradiction. Nations apply only natural law and yet something else than "pure" natural law. But this "something else" is not positive (stipulative, contractual) law, either. The point here is that Wolff's voluntary law is a law between the fully natural and the fully consensual. It is a *strategy of reconciliation*. It is not apologetic as it maintains its connection with natural law maxims. The "interpretations and deductions" are not arbitrary.[150] As Wolff explains:

> ... natural law itself prescribes the method by which voluntary law is to be made out of natural law.[151]

It is different from the fully arbitrary stipulative law.[152] And yet, it is not utopian, either, as it incorporates the real character of the international society within itself.

---

[144] *Wolff* (Jus Gentium) ch. I § 27 (p. 20) *et seq.*   [145] *Ibid.* ch. II § 206 (p. 107).
[146] See also *Midgley* (Natural Law) pp. 176–179.
[147] *Wolff* (Jus Gentium) Preface (pp. 5–8), ch. I § 22 (pp. 17–18).
[148] *Ibid.* Preface (p. 5).   [149] *Ibid.*   [150] *Ibid.* Preface (p. 6).   [151] *Ibid.*
[152] *Ibid.* ch. I §§ 22–26 (pp. 17–19).

Modern lawyers have found it difficult to understand what purpose is served by the voluntary law of nations which is neither fully natural nor fully consensual.[153] Indeed, Wolff himself has difficulty keeping them apart.

In the first place, voluntary law sometimes seems to collapse into a fully consensual law, a "will of nations" as Wolff himself says.[154] To maintain distance between consent and voluntary law, however, Wolff is forced to "objectify" this "will": it is *presumed*, not *actual* will he means thereby.[155] Having recourse to what amounts to an early tacit consent construction enables Wolff to avoid making definite priority between a fully descending and a fully ascending argument. For had he envisaged merely two kinds of law – natural and consensual – he would have had to explain which has priority in conflict. This would have seemed to lapse him either into early utopianism or simple apologism. He needed a third kind of law in order to avoid the objection that he was arguing only on the basis of abstract and unprovable natural law maxims and the charge that his law was merely what States happened to will at any moment.[156]

---

[153] The strategy of constructing a "realistic" natural law which would not become simply consensual goes back at least to Stoic philosophy which assumed that due to man's imperfections natural law could not be applied in its purity but that it must be adapted to the political and social circumstances of the *polis*. See generally *Strauss* (Natural Right) pp. 148–156; *Corbett* (Law and Society) p. 29.

[154] *Wolff* (Jus Gentium) Prolegomena § 25 (p. 19). Later lawyers have sometimes criticized Wolff's inability to distinguish his voluntary law from simple consent. See e.g. *Ruddy* (International Law in the Enlightenment) pp. 35–38; *Twiss* (Droit) pp. 135–139; *Wheaton* (Elements) p. 13. This criticism, however, fails to explain why Wolff also groups natural and voluntary law together and contrasts them to consensual (and enforcible) law.

[155] Wolff himself uses the term "presumed will" when he speaks of the normative character of the *civitas maxima*. This is, for him, a hypothetical community of States. *Wolff* (Jus Gentium) Prolegomena §§ 9–22 (pp. 12–18). In Wolff's system, the normative (descending) principles are drawn from the will of this community, a will, however, which is not real but something which he assumes States *would* have if they understood their own self-interest (that is, their need to join together) correctly. In all relevant respects, this is a tacit consent construction and leads to the corresponding difficulties. See *infra* ch. 5.1.2.

[156] Voluntary law allows him, on the one hand, to mitigate the harshness of natural law in war and to seek pacific solution in a "realistic" way. Moreover, it lets him escape from the dilemma that by natural law only one belligerent is just while the law seldom clearly indicates which one. Voluntary law equalizes the belligerents' positions, makes it possible to treat war as an act of self-help and recommends neutrality for third States. See *Wolff* (Jus Gentium) ch. IV § 378 (p. 195), ch. VI §§ 633–634, 636 (pp. 324–325), ch. VII §§ 889–900 (pp. 454–456). On the other hand, voluntary law

But Wolff loses this balance during his argument and also fails to make distance between voluntary and natural law. For both are now grouped together as imperfect law in that as States are equal no State has the right to impose its own interpretation of natural law over another.[157] In contrast to early writers, Wolff cannot accept such asymmetry between sovereigns. Even his *civitas maxima* is unable to resort to enforcement action in the absence of a contract to this effect.[158] International order is characterized by a factual balance of power (also the normative ideal)[159] in which each State has the right to interpret the law as it wishes with only the imperfect obligation on its conscience that it must do this in good faith.[160]

The plausibility of such a system is based on the assumption that there is generally no reason to doubt States' good faith. This is based on the further assumption that "obligations on conscience" do have some constraining reality and that maintaining the equilibrium is in the self-interest of most States.[161] Inasmuch as *these* assumptions show

---

may also be opposed to consent so as to guarantee the law's normativity. Thus it prevents consensual legislation from attaining normative force if it disclosed mere "unbridled licence" or if legislator's will had "gone off the track", *ibid.* ch. VI § 887 (pp. 453–454).

[157] *Ibid.* ch. II §§ 157–158 (pp. 84–85). Imperfect rights may be invoked only if there is a contract to that effect – that is, if they turn into consensual ones, *ibid.* ch. I § 191 (p. 100), ch. IV §§ 377, 378 (pp. 194, 195), ch. VI § 888 (pp. 454–455). The distinction between perfect/imperfect rights and duties contains, of course, the seeds of the liberal distinctions between law/morality and public/private obligations, sometimes referred to by Wolff as the distinction between justice and charity. Thus, failing to respect its imperfect duties against another State goes "against charity and not justice … Therefore, although it does no wrong, it sins", *ibid.* ch. II § 159 (p. 86). For Wolff, the unjust party's natural obligation is not extinguished by his external compliance with perfect law. Though he cannot be punished, he remains internally bound, *ibid.* ch. VII § 891 (p. 456).

[158] Thus, the coercive power of the *civitas* on which *Wolff* grounds his Prolegomena (§ 13 (p. 14)) is backed only by an imperfect right. See also *ibid.* ch. II §§ 159, 169 (pp. 85, 89).

[159] *Ibid.* ch. VI §§ 642–652 (pp. 330–336). The coercive power of the *civitas*, moreover, seems to have legitimacy only in order to enforce the balance. See *ibid.* ch. VI § 652 (p. 336).

[160] *Ibid.* ch. IV §§ 550–554 (pp. 282–284).

[161] As the system lacks an operative, substantive natural law, disagreements are referred into self-administered legal procedure. In fact, most of Wolff's law is law of procedure in this sense. See *ibid.* ch. V § 526 (p. 288) *et seq* and VIII § 959 (p. 486) *et seq.* For comment, see *Schiffer* (Legal Community) pp. 55–59, 67–68. The assumption here is, of course, that the system itself is reliable and impartial and that States have good reason to genuinely attempt a solution.

themselves doubtful, Wolff's construction loses its credibility – the whole system will then appear as a manipulable façade.

The early classical argument is best illustrated in the work of Emer de Vattel (1714–1767) whose *Droit des Gens ou principes de la Loi Naturelle appliqués à la conduite & aux affaires des Nations et des Souverains* (1758) became the most widely used treatise until the late 19th century.[162] His success, though dependent on several factors, is certainly not unrelated to the manner in which he had absorbed the liberal doctrine of politics and applied it in inter-sovereign relations.[163] Growing directly out of the ideological environment of the Enlightenment, Vattel's work was purged from Christian morality and theological authorities.[164] It was a "realistic" book, especially useful for diplomats and practitioners, not least because it seemed to offer such compelling rhetorics for the justification of most varied kinds of State action.

Vattel's professed programme is to concretize Wolff's abstract theories for the use of sovereigns to whom he expressly writes.[165] His concern is to overcome the utopian nature of his predecessors' work, identified with their excessive use of abstract deductions from general principles.[166] Instead, he defends his views by referring to contemporary State practice. The identity of his work lies in the idealism/realism distinction which is transformed therein into the all-important differentiations between necessary and voluntary law and internal and external duties.

Vattel starts from an ascending argument. Contrary to the early conception, the human being is not drawn to society by natural inclination. Nor is there any material law in the natural state. Though Vattel

---

[162] The book became especially popular among practising lawyers and diplomats of the time as well as of international tribunals. For a statistics of quotations by tribunals of Vattel's book, see *Nussbaum* (History) p. 162. For the reasons of the book's popularity in general, see *Ruddy* (International Law in the Enlightenment), tracing these to its immediate practical relevance, readability and systemic character, pp. 281–310. See also *Remec* (Position) pp. 55–56; *Butler* (Donelan: Reason) pp. 45–63; *Hinsley* (Sovereignty) pp. 200–202; *Lapradelle* (Maîtres) pp. 148–154.

[163] The First Book of the work directs the State's duties towards itself and reads in fact like an extended theory of the liberal State. Political power and economic organization are justified exclusively as functions for the needs and wills of the citizens. *Vattel* (Droit des Gens), L. I (p. 17 *et seq*).

[164] In a standard liberal argument, he proposes that the Church as well as the public conduct of religious rite be controlled by the State, *ibid*. L. I, ch. XII (p. 116 *et seq*). The argument is received from *Rousseau* (Social Contract) Bk IV, ch. 8 (pp. 176–187). For comments, see *Midgley* (Natural Law) pp. 192–195.

[165] *Vattel* (Droit des Gens) Préface, pp. xii *et seq*, xxii–xxv.

[166] See generally *Ruddy* (International Law in the Enlightenment) p. 47 and *passim*.

uses individualistic and communitarian rhetoric in his description of the natural state, he finally adopts a Hobbesian view which he then carries through his book.[167] Civil society arises from the need of human beings to protect themselves and secure wealth and other desirabilities: "La fin de la société civile est de procurer aux Citoyens toutes les choses dont ils ont besoin."[168] The sovereign exists to provide material goods, spiritual welfare and security to his subjects.[169] There is no objective conception of the good life. All that exist are subjective desires and society is based on them.[170]

The law between States is analogous to the law between individuals in the natural state.[171] Vattel adopts the domestic analogy in a manner which characterizes all classical discourse. States are super-individuals, thrown in the world to seek their self-interest. The international community is only an aggregate of such States and, by itself, has no claim on them.[172]

Vattel's *préface* is consecrated to an explanation of what is specific in it and better than early doctrine. Grotius, Hobbes or Barbeyrac had ignored that natural law was originally intended to be applicable between individuals and cannot, therefore, be applied as such between States.[173] They worked with a utopian system which ignored the realities of international life. This leads him into taking up Wolff's distinction between two kinds of non-consensual law, "necessary" and "voluntary" international law. The former consists of immutable natural law. The latter is based on natural law but modifies it so as to correspond to the concrete character of inter-State relations.[174]

Like Wolff, Vattel adopts voluntary law as a strategy of reconciliation. It is more concrete than pure natural law. But it is not consensual, either. A will-based ("arbitrary") law of nations is separated as a distinct, third category of law.[175]

---

[167] *Vattel* (Droit des Gens) Préliminaires § 10 (pp. 5–7). See also comment in *Corbett* (Law and Society) pp. 29–31.

[168] *Vattel* (Droit des Gens) L. I, ch. II § 15 (pp. 23, 24), L. II, ch. I § 3 (p. 258).

[169] *Ibid.* L. I, ch. VI (p. 73 *et seq*), ch. XI (p. 101 *et seq*), ch. XIV (p. 171 *et seq*).

[170] See also *Ruddy* (International Law in the Enlightenment) pp. 84–88; *Remec* (Position) pp. 134–135.

[171] *Vattel* (Droit des Gens) Préliminaires §§ 4–5 (pp. 2–3). For commentary, see *Remec* (Position) pp. 183–189.

[172] *Vattel* (Droit des Gens) Préliminaires § 11 (pp. 7–8).   [173] *Ibid.* Préface, pp. vii–xii.

[174] *Ibid.* Préface, pp. xiv, xix–xx, Préliminaires §§ 7–21 (pp. 4, 11–12).

[175] *Ibid.* Préface pp. xxi–xxii, Préliminaires §§ 24–26 (pp. 13–15).

How is voluntary law derived? Vattel disputes Wolff's point that it could be derived from the nature of the *civitas maxima* – that it consisted of rules *presumed* to have been accepted by the world society.[176] For Vattel, this is pure fiction. Instead, the rules of voluntary law of nations:

> ... se déduisent de la Liberté naturelle des Nations, des intérêts de leur salut commun, de la nature de leur correspondance mutuelle, de leurs Devoirs réciproques ...[177]

Voluntary law of nations is more ascending and realistic than the necessary law of nations as it takes account of the liberty of States. It is more descending and morally acceptable than arbitrary law of nations because it is independent from subjective consent.[178] It allows Vattel to avoid the criticism of his work being utopian or apologist.

The necessary law of nations encapsulates liberalism's assumption about the basis for rational action. It contains two relevant maxims: 1) Each State has the duty to act in accordance with its nature (and not some pre-existing teleology);[179] 2) as its nature is asocial (seeking self-fulfilment), it follows that its duty is to do all that contributes to the "conservation et perfection" of itself.[180] It has duties towards other States, too,[181] but only insofar as these duties – like society in general – are in its own interest (as they are assumed to be). But the duty towards itself is conceptually primary. It is also normatively superior: No State is obliged to aid another State if it would thereby endanger its own self-perfection.[182] Thus, necessary law of

---

[176] *Ibid.* Préface, p. xvii.   [177] *Ibid.* Préface, p. xx.

[178] *Ibid.*, points out that both necessary and voluntary law are established by nature. "... mais chacun à sa manière: Le premier, comme une Loi sacrée, que les Nations & les Souverains doivent respecter et suivre dans toutes leurs actions; le second, comme une règle, que le bien & le salut commun les obligent d'admettre, dans les affaires qu'ils ont ensemble". Préface, p. xxi. Moreover, necessary law *recommends* the observation of voluntary law. The latter is not, however, consensual. It is: "... fondé sur les Principes certains & constans, (et, MK) susceptible de démonstration ...", *ibid.*

[179] *Ibid.* L. I, ch. II § 13 (p. 22).

[180] "... une nation a droit à toutes les choses sans lesquelles elle ne se peut se perfectionner elle-même et son état", *ibid.* L. I, ch. II § 23 (p. 28). See *ibid.* Préliminaires § 14 (23), L. I, ch. II § 18 (p. 26).

[181] *Ibid.*

[182] *Ibid.* Préliminaires § 14 (pp. 8–9). The first volume of his work is divided into two Books: obligations to the State itself and obligations to others. Vattel makes perfectly clear, however, that the duties towards others are secondary; they are operative only if they do not endanger the fulfilment of duties to oneself. See also L. II, ch. I § 3 (pp. 258–259). This corresponds to what is said by *Rousseau* (Social Contract) Bk I, ch. 7 (p. 63). For the background of this view in the rationalist ethic of Leibnitz, see *Lapradelle* (Maîtres) pp. 135–136.

nations lays down what we would call an absolute freedom of the State to pursue its self-interest.[183] This exhausts its function.

There are two further distinctions which serve to make Vattel's law more concrete than that of the early lawyers while not detracting from its normativity. For Vattel, each obligation implies a corresponding right. An obligation-right relationship can be either *internal* or *external*. It is internal when the obligation and the right are located in the same person. This is the case of necessary law of nations. It is external when they are located in different persons.[184] In both cases the right and the obligation are equally real. The point is only that nobody has the right to demand the fulfilment of an internal obligation, "imposée un à chacun dans sa Conscience".[185] This grounds the distinction between private morality and public duty.

The same point is taken further by the distinction between *perfect* and *imperfect* duties.[186] The former are accompanied with an enforceable claim. Such claim can only be established through contract. Even an external duty towards another State cannot be enforced unless there is treaty to that effect. A right corresponding to an imperfect duty is only a "right to ask".[187]

In other words, only a concrete convention makes enforceable law. No intervention is allowed to enforce natural law.[188] It is not difficult to see that a binding world order is not easily justified on such premises.

---

[183] This is particularly evident in Vattel's manner to posit liberty in a controlling position inasmuch as its demands converting the rigid morality of necessary law into the flexible legal standards of voluntary law. *Vattel* (Droit des Gens) Préface, p. xx. See also the comment in *Lapradelle* (Maîtres) pp. 128–130.

[184] *Vattel* (Droit des Gens) Préface, p. xx, Préliminaires § 17 (p. 10).

[185] *Ibid*. Préface, p. xx.

[186] For comment, see *Remec* (Position), pp. 129–140.

[187] *Vattel* (Droit des Gens) Préface, p. xx, Préliminaires § 17 (p. 10). For critical comment, see *Midgley* (Natural Law) p. 188; *Corbett* (Law and Society) pp. 31–32; *Verdross-Koeck* (Macdonald-Johnston: Structure and Process) p. 38; *Lapradelle* (Maîtres) pp. 135–138, 164.

[188] *Vattel* (Droit des Gens) L. II, ch. IV §§ 54–55 (pp. 297–298). An exception is made in respect of tyrannical government. Some have seen here an inconsistency with the rest of Vattel's thought. The private realm of the State is then not, after all, fully secured. *Ruddy* (International Law in the Enlightenment) pp. 184–185; *Remec* (Position) pp. 232–233. This sense of inconsistency is, however, diminished if one thinks of the right to intervene in case of tyrannical government as a means to restore a rule which would better correspond with the liberal ideas outlined in the First Book of the work. For clearly, a manifestly tyrannical government cannot claim the kind of protection which a popular government can under Vattel's assumptions. The other exceptions which Vattel allows to the non-intervention principle are all related to the need to

Natural law posits States as equals. As they are equals, no State can criticize the manner in which another State looks for its self-perfectionment – otherwise it would impose itself as the latter's superior.[189]

Vattel's system differs from that of early lawyers in that he is logically led to making a boundary between international and municipal law. Hence, the possibility of conflict between the two is created. It is solved in favour of municipal law – the "private realm".[190] Any interference with the the latter is contrary to the postulate of equality. The sole justification for interference is received from the harm principle:

> Chacune est maîtresse de ses actions quand elles n'interessent pas le droit parfait des autres.[191]

Like Wolff, Vattel faces the danger of being unable to preserve distance between voluntary law and simple consent. He does argue that modifying the necessary law of nations is not a matter of will. Voluntary law is "établi ... par la Nature".[192] And yet, he argues also that it is for each State itself to decide what the correct modifications or interpretations are.[193] In this way voluntary law – the bulk of Vattel's international law – comes very close to his arbitrary law while yet allowing the argument that a particular voluntary rule is not "merely" consensual but somehow related to important moral-political maxims. He ends up in a diversity of auto-interpretative legal systems while assuming that the interpretations are somehow controlled by the natural law to which they are addressed. The crucial question "what happens if the interpretations are manifestly contrary to natural law" is neither raised nor answered.

preserve the balance of power. They are, in other words, procedural safeguards. See *ibid.* Préliminaires § 22 (pp. 12–13), L. II, ch. V § 70 (pp. 307–308), L. II, ch. XV § 222 (pp. 434–435). See also *Lapradelle* (Maîtres) pp. 147–148.

[189] *Vattel* (Droit des Gens) Préliminaires §§ 18, 21 (pp. 11–12). On Vattel's egalitarianism generally, see *Remec* (Position) pp. 183–186.

[190] *Vattel's* (Droit des Gens) law is, thus, exclusively a law between sovereigns. It does not penetrate into municipal law. Préliminaires § 3, 11 (pp. 1–2, 7–8), L. I, ch. I § 12 (p. 21), ch. II § 40 (p. 42). For a commentary on the formal-legal idea of the State in Vattel, see also *Verzijl* (I) p. 342; *Remec* (Position) pp. 166–173. Vattel constructs a very strict principle of non-intervention. See e.g. L. II, ch. IV §§ 54–55 (297–298). This is made to apply in matters of religion, too, *ibid.* § 59 (p. 302). Also, acts of private individuals are no longer attributed to the state (without the latter's contributory negligence), L. II, ch. VI (pp. 309–313).

[191] *Ibid.* Préliminaires § 20 (p. 11).   [192] *Ibid.* Préface, p. xxi.
[193] *Ibid.* Préliminaires § 21 (p. 12).

Voluntary law comes very close to *tacit consent*.[194] It seems to allow opposing a State with a norm which it does not now accept and which it has never accepted as an explicit commitment. It can always be said that the State had "tacitly" consented. Its sovereignty seems protected while the law's binding force is preserved.

But the argument is fragile. May a State be held to have consented if it denies it has? Vattel does not pose this question. Two arguments could be advanced for an affirmative answer. First, it could be argued that someone else can know better what the State *really* has consented to. But this argument is not open for Vattel who explicitly denies that an external observer could judge or interpret State obligations.[195] Second, it could be argued that the State has consented to a set of criteria under which certain conduct may be deemed "expressive of consent". But what if the State denies this? Then we are back at the beginning.

The problem is that voluntary law (tacit consent) cannot be opposed to a State except by accepting a fully descending position – that is, by constructing a theory of justice which can override its present consent. As Vattel distinguishes himself from early lawyers precisely by denying the enforceability of theories of justice, he cannot consistently make this argument. He seems either doomed to apologism or faces the charge of having failed to explain how or why the necessary "modifications and interpretations" can be controlled by something external to State will.

Treaties, for example, are in principle sacred and the one who violates them violates the natural law of nations.[196] However, treaties which conflict with the State's duty towards itself and treaties which are "pernicious" are void.[197] The conflicting or pernicious nature of the treaty is left for each State's own evaluation. Thus the risk arises that the State remains bound only if that is what it wills.[198] Vattel attempts to

---

[194] *Ibid.* Préliminaires § 21 (p. 12). See also *Ruddy* (International Law in the Enlightenment) p. 95; *Woolsey* (Introduction) p. 25; *Corbett* (Law and Society) pp. 30–31.

[195] See *supra* n. 189.

[196] *Vattel* (Droit des Gens) L. II, ch. XV § 219 (pp. 433–434), L. II, ch. XII § 163 (pp. 374–375). Nevertheless, non-observance of treaty is only a breach of an imperfect (and thus unenforceable) obligation unless the treaty itself contains provisions for its enforcement. L. II, ch. XII § 169 (p. 377).

[197] *Ibid.* L. II, ch. XI § 160 (pp. 372–373), L. II, ch. XII § 170 (p. 378).

[198] *Ibid.* L. II, ch. XV § 222 (p. 435). Vattel does refer to the rule of interpretation according to which no-one may interpret a treaty according to his own will. L. II, ch. XVII § 265 (pp. 462–463) and he assumes that treaties made for unjust causes are

mitigate this threat by two constructions. In the first place, this exception is treated as an implied condition in the treaty. Non-observance in case of the treaty's conflicting or pernicious nature is based on the treaty and thus on the other party's consent as well.[199] In the second place, the potential conflict between the treaty's objectively binding nature and the State's freedom is referred away from discourse, into conscience. There remains the imperfect duty of the State to interpret treaties equitably and in good faith.[200]

Vattel's discourse creates a potential for conflict between private morality (imperfect duty) and public law which could not arise under early doctrine. The suggested resolution takes place within conscience. The unsaid assumption is that States do act in good faith. Once that assumption is questioned, the system appears apologist. For Vattel, however, the assumption seems justifiable considering that the law is, by definition, based on the State's duties towards itself. Obligations have reality because fulfilling them is assumed to be in the State's own self-interest.

Also conflicts between the freedoms of several States are unavoidable in Vattel's system and ultimately unresolved in a material way. Take, for example, war. The early doctrine of just war falls in all but name. In principle, the sole just cause for war is the defence of the State's own rights.[201] By necessary law of nations, war cannot be just on both sides. It is logically impossible that conflicting views on what a State's rights are could be equally correct.[202] However, there is no objective manner in which to decide which State has justice on its side. Each State possesses the exclusive right to decide this matter for itself.[203] From this, says Vattel, it follows that in cases of doubt the war must be considered as legitimate on both sides. Insisting on the justness of the other party

---

void L. II, ch. XII § 161 (p. 373). How can these statements be reconciled with his view that each state is the sole judge of its obligations? Now, it must be remembered that for Vattel "justice" is not the material justice of early lawyers but the justice which provides for state freedom. Far from being inconsistent with the system, the view that treaties should not be interpreted arbitrarily or so as to conflict with justice merely restates this point.

[199] *Ibid.* L. II, ch. XII § 170 (p. 370).
[200] *Ibid.* L. II, ch. XII § 159 (p. 372), L. II, ch. XVII (p. 460 *et seq*).
[201] *Ibid.* L. III, ch. III § 26 (pp. 21–22). See also L. III, ch. IV §§ 49–52 (pp. 295–296).
[202] *Ibid.* L. III, ch. III § 39 (p. 30).
[203] *Ibid.* L. III, ch. III § 40 (pp. 30–31). See also *Verzijl* (I) p. 406.

would only extend fighting. Therefore, voluntary law assumes that each party is right.[204]

For Vattel, war is literally the continuation of politics by other means. It is not waged to enforce the demands of the normative order but to protect the State's own interpretation of its rights. A procedural solution – neutrality – is not only allowed for third parties but also recommended if they wish to stay out from the conflict. War becomes a private contest between nations.[205] Vattel picks up where Grotius left off. He resigns the elaboration of the just causes of war and moves on to further proceduralization of the laws of war, regulating the initiation and conduct of fighting, the acquisition of possessions and the position of the individual with the assumption that what is permitted for one is permitted for the other as well. In other words, he distinguishes between the *jus ad bellum* (substance) and the *jus in bello* (procedure), or ends and means,[206] and locates the former at the level of conscience and the latter in positive law which his treatment clearly privileges. Vattel's is a law of war as procedure. He is therefore able to focus on the conduct of peace negotiations and the peace treaty[207] – matters of increasing importance after the rejection of the idea of war as enforcement of material justice.

Vattel's discourse creates a tension between State freedom and the international order. Clearly, he has difficulty in finding a convincing conception of the latter. This is illustrated in his discussion of the case of two States one of which has been struck by famine. Such a State has the right to demand aid and determine for itself when and how much aid is needed. But no State has the obligation to aid it or to submit to its determination of the existence of famine.[208] The conflict is brought out in the open but no resolution is offered. Rather, the conflict is transformed into an opposition between private morality (the imperfect duty to interpret facts and law in good faith) and public law (enforceable

---

[204] *Vattel* (Droit des Gens) L. III, ch. III, § 39 (p. 30), ch. XII § 188 (pp. 163–164). This is, of course, supposed to have no bearing on the war's intrinsic character as either just or unjust. It is only external (legal) justice which is secured by the conception. The construction is realistic and useful as it legitimizes the acquisitions in war, *ibid.* §§ 189–192 (pp. 164–169). On the other hand, it now makes possible the modern criticism that the system is simply apologist, see e.g. *Nussbaum* (History) pp. 158–159; *Corbett* (Law and Society) pp. 32–33.

[205] *Vattel* (Droit des Gens) L. III, ch. VII (p. 79 *et seq*).

[206] For the significance of this distinction in liberal theory of war, see *Walzer* (Just War) pp. 21–47.

[207] *Vattel* (Droit des Gens) L. IV, ch. I–II (pp. 249–291).

[208] *Ibid.* L. II, ch. I §§ 5, 8–9 (pp. 260–261, 263–264).

duty) and the construction is held together by the assumption that States
will act in good faith as this is ultimately in their self-interest.

Vattel focuses attention away from the fragility of his assumption by
his strategy of proceduralization of the law. The idea of balance of power
emerges as a master principle for international order.[209] Vattel counter-
balances the anarchistic consequences of his preference for State freedom by arguing for a system of alliances whereby smaller States would
gain security in joining together so that ultimately no State could hope
to receive a dominating position by subjugating others. Also, Vattel
discusses different dispute-settlement methods at length implying
thereby that if international law is to have a beneficial effect on world
order it cannot be by postulating material solutions but by providing
procedures for States to overcome their differences.[210]

This procedural aspect is perhaps the most obvious difference
between Vattel and the early scholars. The success of such law is no
surprise. It gave identity and legitimacy to the 18th and 19th century
States-system by formalizing the concept of the State.[211] It was useful for
sovereigns as it contained formal rules for the regulation of inter-
sovereign conduct at war, at conferences and through diplomatic
envoys. It was acceptable because it lacked material obligations and
directed the State's duties towards the State itself. The liberal assumption behind it was that individualism coalesced with the needs of the
community[212] although how this would happen was left obscure.
Discourse stops, or refers to procedure, each time a conflict is opened
up. Nevertheless, the consistency of his argument is maintained by the
assumption that the international society was a market community in
which rational action was self-interested action. Vattel was urging
statesmen to become Hobbesian "market men".[213] This grounds the
distinctively modern flavour of Vattel's argument.

---

[209] *Ibid.* L. III, ch. III §§ 47–49 (pp. 39–42). On the importance of the balance of power
idea for legal writing since the rejection of the just war doctrine, see e.g. *De Visscher*
(Theory) pp. 23–33.

[210] *Vattel* (Droit des Gens) L. II, ch. XVIII § 323 (p. 515 *et seq*). Recourse to peaceful
settlement methods, too, is a matter to be decided by each State itself, *ibid.* L. II,
ch. XVIII § 335 (pp. 525–527).

[211] See generally *Keens-Soper* (Donelan: Reason of States) pp. 33–39.

[212] "La nature oblige tout homme à travailler à sa propre perfection, & par là déjà il
travaille à celle de la Société Civile". *Vattel* (Droit des Gens) L. I, ch. II § 21 (p. 27). See
also *Butler* (Donelan: Reason of States) pp. 59–60.

[213] See *Macpherson* (Possessive) p. 105.

Vattel has lost belief in the unproblematic nature of the early dichotomy of faith/sin. He abandons the assumption that a normative order could be based on it. He opts for the assumption of the initial, unquestioned liberty of the State, manifested in the distinctions internal/external duties and perfect/imperfect obligations.[214] The proper place of material duties is conscience. In law, form is preferred over content.

Vattel's programme is to create an objective system of law by excluding natural law from it. In relation to his own work, natural law is made to look subjective: each State has its own conception of it.[215] Therefore, its proper place is conscience. Many would say, however, that this programme has been curiously reversed. Vattel seems to end up in a system which is distinguished from early writers precisely by its emphasis on the subjective consent of the State, or the subjective nature of inter-State relations over the objective character of international order. Law becomes determined subjectively, through State consent or State interpretations of natural law. What are we to think of this reversal?

The point is that both interpretations of Vattel's work rest on a set of assumptions not directly discussed in them. These are assumptions about the mode of existence and possibility of knowing about norms. If norms exist "out there", independently of our cognizance of them, then the early lawyers' work seems clearly more objective than Vattel's. If norms have no such independence from what we think about them, then the early lawyers' argument appears as disguised subjectivism and Vattel's comes to seem as rigorously objective as possible. What is puzzling about this is the difficulty to say which of the assumptions is correct as they rely on each other. To support the view that norms exist "out there" we can only refer to what we know about them, subjectively. Here it might be retorted that it is really our knowing which creates these norms. To which we could again answer that "knowledge" is by definition grasping something which is external to the process of knowing itself. Unless we believed so, then there would be no way of distinguishing knowing about norms from attempts to create them.

Such an argument could be continued at length without solution. Depending on which of the initial assumptions we would accept, we

---

[214] The use of these distinctions as a method for attempting reconciliation between descending and ascending discourses is emphasized also by *Lapradelle* (Maîtres) p. 165.

[215] *Ehrlich* 105 RCADI 1962/I points out that Vattel no longer speaks of "sin" in order to establish the definite legal status of an act but in order to emphasize that the matter belongs to the realm of moral, not legal obligation, p. 236.

could produce alternating descriptions and criticisms of any legal doctrine. None of them could, however, remain permanent as we could
always produce a competing perspective from which what earlier
seemed like objectivity will appear as subjectivity.

I have not attempted to produce "correct" interpretations about the
law or the doctrines which stand behind it. I have tried to describe the
way in which one system of argument was replaced by another through a
re-interpretation of what the earlier system was about. From the perspective of the classical jurist, the work of his predecessors seemed
metaphysical and failed to give answers to the questions he felt were
relevant. In this way, the purpose and identity of the classical project was
constituted in a criticism of early writing. To be sure, moderns
frequently view the relationship between early and classical doctrines
in a different light. They often applaud the sense of justness and
communitarian spirit of the early lawyers while deploring what in
classicism has seemed like narrow-minded chauvinism.[216] But these
interpretations arise from controversial assumptions about what we
are allowed to take as self-evident and what we may reasonably regard
open for doubt in matters of law, State practice and international
justice. As we lack a unifying perspective for grading the relevant
assumptions (whether norms exist by virtue of a theory of justice or
through State will, interest or behaviour), we really have little reason
to claim for our re-interpretations a status of truth which they
cannot sustain beyond the (controversial) system of assumptions in
which we move.

2.3.2   The professionals

By early 19th century, international law has become a science, an
academic discipline taught separately from, on the one hand,
theology, philosophy and natural law[217] and, on the other hand,
civil law.[218] It is now written about by professional university teachers

---

[216] Many non-naturalist writers, too, like *Schücking* (Preface to Pufendorf: De Officio)
emphasize the healthy effect of "philosophical right" on "valid right" while stressing
the objective character of the latter, pp. 11a, 26a–27a.

[217] See e.g. Klüber (Droit des gens) pp. 21–22a; *Woolsey* (Introduction) pp. 11–13.

[218] See e.g. *F. de Martens* (Traité, I) pp. 243–244. This includes usually also a delimitation
between international *public* and *private* law only the latter of which is understood to
govern relations between States or holders of public power in different States. See e.g.
Merignhac (Traité, I) pp. 6–7.

and diplomats.[219] The liberal programme of understanding it as a matter of objective law rather than ultimately subjective opinions about divine or natural law is being carried out. Increased professionalism is manifested in the increased self-consciousness of lawyers, in the manner in which they reflect on scholarship itself and worry about its scientific character.[220] The first histories on international law and doctrine are published.[221] Treatises are regularly invested with a preliminary "methodological" section including a definition of international law, a discussion of "sources"[222] and history and a delimitation

---

[219] For general overviews of 19th century scholarship, see *Nussbaum* (History) pp. 232–250; *Lachs* (Teacher) pp. 68–90; *Ehrlich* 105 RCADI 1962/I pp. 242–251; *Kosters* (Fondements) pp. 145–273.

[220] *Moser* (Versuch) makes the point that non-professional lawyers such as Grotius, Pufendorf, Wolff and Vattel each came up with different ideas about the law. A positive science, one which concentrated on actual facts was needed, pp. 22–25. *G.-F. de Martens* (Précis), likewise, opens up his popular textbook by discussing the insecurity which followed from the way these lawyers ended up with different kinds of natural law, pp. 31–32, 36–37. Writing in 1847, *Kaltenborn von Stachau* (Kritik des Völkerrechts) perceived the close of a period of constructing subjective systems and theories of international law and the beginning of a new era in which law was grounded in the objective conditions of life between States, p. 11. To a great measure, he argued, this was a result of protestantism, religious freedom and the separation of law and religion from each other, *ibid*, pp. 24–25. In 1858, *von Bulmerincq* begins his "Systematik des Völkerrechts von Hugo Grotius bis auf die Gegenwart" with making the distinction between law as it is and as it ought to be and projecting upon Grotius and his immediate followers the charge of having "confused" the two. This is why, he argues, they failed to ground a scientific study of international law and identified and classified their materials in an arbitrary and indiscriminate way, pp. 14–63. These and other similar arguments emphasize the need for concreteness and verifiability. As *Walker* (Science of International Law) argues in 1893, the law's scientific character lies in that "it must take as its foundation facts as they are", p. 91. Similarly, *Lawrence* (Handbook) pp. 5–6.

[221] See e.g. *Ompteda* (Literatur des gesammten Völkerrechts 1785); *Kaltenborn von Stachau* (Kritik des Völkerrechts, 1847); *Hosack* (On the Rise, 1882) (a review of diplomatic history, ignoring legal scholarship); *Griffith* (History, 18.); *Walker* (History, 1899). See also the review of professional histories in *von Bulmerincq* (Praxis) pp. 84–93.

[222] The doctrine of sources, as will be discussed *infra* (ch. 5) has independent significance only if one thinks that the law cannot be validated by comparing its content to a pre-existing morality or State will – in other words, a "sources" doctrine must become a system which makes validity a *formal* question. The first works to include a listing and a separate discussion of "sources" were *Wheaton* (Elements, 1836 edition); *Kaltenborn von Stachau* (Kritik des Völkerrechts, 1847). For standard discussions of the issue thereafter, see e.g. *Wheaton* (Elements) pp. 20–25; *Phillimore* (International Law, I) pp. 14–75; *Lorimer* (Droit) pp. 17–61; *Nys* (I) pp. 152–173; *Klüber* (Droit des gens) pp. 4–9; *Merignhac* (Traité, I) pp. 80–94; *Halleck* (International Law) pp. 54–62.

of international law *vis-à-vis* morality (too abstract) and diplomacy (too concrete).[223]

Professional discourse builds on Vattel. Despite doctrinal classification of professional writers as "positivists", "naturalists" and "eclectics"[224] the professional argument's coherence is constituted, on the one hand, by the distance it creates between itself and early writing and, on the other hand, by its attempt to create a more convincing conception of international order than Vattel had been able to do. Professionalism proceeds as a series of attempts to avoid adopting a fully ascending (apologist) and a fully descending (utopian) conception of international law.

Later lawyers were unable to appreciate the point in Vattel's "voluntary" law. Some lawyers saw in it too much medieval speculation about natural law[225] while others attacked it as a thinly disguised attempt to legitimize anything that States will as having the status of natural law.[226] Clearly, a new strategy to maintain both critical distance to and realist connection with State practice seemed called for.[227]

---

[223] Austin does not deny that a science of morals, too, could be likewise descriptive. It could simply record people's opinions. But even then it would not fulfil the second condition posited, namely, the superior-inferior relation, *ibid.* pp. 122–129. 1–33.

[224] On these classifications, see F. *de Martens* (Traité I) pp. 198–234; *Oppenheim* (International Law) pp. 89–94. Similar classifications are regularly used for similar reasons by "modern" lawyers as well. See e.g. *Jacobini* (Philosophy) p. 39 *et seq*; *Coplin* (Functions) pp. 15–18.

[225] See e.g. *von Bulmerincq* (Systematik) p. 41. *Corbett* (Law and Society), too, makes the point that Vattel made the "age-old confusion of law and ethics", p. 31. Consequently many professionals associated their law simply with custom and treaty. See e.g. *Wheaton* (Elements) p. 13; *Woolsey* (Introduction) pp. 25–26. These seemed, as *Schücking* (Preface to Pufendorf: De Officio) pointed out, law "objectively produced" and not mere naturalistic imagination, p. 11a.

[226] This point is made by the naturalist *Rayneval* (Institutions) pp. xi–xii (not, however, mentioning Vattel by name). To the same effect, see *Brierly* (Law of Nations) p. 38. *Carty* (Decay) is puzzled by the fact that Vattel has been classed both a naturalist and a positivist, p. 90. My view is that this is explained by both strands being present in his work without either having definite priority. Because naturalism and positivism, however, are usually understood as contradictory, the duality in Vattel's work makes it possible for an interpreter to make Vattel seem consistent by ignoring either of the strands (or holding it simply as an external inconsistency) and representing him as either one or the other. Removing the contradiction in this way, however, makes Vattel vulnerable to valid criticisms – criticisms which his reconciliatory rhetorics tries to deal with. Thus, it ultimately misunderstands Vattel and fails to appreciate the internal coherence of his work.

[227] See e.g. F. *de Martens*' (Traité, I) discussion of the defects in pure naturalism and positivism and his attempt to create a "contemporary" synthesis out of these,

2.3.2.1   Two deviationists: Austin and Jellinek

It is easiest to understand mainstream professional argument's inner coherence by reference to two deviationist strands within it. For mainstream professional discourse fights a battle, as it were, on two fronts. It opposes the attempt to draw from Vattel's system the conclusion that international law is "only" a form of moral argument, as was done by the Englishman John Austin (1790–1859), as well as the conclusion that it is "only" external municipal law, as argued by the Austrian Georg Jellinek (1851–1911).

Austin's point is really very simple.[228] In the *Province of Jurisprudence Determined* (1832) he sets himself the task of delimiting the proper object of the legal science. There are four categories of law, he says: divine and positive law, positive morality and laws metaphorical or figurative.[229] Only positive law is a proper object for jurisprudence.[230] This is human law, set by a political superior to political inferiors in the form of commands.[231] The decisive point here is the idea of "political superior". Laws may be formulated by those, too, who are not political

---

pp. 198–230. In a similar way, *Lorimer* (Droit) criticizes both early naturalists for having neglected the study of the practice of law-application and post-Grotian positivists for having concentrated merely on State practice without any conception of the relation of that practice to natural morality, pp. 53–54. *Woolsey* (Introduction) likewise undertakes a criticism of naturalist and positivist positions and points out that there are always two questions to be asked: "What is the actual understanding and practice of Nations?" and "On what rational and moral grounds can this practice be explained and defended?" Unless *both* questions are asked, the law will become either "subjective speculation" or "mere fact" – "divorced from truth and right", p. 14. Some lawyers, however, still persist in making the Vattelian distinctions between a fully descending natural law, "modifications" to it and positive law. See e.g. *Halleck* (International Law), endorsing the Vattelian solution, pp. 45–46, 49–50. To the same effect, see *Merignhac* (Traité I) pp. 12–13.

  Not all, however, regarded this synthesis as possible. In a delightful and perceptive but little known criticism of the positions of the naturalist Bluntschli and the positivist Hall, *Stephen* (International Law) points out that just as the former is unable to demonstrate the content of his general principles, the latter arrives only at uncritical expositions of State pratice. For Stephen, this dilemma is inherent in any attempt to apply legal metaphors to a study of international relations. If such a study wishes to be critical, it must be a moral science. If it seeks description, it must be history. Either way, there is no independent room for a specifically "legal" science of international relations at all, pp. 18–54.

[228] For the background of Austin's work, see *Hart* (Introduction to Austin: Province) p. vii *et seq.* On Austin's and Bentham's concept of sovereignty as the starting-point of law, see *idem* (Essays) pp. 222–243. On Austin and international law, see *Nussbaum* (History) pp. 233–234; *Nys* (I) pp. 138, 263.

[229] *Austin* (Province) p. 1.   [230] *Ibid.* p. 9 and *passim.*

[231] See generally *ibid.* pp. 11, 13–14, 17–18. For him, the idea of command includes the notion of sanction.

superiors. But such laws are indistinguishable from "mere opinion".[232] To become scientific, jurisprudence must possess a more concrete object. That is, it must direct itself towards actual commands expressed within a superior-inferior relation – a relation characterized by "habitual obedience" which is a matter of simple observation.[233] International law does not fulfil these conditions. Its precepts are but opinions of States. Therefore, writing about international law is, even at its best (i.e. when descriptive and positivistic) writing about positive morality.[234]

In Austin's system international law is not law "properly so-called". This follows from the unstated Vattelian premise of the equality of States – the non-existence of any superior-inferior relation.

Austin's solution follows directly from an attempt to follow through Vattel's idea that the determination of obligations is matter for the obligated State itself. It is only his conclusion which differs – a conclusion derived from another method of drawing the boundary between "moral" and "legal" expressions. Apart from arriving at a different classification, Austin's argument is no different from Vattel's as regards the assumed form of existence of international order and obligation.[235]

It is hardly surprising that most professionals resented the idea of being re-classified as moralists. As the Austinian definition seemed to locate their subject-matter into matters of subjective opinion they had to find a way of explaining why it still was objective and could produce a scientific discipline and an international order.[236] Therefore,

---

[232] *Ibid.* pp. 11–12.

[233] Austin does not deny that a science of morals, too, could be likewise descriptive. It could simply record people's opinions. But even then it would not fulfil the second condition posited, namely, the superior-inferior relation, *ibid.* pp. 122–129.

[234] That is, a human morality, considered without reference to the question of its intrinsic goodness or badness, *ibid.* p. 126. He points out elsewhere (Lectures) that early lawyers such as Grotius and Pufendorf did not succeed in studying international law even as positive morality. They "confounded ... the rule which actually obtains among civilized nations ... with their own vague ideas of international morality *as it ought to be*", pp. 74–75.

[235] Austin was not alone in his conclusion. From the same premises certain other lawyers drew the conclusion that international law is not law in the same sense as municipal law, but "imperfect" law and as such associable with morality. See *Savigny* (System, I) Buch I, Kap. II § 11 (pp. 32–33); *Rayneval* (Institutions) pp. vii–viii. See also *Stephen, supra* n. 227.

[236] For an extended review and criticism of Austin's position, see *Walker* (Science of International Law), arguing that Austin's point is only an attempt to impose an arbitrary definition of "law" which ignores the term's history and etymology, pp. 9–40. He goes on to argue that international law is "law" as it is no different from the focal case of municipal law as it emerges by way of national legislative acts, is adjudged in municipal courts and has war as its final sanction, pp. 41–56. For a similar defence, see *Scott* 1 AJIL 1907 pp. 837–866.

mainstream professional discourse usually contains a discussion about the "legal" character of international law despite the lack of legislation or government-backed sanctions in it. The conclusion is, either, that it does not need these to be objective, i.e. "law", or that they are present within it, albeit in a rudimentary form.[237]

This is also the core of the other deviationist strand, namely the so-called *Selbstverpflichtungslehre*, or autolimitation view of German-language public law theorists. In his *Die Rechtliche Natur der Staatenverträge* (1880) Jellinek expresses his concern: to see whether international law corresponds to an (objective) juristic conception of law.[238] He starts out by making the distinction between early naturalists and himself: one can build a conception of international law either on principles *above* the State or one can use a formal definition which incorporates also uncontroversial cases of law (that is, civil, criminal etc. law) within it.[239] For Jellinek, the latter course:

> ... ist für die juristische Begründung des Völkerrechts der einzig mögliche Weg gewiesen.[240]

Now, the uncontroversial cases have in common that they emerge from the State's or the nation's will. If international law is to be law in the "juristic" sense, it, too, should emerge from such will. The question is: can State will bind itself? Is *Selbstverpflichtung* possible?[241]

Basing law on State will is necessary if one attempts to ground an objective, juristic conception of it. But Jellinek does not think that this leads into apologism. Although law arises from State will it is still not a matter of opinion, or of *arbitrary* State will.

Jellinek rejects the naturalist position that autolimitation is impossible.[242] How could it be impossible if even uncontroversial cases of law are instances thereof?[243] The very idea of the *Rechtsstaat* follows from the

---

237 For this discussion, see e.g. *Twiss* (Droit I) pp. 139, 162–163; *G.-F. de Martens* (Précis) pp. 31–32; *Nys* (I) pp. 139–151; *Bluntschli* (Völkerrecht) pp. 2–12; *Klüber* (Droit des gens) pp. 3–4; *F. de Martens* (Traité, I) p. 24; *Merignhac* (Traité, I) pp. 19–26; *Lawrence* (Handbook) pp. 7–8; *Halleck* (International Law) pp. 51–53; *Creasy* (First Platform) pp. 70–72.

238 *Jellinek* (rechtliche Natur) p. 1. In other words, he attempts to show "... dass die Völkerverträge etwas sind", p. 5.

239 *Ibid.* pp. 1, 4.

240 *Ibid.* p. 2. He makes express reference to the Hegelian theory of the State, p. 3.

241 *Ibid.* pp. 5–6.   242 *Ibid.* pp. 10–12, 14–18.

243 *Ibid.* pp. 18–21. For him, "sovereignty" means self-determination and self-determination precisely the capacity to bind oneself, p. 18.

anti-Hobbesian premise that law binds the sovereign though it also emanates from his will. The existence of law should not be confused with the existence of sanctions. Though there may not exist means to enforce the law upon State organs, this does not mean that these organs would be free to behave as if no law existed.[244]

The same applies to treaties and other international rules. They express the sovereign's will to become bound.[245] By entering into relations with other States, the sovereign recognizes these as bearers of rights.[246] There is no relevant distinction between international and municipal law in this respect. In the latter, the State recognizes legal subjects as such. Besides, not always are the addressant and the addressee of the norm-creating will different even in municipal law. This is the case of constitutional law, for example.[247]

But nothing said so far is really convincing for the normative character of *Selbstverpflichtung*. And many lawyers have not been convinced.[248] For them, the idea of will limiting itself remains a logical impossibility, or outright absurdity. Like Austin's, most mainstream lawyers regard Jellinek's system a failure. No coherent explanation of world order can be found in it.

Such criticisms stem from a one-sided interpretation of Jellinek's work. In commentary, Jellinek is made to seem like an extreme apologist, moving within a fully ascending argument. In a sense, commentators *had to* adopt this interpretation in order to divert criticism away from their own constructions. For Jellinek's conclusions are truly threatening for international order. But this follows from the coherence of his argument – its protoliberal nature – and the manner in which it is the liberal programme *itself* which remains unconvincing.

Jellinek clearly realized that had his argument remained purely ascending – as I have presented it above – no order could arise from it. So he combines his voluntarism with something beyond that

---

[244] *Ibid.* pp. 16–17, 32–34.   [245] *Ibid.* pp. 46–47, 52.   [246] *Ibid.* p. 48.

[247] *Ibid.* pp. 34–37. In this sense, also an important part of municipal law is imperfect law, p. 35.

[248] For conventional criticism of Jellinek's position as apologist, see *Politis* 6 RCADI 1925/1 p. 14; *François* 66 RCADI 1938/IV pp. 14–15; *Verdross* (Verfassung) pp. 12–20; *Twiss* (Droit I) pp. 162–163; *Lauterpacht* (Function) pp. 409–412; *Brierly* (Basis of Obligation) p. 14; *Friedmann* (Legal Theory) pp. 379–380; *Günther* (Völkergewohnheitsrecht) pp. 16–17; *Gihl* (Scandinavian Studies) pp. 55–57; *Chen* (Recognition) p. 23. But see also *Spiropoulos* (Théorie) pointing out the invulnerability of Jellinek to this standard criticism pp. 48–50; similarly *Djuvara* 64 RCADI 1938/II pp. 556–557.

voluntarism itself. He first takes up the objection that will cannot limit itself in a binding manner. The criticisms would be justified if State will were really free. But it is not.[249] Not all will can create law. Only such will may do this which corresponds to *natural State purpose (Staatszwecke).*[250] There must be a reasonable motive (*vernünftliche Motive*) behind normative will, a motive which seeks to fulfil a permissible *Staatszwecke.* A will not accompanied with such does not have normative effect.

Conversely, voluntary obligation can remain binding as the State cannot make an arbitrary decision (*Willkür*) to revoke it. Revoking original will would go against natural State purpose. A voluntary obligation remains binding as long as it corresponds to the objective State purpose – that is, it binds independently of will.[251]

This is a standard form of reconciling an ascending and a descending argument: law arises from will but will is not free. Jellinek makes clear that if law were based on pure will, it could not be binding:

> ... der letzte Grund des Rechts nur in einem objektiven Principe gefunden werden könne.[252]

This is the principle of State purpose, itself derived from the nature of social life among States (*Natur der Lebensverhältnisse*). This forms the objective constraint on State will.[253]

---

[249] *Jellinek* (rechtliche Natur) p. 16.   [250] *Ibid.* pp. 38–39.

[251] *Ibid.* p. 42. Consequently, the *pacta sunt servanda* norm is valid even under the autolimitation view. Its binding character is derived in a standard liberal fashion, on the one hand from being a tacit condition in State will and, on the other hand, from the nature of the State, pp. 57–58. Thus, the criticism that will cannot limit itself is simply missing the point. For Jellinek is *not* claiming that will limits itself. Will is limited by an *extravoluntary* idea about the *Staatszwecke*. This is no "inconsistency" in his work, as suggested by *Verdross* (Einheit) pp. 7–8 and *Corbett* (Law and Society) p. 39. Quite the contrary, it makes his work coherent and at the same time corresponding to the strategies whereby mainstream liberal professionals have attempted to argue the same point. On the other hand, it is not true, either, that simply arguing from self-interest into obligation will make the latter illusory. It is always open to argue that while momentary self-interest does not support the existence of an obligation, a long-term interest will. See also *Macpherson* (Possessive) p. 293 n. C. The obligation *does* become illusory if we believe that "interests" cannot be distinguished from their definition by the political organs of the State at every moment. Of course, nothing like this was suggested by Jellinek nor by the historical school in general. Quite the contrary, the latter was specifically opposed to such an unhistorical and voluntaristic perspective.

[252] *Jellinek* (rechtliche Natur) p. 43.

[253] *Ibid.* The positive character of the law is preserved by postulating that this condition is simply non-legal, *ibid.* p. 49.

Thus it follows, for example, that not any will can create a treaty. A treaty must have a permissible *causa*: States can will only what is legally possible. Otherwise any treaty could be ended at any time and the whole of the law of treaties would be illusory. This would go against the nature of State relations, State purpose and the (objective) nature of treaties.[254] Only *Notrecht* can allow unilateral termination.[255] The argument differs in no significant way from what Jellinek's contemporaries or successors have said about the same thing. An objective law exists beyond State will which sets out the conditions under which treaties become binding and terminate. This allows the co-existence of the *rebus sic stantibus* rule and the *pacta sunt servanda* rule. The argument attempts to combine the two, in Jellinek's case by referring to State purpose and the nature of international relations – justifications which are standard also within modern doctrines.[256]

To sum up: Austin and Jellinek develop two strands already contained in Vattel's argument and the liberal framework of ideas. Their systems have seemed unacceptable because so subjective: Austin's because it assimilated international law with morality (and morality is subjective), Jellinek's because it identified the law with State will (and State will is subjective). In fact, Austin was a moral cognitivist and Jellinek used State purpose as an objective *telos*. Neither of these descending views have, however, been appreciated, let alone developed by their successors. This is so because they will ultimately lead beyond liberalism – into the kind of naturalism which liberalism intended to do away with. Mainstream professionals created space for themselves by ignoring the descending strands in the arguments of the two deviationists. They attempted to explain that there was room for a law which was not "mere" morality nor simply *äusseres Staatsrecht*.

2.3.2.2   Professional mainstream

In principle, the professionals could have elaborated on the naturalist strand in Vattel's argument and insisted on the objective character of the

---

[254] *Ibid.* pp. 59–60.   [255] *Ibid.* p. 62.

[256] At the outset, there seems to be a difference between Jellinek and *Zorn* (Grundzüge). For having based law on State will the latter leaves undiscussed the question of what may limit such will, pp. 5–9. Therefore, he is sometimes discussed as an "extreme" adherent of the autolimitation school. Yet he, too, constructs a non-voluntary principle which is made reference to in order to explain that treaties are binding. This is the principle of *Rechtsnotwendigkeit* which is postulated to "exist" in the realm of legal philosophy, in order to preserve positive law's positive character, pp. 141–142. Zorn's argument remains dualistic (descending-ascending).

process whereby natural reason grasps natural law. But this solution was not really open for them as it would have signified abandoning the liberal distinctions between morality/law, or imperfect/perfect rights, and reopening the early faith/sin debate which it was the purpose of the classical discourse to close. As we shall see, many professionals did conserve the idea of natural law – some even insisted on the natural character of most international law. But they defined natural law so as to conform with State behaviour and did not, therefore, need to build a fully descending argument behind it. Their argument has a structure identical to that of professional positivists or eclectics, the difference being in syntax, or order of making the descending and ascending points.

It is often thought that the 19th century is the golden age of international legal positivism.[257] If by this is meant that the professionals moved within a fully consensualist or otherwise ascending argument the point is simply wrong.[258] In the first place, most professionals expressly preserved some idea of natural law in their system which, though usually termed "secondary" in respect of positive law, fulfilled the important function of offering arguments when positive ones were not available.[259] Secondly, positivism and naturalism are not really so

---

[257] See e.g. *Nussbaum* (History) p. 232.

[258] Of course, the very term "positivism" is ambiguous. For a listing of some of the senses given to that term, see *Hart* (Essays) pp. 57–58 n. 25; *Olivecrona* (Rättsordningen) pp. 76–83. In international legal writing, the term is sometimes associated simply with "voluntarism", see e.g. *Fitzmaurice* 92 RCADI 1957/II p. 36 *et seq*. For discussion, see also *Remec* (Position) pp. 18–20; *Lauterpacht* (Function) p. 3 and *passim*; *Schiffer* (Legal Community) pp. 79–96. Sometimes "positivism" is associated with the analytico-historical method of arguing about the law, see *Pound* (Philosophical) p. 87. At other times, it is associated with scientism and especially the view that metaphysical or aprioristic statements must be excluded from scientific discourse, see *Morgenthau* 34 AJIL 1940 p. 261. Conventionally, a distinction is made between the sociological (McDougal) and normativist (Kelsen) strands in positivism. See e.g. *Sur* (L'Interprétation) pp. 39–47. Sometimes the term is used very indiscriminately to denote anything which can be negatively labelled as "formalism", see *Boyle* (World Politics) pp. 59, 194 and *passim*. For a discussion of the use of the term "positive law" by international lawyers from its sense of law "laid down" to all law which is "valid", see *Ago* 51 AJIL 1957 pp. 691 *et seq*, 707–714. *Onuf* (Onuf: Lawmaking) points out, correctly, that if we hold "positivism" simply to mean that "law is made by man and, by extension, human collectivities called states", then we shall have to concede that "positivism", and behind it "Western liberal rationalism" continues to dominate the way we think about law between states, p. 2 and *passim*.

[259] See e.g. *Klüber* (Droit des gens) pp. 4–6; *Nys* (I), pp. 138 *et seq*, 153–156. Even writers associating natural law with "imperfect" or "moral" law (in contrast to enforceable and fully real law) usually did conserve this law "within the system" in this secondary sense,

separate as it is made to seem. In the professionals' argument initially "positivistic" points about consent turn regularly (though silently) into naturalist ones under the argument from tacit consent, systemic (purposive) coherence or generalization from treaty.[260] Furthermore, the primacy of the State, its "absolute" rights and its will to the law is based on the liberal-naturalist assumption about the primacy of the individual to the society.[261] True, professionals did not class this assumption under necessary natural law as Wolff and Vattel had done. They did not always talk expressly of "fundamental" or "absolute" rights so as to connote naturalism (though often they did). But the descending character of this argument is well manifested in the organization of professional writing which uniformly starts the discussion on substance by discussing the concept of the "State" – or even an enumeration of European States. The State – and a set of rights associated with it – is the professional *a priori*, the transcendental condition from which discourse proceeds and which is not itself subject to discussion.[262]

Professional writing is compatible with "positivism" as well as "naturalism" – indeed builds on both. This not only allows it to use a happy mixture of consensualist and non-consensualist, positivist and naturalist, ascending and descending arguments side by side but requires

see e.g. *Creasy* (First Platform) pp. 11–21; *Davis* (Outline) pp. 24–25; *Lawrence* (Handbook) (pointing out that "ethical" law may, though it is subjective, be turned to when rules cannot be ascertained "by observation") pp. 6–7. See also the point made by *Gidel* 10 RCADI 1925/V pp. 590–592.

[260] On the metamorphosis of initially positivist views about tacit consent or general principles into naturalistic ones in 19th century doctrine, see *Kosters* (Fondements) pp. 182 *et seq*, 218–224. See also *Olivecrona* (Rättsordningen) pp. 34 *et seq*, 63–64 and (on the way Portalis' famous, naturalist Discours Préliminaire laid the groundwork for the extreme positivism of the exegetic school in France) pp. 50–54.

[261] See *van Kleffens* 82 RCADI 1953/I p. 72.

[262] In this sense, standard textbooks appear to construct the international order as an aggregate of the rights and duties which "follow from" the possession of statehood *ipso facto*. See *G.-F. de Martens* (Traité, I) p. 79 *et seq*; *Woolsey* (Introduction) p. 34 *et seq*; *Merignhac* (Traité, I) pp. 114–116, 117 *et seq*; *Halleck* (International Law) p. 63 *et seq*; *Klüber* (Droit des gens) p. 25 *et seq*; *Twiss* (Droit, I) pp. 1–132; *Heffter* (Völkerrecht) p. 41 *et seq*; *Phillimore* (I) p. 79, *et seq*; *Wheaton* (Elements) p. 25 *et seq*; *Holland* (Studies) makes explicit this organization of professional discourse: the law exists in three forms: 1) as a "law of persons" which enumerates the States; 2) as a "law of substance", which outlines the rights which States have and 3) as "adjective law" which provides the procedures of redress in case rights are violated, p. 152. However, usually the assumptions behind this organization remain hidden. The aprioristic character of the State which emerges as the controlling assumption seems to have been an object of discussion within the German public law theorists' circle. See generally *Tuori* (Valtionhallinnon) pp. 7–34, 51–54.

their combination in order to avoid the twin dangers of utopianism and apologism. In the rest of this section I shall discuss the professional argument's inner coherence by reference to its dual nature, the attempt to integrate both strands within itself.

To illustrate the unity of professional scholarship I shall take a look at the structure of argument of two mainstream lawyers who first seem to start from mutually opposing positions, one ascending, the other descending, but who end up in similar doctrinal outcomes.

A popular treatise of the early 19th century which starts from States as the sole legitimate international actors is J. L. Klüber's (1762–1836) *Droit des gens moderne de l'Europe*.[263] The book opens up with a brief section on method, including a definition of international law, a list of sources and a historical overview.[264] The substance of the work is divided into two sections: the first posits States as the subjects of international law,[265] the second outlines the rights which form the corpus of the law between (European) States.[266] This latter section is again divided into two parts: the "absolute" rights which follow from statehood *ipso facto* and the "conditional" rights which are grounded in the particular situation between two or more States (e.g. conventional law, law of war etc.). The argument looks fully ascending: its unquestioned starting-point is the existence of a number of States posessed with a set of rights. The law is nothing but an aggregate of these rights, applied in the particular relations between States.

Klüber's discussion of method reinforces the ascending nature of his discussion. To be proper law, international law must be distinguished from politics, morals and courtesy, as well as from Roman law, Canon law and theology.[267] Early lawyers are criticized for having failed to maintain these distinctions. A study of international law must be simple and systematic.

All statements must be validated as against the sources and not against ambiguous authority, such as "hypotheses ... formes dialectiques ou des speculations métaphysiques".[268] A scientific study of law must be realistic and focus on the rights which (European) States habitually grant to each other.[269]

---

[263] The work was originally published in 1819. The version referred to in the text is the French text of 1861. For Klüber's biography and evaluation, see Preface to the French text, pp. ix–xv and e.g. *Nussbaum* (History) p. 243; *Lapradelle* (Maîtres) pp. 183–193; *Oppenheim* (International Law) p. 98.

[264] *Klüber* (Droit des gens) pp. 1–24.   [265] *Ibid.* pp. 25–55.   [266] *Ibid.* p. 57 et seq.

[267] *Ibid.* pp. 3–4, 16, 25 *et seq*, 40–55.   [268] *Ibid.* pp. 10–11.   [269] *Ibid.* pp. 2–3.

The relationship State–international law is constructed in what seems a fully ascending fashion. The starting-point is the State's sovereignty, understood as its independence.[270] This is associated with the possession of rights which are necessary for the attainment of State purpose. These coalesce with the goals of national policy.[271] In this respect States live in a state of nature:

> ... il s'ensuit que leurs droits réciproques ne sont autres que celles des hommes isolés dans l'état de la liberté naturelle.[272]

Having thus outlined what seems a fully ascending argument, Klüber moves on to discuss the bulk of the law, namely the "absolute" and "conditional" rights of States. Strangely, however, he fails to explain the status of this law. Is it natural or positive? His discussion of sources does not give a reply.[273] In some way, this law simply "exists" by virtue of statehood so that it cannot be discussed within "sources" at all. It is simply *a priori*. There is what seems like a contradiction. On the one hand, the discussion of sources privileges consensual over natural law. On the other hand, the discussion of the law's substance privileges naturalist assumptions over consent.

The "absolute" rights (independence, self-preservation and equality) exist in what seems a purely descending fashion, by virtue of statehood.[274] And so do those of the "conditional" rights which are not based on State consent. For example, rights of property as well as rights of peaceful (diplomacy, negotiations) and non-peaceful intercourse (war) are derived from the State's natural freedom and exist independently of other (for example, consensual) support.[275]

Behind the express but vague distinction between absolute and conditional rights works another distinction, that between the law argued in a descending way and treaties. In order to see whether Klüber is really preferring a naturalist or a positivist conception of the law, we should enquire how he proposes to deal with possible conflicts between these.

---

[270] *Ibid.* pp. 28–30. He expressly denies the idea of a natural community between States: order emerges only from the way in which States grant rights to each other, pp. 2–3.

[271] *Ibid.* pp. 28–34, 156–157.   [272] *Ibid.* p. 58.

[273] See generally *ibid.* pp. 4–11. There is a clear preference to positive sources, express and tacit conventions. Analogy or natural law may be used only if the former are lacking.

[274] *Ibid.* p. 57. The function of these absolute rights is, of course, to carry the domestic analogy through. They establish the State's private realm (the freedom to organize the State in accordance with its own will, *ibid.* pp. 65–116 and the right to do anything necessary for self-protection, *ibid.* pp. 59, 64–65).

[275] *Ibid.* pp. 57–58, 155 *et seq.*

In his discussion of sources Klüber holds natural law secondary to positive law. The discussion of treaties further supports this view:

> En vertu de l'Indépendance de sa volonté, l'Etat peut renoncer à ses droits primitifs et à ceux postérieurement acquis, ou bien les limiter à son gré.[276]

There are no limits to what may be lawful objects of a treaty. A treaty is valid immediately once formal conditions (correct authority, reciprocity, consent and possibility of execution) are fulfilled.[277] Also, though Klüber does not say it directly, it is clear from his discussion that each State is the sole judge of what it has agreed.[278] Treaties are auto-interpretative.

However, such a system would seem to lead into complete apologism. Surely not all treaties (of attacking a third state, for example) can be binding? What is the point of calling absolute rights "absolute" if they can be derogated from by simple agreement? And of course, Klüber does assume that absolute rights cannot be derogated from as they describe what is essential to the State.

Klüber avoids discussing this conflict. Indeed, he can really prefer neither treaties nor natural law. If he preferred the former, he would have to renounce his strong view on absolute rights. If he preferred the latter, he would have to renounce his equally strong view on the importance of consent.[279]

It is not, therefore, surprising that his discussion of procedure (diplomacy, war, neutrality) is almost twice as long as his review of substance.[280] For Klüber, the law is less something that solves material conflicts than a procedure through which States themselves can ultimately arrive at settlement. Possible conflicts between natural rights/treaties are left unresolved. Treaties are inviolable but each State has the

---

[276] *Ibid.* p. 179.   [277] *Ibid.* pp. 181–187.

[278] See, in particular, the discussion on independence and equality, *ibid.* pp. 65, 117.

[279] In this respect, Klüber seems less candid, or less perceptive than Vattel. The obvious problems concerning the validity of competing interpretations of treaties or the extent of absolute or conditional rights are left undiscussed. So are conflicts between international and municipal law, between absolute and conditional rights etc. Each time he comes close to these issues he simply stops. For a modern lawyer, Klüber's discussion very often seems irrelevant, or beside the point (as, for example, when discussing equality he refrains from discussing allocation of rights or settlement of conflicts but focuses on matters of diplomatic etiquette, *ibid.* pp. 116–154). The answer is that Klüber really does not think that law has to do with conflict settlement at all: all it must do is to provide procedures whereby States can agree.

[280] *Ibid.* p. 216 *et seq.*

right to do whatever it thinks necessary for its self-preservation or the protection of its equality and independence. The Party violated against can also do everything to enforce its rights. Only the practice of European States – on which the laws of war are based – has somewhat limited this right.[281] In other words, conflicts between sovereigns about their material rights are brought in the open but left unresolved. They are pushed into procedure and ultimately war (in which, curiously, only the other party can be just despite the fact that their rights and duties are symmetrical).[282]

A similar structure is arrived at by the Baltic-Russian F. de Martens' (1845–1909) treatise *Traité de droit international I–III* despite the fact that de Martens builds on the idea of an international community to which States are "members".

The work starts again with a self-reflective section in which Martens first delimits international law against municipal law, politics and morality.[283] Criticizing both naturalist and positivist writers he expressly opts for a programme of reconciliation by calling himself a "contemporary" writer.[284]

Unlike Klüber, Martens starts out with what looks like a descending perspective on international order. There exists an objective international community which is based on the reciprocal nature of State interests.[285] There is a sociological explanation: international law reflects the reality of international relations and changes with them.[286]

---

[281] *Ibid.* pp. 59, 186–187.
[282] *Klüber's* dicussion of war is an elaborate attempt to reconcile ascending and descending points, points about moral legitimacy and consensual lawfulness, natural justice and custom. See *ibid.* pp. 313, 314, 353–354. See also the comment in *Lapradelle* (Maîtres) pp. 188 *et seq*, 192–193.
[283] *Martens* (Traité, I) pp. 2–20, 24, 245–246.
[284] *Ibid.* pp. 189–234. Being "contemporary" means not accepting either a purely descending or a purely ascending perspective. Instead legal arguments must be grounded *both* "inductively" and "deductively", by empirical investigation and theoretical reflection, p. 199. Naturalism is rejected because it was too abstract and devoid of convincing power over statesmen, positivism is rejected while it protected abuses of law, p. 219.
[285] *Ibid.* pp. 265–269. He expressly criticizes Klüber's approach as unscientific because this does not infer his law in a "scientific" way, from the character of the community but derives it, Martens assumes, from Roman and natural law, pp. 235–236.
[286] *Ibid.* pp. 213–232. This is easy to combine with his scientism; as law is based on sociological facts and history (there is a lengthy historical overview on the development of international relations, assumed to be determining of the law, pp. 32–197), it does not fall into pure (voluntary) politics: "Dans un système scientifique il n'y a pas de place pour des considérations politiques", p. 233.

The laws of diplomacy, economic relations, private international law and the laws of war are termed by Martens the "administrative law" of the international community. The system looks like municipal public law.[287]

But Martens' community is no *Weltstaat* nor even Wolff's *civitas maxima*. State interests do not transform into community interest. International law has no power to enforce community views or interests on individual States.[288] All it can legitimately do is to attempt to satisfy the "essential and reasonable" interests of States.[289] The overriding principle is the legitimacy of the pursuit of self-interest:

> Chaque Etat est obligé, avant tout, de penser à son propre avantage et de défendre de toutes ses forces son pouvoir autonome.[290]

It follows that States have a position analogous to that of individuals in the liberal State. In particular, they possess fundamental rights which are:

> ... inhérents aux Etats; ils sont inalienables et demeurent toujours en vigeur.[291]

Consequently, his system contains the same dialectical movement as that of Klüber's. Though it starts out with a communitarian outlook, it moves therefrom into thinking about such community as a simple aggregate of States' fundamental rights and procedures for their realization.[292]

---

[287] *Idem* (Traité, II) p. 1 *et seq.*

[288] *Idem* (Traité, I) points out that the community has no legislative, administrative or judicial organs. It is simply a set of procedures (in particular, conferences and congresses) under which States can agree on coordinated action, pp. 288–305.

[289] *Ibid.* pp. 274–279.   [290] *Ibid.* p. 273.   [291] *Ibid.* p. 378.

[292] *Ibid.* p. 307 *et seq.* Fundamental rights are the right of self-preservation, territoriality, independence, respect and communication, pp. 387–405. They establish, as it were, what it is to be a State and lay down, in an abstract manner, the boundary between the State and others. The difficulty which ensues from this construction stems precisely from their abstract character. There is no way to solve conflicts between these rights. For conflict-solution would entail giving a *concrete* content to them and preferring some contents over others. But this would entail assuming that a State's self-interpretation can be overridden by some external hierarchy of rights. Such hierarchy would, however, conflict with a constitutive assumption of the system; that is, the assumption that particular rights exist only as derivations from the fundamental ones and which remain controlling. Ultimately, the system can only refer problems to procedure.

Thus, Martens rejects the just war doctrine. War is only continuation of politics.[293] It is a method of realizing State interest. Though he calls war a form of "forcible administration" within the community, this bears no relation to the early lawyers' conception of war as public enforcement of the law. For him, starting a war is a legitimate political choice. The threat this poses to international order is not discussed. However, the procedure of war is regulated. This stems from no overriding humanitarian or naturalistic demands but from a *historicist* argument.[294] The objective constraints on methods of warfare arise from the development of civilization towards increasing respect for human life, development of human institutions and military methods.[295] But his discussion of the laws of war presents no material code. It is a history of the development of warfare. There is the unsaid assumption that history is beneficial and that States are somehow bound by it.[296]

The argument from history is a useful strategy of reconciliation because history is made to look both ascending and descending. It is, on the one hand, an accumulation of State practice and, on the other, invested with a spirit towards the realization of moral ideas. The question why a State which has not previously participated in this development should be bound by it is neither raised nor answered. Nor is the position of a State discussed whose interests would not be served by participating in this development. This would require Martens to adopt either an ascending or a descending position – a choice he cannot make as he attempts to be "contemporary", that is, avoid falling into naturalism (holding the State bound) or positivism (releasing it).

A similar strategy is visible in Martens' discussion of sources. This time he joins with Klüber in that all his sources seem initially ascending. Natural law, reason or morality are omitted from the list.[297] But in fact, his sources admit an ascending as well as a descending interpretation. Custom and treaty – his main sources – arise from subjective consent. But they do not *create* the law. They only manifest the "sentiment de la nécessité d'un ordre juridique dans le domain des relations entre les peuples".[298] Law emerges as an objective, historical process within human consciousness. This becomes the real, descending justification of law and allows recourse to generalizing moral argument. As this

---

[293] *Ibid.* pp. 177–183.   [294] *Idem* (Traité, III) pp. 186–194.   [295] *Ibid.* p. 186.
[296] *Ibid.* p. 199 *et seq.* See also *ibid.* pp. 33–34, 41 *et seq.*
[297] *Idem* (Traité, I) pp. 247–254.   [298] *Ibid.* pp. 250, 247–248.

consciousness manifests itself in what States do, on the other hand, also ascending points remain legitimate. This is, of course, a variation of the liberal theme: consensual (ascending) points are legitimized by non-consensual (descending) ones while the latter manifest themselves in the former. The reconciliation is possible because of the assumption that State practice – history – *does* manifest peoples' legal/moral ideas.

Like Klüber's, de Martens' law is procedural. It creates constant conflict between States but provides no material criteria for solution. On the one hand, the High Seas are free because this is in the general interest. On the other, each State has a right to a territorial sea, grounded in its need for security. But there is no rule for drawing the limit. Obviously, States have different security needs and the strength of the general interest varies in different maritime areas. No criteria are, however, proposed to solve threatening conflicts. Resolution is pushed into treaties negotiable on a case-by-case basis.[299]

The discourses of Klüber and Martens present a parallel structure despite the apparent divergence in their starting-points. Both create strategies of reconciling ascending and descending justifications. To class these writers simply as "positivists", for example, would lose the dualistic character of their argument.[300] The argument from fundamental or absolute rights, for example, is both ascending and descending, positive and naturalist. It allows arguments about consent and interest as well as arguments from inherent rights, the nature of the State etc. The controlling assumption relates to the parallel nature of State interest and objective morality – an assumption at the core of professional historicism.

Similar arguments emerge also in the writings of professionals who have been usually classed as "naturalists" or in whose work naturalist rhetorics seem predominant.[301] The Scottish lawyer James Lorimer (1818–1890) for example, advances the argument that natural law is primary and overrides positive law in cases of conflict.[302] But, he admits,

---

[299] *Ibid.* pp. 491 *et seq*, 501.

[300] Even a straight-forward "positivist" such as *Merignhac* (Traité, I) lists sources into "direct" and "indirect" and classes within the latter classical natural law theories, pp. 92–113.

[301] For a useful discussion of the character of 19th century naturalism, see *Kosters* (Fondements) pp. 158–181.

[302] *Lorimer* (Droit) pp. 19–22. He, too, makes the standard professional point of criticizing both positivists and earlier naturalists, the former because of their inability to create a normative doctrine, the latter for their disregard of State practice, pp. 53–58.

it is often difficult to discover the correct content of natural law. It must be "positivized" in two ways. First, Lorimer assumes that when sovereigns establish positive rules they do not intend these to conflict with reason or natural law.[303] By developing into custom positive law approaches natural law to the extent that it can be interpreted so as to be in accordance with this. The difference between the two is defined away.[304] Secondly, natural law, Lorimer writes, recognizes *de facto* situations such as, for example, the emergence of new States and the existence of non-equal amounts of power and culture in States. By imposing on States a duty to recognize such factual situations natural law remains in harmony with what States do in practice.[305]

Such writers as Henry Wheaton (1785–1848) and Robert Phillimore (1810–1892) both recognize that law is derived in a descending manner, from reason or natural law. But they fail to draw determinate normative conclusions from these and argue by reference to State practice. Wheaton, for example, starts out with utilitarian objectivism: law is derived from its capacity of providing the "general happiness of mankind".[306] But he does not pursue any utilitarian calculus. He accepts that the term "law" is usually applied in respect of inter-State rules which States have established, despite the absence of a common superior, and gives a descending-ascending definition of it:

> International law, as understood among civilized nations, may be defined as consisting of those rules of conduct which reason deduces, as consonant with justice, from the nature of the society existing among independent nations; with such definitions and modifications as may be established by general consent.[307]

Such construction allows recourse to descending arguments about justice, reason etc. as well as to ascending points about consent, independence etc. which can always be presented as "modifications" of the former. No primacy between the two is established but harmony between them is assumed. The system is infinitely flexible. Anything

---

[303] *Ibid.* p. 32 *et seq.*   [304] *Ibid.* pp. 24–25.

[305] *Ibid.* pp. 72–73. See also comment in *Nys* (I) pp. 154–155. In a similar fashion, *Twiss* (Droit international, I) argues that the customs of civilized nations are best evidence of the content of natural law, pp. xxix–xxx.

[306] *Wheaton* (Elements) § 4 (p. 6).

[307] *Ibid.* § 14 (p. 20). Wheaton is, however, ambiguous. His discussion of the "definition and sources of international law" is organized as a commentary to earlier lawyers and it is often difficult to disentangle his own conclusions from those of the lawyers he deals with.

goes as anything may be referred back either to justice or consent. The substance of the work hides this indeterminacy as it amounts to an impressive historiography of State behaviour.[308] Just like Vattel's system of voluntary law, it attempts to avoid the accusation of being utopian (after all, it is "realistic" in its emphasis on what States have done) or apologist (after all, State practice is not binding *per se* but as modification of natural law).

Phillimore grounds international law on divine law.[309] This is said to delimit the validity of positive law and be directly applicable between Christian States.[310] The nature of the thing is a second source. Just like Wheaton, however, Phillimore uses neither in his argument about the substance of the law. He simply assumes that international law is:

> ... enacted by the will of God; and it is expressed in the consent, tacit or declared, of independent nations.[311]

The descending is expressed in the ascending. The work becomes a history of diplomatic practice, assumed to be the correct – or at least the only accessible – manifestation of God's will. Travers Twiss (1809–1897) expresses the same assumption. Natural law is so defined as to become indistinguishable from positive law. Natural law:

> ... est le résultat des relations observées comme existant naturellement entre les nations comme communautés indépendantes.[312]

All such points derive from the liberal attempt to imagine a *law which would be simultaneously concrete and normative*. Speculations about God's will, reason or natural law are rejected in favour of descriptive

---

[308] See also *Stephen's* (International Law) criticism of Hall's similar strategy to define international law in terms of the (descending) dictates of conscience and (ascending) considerations of State practice. This is constantly betrayed by his argument becoming a descriptive account of State behaviour – which can only be reconciled with the argument's starting-point by assuming that behaviour reflects conscience, pp. 39–44. The difficulty which Wheaton experiences in reconciling the two strands in his argument is reflected in later lawyers', comment about his tendency towards descriptivism. Thus, *Ehrlich* 105 RCADI 1962/I argues that Wheaton started "an entirely new approach" by becoming "concrete" and "anti-metaphysical", p. 284 while *Lorimer* (Droit) sees him simply as uncritical, pp. 55–56.

[309] *Phillimore* (I), pp. 15–29.   [310] *Ibid.* Preface.

[311] *Ibid.* Preface; *Halleck* (International Law) p. 47.

[312] *Twiss* (Droit international, I) pp. 134, 142–143. *Rayneval* (Institutions), too, a strict naturalist, points out that even if "facts" normally have no normative character, they are still useful "pour faire connaître l'application des principes consacrées par la raison ...", pp. xii–xiii.

analyses about State behaviour. This is legitimized by assuming State behaviour to reflect God's will, reason or natural law. Possible conflict between natural law and behaviour is thus defined away.

The indeterminate character of such a system is evident once we realize that both cannot be simultaneously preferred. The *raison d'être* of an argument about God's will, natural law or reason is that it is better than, or capable of overriding any argument referring to State behaviour, consent or interest. There is no point in a morality or a rule which assumes that what a State does is always the correct manifestation of what it should do. Similarly, if a conduct or will is normative only when it corresponds to some external rule, then making reference to such conduct or will is superfluous. To check whether a conduct corresponds to God's will, reason or natural law, we should be in possession of a method which allows the identification of God's will, reason or natural law *independently of the conduct* we are looking at – in which case it is that rule, and not the conduct, which is binding. But, of course, the whole liberal argument was premised on our not being able to know God's will, reason or natural law in an other way than by referring to behaviour, will or interest. There is a circle: the professional argument justifies its reliance on State practice by assuming that this practice corresponds to some external norms. But it has defined itself unable to know the content of those external norms except by looking at State practice.

In discourse, this means that any conclusion will ultimately seem uncertain as it needs to be justified by reference to an additional point which, however, can no longer be justified at all. For example, saying that a particular practice is normative as it reflects a natural norm (of history, for instance) immediately invites the objection that it doesn't or that the norm it reflects is not valid. Answering such objection would require making explicit and defending one's theory of justice. But justice can be discussed on professional premises only as it appears in behaviour. And it is no longer open to refer back to a behaviour whose normative sense was the very object of the controversy. Writing histories about diplomatic practice and basing norms on what States have done is all right until the objection is made that the practice is precisely where the problem lies. Discussing God's will, the nature of the thing or natural law is all right until somebody claims that such discussions concern only matters of indemonstrable subjective opinions. Neither objection is answerable except by switching the perspective. To defend one's view on the normative character of a practice so as to avoid apologetics one needs to discuss justice. To defend one's theory of justice without lapsing into utopias one needs to show that one's rule accords with some relevant practice. In both cases one's defence will remain vulnerable to the reverse objection. And so on, *ad infinitum*.

2.3.2.3   The coherence of professional writing: historicism and proceduralization

To understand why, despite the points made above, professional scholarship was able to understand itself as coherent, we need to look further into two controlling assumptions, namely that 1) (descending) norms and (ascending) behaviour coalesced in the inevitable march of history towards progress and enlightenment; and 2) the latent conflict between natural law and State will disappears if only law is conceived in a procedural manner.

Professional writing absorbed the domestic analogy. The law of nations was, in Holland's oft-quoted words:

> ... but private law "writ large". It is the application to political communities of those legal ideas which were originally applied to relations between individuals.[313]

For the professionals, it was an uncontested truth that the world was naturally divided into States, possessing, by the very nature of their statehood, a set of rights the totality of which constituted the normative order between them.[314] That standard text-books open up with a discussion of "statehood" or independence and absolute rights manifests this assumption. The argument it grounds is both ascending and descending. It starts from States and tries to construct a normative order out of their rights which are not deduced from anywhere but simply posited. Simultaneously, these rights come to work as a pre-existing normative base which is not discussed within discourse itself and which delimits what States can legitimately will or have an interest in.[315] States

---

[313] *Holland* (Studies) p. 152. For similar statements, see also *Phillimore* (I) p. 3; *Twiss* (Droit, I) pp. 7–9. See also *supra* n. 66.

[314] After his discussion of the character of statehood, *Phillimore* (I) is able to point out that: "From the nature then of States, as from the nature of individuals, certain rights and obligations necessarily spring", p. 3. As States in fact possessed different rights, the distinction between "absolute" and "conditional" rights was introduced to explain these differences and to make the law "realistic". For this distinction, see *G.-F. de Martens* (Précis) pp. 124, 317 *et seq*; *Twiss* (Droit, I) pp. 164–165; *Wheaton* (Elements) p. 75.

[315] See also *Bruns* 1 ZaöRV 1929 pp. 12–25.

cannot contract out their fundamental rights without thereby losing their status as States, the exclusive players in the game.

But how is it possible that these States, posited as autonomous entities whose primary duties are to the "self" can form a law which is binding on them? Here professional argument bases itself on a *historicist assumption*. This allows moving from an abstract and unhistorical natural law to a study of the concrete.[316] The independence and the rights and interests of States coalesce with a historical development towards higher forms of culture and organization between and within the States. Or as Phillimore puts it: "Duty and true self-love point to the same path."[317] Under such an assumption it is possible, on the one hand, to reject the idea of an immutable natural law and, on the other, to avoid basing law on (arbitrary) State will.[318]

The professional view replaced a universal natural law with the idea that human history consisted of an objective development towards the fullest realization of human freedom, manifested internationally in the freedom of the nation to fulfil its "spirit" or purpose. Law manifests history in the way it allows each nation the degree of freedom corresponding to its stage of development in history's objective progress.[319] To be objective and scientific in the professional era was to understand the central role of history in the development of international law.[320]

This is exemplified in the distinction made between European and other States and in the location of different kinds of international law to apply within and between these groups, in arguments about the custom and tradition of European peoples and nations, about the central role of the ethnic and cultural uniformities in law (manifested, in particular, in the "principle of nationalities")[321] and about economic

---

[316] For discussion, see generally *Strauss* (Natural Right) pp. 12–34.

[317] *Phillimore* (I) p. 9.   [318] *Strauss* (Natural Right) p. 13 *et seq.*

[319] See *Kaltenborn von Stachau* (Kritik des Völkerrechts) p. 243. For a review, see *Carty* (Decay) pp. 30–35.

[320] See e.g. *von Bulmerincq* (Systematik) p. 246; *idem* (Praxis) pp. 82–83 *et seq*; *Oppenheim* 2 AJIL 1908 pp. 315–318.

[321] On the "nationalities principle", each nation was understood as a single individual, a person invested with a right to the greatest subjective freedom. On the meaning and importance of the nationalities principle, see further e.g. *Nussbaum* (History) pp. 241–242; *Nippold* 2 RCADI 1924/II pp. 36–41; *Redslob* 37 RCADI 1931/III (discussing the relationship between liberty and nationalism, the psychologism involved in the latter and possible ways to hold it a legal principle) pp. 5–78; *Catellani* 46 RCADI 1933/IV (a review of the Italian school in this respect) pp. 709–739.

and technological progress. Each factor was interpreted as a part of history's inevitable progress towards increased human freedom.

In the diplomatic field, belief in the ultimately beneficial role of increasing "freedom" was manifested, for example, in the inclusion of the principle of free navigation in international rivers at the Congress of Vienna, in the declaration of maritime law of 1856, in the Treaty of Abolition of slave trade of 1841 and in the establishment of consular law to guarantee the freedom of trade. The relatively peaceful political developments of the 19th century, the rise of Capitalism and the spread of belief in the intrinsically sociable nature of increasing economic contacts further strengthened the assumption. Peace and order were discoverable through commercial liberty.[322] As Charles Vergé observed: "l'argent n'avais jamais eu de la patrie".[323] The task of international law was, under such system, to enforce the Kantian maxim which allows for each nation the freedom compatible with the equal freedom of each other nation: the "harm principle" is the sole justification for intervention by the international order.

We have seen how Jellinek was able to combine arguments from State will with points about a non-consensual *Staatszwecke*. Historicism uses the same strategy throughout. It refers to the nation as a subjective actor and to the objective character of the nation's historical "essence". Von Kaltenborn, for example, points out that a truly scientific international legal doctrine must renounce naturalism. Valid law arises from the *Volkbewusstsein* – national consciousness – and this either may or may not correspond to articulated State will.[324] There may be a presumption to the effect that what the State as the political organ expressly wills corresponds to the national consciousness. For the historicist, however,

---

[322] See e.g. *Walker* (Science of International Law) pp. 111–114. On these developments and the ideas about international politics accompanying them, see generally *Kosters* (Fondements) p. 147 *et seq*; *Nussbaum* (History) pp. 186–211; *Nippold* 2 RCADI 1924/II pp. 58–71; *Schiffer* (Legal Community) pp. 165–186.

[323] *Vergé* (Introduction, G.-F. de Martens: Précis) pp. xxiii–xxxviii.

[324] *Kaltenborn von Stachau* (Kritik des Völkerrechts) pp. 232–235. See also *von Bulmerincq* (Systematik) arguing that the "real" source of international law is international legal consciousness. Custom and treaty have normative force only insofar as they manifest such consciousness, pp. 227–228. *Bluntschli* (Völkerrecht) grounds international law on human nature. Therefore, it does not depend on human will, pp. 4, 58–59. *Heffter* (Völkerrecht), too, assumes that the law – his *consensus gentium* – is not reducible to State will – it is based on the common cultural background of European peoples and their interdependence and therefore exists independently of actual will, by the force of European ideas and concepts, pp. 5–6, 21–22.

such presumption is rebuttable. In other words, order may be normative if only it reflects national consciousness and even against express State will.[325] As von Gierke puts it:

> ... der Staats. resp. Herscherwille nicht die letzte Quelle des rechts (ist, MK), sondern nur das berufene Organ des Volkes für den Anspruch des vom Volkes hervorgebrachten Rechtsbewusstseins.[326]

State will is not constitutive of law but only (at best) declaratory of it. It can only manifest a deeper descending principle of national consciousness. Consequently, it now becomes possible to use custom in place of natural law to hold a State bound even against its will without apparently becoming vulnerable to the objection of utopianism. Custom is not simply agreement but expressive of the nation's objective, historical essence.[327]

Historicism opposed voluntaristic ideas about legislation to which developments since the French Revolution had given currency. It sought support from theories about the organic character of legal evolution which profited from fashionable analogies from physical sciences.[328] In England, Sir Henry Sumner Maine (1822–1888) – arguing against natural lawyers as well as Benthamite voluntarists – presented legal evolution (in "progressive societies") as a lawlike movement from "status to contract".[329] Maine's successor as Professor of Jurisprudence at Oxford,

---

[325] It is precisely this "ascending-descending" character of the historicist argument which explains why it has been criticized both as too naturalist and too positivist. *Triepel* (Völkerrecht), for example, points out that inasmuch as historicism assumes a natural direction of history, it is simply a form of utopian naturalism, pp. 30–31. To the same effect, see *Pound* (Philosophical) pp. 84–86. See also *Hatschek* (Völkerrecht) pp. 1–3 (making a distinction between voluntarists and those who base law on the *Rechtsüberzeugung*). Both criticisms are included in *Spiropoulos* (Théorie) (pointing out that if such "consciousness" is referred to as a historical fact, it lacks binding force, if not, it seems unscientific because indemonstrable) pp. 41–45. See also *Kelsen* (Souveränität) (for a criticism of this dualist – ascending/descending – character of Kaltenborn's argument) pp. 243–245. See also *Lasswell-McDougal* (Essays Rao) pp. 75–77.

[326] *von Gierke* (Grundbegriffe) p. 31. Because the *Willensakt* by the State is only an external manifestation of law and not constitutive of it, von Gierke finds it unproblematic to ground international law on common consciousness whose existence is not threatened by the apparent diversity of what States actually will, pp. 32–33.

[327] For the "two-element theory" of custom, see *infra* ch. 6.3.

[328] See generally *Stein* (Evolution) *passim*, and (with reference to the analogy in Maine) pp. 88, 99–100. See also *idem* pp. 76–78 (for the connection between Comte's and Savigny's positivism).

[329] *Maine* (Ancient Law) p. 100, *passim*.

Sir Paul Vinogradoff (1854–1925), carried the argument into international law by publishing a work on the "Historical Types of International
Law". This work – opening with a criticism of the unhistorical character
of Montesquieu's "Esprit des Lois"[330] – stressed the relationship of types
of law with stages in social organization. It argued that there had
appeared, also internationally, "certain definite formulas which have
governed particular epochs"[331] and that it was possible to outline the
development of international law through four historical stages (the
character of which strongly resembled the first four types in his classification of national laws as well).[332]

One off-shoot of the historicist argument was the concentration by
international lawyers on the customs and traditions of European
nations.[333] There was no question about European culture not being
higher in quality, or more advanced, than the forms of life which were
perceived among non-European peoples. It seemed unnatural – indeed
harmful – to apply the European-origined international law "in all its
rigour" in respect of non-Europeans[334] and it was understood as a historical task for the Europeans to educate and prepare the less civilized
nations for the adoption of European international law.[335]

Though some professional historiography looks quite similar to the
collections of practice by early positivists, such as Richard Zouche
(1590–1660) or J. J. Moser (1701–1785),[336] it is important to see that

---

[330] *Vinogradoff* (Historical Types) pp. 3–4.   [331] *Ibid.* p. 69.

[332] He discerned five types (stages) for legal development and named these after the type
of social formation which they were to correspond to: tribe, city, Church, contractual
association, collective organization, *ibid*, pp. 5–7. His four types of international law
practically repeat the character of the first four general types – contractual association
bearing an obvious resemblance to how he explains the "law between territorial states",
pp. 46–57.

[333] See e.g. *Heffter* (Völkerrecht) pp. 19–21; *Nys* (I) pp. 3–6, 126–137; *Klüber* (Droit des
gens) p. 56 and *passim*; *Wheaton* (Elements) pp. 15–16; *F. de Martens* (Traité, I) 239
and *passim*; *Twiss* (Droit, I) pp. xxvi–xxviii; *Lorimer* (Droit) pp. 69–71. For comments,
see *Nardin* (Law, Morality) pp. 63–68. See also the discussion in *Bozeman*
(Multicultural) pp. 35–49; *Kennedy* (The Influence of Christianity) p. 21 *et seq*. This
concentration on European history and culture was also a noteworthy factor in the
historical school of law generally. Because of the assumption of the superiority of
European culture (and, in particular, Roman law), it seemed possible to assume that
the lawlike evolution of "primitive" or "stationary" cultures would follow the same
path. See generally *Stein* (Evolution) pp. 91–93, 99 *et seq*.

[334] *Hurtige Hane* Case (Scott-Jaeger: Cases) pp. 62–64. See also *Kennedy* (The Influence of
Christianity) p. 139 *et seq*.

[335] *Bluntschli* (Völkerrecht) p. 59.

[336] See, in particular, *Walker* (History); *Laurent* (Histoire).

professionals do not collect facts merely to achieve full description. For them, the world of facts encloses a deeper *normative* meaning of historical purpose.[337] Hence, it may combine its discussion with abstract references, as we have seen, to natural or divine law, popular consciousness etc. which, though remaining on the background, serve to legitimize State practice. Facts have authority because and insofar as the objective trends of history are manifested in them. The State is an instrument of history's natural development towards freedom and progress.[338]

The optimistic historical determinism of professional lawyers is mediated through a *procedural* conception of the law. Early peace proposals were labelled utopian because of their reliance on theories of natural justice.[339] In the eyes of the professionals, the European Concert had already provided an exemplary – though rudimentary – procedural peace-system. Due to increasing cultural and economic contacts it would in a later age develop into a universal international peace procedure through increasing codification, use of arbitration, Conferences between Heads of State, diplomatic contacts and in general strengthening international law.[340]

---

[337] See *Strauss* (Natural Right) p. 17.

[338] As *Stein* (Evolution) puts it, social and legal evolution were seen as a "part of an inexorable ascent to Utopia", p. 124.

[339] See e.g. *G.-F. de Martens* (Précis) pp. 86–90; Lorimer (Droit) pp. 308–325. See also *Vinogradoff* (Historical Types) (opposing plans for "eternal peace" for their unhistorical character) pp. 58 *et seq*, 69–70.

[340] See e.g. *Bluntschli* (Völkerrecht) pp. 3–12. Having reviewed the increasing use of Congresses and Conferences, *Baldwin* 1 AJIL 1907 concludes by noting: "Nations have been brought together by material forces, starting into action greater immaterial forces. Electricity is finishing what steam began. Men come close together who breathe a common atmosphere; who are fed daily by the same currents of thought; who hear simultaneously of the same events . . . It is from these conditions of human society that international Congresses and Conferences have come to assume so large an importance; and it is an importance which must steadily increase rather than lessen, unless these conditions essentially change." pp. 577–578, 565 *et seq*. Later lawyers have not failed to point out that such optimism could only grow in the relatively peaceful conditions of the 19th century – conditions which were no longer present in the following decades. See e.g. *De Visscher* (Theory) pp. 51–52. It is interesting to note that the European Concert has been interpreted in two distinct ways by later lawyers. It has been seen as an attempt at supra-national organization as well as a procedure for intersovereign cooperation. Both interpretations may be associated with contrasting evaluations. The former may be applauded as an effort away from narrow nationalism or criticized as imperialistic means to strengthen foreign domination. For the former, see *Bourquin* (Festschift) pp. 89 *et seq*, 96–98. For the latter, see *Anand* 197 RCADI 1986/III pp. 60–63. Conversely, the "procedural" interpretation may either be accused

The problem of order becomes a procedural problem. If only advanced mechanisms for sovereign cooperation and settlement are developed, material disagreements can be prevented from threatening the system. The balance of power is one such mechanism. The creation of international "Unions" is another. The culmination of this view takes place in the Hague Conferences of 1899 and 1907, in the establishment of the Permanent Court of Arbitration and the proposal for an international prize court. All these were understood as positive, order-strengthening phenomena. Only when belief in procedure was shattered at the First World War, also the credibility of professional doctrines was lost.[341]

But belief in procedure makes professional argument vulnerable from the inside, too. In the professional lawyers' system any conflict between States is a conflict between their initial freedoms. To solve conflicts one would need a viewpoint external to the freedoms themselves. But professional discourse lacks such a viewpoint. This leads it into interminable descriptions of past practice with little or nothing to emerge as a controlling rule.

Take, for example, the question of legality of intervention. In principle, of course, there is a strong rule against external intervention as this is a violation of the State's independence and equality.[342] But it might sometimes be necessary to intervene in order to preserve the balance of power – itself based on independence and equality.[343]

---

of inefficiency (of not going far enough) or applauded for its realism. The point is, of course, that the interpretations stem rather from the interpreter's perspective than from the object of interpretation. For such interpretations, see e.g. Nardin (Law, Morality) pp. 86–97.

[341] This is exemplified in the complete collapse of the professional construction concerning rules of neutrality immediately at the beginning of the war. As the professionals' law of war was a law of procedure, neutrality took a central part of it. For standard discussions, see e.g. Klüber (Droit des gens) pp. 353–404; Bluntschli (Völkerrecht) pp. 413–480; Heffter (Völkerrecht) pp. 303–377; Wheaton (Elements) pp. 426–593; Lorimer (Droit) pp. 233–277. For the collapse of this system, see e.g. Örvik (Decline) pp. 38–118; Boyle (World Politics) pp. 44–51; Nussbaum (History) pp. 230–232.

[342] The sole exception usually admitted is that of self-defence. See e.g. Walker (Science) pp. 134–158. An apparent exception to the liberal character of the doctrine is Woolsey's (Introduction) argument according to which intervention might be allowed against a sovereign committing crimes against his subjects, p. 44. However, inasmuch as this construction may be legitimized by the argument that the sovereign has lost its representative character through these crimes and the social bond which holds the State together has thereby been dissolved, it might seem plausible to include this kind of intervention within the system.

[343] Griffith (International Law) pp. 28–29. See also generally Aron (Paix et Guerre) pp. 120–121.

Typical professional discussions usually list past instances of intervention with much detail. Wheaton, for example, discusses at length the widely spread practice of intervention by the Great Powers in the Holy Alliance, pointing out factors both supporting and militating against intervention. He concludes:

> Non-interference is the general rule, to which cases of justifiable interference form exceptions limited by the necessity of each particular case.[344]

In other words, the rule vanishes into context. The system simply does not allow the hierarchization of the freedom to intervene and the freedom of not to be intervened against. The professional lawyers' system posits State freedom as the metaprinciple – just like liberalism does with individual freedom – but remains at a loss when freedoms conflict. In the absence of material standards, it can only describe past instances of conflict and offer procedures for settlement.[345]

It was accepted, for example, that there were no material criteria – or if they exist, they are not legal – for judging the causes of war:

> The voluntary or positive law of nations ... makes no distinctions ... between a just and an unjust war. A war in form, or duly commenced, is to be considered, as to its effects, as just on both sides. Whatever is permitted by the laws of war to one of the belligerent powers is equally permitted to the other.[346]

As Twiss conceives it, war is a clash of a State's inherent right to enlarge its domain and the inherent right of security and self-preservation of the other State. As there is no standard whereby precedence between these rights (freedoms) could be ascertained, the discussion turns inevitably away from seeking a material solution to suggesting procedures for avoiding the clash or limiting its impact.[347] The justness of war has no

---

[344] *Wheaton* (Elements) p. 100.

[345] That the argument from equality leads almost automatically to a shift from materially constraining to procedural norms – "Conferences" among sovereigns – is well evidenced e.g. by the discussion in *Olney* 1 AJIL 1907 pp. 418–430.

[346] *Wheaton* (Elements) pp. 313–314. See also *Phillimore* (I) pp. 5–8. Even naturalists may renounce the just war doctrine. See e.g. *Rayneval* (Institutions) p. 206.

[347] *Twiss* (Droit, I) pp. 173–175. See also *Griffith* (International Law) pp. 28–29. Also in the realm of peaceful relations, professional discourse proceeds so as to achieve conflict-avoidance procedures by delimiting jurisdictions, not by attaining material solutions. The establishment of consular jurisdiction is one example. See e.g. *G.-F. de Martens* (Précis, I) pp. 381–393; *Wheaton* (Elements) pp. 149–150; *Lorimer* (Droit) pp. 148–153.

bearing on the status of the belligerents, on the authority of the sovereigns involved or on their acquisitions. If any justification for war was invoked, it restated the harm principle: a war was just only if in pursuance of a wrong done against the independence of the State.[348] But each State was the sole judge on whether or not such "wrong" existed – of course, any other solution would have assumed the existence of a material natural law. Woolsey puts the matter adroitly:

> By justice, however, we intend not justice objective, but as it appears to the party concerned or, at least, as it is claimed to exist. From the independence of nations it results that each has a right to hold and make good its own view of right in its own affairs.[349]

If a third State wishes to avoid becoming a belligerent itself, it must consider the war as just on both sides and adopt a neutral attitude.[350] Having dismissed the question of justness, professional scholarship can now move on to regulate conflict, instead of prohibiting it.

Professional writing concentrates on the formalities of warfare – whether a declaration of war is required, who can wage war, what acts are allowed in war and what not, etc. Particular importance is given to the establishment of balance of power to prevent war and to neutrality at war.[351] But whether or not to engage in conflict remains a sovereign privilege. As Nippold writes:

> ... sans même qu'ils aient pour eux une *justa causa belli*, il est évidemment nécessaire de déterminer une procédure préalable et de la mettre à la disposition des parties d'une façon obligatoire.[352]

In an illustrative example, the Hague Peace Conferences failed to attain their original, material goal – the reduction of armaments – and came up, instead, with a Convention on the Pacific Settlement of Disputes (providing procedures for mediation, good offices, fact-finding and arbitration) and a set of Conventions to regulate the procedure of warfare.[353]

---

[348] See e.g. *Klüber* (Droit des gens) pp. 300–301; *Lorimer* (Droit) pp. 190–198.
[349] *Woolsey* (Introduction) p. 183.   [350] *G.-F. de Martens* (Précis, II) pp. 206–208.
[351] See *G.-F. de Martens* (Précis, I) pp. 322–336; *Heffter* (Völkerrecht) p. 10. But see *Klüber* (Droit des gens) pp. 61–63. On the importance of the "equilibrium principle" in 19th-century writing, see *Nippold* 2 RCADI 1924/I pp. 25–30.
[352] *Nippold* 2 RCADI 1924/I p. 79.
[353] On this procedural orientation generally, see also *Potter* 64 RCADI 1938/II pp. 98 *et seq*, 108–136; *Nippold* 2 RCADI 1924/I p. 79 *et seq*. For a discussion of the beneficial character of the result of the Conferences by a contemporary, see *Scott* 2 AJIL 1908 p. 28. See also generally the articles in that volume.

A further strategy of proceduralizing conflict is the use of abstract categories in order to create boundaries between sovereigns. Discussion focuses, for example, to the definition of "State", "belligerency" and "neutrality" and relates a predetermined set of rights and duties to them. For instance, the distinction between civilized/non-civilized states controls discussion about conflicts of territory.[354] The distinction State/ non-State is used to deal with the most varied issues of jurisdiction, representation, ownership etc.[355] The distinction public/private is used to class, for example the rights which belligerents have at war and whether rules of neutrality are applicable.[356] In conflicts of jurisdiction, the same distinction works to allocate territorial jurisdiction in respect of foreign private acts but exempts foreign public acts from such jurisdiction.[357] In such cases, conflict-solution becomes a matter of determining whether the acting entities fulfil the qualities in the definition. Taking a stand on the material issue involved becomes unnecessary.

However, sometimes it is clear that these categorizations lack normative force. Take, for example, Lorimer's discussion of intervention. Intervention between States which have recognized this status in each other – that is, States between which there is a "normal relation" – is inadmissible.[358] But recognition is subject to withdrawal when the State thinks that conditions for it have been extinguished. In such case, an abnormal situation is created which allows intervention.[359] Though this discussion seems controlled by the formal distinctions of recognized/non-recognized State and normal/abnormal relations, the system is normatively very fragile as it depends on the good will and honesty of the State not to use its recognition – or absence thereof – as a means for its political ends. What status a State is deemed to have is dependent on the projection of the *other* State, a projection constantly liable to

---

[354] Civilized "statehood" functions in the allocation of territory by denying possession from entities – such as the American Indians – not understood as having organized as States. Areas occupied by them were therefore *terrae nullius*. See e.g. *Twiss* (Droit, I) pp. 201–207; *Wheaton* (Elements) p. 51n; *Bluntschli* (Völkerrecht) p. 67.

[355] Typically, this distinction grounds the difference between the law applicable in respect of European sovereigns *inter se* and these and non-European sovereigns.

[356] See e.g. *Klüber* (Droit des gens) p. 305; *G.-F. de Martens* (Précis, II) pp. 201–205; *Wheaton* (Elements) p. 314.

[357] See e.g. the *Schooner Exchange* Case (Scott: Cases) p. 300. See also *Wheaton* (Elements) pp. 128–131; *Twiss* (Droit, I) pp. 251–253; *Lorimer* (Droit) pp. 134–137. On the development of the doctrine of the immunity of the foreign sovereign, see also *Badr* (Sovereign Immunity) pp. 10–13.

[358] *Lorimer* (Droit) pp. 119–121, 126–128, 203–204.   [359] *Ibid.* pp. 74–77.

change. The same is true of the other professional categorizations as well. In one way or another, the disputing State's perception of the possession by the other entity of the required status must be taken into account. In such cases, as demonstrated by the *Schooner Exchange* Case (1811), recourse to the tacit consent construction may seem a useful way to arrive at a solution without having to overrule a State's subjective projection.[360]

To summarize: professional discourse presents a unity which combines a descending and an ascending argument in apparent harmony and thus avoids the objection that it is either utopian or apologist. This is possible within a historicist assumption which takes State freedom to be in harmony with general interest and understands State practice to manifest an inevitable historical development towards increasing freedom. States are the creators of the international order and in this capacity act in historically determined ways. However, this assumption is incapable of providing material solutions to conflicts of freedoms. Therefore, it uses the strategy of proceduralization. The law

---

[360] See *supra* n. 357. *Triepel* (Völkerrecht) makes an illustrative argument. He dissociates himself from the naturalist position; law is not something externally given but rises from consent. This distinguishes it from morals, pp. 28–29. But the will of a single State cannot ground a binding obligation. *Selbstverpflichtung* is impossible. Nor can obligation be based on contract for here the wills do not coincide but are mutually opposed, *ibid*, pp. 35–45. Only a *Vereinbarung* can create law as now the wills are directed at the same object. It is the fusion of several wills into one which can be objected against any individual will and thus grounds binding obligation, *ibid*, pp. 49–62. This is a mediating strategy: *Vereinbarung* is ascending (will-based) and descending (opposable to will) simultaneously. In custom, it manifests itself as a tacit agreement. True, uniform behaviour does not create law. Only common will can. But common will can be *inferred* from behaviour. Custom, too is a reconciliation, descending as it is constraining and applicable against a non-assenting State, ascending as it is assumed to manifest will, *ibid*, pp. 97–103.

Obviously, as *Nussbaum* (History) argues, Triepel left the "cardinal question" of whether tacit consent may be *revoked* "unanswered", p. 235. See also *Brierly* (Basis of Obligation) pp. 15–16. But what could he have done? Had he admitted it to be revocable, he would have lost the difference between himself and his interpretation of Jellinek's *Selbstverpflichtung*. Had he denied it, this would have required him to explain how external observers can "infer" consent from external behaviour and "know better" on this basis than the State whether it had consented or not. – In other words he needs to have a theory of "objective interests" or justice which enables this construction. This is how *Spiropoulos* (Théorie) reads him, pp. 53–54. But inasmuch as objective interests must be independent of will, the argument loses the difference between Triepel and his interpretation of the "naturalists". There is nowhere to go. On tacit consent, see further *infra* ch. 5.1.2.

becomes, as Terry Nardin has argued, not an order of material goals or values, but:

> ... a distillation of diplomatic, military and other international usages.[361]

That these procedures are sometimes outright disappointing, is evident for such a mainstream professional as Sir Travers Twiss:

> ... en plusieurs circonstances une nation est dans l'obligation de laisser faire certaines choses par une autre nation, quoiqu'elle les désapprouve, parce qu'elle ne pourrait les empecher par la force sans violer l'indépendence et l'égalité de cette nation, et détruire ainsi le fondement de la société naturelle entre les nations.[362]

2.4   Conclusion

Liberalism, Rawls writes, prefers "rights" to what is "good".[363] It privileges personal freedom and inviolability over substantive goals of social organization. I have argued that these assumptions characterize classical international law as well. Its starting-point is scepticism about human capacity to know the good. Values are subjective. In the absence of a universally valid code of values (or at least a method of knowing it), there is no justification to override the values held by some with those held by others. Hence the postulate of sovereign equality.[364] The problem is that social organization – constraint – is necessary. Otherwise, as Hobbes noted, life becomes "solitary, poore, nasty, brutish and short".[365] But as values are subjective, social organization cannot justify itself by referring to them. It can only seem justified (legitimate) if it is

---

[361] Nardin (Law, Morality) p. 115. This is usually expressed by the professionals themelves by calling their law "Koordinationsrecht". See e.g. Kaufmann (Wesen des Völkerrechts) p. 128 et seq; Hatschek (Völkerrecht) pp. 4–6.

[362] Twiss (Droit, I) p. 14.   [363] Rawls (Theory) p. 31.

[364] Oppenheim (International Law I) observes that equality among States is a "consequence of their sovereignty and of the fact that the Law of Nations is a law between, not above, the States", p. 20. Dickinson (Equality) points out that the idea of equality of States could emerge only when political legitimacy started to be inferred, not from a material natural law but from a pre-normative natural state in which States were understood to exist as so many individuals. The two conditions – state of nature and the domestic analogy – were present simultaneously only in post-Grotian thought: "it was not until the middle of the eighteenth century, in the period of Burlamaqui, Vattel, Wolff, and Moser, that publicists of all schools included the equality of States among their leading principles", pp. 334, 68 et seq.

[365] Hobbes (Leviathan) ch. 13 (p. 186).

understood to exist for the protection of the rights of its members – understood as invisible spheres of inviolability (sovereignty, domestic jurisdiction, self-determination etc.) around them.

The important question now relates to the determination of the State's sphere of inviolability. The initial liberal solution – used by Wolff and Vattel – was to rely on the State's own self-definition thereof. But this left the law unable to solve any conflicts in which these spheres seemed to overlap – it merely posed the problem (described the conflict as a divergence of views about subjective rights) but offered no solution (apart from the procedural solution of suggesting further negotiation).

To provide material solutions, a viewpoint external to the States was needed. This, as we have seen, was taken variably from natural law, good faith, the principle of the invisible hand, the principle of the national spirit or historical inevitability, etc. Each served to explain why it was sometimes legitimate to oppose the State's self-definition of its rights with something else in order to proceed to a material norm. But these principles undermine the original liberal assumptions. If the State's rights are to be determined by some rule external to the State itself, then this must be based either on natural law or majority legislation. The former assumption conflicts with the principle of subjective value, the latter with sovereign equality.

To avoid this consequence, classicism proceduralized the law. Instead of proposing material rules for delimiting sovereign rights, classical lawyers concentrated on *ius in bello*, diplomacy, neutrality, international conferences and congresses and so on. The success of this strategy is dependent on the well-foundedness of the assumption that States *will* use these machineries to solve their conflicts and to maintain international order. This assumption may seem justified if one believes in the invisible hand and in the inevitable development of world organization, peace and prosperity. But the assumption meets with two difficulties.

First, it undermines the sense of conflict in the States themselves. By directing States towards procedure, the law tells them that their controversy is only a minor misunderstanding which can be cleared once the States come to know and understand each other's views. Proceduralization ignores the fact that resources are scarce and that conflict-solution entails giving to some by taking away from others (or from others' reach). And it ignores the reality and importance to the States and their populations of the national, political, ideological, ethnic etc. values through which they look at the conflict and justify their own position. If deep antagonisms are at issue, it is hardly likely that the

States will lay down their swords and enter the offered procedure *bona fide*; all the less if they feel that the other's claim is so unjustified that merely to discuss it on the basis of equality is to submit to injustice.

Second, the procedural solution really assumes the ready presence of the conditions which it aims to create. To assume that States will agree on their rights (including allocation of resources) is to assume that States are not, after all, so selfish as they seem but that they can agree on principles (of delimitation and allocation) whereby conflicts can be solved. But this makes superfluous our original emphasis on the need to think of inter-State conflict in terms of subjective rights rather than some principles of (distributive) justice. If States can agree on principles of allocation, why could the law not take those substantive principles as its starting-point?

In this chapter I have attempted to explain what is involved in the truistic claim that international law is a Western heritage. I have argued that the international legal argument is constructed upon pluralistic and individualistic ideas which I associated with the liberal doctrine of politics. The idea of social conflict as a conflict between individual (sovereign) rights is a conceptual matrix relative to the historically specific intellectual climate of Europe from the seventeenth century onwards.[366] It is a paradox that many writers or statesmen who most deplore the Western intellectual heritage are most anxious to universalize it under a rigid international system of sovereign equality.[367] They simultaneously undermine the intellectual principles of their own cultures. For an international law of sovereign equality is a law of religious

---

[366] For an analysis of the kind of consciousness and social organization which need to be present in order for a liberal system of ideas and of society to emerge, see *Unger* (Modern Society) pp. 66–86, 143–147.

[367] See e.g. *Hingorani* (Modern) (making explicit the domestic analogy and that States have fundamental rights – of sovereignty and self-preservation – "in the same way in which an individual has in municipal law") p. 117. Likewise, *Anand* (New States), for example, thinks it worth arguing that this system of ideas and social organization prevailed beyond Europe already *before* colonization and that the latter merely destroyed the already present pluralist social system, pp. 7–44. Similarly, *Hingorani* (Modern) pp. 12–15. Far from being questioned, then, the system is strengthened in this claim for multiple paternity. Further, in *Anand*'s discussion of the ICJ, it is neither the legal procedure nor the bulk of the law which are challenged – what he claims is that the Europeans have *abused* the originally beneficial (liberal) system which now needs to be restored, (Gross: Future) pp. 1–21. See also *idem* 197 RCADI 1986/III *passim*, (a discussion on the principles of sovereignty and equality which well portrays the tensions of the liberal *problématique* – though, of course, Anand's argument denies its liberal heritage).

and ideological pluralism, moral scepticism, economic instrumentalism and legal objectivism. These values are fundamentally alien to the values professed by many writers and statesmen. For better or for worse, reliance upon the classical law of sovereign equality entails accepting the liberal doctrine of politics. And accepting that doctrine will either mean that one's professed national values should not be taken too seriously or that one's use of the common legal language is based on error or something less than good faith.

3

The structure of modern doctrines

I shall not attempt an exhaustive review of modern international legal doctrines or theories advanced by modern lawyers to explain why international law is something other than politics. My focus will remain with the argument's "deep-structure", that is, the conditions within which express argument is possible. I am less concerned about what lawyers have said or assumed than what they *need to say or assume* in order to think their work coherent. From this perspective, modern discourse will appear as the constant production of strategies whereby threats to the argument's inner coherence or to its controlling assumptions are removed, or hidden from sight, in order to maintain the system's overall credibility.

Modernism shares the classical *problématique*, involved in its adoption of the liberal theory of politics. It tries to explain why the law it projects is both normative and concrete – that is, not vulnerable to the criticism of being apologetic or utopian. But these explanations threaten each other. To remove – or explain away – the threat, doctrine may adopt four strategies. It may prefer normativity or concreteness, renounce both or explain them as compatible. These are *exhaustive and logically exclusive positions* and will count as a full description of the modern argument's structure.

I shall first describe the method whereby it has been possible for a distinctly "modern" discourse to emerge from a criticism of classical doctrines as subjective because either apologetic or utopian (3.1). I shall then describe two divergent strands within modernism to explain why their law is "relevant" for international life (3.2). Finally, I shall outline modernism's structure by means of an opposition between four reformist strands within it none of which seems able to explain the relevance of international law in a convincing fashion (3.3).

3.1 Modern interpretations of doctrine: descending and ascending arguments confirmed

The inability of 19th century international law to prevent war or even to regulate its conduct has been explained as a result of professionalism's failure.[1] What this failure consisted of has been interpreted from two perspectives.

On the one hand, the professional period is accused of *apologism*. It seemed to legitimize whatever was in a State's self-interest.[2] Reference is

---

[1] Much of international legal writing in the 1920s and the 1930s was oriented towards a reconstruction, associated with a feeling of social and political transition due to the Great War and the establishment of the League of Nations. To re-establish itself, battered legal doctrine took on the task of explaining what was needed in order to establish its constraining relevance. The sense of a common programme is evident in professor *Brierly*'s inaugural lecture (reprinted in "Basis of Obligation") in 1924: "... the world regards international law today as in need of rehabilitation". It was felt that "the comparatively small part that it plays in the sphere of international relations as a whole is disappointing", p. 68. Such sentiments were expressed throughout the European legal community. In the leading British work of reconstruction, *Lauterpacht* (Function) directed his criticism against 19th century views about sovereignty which allowed international law to exist only as a law of "coordination" and reserved a very limited role to the judicial function. He argued that it was impossible to distinguish between "legal" and "political" matters without this leading precisely to the weaknesses of professionalism. It was necessary to see international law as a "complete system" whose application was not precluded by the presence of political interests in a dispute, pp. 3–4, 9–25 *et seq*. In France, criticism was directed in particular against views deriving law exclusively from the fictions of sovereignty or State will. *Politis* (Nouvelles) and *Scelle* (Précis) followed Duguit's views and found the basis of law in social solidarity – the latter ultimately from biological necessities. The legislator did not "create" the law, only "declared" it. Statehood was a fiction, ultimately "les individus seuls sont sujets de droit en droit international public", (Précis I) p. 42. See also *Politis* 6 RCADI 1925/I p. 5 *et seq*; *Scelle* 46 RCADI 1933/IV p. 331 *et seq*. In Germany, a similar ethos stood behind the establishment of the Institute of Foreign Public Law and International Law in Heidelberg in 1924. The idea stressed was, again, the completeness of the international legal system. See e.g. the programmatic article by *Bruns* 1 ZaöRV 1929 p. 1 *et seq*. In the Netherlands, *Krabbe* 13 RCADI 1926/III applied his influential distinction between *Staats-/Rechtssouveränität* in international law and based international law on a "conscience juridique de l'homme", pp. 577, 513 *et seq*. The "Vienna School" in Austria, again, saw law alternatively in terms of a systematic unity, traceable back to a logical juristic hypothesis or to structural values. International law was understood to be prior to the State and sovereignty was seen as simply the sum total of the (limited) competences which the law had allocated to the State. See *Kelsen* (Souveränität) *passim*; *Verdross* (Einheit) *passim*; *idem* (Verfassung) *passim*.

[2] Thus, for example, *Schwarzenberger* (Frontiers) argues that 19th century international law "... was subservient to international politics ... or limited to fields which, from the point of view of the rule of force, were irrelevant", p. 300. Similarly *Fenwick* (International Law) notes that the professionals' law had "lost almost entirely its critical

made to the incorporation, in professional doctrine, of "absolutist" views on State sovereignty, based on Hegelian philosophy and expressed, in particular, in the *Selbstverpflichtungslehre*. These, it is argued, were incapable of grounding a reliable international order. By associating the law with what States willed or did, the professionals had, on this view, merely legitimized the narrow nationalism and imperialistic pursuits of European States which ultimately led to the 1914 cataclysm.[3]

But the professionals have also been accused of lacking contact with the reality of evolving international relations. Their historicism is interpreted as a naïve *utopianism*, variously presented as a conservative or a progressive one. The argument that professional doctrines were characterized by conservative utopias points out, for example, that the forms of international organization in 1914 no longer corresponded to international reality. They were inherited from the Vienna conference and the Holy Alliance and carried within themselves outdated ideas about intervention and international legality. In particular, they lacked ways of incorporating peaceful change into the law.[4] The charge of conservatism is frequently directed against the "metaphysical" doctrines of sovereignty or fundamental rights.[5] From another perspective, professional

and constructive character" and that there "was strong tendency on the part of publicists to rally to the defence of national interests", p. 70.

[3] See e.g. Nippold 2 RCADI 1924/I pp. 13, 20–21, 100–117 and *passim*. His argument was that the doctrines of "sovereignty", "equilibrium", "legitimacy" etc., espoused by mainstream professionals, were "political" ones and must be left aside in an objective, legal doctrine of international law, *ibid.* pp. 22–57. The political absolutism of 19th century theories about sovereignty and States' "fundamental rights" is stressed e.g. by *Verdross* (Einheit) pp. 4–8; *Kelsen* (Souveränität) pp. 151–204, 314–320 and generally in works cited *supra* n. 1. See also e.g. *Gidel* 13 RCADI 1925/V (a historical review and criticism) p. 541 *et seq*; *van Kleffens* 82 RCADI 1953/I pp. 68–74. A criticism of the autolimitation view is included in standard post-war writing as a matter of course. This is accompanied by a criticism of the professionals' use of the *rebus sic stantibus* doctrine and the referral of important issues outside law through the legal/political matters distinction. See e.g. *Lauterpacht* (Function) pp. 6–48; *Menzel-Ipsen* (Völkerrecht) p. 33. *Cassese* (Divided) makes the standard point that legal regulation of the time merely reflected Great Power interests, pp. 47, 55. See also *Charvin* (Benchikh-Charvin-Demichel: Introduction) pp. 30–38. Modern third world lawyers, in particular, stress the imperialistic character of 19th century professional doctrines. See e.g. *Bedjaoui* (New International Economic Order) pp. 51–57; *Anand* (New States) pp. 20–24, 25 *et seq*; *idem* 197 RCADI 1986/II pp. 58–65.

[4] See e.g. *Potter* 64 RCADI 1938/II p. 147; *Brierly* (Basis of Obligation) pp. 72–80; *Nippold* 2 RCADI 1924/I p. 35.

[5] Thus, *Politis* 6 RCADI 1925/I observes that the fundamental rights theory "repose sur une simple hypothèse, car elle ne démontre pas l'existence des droits fondamentaux sur laquelle elle se base", p. 15. See also *idem* (Nouvelles) pp. 36–45. Its "metaphysical character" is similarly criticized by *Gidel* 13 RCADI 1925/V pp. 543–545 and *passim*.

doctrines have been accused of progressive utopias. Attention is then focused on its unwarranted belief in the beneficial effect of arbitration and on its reliance on "Conferences", codification and work by scholars and private organization as means for securing peace.[6]

These contradicting interpretations through which moderns view the work of their 19th century predecessors reveal the modern argument's structure. Again, doctrine oscillates between a descending and an ascending perspective in its effort to avoid apology and utopia, associated with mistakes in previous doctrines. Modernism becomes possible – receives identity and acceptability – only by taking a critical distance from professionalism. That professional doctrines have been interpreted as one-sidedly apologetic or utopian has followed less from an effort to understand classicism's inner coherence than a wish to make modernism seem different from it and, as such, more credible.[7]

See further *Brierly* (Basis of Obligation) pp. 3–9. *Nussbaum* (History) accuses professionalism of incorporating "speculative trends" within itself, pp. 236–237 (with particular reference to professional naturalism). Similarly *Pound* (Philosophical) notes that in becoming historical and analytic, professional jurists worked with an old, frozen picture of the law which "no longer sufficed" to meet the requirements of the day, pp. 88–89. Some who take this view, however, hold that 19th century law had a moral standard which was lost from modernism. This view applauds professionalism's concern for the objective values of "sweetness, beauty and harmony" and interprets its demise as a result of its corruption by modern sceptical rationalism, *Baty* (Twilight) pp. 9–15, 269–300.

[6] Criticism focuses particularly on the results of the Hague Peace Conferences and the abortive plan for the International Prize Court. See e.g. *Fenwick* 79 RCADI 1951/II pp. 5–11; *De Visscher* 86 RCADI 1954/II pp. 521–523; *Murphy* (Search) pp. 105–113.

[7] Interestingly, as is recently pointed out by *Kennedy* 27 Harv.ILJ 1986 this duality within modern doctrines is also reflected in modern interpretations of early doctrine, pp. 10–12, 14, 58–118. For one group of moderns, in particular the modern positivists, there is a distinct break between early and classical scholarship, manifested especially in the "indiscriminate" mixing of theological and legal argument within the former, to be replaced by a more scientific classical period. See e.g. *Nussbaum* (History) pp. 79–81; *Corbett* (Law and Society) (pointing out the "ideological" world-picture of early lawyers) p. 6. For these lawyers, the movement from early to classical doctrine was an eminently healthy development towards realism and classicism's failure resides only in its not going far enough. For another group, early lawyers are rather the forerunners of modern scholarship as their work contains the ideals of universal organization and common values. This is the perspective of the modern naturalist, frequently expressing his nostalgia towards early writers such as Suarez, Grotius and Vitoria. See e.g. *Scott* (Spanish Origins) pp. 33, 67–68, 112–116 and *passim*; *idem* (Law I) p. 241 *et seq*; *Trelles* 43 RCADI 1933/I pp. 415–421; *Schiffer* (Legal Community) *passim*; *Nippold* 2 RCADI 1924/I pp. 10–12; *Murphy* (Search) *passim*. *Verdross* (Einheit) pp. 39–45; *Weiler* Rechtstheorie, Beiheft 6 pp. 70–78. But the same evaluation may also be taken from a positivist perspective. Then one emphasizes early lawyers' stress on sovereignty, as manifested in their refusal to recognize papacy's or the Emperor's universalist claims.

Achieving a discourse which would be both normative and concrete seems, however, difficult. The conflicting interpretations about professionalism's failure manifest modern lapses into either direction. To accuse professional doctrines of apologism reveals in the critic the assumption that what is needed is to increase the law's normative-critical nature, its association with moral-political or other supranational demands.[8] To explain professional failure by its utopianism reveals the critic's preference for a law which is concretely manifested in the political context – i.e. in the sociological "facts".[9] Both positions are constantly present in modern doctrine.

See *Walker* (History) pp. 148–150, 213 *et seq.* These interpretations attribute classicism's failure to its specificity, its attempt to be different from its early predecessors.

[8] See e.g. *Le Fur* 18 RCADI 1927/III observing "le discredit dans lequel était feuillé le droit international" in the 19th century and arguing that: "Nous assistons aujourd'hui à la naissance d'un nouvel ordre international, ou on tente de remplacer la notion de souveraineté absolue d'Etat ... par un droit international à la base de justice", pp. 400–401. *Trelles* 43 RCADI 1933/I observes that much of the unity of post World War I scholarship is constituted by a movement away from sovereignty into international organization (that is, from an ascending into a descending position) pp. 397–398. To the same effect, see *Spiropoulos* (Théorie) pp. iv–v. This movement is visible in naturalist as well as positivist writing. For example, both *Verdross* (Einheit) pp. 4–8, 120–135 and *Kelsen* (Souveränität) p. 102 *et seq*, accuse professional doctrines of apologism but while the former constructs the binding principle on material natural law, the latter does this by reference to a juristic hypothesis.

[9] Thus *Scelle* adopts the position which infers law from the "objective causality" of biological necessities. "Le droit positif est donc une traduction des lois biologiques que gouvernent la vie et le développement de la société", (Précis I) p. 5. The significance of this position is that it allows him to avoid the utopianism of classical naturalism and the apologism of positivist voluntarism. He notes expressly that the law is neither metaphysics nor State will. It is "partout et toujours, un phénomène social naturel, analogue à des autres phénomènes sociaux" 46 RCADI 1933/IV pp. 334–335. The same rhetorical strategy is used by *Politis* 6 RCADI 1925/I for whom "will" is only a fiction, an illusion behind the law. Law cannot be inferred from a metaphysical notion of sovereignty but from the "nécessités de la vie qui gouvernent les hommes sans être gouvernées par eux", pp. 29–30. Law depends on "solidarité et ... l'interdépendance économique des peuples" and its emergence is "bien antérieur aux traités, qui se bornent à les formuler", p. 30.

Due to the difficulty to demonstrate the alleged social or biological necessities in a tangible way, another "realist" movement stresses the instrumental aspects of the law. Outlining what was to become the creed of the sociological movement *Pound* (Philosophy) concludes his criticism of 19th century professional views by noting that as the new construction is attempted: "we may demand of him (the lawyer, MK) a legal philosophy that shall take account of the social psychology, the economics, the sociology as well as the law and politics of today ... and above all shall conceive of the legal order as a process and not a condition", p. 89. See further *infra*, ch. 3.3.2.–3.3.3.

The disturbing factor in modern criticisms is that though they seem to have a degree of plausibility, they are also indefensible alone – precisely because the critic always seems to place himself in one or the other position.

If the critic accuses classicism of being apologetic, i.e. too concerned about what States did or willed, he can be answered that State practice was studied *because* it was the best manifestation of justice. Unless the critic is able to show what other evidence of justice there might be apart from State practice, the criticism seems pointless. If such evidence bears no relation to State practice, the critic's position will seem utopian. If he concedes that justice indeed manifests itself in behaviour, his own position will become indistinguishable from that of his opponent[10] and discussion must focus on the criteria of justice which give us the conflicting interpretations of what went on.

If the critic accuses classicism of being utopian, i.e. based on abstract principles such as "fundamental rights" or "national spirit" he can be answered that some such principles of justice *must be assumed* in order to distinguish permissible and prohibited forms of behaviour from each other. If the critic cannot accept these – or some other – principles of justice as valid, then his position will seem apologetic.[11] If he concedes that some principles must indeed be assumed if law is to be binding, then the criticism is, again, about the correct theory of justice.

The continuity from classical to modern doctrines is hidden by modern criticisms. But the criticisms remain partial and unable to justify themselves unless they accept something from the object of their criticism. In particular, they would need to accept that the difference lies actually in theories of justice and not on some epistemological or methodological assumptions. To proceed from this, however, moderns would have to assume that theories of justice can be compared in a rational manner. Otherwise the criticism would seem pointless. But this would lead modern lawyers into the position of their early

---

[10] See e.g. *Quadri* 80 RCADI 1952/I (observing the dangers of such a naturalist criticism becoming either utopian or – if it simply invests practice with moral meaning – apologist) pp. 600–601. See also *Ago* 90 RCADI 1956/II (criticizing Scelle's biological objectivism of the same – it is either based on an indemonstrable hypothesis or forced to abdicate itself in its assumption that positive law coincides with biology) pp. 906–907.

[11] This is the core of *Le Fur*'s 18 RCADI 1927/III criticism of modern points against theories of fundamental rights, pp. 421–423. He makes the same point against the "realist" views of Duguit and Scelle in 54 RCADI 1935/IV pp. 88–94, 96–98. Likewise, *Djuvara* 64 RCADI 1938/II observes that the choice of the relevant social or biological "necessities" is a conceptual, value-dependent one, pp. 525 *et seq*, 539–542.

predecessors – assuming the existence of a natural morality. This, as we have seen, would conflict with the liberal Rule of Law.

Consequently, just like their predecessors, modern lawyers are forced into combining their ascending arguments with descending ones. There is no distinction as far as the argument's structure or the character of its outcomes are concerned. The distinction lies in rhetorics, in what associations are chosen to fulfil the ascending and descending spaces.[12] This makes it easier to understand why present controversies so easily seem like modernized versions of the naturalism/positivism dichotomy, even if they appear in the language of such doctrinal oppositions as idealism/realism, rules/processes, law/policy and so on. The classical *problématique* lies at the bottom.

However, it is imperative to notice, and follows from what I have said so far, that these oppositions cannot be attached to the utopianism/ apologism dilemma in any permanent way. Naturalism may look utopian (as presented in classical criticisms of the early scholars) or apologist (as suggested by modern criticisms of the fundamental rights theories). Positivism may seem apologist (as argued in many modern criticisms of 19th century scholars) as well as utopian (as suggested by critics of Kelsen). No position, argument or doctrine is by itself utopian or apologist. These characterizations relate to a position only as a result of interpretation, projection from an opposing perspective – another view about what it is for an argument to be "subjective" or "objective".

Similarly, "naturalism" and "positivism", too, are purely relational terms which have significance only in opposition to each other. A position may look "naturalistic" in its relation to one but "positivistic" in its relation to another position. This is what made the contrasting

---

[12] The modern programme is one of reconciliation. This takes place by a "double denial". To create identity for themselves, modern lawyers advocate a movement away from *both* naturalism and positivism. See e.g. *Falk* (Status of Law) pp. 514–516. See also *supra* ch. 1.1. Such rhetorics are present in earlier moderns as well. We have seen that this was the case of Scelle's and Politis' "realism" (*supra* n. 9). Likewise, *Le Fur* 18 RCADI 1927/ III – classed by later lawyers as a "naturalist" in *their* attempt to distance themselves from him – is in fact opposed *both* to positivism and naturalism. The former is criticized for its excessive reliance on what "is" while the latter is renounced because it sees in international law only "une adaption du droit naturel entre les Etats", pp. 344–345. Consequently, he makes the rhetorical move towards what he calls a "synthesis", pp. 379–399. This strategy – the initial identification and criticism of positivism *and* naturalism and the option for an intermediate position is precisely what provides the modern argument's identity. See further *infra* n. 72.

interpretations of professionalism's failure possible. But this will ultimately make the modern project impossible to carry out.

Modern lawyers too, are concerned with an attempt to create a law
simultaneously normative and concrete. But if a doctrine or position is
"utopian" or "apologist" only in its relation to another doctrine or position,
then the project would seem succesful only if the moderns shared a
common perspective for undertaking these classifications coherently.
They should occupy a position *beyond* the dichotomy of apologism/uto-
pianism. But they do not. The very perspectives from which modern lawyers
look at each other remain *within* the very controversy. Therefore, even the
*possibility of genuine agreement over what count as correct interpretations of
classicism and what should be done to avoid its "mistakes" is excluded.* In the
absence of a shared position from which to look at other doctrines, even
their characterization as unacceptable because too apologist or too utopian
remains just an exchange of empty words. On the other hand, if the persons
share the same perspective, then they have *already* agreed on how to
characterize the position under scrutiny. There is no argument which
would lead into interpretation. The interpretation is either simply accepted
a priori or it will remain disputed.[13]

Modernism is best understood as a continuing series of *differentiations* which utilize the utopianism/apologism opposition in order to
create space for a doctrine which will not be fully either. Other doctrines
are constantly projected in these categories and seem therefore something "other" than what modernism is about. As utopianism/apologism,
however, have no fixed content but are recognizeable and exist only in
their mutual exclusion, no space is open for reconciliation. Modernism
will dissolve itself into a series of differentiations, a procedure for
making arguments but not one for adopting positions.

The Rule of Law is premised on radical scepticism about values
(justice). Only such values can have a place in the system which can be
linked to demonstrable facts of State behaviour.[14] In the absence of

---

[13] See also *Kennedy* 23 GYIL 1980 pp. 374–376.

[14] *Oppenheim* (International Law): "We know today that a Law of Nature does not exist",
p. 99. See also *idem* 2 AJIL 1908 pp. 328–330. Usually this point is dressed in epistemological terms: even if it exists, we cannot *know* it. See e.g. *Kelsen* (Principles)
pp. 442–443. Similarly *Spiropoulos* (Théorie) p. 110; *Erlich* 105 RCADI 1962/I
pp. 657–659. *Rousseau* (Droit international, I) makes the standard point that natural
law is merely a "theoretical" ideal which is too far removed from actual practice to be a
reliable guide for international law. Accepting it will inevitably lead into subjectivism:
"... elle aboutit à faire dépendre une solution arbitrale ou judicaire de conceptions
subjectives de l'interprète," p. 31.

common values, normative constraint is justified only on the "harm principle"; intervention (interference) becomes the ultimate vice. The law's business is to prevent intervention. To do this in a neutral way, without in fact enhancing some States' values, legal rules must be objective. The doctrine of "sources" serves to delineate in a formal and abstract fashion what count as legal rules and what do not. It points out those avenues whereby State behaviour is transformed into objective rules of law.

But what if a State denies that some rule or proposed application is objective? If we simply admit that State's position, then we fall into apologism. Objectivity requires that the law can be opposed also to a State which does not accept it or does not think it corresponds to its interests.[15] We need a descending argument to justify the rule or the proposed application. But we cannot receive this from any material theory of justice. The sole premise which we have to fall back on is the scepticism-related formal premise about sovereign equality. We are led to consider whether the proposed rule or its application conflicts with it. This will, however, require that we have a material conception of what rights, liberties or competences are included in "sovereignty" or in what respect States are "equal". Moreover, we need to think that *our* position on this matter can override the State's own position. And this seems indistinguishable from arguing on the basis of a purely descending theory of justice.

Of course, modern lawyers continue to maintain that rules must be just or equitable and make points about "elementary considerations of humanity", common interests, legislative purposes, the needs of the international community etc.[16] The modern argument refers constantly back to ideas beyond what States do or will. Such arguments seem

---

[15] *Salvioli* 46 RCADI 1933/IV makes the useful point that whichever way we decide in such situation, the *choice* – unless we wish to violate sovereign equality – can only be made by criteria external to the wills or interests of the States involved, p. 6. *Nippold* RCADI 1924/I notes the need for a "point de vue objectif". Moreover: "Si la science est objective, elle doit pouvoir distinguer le juste et l'injuste, en quelques nations que l'un ou l'autre se manifeste", p. 13. In reconstructive doctrines, the idea that one could be bound only through one's will was emphatically – and from all sides – rejected. See further *infra* n. 72.

[16] Thus, it is argued that it is of the essence of the law that it constitutes a "system" and not merely an aggregate of what States happen to will at any time. This "system" can be grasped, it is suggested, by the construction of "general principles" which grasp the law's systematic coherence. See e.g. *Bruns* 1 ZaöRV 1929 pp. 1–56 and, for example, *Verdross* (Einheit) p. 98 *et seq*; *idem* (Vefrassung) pp. 1–12, 42 *et seq*. See also *supra*, ch. 1.2.3.

defensible because they imply a theory of justice which is *dressed in such general terms that it is possible to refer it back to subjective acceptance by States themselves.* No State would, for example, deny that it has accepted "elementary considerations of humanity" as a standard to be applied in its relations with another State. But the more concrete such principle is made, the more controversial it will seem and the more need there is to make explicit the theory of justice on which it is based. And here is the dilemma: we can make the law seem defensible (that is, ascending-descending) only when there is no conflict of interpretations – in which case, of course, no substantive defence of our position is needed. But immediately when such defence is called for – that is, when there is a normative problem – we are forced to take a position which will immediately seem either apologetic (because we accept the State's own self-definition) or utopian (because we use a material theory of justice).[17]

Modernism cannot solve this dilemma. It continues at the level of generalities. Nippold points out that lawyers should avoid falling either into impatience or scepticism.[18] Merrills argues that the task is to avoid becoming either a "cynic" or a "naive idealist".[19] Similar citations could be continued at length. The Permanent Court of International Justice reconciles the two in its famous statement about the nature of international law in the *Lotus* Case (1927):

> International law governs relations between independent States. The rule of law binding upon States therefore emanates from their own free will as expressed in conventions or usages generally accepted as expressing principles of law and in order to regulate the relations between these co-existing independent communities or with a view to the achievement of common aims.[20]

In other words, the law is concrete as it arises from the States themselves and not some pre-existing morality. But it is normative, too, as it governs inter-State conduct by "binding" rules, ultimately "with a view to the achievement of common aims".

This dualism can be detected in all doctrinal areas. In the characterization of international society we move between the visions of coordination and subordination. We think of State sovereignty as something preceding the law and something delimited by it. We think of international

---

[17] See also *Unger* (Knowledge) p. 85.   [18] *Nippold* 2 RCADI 1924/I p. 19.
[19] *Merrills* (Anatomy) p. 1.   [20] PCIJ: *Lotus* Case, Ser. A 10 p. 18.

organizations as forms of struggle and cooperation between States and persons in their own right with "implied powers" to fulfil their aims. We hold a consensualist as well as a non-consensualist view about sources, think of treaties, custom and general principles as binding because they express consent and because they express justice. And so on. Each dispute involves, in one way or another, the opposition between a descending and an ascending way to argue about order and obligation and varying emphasis on the ideas of normativity and concreteness.

Let me describe some of the ways in which modern lawyers have attempted a reconciliation.

The manner in which J. L. Brierly (1881–1955) introduces his popular text-book is a good example of the modern argument. He starts out by describing what he understands by a fully ascending position. This is related to the legitimation of the nation-State through the doctrine of sovereignty. It "reached its culmination" in Hobbes' effort to identify the law with the word of the strongest power in the commonwealth.[21] But this is unacceptable:

> No democrat if he is true to his principles can believe that there ought somewhere in a state to be a repository of absolute power ...[22]

Internationally, too, the consequences of such a position are grim. As it legitimizes anything that States wish to do it will lead into "international anarchy".[23]

The descending position is manifested in classical naturalism. Though this is treated in a somewhat more positive tone than the ascending argument – owing to Brierly's own intuitive preferences – it does not escape criticism.[24] It was sometimes developed in "ways both fanciful and tedious".[25] Natural law is untenable: law does not always arise from what seems rational. Nor do we entertain the same idea of what is rational or just. Differences of time and place count. Moreover, an absolutely binding conception of natural law would, like the fully ascending argument, only lead into international anarchy: as there is no final certainty about it, it would merely allow each State the freedom to think of its own political views as law.[26]

Brierly presents doctrinal history so as to manifest the tension between the two views and to separate himself from them. Grotius is presented as a proponent of the descending position, utopian because

[21] *Brierly* (Law of Nations) pp. 1–16.   [22] *Ibid.* p. 15.   [23] *Ibid.* p. 45.
[24] See generally *ibid.* pp. 16–20.   [25] *Ibid.* p. 18.   [26] *Ibid.* pp. 20–22.

unable to establish a convincing conception of the just war.[27] Vattel is made to exemplify the ascending argument, apologist and "disastrous" in its overemphasis on independence.[28]

Brierly's own reconciliation takes place in two phases. First, neither natural nor positive law is fully rejected. Though the latter, when it exists (that is, in "easy cases") may be primary, the former has an important role as it encapsulates the law's purpose (useful when hard cases appear).[29]

The rest of the reconciliation is dealt with under the topic "basis of obligation".[30] Brierly notes first that the problem is not one of law at all but one of philosophy.[31] Still, he discusses it at some length. Why does law bind? Neither because it expresses consent nor because it expresses justice. It binds because:

> ... man ... is constrained, insofar as he is a reasonable being, to believe that order and not chaos is the governing principle of the world ... [32]

There is, then, an objective order which is independent of "man" himself. But it can manifest itself only through what human beings believe. Though originally declaratory, human belief becomes the argumentative justification of order. A descending and an ascending argument are made to coincide: order is binding because no social life can exist without it. This is presented as an objective truth, independent of human will or perception. But it is also binding because human beings believe it is. It is now subjective conviction which is primary. This is a simple restatement of the liberal circle: Law must be based on justice and common interest and not somebody's personal opinions. Personal convictions are what count because justice, common interests etc. manifest themselves in them.

Other reconciliation strategies exist. One is the introduction of the descending and ascending arguments under the guise of "general principles" and "custom", respectively. More will be said of this opposition and its reversibility in chapter 6. Suffice it here to refer to D. P. O'Connell's (1925–1979) popular treatise. The descending principles (e.g. he must restore that which does not belong to him, a man may not be judge in his own case) are valid because "they are in themselves law".[33] Alongside these, there exists custom which is contingent and

---

27 *Ibid.* pp. 33–35.   28 *Ibid.* pp. 37–40.   29 *Ibid.* pp. 23–24.
30 *Ibid.* pp. 49–56. For a more extended treatment, see *idem* (Basis of Obligation) pp. 1–67.
31 Brierly (Law of Nations) p. 54; *idem* (Basis of Obligation) p. 16.
32 Brierly (Law of Nations) p. 56. See also *idem* (Basis of Obligation) pp. 66–67.
33 O'Connell (International Law, I) pp. 7, 5–7.

ascending in that it embodies a "coincidence of wills".[34] But there is a danger of conflict. Which is superior? O'Connell does not discuss this. A consistent hierarchy between the two cannot be established without lapsing either into utopias or apologism.[35] Therefore, he makes it seem as if no real conflict existed:

> ... the notions of "general principles of law" and "customary law" are not disjunctive. The former generate concrete rules for contingent instance; the latter is a body of rules actually formulated.[36]

In other words, general principles and custom emerge into one another: the former manifest themselves in the latter – the latter express the former. Indeed:

> ... one is not permitted to set up any antithesis between (the two, MK) but to regard them as concordant elements of the same system.[37]

O'Connell's discussion proceeds from creating a difference into making that difference disappear. First, the descending and ascending arguments are confirmed, then made to seem indistinguishable.

The curious dilemma in modern doctrines is that they create identity for themselves precisely by creating and making disappear the opposition between a descending and an ascending model of argument. The former is projected onto early doctrines (and sometimes on classicism, too) so that they can be made to seem unacceptably utopian. The latter is projected onto classical doctrines, portrayed as unacceptably apologist. The identity of modernism *vis-à-vis* non-modern doctrines is created

---

[34] *Ibid.* p. 6.

[35] *O'Connell* (International Law, I) does outline the positivist's and the naturalist's answers to the problem of relative supremacy but refrains from taking a stand. Instead, he observes that there is the tendency to use "general principles" to denote both standards subjectively accepted by States (under municipal law) but given no definite international form as well as those valid in an objective way, without specific consent. He assumes that there is no reason to choose between these alternative approaches and suggests that a reconciliation may be achieved by assuming identity between them, pp. 9–10, 13. This is, however, simply a *non sequitur*. For the point of the two understandings is that they are capable of overruling each other. To hold a general principle as a consensual norm is meaningful only if we accept that "consensual" means that it can override any non-consensual explanations and *vice-versa*. Inasmuch as there is a normative problem about the content and/or application of a "general principle", we must choose between the ascending (consensual) and descending (non-consensual) understandings. Either we hold the State bound by it because it has consented to it or regardless of its consent. See further *infra* ch.5.

[36] *Ibid.* p. 6.   [37] *Ibid.* p. 7, see also p. 10.

upon assuming a difference between the descending and the ascending argument. But during the moderns' own project, that distinction vanishes. Descending points about justice are made to seem parallel to ascending arguments about State will, behaviour or interest, for example. Threatening conflicts are treated so as to make them disappear.[38] This is so because privileging either would remain vulnerable to the moderns' own criticisms against early and classical doctrines.

3.2 Modern interpretations of practice

Modern lawyers have set themselves the task of explaining the "relevance" of international law. This is another way of expressing the need to imagine the law as both concrete and normative. It is generally held undisputed that the focal case of law – municipal law – fulfils these conditions. The question of the relevance transforms itself into the question whether the subject-matter of modern international legal text-books bears sufficient resemblance to municipal law in the relevant respects.

Since Grotius wrote his *De Jure belli ac pacis* in order to refute the views of those who held international law as non-existent or irrelevant it has been common for writers to dedicate a page or two to a comparison of municipal and international law and to a discussion of the specific nature (primitiveness, weakness) of the latter. The point of such discussion is to oppose critics who believe that international law is irrelevant because it lacks legislative, judicial or enforcement procedures.[39]

---

[38] See e.g. *Bernhardt* 36 ZaöRV 1976 pp. 61, 62. See also *Finch* (Sources) pp. 26–29.

[39] For standard treatments, see e.g. *Levi* (Contemporary International Law) pp. 17–18; *Bleckmann* (Grundprobleme) pp. 152–160; *Carreau* (Droit international) pp. 34–35; *Cavaré* (Droit international I) pp. 146–159 (insufficient and exceptional character of sanctions), pp. 264–267 ("primitiveness"); *Reuter* (Droit international public) pp. 18–21; *Lauterpacht* (International Law I) p. 11 *et seq*; *Ross* (Text-book) pp. 54–59; *Akehurst* (Modern Introduction) pp. 1–11; *Wallace* (International Law) pp. 2–4; *Pinto* (Relations) p. 51 *et seq*. The criticism restates the Austinian point that to call "law" something which lacks the character of sovereign command, backed by habitual obedience, distorts the very concept of law because it becomes indistinguishable from "opinion". This (liberal) criticism can be found in e.g. *Hayek* (Road to Serfdom), arguing that in the absence of an external (objective) authority, "we must not deceive ourselves that in calling in the past the rules of international behavior international law we were doing more than expressing a pious wish", p. 173. See also *Somló* (Juristische) (arguing that though "Great Powers" *do* possess coercive power, international law falls short of "law" as its norms cannot *legitimately* be imposed on recalcitrant states – they are mere wishes – moreover wishes which are continuously disregarded) pp. 153–178.

To appreciate the value of these standard criticisms and responses we need to look closer into the assumptions behind them. Why would lack of certain procedures, present in municipal law, make international law impossible as law? Answering this requires that we possess a *theory about the character of social life among States*. The criticism itself is based on a distinctly Hobbesian theory: there is no natural society among States just as there is none among individuals. Society is artifical and created by human beings (and States) themselves. Moreover, there is the psychological premise: men (and States) can maintain society only if they are forced to do this – by legislative, judicial and enforcement procedures.[40] The legal nature of municipal law rests on this. It is something other than (a speculative) morality precisely as it is able to constrain. Lacking such procedures, international law can only be a hopelessly irrelevant utopia or an interminably flexible apology.

Modern lawyers have attacked this criticism from two perspectives both of which involve a certain interpretation of State behaviour and a certain theory of the character of social life among States. The problem, as we shall see, lies in the fact that these controlling interpretations will, on the *doctrine's own premises*, seem only like conventional ways of conceptualizing the world neither of which can be rationally preferred to the other nor to the assumptions behind the "deniers'" criticism.[41]

An *individualist strategy* accepts the critic's theory but not his analysis. It is true that individualism prevails and that a relevant law can only exist in the presence of legislative, judicial and enforcement mechanisms which force individuals into community. But such mechanisms do exist in international law, albeit in a modified, primitive way. On this view, custom and treaty appear as legislation, adjudication is performed by municipal and international bodies and self-help and reprisals work as mechanisms of enforcement.[42]

---

[40] The assumptions and the conclusion are clearly – and well – expressed in *West* (Psychology, Part 2) pp. 188–193, 203–212 and *passim*. *De Visscher's* (Theory) argument against Jellinek is based precisely on these assumptions: *Selbstverpflichtung* is imaginable only in a community where natural solidarity among persons *already* exists – this is not the case between States, p. 50.

[41] On these two conceptual schemes, see e.g *Bull* (Anarchical Society) pp. 130–136; *Kratochwil* 69 ARSP 1983 pp. 22–27.

[42] For a full, early statement of this position, see *van Vollenhoven* (Scope) which contains an exposition of "international constitutional law", consisting of a theory of international legislation, administration, government and police, pp. 7 *et seq*, 39–107. In its most developed theoretical formulation, this view stresses the role of *dédoublement fonctionnel* of individuals. They are simply sometimes given capacity to act by national

Now, this might seem intuitively plausible in respect of treaties and international judicial bodies. However, the argument does not restrict itself to claiming that only treaties or adjudication are relevant as law. In the first place, they cover only a very small amount of inter-State activity. If they were all that is distinctly legal in such activity, then the law could not seem very relevant. Secondly, it is uncertain to what extent treaties can really be called "law".[43] In any case, they do not normally have effects for third States. So, the argument that international law is relevant because it contains the procedures allegedly lacking from it must refer beyond treaties and adjudication to many kinds of State activity which are assumed to be "legislative", "judicial" or "sanctioning" in character.

law, sometimes by international law. In the former case, they are national, in the latter international "organs" – whether in legislative, judicial or administrative capacity. See *Scelle* (Précis II) pp. 10–12 and *passim*; *idem* 46 RCADI 1933/IV pp. 422–427. From this it follows that the whole body of international law can be expressed – as Scelle does – in terms of legislative, judicial and administrative competences which the law has allocated to certain groups of persons, organized as "States", (Précis II) *passim*. This way of understanding the bulk of the law is very common. See e.g. *Rousseau* 93 RCADI 1958/I pp. 394–396 *et seq*; *Cavaré* (Droit international I) pp. 185–209 *et seq*; *Carreau* (Droit international) p. 302 *et seq*. See further *infra* ch. 4. Obviously, the same result is achieved by Kelsenian monism: all law is simply a set of competences whose source lies outside the State. See e.g. *Kelsen* 42 RCADI 1932/IV (international law providing the "domaine de validité" of municipal acts) p. 182 *et seq*. For the argument that States themselves act as "legislators", see e.g. *Reuter* (Droit international public) p. 14; *Merrills* (Anatomy) pp. 1–5.

For the argument that there is a system of sanctions, applicable in the form of self-help, reprisals or war, see e.g. *Oppenheim* (International Law, I) pp. 13–14. The classical position is, of course, contained in *Kelsen* 14 RCADI 1924/IV pp. 244, 317–318; *idem* 42 RCADI 1932/IV pp. 124–137; *idem* 84 RCADI 1953/III pp. 31–34; *idem* (Principles) pp. 3–4, 16 *et seq*; *idem* (Deutsch-Hoffmann: Relevance) pp. 115–118. Others share this view. *Merrills* (Anatomy) holds that self-help is "quite basic to the enforcement of international law", pp. 21–24. See also *Akehurst* (Modern Introduction) pp. 6–7. See also *Air Transport Services Agreement* Arbitration (1978) in which the suspension of air flights was held as a legal form of self-help, 54 ILR 1979 §§ 80, 84–99. See also ICJ: *Corfu Channel* Case, Reports 1949 pp. 30, 35. For a review, see *Elagab* (Counter-measures) *passim*. Forcible self-help (in contrast to self-defence), however, is usually held prohibited under modern law of the UN Charter. See *Bowett* (Self-defence) p. 11; *O'Connell* (International Law I) p. 304; *Schwarzenberger-Brown* pp. 150–151; *Verdross-Simma* (Völkerrecht) pp. 653–654; *Alibert* (Droit de . . .) p. 22. For a view which reserves a limited right to use force as sanction to the State, see *Schachter* 178 RCADI 1982/V pp. 167–175. See also *Brierly* (Law of Nations) pp. 399–402; *Carreau* (Droit international) pp. 35–36.

[43] For clearly, treaties seem to create *obligations* while the law intervenes only to guarantee that they are binding. See e.g. *Fitzmaurice* 92 RCADI 1957/II pp. 40–43; *idem* (Symbolae Verzijl) pp. 153–176.

The soundness of this strategy hinges on the correctness of the interpretation it implies about the *meaning* of certain forms of State behaviour. How do we know that in making treaties or adopting certain patterns of behaviour a State in fact "legislates" and not merely furthers its national interest in individual circumstances? When does a pattern of behaviour amount to law? Further, how do we know in which function a municipal authority is acting at a particular moment?[44] How do we know that a State's or an international organization's decision in a matter involving law-application is really made in a judicial capacity, that is, by reference to legal rules, and not in furtherance of private interests? Finally, the combined effect of the autointerpretative nature of international law and the doctrine of self-help/reprisals as enforcement seems singularly question-begging. How can we tell which side in a conflict is the "punishing" one and which sanctioned against? Each of these questions relates to the justification of adopting a certain interpretation of the meaning of state conduct: is the conduct or act a "legal" one or a purely political manoeuvre, comity or custom, political rationalization or adjudication, violence or sanction?[45]

Obviously, we cannot simply say that all understandings or usages by States create law. Not all State views about law amount to adjudication.

[44] The problem relates to whether we consider municipal applications of standards originating in international law as straightforward applications of international law or as applications of municipal standards after the relevant international standards have been incorporated into municipal law. This, of course, is the core of the classical monism/dualism dichotomy. The disturbing factor here is that both interpretations of municipal acts seem equally possible. A municipal act of incorporation may appear in a declaratory as well as in a constitutive light. It may have been enacted because international law was binding; or international law may have become binding only by virtue of the act. The mere "fact" of incorporation is powerless to tell which of these interpretations of its meaning is correct. The standard attempt to argue the primacy of one or the other position by focusing on the practice or international/municipal tribunals involves a *non sequitur*, the very choice of the relevant tribunal (international or domestic) already assumes the correctness of one or the other position.

[45] See e.g. *Friedmann* 127 RCADI 1969/II (against interpreting municipal action as *dédoublement fonctionnel* because of national bias) pp. 72–73. The combined effect of the law's autointerpretative character and the doctrine of self-help appears destructive: it offers legal rhetoric for the service of most varied kinds of self-interested violence. That such violence can be masked as legally authorized "sanction" tends to increase popular, and perhaps professional, too, scepticism about the law's relevance. A standard example is the Franco-British "police operation" at Suez Canal in 1956. See e.g. *Henkin* (How) pp. 250–268. For an analysis of the various forms of "private justice" between States and the various justifications about self-defence, defence of national sovereignty, self-determination, humanitarian causes etc. see *Alibert* (Droit de ...) pp. 27–466.

All violence is not enforcement. Unless a distinction between conduct which amounts to law-creation, adjudication and enforcement and conduct which does not is made, we shall fall into pure apologism. Two kinds of criteria seem available to distinguish a State's legal from its purely political behaviour: we might either look at the State's own self-understanding of the character of its action, or we might examine the intrinsic nature of the acts it has performed.

The former – internal – criterion guides us to look at how the State itself understood the character of its conduct. Its behaviour amounts to legislation, adjudication or enforcement if it itself thinks so. Surely it looks like an important element in municipal doctrines of legislation, adjudication or enforcement that these activities embody the acting organ's realization that it is acting in the said capacity. This approach seems to go well with modern theories about social explanation. To understand the meaning of social behaviour, we must include the behaving person's self-understanding of that meaning into our account.[46] But it will lead normatively into simple apologism. The State can always say its activity was such and thus escape criticism. Far from being a demonstration of the law's relevance, the fact that asocial activity can mask itself as legally authorized self-help merely reinforces the critic's view of the law's manipulability and ultimate irrelevance.[47]

---

[46] See *Winch* (Idea) pp. 86–89, 121 *et seq*. The specificity of social institutions lies, it seems, in that they are (at least partly) constituted through the way participants understand them. Thus "it is impossible to identify the institution except in terms of the beliefs of those who engage in its practices", *MacIntyre* (Self-images) p. 264 (against pure behaviourism). For a classic, see *Taylor* (Philosophy) (for a hermeneutic approach which aims at grasping intersubjective "common meanings") pp. 15–57. For an early appeal to include a subjective, internal perspective in any attempt to "know" about the State, see *Jellinek* (Allgemeine) pp. 136–137 *et seq*. That the "subjective test" is needed to distinguish binding from non-binding standards ("law" from "non-law") is simply a restatement of the consensualist position; law is not "natural". This point is contained in the inclusion of the *opinio juris* in the doctrine of custom and, for example, in the difficulty to distinguish "treaty" from other written understandings by other means than through what the parties had intended. For the latter point, see further *infra* n. 48.

[47] Some have indeed claimed that the fact that States regularly do legitimize their actions by reference to international law is a "proof" of its relevance. See e.g. *Oppenheim* (International Law, I) p. 15; *Henkin* (How) p. 45; *Bull* (Anarchical Society) pp. 45, 138; *Fawcett* (Law and Power) pp. 117–118; *Pinto* (Relations) pp. 72–73. But this view may only support the law's manipulability, not its relevance. *D'Amato* 79 Northwestern University Law Review 1984–85 pp. 1301–1303. The manipulability of the doctrine of self-help is frequently pointed out. See e.g. *Schwarzenberger* (Frontiers) p. 39; *idem* (Power Politics) p. 210; *Schmitt* (Nationalsozialismus) pp. 21–22; *de Lacharrière* (Politique) pp. 191–197; *Carreau* (Droit international) p. 36.

But it also seems evident that no act is by its external nature "legal" or "political". Extending coastal jurisdiction, for example, may be a political act, even involving breach of present law. But it may also be legislative and initiate new custom. A written and signed document may involve the adoption of legal obligations but equally well may not. If it is not the acting State(s)' belief which determines the act's legal/political character, then we can only assume that everything depends on the context.[48]

We now have to interpret context. But how do we know which context is relevant and why? If the act's contextual meaning is

---

[48] The opposition of an internal and external perspective is nicely present in the discussion concerning which acts amount to the conclusion of treaties. Is the presence of a binding agreement a matter of party intentions or of some (formal) criteria external to them? In his first Report on the Law of Treaties, *Brierly*, YILC 1950, vol. II, took the view that the definition of a "treaty" should comprise all agreements which establish relations of international law between the parties, pp. 226–229 (§§ 13–34). But this states the conclusion rather than the criterion. What we want to know is *which* acts are such as to establish binding relations under international law. *Lauterpacht*, Report, YILC 1953, vol. II, took an internal view: it was impossible to establish any external criterion. Any conduct might constitute treaty "regardless of (its, MK) form" if only "the intention to assume an obligation was reasonably clear", pp. 101, 102. But to avoid apologism he needed to construe this intention through an external perspective: "intentions must be implied from the fact of the formality of the instrument", YILC 1954, vol. II p. 125 (§ 111). Both subsequent Special Rapporteurs agreed with the initial internal view: a treaty was made when there was *intention* to establish binding rules. See *Fitzmaurice*, First Report, YILC 1956, vol. II p. 117 (§ 6); *Waldock*, First Report, YILC 1962, vol. II p. 31. Form (external criterion) was irrelevant. The restriction to "written" materials was a matter of convention – "of terminology rather than substance" – non-written agreements would be just as binding. See ILC: Report 1959, YILC 1959, vol. II pp. 92–93 (§§ 1–5). Yet, the Commission deleted the rapporteur's reference to "intent" – it would not be for the States to decide whether some agreement between them would be covered by international law or not. See commentary by *Waldock*, Fourth Report YILC 1965, vol. II p. 12 (§16).

In doctrine, too, one usually takes the internal perspective: an instrument is a "treaty" if it is intended to be binding. See e.g. *McNair* (Treaties) p. 6; *O'Connell* (International Law I) p. 195; *Widdows* L BYIL 1979 pp. 117 *et seq*, 121, 149; *Bothe* XI Neth.YBIL 1980 p. 94. Yet, difficulties emerge once a State denies its intent. At that point, we must either accept the State's own report – which leads into apologism – or we must have some formal criterion with which we can ascertain the (constructive) intent of the State(s) involved. *Widdows* L BYIL 1979, for example, after having taken the internal view, goes on to argue that "intent" is to be inferred from the text and the context, p. 137 *et seq*. Likewise *Reuter* (Traités) pp. 36–37. The problem is now how we can justify our construction: either there must be some formal criterion which tells us which kinds of texts or contexts can be taken to manifest intent and which can *overrule the State's own report* or then the State will remain the final arbiter. The first solution seems utopian and contradicts the initial, intent-based explanation of treaties; the latter is devoid of normativity: the State is bound if it wishes to report that it once had the intention to become bound.

constructed without reference to what the State(s) involved believed its meaning was, then we face the difficulty of justifying our construction. Why should a State which disagrees with our contextual evaluation be bound by it? The only argument open for us is now that the State is bound because *contextual justice* (for example the protection of *other* States' expectations) requires this. But how do we know whether legitimate expectations were involved without scrutinizing the motives of these other States? In which case our solution will be either apologetic (because it takes as given the other State's report of the expectations it had) or utopian (based on the assumption that a norm of justice settles the question of contextual meaning without regard to how *any* of the States has experienced the act). This argument could be continued. The point is only that it seems impossible to formulate an understanding of State conduct (legal or political?) without either relying on the State's self-evaluation (and becoming vulnerable to the charge of apologism) or on a naturalistic theory of the intrinsic character of such conduct (and facing the the objection about utopianism). Neither an internal nor an external perspective seems to grasp the meaning of a conduct objectively.

In other words, the individualistic strategy – the argument that though international society *is* asocial, the law still has relevance because there *do exist* machineries of legislation, adjudication and enforcement – fails as it cannot demonstrate the plausibility of explaining State behaviour in those terms.

The other possibility is to adopt a *communitarian strategy* and deny the well-foundedness of the critic's assumption of the unsocial character of international relations and hold that the existence of formal machineries is not at all necessary for a normative system to be legal and relevant.[49] The non-existence of such mechanisms may be associated with the primitive nature of international law.[50] But, the argument goes,

[49] This is a very frequently made point by modern lawyers. See e.g. *Strupp* 47 RCADI 1934/1 pp. 269–273; *Bishop* 115 RCADI 1965/III pp. 167–168. See also *Nardin* (Law, Morality) arguing that the converse view confuses the features of a legal system with its conditions of existence, pp. 119–121; *D'Amato* (Onuf: Lawmaking) pp. 84–85; *Fried* (Deutsch-Hoffmann: Relevance) pp. 133–144. The standard point against the existence of sanctions as a necessary condition of legal system is that this fails to include most power-conferring norms into the law. See *Hart* (Concept) pp. 33–35.

[50] See e.g. *Hall* (International Law) pp. 14–16; *Henkin* (How) p. 32; *Verzijl* (I) pp. 398–399. See also *Barkun* (Law without Sanctions) *passim*; *Bull* (Anarchical Society) pp. 62–65. *Hart* (Concept) associates the "primitive" character of international law with its lack of a rule of recognition which leads to each rule having to be supported by an acceptance directed at it, p. 209. For criticism of the association of the notion of "primitiveness"

what makes law constraining is that the human being is a social animal. His objective need is to live in society and cooperate with others. The reality and relevance of international law is based on the fact that States have a common need to create and use a law between them.[51]

This seems a more plausible objection to the critic's claim that international law is irrelevant. Most modern lawyers argue that the constraining nature of international law is independent from the existence of legislative procedures, widespread adjudication or public enforcement. The "invisible hand" makes it that self-interest is best enhanced in cooperation. They argue that in international as well as municipal law most rules are followed by most legal subjects most of the time.[52] States themselves recognize the existence of binding international law and have constant recourse to its rules and principles. One should not look only for visible events or great crises. Behind these is a large invisible network of non-spectacular State action: diplomatic routine, postal and commercial connections, tourism etc. In this multitude of interdependencies States need regularities and expectations about how other States will behave.[53] They need rules. Through reciprocity, rules crystallize as binding. Just like municipal law does not only deal with the policeman and the thief, neither is international law simply a matter of punitive rules or enforcement,[54] Law-observance is usually less costly

---

with international law, see *Nardin* (Law, Morality) pp. 150–166 and especially *Lauterpacht* (Function) p. 399 *et seq*. See also *Campbell* 8 Oxford JLS 1988 pp. 169–196.

[51] See generally *Kaplan-Katzenbach* (Political Foundations) pp. 5–11, 20–21. For a concise statement of this view, see also *O'Connell* (International Law, I) pp. 3–5; *Lissitzyn* (Divided) pp. 68–69; *Bleckmann* (Grundprobleme) (stressing the character of international law as representative of common interest) p. 162 and *passim*. *Baty* (Twilight) argues that international law is proper law precisely in that it is based on a common consciousness of nations and not the existence or fear of sanctions, pp. 5–7.

[52] *Jessup* (Modern) pp. 6–8; *Henkin* (How) pp. 39–49; *Merrills* (Anatomy) pp. 26–27, 61–64; *Schachter* 178 RCADI 1982/V pp. 28–29; *Fisher* (Improving Compliance) p. 12; *de Lacharrière* (Politique) pp. 112–113; *Akehurst* (Modern Introduction) pp. 2–5, 8–11; *Wallace* (International Law) pp. 2–3.

[53] This has led into a marked change of focus among writers from the concern with the regulation of war towards the regulation of peace in the 20th century which may have something to do with the modern emphasis on "pragmatism". For a comparison, see *Kegley* (Onuf: Lawmaking) pp. 182–186. *Boyle* (World Politics) associates this with the emergence of the sociological approach which tends to downplay the law's relevance in matters of political importance, pp. 5–7 and *passim*. For a criticism of this "humility", see *Lauterpacht* (Function), making the point that to assert the possibility of a legal system in which *all* externally constraining factors (legislation, adjudication, enforcement) are lacking "is to reduce the conception of law to a shadow of its own self", p. 433, and generally pp. 139–201 and *idem* (International Law, 2) pp. 11–12, 31–33.

[54] *Henkin* (How) pp. 12–22; *Castberg* 138 RCADI 1973/I pp. 12–14.

than law-breaking.[55] Domestic pressures may make it expedient for the ruling elites to follow the law.[56] And so on.[57] The relevance of the law is grounded in that States do comply with it.

These arguments may seem convincing but in fact are not. It is not enough to refer to what seems like a factual concordance between legal rules and State behaviour to demonstrate the relevance of the former. For it may be that conduct is concordant with rules only because the latter are infinitely flexible. On this argument, a fully apologetic law would be the most "relevant" one. But this is nonsense. True, States find it regularly useful to refer to rules and principles of international law. But this may only be evidence of its manipulability, not its relevance.

In order to answer the sceptical criticism we should demonstrate that international law has an effect on the *motivations* of States for adopting particular forms of behaviour. There is, however, a strong argument to the opposite effect.

It is frequently argued that if rules are followed this is not necessarily due to any reasons internal to the legal system. That States adopt predictable patterns of behaviour results, not from the law's constraining force but from such factors as the logic of deterrence, balance of power etc.[58] Once the peaceful continuation of such patterns is

[55] On these points, see e.g. *Akehurst* (Modern Introduction) pp. 8–11; *Henkin* (How) pp. 49–56, 69–74; *Menzel-Ipsen* (Völkerrecht) p. 17; *Moore* (Falk-Kratochwil-Mendlowitz) p. 53; *D'Amato* 79 AJIL 1985 (with reference to the Nicaragua–U.S. dispute) pp. 401–405.

[56] *Schwarzenberger* (Frontiers) pp. 39–40; *Henkin* (How) pp. 60–68, 74–76; *Menzel-Ipsen* (Völkerrecht) p. 18.

[57] See generally, *Levi* (Contemporary International Law) pp. 15–18; 21–22; *Henkin* (How) pp. 94–95. *Coplin* (Functions) argues this point by emphasizing how international law works to communicate to States the rules and structures of the "international system", p. 170. The same argument is made by *Bull* (Anarchical Society) pp. 140–141. For *Kratochwil* 69 ARSP 1983 international law's relevance is based on its being a useful "rhetorical tool" to exercise pressure, pp. 40–43. See also *Fawcett* (Law and Power) pp. 35–47; *Gould-Barkun* (Social Sciences) p. 181; *Boyle* (World Politics) pp. 80–81. *Fisher* (Improving Compliance) argues that physical coercion against a State is neither an effective nor acceptable means of ensuring the law's effectiveness, pp. 39–101. The law's compliance aspect can be strengthened primarily by increasing its instrumental usefulness.

[58] See e.g. *Aron* (Paix et Guerre) pp. 717–722; *Deutsch* (Deutsch-Hoffmann: Relevance) pp. 98–102; *Bell* (Conventions) pp. 68–69. When writers such as Henkin expand their law so as to include virtually all inter-State understandings into it, they lose its critical content. It is frequently doubted whether, for example, the tacit agreements and behavioural patterns induced by super-power nuclear deterrence, though their being "sanctioned", should be included into "law". On this latter problem generally, see *Stone* (Visions) pp. xxiv–xxvii. On the status of tacit agreements by super-power leaders

disturbed, the resulting crisis settlement techniques have been "strikingly non-legal, even anti-legal in quality".[59] According to this view, international law cannot constrain because it is devoid of moral authority, does not create fear of authority nor is based on utilitarian calculations.[60] Even if it is true that some rules for inter-State conduct are necessary, it is not thereby demonstrated that they have to be legal and, in fact, usually are not. Finally, it does not seem certain that reference to long-term gains is effectual in respect of States wishing to overthrow the *status quo*. Nor do such gains outweigh immediately even less significant short-term gains if these only materialize during the reign of the decision-makers.[61]

On this view, nothing is gained by thinking about factual regularities in State behaviour as observance (even less administration) of legal rules. Such approach involves "wasteful self-deception"[62] as it leads into believing that these regularities bind in a way they clearly do not. What is decisive is whether the law influences motivations. And this the realist critic denies.

But how can we receive information about motivations in order to find out which argument is correct? The easy way would be to go and ask the State itself: "Why did you behave as you did?" But this will lead into

rather as non-committing coordinating positions than legal rules, see *Merrills* (Anatomy) pp. 83–92 and generally *Dore* (Superpowers) *passim*.

[59] *Bell* (Conventions) p. 2. She also emphasizes the spontaneous, "off-the-cuff" character of contemporary crisis management, not easily subsumable under legal technique, pp. 73–98. *Fawcett* (Law and Power), too, points out that the settlement of major contemporary international crises has never been a distinctly legal matter – even despite the apparent applicability of legal rules, pp. 60–79. *Bozeman* (Multicultural) predicts that the increasing role of non-Western international actors and conflicts involving them will further diminish the need for distinctly legal settlement, pp. 169–172, 182 and *passim*. On the other hand, it is sometimes pointed out that when legal obligations conflict with State interest, there are several strategies of avoidance, non-compliance and simple defiance which have allowed States to escape their constraining force, see *Kim-Howell* (Conflict of Obligations) making this point about the law of the UN, *passim*. For standard (optimistic) discussions of the effect of deviance, see *Merrills* (Anatomy) pp. 73–81; *Henkin* (How) pp. 22–27. For a less optimistic one, see *Corbett* (Law and Society) p. 9, *passim*.

[60] *Corbett* (Law and Society) pp. 9–10, *passim*. *Hoffmann* (Deutsch-Hoffmann: Relevance) pp. 39–40. Lacking thus an "internal point of view", international law would become indistinguishable from factual behaviour and thus fail to meet *Hart's* (Concept) criterion of a legal system, pp. 95–96, *passim*.

[61] Thus, the "invisible hand" argument – or at least the assumption of the "enlightened" perspective of statesmen – seems open for doubt. See e.g. *Hoffmann* (Deutsch-Hoffmann: Relevance) pp. 54–60; *Bull* (Anarchical Society) pp. 141–145.

[62] *Corbett* (Law and Society) p. 11. See further *Onuf* (Onuf: Lawmaking) pp. 49–50.

apologism. The State will inevitably claim that its action was motivated by considerations of law. There should exist external criteria for determining whether the State's motivations were influenced by law or not. Again, these criteria may be related either to the nature of the act itself or to the context in which it was carried out. It seems clear, however, that merely by taking an external look at behaviour we do not get to the motivations behind it. The same behaviour may be induced by different, indeed conflicting motives. Intervention, for example, may spring from friendship as well as hostility. The act itself is incapable of showing its meaning. A reference to context is needed. But can context be evaluated without regard to the subjective evaluation of its significance by the State itself? To escape from apologism we should be in possession of a rule whereby the evaluation of context could be undertaken, regardless of subjective perceptions. It can hardly be claimed that such rules exist. But even if they did, they would lead nowhere as proof of the law's relevance. For we have defined relevance as having to do with *real motivations*. By advancing a presumptive rule about motivations in a certain context we need to justify the presumption itself. And the critic's point was precisely to *deny* the presumption that uniformities of conduct manifest motivations to behave in accordance with the law. In other words, to prove the relevance of international law, *reference cannot be made to the factual uniformities whose meaning (legal or political) was the object of the very controversy.*

We have seen that neither the individualistic nor the communitarian strategy seems able to convince the critic of the relevance of international law. There were two reasons for this. First, we fail to be convincing because even if we share the critic's individualistic theory of the nature of social life among States we cannot prove that State behaviour must be so interpreted as to disclose a recurring pattern of constraint in the form of legislation, adjudication and enforcement. Second, we fail because we cannot demonstrate that the individualistic theory is wrong and a communitarian theory better describes what is going on. There is an important lesson to be drawn from our failure. Having denied what Roberto Unger has called the doctrine of "intelligible essences",[63] liberalism will have to accept the *indeterminate character of interpretation.* That is, it will have to accept that the way in which we interpret the world is not controlled by the world's intrinsic structure but by convention, conceptual matrix. If the matrices differ, then it becomes very difficult to decide on which criteria the choice between differing interpretations

---

[63] *Unger* (Knowledge) pp. 79–80.

they have produced can be made. In particular, no choice can be made by simply looking more carefully at a behaviour as it is those matrices which single out to us what we can see in it.

I shall later speak more of this dilemma. Here it is enough to say that liberalism will inevitably assume that neither theory is "objectively" correct. It will have to treat them simply as conventional ways to characterize some aspects of State behaviour. But if this is so, then there is simply no justification to impose one or the other as a correct *description* of the nature of social life among States. If a choice is to be made, it must be made on other grounds than description. But this makes it look like a fully political choice.

To sum up the argument in this section. What position the moderns have taken in regard to the problem of relevance depends on what interpretation about observable State conduct they have assumed. For the mainstream international lawyer, State behaviour either manifests a continuous process of legislation, adjudication and enforcement of the law by States or a regular pattern of rule-observance, pure and simple. Occasional deviations are dismissed as non-consequential for the law's overall relevance. The critics, however, point out that this interpretation succeeds only because the mainstream uses such a flexible conceptual legal matrix as to be able to accommodate any major trends within it. Because infinitely flexible, the law has itself proved its irrelevance. On the other hand, if the lawyer's scheme were not so flexible, it would then have to demonstrate its correctness in other ways than by its descriptive properties. But this would make it seem like a theory of justice which cannot, on the lawyer's own premises have any claim for "correctness" at all.

3.3 The relations of doctrine and practice reconsidered: four versions of modern doctrine

A curious fact is that a whole branch of international doctrine, namely international political science (International Relations), seems capable of addressing the same object as international law in virtually complete abstraction from any idea of law between States.[64] While this is no proof of the non-existence or irrelevance of the law it shows, at least, that interpreting and understanding State behaviour in some relevant respect seems possible without any assumption of international law as a

---

[64] For a review, see *Boyle* (World Politics) pp. 11–16.

controlling factor. Of course, many standard textbooks on international law exhibit the converse tendency: references to the political aspects of State conduct are incidental and capable of being dismissed without consequence for normative analysis.

The point is that the two ways of looking at State behaviour are inherent in the perspectives of political science and law themselves. They are not imposed upon the observer as objective facts but follow from adopting conceptual schemes through which isolated facts of behaviour are linked together and given meaning.[65]

Notice the shift in perspective. Originally, it seemed that the problem of relevance could be solved by just looking closely enough, and long enough, at State practice. Now the matter stands otherwise. If State practice appears only through a conceptual matrix and the matrices of political science and law differ, then we cannot simply postulate a further innocent (non-theory-related) perception which could tell us which is better. From this perspective, the problem of relevance turns out not to be one of finding out whether State behaviour "really" is "political" or "legal" (such "real" character being inaccessible as description hinges upon the conceptual matrix) but whether we have good reason to adopt one or the other way of looking at behaviour. On which criteria can such choice be made?

If the two systems of political science and law cannot claim preference because of their descriptive qualities (involving equally possible but mutually exclusive descriptions) we must look at their non-descriptive qualities.

It is trite to point out that all social science is normative. Also choice between a political and a legal way of interpreting State behaviour involves choice between different models about what States should or should not do. The very claim of "relevance" is a normative claim. It implies an attempt to construct a doctrinal system with factual grasp and impact on State behaviour in light of its significant features.[66] I shall not

---

[65] *Spiropoulos* (Théorie) makes the point: "Rien de plus erroné, en effet, que la croyance, que les critères distinguant le droit des autres règles de conduite normatives, s'imposent à l'observateur par la suite de l'analyse des réalités sociales", pp. 63–64 and generally, 63–69. See also *supra* n. 11. See also *Ross* (Text-book) pp. 51–52. How we choose to view international behaviour is, somehow, dependent on the perspective which we occupy. The problem is whether or not this necessitates accepting Spiropoulos' conclusion, namely that the choice of the conceptual scheme would itself be "arbitrary".

[66] On normativity and choosing "significant" features for description, see e.g. *Finnis* (Natural Law) pp. 3 *et seq*, 9–18.

attempt to evaluate the respective normative merits of political science and law. Instead, I shall reconstruct the normative claims of legal doctrine by reference to four doctrinal strategies.

Initially, the international lawyer may adopt two ways of explaining the relevance of his discipline. He may insist that the law be normatively strong – that it is binding. Or he may argue so as to imply a law which is easily demonstrable as it is supported by a wide range of State activity.[67]

The argument which emphasizes the law's normative strength will imply a clear-cut distinction between law and politics, binding and non-binding standards. A standard either binds or does not. If it does – and *only* then – it is valid as law. If it doesn't, it is something else, for example political opinions *de lege ferenda*. But by implying strict tests of pedigree and dismissing quasi-binding standards from "law", this approach will enable us to see only very little law in State behaviour. Conduct which takes place outside the frame of "strictly binding" rules will seem purely political. The more one lays stress on binding force, the less behaviour one is able to cover with one's system.

The argument which emphasizes the wide applicability of legal standards stresses the close connection between law and State behaviour. It includes within law the most varied kinds of more or less binding standards and processes and allows seeing law in action in many places. But this view will inevitably imply a law which is normatively weak, or uncritical of behaviour. Doing away with clear distinction between binding and non-binding standards and emphasizing each obligation's contextual nature it will lead into law which seems to exist everywhere but which lacks constraining force.

Two versions of doctrine emerge:

1. the rule-approach position (law is normatively strong but restricted in scope);
2. the policy-approach position (law is normatively weak but wide in scope).

The rule-approach contains a successful criticism of the policy-approach inasmuch as this implies a confusion of law with politics in what amounts to an apologist manner. By seeing law in every "process" the policy-approach lawyer will create a law which seems uncritical, useful only to legitimize *de*

---

[67] See also *Kennedy* 23 GYIL 1980 pp. 359–361, 380–382.

facto situations.[68] The policy-approach lawyer will, again, successfully accuse the rule-approach lawyer of being obsessed with an abstract and unreal binding force and creating a utopian doctrine without connection to actual State behaviour.[69] Neither position seems capable of doing away the critic's intuitive feeling of the irrelevance of international law. Either the law is trivial because so narrow or because so uncritical.

It is possible to discern two further positions to these issues. One adopts the kind of scepticism which has been developed particularly among political scientists. This view shares the rule-approach lawyer's idea of the law's restricted material scope but is sceptical also about its binding force. It renounces altogether the attempt to explain international law as a normatively meaningful discipline. A final "idealist" approach attempts to combine the virtues of the rule and policy approaches. It adopts the modern project in its original form and attempts to reconcile the law's binding force with its wide material scope. Thus, there are two more positions:

3. the sceptical position (law is both normatively weak and materially restricted);
4. the idealistic position (law is both normatively strong and materially wide).

The four positions outlined do not entail any particular views about substantive norms. Each is defined exhaustively by its attitude towards the problems of normative force and material scope. The positions are also purely relational: they involve no fixed views about binding force or applicability. They are meaningful only *vis-à-vis* each other (like "long"/ "short"). We can identify a view as a rule-approach position only in that it lays more stress on binding force than another position which, in relation to the former, will appear as a policy-approach position. Correspondingly, a position is either sceptical or idealistic only in its relation to (distance from) the former two positions. Altogether, the four positions are *exhaustive*. Each doctrinal system or argument may, by relating it to other systems and arguments, be classed under one or another. Similarly, any position may shift from one approach to another

---

[68] "Si le droit est un pur fait, il n'est pas obligatoire", *Le Fur* 18 RCADI 1927/III (making this point against "social solidarity" theories) p. 402; *idem* 54 RCADI 1934/IV pp. 96–98. Similarly *Guggenheim* 80 RCADI 1952/I (against the "realism" of the policy-approach) pp. 19–24; *Chaumont* 129 RCADI 1970/I (against Quadri's "realist" theory of effective will as law's basis) p. 362.
[69] See e.g. *Kaplan-Katzenbach* (Political Foundations) p. 6 and generally *infra* ch. 3.3.3.

if the perspective is changed. A position which looks like a policy-approach position from a rule-approach perspective, may appear like scepticism from an idealistic point of view, for example.

Consequently, my intention is not, and cannot be, the labelling of particular "schools", lawyers or arguments under any of these four categories in a fixed fashion. I shall concentrate on the way in which the lawyers *themselves* have made the distinction between themselves and others and explained their system as better than that which they have criticized. This makes it possible to establish relational links which allow my classification. However, care should be taken not to understand that the categorizations have validity beyond the doctrinal disputes whereby lawyers have established their identities as against others.

Doctrine cannot move into any of the four positions and simply stay there as each position seems vulnerable to valid criticism from the remaining three. Mainstream rule-approach and policy-approach seem either utopian or apologetic. Scepticism is frustrating and idealism is self-contradicting. This explains the movement by modern lawyers constantly towards a middle position – a position from which it would be possible to reject the utopias of those who think the world is or is in the process of becoming a law-regulated community and the apologies of those who engage themselves in law's infinite manipulation in favour of political ends.[70] This means, in other words, making constant difference between oneself and all the four positions outlined. But as these positions are *logically exhaustive*, there is no space between them. The modern project works in vacuum, lacking identity, containing nothing else apart from a code of making *differences*, a manner of escaping without arriving anywhere, a constant flight from material stand.[71]

---

[70] See *supra* n. 12 and ch. 1.

[71] *Rousseau* (Droit international, I), for example, discusses the topic "basis of obligation" in terms of the opposition between "voluntaristic" and "objectivistic" theories. Neither seems acceptable. The former will do away with the law's binding character. The latter are unable to show how norms could be objectively deduced from them. He comes up with no substantive solution and finally refers the whole issue beyond discourse altogether: it is "extralegal" and insoluble by juristic reflection, pp. 35–37. As this topic exhausts what Rousseau has to say about "theory", he is simply led into adopting an unreflective pragmatism. See also *Charvin* (Benchikh-Charvin-Demichel: Introduction) pp. 48–51. The modern argument is also well present in the discussion by *Sur* (L'interprétation), concerned to establish between normativism and politics "une position à la fois synthéthique et éclectique", p. 20. Naturalism and scepticism are rejected as these "confuse" the law with politics, pp. 24–38. This leaves him with two kinds of positivism: "normativism" and "realism". Both are insufficent alone. The

This is why the modern international lawyer has rejected theory, reflection on the field of positions available to him.[72] He is paralyzed by the fear that reflection would force him to adopt one of the four positions outlined, none of which is able to ground a relevant concept of

former is too abstract, the latter mixes law with fact, pp. 43–47. What is needed is a synthesis, a synthesis which, for Sur, is created by his theory of interpretation which marks the "point de passage obligé entre le fait et le doit, entre le droit et la politique", p. 60.

[72] The turn to pragmatism in modern doctrines is nowhere better reflected than in the stylistic and thematic development of the general courses given at the Hague Academy.

During the inter-war era, the courses were predominantly written in the spirit of reconstructive doctrine. Many were dedicated to completely theoretical or philosophical topics, such as the "basis of obligation" (see *Verdross* 16 RCADI 1927/I pp. 251–321; *Brierly* 23 RCADI 1928/III pp. 467–551; *Djuvara* 64 RCADI 1938/II pp. 485–625), the place and development of natural law or the fundamental rights of States (see e.g. *Le Fur* 18 RCADI 1927/III pp. 263–441; *Gidel* 10 RCADI 1925/V pp. 541–599) and so on. Most of them were really at least as much works of philosophy or legal theory (and some even much more so) than expositions of valid norms. They were characterized by the author's initial elaboration of a "theory" (usually containing a rhetoric of "double dissociation" or reconciliation: naturalism and voluntarism are rejected in favour of some mediating, "realistic" or "synthetic" view) and his use of specific doctrinal areas as testing-grounds or exemplifications of his theory. See e.g. *Politis* 6 RCADI 1925/I pp. 5–117; *Kelsen* 14 RCADI 1926/IV pp. 231–329; *Verdross* 30 RCADI 1929/V pp. 275–505; *Scelle* 46 RCADI 1933/IV pp. 33–697; *Le Fur* 54 RCADI 1935/IV pp. 5–307; *Kaufmann* 54 RCADI 1935/IV pp. 5–307.

In the past forty years, however, this has changed. Gone are "purely theoretical" lectures (with the significant exception of those by *Ago* 90 RCADI 1956/II pp. 851–958 and *Ziccardi* 95 RCADI 1958/III pp. 263–407 and, to some extent, *Quadri* 80 RCADI 1952/I, though his is really an "anti-theory", stressing the link between law and effectiveness, pp. 579–633). Nobody has bothered to discuss "foundations" in a separate course. The style of the general course has drastically changed. It is possible to summarize this change – and the resulting character of modern pragmatism – by reference to four distinguishing traits: 1) Reliance on strictly juridical-technical topics and style; 2) No express theory to connect these topics – doctrinal subjects live on their own as divisions produced by textbook tradition are taken as given; 3) Discussion with *other* lawyers and critical exposition or deviating theories virtually non-existent; 4) Heavy reliance on the traditional listing of "sources" which also organize doctrinal discussion. Already in the first post-war course, *Rolin* 77 RCADI 1950/II holds that theoretical work was insignificant as it failed to have a bearing on State practice. What was needed was "une rigoureuse observation des faits", p. 309. *Bishop* 115 RCADI 1965/II calls for taking a "user's" standpoint which requires that one keeps one's "feet on the ground", p. 151. A search for "principles" might only positively distort the understanding of legal process, p. 170. Similar hostility towards "abstract" theory permeates, of course, the course by *McDougal* 82 RCADI 1953/I pp. 137–259 (see further *infra* ch. 3.3.3.). It may be helpful to distinguish three rhetorical strategies through which pragmatism proceeds to introduce the bulk of the law. The *first* – and the most "theoretical" – of these is an express rhetoric of reconciliation: this consists usually in a rejection of naturalism and Kelsenian normativism as too "abstract" and/or some kind of appeal to take account

international law. Hence, his middle position is an *ad hoc* position: it works so as to produce the most varied kinds of arguments from precedents, treaty-texts, lawyers' writings, policies, functionalistic theories etc. Being inherently uncertain about what the law actually is (is it binding standards, is it effective standards?) he mixes elements borrowed from all possible styles of legal and quasi-legal argument: classical positivism, naturalism, sociology, fundamental rights theories etc. – degenerating sometimes into a sophisticated hotchpotch of learned citation and naïve historicism.[73]

Such scholarship survives only because it is *ad hoc*. It poses and answers normative problems of the most limited kind emphasizing the contextuality of each solution. The solutions it reaches are constantly challenged by other scholars and practice alike. But it remains perplexed about the reasons for the constant variations in normative doctrines. It

of the "process" or "political" aspect of the law. See e.g. *De Visscher* 86 RCADI 1954/II p. 451; *Rousseau* 93 RCADI 1958/I (law both system of normative standards and a factor of social organization) pp. 388–393; *Monaco* 125 RCADI 1968/III (a coté l'aspet normatif, également un aspet social") p. 109; *Barile* 161 RCADI 1978/III ("reality" as the starting-point, not some abstract definition thereof – emphasis on "effectiveness") pp. 22, 23–26. See also *Quadri* 113 RCADI 1964/III (traditional naturalism and voluntarism both "fictitious" – law based on the effective and imperative will of the majority; it is not a matter of abstract "consent" but of its capacity to enforce itself) pp. 267–279. Similarly, theory in the courses by *Schachter* 178 RCADI 1982/V and *Virally* 183 RCADI 1983/V is, as we have seen, a theory of reconciliation – appealing to a combination of the "rule" and "process" aspects of the law, see *supra* ch. 1.1. The *second* strategy is to assume, simply, that "law reflects society" and to introduce different doctrinal topics after a discussion of the character of the international society or some history thereof. See e.g. *Waldock* 106 RCADI 1962/II (a discussion of the "constitutional" aspects of international society – the League and the UN) pp. 5–38; *Bishop* 115 RCADI 1965/II (a discussion of the character of present international society) pp. 153–166. *Mosler* 140 RCADI 1974/IV pp. 17–44 and *Anand* 197 RCADI 1986/III pp. 18–20 *et seq* introduce the law through an argument about the "great changes" in the international society and the resulting factual interdependence in the world of facts. The *third* strategy is to renounce all discussion of areas beyond specific doctrines and start simply with an exposition of the law within the different sources. *Sørensen* 101 RCADI 1960/III makes this choice expressly, following his "realist" view of law as what authoritative organs μse to decide cases. For him, what is needed is a "méthode empirique basé sur une analyse de la jurisprudence des tribunaux internationaux", p. 11. Others do not elaborate the point. The law is, simply, what the textbook sources come up with. That this method fails to explain why there is still so much disagreement about what law sources produce is its greatest weakness. In its pragmatism, it must assume that deviant doctrines are simply "false" – though it fails to explain why they should be so. For this style, see *Jennings* 121 RCADI 1967 pp. 327–600; *Jiménez de Aréchaga* 159 RCADI 1978/I p. 9 *et seq*; *Fawcett* 132 RCADI 1971/I (delimiting his discussion to issues of jurisdiction) pp. 369–557.

[73] See e.g. *Lachs* 169 RCADI 1980/IV.

tries to cope with the indeterminacy of the law as a "normal" pheno-menon pointing out that there is nothing particularly worrying in the fact that reasonable lawyers constantly disagree about the law and produce differing solutions to normative problems. After all, law cannot completely detach itself from values (it is "relatively indeterminate") and values are arbitrary.

In the following sections I shall look at each of the four versions of modern scholarship. I shall demonstrate how they differ in respect of their approach to the law/politics delimitation and how this affects their approach towards certain other doctrines and why the solutions proposed will always appear partial and open for criticism from the other positions. In order to keep discussion as brief as possible, I have identified each position with a particular international lawyer. As I have said, this is not intended to be a fixed, permanent classification but only to demonstrate typical ways of trying to construct better doctrines by lawyers who have been relatively "theoretical" and consistent. The point is in the distinc-tions established, not in the substantive doctrines invoked.

3.3.1 Rule-approach: Schwarzenberger

The rule-approach may be associated with the Austinian conception of law as rules, identifiable by reference to an objective test of pedigree (sources) which will exhaustively tell which standards qualify as law and which do not. The basis of the rule-approach is in the standard criticism of early and classical doctrines as "subjective", that is political, because they identified the law by reference to someone's political opinions (justice) or simple State will. The test of pedigree is insisted upon to allow a determinate delimitation between objective law and subjective politics.[74]

The standard rule-approach discussion opens up with a definition of international law in terms of rules:

> International law is the body of legal rules which apply between sovereign States and such other entities as have been granted international personality.[75]

---

[74] For a recent, succinct statement of the rule-approach view, see *Weil* 77 AJIL 1983 p. 413 *et seq.*

[75] *Schwarzenberger-Brown* (Manual) p. 3. For classical definitions of the same type, see e.g. *Oppenheim* (International Law, I) p. 3; *Hall* (International Law) p. 1; *Hackworth* (International Law, I) p. 1; *Brierly* (Law of Nations) p. 1. See also *Coplin* (Functions) p. 7; *Starke* (International Law) p. 1; *Reuter* (Droit international) pp. 35–36.

The corpus of international law consists of an exhaustive statement of such rules. Thus is established the distinction between law and politics. Law is what can be identified as "rules". All else is politics, whether in the guise of power or morality. The distinction is also about what is objective and what is subjective. The specifically "legal" character of legal problem-solution and doctrine's "scientific" nature are based on this.

The doctrine of sources contains the rule-approach lawyer's objective test of what can be admitted as "rules". Though there is, among the rule-approach lawyers themselves, constant disagreement about the correct sources – the more positivistically oriented lawyer emphasizing treaties and custom, the more naturalistically inclined lawyer stressing general principles, systemic values etc. – there is no dispute about the primary importance of the test[76] and the consequent distinction between law/ non-law, or *lex lata* and *lex ferenda*.[77] Though the latter may have value in doubtful cases or in the political analyses of law, only the former may be used as rules in the above, source-related sense. Similarly, the distinction between "hard" and "soft law" may be used in non-normative descriptions but has no bearing on the law's binding force. A legal rule is either "hard" or then it is no legal rule at all.[78]

There is also a clear-cut distinction between legal and political procedures. The focal case of the former is the judicial process which is taken to enshrine the ideal of objectivity.[79] Here legal rules work in their purest sense. Other procedures, activities of international organizations, advancement of claims by States against each other etc. may be significant as the social environment of rules. But in the ascertainment of valid law they are secondary to the judicial process.

A rule-approach lawyer makes an analytical distinction between legal and political disputes. True, he admits that many disputes contain elements of both. But he must insist on the principled distinction

---

[76] *Oppenheim* 2 AJIL 1908 (for a statement of the "positive method" – admitting only treaty and custom as "sources") pp. 333–336.

[77] See *Oppenheim* 2 AJIL 1908 p. 335. The principle which distinguishes what "is" and what "ought to be" law is described by *Virally* (Mélanges Reuter) as: ". . . l'une des règles les plus fondamentales de la science du droit et un acquis de la pensée juridique qui ne saurait être remis en question", pp. 519, 532–533. The same point is emphasized by *Jennings* (Festschrift Lachs) p. 128; *idem* (Acquisition) pp. 69, 71–73.

[78] This is what *Weil* 77 AJIL 1983 describes as the "normativity threshold", pp. 415–418.

[79] Thus, many (particularly British and American) lawyers prefer to discuss international law in light of what courts and tribunals have said about it.

between these aspects in order to determine the proper object of judicial function as well as that of his own doctrine against political science.[80]

The law/politics distinction does not necessitate the adoption of a formalistic attitude by the rule-approach lawyer. He may – and often does – recognize the significance of historical, sociological or political factors in law-creation and application.[81] A rule-approach lawyer may himself conduct extensive research in these areas.[82] The point is only to insist on the distinction between a normative analysis of rules and other, descriptive analyses of "facts":

> ... facts, however undisputed, which are the result of conduct violative of international law cannot claim the ... right to be incorporated automatically into the law of nations.[83]

In normative analyses, historical facts or physical power may have relevance only if this is admitted by a rule. Facts cannot be normative by themselves.

Neither does the rule-approach necessitate the adoption of any form of positivism. A naturalist lawyer may be – and often is – equally adamant about the law/politics distinction and the need to think about the law in terms of rules rather than behavioural facts. It is only that his idea of sources differs from that of the positivist's.[84]

Let me now illustrate how the rule-approach is present in the work of Georg Schwarzenberger and how, ultimately, the approach is

---

[80] In classical doctrine, this distinction coalesced with the doctrine separating legal and political disputes by their subject-matter or importance: some disputes were simply so connected with national interests that they could not be beneficially dealt with under a judicial process. To be sure, this distinction is still reflected in the Statute of the ICJ and many jurists advocate a distinction similar to or equivalent with it. There has been, however, an important reformist trend, exemplified in particular in *Lauterpacht* (Function) which refuses to make this distinction so clearly and at any rate on the basis of the "importance" of the issue. According to this view, to leave a matter undecided by law is ultimately a legal decision as well, pp. 6–21, *passim*. See also *De Visscher* (Theory) pp. 75–78 *et seq.*

[81] See e.g. *Guggenheim* (Lipsky: Law and Politics) pp. 26–27; *Jennings* (Acquisition) p. 69.

[82] As exemplified in *Schwarzenberger* (Power Politics).

[83] *Lauterpacht* (Recognition) p. 413. For an analytical review of the role of "effectiveness" in rule-approach theory, see *Tucker* (Lipsky: Law and Politics) p. 31 *et seq.*

[84] The voluminous work of Georg Schwarzenberger provides a good illustration of the rule-approach not only because of its consistency and the explicit character of its assumptions but also because of its concern for "realism" and social environment. It shows, then, that rule-approach is *not* confined to narrowly formal or legalistic analyses. It may be that the work's idiosyncratic style and terminology detract somewhat from its illustrative character. See e.g. the criticism by *Jenks* (Prospects) p. 115 n. 28. But terminology notwithstanding, I shall assume that most traditionally educated lawyers would agree with most of what he says although not perhaps with how he says it.

unconvincing as it ends up with a very narrow field of application for international law and and fails to maintain the law/politics distinction in as clear-cut a manner as it assumes.[85]

Schwarzenberger's conception of the conditions of social life among States is distinctly Hobbesian. States exist to pursue power politics for the advancement of self-interest. There is no natural community, only artificial society between them. The law is based on this:

> In a society in which power is the overwhelming consideration, the primary function of law is to assist in maintaining the supremacy of force and the hierarchies established on the basis of policies . . .[86]

The social determines the law and not *vice-versa*. In order to grasp full understanding of law, one must have sufficient knowledge of its social and historical background.[87] Here lies the perspective from which Schwarzenberger can explain his work as objective. The law's objectivity lies in its being separable from naturalist "oughts" and grounded in the hard – but verifiable – facts of power politics.

This initial "realist" perspective, however, serves only to explain the ground from which rules emerge and to separate Schwarzenberger from legal utopia-builders. Sociological or historical analyses lose their role in what Schwarzenberger sees as the main tasks of doctrine, the analysis and systematization of rules. The former can only be *supplementary* to this main task. They differ by object and by method and must not be confused but held "in watertight compartments".[88]

---

[85] A naturalist rule-approach lawyer would, obviously, share the *opposing* conception to that of Schwarzenberger's as to what makes a rule "objective" – that is, what makes it a legal rule. Therefore, his rhetoric would reverse that of Schwarzenberger's and insist on the irrelevance of "power politics" to the law. Yet, the insistence on the importance of the distinction between "law" and "politics" would be the same. For the test of pedigree in a naturalist form, see e.g. *Kopelmanas* XVIII BYIL 1937 p. 127; *D'Amato* (Onuf: Lawmaking) p. 90. See also the argument in *Le Fur* 54 RCADI 1935/IV pp. 141–143.

[86] *Schwarzenberger* (Power Politics) p. 199; *idem* (Frontiers) pp. 23–25.

[87] *Schwarzenberger* (Power Politics) p. 198; *idem* (Law and Order) p. 1. Indeed, he points out that each legal doctrine is bound to contain at least an implicit theory of these, *idem* (Frontiers) p. 21. He makes his own theory explicit by outlining different "models" of law, corresponding to the different social environments in which these work. These are "power law", "reciprocity law" and "coordination law", each supposed to be reflected in a typology of social systems on a scale from society to community. See *idem* (Frontiers) pp. 25–36; *idem* (Power Politics) pp. 199–209; *idem-Brown* (Manual) pp. 9–10. See also *idem* (Dynamics) in which this analysis is taken further, pp. 32–55.

[88] *Schwarzenberger* (Inductive) p. 40. See also *ibid.* pp. 7–8, 56–59, 63–64; *idem-Brown* (Manual) pp. 19–20.

Yet, in the identification of rules the realist perspective re-emerges. For Schwarzenberger, the proper legal method is the "inductive approach". This insists on not confusing the objective *lex lata* with the subjective *lex ferenda*.[89] The inductive approach may be summarized in four tenets (using Schwarzenberger's own formulations):

1. emphasis on the exclusive character of the three primary law-creating processes . . .
2. establishment of the "means of determination of rules of law" . . . in accordance with rationally verifiable criteria;
3. awareness of the character of the rules of international law as the only binding norms of international law . . .
4. realisation of the differences (of, MK) international law as applied in unorganised, partly organised and fully organised international societies.[90]

The most important message is this: only "rules" are binding and they must be established by objective criteria ("law-creating processes"). Attempts to create different categories of rules or to grade normativity according to some scale of evaluative significance are normatively irrelevant. *Jus cogens* is merely a name for a set of rules which – like other rules – arise from consent and which are binding like any other, "ordinary" rules.[91] "Soft law" is no law at all.[92] "General principles of international law" or "fundamental principles" are merely descriptive generalizations from a chosen set of rules. They have no normative status independent of the status of the rules from which the generalization started.[93]

The objectivity[94] of the inductive approach is established by creating a contrast between it and two subjective tendencies: deductivism and

---

[89] *Schwarzenberger* (Inductive) pp. 47, 51, 65–66, 71, *passim*.

[90] *Idem* (Dynamics) p. 2. The formulation repeats that of his earlier works. See *idem* (Inductive) pp. 5–6; *idem* (Law and Order) pp. 4–5.

[91] Its quality as *jus cogens* relates solely to the (extralegal) importance which is attached to it. To be otherwise would be to assume the existence of an objective code of values – a possibility excluded *ex hypothesi* from his system. See *idem* (Law and Order) pp. 27–56; *idem* (Inductive) pp. 100–101; *idem* (Dynamics) pp. 124–125.

[92] *Ibid*. pp. 9–10.

[93] *Idem* (Inductive) pp. 72–84; *idem-Brown* (Manual) pp. 33–36. For a discussion, see Koskenniemi XVIII Oikeustiede-Jurisprudentia 1985 pp. 126, 142 *et seq*. This is not affected by the character of some principles as "fundamental" for this quality is related only to the character of some princples on a relatively "high degree of abstraction".

[94] *Schwarzenberger* (Inductive) concedes that "full" objectivity is impossible – what is important is to "maximize" the objectivity of doctrine to counter the extreme subjectivism of diplomatic practice pp. 56, 65.

eclectism. The former is subjective as it uses naturalistic maxims with which "any one could prove whatever he wanted to prove".[95] It is "law-making in disguise". Many modern lawyers share such deductivism, manifested in their reliance on general principles, such as, for example, permanent sovereignty, human rights, national self-determination. But "the more general the maxim, the more suspect it necessarily is".[96] The principles mark an "unholy mixture of law and politics".[97] They can be used only to the extent they find inductive support from State practice in the form of "rules".[98] On the other hand, "eclectism" is suspect as it makes arbitrary use of randomly selected fact-materials with which, too, anything could be proved.[99] The inductive approach avoids such eclect-ism by using "deep-going historical and sociological analyses" from which really reliable inferences can be drawn.[100]

The objectivity of doctrine is based on its effort to create verifiable or falsifiable hypotheses on perception of the functioning of "law-creating processes".[101] Law is created by legal subjects – not by deductions from abstract principles.[102] This is done through the social processes of custom, treaty and general principles (understood as convergences in municipal law).[103] Law-creation is to be strictly distinguished from law-ascertainment by "law-determining agencies" (courts, writers, States themselves). This distinction further strengthens the law/politics dis-tinction. Law exists objectively, through the regular functioning of the law-creating processes. Its ascertainment can be more or less objective, depending on the "degree of the skill and technical qualification of each law-determining agency".[104]

The significance of the different law-determining agencies is based on how objective they are, in other words, how they rank on the scale law-politics. Naturally, courts are the most significant ones, followed by text-writers of competence and States themselves, but the order is not

[95] *Ibid.* pp. 12, 9–13. The just war doctrine, for example, is understood as a manipulable ideology as it contains no objective criteria for judging the justness of the belligerents' acts, *idem* (Frontiers) pp. 236–240.
[96] *Idem* (Inductive) pp. 48, 186.
[97] Consequently, doctrine must be "immunized" against them, *ibid.* p. 50.
[98] *Ibid.* pp. 38, 154.   [99] *Ibid.* pp. 13–19.   [100] *Ibid.* pp. 39, 50–51.
[101] *Idem-Brown* (Manual) p. 17.
[102] All law is based on consent. Here lies its objective character. Consent – unlike value – can be verified, *idem* (Inductive) p. 19, *idem* (Frontiers) pp. 36–37.
[103] *Idem* (Inductive) pp. 19–21 *et seq*, 33–37; *idem-Brown* (Manual) pp. 21–28.
[104] *Idem* (Inductive) p. 23.

given. Everything depends on the actual objectivity of the agency in question.[105]

The distinction between legal and political disputes follows as a matter of course. Schwarzenberger admits that it may sometimes be difficult to distinguish the political and legal elements in a given case. This is made easier by the optional character of the judicial process: it depends ultimately on the States themselves whether they choose to regard a dispute legal (justiciable) or not.[106]

The principal legal procedure is the judicial process. The law of international institutions is discussed by reference to the "overriding realities" of power politics.[107] To see in such institutions the rudiments of an international community is "wishful thinking or escapism".[108] The UN is a "quasiorder", dominated by great power antagonism and "power politics in disguise", lacking legislative capacity or governmental functions.[109]

From this it appears, as Schwarzenberger admits, that:

> ... in our time, the role of international law in the relations between the world camps is more limited than in the relations between potential enemies in any pre-war period since the rise of contemporary international law.[110]

Law exists mainly away from the centres of power politics.[111] Even when some law undeniably exists in such areas – for instance, on the illegality of nuclear weapons – insistence on its binding force is "hopelessly inadequate".[112] The ultimate test for law is to what extent it is capable of sustaining a *de facto* order. On this test, international law fails.[113] It will have relevance beyond marginal areas only once the conditions for international social life have changed.

---

[105] The primary position of courts is based on the "greater degree of responsibility and care" which lawyers show when dealing with an actual case, *ibid.* p. 24. In comparison, officials, especially diplomats, are "suspect of bias and subjectivism", *ibid* p. 28. See also *ibid* pp. 23–33, *idem-Brown* (Manual) pp. 28–32.

[106] *Idem* (International Law I) pp. 389–391.

[107] *Idem* (Frontiers) pp. 279–280; *idem* (Law and Order) pp. 78–81.

[108] *Idem* (Frontiers) p. 281.

[109] *Idem* (Power Politics) pp. 334 *et seq*, 510–512; *idem-Brown* (Manual) pp. 222, 259–260, 309–311. The New International Economic Order, for example, has no status as *lex lata*. The reality of power politics makes utopia of the ideal of community which would sustain such an order, *idem* (Dynamics) p. 25.

[110] *Idem* (Inductive) p. 79.   [111] *Ibid.* p. 105.   [112] *Idem* (Law and Order) p. 216.

[113] *Ibid.* pp. 161–168.

By insisting on a strict test of pedigree – that is, a clear-cut distinction between law and non-law – the rule-approach will end up with a law with only a marginal role in international affairs. But this is not its only problem. A more serious one concerns its inability to provide a convincing account of how law and politics can be held so sharply distinct as assumed by it. This is a problem which concerns the very basis, or justification, of the rule approach itself.

Ascertaining the law is often difficult however technically qualified the agency may be. Constructing the applicable law requires, as we have seen, balancing and evaluative considerations which cannot easily be fitted into a pedigree-dependent concept of law. Moreover, views about the correct pedigree test, too, remain conflicting. The rule-approach lawyer needs to concede that the law is "relatively indeterminate" and that there is a margin of (political) discretion involved in legal activity. But as we have seen in the first chapter, the margin of discretion is uncertain and conflicting views about the correct norms seem capable of decision only by assuming a position on rival theories of justice. In other words, because rules cannot be applied automatically, the rule-approach lawyer is constantly faced with the objection that his inevitable interpretations are merely political constructions. Unless he can explain that his interpretation is non-political, his emphasis on the law/politics distinction will seem misplaced.[114]

From a non-rule-approach perspective, to speak of relative indeterminacy is to undermine the very starting-point of the rule-approach. It is to concede that the law/politics distinction *cannot* be made in such a simple manner. Legal norms and their applications remain controversial. Competent lawyers constantly disagree. *De lege lata* and *de lege ferenda* appear indistinguishable. Legal and political disputes merge into one another. Constant recourse to balancing, equity, "humanitarian considerations" etc. by legal and political organs blurs the distinction between them. The law is administered by political bodies under political procedures – making it increasingly difficult to maintain that behind differing interpretations of the law there is an "objective" rule

---

[114] The modern rule-approach lawyer writes about the "blurring of the normativity threshold", about increasing uncertainty in respect of the correct legal sources and about what count as authoritative law-making agencies. For him/her, the important task now is to re-establish the clarity of the law/non-law distinction. Apart from the article by *Weil* 77 AJIL 1983 p. 413 *et seq*, see also e.g *Kunz* 51 AJIL 1957 pp. 77–83; *Jennings* XXXVII Schw.JB 1981 p. 59 *et seq*; *idem* (Cheng: Teaching) pp. 3–9.

which can be contrasted to the subjective interpretations in which it appears.

3.3.2   Scepticism: Morgenthau

Modern scepticism about international law constitutes itself by means of a twofold distinction. On the one hand, it emerges as a reaction against the "collapse of international law of Geneva".[115] It attacks early 20th century doctrines as utopian, self-betrayingly unaware of the overriding realities of politics.[116] Like the rule-approach, scepticism believes law to have only a restricted field of application. On the other hand, scepticism does not believe that the rules of international law are uniformly and absolutely binding, either. In addition to being marginal in scope, international law is also normatively flexible, binding only "more or less", as determined by political realities. As a result, scepticism is suspicious about the law/politics distinction which created the identity of the rule-approach. But contrary to the policy-approach, scepticism does not wish to abolish this distinction altogether. It holds it as a normative ideal but is doubtful about the possibilities of its international realization.

It is uncertain whether any scholar has ever espoused the sceptical position in its purest form. Most writers prefer to leave some scope for international law or concede that it is binding at least in some marginal sense. Many of the distinctions which create the sceptical position's identity are, however, present in the work of Hans Morgenthau. Accordingly, I shall illustrate this position by reference to him.[117]

The first leg of scepticism stresses the significance of the political context and criticizes mainstream lawyers for their "metaphysical" abstractions. Morgenthau attacks classical discourse in the following way: Classicists defined "law" too narrowly as rules emerging by agreement between States. They have also defined it too broadly by holding

---

[115] *Morgenthau* 34 AJIL 1940 p. 264.

[116] The sceptical argument is that utopianism is not only irrelevant but outright harmful. See e.g. *ibid.* p. 283; *idem* (Politics among Nations) pp. 12–14, 281–283.

[117] Many of the sceptic's points are expressed also in *De Visscher* (Theory), arguing that the law cannot work in times of high political tension because such tension tends to blur the legal issues and create an all-encompassing antagonism within which the use of law will appear as counter-productive formalism, pp. 78–87. See also *Corbett* (Law and Society) pp. 36–89, *passim*.

that all legally formulated agreement results in binding rules.[118] It is true, he concedes, that classicism was beneficial in its creation of distance towards early, naturalistic writing. But by concentrating on written agreements as an abstract test and by assuming that from these emerges a logically consistent body of law, it became metaphysical itself.[119] It lost its ties to social reality in:

> ... an attempt to exorcise social events by the indefatigable repetition of magic formulae.[120]

Morgenthau accuses mainstream lawyers of having defined legal study so as to exclude elements vital to it: sociological, ethical and other factors constantly penetrate into the legal rules, establish new ones, change old ones and so on.[121] Contrary to Schwarzenberger, he assumes that these factors have direct significance in the *normative* study of law, not merely in the description of the law's environment. Politics is focal and law secondary. Even where the latter exists, its content cannot be ascertained independently from political analyses.

To appreciate the sceptic's second point – that international law is not very binding, either – it is first necessary to realize that the sceptic does not deny the need for a test of pedigree for law. In this sense, he shares a municipally influenced, "legalistic" idea of law.[122] But the sceptic's test does not refer to an abstract doctrine of sources. It refers to the presence or absence of sanctions. The sceptic insists on the objective and scientific nature of this test. Hypotheses about valid law must be tested in State practice just as those of natural sciences must be tested in natural reality.[123] Rules which are unaccompanied by sanction amount to mere subjective wishes.[124]

This will lead the sceptic into disappointing conclusions about the relevance of international law. Raymond Aron writes that the test of law is in time of crisis. And it is precisely in such times that the rules of international law break down.[125] International law is not binding in any uniform or absolute manner because sanctions do not exist in such manner either. Here lies the difference between the sceptic's and the rule-approach lawyer's (such as Kelsen) concept of "sanction": For the latter, sanction is a matter of the existence of a rule providing for

---

[118] *Morgenthau* 34 AJIL 1940 p. 265.   [119] *Ibid.* pp. 262–263.
[120] *Ibid.* pp. 260.   [121] *Ibid.* pp. 267–273.
[122] See also the criticism by *Sur* (L'interprétation) pp. 33–38.
[123] The analogy is made explicit in *Morgenthau* 34 AJIL 1940 p. 260, see also pp. 283–284.
[124] *Ibid.* pp. 276–278.   [125] *Aron* (Paix et Guerre) p. 705.

sanctions. For the sceptic, this is a matter of observable fact. What is important is not whether such rule exists or not but what is the likelihood that actual sanction will follow. And this is a likelihood that varies due to differences of political context.[126] Rules bind "more or less" as the likelihood of sanction grows or diminishes.

A second criticism points out that mainstream jurisprudence has overlooked the fact that the sociological contexts of international rules are highly individualized. Generalization from treaties into custom lacks foundation.[127] Each rule is relative to social context – the common interest or balance of power which supports it.[128] Beyond such context, the rule has no reality. The pedigree for law is a complex and highly precarious pedigree, changing with the variations of the political context.

The sceptic's argument is curious because it both maintains and denies the law/politics distinction. The distinction is maintained through the assumption that law can be separated from non-law through a criterion (the likelihood of sanction). But the distinction is denied as the question of the likelihood of sanction becomes a sociological one. Binding force emerges with factual coercion. Law is merely a division of power politics. The distinctions between law and society, legal and political disputes and legal and sociological methods vanish. What is binding is determined by what is politically effective.

The law's universality (generality) is lost. As binding force is a matter of degree and context, it happens regularly that what law is effectual (i.e. valid) against one State is not *vis-à-vis* another.[129] Consequently, on many areas "obscurity and confusion frequently reign".[130] The lack of precision of rules makes it possible for governments to interpret the law so as to suit their own purposes.[131]

Morgenthau never started the "functionalist" science of international law which, he argued, could produce statements about the law through a purely sociological study.[132] Understandably, his strong preference for the political must have made any specifically legal doctrine seem irrelevant. As law is anyway minimal in scope and only more or less binding,

[126] *Morgenthau* 34 AJIL 1940 pp. 278–281.
[127] *Ibid.* pp. 270–272. For *Aron* (Paix et Guerre), it is precisely the heterogeneity of the international system which renders international law ultimately powerless, pp. 126–132, 718–722.
[128] *Morgenthau* 34 AJIL 1940 p. 275; *idem* (Politics among Nations) p. 278.
[129] *Morgenthau* 34 AJIL 1940 pp. 278–282.
[130] *Morgenthau* (Politics among Nations) p. 280.   [131] *Ibid.* p. 281.
[132] See also *Boyle* (World Politics) p. 12.

there remains little justification to waste one's time in attempting reform.[133]

Scepticism may have treated unjustly many of the traditional doctrines against which it constituted itself.[134] The concern for "realism" had been there since Wolff, as we have seen. The arguments on which Morgenthau or Aron criticize international law are no different from the arguments which Vattel used to criticize his predecessors or those on which Oppenheim based his voluntarism. That Morgenthau and Aron are lead into scepticism while Oppenheim moves within the rule-approach results from assumptions *outside the system itself.* The former assume States to be inherently hostile and in bad faith. The latter assumes that enlightened self-interest will make States want the existence of binding order.

Scepticism argues, then, that international law is irrelevant as neither extensive nor normative. The immediate problem with scepticism is its reliance on an external point of view. Associating law with factual sanctions fails to count for the internal aspect of rules – the feeling with many statesmen and diplomats that rules exist and are binding upon them and their States. By simply looking at behaviour it fails to answer the relevant question of whether and to what extent legal rules worked behind that behaviour (at the level of motivations, by structuring decision-contexts, delimiting alternative ways of action etc.). It works on the assumption that legal rules will always be overridden when important State interests are at stake – and thus ignores that such are usually given legal protection. Its criticism may seem successful against constructions which separate legal rules from the ways statesmen and States think about them. Once law is understood in a more flexible,

---

[133] Raymond *Aron*'s (Paix et Guerre) scepticism shares the idea of a unitary test for law and ends with dismissing law as irrelevant because both minimal and non-binding. Law is defined by the existence of legal procedure. But international legal procedure is fictitious. Nothing is gained from applying the idea of "legislation" to treaty or custom or "enforcement" to the use of force. There is no distinction between international law and ethics. Like ethics, it is based on the subjective freedom of the State and, like ethics, remains incapable of restraining force pp. 710–712. In its strong preference for sovereignty it is incoherent. No State's interpretation of the law can be preferred over another's pp. 706–707. Change cannot be effected without breach. In brief: "Toute théorie qui prend pour point de départ la Souveraineté des Etats et, d'une manière ou d'une autre, rattache le droit à cette Souveraineté dépouille le droit international de certains caractères constitutifs du droit," pp. 709–710. In core areas of international conduct, the law is fictitious. Either it condemns the use of force and remains silent on how force could be contained or it legitimizes force as "enforcement" in a way which conflicts fundamentally with the belligerents' self-understanding, p. 705.
[134] See also the evaluation in *Boyle* (World Politics) pp. 17–41.

"political" way, however, it might seem that its relevance may be safeguarded.

3.3.3 Policy-approach: McDougal

Like scepticism, the policy-approach finds identity by contrasting itself to the rule-approach. The latter is criticized for being obsessed with the abstract question of the legality or illegality of State action. Binding force is not an on/off affair of applying formal rules but a more-or-less problem related to the factual authoritativeness of legal decision. But the policy-approach distinguishes itself also from scepticism's ideas about the law's marginal scope.[135] As authoritative decision-making goes on at all levels of international conduct, law, too, has relevance at all such levels. Though the law's normative force may not always be great, its scope is very wide.

I shall discuss the policy-approach by reference to the work of Myres McDougal. I believe that while many find it difficult to accept his theoretical expositions and feel especially alien to his idiosyncratic language,[136] his assumptions about the relatedness of law and politics are shared by perhaps a majority of modern international lawyers.

The concerns of the policy-approach were expressed over 60 years ago by Roscoe Pound in an article where he criticized 19th century naturalism and positivism. The former was too far removed from State practice, the latter too uncritical. What was needed was a strategy:

> ... whereby the conflicting or overlapping interests and claims and demands of the peoples of this crowded world may be shared or satisfied so far as may be within a minimum of friction and a minimum of waste (in other words, MK) a functional critique of international law in terms of social ends.[137]

A teleological jurisprudence was needed, aware of the social context and the values of participants therein and which would apply utilitarian

---

[135] See *McDougal* 82 RCADI 1953/I pp. 157–160. See also *Moore* (Reisman-Weston: Toward) pp. 325–327.

[136] For a delightful criticism on this point, see *Fitzmaurice* 65 AJIL 1971 pp. 360–367.

[137] *Pound* (Philosophical) p. 19. See also *McDougal's* citation of Pound in 82 RCADI 1953/I p. 140. On the relationship between *McDougal* and the American sociological movement, see e.g. *Onuf* (Lawmaking) pp. 5–6; *Morison* (Reisman-Weston: Toward) pp. 10, 13 and *passim*; *idem* (Macdonald-Johnston: Process and Structure) pp. 162–171; *Rosenthal* (Etude) p. 31–33.

calculations to maximize global well-being through legal decision.[138] While the rule-approach relied on formally neutral "rules", this approach was to rely on value-dependent "policies" or "processes" to construct a relevant international law.[139]

The starting-point is a criticism of a definition of law in terms of "rules":

> ... rules are merely accumulated trends of past decision which do not identify the variables that led to those decisions, nor relate them to the changed conditions of today's problems, nor indicate preference for the future.[140]

A policy-approach can have little or no place for formally neutral rules. Rules have value only as instrumentalities for the controlling values.[141] Indeed, concentration on rules:

> ... causes too many people to make sharp and unreal distinctions between law and policy, between formulations *de lege lata* and *de lege ferenda*.[142]

The idea of "binding force" associated with a rule's formal validity is rejected as "mystical".[143] McDougal makes the distinction between formal authority and effective control. While the rule-approach lawyer prefers the former, a policy-lawyer will focus on the latter.[144] From this emerges the definition of international law as:

---

[138] See generally, *Allott* XLV BYIL 1971 pp. 124–126.

[139] *Schachter* 178 RCADI 1982/V argues that this preference reflected McDougal's wish to overrule law in favour of politics, pp. 44–54. More accurate is, perhaps, that the concept of "law" is extended so as to cover much of "politics" as well.

[140] *Higgins* (Cheng: Teaching) p. 38. For general analysis of McDougal's criticism of "rules", see *Rosenthal* (Etude) pp. 61 *et seq*, 69–83.

[141] See *Nardin* (Law, Morality) pp. 209–210. See also *supra* ch. I.

[142] *McDougal* 82 RCADI 1953/I p. 144. On this point generally, see also the evaluation in *Schachter* (Schwebel: Effectiveness) pp. 11 *et seq*, 15–16.

[143] *McDougal* 82 RCADI 1953/I p. 185.

[144] *Ibid.* pp. 172–173, 194–198. See also *Higgins* (Reisman-Weston: Toward) p. 79 *et seq*; *Morison* (*ibid.*) pp. 19–30. *D'Amato* (Jurisprudence) argues that McDougal in fact applies the classical test of law as standards backed by sanction, p. 189. But McDougal does not think that actual sanction is necessary to ground effective authority. Power may be effective also due to community expectations. This allows McDougal to avoid the charge of apologism. But the problem also emerges of how to know whether expectations exist. D'Amato's interpretation becomes plausible if one thinks that expectations arise only if sanction is provided for – in which case we are back in apologism. See *McDougal-Reisman* (Macdonald-Johnston: Structure and Process) pp. 105–106.

... flow of decision in which community prescriptions are formulated, invalidated and in fact applied.[145]

Rule-approach law is too narrow. It fails to grasp that contemporary normative process has shifted "from formal, legally binding accords into other form of commitments".[146] It is not the rule's (or other "community prescription's") formal validity which is important but the degree of effective control which can be associated with it.

But the effectiveness of community prescriptions varies. This is a consequence of the lack of common values and the individualized nature of situations in international life. To avoid utopianism, international law must be responsive to such variations.[147] Reliance on the general and abstract formulation of rules only creates "further uncertainty within an already fragile and delicately balanced system".[148]

Emphasis is on law as "comprehensive global processes of authoritative decision".[149] Hence its wide scope. But these processes are not merely naked power (as the sceptics assumed). There is the internal perspective: within processes "people strive to maximize values by applying institutions to resources".[150] Legal processes seek to realize peoples' values – namely certain "goal values of international human dignity".[151]

In McDougal's vocabulary, the policy-approach proceeds from the "clarification of values" towards the "identification of participants" and "arenas of decision" in which available "procedures" are manipulated to achieve social "effects".[152] All these elements are relevant as parts of the process and as "law". In this way, the policy-approach law becomes:

---

[145] *McDougal* 82 RCADI 1953/I p. 181.

[146] *Gottlieb* (Onuf: Lawmaking) p. 109 and generally pp. 109–130. See also *Sheikh* (Behavior) pp. 308–310.

[147] *Kegley* (Onuf: Lawmaking) points out that a policy-approach will study law precisely as a function of social change, pp. 177–181, 189–190. Still, it invariably starts out with a description of the law's social environment, assumed to be determinant of the law's content. For a programmatic approach to this effect, see e.g. *Sheikh* (Behavior) pp. 23–45 and pp. 321–327 (on the strategy of constructing determining "models").

[148] *Dore* (Superpowers) p. 134.

[149] The term "process" is used in various senses in McDougal's work. It is perhaps easiest to understand in its widest meaning denoting any form of social interaction. See *Morison* (Reisman-Weston: Toward) pp. 30 *et seq*, 34–35; *Rosenthal* (Etude) pp. 83–89.

[150] *McDougal* 82 RCADI 1953/I p. 167.

[151] *Ibid.* pp. 168, 190–191.

[152] For an elaboration of the "framework of enquiry", see *ibid.* pp. 165–191, esp. pp. 172–179; *McDougal-Reisman* (Macdonald – Johnston: Structure and Process) pp. 116–120.

... extremely broad, taking in apparently everything that nation-State officials do (in other words, MK) policy and law are indistinguishable.[153]

By relying on a formal and abstract test the rule-approach lawyer was capable of seeing only very little law in international life. Thereby, writes McDougal, he also failed to achieve a complete description of what goes on. By using an arbitrarily restrictive doctrine of legal subjects he failed to produce an exhaustive account of the relevant actors.[154] By concentrating on formal sources he failed to achieve full description of the techniques of authoritative international decision-making.[155]

By widening the law's scope, McDougal will inevitably decrease its normative force. Indeed, he admits this by his criticism of rule-approach emphasis on the latter issue.[156] On the other hand, McDougal believes he can avoid scepticism by integrating values in his description of law as decision-processes.

Policy-approach lawyers base their claim to objectivity on scientist assumptions.[157] They believe they are objective as they focus on observable decision-making, authority and effectiveness and not on rules and their abstract validity.[158] Their interdisciplinary orientation[159] – the links with legal realism and sociological behaviourism – suggests a claim for scientific objectivity which a rule-approach would seem unable to make.

---

[153] *D'Amato* (Jurisprudence) p. 189.

[154] *McDougal* 82 RCADI 1953/I pp. 160–162. The policy-approach lawyer, by contrast, will include decision-making by virtually any entity, person or group of persons within its framework of enquiry. See e.g. *ibid.* pp. 174, 227–256. On this emphasis on "comprehensiveness", see also *McDougal-Reisman* (Macdonald-Johnston: Structure and Process) pp. 111–112.

[155] *McDougal* 82 RCADI 1953/I pp. 162–164. See also *Higgins* (Cheng: Teaching) p. 27 *et seq.*

[156] As *Kratochwil* 69 ARSP 1983 points out, McDougal's criticism of the rule-approach implies such a formalistic interpretation of it that it is doubtful whether the criticism has real bite on a standard rule-approach lawyer's work, pp. 33–34.

[157] See also *Rosenthal* (Etude) pp. 30–31.

[158] McDougal criticizes rule-approach lawyers for not living up to their own idea about objectivity as they inevitably come to treat "fact" and "value" in what seems like an indiscriminate fashion. This is particularly visible in their approach towards legal interpretation. By contrast, the policy-approach argues that it makes a clear distinction between its descriptive and normative strands. See generally the critical exposition in *Allott* XLV BYIL 1971 pp. 115–121. For McDougal's criticism of the "unscientific" character of modern naturalism, see *McDougal-Reisman* (Macdonald-Johnston: Structure and Process) p. 110.

[159] This aspect is emphasized by *Lachs* (Teacher) pp. 150–162.

But the policy-approach remains ultimately unable to maintain its claimed objectivity. Its project will be vulnerable to the objection of lapsing either into uncritical apologism or naïve utopianism.

McDougal loses the distinctiveness of legal doctrine. Law becomes a technique of social engineering. The study of law will concern itself with sociological descriptions ("model-building") and probabilities with which legal processes will reach desired results. It asks sociological questions such as "why", "how", "when" and "to what effect",[160] ignoring questions about the validity or content of law – analysis and systematization, the core of Schwarzenberger's legal paradigm.

But this is no significant objection to the policy-approach. Analysis and systematization of rules are set aside quite deliberately – this follows from the criticism of the rule-approach. But the point about ignoring the internal aspect is applicable against McDougal – just as he applied it against Morgenthau. On the one hand, descriptions of legal decision-making should not ignore the way in which decision-makers occupy themselves with the formal validity, or binding force, of the standards they apply. If it is the case that most decision-makers share a rule-approach conception of the law and hold the boundary between law and politics as relevant, then one cannot explain their behaviour merely as a community process of value-enforcement. On the other hand, for such decision-makers the policy-approach seems like a useless exercise in academic theory. What they are interested in is not which decisions will fulfil which values but which rules are valid and which are not. As the policy-approach provides no answer to this question, it undermines its own claim for instrumental usefulness.[161]

The most significant objection is that to avoid apologetics, the policy-approach will have to take a position which undermines its scientist assumptions and seems utopian on its own premises.

If law were concerned only with describing processes or predicting outcomes and not with the ends to which they are used, it would remain unable to criticize particular State policy. Yet, to describe such ends in terms of "community policy" (maximization of welfare) fails to guarantee the protection of State rights if cost-benefit effectiveness will provide for overruling them (not to say anything of the

[160] See e.g. *McDougal-Reisman* (Macdonald-Johnston: Structure and Process) pp. 123–128.
[161] *Sheikh* (Behavior) pp. 5–8.

difficulties in making such calculations or deciding between differing ones).[162]

Nothing could be further away from the mind of McDougal than constructing an apologetic doctrine. To avoid it, he postulates that the policy-approach should also be concerned with the enhancement of certain "goal values of international human dignity" (such as power, respect, enlightenment, wealth, well-being, skill, affection and rectitude). The problem is only how to demonstrate the correctness of such base-values and the deductions made from them.[163]

Several critics have pointed out the extreme subjectivism in McDougal's discussion of goal values. There is an implicit assumption that reasonable men will agree on such values and adopt those held by McDougal himself.[164] Recurring use of the term "reasonable" in his argument always immediately preceding the conclusion testifies to the same effect.[165] Lacking a system of demonstrating the correctness and

---

[162] On this criticism, see *Schachter* 178 RCADI 1982/V pp. 25–26; *Nardin* (Law, Morality) pp. 194–197.

[163] The policy-approach attempts to grasp law both as power and value, the former aspect being concerned with "actual effectiveness", the latter – initially – conceptualized relativistically as "community expectation". See e.g. *McDougal-Reisman* (Macdonald-Johnston: Structure and Process) p. 112. The "intellectual's" task is to clarify (describe) the value-systems different people possess, *ibid.* p. 122. But the relativistic character of value disappears in McDougal's treatment of "human dignity" values which are inferred from existing human rights instruments and other documents as well as a community recognition which can be grasped by (a somewhat mystical) "identification with the whole of humankind". See e.g. *ibid.* pp. 114–116, 122–123. As *Rosenthal* (Etude) points out, McDougal does not make explicit what he means by "human dignity" values, associating them variably with community consensus and with some "internal" or systemic values of democratic decision-processes, pp. 54–57. For a more detailed analysis of the connection between McDougal's "human dignity" values, classical utilitarianism and the American foreign policy credo, see *Krakau* (Missionsbewusstsein) pp. 474–504; *Rosenthal* (Etude) pp. 127–144. The function of such values within McDougal's discourse is, in any case, to control decision (power). They are, in a sense, the rule-approach law within his own system. The distinction human dignity value/actual decision has precisely the same function in McDougal as law/politics in rule-approach discourse. McDougal's problem, of course, is that his doubts about the clear-cut character of the latter distinction are equally applicable in respect of the former.

[164] For criticisms, see *Allott* XLV BYIL 1971 pp. 123–125; *Boyle* (World Politics) pp. 63–67; *Boyle* 26 Harv.ILJ 1985 p. 349; *Fitzmaurice* 65 AJIL 1971 pp. 370–373 and the studies by Krakau and Rosenthal, *supra* n. 163. See also *Dorsey* 82 AJIL 1988 (making the liberal point that this kind of claim for a set of values to universal validity poses "the greatest danger" to peace and world order) pp. 41–51.

[165] On McDougal's use of "reasonableness", see also *Rosenthal* (Etude) pp. 123–127; *Krakau* (Missionsbewusstsein) pp. 505–508.

content of his values, however, he will remain vulnerable to the objec-tions advanced against any other kind of naturalism.[166]

There is this problem: blurring the law/politics distinction will result in a law which seems to exist everywhere but which is devoid of critical, normative force. To escape apologism, one has to postulate the existence of objective values.[167] But as there is no test to demonstrate the correct-ness of these values, this strategy will turn against the policy-approach the objection it advanced against its rivals, namely that of metaphysical subjectivism. This is fatal for the policy-approach on its own scientist standards. It will also undermine its claim for instrumental usefulness. For as the base values remain generally formulated and controversial, they do not provide the kind of standards which lawyers and diplomats could use in order to decide what might count as permitted or prohibited behaviour.[168]

Let me briefly illustrate this dilemma by reference to Francis Boyle's *World Politics and International Law* (1985). Boyle starts out with an attack on positivism, "obsessed" with the legal/illegal distinction which only enhances popular belief in the irrelevance of international law.[169] State activity should rather be looked at through a spectrum varying from the "egregiously illegal" to "perfectly legal".[170] The distinction between law and politics is suspect:

> ... it is a logical and historical fallacy to believe that law and politics are essentially independent of each other. In the realm of international relations, they are highly interdependent so as to be almost indistinguishable.[171]

Boyle proposes to base a relevant doctrine on a *mélange* of traditional doctrine and political science.[172] Concern should not focus on the

---

[166] The use of platitudes such as "the application of legal rules must be politically acceptable" (*Sheikh* (Behavior) p. 69) in standard policy-approach writing makes, of course, that approach particularly vulnerable to the same criticisms which it itself directed against the mixing up of fact and value by its predecessors. A statement such as the above is meaningful in a system containing an explicit theory of political value. I know of no policy-approach lawyer who would have taken this openly political strand: indeed, taking it would immediately undermine the scientist premises on which the policy-approach criticized rule-approach naturalists and their assumption of a clear-cut distinction between binding (that is, acceptable) and non-binding (that is, non-acceptable) standards.

[167] As *Rosenthal* (Etude) demonstrates, McDougal ends up in assuming a theory of common interests which has normative force against individual States, pp. 133–134.

[168] *Allott* XLV BYIL 1971 pp. 127–128; *Nardin* (Law, Morality) pp. 194–197; *D'Amato* (Jurisprudence) p. 190.

[169] *Boyle* (World Politics) pp. 59–60. [170] *Ibid.* pp. 164–167.

[171] *Ibid.* p. 81. He leaves undiscussed the sense of "almost". [172] *Ibid.* pp. 58–61.

legal/illegal distinction. Instead, a 5-stage methodological programme is proposed: 1) description of cases; 2) formulation of hypotheses on the role of law on the basis of the cases analysed; 3) testing of these hypotheses by reference to other cases; 4) making predictions; 5) formulation of prescriptive standards.[173] By this method he proposes to prove the instrumental relevance of international law.[174] But in fact the contrary takes place as the identity of law *vis-à-vis* sociology and politics is lost altogether.

If law is to have instrumental value, its content should be reasonably clear. But Boyle proposes no other test for recognizing what might count as "law" beyond the "diplomatic consensus" at each moment. Now, this is hardly a determinate test – even less so if what one seeks is not to prove whether an action is legal or not but how it ranks on the scale from manifestly illegal to the manifestly legal. It is very doubtful whether diplomatic practice can be studied in those terms at all.

Boyle aims to prove the relevance of international law by reference to the frequent use of legal arguments in "high international politics". Looking at these arguments – and *not* at their validity (indeed, condemning the very question about validity as "positivistic") – Boyle draws the conclusion that Governments generally act in the way they perceive to be "least violative of the international legal order".[175] But this conclusion is simply meaningless as "legal order" under Boyle's premises does not denote any normative standards at all. If, as Boyle writes,[176] Governments interpret the law – the legal order – so as to render it compatible with their interests, then surely that Governments usually act in ways which they see least violative of international law is only a truism: Governments follow their interests and habitually dress their policies in the garb of legal rhetoric.

In fact, this conclusion is the only one which can be made on policy-approach premises about the relevance of international law. The problem lies in the core of the policy-approach. Attempting to prove the law's relevance by denying its independence from politics is absurd: the very programme of proving the law's relevance coalesces then with proving the relevance of politics!

---

[173] *Ibid.* pp. 67–70; 155–164.
[174] *Ibid.* pp. 165–167. His "functionalism" is in fact only a form of political science – and a fairly simplistic one at that. Even his "prescriptive statements" claim to be statements about utility.
[175] *Ibid.* p. 160.   [176] *Ibid.* p. 79.

Boyle thinks his law is relevant as it will, by definition, protect "vital security interests".[177] But this also affirms its uncritical character. For Boyle, any use of legal rhetoric by some international body is "law". Indeed, other tests are dismissed as irrelevant: *de lege ferenda*, too, may be "law".[178] The very idea of verifying the law's content is dismissed as "formalism". But is this really proof of the law's relevance? If decision-makers cannot – and should not – verify the law's content but should use their own *de lege ferenda* views, then surely any present law cannot be held as a constraining factor in social practice.

But Boyle is also a political partisan and cannot be content with the apologist consequences of his method. The greater part of the book contains a critical analysis of the lawfulness of recent United States international action.[179] The book ends in the appeal that the US should "rely exclusively on the panoply of rules, techniques and institutions of international law".[180] But this *normative* analysis conflicts with the methodological programme. The legal/illegal distinction is now taken as unproblematic and issues concerning the legality of US action are assumed capable of being determined in abstraction from the American self-understandings, rhetoric or its (controversial) interests. Boyle's methodological exposition does not warrant his normative conclusions. On his own standards, views of US action as "illegal" are only political opinions dressed in legal language.

To sum up: the policy-approach creates a law which is wide in scope but weak in normative force. To correct the latter defect, it uses naturalistic or unexplained ideas of justice which are, however, undermined by the scientism through which it criticized standard naturalism and positivism. The relevance of international law is not demonstrated within it.

3.3.4   Idealism: Alvarez

The previous three were already watered-down versions of the modern programme. Each accepts that it is contradictory; law cannot be concrete and normative at the same time. Thus they attempt to preserve one part of it and downplay the other or simply adopt a sceptical attitude. But the result is unsatisfactory: The rule-approach has difficulty to demonstrate the binding force of what little amount of law it is left with.

---

[177] *Ibid.* p. 164.   [178] *Ibid.* pp. 83–84.
[179] *Ibid.* pp. 171–200.   [180] *Ibid.* p. 179.

The policy-approach avoids apologism only by drawing an objective morality from a magician's hat. Scepticism is cynical.

Consequently, lawyers have been unable to stay within any of these positions permanently. Unless they have become cynics, they characteristically move from their initial rule or policy-approach position towards a reconciliation. Many rule-approach lawyers simply by-pass deviant doctrines and write as if there were, in fact, a wide range of uncontroversial rules constantly applied between States. Standard policy-approach lawyers write as if everybody agreed on their preferred values. Both aim at ensuring that their law be as far as possible both wide and normative. Yet, both contain a successful criticism of the subjectivism in the other.

"Idealism", the fourth available position, is simply the modern programme in its original form – the position towards which standard rule- and policy-approach lawyers constantly move. I shall describe it here with particular reference to the genre of legal writing which sees law to exist especially in and through the United Nations and manifest itself in the "new" areas of economic and human rights law, law of natural resources and environment and so on. This variation of modernism relies on the assumption that "new developments" in international society have vastly enlarged the law's material scope. That law is absolutely binding is usually taken as an implicit, unproblematic assumption.[181]

Idealism contrasts itself to both traditional rule-approach and policy-approach theorizing. Old doctrines are attacked as obsolete apologies. Classical positivism is seen as conservative formalism[182] while reliance on naturalistic "policies" is seen either as a powerless form of moral criticism or outright reactionary imperialism.[183]

An analysis of the idealist argument is made difficult because it avoids express theorizing and is usually dressed in untangible generalities.[184]

---

[181] Thus, the paradigmatic idealist, Judge *Alvarez* both emphasizes the relatedness of law and politics – indeed, the imperative need of the former to correspond to the latter – while still arguing for the need "to differentiate between judicial and political elements" in legal decision, diss. op. ICJ: *Admission* Case, Reports 1948 pp. 69–70. See also *idem*, diss. op. ICJ: *Status of South West Africa* Case, Reports 1950 pp. 177–178; *idem*, diss. op. ICJ: *Anglo-Norwegian Fisheries* Case, Reports 1951 p. 149.

[182] See e.g. *Bedjaoui* (New International Economic Order) pp. 98–103, *passim*.

[183] *Ghozali* (Mélanges Chaumont) holds natural law a camouflage for attempts to further economic interests or zones of influence, p. 303.

[184] Lawyers are unable to formulate it as a concrete programme because of its self-contradictory character. This creates difficulties for the discussion above. How do we know whether a point about, for example, the need to make law better "reflect" the

However, it is possible to isolate two assumptions behind it: On the one hand, law is understood as a reflection of society. This serves to explain the law's material scope. On the other hand, it is also critical of existing structures of international dominance. This explains the law's normative nature. But these assumptions contradict each other. Thus, idealism creates strategies for explaining away the contradiction, moves back towards a rule-approach or a policy-approach position or succumbs to the temptation of scepticism.

The first leg of idealism explains the law's wide material scope and resembles the policy-approach. Old law of coordination which remained silent on many important issues in inter-State relations is contrasted with a modern law of cooperation which transforms into normative language the needs of interdependence, created by recent economic and technological progress.[185] The law has expanded from lateral coordination into regulating the most varied economic, humanitarian and social fields:

> ... the emphasis of the law is increasingly shifting from the formal structure of the relationships between States and the delimitation of their jurisdiction to the development of substantive rules on matters of human concern vital to the growth of an international community.[186]

The changes in international economic, social and technological "systems" have created an expanded need for legal regulation. As law mirrors

international society has been made by an idealist or a policy-approach lawyer? Indeed, this cannot be known otherwise than by taking seriously the argument whereby the lawyer distances himself/herself from others. Inasmuch as the totality of the argument strives towards preserving a distance to standard rule and policy-approach writing it can plausibly be inferred that the lawyer's argument is an "idealist" one. Remember, however, that my interest is *not* in a description and/or classification of positions actually held by lawyers but to illustrate *positions logically available*, that is, the structure which controls modern discourse.

[185] *Friedmann*'s (Changing) argument is illustrative. His discussion builds on the assumed expansion of international law on the most varied fields of human rights, social cultural and economic fields, pp. 3–30, 61–63, 67–70, 152–187. See also *idem* (Essays Jessup) p. 113 *et seq*; *idem* XIX BYIL 1938 pp. 130–141. Indeed, the idealist argument generally dwells at length on the "expansion of the international society". See e.g. *Falk* (Reisman-Weston: Toward) pp. 133–147; *Buirette-Maurau* (Tiersmonde) pp. 19–36. But this is not simply a standard argument among Western liberals. Lawyers identifying themselves with third world policy often take the same track. See, in particular, *Alvarez* (Droit international nouveau) pp. 455–603 (reviewing the "new domains" of international law).

[186] *Jenks* XXXI BYIL 1954 p. 9. For the needed change of perspective, see also *idem* (Common Law) pp. 62–89, *passim*.

society, it also reflects these changes.[187] The obsoleteness of traditional law lies precisely in its failure to integrate them into itself.

For idealism, the test of law is its correspondence to the objective character (interests, needs etc.) of the international society. As the test is a loose, almost intuitive one, idealism often expresses itself in terms of general principles or broadly conceived "rights" to development, peace etc.[188] Restricting legal sources to those mentioned in Article 38 of the ICJ Statute is seen as narrow formalism.[189] The law-creative functions of consensus at the UN and other international bodies is emphasized. Consensus, interdependence, "needs of the international society" all serve as grounds for legal argument – securing thus the breadth of the idealist's law.[190]

Like the policy-approach, this strand within idealism runs the risk of apologism. If law always mirrors society, what basis is there to adopt a critical posture? A second argument is needed which can explain law also as *an instrument of change.*[191]

But how can the law both reflect society and be critical of it? Let me illustrate this tension in the work of Alejandro Alvarez, a South-American legal scholar and a long-time judge at the ICJ. His writing starts out with assuming that international law both reflects the changes in the international society and is critical of that society. In the course of the argument, however, the critical strand is devoured by the socio-logical one.

Alvarez' argument opens up with extended descriptions of the changes in the "life of peoples" which have emerged especially since the Second World War.[192] New political, psychological, social and scientific problems have arisen which call for urgent treatment. But

---

[187] "... international law is a dependent variable rather than an autonomous and deter-mining factor". *Bedjaoui* (New International Economic Order) p. 111. For this stan-dard point, see also *Anand* (New States) pp. 46, 113–116, *passim.*

[188] For a plea for the "human right to development", see *Bulajić* pp. 332–358 and *passim.* See further e.g. *Wassilikowski* (Essays Lachs) p. 308; *Mbaye (ibid.)* pp. 167–177. See also UNGA Res.41/133, 4 December 1986 (Declaration on the Right to Development).

[189] See e.g. *Slouka* (Onuf: Lawmaking) pp. 131–171. See also *Elias* (Essays Jessup) pp. 37–57.

[190] See also *Ghozali* (Mélanges Chaumont) p. 297 *et seq.* On lawyers emphasizing "consensus" over traditional law-making, see e.g. *Gottlieb* (Onuf: Lawmaking) p. 109 *et seq*; *Bedjaoui* (New International Economic Order) pp. 169, 177–192.

[191] See, in particular, the discussion in *Bedjaoui* (New International Economic Order) pp. 109–115.

[192] See *Alvarez* (Droit international nouveau) pp. 11–30.

traditional science, including law, has shown itself incapable of dealing with them.[193]

These changes have transformed the basis of society.[194] A State-centred individualism can no longer guarantee society's survival. A new global interdependence has emerged, reflected in the creation of supranational organizations and, in particular, the United Nations:

> As a result of the increasingly closer relations between States, which has led into their ever greater interdependece, the old community of nations has been transformed into a veritable international society.[195]

This social change has been accompanied with a transformation in international law. A "new" international law is not merely a set of political desiderata. It is law *now* as it reflects the new "juridical conscience of peoples".[196] In the *Competence of the General Assembly* Case (1950) Alvarez points out:

> There is no doubt that the Court must apply the existing law to the case which has been referred to it.[197]

The starting-point looks like that of a rule-approach lawyer. "What is this law to-day?",[198] Alvarez asks. And he answers by referring to the social developments outlined above:

> ... a new universal international conscience is emerging, which ... has opened the way to a new international law.[199]

Consequently, the powers of the General Assembly must be decided, not on a narrow or legalistic construction of the *travaux préparatoires* or of the text of the Charter. It must be interpreted so as to reflect the new

---

[193] *Ibid.* p. 38 *et seq.* Consequently, he proposes the establishment of a "new" science; a science on the evolution of the lives of peoples, on popular psychology and on the reconstruction of the basis of social life, *ibid* pp. 57–380.

[194] *Ibid.* p. 277 *et seq.*

[195] *Alvarez*, diss. op. ICJ: *Admission* Case, Reports 1948 p. 68 (note that Alvarez has reversed the terminology by Tönnies).

[196] For the sources of this new law, see *Alvarez* (Droit international nouveau) pp. 430–433. They are, again, ascending and descending, they reflect simultaneously peoples' (subjective) consciences and spontaneous (objective) conditions of social life, *ibid* pp. 431, 432, 445.

[197] *Alvarez*, diss. op. ICJ: *Competence of the General Assembly* Case, Reports 1950 p. 12. To the same effect, see *idem*, diss. op. *Admission* Case, Reports 1948 pp. 69–70; *idem*, diss. op. *Status of South West Africa* Case, Reports 1950 pp. 175–177.

[198] *Alvarez*, diss. op. ICJ: *Competence of the General Assembly* Case, Reports 1950 p. 12.

[199] *Ibid.*

conditions of international life and in particular the purposes and nature of the UN as an organized representative of mankind.[200]

The "new" international law is law *ex nunc* as it corresponds to the nature of present international society and peoples' cognition of it in their juridical conscience. It is not merely a set of *de lege ferenda* wishes. On the contrary, there is no difference between the *de lege ferenda* and the *de lege lata* in this respect.[201]

But Alvarez does not think his new law is a political programme among others. He holds it a scientific truth, verifiable by recourse to the actual living conditions, needs and interests of peoples. It is objective and therefore applicable as law.

Despite its progressivist style, Alvarez' work lacks critical bite. This may not be evident as long as he remains with generalities.[202] To be sure, his position as a dissident at the ICJ and his South American background cast him inevitably as a critic. But in fact his programme is virtually empty of social criticism. Criticism is directed, as it were, backwards, towards a law and politics of a superseded era.[203] The present is portrayed as one of all-encompassing interdependence where people are in agreement about the fundamentals of social life. Existing conflict is wiped away or presented as "error" which can be corrected when everybody understands his real interest, this being demonstrable

---

[200] *Alvarez*, diss. op. ICJ: *Competence of the General Assembly* Case, Reports 1950 pp. 16–19. See also *idem*, diss. op. *Admission* Case, Reports 1948 pp. 68–69; *Azevedo*, diss. op. ICJ: *Competence of the General Assembly* Case, Reports 1950 pp. 23–24. On the corresponding position of the developing States in regard to the interpretation of the UN Charter in general, see *El-Erian* (Essays Jessup) pp. 96–98.

[201] *Alvarez*, diss. op. ICJ: *Competence of the General Assembly* Case, Reports 1950 pp. 13–14; *idem*, diss. op. *Admission* Case, Reports 1948 pp. 69–70. In the *Anglo-Norwegian Fisheries* Case, Reports 1951, he argues, emphatically, first, that the "Court must *develop* the law of nations, that is to say, it must remedy its short-comings". Immediately thereafter, however, he goes on to argue that the Court must give effect to general principles of law as they are expressed in *present* peoples' consciousness, expressed e.g. in UN resolutions because, it seems, these are law *now*, pp. 146, 148–149. This makes the Court's task both constitutive and declaratory: the argued norm is both based on the Court's decision and on something beyond it (peoples' consciousness). The same ambiguity is reflected in the *Status of South West Africa* Case, Reports 1950, in which he argues that the Court "must apply the law which already exists to-day", p. 176. In another passage, however, he argues that in applying this "new" law, the Court "creates the law", p. 177.

[202] Indeed, as other idealists, he, too, relies expressly on arguments from general principles instead of "narrowly" conceived rules, see *Alvarez* (Droit international nouveau) pp. 437–453.

[203] See e.g. *ibid*. pp. 57–159.

scientifically. Alvarez' construction does provide a law which is materially wide as it regulates nearly everything in society. But it does this with too much cost to its critical nature. The only criticism it allows is that against a State which has not followed its time. Moreover, Alvarez does not succeed in treating "interdependence", "social needs" or "juridical conscience" in a concrete way. His argument makes constantly controversial interpretations and appears inevitably as political.[204]

Alvarez' work may be contrasted to that of the Algerian lawyer and diplomat, Mohammed Bedjaoui. He shares a similar outlook and programme as Alvarez. Also, his argument has real critical bite. But it has this at the cost of the applicability of his law.

Bedjaoui's work is openly political. He attacks international law together with other features of present international society.[205] His own preferred law is expressly *de lege ferenda*.[206] It is not derived from the present society, characterized by imperialism and oppression. On the contrary, it attempts to transform the present society and its law. This is in no way altered by Bedjaoui's refusal to hold his own programme as a merely moral (naturalistic) critique. He thinks his opinions share in the quality of objective truth. But he differs from Alvarez in that he does not claim these opinions to be law *ex nunc*, only in a better society. His law is critical but lacks applicability.

Alvarez and Bedjaoui illustrate opposite ways to deal with idealism's internal tension. If stress is laid on the law's capacity to reflect society, it will be uncritical. If emphasis is on criticism, the idealist must concede that his principles have no present applicability as law. I shall now look at three strategies of hiding the tension within idealism.

The first strategy is distinguishing between social needs and values and the social power-structure. The idealist argument might be understood so that its first strand (material scope) referred to the former while the second strand (criticism) referred to the latter. In other words, the

---

[204] This is an inevitable consequence of a view which does not think that a test of pedigree of norms is relevant or necessary. For example, *Sheikh* (Behavior) presents a "sociological" programme which is explicitly anti-positivistic and anti-naturalistic. But as he proceeds to infer norms from his description of the international society he overlooks the fact that society is regularly interpreted in differing and conflicting ways. See esp. pp. 113–149. His normative result remains as controversial as his description. The matter is aggravated by the way in which his norms claim the validity of a sociological description: the result will look like an attempt to impose norms under non-normative (non-political) arguments.
[205] *Bedjaoui* (New International Economic Order) pp. 23–97.
[206] *Ibid.* pp. 15–16, 97 *et seq*; 109–115.

argument might be that existing needs and values no longer correspond to existing power-structures.

But idealism cannot simply argue on the basis of needs and values as it tries to avoid what it understands as a "merely" moralistic criticism. It does not wish to present political arguments but insists that these are in some sense already applicable law.[207] When idealist lawyers have criticized the ICJ, for example, for having taken a conservative position they have not meant that the law was conservative but that the Court failed to take account of new developments *in* the law, that it did not apply valid law at all.

To make this argument, idealism needs to assume that "needs and values" of States can be separated from observable State behaviour or will – these latter being manifestations of an oppressive power-structure. In other words, it needs to assume that they have, as such, an objective character so as to be applicable as law. But this seems indistinguishable from standard naturalism.[208] It is open to a familiar objection: There has been no theory of values or needs which would have commanded a significant degree of consensus. Any view on them seems to encapsulate controversial political ideas. If the possibility of verifying needs and values by reference to what goes on in society is excluded (and this was the argument's starting-point), how can they at all be verified? The position that one can base law on needs and values which are differentiated from structures of international practice seems unacceptable because naturalistic. It does not have distance from the arguer's political opinions.

There are two further strategies to make the conflict disappear. One consists in admitting that a social change has not yet taken place but that it is "on the way" and that the law's task is to aid in this. McWhinney argues:

> We live today in an era of transition in the world community, from an old system of public order to a new one.[209]

---

[207] Of course, most idealists hold quite a simple form of economic determinism: values, that is politics and law, are derived from an economic infrastructure. The strategy of allocating to needs and values a status distinct from power-structures is usually excluded by the idealist's own assumptions.

[208] *Jenks* XXXI BYIL 1954, for example, explicitly denies having presented a new naturalistic theory of law, p. 9.

[209] *McWhinney* (UN Law-making) p. 3. See also *ibid.* pp. 22–23; *idem* (Conflict) p. 118 *et seq.*

The argument about the international system being "in transition" has been voiced throughout the 20th century.[210] Its use implies that law can be tested not only against present-day reality but some future trends. We notice here a strategy similar to the classical lawyers' recourse to historicism. Here, too, one tries to avoid apologism by opposing to States a law based on objective historical trends. This would, of course, require a reliable theory about such trends. But there is not only disagreement about trends of social organization. There is also deep-going disagreement about what such trends *should be* like. To test the law against hypothesized and value-laden historical trends is indistinguishable from a naturalist test – and just as unacceptable.

A third strategy is to claim that society and law have already changed but that juristic theory has failed to reflect this:

> The crux of our present problems is that the profound transformation of law already achieved in practice, which is proceeding continuously, though generally recognized and welcomed by contemporary international lawyers, has not been sufficiently assimilated into their instinctive thinking to reflect it adequately ... [211]

In other words, what needs criticism is juristic instinct, controlled by obsolete concepts and categories, not the law which has aready changed to reflect the realities of a new society.[212] But many would not share this view. It directs criticism away from social institutions and law into juristic concepts and categories. Most idealists wish not to be bothered with the latter. They wish to aim directly at the structures of power and politics. Morover, what is the test of the "adequacy" of juristic concepts? It is hard to see what other test a critic would use apart from that of correspondence with his *de lege ferenda* views or the character of society. In the former case we are back at the objections advanced against naturalism. In the latter case, we shall either fall into apologism (if "society" is understood in terms of its power-relations) or utopianism (if "society" is understood in terms of objective values or needs).

Everywhere, the idealist argument will either dissolve in contradiction or turn out to be a rule-approach or a policy-approach argument in disguise. The idealist will try to argue that his law is based on

---

[210] See also *Röling* (Expanded World) pp. vii–xxv and *passim; Falk* (Reisman-Weston: Toward) p. 148 and *passim.*

[211] *Jenks* XXXI BYIL 1954 p. 9.

[212] See also *Bedjaoui* (New International Economic Order) pp. 106–109.

international society and critical of it. If he insists on the former, he will lose the justification of his criticism. If he insists on the latter, he cannot claim that his law is widely applicable without becoming a naturalist. It is hardly surprising, then, that some idealists have turned sceptics in regard to the relevance of law as an instrument of change.[213]

Lack of independent standing from the idealist approach has contributed to the apparent paradox that despite its critical tone, idealism has been forced to adopt some of the most classical ideas in the classical lawyer's vocabulary. As Charles Chaumont notes:

> Si le droit classique est en voie de disparition comme phase historique, il n'est pas aboli comme méthode et vision.[214]

But even this suggests too much. The content of the law put forward by its most ardent critics seems curiously familiar: it builds on sovereignty, independence, equality, territorial integrity and consent.[215] Emphasis on non-intervention over humanitarian values is striking.[216] The State is presented as the natural organization and the normative principle. The sole difference lies in *which* States, which policies, are pointed out as deserving protection. But to argue openly on these terms, the idealist would seem to make a political point and lose his claim to legal neutrality.

3.4   Conclusions: descriptivism

The four positions count as an exhaustive description of the possibilities of modern argument about international law. As normativity and

---

[213] See e.g. *Borella* (Mélanges Chaumont) pp. 87–88; *Ghozali* (Mélanges Chaumont) pp. 311–314. See also *Falk* (Reisman-Weston: Toward) (noting the tendency of international law to reflect the values of the élites of the most powerful countries) pp. 148–149. His analysis is pessimistic: "international law works largely as an opiate", pp. 158–161. See also the sceptical analysis in *Colin* XVIII RBDI 1984–85 pp. 776–793.

[214] *Chaumont* 129 RCADI 1971/I p. 345. To the same effect, see *Henkin* (How) pp. 122–125; *Gray* 3 Legal Studies 1983 pp. 270–271; *Prott* (Culture) pp. 225–226; *Anand* (Gros: Future) p. 6.

[215] On this point, see e.g. *Buirette-Maurau* (Tiers-monde) pp. 35–36; *Elias* (IIL 1973) p. 371; *Röling* (Expanded World) pp. 73–86; *Henkin* (How) pp. 125–134; *Fitzmaurice* (IIL 1973) pp. 214–215. See also *Anand* (New States) pp. 48–52, 62–73 and *passim*. On Third-World emphasis on sovereignty, see *Akehurst* (Modern) pp. 19–22; *Ginther* (New Perspectives) pp. 236–237. On Third-World position about equality, see *Starke* (International Law) p. 6; *Mayall* (Donelan: Reason) pp. 126–136; *Verzijl* (I) pp. 444–447.

[216] See *Tucker* (Inequality) pp. 57–65.

concreteness have been assumed as necessary and sufficient conditions for an objective, that is, relevant doctrine, no other positions are available. Each is distinctly *modern* in its attempt to distance itself from earlier naturalism and positivism, understood as subjective because utopian or apologist. Each aims to construct a law which would be binding while not implying a stand on rival theories of material justice. This is simply the classical project continued. It was a classical insight which brought the problems of objectivity and relevance to the fore and made it seem imperative to reconcile normativity with concreteness. If the reconciliatory strategies have differed, the need to undertake them reflects an identical concern and argumentative structure – with as much or little likelihood for success – behind classicism and modernism.

We can now perceive the structuring effect of the tension between the descending and ascending modes of argument in modern doctrines. The former aims to prove the law's normativity, its binding character, the latter tries to ensure the law's concreteness, its relatedness to State behaviour, will and interest. Emphasizing one will lead into a de-emphasis on the other. The positions remain exhaustive and exclusive: each is defined by its opposition to the others, by its being on the scales of normativity and concreteness what the others are not. Normativity implies capability of overruling concreteness. A rule is truly normative only if it can be successfully opposed to a concrete fact-description (including a description of what somebody "wants"). Concreteness implies correspondence to a fact-description (including a description of "wants"). This makes intermediate doctrines inevitably fail. An argument, doctrine or position, "intermediate" or not, can justify itself only by claiming normativity or concreteness. It cannot make reference to both without self-contradiction. But this makes it possible to project it, from an opposing perspective, *as too weak on either of the two scales and unacceptable as such.*

In this way, each of the four positions will remain only a partial solution and fails to produce a fully convincing doctrine. Hence, few lawyers have adopted them quite in the manner discussed. The structure of modernism is not static but fluid. Lawyers are in constant movement from one position to another without being able to stay permanently in any. Adopting any of the positions seems possible on the basis of the valid criticism it produces of the others. But none of them can successfully maintain a positive programme of its own.

As a result, many lawyers have come to support views which point beyond modern (liberal) doctrines. These lawyers have argued on the basis of the justice or equitableness of their preferred norms. It is difficult to know what to make of this development, also manifested in recent judicial and arbitral practice. Such arguments seem to assume either that justice is, after all, in some sense objective, or that there is room for legal argument beyond objective rules. Neither assumption can be reconciled with the reviewed structure. In chapter 8 I shall look into how such arguments need to be taken seriously – even if this will require abandoning the ideal of legal objectivity with which modern law constructs its identity. Let me finish this chapter by taking another perspective on this development.

The unity of modernism lies in its opposition to early theories. Each of the four approaches reviewed refuses to develop its concept of law in terms of a material theory of justice. Each attempts to develop a conception of international law on a neutral, objective view over what seems to take place in the social world where States live. In other words, what modern doctrines have in common is that they share a *social conception of law*. They believe that the law is determined by social events, that is, treaties, customs, precedents, policies, "authority" or more general patterns of history, in particular economic and technological development. They believe the law to be a "social fact" and that an adequate concept of law is one which accurately describes those "facts". Moreover, each bases its claim to superiority *vis-à-vis* the other approaches on the accuracy of *that very description*.[217]

---

[217] This is best reflected in the standard modern style of preceding normative analyses with a description of the "international society" or a history of international relations. The assumption is then that: "A la base de tout effort vraiment constructif en droit international se trouve un certain conception des rapports du droit et du pouvoir. C'est à une conception fonctionnelle du pouvoir, à une conception sociale du droit que s'attache notre enseignement", *De Visscher* 86 RCADI 1954/II p. 451. Similarly, *Monaco* 125 RCADI 1968/III affirms: "notre point de départ est une conception sociale du droit", p. 109. To the same effect, see also *Cavaré* (Droit international I) p. 167. *Jessup* (Modern) makes the methodological point: "The significant question to ask about international law is whether the use of that term is in accordance with an accurate observation and study of the conduct of states ...", p. 6. Beside actual conduct of States, history and society may also be taken to include objective tendencies which are useful for the construction of the descending argument. Thus *Fenwick* 79 RCADI 1951 directs the social conception beyond statehood or State will, towards understanding that the law "is based on the fact of the interdependence of States", p. 13. Frequently, the social conception of law is expressed in views which hold "effectiveness" as the "basis" (or the real content) of the normativity of international law. See, in particular, *Quadri* 80 RCADI 1952/I p. 618 *et seq*; *Barile* 161 RCADI 1978/III pp. 23–26. Similar statements could of course, be continued at length. The point is

The obvious problem here is that the facts which constitute the international social world do not appear "automatically" but are the result of choosing, finding a relevant conceptual matrix.[218] This is a conceptual choice, a choice which cannot be evaluated in terms of facts because it *singles out those very facts* on which it bases its "relevance".[219]

The four versions achieve different descriptions of what goes on because they involve differing conceptual matrices. The rule-approach lawyer looks at international social life through his doctrine of sources. The policy-approach lawyer constructs what count as "processes of authoritative decision" by an anterior criterion of authority, base-values and relevance. The sceptic looks at State behaviour as a continuing pattern of self-interested violence while the idealist sees the social life among States in terms of common needs and solidarity values. Each bases its superiority on its capacity to describe more accurately the social environment of international politics.

Modern lawyers criticize their predecessors for having started out by a conceptual system which is taken to be prior to the social events in which that system is to be applied. The "realist" approaches have mocked the strategy to start out by a "definition of international law".[220] Yet, even if

[218] only to emphasize the reliance of modern writing on the assumption that if only the "facts" of statehood and history are properly described the law will be properly described, too. For two standard discussions see e.g. *Mosler* (Legal Community) pp. 1–28; *Cassese* (Divided) pp. 1–73.

Conceptual matrices destroy the descriptivist dream in two ways. First, inasmuch as social action receives meaning through the concepts through which participants view what they are doing, any understanding of such action must go further than mere observation of behaviour. It needs to become conceptual analysis. Second, in attributing meaning to social action any observer does this through his conceptual apparatus. His observation and analysis are part of his being a participant as well. That the two matrices are non-identical and that the former can only manifest itself through the latter makes it impossible to uphold the descriptivist's dream of objectivity. The first point leads into hermeneutics, the second into Critical Theory. These matters are systematically discussed e.g. in *Taylor* (Philosophy) pp. 15–115; *Bernstein* (Beyond Objectivism) pp. 165–169, 171 et seq. For the second point, see also *Giddens* (Central Problems) pp. 243–245, 251–253. An international lawyer to have consistently opposed the descriptivist project is *Kelsen*. In General Theory he makes this explicit: "Cognition cannot be passive in relation to its objects, it cannot be confined to reflecting things that are somehow given in themselves ... Cognition itself creates objects," pp. 434–435. See also *Ago* 90 RCADI 1956/II pp. 908, 912–913.

[219] As *Carty* (Decay) observes: "One cannot simply study the practice of States as evidence of law because it is logically inconceivable to examine any evidence without *a priori* criteria of relevance and significance – in this case a prior conception of law", pp. 95–96.

[220] See e.g. the very useful anti-conceptualist argument by *Williams* XXII BYIL 1945 pp. 146–163. See also *Olivecrona* (Rättsordningen) pp. 11–12.

no such express definition is made, a prior conceptual choice is involved in the accounts of the realists themselves.[221] But the inevitablity of the prior conceptual choice undermines the modern criticisms of early doctrine.[222]

Here lies the indeterminate character of modernism. The four approaches involve different "conceptual schemes" – alternating descriptions of the social world of State behaviour. As their normative projects are based on different descriptions of what actually takes place and as they assume that the superiority of these projects can only be decided on the basis of description, there is no hope to make a rational choice. We cannot decide between the four versions on the basis of criteria which they themselves offer because accepting those very criteria will *already assume that we have made a choice*. Comparing them in a rational manner assumes that we can occupy a perspective *beyond* those descriptions. This involves either knowing the "true nature" of social life among States – a possibility denied by the very existence of disagreement – or basing the choice on a non-descriptive principle of relevance, that is, a theory of justice.

The four versions claim that they will provide a description of facts which renders a relevant conception of international law. Using apparently neutral (descriptive) language they hope to preserve the liberal theory of politics. But in their mutual criticism, they reveal the material theories of justice hidden in them.

The moderns describe State behaviour sometimes in terms of States consenting to or protesting against rules, sometimes in terms of egoistic power policy and sometimes as a function of more deep-lying ideological, economic or historical determinants, the logic of needs and interests or institutional structures. Clearly, each such description has some degree of plausibility.[223] How can a choice between them be made? If the assumption is excluded that the "true nature" of the social life among States can be known independently of those descriptions, then

---

[221] See e.g. *Le Fur*'s 54 RCADI 1935/IV criticism of the sociological approaches of Duguit and Scelle, pp. 88–94, 96–99.

[222] Thus *Monaco* 125 RCADI 1968/III, for example, having first criticized normativism and chosen to pursue a social conception of law is forced to outline a set of "principes constitutionelles" which determine what acts by States may count as "production juridique". These principles (equality, independence, self-defence) however, remain simply postulated, pp. 131–134. Though they ground a recognizably liberal discourse, their justification is made impossible by the adopted "sociological" method.

[223] Compare e.g. *MacIntyre* (Miller-Siedentop: Nature) pp. 19–33.

the decision can only be made by comparing the kinds of law which the approaches will render *vis-à-vis* each other. Clearly, reliance on "sources", for example, will render a different law from that rendered by reliance on "authority". The assumption that States have reason to be suspicious against each other will render a law which differs from a law produced by a perspective which sees everywhere interdependence. To say that one law is utopian while the other is apologist ultimately begs the question. Those criticisms assume what was to be proved – namely that we already know the character of social life among States.

The point is that reliance on "sources", "authority", "sanctions" or "interdependence" will sometimes give us a law which is simply unacceptable in view of the ideals of social organization we possess. The criticism that "sources" gives us a law which is inadequate reflects a pre-theoretical view that some principles of justice will not be adequately reflected by the law we thereby receive. It singles out some "events" which should not be held law-determining while missing other facts which should be given authority. Correspondingly, reliance on "authority" (or sanctions, or interdependence) will do the same. The core problem is not that these matrices should be defective as such. If they seem defective, it is only because they fail to give us norms which we consider as "just" – which best reflect our ideal of social organization among States.

The assumption that legal justice can be inferred from social facts proves false. Facts do not stand "there" as impartial arbiters of our legal-theoretical controversies. They are, as Nelson Goodman puts it, "fabricated"[224] as we go along to construct a law which would meet our social ideals. Reliance on the self-evidence of our views about "facts" is unwarranted. Indeed: "Facts, like telescopes and wigs for gentlemen, were a seventeenth century invention."[225] So was the idea that a just society could be established without discussing justice. Hence the interminable character of modern criticisms and the inability of lawyers to stay within any of the available positions. Hence the inevitable recourse to justice – a justice, however, which will either have to be condemned as mere "subjectivism" or it will undermine the modern project altogether and ultimately the liberal theory of politics.

---

[224] *Goodman* (Worldmaking) pp. 91–107 and *passim*.
[225] *MacIntyre* (Whose Justice?) pp. 357, 332–333.

4

Sovereignty

The international doctrine of State sovereignty bears an obvious resemblance to the domestic-liberal doctrine of individual liberty. Both characterize the social world in descriptive and normative terms. They describe social life in terms of the activities of individual agents ("legal subjects", citizens, States) and set down the basic conditions within which the relations between these agents should be conducted.

But the relations between individual liberty and normative principles might be figured in alternative ways. We have seen that a pre-classical scholarship started out with assuming the existence of a normative code – a set of rights and duties in different areas of the Prince's conduct. That code was normative in its own right. Sovereignty – the Prince's sphere of liberty – had no independent normative status. It was simply a description of the powers and liberties which the Prince was endowed with by the normative code. A reverse perspective was developed by the classical lawyers. For them, the State's sphere of liberty was prior, and normative, and the principles of conduct between States simply followed as a description of what was required to safeguard the anterior liberties. It should not be difficult to recognize the opposition between a descending and an ascending outlook in this explanation of the contrast between early and classical doctrines.[1]

The problem with the classical position is how to explain what is involved in a State's sovereignty – its sphere of liberty – without lapsing

---

[1] Many have recognized the existence of these two alternative viewpoints. Often, however, the arguments on which the choice between them has been made, have been such as to already assume the correctness of one or the other. Thus, for example, as *Verdross* makes a naturalist "choice" to prefer the descending perspective, this is predetermined already by the way in which he looks at the problem from a perspective external to "pure facts". See e.g. *Verdross* (Verfassung) p. 118 *et seq* and *passim*. One lawyer to have clearly realized that the choice between the viewpoints cannot be made by criteria determined by the viewpoints themselves is *Kelsen* (Souveränität) for whom the choice remains an extralegal (political) one, pp. 317–319; *idem* 14 RCADI 1926/IV pp. 321–326.

into apologism; the conclusion that a State's liberty extends to anything the State itself thinks appropriate to extend it to. A fully formal idea of "freedom" is incapable of constructing a determinate, bounded conception of statehood as well as giving any content to an international order. Therefore, classical lawyers developed theories of "absolute rights", for example, which, by giving content to what it was for a State to be "free", also delimited liberty so as to achieve determinate descriptions. By this movement, however, they constructed a descending argument which stood in tension with their ascending denial of a pre-existing (natural) normative code and the very justification for assuming that States were "free" in the first place. Just like individuality can exist only in relation to community – and becomes, in that sense, dependent on how it is viewed from a non-individual perspective – a State's sphere of liberty, likewise, seemed capable of being determined only by taking a position *beyond* liberty.[2] The paradox is that assuming the existence of such a position undermines the original justification of thinking about statehood in terms of an initial, pre-social liberty.

The ambiguity about the modern doctrine of sovereignty follows from this paradox. On the one hand, we seem incapable of conceptualizing the State or whatever liberties it has without reflecting on the character of the social relations which surround it. The sphere of liberty of a member of society must, by definition, be delimited by the spheres of liberty of the other members of that society. But the delimitation of freedoms in this way requires that we do not have to rely on the self-definition of the members of their liberties. In other words, a State's sphere of liberty must be capable of determination from a perspective which is external to it. On the other hand, we cannot derive the State completely from its social relations and its liberty from an external (and overriding) normative perspective without losing the State's individuality as a nation and the justification for its claims to independence and self-determination.

Consequently, modern doctrine constantly oscillates between an ascending and a descending perspective on statehood. The former is expressed in the manner in which recourse to "sovereignty" seems always available, in one form or another, to legitimize what first appear like clear breaches of the State's international obligations. Not infrequently both parties in a dispute put their conflicting claims in terms of their sovereignty. To solve such disputes, doctrine is forced to look beyond

---

[2] See e.g. *Unger* (Knowledge) pp. 191–235.

any simple description of sovereign power into the norms which convey or delimit such power. But in order to be justifiable, these latter norms will have to be traced back to the sovereigns themselves. And from this emerges the problem of how they can be used to achieve such delimitations. In this chapter I shall argue that this intuitively felt ambiguity follows from the way in which discourse attempts to preserve the descending and ascending perspectives within itself. Moving thus within contradictory premises, it fails to provide substantive resolution to disputes involving arguments about sovereignty.

4.1   The structure of the problem: Schmitt v. Kelsen

This contradiction may be illustrated by reference to the positions of Carl Schmitt and Hans Kelsen in regard to the relationship between law and power within the State. For Schmitt law is secondary to factual decision. Making and applying law involve decision. The legal idea cannot translate itself into social action automatically, independently of decision: "... in any transformation there is present an *auctoritatis interpositio*".[3] Everything depends ultimately on factual decision, not on the abstract norm. To look for the place of sovereignty – the highest authority within the State – we should not ask "what controls legal decision-making under regular circumstances?" but "who shall decide on the exception?"[4] And this is a question of power, not of law. This looks like a purely ascending position. State's power is normative and that power is itself external to and constitutive of the law.

Kelsen works in the opposite direction. Factual power cannot establish what ought to be. The State as a juridical concept is separate from the State as a sociological concept.[5] Juridically, that is in the realm of the "ought", "State" is simply another name for the (municipal) legal order. As the validity of the latter – being a matter of "ought", not "is" – can only be derived from a further norm and ultimately a hypothetical *Grundnorm*, the State's (juridical) identity, too, becomes dependent on it.[6] For Kelsen, the question of the "place" of sovereignty is unanswerable in legal terms as

---

[3] *Schmitt* (Political Theology) p. 31.
[4] For *Schmitt* (Political Theology), the location of factual power remains usually hidden. Things happen as if impersonal laws were governing. Only when the legal order is threatened, that ultimate repository of power will manifest itself. It will then take on the character of the ultimate "source of validity" of the order, pp. 5–15, 29–35.
[5] See, generally, *Kelsen* (Soziologische) *passim*; *idem* (Souveränität) pp. 1–101.
[6] *Kelsen* (Rechtslehre) pp. 67–89.

it concerns a simple sociological fact. Legally, "sovereignty" is really only another way of saying that the legal order is valid. The argument seems purely descending. The legal order is prior to factual power.

These two positions have an immediate connection with modern ideas about objectivity in the law. Schmitt's system seems objective because "realistic" and directed towards concrete, observable facts. For Schmitt, Kelsen appears utopian: his is only a scholar's subjective construction which "has no connexion with positivity (*Positivität*)".[7] In Kelsen, these associations are reversed. His system seems objective as he shares the *opposite* view of what it means for a system to be "objective". Decision and power are relegated into the realm of sociology precisely because so subjective. Kelsen's own ideas seem objective because detached from such considerations.[8] His objectivity is constituted by the controlling force of his normative premises. From this perspective, Schmitt's system is subjective because apologist, because it assumes that might makes right. As Schmitt and Kelsen argue from opposite perspectives, they are capable of dismissing each other as too subjective. But because the perspectives differ, there is also no hope of rational agreement until the prior question – whether "objectivity" should mean relatedness to facts or relatedness to norms – is solved. And agreement on this is hardly forthcoming.

In Schmitt's system, sovereignty is a matter of fact-description and law a normative consequence thereof. In Kelsen, the law is normative and "sovereignty" merely a descriptive shorthand for the rights, liberties and competences which the law has allocated to the State. Though the positions are contradictory, they both move within a distinctly modern *problématique*. Both project a normative model about how the relations between statehood and law should be understood without taking a stand on material justice.

But neither position can be fully accepted and yet not fully rejected, either. Though mutually exclusive, empiricism and conceptualism also rely on each other. Hence, international sovereignty doctrine oscillates constantly between arguments such as Schmitt's and Kelsen's.[9] It works

---

[7] *Schmitt* (Political Theology) pp. 18–22.

[8] *Kelsen* (Souveränität) repeatedly distinguishes between legal "objectivism" and "subjectivism", associating the latter with doctrines allowing the State's factual position or power to influence the law's content, pp. 241 *et seq*, 314–319. See *idem* (Soziologische) pp. 136–140.

[9] The Schmitt/Kelsen contrast is, of course, only a relatively modern surface of a long-continued discussion in German *Staatstheorie* about whether the State was a *Rechtsvoraussetzungsbegriff* – a sociological fact preceding the law – or a *Rechtsinhaltsbegriff* – a concept determined from "within" the legal system. For the former view, see e.g. *Jellinek* (Allgemeine) pp. 337 *et seq*, 364–367. For the latter, see

with a fluid conception of sovereignty which assumes the correctness of both. Full rejection of Schmitt's realistic emphasis on decision would make doctrine seem utopian. Moreover, it would fail to give protection to the State's assumed initial freedom and independence.[10] Full rejection of Kelsen's argument would make doctrine look apologist; it would fail to distinguish between actual and legitimate decision. It would also fail to protect the equality of other States and to explain the legitimacy of external constraint to State power.[11]

Disputes involving sovereignty organize themselves in a similar way. One State argues in terms of effective power. The other argues in a way which assumes the precedence of constraining norms to actual power. Neither position can be consistently preferred. Therefore, disputes about sovereignty remain incapable of material solution by law.

4.1.1   The "legal" and the "pure fact" approaches

According to the Kelsenian view, "sovereignty" is a systemic concept – not something external to but determined *within* the law.[12] The legal order pre-exists the sovereignty of the State and remains in control thereof. I shall call this the *"legal approach"* to sovereignty.

e.g. *Kelsen* (Soziologische) p. 75 *et seq*; *idem* (Rechtslehre) pp. 117–121. On this contrast, see e.g. *Kunz* (Anerkennung) pp. 15–19. A similar contrast is apparent in Austin's and Hart's treatment of sovereignty. For the (initially Hobbesian) argument that the sovereign is external to the rules which emanate from him, see *Austin* (Province) pp. 193–195 *et seq*. For the view that "rules are constitutive of the sovereign", see *Hart* (Concept) pp. 49–76.

[10] *Carty* (Decay) notes that the Kelsenian view fails to give independent normative sense to a principle of self-determination, p. 47.

[11] The difficulty of making a preference is perceived by *von Gierke* (Grundbegriffe), who argues that the State must (juridically) be understood *both* as a factual centre of power and a legal construction, pp. 30–31. For a critical review of these "two-sides theories", see also *Kelsen* (Soziologische) p. 105 *et seq*. Modern international lawyers are similarly trying to take a dual perspective. *Bleckmann* (Aufgabe), for instance, points out that the opposition between the two perspectives is analogous to the ideals of individual liberty and the *Rechtsstaat* and that neither can be allowed to fully overrule the other, p. 38; *idem* ÖZöRV 1978 pp. 194–196. But it is probably more correct to associate the dual perspective with the opposition between liberty and equality or free market and the social (democratic) welfare State.

[12] *Kelsen* expresses this in the argument according to which it is the essential function of international law to determine the "sphere of validity" of municipal law, that is the boundaries of the State's internal competence. See e.g. 42 RCADI 1932/IV p. 182 *et seq*; *idem* (Principles) p. 177 *et seq*. For a recent restatement of the Kelsenian position, see *Carreau* (Droit international public) pp. 304, 314.

The legal approach dominated the early lawyers' system.[13] "Sovereignty" denoted the Prince's authority which was derived from a postulated, superior normative code. It may best be understood as his legally limited "competence".[14] The Prince cannot legitimize his action by referring to his sovereignty if this action conflicted with the law. A war is not just simply because waged by a legitimate sovereign. It is just only if waged as enforcement of the law. Even if Bodin did stress the scope of the Prince's authority, he did not give up the idea that such authority was derived from a normative code which remained controlling. That it was "absolue et souveraine" meant only that:

> ... elle n'a autre condition que la loy de Dieu & de la nature commande.[15]

According to this approach, sovereignty is a quality which is allocated to certain entities by international law which, in this sense, is conceptually anterior to them. Many modern lawyers, too, share this view. They argue, with Kelsen and Hart,[16] that the criteria for the emergence and dissolution of States are not simply questions of fact but established by a rule of law. The law delegates to certain entities the quality of statehood as a sum of rights, liberties and competences:

> Souveränität ist gerade die besondere Kompetenz, die die Staaten auf grund des Völkerrechts besitzen. 'Staatliche Souveränität' und die 'unmittelbare Völkerrechtsunterwerfenheit' bedeuten daher ein und dasselbe.[17]

---

[13] See *supra*, ch. 2.2.

[14] For reviews, see *Verdross* (Einheit) pp. 13–29; *Sauer* (Solidarität) pp. 18–26.

[15] *Bodin* (Six Livres) L.I, ch. VIII (p. 129).

[16] *Hart* (Concept) pp. 215–218. Similarly *Olivecrona* (Rättsordningen) pp. 89–106.

[17] *Verdross* (Einheit) p. 35. *Idem* 16 RCADI 1927/1 pp. 311–319. See also *Kunz* (Anerkennung) pp. 17–19. This view was adopted by many early 20th century lawyers as a part of their criticism of the professionals' excessive emphasis on sovereignty. See e.g. *Politis* 6 RCADI 1925/I p. 5 *et seq*; *Krabbe* 13 RCADI 1926/III pp. 576–581; *Le Fur* 18 RCADI 1927/III pp. 412–419; *Scelle* (Précis I) pp. 7–14 and *infra* n. 18. Frequently, this view is expressed by holding the "international community" as conceptually anterior to the individual State whose sovereignty is seen as its organ-status. See e.g. *Sauer* (Solidarität) p. 163. *Nippold* 2 RCADI 1924/II argues that sovereignty is a principle of municipal law, paralleled internationally by the principle of the international community. Internationally, the only relevant sense of sovereignty is the systemic one; the one endowing the State with the quality of "subject" of international law, pp. 22–24, 51–57. Similarly, *Bruns* 1 ZaöRV 1929 pp. 10–12; *Mosler* 36 ZaöRV 1976 pp. 11–21; *Verdross-Simma* (Völkerrecht) pp. 48–49; *Alvarez*, diss. op. ICJ: *Corfu Channel* Case, Reports 1949 p. 43. For the "systemic" character of sovereignty, see also *Lauterpacht* (Function)

The same point is formulated in another way by Rousseau:

> La fonction essentielle du droit est de conférer, de répartir et de réglémenter des compétences – et le droit international public ne fait pas exception a cette donnée fondamentale de la vie sociale.[18]

International law allocates competences and legitimate spheres of action to entities it chooses to regard as legal subjects. No subjects, no sets of rights, competences or liberties are externally given. They are constituted by the law itself.

Many kinds of argument imply an acceptance of the legal approach, epitomized in the idea of "relative sovereignty".[19] It is implied in the view which holds domestic jurisdiction as a "relative" question, in the view which chooses the monistic conception of international law with the primacy of international law, in the view which draws boundaries between conflicting jurisdictions by recourse to "equitable principles"

---

pp. 95–96; *Chen* (Recognition) p. 20; *Fitzmaurice* XXX BYIL 1953 pp. 8–18; *Coplin* (Functions) pp. 26–27, 30–31; *Higgins* (Reasonable) p. 10; *Merrills* (Anatomy) pp. 30–31; *Virally* 183 RCADI 1983/V pp. 78–79. See also *Ross* (Text-book) pp. 40–43; *D'Amato* 79 Northwestern University Law Review 1984–85 pp. 1305–1308.

[18] *Rousseau* 93 RCADI 1958/I p. 394. See also generally *ibid.* pp. 397–426. See further, *Scelle* 46 RCADI 1933/IV, for whom "le droit positif n'est qu'un faisceau de règles de compétence", p. 367. This view follows from Scelle's methodological individualism which systematically breaks "moral persons" down to the rules of competence which are directed at individuals. "Sovereignty" – like "State" – are only fictitious ways of speaking about groups of individuals invested with specific types of competences, *idem* (Précis I) pp. 7–14. Similarly *Bourquin* 35 RCADI 1931/I p. 101 *et seq*; *François* 66 RCADI 1938/IV pp. 65–68; *Cavaré* (Droit international I) pp. 185–189 *et seq*; *Reuter* 103 RCADI 1961/II pp. 512–516; *idem* (Droit international public) affirms, in a somewhat circular argument, that as no State can unilaterally extend its competence, it must be assumed that such competences derive from international law – though the competence-conferring rules remain few and fragmentary, pp. 156–157. The idea that the law is simply a set of competences is associable with the ideal of the "completeness" of the legal system. Everything is regulated because either someone has the competence or he has not. For a recent, critical discussion of the idea of the State as an "order of competences", see *Carty* (Decay) (tracing this idea to 19th century German public law theories) pp. 43–48 *et seq*.

[19] For the standard point about "relative sovereignty" as supreme power controlled by the law, see e.g. *Guggenheim* 80 RCADI 1952/I pp. 84–85; *Jenks* (Common Law) pp. 123–129; *Schwarzenberger* 10 CLP 1957 pp. 269–271; *Nincić* (Sovereignty) pp. 6–15; *Wildhaber* (Macdonald-Johnston: Structure and Process) p. 437, *passim*. *Kelsen* 14 RCADI 1926/IV points out the dilemma: "relative sovereignty" involves a contradiction. The term's original sense is that of supreme power. If power is limited by the law, it cannot be supreme. To use the term is to distort "sovereignty's" proper, original sense, pp. 311–313; *idem* 84 RCADI 1953/III pp. 83–85.

and in the view which holds international organizations as functional bodies whose rights and duties may be inferred from their purpose.[20]

Ultimately, the very concept of sovereignty loses its normative significance under the legal approach. If a State cannot refer to its sovereignty to justify its action but has to find a rule of law which has given it the right, liberty or competence to act in a certain way, then to speak of "sovereignty" at all is merely superfluous or, at best, a description of the norms whose normative force is in their being incorporated in some legal act, not in their being inherent in statehood.

Under the legal approach, the law's objectivity is based on the assumption that facts of State practice, power and authority will disclose merely subjective politics. To rid law from the danger of apologism, a higher normative code needs to be assumed. This may be thought of as a code of natural law. But it is clearly more common for modern lawyers to envisage it in terms interdependence, common interests, a shared progressive morality or legal logic.

In Schmitt's argument, sovereignty is external to international law, a normative fact with which the law must accommodate itself. I shall call it the *"pure fact approach"*.

An independent idea of sovereignty which precedes the law emerged with classical scepticism about the objective character of Natural or Divine law.[21] In order to find out what is normative and what is not, you must not look at abstract speculations about justice but at what

[20] Much UN rhetoric, quite understandably, implies the legal approach. Thus, in the Draft Declaration on the Rights and Duties of States it is pointed out that: "Every State has the duty to conduct its relations with other States in accordance with international law and with the principle that the sovereignty of each State is subject to the supremacy of international law", UNGA Res. 375(IV) 6 December 1949. More recently, in the Friendly Relations Declaration, it is argued that: "All States ... are equal members of the international community." UNGA Res. 2625 (XXV) 24 October 1970. The idea is taken into Article 2(3) of the 1982 UN Convention on the Law of the Sea: "The sovereignty over the territorial sea is exercised subject to this Convention and to other rules of international law."

[21] Indeed, as *Hobbes* (Leviathan) noted, if the law arises from the sovereign, it seems logically necessary to leave the sovereign itself unregulated by it, ch. 18 (pp. 230–231). For this position in Vattel, see *Ruddy* (International law in the Enlightenment) pp. 125–127. The same point underlies Hegel's views about the relation between the State and law. See e.g. *Hegel* (Grundlinien) § 331 (p. 284). The point encapsulates what 19th century German theorists argued as the "normative force of the factual", see *Jellinek* (Allgemeine Staatslehre) pp. 337–339, 364 *et seq.* For a review, see *Kunz* (Anerkennung) p. 18n. 10. For this position generally, see *De Visscher* (Theory) pp. 166–169; *von Simson* (Souveränität) pp. 31–53. See also *Raphael* (Problems) pp. 55–58 (generally), 59–75 (a criticism).

takes place in the real world.[22] An objective concept of statehood had to be unrelated to any views about, for instance, the constitution, religion or policy of the State.[23] To be a State was to hold certain factual, not evaluative properties. If non-European entities did not qualify for statehood this was not because of the existence of a material code which would, for all time, have prevented their qualification as such. It was simply because their subjective essence (degree of civilization) did not correspond to that of European States: they were simply too different. For the classical jurist, this difference was a matter of fact, not of political opinion.[24]

To be a State is, according to this position, a question of fact which the law can only recognize but cannot control. In principle, it would be possible to speak of a sovereign State only when the entity is "peace-loving", "democratic" or fulfils some other such criteria. This, however, presupposes the existence of a normative code which is superior to statehood. What criteria would it contain? How do we know its content or whether a particular entity fulfils the criteria included in it? Because these seem such difficult questions the answers to which seem dependent on political views, moderns do not assume the existence of such a code.[25] As Anzilotti points out:

> ... il n'y a pas d'Etats légitimes et d'Etats illégitimes; la légitimation de l'Etat réside dans son existence même.[26]

The analogy with liberal individualism is evident: an individual's rights must be independent of creed, colour or politics. The fact of your being a human being is sufficient to ground your human rights and your status

---

[22] *Lansing* (Notes) attacks Bluntschli's naturalism by the point that sovereignty cannot be made a "public law conception" because this would make it unable to comprise the factual, objective power on which public law itself stands. A meaningful concept of sovereignty must, in this sense, be external to the law, an objective reason for it, pp. 8–11.

[23] For this view among professional lawyers, see e.g. *Klüber* (Droit des gens) pp. 28–30; *Merignhac* (Traité, I) pp. 130–132; *Hall* (International Law) pp. 20–21.

[24] See e.g. *Westlake* (Chapters) pp. 137 *et seq*, 141–143.

[25] See, however, ICJ: *Namibia* Case, Reports 1971 in which it seems implied that if the UN Security Council held a State "illegal" (as it has done e.g. in respect of Rhodesia or South Africa's Bantustan homelands), the members of the UN (and possibly other States, too) would be under an obligation not to recognize that entity's statehood, pp. 54–56 (§§ 117–126).

[26] *Anzilotti* (Cours, I) p. 169.

as a legal subject. The existence of that fact is beyond the control of the law. It is simply given to it.[27]

Perhaps the most frequent version of the pure fact approach is expressed in voluntarism, the view that international law emerges from the will of the State. This view accepts as given the existence of an authoritative will and proceeds to construct law from it.[28] But many other arguments, too, presuppose the pure fact view. It is present in the argument that the State has a given sphere of domestic jurisdiction, or that monism with the primacy of municipal law is correct, or that conflicts between jurisdictions must be solved by looking at what rights are entailed in "sovereignty" and statehood *per se*, or that the functions of international organizations are dependent on what States have agreed about them etc.

The two approaches involve opposing views on how to establish whether a State is free in some particular relationship or not. The legal approach assumes such freedom to exist when there exist legal rules which have allocated it to the State. The pure fact view thinks that a State is free *ipso facto* unless specific rules restrict its freedom. To solve a normative problem about State freedom – even to approach the problem – this question would seem to require prior solution. Making a preference, however, is not at all an easy task.

4.1.2 The continuing dispute about the extent and relevance of sovereignty

The legal and pure fact approaches are contrasting ways to *justify* sovereignty – the State's sphere of liberty. This opposition is often confused with the distinct contrast between two views about the *extent*

---

[27] The analogy is clearest in the non-problematic application of the idea of "fundamental rights" at the inter-State level. The argument about sovereignty being such a right, "inherent" in statehood has a structural function identical to the human rights argument at the municipal level. See e.g. *Vattel* (Droit des Gens) L. I, ch. I § 1 (p. 17); *G.-F. de Martens* (Précis, I) pp. 100–101; *Wheaton* (Elements) p. 27. For a more recent formulation, see *Korowicz* 102 RCADI 1961/I p. 102. For a review of the analogy between the conception of the individual with an "automatic" (natural) right of property and the State with sovereignty over its territory through its simple existence as a State, see *Carty* (Decay) pp. 44–46, 55–56.

[28] For the classic, see *Jellinek* (Allgemeine) pp. 274–275. Indeed, *Hart* (Concept) holds the two views as indistinguishable, pp. 218–219. The voluntaristic conception is taken as the "real" sense of sovereignty also by *von Simson* (Souveränität) pp. 31–53.

of sovereignty. One view is highly critical of sovereignty and seeks to restrict it as much as possible.[29] Another view stresses the continued relevance of sovereignty and its wide material scope.[30] Discussion about sovereignty constantly takes up these latter views and seeks to relate them to the opposition between the legal/pure fact approaches in order to make either seem unacceptable. While the legal approach is usually associated with views seeking to restrict sovereignty and the pure fact approach with arguments stressing the State's freedom, there is no reason not to assume that while the normative order could allocate very extensive rights to States, the rights which they possess *ipso facto* are only few in number. Views about the material extent of sovereignty cannot be related to the available justifications in a permanent way. This makes it possible for an adherent to either position to interpret any present situation as manifesting his preferred perspective. It is not possible to argue for the relative correctness of either justification by simple "observation". Choosing either one is a conceptual, not an empirical matter – because it is so, modern doctrine is puzzled about how to establish preference.

Three sets of criticisms have been presented against the very idea of sovereignty: sociological, moral and logical-systematic.

According to the sociological criticism, no State is able to exist in such autonomous fashion as suggested by traditional theories of sovereignty. The criticism stresses the many forms of economic, political and social interdependencies between States and finds support from the establishment of international organization.[31]

A moral criticism, often indistinguishable from the sociological one, points out that State sovereignty serves to strengthen State egoism, interpreted as one of the chief reasons for the cataclysms of the present

---

[29] In fact, quite a few lawyers have, for one or another of the reasons stated below, proposed a "rejection" of the concept altogether. See e.g. *Kelsen* (Souveränität) p. 321; *idem* 84 RCADI 1953/III p. 82; *idem* (Principles) p. 194; *Politis* 6 RCADI 1925/I p. 5 *et seq*; *Scelle* (Précis, I) 13–14; *Morellet* XXXIII RGDIP 1924 pp. 116–119; *Eagleton* 36 AJIL 1942 p. 234; *Ross* (Text-book) pp. 33 *et seq*, 44–45.

[30] These lawyers have accused the former of "ideological escapism" and neglecting the positive "functions" of sovereignty. See e.g. *Bull* (Falk-Kim-Mendlowitz) pp. 60–73; *Hinsley* (Sovereignty) pp. 221–236; *Schwarzenberger* 10 CLP 1957 pp. 264–266 and *passim*.

[31] For early statements, see e.g. *Olney* 1 AJIL 1907 pp. 418 *et seq*, 429–430; *Reinsch* 23 AJIL 1909 pp. 1–19 *et seq*; *Morellet* XXXIII RGDIP 1926 pp. 113–114; *Bourquin* 35 RCADI 1931/I pp. 9 *et seq*, 23–26. See further *Jessup* (Modern) pp. 13, 36–42; *Fried* (Deutsch-Hoffmann: Relevance) pp. 124–127.

century.[32] It has become the hall-mark of Western-liberal doctrines to challenge absolutist views of sovereignty, imputed to Hegel's philosophy and political nationalism. In this spirit, for example, the former United States Secretary of State, Robert Lansing, published a series of articles in the first decade of the past century dealing with a perceived transition from State sovereignty to "world sovereignty".[33] As a recent writer puts the moral point: "Free, pluralistic democracy" requires the harnessing of sovereignty.[34]

The logical-systematic criticism has already been referred to. For Kelsen, sovereignty can have no independence from the more general and fundamental question of the primacy of international or municipal law within a monistic conception of law. An "absolutist" view on sovereignty is merely another way to express the primacy of municipal over international law.[35] For Kelsen, such a conception will ultimately deny the reality of international law and lead into apologism.[36] Therefore, he reduces sovereignty to a description of the State's competence, determined by international law.[37] For Alf Ross, sovereignty emerges as a tû-tû concept – a word without a meaning independent from a full description of the duties and rights which the law ascribes to the State.[38]

These criticisms have some intuitive plausibility. Initially, they seem to stem from the legal approach. What seems common to them is an effort to look at sovereignty from the perspective of a normative code,

---

[32] See *supra*, ch. 3 n. 1 and e.g. *Van Kleffens* 82 RCADI 1953/I pp. 70–71; *Schiffer* (Legal Community) pp. 193–201. Frequently "sovereignty" has been held an irrational and essentially psychological – or psychopathological – idea, a "mystic sentiment expressed in abstruse legal doctrines", *Howard-Ellis* (Origin) p. 120. To the same effect, see *West* (Psychology) pp. 29–37, 180 *et seq*, 200–202; *De Visscher* (Theory) p. 64; *Kaplan-Katzenbach* (Political Foundations) p. 135; *Stone* (Conflict) p. 109; *Ross* (Text-book) pp. 37–39.

[33] See *Lansing* 1 AJIL 1907 p. 105 *et seq*. Articles published also in *Lansing* (Notes).

[34] *Wildhaber* (Macdonald-Johnston: Structure and Process) p. 436. On these points, see also *Brierly* (Law of Nations) p. 15; *Ross* (Text-book) pp. 45–46 and the strong criticism in *Falk-Kim-Mendlowitz* (Toward) pp. 55–139.

[35] For Kelsen, the juridical concept of "State" coalesces with the concept of the legal order. Juridically, to call the State "sovereign" is to attribute a quality to the legal order, not to the "sociological conception" of the State as a factual centre of power. This quality refers to the legal order's formal validity *vis-à-vis* other legal orders. See *Kelsen* (Souveränität) pp. 9–16 and *passim*.

[36] *Ibid.* pp. 314–319.   [37] See *supra* n. 12.

[38] See *Ross* 70 Harvard L.R. 1957 pp. 812–815; *idem* (Text-book) pp. 33 *et seq*, 40–45. See also *Politis* 6 RCADI 1925/I pp. 15–23.

assumed to be prior to any initial liberty and conceptualized variably through a descending approach to interdependence, morality or plain legal logic.

But this way of understanding the criticisms has a bite only if one *has already accepted* the correctness of the legal approach; the assumption that the law precedes the State. If one does not share it, then the criticism simply misses the point. From the pure fact perspective it may always be retorted that the very idea of interdependence starts out from a prior conception of the State between which relations of dependence have been formed, that morality – democracy, for instance – is relevant only insofar as States have freely accepted it and that legal logic really requires only making a choice between the two perceptions but not what that choice should be.[39]

The criticism may as well be voiced from a pure fact approach. It may be argued that the liberty which States "inherently" possess is not extensive in scope or that States have used their freedom so as to construct a normative code which now greatly restricts their liberty.[40] From the legal approach, of course, *this* criticism seems unconvincing as it seems to leave a door open for the State to deny the law's binding force. What is important, however, is that both approaches can accommodate these criticisms in themselves. Neither justification implies anything determinate concerning the material extent of sovereignty. Correspondingly, stressing the wide material scope of sovereignty is possible from both approaches.

It is not at all difficult to make the case for an extensive concept of sovereignty. As Rosalyn Higgins pointed out in her inaugural lecture in 1982:

> States are still the most important actors in the international legal system and their sovereignty is at the core of that system.[41]

[39] *Kelsen* (Souveränität) himself recognizes that the choice between the two "monisms" remains a *political* one – a choice regarding one's "Welt- und Lebensanschauung", p. 317.

[40] Thus *Kaufmann* 54 RCADI 1935/IV is able to argue on explicitly Hegelian premises against "absolutist" ideas of sovereignty. Recognizing sovereignty as the supreme will and power does not mean that the sovereign could use that will and power in an "arbitrary" way. For sovereignty includes also the idea of the State's responsibility towards itself and its duty to have regard to the objective commands of morality and interdependence as well as to the duties accepted by it. Though "inherent", sovereignty is also "elastic", pp. 352, 359 and generally 351–364. It is easy to see the Jellinekian construction at work here. See *supra* ch. 2.3.2.1.

[41] *Higgins* (Reasonable) p. 3. See also *Island of Palmas C*ase, II UNRIAA p. 839; *Deutsch* (Deutsch-Hoffmann: Relevance) pp. 83–85; *Bleckmann* (Grundprobleme) p. 84.

Indeed, many international developments seem to support the view that sovereignty is essentially beneficial and that what is needed is not its abandonment but its realization on the most varied fields of international conduct.

In the first place, the State's exclusive right to decide what acts shall take place in its territory is virtually undisputed and functions as an independent, overriding justification. The very term "intervention" suggests the idea of the wrongfulness of the act – sometimes, as in 1960 when the UN Security Council condemned the capture of Adolf Eichmann by Israeli security foces in Argentinian territory, even against *prima facie* strong moral reasons for approval.[42] Many have argued that humanitarian considerations are irrelevant in judging whether or not an act amounts to illicit intervention.[43] No reference was made to competing justifications or the intervener's motivations when the General Assembly condemned the recent interventions in Kampuchea, Nicaragua, Afghanistan and Grenada, for example, as violations of the "independence, sovereignty and territorial integrity" of the respective States.[44]

It should not be forgotten that sovereignty was originally taken as a progressive, egalitarian principle and that it still carries these connotations. Claims for "economic sovereignty" attain strong moral support from the rhetorics of the New International Economic Order. The State's permanent sovereignty over national resources is supported by countless UN General Assembly resolutions from 1962 onwards.[45] Use of natural resources is a general sovereignty issue. Typically, in cases of international pollution both the source-State and the target-State

---

[42] See generally SC Res. 138/1960 (24 June 1960). See also *Whiteman* (Digest, V) pp. 208–214 and e.g. *Henkin* (How) pp. 269–278. The examples are, of course, many. Thus, for example, the UNGA condemned Indian intervention in Bangladesh in 1971 as a violation of Pakistani sovereignty despite the fairly uncontroversial humanitarian justifications applicable. See UNGA Res. 2793 (XXVI), 7 December 1971. Also, only US veto in the Security Council in 1976 prevented the Council from condemning the Israeli rescue operation at Entebbe airport in Uganda. For a discussion, see *Schachter* 178 RCADI 1982/V pp. 147–148; *Boyle* (World Politics) pp. 77–167.

[43] ICJ: *US Military and Paramilitary Activities* Case, Reports 1986 pp. 106–110, 111–112 (§§ 202–209, 212–214).

[44] See UNGA Res. 34/32, 14 November 1979 (Kampuchea); 38/10, 11 November 1983 (Nicaragua); ES-VI, 14 October 1980 (Afghanistan); 38/7, 2 November 1983 (Grenada). See also the discussion in *Franck* (Nation against Nation) pp. 224–231.

[45] *Ghozali* (Mélanges Chaumont) argues about "sovereignty" in the economic context: "... l'arme de l'impérialisme s'est transformée en arme centre l'impérialisme", p. 313. Similarly *Demichel* (Benchikh – Charvin – Demichel: Introduction) p. 57.

legitimize their claims by reference to their sovereignty.[46] Also claims of sovereignty beyond State territory, whether in air space or maritime areas receive strong, perhaps increasing support. A process was started from the 1945 Truman proclamation which did not stop at extending sovereignty over the continental shelf. The 1982 UN Convention on the Law of the Sea legalized a system whereby 40% of the Oceans' surface was brought under national control.[47]

These developments are, of course, well-known and manifest the view that what is needed is not to do away with national barriers but to strengthen them against external, imperialistic pursuits of other States.[48]

But it would be simply wrong to associate the view which emphasizes the wide scope of sovereignty with the pure fact approach, solely. As the experience of the III UN Conference on the Law of the Sea has taught us, each extension of sovereignty may always be explained as a new allocation of rights, liberties and competences by the law. By looking at these arguments or developments it is impossible to decide whether it is the pure fact or the legal approach which correctly grasps the relations between the State and international law.

In many, if not most, international disputes what seems to be at issue is precisely the *extent* of a State's sovereignty. The normative sense of sovereignty seems to lie in what view we take of its extent. In this sense, the question about the *justification* of sovereignty may seem simply superfluous or "academic". Why bother with the latter – seemingly inconsequential – matter if it is the question of extent which has practical importance? But it does not seem possible to take a view about the extent of sovereignty without forming an anterior stand on the question of its justification. This is so because there is no "natural" extent to sovereignty. *Its extent can only be determined within a conceptual system and the systems provided by the two approaches are not only different but contradictory.*

As long as there exists no disagreement about the legitimacy of State action, the legal and pure fact approaches may be left in abeyance. But as

---

[46] See *Koskenniemi* XVII Oikeustiede-Jurisprudentia 1984 p. 100 *et seq.* The Canadian claim for damages resulting from the fall of the Kosmos 954 satellite on Canadian territory and the small radioactive fall-out was dressed in terms of violation of sovereignty. See 18 ILM 1979 p. 907. Similarly, in the *Nuclear Tests* Cases, the Australian claim was concerned with, *inter alia*, violation of sovereignty, Pleadings I p. 14.

[47] *Friedmann* 65 AJIL 1971, for example, holds that the new Law of the Sea marks the final victory of Selden over Grotius, pp. 757–770.

[48] See further *infra* ch. 7.

soon as disputes arise, position needs to be taken on whether a State has a sphere of liberty which is "inherent" in its statehood or whether it possesses rights, liberties or competences only inasmuch as allocated by the law. This is needed in order to know what sort of arguments one should make to defend one's position.

A State argues that it has a sovereign right. Another State denies this. The dispute seems to be about the extent of sovereignty in a concrete circumstance. But the term "sovereignty" is ambiguous and open to interpretation. The decision in such dispute seems completely dependent on what the interpretation will be. And the interpretation, again, hinges on the crucial question: What should it aim at?

In the pure fact view, law is a means to fulfil the liberty of the State. This may sometimes require the restriction of liberty. But liberty can be restricted only through an unambiguous rule of law. If such rule is lacking, then interpretation must give effect to the original liberty in its authenticity. A problem-solver can have no authority, no justification to decide otherwise.

In the legal approach, there is no such anterior liberty. Behind law, there is only – law. If the law is ambiguous, we cannot solve the problem otherwise than by constructing from the legal materials available the best (most useful, most coherent, most "just") solution possible. The point is not to give effect to some hypothetical, initial "liberty" but to what the law says, even if this can be determined only "constructively".

But a choice between these two positions cannot be made. The former will ultimately end up in apologism, affirming the State's self-definition of the extent of its sovereignty. The dispute will remain unsettled. The latter will lead into utopianism, fixing the extent of sovereignty by reference to a natural, non-State-related morality. Neither solution seems acceptable. Rather, both seem needed because they limit each other's negative consequences. This, again, requires that both can be used to justify situations in which States have few or no obligations as well as situations where there exist a wide extent of duties restricting the State's present liberty.

Here is the structure of sovereignty discourse: First, arguments will arrange themselves so as to manifest the opposition between the legal and the pure fact views. Because a preference cannot be made, however, arguments have to proceed so as to make this initial opposition disappear. Second, this requires that any fact-situation can be explained from both approaches. The presence and absence of obligation are explained as consequences of an initial liberty as well as a legislative act by an initial normative code. But if both approaches justify any situation, then there is no determinate extent to sovereignty at all. Anything can be explained as in accordance with or contrary to sovereignty. Disputes about whether a State is free or not remain incapable of material resolution.

In the following section (4.2) I shall show what it means that sovereignty lacks fixed, determinate content. I shall then outline the legal approach to construct a meaning to sovereignty (4.3) and the corresponding attempt from the pure fact perspective (4.4) as well as the reasons for why they fail. I shall then show how modern "constructivism", also, will remain ultimately unacceptable (4.5). The remaining sections are devoted to an illustration of the conflict between the two approaches within doctrines about statehood and recognition (4.6) and territorial disputes (4.7).

4.2   The meaning of sovereignty

If the term "sovereignty" had a fixed, determinate content, then whether an act falls within the State's legitimate sphere of action could always be solved by simply applying it to the case. This is the way much legal discussion proceeds. Though it is notoriously difficult to pin down the meaning of sovereignty[49] literature characteristically starts out with a definition. "Sovereignty" is usually connected with the ideas of independence ("external sovereignty") and self-determination ("internal sovereignty").[50] A classical definition can be found in the

---

[49]   On the different constructions of the "meaning" of sovereignty in 19th century professional doctrines, see *Morellet* XXXIII RGDIP 1926 pp. 106–108. *Kelsen* isolates altogether eight different meanings to the term (Staatslehre) p. 102 *et seq. Wildhaber* (Macdonald-Johnston: Structure and Process) identifies four pp. 435–437. See also *Dennert* (Ursprung) pp. 5–6 n.9; *Basdevant* 58 RCADI 1936/IV p. 579; *von Simson* (Souveränität) pp. 24–31. *Schwarzenberger* regards attempts at definition as "shadow-fighting", 10 CLP 1957 p. 264. Similarly *Ross* (Textbook) pp. 33–34. *Akehurst* (Modern Introduction) comments: "It is doubtful whether any single word has caused so much intellectual confusion and international lawlessness", p. 15.

[50]   The distinction between "external" and "internal" sovereignty reflects an attempt to include a descending and an ascending argument into the construction of the identity of the State: its point is to explain how States can be both internally free and externally bound. The distinction is commonly traced back to *Bodin* (Six Livres) ch. IX (esp. p. 221 *et seq*). Significantly, Grotius does not make it. Indeed, in the early lawyers' system it would be pointless as there is no distinction between external and internal legitimacy. The distinction re-emerges in *Vattel* (Droit des Gens) L. I, ch. I § 4 (p. 25). It is then taken as a matter of course in the professional system. See e.g. *Wheaton* (Elements) p. 25; *Klüber* (Droit des gens) pp. 28–34. For the distinction in modern writers, see e.g. *Oppenheim* (International

statement by Judge Huber in the *Island of Palmas* Case (1928), connected with a dispute between the Netherlands and the United States
over sovereignty on the Island of Palmas (Miangas) in the Pacific:

> Sovereignty in the relations between States signifies independence, independ-
> ence in regard to a portion of the globe is the right to exercise therein, to
> the exclusion of any other State, the functions of a State.[51]

The idea of independence was, again, defined by the PCIJ in the *Austro-
German Customs Union* Case as:

> ... the continued existence of (a State, MK) within her present frontiers
> as a separate State with the sole right of decision in all matters economic,
> political, financial or other ...[52]

Both definitions speak of what is usually called external sovereignty, the
legal position of the State *vis-à-vis* other States. In most international
disputes it is the content of this position which emerges as the central
problem.

But other lawyers have pointed out that such definitions are useless as
it seems impossible to infer individual norms, or solutions to particular
disputes from them.[53] How should one, for example, solve a dispute in
which *both* disputing States refer to their sovereignty?

In the *Right of Passage* Case (1960), a dispute arose between India and
Portugal with regard to the the latter's alleged right to move persons and
goods, including military personnel, arms and ammunitions, from the
Portuguese colony of Damaõ on the Indian coast to its enclaves deep
inside Indian territory. In the Portuguese request it was argued that such
right of transit was:

> ... comme une nécessité logique, impliquée dans la notion même du
> droit de souveraineté ...[54]

Law, I) pp. 113–115; *Lansing* (Notes) pp. 29–32; *Strupp* 47 RCADI 1933/I pp. 493–496;
Suontausta (Souveraineté) p. 41; *Van Kleffens* 82 RCADI 1953/I pp. 88–89, 94–115;
Schwarzenberger 10 CLP 1957 pp. 268–271, 276–283; *Korowicz* 102 RCADI 1960
pp. 11–14, 39; *von Simson* (Souveränität) p. 19; *Wildhaber* (Macdonald-Johnston:
Structure and Process) pp. 435–437, 440–444; *Virally* 183 RCADI 1983/V p. 77; *Anand*
197 RCADI 1986/II pp. 28–29.
[51] *Island of Palmas* Case, II UNRIAA p. 829. See also *Westlake* (International Law, I)
p. 308; *Hinsley* (Sovereignty) p. 158; *Coplin* (Functions) p. 172. On "independence"
generally as a condition for statehood, see *Crawford* (Creation) pp. 48–71.
[52] PCIJ: *Austro-German Customs Union* Case, Ser.A/B 41 p. 45. See also *Anzilotti*, diss. op.
ibid., p. 57.
[53] *Ross* (Text-book) pp. 36–37.   [54] ICJ: *Right of Passage* Case, Pleadings I pp. 6, 26.

Portugal's judge *ad hoc* sought further to drive the point home:

> Sovereignty over any territory implies the capacity to exercise public
> authority in that territory. It implies the right and the obligation to
> maintain order there, if necessary *manu militari* ... how could that
> authority, that right and obligation and those duties be exercised if a
> right of access as to the enclaves were not recognized?[55]

India disputed this and, instead, made a mirror-image argument:

> These alleged rights of passage must evidently impinge upon and dero-
> gate from India's sovereign rights over the territory concerned.[56]

And the Indian judge *ad hoc* agreed:

> To the extent that India is sovereign she must have complete, absolute and
> unrestricted right to regulate the passage of goods, men and traffic ...[57]

Both States argued on the basis of their sovereignty. But their arguments
reflected differing interpretations of the meaning of the term "sovereignty" – that is, on the extent of their sovereignty. Which was correct?

It is obvious that the definitions set out above do not provide an
answer. To define "sovereignty" as "independence" is to replace one
ambiguous expression with another. To explain it in terms of a "sole
right of decision" seems more concrete but that, too, creates difficulty.
For does not any international obligation entail a restriction of that "sole
right"? And if restrictions are admitted without this depriving the State
of its sovereign status, how do we know whether they are those implied
in the Portuguese or the Indian view?

The expression "sovereignty" or any definition thereof cannot have
such fixed content as to be "automatically" applicable. It is not only that
they are ambiguous or have a penumbra of uncertainty about them.
There simply is no fixed meaning, no natural extent to sovereignty at all.
Moreover, assuming that sovereignty had a fixed content would entail
accepting that there is an antecedent material rule which determines the
boundaries of State liberty regardless of the subjective will or interest of
any particular State. But this is incompatible with the liberal doctrine
of politics. For it, "liberty" is a purely formal notion. Any attempt
to impose material boundaries to it which do not stem from the free

---

[55] *Fernandes*, diss. op. ICJ: *Right of Passage* Case, Reports 1960 p. 124.
[56] ICJ: *Right of Passage* Case, Pleadings II p. 113 (Counter-memorial).
[57] *Chagla*, diss. op. ICJ: *Right of Passage* Case, Reports 1960 p. 119.

choice of the individual or entity in question will appear as unjustified coercion.

This explains the apparently puzzling phenomenon that "sovereignty" seems compatible with the situation of a State living in hermetic isolation from others as well as for one which has surrendered all its decision-making power to supranational bodies. This is easiest to see by way of an example which shall also introduce the need to move away from the question of the fixed content of sovereignty to the *assumptions* which control arguments about it.

In the *Austro-German Customs Union* Case (1933), the PCIJ was requested an advisory opinion by the Council of the League of Nations regarding whether a customs union established between Austria and Germany on 19 March 1931 violated Austria's obligations under the Treaty of Saint-Germain (10 September 1919) and the related Geneva protocol (4 October 1922).[58] In these instruments France, Italy, Czechoslovakia and the United Kingdom had guaranteed Austria's independence in exchange for the latter's undertaking not to alienate it. In Article 88 of the Treaty of Saint-Germain it was stated:

> The independence of Austria is inalienable otherwise than with the consent of the Council of the League of Nations.[59]

In the Geneva protocol, Austria undertook:

> ... not to alienate its independence; it will abstain from any negotiation or from any economic or financial engagement calculated directly or indirectly to compromise this independence.[60]

The guarantor States argued that Austria had violated these provisions. By making the customs union arrangement Austria had alienated its sovereignty.[61] Austria denied this. It held that the faculty of binding itself was inherent in its sovereignty. By making the customs union Austria had taken a sovereign decision in order to further its own commercial interests.[62] The Court was similarly divided. The majority held that it was difficult to maintain that the customs union was not

---

[58] PCIJ: *Austro-German Customs Union* Case, Ser. A/B 41. For the terms of the request, see *ibid*. p. 38. For the content of the Protocol and the Court's analysis, see *ibid*. pp. 50–51.

[59] *Ibid*. p. 42.   [60] *Ibid*. p. 43.

[61] See e.g. written statement by the Government of France, *ibid*. Ser. C 53 pp. 119–152.

[62] Written Statement by the Government of Austria, *ibid*. Ser. C. 53 pp. 86 *et seq*, 94–101.

calculated to threaten Austria's economic independence.[63] But a strong minority held that making such unions had been a frequent practice and never had the question arisen that States involved in them would have renounced their independence.[64]

The strangeness of the argumentative positions in this case relates to their pointing beyond the liberal doctrine of politics. The guarantor States' position was equivalent to Rousseau's point about "forcing men to be free". It sought to impose a determinate *material* content of sovereign freedom on Austria which claimed to overrule Austria's own sovereign will. It was based on a theory of objective interests. Austria's point captured the insight that sovereign liberty can only be determined in a subjective way, that a State's interests cannot be dissociated from what it "wants" and that it now "wants" the establishment of the union. But if this is true, then there is no justification to overrule guarantor States' "wants" – that is, their will to exclude the threat posed by the extension of German influence – in favour of Austria's. The case will simply have to remain undecided.

The same arguments are available in respect of any integration or, in fact, any consensual obligation. From one perspective, undertaking obligations seems a limitation of the State's "sole right of decision" and in this sense its independence and sovereignty. From another perspective, the capacity to enter into such binding arrangements seems one without which a State could hardly be said to be truly sovereign at all.[65] By arguing in this way, however, no solution can be found. The very problem-setting seems as frustrating as the little boys'

---

[63] The Court held that only the Geneva Protocol was violated – and not the Treaty of Saint-Germain – because only the former made express reference to economic arrangements. *Ibid.* Ser. A/B 41 p. 52. The inarticulate character of the conclusion is aptly criticized by *Lauterpacht* (Development) pp. 48–49. See also *Crawford* (Creation) pp. 49–51.

[64] PCIJ: *Austro-German Customs Union* Case, Ser A/B 41 pp. 76–78, 82.

[65] ". . . the right of entering into international agreements is an attribute of sovereignty", PCIJ: *Wimbledon* Case, Ser. A 1 p. 25. See further generally *McNair* (Treaties) pp. 754–766. Recently, in his preliminary Award in case No. 2321 at the ICC, the Sole Arbitrator observed that a State could not invoke its immunity to avoid judicial proceedings based on an agreement which it has made. For: "A sovereign State must be sovereign enough to make a binding promise both under international and municipal law", 65 ILR 1984 p. 452. Similarly *Dispute between Texaco Overseas Petroleum Company/California Asiatic Oil Company v. the Government of the Libyan Arab Republic*, XVII ILM 1978 p. 24 (§§ 63–69). This matter is at the heart of the debate about whether States remain bound by concession contracts. The irony of the doctrine of "permanent sovereignty" – if it is taken to mean that the State is *not* bound, as implied in the Libyan

dispute about whether God Almighty can create a stone so big He Himself cannot lift up.

It is impossible to define "sovereignty" in such a manner as to contain our present perception of the State's full subjective freedom and that of its objective submission to restraints to such freedom.[66] If we start by associating sovereignty with an initial, aprioristic freedom of the State, we shall either have to conclude that no State is free or that the international order is not really binding. If sovereignty is associated with the momentary set of rights, liberties and competences given by the normative order to the State, then we shall have to reject the idea that the State would be free to do anything which it is not specifically empowered to do.

These conclusions seem both mutually exclusive and equally incapable of being accepted as such. Clearly, we need to think that the State is both free in areas where it has no engagements as well as restrained by the engagements it has. Whatever we think sovereign statehood to mean, it should be compatible with both. But States have undertaken different obligations and have widely differing spheres of freedom and restraint in this respect.

Therefore, by a simple reference to "sovereignty" or statehood no determinate consequences arise so as to indicate whether the State in some particular relation is free or not.

arguments in the above case – is that it denies the State's capacity to make such promises and has an adverse effect on the State's commercial relations. For this latter point, see *Revere Copper v. OPIC* (District Court, US, December 1978) 56 ILR 1980 pp. 279–284 (using a good faith standard to hold the sovereign bound).

[66] The painful attempts by doctrine to distinguish between "sovereignty" on the one hand and, for example, "sovereign rights" or "freedoms" on the other or between "alienation" and "restriction" of sovereignty all stem from its inability to adopt a "pure fact" or a "legal" perspective on statehood. For these distinctions, see e.g. *Van Kleffens* 82 RCADI 1953/I p. 87; *Arangio-Ruiz* (Friendly Relations) pp. 275–278; *Blix* (Sovereignty) p. 11; Joint diss. op. PCIJ: *Austro-German Customs Union* Case, Ser. A/B 41 p. 77. *Dispute between Texaco Overseas Petroleum Company/California Asiatic Oil Company v. the Government of the Libyan Arab Republic*, XVII ILM 1978 (concession contract not an alienation of permanent sovereignty but a partial and temporal limitation of its exercise) p. 26 (§§ 77, 78). Somehow, doctrine needs to assume that statehood has an inner "essence" (described as the State's inalienable sovereignty) as well as an external, historically relative actuality (described as a limited set of rights, or freedoms, or restrictions on sovereignty's variable surface). Doing away with the former would seem to leave the system "hanging in the air". It would involve assuming that there is some material code "behind" statehood which the law seeks to ensure. Doing away with the latter would achieve a non-normative law, a description of the essence of statehood from a solipsistic perspective. See also *Kelsen* (Souveränität) p. 247 and *passim*.

4.3 The rise and fall of the legal approach: the temptation of analysis, domestic jurisdiction and the dilemma of interpretation

If "sovereignty" entails no determinate amount of freedom or constraint, then it looks like a generic description of the particular rights, liberties and competences which are applicable to the State, each of which needs to be grounded in a distinct legislative source. This will make the law prior to the State and allows a determinate delimitation of its sphere of liberty.

From an analytical, "Hohfeldian", perspective, "sovereignty" looks like a generic term – a "general principle" in Schwarzenberger's sense – which only describes the cluster of power-conferring norms which address themselves to the State and is devoid of independent normative authority.[67] A claim of sovereignty would be reduced to a claim concerning the existence of individual rights, liberties and competences. Initially, such analysis would seem to shed light on cases such as the *Right of Passage*, for example. The conflicting views about sovereignty could be translated into claims about the existence or non-existence of a customary right of passage to a State's enclaves and positive restrictions to such a right. This is the way the ICJ discussed them.[68]

There are analogous cases. In the *Nuclear Tests* Case (1974) Australia and New Zealand argued that French nuclear weapon tests caused radioactive fall-out which violated their sovereignty.[69] France, relying

---

[67] *Schwarzenberger* 10 CLP 1957 p. 284. *Schwarzenberger-Brown* (Manual) regard "legal sovereignty . . . an abstraction from a number of relevant rules", p. 52. See also e.g. *Ross* (Textbook) pp. 40–45. For a discussion of Schwarzenberger's "descriptive" concept of general principles, see *Koskenniemi* XVIII Oikeustiede-Jurisprudentia 1985 pp. 126–127. The idea of sovereignty as an "omnibus word" stems, obviously, from the criticism which argues that "sovereignty" can have no essential content but is relative or "rule-determined". Thus *Hart* (Concept) is able to argue that to find out what rights and duties States have by looking at what kind of sovereignty States have is to "invert . . . the order in which questions must be considered". We can know sovereignty only if we *first* have an idea of what rights and duties the normative order gives States, p. 218. This outlook is widely shared by Anglo-American lawyers. See e.g. *Brownlie* (Principles) p. 19; *Brierly* (Basis of Obligation) pp. 350–351, 373; *idem* (Law of Nations) p. 47. See also the analysis by *Starke* (International Law) of "sovereignty" into 1) power to exercise control over domestic affairs, 2) power to admit and expel aliens, 3) privileges of a State's diplomatic and consular representatives, 4) exclusive territorial jurisdiction pp. 113–121. To the same effect, see further *Crawford* (Creation) pp. 26–27n. 105; *Blix* (Sovereignty) p. 12.

[68] ICJ: *Right of Passage* Case, Reports 1960 pp. 36–45.

[69] According to the Australian Application, the resulting radio-active fall-out ". . . a) violates Australian sovereignty over its territory . . ." ICJ: *Nuclear Tests* Case,

on the exception concerning matters of national defence in its acceptance of the Court's jurisidiction also relied on a sovereignty-based
claim.[70] The judges were quick to notice the mirror-image nature of
the claims:

> Of course, Australia can invoke its sovereignty over its territory and its
> right to prevent pollution caused by another State. But when the French
> Government also claims to exercise its right of territorial sovereignty, by
> proceeding to carry out tests in its territory, is it possible legally to deprive
> it of that right, on account of the mere expression of the will of
> Australia?[71]

Had the Court entered into a discussion of the substance of the Parties'
views, it would have been obliged to look "beyond" abstract sovereignty
and take a view on the customary law status of atmospheric nuclear-
weapon testing.[72]

In the *Asylum* Case (1950) Peru and Colombia disputed about the
right of a person who had taken asylum in the Colombian Embassy in
Peru to safe exit from Peru. Both States argued on the basis of their
sovereignty, Colombia to support this right, Peru to deny it.[73] Again, the
Court avoided discussing the "nature" of sovereignty or statehood and
concentrated on the customary law status of, on the one hand, the
alleged rights of Colombia to qualify the person as a political refugee
and the alleged right of Peru to prevent his exit through Peruvian
territory.[74]

In these cases – as in many others[75] – what are originally presented as
claims about sovereignty turn out as disputes about the existence of
certain individual rights, liberties and competences. Moreover, disputes

---

Pleadings, I p. 14. See also the Request for Interim Measures, *ibid.* p. 43. Though
Australia *also* argued that the fall-out violated its "independent right to decide what
acts shall take place in its territory", this was not to distinguish such right from
"sovereignty". The formulation followed that in Article 2(4) of the UN Charter and
was treated in Australian arguments as an "aspect" of its sovereignty. See oral argument
by Mr Elliott, *ibid.* pp. 186–188; Mr Byers, *ibid.* pp. 479–483.

[70] France never participated in the formal proceedings. For its views, see *ibid.* Pleadings II pp. 339, 347–348.
[71] *Ignacio-Pinto*, diss. op. ICJ: *Nuclear Tests* Cases, Reports 1974 p. 131.
[72] On the Court's treatment of the claims, see *infra* ch. 5.3 and 6.5.1.
[73] See esp. Memorial of Columbia, ICJ: *Asylum* Case, Pleadings I p. 29; Counter-Memorial of Peru, *ibid.* p. 146.
[74] *Ibid.* Reports 1950 pp. 274–275.
[75] See e.g. ICJ: *Corfu Channel* Case, Reports 1949 (on the question of whether the British Naval operation "Retail" violated Albania's sovereignty), pp. 26–35.

in which both parties base their arguments on sovereignty would seem capable of solution *only* if they are so treated. "Sovereignty" would then seem only a more or less convenient shorthand for a total of such rights, liberties and competences each of which needs support from a distinct legislative source.

This conclusion seems supported by much that has been said about the determination of a State's "domestic jurisdiction" – a concept which translates the liberal distinction between the "public" and the "private" realms into international legal language. Let me now illustrate the difficulties in constructing a determinate concept to sovereignty by reference to that doctrine which, as Brierly argued in 1925, had become a new catchword to replace "the somewhat battered ideas of sovereignty, State equality, and the like".[76]

Reference to domestic jurisdiction was included in Article 15(8) of the League Covenant and Article 2(7) of the United Nations Charter. In both instruments, it was included to safeguard member States' freedom against excessive adoption of international jurisdiction by the two organizations.[77] But the formulation of that concept differed and the difference reflects what seem like two distinct ways of constructing the State's "private realm".

What was to be included in domestic jurisdiction in the League system was to be determined by the Council or the Assembly and the determination was to be made "by international law". Domestic jurisdiction was constructed from a *descending* perspective *external* to the State; it denoted hardly more than the sphere of (negative) liberty left to the State by the law – as interpreted by League organs – at any moment.[78] As

---

[76] *Brierly* VI BYIL 1925 p. 8.

[77] In both instruments, the provision was included at the insistence of the United States in order to protect its tariffs and immigration policy. For the background on the Covenant provision, see *Nincić* (Sovereignty) pp. 138–141; *Waldock* XXXI BYIL 1954 pp. 103–104. Article 15(8) of the Covenant read: "If the dispute between the Parties is claimed by any one of them, and is found by the Council, to arise out of a matter which by international law is solely within the jurisdiction of that Party, the Council shall so report, and shall make no recommendation as to its settlement." For the background of the corresponding (but different) Charter formulation, see *Waldock* XXXI BYIL 1954 pp. 127–128; *Kelsen* (The Law of the United Nations) p. 769 *et seq.* A similar safeguard clause is included in the constituent instruments of many international organizations (OAS, OAU, Arab League). See *Trindade* 25 ICLQ 1976 pp. 721–722.

[78] *Waldock* XXXI BYIL 1954 argues that it was held as self-evident by the League organs that they had the competence – and not the State itself – to decide on the validity of domestic jurisdiction claims, pp. 106–107. To the same effect, see *Kim-Howell* (Conflict of Obligations) pp. 36–38; *Rajan* (Expanding Jurisdiction) pp. 4–5.

such, however, it fails to provide the security for which it was introduced. It makes the sphere of the State's liberty completely relative to what is externally decided.

The Charter remains silent on who is to undertake the determination and whether it should be made by international law or the municipal law of the respective State. The Charter formulation suggests an *ascending position*: this sphere can be determined by the State itself. As such, however, it threatens to make international jurisdiction illusory: if what lies in the private sphere can be decided by the State itself and this decision can be effectively opposed against international action, then the legitimacy of such action is dependent on the good will of the State against which the action is taken.[79]

Much discussion has focused on the difference between the Covenant and the Charter formulations.[80] Yet, as both positions tend towards unacceptable consequences, they have in argument lost their initial polarity. League organs never interpreted the Covenant so as to assume unrestricted legislative powers. As the PCIJ pointed out in the *Nationality Decrees* Case (1923) there are matters – such as questions of nationality – which are "in principle within this reserved domain".[81] These are matters which do not come under domestic jurisdiction simply by virtue of a legislative act but as a consequence of statehood and they establish a barrier *against* international legislation.

On the other hand, UN organs have constantly assumed jurisdiction in matters which with some justification have been understood to be covered by the functions of the organization.[82] Though the plea of

---

[79] For a strong recent defence of this view, see *Watson* 71 AJIL 1977 p. 62 *et seq* (pointing out that the "relativist" approach goes against the letter and spirit of Article 2(7) and that a contrary interpretation is utopian and counter-productive as such). A similar interpretation has been taken by others who, however, worry about its consequences, see *Kelsen* (The Law of the United Nations) pp. 777–784; *Preuss* 74 RCADI 1949/I pp. 597–604; *Gross* (Essays II) has taken the "intermediate" interpretation that *both* the State and the organization are empowered to make the determination which remain valid, respectively, in the national and the organization's legal order, p. 1179.

[80] See e.g. *Brownlie* (Principles) pp. 293–294; *Cavaré* (Droit international I) pp. 192–193; *Nisot* 43 AJIL 1949 pp. 776–779.

[81] PCIJ: *Nationality Decrees* Case, Ser. B 4 p. 24.

[82] Hence, many commentators have concluded that there is no essential difference between the Covenant and the Charter formulations but that *both* provide the determination by the organs themselves and by reference to rules of international law. See, in particular, *Rolin* 77 RCADI 1950/II pp. 381–393; *Waldock* XXXI BYIL 1954 p. 129; *Trindade* 25 ICLQ 1976 pp. 719–720. For a review and criticism of their arguments, see *Watson* 71 AJIL 1977 pp. 60–83.

domestic jurisdiction has been occasionally made – with decreasing frequency, it seems – it has been remarkably unsuccessful.[83] The organization has extended its jurisdiction by referring to its "purposes and principles" especially under chapters IX and XI of the Charter to nearly all areas of life, including questions of internal régimes,[84] economic and social conditions,[85] human rights,[86] self-determination,[87] *apartheid* and protection of minorities, for example. This has led commentators to conclude that domestic jurisdiction is "undergoing a continuous process of reduction".[88] In particular, it has seemed to possess no "inherent" or natural content which could be opposed to international action. Its content seems to have been determinable only by taking a legal approach; by looking at present regulation and what areas it leaves open for States to regulate by municipal law.

The plea of domestic jurisdiction has had likewise little success in international adjudication. In particular, courts have held that making it is no bar to dealing with the merits of the claims advanced.[89] This

[83] During the first years of the organization, the matter came up in relation to the Spanish, Indonesian and Greek questions as well as in connection with South Africa's policy of *apartheid*. Later, it has occasionally been raised in respect of e.g. Hungary, Czechoslovakia, Dominican Republic and Afghanistan. Unless the matter has come before the Security Council and a permanent member has vetoed it because of its own stake in the matter, the plea has regularly been rejected. For general overviews, see *Rajan* (Domestic Jurisdiction) p. 145 *et seq*; *idem* (Expanding) (an updated addition to the former). See also *Kim-Howell* (Conflict of Obligations) p. 34 *et seq*, and (for analysis of the Spanish, South African and Rhodesian cases) pp. 48–56; *Higgins* (Development) pp. 58–230; *Trindade* 25 ICLQ 1976 pp. 722–744.

[84] See e.g. *Rajan* (Domestic Jurisdiction) pp. 146–179; *idem* (Expanding) pp. 11–34; *Nincić* (Sovereignty) pp. 186–192.

[85] *Rajan* (Domestic Jurisdiction) pp. 397–418; *idem* (Expanding) pp. 85–97.

[86] *Rajan* (Domestic Jurisdiction) pp. 298–397; *idem* (Expanding) pp. 98–123; *Nincić* (Sovereignty) pp. 193–218.

[87] *Rajan* (Domestic Jurisdiction) pp. 179–298; *idem* (Expanding) pp. 35–84; *Nincić* (Sovereignty) pp. 219–259; *Trindade* 25 ICLQ 1976 pp. 729–734.

[88] *Trindade* 25 ICLQ 1976 p. 765. *Higgins* (Bull: Intervention) concludes her survey: "One is led very near to saying that most things short of actual action by the United Nations are in fact now permissible intervention", p. 36. See also *Waldock* 106 RCADI 1962/II (arguing that Article 2(7) of the Charter only guarantees that the UN will not interfere with the State's exclusive authority on its territory) pp. 182–191.

[89] See e.g. PCIJ: *Losinger* Case, Ser A/B 67 pp. 23–25 (a reservation about matters of domestic jurisdiction not "automatically" a bar to discussion of merits); *Electricity Company of Sofia* Case, Ser. A/B 77 pp. 78, 82–83 (the fact that a concession was granted in accordance with municipal law did not exclude the involvement of international obligations). To the same effect, see ICJ: *Anglo-Iranian Oil Company* Case, Reports 1951 p. 92. *Scelle* 46 RCADI 1933/IV summarizes: domestic jurisdiction "est par lui-même,

suggests immediately that whether or not a matter concerns a State's domestic jurisdiction seems capable of determination only once it is known what obligations the State has. In the *Polish Nationals in Danzig* Case (1932), for example, the PCIJ pointed out that while the Constitution of Danzig was an internal matter, its application might still involve Danzig's international obligations and assumed jurisdiction concerning minority protection.[90] A similar point was made by the ICJ in the *Peace Treaties* Advisory Opinion (1950) where it noted that although the matter related to the constitutional régimes of Bulgaria, Hungary and Romania, the fact that it involved the interpretation of treaties to which these States were parties detached it from the reserved domain.[91] As the Court argued in the *Right of Passage* Case, against India's preliminary objection, the fact that such passage related to India's sovereignty did not preclude the Court from dealing with the issue as by formulating its claim as a right against India's duty, Portugal had placed itself "on the plane of international law".[92]

Now, it would seem that once sovereignty is understood as "domestic jurisdiction" it would lack any inherent or natural content. Its content would be, as the PCIJ pointed out in the *Nationality Decrees* opinion (1923), "an essentially relative question" and dependent on "the development of international relations", i.e. of the prevailing corpus of law at each moment.[93] But this creates unacceptable consequences.

In the first place, it destroys the normative meaning of words such as "sovereignty", "self-determination", "non-intervention", "independence" or "exclusive jurisdiction". None of these could be successfully invoked against a State which succeeds – like Portugal succeeded in the *Right of Passage* Case – in formulating its claim so as to bear a relation to the

sans significance" – it cannot be determined independently of a survey of the State's rights and duties, p. 415.

[90] PCIJ: *Polish Nationals in Danzig* Case, Ser. A/B 44 p. 24. To the same effect, see *German Interests in Polish Upper Silesia* Case, Ser. A 7 p. 19 (the application of municipal law might conflict with international obligations); *Greek and Turkish Populations* Case, Ser. B 10 p. 17 (the matter related to construction of treaty).

[91] ICJ: *Peace Treaties* Case, Reports 1950 pp. 70–71. For commentary, see e.g. *Briggs* 93 RCADI 1958/I pp. 321–324.

[92] ICJ: *Right of Passage* Case, Reports 1957 p. 33.

[93] Most lawyers argue in this way. See e.g. *Politis* 6 RCADI 1925/I pp. 47–48 *et seq*; *Scelle* 46 RCADI 1933/IV pp. 414–420; *Strupp* 47 RCADI 1934/I pp. 502–504; *Sørensen* 101 RCADI 1960/III pp. 165–166; *Cavaré* (Droit international I) pp. 200–201; *Waldock* XXXI BYIL 1954 p. 111; *Brownlie* (Principles) pp. 292–293; *Jacqué* (Elements) pp. 57–60; *Virally* 183 RCADI 1983/V pp. 81–82. See also IIL Resolution of 1954, IIL Yearbook 1954 pp. 150, 299. See also *supra* notes 82–83.

international rights and duties of the States involved. And nothing could be easier than formulating a claim in such a way. In the absence of a "natural" private realm, *any* act can plausibly be said to violate another State's rights if only that State so thinks.[94] To deny *prima facie* violation we should be in possession of a naturalist test of domestic jurisdiction (an "absolute rights" test) – a hypothesis excluded by the legal approach.[95]

The legal approach denies that States have a natural realm of liberty which would exist through the simple fact of their being States. There is no general principle investing a State with a *prima facie* legitimate sphere of action. To do something, the State will always have to show a specific rule of international law entitling it to act or at least the absence of a prohibiting rule.[96]

On many areas of international conduct, however, there are only few detailed rules. Moreover, and here is the paradox, the most important rules of general application seem to be precisely the rules laying down the right of self-determination, non-intervention, independence or exclusive jurisdiction. It is virtually impossible to imagine an international law in which such concepts would be reduced to non-normative abstractions. If they were such, then international law would appear as a huge *lacuna*, consisting of a few scattered, mainly treaty-based individual rules and we would be at a loss about how to justify our abstractions.

---

[94] This is so because, as *Virally* 183 RCADI 1983/V observes, sovereignties delimit each other, p. 78. In a system in which each participant's freedom ("private realm") is delimited only by the equal amount of freedom of others, any claim about *my* freedom, right, competence etc. will automatically involve a claim about others' obligations. In such system, each participant's freedom is relative to assessments about what is "equal" amount of freedom in particular respects – assessments for which "objective" standards seem lacking.

[95] Thus, in the *Nationality Decrees* Case, the British case was also formulated in terms of the French acts being violative of British sovereignty. Ser. C 2 suppl. p. 60 (British Government Case). To decide on this claim, it is obviously insufficient to formulate the domestic jurisdiction test in the way the Court did as concerning France only. *Waldock* XXXI BYIL 1954, for example, argues that the *prima facie* test works in the reverse direction, that is to the determination of the respondent's reserved domain, pp. 107–114. This may be a correct description of what took place in the *Nationality Decrees* opinion but it leaves unexplained how it is possible to start out from the *respondent*'s (instead of the applicant's) perspective and prefer its private realm to the allegedly violated private sphere of the applicant.

[96] Because of these difficulties, some have concluded that the domestic jurisdiction doctrine is not a "legal" doctrine at all but represents only the various political claims – a view which is taken to explain the widely differing interpretations of its extent and character. See *Trindade* 25 ICLQ 1976 pp. 728–729.

The legal approach, however, is untenable also as it will either have to accept that the individual rules which lay down rights, liberties and competences have "natural" meanings which are applicable without interpretation or it will have to use a theory of interpretation which contradicts its own premises.

According to the legal approach, only individual rules have normative force. But fixing the sense of rule-formulations requires interpretation which connects them to the system in which they appear. Now the problem is that *it is precisely the nature of the system which is disputed in the opposition of the legal and the pure fact approaches* to sovereignty. We can construct the sense of individual rules only if we already know whether the freedom of the State is prior to the normative order or *vice-versa*.

There are two systems of interpreting ambiguous rules. In one system, each rule is regarded as an obligation which limits State freedom and needs therefore to be *restrictively* construed. In another system, rules may establish not only duties but also rights, liberties and competences and the sense of rules is determined by linking them to the "systemic" properties of the legal order. Quite apart from other difficulties, neither system is open for the legal approach to derive its principles of interpretation from.

The legal approach cannot adopt the principle of restrictive interpretation because that principle is based on the assumption of an initial, unrestricted liberty of the State. This is simply the pure fact approach restated. As the point of the legal approach is to reject the pure fact view, it cannot, without self-contradiction, give effect to such initial liberty.

But the legal approach cannot accept the idea of systemic interpretation, either, for this will lead into the assumption that values are objective or back into the pure fact approach.

Systemic interpretation construes rules by linking them to the values (purposes) of the legal order as a whole. What are those values? A first possibility would be to associate them with the States' preferred values. But associating systemic value with the States' values is *premised on the acceptance of the pure fact approach*. It assumes that States have the initial liberty to introduce their subjective values as law and once law is ambiguous, that liberty must be given effect to – precisely the assumption against which the legal approach constituted itself.

The second possibility is to assume that systemic values are independent of States' values. They could exist, and be discoverable, through their "coherence" with the rules of the legal order as a whole. But one man's coherence is not necessarily that of another's. To overrule one interpretation of systemic value with another is justifiable only if there is an external (objective) standard whereby these can be measured. But then it must be assumed that these values – the "principles of coherence" – are valid regardless of whether anybody has accepted them. In other words, they must be assumed to exist as a natural morality.[97] This looks like a utopian position. Moreover, it fails to explain why the initial rules from which inferences about coherence started should be regarded as valid simply because they have been enacted in a formal-legal procedure. For the justification of such a procedure is a pure fact justification: legislation is a valid way of creating rules only if there are no objective values.

The legal approach cannot be coherently held. *Its interpretative principles cannot be justified without either assuming the correctness of the pure fact view (and thus accepting self-contradiction) or some form of moral objectivism which cannot be justified within the legal approach itself.* The approach which would do away with an independent concept of sovereignty fails to explain why the rules which it assumes to exist are valid in the first place. It cannot construct a meaningful "system" out of the totality of individual rules it perceives at all without either assuming the correctness of its opposite: the view that rules exist to protect the State's initial freedom, or by taking an objectivist view on values.

It may have been these reasons for which the PCIJ formulated its approach in the *Nationality Decrees* opinion in such careful terms. The question was whether certain French nationality decrees which had been promulgated in the French Protectorates of Morocco and Tunis were applicable to British citizens residing therein.[98] France argued that this was a matter of domestic jurisdiction. United Kingdom held that the matter related to France's international (treaty and other) obligations.[99] Initially, the French relied on a pure fact, the British on a legal approach.[100] The Court was careful not to take a definite view either way. It admitted that "questions of nationality are ... in principle

---

[97] That is, valid as a (background) theory of justice – irrespective of whether anybody accepts it. See *supra* ch. 1.2.2.2.

[98] PCIJ: *Nationality Decrees* Case, Ser. B 4 p. 21.

[99] According to the British case: "... every contention put forward on either side depends principally, at least, upon treaty obligations, on international law, and therefore obviously not on French domestic jurisdiction." *Ibid.* Ser. C 2 (speech by Sir Douglas Hogg) pp. 49–50. According to the French case, nationality was a matter which was an essential attribute of sovereignty as it related to the State's very organization and constitution, *ibid.* Ser. C suppl. (French Government Case) pp. 20–23.

[100] The French case resting on French territorial sovereignty (*ibid.* Ser. B 4 pp. 14–15), the British case resting on treaty obligations which set limits to such sovereignty (*ibid.* p. 16.)

within the reserved domain".[101] It thus recognized the existence and normative significance of such a domain. However, it could be "restricted by the obligations which (France, MK) may have undertaken towards other States".[102] But whether this was so was a matter of substance. Hence, the "relativist test" was a *prima facie* test, a preliminary view as to whether the matter might plausibly involve some of France's international obligations.[103] The Court never touched the substance as the Parties agreed outside of Court. But if it had, then it might have fallen on the applicant to prove the existence of such obligation with the assumption that unless such proof could be adduced, then France's initial freedom might have been given normative effect – a decision which would have violated British sovereignty.

4.4   The rise and fall of the pure fact approach: Lotus principle

We have seen that the meaning of sovereignty seems determinable only in a contextual way, having regard to the rights and duties the State possesses at each moment. But also attempts to reduce it fully to such individual rules seem unworkable as rules require construction through the use of interpretative principles. A residual rule, or a principle of interpretation is needed which can both serve to explain the binding force of existing rules and provide a basis for decision when individual rules are ambiguous or lacking. Here "sovereignty" re-emerges as a normative principle in its own right.

In the *Lotus* Case (1927), the PCIJ observed that there were no rules governing the exercise of jurisdiction by Turkey over foreign vessels in the High Seas.[104] To avoid a *non liquet* the Court relied on the assumption that unless specific prohibiting rules exist, State sovereignty – the sphere of its legitimate action – is unlimited.[105] In the absence of a positive prohibition Turkey was presumed to possess jurisdiction. The Court had previously resorted to a similar argument in the *Wimbledon* Case (1923) and was again to do so in the *Free Zones* Case (1932).[106]

The principle according to which State sovereignty must be presumed as extensive as possible may be called the "Lotus principle" in

---

[101] PCIJ: *Nationality Decrees* Case, Ser. B 4 p. 24.   [102] *Ibid.*

[103] On the "provisional" character of the conclusion and the manner in which the Court refrained from assuming that it prejudices anything on the merits, see PCIJ: *Nationality Decrees* Case, Ser. B 4 pp. 24–26.

[104] PCIJ: *Lotus* Case, Ser. A 10 p. 30.   [105] *Ibid.* pp. 18–19.

[106] PCIJ: *Wimbledon* Case, Ser. A I p. 24; *Free Zones* Case, Ser. A/B 46 p. 167.

accordance with the above mentioned decision. It expresses the assumption that State sovereignty is the starting-point of international law in the same way as individual liberty is the basis of the municipal legal order.[107] Both can be restricted only by a law which is enacted in the correct legal procedure.

This is nothing else than a restatement of the pure fact approach. States are vested with a natural liberty which must be given effect to when individual rules are lacking or ambiguous. The essence of the law is not to allocate competences but to establish duties as exceptions to the initial liberty.[108]

Much international jurisprudence encapsulates this assumption. It is visible, for instance, in the *Anglo-Norwegian Fisheries* Case (1951). The *dispositif* of the judgement is dressed in revealing language: the Norwegian method of drawing straight baselines was "not contrary to international law".[109] In other words, the Court was not concerned with whether or not there existed a positive rule entitling Norway to use this method. Such competence was assumed to exist *ipso facto* by the fact that no prohibiting rules existed. The same assumption was present also in the Court's discussion, in the *North Sea Continental Shelf* Cases (1969), of whether the equidistance rule was binding on the Federal Republic of Germany. The Court did not pose the issue so as to enquire whether

---

[107] As *Kaltenborn von Stachau* (Kritik des Völkerrechts) puts it, the international normative order: ". . . auf der basis der Souveränität der einzelnen Staaten in ähnlicher Weise aufgebaut wie die staatliche Gemeinexistenz, der Staatsorganismus auf dem Fondament individueller Freiheit", p. 267.

[108] For a recent discussion of the opposition between a ("subjectivistic") view which looks at international law through restrictions to an antecedent liberty and a ("objectivistic") view which takes international law to establish competences, see *Bleckmann* ÖZöRV 1978 pp. 174–183. For the view that international law consists mainly of liberty-limiting obligations and only in rare cases establishes specific competences, see e.g. *Fitzmaurice* XXX BYIL 1953 pp. 9–10; *Marek* VI RBDI 1970 pp. 46–47. See also *Dore* (Superpowers) pp. 128–130. Of course, the argumentative structure which opposes "law" with "sovereignty" assumes that the purpose of the former is precisely to restrict the latter. For this point, see e.g. *Van Kleffens* 82 RCADI 1953/I p. 84; *Suontausta* (Souveraineté) p. 41; *Wildhaber* (Macdonald-Johnston: Structure and Process) p. 442; *West* (Psychology) p. 29 *et seq*. As *Strupp* 47 RCADI 1934/I points out, the Lotus principle is simply a modernized version of the fundamental rights doctrine. Both start out from the non-existence of a set of natural duties and affirm obligation only in the presence of positive undertakings, pp. 497–498.

[109] ICJ: *Anglo-Norwegian Fisheries* Case, Reports 1951 p. 143. See also the Norwegian formulation of its view, *ibid*. p. 123 and the Court's discussion on pp. 132, 138–139. For a discussion of this point, see also *Fitzmaurice* XXX BYIL 1953 pp. 8–11; *idem*, sep. op. ICJ: *Fisheries Jurisdiction* Case, Reports 1973 pp. 25–30.

Denmark and the Netherlands were entitled to use this method but whether the Federal Republic was under an obligation to accept it.[110] In a more general fashion, the opposability doctrine, endorsed by the Court in, for example, the *Fisheries Jurisdiction* (1974), *Nuclear Tests* (1974) and *U.S. Military and Paramilitary Activities* (1986) Cases reveals the same assumption.[111] The issue is not whether there exist rules providing competences but whether there are obligations restricting the State's initial freedom.

A pure fact approach reveals itself also behind such doctrines as those according to which restrictions of sovereignty must be established by "clear and convincing evidence",[112] cannot be made by analogy[113] and must be interpreted restrictively.[114] Each is based on the assumption that there exists an initial liberty of the State which must be given normative effect if clear obligations are absent. The problem with such doctrines is, however, that they do not provide grounds for decision in cases which involve a *conflict* of liberties.[115]

In the *Right of Passage* and *Asylum* Cases, preference for interpreting sovereignty restrictively lead nowhere because we do not know which of the two States' sovereignty to prefer. Moreover, it is not difficult to dress *any* dispute in language which implies a conflict of liberties, or sovereignties. This is so because under the pure fact view itself, the ultimate *ratio* of any legal regulation is to prevent violations of liberty – "harm" – and each State has the final say about what constitutes "harm" to it, what

---

[110] ICJ: *North Sea Continental Shelf* Cases, Reports 1969 p. 23 (§§ 21–23). See also *Marek* VI RBDI 1970 pp. 46–47.

[111] See *infra* ch. 6.5.1.

[112] *Schwarzenberger* (Dynamics) expresses this in terms of the presumption of good faith of the sovereign, p. 64.

[113] *German Reparations* Case, I UNRIAA p. 76.

[114] See e.g. PCIJ: *Free Zones* Case, Ser. A/B 46 p. 167; *Certain German Interests in Polish Upper Silesia* Case, Ser. A 7 p. 30; *Nationality Decrees* Case, Ser. B 4 p. 25; *Interpretation of the Status of Memel Territory* Case, Ser. A/B 49 pp. 295–296, 314. See also the *Kronprins Adolf* Case, II UNRIAA p. 1285; *Radio Corporation of America* Case, III UNRIAA p. 1672; ICJ: *Libya–Malta Continental Shelf* Case (Application by Italy to Intervene) Reports 1984 p. 22 (§ 35); Iran-US Claims Tribunal: *Golpira v. Iran* (Case No. 211), diss. op. *Shafeiei*, 72 ILR 1987 p. 534. For literature, see *Strupp* 47 RCADI 1934/I pp. 495–496; *Lauterpacht* (Development) pp. 300–306; *Rousseau* (Droit international public I) pp. 273–274; *Zoller* (Bonne foi) pp. 218–220.

[115] For criticism of the Lotus principle, see *Bruns* 1 ZaöRV 1929 pp. 31–40, 50–56; *Brierly* 84 RCADI 1936/IV pp. 146–148; *Lauterpacht* (Function) pp. 94–96; *Mann* (Studies) pp. 25–27; *Bleckmann* (Grundprobleme) pp. 198 *et seq*, 201–202; *Fitzmaurice* 92 RCADI 1957/II pp. 55–59. See also *Koskenniemi* XVII Oikeustiede-Jurisprudentia 1984 pp. 103–105.

violates its liberty. To hold otherwise would be to assume the presence of a material criterion which would overrule liberty – a criterion which the pure fact approach has excluded. Hence, any claimed right, liberty or competence is bound to encroach upon another State's rights, liberties or competences.[116] The pure fact view is powerless to do more than acknowledge this fact. Inasmuch as dispute-solution involves undertaking a delimitation of or establishing a "balance" between liberties, it cannot be conducted under the pure fact view at all.

The difficulty with the pure fact view is that it will do away with the law's binding force altogether. For if norms have no natural meaning but require interpretation and if the interpretative rule calls simply for respect to liberty, then hard cases can only be decided by letting each State do what it wishes.

If dispute solution entails the establishment of a balance between freedoms, then we must move beyond the pure fact approach. For in order to prefer liberties, or self-understandings about liberties, *vis-à-vis* each other or to establish a balance between them, a code of material value is needed which is independent from the conflicting liberties themselves and which must be superior to the liberties in providing a way to evaluate them. Thus we come back to the legal approach, once again.

4.5 Constructivism: recourse to equity

It is common for lawyers to attempt to escape from the unacceptable consequences of the Lotus principle by appealing to evaluative, constructivist considerations or to the "spirit of the system".[117] If two liberties, for example, two jurisdictions, seem to conflict, then:

> ... le conflit ... ne saurait être décidé par une règle absolue qui accorderait, d'une manière génératе la préférence, soit à l'une, soit à l'autre des deux juridictions concurrentes.[118]

---

[116] See *supra* n. 94. See also *Levine* (Liberal Democracy) pp. 128–129 and *Unger* (Knowledge) pp. 84–85.

[117] *Fitzmaurice* 92 RCADI 1957/II p. 51.

[118] PCA: *Casablanca* Case, XI UNRIAA p. 128. The case involved a conflict between German consular jurisdiction and French military jurisdiction in Moroccan territory. The tribunal concluded that the conflict must be solved by taking account of the "circonstances de fait qui sont de nature a déterminer la préférence", *ibid*.

One must, rather, look behind abstract presumptions for the general system of goals and values in international law and attempt to construct a solution which is best in harmony with them.[119]

This approach may be illustrated by reference to the *Anglo-Norwegian Fisheries* Case (1951). Here the ICJ observed that there existed no unambiguous rules for drawing the baselines of the territorial sea. Nevertheless, the Court observed:

> It does not at all follow that, in the absence of rules having the technically precise character alleged by the United Kingdom Government, the delimitation undertaken by the Norwegian Government in 1935 is not subject to certain principles which make it possible to judge as to its validity under international law.[120]

Despite the absence of detailed obligations, Norway still could not rely on an overriding liberty principle:

> The delimitation of sea areas has always an international aspect; it cannot be dependent merely on the will of the coastal State ... the validity of the delimitation with regard to other States depends on international, not municipal law.[121]

The Court proceeded to construct the applicable law by recourse to what today would be called "equitable principles", including for example, "certain economic interests, peculiar to a region, the reality and importance of which are clearly evidenced by long usage".[122] The Court avoided a *lacuna*, not by resorting to the Lotus principle but by balancing. The extent of Norway's sovereignty was made dependent on considerations about the economic justice of alternative solutions.

Delimitation cases are clearly exemplary cases in which a State's sphere of liberty must be determined. Legal practice here overwhelmingly follows

---

[119] See e.g. *Bleckmann* (Grundprobleme) pp. 164–166. Thus, we are led into the discussion reviewed in chapter 1.
[120] *Anglo-Norwegian Fisheries* Case, Reports 1951 p. 132. Norway had originally argued that the coastal State does have an extensive right to delimit its territorial sea according to its will – the sole restrictions to such right being provided by "reasonableness", *ibid.* Pleadings III (Rejoinder of Norway) p. 11.
[121] ICJ: *Anglo-Norwegian Fisheries* Case, Reports 1951 p. 132.
[122] *Ibid.* On the "equitable" nature of the Court's reasoning, see also *Koskenniemi* XVII Oikeustiede-Jurisprudentia 1984 pp. 131–152.

the constructivist position.[123] The problem is whether constructivism can be reconciled with doctrine's self-constitutive assumption about the objectivity of law.

In the *North Sea Continental Shelf* Cases (1969), the ICJ first observed that the parties were neither under an obligation to apply the 1958 Convention nor a customary equidistance rule. This did not mean that the situation was one "for the unfettered appreciation of the Parties".[124] It noted that there was an obligation to negotiate in good faith and that the ideas of delimitation by agreement and in accordance with equitable principles "have underlain all subsequent history" of continental shelf law since the 1945 Truman Proclamation.[125] It pointed out that there was:

> no legal limit to the considerations which States may take account of for the purpose of making sure that they apply equitable procedures, and more often than not it is the balancing-up of all such considerations that will produce the result ... [126]

In its own judgement it listed four such factors which it thought relevant for achieving an equitable delimitation: geological and geographical factors, the unity of mineral deposits and a "reasonable degree of proportionality" between the shelves allocated to the States and their respective coastlines.[127]

Maritime delimitation since the North Sea judgement has proceeded by way of aiming at equitable solutions by balancing the different factors involved. It is true that in the *North Sea* Cases the Court still experienced some hesitation about this. It attempted to preserve the idea that it was a pure fact which area belonged to which of the disputing States. Their rights were assumed to exist, as the Court put it, *ab initio* and *ipso facto*. It expressly rejected the German view that delimitation would be a matter of equitable apportionment.[128] As Judge Oda noted, delimitation was to consist of:

> ... discerning and bringing into light a line already in potential existence.[129]

---

[123] For an early "equitable delimitation", see PCA: *Grisbadarna* Case, XI UNRIAA esp. pp. 161–162. See also *Munkman* XLVI BYIL 1972–3 pp. 59–60 *passim*, and the discussion in *Koskenniemi* XVII Oikeustiede-Jurisprudentia 1984 pp. 136–148.

[124] ICJ: *North Sea Continental Shelf* Cases, Reports 1969 p. 46 (§ 83).

[125] *Ibid.* p. 33 (§ 47).   [126] *Ibid.* p. 50 (§ 93).   [127] *Ibid.* pp. 50–52 (§§ 94–98).

[128] *Ibid.* pp. 22–23 (§§ 19–20).

[129] *Oda*, diss. op. ICJ: *Tunisia–Libya Continental Shelf* Case, Reports 1982 p. 254. See also *Lang* (Plateau continental) pp. 18–20.

But the attempt to safeguard the pure fact view in this way and to avoid the objection that balancing the equities is a matter of subjective evaluation has proved practically meaningless. What rights the parties have – what the extent of their sovereign liberty is – follows from the Court's act of balancing and is not inscribed in some transcendental code *ex ante*. In the *Anglo-French Continental Shelf* Case (1977), the Court of Arbitration pointed out that the principle of "natural prolongation" – with which the ICJ had originally associated its view about the *ab initio* and *ipso facto* existence of the boundary – "may be subject to qualifications in particular circumstances".[130] The delimitation was to be undertaken:

> ... in the light of all relevant geographical and other circumstances.[131]

In other words, that rights are said to pre-exist the actual act of listing and evaluating the various circumstances appears only as a strenuous fiction: for practical purposes, they become dependent on the act of establishing the balance, on taking a view on equity by the Court.

Later delimitations have completely set aside *ab initio* rights in favour of equity as the goal of delimitation. This idea was present already in the *North Sea* Cases[132] but became overriding in the Anglo-French and the *Tunisia–Libya Continental Shelf* (1982) Cases. In the former, the presence of the British Channel Islands close to the French coast and the position of the Scilly Isles with a potential for distorting the median line were taken account of as "special circumstances" which required a modification of the otherwise privileged equidistance rule.[133] The purpose, as the Court of Arbitration noted, was to make:

> ... a more appropriate and a more equitable balance between the respective claims and interests of the Parties.[134]

---

[130] *Anglo-French Continental Shelf* Case, XVIII UNRIAA p. 91 (§ 191).

[131] *Ibid.* p. 92 (§ 194). Thus *Herman* 33 ICLQ 1984 argues that delimitation is an "evaluative process of fact assessment", pp. 853–858. It escapes, he assumes, pure "subjectivism" in that it takes account of the pertinent "facts". But, of course "facts" do not (under liberal assumptions) possess intrinsic value. The problem remains to justify the axiology from which value is projected onto "facts".

[132] ICJ: *North Sea Continental Shelf* Cases, Reports 1969 p. 49 (§ 90).

[133] *Anglo-French Continental Shelf* Case, XVIII UNRIAA p. 93 (§ 197) and pp. 98–99 (§§ 207–210).

[134] *Ibid.* p. 94 (§ 198).

In the *Tunisia–Libya* Case, the Court expressly rejected the idea of antecedent rights and made everything subservient to equity:

> The result of the application of equitable principles must be equitable . . .
> The equitableness of a principle must be assessed in the light of its usefulness for the purpose of arriving at an equitable result.[135]

The same approach is visible in other recent delimitations. In the *Gulf of Maine* Case (1984), the Chamber of the Court observed that there were no conventional or customary rules regulating the delimitation of a single maritime boundary between Canada and the United States. But this did not mean that no delimitation was possible. The Chamber merely noted that it was not bound by any "special law" applicable between the Parties and went on to construct an equitable, contextually evaluated balance from the different factors involved.[136] In the *Libya–Malta Continental Shelf* Case (1985) the Court rejected the Libyan emphasis on the close relations between the concept of the shelf and that of "natural prolongation". Likewise, it rejected Malta's argument for equidistance.[137] It observed that it was "the goal – the equitable result – and not the means used to achieve it" which was decisive.[138] Everything turned on the act of balancing.

Constructivism extends beyond maritime delimitation to all disputes involving sovereignty. Take, for example, disputes about territory. In the *Island of Palmas* Case (1928) the Arbitrator was faced with conflicting claims of the Netherlands and the United States on the small Pacific Island of Palmas (Miangas). The final decision in the case was made by applying the rule about continuous and peaceful display of authority.[139] But had this rule not been applicable, what would have been the decision? Judge Huber felt it necesary to point out that in such case:

> . . . the decision of the Arbitrator would have to be founded on the relative strength of the titles invoked by each Party.[140]

The power to establish "relative strengths" was inherent in the judge's function. International law, noted Judge Huber, demands an evaluation of the worths of conflicting interests. Indeed, the decision to privilege effective possession came about precisely through such evaluation: it was

---

[135] ICJ: *Tunisia–Libya Continental Shelf* Case, Reports 1982 p. 59 (§ 70).
[136] ICJ: *Gulf of Maine* Case, Reports 1984 p. 312 (§ 155).
[137] ICJ: *Libya–Malta Continental Shelf* Case, Reports 1985 pp. 34–38 (§§ 35–44).
[138] *Ibid.* pp. 38–39 (§ 45).   [139] *Island of Palmas* Case, II UNRIAA pp. 867, 870–871.
[140] *Ibid.* p. 869.

the correct rule as it best enhanced the protection of the population of the island and the interests of other States.[141] Later on, the method of "relative strengths" has been used in many other territorial disputes.[142]

Recourse to balancing has been used to avoid *non liquet* situations whether or not there has been an express authorization to rule *ex aequo et bono*.[143] In the *Guatemala-Honduras Boundary* Case (1933), for instance, the power to modify the *uti possidetis* rule was taken by the arbitrators to authorize them to determine the boundary "as justice may require".[144] In the *Rann of Kutch* Case (1966) the Tribunal expressly noted that it did not have the power to decide *ex aequo et bono*.[145] Nevertheless, Judge Lagergren felt free to strike a balance between Indian and Pakistani interests by refusing to recognize those parts of the Rann which penetrated deep into Pakistani territory as Indian together with the rest (about 90%) of the area. He pointed out:

> ... it would be inequitable to recognize those inlets as foreign territory. It would be conducive to friction and conflict. The paramount consideration of preserving peace and stability in this region compels the recognition that this territory which is wholly surrounded by Pakistani territory also to be recognized as such.[146]

In the recent *Burkina Faso-Mali Frontier* Case (1986) the Chamber of the ICJ bluntly observed that the kind of equity *infra legem* which had been used in maritime delimitations was applicable in terrestial disputes as well.[147]

Constructivism is the sole available means to deal with any kinds of conflicts which seem to involve a conflict of liberties. This is easiest to illustrate by reference to the law of natural resources.

Transboundary pollution, for example, involves the juxtaposition of the freedoms of the source-State and the target-State: on the one hand, there is the former's sovereign right to exploit its natural resources in

---

[141] *Ibid.* pp. 869–870. Se also *De Visscher* (Equité) p. 102; *Jennings* (Acquisition) p. 75.
[142] *Clipperton Island* Case, II UNRIAA p. 1110; PCIJ: *Eastern Greenland* Case, Ser. A/B 53 p. 46; ICJ: *Minquiers and Ecrehos* Case, Reports 1953 pp. 57, 60–67.
[143] See also the discussion in *Munkman* XLVI BYIL 1972–3 p. 1 *et seq* and esp. pp. 96–116; *Bardonnet* (Mélanges Reuter) p. 35 *et seq* and further *Koskenniemi* XVII Oikeustiede-Jurisprudentia 1984 pp. 142–148.
[144] *Guatemala-Honduras Boundary* Case, II UNRIAA p. 1352.
[145] *Rann of Kutch* Case, XVII UNRIAA p. 11.   [146] *Ibid.* pp. 569–570.
[147] ICJ: *Burkina Faso-Mali Frontier* Case, Reports 1986 pp. 567–568 (§ 28).

accordance with its own environmental policies; on the other hand, there is the victim's sole right to decide what acts shall take place in its territories.[148] The former's liberty to pursue economically beneficial uses of its territory is contrasted with the latter's liberty to enjoy a pure environment. The conflict is insoluble by simply preferring "liberty". Balancing seems inevitable in order to reach a decision.[149]

The law regarding the uses of international watercourses is based on a principle of "equitable utilization", enshrined in the International Law Association's Helsinki Rules of 1966, a resolution by the Institute of International Law of 1979 and in the ILC project on non-navigational uses of international watercourses.[150] The law concerning fishery

---

[148] See e.g. Principle 21 of the Stockholm Declaration, UN Conference on the Human Environment, Stockholm 5–16 June 1972, UN Doc. A/CONF.48/14.

[149] The project of the ILC concerning "liability for the harmful effects of activities not prohibited by international law" provides an illustration. The very definition of this item by the ILC locates it in that realm of the law where there exist no prohibitory rules (i.e. where responsibility as a consequence of the wrongfulness of the act is not triggered). In the absence of prohibiting rules, however, the question arises *on what basis liability would follow?* The answer given by both Special Rapporteurs (and indeed, the only possible answer) refers, 1) to the need to create procedures ("regimes") which the States involved could use to settle their conflict (duty to cooperate and negotiate in order to reach agreements); and 2) to equity and the need to "balance" the interests of the source-State and the affected State. Whatever content "liability" is to have shall be determined in an equitable evaluation. See, in particular the "Schematic Outline" in *Quentin-Baxter*, Third Report, YILC 1982, vol. II/I. pp. 62–64. The material rule in this "twilight zone" of non-prohibited but injurious activities is always an equitable construction. Having reviewed the balancing standard in the practice of the ICJ, the Special Rapporteur concludes: "The equitable principle can be seen to operate . . . in circumstances in which wrongfulness is precluded", *idem* First Report, YILC 1980, vol. II/I p. 261 and generally pp. 156–162. On the balancing standard, see further *idem* Second Report, YILC 1981, vol. II/I p. 112 *et seq*, and section 6 of the Schematic Outline, *supra*. See further *infra* ch. 7 n.101.
   The typical case here concerns a State's obligations regarding transfrontier pollution. In the absence of specific duties, the content of these obligations seems determinable only through an equitable evaluation. See e.g. *Koskenniemi* XVII Oikeustiede-Jurisprudentia 1984 pp. 152–164; *Lammers* RCADI Coll. 1984 pp. 153–165; *Handl*, XVI Neth.YBIL 1985 pp. 68, 76–77; *Goldie ibid.* pp. 175, 204–238.

[150] For the centrality of equity in water resource law, see ILA: Report of the 52nd Conference, Helsinki 1966 pp. 486–494 ("Helsinki Rules"). See further, ILA: Report of the 58th Conference, Manila 1978 pp. 222, 228. See also Report by *Salmon* to the Institut de Droit International, Annuaire 1979-I pp. 201–210 and esp. pp. 202–203 (on the *sic utere* and abuse of rights principles). The principle of equitableness lies also at the core of the ILC project on the Non-navigational Uses of International Watercourses. See, in particular, *Schwebel*: Third Report, YILC 1982, vol. II/I pp. 75–110 (Draft Articles 6–8 and esp. pp. 82–85 (state of doctrine on equity). See further *Evensen*: First Report, YILC 1983, vol. II/I pp. 169–174 (Draft Articles 6–9); *idem* Second Report,

resources amounts to little else than a general statement to the effect that a coastal State's "preferential rights" must be balanced against the "historic rights" of other States. Neither right (liberty) is given absolute preference but reconciliation is looked for.[151] In the *Fisheries Jurisdiction Case* (1974), the Court noted that adjustment between the two sets of rights was to be made "in as equitable manner as possible."[152] Nationalisation of foreign property provides a further example. The law regarding compensation for the taking of alien property, in particular concessionary rights, has developed into the direction of equitable, or "just" compensation in an effort to balance the interests of the nationalizing State and the home State.[153]

YILC 1984, vol. II/I pp. 110–112 (Draft Articles 6–9). For a review and further references, see *Koskenniemi* XVII Oikeustiede-Jurisprudentia 1984 pp. 153–156.

[151] See ICJ: *Fisheries Jurisdiction* Case, Reports 1974 pp. 24–27 (§§ 55–60), 28–29 (§§ 63–67). The Court noted that "in order to reach an equitable solution ... it is necessary that the preferential fishing rights of Iceland ... be reconciled with the traditional fishing rights of the Applicant", p. 30 (§ 69).

[152] *Ibid.* p. 30 (§ 70).

[153] Such balancing is best evidenced in the law concerning compensation for expropriation. On the one hand, nationalization is generally held lawful. But there must be "appropriate compensation". Thus, in the *Libyan American Oil Company (LIAMCO) v. the Government of the Libyan Arab Republic*, XX ILM 1980, the Arbitrator reviewed the status of the "prompt, adequate and effective compensation" rule and concluded that such compensation was "no more imperative" and that it had been replaced by the need for "convenient and equitable compensation". This, he noted, was justified by "taking into consideration not only the interests of the owner of the property nationalized, but also those of the Society ... and of the nationalizing State", p. 74 (§ 145) – a balancing standard. He noted, however, that no definitive rule had emerged. It was therefore necessary to have regard to "general principles". The applicable principle in this case was – equity. The inferred rule (or non-rule) was that of "equitable compensation", pp. 76–77 (§§ 150–151). In the *Dispute between the Government of Kuwait and the American Independent Oil Co. (AMINOIL)*, 66 ILR 1984, again, the Tribunal first observed that the law applicable to compensation could not be determined by "abstract theoretical discussion". It had to be determined contextually, p. 602 (§§ 144–145). This led it to give effect to a principle of "effective compensation" – one which "would not make nonsense of foreign investment", pp. 602–603 (§§ 146–147). It noted that its task was to assess a "contractual equilibrium", pp. 603, 607 (§§ 148–149, 159). It thus rejected the claimant's view about full profit until the concession would have ended and the plaintiffs view about "net book value", opting for a middle – a "reasonable rate of return", pp. 607–609 (§§ 160–164). Of course, the (perhaps now majority) view that compensation must be "appropriate" (or "just", "equitable"), rather than "prompt, adequate and effective", is precisely a balancing standard – a rule the content of which depends on the circumstances. See further *Schachter* 178 RCADI 1982/V pp. 323–326; *Pellonpää* 3 KOIG 1986 pp. 334 *et seq*, 361–363. See, however, also the *Dispute between Texaco Overseas Petroleum Company/California Asiatic Oil Company v. the Government of the Libyan Arab Republic*, XVII ILM 1978 (for *restitutio in integrum*) pp. 32–36 (§§ 97–109). The

Even the seemingly clear-cut norm against external intervention turns
out to require balancing. Waldock observes, in a classic formulation,
that intervention might be lawful in case of immediate threat of injury,
failure by the territorial sovereign to protect the interests of other States
and the intervention is limited strictly to achieving such protection.[154]
The formulation manifests an effort to achieve a balance between more
and less important State interests. If there is no natural meaning to
sovereignty, then its counterpart – intervention – is capable of determination only through such a contextual test. The same is true of the
Webster formulation of the extent of the right of self-defence which
places an evaluation of proportionality and urgency at the heart of the
law.[155] The obvious problem is that a system which regards evaluation
"subjective" seems incapable of making justifiable criticisms of the
views States themselves have taken on the admissibility of intervention
or self-defence in some actual circumstance.[156]

The applicability of the Lotus principle seems now quite thin indeed.
Applying it would seem manifestly unjust as it takes account only of the

defendant ignored the Award. For the element of equity in compensation cases, see
also *Zoller* (Bonne foi) pp. 242–243. The case of extraterritorial jurisdiction is similar.
Here, two States' subjective freedoms clash and legal practice can only resort to some
balancing of interests test – a solution which is vulnerable to the standard criticism
against equity that it creates a "vague system, operated by inappropriate tribunals, with
unpredictable results", *Lowe* 34 ICLQ 1985 pp. 730–731. See further *infra* ch. 7 n. 44.
For the view that inter-sovereign conflict in antitrust cases, too, must be solved by an
evaluation of the interests at stake, see *Meessen* 78 AJIL 1984 pp. 783 *et seq*, 802–810.

[154] *Waldock* 81 RCADI 1952/II p. 467.

[155] Indeed, a rule which calls for an evaluation of proportionality – like the rule about
equity in general – rather *poses* the problem than solves it. An assessment of "proportionality" involves highly controversial evaluations about the admissibility of defensive action in anticipation of an attack, about how personal and material losses should
be "counted", whether the victim's own behaviour should be taken into account,
whether there might have been a justifying cause (aiding a minority which fights for
self-determination, for example) and so on. That these are complex issues which can
hardly be decided without taking reasoned *moral* positions is evident if one reads, for
example, the appropriate chapter in *Hoffmann* (Duties) pp. 55–85. See also *Navari*
(Mayall: Community) p. 24. For a recent discussion, see *Schachter* 178 RCADI 1982/V
pp. 133–166. On the *Caroline* Case and the formulation of the conditions for
self-defence therein, see *Bowett* (Self-defence) pp. 58–60 and *passim*. Discussing
humanitarian intervention in relation to self-defence under Article 51 of the UN
Charter *Higgins* (Bull: Intervention) concludes that leading cases seem always to
refer to "... a contextual case-by-case appraisal of all the circumstances", p. 38.

[156] The problem is not, as some appear to think, that there is no third-party determination
of these matters. See e.g. *Jessup* (Modern) pp. 164–169, 196 *et seq*. The problem is that
there are no specifically legal criteria which would be determining.

liberty of one of the States concerned. As McNair points out, discussing the Lotus principle in the interpretation of contractual provisions:

> ... it reduces the reciprocal benefit ... due to the other Party, also a sovereign State, which seems to me to be absurd.[157]

Indeed, if we apply the rule set out by the ICJ in the *Asylum* Case, according to which the party which relies on a customary rule must prove its existence[158] so as to be in harmony with the Lotus principle, we notice the absurdity. For surely, if conventional norms or general principles are lacking, then *both* parties rely on custom, one on a prohibitory, the other on a permissory rule. If it were always the former who would bear the burden of showing the existence of the rule (an idea containing an implicit acceptance of the Lotus principle), then the outcome of the dispute would be substantially dependent on the way in which a party can manipulate itself in the position of the defendant, as arguably illustrated by the *Anglo-Norwegian Fisheries* Case.[159]

Much judicial practice supports the constructivist approach. A State's rights and duties are not determined by abstract presumptions based on sovereignty but by "balancing the equities". It is not sovereignty which

---

[157] McNair (Treaties) p. 765; Iran-US Claims Tribunal: *Case A/1*, 68 ILR 1985 p. 537. Similarly *Salmon* (Perelman: Problème) p. 317. For a discussion of the opposition between the "restrictive" (that is, incorporating the Lotus principle) and "liberal" (equitable) interpretation of treaty provisions in municipal practice and in the *travaux préparatoires* of the Vienna Convention on the Law of Treaties and the inconclusive character of doctrine and practice in this respect, see *Schreuer* XLV BYIL 1971 pp. 282–301.

That a requirement of balancing follows from sovereign equality is also usefully discussed in *Barboza*, Second Report on International Liability for Injurious Consequences arising out of Acts not prohibited by International Law, UN Doc. A/CN.4/402 (16 May 1986), pp. 26–27 (§§ 52–54). See also Draft Article 6 (Freedom of Action) and comment in *idem*, Fourth Report, A/CN.4/413 (6 April 1988) pp. 8 and 32–33 (§§ 92–95).

[158] ICJ: *Asylum* Case, Reports 1950 pp. 276–277. See also comment in *Baxter* XLI BYIL 1965–66 pp. 296–297; *Marek* VI RBDI 1970 p. 63; *Brownlie* (Principles) pp. 6–7.

[159] *Fitzmaurice* XXX BYIL 1953 pp. 12–13. The Parties argued at length about the correct position of the burden of proof. See ICJ: *Anglo-Norwegian Fisheries* Case, Pleadings I (Memorial of the United Kingdom: the Party relying on historic right must prove its existence) pp. 94–97, *ibid.* (Counter-Memorial of Norway: the one who relies on prohibitory custom must prove its existence) pp. 378–379. It is submitted that the Court avoided discussing this question because of the plausibility of the Parties' alternative descriptions of what was in issue. Establishing a priority between the rules would have meant establishing a priority between these descriptions, the perspectives from which the two States looked at the matter.

determines the extent of a State's legal rights, liberties and competences – it is the latter which determine the extent of its sovereignty. But if this is so and if the law constantly refers us to look for a contextual equity (either by an express rule or an interpretative principle), then we must assume that equity overrides and delimits State liberty, that there exists a general principle which obliges States to take reasonable regard of others, that:

> Any conflict between the opposing rights of two States is to be settled on the basis of reasonable adjustment or compromise.[160]

This, of course, takes us quite far from what was expressed as the identity of the judicial process – applying rules in an objective way. For, as Reuter writes:

> ... il y'a toujours plusieurs équités possible et chacune d'entre elles est soustendue par une conception politico-philosophique différente.[161]

If State freedoms can be delimited by evaluative balancing, then this initial scepticism about the objectivity of values was either mistaken or we have simply renounced the identity of the legal process in favour of making political compromises.

The constructivist approach cannot be consistently held as it fails to explain how the established balance – the judge's conception of equity – can be opposed to a State not accepting it. It is ultimately just another version of the utopian position, assuming the objectivity of a natural morality. If inter-sovereign conflict is dealt with by rules which refer further to reasonableness, equity, proportionality and the like, then, as Philip Allott writes,

> ... the specifically legal character of the law would have ceased to exist. All would have become politics.[162]

---

[160] *Stowell* (International Law) pp. 123 and generally 122–130. Indeed, such an extension of compromise, or equity *infra legem* into any conflict where clear-cut legal rules are lacking has been increasingly suggested. Thus, in the *Decision of the ICSID ad hoc Committee Setting aside the Award Rendered on the Merits in the Arbitration between AMCO Asia Corp et al. and Indonesia*, XXV ILM 1986 it was suggested that recourse to "equitable principles" by the ICJ in maritime delimitations was not a course open only in such cases and that there would be no question of an *ex aequo et bono* judgement – and consequently any *ultra vires* decision – if such principles were used to determine compensation, for instance, p. 10 (§§ 27–28). See further e.g. *Schachter* 178 RCADI 1982/V pp. 82–90.

[161] *Reuter* XV RBDI 1980–1 p. 179.

[162] *Allott* XLV BYIL 1971 p. 127. The same point is made by *Bourquin* 64 RCADI 1938/II (application of equity is to go beyond objective law and to "legislate" for the parties)

The same consequence follows from suggestions to delimit conflicting sovereignties by reference to a principle of good faith or abuse of rights. Either such concepts refer to the subjective, mental states of the acting organs – in which case they cannot be normatively controlling because we cannot assume to know these states better than those organs themselves – or they refer to a non-subjective thery of justice – a theory which conflicts with the principle of the subjectivity of value.[163] To this extent statements such as "responsibility is the necessary corollary of right"[164] appear as healthy admissions that constraining rules cannot be constructed simply from an initial liberty. But they fail to give direction as to how this could be done.

If we wish to stay within modern discourse – that is, if we continue to deny the existence of natural justice – the crucial question we shall face will be this: What basis is there to impose a balance, some conception of equity, "reasonableness" or good faith, on a State which has not accepted it? To argue that it is binding because *other* States have accepted it fails to explain why a State should be bound by other States' subjective values. This is manifestly contrary to its sovereign equality.[165] From the perspective of the State against which the balance is invoked this seems an attempt to impose others' political views on it.[166] As we have seen, modern doctrine attempts to avoid this by appealing to an impersonal

---

pp. 422–423. Similarly *Scelle* 46 RCADI 1933/IV pp. 566–567. See also *Akehurst* 25 ICLQ 1976 p. 811.

[163] For the suggestion of good faith as the constraining principle (noting, however, the difficulties of verification), see e.g. *Gounelle* (Motivation) pp. 192–222. See also *Revere Copper v. OPIC* (Arbitration Tribunal, 24 August 1978) 56 ILR 1980 pp. 279–284. For a critical view see *Zoller* (Bonne foi). For her, good faith either refers to a state of mind or a moral principle. In both cases it is objectively unverifiable, pp. 335–354 and *passim*.

For the suggestion of "abuse of right" as a controlling rule, see e.g. *Politis* 6 RCADI 1925/I pp. 77–109; *Lauterpacht* (Function) pp. 286–306; *Jacqué* (Elements) pp. 171–176; *Zoller* (Bonne foi) (a critical view) pp. 96 *et seq*, 109–122. For criticism, see also *Koskenniemi* XVII Oikeustiede-Jurisprudentia 1984 pp. 113–116.

[164] ICJ: *Barcelona Traction* Case, Reports 1970 p. 33 (§ 36). The same principle has been much belaboured in respect of international environmental conflict in which it has essentially led to an attempt to search for the equitable solution. See *supra* n. 149.

[165] For the argument that liberties cannot be preferred *vis-à-vis* each other because this would contradict with sovereign equality, see *Schwarzenberger* (Dynamics) p. 72; *Kooijmans* (Equality) p. 126 *et seq*.

[166] Thus, it was argued by Judge *McNair* in the *Anglo-Norwegian Fisheries* Case that: "... the manipulation of the limits of territorial waters for the purpose of protecting economic and social interests finds no justification in law," diss. op., Reports 1951 p. 169. Similarly, Degan (l'Equité): "Il ne fait aucun doute que ce raisonnement de la Cour n'est pas purement juridique" p. 225.

systemic value. But this is merely another version of the (utopian) position which accepts that some norms are valid irrespective of anybody's acceptance. Not surprisingly, many international lawyers have objected against the growing practice by international tribunals to use "equitable principles" because those principles seem so subjective and political.[167] Reference to them (or reasonableness, good faith etc.) has only restated the problem of justice which it was the task of formal rules to dispose of. It has seemed, as Judge Oda writes, to "suggest the principle of non-principle".[168]

To conclude: modern discourse about sovereignty shifts constantly between a pure fact and a legal approach. When the positions are traced to their logical conclusion, they will show themselves in conflict with their constitutive assumptions. At that point, argument will try to rescue itself by relying on the opposite approach. The pure fact view will justify itself as a legal one: State sovereignty is given preference because the law says so. The legal approach will ultimately find that the systemic value which provides the law's coherence is the liberty of the State.

Sovereignty discourse silently *changes the meanings it gives to objectivity and subjectivity*. The legal view claimed to be better than the pure

---

[167] This concerns especially its delimitation practice. See e.g. *Gros*, diss. op. ICJ: *Tunisia–Libya Continental Shelf* Case, Reports 1982 pp. 147–156; *idem*, diss. op. ICJ: *Gulf of Maine* Case, Reports 1984 (arguing that the search for equity allocates a new function to the judge "as freed from the positive law it is charged to apply") p. 388; *Ruda, Bedjaoui, Aréchaga*, joint sep. op. ICJ: *Libya–Malta Continental Shelf* Case, Reports 1985 (pointing out the "pretorian subjectivism" in delimitation by equity) pp. 90–91; *Oda*, diss. op. *ibid.* (deploring the subjectivism in the Court's search for equity) pp. 125, 159. See also *Pirotte* LXXVII RGDIP 1973 pp. 130–133; *Bowett* XLIX BYIL 1978 (criticism of the effect of equity on the predictability of the law – with reference to the *Anglo-French Continental Shelf* Case) pp. 13–14 *et seq*; *Charney* 78 AJIL 1984 (a review of criticisms) pp. 589–591; *Rosenne* (Festschrift Bindschedler) (noting that "very frequently" a reference to equitable principles contains no "*real* substantive rule of law") pp. 407–425.

   Of course, the Court itself has argued that its equity is not really the kind of "subjective equity" – "a matter of abstract justice" – which it thought was entailed by the German argument about "equitable shares" in the *North Sea Continental Shelf* Cases. It has made the distinction between equity *ex aequo et bono* and equity *infra legem* and assumed that it has kept itself well within the boundaries of the latter, Reports 1969 p. 48 (§ 88). See also *supra* n. 128 and the discussion in *Koskenniemi* XVII 1984 pp. 134–136.

[168] *Oda*, diss. op. ICJ: *Tunisia–Libya Continental Shelf* Case, Reports 1982 p. 157. Similarly, *Tanaka*, diss. op. ICJ: *North Sea Continental Shelf* Cases, Reports 1969 pp. 195–196.

fact view because it was more objective than this. It was more objective because the view that States had an initial freedom led into apologism. To think that the law precedes the State, however, will ultimately lead to the assumption that values are objective. As the legal approach cannot hold such a position it maintains that the relevant sovereignty-determining standards are valid because accepted by States themselves. But this entails assuming that subjective acceptance has a validity and an objectivity which natural morality lacks. It is now the State's initial freedom to accept or reject norms which grounds the objectivity of the legal approach – the very assumption against which it constituted itself.

A reverse shift takes place in the pure fact argument. For it, originally, the legal approach seemed subjective as this did not base itself on the objective fact of a State's existence as a centre of effective authority. But to justify itself, the pure fact view will ultimately have to assume the existence of a set of criteria for legitimate authority which are external to the pure fact of effectiveness. It will have to rely on an antecedent conceptual system which tells which facts are legally relevant and which are not. These criteria come to form the normative system which now overrides statehood and delimits the State's sovereign sphere.

Both approaches, while originally exclusive, lose their identity during argument and come to rely on each other – indeed, start to appear indistinguishable. The structure of modern discourse about sovereignty is provided by the continuous re-affirmation of the initial opposition between the two views and its gradual dissolution during argument. Lawyers commonly argue about the limits of sovereignty as if they assumed the existence of objective values. They ground their propositions on equity, "peace and stability", economic efficiency, vital interests etc. They assume that liberties can be limited objectively, by recourse to such ideas. But they remain at a loss in respect of the justification of such objectivities and ultimately justify them by subjective acceptance – behind which looms the metavalue of liberty. And lawyers argue about sovereignty as the need to honour the State's subjective consent, domestic jurisdiction or self-determination. To justify this, they appeal to the law which, they assume, contains these within itself and thus remains anterior to them.

In the following sections I shall attempt to show how this discursive structure leads to the impossibility of justifying, in a determinate manner, solutions to disputes about sovereignty. Instead, discourse has developed "strategies of evasion" which make it seem as if decisions could be justified without taking a stand on the relative superiority of the legal and pure fact approaches. These strategies, however, use projections and interpretations which cannot ultimately be justified within modern assumptions about legal objectivity.

4.6   Example: statehood and recognition

The structure of argument created by the opposition of the two approaches to sovereignty may be illustrated by reference to the doctrinal disagreement on whether the creation of States is a "factual" or a "legal" occurrence and whether recognition is "declaratory" or "constitutive".[169] None of the positions can be consistently held. Although they at first seem contradictory, they lose this contradictory character during argument and come to rely on each other in a way which makes preferring either one impossible. As standard disputes about statehood and recognition organize themselves by assuming a contrast between these positions, such disputes become insoluble.

According to the pure fact view, the emergence of the State is an extralegal, sociological event which is not controlled by the legal order but is something externally given to it.[170] Those who have taken this view support it regularly by an interpretation of diplomatic history. Surely, they argue, most States have emerged through political and military struggles, factual concentrations of power and consolidation of Government. To say that States such as France, the United Kingdom or Sweden, for example, were created in some legally controlled process would seem a curious position. What we have witnessed are sociological processes which sometimes direct themselves against prevailing legal structures. That an entity starts to behave and becomes treated like a

---

[169] For general reviews of this classical and all-but-resolved debate, see e.g. *Kunz* (Anerkennung) pp. 65–84; *Strupp* 47 RCADI 1934/I pp. 425–442; *Chen* (Recognition) pp. 13–17; *Bindschedler* 9 Arch.VR 1961–62 pp. 385–394; *Charpentier* (Reconnaissance) pp. 190–200; *Blix* 130 RCADI 1970 /II pp. 603–610; *Crawford* (Creation) pp. 16–25; *idem* XLVIII BYIL 1976–77 pp. 95–107; *Brownlie* (Principles) pp. 91–93; *Gilson* (Sovereign Equality) pp. 196–201. My analysis here is inspired by *Kennedy* (Structures) pp. 129–151.

[170] As *Chen* (Recognition) puts the point: "The source of rights and duties of an entity in international law is the fact of its actual supremacy within a specified area of territory ... This fact is the basis of international law" p. 3. Because the law emerges from the State, it would be illogical to think of the emergence of States as a legally regulated process. See also *Jellinek* (Allgemeine) pp. 270–283.

State is a political process and not something created or controlled by the law.[171]

Clearly, such argument supports a declaratory view on the effects of recognition. A State's emergence is a factual event. The legal significance of recognition becomes marginal; its sense is to establish a formal basis for the relations between the recognized and recognizing States.[172] But admission to statehood and the acquisition of the rights and duties which follow from it are independent of recognition.

On reflection, however, this position seems untenable because too subjective. Consider de Lapradelle's position in the *Nationality Decrees Case* (1923):

> ... la question de la formation de l'Etat est-elle la question fondamentale du droit international. Mais comment la régle-t-il? En laissant à l'Etat le soin de s'organiser lui-même: à lui de décider comment il se forme, et se recrute: à lui de créer sa propre substance, puis de la développer; à lui de promulguer, par la jeu de sa puissance et dans l'étendue de cette puissance, les lois qui sont celles de sa croissance et, par suite, de sa vie.[173]

This view sets the entity's own subjective power and will to exist as a State before any act of recognizing it as a State by the legal order. But it looks apologist in its reliance on the self-assessment of the entity itself. Surely, even if the process which leads to the establishment of the State may be a sociological one, it cannot be wholly dependent on what the emergent entity does and how it itself views what it is doing. The cases of Hyderabad and Rhodesia, among others, testify to the effect that whether an entity is a State or not cannot be a simple matter of the entity's self-definition but that this definition, in order to create legal consequences, must correspond to some external criteria. Other States could hardly be expected to accept the

---

[171] See e.g. *Corbett* (Law and Society) p. 63; *Strupp* 47 RCADI 1934/I pp. 425–426; *Briggs* 43 AJIL 1949 pp. 115–117; De *Visscher* (Theory) pp. 103–104; *Lansing* (Notes) pp. 11–13; *Cavaré* (Droit international I) pp. 342–349; *Barile* 161 RCADI 1978/III pp. 26–27, 30; *Anand* 197 RCADI 1986/II p. 22; *Carty* (Decay) (defending his view that international law is not a "complete system") p. 57 and *passim*.

[172] See e.g. *Kato* 10 IJIL 1970 pp. 305–307, 322–323; *Bindschedler* 9 Arch.VR 1961–62 pp. 389, 393–394; *Ross* (Text-book) pp. 114–116; *Erich* 13 RCADI pp. 30–38; *François* 66 RCADI 1938/IV pp. 72–74; *Rolin* 77 RCADI 1950/II pp. 327–328: *Blix* 130 RCADI 1970/II pp. 609–610; *Briggs* 43 AJIL 1949 pp. 113–121; *Hingorani* (Modern) pp. 96–97. *Chen* (Recognition) affirms the minimal international importance of recognition under this view. Its sole significance is relative to national courts, p. 7.

[173] *Lapradelle*, PCIJ: *Nationality Decrees* Case, Ser. C 2 p. 83. *Jellinek* (Allgemeine) summarizes: "Der Staat ist Staat kraft seines inneren Wesens", p. 273.

entity's self-definition. Its statehood must manifest itself by reference to an external – and in this sense non-subjective – set of criteria for statehood.

The factual approach must rely on a legal approach concerning the existence of a set of criteria which pre-exist the sociological process and determine the sense and consequences of that process. The criteria for statehood – territory, people, Government, capacity to enter into relations with other States[174] – need to be regarded as constitutive of statehood. They form the normative code which regulates the attainment of statehood. This has made it possible for many legal approach lawyers, such as the naturalist Bluntschli[175] or the positivist Kelsen[176] to endorse the declaratory view of recognition while still attaching constitutive effects to the rule which provides for the criteria of statehood. A purely declaratory view seems to "confuse" facts with law.[177] Facts alone are powerless to create law. For facts to have significance an anterior legal system must be assumed to exist which invests facts with normative sense.[178]

But this "declaratory-constitutive" view, too, creates difficulties. In the first place, it has to explain the status of the rule providing the criteria for statehood. If this rule precedes any individual State then it looks like a rule of natural law. A justifiable rule about statehood needs to have some relation to subjective acceptance by States.[179] We might argue, for instance, that any present criteria have emerged through a political, legislative act by the existing States while the creation of the first State(s) remains a matter of fact, only.

---

[174] For these criteria, see e.g. *Kunz* (Anerkennung) p. 15; *Kelsen* (Principles) p. 388; *Brierly* (Law of Nations) p. 137; *Corbett* (Law and Society) p. 61; *Blix* 130 RCADI 1970/II pp. 622, 632–638. *Crawford* (Creation) interprets the traditional criteria so that they *all* aim to prove the factual effectiveness of the entity, pp. 31–76.

[175] *Bluntschli* (Völkerrecht) p. 71. For the association of the declaratory position with naturalist theories of self-determination, see also *Chen* (Recognition) pp. 18–19; *Blix* 130 RCADI 1970/II pp. 609–610.

[176] *Kelsen* 14 RCADI 1926/IV pp. 309–310. See also *Fitzmaurice* IIL 1973 p. 216; *Kunz* (Anerkennung) holds that while recognition is declaratory in respect of the "membership" of the State in the international community, it is constitutive in respect of the relations between the recognizing and recognized States, pp. 80, 86, 88.

[177] *Kelsen* 42 RCADI 1932/IV pp. 260–266; *idem* (Principles) pp. 420–421; *Tucker* (Lipsky: Law and Politics) pp. 31–48. See also *Lauterpacht* (Recognition) pp. 45–51; *Ago* 51 AJIL 1957 pp. 702–703. Later, in fact, *Kelsen* labelled his view "constitutive" – in the sense that he held the law to "constitute" the state (Principles) p. 394. On this apparent change of position, see also *Gilson* (Sovereign Equality) pp. 203–206; *Kunz* 44 AJIL 1950 pp. 713–714.

[178] *Crawford* XLVIII BYIL 1976–77 p. 95.

[179] See also *Kelsen* 14 RCADI 1926/IV pp. 309–310; *idem* 42 RCADI 1932/IV p. 182 *et seq.*

Secondly, facts do not, as it were, automatically compare themselves with the rule containing the criteria for statehood. To hold otherwise would be to accept the naturalistic view that perception is "pure" in the sense of being unrelated to what I have called conceptual matrices.[180] But there is always an amount of theory, or construction, involved in the perception of facts. Similarly, to compare facts with some criteria about them is possible only through the comparing person's conceptual matrix which, in this sense, has a constitutive effect on whether correspondence is perceived or not.[181]

Thirdly, even if facts were objective in the sense discussed, they could hardly be allowed to impose themselves on an existing State in the way the declaratory theory assumes. For the emergence of States entails the creation of new duties on the old States. To hold that these States can be opposed with duties which they have never consented to would violate *their* initial liberty as well as their equality *vis-à-vis* the new State whose subjective power would now determine their duties.[182]

For these reasons, the pure fact view needs to be rejected and with it the declaratory theory. It is ultimately based on unacceptable assumptions about the overriding normative force of the new entity or of the objectivity of "facts". Doctrine seems compelled to move towards the legal approach and a (pure) constitutive theory about the effects of recognition. It needs to assume that a State's emergence is controlled by the legal order as represented by the existing States.[183]

The legal approach – the idea that law is anterior to statehood – may equally well be supported by reference to diplomatic history.[184] For it does not seem to be the case that simply by attaining some actual

---

[180] Thus *Scelle* 46 RCADI 1934/IV, a "declarativist", must insist on the cognitive character of recognition as a "pur constatation" of fact – an "acte juridictionnel", pp. 387, 388. But it seems doubtful whether we have reason to rely on such "purity of perception". The point against declaratory theory's "automatic test of existence" is made by *Lauterpacht* (Recognition) pp. 48–51. *Anzilotti* (Cours, I) connects the "automatic" test with indefensible naturalism, pp. 163–164.

[181] As *Kelsen* (Principles) puts it: "In the realm of law, there is no fact 'in itself', no immediately evident fact; there are only facts ascertained by the competent authorities in a procedure determined by law", p. 388. *Wright* 44 AJIL 1950 captures this insight in the following: "Recognition is in principle declaratory but in practice constitutive", p. 557.

[182] This is, arguably, *Oppenheim*'s (International Law, I) reason for his espousal of the constitutive view, p. 117. See also *Anzilotti* (Cours, I) pp. 163–164.

[183] For the constitutive position generally, see *Oppenheim* (International Law, I) pp. 116–121; *Cavaglieri* 26 RCADI 1929/I pp. 351–353.

[184] See e.g. *Verdross* (Verfassung) pp. 131–137; *Kunz* (Anerkennung) pp. 88–89.

degree of effectiveness an entity would have *ipso facto* been considered
a State.[185] Communities which have lacked the actual effectiveness
normally connected with statehood have been regarded as States
(Monaco, Tuvalu, The Holy See etc.) while communities with much
greater effectiveness have been denied it (Rhodesia, Transkei, Taiwan).[186]

Much practice seems to support the view that statehood is independent of any fixed set of factual criteria. Many States have, for example,
been forced to accept important restrictions to their legislative powers,
even against their will, without thereby having lost their character as
sovereign States in the eyes of other States.[187] Sometimes the preservation of sovereign statehood has been linked to the mere absence of
will by a *de facto* occupying power to annex the territory in question.[188]
Nor has the exercise of administrative – even "supreme" – powers
by a foreign State or lack of effective authority altogether been
thought to involve loss of sovereign statehood.[189] Finally, examples are
not lacking of situations where the attainment of independence has

---

[185] The argument of the historical character of notions of statehood is presented against
the pure fact view by *Hart* (Concept) pp. 216–217; *Brierly* (Basis of Obligation) p. 125.

[186] See generally *Crawford* (Creation) pp. 103–106, 149–169, 225–227; *James* (Sovereign
Statehood) gives several examples of the differences in factual effectiveness in entities
considered "States" and argues that the sole test of statehood can be a "legal" one –
namely the test of constitutional dependence, pp. 39–45, 99–130 and *passim*.

[187] A classical example being the system of Minorities Treaties, established on the basis of
Article 256 of the Versailles Peace Treaty. Under this system, and more specifically
Article 93 of the Versailles Treaty, Poland, for example, was held bound to honour the
principle of equality of all Polish citizens. See generally, PCIJ: *German Settlers in
Poland* Case, Ser. B 6 pp. 19–21, 36–37.

[188] For example, the complete collapse of effective Government in Germany by 5 June
1945 was not taken to mean the dissolution of Germany as a sovereign State as the
Allied powers had not expressed their wish to annex it. For discussion, see e.g.
Crawford (Creation) pp. 274–275; *Jennings* XXIII BYIL 1946 pp. 113–114; *O'Connell*
(International Law, I) pp. 441–442; *Fawcett* (Law and Power) p. 19. See also *Korovin* 40
AJIL 1946 p. 744. The idea that absence of will to annex will suffice to prevent transfer
of sovereignty from the vanquished to the victor State follows also from the principle
according to which the *establishment* of sovereignty requires the presence of an *animus*
to that effect, see PCIJ: *Eastern Greenland* Case, Ser. A/B 53 pp. 45–46.

[189] There is an abundance of case-law on this. See e.g. PCIJ: *Wimbledon* Case, Ser. A 1
p. 25; *Exchange of Greek and Turkish Populations* Case, Ser. B 10 p. 21. In the
Lighthouses of Crete and Samos Case, the PCIJ held Turkey to possess sovereignty
over the islands despite the "theoretical" character of its control over them, Ser. A/B 71
p. 103 and the criticism by *Hurst*, diss. op. *ibid.* p. 127. See also ICJ: *Status of South West
Africa* Case, Reports 1950 p. 132; *US Nationals in Morocco* Case, Reports 1952 pp. 185,
188 and *James* (Sovereign Statehood) pp. 100–104; *Crawford* (Creation) pp. 186–214.
See also e.g. *Whiteman* (Digest, I) pp. 248–251. In some cases, such as Burma in late
1970s and contemporary Lebanon, complete absence of effective Government has not

taken the character of a legal transaction or been otherwise controlled by a community process, for example, United Nations' decolonization policy.[190] Recent attempts to reinvigorate the time-honoured practice of non-recognition of illegally created title speaks in favour of a legal, constitutive view of recognition.[191] However, this view, too, turns out to be unacceptable as too political.

The standard view does not accept a duty to recognize.[192] The "political" nature or recognition can also be inferred from the inability to

been taken to involve loss of statehood. For discussion, see *James* (Sovereign Statehood) pp. 123–129. For such doubtful cases as those of Danzig, Cyprus, Guinea-Bissau and some other mini-States, see *Crawford* (Creation) pp. 163–169, 188–194; *James* (Sovereign Statehood) pp. 53–71, 99–130, 142–160, 188–194, 238–246. For cases where administration and sovereignty are separate, see also *Whiteman* (Digest, II) pp. 1104–1111. For the point that sovereignty may be "qualified", see e.g. *Aliq v. Trust Territory of the Pacific Islands* (US High Court, Appellate Div. 24 Nov. 1967) 61 ILR 1981 pp. 89 *et seq*, 96, 99.

[190] Thus, States emerging from the Vienna Conference of 1815 or through such contractual arrangements as the Versailles Peace Treaty, seem to be constituted through a "legal process". See also the Austrian State Treaty of 1955, 217 UNTS p. 223. On this point further, see *Crawford* (Creation) pp. 310–311; *Blix* 130 RCADI 1970/II pp. 605–606. See also *Dugard* (Recognition) (reviewing the collective recognition practice in the League and the UN) pp. 14–24, 41–80.

[191] On the UN policy of non-recognition in respect of Rhodesia, see UNGA Res. 2024 (XX) 11 November 1965 and SC Res. 216, 217, 12 November 1965, 232, 16 December 1966 and 253, 29 May 1968. For discussion, see *Fawcett* (Law and Power) pp. 19–20, 92–103; *Okeke* (Controversial Subjects) pp. 104–105. On this policy *vis-à-vis* South Africa's Bantustan homelands (Transkei, Bophuthatswana, Venda, Ciskei), see e.g. UNGA Res. 344 D (XXX), 28 November 1975 and 32/105, 14 September 1977. See also SC Res. 402, 22 December 1976, 407, 25 May 1977. See also the Statement by the President of the Council in 1982 (Doc. S/14794). For these cases, see further *Dugard* (Recognition) pp. 90–108 and (on UN non-recognition of the Turkish republic of Northern Cyprus) pp. 108–111. On the different considerations of illegality which have affected this policy, see *James* (Sovereign Statehood) pp. 133–161. It is probably a majority view that no *duty* of non-recognition exists. This view has been somewhat challenged by the opinion in ICJ: *Namibia* Case, Reports 1971 pp. 51, 54 (§§ 112, 117, 119). See also UNGA Res. 42/22, 18 December 1987 (Declaration on the Enhancement of the Effectiveness of the Principle of Refraining from the Threat or Use of Force), operative para. 10 & Annex. See also *Crawford* (Creation), holding that there is a duty of non-recognition in respect of fundamental breaches, pp. 123–124. See also *Virally* 183 RCADI 1983/V pp. 56–57; *Dugard* (Recognition) pp. 135 *et seq*, 152–163. For a review of the history of the non-recognition doctrine (apart from the useful work by Dugard, *supra*), see *Bierzanek* VIII AFDI 1962 pp. 119–124 (containing also a criticism of the doctrine as contrary to the aim of peace and security), pp. 119–132; *Bindschedler* 9 Arch.VR 1961–62 pp. 391–393.

[192] *Oppenheim* (International Law, I) p. 118; *Charpentier* (Reconnaissance) pp. 291–294; *Bierzanek* VIII AFDI 1962 p. 130 (but see also pp. 131–132). See also the discussion of the change in US policy from a "right" to recognition to holding recognition

justify a naturalist view on the rule providing the criteria for statehood. But if recognition is constitutive and political,[193] then the system fails to protect the initial liberty and equality of the new entity, its right of self-determination. The entity's identity as a State becomes wholly dependent on the political views of old States. This would also threaten the Rule of Law. A situation would be created in which any emergent entity, however effectively in possession of territory, people and Government, could be considered a legal nothing by the non-recognizing States.[194] Each entity's status would become infinitely variable depending on whether a State has recognized it or not. It would lack coherent legal identity altogether.[195]

These are precisely the kind of difficulties for which the pure fact view and the declaratory theory were conceived in the first place. For the declarativists, 19th century European practice of admitting non-European states to the "community of civilized nations" was a form of political subjectivism which failed to do justice to the objective character and individuality of the non-European entities.[196] It failed to give effect to their liberty as persons similar to European States and equal in this sense with them. Most importantly, it failed to give effect to what had seemed like objective facts:

> To ignore such objective facts is to allow subjectivity to prevail over objective reality and thus to introduce a dangerous myth.[197]

essentially a "political" act, Corbett (Law and Society) pp. 68–78; Brownlie (Macdonald-Johnston: Structure and Process) pp. 637–638; Wright 44 AJIL 1950 pp. 556–557; Brown 44 AJIL 1950 pp. 620 et seq, 639–640; Coplin (Functions) pp. 58–60. See also Crawford (Creation) pp. 258–266.

[193] See especially Kato 10 IJIL 1970 pp. 305, 307–318 (a review of the "political" character of recognition).

[194] See Brierly (Law of Nations) pp. 138–139; Charpentier (Reconnaissance) pp. 193–194; Corbett (Law and Society) p. 61. See also Brownlie (Principles) p. 94.

[195] Kelsen (Principles) pp. 393–394; Bindschedler 9 Arch.VR 1961–62 p. 386; Erich 13 RCADI 1929/III pp. 34–35; Blix 130 RCADI 1970/II p. 608; Briggs 43 AJIL 1949 pp. 117–119. Charpentier (Recognition) p. 203 et seq, and Cheng (Macdonald-Johnston: Structure and Process) pp. 516–518 see no difficulty in this consequence; for them, the "voluntary" character of the international society makes this "relativist" conclusion inevitable.

[196] Kato 10 IJIL 1970 pp. 320–321. Chen (Recognition) deplores what he calls the "Machiavellian" consequences of the constitutive view, p. 3.

[197] Kato 10 IJIL 1970 p. 302. Brownlie (Principles) prefers the declaratory view for the same reason, because "it militates in favour of a legal and objective method of analyzing situations", p. 635.

To counter these objections the legal-constitutivist view has sometimes assumed the existence of a *duty* to recognize and a corresponding right to be recognized once factual criteria for statehood have been fulfilled.[198]

But this view loses the very distinctiveness of the constitutive approach altogether and, if taken seriously, becomes vulnerable to the criticisms advanced against the declaratory view.[199] For the question now arises how the "objective" facts of territory, population, Government and capacity to external relations can automatically impose such a duty on the existing State. Even if the criteria were uncontroversial (which they are not and never have been), their application in particular circumstances will remain a matter of subjective assessment. If a State refuses to recognize an entity because it thinks that this has not fulfilled the criteria for statehood, there is no point in insisting that it has a duty to recognize and that the existence of this duty makes the matter something other than subjective choice. Of course, the State can deny that the entity fulfilled the criteria for statehood *mala fide*. Maybe it secretly held that it did fulfil the required conditions. But the point is that *nobody can know the State's motives better than the State itself.* Under liberal assumptions, as I shall argue in more detail later (chapter 5), nobody has the right to claim that he "knows better". If this were not so, then we could simply posit that "somebody" as the super-legislator.[200] We would lose the justification for basing law on legislative State policies. To "know better" is an argument about objective interests.

[198] *Lauterpacht* (Recognition) pp. 6, 25, 72–78 and *passim.* Lauterpacht's theory is devised to avoid the consequences of pure constitutivism which "divorces" questions of statehood "from binding considerations of legal principle", p. 41. See also *Guggenheim* (Traité, I) pp. 150–151. For a criticism, see e.g. *Kunz* 44 AJIL 1950 pp. 713–719.

[199] "... si la reconnaissance est obligatoire, elle n'est plus constitutive", *Charpentier* (Reconnaissance) p. 194. To the same effect, see *Brownlie* (Macdonald-Johnston: Structure and Process) p. 627.

[200] *Wright* 44 AJIL 1950 suggests that a tribunal might be able to oppose the statehood of an entity against a non-recognizing State if only the former had secured "general recognition", pp. 550–551. This is another way of saying that the duty to recognize or accept the entity's statehood becomes operative when a majority has recognized. For the popular argument about "collective recognition", see *Jessup* (Modern) pp. 44–51. The kind of majority legislation assumed by both suggestions, however, contradicts the sovereign equality of *both* the State which is the object of recognition and the State which has not recognized. It is indefensible within the liberal system as it ultimately assumes that communal goals are always expressed in majority vote and must override individual States' freedom.

The attempt to achieve reconciliation by assuming a duty to recognize adds nothing to the system. It will remain vulnerable to the objections presented either against pure declarativism or pure constitutivism.

Neither of the two views seems defensible alone and neither provides a satisfactory interpretation of State practice. From one perspective, such practice seems to support declarativism, from another, constitutivism. Statehood seems dependent on both facts and an external cognition of facts. But neither alternative seems fully acceptable. To lay stress on "pure facts" seems necessary so as to overrule the subjectivism in external cognition. To emphasize the importance of external cognition seems necessary to avoid relying on a naturalistic view about the "self-evidence" of facts or on the new entity's self-definition.[201] Yet, no third alternative seems available. The attempt at reconciliation by postulating a duty to recognize will reveal itself as either pure declarativism or pure constitutivism in disguise.

Imagine a dispute between entity A and State X about the former's statehood. A argues that it is entitled to statehood because it possesses a piece of territory, has a Government which exercises effective control on the territory and the population residing there and is capable and willing to enter into relations with other Governments. X denies that A can be State because of the undemocratic nature of its internal régime.

Initially, A relies on a pure fact argument. It denies that other States' recognition is needed. Its statehood exists *ipso facto* and other States simply have to accept this. Reference to "democracy" is merely an

---

[201] Some lawyers have attempted to escape this difficulty by distinguishing between recognition as a "cognition of fact" and recognition as "political act". See e.g. *Rolin* 77 RCADI 1950/II pp. 327–328; *Brownlie* (Macdonald-Johnston: Structure and Process) pp. 633–634; *Briggs* 43 AJIL 1949 p. 120; *Blix* 130 RCADI 1970/II pp. 607, 609, 623–624; *Crawford* XLVIII BYIL 1976–77 p. 95. The former would involve a simple perception that the required conditions for statehood exist, the latter would denote the State's willingness to attach legal consequences to it. The distinction rests on being able to differentiate between the State's (impartial, objective) acts of cognition and (partisan, subjective) volition. It then uses the former to explain the State's emergence and the latter to explain the different consequences attached to it. But the construction is a failure. In the first place, it is quite unclear whether there exists a "pure" cognition which can be opposed to "pure" volition. Indeed, one of the assumptions behind this book is that the distinction cannot be made. Secondly, the point really is that it seems impossible to oppose to a State a view about what it has or has not taken cognizance of. If the State simply denies the presence of the (objective) cognitive criteria, we seem unable to argue that such cognition *had* taken place though the State now denies it. By denying "cognition", the State will achieve precisely the same effect as denying a recognition in a constitutive system.

attempt to introduce a political right for existing States to decide freely which entities they will or will not accept. To make statehood dependent on the will of old States fails to give effect to the right of self-determination and creates an inegalitarian law in which each entity's identity would be relative to other entities' wills. However, to pursue this argument A will have to show why it is that precisely its criteria are relevant and not, for example, the alleged criterion of the democratic nature of A's regime. It will, in other words, have to assume the existence of a rule about the criteria of statehood which is anterior to it and which cannot be justified by reference to its own consent. A's argument is now *both* a pure fact and a legal one.

In answering these points, X will have to present its own views in a similar light. It will oppose A's initial point (that A's statehood is dependent only on pure facts) by noting the need for an external rule about the criteria of statehood. At this stage, the dispute seems structured by A's being a pure fact position and X's a legal position. But when A's position reveals itself to be also a legal one, X will have to argue why it is that *its* view of the criteria is better than that of A's. This forces it to make a reverse shift. It will now occupy A's initial position. It will argue that it can be opposed only by criteria which it has accepted. To hold otherwise would be either to assume that the criteria exist as natural law or by virtue of *other* States having preferred it. The former argument would seem utopian, the latter would violate X's sovereign equality. In other words, its initial liberty would be violated by another solution. X's argument is now *both* a legal and a pure fact one.

During this imaginary dispute, A will have changed its position from a factual to a legal one and X from a legal to a factual one. Moreover, this is what they were compelled to do by the logic of the discourse in order to present a coherent case. The pure fact view will involve a claim to override the other disputant's inital freedom and sovereign equality. Such a view seems manifestly untenable. To insist that *my* view is better *because* it is mine or that *my* interpretation of facts is better simply because *I have put it forward as a sovereign* provides no grounds for decision. A rule external to both sovereigns is needed. But the determination of the *content* of that rule and whether some facts fit the criteria contained therein will immediately re-emerge an identical dispute. Whose rule, or whose interpretation thereof is to be given preference?

Both positions involve a combination of the pure fact and legal approaches. But this involves contradiction. The two cannot be put together in a way that seems called for. For they are based on mutually exclusive assumptions. The factual approach assumes that a State's liberty, its will and interest must be effective: these must override external constraint. The legal approach assumes that the legal order must be effective: that it can overrule the State's subjective liberty, will or interest. Sometimes, of course, "facts" and "rules" may point to the same direction. In such cases, there is no need to establish preference. But the very essence of the dispute in our example – as well as in *any* dispute about recognition – is that facts and the law seem to conflict and that the decision-maker is asked to establish which of these is prior to the other.

The pure fact and the legal approach to sovereignty seem indefensible because both dissolve into politics. The former fails to draw a line between force and law. The latter will legitimize the imperialism of existing States. The pure fact approach is, moreover, indefensible as facts alone cannot create law. Rules are needed. But rules are not automatically applicable. They need interpretation and interpretation seems subjective. This is not merely a "practical" difficulty of interpretation. The doctrine of sovereign equality makes it impossible to decide between competing interpretations. If the validity of the interpretation cannot be checked against the rule itself (which it, of course, cannot, as this would require that we could know the meaning of the rule independently of the interpretations – in which case no interpretation would be needed), then there is no other basis to make the choice than either by referring to a theory of justice or to the identities of the States involved: one interpretation is better either because it is more just or because it is produced by this, and not that, State. And the former solution is utopian, the latter violates sovereign equality. Both seem purely political.

4.7   Example: territorial disputes

The structure of creating and losing the contradiction between the pure fact and the legal approaches to sovereignty may be illustrated also by reference to the question whether sovereignty on a piece of territory is dependent on effective possession or external recognition. As dispute-solution is unable to prefer either of these alternatives it will have to proceed by way of adopting interpretations about facts and the disputing States' positions which – together with the ultimate solution – will remain undetermined by the legal arguments available.

Textbooks commonly list four or five modes of acquisition of territory: occupation, (adverse)prescription, cession and accretion (and sometimes conquest).[202] However, it is notoriously difficult to keep these analytical categories separate. Occupation and prescription, for example, seem overlapping and may have a relation to some cessionary instrument or natural accretion.[203] Moreover, other "modes", such as contiguity or adjudication may seem relevant as well.[204] International tribunals have usually refrained from applying any of these modes expressly. Therefore, lawyers have been tempted to look at territorial acquisition from a wider perspective from which each of the claimed "modes" would be seen as an expression of a more fundamental rule or principle. Two candidates frequently present themselves: effective possession and "consolidation".[205]

It often seems as if each of the classical modes only constituted an attempt to rationalize, or justify, what presently or in the past existed as effective possession of a piece of territory. Occupation, accretion and contiguity have an obvious relation with the physical control which the State has exercised or can exercise on the territory.[206] Prescription and historic right refer to the temporal aspects of such control. To an extent, cession and adjudication seem different as they look beyond continued

---

[202] See e.g. *Oppenheim-Lauterpacht* (International Law, I) p. 546; *Fauchille* (Traité) p. 532; *Sørensen* (Manual) pp. 321–324; *O'Connell* (International Law, I) pp. 405–443; *Fenwick* (International Law) p. 404; *Strupp* 47 RCADI 1934/I pp. 533–534; *Virally* 183 RCADI 1983/V pp. 142–147.

[203] See *Shaw* (Title) p. 17; *Brownlie* (Principles) pp. 134–135; *O'Connell* (International Law, I) pp. 405–407. *Johnson* XXVII BYIL 1950 distinguishes occupation and prescription by applying the latter term only to maritime territory, pp. 348–353. The status of conquest, or subjugation, is uncertain. *Lauterpacht* (International Law, I) denies its present validity, pp. 380–381 while *O'Connell* (International Law, I) sees no reason to exclude it as a basis of title if only accompanied with acquiescence or recognition, pp. 431–436. Clearly, both arguments have some plausibility. If *any* conquest were held capable of conferring title, then the law on acquisition would seem apologist. If *all* conquest-related present titles were regarded as illegitimate, then the gap between law and fact would make the former seem utopian. Reconciliation may be sought by legitimizing acquisition by conquest by some cessionary act, even if this might raise problems in respect of the conditions of validity of such instrument under Article 52 of the Vienna Convention on the Law of Treaties. See also *Chemillier-Gendreau* XI RBDI 1975 pp. 44–45.

[204] On contiguity as basis for title, see *Koskenniemi* 82 LM 1984 pp. 446–449 and *passim*.

[205] See *Shaw* (Title) (effective possession) pp. 17–24; *De Visscher* (Theory) (consolidation) p. 200. See also *Jacqué* (Elements) pp. 220–221.

[206] Inasmuch as geological or geographial contiguity has been relevant, its justification has related to its link with effectiveness of control. See *Waldock* 36 Transactions of the Grotius Society 1950 p. 141.

effectiveness. In this respect, they need to be discussed separately. But inasmuch as they too imply acts of renouncing or taking possession, they have a relation with effectiveness as well.

Much discussion has centred upon the question what constitutes effective possession, or as Max Huber formulated it "continuous and peaceful display of territorial sovereignty".[207] Much of the relevant case-law turns on an evaluation of whether the acts relied upon have or have not constituted possession.[208] The law does not allocate sovereignty irrespective of considerations of effectiveness. Symbolic acts or discovery are not usually assumed to create a valid title. The reason for this was explained by Judge Huber in the following way: Territorial sovereignty does not only involve rights but also duties in respect of third States and local populations. Without effective manifestations of sovereignty, such duties could not be adequately fulfilled. The law would lack required concreteness.[209]

However, it is immediately evident that effective possession cannot constitute an exhaustive rule on what is needed to show title. Not *all* factual possession results in sovereignty. It seems reasonably clear that illegal occupation, however effective, *cannot per se* create title.[210] But law cannot interminably divorce itself from fact. Therefore, it is assumed that original illegality may be corrected in a process of consolidation, that is, the passing of time during which it becomes generally accepted to be best to let the sleeping dogs lie – *quieta non sunt movere.*[211]

[207] *Island of Palmas* Case, II UNRIAA p. 839. For doctrinal discussion on the conditions of "effective possession", see e.g. *Fenwick* (International Law) pp. 405–407; *O'Connell* (International Law, I) pp. 409–419.

[208] For the *Eastern Greenland* Case, see *infra* ch. 4.7. See also ICJ: *Minquiers and Ecrehos* Case, Reports 1953 p. 57 *et seq*; *Frontier Lands* Case, Reports 1959 pp. 227–230; *Temple* Case, Reports 1962 pp. 29–33; *Western Sahara* Case, Reports 1975 pp. 45–48 (§§ 99–107).

[209] *Island of Palmas* Case, II UNRIAA pp. 839, 843–846. See also *Fenwick* (International Law) pp. 410–411.

[210] *Lauterpacht* (International Law, I) pp. 341–344. *Sørensen* 101 RCADI 1960/III (noting the insufficiency of mere effectiveness in adverse prescription) pp. 147–148. See also ICJ: *Namibia* Case, Reports 1971 in which the Court distinguished between sovereignty and effective control, p. 54 (§ 118).

[211] This principle serves to maintain the law's concreteness. On the validation of illegally attained title through acquiescence, see *Lauterpacht* (International Law, I) pp. 344–345. The principle according to which things should be left as they are – the "principle of stability and finality" – is present in *Vattel* (Droit des Gens) L. II, ch XI §147 (p. 364). It has been frequently referred to in case-law. See e.g. *Grisbadarna* Case, XI UNRIAA p. 161; ICJ: *Temple* Case, Reports 1962 p. 34. For discussion, see

Sometimes such considerations may justify territorial title even in the absence of proof on full effectiveness of possession.[212]

Consider the case of adverse prescription (historic right). If this is a valid mode of acquisition, it seems clear that something more than mere factual occupation and passing of time must be involved. What is needed is a general consensus or at least a long-standing absence of protest indicating that title has shifted from the original to the derivative possessor.[213] The very process of decolonization and the continuing disputes about, for instance, British sovereignty in the Falklands or Gibraltar, show that even long-continued possession may seem insufficent for title to emerge or be maintained. The very claim of self-determination is premised on the assumption that however long, mere possession cannot suffice to justify sovereignty.[214] Whatever historic rights there may exist, their existence seems less dependent on actual possession than on general acquiescence or recognition of the exceptional treatment which such rights entail.[215]

In such cases it is less actual effectiveness of possession than general views about sovereignty which seem determining in whom the title should be vested.

Cukwurah (Boundary Disputes) p. 123; *Bardonnet* (Mélanges Reuter) pp. 46–47; *De Visscher* (Confins) p. 28; *Johnson* XXVII BYIL 1950 pp. 333, 335 and *passim*.

[212] See cases *supra* n. 142. In these cases, the tribunals have been content with very little by way of showing effectiveness. The matter has turned on an evaluation of the *relative* strength of the claims when neither Party has been able to show full effectiveness. See also *Island of Palmas* case, II UNRIAA p. 869. For commentary, see *O'Connell* (International Law, I) pp. 408–409, 411–413; *Lauterpacht* (International Law, I) pp. 379–380; *Fitzmaurice* XXXII BYIL 1954–5 pp. 34–36, 64–66; *Waldock* XXV BYIL 1948 p. 336.

[213] Or at least silence (absence of protest) which is capable of interpretation as acquiescence. As *Vattel* (Droit des Gens) puts it, "une très-longue possession non contestée", L.II, ch. XI § 149 (p. 365). See *O'Connell* (International Law, I) pp. 423–424; *Johnson* XXVII BYIL 1950 p. 347.

[214] The problematic character of fusing the law of self-determination together with the traditional law on territorial title is discussed in e.g. *Shaw* (Title) p. 149 *et seq. Carty* (Decay) notes that reliance on private law concepts such as possession, for example, makes it very difficult to deal with nationalism and self-determination in an adequate way. The juristic tendency to think about territorial matters in private law terms reflects, he observes, the 19th century lawyer's wish to exclude tackling with those issues directly because they were seen as too political, p. 43 *et seq.*

[215] Thus in the *Anglo-Norwegian Fisheries* Case, Reports 1951, the ICJ legitimized Norwegian rights on maritime territory by reference to the "general toleration" of States, pp. 138, 139. See also comment in *Fitzmaurice* XXX BYIL 1953 pp. 26–29, 32–33 and generally *Blum* (Historic Titles) pp. 38 *et seq*, 59–98.

Likewise, the "pure facts" of geography or geology have seemed powerless for creating title unless accompanied by general recognition. The role of contiguity is an example. In a sense, as Kelsen points out, everything is contiguous to everything else. To recognize claims based on physical closeness seems a dangerous way of justifying interminable extensions of national jurisdiction.[216] That contiguity has been accepted as a valid basis for title in, for example, maritime areas is beyond dispute. But this may be less an expression of the intrinsically normative character of physical closeness than of the wish to give effect to the gradual acceptance, by States at large, of the extensions undertaken by individual States.[217]

Both cession and adjudication refer beyond effectiveness of power to external recognition of a State's title as valid. In making reference to the origins of possession they imply a denial of the sufficiency of mere possession to create title; there must be a permissible *causa* to possession which is independent of the act of taking possession itself, be this in an objectively binding rule or an external process of acquiescence or recognition.

The law of territorial acquisition oscillates between basing title on effective possession (and its derivatives) and on external recognition (acquiescence). It should not be difficult to perceive here the opposition between a pure fact and a legal approach to sovereignty. The problem is to construct a law which would neither associate title with effective power nor assume that title is received from what other States think about it. In other words, the system should be such as to guarantee the normativity and concreteness of the law without derogating from sovereign equality.[218] But this seems impossible.

The standard argument from effective possession seems *apologist* in that it attempts to impose one State's subjective power and will to sovereignty on other States in a way which cannot explain the objectivity of the criteria whereby effectiveness can be ascertained. It violates other States' sovereign equality. In the *Eastern Greenland* Case (1933), the PCIJ pointed out that sovereignty required "intention and will to act as a sovereign and some actual exercise or display of such authority".[219]

[216] *Kelsen* (Festschrift Wehberg) pp. 203–205. Similarly *Lauterpacht* XXVII BYIL 1950 pp. 429–430.
[217] *Lauterpacht* XXVII BYIL 1950 legitimizes such claims precisely by reference to the aspect of tolerance, or acquiescence in *other* States, p. 393 *et seq.*
[218] For a discussion of the tendency to emerge the law with power under the doctrine of effectiveness, see e.g. *Chemillier-Gendreau* XI RBDI 1975 pp. 38–46.
[219] PCIJ: *Eastern Greenland* Case, Ser. A/B 53 p. 46.

The Court's express distinction between the aspects of *animus/corpus* of possession aimed at reconciliation. On the one hand, the State's own self-interpretation (*animus*) had to be effective. On the other hand, there had to exist an external criterion (*corpus*) to control such self-interpretation.

Both elements seem needed. Relying on *animus* – the will to sovereignty – violates the wills of other States. Relying on *corpus* – acts of possession – fails to deal with the case where there are conflicting interpretations about whether some acts count as "possession" or not. The latter is, of course, the single most important issue in territorial disputes. One State's interpretation of the facts stands against that of another's. This conflict is not soluble by referring back to the facts "in their purity" as this would assume that we can know the meaning of "possession" without interpretation. The problem is how to justify overruling a participant State's interpretation. The standard solution is to refer to third States' views as to the content of the rule and its application, that is to their recognition or acquiescence.[220]

But external recognition (acquiescence), too, seems unacceptable alone. To derive territorial sovereignty from general consent fails to protect the initial liberty of States, their right of self-determination. It fails to give effect to the nation's subjective *animus*. From the claimant State's perspective, such a view merely gives effect to the subjective politics of other States. Hence it fails, ultimately, to give effect to the *corpus* of possession as well.[221]

In other words, to be acceptable, both arguments need to rely on each other. To demonstrate effective possession we must refer to a generally accepted rule and a generally accepted interpretation thereof. To escape politics, we must assume that the adequacy of general recognition or acquiescence can be checked against actual effectiveness of possession. We must assume that the justification for territorial title lies both in facts as well as in an interpretation of those facts by States at large.

But the positions cannot be linked together in this way without losing the sense in them. They imply a capacity to overrule each other. The argument about effective possession assumes that territorial title

---

[220] On the role of external (third States') recognition or acquiescence in the law of territorial acquisition, see e.g. O'Connell (International Law, I) pp. 424–426.

[221] The position is equivalent to the declarativist's criticism of the constitutive position regarding the recognition of States.

emerges from pure fact. Facts overrule views about them. This seems
necessary so as to avoid political subjectivism. The argument from
recognition assumes that whatever titles States may have depends
on what view States have taken on them. These views give facts their
legal sense. This seems required in order to maintain distance between
political power and legal right. Either pure fact (and State liberty)
is effective (in which case general consent is overruled) or general
recognition is effective (in which case pure facts and State liberty are
overruled).

The argumentative structure of disputes about territory is provided
by the constant affirmation of the opposition between these two approaches and its dilution within argument. What happens in dispute-
solution is that *disputing States' positions are interpreted so as to lose
the conflict between them*. Effective possession and general recognition
are so interpreted as to point to the same solution. Either both are
present or both are absent. The question what *if* they were to point to
differing solutions is neither raised nor answered. Nor can it be because
this would emerge the need to establish priority between them – a
priority which cannot be made. The embarrassing dilemma is that by
failing to indicate a preference between fact (possession) and views
about fact (recognition), dispute-solution fails to be guided by any
rule at all.

Let me now illustrate this structure by reference to three cases from
the jurisprudence of the World Court.

The *Eastern Greenland* Case (1933) arose out of a Norwegian royal
resolution of 10 July 1931 in which Norway declared its sovereignty over
a small portion of Eastern Greenland (Eirik Raudes land). Denmark
disputed the validity of this act, arguing that its sovereignty extended
over the whole of Greenland. Norway denied Danish title on the territory occupied by it which it regarded a *terra nullius*.[222]

Denmark's initial argument is that Danish sovereignty was based on
general recognition and acquiescence. It:

> ... a été exercée en fait pendant des longues périodes, d'une manière
> entièrement publique et avec la recognition et l'adhésion de tous les
> autres Etats.[223]

---

[222] For the parties' final submissions, see PCIJ: *Eastern Greenland* Case, Ser. A/B 53
pp. 24–26.
[223] *Ibid.* Danish Memorial, Ser. C 62 p. 101.

This was further elaborated in the Danish reply:

> Le statut juridique d'un région déterminée est fixé en droit international
> par la conviction générale ou *communis opinio* des Etats qui forment la
> communauté internationale.[224]

Denmark refrained expressly from relying on isolated acts of occupation
or other evidence of effective possession.[225] The rule, it argued, is that of
general recognition, not effective possession. As sovereignty on a
piece of territory concerns the international community as a whole, it
therefore must depend on community recognition. Mere subjective
acts are insufficient for validating title *erga omnes.*[226]

Recognition of Danish claims was said to be evidenced by continued
absence of protest towards Danish sovereignty on Greenland. Denmark
invoked, in particular, the Treaty of Kiel of 14 January 1814 in which it
had ceded Norway to Sweden with the express mention that Greenland
did not constitute a part of this cession, several commercial conventions
in which other States had admitted Denmark's right to exclude
Greenland from the application of those conventions and a series of
diplomatic overtures between 1916 and 1921 during which many
third States (USA, France, Sweden, Japan, UK) had recognized Danish
sovereignty over the whole of Greenland.[227]

Norway replied with an argument about effective possession. Title
to territory is independent of general recognition and constituted by
constant and peaceful display of authority.[228] The Norwegian case
belabours at length the content of effective occupation and concentrates
on showing the Danish claim as "fictive" and based on repudiated
doctrines about discovery or contiguity.[229] For Norway, the territory
had been *terra nullius* until it had established effective occupation on it.

The validity of recognition was expressly denied:

> "La Norwège n'est évidemment engagé en rien par des déclarations
> données par des Etats étrangers.[230]

---

[224] *Ibid.* Danish Reply, Ser. C 63 p. 712.

[225] *Ibid.* Danish Reply, Ser. C 63 pp. 726–729 and argument by *De Visscher*, Ser. C 66 p. 2797.

[226] *Ibid.* Ser. C 66 pp. 2794–2795.

[227] *Ibid.* Danish Memorial, Ser. C 62 pp. 101–107; *ibid*, Danish Reply, Ser. C 63 pp. 712–713 and argument by *De Visscher*, Ser. C 66 pp. 2798–2857.

[228] *Ibid.* Norway's Counter-Memorial, Ser. C 62 pp. 373–430.

[229] *Ibid.*, oral argument by *Gidel*, Ser. C 66 p. 3220 *et seq*; and Norway's Rejoinder, Ser. C 63 pp. 1190 *et seq*, 1331–1372.

[230] *Ibid.* Norway's Counter-Memorial, Ser. C 62 p. 538.

For Norway, general recognition was only a *res inter alios acta*.[231] There is no majority rule in international law.[232] Reliance on recognition will inevitably violate Norway's sovereign equality.

At this stage, the two rules are presented as mutually opposing. Preferring general recognition would seem to support the Danish claim and preferring effective possession the Norwegian view. But both States succeeded in making their opponent's view seem untenable. Title based on general recognition seemed fictitious as devoid of factual, objective criteria. Title based on effective possession violated community consent. And there was the difficult issue of sources: could Norway be held bound irrespective of consent? Could Denmark be so bound? Therefore, both Parties needed to complement their initial arguments with additional points.[233]

Denmark argued also that it exercised effective control on the disputed territory and had exercised it "for centuries".[234] Its title was not fictitious. By contrast, it held that Norway had not succeeded in showing effective possession. For this contains a dual structure: actual acts of sovereignty (*corpus*) and the will to act as sovereign (*animus*). Denmark denied the presence of *animus* in the Norwegian acts as Norway had, according to Denmark, expressed its contrary *animus* in its recognitions of Danish sovereignty.[235]

Norway argued also from general recognition. The rule about effective possession was argued as a customary rule which was binding on

---

[231] In his oral argument, professor *Gidel* pointed out that giving effect to third States' views would be to concede to a policy of "spheres of influence" – one which could not be binding on Norway, *ibid*. Ser. C 66 pp. 3229, 3259–3260. Norway's Rejoinder stressed that reliance on foreign consent was a colonialist rule, *ibid*. Ser. C 63 pp. 1373–1380.

[232] *Ibid*. Oral argument by *Gidel*, Ser. C 66 pp. 3220–3226.

[233] Both Parties argued that the other was bound because it had consented to the other's position. This seemed necessary to preserve sovereign equality. Thus both came to assume that their right is based on the other's consent. See *ibid*. Danish Memorial C 62 pp. 107–114; Norwegian Counter-Memorial C 62 pp. 428–493.

[234] *Ibid*. Danish Reply, Ser. C 62 pp. 726 *et seq*; 732–744, 810–825. The Danish Memorial made express reference to the "continous and peaceful display of sovereignty" rule, *ibid*. p. 104.

[235] Norway's consent was held based on 1) the Treaty of Kiel of 1814; 2) general multi-lateral conventions to which Norway was a Party and which recognized Danish rights; 3) the Declaration by the Norwegian Foreign Minister to the Danish Foreign Minister on 22 July 1919 according to which Norway would "make no difficulties" in respect of Danish extension of sovereignty over Greenland. See *ibid*. Danish Memorial, Ser. C 62 pp. 107–114, Danish Reply, Ser. C 63 pp. 850–900.

Denmark irrespective of Danish consent.[236] A similar assumption worked behind its view that sovereignty could also be based on a comparison of interests.[237] Both involve the assumption that sovereignty does not emerge from merely subjective acts or will of the territorial State. There is an external criterion – a customary rule or a hierarchy of interests – which regulates the acquisition of title. Inasmuch as such criterion cannot be one of natural law, it must be assumed to be grounded in general recognition. Finally, in order not to undermine Danish sovereignty, Norway also relied on Danish recognition of the Norwegian claim – assuming thus that the limits of its own sovereignty might be dependent on Danish consent.[238]

Both disputants relied on effective possession and general recognition. And both assumed that their sovereignty also depended on what the other had recognized. More generally, both adopted an ascending and a descending argument about sovereignty. As the approaches are contradictory, both sets of arguments were contradictory, too. Such maximalist advocacy may be commonplace in any litigation. But the point is that contradiction seems inevitable as each position is defensible only by confirming its opposite.

Two reasons make it impossible for the Court, too, to proceed by way of giving preference either to effective possession or general recognition: first, neither position is defensible alone; second, both disputants have occupied both positions. Instead, the case turns on a series of interpretations. Can third States' conduct be interpreted as a recognition of either disputant's position? Can either State's acts be so interpreted as to amount to effective possession with both the *corpus* and *animus* factors included? The question of possible conflict is not raised. Nor is the question of possible preference should both States have had effective possession.

In the first part of the judgement, the Court bases Denmark's sovereignty on effective possession as well as general recognition.

The King of Denmark had, at least since 1721, manifested his sovereignty over parts of Greenland with the intention that his sovereignty

---

[236] *Ibid.* Norwegian Counter-Memorial, Ser. C 62 pp. 382–394 and argument by *Gidel*, Ser. C 66 p. 3226 *et seq.*

[237] Norway held that such comparison would immediately lead to prefer the interests of Norwegian hunters and fishermen, *ibid.* Norwegian Counter-Memorial, Ser. C 62 pp. 174–243 and argument by *Rygh*, Ser. C 66 pp. 2948–2970.

[238] *Ibid.* Norwegian Counter-Memorial, Ser. C 62 pp. 482–493; Rejoinder, Ser. C 63, pp. 1324–1327.

take effect over the whole of Greenland.[239] The conditions for effective occupation were fulfilled. There was no dispute about the possessions of the Danish-Norwegian King being transferred to Denmark in the Treaty of Kiel of 1814. There was, then, no *terra nullius* for Norway to occupy.[240]

But Danish title was also based on general recognition, evidenced in several bilateral commercial treaties in which Denmark's stipulating over Greenland had encountered no protests, in the practice of requesting grants of concession from Denmark to foreign nationals which were to apply over whole Greenland and in the diplomatic overtures of 1915–1921.[241]

Consequently, the Court could affirm the equal validity and effectiveness of the Parties' two rules by making these point to the same direction. Both supported Danish sovereignty.

It might be objected that the Court turned to general recognition only as *evidence* of effective possession, this latter being the overriding and determining rule. But it is difficult to make a distinction between the rule and the ways of manifestation of the rule. One seems unable to argue about the presence of a rule in some behaviour without at the same time referring to the external manifestations, the evidence there is for such rule. The rule as a pure idea is always inaccessible. All we can grasp are its "traces" in external manifestation. To hold otherwise would be to assume the presence of natural meanings in social action. But this is a utopian idea.

Now, to have affirmed both effective possession and general recognition leaves still open the problem about sources: how can Danish acts or even general recognition be opposed to Norway without violating the latter's sovereign equality? Therefore, in the second part of the judgement, the Court proceeded to show "that Norway had given certain undertakings which recognized Danish sovereignty over all Greenland".[242] Such recognition was based on: 1) Norwegian statements during the termination of the Union (1814–1819); 2) a series of bilateral agreements in which Greenland had been referred to as a Danish colony; 3) on the reply of the Norwegian Foreign Minister, on 22 July 1919 to the

---

[239] *Ibid.* Ser. A 53 pp. 45–51. The Court argued that very little sufficed to show sovereignty on polar regions, p. 46. Danish "animus" was not derived from any psychological considerations. It resulted from an interpretation of the term "Greenland" as it was expressed in official Danish-Norwegian documents of the time, pp. 49–50.

[240] *Ibid.* pp. 51, 62–64.   [241] *Ibid.* pp. 51–62.   [242] *Ibid.* pp. 64–74.

Danish Minister in which he had stated that Norway "would make no difficulties" in respect of Danish claims on Greenland.

This argument may be approached from different points of view. As Judge Anzilotti conceived it, the Norwegian recognition constituted an agreement between the two States.[243] It can also be discussed as a unilateral act, by laying weight on the declaration of the Norwegian Foreign Minister.[244] For our purposes it is enough to point out that this argument served to deny Norwegian *animus occupandi* (and effective possession) as well as to maintain Norwegian sovereign equality. By this argument, the conflict between two equally effective possessions could be avoided without going into an evaluation of the acts themselves. The solution appears derived from the sovereign will of *both* disputants. No violation of sovereign equality is involved.

To sum up: the Court avoided taking any stand in the apparent conflict between the two rules invoked. It thus followed the same strategy as the parties themselves. And it laid equal weight to their sovereign wills. Every argument was interpreted so as to point in the same direction: the conduct of third States implied recognition of Danish sovereignty; Danish conduct constituted effective possession; Norway had recognized Danish sovereignty; as it had recognized Danish sovereignty its own acts could not amount to effective possession.

The decision was overdetermined: the same conclusion was drawn from conflicting premises. The embarrassing dilemmas involved in an effort to make a preference were avoided by presuming that there was no conflict. Similarly, formal equality and sovereign authority were preserved by making no preference between the parties' positions. *The message of the Eastern Greenland case was that there was no dispute, no disagreement between Denmark and Norway at all*: both parties – like all other States – had agreed to Danish sovereignty. Only Norway attempted to deny this.[245] But as it itself had recognized Denmark's sovereignty, the solution could give effect to Norway's sovereignty as well. It is not difficult to see why such an argument cannot seem very convincing to the parties which lived on their claims being conflicting.

A similar structure of argument reveals itself in the *Anglo-Norwegian Fisheries* Case (1951). Here the ICJ was asked to decide whether the Norwegian system of applying straight baselines exceeding 10 miles in the delimitation of its territorial sea – a method which enclosed large

---

[243] *Anzilotti*, diss. op. *ibid.* pp. 76–95.   [244] See *infra* ch. 5.3.
[245] See PCIJ: *Eastern Greenland* Case, oral argument by *Gidel*, Ser. C 66 pp. 3193–3218.

maritime areas within Norway's internal waters – was in conformity with international law.[246] Both parties – Norway and the United Kingdom – made points about sovereignty over maritime areas arising as a pure fact of effective possession and geographical relatedness to non-controversial land-territories. And both argued about the need to establish external recognition to claims of sovereignty over these areas.

The United Kingdom argued that the Norwegian decree of 1935 could only be valid if the system established in it had been generally recognized through historic right or custom. The Norwegian system had failed to receive such recognition. It also disputed the consistency – effectiveness – with which Norway had applied its method. There was no effective occupation of the sea-areas claimed.[247] Norway put forward opposing arguments on both issues. It argued that it had applied its method consistently and that the waters had been in effective use by Norwegian fishermen and that its legitimate interests further supported the validity of its decree. And it also argued on the basis of a recognized custom or, at least, historic right.[248]

Again, the relevant section of the judgement is in two parts: one deals with the consistency with which Norway had applied its system (effectiveness), the other with the general recognition of that system by States in general.[249] In order not to violate the sovereign consent of the United

[246] The Norwegian system had been promulgated by a Royal Decree of 12 July 1935. The case concerned the conformity of this Decree with international law. For the background, see ICJ: *Anglo-Norwegian Fisheries* Case, Reports 1951 pp. 121–126. See also *Waldock* XXVIII BYIL 1951 pp. 117–126. For the ensuing analysis, see also *Kennedy* (Structures) pp. 82–90.

[247] It was held that for the existence of historic right, two conditions must be fulfilled: there must be 1) actual acts of effective authority and 2) acquiescence by other States, ICJ: *Anglo-Norwegian Fisheries* Case, Reply of the United Kingdom, Pleadings II p. 303. For the argument against the consistency of the enforcement of the system, see *ibid.* pp. 591–597. For the lack of recognition of the system in general custom, *ibid.* pp. 603–604 and generally p. 426 *et seq* and Memorial of the UK, *ibid.* Pleadings I pp. 60–84. For lack of acquiescence, see also *ibid.* Reply of the UK, Pleadings III pp. 602–604.

[248] For the Norwegian argument about the general recognition of its system, see *ibid.* Counter-Memorial of Norway, Pleadings I pp. 351–361, 370–373. For the argument that custom does not bind Norway as this possesses a historic right, *ibid.* pp. 381–384. For the justification of the Norwegian right as based on possession, economic interests, security and general recognition, *ibid.* pp. 571–573 and esp. Rejoinder of Norway, Pleadings III pp. 462–490. For critical commentary, see *Waldock* XXVIII BYIL 1951 pp. 128–129, 160.

[249] The Court concluded its discussion of the substance by observing that the Norwegian system: "... was consistently applied by Norwegian authorities and ... encountered no opposition on the part of other States", ICJ: *Anglo-Norwegian Fisheries* Case, Reports 1951 pp. 136–137.

Kingdom, the Court further interprets its inactivity as acquiescence. As a result, the dispute becomes non-existent: each rule as well as each State's will renders the same conclusion.

First, the Court bases Norwegian sovereignty on the claimed seas on *possessio longi temporis*.[250] The Court finds Norway applying its system consistently since 1869.[251] The Court's discussion of geography and economics contribute to strengthen the effectiveness of Norway's possession.

The "dependence of the territorial sea on the land domain", the "close relationship existing between certain sea areas and land formations" and the "economic interests peculiar to a region, the reality and importance of which are clearly established by long use"[252] each support Norwegian possession. They are the pure facts on which Norway's sovereignty may be based.

Having established the presence of effective possession, the Court observed that:

> From the standpoint of international law, it is now necessary to consider whether the application of the Norwegian system encountered any opposition from foreign States.[253]

It concluded that the "general toleration of foreign States" of the Norwegian system was "an unchallenged fact".[254] Absence of protest bore "witness to the fact that they did not consider it to be contrary to international law".[255]

In other words, Norway's sovereignty arose from an ascending as well as a descending point; from the subjective behaviour, will and interests of Norway itself as well as from the general recognition of the international community. No preference between these two is established[256] as they are interpreted so as to point in the same direction. Norwegian acts were interpreted as effective occupation, general silence as absence of protest (despite the well-argued point by the UK that very few States *could have known* of the Norwegian system as its details had been available in foreign languages for only a very brief period).

---

[250] *Ibid.* pp. 127, 130.   [251] *Ibid.* pp. 134–138.   [252] *Ibid.* p. 133.

[253] *Ibid.* p. 138. *Waldock* XXVIII BYIL 1951 argues that the Court thus implied that the Norwegian system had its "legal basis in the consent of States", p. 162. See also *Fitzmaurice* XXX BYIL 1953 pp. 27–42.

[254] ICJ: *Anglo-Norwegian Fisheries* Case, Reports 1951 p. 138.   [255] *Ibid.* p. 139.

[256] That both points were needed is not disputed even in the dissenting opinions. Judge *Read* affirms them expressly, *ibid.* p. 194, while Judge *Alvarez* discusses the twin conditions of actual possession and "reasonableness". In his objectivist view of morality, obviously, "reasonableness" plays the same ("descending") part which general recognition does under mainstream non-cognitivist assumptions, *ibid.* pp. 152, 150.

The remaining task is to protect the sovereign consent of the United Kingdom. This is achieved by interpreting its conduct as acquiescence. The Court points out:

> The notoriety of facts ... Great Britain's position in the North Sea, her own interest in the question, and her prolonged abstention would in any case warrant Norway's enforcement of her system against the United Kingdom.[257]

According to the Court, the UK could not have failed knowing about the Norwegian decree of 1869. Therefore, its inaction could only be interpreted as acquiescence in the Norwegian system.

The Court arrived at a solution by a series of interpretations which defined the material dispute away. Norway's sovereignty was established by Norway's own acts, general recognition and UK consent. None of these was preferred. Sovereignty followed from all of them. The critical issue of possible conflict is neither raised nor answered. And, as pointed out, it cannot be answered without engendering unacceptable consequences. But this loses the sense of the original need to make reference to anybody's acts or consent in the first place. The distinguishing feature of a claim about Norwegian sovereignty (or British or general consent) is that this can be *effectively* opposed to other States. If Norwegian sovereignty is to have a sense, it must be capable of overruling any general views or another State's particular views which conflict with it. This applies, obviously, to British sovereignty or the argument from general recognition as well. By discussing them as if they were equally relevant to the emergence of sovereignty the Court loses the sense in all of them. The solution comes out through a strategy of evading material choice. No material solution is needed because there is no dispute. No wonder British lawyers have found it hard to accept the Court's solution.[258] The argument from British acquiescence (tacit

---

[257] *Ibid.* p. 139. The protection of British sovereignty was an important consideration as the Court had earlier given protection to Norwegian sovereignty through the persistent objector rule, *ibid.* p. 131. Failing to give equal importance to British consent would have violated sovereign equality. The relevance of possible British acquiescence was anticipated in the Parties' arguments. See its affirmation in *ibid.* Rejoinder of Norway, Pleadings III pp. 484–487 and denial in *ibid.* Reply of the UK, Pleadings II p. 591 *et seq.*

[258] For an extended, critical discussion of the Court's construction of British consent, see *Fitzmaurice* XXX BYIL 1953 pp. 163–172. He argues that the test of consent was in fact based on a non-consensual presumption. The British, he says, were put in a position of having to show the *absence* of consent on their part. Likewise, *Waldock* XXVIII BYIL 1951 pp. 164–166.

consent), in particular, seems to be based on the assumption that
the Court can know better than the British themselves to what they
have consented – an assumption which is indistinguishable from full
naturalism and vulnerable to the objections against it.[259]

My third example is provided by the *Western Sahara* Advisory opinion (1975). Here the ICJ was requested by the UN General Assembly to
determine, firstly, whether the area of Western Sahara (Sakiet el
Hamra and Rio de Oro) had been, at the time of its colonization by
Spain (1884), a *terra nullius* and secondly, if not, "what were the legal ties
between this territory and the Kingdom of Morocco and the
Mauritanian entity"?[260]

The issue had come before UN organs as one of decolonization. The
apparently primary issue of the right of self-determination of the
Saharan population had become complicated by the:

> ... pretensions put forward, on the one hand, by Morocco that the
> territory, was then (i.e. at the time of Spanish colonization, MK) a part
> of the Sherifian State and, on the other, by Mauritania that the territory
> then formed part of the ... Mauritanian entity.[261]

In other words, the Court was required to take a stand – if the answer to the
first question was in the negative – on whether Morocco and Mauritania
had possessed sovereignty on the disputed area before Spanish colonization and were now in a position to reclaim that lost legal title.[262] Though
advisory, the case came very close to a contentious procedure. The claims
of sovereignty advanced by Morocco and Mauritania and the Spanish
reliance on the right of self-determination of the West Saharan population
conflicted in a manner resembling a territorial dispute. The Court held the
advisory procedure appropriate inasmuch as the matter involved a determination of the proper courses of action of UN bodies.[263]

---

[259] See further *infra* p. 278.   [260] ICJ: *Western Sahara Case*, Reports 1975 p. 14 (§ 1).
[261] *Ibid.* p. 40 (§ 85).
[262] The Court pointed out that the question about the "legal ties" needed to be "understood as referring to such 'legal ties' as may affect the policy of decolonization of
Western Sahara", *ibid.* p. 41 (§ 85). Spain opposed the Court's jurisdiction on the
grounds that the question was simply of academic or historical nature, *ibid.* Pleadings I
(Spanish Written Statement) pp. 187–205. For the Court's reply, see *ibid.* Reports 1975
pp. 19–21 (§§ 16–19, 24) and 29–31 (§§ 48–53). For a discussion of the way in which
the Court's treatment allowed it to deal with a historical issue as one of contemporary
law and doctrine, see *Shaw* XLIX BYIL 1978 pp. 125–127.
[263] ICJ: *Western Sahara Case*, Reports 1975 pp. 26–27 (§§ 39–41).

Morocco argued its sovereignty on the basis of effective possession and general recognition. It pointed out that Spain had failed to establish effective possession immediately after the colonization and at least before 1916.[264] Until that time, Morocco had continued to enjoy its immemorial possession of Western Sahara. It referred to acts of jurisdiction by the Sultan to whom the Saharan tribes paid allegiance. According to Morocco, those acts established both the *corpus* and *animus* of its effective possession.[265] Its argument about general recognition related to numerous bilateral treaties which Morocco had concluded in the 19th century and in which its authority had been tacitly consented to by States at large.

The central part of Mauritania's argument was based on contiguity, namely its view that Western Sahara had been a part of the Bilad Shinguitti which, at the time of colonization, had formed what was called the "Mauritanian entity".[266] It was pointed out that the Moroccan acts of jurisdiction had been of isolated nature and could not break the geographical, ethnic and cultural ties which bound that area to the Bilad Shinguitti.[267] The aspects of effective possession and general recognition were not treated separately in this argument.

Spain rejected both sets of arguments and advanced an ascending and a descending argument to support its view on the independence of Western Sahara. Such independence was a direct consequence of the inherent right of self-determination of the Saharan population.[268] It followed also from the recognition of that right by States in general as well as Morocco and Mauritania in particular.[269]

The Court began with an examination of the two Moroccan views, namely the "internal acts invoked by Morocco" and the "international acts said by it to show that the Sultan's sovereignty was directly recognized".[270] It dismissed neither argument as *a priori* invalid and thus implied that Morocco's sovereignty could be based on both. Again, the possibility of conflict between them was left undiscussed. This was possible because both were interpreted so as to produce the same consequence.

---

[264] Oral argument by *Slaoui, ibid*. Pleadings IV pp. 125–127.
[265] Oral arguments by *Isoart* and *Dupuy, ibid*. pp. 264–271, 301–305.
[266] Oral arguments by *Maouloud* and *Salmon, ibid*. pp. 355 *et seq*, 429–438.
[267] Oral argument by *Cheikh, ibid*. pp. 393–420.
[268] Written argument by Spain, *ibid*. Pleadings I pp. 206–208.   [269] *Ibid*. pp. 87–108.
[270] *Ibid*. Reports 1975 p. 49 (§ 108).

First, the Court held the evidence inconclusive to establish Moroccan "immemorial possession". The Sultan did exercise some jurisdictional authority but evidence of the effectiveness of this authority was insufficient. The analogy with the Eastern Greenland case, invoked by Morocco, was rejected.[271] Here the question concerned a territory actually populated. The Sultan's acts were interpreted so as not to establish effective possession.[272]

Second, the argument from general recognition of Moroccan sovereignty focused on a series of bilateral treaties between Morocco and third States from 1767 until 1911.[273] But the Court did not construe these so as to amount to collective recognition. A distinction was made between the Sultan's authority and his sovereignty. While the invoked treaty formulations (recognizing Western Sahara as "a part of Morocco" or "comprised" in Morocco) did contain a recognition of the former, they did not imply a recognition of the latter.[274]

The Mauritanian claims were rejected in a brief discussion in which the Court found that the Bilad Shinguitti lacked the "common institutions or organs" which would have justified treating it as an area under unified sovereignty.[275] The Mauritanian view is treated as partly one about direct effective possession ("political authority"), partly as a point about cultural, ethnic and religious ties,[276] that is, of indirect possession. None of these were demonstrated with sufficient clarity or intensity.[277] The question of external recognition is not discussed as it was absent from Mauritanian argument (a fact which shows the weakness of the Mauritanian case).

The Court ended up denying Moroccan as well as Mauritanian sovereignty. Some legal ties had existed but these did not amount to ties of sovereignty. The Court did not have the occasion to pronounce more on the right of self-determination of Western Sahara as this was not included in the question formulated to it. Had it gone into this matter more deeply – as some of the judges did – it would in all probability have argued – as Spain had – about the "inherent" character of such right (ascending argument) and about the recognition of that right generally (the descending point).[278]

---

[271] *Ibid.* pp. 42–43 (§§ 91–92).

[272] *Ibid.* pp. 43–48 (§§ 94–106). See also *Shaw* XLIX BYIL 1978 pp. 140–141, 143.

[273] ICJ: *Western Sahara* Case, Reports 1975 pp. 49–57 (§§ 108–129).

[274] *Ibid.* pp. 53, 54, 56–57 (§§ 117, 118, 120, 126, 129).   [275] *Ibid.* p. 63 (§ 149).

[276] *Ibid.* pp. 58–61 (§§ 133–138).   [277] *Ibid.* pp. 63–65 (§§ 147–152).

[278] Written Arguments by the Government of Spain, *ibid.* Pleadings I pp. 78–136.

The Court's treatment of the Moroccan claims, in particular, is a further illustration of its acceptance of two contradictory assumptions: namely that sovereignty may follow "from the inside" of a State's subjective acts as well as "from the outside", through general recognition. As neither position can be preferred the Court must move so that they seem compatible. In this way, considerations of factual power and normative constraint seem balanced while each State's sovereign consent goes unviolated. But this is done at the cost of determinate rule about territorial acquisition. Territorial title seems capable of being argued both without any actual acts of possession, by simple reference to general recognition (which could well be "tacit") as well as without any general recognition, by reference to the State's own acts (which might well have been held illegal by other States). Neither argument seems preferable because they both need each other in order to avoid immediate criticism. But once they rely on each other, neither can be used to overrule the other. They are ultimately the same.

4.8   Conclusion on sovereignty

In modern international law "sovereignty" plays a role analogous to that played by "liberty" in domestic liberal discourse. It works as a description and a norm. It characterizes the critical property an entity must possess in order to qualify as a State. And it involves a set of rights and duties which are understood to constitute the normative basis of international relations. But lawyers have difficulty to envisage how the relations between the descriptive and prescriptive parts of sovereignty doctrine should be understood.

Modern lawyers start out by emphasizing description in order to distinguish their system from that of the early lawyers. They adopt the "pure fact approach". Sovereignty is related to *de facto* independent power. Any other solution would fail to give effect to the assumption that liberty is basic – that there is no justification to impose restrictions on liberty which cannot be derived from liberty itself (for instance, from free consent). But difficulties emerge when we want to explain which facts count and what the boundaries of liberty are.

If we rely on the self-definition of the entity, we shall lapse into apologism and other entities' sovereignty seems violated. There must be an anterior rule about the conditions for sovereignty. This creates the difficulty of explaining the status and content of that rule. Two possibilities seem open: either it is a rule of natural law or a rule created by *other* States. Neither seems acceptable. If the conditions and extent of liberty were defined by a naturalistic rule, then the distinction between early and modern doctrines vanishes. If the conditions and extent of liberty are derived from what others say, then there is no initial liberty at all. An entity's sphere of legitimate action would be completely relative to what is externally decided.

In more general terms, the difficulty relates to holding the facts/law ("is"/"ought") opposition intact. For one seems capable of determination only in terms of the other. To see which facts are relevant, we must look for a legal rule. To establish the content of that rule without assuming the existence of a natural justice (and without abandoning the modern project), we must refer to facts.[279] The pure fact approach relies on the legal approach and *vice-versa*. Because both standpoints alone are vulnerable to criticism, neither can be maintained and argument is forced into constant movement between them. But as disputes about liberty organize themselves by polarizing legal views with pure fact views, their solution in these terms becomes impossible. In legal practice, solutions are arrived at only by means of evasion: by making it seem that no polarity exists in the first place. State behaviour is so interpreted as to manifest agreement.

This problem may be described in another, more familiar way. The moderns have admitted that there is nothing automatic about either facts or norms concerning sovereign statehood. No simple fact-description has seemed to allow an automatic inference about State rights and duties. Likewise, the norm "sovereignty" has been capable of accommodation with the most various rights and duties. To arrive at a determination of whether an entity is "sovereign" in some particular respect, it has seemed necessary to interpret the factual or normative materials available. The solution of normative problems concerning sovereignty has required choosing between several competing interpretations.

Discourse has typically opposed the self-interpretation of the State whose statehood or title has been the object of disagreement with a conflicting interpretation by another State. In addition, third States' interpretations have been held relevant as well. The difficulties courts (or other problem-solvers) have experienced in such cases have related to the justification of overruling any participant interpretation in favour of another one. Because the problem-solver cannot go beyond the

---

[279] This circularity is also pointed out by *Ross* (Text-book) (noting that to define "State" we refer to international law while to define the latter we refer to "States") p. 12.

interpretations to see what invoked facts or norms "really" say, any proposed solution has seemed to involve preferring sovereign interpretations *vis-à-vis* each other in an unjustifiable manner. Therefore, as we have seen, the ICJ has tended to assume that there was no material dispute in the first place; that there had, at some point, been an interpretation on which everyone had agreed.

But this solution looks like an outright distortion of participant understandings. Disputes arise because resources are scarce. Affirming one State's liberty to use resources means denying this liberty from another State. And States do disagree on how resources should be allocated between them. But the doctrine of sovereignty seems unable to cope with this disagreement without either making what seems like illegitimate preference or doing away with the dispute altogether.

A better way would be to uphold one claim and overrule others. This seems compelled by the quest for a truly normative law. Whether modern doctrine in fact contains such a law is a question to which we shall turn in the next chapter.

5

Sources

We have seen that it is, in principle, perfectly possible to conceptualize the totality of international legal norms as a consequence of the doctrine of sovereignty. In a sense, all legal norms are merely descriptions of what it is for each State to be sovereign. This is the way many classical lawyers presented their international law. Statehood was assumed given and the law followed in terms of the "absolute" and "conditional" rights which accompanied it. This approach seemed unworkable because of the abstract and ultimately subjective way that such rights were conceived. Moreover, it failed to explain the phenomenon that sovereignty was associable with the most varied kinds or rights and obligations. When modern lawyers were compelled to admit that sovereignty had no natural content, they also had to recognize that it did not serve as a reliable starting-point for deductions about the law.

The modern doctrine of sources of international law attempts to deal with the problem of the indeterminate character of the doctrine of sovereignty. On the one hand, it tries to provide for the concreteness of the law by refusing to accept any norms as simply given, either by virtue of statehood or some anterior normative code. It tells the lawyer where he can find the law in an objective fashion. On the other hand, sources doctrine also attempts to provide for the law's normativity by detaching it from the momentary views and interpretations which States might hold of its content. The doctrine of sources includes an attempt to reconcile the law's concreteness with its normativity. This is easiest to see if we realize that a distinct doctrine of sources becomes superfluous in a purely descending or a purely ascending argument about international law.

In the first place, it has not always been held necessary to separate a distinct doctrine of sources from the different substance-areas of the law. If one were to delineate the norms of international law by reference to their *content*, then there would be no place for a sources doctrine. One would simply assume the existence of some standards as normative and then deduce the rest of the norms from their conformity with these.[1] At best, something like a sources doctrine would only tell us how those deductions are correctly made.

Secondly, many lawyers think that the doctrine of sources is exhausted by the statement: the consent of States is the ultimate source of international law.[2] These lawyers have tended to regard sources doctrine as a formalistic dogma of by-gone analytic positivism.[3] They point out that anything can count as law as long as it emerges from *consent* and nothing which is not consensually supported can count as such. Alf Ross notes:

> The basis of the doctrine of legal sources is in all cases actual acceptance and that alone.[4]

---

[1] This is the reason why those whom I have called "early" writers never developed a distinct doctrine of sources: normativity was a matter of origins only in the most obvious sense – all law derived from God (or nature). Finding the law became a matter of content analysis: whether the potential standard corresponds to God's will or natural reason.

[2] *Wright* 7 IJIL 1967 (arguing that agreement, custom, reason and even authority *all* express consensual arguments, respectively expressed, tacit, presumed and implicit) p. 5. Indeed, some form of consensualism is the professed creed of most mainstream international lawyers. For example, *Brownlie* (Principles) asserts that sources are what count as "evidence of the existence of consensus among States ..." p. 2. To the same effect, see e.g. *Merrills* (Anatomy) holding international law "essentially an agreement" between States, pp. 1–5. Likewise, *Hingorani* (Modern) p. 15. *Henkin* (How) claims that it is built on "the principle of unanimity", p. 33.

[3] See e.g. *McWhinney* (UN Law-Making) p. 43. Significantly, many critics of the sources doctrine making this point take a "progressive" view on the law's content. According to them, a rigorous sources doctrine only serves to prohibit change and perpetuate the normative *status quo* – assumed to go against what most States now "accept". See e.g. *Ghozali* (Mélanges Chaumont) pp. 305–314. This view is reflected in theories which hold States as "Herren des Völkerrechts". These are driven to conclude that there is no basis to deny any formless consensus among States the status of law. See e.g. *Simma* (Reziprozität) pp. 40–43 and discussion in *Ballreich* (Festschrift Mosler) pp. 16–24. Sources doctrine no longer adequately reflects the various ways in which States create norms in informal, often "spontaneous" processes. See e.g. *Onuf* (Onuf: Lawmaking) pp. 14 *et seq*, 29–31, *passim*. For criticism of these approaches, see e.g. *Schachter* (Schwebel: Effectiveness) pp. 11–12.

[4] *Ross* (Text-book) p. 195. For Ross, the validity of the law is a psychological condition, a "feeling of validity". A theory of sources is merely a theory of what gives rise to such "feeling" and is, in that sense, "accepted". From this perspective, "sources" are less related to law's systemic properties than to the impulses under which judges work. This doctrine is adopted to international law by *Sørensen* (Sources) arguing that: "La doctrine des sources de droit s'occupe exclusivement des éléments généraux qu'entrent dans la motivation judiciaire et qui se présentent à l'esprit du juge d'une manière obligatoire ou comme imposés par une nécessité sociale", p. 24. To the same effect, see also *van Hoof* (Rethinking) pp. 198–199. The common criticism against such a

Under this view, a distinct doctrine of sources becomes unnecessary. At best, it will now work as a non-normative description of standard ways whereby States express their consent.

A distinct, normative doctrine of sources can emerge only after these two views have been rejected. Something should not be law simply because its content corresponds to some *a priori* normative standards or State consent. The very idea of a doctrine of sources is, in this sense, opposed to a purely descending or a purely ascending conception of international law. To carry out its task, sources doctrine must become *formal*. That is, it must assume that something is not norm *merely* by virtue of its content reflecting natural justice or State consent.[5] If sources doctrine did not contain such assumption, then it could not maintain law's distance from States' subjective, political views – the task for which it was created.[6] Only if the criterion for law is formal, a decision applying it does not involve the implication that one sovereign's political views are preferred to those of another's.

Because of its logical priority, the doctrine of sources tends to become abstract and, despite its methodological pretensions,[7] look like a foundational philosophy of international law. But if it were fully foundational, lawyers would have difficulty in justifying it. It would look like a fully descending, aprioristic set of normative demands and be vulnerable to the charge of being utopian. Sources doctrine must, in some way, link itself to concrete State behaviour, will and interest. This tension is reflected in two contrasting ways of understanding what the doctrine of sources is about. On the one hand, it is portrayed as a description of the processes whereby States create law. In this perspective, sources doctrine is concrete as it merely reflects, or describes, anterior social developments. On the other hand, it is understood to tell us in which places law can be found. From this viewpoint, it works as an

---

perspective is, of course, that it fails to account for the law's normativity. It includes no theory on what factors judges *should* take into account.

[5] See further *Kennedy* (Structures) pp. 101–104.

[6] As *Schachter* 178 RCADI 1982/V points out, the function of the sources discourse is to guarantee the law's objectivity, p. 60. See also *Onuf* (Onuf: Lawmaking) pp. 9–13.

[7] As *Bleckmann* (Grundprobleme) notes, most of modern discussion of "method" takes place under the sources doctrine, pp. 15–17. This is understandable as "method" is conceived through the analogy with natural sciences: its task is not to *create* the object, only to indicate where it is to be found (i.e. precisely what many consider the function of "sources"). Typically *Rosenne*'s book on the "Practice and Methods of International Law" opens up with the explanation that the task of method is to show "where-to-find-your-law-and-how-to-read-it", p. ix. Consequently, the book becomes a review of where to "find" treaties, judicial decisions, custom and so on.

independent methodology which can produce normatively constraining results.[8] In other words, it contains a theory of legislation and a theory of adjudication within itself. Treaties, custom and general principles of law recognized by civilized nations seem, on the one hand, like descriptions of law-creating processes and, on the other, like the objectified results of those processes. In this way sources doctrine includes a concrete and a normative perspective within itself: the law it projects is a result of concrete State action and yet something independent from it.

My purpose is not to achieve full description of how lawyers have discussed sources but to expose the *structure* of sources argument. I shall illustrate the opposition of ascending and descending arguments about international law by reference to the tension between a consensual and a non-consensual understanding of what sources doctrine is about. I shall discuss this tension first within the orthodox theory of sources (5.1) in two parts. The first part (5.1.1) shall outline the basic structure of sources doctrine, opposing ascending arguments about "consent" to descending ones about "justice". In the second part (5.1.2) I shall argue that sources doctrine contains a master principle of tacit consent. I shall illustrate the discursive functioning of this master principle in three doctinal areas: treaty interpretation (5.2), unilateral declarations (5.3) and acquiescence-estoppel (5.4). This will be followed by a discussion of five cases from the practice of the ICJ (5.5). I shall conclude the chapter by the argument that sources doctrine has failed to provide a determinate means for identifying the law as it is based on the assumption that neither "justice" nor "consent" can be known without engendering the objections about utopianism and apologism.

---

[8] For modern discussion of the ambiguous character of the idea of a legal "source", see e.g. *Jennings* (Cheng: Teaching) pp. 3–4; *Fitzmaurice* (IIL 1973) pp. 249–251. For the classic debate, see *Corbett* VI BYIL 1925 pp. 29–30; *Sørensen* (Sources) pp. 13–14; *Parry* (Sources) pp. 1–5; *van Hoof* (Rethinking) pp. 57–60; *Fitzmaurice* (Symbolae) p. 153; *Kunz* 47 AJIL 1953 p. 663. Many have suggested to do away with the term altogether. See e.g. *Corbett* VI BYIL 1925 p. 29; *Wolfke* (Custom) p. 11; *D'Amato* (Custom) pp. 264–268; *Onuf* (Onuf: Lawmaking) pp. 14–31. Sources doctrine is riddled with dualisms which in one way or another transform the opposition between (subjective) legislative politics and (objective) adjudicative ascertainment. These oppositions include the contrasts between "material" and "formal" sources, "sources" and "evidences" as well as "law-making processes" and "law-determining agencies". For conventional discussion, see e.g. *Gihl* (Scandinavian Studies) p. 72; *Rousseau* (Droit international public I) pp. 57–58; *Sørensen* (Sources) pp. 13–14; *Parry* (Sources) pp. 4–5; *Fitzmaurice* (Symbolae) pp. 153–154; *Schwarzenberger* (International Law I) pp. 26–28; *idem* (Dynamics) p. 6 and comment on the latter by *Parry* (Sources) p. 92. See further *Wolfke* (Custom) pp. 116–118; *Suy* (Actes) p. 217. For perceptive commentary, see *Floum* 24 Harv.ILJ 1983 pp. 270–272.

5.1 Sources theory

Much of sources theory has been consecrated to the topic of the *basis of obligation*. This seeks to give the ultimate reason for why law binds, or the *a priori* from which legal argument is thought to proceed. Standard debates have organized themselves around such dichotomies as naturalism/positivism, sociological(biological!)/voluntaristic explanations, for example. The law's binding character is sought from either somewhere beyond the State (in a natural morality, community interest, legal logic etc.) or within the State (its will, interest, fundamental rights, self-determination etc.). Doctrine's awareness of the importance of these dichotomies is reflected in the way it uses them to organize its own history. A period of naturalism is contrasted with a period of positivism and these again with some "eclectic" period. Yet, the contrasts re-emerge within modernism as it understands different sources (treaty, custom, general principles) variably from both perspectives. Their binding force is thought to reflect sometimes justice or social necessity, sometimes State consent or interests.[9] No period has been able to impose itself in a permanent manner on others.

---

[9] I have been inspired for the argument in this chapter by *Kennedy* (Structures) pp. 11–107. He reconstructs sources discourse through its constant opposition and association of consensualist ("hard") and non-consensualist ("soft") rhetorics. Though these are exhaustive and mutually exclusive ways of arguing about sources, neither can be fully accepted: "When pressed, the hard defender of a norm can be forced to concede that the norm can only be binding if it is soft. Likewise, the defender of a soft norm can be forced to defend his norm in hard terms. Because neither set of arguments can be convincing by itself and neither can trump the other, argument within this structure could go on endlessly without resolution", p. 31. The inability to achieve a resolution reflects the need to imagine an authoritative order within a world of autonomous sovereigns. Kennedy discusses various strategies for including both hard and soft rhetorics in the arguments distinguishing between the different classes of sources (treaty/ custom, custom/general principles etc.) as well as in the areas of unilateral declaration, *rebus sic stantibus* and custom, *ibid.* p. 33 *et seq.* Each portrays the basic tension behind the various "strategies of closure" which make it seem as if consensual justification could co-exist with non-consensual justification in a non-problematic manner. This argument is also contained in *idem* 2 Am.U.J.Int'l L.& Pol'y 1987 pp. 1–96. See also *idem* 23 GYIL 1980 (discussing the tension between "consent-based" and "external" arguments within sources discourse by reference to the "fundamental contradiction" of individuality and community in international life) pp. 361 *et seq*, 370, 378–379.

A similar outlook towards international legal argument has been used by some others as well (presumably under the influence of Kennedy and Critical Legal Studies scholars). Thus *Koh* 23 Harv.ILJ 1982 identifies the opposition between "subjectivity" and "purposiveness" as controlling the discourse on the permissibility of reservations to multilateral

Modernism acknowledges that neither contrasting position can be consistently preferred because they also rely on each other. Naturalism needs positivism to manifest its content in an objective fashion. "Justice", "common interest" or "reasonableness" seem to be arguable in a tangible way only by linking them to what States have thought them to mean – to what they have *consented* to. Positivism needs natural law in order to answer the question "why does behaviour, will or interest create binding obligations"?

To avoid arguing in a circle, it needs a *non-consensual* principle. Because neither position is sustainable alone, doctrine must attempt a reconciliation.[10] However, each reconciliation will remain temporary.

---

treaties, pp. 71, 73–76 *et seq. Floum* 24 Harv.ILJ 1983 discusses the effect of will/non-will approaches to the indeterminacy of international legal and diplomatic argument in general, pp. 278–283 and *Boyle* 26 Harv.ILJ 1985 observes the indeterminate and structuring character of the attempt to define international law by reference to some "essential" attributes in it while each definition will turn out to include contested, political ideas. The result, he argues, is a reifying legal discourse which cannot live up to its expectations of rational objectivity and constantly reinforces the sceptic's intuition about the system's ultimate irrelevance, pp. 327–359.

Useful discussions outside international doctrine include also *Unger* (Modern Society) (discussing the opposition between an instrumental and a non-instrumental view of rules as explanations of what holds society together) pp. 262–265; *Collins* (Twining: Legal Theory) (discussing the opposition between "choice theory" and "interests theory" as rival explanations of the enforceability of contracts) pp. 136–151 and *Dalton* 94 Yale L. J. 1985 (discussing contract doctrine by reference to the dichotomies of public/private, objectivity/subjectivity (intent) and form/substance) pp. 1010–1095 *et seq.*

[10] The fact that positivism and naturalism rely on each other has been frequently observed. See e.g. *Kosters* (Fondements) (for an analysis of this point in 19th century doctrine) pp. 212–217. See also *Schiffer* (Legal Community) (tracing the non-consensual assumptions behind Oppenheim's apparently consensual discourse) p. 86 *et seq. Lauterpacht* XXIII BYIL 1946 pp. 22–24. This is also the source of much modern frustration with the standard way of opposing naturalism and positivism to each other. See e.g. *Floum* 24 Harv.ILJ 1983 pp. 271–272 and further *infra* n. 31. A typical, illustrative rhetoric of reconciliation is contained in *Séfériadès* 34 RCADI 1930/IV, establishing his position by a criticism of Jellinekian "subjectivism", on the one hand, and naturalism as well as Kelsen's positivism, on the other. Each seems capable of being manipulated to support political purposes, pp. 188–189, 191–200. A realist ("objective", non-manipulable) theory must start from affirming that law emerges from "will". In contrast to Jellinek, however, one State's will is insufficient. What is needed is a *volonté générale* (surprisingly, there is no reference to Triepel!). Yet, this is not an "arbitrary" will – it is "nullement la consequence du hazard ou d'un caprice du moment", p. 184. It expresses basic moral and social needs. Will creates laws but (as if this were simply an innocent correction) only "dans la mesure ou ils ne heurtent pas la morale internationale", p. 205. The argument is capable of opposing earlier "mistaken" views because it is voluntaristic and non-voluntaristic simultaneously. As such, however, it is ultimately vulnerable to criticism from both perspectives. See further *supra* ch. 3 n. 72.

When pressed by argument, the lawyer is forced to rely either on consent or something that overrules consent in a way which makes his argument seem either utopian or apologist. Chen puts the dilemma clearly. Doctrine is:

> ... faced with two alternatives, either to presuppose an objective juridical order, above the State, thereby renouncing its claim as a legal theory, or to reject the binding force of international law, thereby amounting to a rejection of international law qua law.[11]

As a result, two strands of argument, or rather two movements, characterize modern sources discourse. One starts from an ascending justification and proceeds so as to deny it in application. The movement is from pure consent into something more, or other, than it. A second strand starts with a descending, non-consensual theory of binding force and moves to demonstrating its correctness by its closeness to consent. The strands are vigorously opposed and accuse each other, respectively, of apologism and utopianism. But their movement is towards the same point; the point at which justice emerges with consent to create a norm which would be both concrete and normative.

5.1.1   Consent v. justice

To quote Kelsen:

> ... toute cette théorie de 'sources' n'est qu'une paraphrase de la théorie bien connue de l'autolimitation de l'Etat, suivant laquelle l'Etat ne pourrait être obligé que par sa propre volonté.[12]

Twentieth-century theorizing about sources constructs itself by its opposition to the autolimitation view which it understands to claim that an obligation is binding on a State only if the State has voluntarily consented to it. This, in orthodox interpretation, is an apologist doctrine, incapable of securing a binding international law.[13]

At least four standard objections have been voiced against full consensualism.[14] First, to say that law is identical with consent argues too much

---

[11] *Chen* (Recognition) p. 26.   [12] *Kelsen* 14 RCADI 1926/IV p. 285.

[13] See *supra* ch. 2.3.2.1.

[14] By "consensualism", obviously, different ideas might be meant. *Schachter* 178 RCADI 1982/ V distinguishes between five meanings: 1) the view that international law in general is accepted by States; 2) that a State may opt out of it; 3) that the creation of new rules requires the consent of all; 4) that a State which has not consented to custom may reject it;

because anything that States will at any moment would then be law to them. This not only creates tremendous difficulties of law-ascertainment but it would be a fully apologist doctrine: If there is no distance between "will" and "law", then there is no justification to impose a standard on a non-consenting State. Limits on State freedom which are merely willed and capable of being altered at any change of will are no normative limits at all.[15] Pure consensualism distorts the law's instrumental purpose as it merely enregisters existing *status quo*.[16] Behind a relativist and tolerant disguise it betrays an inherent inability of criticizing odious instances of State practice.[17]

Second, consensualism argues too little as it does not tell us from where to find consent. It is one thing to argue that law emerges from consent and another to say that UN General Assembly resolutions, for example, express consent. Even if the former were plausible it would be too abstract. The latter is concrete but probably false. In addition to what Fitzmaurice and Thirlway have said about the imperative need for a rule which provides an exhaustive enumeration of sources from a logical point of view, a meaningful theory of sources must go beyond general statements about the priority of consent to indicating

5) that a State which has objected to custom may reject it, pp. 33–39. I shall however, refrain from a stipulative definition and regard as "consensualist" any doctrine, argument or position which *sets itself in opposition* to a doctrine, argument or position which claims to override State will. For me, the normative sense of "consensualism" is simply – and exhaustively – in its claim to override some other view *because* this does not give required effect to what States will. This choice gives effect to the insight that words or arguments do not have any intrinsic meaning but that they possess sense only to the extent they differ from other words or arguments. It respects the self-understandings of programmatic consensualists as these have grounded their position in a *criticism* of non-consensualistic (naturalistic, sociological, psychological) views. See e.g. *Triepel* (Völkerrecht) pp. 28–32; *Oppenheim* 2 AJIL 1908 pp. 327–336. For useful, short accounts of consensualism as a theory of political legitimation, see e.g. *Raphael* (Problems) pp. 85–102; *Simmons* (Moral Principles) p. 57 *et seq.*

[15] Among many general "refutations" of consensualism, stressing this point, see e.g. *Le Fur* 54 RCADI 1935/IV pp. 21–32; *Brierly* (Basis of Obligation) pp. 11–12; *Djuvara* 64 RCADI 1938/II pp. 552–559; *Fitzmaurice* 92 RCADI 1957/II pp. 36–47. See further e.g. *Verdross* (Einheit) p. 37; *Ross* (Text-book) pp. 39–40; *Rousseau* (Droit international public I) p. 36. See also *Boyle* 26 Harv.ILJ 1985 p. 337.

[16] *De Visscher* (Theory) p. 21. The paradox is that a purely consensual theory would fail to explain legal change in a situation where 1% of the community opposes it. In such case, it will have to accept that it is this opinion which is the collective choice – in which case, of course, the consent of 99% seems violated. *Levine* (Liberal Democracy) p. 30.

[17] *Strauss* (Natural Right) pp. 3–6.

which acts express consent and which do not.[18] A pure consensualism does away with any significant sources doctrine. If simple consent were enough to establish law, why would the specific form of a treaty or the requirement of material practice in custom be necessary at all?[19] But many – though not all – consensualists do think that these requirements (like the sources doctrine) have significance.

Third, consensualism is logically flawed. The emergence of a consensual norm assumes the existence of a non-consensual norm according to which consent is to have law-creating effect. As Hart puts it, voluntary obligations presuppose the existence of power-conferring rules; rules which invest the agents with the power to bind through will. This rule cannot, however, itself be based on consent because we would then have to explain why that consent is binding. And so on *ad infinitum*.[20] The rule which explains the binding force of consent – call it, for example, *pacta sunt servanda* – must be presumed to exist irrespective of further consent.[21]

---

[18] The point is that the idea of exhaustiveness is implicit in the very notion of "source" whose function is to establish certainty in law-application. See *Thirlway* (Customary Law) pp. 37–39; *Günther* (Völkergewohnheitsrecht) pp. 75–76.

[19] *Thirlway* (Customary Law) pp. 37–39, 75; *Deutsch* (Deutsch-Hoffmann: Relevance) points out that a purely consensualist sources doctrine would only contain a methodology for opinion-analyses, pp. 87–88.

[20] See *Hart* (Concept) pp. 42–43 and 219–220. See also *Ago* 51 AJIL 1957 pp. 702–707. Even early liberals did think that the binding force of the social contract must rest elsewhere than in the contract itself. For this point, see *Hume* (Of the Original Contract, in: Hume: Essays) pp. 467–468. For the argument in international law, see e.g. *Verdross* 16 RCADI 1927/I pp. 277–278; *Djuvara* 64 RCADI 1938/II pp. 542–559; *Sørensen* (Sources) pp. 14–15; *Lauterpacht* (Function) pp. 418–419; *Fitzmaurice* 92 RCADI 1957/II pp. 36–37, 38 *et seq*; *idem* (Symbolae Verzijl) pp. 163–164; *Verdross* (Einheit) pp. 8, 10, 37–38, 104–105; *Remec* (Position) pp. 32–33; *Nardin* (Law, Morality) pp. 214–216; *Mosler* 36 ZaöRV 1976 (on the "structurally conditioned" character of the Völkerrechtsverfassung) pp. 31–37; *Corbett* (Law and Society) pp. 71–72. See also *Jacqué* (Eléments) (noting that though a theory of "legal acts" (actes juridiques) needs to refer to the subjective will of the actor, it must also assume the existence of a legal "base" which allows will to transform into a legal act) pp. 27–33 and *passim*. See further *Gounelle* (Motivation) pp. 23–31 and *passim*.

[21] Obviously, lawyers have been at pains to demonstrate how the *pacta* norm can be both non-consensual and objective (that is, non-political) at the same time. For some, it is a logical hypothesis. See e.g. *Kelsen* 14 RCADI 1926/IV pp. 256, 265. Kelsen later reformulated his view so that the hypothesis obligated States to behave as they customarily have behaved (Principles) p. 446. *Anzilotti* (Cours du Droit International I) holds the *pacta* norm as indeed hypothetical but – contrary to Kelsen – constructs the normative order on a factual social contract whose binding force this norm intends to secure, pp. 42–45. Others list the *pacta* norm into the "minimum content of natural law". See e.g. *Hart* (Concept)

Fourth, many doctrines which consensualists have had no difficulty to accept run against pure consensualism. Even the most ardent supporters of consensualism concede that not *all* consent – for instance uncommunicated consent or consent to attacking a third State – creates binding obligation.[22] Moreover, if it is the case that new States are bound by existing law – or old States in their relations with the new – then at least to that extent their consent is irrelevant. The obligation comes from elsewhere than consent – for example, from the "pure fact" of coming into existence of the new State.[23]

pp. 189–195; *idem* (Essays) pp. 112–116; *D'Amato* (Onuf: Lawmaking) pp. 96–98. *De Visscher* (Theory) holds it a moral norm, pp. 97–99. So does *Suy* (Actes), adding that it nevertheless has truth value (valeur objectif) as it is needed to "réaliser la sécurité et l'harmonie des rapports sociaux", p. 14. *Verdross* (Festschrift Wehberg) points out that even the Kelsenian hypothetical norm must assume the presence of certain objective values (namely those of social peace), pp. 386–387; *idem* 16 RCADI 1927/I pp. 284–286; *idem* (Verfassung) pp. 28–33. See also *Jacqué* (Eléments) p. 36. Other versions envisage the *pacta* or the corresponding basic norm as simply an "objective", "structural" or "logical" necessity. See e.g. *Bourquin* 35 RCADI 1931/I pp. 77–80; *Fenwick* (International Law) pp. 36–37; *Crawford* (Creation) pp. 79–80; *Skubiszewski* 31 ZaöRV 1971 p. 846; *van Hoof* (Rethinking) pp. 72–73; *Henkin* (How) pp. 89–90; *Bos* (Methodology) pp. 221–222. *Friedmann* (Changing) holds it a customary rule p. 300. But *Lavalle*, 33 ÖZöRV 1982, notes – and it follows from what is said in the text – that this cannot be so as it is used precisely to explain custom's binding force pp. 9–28.

   As *Floum* 24 Harv.ILJ 1983 notes, this is not the end of difficulties. For absent an "objective" test for what such non-consensual explanation might be, it is difficult to avoid the conclusion that the law binds simply because States think so – in which case we are back where we started and fail to come up with a reason for holding a norm binding on a State which does not agree to it p. 27. Some have despaired and renounced altogether the attempt to create a workable, non-consensual explanation. They believe the matter of "foundation" to be an "extralegal question" which cannot be solved within the legal system at all. See e.g. *Rousseau* (Droit international public I) p. 37; *Strupp* 47/4RCADI 1933/I p. 258 *et seq*; *Kunz* 47 AJIL 1953 p. 663; *Remec* (Position) p. 33; *Günther* (Völkergewohnheitsrecht) pp. 77–78; *Onuf* (Onuf: Lawmaking) arguing that this question can be only solved by a sociological or psychological study, pp. 29–31. For a criticism, see *Finnis* (Natural) pp. 357–359. Clearly, such pragmatism is self-defeating. To avoid apologism, an explanation about why non-consenting States should be bound is needed.

22 Contract lawyers have been clear about the fact that mere "will" is insufficient to create binding obligation. Some external act, at least, is needed to make a promise binding. See generally *Atiyah* (Promises) pp. 20–21 and *passim*. The point is that one cannot simply equate the law with consent without losing the idea of a "rule" as a standard for conduct, not a simple description of will. See *Nardin* (Law, Morality) pp. 195–198. See also *Schachter* (Schwebel: Effectiveness) pp. 21–22.

23 There is, of course, dispute about whether new States are bound by existing international law or not. A vast majority of (Western) lawyers have rejected full consensualism and believe the State to be bound – often by some argument from "social necessity". See e.g. *Scelle* 46 RCADI 1933/IV pp. 433–434; *Fitzmaurice* 92 RCADI 1957/II p. 98 *et seq*; *Thirlway*

The problem is how to create distance between consent and binding force without having to assume a fully naturalistic position – a position which regards consent as wholly irrelevant and thus seems vulnerable to the charge of being utopian and manipulable at will.[24]

Now, we have seen that classical lawyers attempted to avoid the above objections by assuming that consent was not simply arbitrary (Willkür). They took it to mean a rational principle which reflected the nation's spirit and history.[25] Similarly, many 20th century jurists have attempted to avoid the unacceptable consequences of full consensualism by basing law on ideas about social or biological necessity. The law is binding not because it reflects what States happen to will but because this is compelled by the objective need to live in society.[26] This would seem to allow overruling a State's consent without engaging in moral theory.

(Customary Law) p. 55; *Rousseau* (Droit international public I) p. 313; *Sørensen* 101 RCADI 1960/III p. 45; *Barberis* XIV NTIR 1967 p. 373. See also ILC: Report to The UN General Assembly 1974, YILC 1974 vol. II/I p. 212 (by implication). Some critics have held that new States have the right to "pick and choose". See e.g. *Anand* (New States) pp. 71–72. The difficulty with such a fully consensual position is that it frees *existing* States from their duties towards the new entities. For it cannot be argued that new States are bound by their consent while existing States' consent is irrelevant without violating sovereign equality. The advantage gained by new States by their right "to pick and choose" is countered by the non-existence for existing States of duties towards them. *Sørensen* 101 RCADI 1960/III p. 45 *et seq*; *Waldock* 106 RCADI 1962/II p. 52; *Unger* (Völkergewohnheitsrecht) p. 63; *Bernhardt* 36 ZaöRV 1976 p. 69. Therefore, some lawyers have held that new States are bound regardless of their consent to the basic, structural principles of international law, while their consent is needed to make regular customary norms binding against them. See e.g. *McWhinney* (UN Lawmaking) pp. 47–48. But a fully non-consensualist explanation seems vulnerable to the objection of being utopian – what would the relevant "social necessity" be or the non-derogable structural principle and who would be the judge thereof? This has led others to adopt a tacit consent construction. New States are bound because, by their entry into the "family of States", they *consent* to being bound. See *Crawford* (Creation) pp. 4–5. This argument bears an affinity to the liberal point about "residence" grounding political obligation and its ultimate failure lies in the absurdity of even suggesting that a State might opt for not giving its consent in this sense. But a tacit consent argument also fails to explain why *existing* States should be bound. If we take it seriously as a consensual argument, then we must either violate old States' sovereign equality or accept the embarrassing consequence that they may at least in principle withhold their consent and thereby gain the right to treat the new entity as non-existent. *None* of the available constructions seems to avoid objections compelled by the system itself.

[24] *Stone* (Falk-Black: Future) notes that unless the law departs from abstract doctrines of justice it is bound to become irrelevant and perish as a normative order altogether, pp. 382–399.

[25] See *supra* ch. 2.3.2.1. and 2.3.2.3.

[26] *Duguit* (Traité) pp. 276 *et seq*, 316 *et seq*. For criticism, see e.g. *Friedmann* (Legal Theory) pp. 159–171. For more recent attempts to argue about international law from "man's basic attributes", see *Landheer* (Sociology) pp. 17–19. *Verdross*

But modern lawyers have been no more succesful than their predecessors in this. They have been unable to explain their assumed objective
needs so as to avoid the criticism of arguing from an essentially political
position.[27]

Generalizations from economic or social necessities, psychology,
mass consciousness etc. have not been accompanied with explanations
about how to derive reliable normative consequences from them.[28]
Modern sociological theories end up in demonstrating their content

(Festschrift Wehberg) calls for studies in "philosophical anthropology", p. 388.
D'Amato (Onuf: Lawmaking) appeals for studies on the "nature of the system",
pp. 93–94, 98 *et seq*. The former treads on very disputed ground: indeed, the argument
from man's "essence" can only be defended on assumptions which are among the most
contentious ones in politics or human sciences. D'Amato, on the other hand, fails to
explicate what the "nature" of the system is. As we shall see in chapter 7, there are at least
two radically different – indeed mutually opposed – ways of conceptualizing it.

[27] Thus *Scelle* 46 RCADI 1933/IV, for example, concedes that though positive sources do
not *create* the law, they are the best available evidence of its content – of what the "fond
juridique première" requires. There is a "hypothèse de base nécessaire" that legislation
expresses the assumed biological necessities in a trustworthy fashion, p. 428 *et seq*; *idem*
(Précis II) pp. 298–299. This, of course, makes justifiable *Le Fur*'s 54 RCADI 1935/IV
criticism according to which drawing the legitimacy of positive laws from social or
biological necessities tends to degenerate into an apology of absolutism, pp. 96–98.
    The same criticism is equally applicable against the soviet doctrine which assumes
that State will – the immediate source of law – reflects inescapable economic necessities.
Tunkin's (Theory) argument is crystal-clear. International law emerges from "agreement". But the wills which "concord" to make the agreement are not arbitrary (as in
bourgeois doctrine). The will of the State has a class character – it is "determined by the
nature of the state", p. 211. But this is not the end of the matter. For: "economic
structure determines the class character of a state", p. 236. In the formation of the will as
well as in the formation of the "agreement" (or "concordance") the society's economic
base, its social laws "exert a determinative influence", p. 236. The argument is both
consensualist and non-consensualist simultaneously. The two strands are held together
by the assumption that will always "reflects" some non-voluntary reality. The State's
will is always assumed to be the correct manifestation of the determining economic
base. The same argument is present in *Kartashkin* (Macdonald-Johnston: Structure and
Process). He observes, first, that law is determined by "economic foundation", p. 80.
Then comes the assumption that "the will of the ruling class is primarily determined by
the economic structure of society", *ibid*. Finally he tells us that "contemporary international law" comes about by way of "compromise leading to numerous agreements",
p. 83. By this chain of arguments, his position – like Scelle's – is consensualist and non-
consensualist at the same time. The integrity of the (normative) assumption of a
determining base is preserved while it remains possible to argue the law from (concrete)
State will. "Will" is absolutized as is also the non-voluntary "base". But the argument's
normative assumptions turn themselves into an apology for any existing ruling class;
any *status quo* can claim consensual support merely because it exists.

[28] Many have lamented the fact that the social conception of law has not been accompanied with sociological studies in international relations on which the law's "ought"

by reference to State consent, sometimes with an inordinate degree of closeness to particular State policy.[29] If they were left at a fully non-consensual level, they would become vulnerable to the same criticism which early liberals voiced against their predecessors. Their generalities would not be able to ground an objective law-ascertainment practice because "the criteria according to which those who apply international law must interpret it are so vague".[30] Consequently, as was noted already by Hall, naturalists (non-consensualists) tend to become positivists (consensualists) when they seek evidence for their norms.[31] They refer back to consent. Only those economic or sociological facts are relevant which States think are so. In other words, even professed non-consensualists seem forced to argue in a consensual way to avoid politics.

For the modern lawyer, it is very difficult to envisage, let alone to justify, a law which would divorce itself from what States think or believe to be law. Liberal lawyers started from the assumption that questions of justice (normative necessities, objective interests) are ultimately matters of subjective opinion. They opted for a consensualism which is constantly on the move towards a principle which would enable it to avoid the criticism about its apologistic character. But if modernism takes this search seriously, it will have to abandon its initial consensualism altogether – which will

could be based. See e.g. *van Kleffens* 82 RCADI1935/I pp. 77–78; *Stone* (Visions). This is, of course, an incident of the much larger irony of liberal reason which initially believed in the construction of a practical reason along the lines of the epistemological revolution in the natural sciences but which remained, despite attempts, unable to provide for a moral science in which certainty would be based on self-evident axioms or physical sensations. For a discussion of these attempts (especially in Locke and Hume) and the consequent move from initial optimism to moral irrationalism, see *Spragens* (Irony) pp. 50–75, 196–255; *MacIntyre* (After Virtue) p. 36 *et seq.*

[29] See *supra* ch. 3.3.3.   [30] *Nardin* (Law, Morality) p. 210.

[31] *Hall* (International Law) pp. 1–2. The same point is made by *Djuvara* 64 RCADI 1938/II pp. 498–500; *Fitzmaurice* (IIL 1973) pp. 308–309. *D'Amato* (Onuf: Lawmaking) is a good example of a modern naturalist in this respect. For him, natural law resides not in some immutable "essences" but in changing human "purposes, or ends", p. 89. By this movement D'Amato can make his law seem concrete and escape modern criticisms against innate ideas or natural essences. But the really important point here is whether such "purposes" may, or may not, be opposed to States which deny that they share, or have ever shared, them. If they cannot, then the position is indistinguishable from a positivist one and D'Amato's objections against it become applicable against himself. If they can, then D'Amato should either present a theory about what it is that allows him to know better than the State itself what its "purposes" are or hold a fully non-consensual theory about essential human purposes – a theory vulnerable to the objection of utopianism which his argument was originally intended to avoid.

make it vulnerable to the criticisms through which it distanced itself from early naturalism. Two strategies by consensualists to guarantee the law's binding force illustrate this.

Having established themselves as non-naturalists, consensualists are led to assuming that law arises from individual wills. But people (and States) will different things. How can social order maintain itself if it can only be justified by reference to individual wills and there is no anterior standard of what one is allowed to will and what not? One solution is to postulate, along with Rousseau, that once different individual wills emerge as a *volonté générale*, they can be treated as a *Vereinbarung* of several wills into one coherent, normative will,[32] a consensus.[33] Initially, it is difficult to see why this would enable the consensualist to avoid the

---

[32] The application of this *Rousseauesque* idea (see *infra* nn. 35–37) in international law is generally attributed to *Triepel* (Völkerrecht) pp. 27 *et seq*, 51–53, 65 *et seq*. It is also present in the many contemporary doctrines which regard international law as a projection of "common consciousness". For *Barile* 161 RCADI 1978/III for example, the law is not a "conviction individuelle des membres de la communauté, mais seulement une convergence de ses convictions", pp. 48–49 *et seq*, 54–56. While it is possible to interpret "conscience" as a psychological or even metaphysical entity, it is difficult to see what other basis there is to maintain its concreteness than regarding it as a concordance of established State wills. Yet, the difference between this position and full, individualistic consensualism is uncertain.

[33] It is frequently held that international law emerges as a "formless consensus", out of an informal acceptance manifested in acts of several States which are directed at the same object. But this is not a recent perspective. It was expressed clearly by *Heffter* (Völkerrecht) in 1882. For him, the law was something more than, or behind, express agreements or customs. It was: " ... einen allseitigen ausdrücklichen oder doch mit Gewissheit voraussetzenden Einverständnis (consensus) innerhalb eines Gewissen Staatskreises, auf das Überzeugung, dass jener seiner Theile unter gleichen Umständen dieselbe Nöthigung so und nicht anderes zu handeln empfinden werde ... ", pp. 3, 5–6. Despite its apparent modernity, consensus theory essentially repeats the classical view that the law's ultimate foundation lies neither in natural morality nor in any formally expressed (and thus also formally retrievable) "will" but in a feeling, a sentiment of being bound, a "conscience juridique commune". Its rhetorical function is precisely to avoid the former associations so as to hold the law both concrete (after all, it is actual people's feelings which count) and yet flexible simultaneously. *François* 66 RCADI 1938/IV makes this explicit. Treaties or custom do not really make law, they only declare some part of it: "Ce qui importe, c'est que la communauté internationale d'une manière ou d'une autre, considère effectivement la norme comme formant partie du droit positif" p. 23. For modern consensus theories, see e.g. *Lissitzyn* (International Law) p. 35 *et seq*; *Zemanek* (Macdonald-Johnston: Structure and Process) p. 857 *et seq* (stressing the difference between consensus and unanimity and thus making explicit the not altogether consensual character of consensus) pp. 874–875, 877. For the view that "sources" are only manifestations of consensus, see also *Quadri* 113 RCADI 1964/III p. 319 *et seq*; *Simma* (Die Reziprozität) pp. 34, 40–43; *Wright* 43 AJIL 1948 (associating law with the

criticisms outlined above. A *volonté générale* stays one only so long as individual wills are directed at the same object. If there is disagreement, there is no such common will and the putative standard remains not binding.[34] As a practical matter, it is doubtful whether a community of opinion prevails among States to the extent that one could speak of a *volonté générale* among them. But the problem is clearly much less to explain why States which have agreed are bound than why also those States should be bound which have not. And this explanation is not easily attainable if one sticks to a purely consensualist understanding of the *volonté générale*.

For this reason, adherents to this view must move beyond its consensualist interpretation. Rousseau's own position is illustrative. The common will is not identical with the (arbitrary) "will of all".[35] It is a normative principle, denoting what people *should will* in order to enhance their own good. It corresponds to what is just, not what people actually consent to. This makes it consistent for Rousseau to argue that man can be "forced to be free" and cannot consent to slavery, for instance.[36] He is *non-consensually* bound by a theory of his *real interests*. This theory overrules his actual will. The position becomes fully non-consensualist.[37]

"predominant opinion of the legal community") p. 414. To the same effect, see *Falk* (Future) pp. 55–58; *D'Amato* (Onuf: Lawmaking) pp. 99–100; *Ballreich* (Festschrift Mosler) pp. 1 *et seq*, 16–24. The standard criticism, of course, points out the intangible, manipulable aspects of arguing from such "feelings" or a common consciousness.

[34] For these and other criticisms, see e.g. *Heilborn* 11 RCADI 1926/I p. 19; *Brierly* (Basis of Obligation) p. 16; *Günther* (Völkergewohnheitsrecht) pp. 30–32.

[35] See *Rousseau* (Social Contract) Bk II, ch. 3 (pp. 72–73); *idem* Bk IV, ch. 1 (pp. 150–151). See also comment in *Cranston, ibid.* (Introduction) pp. 37–38.

[36] For this famous argument, see *Rousseau* (Social Contract) Bk I, ch. 7 (pp. 63–64). Indeed, Rousseau contends that the general will "derives its generality less from the number of voices than from the common interest which unites them". Bk II, ch. 4 (p. 76). The *volonté* becomes a non-consensual theory of objective interests. How does Rousseau think that such interest can be known? It "... makes itself so manifestly evident that only common sense is required to discern it". Bk IV, ch. 1 (p. 149). The problem here is, of course, what happens if there is disagreement? In such case the very existence of self-evidence seems excluded. But if mere denial is sufficient to prove the absence of the interest, then the very purpose for which it was introduced is frustrated. We shall result in apologism. The argument from such interest must be assumed capable of *overriding* subjective wants or perceptions of interest. For the paradoxically non-liberal character of Rousseau's argument, see e.g. *Raphael* (Problems) pp. 99–102. Internationally, this poses the problem of how one can impose on a State an interest which is separated from its articulated wants without either violating sovereign equality or assuming the binding force of a natural morality.

[37] This is easy to see in, for example, the argument by *Bleckmann* (Grundprobleme). For him, international law rests on a consensus – albeit a "hypothetical" one, pp. 81,

Inasmuch as it means that the will of any *particular* State is negligible, then it is only another way of saying that States are bound irrespective of consent.[38]

But this movement by consensualists away from consensualism is vulnerable to the very criticism which consensualists originally directed at their naturalist opponents. How can a theory of objective interests, that is a theory about someone else *knowing better* what my interests are or what it is that I will or have willed, be defended in an objective way? Does it not, under the consensualist's own assumptions, look suspiciously like political opinions in disguise? Moreover, in order to "know better" we should have to accept that there exists a manner in which we can penetrate the subjectivity of the State to receive knowledge of the meaning, to the State itself, of its actions. But this would be an indefensible position within the liberal doctrine of politics. It would make legislation unnecessary. We could simply posit ourselves as dictators because we "know better" what States will or what lies in their interest – even better than what States have expressly said. It would make us Leviathans.[39] But any such theory seems indefensible as it loses the justification for which liberal theory based its superiority to early naturalism.

184–189. This is not "discovered" by looking at what States actually have consented to. It is constructed through a balancing of interests test. It is what, he assumes, States *would* (have reason to) consent to (if they were asked). See also *idem* (Funktionen) pp. 44–45. To call this construction "consensual" is a rhetorical move to make it seem more acceptable than if the balancing test would be argued on purely evaluative grounds.

[38] *Chen* (Recognition) p. 26. For an argument identical with Rousseau's insistence on holding separate "the will of all" and "general will" and ending up in recognizing the (non-consensually) normative character of "objectively existing . . . common interests" by a Soviet writer, see *Alexidze* 172 RCADI 1981/III p. 245.

[39] It has sometimes been argued that a State has violated international law by acting in deviance of its *own* interest. Thus, in the *Dispute between Texaco Overseas Petroleum Company/California Asiatic Oil Company v. the Government of the Libyan Arab Republic*, XVII ILM 1978, the plaintiff argued that the Libyan nationalizations were not taken in view of public interest but were a political, discriminatory measure. The tribunal noted that "it must regard the Libyan Government as having acted in accordance with its own sovereign appreciation of the national interest", p. 25 (§ 74.1). That settled the matter. Similarly *Libyan-American Oil Company (LIAMCO) v. the Government of the Libyan Arab Republic*, XX ILM 1981 p. 58 (§ 114). The denial of the argument of knowing better what a State's interests are follows from the inability of (liberal) doctrine consistently to justify a theory of objective interests (or *any* material principle of justice which would claim preference over a person's/State's wants). See generally *Levine* (Liberal Democracy) pp. 39, 43, 49, 65–66; *Raphael* (Problems) pp. 100–102, 139–140. See also *Mill* (On Liberty) ch. 3.

The sole way to avoid this objection would be to join in with Oppenheim's majoritarian opinion: "Common consent" binds not as the "will of all" but as that of an "overwhelming majority".[40] But this violates sovereign equality and thus conflicts with another of con-sensualism's main premises. Why should the (arbitrary) will of the majority bind a non-assenting minority?[41] This seems both utopian and apologist at the same time. It seems utopian as it is based on a (highly questionable) moral position according to which majority will shall always prevail. It seems apologist as it offers no standard for the majority.[42]

Another movement from consensualism towards binding law is the contract theory which claims to differ from the former view in that it does not assume State wills to be directed at the same object. In the contract, different wills oppose each other. Different sovereigns renounce some of their liberty to gain advantages from other States in return.[43]

The initial difficulty with this view, often noted, is that it seems to rest on a fiction. It has not been able to demonstrate the historical existence of such a contract on which it bases itself. Likewise, its con-ception of "State will" seems like an anthropomorphic metaphor without

---

[40] *Oppenheim* (International Law I) p. 16.

[41] The liberals never explained this so clearly. If the main premise is that obligation may arise only from consent, why should majority will bind the minority? The standard answer refers to tacit consent. See *Locke* (Two Treatises), Second Treatise, sect. 119 (p. 177); *Rousseau* (Social Contract) Bk IV, ch. II (pp. 153–154). For the weakness of this construction which assumes "residence" (not migrating) to suffice as evidence of consent, see *Simmons* (Moral Principles) pp. 71–74. Obviously, mere "residence" is irrelevant as an argument about consent in inter-State relations. States can hardly be expected to migrate from the planet in order to deny consent effectively. In any case, it seems clear that majority legislation may seem legitimate only in a system which shares basic values and a broad adherence to minority rights – conditions the presence of which internationally may seem doubtful. See *Zemanek* (Macdonald-Johnston: Structure and Process) pp. 869–871.

[42] A recent attempt to resuscitate Rousseau's reconciliation is contained in *Onuf* (Onuf: Lawmaking). He argues that law-emergence is a process which focuses on a common interest around which a formless consensus is gradually formed by a spontaneous but yet goal-directed psychologico-social process, pp. 28–31. But the construction does not – indeed cannot – establish a hierarchy between articulated individual will and the common interest from which it deviates. To prefer the former will lead into apologism, to prefer the latter would require a theory of "objective interests" which seems utopian. Onuf's may be an adequate description of norm-emergence but it is singularly useless as a *normative* theory about which rules may be opposed to a non-consenting State.

[43] See e.g. *Strupp* 47 RCADI 1934/I pp. 298–304 *et seq.* For modern adherents, see *van Hoof* (Rethinking) pp. 71–82, 153–154.

psychological reality.[44] Contractarian liberals have, therefore, moved to argue about the "hypothetical" nature of the contract.[45] But why should such a hypothesis be binding (*a fortiori* as law)? To be sure, some have argued that this question is unanswerable.[46]

But this is clearly unsatisfactory as apologist. Its binding force can be explained by reference to the *non-consensual* element of *pacta sunt servanda*, or confidence, or good faith, or reciprocity in a contract, community interest, social necessity or whatever.[47] In brief, one must assume a principle of "fairness", or justice, which makes the contract binding.[48]

But whose idea of what is fair or just should prevail in case there is disagreement about the existence or the validity of the contract? The law

---

[44] See e.g. *Sørensen* (Sources) p. 16; *Kunz* 47 AJIL 1953 p. 664; *Green* 74 RGDIP 1970 pp. 81–82; *Skubiszewski* 31 ZaöRV 1971 p. 840. For this and further criticism, see also *Günther* (Völkergewohnheitsrecht) pp. 25–27; *Unger* (Völkergewohnheitsrecht) pp. 11–16.

[45] This is sometimes done by constructing a theory on a hypothetical "original position" in which a group of persons would have to agree on the principles of social organization between themselves from behind a "veil of ignorance" about their own and others' particular capabilities, wants etc. See *Rawls* (Theory) pp. 11–22, 118 *et seq*, 136–142. The Rawlsian model is discussed and partly accepted as an adequate basis for a theory of international obligation by *Bleckmann* (Grundprobleme) pp. 266–268. The argument that justice emerges from decisions which rational agents in such circumstances would agree upon involves an attempt to combine ascending and descending justifications so as to avoid apologism (the use of empirical power in order to extract unequal advantages in the contract) and utopianism (the adoption of a transcendental (Kantian) rights theory). See the discussion in *Sandel* (Liberalism) pp. 16–17, 38–39. See further comment by *Lyons* (Ethics) pp. 136–139. *Dworkin's* (Taking) attempt to construct justice through a best possible theory justifying present social institutions is similar. He, too, attempts to combine an ascending and a descending vision of justice by presuming that a hypothetical person ("Hercules") can develop from existing institutions the conception of justice which is embedded in them and which in this sense can be confirmed consensually (by their embeddedness in those institutions) as well as non-consensually (in that nobody's consent is relevant to verify the attained conception of justice), pp. 105–130.

[46] See *supra* n. 21.

[47] For an elaborate argument according to which international law binds because of the justice-based need to protect legitimate expectations, see *Müller* (Vertrauensschutz) pp. 2, 78, 258 *et seq* and *passim*. For the argument that the law is based on the non-consensual principle of non-contradiction, see *Günther* (Völkergewohnheitsrecht) p. 156 *et seq*. For "reciprocity" as explanation of obligation, see further *Bleckmann* (Grundprobleme) pp. 162–163.

[48] On the principle of fairness which demands that people (States) which freely enter cooperative arrangements also abide by their rules, see *Rawls* (Theory) pp. 3 *et seq*, 111–114.

recognizes situations where contracts should no longer be binding because of, for example, changed circumstances (*rebus sic stantibus*). It is impossible to oppose an evaluation of circumstances on a State which does not share it without either assuming that the evaluation is the correct one as a matter of natural justice or because *other States* have accepted it. But the former is a utopian position, the latter violates sovereign equality.

The *volonté générale* and contractarian movements may, of course, be supplemented by other attempts to objectify consent. Without going into them,[49] it may be concluded that in order to avoid the objection about apologism, consensualism needs a principle beyond itself[50] – and it is a principle which consensualism cannot justify on its initial assumptions. To justify it – be it either a theory of objective interests or a conception of justice or fairness – consensualism must become (pure) non-consensualism. It is not a reconciliation that is achieved but a change of position. It is now held that the non-consensual standard *overrules* conflicting consent.

So, we seem to be in an interminable circle. Consensualism is needed because this seems the only way to guarantee the law's concreteness. Non-consensualism seems needed to provide for its binding force. And yet, both positions seem to exclude each other. Consensualism is justifiable only if non-consensualism is not. And *vice-versa*. In order to find out, in a given case, whether preference should be given to consent or a non-consensual principle of justice a meta-theory is needed to establish the preference. But this would have to be justified in either a naturalistic or a positivistic manner. In which case it could be opposed by a

[49] One of them is, however, worth a mention because of its initial plausibility. *Ago* 51 AJIL 1957 has argued that both (pure) naturalism and (pure) positivism seem flawed as attempts to explain the law's emergence: international law is neither a matter of pre-existing norms, nor one of "laying down" norms in a legislative process. Its emergence is a spontaneous process, a projection of "legal consciousness" on actual events and actions. For him, "legality is a qualification which legal science attributes to definite opinions", p. 729, see also pp. 700–707, 714 *et seq*. In other words, the law is controlled by and emerges from a sociologico-psychological process, conditioned by factual power and value-perceptions, as projected onto normative views by the legal profession. But it is difficult to see why such projections should be accepted as normatively controlling. It may explain something of how we come to think of certain propositions as "law". But it is silent on which norms are valid at particular moments and which not; it is useless as a normative (problem-solving) vision. For criticism, see also *Günther* (Völkergewohnheitsrecht) p. 76.

[50] It needs what *Fishkin* Nomos XXVIII has called a "perspective of impartiality", p. 215, *passim*.

contrasting view. And so on.[51] This explains why some have wished to exclude this whole discussion from legal argument. They think that basis of obligation is not a legal issue at all. These lawyers have assumed that for practical purposes it suffices for the lawyer to look at consent.[52]

But this discussion is not merely of purely philosophical or academic interest. For even if we refrain from discussing basis of obligation in the abstract, we are led into it in any standard argument about opposing norms on non-consenting States. On the very assumptions of standard doctrine, the relevance of international law, even its character as law depends on whether or not such States are bound by it.

Normative problem-solution demands taking a stand on the basis of obligation. We cannot get very far by unreflective consensualism when having to explain, for instance, when an existing rule may be deviated from or terminated because of change of circumstances or other intervening equitable factors. To regard the references by the ICJ to such considerations as "social progress", "humanitarian values", "elementary considerations of humanity" or "good faith" as references to consensual norms not only disregards the manner in which the Court itself treated these differently from purely consensual norms but makes them dependent on changing State wills in a manner completely at odds with the way in which such norms have been used for the purpose of restricting the ambit of consensual ones.[53]

Let me illustrate the functioning of the structure of sources discourse within the debate about *jus cogens*.

According to article 53 of the Vienna Convention on the Law of Treaties, a peremptory norm, that is a norm which cannot be deviated from by States even by consent, is:

> a norm accepted and recognized by the international community of States as a whole.

---

[51] *Boyle* 26 Harv.ILJ 1985 pp. 337–338. The ultimate fruitlessness and circularity of the positivism/naturalism dichotomy has been frequently noted. See also *Kennedy* (Structures) p. 32 *and passim*; *idem* 23 GYIL 1980 pp. 378–382; *Floum* 24 Harv.ILJ 1983 p. 265. *Onuf* (Onuf: Lawmaking) points out that positivists have escaped from having to make explicit their non-consensual assumptions only by de-emphasizing theory in general and by focusing on the taxonomic tasks of doctrine, pp. 12–13.

[52] See e.g. *Strupp* 47 RCADI 1934/I pp. 298–300, 301 *et seq.*

[53] See e.g. ICJ: *Guardianship of Infants* Case, Reports 1958 p. 71; *Reservations* Case, Reports 1951 p. 15; *Corfu Channel Case*, Reports 1949 p. 22 and *Nuclear Tests* Cases, Reports 1974 p. 268.

Initially, *jus cogens* seems to be descending, non-consensualist. It seems to bind States irrespective of their consent.[54] But a law which would make no reference to what States have consented to would seem to collapse into a natural morality. It would appear as an indemonstrable utopia – a matter of subjective, political opinion.[55] Hence the reference to recognition by "the international community of States". To that extent, *jus cogens* becomes ascending, consensualist.[56] Moreover, every State's subjective consent seems necessary as the

[54] Thus, many lawyers hold the *jus cogens* to be a kind of modern natural law. *De Visscher* 75 RGDIP 1971 for example, notes that it sets certain superior values whose significance lies in that they overrule consent. These values can only be identified by non-positivist methods, pp. 9–11. Likewise, *Virally* 183 RCADI 1983/V notes that *jus cogens* has no place in a fully voluntaristic system. It posits a non-consensual, "fundamental" rule, p. 176. Some try to avoid connoting naturalism so expressly and argue that the concept reflects certain "structurally necessary" norms of the legal order or an international "order public". See e.g. *Monaco* (Festschrift Mosler) p. 613; *Münch* (*ibid.*) p. 617; *Carreau* (Droit international) p. 69; See also *Jacqué* (Eléments) pp. 154–155. However, the point of all such understandings is to envisage a (non-apologist) law which would be capable of overruling particular State wills. In that respect, any such argument's identity lies in its descending character.

[55] It is precisely the utopian – and as such subjective – character of *jus cogens* which has led many lawyers to take a critical view towards it. *Virally* 183 RCADI 1983/V, for example, having first noted that a meaningful concept of *jus cogens* can only be a naturalist one, goes on to observe that this creates difficulties of identification because "la supériorité intrinsèque de telle ou telle règle est, en effet, une affaire d'opinion, liée à une appréciation de l'échelle des valeurs morales et sociales", p. 176. *Rousseau* (Droit international public I) notes that *as jus cogens* is indistinguishable from naturalism and naturalism tends to degenerate into political, ideological views, the concept is threatening p. 151. Critics of *jus cogens* have been unable to see it as much more than subjective opinions in naturalistic disguise. Moreover, introducing subjective opinions into the system under the *jus cogens* doctrine distorts the binding force of other, regular norms. For this criticism, see e.g. *Lauterpacht* 62 RCADI 1937/IV p. 357; *Jacqué* (Eléments) p. 158; *Weil* 77 AJIL 1983 pp. 423–429; *Wengler* (Mélanges Rousseau) p. 337; *de Lacharrière* (Politique) p. 200; *Nisot* 76 RGDIP 1972 pp. 694–696; *Jennings* 121 RCADI 1967/II p. 564; *O'Connell* (International Law I) p. 245; *Carreau* (Droit international) pp. 73–75. *Sur* (L'interprétation) thinks that the concept "soulève d'avantage de problèmes d'interprétation qu'elle n'en resout", p. 179. *Sztucki* (Jus Cogens) notes that the absence of verifiable content to *jus cogens* and the difficulty to see how it could be identified, renders it "inoperative or subject to misuse", p. 123 and generally pp. 59–62, 125–142.

[56] *Gomez Robledo* 172 RCADI 1981/III notes the compromise character of the formulation and observes that "grace à celui-ci le *ius cogens* était incorporé de manière totale au droit international positif", p. 105. See also *McWhinney* (UN Law-Making) pp. 73–76. But though the formulation certainly achieves a distinction between natural law and *jus cogens*, it tends to coalesce the latter with any regular positive norm. And it has been difficult to keep it as a separate category. *Akehurst* XLVII BYIL 1974–75 makes the observation that the concept (in its "positive" understanding) has been connected with customary and treaty rules as well as general principles of law, p. 283. By linking *jus*

article speaks of the community as a whole and not just some representative part of it. Indeed, any other position would seem to violate sovereign equality.[57] Finally, *jus cogens* doctrine shows itself as a compromise. It accommodates a descending with an ascending perspective: peremptory norms bind irrespective of consent (indeed, this must be so if they purport to limit what one may consent to) but what those norms are is determined by consent.

But the reconciliation is only apparent. While naturalism and positivism, justice and consent, are combined in the definition, they will break separate in any attempt to *oppose* the *jus cogens* on a non-consenting State. For a State may argue that a norm cannot be opposed to it because it has never recognized it as *jus cogens*. To counter this, we must prefer either the consensualist or the non-consensualist strand in *jus cogens*. Either the State's subjective consent is necessary or then it is not. If it *is* necessary, then we lose the distinctiveness of *jus cogens vis-à-vis* ordinary custom, or treaty, altogether. Moreover, we seem to collapse into what seems like full apologism. If it is not, then we must accept *jus cogens* either as form of majority legislation or a natural morality. The former solution seems unacceptable because it violates sovereign equality, the latter because utopian in a system premised on the subjectivity of value. Either way, our expectations of objectivity will be failed: *jus*

---

cogens with positive sources, one avoids the subjectivism inherent in identifying it as natural law. *Brownlie* (Principles) regards *jus cogens* simply as custom, pp. 10–11, 513. Similarly *Kelsen* (Principles) p. 483; *McNair* (Treaties) p. 215; *Pinto* (Relations) pp. 87–88; *Tunkin* (Theory) pp. 158–159; *James* (Sovereign Statehood) p. 213; *Dugard* (Recognition) pp. 148–150. This argument implies that *jus cogens* differs from "ordinary" custom only in that it is regarded more binding or "fundamental". See further e.g. *Anzilotti* (Cours I) pp. 96–98; *Schwarzenberger* (Dynamics) pp. 124–125. See also the review of positions in *Gomez Robledo* 172 RCADI 1981/III pp. 70–80, 94–104. The point of this movement is, as *Chaumont* 129 RCADI 1970/I makes explicit, that a "scientific" (that is, "objective") concept of *jus cogens* can hold as such only rules which States agree that are such, pp. 370–377. Similarly *Wallace* (International Law) p. 29. Yet, this loses the distinction between *jus cogens* and consent and simultaneously the very meaning of the former.

[57] *Well* 77 AJIL 1983 pp. 426–427; *Sur* (L'interprétation) p. 177. See also *Charney* LVI BYIL 1985 (attempting to salvage a meaningful – that is, non-derogable – non-naturalist conception of *jus cogens* on the argument that majority legislation *does* exist in international law) pp. 19–20 n. 81. This view is also taken (implicitly) by *Cassese* (Divided) (noting that consent by the "three main groupings" of States suffices – though leaving scope for the persistent objector) p. 178. Likewise, *Gomez Robledo* 172 RCADI 1981/III pp. 105–108; *Alexidze* (*ibid.*) pp. 246, 256–258.

cogens is either based on a theory of justice or it cannot be opposed to a non-consenting State.[58]

5.1.2 Tacit consent: a reconciliation?

The common attempt to avoid the difficulties outlined at the end of the previous section is to escape into the tacit (presumed) consent construction. This is, of course, the standard liberal argument, present since Hobbes, Locke and Hume,[59] for ensuring the normative force of social order while preserving its political legitimacy.[60] The structure of the tacit consent argument – the way of transforming the concerns for normativity and concreteness – is nicely present in the opposition between Austin's argument about "habitual obedience" and Hart's "internal aspect". For Austin, habitual obedience serves to distinguish law from other commands.[61] The test is objective as habitual obedience is an empirical fact. But this, as Hart points out, leads into apologism; it fails to distinguish between force and law, the gunman and the legislator. In addition to conforming behaviour, rules need an "internal aspect", a motive for acceptance as legal rules as well.[62]

---

[58] A similar point has been made by *Fishkin* Nomos XXVIII. He notes that liberalism cannot consistently use an "external strategy" of moral justification (what I have been calling a "descending pattern") because such strategies have been defined by it as negative absolutism. But if there is only an "internal strategy" (what I have been calling "ascending pattern") open for the liberal, then the kinds of expectations of objectivity which liberalism itself grounds cannot be met: justification will remain controversial, pp. 207 *et seq*, 225–227. He concludes: "Given those ground-rules, those who probe the foundations of liberalism will find only subjectivism. But a moral ideology that is not objective – one that supports claims to its own subjectivity or arbitrariness – strips itself of legitimacy and authority. In that sense, liberalism self-destructs as a coherent moral ideology in a culture embued with such expectations", p. 227.

[59] *Hobbes* (Leviathan) ch. 20 (pp. 253–256); *Locke* (Two Treatises) Second Treatise, ch. VIII (pp. 177–178). *Hume* (A Treatise) grounds justice on a "convention" which, nevertheless, "is not of the nature of promise". It arises through general acquiescence in the prevailing property system, from a "general sense of common interest". Rather like language, it is created by an unconscious participation. Bk III pt. II sect. II (pp. 539–541).

[60] For general discussion, see *Simmons* (Moral Principles) pp. 79–100; *Raphael* (Problems) pp. 85–96. For critical discussion of this view of tacit consent in legal doctrine, see e.g. *Mensch* (Kairys: Politics) pp. 22–23; *Dalton* 94 Yale L. J. 1985 pp. 1039–1066.

[61] *Austin* (Province) in fact characterizes habitual obedience as one type of consent, Lecture VI pp. 296–298, 302–303.

[62] *Hart* (Concept) p. 91 *et seq*. Hart doubts the existence of a rule of recognition in international law. He assumes that the rules of international law are valid like those of a primitive legal system, by recognition of each individual rule separately, *ibid*.

For Hart, the rule of recognition is the ultimate validating rule of the legal order. As it validates the law by reference to what people have actually recognized, the law's justification is preserved; the gunman situation is avoided. But how are internal motivations ascertained? Hart assumes that ascertaining the content of the rule of recognition is an "empirical, though complex question of fact".[63] In other words, he assumes that the psychological element in rules can be ascertained by other means than psychological enquiries; that it can be inferred from external behaviour. The question is, now, does this really succeed as a reconciliation?[64]

Tacit consent seems ascending and descending, consensualist and non-consensualist *simultaneously*. It seems useful as it seems to avoid the objections of being either apologist or utopian.[65] It is present in the most varied international legal doctrines including, for example, the relations between custom's two elements (material practice and the *opinio juris*), the doctrines of acquiescence and estoppel, the idea of the *rebus sic stantibus*, or equitable application, as an implied condition in a treaty, among others.[66]

---

pp. 90–92, 225–226. For critics who think that there *is* a rule of recognition also in international law, see *van Hoof* (Rethinking) pp. 46–55; *D'Amato* 59 AJIL 1965 pp. 321–324. Hart's conception – *with* a rule of recognition – is applied to explain the basis of international obligation by *Schachter* (Schwebel: Effectiveness) pp. 19–20 *et seq.*

[63] *Hart* (Concept) p. 245.

[64] This, I shall argue is not the case. A similar point has been made by *Duncanson* Juridical Review 1987, pointing out that Hart's definition makes the legal order depend on what those in official positions think ("internally"). Thus it, too, tends towards apology as being an official becomes the criterion of whether your (internal) views count, pp. 117–125.

[65] *Bleckmann* (Aufgabe) observes that (purely) non-consensual norms are frequently formulated in such a manner as to appear as tacit consent rules, pp. 21–22. Thus they seem less utopian because closer to subjective acceptance. Similarly *Sur* (L'interprétation) p. 117. The rhetorics of reconciliation in tacit consent arguments is nicely present in *Jacqué* (Eléments). In his discussion of the elements of the international "acte juridique" he first notes that neither the *Willens* nor the *Erklärungstheorie* can be held alone. Neither subjective consent nor an external act are sufficient. Both need to be present. Thus, Jacqué defines the "acte juridique" in terms of the *negotium* (the act's psychological content) and the *instrumentum* (the text, the behaviour) which incorporates it, pp. 29–33, 36–37, 47–51, 113 *et seq.* What this discussion leaves open, of course, is that in any standard dispute the two will break separate: one State will argue on the basis of a text or a behaviour, the other on the basis of the (different) subjective meaning to it of that text or behaviour.

[66] The classic statement is by Cocburn, C. J: "To be binding, the law must have received the assent of the nations who are to be bound by it. This assent may be expressed, as by treaty or by the acknowledged concurrence of governments, or may be implied from

According to the tacit consent construction State consent is inferred from *past behaviour*. This escapes the objection about the fictitious nature of ordinary consensualism. Torsten Gihl, for example, writes that the law cannot be ascertained by reference to any "real" will but must be established by "empirical means".[67] Such empirical means seem available in the ascertainment of how States have behaved. But there are two contrasting ways of understanding past behaviour, a subjective and an objective one: Past behaviour might be held binding either because it reflects consent or because it reflects some non-consensual principle of justice. As these alternatives appear exclusive, a choice seems called for.

According to the *subjective* understanding, past behaviour may be understood as tacit consent because it incorporates a subjective experience (will or belief) of being bound. This argument seems concrete as the *justification* for having recourse to past behaviour is received from the assumption that it reflects subjective consent.[68] It seems normative because behaviour is something external to psychological consent, something against which the law can be *ascertained* in an objective fashion.

The subjective approach understands past behaviour as a promise about future action. Indeed, this assumption is seen as the *only justification* for having recourse to past behaviour. But surely not *all* behaviour reflects consent or can be understood as promise. A State may have behaved as it did because of external pressure or because it wished to make a political gesture, for example.[69] We cannot know whether a State expressed its (subjective) consent or not *merely by looking at external behaviour*. This is, of course, the basis of Hart's criticism of Austin. We need an "internal aspect". How do we achieve it?

---

established usage . . .", *R. v. Keyn* (7) (1776) 2 Ex. D. p. 202. See also PCIJ: *Free Zones* Case Ser. A/B 46 p. 166.

[67] *Gihl* (Scandinavian Studies) p. 69. See also *Venkata Raman* (Reisman-Weston: Toward) p. 390; *Simmons* (Moral Principles) p. 79.

[68] "La jurisprudence attache des conséquences juridiques aux attitudes, aux comportements des Etats parce qu'elle y voit des manifestations de volonté imputable à des sujets du droit international", *Zoller* (Bonne foi) pp. 274, 280–281. For a review of cases which *Jacqué* (Eléments) holds to illustrate that the State has been held bound because its behaviour has been interpreted as subjective consent, see pp. 210–226. As *Simmons* (Moral Principles) points out, any non-naturalist principle of tacit consent must ultimately rely on the subjective construction, pp. 80–83.

[69] See also *infra* ch. 6. For such reasons, *Raphael* (Problems) denies that acquiescence may create obligation, pp. 95–96.

One solution would be to ask the State itself. But this is an apologist solution. It is likely that the State would simply deny that its conduct incorporated any consent.[70] Another solution would be to argue that we *know better* than the State itself what it has consented to. But consent is a purely subjective thing. The argument from "knowing better" is, as we have have seen, inadmissible under the liberal theory of legislation; it appears as a strategy of introducing authoritarian opinions in a democratic disguise.[71]

There is an additional, and apparently decisive reason for why the subjective understanding cannot be consistently held as it leads into simple apologism. Atiyah points out:

> A man may *think* he ought to fulfil a promise (or behave in the way he did, MK), but his thinking that he has an obligation cannot actually *be* the (sole) source of the obligation; if it was only honest men would be bound ...[72]

In short, any theory of the binding character of past behaviour must explain why a State is bound even against its own intention.

A variation of the subjective understanding rejects the psychologism inherent in it. It is not real but hypothetical or presumed consent which is relevant.[73] Participation in some activity – "using the highways" – or

---

[70] For this reason, some have criticized the subjective understanding of tacit consent. *Schachter* (Schwebel: Effectiveness) notes that it threatens established rules of law as it contains the suggestion that a State is not bound "if it no longer agrees ... or has never expressly manifested its agreement", p. 21. *Unger* (Völkergewohnheitsrecht) points out that estoppel doctrines fail to give effect to considerations of justice and reasonableness, pp. 27–29. But clearly, this is so only if estoppel is defined subjectively; the objective understanding takes estoppel to be based on considerations of justice and good faith. See further ch. 5.4. *infra*.

[71] See *supra* at n. 39.

[72] *Atiyah* (Promises) p. 18. When, for example, the International Military Tribunal included among Nazi Germany's crimes the "violation of international treaties, agreements and *assurances* (emphasis MK)" – the latter covering promises to Austria, Belgium, Holland and Czechoslovakia – the Tribunal took a non-subjective view of the binding character of "assurances". Had Germany's actual will been decisive, then there would probably have been no obligation at all. See International Military Tribunal: Trial of Major War Criminals, vol. I (1947) p. 171. See also *ibid.* pp. 186 *et seq*, 224–226 (on the premeditated character of German attacks).

[73] *Virally* 183 RCADI 1983/V notes: "la volonté exprimé ... compte toujours pour la volonté réelle", p. 179. By thus assimilating consent with external conduct the objections regarding the fictitious or indemonstrable character of consensualism may be avoided. However, many have objected against speaking in terms of consent at all in such cases. See e.g. *Nardin* (Law, Morality), pp. 212–213. Similarly, *Lenoble-Ost* (Droit,

accepting benefits suffice for consent to be inferred.[74] But on what basis can we oppose a presumed consent to a non-consenting State? Either we should adopt the position that we know better – in which case the above objections become pertinent – or we should be in possession of a theory according to which some forms of behaviour create binding norms regardless of whether they express real consent or not (although we curiously classify those forms of behaviour under "tacit consent"). For we cannot simply hold that *all* forms of behaviour allow the presumption of consent and thus become binding. But neither do we possess a list of those forms of behaviour which States are bound to follow if they have once adopted them, regardless of whether they did it out of consent. Even if we possessed such a list, we could hardly oppose it to a State which does not accept it without assuming that it is based on a non-consensual theory of justice – an assumption vulnerable to the objection of being utopian.

Thus, we seem compelled to move into an *objective* understanding which regards past practice relevant, *not* because it reflected the State's subjective consent but because *other States* have the right to rely on the State continuing its once-adopted conduct.[75] Whether this is stated in terms of the

---

Mythe) point out that the construction is based on (an unfounded) myth of the rationality of the legislator, *passim*, and pp. 66–73, 75 *et seq*. The same point is made by *Pateman* (Political Obligation), arguing that tacit consent is propagandist as it maintains an illusion of consent where there in fact is none, pp. 15–17, 81–91, 103 *et seq*, 150–162. Such criticisms, however, are valid only against the *subjective* understanding of why past behaviour binds. If we regard past behaviour binding irrespective of consent, because justice seems to demand this, then the charge of fictitiousness does not apply and the construction's basis in a theory of justice – instead of any indemonstrable hypothesis about consent – will become apparent.

[74] This is a classical way of understanding tacit consent. It amounts, as *Tammes* II Neth.YBIL 1971 notes, to a calculation of probability – of how probable it is that the State in question would have consented in such circumstances, pp. 13, 19–21. Arguably, it was present in *Wolff*'s and *Vattel*'s concept of "voluntary law", posited between the fully non-consensual necessary natural law and the fully consensual positive law. See *supra* ch. 2.3.1. The argument became widely used only under liberal doctrines. It was useful as it allowed the consensual justification of the most varied present social conditions. See *Simmons* (Moral Principles) pp. 83–94. See also *Shapiro* (Evolution) pp. 287–289 and *passim*.

[75] This is a very frequently made justification. See especially *Müller* (Vertrauenschutz) *passim*; *Günther* (Völkergewohnheitsrecht) pp. 155–165; *Schachter* (Schwebel: Effectiveness) pp. 22–27; *Jacqué* (Eléments) pp. 113–114, 119–120; *Decaux* (Réciprocité) pp. 117–118; *Reuter* (Droit international public) p. 142; *Martin* (L'Estoppel) pp. 304–306, 313–314. Quite frequently, early liberals took this move which transferred them into assuming a *naturalistic* duty (based on, for example, paternal affection or monarchical honour) to fulfil expectations. See *Simmons* (Moral Principles) p. 101 *et seq*.

principle of non-contradiction, good faith, justice, legitimate expectations, reciprocity, fairness or *Vertrauensschutz* is irrelevant.[76]

But if reliance is a *condition* of binding force, the problem arises why anyone should be entitled to rely on the continuance of a behaviour *before* it became binding. The behaving State is now left at the mercy of other States' decision whether or not to rely.[77] It might be argued that behaviour created its binding character by the way it apparently signalled the behaving State's consent (even if it did not). But this creates the problem of how to oppose one State's subjective interpretation of the meaning of another State's conduct on that latter State. The problem is identical with the problem of knowing about the behaving State's subjective intentions. We might simply ask that other State. But this will lead into apologism. It will inevitably say that it relied. Basing the decision on what it says – instead of what the behaving State itself says – would seem to violate the latter's sovereign equality. The difficulty is that if we rely on either of the subjective understandings, we shall have to do this by relying on a State's *present* account of what it had experienced in the *past*. The objectivity which we hoped to gain by focusing from real consent into tangible behaviour is lost by the fact that in *interpreting the meaning of that behaviour we fall back on subjective accounts* thereof. Ultimately, the binding character of past behaviour cannot be a matter of reliance. The question is: whether there was any *justification* for such reliance or not?[78]

The sole way of avoiding a preference between the subjective understandings of the behaving and other States is to fall back into assuming that certain forms of behaviour are such as to become binding automatically, on a "reasonable man" standard,[79] regardless of whether there

---

[76] The following are typical examples of such justifications. A State could not challenge another State's maritime boundaries as it used the same method to establish its own boundaries. *South Atlantic Islands Development Corp. v. Buchan*, 55 ILR 1979 p. 5. Compensation for nationalization was to be measured by having regard to the legitimate expectations created through written communications and party behaviour. *Dispute between the Government of Kuwait and the American Independent Oil Co.* (*AMINOIL*), XXI ILM 1982 1034 *et seq.* See further *infra* ch. 5.5.

[77] *Atiyah* (Promises) pp. 37–39, 63–69.

[78] *Ibid.* pp. 66, 127–129; *Martin* (L'Estoppel) pp. 313–314. See also *Zoller* (Bonne foi) (noting that only *some* expectations are protected and which are can only be solved by an anterior theory of *legitimate* expectations) pp. 346–349.

[79] As pointed out earlier, it cannot be the case that *all* past behaviour is binding. This would not only make legal change impossible but would conflict with the law's subjective justification; States simply do not regard themselves bound by previous behaviour as an unexceptionable rule.

was any intent to become bound or reliance involved.[80] But this seems an awkward suggestion for at least two reasons. In the first place, it is difficult to think of other justifications for holding a State bound by what it has done than the need to protect its consent or other States' reliance.[81] If neither is present, why should the State be bound? We might assume that it is bound by certain forms of behaviour simply because that is *just* (reasonable, in accordance with good faith etc.). But it is difficult to see what other reason there would be to hold it as a just solution than to protect legitimate expectations, that is, reliance. And reliance, as we have seen, is a subjective experience which can – unless we hold an objective interests theory – only be ascertained by asking the State itself.[82]

Secondly, the very assumption of automatically binding forms of behaviour seems unacceptable because utopian. Such a purely non-subjective justification could only be based on a natural morality, in this case a (conservative) theory about right behaviour being the kind of behaviour which a State once has chosen to adopt. The oddness of this suggestion lies in that it makes the fact that the State once behaved in a certain manner the *decisive* criterion for its having to behave in a similar way in the future. Apart from emanating from an almost incomprehensible moral theory, such a theory is, on the doctrine's own premises, simply utopian in that by excluding subjective understandings it defines itself as unverifiable.

If past behaviour binds because that seems just, the justice of it lies in the protection of subjective understandings. Nothing is gained by referring to some utilitarian principle because these boil down to the protection of State interests which cannot be dissociated from their articulated (subjective)

---

[80] *Tammes* II Neth.YBIL 1971, for example, suggests that "real" consent might be overridden with a constructive one if the "interests of the smooth functioning of the international legal order" require this, pp. 12, 11 *et seq. Charney* LVI BYIL 1985 expressly rejects the consensual view and holds the State bound by a pattern of behaviour if this is what the "societal context" requires, pp. 16–18. For a discussion of binding force regardless of expectations, see *Atiyah* (Promises) pp. 52–63.

[81] Indeed, I know of no modern lawyer who would have justified the binding force of past behaviour by reference to *other* considerations than the consent of the behaving State or the expectations of other States.

[82] Discussing the possibility to base obligation on good faith *Zoller* (Bonne foi) accepts Lauterpacht's view according to which an obligation whose content would be left to the determination of the obligee does not constitute a legal bond. This is the case of good faith. It cannot be ascertained objectively. Consequently: "C'est pourquoi le principe de bonne foi est un principe moral et rien de plus", p. 345. Similarly *Sur* (L'interprétation) pp. 76–78.

wills.[83] The difficulty lies in that subjective understandings seem verifiable only by falling into apologism – having to rely on what States presently say.

These problems, well-known to liberal moralists, are very important in structuring international legal argument. They will be elaborated more fully below. The point I wish to make here is that the unresolved dispute about the basis of obligation emerges each time a State denies that a rule can be applied to it, that is, in any international *dispute*. There is an opposition between a descending (naturalist, non-consensual) and an ascending (consensualist) argument. But neither can be preferred. The former would fail to demonstrate the content of its norms. The latter would legitimize what each State wills at each moment. The tacit consent reconciliation will break down at the moment of application. To answer the immediate objections of disputing States we shall have to choose. Past behaviour either binds because it expresses justice, reciprocity, legitimate expectations etc. and these can *override actual will or reliance*. In this case we succeed in applying the standard but remain vulnerable to the charge of utopianism. Or it binds as it expresses actual will or actual reliance and these *override justice, good faith etc*. In this case we succeed to demonstrate the content of the standard but fail to apply it against the State and thus remain vulnerable to the charge of apologism.

In the practice of legal problem-solution this dilemma expresses itself in the following way. The position expressed by one's opponent is interpreted so as to manifest either consensualism or non-consensualism and be unacceptable as such. This is possible because each position may be argued from both approaches. Moreover, they need to be capable of being so argued to avoid the charge of being either utopian or apologetic. After projecting this interpretation on its adversary's position, one can develop the appropriate counter-position. The dispute starts to look as if its solution required making a preference between consensualism and non-consensualism. As such preference cannot be made, the dispute-solver needs to have recourse to strategies of evasion, for example the proceduralization of the dispute, the contextualization of the dispute or the re-interpretation of the parties' positions so as to make them seem compatible and point towards the same solution.[84]

Consensualism and non-consensualism cannot be reconciled as assumed in the tacit consent argument. For these are mutually exclusive positions whose sense lies precisely in this exclusion. A consensual point

---

[83] For a discussion of the utilitarian case in this respect, see *Atiyah* (Promises) p. 29 *et seq.*
[84] See further *Kennedy* (Structures) pp. 82–99, 107.

is meaningful only under the assumption that it can override a non-consensual one and *vice-versa*. Past practice may be understood as relevant because it expresses consent or because it expresses justice. But if it is understood to express *both*, then we make the unwarranted assumption that consent is identical with what is just. The unwarranted nature of the assumption is demonstrated by the simple fact that a dispute has emerged. The dilemma is that we seem to lack means of ascertaining "consent" or "justice" independently from each other without either falling victims of apologism (that is, relying on what the State says) or utopianism (that is, relying on a theory about natural morality).

5.2 Treaty interpretation

The conflict between consensualism and non-consensualism and the ultimately unsatisfactory nature of both is clearly visible in two competing understandings of why treaties bind. According to a subjective approach treaties bind because they express consent. An objective approach assumes that they bind because considerations of teleology, utility, reciprocity, good faith or justice require this. The history of the doctrine of treaty interpretation is the history of the contrast between these two approaches.[85]

Doctrinal expositions and case-law on treaty interpretation usually start out by emphasizing that a text must first be so construed as to give effect to its "normal", "natural", "ordinary" or "usual" meaning.[86] This seems supported both by the subjective as well as the objective understanding. "Natural" meaning seems relevant as the most reliable guide to what the parties had consented to as well as what justice requires. But this position is not really a rule of interpretation at all. It assumes what was to be proved;

---

[85] See e.g. *Rousseau* (Droit international public I) pp. 135–137; *Zoller* (Bonne foi) pp. 205–244; *Bleckmann* (Grundprobleme) pp. 89–110. See also the useful discussion by *Dalton* 94 Yale L. J. 1985 of the parallel dichotomy in municipal contract doctrine, pp. 1039–1066.

[86] See e.g. PCIJ: *Acquisition of Polish Nationality* Case, Ser. B 7 p. 20; *Employment of Women during Night* Case, Ser. A/B 50 p. 373; ICJ: *Competence of the UN General Assembly* Case, Reports 1950 pp. 7–8; *Ambatielos* Case, Reports 1952 p. 45 (interpreting the declaration of acceptance of the Court's jurisdiction); *Anglo-Iranian Oil Company* Case, Reports 1952 pp. 104–105 (declaration of acceptance); *Temple* Case, Reports 1961 p. 32. For further references, see *McNair* (Treaties) pp. 368–380. Standard quotations include *Grotius* (De jure belli) Bk II, ch. XVI, sect. ii (pp. 409–410); *Vattel* (Droit des Gens) Bk II, ch. CVII § 263 (p. 461). See also *Rousseau* (Droit international public I) p. 269; *De Visscher* (Problèmes) pp. 52–58; *Degan* (L'interprétation) pp. 78–84; *Jacqué* (Elements) pp. 115–120.

that the expression has a certain meaning instead of another one. The doctrine of "normal" meaning fails to deal with the fact that already the ascertainment of the "normal" requires interpretation and that the very emergence of the dispute conclusively proves this.[87]

It is doubtful whether the "normal meaning" doctrine really has the overriding force attributed to it. If we accept the subjective understanding, it follows that normal meaning is relevant only as (rebuttable) evidence of intent.[88] Under this understanding, original intent is primary and overrides normal meaning if shown to conflict with this. The Vienna Convention on the Law of Treaties, for example, suggests expressly that if the Parties' intent is ascertainable, then it overrides any other point, including normal meaning.[89] If we accept the objective

---

[87] ". . . the real *raison d'être* of the hallowed rule of the textual interpretation of a treaty lies precisely in the fact that the intentions of the parties are supposed to be expressed or embodied in – or derivable from – the text." *Fitzmaurice* sep. op. ECHR: *Belgian Police Case*, Ser. A 19 p. 33. Similarly, *Young Loan* Case (Arbitral Tribunal for the Agreement on German External Debts, 16 May 1980) 59 ILR 1980 p. 531.

[88] *Sur* (L'interprétation) pp. 74, 258.

[89] It is frequently noted that Article 31 of the Vienna Convention is of the nature of a compromise: it refers to virtually all thinkable interpretative methods. First, it seems to take an objective perspective, what counts is the text: "A treaty shall be interpreted in good faith in accordance with the ordinary meaning to be given to the terms of the treaty in the context and in the light of its object and purpose", Paragraph 1. The text and the context – together with good faith – shall be decisive. However, this is so, as *Waldock* (Third Report on the Law of Treaties) points out, because text is the primary evidence of what the parties had subjectively intended, YILC 1964/II p. 56. The justification of the (objective) textual approach is (subjective) consensual. Therefore, it was logical for the Commission to add in paragraph 4 the provision that "A special meaning shall be given to a term if it is established that the parties so intended". If intent is what counts, then any special meaning must overrule the obvious textual one. The difficulties which this creates become evident when a party argues that it had a special meaning in mind. At that point, any problem-solver must either privilege that State's view, argue that he knows better what the State had in mind or hold that whatever it had in mind is of no consequence to the interpretation. That is, he becomes vulnerable to the objection of making an apologist or a utopian decision. This is what happened in the *Nuclear Tests* Cases, Reports 1974 in which the ICJ interpreted the texts of the two Applications so as to overrule normal meaning by a construction regarding the "Application as a whole", pp. 263–265 (§§ 30–33). It is hardly surprising that Australia found it difficult to accept such reasoning. After all, the Court had not bothered asking it what its intent had been and it should have been doubtful whether mere cessation of the tests was the sole object of the claims. Indeed, Australia (and New Zealand) were faced with the Court's view that it "knew better" than those States themselves what they had intended by their Applications. See also *Barwick*, diss. op. *ibid.* pp. 441–443. For critical comment, see *Sur* (L'interprétation) pp. 270–273, 276–285; *Zoller* (Bonne foi) pp. 208–214; *Jacqué* (Eléments) pp. 117–119. For an illustrative example of the indeterminateness of the Vienna Convention interpretation system, see *Young Loan* Case (Arbitral Tribunal on German

understanding – that intepetation must give effect to justice, reciprocity, good faith etc. – then it follows that normal meaning is secondary and relevant only as (rebuttable) evidence of what the Parties held as just between them. In this case, justice overrides normal meaning.[90]

The problem is not whether or not to give effect to a normal meaning. This is a question-begging perspective. For what is "normal" cannot be ascertained independently of taking a stand on whether the expression's normal sense is the sense it had for the parties or which is reasonable (in accordance with justice, good faith, etc.).[91] Normal meaning has no independently normative character. It is relevant only inasmuch as it gives access to original intent or to something beyond it (for example, legitimate expectations, justice etc.). If a dispute arises (that is, in any normative *problem*), the issue is not what is "normal" but which of the competing conceptions of normality – the subjective or the objective – must be given precedence.

It is often held that the principal goal of interpretation is to give effect to (subjective) party intentions.[92] But it is virtually impossible to ascertain

External Debts, 16 May 1980) 59 ILR 1980 (in which the Tribunal followed the Vienna Convention by interpreting the 1953 Agreement on German External Debts in accordance with the normal meaning, context, object and purpose, subsequent practice and *travaux préparatoires*. By a 4–3 vote, the majority held that each method supported its conclusion while the minority constructed each supportive of the opposing conception) pp. 529–590. Both majority and minority claimed to use these (initially objective) methods in order to get at the drafters' (subjective) intent. But if subjective intent was what the difference in the interpretations was about, then there was no way to solve the conflict; for the interpretation started from the assumption that real intent could not be known independently of its manifestations.

[90] "Justice" being conceptualized in terms of e.g. reasonableness as in PCIJ: *Polish Postal Service in Danzig* Case, Ser. B 11 p. 39, "spirit, purpose and context" as in ICJ: *South West Africa* Case, Reports 1962 p. 336 or some idea of "stability and finality" as in ICJ: *Temple* Case, Reports 1962 p. 34. It is, in fact, not infrequently argued that all interpretation simply aims at arriving at what is in accordance with equity or good faith. See e.g. *Friedmann* (Changing) pp. 197–199. See also Iran–US Claims Tribunal: *Interpretation of the Algerian Declarations of 19 January 1981*, 62 ILR 1982 pp. 605–606. As we have seen, Article 31 of the Vienna Convention, too, begins with a reference to good faith. However, as others have argued, this seems to restate the problem rather than solve it. Now it is "good faith" (or "justice") which needs to be given content – a matter of subjective preference under liberal assumptions. See *Sur* (L'interprétation) pp. 76–78; *Zoller* (Bonne foi) pp. 87–95, 229–244, 334–340. Therefore, some have held that the good faith merely refers back to subjective consent and the object and purpose test. See *Reuter* (Traités) p. 124.

[91] *Bleckmann* (Grundprobleme) p. 94.

[92] For *Lauterpacht* (Development), "the function of the interpretation of treaties" consists of "ascertaining what was the intention of the parties", p. 27. To the same effect, see e.g. *De Visscher* (Problèmes) p. 18; *Reuter* (Droit international public) p. 124; *Brierly* (Law of Nations) p. 325; *Schwarzenberger* (International Law I) p. 208. *Sørensen* 101 RCADI

real, subjective party intent. In particular, doctrine lacks means to oppose its conception of party intent on a deviating conception proposed by the party itself. Besides, sometimes intent may seem like a relatively minor matter – peace treaties or human rights instruments being the obvious examples. The important point is, however, that if intent is to be the *goal* of interpretation, it cannot be used as a *means* for attaining it.[93] A *Willenstheorie* stands on the shoulders of an *Erklärungstheorie*.[94] If the problem is finding out what States had consented to, then we cannot argue from consent to support our interpretation. All we have are non-subjective points about text, subsequent conduct, teleology, good faith etc. Intent can only be what the available textual, systematic, historical etc. analyses suggest. It can be known only in its (objective) manifestations. The subjective view is, in this way, indistinguishable from the objective one.[95]

But moving into the objective approach provides no solution. How can we know which interpretation (which behaviour, which teleology) manifests consent? The problem-solver should be capable of justifying his view about what it is that the text (party behaviour, contractual equilibrium) requires.[96] Inasmuch as he cannot justify it by referring to intent (because the argument started from the assumption that intent was not known) he must refer to some non-subjective criterion. The irony is, of course, that the system simultaneously denies there to be such a thing as an "objective normality" or any other non-subjective criterion by which the contractual relationship could be evaluated. It tells us only that we cannot proceed beyond our

1960/III (form never important in other ways than as evidence of subjective will) p. 55; *O'Connell* (International Law I) p. 251; *Guggenheim* 80 RCADI 1952/I p. 56; *Zoller* (Bonne foi) pp. 216–223; *Barile* 161 RCADI 1978/III pp. 85–87; *Reuter* (Traités) p. 84; *Bleckmann* (Grundprobleme) p. 89; *McDougal-Lasswell-Miller* (Interpretation) pp. xvi, 6–11, 82–87.

[93] *De Visscher* (Problèmes) p. 50.

[94] "Rechercher *les volontés* des Parties, c'est interpréter leurs manifestations", *Strupp* 47 RCADI 1934/I p. 380. See also *Jennings* 121 RCADI 1967/II p. 545; *Zoller* (Bonne foi) (A review of the move from an initial *Willenstheorie* to an *Erklärungstheorie* in the Vienna Convention) pp. 206–214; *Bleckmann* (Grundprobleme) pp. 92–98, 100–102; *Sur* (L'interprétation) pp. 259, 272–273; *Reuter* (Traités) pp. 84–85.

[95] Thus, for the ICJ, objective arguments about "object and purpose", context, effectiveness etc. have been held relevant because the drafters had (subjectively) intended them to be. See *Reparation for Injuries* Case, Reports 1949 p. 179; *Effect of Awards of Compensation* Case, Reports 1954 pp. 56–57 and comment in *De Visscher* (Problèmes) pp. 140–150. See further ICJ: *South West Africa* Case, Reports 1962 p. 329; *Namibia* Case, Reports 1971 p. 31 (§ 53).

[96] For the "contractual equilibrium" argument, see *Dispute between the Government of the State of Kuwait and the American Independent Oil Company (AMINOIL)*, XXI ILM 1982 pp. 1034–1038.

subjective views about such matters and that nobody has any duty to defer to another's subjective views. By this simple assumption – the rejection of natural law and intelligible essences – the liberal system of treaty interpretation deconstructs itself. It assumes that real (subjective) intent cannot be known and refers us to the external manifestions which it takes to be evidence of consent. But it lacks a theory about the evidentiary value of different possible manifestations. It refers back to subjective views (that behaviour, that teleology etc. counts which manifests intent) which, however, it already assumed to be unknowable independently of their external manifestations. By denying knowledge of *both* subjective and objective meanings, theories of treaty interpretation become a *perpetuum mobile* which allow challenging each proposed interpetation as "subjective".

The fusion of the subjective and objective understandings in this way resembles the tacit consent strategy. The subjective theory seems necessary to preserve the treaty's legitimacy. The objective view is needed to preserve the treaty's binding force. Neither can be maintained alone. Intent can be known only in its manifestations – which manifestations (text, behaviour, teleology etc.) count depends on whether they express intent. The subjective argument can be supported only by moving into an objective position. The objective argument can be held only on subjective premises. The argument is hopelessly circular.

The difficulty is that conflicting interpretations are, on doctrine's own premises, incapable of legal decision. Controversial points about consent merely refer to equally controversial points about justice and *vice-versa*. In the *Case Concerning the Interpretation of the Algerian Declarations of 19 January 1981*, the Iran–United States Claims Tribunal was to decide whether Article II of the Claims Settlement Declaration included a right for Iran to press claims against United States' nationals. The majority held that it could not be so interpreted. A "clear formulation" of that Article excluded Iranian claims from the Tribunal's jurisdiction. This clear formulation had authority because it was clearest evidence of Party consent.[97] The minority argued that a literal construction failed to give effect to the settlement's reciprocal character. According to the minority, reciprocity had been the very basis on which Iran had entered the agreement. By excluding reciprocity, the majority had violated Iranian consent and unjustifiably preferred the justice of literality to the justice of reciprocity.[98] Both sides

---

[97] Iran–US Claims Tribunal: *Interpretation of the Algerian Declarations of 19th January 1981*, 62 ILR 1982 pp. 599–600.
[98] *Ibid.* pp. 603–606.

invoke subjective consent and non-subjective justice but are unable to address each others' views directly. Neither side argues on the basis of "real consent". But while the majority sees consent manifested in the text, the minority sees consent in reciprocity. Both sides say their interpretative principle is better as it better reflects consent. But deciding the dispute on these arguments would require a means of knowing consent independently of its manifestations – a possibility excluded as reference was made to manifestations because of the assumption that real consent could not be known. Moreover, neither can the two sides argue that their justice – the justice of literality or the justice of reciprocity – is better without arguing from a theory of justice which seems indefensible under the Rule of Law. Ultimately, both interpretations are unargued. A doctrine which excludes arguments from "knowing better" and natural justice has no means to decide on the superiority of conflicting interpretations.[99]

Legal text-books habitually review several methods of interpretation whereby the ambiguous expression can be linked to a meaning external to itself. Reference is made to teleological, grammatical, logical, systematic, historical, functional and authoritative methods, the need to consult the *travaux préparatoires* etc.[100] But more often than not they point at differing meanings. In practice, interpretation tends to refer to several such considerations in a "controlled confusion".[101] The point is that there is no constraining

---

[99] *Fitzmaurice*, sep. op. ECHR: *Golder* Case, Ser. A 18, expresses well this dilemma. He notes that different interpretations do not so much arise from disputes regarding the sense of terms but from a different mentality, or "attitude or frame of mind" with the parties. The parties are speaking "on different wavelengths, – with the result that they do not so much fail to understand each other as fail to hear each other at all. Both parties may, within their own frames of reference, be able to present a self-consistent and valid argument, but since the frames of reference are different, neither argument can, as such, override the other. There is no solution to the problem unless the correct – or rather acceptable – frame of reference can first be determined; but since matters of acceptability depend on approach, feeling, attitude, or even policy, rather than correct legal or logical argument, there is scarcely a solution on these lines either", pp. 42–43 (§ 23). This expresses well the point that the parties' interpretations are ultimately justifiable only by reference to their "attitudes" about justice. Either you accept what I consider just – and agree with the interpretation – or you do not – in which case the disagreement will persist.

[100] See generally *Oppenheim-Lauterpacht* (International Law I) pp. 951–957 *Schwarzenberger* (International Law I) pp. 209–233; *Rousseau* (Droit international public I) pp. 269–305; *De Visscher* (Problèmes) pp. 59–127; *Degan* (L'interprétation) pp. 55–57, 69–148.

[101] *Schwarzenberger-Brown* (Manual) p. 135. For an attempt to create a hierarchy, see *Degan* (L'interprétation) pp. 151–156. Examples of Tribunals using all thinkable

hierarchy among them.[102] Nor can there be because the "methods" do not have any independence from the subjective and objective constructions. Their use is justifiable only as a means of finding original intent or justice. But whether their use is justified by either a subjective or an objective argument, any such justification can be validly criticized from the opposing position.[103]

Imagine a court making use of the "contextual method" in a dispute between States A and B and arriving at the interpretation suggested by A. It argues that the unclear expression must be interpreted in this way so as to make it coherent with the treaty as a whole. State B thinks that the interpretation fails to give effect to original party intent. The court must now justify its "contextual method" either in a subjective or an objective way.

The court might say that context is relevant because only it brings out what the parties originally willed. But can the court oppose its interpretation of party intent against that of a party itself? It can if it possesses a method of "knowing better". But surely it possesses no such method. More importantly, however, the assumption that it possesses such a method runs contrary to its very argument about context. Why refer to context at all if the court can directly say what the party really willed? But it did not know what the parties had willed *before* it undertook its study of the context. Therefore, it is not open to it to justify its recourse to context by reference to party intentions.

The court's argument turns out to be an objective one. It is not really speaking about real will but of *presumed* will. But if this presumption may overrule possible real will, then it is equivalent to saying that a provision

---

methods of interpretation in a happy confusion are abundant. For a recent case, see *Frigerio v. Federal Department of Transport* (Federal Tribunal, Switzerland) 72 ILR 1987 pp. 683–687. Practising lawyers easily perceive the difficulty. It seems difficult to maintain strict hierarchy, as the ECHR notes, because the different methods do not function separately: "the process of interpretation of a treaty is a unity, a single, combined operation" which "places on the same footing" the different considerations involved, *Golder* Case Ser. A 18 p. 14 (§ 30). If original intent is held as the goal, then, clearly, there is no justification to exclude any item which might evidence it.

[102] See generally *McDougal-Lasswell-Miller* (Interpretation) (hierarchy cannot be established – the importance of a canon varies through variations in context) pp. 111–118. Thus *Hussain* argues that the choice of the "canon" is dependent on legal-philosophical grounds, pp. 75–76 and *passim*, and *Peczenik* (Metodproblem) points out that the choice is ultimately a question of evaluative preference, pp. 61, 190–197. But it is not really that the "canons", once chosen, would be determining. For, as pointed out in the text, each canon may ultimately be understood in a subjective or an objective way. The solution seems more connected to the "philosophies" or evaluations – while reference to a canon only adds apparent neutrality to the choice.

[103] *Bleckmann* (Grundprobleme) p. 94.

binds *independently of consent*. The court's argument is not only about "objectified consent". It is completely non-consensual, objective. It assumes now that consent can be overridden by something which is not consent. Why should context have such strong force? Now the court must make explicit its non-consensual theory. It can argue, for example, that context protects the other party, or that it gives effect to the (non-consensual) purpose of the treaty, or that it is simply just or logical that expressions are read so as to conform with context and justice or logic must override real intentions. But how can the court *justify its non-consensual theory*? Mere reference to protecting the other State (its original intent or reliance) is insufficient because that would put consenting A and non-consenting B in an unequal position.[104] The court must argue from a theory of justice which is independent from and capable of overriding *any* consent – a *purely objective* theory. But this, of course, is vulnerable to the objection of being a utopian theory. The court is in a dilemma. Whatever it will do, it will be accused of subjectivism. If it relies on consent, it will overrule sovereign equality by an argument which looks apologist. If it argues from a non-consensual theory, it fails to justify its decision in an objective way.

Modern international lawyers are sceptical about the determinate nature of treaty interpretation.[105] They point out, for example, that "l'interprétation est un art, non un science",[106] that it "partly depends on intuition"[107] or that "the plain reality is that the interpretation of broad international agreement is operating in a largely indeterminate

---

[104] *Salvioli* 46 RCADI 1933/IV p. 7. *Gounelle* (Motivation), for example, argues that the provision in Article 18 of the Vienna Convention on the Law of Treaties which puts upon the signatory an obligation not to act in such a way as to defeat the object and purpose of the treaty cannot really require a scrutiny of such object and purpose *in abstracto* – a matter of fruitless speculation. It must rather be taken as a standard to protect other States' legitimate expectations, pp. 205–206. But this leaves the signatory at the mercy of how others choose to interpret its conduct. Hence, Article 18 is usually explained as a good faith standard. See *Brownlie* (Principles) p. 603; *Reuter* (Traités) pp. 62–63. This view, of course, leaves open how one participant's interpretation of "good faith" can be overridden by that of another's without either taking a naturalistic view on good faith, or violating sovereign equality.

[105] *Atiyah* (Introduction) sums up the contract lawyer's dilemma: "Perhaps nowhere does the law of the twentieth century seem more inadequate to its purposes than in the rules for the interpretation of written documents", p. 166.

[106] *Sur* (L'interprétation) p. 83. Similarly *Jennings* 121 RCADI 1967/II p. 544. For other statements regarding the "artistic" character of interpretation, see *Rousseau* (Droit international public I) p. 291; *Degan* (L'interprétation) pp. 163–164. See also *Anzilotti* (Cours) pp. 112–114.

[107] *De Visscher* (Problèmes) p. 13.

setting".[108] The one thing that unites Kelsen and McDougal, the rule and the policy-approach, is their insistence on the indeterminate, subjective, political character of interpretation.[109] They, as well as Richard Falk, for example, criticize disguising the arbitrariness of interpretation under the fictions of textual clarity or juristic method. They propose that interpretation be conducted openly by reference to important values.[110]

Such appeals to "openly evaluative" argument are a commonplace in modern liberal theories of adjudication. It is widely accepted that treaty expressions are ambiguous and that interpreting them is no automatic process.[111] But I have tried to argue more. The problems of treaty interpretation lie deeper than in the unclear character of treaty language. They lie in the contradiction between the legal principles available to arrive at an interpretation. Critics' suggestion to use "openly evaluative" argument fails to perceive that it shares in this basic dilemma. The tension between evaluative arguments from community policy and legitimate interests, for example, merely reformulates the tension between the objective and subjective positions. Liberal politics ("evaluation") is just as incapable of coping with this tension as liberal law is. Appeal to evaluation in a system which is premised on the subjective character of value means either capitulation in front of arbitrariness or radical departure from the system itself. For if evaluation is non-arbitrary, then we lose the sense of the distinctions between law/politics, adjudication/legislation and move beyond the conceptual system of liberal politics altogether.[112]

---

[108] *Falk* (Status of Law) p. 372.

[109] *Kelsen* (Rechtslehre) notes that interpretation is not at all an activity of intellect but of will: "Die Frage, welche der im Rahmen einer Norm gegebenen Möglichkeiten die "richtige" ist, ist – voraussetzungsgemäss – überhaupt keine Frage der auf das positive Recht gerichteten Erkenntnis ... sondern ein rechtspolitisches Problem" p. 98. See also *McDougal* 82 RCADI 1953/I pp. 149–157; *Schwarzenberger-Brown* (Manual) pp. 135–137.

[110] *Falk* (Status of Law) pp. 370–376, 344–348; *McDougal-Lasswell-Miller* (Interpretation) ("postulated goals of interpretation") pp. 39–45.

[111] This is but one basic consequence of the problem of the ambiguity of meaning, so conclusively established by modern linguistics, hermeneutics and structuralism and so threatening to the liberal ideal of the objectivity of law-ascertainment. For one criticism of the legal myth that legal interpretation might be extra-linguistically controlled, see e.g. *Lenoble-Ost* (Droit, Mythe) pp. 86–90, 102–114 and *passim*.

[112] Therefore, many lawyers have criticized the policy approach to treaty interpretation as unacceptably subjective. See e.g. *Fitzmaurice* 65 AJIL 1971 pp. 370–373; *Allott* XLV BYIL 1971 pp. 123–125. See also *supra* ch. 3.3.3.

The indeterminacy of treaty interpretation follows from doctrine's inability to prefer consistently subjective and objective points. The structure of treaty interpretation is governed by the *constant shift from a subjective into an objective position and vice-versa*. Argument either stops at a position where it will look apologist or utopian or continues interminably. This is hidden by doctrine's use of *strategies of evasion* which make it seem as if the subjective and objective were not conflicting and as if a resolution gave effect to what everybody had already consented to.

Consider a dispute about the binding force of a treaty provision. State X argues that State Y has breached its obligations by not carrying out a provision included in a treaty between them. This position can be interpreted as subjective: a State must carry out treaty provisions because treaties express sovereign consent and consent binds. But it can also be interpreted as an objective one: treaties bind because non-consensual standards of justice, good faith or the natural law principle *pacta sunt servanda* require this. State Y now chooses either one of these to interpret its opponent's claim. Let us say Y chooses the subjective one. It can now develop an objective argument to challenge this. The provision is not binding because it would be inequitable if it were so. It relies on the *rebus sic stantibus* rule.[113]

From a problem-solver's perspective it now looks as if he would have to decide whether treaties bind because they express consent or because they express justice. The situation would have been the same had State Y chosen the alternative route and interpreted State X's position as an objective one and developed a subjective point to challenge this. It could simply have denied that the provision – or X's interpretation thereof – really expresses what Y has consented to. State X's position would in such case appear as an objective point about tacit consent instead of authentic party will. In both situations making a decision one way or another would seem to involve taking a stand on the relative superiority between the subjective and objective approaches. Such superiority cannot, however, be consistently made.

If one were to choose a purely subjective position one would have to look at original intent. But original intent cannot be opposed to a State denying such intent unless one accepts a non-consensual (descending) position: intent binds in the form it is declared in the *travaux*

---

[113] Notice that the Vienna Convention on the Law of Treaties does not regard the *pacta* as an absolute rule. Article 26 brings in "good faith" as a relevant standard. This restates a Vattelian perspective which seems vulnerable to the criticism of "whose good faith", "whose justice" it is it that counts. See also comment by *Virally* 183 RCADI 1983/V pp. 188–191. The *rebus* rule is included in Article 62 of the Vienna Convention.

préparatoires. Reliance on declared instead of actual intent is non-consensual: its point is not to give effect to real will but to the legitimate expectations of other States. It is a standard of justice.[114]

But the content of standards of justice cannot be known without looking into what the States themselves regard as "just", "equitable" or "legitimate". Reliance on them will become consensual. If it were not, then the assumption should be accepted that written standards can be opposed to a State regardless of whether they express State will. But this loses the identity of treaty as consensual *vis-à-vis*, for example, the Decalogue and runs against accepted doctrines concerning the vitiating effect of error, or duress.[115] Preferring non-consensualism will either result in holding the State bound irrespectively of its will, in which case the problem-solver will lack criteria for justifying the adopted standard, or it will result in consensualism, holding the standard binding only to the extent that it expresses the real consent of the parties. The former seems too utopian, the latter too apologist to be acceptable.

The problem-solver must have recourse to a strategy of evasion. Let us take the imaginary dispute between State X and State Y once more. State Y has referred to the *rebus sic stantibus* rule to free itself from the treaty. This looks like an objective point and was presented as such by State Y itself. The problem is that accepting it would violate the consent of State X. It would become bound by a standard of justice as interpreted by Y. But the *rebus* doctrine can also be understood from a subjective perspective. Many doctrines present it as an "implied condition" in a treaty. The parties are assumed to have consented to its application. Taking such an interpretation of Y's position would allow X to oppose it by a non-consensual principle such as the *pacta sunt servanda.* It would alternatively allow X to deny that it had ever consented to the *rebus* norm, at least in the form now invoked by Y against it.[116]

---

[114] See also *Atiyah* (Promises) pp. 21–22 and *supra* at n. 76.

[115] For the grounds of invalidity of Treaties, see Vienna Convention on the Law of Treaties, Articles 46–52. Most of these grounds relate to the non-authenticity of consent (indeed, they are termed "vices de consentment" in French. See also *Reuter* (Traités) pp. 145–151). Acting *ultra vires*, in error or as a consequence of fraud, coercion or corruption seem good grounds for denying binding force because consent was not really present. Yet, because concentrating simply on the authenticity of one party's consent threatens the other party, these vitiating effects have also been taken to express demands of justice.

[116] The *rebus* norm has been argued in both a consensual and a non-consensual way. Early writers such as Grotius or Gentili seem to have regarded it as an implied condition in treaties. At the influence of the German historical school in the 19th century, the

These arguments would put the problem-solver in the difficult position of having either to ascertain the non-consensual value of the two principles (utopianism) or privileging one or the other of the conflicting wills (violating sovereign equality).[117] But the "implied condition" construction will let the problem-solver temporarily escape from this hook. For he can interpret the conduct of one or other of the States so as to be consistent with the other's opinion and thus to *make the material dispute disappear*. Accepting the *rebus* norm as an implied condition makes it possible to impose it on State X without having to formally overrule its consent. The solution is consensualist and non-consensualist at the same time. It gives similar weight to both States' sovereign consent. And taking account of changed circumstances also gives effect to important requirements of justice.[118]

But such strategy leaves unexplained why the interpretation of the content of this rule by Y was given preference to the interpretation of it by X. To be sure, it was argued that X had consented, albeit tacitly. But how do we justify the point that its conduct was such as to allow this presumption? This could be done if there existed a rule to the effect that

concept became related to the "nature of the State" which was assumed not to allow the continuing force of obligations which countered the State's vital interests. Though at present perhaps a majority of writers hold it as an element of justice, it is not uncommon to see it referred back to (implied) party will. See *Kaufmann* (Wesen) pp. 79–82 *et seq*; *Vamvoukos* (Termination) pp. 11–30, 186–187 *et seq*; *Müller* (Vertrauenschutz) pp. 211–217. *Lissitzyn* 61 AJIL 1967 argues the doctrine from "genuine expectations" (subjective) and "burdensomeness of the performance of obligations" (objective), pp. 897–898 *et seq*. He then infers "expectations" from some theory of "burdensomeness" and "burdensomeness" from party expectations. In fact, this circularity *cannot be avoided* without implying, either, that one can "know better" (expectations) or that one has access to objective justice (burdensomeness). Continuing this play of referrals is the only way to avoid making these claims while upholding a normative voice. For the recognition of the *rebus* norm by international writers (from both perspectives), see *Lauterpacht* (Function) pp. 272–283; *Reuter* (Droit international public) pp. 137–140; *Decaux* (Réciprocité) pp. 207–219; *Rousseau* (Droit internatonal public I) pp. 224–230. For a review of cases, see *Vamvoukos* (Termination) pp. 60–126. Presently, both doctrines have been affirmed in Article 62 of the Vienna Convention on the Law of Treaties. For the background and interpretation of this provision, see *ibid.* pp. 57–59, 126–151.

[117] *Carty* (Decay) points out, correctly, that the impossibility to decide between the *pacta* and *rebus* rules results from the way doctrine has conceptualized international treaties as analogous to municipal contracts and attempted to deal with their binding force in a purely formal manner. Because it cannot consistently evaluate political circumstances, it can ultimately establish no preference, pp. 65 *et seq*, 79–81.

[118] Thus *Atiyah* (Promises) points out that the "... technique of 'implying' conditions ... is often a fictitious device for giving effect to the judicial sense of justice", pp. 24, 89 – and, he might have added, to the parties' subjective wills.

a certain conduct, namely that adopted by X during the negotiations, is deemed to express consent. Quite apart from the fact that no such rules exist – indeed no such rules can exist as the same conduct might have a different meaning in a differing context – even if it existed it would still have to receive ascending justification from both X and Y. But also this rule could be challenged. The problem-solver would then need to construct a tacit consent also behind it. And so on, *ad infinitum*.

The decision in our imagined problem rests on an interpretation of the meaning of the parties' conduct and of the *rebus* rule. During the argument, both were interpreted alternatively in a subjective (ascending) and objective (descending) way. But none of the interpretations could remain permanent as they could always be opposed by a further point to challenge the previous one.[119] The solution remains open to challenge by what look like valid legal arguments. It was located at the point of choosing to interpret one party's conduct as consent to the other's position. This made it possible to seem as if nobody's consent were overruled and justice were given effect to. But this interpretation remained ultimately open to challenge. If real consent was what was meant, then X's own knowledge of its consent was overruled in an unacceptable way. If justice-based consent was meant, then the argument failed to indicate why the justice of changed circumstances could overrule the justice of *pacta sunt servanda*.

The process can continue interminably. In order for closure to emerge priority should be established between the subjective and objective approaches, or the ascending and descending models of argument. This, however, is impossible within the conceptual structures of the liberal doctrine of politics which requires, on the one hand, that law be justified by recourse to the legal subjects' subjective behaviour, will or interest and that its application must be divorced from them. The distinction between a level of justification and a level of ascertainment does not hold within argument.

5.3   Unilateral declarations

In this section I shall argue that doctrine has been unable to provide a coherent explanation for why certain statements bind as unilateral assumptions of an obligation. Doctrine oscillates between a subjective and an

---

[119] The opposition and fusion of consensual and non-consensual points within the *rebus* doctrine is further discussed by *Kennedy* (Structures) pp. 66–80.

objective understanding of such statements neither of which seems capable of being consistently preferred. To preserve sovereign independence and equality effect must be given to the subjective understanding of the statement by the declaring State as well as by the States to whom the declaration was made.[120] To solve differences of interpretation, appeal must be made to a non-subjective standard. The tension between subjective interpretations and the non-subjective standard is wiped away by assuming that each renders the same result. But this fails to explain why any dispute ever arose and loses the sense of the whole interpretative project.

In the *Nuclear Tests* Case (1974) the ICJ remarked:

> It is well recognized that declarations made by way of unilateral acts, concerning legal or factual situations, may have the effect of creating legal obligations.[121]

Initially, it seems that this is the basic case of a State incurring a legal obligation in a purely *subjective* way, by simple act of will.[122] But such a fully consensual understanding is manifestly untenable as an explanation of its *binding* nature. First, as we have seen, doctrine needs to

---

[120] See further *ibid.* pp. 54–66 (analysis of consensual and non-consensual rhetorics in the *Nuclear Tests* Cases). See also *Bederman* 82 AJIL 1988 (reviewing the indeterminacy of a doctrine which opposes the *pacta* norm with the *rebus* norm while remaining controlled by the "primitive" view of sovereign statehood as the law's discursive centre) pp. 1–40.

[121] ICJ: *Nuclear Tests* Cases, Reports 1974 p. 267 (§ 43). Standard examples which have been taken to involve the assumption of obligations by unilateral statements include e.g. declarations on the protection of minorities, the "Ihlen declaration" in the *Eastern Greenland* Case on 22.7.1919, the Egyptian declaration on the Suez canal of 24.4.1957 and the South African declarations in 1947 affirming its responsibility in respect of South West Africa as well as the acceptances of ICJ jurisdiction. For critical discussion, see e.g. *Suy* (Actes) pp. 115–147 (noting the difficulty to separate these from "agreement"); *Rubin* 71 AJIL 1977 pp. 3–7 (assimilating these with estoppel and third party beneficiary treaties); *Sicault* 83 RGDIP 1979 p. 635. See also *Jacqué* (Eléments) pp. 250–255.

[122] This seems particularly evident in the way in which the World Court has interpreted the declarations accepting its compulsory jurisdiction. See e.g. PCIJ: *Free Zones* Case, Ser. A 22 p. 24; *Chorzów Factory* (Jurisdiction) Case, Ser. A 9 p. 32. See also *Schwarzenberger* (International Law I) p. 226. It is regularly added that this does not mean that "will" would be normative by itself but that its normative character results from an anterior rule: in French doctrine, the distinction is made between "faits" and "actes juridiques". See e.g. *Suy* (Actes) pp. 16 *et seq*, 19, 34; *Jacqué* (Eléments) pp. 46 *et seq*, 121–128 (arguing that though subjective intent is a necessary condition to create a norm, it is not a sufficient one – some external (objective) element is needed) 187–193, 255–257, 321 *et seq*; *idem* (Mélanges Reuter) p. 330; *Zoller* (Bonne foi) pp. 280–281. The same idea is expressed by explaining the binding character of unilateral declarations by a customary rule. See *Fiedler* (Encyclopedia 7) p. 518.

assume that psychological will is inaccessible to an external observer. A purely consensual view on unilateral declarations would – as the "knowing better" argument is not available to it – need to rely on the State's own account of what it was that it willed.[123] Second, if the termination or modification of the obligation were matters of subjective will, then the State could escape being bound by a further act of will – the existence of which would seem to be determinable only by the State itself.[124] A purely

---

[123] *Supra*, at n. 39.

[124] This aspect has been particularly discussed in respect of the unilateral declarations conferring compulsory jurisdiction on the ICJ. The first issue has been whether it is possible to hold such declarations binding on a State *against* a State's interpretation according to which a particular dispute is not covered by it when that State has specifically reserved the right to judge the matter for itself. For the extensive discussion of the matter and especially of the "Connally amendment" in the United States declaration, see generally *Briggs* 93 RCADI 1958/I pp. 328–363; *Zoller* (Bonne foi) pp. 131–140; *Elkind* (Non-appearance) pp. 124–168. In one (subjective) view, there is no ground to oppose a differing interpretation by a Court on the State. As it was put for the United States in the *Interhandel* Case: "The determination of the United States is not subject to review or approval by any tribunal. It operates to remove definitely from the jurisdiction of the Court the matter which it determines." Pleadings p. 320. Such a purely subjective view, however, conflicts with the principle that a Court should decide itself its scope of jurisdiction. On this principle, see e.g. ICJ: *Nottebohm* Case, Reports 1953 pp. 119–120. The most consistent opposition to it has been expressed by Judge Lauterpacht, according to whom a self-judging reservation makes the binding force of the declaration illusory. Consequently, he holds that declarations containing such reservations ground no jurisdiction at all. See *Lauterpacht* (Function) p. 189; *idem*, sep. op. ICJ: *Norwegian Loans* Case, Reports 1957 pp. 48, 53; *Interhandel* Case, Reports 1959 p. 95. For a review of Lauterpacht's position, see *Hussain* (Opinions) pp. 134–142. Others have taken the view that subjective determination may be valid if made in good faith. See *Read*, sep. op. ICJ: *Norwegian Loans* Case, Reports 1957 p. 94; *Strupp* 47 RCADI 1934/I p. 507; *Jacqué* (Eléments) pp. 125–126. But this surfaces the problem of how anybody can determine whether or not a State has made its determination in good faith without making an argument which engenders the objection of utopianism. *Zoller* (Bonne foi) pp. 134 *et seq*, 137–140. In regard to "ordinary" reservations, the matter is not significantly different. Here as well the Court faces the problem of how it can overrule the declarant's own view of the scope of its declaration. The Court hovers between a subjective and an objective view. It observes that subjective intent is what counts but then goes on to make that intent defer to a "normal meaning" interpretation. See e.g. ICJ: *Anglo-Iranian Oil Co.* Case, Reports 1952 p. 104 ("having due regard to the intention of the Government of Iran) and p. 105 ("having regard to the words actually used"). An objective construction is also evident in the Court's refusal to accept unilateral withdrawal in the *US Military and Paramilitary Activities* Case, Reports 1984 pp. 418–421 (§§ 59–65). See also *Rosenne* (Law and Practice) p. 417. Ultimately, of course, this leaves open whether the Court thinks it can "know better" or whether its construction is justified by reference to non-subjective justice. Both justifications, as we have seen, remain problematic and point

subjective view collapses into simple apologism. A State is bound only if it so wills.

Consequently, something else is needed than the establishment of what the State has willed to regard its statement as a binding unilateral declaration. What this "else" is has been formulated in different ways. Common to these is the attempt to interpret a statement as a unilateral declaration only if it has been made publicly and/or so that other States have either relied or acted upon it or at least had the possibility of so doing. All this works to add an *objective* element in the interpretation of unilateral statements.[125]

Publicity, reliance or "acting upon" serve to explain that statements can become binding not simply because they reflect real will but because the need for security in legal relationships, protection of legitimate expectations or "good faith" requires this.[126] Rather than as acts of will, declarations are understood in the light of the interpretations taken by *other* States or from the perspective of a non-subjective standard of justice. That they cannot be modified or terminated by a further act of will results from this distance which has now been established between the statements and any possible declarant will behind them. Whether and to what extent they are binding becomes a matter, not of subjective intent but of external (subjective) interpretation or objective justice – their termination or modification becomes a matter of applying the *rebus sic stantibus* rule.[127]

---

beyond the liberal doctrine of politics (implying that texts or good faith might have "essential meanings").

[125] Standard argument refers to "declared" instead of "real" will. See e.g. *Sicault* 83 RGDIP 1979 pp. 647–648. *Jacqué* (Eléments) pp. 115 *et seq*, 129; *Günther* (Völkergewohnheitsrecht) p. 161.

[126] *Rubin* 71 AJIL 1977 constructs their binding force on a good faith position, pp. 10–11. Similarly, *Jacqué* (Eléments) pp. 256–257. See also *Suy* (Actes) p. 270; *Venturini* 112 RCADI 1964/II pp. 403–404. *Fitzmaurice* XXXIII BYIL 1957, for example, regards that unilateral acceptances of ICJ jurisdiction are merely unilateral in form while in substance they create a reciprocal agreement between the declarants, p. 231. The position is made clear in the *US Military and Paramilitary Activities* Case, Reports 1984 in which the ICJ observed that: "the unilateral nature of the declarations does not signify that the State making the declaration is free to amend the scope and the contents of its solemn commitment as it pleases", for, "even though they are unilateral acts (they, MK) establish a series of bilateral engagements", p. 418 (§§ 59, 60).

[127] *Sicault* 83 RGDIP 1979 pp. 654–655. As the ICJ in the *Nuclear Tests* Cases held that other States' reliance is not a necessary condition for the validity of the declarations, it left open how they then could be terminated. Having ruled out the possibility of "arbitrary" termination and the relevance of third States' views the only standard left

This raises an embarrassing issue about the very existence of "unilateral declarations" as a specific category of legal obligations. They become indistinguishable from offers or acceptances in a bilateral transaction involving the creation of (tacit) agreements. Some lawyers have, indeed, argued that this is the case and that there is no reason to distinguish unilateral declaration as a distinct class of normative acts.[128] But this is a moot issue. As we have seen "agreement", too, is a fluid category. Whether or not it exists can be determined either in a subjective or an objective way, that is, by either focusing on the "real" or the "declared" will of the Parties.

More important is which of the three possible understandings – that based on declarant will, reliance or non-subjective justice – we choose to prefer. I have already observed that to prefer the former will end up in apologism. But neither can the second – subjective reliance – be consistently preferred. It would seem odd if a statement could be understood so as to overrule the declaring State's own subjective interpretation in favour of another State's subjective interpretation. Such solution would violate the declaring State's sovereign consent.[129] Therefore, it is necessary to look, not at what other States subjectively experienced, but how a "reasonable man", acting in good faith, would have understood the declaration. Some statements are, by *their nature*,

---

would seem to be an objective standard about fundamental change. See also *Bollecker-Stern* XX AFDI 1974 p. 333.

[128] *A fortiori* this might seem so as Article 38 of the ICJ Statute makes no mention of unilateral declarations. This makes *Rubin* 71 AJIL 1977 argue that the decision in the *Nuclear Tests* Cases was in fact *ultra vires*, pp. 28–29. For a view interpreting unilateral declarations in terms of contractual relations, see *Quadri* 113 RCADI 1964/III p. 363. The same view has been taken of the Ihlen declaration in the *Eastern Greenland* Case by *Anzilotti*, diss. op. PCIJ, Ser. A/B 53 pp. 86–91. Similarly, *Suy* (Actes) pp. 123–124 and generally 196–201, 114–121. For further discussion, see *Fiedler* (Encyclopedia 7) pp. 519–520; *Jacqué* (Mélanges Reuter) p. 327 *et seq*; *idem* (Eléments) pp. 321–329; *Sicault* 83 RGDIP 1979 pp. 635–645; *Reuter* (Droit international public) pp. 80–81; *Zoller* (Bonne foi) pp. 282–285. See also *supra* n. 126.

[129] This problem lies at the heart of the judgement in the *Nuclear Tests* Cases. Inasmuch as the Court rejected the need for other States' reliance (the applicant States had expressly denied their reliance – they did not consider the French declarations as creative of obligations), it seemed not to think of the relationship as contractual and to lean towards a declarant's intent-based explanation of why unilateral declarations bind, Reports 1974 pp. 267, 269 (§§ 43, 50). See also *Bollecker-Stern* XX AFDI 1974 pp. 329–330; *Sicault* 83 RGDIP 1979 pp. 675–676; *Jacqué* (Mélanges Reuter) p. 334; *Franck* 69 AJIL 1975 pp. 617–618; *de Lacharrière* (Politique) pp. 61–62. On the other hand, however, it also rejected a purely intent-based argument in pointing out that the declaration's binding force could be construed on "trust and confidence", ICJ: *Nuclear Tests* Cases, Reports 1974 p. 268 (§ 46). See also text below.

or context such as to become binding. The difficulty here is that statements or contexts do not demonstrate their objective nature automatically. Their character is, under the assumptions of the liberal doctrine of
politics, indistinguishable from the way States subjectively experience
them. To think otherwise would be to assume the idea of intelligible
essences and to become vulnerable to the charge of utopianism.

For these reasons, doctrine includes *both* a subjective and an objective
understanding into itself. A unilateral declaration becomes binding on
two conditions:

> ... if clearly intended to have that effect (subjective, MK) and held out, so to
> speak, as an instrument on which others may rely (objective, MK).[130]

The problem is that that the two understandings *cannot be simultaneously recognized* in this way. For the point of the subjective understanding is to overrule the objective one and *vice-versa*. Let me explain
this by reference to the *Nuclear Tests* Case (1974). Here the Court
enquired whether certain statements by French authorities (President,
Foreign Minister, Minister of Defence) regarding the cessation of the
atmospheric nuclear weapon tests in the Pacific had established an
obligation on France to carry out no more of such tests. It observed, first:

> When it is the intention of the State making the declaration that it should
> become bound according to its terms, that intention confers on the declara-
> tion the character of a legal undertaking, the State being thenceforth legally
> required to follow a course of conduct consistent with the declaration.[131]

In other words, unilateral declarations bind insofar as they express subjective intent.[132] This, the Court noted, was precisely what distinguished
binding from non-binding declarations.[133] But had France in fact had the

---

[130] *Fitzmaurice* XXXIII BYIL 1957 p. 230. *Sicault* 83 RGDIP 1979 observes, first, that
subjective intent of the declarant is a necessary condition of the binding character of
the declaration, pp. 665–668. He goes then on to construct this intent "objectively", as
declared will, and ends up arguing that unilateral declarations bind on the basis of
good faith, pp. 677–686. Similarly *Fiedler* (Encyclopedia 7) starts out by the point that
"(d)ecisive for the binding force of (unilateral, MK) act is the intention of the declaring
State to be bound" but continues that "the decisive ground for the binding force of
such acts can be found in this principle (of good faith, MK)", pp. 521 and 520; *Decaux*
(Réciprocité) p. 207 (unilateral declarations bind because of "bonne foi, la securité des
transactions juridiques et la réciprocité") p. 213 ("Il faut que la partie déclarante ait eu
l'intention de se lier").
[131] ICJ: *Nuclear Tests* Cases, Reports 1974 p. 267 (§ 43).
[132] See also *Jacqué* (Mélanges Reuter) p. 334; *Bollecker-Stern* XX AFDI 1974 p. 329.
[133] ICJ: *Nuclear Tests* Cases, Reports 1974 p. 267 (§ 44).

intent? None of the statements contained an express assumption of obligation. The closest they came to having some finality was to inform that this round of the atmospheric tests "would be the last".[134] Many commentators have stressed the extreme unlikeliness that France would have really intended to assume an obligation – not least because it had itself in another connection denied that unilateral statements of this kind would be binding.[135]

But the Court did not simply conclude that France was not bound. It went on to construct the sense of the French statements from a non-consensual perspective. In the first place, it observed that the statements could not:

> ... be interpreted as having been made in implicit reliance on an arbitrary power of reconsideration.[136]

This is an ambiguous statement: it still connotes a subjective understanding. It does not refer to other States' beliefs or justice. It contains an assumption about intent. But the effect is objective: France's subjective will is now construed in terms of a hypothesis – moreover a hypothesis for which the Court seeks no support from other consensual sources. A second step is more revealing:

> One of the principles governing the creation and performance of legal obligations, whatever their sense, is the principle of *good faith*. Trust and confidence are inherent in international cooperation ... Thus interested States may take cognizance of unilateral declarations and place confidence in them, and are entitled to require that the obligation thus created be respected.[137]

Now the French statements bind objectively, regardless of intent and by virtue of good faith and other States' reliance. Moreover, the normativity of French statements:

> ... must be considered within the general framework of the security of international intercourse, and the confidence and trust which are so essential in the relations of States. It is from the actual substance of these statements, and the circumstances attending their making (which are relevant, MK).[138]

---

[134] *Ibid.* pp. 265–267 (§§ 34–41).
[135] See *Rubin* 71 AJIL 1977 pp. 26–30; *Franck* 69 AJIL 1975 p. 616; *Sicault* 83 RGDIP 1979 pp. 687–688; *Jacqué* (Mélanges Reuter) pp. 328–329.
[136] ICJ: *Nuclear Tests* Cases, Reports 1974 p. 270 (§ 51).
[137] *Ibid.* p. 268 (§ 46).   [138] Ibid. p. 269 (§ 51).

It was now not, after all, French intent which was decisive but good faith, trust and confidence, the objective nature ("substance") of the statements and the circumstances of their making which resulted in France being bound.[139]

None of the judges disagreed with this construction. It allowed holding France bound in a subjective as well as an objective way. It allowed basing French obligation on France's intent without having to rely on French self-interpretation about that intent. The judgement followed the strategy of tacit consent. French intent was construed on the basis of the status of the authorities involved, the "general nature and characteristic of these statements" and the fact that they were addressed to the public at large. These same facts also made it possible to appeal to the subjective reliance of other States and to non-subjective considerations about good faith, trust and confidence etc.[140]

The difficulty is that this way of combining the different considerations tends to lose the sense of having appeal to any of them. The argument about subjective French intent is based on the assumption that such intent is normative. That is, it must be capable of overriding *other* considerations. French sovereignty seems to require this. Making reference to subjective reliance by other States or to objective points

---

[139] Hence, many have felt that the Court in fact applied a good faith standard. See *Sicault* 83 RGDIP 1979 pp. 677–686; *Rubin* 71 AJIL 1977 pp. 2, 10. For a critical view, see *Zoller* (Bonne foi) pp. 12–13, 340–354. The switch from a consensual to a non-consensual argument is, of course, the core of the tacit consent strategy. Thus, in the *Burkina Faso-Mali Frontier* Case, Reports 1986, the Chamber of the Court was faced with the argument that certain statements by Mali authorities constituted acquiescence in the Burkinabe claim. The Court first took a consensual stand; a statement binds only if intended to be binding. "It all depends on the intent of the State in question", p. 573 (§ 39). But this intent is nowhere to be found. It must be "constructed". And the construction must pay regard to "all the factual circumstances in which the act occurred", p. 574 (§ 40). The absence of acquiescence was inferred from the (objective) fact that there would have been open more adequate channels for Mali to communicate its intent if it would really have wished to do so, *ibid*. See also ICJ: *Anglo-Norwegian Fisheries* Case, Reports 1951 (British consent to the Norwegian system of straight base-lines "inferred" from Britain's (objective) position in the North Sea) p. 139.

[140] ICJ: *Nuclear Tests* Cases, Reports 1974 pp. 267, 269 (§§ 43, 50, 51). The Court observed that "intention is to be ascertained by interpretation", *ibid*. p. 267 (§ 44) – a statement which has been interpreted as implying a tacit consent construction. See e.g. *Sicault* 83 RGDIP 1979 pp. 647–650; *Bollecker-Stern* XX AFDI 1974 pp. 329, 331; *Franck* 69 AJIL 1975 p. 616; *Jacqué* (Mélanges Reuter) pp. 341–342. *Rubin* 71 AJIL 1977 observes that this seemed "to shift the basis of the obligation from the intention of the declarant . . . to the reaction of other States", p. 11. *Zoller* (Bonne foi) notes that the Court never made up its mind about whether to prefer the *Willens-* or the *Erklärungstheorie*, pp. 342–343. See also *Kennedy* (Structures) pp. 56–66.

about good faith is superfluous. The point about subjective reliance assumes that other States' sovereignty should be overriding. And the appeal to good faith assumes that justice should be overriding. Each involves the assumption that it is capable of overriding competing considerations. If each consideration points in the same direction then there simply is no dispute.

Now, the Court may have tried to avoid contradiction by implying that one of the considerations was overriding while the others were only supportive. At one point it came back to arguing that it was really French will which was decisive while the other considerations were relevant as evidence thereof. In regard to the French declarations, it stated that:

> ... the question of form is not decisive ... the sole relevant question is whether the language employed in any given declaration does reveal a clear intention.[141]

But this involves a familiar circularity. The starting-point is that subjective intent is decisive but that intent is inferred from material acts. How can the inference itself be justified? There was no additional "test" of whether the statements corresponded to intent. Indeed, such test would have assumed that the Court could know French intent *independently of the statements* – in which case, of course, recourse to the statements would have been superfluous. In other words, it is not open for the Court to argue that the statements were relevant *because* they reflected real French intent.

The Court might have assumed that there existed a general rule to the effect that certain statements, given in certain contexts, allow the presumption of intent and that these conditions were present in this case. But there is no such rule. Subjective intent can be expressed in the most varied ways. Conversely, many statements rather hide than express real intent. Everything, as Fiedler points out, turns on a contextual determination of the "place, type, manner and form of the declaration".[142] There is, Sicault notes, "assez grande souplesse" in this.[143] But if the

---

[141] ICJ: *Nuclear Tests* Cases, Reports 1974 pp. 267–268 (§ 45). Similarly *Jacqué* (Mélanges Reuter): "... l'essentiel est de pouvoir établir l'intention de l'auteur, la forme dans laquelle s'exprime cette intention est secondaire", p. 341. See also *idem* (Eléments) pp. 111 *et seq*, 121–128, 322. But see also *ibid*. p. 256 in which unilateral promises are held binding if there is reliance. Here, as elsewhere, Jacqué fails to accord priority to a consensual or a non-consensual understanding of the *acte juridique* – with the result that his argument repeats the doctrine's indeterminacy.

[142] *Fiedler* (Encyclopedia 7) p. 52.   [143] *Sicault* 83 RGDIP 1979 p. 660.

test was contextual, then the Court's presumption that *this* context did disclose French intent was left unargued.

Another understanding would hold the statements, and the context, relevant because of considerations unrelated to French intent. Quite apart from the threat this suggestion tends to pose for French sovereignty, in this case, neither Australia nor New Zealand had relied on the statements.[144] Both expressed the view that the French declarations were not binding. Thus, the standard must relate to some fully non-consent-related criteria of justice, or good faith, trust etc. But this contradicts the Court's original, subjective understanding of unilateral declarations. Moreover, it emerges the objection of utopianism: if the Parties' subjective understandings are excluded, how can the Court justify its objective criterion?[145]

The strategy of the ICJ in the *Nuclear Tests* Case is to give effect to all three considerations: subjective French intent, subjective reliance by Australia and New Zealand and objective justice. Each renders the same solution: France is bound. No preference is made. But the argument leaves unexplained how the Court can maintain that it gives effect to French intent in face of the fact that France has denied it. It leaves unexplained how it can protect the Applicants' reliance as they deny having relied. And it leaves unexplained its theory of justice which says that certain statements bind by virtue of good faith. Moreover, having recourse to the three arguments is contradictory. Each of them makes the other two superfluous. If giving effect to French intent is what counts, then it must suffice as the sole criterion: its point is to override other States' intent or objective justice. If other States' reliance is what counts, then it must override French intent or justice. And if justice is effectual, then it must override any subjective intent or reliance.

Briefly: The doctrine of unilateral declarations cannot provide the law with the kind of objectivity which is taken to distinguish it from political argument. This is so because it must ultimately rely on a consensual or a non-consensual interpretation of such acts. But a consensual interpretation will lead into apologism. A non-consensual interpretation will lead

---

[144] See ICJ: *Nuclear Tests* Cases, Reports 1974 pp. 261, 268–269, 465–466, 473–474 (§§ 27, 47–48, 27–28, 50).

[145] This is the basis of *Rubin's* 71 AJIL 1977 criticism of the Court's standard of security and good faith, pp. 15–16. See also *Zoller* (Bonne foi) (the Court's good faith was "subjective") pp. 345, 353–354.

into utopianism. We shall either have to rely on what the States themselves say or argue on the basis of a non-consensual theory of justice. The
doctrine's *own assumptions* undermine its expectations about
objectivity.

5.4 Acquiescence and estoppel

In this section I shall expand upon my argument concerning the structuring character of the master principle of tacit consent. For a State may
become bound not only because its statements are interpreted so as to
amount to unilateral assumption of an obligation. Its other behaviour
may be given a similar interpretation.[146] These cases are usually discussed under the doctrines of "acquiescence" and "estoppel".[147]

There is considerable difficulty to carve out an independent area for
each of the three doctrines of unilateral declaration, acquiescence and
estoppel. They are distanced from the law-making procedures of custom
and treaty by their unilaterality. But this unilaterality is interpreted
in ways which are difficult to keep separate. Should we speak of unilateral

---

[146] Many have noted that these doctrines concern the interpretation of State behaviour.
See e.g. *MacGibbon* XXXI BYIL 1954 pp. 146–147; *Vallée* 77 RGDIP 1973 pp. 964–970;
Müller (Vertrauensschutz) p. 36. For general discussion, see *Cahier* (Mélanges
Guggenheim) pp. 237–265.

[147] These doctrines have been heavily influenced by ideas of Anglo-American law. For
background, see e.g. *Müller* (Vertrauensschutz) pp. 7–8; *Rubin* 71 AJIL 1977 pp. 20–21
and especially *Martin* (L'Estoppel) pp. 9–62. But lawyers have had difficulty in classing
them under the sources referred to in Article 38 of the ICJ Statute. See generally
Müller-Cottier (Encyclopedia 7) p. 80. *MacGibbon* 7 ICLQ 1958 thinks of them as
custom, p. 513. Others see estoppel, in particular, as a general principle of law. See e.g.
Friedmann 57 AJIL 1963 p. 288; *Bowett* XXXIII BYIL 1957 p. 202; *MacGibbon* XXXI
BYIL 1954 p. 148; *idem* 7 ICLQ 1958 p. 470; *Brownlie* (Principles) p. 638; *Dominicé*
(Mélanges Guggenheim) p. 327. Sometimes acquiescence fuses together with tacit
agreement. See *Air Services Agreement* Arbitration (1963) 69 RGDIP 1965 pp. 249,
251. For a review of cases classed under estoppel, see *Müller* (Vertrauensschutz)
pp. 12–35; *Alfaro*, sep. op. ICJ: *Temple* Case, Reports 1962 pp. 43–51; *Dominicé*
(Mélanges Guggenheim) pp. 334–362; *Bowett* XXXIII BYIL 1957 p. 180 *et seq*;
MacGibbon 7 ICLQ 1958 pp. 479–486; *Martin* (L'Estoppel) pp. 78–172. For cases on
acquiescence, see *Müller* (Vertrauensschutz) pp. 39–53; *Suy* (Actes) pp. 63–68. See also
ICJ: *Gulf of Maine* Case, Memorial of Canada pp. 172–179 (§§ 412–426). The insecurity
in classing the concepts under the recognized sources reflects the way they are sometimes understood from a consensual, sometimes from a non-consensual perspective
and while the consensual element is often related to the intent of the acting state, it is
equally often related to the reliance of others. Depending on which aspect one
emphasizes, the doctrines tend to appear simply as manifestations, or sub-classes, of
unilateral declarations, treaties, custom or general (natural) principles.

declaration or acquiescence in, for example, the *Minquiers and Ecrehos* Case (1953) in which the ICJ gave much attention to certain letters of the French Foreign Ministry and the Ministry of Marine which seemed to contain recognition of the British claims on the two islets?[148] What about the statements of authorities without capacity to bind their Governments?[149] Inasmuch as they are "statements" they seem to involve unilateral declaration. But as they lack constitutionally or internationally binding status, they seem rather more like evidence of acquiescence.[150]

Also the distinction between acquiescence and estoppel seems equivocal. Take the *Right of Passage* Case (1960). Was India's inaction in respect of the "constant and uniform practice" by Portugal to transfer non-military personnel and goods through its territory relevant as acquiescence or did it simply estop India from challenging the lawfulness of such passage?[151]

Though doctrine discusses at length these distinctions,[152] making them seems less relevant than choosing the relevant criteria for that purpose. Initially, each of the three concepts contains a description of how a State may become bound by an obligation through adopting a form of behaviour. Broadly speaking, the doctrine of unilateral declarations seems initially to bear a closer contact to intent-based justification of obligations than do acquiescence or estoppel. Basing obligation on non-verbal behaviour seems to have a closer relationship with considerations of reliance, reciprocity and justice. Whatever merit there is in these *prima facie* impressions, it seems clear that just as the binding character of unilateral declarations could not be justified in a purely subjective way, neither can acquiescence or estoppel be held purely objective doctrines.[153] In some way, they need to be understood from both perspectives.

---

[148] ICJ: *Minquiers and Ecrehos* Case, Reports 1953 p. 71.

[149] For a review, see *Cahier* (Mélanges Guggenheim) pp. 242–244.

[150] Also the distinction between unilateral declarations and estoppel is far from clear. For clearly, a declaration may work as a procedural estoppel. See e.g. the discussion in *Jennings* (Acquisition) pp. 42–54. *Müller-Cottier* (Encyclopedia 7), for example, class the *Nuclear Tests* judgement under estoppel, p. 80.

[151] See ICJ: *Right of Passage* Case, Reports 1960 p. 40. Similarly, it might be asked that if a State omits a provision concerning interest from a contract, might this be relevant as tacit agreement or as estoppel. See *Russian Indemnity* Case (1912) XI UNRIAA p. 421 *et seq.*

[152] See e.g. *Jennings* (Acquisition) pp. 45–51; *MacGibbon* XXXI BYIL 1954 pp. 147–150; *Bowett* XXXIII BYIL 1957 pp. 197–201.

[153] *Bowett* XXXIII BYIL 1957 notes of estoppel that "the statement or representation must be voluntary", p. 190.

Attempts to separate acquiescence from estoppel reflect a wish to distinguish analytically between consensual and non-consensual justifications. Acquiescence is contrasted to estoppel by relating it to the establishment of "material law" while estoppel is related to the State's "procedural" obligations – the former being more consensual than the latter.[154] Sometimes both are held "material law" concepts.[155] Acquiescence is then defined as absence of protest, or simply silence, and comes close to tacit agreement.[156] Estoppel seems then more related to conditions of justice. It is taken either to express the principle that a State "may not blow hot and cold"[157] or to refer to situations where

---

[154] *Schwarzenberger* (International Law I), for example, deals with estoppel under "procedural rights", pp. 435–438. A similar view is evident in *Fitzmaurice*, sep. op. ICJ: *Temple* Case, Reports 1962 (linking estoppel with "preclusion" or "foreclusion") pp. 62–63. See also *Müller* (Vertrauensschutz) pp. 10–11, 39. For cases and opinions, see *MacGibbon* 7 ICLQ 1958 pp. 501–512. See also ICJ: *Gulf of Maine* Case, Reports 1984 p. 305 (§ 130) and *ibid*, Canadian reply p. 90 (§ 214).

[155] See e.g. *Vallée* 77 RGDIP 1973 pp. 974–989; *Alfaro*, sep. op. ICJ: *Temple* Case, Reports 1962 pp. 41–42; *Jennings* (Acquisition) pp. 50–51; *MacGibbon* 7 ICLQ 1958 (emphasizing the relation between estoppel and material justice) pp. 478–479; *Blum* (Historic Titles) pp. 90–91.

[156] See e.g. ICJ: *Gulf of Maine* Case, Reports 1984 p. 305 (§ 130); *ibid*. Memorial of Canada, p. 173 (§ 414); *Air Services Agreement* Arbitration 69 RGDIP 1965 pp. 249–250; *MacGibbon* XXXI BYIL 1954 pp. 143–146; *Bowett* XXXIII BYIL 1957 pp. 198–201. Indeed, that acquiescence requires a subjective aspect seems implied by the general view according to which one can acquiesce in something only if one has knowledge of it. See e.g. ICJ: *Anglo-Norwegian Fisheries* Case, Reports 1951 pp. 138–139 and *Suy* (Actes) p. 62. Clearly, the very point of the acquiescence doctrine, as used in territorial disputes, is to base the applicable norm on the consent of the acquiescing State. See *Blum* (Historic Titles) pp. 81–89; *Müller* (Vertrauensschutz) pp. 39–53.

[157] Such a principle of non-contradiction seemed operative in the *Mavrommatis* Case (1924) in which the PCIJ held that Britain was estopped from arguing that Mavrommatis had not respected the time-limits in Protocol XII of the Lausanne Peace Treaty having earlier denied that the disputed concession agreement came under the relevant Articles of the Treaty, Ser. A 2 p. 33. See also *Argentina–Chile Boundary* Case, XVI UNRIAA p. 164. For estoppel as a principle of non-contradiction, see also *Alfaro* sep. op. *Temple* Case, Reports 1962 p. 39 *et seq*; *Zoller* (Bonne foi) pp. 275, 277–278; *MacGibbon* 7 ICLQ 1958 p. 469 and *passim*; *Günther* (Völkergewohnheitsrecht) pp. 140–144, 155 *et seq*. This "wider" sense of estoppel doctrine was expressed in the concurring opinion of *Mosk, Oil Field of Texas Inc. v. Iran*, Iran-US C.T.R. 1981–82 (I) pp. 375–376. *Brownlie* (Principles), too, emphasizes its "non-technical" character, pp. 638–639. Its relation to material justice seems evident. Though the PCIJ never used the word "estoppel" in the *River Meuse* Case, many would probably hold its decision as a typical estoppel-situation when it noted that the Netherlands could not oppose the construction of locks in the Belgian side of the river as it had itself previously constructed similar locks on its own side, Ser. A/B 70

other States have relied upon the State continuing its behaviour and done this in their own detriment or the other's advantage.[158]

But these distinctions are fluid in a way that reflects the difficulty to justify either doctrine in a purely consensual or non-consensual way. Continued inaction may be interpreted as absence of protest – and thus constitute acquiescence – while it may also seem relevant because other States have relied on it – and thus constitute estoppel.[159] As "absence of protest" may relate to positive behaviour, too, any *prima facie* estoppel-related conduct seems capable of being conceptualized as acquiescence as well. Take, for example, the much-belaboured Ihlen declaration in the *Eastern Greenland* Case (1933). It seems quite plausible to hold Norway bound by the statement by its Foreign Minister according to which Norway would "make no difficulties" in respect of the Danish claims because the statement involved agreement or admission of an obligation as well as because it could not "blow hot and cold".[160]

The difficulty to uphold these distinctions results from the fact that if the doctrines were either fully consensual or fully non-consensual, neither could be consistently maintained. If the analytical distinction *is* made, then each argument must show that *both* are present or reconstruct both doctrines so as to contain both strands within themselves. In the *Gulf of Maine* Case (1984), for example, the Chamber of the ICJ was

p. 25. For a review of publicists accepting this wider notion of estoppel, see *Martin* (L'Estoppel) pp. 182–187.

[158] On this more "technical" notion, see *Fitzmaurice*, sep. op. ICJ: *Temple* Case, Reports 1962 p. 63; *Bowett* XXXIII BYIL 1957 p. 200; *Müller-Cottier* (Encyclopedia 7) p. 78; *Spender*, diss. op. ICJ: *Temple* Case, Reports 1962 pp. 143–144; *Blum* (Historic Titles) pp. 96–97; *Müller* (Vertrauensschutz) p. 10; *Zoller* (Bonne foi) p. 275. The element of "prejudice" (change of position) is often included in estoppel to add a distinctly non-subjective requirement to it. See e.g. ICJ: *Gulf of Maine* Case, Reports 1984 p. 309 (§ 145); *Barcelona Traction* Case, Reports 1964 p. 25; *North Sea Continental Shelf* Cases, Reports 1969 p. 26 (§ 30); *US Military and Paramilitary Activities* Case, 1984 p. 415 (§ 51). See further *Holquin*, diss. op. ICJ: *Arbitral Award* Case, Reports 1960 p. 222. For the two conceptions of estoppel in general, see *Martin* (L'Estoppel) pp. 71–72 *et seq* (concluding, from a very large review of cases, that international practice has – contrary to the view of many writers – accepted the more narrow, Anglo-American notion of estoppel) p. 193; *Vallée* 77 RGDIP 1973 pp. 954–963; *Dominicé* (Mélanges Guggenheim) pp. 329–330; ICJ: *Gulf of Maine* Case, Memorial of Canada, pp. 177–178 (§§ 420–423).

[159] See *Jennings* (Acquisition) pp. 45–46.

[160] To maintain an independent conception of estoppel, it seems necessary to distinguish it from a purely consensual "recognition" or admission of an obligation by involving some consideration of (objective) damage or violation of legitimate expectations. See *Martin* (L'Estoppel) pp. 194–204.

concerned with having to interpret the normative sense of United States inaction in regard to the granting of oil and gas permits by Canada in the disputed area. It was argued on the Canadian side that US inaction from May 1964 onwards until the first official reaction in 1969:

> ... constitutes acquiescence in or recognition of the use of the equi-distance method ... and creates an estoppel in favour of Canada.[161]

Initially, the Canadian argument distinguished between the two concepts. The former was equivalent to tacit agreement (by the US), the latter protected (Canadian) reliance. Nevertheless, just as justice and consent rely on each other, Canada argued that estoppel was the *alter ego* of acquiescence.[162] The Chamber of the Court seemed to agree. The same set of facts was capable of making both concepts operative.[163]

The important point lies not in these distinctions and their fluidity but in what they reveal of the underlying structure of argument. It seems impossible to defend a conception which would base the normativity of past behaviour in simple consent or in pure justice. Within argument, acquiescence and estoppel become indistinguishable because of doctrine's need to avoid apologism or utopianism. Lauterpacht's discussion of the significance of absence of protest in the development of the law on the continental shelf captures well this point:

> "In the first instance, the absence of protest on the part of other States may be fairly interpreted as meaning that they 'accepted as law' ... the practice of other States relating to submarine areas ... However, in addition to providing evidence as to the views of Governments on the existing legal position, the absence of protest ... may in itself bring about legal effects ... (I)t may, in addition, in itself become a source of legal right inasmuch as it relates to estoppel or prescription ... (T)he far-reaching effect of the failure to protest is not a mere artificiality of the law. It is an essential requirement of stability – a requirement even more important in international than in other spheres; it

---

[161] ICJ: *Gulf of Maine* Case, Memorial of Canada p. 183 (§ 428).

[162] Initially, Canada associated its acquiescence argument with US "tacit acceptance or recognition" of the Canadian claims and its estoppel point with the fact that "the Canadian Government was placed in a situation of reliance". The former was used in order to argue consensually, the latter to argue non-consensually. On the Canadian argument from acquiescence, see *ibid.* p. 176 (§ 418) and on estoppel, *ibid.* pp. 178–180 (§§ 424–427). Yet, it could not plausibly rely on either of these arguments alone (because the former would have involved "knowing better" and the latter would have either overruled US sovereign equality or involved basing US duties on a theory of non-consensual justice). Therefore, it fused them together.

[163] *Ibid.* Reports 1984 pp. 304–305 (§§ 129, 130).

is a precept of fair dealing inasmuch as it prevents States from playing fast
and loose ... and it is in accordance with equity."[164]

In other words, absence of protest is given normative sense from two
perspectives. One interprets it as manifesting subjective recognition of
an obligation, or a promise.[165] The other looks at it from the perspective
of other States' expectations, stability or good faith.[166] Neither understanding can be resorted to alone. The former will deny the reality of the
obligation and violate the sovereignty of other States. The latter will
make the obligation intangible and violate the acting State's sovereignty.

Take, for example, the *Air Services Agreement* Arbitration (1963). The
Tribunal had to decide whether the two Parties (France and United States)
to an Air Service Agreement of 1946 had modified the agreement so as to
include a right of descent in Tehran on a Pan Am route Paris–Rome, not
originally included in it.[167] The Tribunal started out by examining French
intent. The relevant French authorities had refrained from protesting as
Pan Am had, since 1955, descended in Tehran. This was interpreted as
French subjective acquiescence.[168] But a fully intent-based argument would
have implied that French authorities can also terminate that right at will.
Therefore, the Tribunal turned to argue on the basis of justice, or reasonableness. Making the descent had involved important investments on the
part of Pan Am. It would have been unreasonable to leave those investments at the mercy of continued French consent.[169]

---

[164] *Lauterpacht* XXVII BYIL 1950 pp. 395–396. See also *Vallée* 77 RGDIP 1973
pp. 964–970, 989–999.
[165] Hence, *Vallée* 77 RGDIP 1973 argues that in fact estoppel is frequently resorted to
because it works as "evidence" of consent, pp. 964–970. *Bowett* XXXIII BYIL 1957
observes that obligations undertaken by conduct are, in this sense, no different from
obligations undertaken by treaty, p. 181. Many others, too, think of the acquiescence-
estoppel doctrine in terms of evidence of subjective intent. See *Zoller* (Bonne foi)
pp. 276–278, 280–285; *MacGibbon* 7 ICLQ 1958 pp. 471–473.
[166] For arguments emphasizing the closeness of the acquiescence-estoppel doctrine with
such non-consensual points (often by reference to the need to protect others' reliance),
see e.g. *Rubin* 71 AJIL 1977 pp. 20–21; *Müller* (Vertrauensschutz) pp. 9–10 *et seq*,
38–39, 41; *Schachter* 178 RCADI 1982/V p. 121; *Suy* (Actes) pp. 151–152; *Bowett*
XXXIII BYIL 1957 pp. 193–194.
[167] *Air Services Agreement* Arbitration 69 RGDIP 1965 pp. 249–254.
[168] *Ibid.* pp. 251–252.
[169] *Ibid.* p. 252. Similarly, in the *Barcelona Traction* Case, Reports 1964, the ICJ fused a
consensual with a non-consensual justification as it held that Belgium had not, by
disrupting the procedures at an earlier phase, thereby become precluded from
re-opening the issue. It held that the facts did not demonstrate that Belgium had

But this combination will involve obvious problems. Take the *Gulf of Maine* Case (1984), once more. Canada had argued that the United States was bound by absence of protest on its part because this was, on the one hand, evidence of US intent to be bound and, on the other hand, in accordance with good faith and equity. The Chamber of the Court starts out with the latter, non-consensual one. What is common to acquiescence and estoppel is that:

> ... both follow from the fundamental principle of good faith and equity.[170]

Had it followed this understanding, it should have had to enter a discussion of whether or not the conditions of good faith or equity were present to bind the United States in its silence. But there was no such discussion. This is understandable as arguing from non-consensual justice seems so subjective. Instead, it moved to a consensual understanding of the acquiescence-estoppel rule and went on to discuss whether the invoked "Hoffmann letter" was evidence of United States acceptance of the Canadian equidistance. It was not:

> ... facts invoked by Canada do not warrant the conclusion that the US Government thereby recognized the median line ...[171]

In other words, the United States was not bound because there was no subjective intent to be (regardless of considerations of good faith or equity). How did the Court arrive at this conclusion? It could not simply rely on US denial of such intent. This would have been apologist and violated Canadian sovereignty. The Chamber's conclusion did not concern lack of "real" but of "constructive" US intent. On what principles was that construction based? Mainly on inconsistency in the facts and on the low governmental status of the authorities involved.[172] But what justified this choice of relevant facts and their ensuing interpretation? What made the Court's construction better than the Canadian one?

---

thereby consented not to re-open it (consensual point) and that the Spanish position was not affected in any prejudicial manner (non-consensual point), pp. 24–25. For commentary, see *Müller* (Vertrauensschutz) pp. 31–32; *Dominicé* (Mélanges Guggenheim) pp. 328–329; *Martin* (L'Estoppel) pp. 157–165. See also *supra* n. 158.

[170] ICJ: *Gulf of Maine* Case, Reports 1984 p. 305 (§ 130).

[171] *Ibid.* p. 307 (§ 138). There is a clear assumption that the US could be bound only if somebody actually intended this. The "Hoffmann letter" did not create an obligation as Mr Hoffmann "did not seem aware" that his letter to the Canadian authorities could be understood as acquiescence, *ibid.* (§ 139).

[172] The facts relied upon by Canada revealed "uncertainties and a fair degree of inconsistency" in the US position, *ibid.* p. 307 (§ 138).

The argument stops here. The principles of construction were left undiscussed.

In principle, the Chamber could have used two principles of construction: 1) a construction is justified if it corresponds to intent; 2) a construction is justified if it reflects some non-consensual principle of good faith, legitimate expectations, justice or whatever. These are *exclusive* justifications. But *neither was open* to the Chamber. The former was excluded by the previous argument which ruled out the possibility of knowing real US intent and using it against Canada. The latter was excluded because it would have involved arguing in a fully non-consensual way against Canadian non-consensual justifications. This would have assumed the correctness of an objective justice and would have conflicted with the Chamber's previous refusal to think of acquiescence-estoppel in a non-consensual way. And, of course, it would have conflicted with the liberal doctrine of politics. Consequently, the Chamber simply took another interpretation of US conduct than Canada. Why it was better was not discussed as it could not have been discussed. The decision was, on its own premises, undetermined by legal argument.

Acquiescence-estoppel doctrine will ultimately define itself as simply arbitrary. The argument is in six by now familiar steps.

1. Doctrine starts out with a subjective view: the estoppel-acquiescence rule binds as it reflects intent. But real intent cannot be ascertained in a way which would guarantee the standard's normativity. Moreover, basing a decision on one Party's intent violates the sovereignty of the other.
2. Hence, intent is "inferred" from material behaviour. But not all behaviour allows making this inference. Not all past behaviour constitutes acquiescence or triggers off estoppel.[173] Clearly, criteria for distinguishing binding from non-binding behaviour are needed. Which are these criteria?
3. A first possibility is to assume that such criteria could refer to good faith, reasonableness, or legitimate expectations, for instance. If these criteria make a further reference to other States' reliance or acting

---

[173] Of course, courts have frequently ruled out the possibility that some behaviour would have been capable of such interpretation. See e.g. PCIJ: *Serbian Loans* Case, Ser. A 20 p. 39; ICJ: *North Sea Continental Shelf* Cases, Reports 1969 pp. 26–27 (§§ 30–32); *Gulf of Maine* Case, Reports 1984 pp. 303–308 (§§ 126–141); *US Military and Paramilitary Activities* Case, Reports 1984 pp. 413–415 (§§ 48–51).

upon, we face the difficulty of explaining why such reliance was justified in the first place. If we refer to some fully non-subjective criterion, we end up in holding the State bound by a theory of justice in a manner which is either utopian or violates its sovereignty because justifiable only on the basis of what principles other States have accepted.[174]

4. A second possibility is to argue that such behaviour is relevant which manifests intent in a "clear and unambiguous way".[175] But this assumes what was to be proved: namely that intent is "clear and unambiguous". The point is how we can justify our construction against another State's conflicting construction? We cannot "infer" intent from past acts or omissions and check the inference against whether it corresponds to intent or not because the whole argument started from the assumption that intent was *unknown* to us.

5. Thus, the inference needs to be justified by the character of the acts themselves or the context in which they were made. Many contextual determinants may be held relevant. These may include e.g. the position of the acting authority, the public nature of the act etc.[176] But no such criteria seem decisive. While it has sometimes been relevant that the acting authority had the capacity to bind his Government, at other times no such requirement has been made.[177] Nor have duration or consistency been held to establish acquiescence or estoppel automatically. The standards used have been flexible. The context seems determining.[178] But how to evaluate context?

---

[174] For this reason, those who regard acquiscence-estoppel as an expression of the good faith principle inevitably stress also that the "representation" – express or tacit – must reflect intent to become bound. See *supra* n. 165 and e.g. *Martin* (L'Estoppel) pp. 304–306 (based on good faith), 274–276 (must reflect intent in a clear manner). But see also *ibid*. pp. 307–317 ("intent" is constructed by a tacit agreement argument).

[175] *Bowett* XXXIII BYIL 1957 p. 188; *Martin* (L'Estoppel) pp. 275–276.

[176] In the *Barcelona Traction* Case, Reports 1964, the ICJ held as relevant whether the acting authority had the capacity to bind its government, pp. 22–23. See also ICJ: *Nuclear Tests* Cases, Reports 1974 p. 267 (§ 44); *US Military and Paramilitary Activities* Case, Reports 1986 p. 41 (§ 64).

[177] ICJ: *Minquiers and Ecrehos* Case, Reports 1953 (acts by the Ministry of Marine sufficient) pp. 66–67, 71; *Temple* Case, Reports 1962 (knowledge of "minor officials" sufficient) p. 25. For a review, see *Cahier* (Mélanges Guggenheim) pp. 242–244; *Jacqué* (Eléments) p. 211; *Martin* (L'Estoppel) pp. 277–282.

[178] Even one statement may be sufficient. See PCIJ: *Eastern Greenland* Case, Ser. A/B 53 pp. 69–71. In the *Serbian Loans* Case, Ser. A 20, the Court considered whether there

6. The dilemma is that there *are no criteria left by which the "contextual evaluation" could be made.* The only conceivable criteria would be the capacity of the act to represent intent or its internal nature. But both were excluded by our previous arguments. It was not possible to hold behaviour binding because it reflected intent as this would have required knowing intent independently of the act. And it was impossible to hold the act binding due to its inner essence because we do not know which "essences" are binding. In other words, *the doctrine's own assumptions define the contextual determination as simply subjective, arbitrary choice.*[179]

5.5   The structure of sources doctrine: examples

Sources doctrine is structured by its aim to avoid the objection of being either apologist or utopian. It integrates a descending (objective, non-consensual) and an ascending (subjective, consensual) strand within itself. In the practice of problem-solution this means that final decisions must be justified by reference both to party intent and justice. This takes place by losing the original opposition between "consent" and "justice" and making them rely on each other. To achieve a normative conception of "consent", the latter is looked at from the perspective of justice. To be able to argue concretely about "justice", reference is made to what States have consented to. This is an interminable movement. At the moment our perspective reveals itself as being either "consent" or "justice", it will become vulnerable to valid criticisms. Then the perspective must be changed. And so on. The vulnerability of this structure is hidden by the

had been a "deliberate surrender" of French rights relating to payment in full of certain loans to the Serbian government on the basis of such factors as the large number of private individuals involved, the required time of making a collective protest and regular standards of Government action to protect its citizens, p. 39. In the *European Danube Commission* Case, Ser. B 14, the Court held that participation by a State's representative in the Commission could be interpreted as acquiescence in the Commission's jurisdiction, p. 17. In the *Anglo-Norwegian Fisheries* Case, Reports 1951, the relevant factor was the extent of British maritime interests and its position as a maritime power, pp. 138–139. See also *US Military and Paramilitary Activities* Case, Reports 1986 p. 41 (§ 69). In other words, as the Court itself has noted, the ways in which consent may be expressed (or, rather, inferred) are unlimited, ICJ: *Temple* Case, Reports 1962 p. 31. See also *Jacqué* (Eléments) pp. 128–129; *Cahier* (Mélanges Guggenheim) pp. 244–260.

[179] Thus, though lawyers point out that the "intent" which is relevant is not "real" but "constructive", they remain silent on how its construction should be justified. See e.g. *Müller* (Vertrauensschutz) p. 41; *Akehurst* XLVII BYIL 1974–75 p. 39.

strategies of evasion, by the manner in which dispute-solution denies the reality of the disputes: if "justice" coalesces with what everybody has "consented" to, then no material solution seems needed.

In this section I shall illustrate this constant differentiation and association of points about "consent" and "justice" in the practice of the International Court of Justice. I have decided to include these examples in a separate section rather than in my discussion of the different doctrines above because of the necessity to understand sources doctrine as a whole. Cases which seem to be about treaty interpretation turn on as incorporating significant points about the meaning of unilateral statements or material behaviour. Cases which seem to be about estoppel or acquiescence involve the interpretation of written statements. Discussing the cases within the particular doctrinal areas also loses the possibility of understanding each case as a unified whole, the different parts of which relate to each other so as to achieve the required reconciliations.

5.5.1   Example 1: the Status of South West Africa opinion

In the *Status of South West Africa* Case (1950), the ICJ was asked the question: "does the Union of South Africa continue to have international obligations under the mandate for South West Africa ...?"[180] In other words, were the obligations once entered into by South Africa, as a member of the League of Nations, still binding on it despite the dissolution of the League? In particular, did the League's powers of supervision still persist, albeit transferred to the United Nations?[181] In principle, there were at least two contrasting approaches through which the Court could have entered upon a discussion of this question. It could have understood the question so as to relete solely to the interpretation of Article 22 of the League Covenant and of the text of the Mandate itself. Or it could have studied what kind of an obligation South Africa had originally consented to. The former approach seems to be a rather objective one, being concerned with texts and "systems", the latter a more subjective one, being concerned with South Africa's original intentions. Both strands seem insufficient alone. The "textual" strand seems to neglect South African sovereign will while the "intentionist" strand neglects considerations of justice. Therefore, the

180 ICJ: *Status of South West Africa* Case, Reports 1950 p. 131. See also *McNair*'s discussion of the Mandates system as an objective regime, *ibid.* pp. 147–151.
181 For the background, see *ibid.* pp. 131–136; statement by the representative of the UN, M. *Kerno*, *ibid.* Pleadings p. 160 *et seq.*

Court embarks upon both. It constructs the continuing validity of the South African mandate on objective (non-consensualist, teleological) as well as subjective (South Africa's consent) grounds.

In the first place, that South Africa remained bound by the mandate followed from the mandate's *objective nature*. It:

> ... was created in the interests of the inhabitants of the territory, and of humanity in general.[182]

Obligations relating to the territory – whether those of administration or of supervision[183] – had in no way lost their purpose through the dissolution of the League. Their "raison d'être and original object remain".[184] Even the technical procedures of supervision, originally entrusted to League organs, continued to have normative validity. The Mandates system was to be interpreted objectively, in light of its purpose which:

> ... must have been to provide a real protection for (South West African, MK) right; but no such right could be effectively safeguarded without international supervision and a duty to render reports to a supervisory organ.[185]

During the later phases of the South West African question, the Court continues to stress objective considerations. It emphasizes the humanitarian (instead of contractual) character of the mandate as a "sacred trust" and the continuing presence of the causes which demand that South Africa comply with the mandate.[186]

But the Court did not leave the matter there. Indeed, such an argument seems vulnerable to the objection of being too political. Assuming the existence of an objective teleology seems both controversial and beyond legal methods of ascertainment. Surely obligations based on consensual arrangements such as League mandates must also be justified by reference to consent. So the Court looks into South African

---

[182] *Ibid.* Reports 1950 p. 132.   [183] *Ibid.* p. 133.

[184] *Ibid.* p. 133.   [185] *Ibid.* pp. 136–137.

[186] See ICJ: *South West Africa* Case, Reports 1962 pp. 335–337 *et seq*; *Namibia* Case, Reports 1971 pp. 28–30 (§§ 45–51) *et seq*. The position is not contradicted by the Court's judgement of 1966 in which the question was so formulated as to concern Ethiopia's and Liberia's *locus standi*. True, the Court there held that humanitarian considerations were insufficient to ground the Applicants' right. But this does not mean that the decision would have been differently structured. The Court dwelled at length on the "systemic" nature of the Mandates. This was used as an objective, non-consensual principle which overruled anything that the Applicants might have subjectively intended as League members. *South West Africa* Case, Reports 1966 pp. 23 (§ 18), 19–31 (§§ 9–40). See further *infra* ch. 6.4.2.

behaviour and particularly into its statements at the League Assembly and before UN organs. It concludes that:

> (t)hese declarations constitute recognition by the Union Government of South Africa of the continuance of its obligations under the mandate.[187]

South African conduct and statements were interpreted as recognition by South Africa of the powers of international supervision of the General Assembly.[188] This subjective recognition aspect, too, is consistently held in the Court's later judgements and opinions about the South West African (Namibian) question.[189]

The *South West African* Cases exemplify the Court's need to make its decisions correspond to considerations of justice as well as consent. Such correspondence, however, is achieved only through assuming that these point in the same direction. But this is equivalent to assuming that *there really is no material dispute at all* for the Court to solve. Its business is only to give effect to what justice says and what everybody already agrees upon. In this way, the Court *evades* making an express material solution. The material problem – what if justice and South African consent would *not* have had the same content? – is neither raised not answered. This is so because raising it would reveal the need to prefer either one.

The difficulty with the Court's strategy lies in the ultimately unwarranted nature of the assumption of conformity between justice and consent and the manner in which assuming such conformity loses the sense of making both arguments in the first place. For these are meaningful only in opposition to each other. There is no point to argue, as the Court did in the *Status of South West Africa* opinion, about an objective teleology of the mandate unless it is assumed that this teleology can *override* whatever some States had consented to. The reverse is true of the Court's arguments about South African recognition. These are meaningful only on the assumption that South Africa's obligations really depend on what it has consented to – an assumption which conflicts with the Court's previous argument about teleology. By assuming that South African obligations depend on justice as well as consent the Court constructs a law which is incapable of proving guidance in future cases: any argument will be *prima facie* valid and no argument more than that.

---

[187] ICJ: *Status of South West Africa Case*, Reports 1950 p. 135.

[188] *Ibid.* p. 142.

[189] See ICJ: *South West Africa Case*, Reports 1962 pp. 335, 339–340. *Namibia* Case, Reports 1971 pp. 39–41 (§§ 74–78).

It might be possible to argue that one or the other of the justifications was there only *ex abundate cautela* – a frequent enough occurrence in legal advocacy. In other words, either the teleologial or the consensualist argument was simply superfluous and added there only as a matter of internal aesthetics. But this loses the inner coherence of the Court's argument. It *needed both arguments* in order to avoid the objection that it was arguing on utopian or apologist assumptions. To say that it was "really" the teleological or the consensualist point which was determining violates the all-important balance which the Court aimed to construct.

5.5.2   Example 2: the Reservations opinion

In the *Reservations to the Genocide Convention* Case (1951), the Court discussed the conditions of validity of reservations to the Convention on the Prohibition of Genocide. Again, two types of answers seem possible: a reservation could be valid if other States consent to it or if it corresponds to some non-consensual criterion.

The Court started by considering whether a State which had made a reservation to which others had objected could be considered a party to the treaty. The Court outlined a rule which it held well-established, namely that:

> ... a State cannot be bound without its consent and consequently no reservation can be effective against any State without its agreement thereto.[190]

At first blush, this "basic principle" seems fully consensualist: States whose reservations have been objected to do not become parties. But this is not what the Court is saying. In the first place, it tempers the principle's apparent consensualism by interpreting it from two perspectives. Besides manifesting the contractual nature of conventions it also expresses the principle of the integrity of conventions.[191] The argument from "integrity" is an objective point which explains that "old" parties cannot be objected with the rights of a "new" party if these are not counterbalanced by the latter's reciprocal duties.

In the second place, to conclude that a reserving State does not become a party goes, according to the Court, against certain objective considerations, namely the "universal nature of the Genocide Convention, the wide degree of participation envisaged for it as well as the need for flexibility".[192] Moreover (the subjective point), the faculty

---

[190] ICJ: *Reservations* Case, Reports 1951 p. 21.   [191] *Ibid.*   [192] *Ibid.* pp. 21–22.

of making reservations had been envisaged during the *travaux prépara-toires* and was implicit in the very question by the General Assembly.[193] Thus, mere non-consent to a reservation did not preclude the reserving State from becoming a party – it concerned only the relations between the latter and the objecting States.

The second question related to what kinds of reservations were allowed. This was a trickier one because it seemed to involve justifying different treatment of different reservations on the basis of their content. The Court's argument is again first objective, then subjective.

The Court holds that such reservations are acceptable which are in conformity with the "object and purpose" of the Convention. This seems an eminently objective standard. It is also argued in a non-consensual way, by stressing the universal character of the Convention – its object being unrelated to particular State interests.[194] But it is not *wholly* objective. The Court points out that the "object and purpose test" can also be inferred from the "intention of the General Assembly and of the States which adopted (the Convention, MK)".[195] In fact, disregard-ing the object and purpose test would "frustrate the purpose which the General Assembly and the Contracting Parties had in mind".[196]

The crucial issue, however, is which reservations are in conformity with the object and purpose test and which go against it. It is here that material disputes arise. Notice, first, that the test itself seems objective. Conformity or non-conformity with the object and purpose seem to be independent of any State's opinions on the matter. Second, the Court is not making a point about the reserving State's subjective intentions. These may or may not coincide with the treaty's object and purpose. But inasmuch as the argument assumes that States are *bound by* this test, it assumes that such object exists and can be discovered independently of particular party intentions. But the Court never outlined how such test could be undertaken, nor what criteria were relevant in it. The sense of the assumptions behind the object and purpose test is lost by the manner in which the Court forces a subjective argument into the picture. It says:

---

[193] *Ibid.* pp. 22–23.   [194] *Ibid.* p. 23.   [195] *Ibid.* p. 24.
[196] *Ibid.* p. 24. It is difficult to think what other purposes a treaty might have – at least for its interpretation – except those which the parties intended to attain with it. See also *Fitzmaurice*, sep. op. ECHR: *Belgian Police* Case Ser. A 19 p. 33. *Jacqué* (Eléments) summarizes: "La definition du but est subjective puisqu'elle ne peut être qu'après une analyse des intentions de l'auteur", p. 169.

> ... each State which is a party to the Convention can appreciate the
> validity of the reservation and it exercises this right individually and from
> its own standpoint. As no State can be bound by a reservation to which it
> has not consented, it necessarily follows that each State objecting to it
> will, or will not, on the basis of its individual approval, within the limits of
> the criterion of the object and purpose, stated above, consider the reser-
> ving State to be a party to the Convention.[197]

In a sense, the Court here both affirmed the objectively binding character of the law and then denied it. At one point it expressly objected to
the view put forward by the Soviet Union about it being contrary to State
sovereignty to devise a non-consensual test about whether or not reservations are allowed. The Court pointed out that:

> ... so extreme an application of the idea of State sovereignty could lead
> to a complete disregard of the object and purpose of the Convention.[198]

And yet, its final ruling according to which it was for each State to decide
what was to be considered as conformity and non-conformity seems
equivalent to the view which it attacks here.

In other words, the Court assumed that a Convention's object and
purpose can be assimilated with what States think to be its object and
purpose.

Superficially, the Court seems to have achieved a reconciliation
between a descending and an ascending approach. The argument is
not apologist as it makes reference beyond consent, to object and
purpose. It is not utopian, either, because it establishes the content of
object and purpose by reference to State consent.

But the Court thereby fails to achieve any determinate rule about the
admissibility of reservations. It provides no hierarchy between the
descending and ascending arguments.[199] It merely assumes that the
two point in the same direction. But this is an unwarranted assumption,
contradicted by the very emergence of the dispute. The important point

---

[197] ICJ: *Reservations* Case, Reports 1951 p. 26.   [198] *Ibid.* p. 24.
[199] For a cogent criticism, see *Koh* 23 Harv.ILJ 1982 pp. 84–88. Similarly *Decaux*
(Réciprocité), noting that the Court "écarte la réciprocité au nom de la morale, mais
met en pièces la morale au nom de relativisme", pp. 68–70. This same strategy seems to
have been adopted in the Vienna Convention on the Law of Treaties. It repeats the
need for the "object and purpose test" and then goes on to point out that: "Each State
which is a party to the Convention can appraise the validity of the reservation and it
exercises this right individually and from its own standpoint", Article 19 (c). See also
Koh, supra pp. 97–99.

is, however, that this assumption fails singularly to indicate any solution when States insist on their different views. At that point, the Court's rule fails us. We have no standard to judge which party's position is the better one. We are led into a search of possible tacit consent in one or another party to its adversary's position about the object and purpose. Unless we can ground our decision on tacit consent, we seem either to fall into utopianism (arguing from a non-consent-related object and purpose) or violate sovereign equality (regarding as object and purpose what *other* States hold as such). But this will only lead into the further problem of having to explain why *our* conception of what the party had consented to can be opposed to that party itself. In which case we face the threat of lapsing back into arguing either in a utopian or an apologist way. And so on. Pushed by argument, a problem-solver will have to justify his position on what the object and purpose test by either descending or ascending arguments. At that point, reconciliatory rhetoric will fail.

5.5.3 *Example 3: the* Admission *opinion*

My third example is provided by the *Admission of a State to Membership in the UN* Case (*1948*) which is concerned with an interpretation of Article 4 of the UN Charter. In the course of its discussion, the Court objects both to a purely objective (non-consensualist) and a purely subjective (consensualist) approach and moves so as to include both in its own construction losing, however, thereby the sense of that very provision.

The matter arose out of a difficulty to have new members accepted to the organization in 1946 and 1947. The legal issue concentrated on whether a member State was allowed to make its positive vote on the acceptance of a new State conditional on other States being accepted simultaneously.[200] On 17 November 1947, the General Assembly decided to refer this issue to the ICJ. Only the first part of the question posed by the Assembly needs discussion here:[201]

---

[200] There had been two sets of such applications. In respect of those of 1946 (Albania, Mongolia, Portugal, Ireland, Transjordania), the United States had suggested a decision *en bloc* while the Soviet Union had opposed such procedure. In respect of those in 1947 (Hungary, Romania, Bulgaria, Finland, Italy), the Soviet Union suggested *en bloc* admission. At the time of the request, no admissions had been granted. For a history, see e.g. Statement by the representative of the Secretary-General, M. *Kerno*, ICJ: *Admission* Case, Pleadings pp. 42–58.

[201] ICJ: *Admission* Case, Reports 1948 p. 58. The second part was addressed to the legitimacy of making a State's vote conditional on the admission of other States.

> Is a member of the UN which is called upon, in virtue of Article 4 of the Charter, to pronounce itself by its vote, either in the Security Council or the General Assembly, on the admission of a State to membership in the UN, juridically entitled to make its consent to the admission dependent on conditions not expressly provided for by paragraph 1 of the said Article?

That paragraph provides:

> Membership in the UN is open to all other (i.e. other than original members, MK) peace-loving States which accept the obligations contained in the present Charter and, in the judgement of the organization, are able and willing to carry out those obligations.

At the outset the problem seemed to involve a conflict between a subjective and an objective approach. During discussion, many States had argued that the criteria in Article 4 were not exhaustive but that the admission of a State was a purely political question.[202] In his statement, Dr Lachs, for example, emphasized the subjective freedom of members which, in his opinion, was well manifested in the practice of UN organs.[203] On this argument, States were free to attach any conditions they willed to their positive vote. On the other hand, other States had argued that the question of admission had been exhaustively settled in Article 4.[204] The members were not entitled to base their vote on other criteria except those mentioned therein. Mr Kaeckenbeek argued that this followed from the unambiguous formulation in Article 4(1).[205] Supporters of the former, subjective view rejected the universality principle of the organization which adherents to the objective view sought to uphold.[206] These positions are exhaustive and mutually exclusive. A decision can only give effect to subjective member will or the non-consensually binding character of the Charter. Either will is prior to the text of Article 4 or the text of that Article is prior to will.

---

[202] See e.g. written observation by Yugoslavia, *ibid*. Pleadings p. 23 and the review of positions by M. Kerno, *ibid*. pp. 53–55.

[203] Statement by Dr *Lachs*, *ibid*. Pleadings pp. 100–115.

[204] See written observations by China, El Salvador, Guatemala, Honduras, India, Canada, United States, Greece, Belgium, Iraq, Australia, Siam, *ibid*. pp. 14–33.

[205] Statement by M. *Kaeckenbeek*, *ibid*. pp. 91–92.

[206] For the former, see written observation by Greece, *ibid*. Pleadings p. 21. See also *ibid*. Alvarez, ind. op. Reports 1948 p. 71. For the latter, see *ibid*. statement by Professor *Scelle*, Pleadings pp. 70–73 and *ibid*. joint diss. op. Reports 1948 p. 30.

But both positions are problematic. If a decision on admission were a purely political matter, Article 4 would lose its normative character.[207] A purely subjective construction seems apologist. It makes Article 4 simply superfluous. On the other hand, if the members could not express their affirmative attitude by their vote but that vote would simply register the presence of pre-existing criteria, then this would, as the joint dissent pointed out, be a "strange interpretation" of voting.[208] Inasmuch as pararaph 2 of Article 4 says that admission "will be effected" by vote, it seems to assume that member will, as expressed in the vote, is constitutive of membership.[209] More fundamentally, it would undermine the liberty of existing members to decide on the nature and degree of their legal relations with other States. By the simple presence of the criteria outlined in Article 4, they would have to confront these States as equal members of the organization.

To avoid these problems, both positions are accompanied with arguments from the opposing position. Thus the initially objective-looking argument about the exhaustivity of the criteria in Article 4 is accompanied by subjective arguments according to which the Article must be so interpreted because the drafters originally so intended[210] as well as with the subjective argument according to which a State fulfilling the conditions had a positive right to become accepted as a member.[211] In other words, neglecting to give effect to Article 4 would violate the subjective consent of the drafters and the subjective essence of the statehood of applying States. Conversely, the originally subjective-looking argument about the political character of the admission procedure was supported by objective arguments about the "nature" of the political organs[212] and of the admission decision as well as arguments about the *travaux préparatoires*, this time given an objective interpretation: they overruled any subjective right of the applicant as well as any possibly conflicting present will of the members.[213]

The arguments can be summarized as follows:

---

[207] *Ibid.* pp. 62–63. It was possibly with such consequences in mind that those who expressed the subjective view avoided referring to Article 4 altogether and simply concentrated on denying the Court's competence. See e.g. observations by the Ukranian SSR and the Soviet Union, *ibid.* Pleadings pp. 28, 29.

[208] *Ibid*, joint diss. op. Reports 1948 pp. 82–83; *Zoričić*, diss. op. p. 97.

[209] *Ibid*, joint diss. op. p. 84. The opinion refers expressly to the Lotus principle, p. 86.

[210] Written observations by Canada and Belgium, *ibid.* Pleadings pp. 19, 25–26.

[211] *Ibid.* Reports 1948, *Alvarez*, ind. op. pp. 70–71.

[212] *Ibid. Krylov*, diss. op. pp. 107–108.

[213] *Ibid.* Joint diss. op. pp. 87–90; *Zoričić*, diss. op. pp. 98–100, 101–103.

1. *Article 4 is exhaustive*
   a. subjective support:
      - because this is what drafters intended;
      - because this gives effect to applicant's subjective right.
   b. objective support:
      - because of the unambiguous wording of Article 4(1);
      - because of the "universality principle".
2. *Article 4 is non-exhaustive*
   a. subjective support:
      - because members' will must have effectiveness;
      - because this is what the drafters intended.
   b. objective support:
      - because of the unambiguous wording of Article 4(1);
      - because of the political nature of UN organs and of the admission procedure.

Both positions are supported by subjective and objective arguments. Moreover, similar arguments are put forward to support opposing views. Original intent of the drafters and the text of Article 4 are interpreted in contradictory ways. The same is true of the argument from the nature of the UN. It is interpreted either in terms of universality (in support of exhaustiveness) or in terms of politics (to support non-exhaustiveness). Finally, the argument from subjective liberty (or right) contrasts the liberty of the existing members with the liberty of the applicant once it has fulfilled the conditions in Article 4.

A first thing to notice about these arguments is that they are either superfluous or contradictory. An interpretation of Article 4 cannot follow from *both* subjective and objective arguments. This is so because both are based on the assumption that they are, by themselves, *fully determining*. To argue for the exhaustivity of the criteria in Article 4 on the basis of thinking subjective intent and objective nature of the UN being *both* determining is simply to argue too much. The assumption behind the former point is that consent overrules nature while the assumption behind the latter is reverse. But to concede that the positions must be either subjective or objective is to render them vulnerable to the charge of being either apologist or utopian. Both positions were accompanied by both arguments precisely to avoid this accusation.

A second point is that it seems impossible to decide which of the conflicting arguments should be preferred. This is visible in respect of each of the four pairs of contrasting arguments.

There were conflicting views about original drafter intent. Whether this supports exhaustivity or non-exhaustivity cannot be decided on a fully consensual basis. We lack access to what the drafters "really" willed. Will must be construed objectively, by reference to past behaviour or to the text itself. There is, however, no other relevant past behaviour than the very acceptance of the text in Article 4. So, what the drafters willed can only be construed by looking at the text. But this argument fails. For the indeterminacy of the text – that it was capable of the two contrasting interpretations – was the argument's very starting-point. Original intent does not lead into solution.

There were arguments contrasting member liberty with the subjective right of applicant. Basing the decision on the need to give effect to either one seems impossible because it would violate sovereign equality. Of course, liberties and rights can be prioritized by reference to a superior code of value. But such code must be independent of the liberties or rights themselves. As such, it looks like a natural morality and is vulnerable to the objection of being utopian. If the assumption of a constraining hierarchy is rejected, however, the argument fares no better. For this means that we shall overrule one State's liberty or right in a manner which is simply arbitrary or assumes that one State's liberties or rights are more valuable than those of another State's because they belong to *that* State. This violates sovereign equality. The arguments from member freedom/right of applicant do not provide solution.

Thirdly, it is likewise impossible to prefer either one of the arguments about the nature of the UN or its organs. How does one "know" whether it is in the "nature" of the UN that it have universal membership or that its organs are "political" instead of "legal"? There are two ways in which such arguments can be supported. A purely objective approach argues that the nature of the UN automatically reveals itself to any external observer. But this assumes an indefensibly naturalist position (that things have "essences" which are independent of the conceptual framework of observers) which is utopian as it cannot support itself by arguments from what States believe. Besides, it seems contradicted by the fact that there is disagreement. To base such essence on subjective perception and to assume an ascending (subjectivist) argument fares no better. According to this argument, we can know the nature of the UN only in the manner in which States think about it. But what to make then of the *different* perceptions of States? Surely it cannot be plausibly said that some States understand the nature of the UN better than others. Even if this were the case, it could not be put forward as the decisive legal argument as it is contrary to sovereign equality. If sovereign equality is to be honoured, it is impossible to argue about the nature of the UN without a non-subjective theory in order to compare subjective views on this matter against each other. But a non-subjective theory seems utopian in the most obvious sense. It assumes that we can reach the meaning of social phenomena independently of the subjective experience of the participants in those phenomena.

Finally, there is the opposition between the two interpretations of the text of Article 4. The normal meaning of the paragraph was quoted to support both the exhaustiveness as well as non-exhaustiveness of the criteria listed therein. This dispute seems capable of decision only by either assuming that one meaning is more *intrinsically* "*normal*" than the other or that extratextual considerations, that is either subjective intent or objective justice, support either one. But clearly, none of these arguments leads to a solution. The argument from the intrinsically "natural" character of one or the other interpretation seems contradicted by the very fact that dispute exists. What seems in need of justification is how to prefer one Party's interpretation over that of another's. This can be done by assuming normal meaning to coincide with drafter intent. But, as we have seen, drafter intent can be known only on the basis of a presumption based on the text itself. And it is now the very meaning of the text which is the object of construction. If normal meaning is held identical with "just" meaning, we are led into the difficulty of making a preference between two theories of justice without either moving in a utopian argument or simply preferring one over the other in a way which violates sovereign equality.

None of the conflicting justifications expressed in this case can be preferred. A decision is not found by simply preferring objectivism or subjectivism because *both* positions are both objective and subjective. Nor can the different subjective or objective justifications be preferred as they depend on assumptions which are either utopian (that is, indemonstrable) or apologist (privilege one State's will, perception or understanding over another's in a manner which violates sovereign equality). The Court faces the task of constructing a solution independently of the positions advanced. In this, however, it is constrained by the same considerations which prompted the curiously self-contradicting arguments of the pleading States. To avoid the objection of arguing in a utopian or an apologist manner, the Court must make sure that the judgement includes an ascending (subjective) as well as descending (objective) argument.[214]

In the first place, the Court affirmed the objectively binding character of Article 4. The natural meaning of that Article pointed to the full exhaustiveness of the criteria listed therein.[215] A member:

> ... is not juridically entitled to make its consent to the admission dependent on conditions not expressly provided by paragraph 1.[216]

The Court affirmed that:

> The political character of an organ cannot release it from the observance of the treaty provisions established by the Charter when they constitute limitations on its power or criteria for its judgement.[217]

These points seem purely objective. They imply a view about normal meaning and the nature of political organs. As such, however, they threaten to overrule subjective consent in a utopian manner: for these points about normal meaning and of the character of Article 4 were not really argued at all, they were simply posited. Therefore, the Court supports its findings with subjective points. The text was authoritative as it clearly demonstrates the "intention of its authors".[218] If the drafters had intended to make the criteria non-exhaustive, they "would undoubtedly have adopted a different wording".[219] In this way, the Court could justify its decision subjectively, by rendering original drafter intentions effective.

But this is not really satisfying as it still leaves open the question of why (controversial) original intent of the drafters should be preferred to the (actual) will of present members. This seems a utopian position which simultaneously threatens present members' sovereign equality and the character of the procedure of voting as expressing affirmative will. These considerations are taken account of by the Court in its construction of the content of the criteria in Article 4. The conditions listed there were "wide" and "elastic" and left present members "a wide degree of appreciation".[220] There was no conflict, the Court said,

---

[214] This concern was present already in professor Scelle's ingenious effort to distinguish between "admissibility" and "admission". While the former was determined by the objective formulation of Article 4, the latter remained a matter of political choice, *ibid*, statement by *Scelle*, Pleadings pp. 64–70.
[215] *Ibid*. Reports 1948 pp. 62–64.   [216] *Ibid*. p. 65.   [217] *Ibid*. p. 64.
[218] *Ibid*. p. 62.   [219] *Ibid*. p. 63.
[220] *Ibid*. pp. 63, 64. To the same effect, see *Azevedo*, diss. op. pp. 77–78.

between politics and law. The latter's content is determined by the former. A commentator has observed:

> ... if and when political considerations, considerations of expediency, existed ... it is both possible and likely that the applicant would be excluded on reasoned grounds arising from Article 4(1).[221]

But this looks like an unacceptably apologist position. If the content of the State's obligation can be determined by the State itself, then surely its binding force is merely an illusion. This would render Article 4 superfluous and thus violate drafter intent. Therefore, the Court makes an ultimate attempt to move back into an objective position. For although political considerations were covered by Article 4, this did not mean that political choice was fully free. It was restricted by the members' duty to interpret the criteria in Article 4 in *good faith*.[222] Though the reference to good faith was made by the Court almost in passing, it serves a crucial role in allowing the Court to avoid the objection of apologism.

But the antinomous and indeterminate character of such solution seems evident. No substantive decision, material rule, emerges from it. The decision is without consequence to the problem it is addressed to. Members are bound by the criteria in Article 4 but what those criteria are is up to the members to decide. Member will is restricted by good faith but the content of the good faith standard is left open.[223] Every argument to give content to the good faith standard will raise the original argumentative cycle again: is there a "natural" conception of good faith or does good faith depend on what States will? Article 4 may contain an implicit reference to good faith but good faith, in turn, contains an implicit reference to the criteria in Article 4. It merely poses the original question in another vocabulary.

Though there is constant movement towards reconciling the objective and subjective arguments, there is no final decision anywhere. The argument is constantly avoiding fixing itself at any position. The Court first affirms that objective considerations (normal meaning, character of

---

[221] *Stuart Klooz* 43 AJIL 1949 p. 261.

[222] ICJ: *Admission* Case, Reports 1948 p. 63. See also *ibid.* joint diss. op. pp. 91–92; *Zoričić*, diss. op. p. 103; *Krylov*, diss. op. p. 115; *Alvarez*, ind. op. p. 71. To the same effect, *see Azevedo*, diss. op. p. 80.

[223] *Zoller* (Bonne foi) holds that inasmuch as the reference to good faith had any ascertainable content, it either referred back to the criteria in Article 4 or to the objects and purposes of the organization in general, pp. 164–167. In neither case, however, does it offer any independent criteria for solving interpretative conflicts.

political organs) are decisive and override sovereign will. But it then constructs these subjectively, first by reference to drafter intent. This now determines the sense of the text and the nature of the organs. But drafter intent, in turn, is argued from the objective position about the text's normal meaning. The text now determines drafter intent. But the sense of the text is elusive. It is made concrete by present members' use of their "wide degree of appreciation". Now the text defers to (subjective) present member will. But present member will is not free. It is constrained by an objective but open-ended good faith standard – a good faith whose content is dependent on the (ambiguous) meaning of Article 4 and the interpretations and political decisions taken by members. The objective arguments refer immediately to subjective ones and *vice-versa*. There is no closure, no ultimate reconciliation. Each position dissolves into an unending cycle of subjective and objective justifications.

5.5.4 *Example 4: the* Arbitral Award *Case*

The *Arbitral Award of 1906* Case (1960) is a *locus classicus* on acquiescence-estoppel though the Court never mentioned either concept in it.[224] The case was concerned with a Nicaraguan claim that an Arbitral Award by the King of Spain of 23 December 1906 was null and void because the arbitrator had not respected the terms of the *compromiso* in the 1894 Treaty. The Award was claimed to be invalid also because the *compromiso* had lapsed before the designation of the arbitrator and because of excess of the arbitrator's jurisdiction, essential error and inadequacy of the reasons in the Award.[225]

The judgement is in two parts. In the first part the Court holds the Award opposable to Nicaragua because of its subjective acceptance, in the second it refutes the Nicaraguan claims on their merits.

In the first part, the Court interprets Nigaragua's subsequent behaviour as acceptance of the Award. Several acts by Nicaraguan authorities were discussed. These included absence of protest during the arbitral proceedings, a telegram by the President of Nicaragua to the President of Honduras on 25 February 1906 and a statement before the Nicaraguan

---

[224] For commentary, see e.g. *Müller* (Vertrauensschutz) pp. 63–68; *Blum* (Historic Titles) thinks that lack of reference to estoppel resulted from that doctrine's uncertain status, pp. 93–94.

[225] For the Nicaraguan submissions, see ICJ: *Arbitral Award* Case, Reports 1960 pp. 197–199, 205, 210.

Legislative Assembly on 1 December 1907.[226] These were argued by the
Court to evidence Nicaragua's acceptance of the terms of the Award.[227]
But the Nicaraguan obligation could not be fully subjective, consensual.
Since 1912 onwards, Nicaragua had challenged the Award's validity. If
Nicaragua was nevertheless now bound, this could only be because the
Court "knew better" or because good faith, trust or stability required
that the Award be regarded as valid.[228]

Nicaragua had disputed its initial acceptance. It argued that the early
statements by its authorities had been based on erroneous beliefs about
the Award's content. It pointed out that Honduras had known of
Nicaragua's non-acceptance and that there had therefore been no reason
for it to protest expressly before 1912 when the matter had become
acute.[229] Clearly, these are not manifestly implausible arguments. But
my point is not to challenge the Court's interpretation – only to show
that there was no conclusive argument with which to justify preferring
the Court's interpretation to that of Nicaragua's.

The Court "inferred" Nicaragua's acceptance from certain behaviour
and statements. How could it justify this against Nicaragua's contrary
interpretation? Presumably, it was not making a point about Nicaragua's
real intent. In any case, such an argument could not have been open to it.
But if it was constructive intent, what principles of construction were used?
No such principles were mentioned. The Court simply countered the
Nicaraguan view about error by noting that the "full terms of the Award
must have been available to Nicaragua" (emphasis MK).[230] The Court's
position can either be accepted or not. But its acceptance cannot be the
result of the Court's material argument for no such argument exists. Of the
two available positions (that Nicaragua had consented because the acts
reflect its consent or because they reflect a principle of constructive interpretation) the Court adopts neither one. It presents the conclusion as

---

[226] *Ibid.* pp. 207, 210–211. *Vallée* 77 RGDIP 1973 notes that the case seems to concern estoppel precisely because subjective acceptance was based on inferences from conduct, pp. 968–969.

[227] ICJ: *Arbitral Award* Case, Reports 1960 pp. 213, 219.

[228] It is difficult to think of the judgement in this way because Honduras had not pressed for the carrying out of the Award and, presumably, had not even "relied" on Nicaragua's acceptance. See the oral argument by *Jessup, ibid.* Pleadings II p. 230 *et seq*; *Holquin*, diss. op. *ibid*, Reports 1960 p. 236. Judge *Spender*, however, constructed Nicaragua's continued obligation expressly on good faith, *ibid*, diss. op. pp. 219–220.

[229] Memorial of Nicaragua, *ibid.* Pleadings I pp. 196–204 (§§ 176–190) and oral argument by *Jessup, ibid.* p. 230 *et seq.*

[230] *Ibid.* Reports 1960 p. 213.

self-evident. This is hardly convincing for someone who does not *already* agree with the Court's view.

Having regard to its conclusion in the first part of the judgement, the refutation of the substance of Nicaragua's claim in the second part seems simply superfluous.[231] Why go into this matter if the Award was already valid because of Nicaragua's acquiescence? A possible answer is that the second part directs attention away from the fragility of the Court's construction in the first. It doesn't really matter if the Court's argument about Nicaragua's will is unconvincing as non-consensual law renders the same solution: Nicaragua is bound. The latter part adds justice to support what had already been arrived at through consent. Nicaragua's obligations are not, after all, dependent only on (subjective) speculations about consent.

The judgement operates several reconciliatory strategies. It reconciles consensualism with non-consensualism in the judgement's general structure (the opposition between the two parts). Also both parts contain an internal reconciliation. Nicaragua was bound because it had (subjectively) consented – its consent was inferred from its (objective) behaviour. Nicaragua was bound by (objective) principles regarding the validity of arbitral Awards – this law was applicable because it could be justified by reference to Nicaragua's consent. Each position by the Court can be broken down into a consensual and a non-consensual principle which it has to contain in order to seem justifiable. Moreover, the judgement reconciles Nicaraguan with Honduran sovereignty. The latter is protected by the Court's very acceptance of the Honduran claim. The former is protected by assuming that Nicaragua had consented.

The difficulty is, of course, that no rule emerges from the Court's treatment of the case. We do not know whether the validity of arbitral Awards is a matter of consent or justice nor, if it is either, how consent can be ascertained or what principles of justice are relevant. Each consensual point refers back to a non-consensual one and *vice-versa*. The judgement seems acceptable because consent is made parallel with justice. Why they are so, is nowhere discussed.

---

[231] As suggested by *Martin* (L'Estoppel) p. 119. For the Court's discussion of the substance of Nicaraguan views, see ICJ: *Arbitral Award* Case, Reports 1960 pp. 205–206 (validity of the designation of Arbitrator), 207–209 (lapse of the *compromiso*), 214–217 (the remaining claims).

5.5.5   Example 5: the Temple Case

In the *Temple* Case (1962) the Court was dealing with a dispute between
Cambodia and Thailand over sovereignty in the area of the Temple of
Preah Vihear, situated in a disputed sector in the frontier between the
two countries.[232] A convention of 13 February 1904 had established the
watershed line as the boundary. A Delimitation Commission, accepted
by Siam and France (as the protectory power for Cambodia), had
worked between 1904 and 1907 and drawn a map which had located
the Temple in Cambodian territory. The map had been annexed to the
convention of 1904 and copies had been widely circulated in both
countries.[233] Without having previously protested, Thailand moved,
in 1949, to occupy the disputed area and placed military forces there
in 1954. By this time it argued that the map did not correspond to the
correct watershed line – a line which would leave the temple on the Thai
side of the boundary.

Both Parties argued in an objective and a subjective way. They relied
on the 1904 Convention and to their subjective actions in the territory.[234] Both claimed that the other had acquiesced in its view. Thailand
argued that Cambodia had tacitly reconigzed Thai sovereignty by failing
to protest against the acts of local Thai authorities in the temple area.[235]
Cambodia relied on Thai recognition of the maps and, in particular, the
absence of protest by Prince Damrong of Thailand during an official
visit to the area where he had been saluted by the French resident and the
French flag had been flown.[236] There was no dispute on applicable law.
The case turned on an interpretation of the 1904 Convention and of the
Parties' conduct. Much of the judgement has to do with interpreting the

---

[232] Though this is a sovereignty dispute, it differs from standard territorial disputes
(discussed *supra* ch. 4.7.) as it contains almost no discussion of the general law of
territory. The Court held that the different geographical, historical and archaeological
issues were simply not "legally decisive". ICJ: *Temple* Case, Reports 1962 p. 15. In other
words, the case turned on an interpretation of the normative sense of the Parties'
behaviour. See also *ibid. Alfaro*, sep. op. p. 39 *et seq*; *Fitzmaurice*, sep. op. pp. 62–65;
Spender, diss. op. pp. 142–146. But see also *Jennings* (Acquisition) pp. 49–50.

[233] For the history of the dispute, see ICJ: *Temple* Case, Reports 1962 pp. 16–20.

[234] Cambodia interpreted the Convention in light of the annexed map, see Application,
ibid. Pleadings I pp. 5–11. Thailand interpreted it in accordance with the watershed
principle, based on Article I of the Convention, see Rejoinder, *ibid.* pp. 590–598. For
the arguments about effectiveness (that is, their subjective actions), see Application by
Cambodia, *ibid.* pp. 11–12, Counter-Memorial by Thailand, *ibid.* pp. 188–192.

[235] Counter-Memorial by Thailand, *ibid.* pp. 185–187.

[236] Application by Cambodia, *ibid.* pp. 12–14; Reply, *ibid.* pp. 462–465.

normative sense of Thailand's absence of protest. Did it or did it not constitute tacit acceptance of the Cambodian position?

> The real question ... which is the essential one in this case, is whether the Parties did adopt the Annex I map and the line included in it ... thereby conferring on it a binding character.[237]

Thailand denied that its silence could be interpreted as acquiescence because it had resulted from ignorance, error and the conviction that the temple was situated in Thai territory. The Court took a different view. Ignorance and error were excluded because of the publicity given to the maps in Thailand.[238] The argument that Thailand had erred in the correct place of the watershed line was not open to it because it had also argued from effective occupation of the Temple.[239] For the Court, Thailand's conduct did not "afford *ex post facto* evidence sufficient to show that she never accepted" the boundary on the maps.[240]

There are two conflicting interpretations of the meaning of Thailand's silence. Curiously, the argument does nothing to explain why one interpretation would be better than the other. The Court only observes that even Thai administrative acts in the Temple could not "cancel out the clear impression" of Thai acquiescence.[241] What created this "impression" was nowhere made explicit.

Clearly, the Court was in the presence of a dilemma. What would allow overruling Thailand's *own* interpretation of its behaviour? The Court could not argue that it "knew better". So, the interpretation was based on "constructive knowledge". But what (non-subjective) principles of construction were used? Possible candidates are protection of Cambodian reliance or some abstract principle of justice, legal security or good faith. Only one such consideration was expressly invoked by the Court. This made reference to the benefits which Thailand had accrued from the settlement.[242] During the proceedings, however, opposing justice-based arguments had been invoked. It had been argued that there never was any reliance on the Cambodian side.[243] And what was just in the matter had been made controversial. For Thailand's silence, it had been argued, might only have reflected its situation *vis-à-vis* a

---

[237] *Ibid.* Reports 1962 p. 22.   [238] *Ibid.* pp. 22–26.   [239] *Ibid.* p. 33.   [240] *Ibid.* p. 29.
[241] *Ibid.* p. 30.   [242] *Ibid.* p. 32.
[243] See e.g. *ibid.* Koo, diss. op. p. 97, *Spender*, diss. op. pp. 144–145.

colonial power; protesting might have been detrimental to Thailand's own interests.[244]

The point is not whether these are the decisive or even the most important considerations of justice or good faith which might have been applicable. Others might be envisaged and were presented during the proceedings. The point is that the Court did not and could not argue about such justifications, compare them with each other and then arrive at some conclusion because *going into them would have involved it in an argument about objective justice* – an argument which the Court, under the liberal assumptions, was not in a position to engage in. It had to argue the Thai recognition from its "impression" because there was no other argument available to it.[245]

Though the Court refrained from arguing about justice in respect of its interpretation of Thailand's silence, there was, like in the Arbitral Award case, an additional argument which based Thailand's obligations on something external to its consent. This was the argument about the "stability and finality" of boundaries which precluded Thailand from challenging the boundary now. But though this worked as an independent justification, it received also subjective support in that the Court imputed this principle as an implied condition in the original boundary settlement to the Parties. Though the principle of "stability and finality", thus, worked as an objective criterion, it was justified in a subjective manner.[246]

The structure of the judgement in the *Temple* Case follows that of the Arbitral Award case. Thailand is bound through a (subjective) principle of acquiescence and an (objective) principle of "stability and finality". The fragility of the Court's argument from its "impression" is compensated by its judgement also being in conformity with justice. The weakness of its reliance on one principle of justice (out of the several which were discussed) is compensated by the argument that anyway Thailand had acquiesced. At closer look, both parts of the judgement also contain a further objective and subjective strand within themselves.

[244] *Ibid. Koo*, diss. op. pp. 90–91; *Spender*, diss. op. pp. 125–126, 141. See also *Jessup* (Price) pp. 15–16; *Prott* (Culture) pp. 158–161.
[245] This has made it seem for some commentators that Governments need to be very careful in their dealings so as to avoid that their acts or statements are taken to constitute binding obligation on the basis of the standards set in the *Temple* Case. See *Johnson* 11 ICLQ 1962 p. 1203; *Müller* (Vertrauensschutz) p. 48.
[246] ICJ: *Temple* Case, Reports 1962 pp. 34–35.

Acquiescence reflects Thai will and the justice of having regard to the benefits it had received. "Stability and finality" is a principle of justice which may be traced back to party will.

The decision seems justifiable because it contains both sets of arguments. The subjective argument makes sure that Cambodian and Thai sovereignty are respected. The objective argument makes the decision seem just. The judgement seems coherent because every conceivable argument points in the same direction. Yet, each argument is also insufficient at the point at which it stops. Thai acquiescence is ultimately explained by the Court's "impression". None of the justice-based arguments favouring Thailand is discussed. Neither strand is convincing on its own. And, of course, they cannot really be convincing because the argument starts from the assumption that neither consent nor justice can be argued in a determinate way. There can only be an unending referral from one to the other – a referral which loses the possibility of deriving a rule from the judgement. Cambodian sovereignty is received from Cambodia's behaviour, Thai consent and justice.

5.6 Conclusion on sources

I have argued that the identity of modernism consists in its adoption of what could be called the "social conception of law". According to it, law is not a matter of theorizing about some pre-existent, inherently normative standards. It is something created in an "ascending" way, through the behaviour, will and interests of States. Law is socially determined. However, it cannot be fully determined without losing its normative character. The very conception of law implies at least a marginal distance between it and the social reality to which it is applied ("relative autonomy"). In a world of saints, no law is needed. This creates two problems for international law. First, *which* group of States will be chosen as that whose behaviour, will or interest are overruled? Second, how to justify this choice?

Stated in such a way, the task of modern sources doctrine seems very difficult indeed. For there would be no problem to justify these discriminations if one assumed that the law's normativity is simply a matter of its conformity either with justice or with some States' will. But the first possibility is excluded by modern scepticism about principles of justice and the latter by the ensuing assumption that States are equal. In some way or other, the "social conception of law" must assume that discriminations can be made in a purely formal and neutral fashion, by simply looking at the social processes of law-creation. The problem with the social conception of law concerns the *interpretation of the social processes whereby law is created.*

We have seen that "social facts" do not come before our eyes "an sich". To understand what takes place in the social world, we need to interpret. And in such interpretation we need to include *both* external behaviour (and texts) as well as the subjective understandings of the persons behaving (or having written the relevant texts). To see whether or not law-creation was involved in some behaviour or text, we need to refer both to the subjective understandings of the behaving States and to the intrinsic character of the acts (or the texts). This is simply another way of saying that we need a law which would be simultaneously concrete and normative.

Now a problem emerges. Inasmuch as we rely on the subjective understandings, we come up with a law which has lost its normative character. This is so, because we cannot – if we distinguish will and its external manifestations in the way the liberal theory of politics inevitably does – say that "we know better". The whole point and purpose of the distinction between "external" and "internal" aspects relies on this assumption. If we did not make it, we would have no basis to distinguish "concreteness" from "normativity".

On the other hand, if we choose to rely on the external behaviour, we still need a way of distinguishing between "law-creative" and "political" forms of action. As we cannot make this distinction by reference to the "internal aspect" solely, we must presume that this distinction exists by virtue of a non-subjective theory of justice: some behaviour creates law because of its character (or consequences, for example). But this seems like a utopian assumption. How can it be defended against a State's diverging interpretation of the behaviour?

Now we can see what leads sources discourse into being indeterminate and unconvincing. It tells us that "law" can be delineated objectively from certain social processes of law-creation. But it fails to give us criteria on which we can interpret what takes place in the social world of State behaviour. It refers us to interpreting such behaviour alternatively in terms of "consent" and in terms of "justice". But it does this after having previously committed itself to the two views according to which:

1. we cannot "know better" than the State what it has "really" willed;
2. we cannot know the content of "justice" independently from what States will.

In other words, the very premises of the doctrine of sources explain its indeterminacy. Sources discourse tells us that the law can be found in State behaviour and that this behaviour reflects either "consent" or "justice". But it assumes that neither can be known in a way which could safeguard juristic objectivity – the objectivity which, it assumed, distinguished "law" from "politics".

Sources argument will, on its own premises, remain in continuous flight from having to admit its political character. It explains consent in terms of justice and justice in terms of consent. To avoid criticism compelled by itself it constantly moves position. But its argument will remain open-ended as long as the shifting of positions continues and unconvincing when it stops.

6

Custom

The doctrine of sovereignty seemed too abstract to provide a reliable basis for conclusions about the content of international law. The more concrete it was made, the less normative it became. Similarly, the doctrine of sources was left oscillating between justice and consent based arguments without being able to fully rely on either.

It is possible to make a fresh start and imagine that both sovereignty and sources are only abstract – theoretical – ways to grasp the concrete character of international relations. We might assume that international law is "living" law, constantly shaped by inter-State conduct and normative beliefs which cannot be adequately grasped by abstract, conceptual exercises around "sovereignty" or a formal sources doctrine. What might seem needed to know the norms is, rather, to take a closer look at State practice and State beliefs. Moreover, once that perspective is taken, we might hope to reconstruct the two preceding doctrines so as to avoid the problems encountered in discussing them independently of State practice and beliefs.

For it seems clear that the three doctrines do not have any independence from each other. Once we have clear what the customary practice and normative beliefs held by States are, we seem to have exhaustively defined the normative scope of "sovereignty" and need no formal sources doctrine at all. At best, these would then be simply descriptions of the norms we have "found" and the ways in which we have found them. By concentrating on concrete acts of State practice and on what States think to be valid norms, then, we might assume, the problems encountered in the latter two doctrines could be overcome.[1]

The argument in this chapter is in several steps. I shall first describe two contradicting perspectives towards custom among modern lawyers

---

[1] Compare the discussion in *Kennedy* (Structures) (material norms constantly referred from one discursive realm of international law to another (process-sources-substance). No normative closure emerges), pp. 287–294.

(6.1) and then discuss attempts to develop a sphere for custom between a fully descending and a fully ascending law (6.2) The conventional theory about custom will contrast a materialistic with a psychological understanding but remains unable to prefer either (6.3). I shall illustrate this opposition by reference to the antinomies of general and particular, stability and change (6.4). This will lead into a discussion of the strategies for argumentative closure which use equity and proceduralization to escape from orthodox doctrine's indeterminacy and highlights the dependence of material custom on unexplicated theories of justice (6.5).

6.1 Custom as general law: two perspectives

Since Suarez, at least, it is commonly assumed that the core of international law consists of custom.[2] Custom is the all-important network of non-treaty-based, generally applicable standards. Clive Parry notes:

> One can have a very fair idea of international law without having read a single treaty; and one cannot have a very coherent idea of the essence of international law by reading treaties alone.[3]

Recently, in the *U.S. Military and Paramilitary Activities* Case (1986), the ICJ affirmed this view by listing some of the most important standards of international relations – non-use of force, non-intervention, self-defence and respect for sovereignty – into custom.[4]

The generality of custom seems like an incident of its normativity. All States should be bound by the same law, regardless of their subjective

---

[2] *Suarez* (De Legibus) Bk II, ch. XX, sect. 1; Bk VII, ch. III, sect. 7 (pp. 351, 459). For historical surveys on the role of custom in international law, see e.g. *Nys* (Droit international, I) pp. 157–161; *Kosters* (Fondements) pp. 115–129; 228–251. The explanation for custom's normative character has varied. While up to the 19th century custom's normativity was often linked with its character as evidence of natural law, the professionals based it on the assumption that custom expressed the national spirit. Modern explanations have varied and, as we shall see, custom is resorted to either because of its character as expressive of consent or expressive of some objective ("progressive") historical forces. See also *Carty* (Decay) pp. 2, 25 *et seq*; *Ferrari-Bravo* 192 RCADI 1985/III pp. 244–245.

[3] *Parry* (Sources) pp. 34–35. For arguments emphasizing the centrality of custom, see e.g. *Waldock* 106 RCADI 1962/II pp. 40–41; *Cavaré* (Droit international I) pp. 237–239; *Stern* (Mélanges Reuter) p. 479 *et seq*; *Wright* 7 IJIL 1967 pp. 1–14. For the point that custom is "general law" and as such the only part of international law which corresponds to municipal law see also *Cheng* (Macdonald-Johnston: Structure and Process) p. 548; *James* (Sovereign Statehood) p. 213.

[4] ICJ: *US Military and Paramilitary Activities* Case, *Reports* 1986 pp. 97–112 (§§ 183–215).

will or power. This does not rule out specific conventional arrangements. But just as municipal law requires that the acts of legal subjects
are evaluated from the perspective of a unitary normative structure, it
must be assumed that there exists a general, uniformly applicable law
between States, however abstract or rudimentary, by virtue of which
States have the power to create specific obligations and from which these
obligations can be evaluated and interpreted.[5]

But custom's generality may also be related to its responsiveness to
social context, variations in State will and interest. To emphasize this
aspect of custom, many lawyers envisage it as a "process of reciprocal
interaction" consisting of an aggregate of bilateral relationships, varying
from one inter-State relation to another and expressed in the doctrines of
"opposability", "persistent objector" and particular custom, for example.[6]

There is a tension between the demands for custom's generality and
responsiveness. This is visible in doctrinal treatment of what could be
called custom's "fragmentation". By fragmentation I mean that:

> ... particular norms, limited to a small number of States, often only two,
> are much more common than general norms.[7]

Since Oppenheim,[8] lawyers have emphasized the need for codification
to enhance the law's concreteness. Nowadays codification has rendered
obsolete much abstract custom on several fields of inter-State behaviour.[9] The law has fragmented as different States have become bound
by different legal regimes on areas such as economic development, the

---

[5] As the Chamber of the ICJ pointed out in the *Gulf of Maine* Case, Reports 1984, general
custom is the "background" against which specific obligations are to be interpreted and
applied, pp. 290–291 (§ 83). The distinction between general law and specific obligations
is, of course, normativism's basic tenet. See *Kelsen* (Principles) pp. 437 *et seq*, 455; *Cheng*
(Macdonald-Johnston: Structure and Process) pp. 526–530. For the equivalent distinction in French doctrine between general law and the *actes juridiques* which can create
legal obligations only inasmuch as the (anterior) legal order attaches such consequences
to them, see e.g. *Suy* (Actes) pp. 22–25; *Jacqué* (Eléments) pp. 26–37, 46 *et seq*. See also
supra ch. 5. nn. 20, 122.

[6] See e.g. *McDougal* 49 AJIL 1955 pp. 356–358; *Skubiszewski* 31 ZaöRV 1971 p. 824;
D'Amato (Custom) pp. 18–19; *Wolfke* (Custom) p. 63; *MacGibbon* XXXIII BYIL 1957
pp. 115–117 and in particular, *Venkata Raman* (Reisman-Weston: Toward) p. 368 *et seq*;
Günther (Völkergewohnheitsrecht) p. 155 *et seq*.

[7] *De Visscher* (Theory) p. 135. See also *Huber* (Grundlagen) pp. 40–42.

[8] See *Oppenheim* (International Law I) pp. 35–44.

[9] For the need of codification generally, see e.g. *Thirlway* (Customary Law) pp. 1–15; *Geck*
36 ZaöRV 1976 pp. 96 *et seq*, 99–102; *Villiger* (Custom) p. 63 *et seq*. For historical
surveys, see e.g. *Dhokalia* (Codification) pp. 3–133; *Villiger* (Custom) pp. 63–85; *Onuf*
(Falk-Kratochwil-Mendlowitz) pp. 269–279.

law of the sea, human rights, environmental protection etc. As a result, problems concerning the normative primacy of the two systems – general custom and the specific regime – have emerged.[10]

Another aspect in fragmentation has been the movement towards particularism *within* custom. It is commonplace to read the most varied kinds of contextual determinants into the ascertainment of State's customary obligations. Classically, this has been so in respect of rules of State responsibility and especially the customary standard of due diligence.[11] More recently, the search for equitableness has affected the law on, for example, natural resources, treatment of individuals, State succession or the status of non-State actors.[12] Customary rules tend to be interpreted differently depending on whether they are applied in respect of industrialized or developing States. Typically, the extent of the customary duty of compensation in cases of expropriation of alien property by a developing State tends to be determinable through a search for contextual equity.[13] Although it is incorrect to say that custom now contains a general rule of reverse discrimination, granting special privileges, giving up reciprocity and increasing the influence of "equitable principles" do manifest a tendency to tailor a State's customary obligations so as to take into account its particular situation.[14]

---

[10] Some assert the primacy of custom – as general law – to treaty on logical grounds. See e.g. *Kelsen* (Principles) pp. 445–446; *Bernhard* 36 ZaöRV 1976 p. 51. See also *Nardin* (Law, Morality) pp. 166–173 and *supra* n. 5. Others hold custom as an "undeveloped" form of legislation and emphasize treaty's superiority and greater normative force. See e.g. *Van Hoof* (Rethinking) pp. 113–116, 117–119; *Cheng* (Macdonald-Johnston: Structure and Process) pp. 527–528 (characterizing custom as agreement which is "lacking").

[11] See e.g. *Affaire des biens Britanniques au Maroc Espagnol*, II UNRIAA p. 644 and generally *Koskenniemi* XVII Oikeustiede-Jurisprudentia 1984 pp. 124–127; 162–164.

[12] For a review, see *Fitzmaurice* (IIL 1973) pp. 214–248. See also *Ferrari-Bravo* 192 RCADI 1985/III pp. 250–251 and *supra* ch. 4.5.

[13] See e.g. *Dispute between the Government of Kuwait and the American Independent Oil Company (AMINOIL)*, in which the Tribunal wished to refrain from "abstract theoretical discussion" and determine the compensation "by means of an enquiry into all circumstances relevant in the particular concrete case", XXI ILM 1982 p. 1033. General rules were rejected in favour of a contextually determined one. See also *supra* ch. 4 n. 153.

[14] For the classical position favouring "material" (contextual) equality to "formal" (general) equality, see PCIJ: *Minority Schools in Albania* Case, Ser. A/B 64 p. 19. For special privileges in treaty law, see e.g. Art. XXXVI(8) of the GATT; Art. 155 of the Second Lomé Convention (31 October 1979), XIX ILM 1980 p. 327; Art. 191 c1) and 207(4) of the UNCLOS. For compensatory equality within the UNCTAD, the UN and generally, see *Colliard* (Mélanges Reuter) pp. 160–163, 165, *passim*. For a discussion of the move

A third development consists in the hierarchization of different kinds of custom. Sometimes custom is made to seem indistinguishable from natural law. In the *North Sea Continental Shelf* Cases (1969), for example, the ICJ held that custom "cannot ... be subject of any right of unilateral exclusion"[15] – thus apparently contradicting its previous view in the *Anglo-Norwegian Fisheries* Case (1951). In the discussion of the relations between custom and the UNCLOS, for example, many have argued so as to make custom binding irrespectively of State will. The effort to hammer out *jus cogens* norms from certain customary rules has tended towards the same direction.[16]

Sometimes standards are included into custom regardless of whether they have been backed by a history of general compliance.[17] "Custom" has become a generic name for nearly all non-conventional standards, including acts and decisions of international organizations and conferences. Verdross has listed six types of non-written standards each of which has been a candidate for customary status: 1) norms which constitute the law's structural basis (e.g. *pacta sunt servanda*), 2) norms which guarantee inter-State communication (e.g. diplomatic immunity); 3) norms which are based on the *opinio juris* (e.g. space law); 4) consensus norms, arising from claims and their acceptance; 5) norms arising from conflict-resolution; 6) norms upheld by an informal consensus.[18]

Now, lawyers are deeply divided in their appreciation of these developments. One group of lawyers argues that the creation of specific, context-determined obligations has encroached on the normativity of general law. They point out, in particular, that as a State's obligations become dependent on economic, social and other equitable

---

to particularization in international law, see also *de Lacharrière* (Politique) pp. 63–87. For the "double standard" in UN practice concerning intervention and human rights, see *Franck* 78 AJIL 1984 pp. 811 *et seq*, 819–830. See further *Koskenniemi* XVII Oikeustiede-Jurisprudentia 1984 pp. 124–127, 131 *et seq*; *Nawaz* (Hossain: Legal Aspects) pp. 113–131. On non-reciprocity, see especially *Decaux* (Réciprocité) pp. 41–52. For the effect of equity in custom, see further *infra* 6.5.2.

[15] ICJ: *North Sea Continental Shelf* Case, Reports 1969 p. 38 (§ 63).

[16] Often it is argued that *jus cogens* norms are "customary". This results from the obvious difficulty of explaining how they might be otherwise without assuming that they coalesce either with natural law or with purely consensual arrangements. See *supra* ch. 5 n. 56.

[17] On "instant custom", see *Cheng* 5 IJIL 1965 pp. 23–48.

[18] *Verdross* 29 ZaöRV 1969 p. 642 *et seq*. See also *Simma* (Reziprozität) pp. 34–38; *Barile* 161 RCADI 1978/III p. 52 *et seq*.

considerations, their content becomes very uncertain. The danger of political abuse and non-normative apologism looms large.[19] It destroys custom's character as general law.[20] They argue that the law's hierarchization tends, ironically, to threaten the normativity of *both* the created super-custom and the left-over regular custom.[21] The former becomes vulnerable to the standard criticisms against natural law while the latter simply defines itself as non-binding by reference to the former.

These lawyers argue also that the confusing variety of different kinds of custom makes it hard to identify general law and the sphere of States bound by it at any one moment.[22] Not only are many such standards ambiguous but their relative importance and methods of verification have become uncertain. The distinction between binding and non-binding standards becomes blurred. The tendency of international law-making to move from treaty into instruments of the most varied kinds (decisions, recommendations, reports etc.)[23] has put strains on the ascertainment of valid law. Its normativity has become a matter of "more or less"[24] – an evaluation which traditional methods of law-ascertainment are not well equipped to deal with.

These criticisms are based on a vision of social justice which emphasizes the generality, uniformity and clarity of legal standards and the *formal equality* which such standards establish between States. Put in other words, this vision emphasizes the law's normativity, its power to induce conforming behaviour *regardless* of the particular situation, policy or interest of the State. Deviations from formal equality are allowed, but only by way of special legislation, applicable in respect of all members of a clearly defined class. It should not be done by

[19] For critical comment, see especially *Wengler* (Mélanges Rousseau) pp. 335–338; *Fitzmaurice* (IIL 1973) pp. 230–235; *Weil* 77 AJIL 1983 pp. 413–442; *Villiger* (Custom) p. 37. See also *Ferrari-Bravo* 192 RCADI 1985/III pp. 245–247. *Colliard* (Mélanges Reuter) speaks of "pluralité des normes", p. 179.

[20] See *Unger* (Völkergewohnheitsrecht) *passim* and pp. 54–63; *Sørensen* 101 RCADI 1960/III p. 44; *Bleckmann* (Funktionen) p. 46; *Villiger* (Custom) p. 31. See also *Green* XXIII Can.YIL 1985 pp. 3–32.

[21] See especially *Weil* 77 AJIL 1983 pp. 423 *et seq*, 433–436. See also *supra* ch. 5 n. 55.

[22] *Jennings* (Cheng: Teaching) pp. 3–9; *Idem* XXXVII Schw.JB 1981 pp. 59–88.

[23] For a review of this development, see e.g. *Gottlieb* (Onuf: Lawmaking) pp. 109–130.

[24] *Strebel* 36 ZaöRV 1976 pp. 331–332; *Weil* 77 AJIL 1983 pp. 415–418. *Thirlway* (Customary Law) emphasizes the illusory character of the binding force of such standards – they will be overridden at once if they come to conflict with important State interests, pp. 78 and generally, 71–79.

introducing unclear distinctions or evaluative considerations into law-ascertainment.[25]

Others see fragmentation as a perfectly healthy phenomenon.[26] They regard general custom as a law of an underdeveloped society while treaties and "opposabilities" created on the basis of reciprocity, acquiescence, estoppel, etc. seem like dynamic forms of law-creation which guarantee the harmony between the law and the social context – in other words, the law's concreteness.[27] Theirs is a vision of social justice which rests obligation on each State's specific will and interest (need). The essence of justice is, on this view, that it intervenes to correct material inequalities which exist between States. Flexible standards are a beneficial move away from a custom which is "passéiste et conservatoire" into a "coutume sauvage" which allows the majority to have their say in law-creation.[28] If there is a problem, these lawyers argue, it is a problem of the obsolete character of traditional law-identification methods and of the formalistic distinction between binding and non-binding law. Certainly the distinction between more and less binding norms reflects the natural intuition that some norms *are* more important than others and should be so treated. To speak in terms of a single, uniformly applicable law, they argue, is a utopian manner of looking at the complex reality of inter-State relations and loses the need for the law to intervene to correct existing inequality.

Both views entail partial answers to problems within the doctrine of custom. The former is able to explain custom as general law, applicable in respect of all States regardless of their particular interests or wills. But in order not to make custom seem like a natural morality, it will have to justify its norms ultimately by reference to concrete State practice and

[25] See e.g. *Villiger* (Custom) p. 37. *Fitzmaurice* (IIL 1973) argues that "many believe there is reason to fear that the very foundations of our discipline as international lawyers may be in question", p. 207, see also pp. 230–235. Similarly, *Cheng* (Macdonald-Johnston: Structure and Process) pp. 528–530; *Wolfke* (Custom) pp. 104–109; *Bernhardt* 36 ZaöRV 1976 pp. 51–52.

[26] See *Henkin* (How) pp. 122–123; *Kelsen* (Principles) pp. 451–454.

[27] In particular, lawyers taking a third-world perspective emphasize this aspect. See e.g. *Buirette-Maurau* (Tiers-monde) p. 73; *McWhinney* (UN Lawmaking) p. 47. For lawyers favouring the increased particularization of custom, see also *van Hoof* (Rethinking) pp. 113–116; *Coplin* (Functions) p. 11; *Sheikh* (Superpowers) pp. 62–63; *Wolfke* (Custom) pp. 11–19. See also *Lissitzyn* (Divided) pp. 65–66 and particularly *Venkata Raman* (Reisman-Weston: Toward) pp. 387–388.

[28] *Dupuy* (Mélanges Rousseau) pp. 80–84; *Bedjaoui* (New International Economic Order) pp. 136–138. See also *Lachs* (Festschrift Mosler) pp. 493 *et seq*, 500–501; *Buirette-Maurau* (Tiers-monde) pp. 60–65.

opinio juris. The latter view is able to explain custom as an instrument of State policy. Emphasis lies on the law's concreteness, its correspondence with the social context. However, inasmuch as it does not wish to end up in descriptive apology, it needs a principle whereby custom can be applied against a State irrespective of its particular wishes or interests.

What originally seem like two opposing views on the nature of custom become indistinguishable in their effort to provide for the law's normativity as well as its concreteness. The sole difference lies in the form of the argument. One proceeds from normativity towards concreteness, the other from concreteness towards normativity.[29] Both views need to assume that the law is justifiable by reference to State interests and wills and ascertainable independently of them. Fitzmaurice makes the point explicit:

> As in the case of treaties or other specific international agreements, the element of *consent* or assent (using the terms in their widest sense) is clearly apparent in the *formation* of a customary rule of law . . .[30]

The demand for concreteness reflects a voluntarist theory of legislation. Custom is not imposed on States by any extra-positivistic process. It arises as a consequence of their policies. In the second place, however:

> . . . once it (i.e. custom, MK) exists as law, its binding force does not depend on consent, but on its character as law.[31]

Custom's normativity is based on a non-voluntaristic theory of ascertainment. It can be found and applied regardless of State will, need or interest.

But the two views cannot be held together in normative problem-solution. Either concreteness or normativity must be preferred. Because doctrine is unable to establish such preference it will remain imprisoned by the way arguments constantly oppose these perspectives against each other.

---

[29] *Stern* (Mélanges Reuter) points out, correctly, that the "objectivist" and "voluntarist" visions of customary law reflect initially two opposing visions of social life among States – while the former emphasizes the priority of normative order, the latter starts from stress on State autonomy, pp. 479 *et seq*, 483–494. That neither approach seems capable of being held alone reflects the difficulty to think of social life either in terms of fully social or fully autonomous entities. See further *infra* ch. 7.

[30] *Fitzmaurice* 92 RCADI 1957/II p. 97.

[31] *Ibid.* p. 40. See also *Lauterpacht* (Function) pp. 419–420; *Suy* (Actes) pp. 249–250.

This is reflected in the insecurity about the method for "finding" custom. If custom may arise from formless consensus and "structural" postulates, then surely the classical criteria of State practice and *opinio* are inadequate. If only converging State practice and beliefs may create custom, then in many matters there is no general law at all.[32] This leads to the paradox that there is even:

> ... some difficulty about pointing out an unmistakable example of the emergence of a new customary law of general validity.[33]

It might seem natural to base one's theory of custom-ascertainment on one's view about the reason for the law's ultimate validity.[34] Bleckmann suggests that a test of custom could be based on induction, on how non-controversial customary rules have arisen.[35] But the suggestion is circular and will only lead into the insoluble dilemma of consensualism/non-consensualism. In order to point out a non-controversial customary norm we should *already* be in possession of a theory of custom-ascertainment.

The abundance of studies on custom-ascertainment by the ICJ suggests that a test of custom could be inferred from the Court's practice.[36] But there are only few explicit references by the Court to general custom.[37] Even these have been usually made in an *ex cathedra* manner. In the *Corfu Channel* Case (1949), for example, the Court observed that innocent passage by warships through international straits was "generally recognized and in accordance with international custom".[38] No distinct test was used to confirm this. The conclusion was simply stated, not argued. Usually the Court has refrained from classifying the standards it has used by reference to Article 38 of its Statute. On many issues, therefore, it is impossible to say whether the Court had in mind a customary rule or a general principle or some other type of standard. As one observer remarked, the Court seems to have:

---

[32] See e.g. *Jennings* XXXVII Schw.JB 1981 pp. 65–71.   [33] *Parry* (Sources) pp. 61–62.
[34] *Bleckmann* (Aufgabe) pp. 20–21.   [35] *Ibid.* pp. 23–25.
[36] See *Skubiszewski* 31 ZaöRV 1971 p. 835 *et seq*; *Bos* 25 GYIL 1982 p. 30 *et seq*; *Marek* VI RBDI 1970 p. 55 *et seq*; *Barberis* 45 RDI 1967 p. 563 *et seq*; *Sørensen* (Sources) pp. 105–111; *Akehurst* XLVII BYIL 1974–75 pp. 31–42; *Wolfke* (Custom) pp. 28 *et seq*, 121–130; *Kearney* (Gross: Future) pp. 610–723, especially pp. 696–710; *Jenks* (Prospects) pp. 225–266; *Lauterpacht* (Development) pp. 368–393; *Haggenmacher* 90 RGDIP 1986 p. 5 *et seq.*
[37] The first explicit discussion having been in ICJ: *North Sea Continental Shelf* Cases, Reports 1969 pp. 46–47 (§ 85).
[38] ICJ: *Corfu Channel* Case, Reports 1949 p. 28.

... instituted a system of decision-making in which the legal conclusion reached is determined by the application of rules largely treated as self-evident.[39]

Despite these difficulties, I shall in the following sections concentrate on arguments in and by the ICJ on custom. This is not to suggest that judicial decisions are the "ultimate" source of law. It is merely because the need for consistency and clarity in judicial argument allows better than isolated statements in legal writing to extract the assumptions which go to constitute the discourse about custom.

6.2   The identity of custom: the ascending and descending approaches

A remarkable fact about custom is that it is constantly in danger of collapsing either into tacit agreement or a naturalistic principle. The function of a separate doctrine about custom is to make room for a law between these two; a law understood in an ascending fashion (as agreement) and a law understood in a descending way (as non-consensual principle).[40] This may be attempted by combining both understandings. Custom is argued in a descending way to distinguish it from treaty. Compared with the latter, custom is made to seem less consensual. To distinguish custom from natural law it is made to look more ascending, or more consensual than this. Prosper Weil writes:

> The classic theory of custom depends on a delicate, indeed precarious equilibrium between two opposing concerns: on the one hand, to permit customary rules to change without demanding the individual consent of every State; on the other hand, to permit individual States to escape being bound by any rule they do not recognize as such ...[41]

---

[39] *Kearney* (Gross: Future) p. 653. Similarly *Cheng* (Macdonald-Johnston: Structure and Process) pp. 541–542 (in respect of the North Sea judgement).

[40] As *Cheng* (Macdonald-Johnston: Structure and Process) puts it, custom: "... means really that part of the applicable rules and norms of the international legal system that is not covered by texts ... or the general principles of law", p. 513. For a useful analysis of the discussions about custom in the League of Nations' Committee of Jurists during the drafting of the Statute of the PCIJ, see *Haggenmacher* 90 RGDIP 1986 (pointing out that the "two-element theory" which combined "objective" practice with its "subjective" recognition as law was devised precisely to achieve a mediation) pp. 18–32.

[41] *Weil* 77 AJIL 1983 pp. 433–434. *D'Amato* (Custom) discusses this through the tension between the aspects of "stability" and "change", p. 12.

In what follows I shall examine whether this "classic theory" has succeeded to delimit custom against treaty, on the one hand, and natural law, on the other. To the extent that custom is posited "in between" these two it works as a *strategy of reconciliation*, a strategy for combining the demands for the law's concreteness and normativity.

In the first place, custom is distinguished from treaty by its less consensual character. Custom, it is explained, is less responsive to changing wills and interests than treaty. It emerges through a rigid historical process while treaty arises from instant agreement. Custom is different from treaty precisely by being something other ("more") than agreement. Its identity *vis-à-vis* treaty depends on its being less consensual than this.[42] To the question "why does custom bind?" we must give an answer which is other than "because it expresses the subjective will". The answer may refer to history, legitimate expectations, social justice, necessity or whatever. But – if we wish to preserve an independent category of general custom – it needs to refer beyond simple consent.[43]

This strategy can be illustrated by reference to the *North Sea Continental Shelf* Cases (1969). Here the Court examined, *inter alia*, the relation of Article 6 of the 1958 Geneva Convention on the Continental Shelf with customary law. It observed that the process of conventional norms turning into custom was perfectly possible although not easily to be presumed.[44] This was so because the norms became non-consensually binding as a result of such transformation. The faculty of making reservations was characteristic of treaties while custom:

[42] In the discussion of custom-formation reference is frequently made to the metaphor of path-formation. This is a non-subjective process in that it does not take place by anybody's decision but through a gradual social process. See *Cobbett* (Leading Cases) p. 5; *De Visscher* (Theory) p. 149; *Finch* (Sources) pp. 47–48; *Strupp* 47 RCADI 1934/I p. 331. In introducing his draft to the League of Nations' Committee of Jurists on this point, Baron *Descamps* distinguished custom and general principles from treaty by the formers' more objective character, see Procès-verbaux pp. 324–325 and comment by *Haggenmacher* 90 RGDIP 1986 p. 21. See also *Allott* XLV BYIL 1971 pp. 129–133. *Carty* (Decay) points out that the distinction is rather one of doctrine – diplomatic practice emerging custom regularly with tacit agreement, p. 26.

[43] Even *Cheng* (Macdonald-Johnston: Structure and Process) who associates custom with tacit agreement still does not wish to class it under "agreements not in written form" referred to in Article 3 of the Vienna Convention on Treaties and argues that custom's (objective) "framework" is what distinguishes it from treaties, pp. 528–530.

[44] ICJ: *North Sea Continental Shelf* Cases, Reports 1969 p. 41 (§ 71).

... by its very nature, must have equal validity for all members of the international community, and cannot therefore be the subject of any right of unilateral exclusion.[45]

Later, in the *Gulf of Maine* Case (1984), the Court added that customary principles of maritime law were:

... undoubtedly of general application, valid for all States and in relation to all kinds of maritime delimitation.[46]

This differentiation is implicit in the doctrine which holds that treaties may create custom.[47] In a purely consensual theory about custom such doctrine would be either superfluous (the treaty's extracontractually binding force resting on subjective consent of the third Party – in which case no elaborate argument about the original *treaty*'s binding force is needed) or relate only to "evidence" of the acceptance of the norm by third States. The North Sea cases formulation seems, however, unambigious. If custom is "generated" from treaty in another way than by universal acceptance, then the clear implication is that at least some States are bound irrespective of their consent.[48]

But it seems impossible to think of custom as fully non-consensual. If it were, it would become a set of natural principles and vulnerable to the standard objection about the utopian character of natural law.[49] Historically, the point of custom is to avoid this criticism.

[45] *Ibid.* pp. 38–39 (§ 63). *Lang* (Plateau) sees here a denial of custom's consensual basis, p. 90. Similarly *Marek* VI RBDI 1970 pp. 50, 53–54; *Cheng* (Macdonald-Johnston: Structure and Process) p. 529. The admissibility of reservations to a codifying convention is a tricky problem precisely because it seems to imply taking a stand which would either collapse the pre-existing custom into natural law or tacit agreement. Trying to avoid this, *Jennings* (Mélanges Reuter) argues that reservations might be allowed to the application of the convention but not to the pre-existing custom, p. 352. See also *Villiger* (Custom) p. 264 (expressing the view that such reservation expresses "disapproval" of custom and might thus affect the *opinio juris*); *Thirlway* (Customary Law) pp. 119–124 (appealing to the object and purpose test).
[46] ICJ: *Gulf of Maine* Case, Reports 1984 p. 293 (§ 90).
[47] For this doctrine, see *D'Amato* (Custom) p. 105 *et seq*; *Thirlway* (Customary Law) pp. 81–89.
[48] The Court expressly denied that unanimity was needed. ICJ: *North Sea Continental Shelf* Cases, Reports 1969 pp. 41, 42 (§§ 71, 73).
[49] Hence, commentators have criticized the very categorical formulation of the Court. See *supra* n. 45 and e.g. *Green* XXIII Can.YIL 1985 (the standard carried "in theory" but not "in fact") pp. 11–12. For a discussion of the distinction between the more objective general principles and the more subjective custom, see *O'Connell* (International Law I) pp. 5–7.

Bynkershoek (1673–1743), for example, derived his law of nations from two sources, reason and usage. The latter was distinguished from the former by being closely linked with what States do. Its presence in his system was justifiable, and justified, only under this assumption. Custom was needed to make the law concrete.[50]

But discourse does not maintain a neat threefold distinction between a fully naturalistic principle, custom and fully consensual treaty. The initial differentiation between custom and treaty tends constantly to push the former into natural law. Thus, in the practice of the ICJ, a group of important norms constantly oscillates between custom and natural law. They can be permanently located with *neither* of these categories without this engendering consequences which themselves seem unacceptable. Consequently, they are not justified at all within the system, they are merely "assumed".

In the *Corfu Channel* Case (1949) the Court discussed Albania's obligations in respect of innocent passage through its territorial sea. Having satisfied itself that Albania had known about the existence of a minefield in its waters and neglected its duty to warn international shipping, the Court noted that this duty was based on:

> ... certain general and well-recognized principles ...[51]

These were three: 1) "elementary considerations of humanity"; 2) "freedom of maritime communication" and 3) "every State's obligation not to allow knowingly its territory to be used for acts contrary to the rights of other States".[52]

What was the status of such principles? Were they customary or "general principles recognized by civilized nations" or perhaps something else? The Court did not answer these questions. Such questions may be posed also in regard to the "fundamental general principles of international humanitarian law", discussed in the *U.S. Military and Paramilitary Activities* Case (1986).[53] Making express reference to the Corfu Channel judgement, the Court postulated the existence of humanitarian principles which were related to but independent from the 1949 Geneva Conventions.[54] Though its discussion was included in that part of the judgement which dealt with customary law, the Court refrained

---

[50] See his discussion on contraband, *Bynkershoek* (Quaest.Jur.Publ.) Lib.I ch. 10. (p. 67).
[51] ICJ: *Corfu Channel* Case, Reports 1949 p. 22.   [52] *Ibid.*
[53] ICJ: *US Military and Paramilitary Activities* Case, Reports 1986 pp. 113–114 (§ 218).
[54] *Ibid.* pp. 112–115 (§§ 216–220).

from using the term "custom" in respect of these principles. Nor did it – in contrast to the other rules dealt with – even attempt to ground them in State practice.[55] The status of these principles – were they fully non-consensual, naturalistic principles or perhaps based on long-standing practice or acceptance – was left obscure.

For the purpose of the two judgements it might be enough to postulate the existence of such principles. A theory about custom, however, requires their justification. The choice is, either, that the Court assumed the existence of a class of customary rules which could be justified without reference to material practice and the *opinio juris* or that the principles were not custom at all but natural standards unrelated to the presence of State practice or consent.[56]

The issue is not what the judges had in mind but how we think about principles such as "elementary considerations of humanity". Do we regard them as valid insofar as and to the extent that we find confirmation for them in State views and practice? Or do we regard an exegesis of the latter irrelevant in face of their "fundamental" character?

I can only assume that most lawyers would make an important distinction between customary rules which, for example, lay down the extent of a State's maritime jurisdiction and "elementary considerations of humanity". While the former seem to have a natural connection with what States have done or accepted, arguing the latter by reference to State practice would seem intuitively artificial or even repulsive. But how to reflect this distinction in what we think about sources? Including both within "custom" will either undermine the "fundamental" character of humanitarian principles (apologism) or will require abandoning the standard definition of custom in terms of past behaviour and the *opinio juris* (utopianism).

[55] That they are customary is taken as a matter of course by commentary. See e.g. *Detter-Delupis* (Concept) p. 120. It may be doubted if even the other three rules were simply customary, that is, determined through consistent practice and the *opinio juris*. President *Singh*, for example, expressly left open whether the non-use of force principle was valid as custom or general principle and argued about non-intervention in ways which seemed to coalesce it with natural law ("sanctified absolute rule of law"), *ibid.* sep. op. pp. 151 *et seq*, 146.

[56] The discussion of these principles in the *Corfu Channel* and *US Military and Paramilitary Activities* Cases differed completely from the way the Court tried to ascertain the two elements ("practice"/opinio juris) in, for example, the *Asylum* Case, Reports 1950 pp. 276–277 and the *North Sea Continental Shelf* Cases, Reports 1969 p. 44 (§§ 76–77).

Including "elementary considerations of humanity" within natural law, however, will open the door for argument which seems subjective and inadmissible on the assumptions behind the Rule of Law. To conserve their legal-objective character, such considerations need to be justifiable by reference to some form of tangible practice or acceptance. And this tends to be unacceptable because apologist.

Let me illustrate this dilemma by reference to the discussion on the character of "general principles of law recognized by civilized nations" in Article 38(1)c of the ICJ Statute. Together with custom, these seem to account for what is general about international law. Still, there is much uncertainty among lawyers about the meaning and relevance of such principles, never invoked expressly by the ICJ or its predecessor.[57]

There are two ways of understanding such principles. During the drafting of the PCIJ Statute discussion moved from considering them in naturalistic overtones to thinking of them in a more positivistic manner as principles of national law, applicable by analogy in inter-State relations.[58] Some still associate them with natural law principles.[59] But most lawyers relate them to principles of national law with a sphere of international application. Many uses of the term in fact deny it any specific status beyond generalization from State practice. Such generalizations are either non-normative or, if normative, indistinguishable from customary norms, apart from, perhaps, their greater "importance".[60] But, as we

---

[57] See also *Koskenniemi* XVIII Oikeustiede-Jurisprudentia 1985 pp. 121–163.

[58] For the drafting history, see League of Nations, Committee of Jurists, Procès-verbaux p. 293 *et seq.* For the suggestion by Baron *Descamps* to include principles of "objective justice" in the sources the Court was to apply, see pp. 322–325. For the suggestion to include "justice and equity" by *Lapradelle*, see p. 295. These suggestions were particularly opposed by *Root* and *Phillimore* whose more positive law approach in the end carried the day. See further e.g. *Hergzegh* (Principles) pp. 11–33; *Bogdan* 46 NTIR 1977 p. 45 *et seq*; *Verdross* 52 RCADI 1935/II p. 207 *et seq*; *Le Fur* 54 RCADI/IV pp. 202–204; *Sørensen* (Sources) pp. 124–126.

[59] *Verdross-Simma* (Völkerrecht) pp. 71 *et seq*, 309; *Bernhardt* 36 ZaöRV 1976 p. 53; *Lauterpacht* (International Law I) p. 68. The difficulty of thinking about them in fully naturalistic terms is well reflected in the way standard argument regularly bases them (in an ascending way) on some recognition in the "common consciousness of States" or State practice. Thus, in the *Arbitration Between Petroleum Development (Trucial Coast) Ltd and the Sheikh of Abu Dhabi* 1 ICLQ 1952 Lord Asquith remarked that such principles were: "rooted in the good sense and common practice of the generality of civilized nations or . . . a modern 'law of nature'", pp. 250–251.

[60] Many think of "general principles" as a class of customary norms. See e.g. *Strupp* 47 RCADI 1934/I pp. 335–336; *Scelle* 46 RCADI 1933/IV pp. 436–437; *Reuter* (Droit international public) pp. 100–101; *Monaco* (Festschrift Mosler) p. 611; *Virally* (Mélanges Guggenheim) p. 532; *Detter-Delupis* (Concept) pp. 51–52. Similarly

have seen, it does not seem possible to discard the category of non-consensual norms altogether.

The distinction between custom and a law which is less consensual than custom was implicit in the *Barcelona Traction* Case (1964, 1970) in which the ICJ was faced, *inter alia*, with the Spanish preliminary objection according to which "international law does not recognize, in respect of injury caused by a State to a foreign company, any diplomatic protection of shareholders exercised by a State other than the national State of the company".[61] In answering this, the Court held that:

> ... an essential distinction should be drawn between obligations of a State towards the international community as a whole and those arising vis-à-vis another State in the field of diplomatic protection.[62]

As examples of the former, the Court listed obligations outlawing aggression and genocide as well as certain human rights obligations. These were binding *erga omnes*, without there having to exist evidence that a State would have accepted them in respect of another State. In other words, they were distinguished from "mere" custom by their non-consensual character.[63]

ICJ: *Gulf of Maine* Case, Reports 1984 (equalling "principles" with other norms, albeit more "general, fundamental" ones) pp. 288–290, 300 (§§ 79, 113). The problem is that if we wish to avoid associating principles with naturalistic or systemic norms and link them with custom to highlight their concreteness, we lose the *rationale* of this class of norms altogether. In particular, we become able to apply principles only against States which have participated in the practice which consecrates them and which now recognize them as binding. To avoid this consequence we can only fall back on systemic (objective) arguments. An illustrative treatment is in the *Burkina Faso–Mali Frontier* Case, Reports 1986 in which the Chamber of the ICJ grounded the authority of the *uti possidetis* principle on its acceptance by the parties as well as on events taken place before the two States had even emerged. *Uti possidetis* was the applicable rule because the parties had, in the Special Agreement, accepted it *and* because it had a "logical connexion" with the principle of self-determination and the need to avoid "fratricidal struggles", pp. 564–565, 566–567 (§§ 19–21, 24–26). It was valid consensually as well as non-consensually. The Chamber could use both arguments because nobody had challenged the application of the principle. Had it been disputed, however, the Chamber should have made a preference: was acceptance needed or was it not? (To be sure, it might have resorted to the tacit consent strategy and thereby held the principle valid consensually as well as non-consensually. But this strategy entails the difficulties discussed in ch. 5 *supra*.)

[61] ICJ: *Barcelona Traction* Case, Reports 1964 p. 44.

[62] *Ibid*. Reports 1970 p. 32 (§ 33).

[63] By making this distinction the Court effectively reversed its view in the *South West Africa* Case (1966) where it had excluded the existence of *erga omnes* norms. See *supra* ch.1.1. at nn. 36–42. For comment, see *Gross* (Gross: Future) p. 748.

The Court did not enquire how this distinction should be reflected in the list of sources. We do not know whether the Court had in mind two categories of custom or custom and something separate from it. The Court made, however, express reference to its earlier position in the *Reservations to the Genocide Convention* Case (1951). In this latter case it had discussed the specific character of the convention, remarking that the crime of genocide involved:

> ... a denial of the rights of existence of entire human groups, a denial which shocks the conscience of mankind and results in great losses to humanity which is contrary to moral law ...[64]

For this reason, the principles underlying the convention were:

> ... principles recognized by civilized nations as binding on States even without any conventional obligation.[65]

Thus there seemed to exist a set of norms which could be justified by reference to "moral law" and did not need consensual support. The association of these "general principles" with the *erga omnes* norms in the *Barcelona Traction* Case implies a distinction between two types of law but does not conclusively solve the issue whether these are two types of custom or custom and natural principles. If the Court really made the latter distinction, then the ironical conclusion is that regular custom becomes fully consensual and indistinguishable from (tacit) agreement – a position many would not accept.

Such conclusion is avoided by the distinction which the Court made in the *Barcelona Traction* Case between the "rights of protection" relating to the *erga omnes* norms and which had "entered into the body of general international law" and those which were "enforced by international instruments of a universal or quasi-universal character".[66] Now, if the *erga omnes* norms had the status of purely non-consensual law, as distinguished from treaty and custom, but only a part of the "corresponding rights of protection" had a conventional background, then that part of such rights which lacked conventional basis but belonged to the "body of general international law" had to be somewhere between the fully non-consensual and the fully consensual. This threefold classification allowed the Court to enquire whether the alleged rights of Belgian shareholders were, in the absence of specific conventions, valid as custom without it

---

[64] ICJ: *Reservations* Case, Reports 1951 p. 23.   [65] *Ibid.*
[66] ICJ: *Barcelona Traction* Case, Reports 1970 p. 32 (§ 34).

needing to imply that they were on the same level with norms prohibiting aggression or genocide.

But the problem remains to *know* which norms do not need backing from State practice or consent in order to be valid. The Court gives no indication of this. Its *erga omnes* norms are simply assumed, not argued. Curiously, whenever specific arguments are put forward, then the naturalistic norms lose their purely descending character. Even principles said to be valid without specific assent are traced back to States by supporting them by points about national or peoples' "conscience" or "good sense" or, as Barile puts it, in a fashion reminiscent of 19th century professionals "conscience juridique internationale actuelle".[67] As this takes us back to examining consent, it loses the naturalistic flavour of general principles.

That modern lawyers find it hard to imagine how to argue for norms otherwise than by referring to past practice or consent may be illustrated by the discussion in the *U.S. Military and Paramilitary Activities* Case (1986) of the right of self-defence and its relation to Article 51 of the UN Charter. The right existed independently of this conventional provision. Support for this was found from the formulation of the Article which referred to it as an "inherent right" ("droit naturel" in French).[68] The rule pre-existed and was thus independent from its acceptance by States in the Charter. Nevertheless, the Court did not classify it as natural law. It observed:

> The Court therefore finds that Article 51 of the Charter is only meaningful on the basis that there is a "natural" or "inherent" right of self-defense and *it is hard to see how this can be other than of a customary nature* (emphasis MK).[69]

In view of the fact that the Court made no reference to State practice or the *opinio juris* on this point it can only be concluded that its "custom" was in fact no different from a naturalistic principle. That the Court took

---

[67] *Barile* 161 RCADI 1978/III pp. 58–59. The argument from "conscience" is much used, presumably because it can be taken to denote something which is not "external" (and in that sense utopian) to human ideas while still remaining in control of "arbitrary" will. See e.g. *Verdross* (Mélanges Guggenheim) pp. 523–526; *Alvarez*, ind. op. ICJ: *Anglo-Norwegian Fisheries* Case, Reports 1951 pp. 147–148. Yet, the argument from "consciousness" or "spirit" is vulnerable to the criticism about its indemonstrable, naturalistic character. See e.g. *Triepel* (Völkerrecht) pp. 30–31; *Le Fur* 54 RCADI 1935/IV pp. 145–146. See also *Sørensen* (Sources) p. 250; *Lasswell-McDougal* (Essays Rao) pp. 75–77.

[68] ICJ: *U.S. Military and Paramilitary Activites* Case, Reports 1986 p. 94 (§ 176).   [69] *Ibid.*

pains to deny this can only be imputed to its wish not to be objected with engaging in a utopian construction.

The Court frequently argues so as to distinguish between two kinds of custom. In discussing the law applicable to the drawing of a single maritime boundary in the *Gulf of Maine* Case (1984), the Chamber of the Court observed:

> ... customary international law ... in fact comprises a limited set of norms
> for ensuring the co-existence and vital co-operation of the members of the
> the international community, together with a set of rules whose presence in
> the *opinio juris* of States can be tested by induction based on the analysis of
> sufficiently extensive and convincing practice ...[70]

In other words, there was a "naturalistic" custom which was distinguished from "regular" custom by its being more "vital" and not needing the kind of backing from past practice and consent as this. A similar distinction had been implied by the Court already in the *North Sea Continental Shelf* Cases (1969) in which it studied the customary nature of the equidistance rule. The Court distinguished between a "positive law and a more fundamental aspect" of the matter. The former was accompanied by arguments aiming to show that equidistance was binding as custom because of past practice and the *opinio juris*. The latter related to what the Court called the "natural law of the continental shelf" – whether equidistance was "inherent" in the concept of the shelf, whether it had "an *aprioristic* character of so to speak juristic inevitability".[71] It is difficult to see what the latter have in common with "regular" customary norms whose identity lies in their being supported by the twin criterion of State practice and consent.

Many modern lawyers associate the *Völkerrechtsverfassung* norms, or norms which hold together the "conceptual apparatus" of international law, with custom, albeit less related to State practice than regular custom.[72] Even *jus cogens* is often said to be "customary".[73] I have suggested that this follows from an inability to imagine how else it could be argued

[70] ICJ: *Gulf of Maine* Case, Reports 1984 p. 299 (§ 111).
[71] ICJ: *North Sea Continental Shelf* Cases, Reports 1969 pp. 28–29 (§ 37). For a discussion, see *Marek* VI RBDI 1970 pp. 60–61; *Lang* (Plateau) p. 63 *et seq*; *Reynaud* (Judgement) p. 107 *et seq*. It is clear, as *Haggenmacher* 90 RGDIP 1986 points out, that had the Court taken seriously its natural law argument here and had it actually based a positive finding on it, this would have revolutionized its argumentative practice, pp. 122–123.
[72] See e.g. *Thirlway* (Customary Law) pp. 28–30; *Reuter* (Droit international public) p. 97.
[73] See *supra* ch. 5 n. 56.

in an objective way than by assuming that it is backed by State practice and consent.

Ultimately, however, this betrays the coherence of the doctrine of custom as it includes both too little and too much within it. It makes the class of customary norms empty by pushing "ordinary" custom into the realm of agreements while not being able to distinguish its "super-custom" from natural justice. It includes too much within custom by including norms which are backed by past practice and the *opinio juris* as well as norms which are not so backed, that is every conceivable norm, within it.[74]

But if it is the case that custom is not natural law, then it seems to collapse into tacit agreement. And this is what is implied by the inclusion of "instant custom" as well as the doctrine of persistent objector into custom.[75] In the North Sea cases, the Court bluntly contradicted itself. In order not to imply that its distinction between custom and treaties emerges all custom with *jus cogens*, it tried to make the difference:

> ... (w)ithout attempting to enter into ... any question of *jus cogens*, it is well understood that, in practice, rules of international law can, by agreement, be derogated from in particular cases.[76]

Indeed, it sometimes appears that it is custom, and not treaty, which is supported by a consensual understanding of the law. Clearly, a treaty seems less consensual than custom in its fixation into written form, in its capacity to bind the State by the (objective) sense of its provisions. It is not only that some treaties have been held able to create "objective regimes".[77] Other multilateral treaties, too, seem to gain objectively normative force towards non-parties.[78]

---

[74] *Marek* VI RBDI 1970 notes the difficulty that unless custom were "generally binding", it would lapse into tacit agreement, pp. 53–54. This difficulty leads into further classifications. *Gianni* (Coutume), for example, makes an explicit distinction between custom "dans le sens restraint" and custom "dans le sens large", the latter of which would be more consensual than the former, pp. 119–120, 135. *Skubiszewski* 31 ZaöRV 1971 notes bluntly that a great many customary norms "are not *jus cogens*, yet no reservations are permitted", p. 848.

[75] On "instant custom", see *supra* n. 17. On persistent objector and particular custom, see *infra* ch. 6.4.1.

[76] ICJ: *North Sea Continental Shelf* Cases, Reports 1969 p. 42 (§ 72). For a comment, see e.g. *Skubiszewski* 31 ZaöRV 1971 p. 832.

[77] ICJ: *Reparation for Injuries* Case, Reports 1949 p. 185.

[78] See e.g. *Jennings* (Cheng: Teaching) pp. 7–8; *Weil* 77 AJIL 1983 pp. 438–440. Also, it has been pointed out that certain treaties create "objective obligations" which may allow collective enforcement even when there has been no violation of another State's or its national's right. See ECHR: *Ireland v. the United Kingdom* Case, Ser. A 25 pp. 90–91 (§ 239).

By contrast, custom may look more responsive than treaty as it needs no formal instrument to come about or the passing of strict *rebus sic stantibus* criteria to terminate.[79] It may even emerge by unilateral, political acts.[80] The view, for example, that some of the provisions in the UN Convention on the Law of the Sea (1982) are generally binding irrespective of their acceptance by all States participating in the Conference appears as an attempt to impose a non-consensual standard on States whose consent encompasses a deviating customary norm.[81]

Carving a specific doctrine of custom between naturalistic principles and consent seems difficult. We have difficulty to distinguish custom from natural law because we cannot consistently hold a material theory of the latter. Therefore, "general principles" tend to become positivized as generalizations from past practice, principles of municipal jurisprudence or derivations from what nations or peoples have accepted in their "conscience". If they were not so "positivized", they would seem like mere subjective opinions.

But if important norms (elementary considerations of humanity, prohibition of aggression, of genocide, of racial discrimination etc.) cannot be argued by reference to a conception of material justice, how can they at all be argued? Not many of such norms can be supported by producing impressive lists of past compliance. But few would regard that this derogates from the legal relevance of such norms. To treat them – as mainstream modern doctrine does – as customary (albeit somehow different from regular custom) is a successful strategy only so long as their validity or content is not disputed. Once those questions arise, we need to know whether it is what States have said and done or theories of material justice which settles them. But making this choice will render

---

[79] E.g. *Cheng* (Macdonald-Johnston: Structure and Process) pp. 529, 532; *Skubiszewski* 31 ZaöRV 1971 p. 847; *Villiger* (Custom) pp. 37–38, 128–129; *Baxter* 129 RCADI 1970/I p. 97. Some have pointed out that it is precisely for the rigidity of treaty-making that international legislation directs itself into customary law channels. *McWhinney* (UN Law-Making) p. 101; *Thirlway* (Customary Law) p. 146; *Jennings* XXXVII Schw.JB 1981 pp. 62–63; *Bedjaoui* (New International Economic Order) p. 138. See also *de Lacharrière* (Politique) pp. 32–48.

[80] *Jiménez de Aréchaga* (Essays Lachs) pp. 575–585.

[81] For a discussion of the effect of the 1982 UNCLOS on third States, see *Lee* 77 AJIL 1983 (this effect depends on whether the provision has entered into customary law – a process which must be accompanied by the presence of the criteria of practice and the *opinio*) pp. 553–556, 567–568; *Caminos-Molitor* 79 AJIL 1985 (third States may not be able to claim customary rights in respect of provisions subjected to the package-deal method – apart from rights which crystallized as customary already during the Conference) pp. 882–890.

the resulting norm unacceptable because either utopian or apologist – unless we assume that the world is in fact a heaven in which all important norms are backed by State practice and consent.

The difficulty of separating custom from agreement can be explained in a similar fashion. To think of custom as valid irrespective of consent is to think of it as a kind of behaviour-related natural law. Now, this may look like a verifiable type of natural law. But it runs into difficulties. First, it is incapable of making a distinction between behaviour adopted as a matter of convenience and as compliance. It cannot accommodate change without violation. Most importantly, it would seem like a purely apologist custom: *anything* States do creates custom. To avoid these problems, we must include an internal aspect – *opinio juris* – within custom. But now the problem emerges, why do we need *anything more*? Does it not involve inadmissible formalism or utopianism to deny the status of law from a norm which all States consider as valid? But if it is law, what category of law does it come under? If there is no formal treaty, then the only possibility seems to be to regard it as custom. But this destroys the normative distinction between custom and treaties: both arise now from consent. The sole distinction would seem to be the descriptive one: treaties describe consent in written while custom is consent in non-written form. But as non-formal agreements, too, tend to be written down in recommendations, resolutions, "Final Acts" etc., even this ultimate basis for difference seems lost.

To sum up, modern legal argument lacks a determinate, coherent concept of custom. Anything can be argued so as to be included within it as well as so as to be excluded from it. Many have perceived this. Sir Robert Jennings, for example, notes that much of what we tend to call custom:

> ... is not only not customary law: it does not even faintly resemble a customary law.[82]

This is premised on some (even if intuitive) idea of "real" custom. Such intuition may refer to the long-standing character of custom and its non-concern with naturalist issues. To give justice to that intuition seems difficult because a delimitation of custom on those terms either involves denying the status of law from standards which are usually regarded as such or the creation of a new category of law which seems capable of being argued only in terms of a theory of justice. Achieving a

---

[82] *Jennings* (Cheng: Teaching) p. 5. Similarly, *Detter-Delupis* (Concept) pp. 112–116.

reliable method for custom-identification is not such an innocent decision as it seems. It will raise the question of what we shall do with standards which respond to deeply felt sentiments of justice as well as informal agreements neither of which can be conclusively supported by referring to the intuitively natural test of past practice.

6.3   Conventional theory: the psychological and the material element and the circularity of the argument about custom

Conventional theory attempts to construct a theory of custom between the fully descending (natural law) and the fully ascending (treaty). This would enable it to escape the charge of being either utopian or apologist. Therefore, by a near-unanimous orthodoxy, it includes two elements in its definition of custom:

1. a psychological element – the *opinio juris*;
2. a material element – State practice.[83]

The function of the psychological element is to guarantee that custom does not conflict with the liberal theory of legislation. It counts for the law's "internal aspect" which distinguishes it from simple coercion. The material element aims to ensure that law-ascertainment can be undertaken without having to rely on what States subjectively accept at any moment. Neither element can be dismissed or preferred to the other without this engendering immediately the objection that custom is either apologist (because it makes no distinction between might and right) or utopian (because we cannot demonstrate its norms in a tangible fashion). Because both elements seek to delimit each other's distorting impact, the theory of custom needs to hold them independent from

---

[83] For the acceptance of this "two-element theory" in case-law, see ICJ: *Asylum* Case, Reports 1950 p. 276–277; *North Sea Continental Shelf* Cases, Reports 1969 p. 44 (§§ 76–77); *Libya–Malta Continental Shelf* Case, Reports 1985 p. 29 (§ 27); *US Military and Paramilitary Activities* Case, Reports 1986 pp. 97, 108–109 (183, 207). For the orthodox position in doctrine, see e.g. *Gény* (Méthode) pp. 319–320; *Finch* (Sources) p. 47; *Sørensen* (Sources) pp. 84–111; *Brierly* (Law of Nations) p. 59; *Kelsen* (Principles) pp. 440–441; *Scelle* 46 RCADI 1933/IV pp. 432–434; *Rousseau* (Droit international public I) p. 315 *et seq*; *Reuter* (Droit international public) p. 93; *Thirlway* (Customary Law) p. 46 *et seq*; *Suy* (Actes) p. 217 *et seq*; *Blum* (Historic Titles) pp. 39–46; *Cohen-Jonathan* VII AFDI 1961 p. 132; *Wolfke* (Custom) pp. 20–58; *Schwarzenberger-Brown* (Manual) p. 26; *Marek* VI RBDI 1970 pp. 55–56; *Gounelle* (Motivation) pp. 67 *et seq*, 81–82; *Vamvoukos* (Termination) pp. 248–260. The two-element theory is traced back to Justinian's Digest by *Watson* (Evolution) pp. 44–45. For a useful recent discussion and criticism, see *Haggenmacher* 90 RGDIP 1986 p. 9 *et seq*.

each other. But this it cannot do. Attempting to identify the presence of the psychological element, it draws inferences (presumptions) on the basis of material practice. To ascertain which acts of material practice are relevant for custom-formation, it makes reference to the psychological element (i.e. "those acts count which express the *opinio juris*"). The psychological element is defined by the material and *vice-versa*.[84] This circularity prevents doctrine from developing a determinate method of custom-ascertainment. It is led to determining custom in terms of an equity which it can itself only regard as arbitrary.

6.3.1 The rejection of pure materialism

In order to see why both elements seem necessary, it is useful to consider, as a first move, three deviant theories which, by expressly denying the relevance of the psychological element, manifest an inadmissible materialism.

First, there is the view which holds custom as simply a repetition of similar acts over a period of time. In Kelsen's early work the need for a psychological element was rejected as logically impossible: something could not become a norm for the reason that States thought it *already* was one. Moreover, it was virtually impossible to prove the psychological element. It was, for Kelsen, simply an off-shoot of the autolimitation view which tried to explain custom in terms of consent.[85]

The well-known difficulty with this view is that it includes either too much or too little within custom. If all practice is law-creating, then

---

[84] Interestingly, this is reflected in the often noticed ambiguity in the wording of Article 38 (1) b of the ICJ Statute. This speaks of "custom as evidence of general practice, accepted as law". The wording hesitates between associating "custom" with material practice or the acceptance of that practice by States at large. Finally, it ends up in associating it with neither. "Custom" becomes a *third*, undefined category which is capable of being "evidence" of the presence or absence of the remaining two. But this seems nonsense: either something is relevant because it encapsulates a practice or an acceptance thereof. A third category (such as natural law) seems excluded. See also *Lauterpacht* (International Law I) p. 65. Therefore, modern lawyers read the formulation as simply "unfortunate", rest content with the two-element theory and start going about in a circle by identifying relevant practice through its assumed "acceptance" and inferring that acceptance from material practice. For standard discussion of the "unfortunate" (but, as I argue, significant) formulation of the paragraph, see *Wolfke* (Custom) pp. 22–23, 26–28; *Gihl* (Scandinavian Studies) pp. 76–77; *Bernhardt* 36 ZaöRV 1976 p. 64; *Skubiszewski* 31 ZaöRV 1971 p. 812; *Parry* (Sources) pp. 56–57; *Villiger* (Custom) p. 3; *Günther* (Völkergewohnheitsrecht) pp. 58–70.

[85] *Kelsen* 1 RITD 1939 pp. 263–265; *idem* 14 RCADI 1926/IV pp. 291–292.

everything is regulated and no State can act in a manner different from the way in which it has acted. Conversely, if everything States do is law-creative, then no State can act illegally. This view is incapable, not only of making the distinction between legal custom and conventions of courtesy and of explaining discretion in matters of foreign policy,[86] but it also fails to distinguish between custom and behaviour induced by threat or use of force.[87] A meaningful custom must be something else than an unexceptionable command for States to behave as they have behaved.[88]

Thus a second strategy of doing away with the psychological element tries to identify as relevant practice such behaviour which corresponds to material criteria of justice. It is suggested, for example, that a practice amounts to custom if it is in "conformity with the social needs of a legal order"[89] or if it corresponds to "reasonableness"[90] or "moral utility".[91] To this view it can be objected that even if it is able to distinguish between binding and non-binding usages, it still cannot distinguish custom from norms of courtesy which correspond to some social needs. Not all sense of moral or social obligation, even if in conformity with behaviour, creates law and not all law needs to correspond to such criteria.[92] But the even more important objection is that this view is utopian as naturalistic. Because "justice", "social need", "reasonableness" and "moral utility" are *subjective* notions, they cannot be used in order to achieve a determinate delimitation between practice which is and

---

[86] For this standard criticism, see *Gény* (Méthode) pp. 110–118; *Le Fur* 54 RCADI 1935/IV p. 198; *Sørensen* (Sources) p. 105; *Kunz* 47 AJIL 1953 p. 667; *Thirlway* (Customary Law) p. 53; *Suy* (Actes) pp. 222, 233–234; *Marek* VI RBDI 1970 p. 56; *Fitzmaurice* 92 RCADI 1957/II pp. 103–104; *Skubiszewski* 31 ZaöRV 1971 pp. 837–839; *Akehurst* XLVII BYIL 1974–75 p. 33; *Vamvoukos* (Termination) pp. 248–249; *O'Connell* (International Law I) pp. 8–9, 15–16; *Virally* 183 RCADI 1983/V p. 182.

[87] *Strebel* 36 ZaöRV 1976 pp. 328–330.

[88] The view was later abandoned by *Kelsen*, too. See 84 RCADI 1953/III p. 123; *idem* (Principles) p. 440.

[89] *Kopelmanas* XVIII BYIL 1937 p. 148. To the same effect, *Scelle* 46 RCADI 1933/IV p. 434; *idem* (Précis II) pp. 297 *et seq*, 304–312 and *idem* (oral argument) ICJ: *Asylum Case*, Pleadings I pp. 119–120; *Müller* (Vertrauensschutz) pp. 88–89. See also *Finch* (Sources) p. 44.

[90] *McDougal* 49 AJIL 1955 p. 361.

[91] *Venturini* 112 RCADI 1964/II p. 389 *et seq*. Similarly *Salvioli* 46 RCADI 1933/IV pp. 20–21; *Le Fur* 54 RCADI 1935/IV p. 198. The same idea is implied in *Suarez'* (De Legibus) distinction between "factual" and "legal" customs, Bk VII, ch. I sect. 5 (pp. 445–446).

[92] This (positivist) point is made by *Sørensen* (Sources) pp. 107–108; *MacGibbon* XXXIII BYIL 1957 p. 133; *Akehurst* XLVII BYIL 1974–75 p. 35.

which is not law. Such conceptions can be justifiably opposed to States only if they are linked with what States have thought of as "justice", "social needs" etc. But this will require a study of what States will or believe, in other words, it will have to make reference to the *psychological element* and give up full materialism.[93]

According to a third, and a more apparently plausible strategy, a conduct becomes binding, not because it expresses any *opinio juris* or a principle of material justice but because *other* States have the right to rely on the continuation of the conduct a State has once chosen. In this view, it would be the legitimate expectations of other States – a *Vertrauensprinzip*, or a "principle of fairness" – which combines with material behaviour to make it binding.[94]

Something like this comes close to a view widely held by lawyers before the mid-nineteenth century. Inasmuch as difference was made between custom and tacit agreement, it was made by regarding custom as a presumption about the State's future conduct, based on how it had acted in the past.[95] It was, however, unclear to what extent such presumption grounded a binding rule.[96] For Martens, it required that the State inform others if it contemplated a change in its habitual behaviour. It created an imperfect duty in this respect.[97]

This construction does away with general custom altogether. Under it, custom becomes a set of bilateral relations, dependent of cognizance and reliance on one State's behaviour by another. The problem, however, is that this approach must either rely on a naturalist theory about the kinds of expectations created by a form of conduct (and thus be utopian) or base itself on the scrutiny of the subjective attitudes of the *other* State[98] (in which case it would combine a psychological element

---

[93] *Stern* (Mélanges Reuter) pp. 493–494. See also *Kelsen* 1 RITD 1939 pp. 265–266. In the League of Nations Committee of Jurists, Baron *Descamps*'s naturalistic approach to custom was rejected the Committee's majority. See Procès-verbaux pp. 293–297, 307–321 and commentary in *Haggenmacher* 90 RGDIP 1986 p. 22. See also *Ehrlich* 105 RCADI 1962/I p. 253.

[94] *Müller* (Vertrauensschutz) pp. 77–103; *Günther* (Völkergewohnheitsrecht) pp. 155–159; *Reuter* (Droit international public) pp. 94–95. See also criticism by *Bleckmann* (Aufgabe) p. 22.

[95] *Kosters* (Fondements) p. 115; *Carty* (Decay) pp. 20–30.

[96] *Bynkershoek*, for example, notes that custom is simply a presumption without "any validity in the face of a definitely expressed wish on the part of him who is concerned" (De foro legatorum) ch. XIX (pp. 106–107).

[97] *G.-F. de Martens* (Précis) pp. 191–193.

[98] This is implied by *Suy* (Actes) pp. 261–262.

within itself). The former approach is adopted by lawyers arguing that legitimate expectations or good faith sometimes demand that a State not change its conduct. But this seems similar to the view which based custom on justice. How do we know what expectations are "legitimate" or the content of the good faith principle? Can we impose a conception of legitimacy or good faith on a State which does not accept it? To avoid utopianism, we might focus on *actual reliance*. But this leads us into a study of the psychology of those States and leaves open the question how it is possible to oppose one State's expectations on another State which perhaps never intended to continue its once-adopted conduct.

Doing away with the psychological element will either result in an inability to distinguish fact and law or pure naturalism. The psychological element is needed in order to avoid apologism or utopianism.

6.3.2   The rejection of pure psychologism

A second deviationist strand has taken seriously the criticisms discussed above but has been unable to understand why the material element is needed at all. To explain why a theory of custom cannot rely on the psychological element ("internal aspect") alone is difficult because this element emerges in so many disguises. For a proper understanding of the problems involved, it is necessary to consider different varieties of the claim according to which custom can be defined in a purely psychological fashion (even if a full discussion would require going into some deeply philosophical problems).

There are four versions of the claim that custom is essentially a matter of State psychology. The psychological element is associated variably with:

1. a collective (national, popular) unconscious;
2. tacit agreement;
3. the belief by a State that something is law;
4. the will by a State that something be law.
   In addition, there is a fifth and a much stronger version of this view which grounds the primacy of psychology on the following claim:
5. "law cannot be dissociated from what States will or believe".

In the following sub-sections I shall argue that these views either betray a hidden materialism, enter into contradiction with themselves or, ultimately, fall into crude apologism.

6.3.2.1   The psychological element as the material one: collective unconscious

The *opinio juris* was introduced into the theory of custom by the German historical school of law in the 19th century. Customary law was now portrayed not merely as a repetition, or imitation, of similar acts but as a manifestation of the nation's collective unconscious, emerging from the nation's spirit and history. Similarly, international custom – if distinguished from national customs – was to reflect the spirit and history of the group of nations which it regulated.[99]

From the introduction of such a view it is a short leap into questioning the need for a material element in the first place. If the law is based on a collective, unconscious "spirit", it seems pointless to regard previous behaviour as an *additional* requirement (that is, to make reference to such behaviour in any other way than as *evidence* of this spirit). Bluntschli, for example, writing in 1872, refrained from speaking of "custom" at all. His non-written international law coalesced with the "*Rechtsbewusstsein der Menschheit*". Past usages may or may not have significance but only as evidence of the *consensus gentium*, not because of their independently normative force.[100]

Such an argument, however, is not really a psychological one at all. The argument from a collective unconscious ("spirit", purpose, history, essence, etc.) does not coalesce with an argument about the real – "arbitrary" – psychological will of the nation or its people. The latter are seen as only more or less adequate external manifestations of the normative spirit, residing outside anybody's psychology. Savigny, for example, took pains to demonstrate the internal contradictions of the view which associated custom (as law in general) with conscious will. Such a view could not explain why this arbitrary will should be binding. Will's binding force could rest only on a non-psychological principle of the national spirit.[101]

Such an argument is based on the *naturalistic* assumption that a nation has an intelligible essence. And this is the reason why later

---

[99] For reviews, see *Guggenheim* 94 RCADI 1958/II pp. 36–59; *Wolfke* (Custom) p. 52; *Rousseau* (Droit international public I) pp. 323–324; *D'Amato* (Custom) pp. 44–50; *Carty* (Decay) pp. 30–35; *Kosters* (Fondements) pp. 241–243. For a modern argument to the same effect, see *Barile* 161 RCADI 1978/III pp. 48–51.

[100] *Bluntschli* (Völkerrecht) pp. 3–7, 63–64 (§§ 13, 14). Consequently, usages not in conformity with such unconscious are legally insignificant, p. 64 (§ 15). See also *Heffter* (Völkerrecht) pp. 5–6, 21–22.

[101] *Savigny* (System) Vorrede p. xvi, Buch I, Kapitel I § 7 (pp. 13–16), §§ 12–13 (pp. 34–44).

lawyers have been unable to accept it.[102] For who could tell what the nation's "spirit" or "essence" was? For liberalism, national spirit was a mere myth, a fictitious and utopian construction. To achieve concreteness, liberals have been driven to identify the national spirit in a psychological way, by means of conscious will, a vote.

6.3.2.2   Tacit agreement

Many lawyers have associated the psychological element with a general will among States to be bound. This makes custom lose its specificity in respect of agreement, or consensus. The sole condition now for something to be custom is that States consider it as "legally necessary or legally right", as Oppenheim put it.[103] The traditional requirements of generality, consistency and duration are superfluous or, at best, evidence of the consent behind them. If agreement (consensus) exists, custom exists.[104] Tunkin expresses the view that:

> ... the essence of the process of creating a norm of international law by means of custom consists of agreement between States, which in this sense is tacit, and not clearly expressed, as in a treaty.[105]

Many other modern lawyers, too, accept this view, expressly or implicitly. The doctrine of "instant custom" is the standard example.[106] Its attraction is well expressed by Chaumont:

---

[102] For criticism of the naturalism inherent in arguments from a collective unconscious, see *Triepel* (Völkerrecht) pp. 31–32; *Kelsen* 1 RITD 1939 pp. 360–361. See also *supra* n. 67.

[103] *Oppenheim* (International Law I) pp. 21–22.

[104] This view was taken by *Vattel* (Droit des Gens) who also clearly saw the consequence thereof. For him, custom was based: "... sur une convention tacite des Nations qui l'observent entr'elles. D'ou il paroit qu'il n'oblige que ces mêmes nations qui l'ont adopté et qu'il n'est point universel", L.I ch. I § 25 (p. 14). The modern "classical" proponents of the view are *Anzilotti* (Cours) pp. 73–74; *Strupp* 47 RCADI 1934/I p. 301 *et seq.*

[105] *Tunkin* (Theory) p. 124. Similarly *Kartashkin* (Macdonald-Johnston: Structure and Process) p. 88.

[106] See *Cheng* 5 IJIL 1965 pp. 23–48. See also *Ferrari-Bravo* 192 RCADI 1985/III pp. 314–316; *Bernhardt* 36 ZaöRV 1976 p. 73. Many Thrid-World lawyers have, understandably, adopted this view. For them, and for many others, too, custom is simply informal consensus. See *Bedjaoui* (New International Economic Order) pp. 138 *et seq*, 167–170; *Buirette-Maurau* (Tiers-monde) p. 63. The standard example is the III UNCLOS of which some have argued that the "shared thoughts" of the participants were enough to create custom on some areas of the law of the sea. See *Jiménez de Aréchaga* (Essays Lachs) pp. 576–577. For discussion and criticism, see *Thirlway* (Customary Law) pp. 40 *et seq*, 76–78.

> A notre avis, sauf si l'on considère la coutume comme ayant une mystér-
> ieuse autorité venue soit des hauteurs de la métaphysique, soit des
> profondeurs du subconscient des groupes humains, c'est-à-dire, pour
> reprendre l'expression du professeur Reuter, comme un "phénomène
> irrationnel", on ne peut échapper à la logique de l'accord.[107]

In other words, to associate custom with anything beyond State will
seems utopian. But, of course, this view is vulnerable to the standard
objections against full consensualism. In particular, it fails to explain
why an agreement can bind "generally" or can continue to bind States
which have changed their minds.[108]

To seem acceptable, doctrines manipulate the ambiguity in the idea of
tacit agreement. As pointed out above, tacit agreement may be given an
ascending as well as a descending interpretation. To avoid utopianism
lawyers initially argue that custom is binding as it expresses consent. But
this is vulnerable to the objection of apologism. If custom is binding only
if it expresses consent, then it cannot be opposed to a non-consenting State
without either accepting the validity of the argument from "knowing
better" or constructing the agreement on the *Erklärungstheorie* – the idea
that agreements bind because they involve considerations of reciprocity,
good faith, fairness etc. These latter arguments, however, remain vulnerable to the standard criticisms against full naturalism. Hence, a reference
must be made back to subjective consent. And so on, *ad nauseam*.

6.3.2.3   The psychological element as will and belief

A first thing to notice about the orthodox use of the *opinio juris* is its
ambiguous character. Different views on this may be grouped into two.
The psychological element might either be:

1. the belief or conviction of the State that something is law;
2. the will of the State that something be law.[109]

---

[107] *Chaumont* 129 RCADI 1970/I p. 440.

[108] *Le Fur* 54 RCADI 1935/IV p. 198; *Virally* 183 RCADI 1983/V pp. 181–182. For the
problem is not really to explain why some States are bound which participate in a
"consensus" but why those also should be which do not. In other words, why should it
be "binding"? The unacceptable apologism engendered by the tacit agreement theory
in its purely subjective form is pointed out by *Bernhardt* 36 ZaöRV 1976 p. 62; *Villiger*
(Custom) p. 21 and *Schachter* (Schwebel: Effectiveness) p. 21. For further (standard)
criticism, see *Günther* (Völkergewohnheitsrecht) pp. 25–27.

[109] For different formulations, see *Günther* (Völkergewohnheitsrecht) pp. 40–41;
D'Amato (Custom) pp. 66–72.

The *opinio* might be understood either as pertaining to what the State knows or believes, or it might be thought of as a *voluntas*, a conscious, law-creating will. These could be called, respectively, the declaratory and the constitutive approaches to the psychological element.[110] They are not merely different but mutually exclusive and defined by this exclusion. The declaratory view holds that custom arises independently of any subjective will and that the intervention of the psychological element is necessary only to make the law known, not to create it. The *opinio juris* is, on this view, an effect and not the cause of obligation. The constitutive view, again, grounds custom on State will and denies it any existence independently of such will. The *opinio* is the direct reason for custom's binding character.

But the declaratory view is merely a restatement of the materialist approach to custom while the constitutive view seems to make custom indistinguishable from agreement. In order to escape the objections considered above, standard doctrinal argument makes use of both senses of the *opinio* in a happy mixture, resorting to one when argument would otherwise seem too apologist, to the other when too utopian.

Much judicial practice seems to occupy initially the declaratory position. In the *Lotus* Case (1927), the PCIJ associated the psychological element with "being conscious of having a duty".[111] In the *North Sea Continental Shelf* Cases (1969) the ICJ required that material practice be associated with:

> ... a belief that the practice is rendered obligatory by the existence of a rule of law requiring it.

It observed that:

> ... need for such belief, i.e. the existence of a subjective element, is implied in the very notion of the *opinio juris sive necessitatis*.[112]

In both cases, the Court rejected the claim concerning the existence of binding custom. States were not bound because it was not established

---

[110] *Fitzmaurice* 92 RCADI 1957/II p. 102; *Stern* (Mélanges Reuter) pp. 482, 485–488. See also *Suy* (Actes) pp. 223–229.
[111] PCIJ: *Lotus* Case, Ser. A 10 p. 28.
[112] ICJ: *North Sea Continental Shelf* Cases, Reports 1969 p. 44 (§ 77). See also *ibid.* pp. 28, 46 (§§ 37, 89). This formulation is sometimes criticized as it seems inapplicable to customary rules creating rights or competences. See generally *MacGibbon* XXXIII BYIL 1957 pp. 117, 127–128, 144; *Akehurst* XLVII BYIL 1974–75 pp. 37–38. But see *Thirlway* (Customary Law) p. 49.

that their actions had been motivated by a *belief* in the existence of custom.

Other formulations have been more equivocal. The Court has sometimes required that the practice be "accepted as law" or that it manifest the "view" of States that it is binding.[113] In the *U.S. Military and Paramilitary Activities* Case (1986) the Court based the normative status of certain General Assembly resolutions on the "attitude" taken by States in this matter.[114] It is unclear whether such expressions connote something that the States "willed" or what they "believed" was law. In the latter case, however, the Court's discussion of the relevant UN resolutions tends towards a declaratory view. The customary norms (of non-use of force and self-defence) seemed to exist *ex ante* the resolutions (in particular the 1970 Friendly Relations Declaration) or other documents in which the *opinio juris* – variably treated as a "recognition" by States that a something is law or that they "regard" it to be so – was expressed. Their adoption – and hence the *opinio* – was treated by the Court as confirmation, not creation of custom.[115]

Under the declaratory view, the *opinio juris* is an opinion, or a conviction, of States that something *already* is law, not a will that something *become* law. Haggenmacher summarizes:

> ... tous ces termes ont en commun de relever du domaine de la connaissance; inversement, aucune d'entre eux ne se rattache au domaine de la volonté ... l'*opinio juris* n'est pas une acte de volonté visant à promouvoir une norme autant que *lex ferenda*; elle appréhende au contraire la norme comme déjà existante et pleinement valable.[116]

Only by thus associating the *opinio* with knowledge instead of will it seems possible to preserve custom's more descending, normative character *vis-à-vis* treaty. By implying that custom is valid regardless of State

---

[113] ICJ: *Asylum* Case, Reports 1950 p. 277; *Nottebohm* Case, Reports 1955 p. 22; *Right of Passage* Case, Reports 1960 p. 40. See also ICJ: *US Nationals in Morocco* Case, Reports 1952 pp. 199–200.

[114] ICJ: *US Military and Paramilitary Activities* Case, Reports 1986 pp. 99–100 (§ 188).

[115] *Ibid.* pp. 99–101 (§§ 188–189). For the difficulties which lawyers have had in attempting to draw a definite view from the jurisprudence of the Court in this matter, see *Villiger* (Custom) pp. 25–26; *Verdross-Simma* (Völkerrecht) pp. 277–278; *Fitzmaurice* 92 RCADI 1957/II p. 105; *Wolfke* (Custom) pp. 30–31.

[116] *Haggenmacher* 90 RGDIP 1986 pp. 11. Thus *Scelle* (Précis II) observes that custom (and treaty) "sont des modes de constation et d'expression du droit objectif préexistant ... La valeur obligatoire de la coutume ... ne dérive à aucun degré de la volonté des sujets de droit ..." p. 298.

will doctrine seems able to impose it on States which do not, at the moment of application, accept it.[117]

But a purely declaratory view remains incapable of explaining how a customary rule may arise in the first place. Surely, as Kelsen observed, something cannot *become* law by the belief that it *already is* law.[118] Contrary to what Gihl, for example, suggests,[119] this is not merely an academic's pet dilemma. It shows that the declaratory view is premised on the acceptance of pure materialism. It assumes that the emergence of custom is independent from its recognition by States. As such, it will remain vulnerable to criticisms against other materialist theories.[120] It will either fail to make the distinction between binding and non-binding usages or use unverifiable criteria to make it. To escape these objections, "will" must have some constitutive role as well.

Many lawyers have attempted a compromise between the constitutive and declaratory views by explaining custom-emergence as a gradual process during which the psychological element undergoes gradual transformation. There is first a politically motivated will – an *opinio necessitatis* – which gradually strengthens into *opinio juris*, a belief that the behaviour has become a matter of law. The starting-point is an act of political convenience by a State. This is followed by similar acts by other States – a gradual acceptance of this practice so that it finally "turns into" law.[121] Van Hoof and Meijers believe custom-formation to be a

---

[117] *Haggenmacher* 90 RGDIP 1986 pp. 11–13. A "cognitive" conception of the *opinio juris* seemed present in the *Dispute between the Government of Kuwait and the American Independent Oil Co. (AMINOIL)*, XXI ILM 1982 in which the Tribunal observed that the several agreements cited by the Government to support the existence of a particular *lex petrolea* did not express any *opinio juris* because they had been the result of bargaining and were thus not "inspired by legal considerations". The *opinio*, said the Tribunal, was a "stranger" to such politically motivated (i.e. will-based) agreements, p. 1036. The same stand seems to have been taken by the Iran-US Claims Tribunal. See *Sedco v. National Iranian Oil Co. and Iran* XXV ILM 1986 p. 633.

[118] For discussion, see e.g. *Kelsen* 1 RITD 1939 p. 253 *et seq*; *Kunz* 47 AJIL 1953 p. 667; *Wolfke* (Custom) p. 70; *Akehurst* XLVII BYIL 1974–75 p. 32; *Thirlway* (Customary Law) pp. 47–55; *MacGibbon* XXXIII BYIL 1957 p. 115; *Verdross* 29 ZaöRV 1969 p. 635 *et seq*; *Stern* (Mélanges Reuter) pp. 482–484, 487.

[119] *Gihl* (Scandinavian Studies) p. 83.

[120] Otherwise, one seems compelled to explain custom-emergence by some fully naturalistic conception of social or "biological" necessities or by the "error theory". For the latter, see *Kelsen* 1 RITD 1939 p. 263; *Cheng* 5 IJIL 1965 p. 45 n. 107; *Haggenmacher* 90 RGDIP 1986 p. 108 n. 332; *Watson* (Evolution) p. 46 n. 7. See also *Vamvoukos* (Termination) pp. 255–256.

[121] *Suy* (Actes) noting that the declaratory theory (the *opinio* as cognizance of a pre-existing custom) cannot be held as it fails to explain custom-formation pp. 233–235,

three-stage process during which a practice first delineates the content of the future rule. This is followed by a process whereby State authorities come to regard the practice as binding and, subsequently, the appearence of external manifestations which show that the rule has become generally accepted.[122]

Such explanations may describe better or worse how beliefs about or practices relating to a rule develop. Surely the Truman Proclamation, for example, was not accompanied by any belief that making such a claim was a matter of law. Only after several other States had made similar claims and others had acquiesced in them it was possible for a belief to develop that legal rules had been created.[123] But this brings in nothing to solve the problem. We are still unable to reveal how the transformation from a political *opinio necessitatis* into a legally motivated *opinio juris* was possible. Now, we may believe that the former stage only delineates the content of a rule which is, as it were, proposed for acceptance or rejection. But this merely defines the *opinio necessitatis* as a *de lege ferenda* view – a belief that something is *not* law although it *should be* – and leaves unexplained how it may transform itself into a belief that the proposed rule *already is* law. Thus, we must assume that the rule is already definitely established at the *opinio necessitatis* stage, the stage of political will:[124]

> The *opinio necessitatis* in the early stages is sufficient to create a rule of law, but its continued existence is dependent on the subsequent practice accompanied by *opinio juris*.[125]

The only way to solve the dilemmas involved in a declaratory theory about the *opinio juris* is to reject that theory altogether: the *opinio* becomes a matter of will, not of knowledge.

The constitutive view about the *opinio juris* can also be supported by reference to judicial practice affirming the obligation-creative character

---

238, 260–262. See also *Simma* (Reziprozität) pp. 33–34; *Verdross-Simma* (Völkerrecht) p. 286; *Reuter* (Droit international public) pp. 95–96.

[122] *Van Hoof* (Rethinking) pp. 93–97; *Meijers* IX Neth.YBIL 1978 p. 3 *et seq.* See also *Villiger* (Custom) pp. 29–30; *Cheng* (Macdonald-Johnston: Structure and Process) pp. 539–541; *Skubiszewski* 31 ZaöRV 1971 p. 839; *Fitzmaurice* 92 RCADI 1957/II p. 103; *Klami* (Gewohnheitsrecht) p. 8 *et seq.*

[123] ICJ: *North Sea Continental Shelf* Cases, Reports 1969 pp. 33–34 (§ 47).

[124] Thus *Bos* 25 GYIL 1982 suggests that the *opinio* is simply a conviction that "some rule or other makes good law", p. 30. His views on this matter are, however, confused and he uses three different versions of the *opinio*, see *ibid.* pp. 16–17.

[125] *Thirlway* (Customary Law) p. 56. Similarly *Bleckmann* (Grundprobleme) pp. 120–121.

of consent. The ICJ's refusal to hold the Federal Republic of Germany bound by the equidistance rule as it had not consented to it in the *North Sea Continental Shelf* Cases (1969) encapsulates this assumption.[126] It explains better the case of "instant custom". Here the emergence of a will is a necessary and sufficient condition for custom to emerge. The psychological element is directed at the future, not the past. Stein observes:

> ... *opinio juris* is no longer seen as a consciousness that matures slowly over time ... but instead a conviction that instantaneously attaches to a rule believed to be socially necessary or desirable.[127]

We cannot compromise and hold the psychological element as partly an object of knowledge, partly an object of will.[128] The liberal theory of politics is premised on a dualistic psychology. The categories of will and knowledge are, in it, fundamentally different. Their separation reflects the separation – indeed opposition – of what is subjective and what objective.[129] An object of will exists merely by virtue of having been willed. And, of course, anybody can will anything. An object of knowledge, however, has an existence independent from the process of knowing itself. If we think that rules of law emerge from being willed, then any knowledge about some extravoluntary reality is merely superfluous. If we believe that their existence is grounded in something else than will, then it becomes singularly irrelevant to refer to whatever anyone might will.

For Tunkin, *opinio juris*:

> ... signifies that a State regards a particular customary rule as a norm of international law, as a rule binding on the international plane. This is an expression of the will of a State, in its way a proposal to other States.[130]

To say that a State both believes something to be law and proposes it as an act of will seems contradictory. Either it is law – in which case a State is not in a position to "propose" it however much it might correspond to what it wills. The duty of other States is unaffected by any such "proposal". Or it is not yet law – in which case the State is as free to propose it as other States are to reject it. If Tunkin's first sentence is correct then the second is superfluous and *vice-versa*.

---

[126] ICJ: *North Sea Continental Shelf* Cases, Reports 1969 pp. 25–27 (§§ 27–32).

[127] *Stein* 26 Harv.ILJ 1985 p. 465. See also *Cheng* (Macdonald-Johnston: Structure and Process) pp. 531–532; *Dupuy* (Mélanges Rousseau) pp. 83–87.

[128] As seems implied by *Barile* 161 RCADI 1978 pp. 49–50 and *Finch* (Sources) p. 44.

[129] See generally *Unger* (Knowledge) pp. 29–62.   [130] *Tunkin* (Theory) p. 133.

The attempt to distinguish between an initial stage at which "will" would be sufficient and a subsequent stage at which something more – a "belief" – would be needed is just as implausible. It leads, for example, into the absurdity of having to accept that something has ceased to be law because States have not, during some period of time, developed a "belief" while they – perhaps all of them – still continue to "will" it. Speaking of different stages only puts into another vocabulary the fundamental issue, namely the transition from "ought" to "is". The gap between the two will remain unless we accept pure materialism (that is, that facts are binding in their own right) or pure psychologism (that is, that nothing which is not willed can be binding). And this will make us vulnerable to the objections of apologism and/or utopianism, once more.

At least two objections could be made against the above arguments. In the first place, it seems overburdened with anthropomorphism. How can we speak of "will" or "belief" or make a meaningful distinction between the two in respect of such corporate entities as States? And secondly, does not the association of the psychological element with "will" rather than "belief" make it impossible to separate between *lex lata* and *lex ferenda*?[131]

The argument does rest on anthropomorphism. But if this is objectionable it is resorted to only because this is the manner we discourse about international law. The different forms of consensualism, imputability as well as doctrines about the vitiating effect of duress or error, for example, are premised on assuming the reality of State psychology. The domestic analogy makes it necessary to think of custom in terms of mental acts by States – however much this conflicts with liberalism's methodological individualism.[132]

It may be true that it is difficult – even impossible – to distinguish between what States will and what they believe. But the point is that *the very structure of liberalism (the common distinctions between legislation/ adjudication and law/politics, for example) leads into making the difference between will and belief and holds it as crucial* The assumption that law is different from politics by being more "objective" than this carries

---

[131] A concern expressed by *Akehurst* XLVII BYIL 1974–75 p. 37 and *Jennings* XXXVII Schw.JB 1981 p. 67.

[132] For suggestions to develop techniques for the identification of the relevant policymakers and *their* beliefs, see *Verdross-Simma* (Völkerrecht) p. 284; *Sørensen* (Sources) pp. 108–109; *Schachter* (Schwebel: Effectiveness) pp. 24–26. See, however, also the sceptical remarks by *Bourquin* (oral argument) ICJ: *Right of Passage* Case, Pleadings IV p. 507; *D'Amato* (Custom) pp. 35–41. See also *Haggenmacher* 90 RGDIP 1986 p. 17.

with it the distinction between (subjective) will and (objective) knowledge. If we believe that international law is law, then we must assume
that the processes whereby States will something and know something
are different. States must be assumed capable of leading a schizophrenic
existence – being legislators in a "private", subjective capacity and judges
in a "public", objective one.

The association of the psychological element with "will" does affect
the possibility to distinguish between emerging and valid law.[133] If
anything can be law by the mere fact that States will it then there is no
basis for the distinction. *Lex ferenda* is merely a description of a State's
subjective hope that what it wills (and what thus is law to it) will become
generally willed (that is, general law). If this seems like sheer apologism,
it is also a logical consequence of what has been said so far.

6.3.2.4   The phenomenological claim and the consequences of psychologism

There is a final, strong version of psychologism, expressed in D'Amato's
argument according to which international law:

> ... is entirely phenomenological; it does not exist apart from the way
> representatives of States see it.[134]

It is the apparently unobjectionable character of this claim which leads
modern doctrine to privilege the psychological element in its theory of
custom. What basis would there be to hold something as law which States
would not so hold? This is a variant of the "realist" criticisms of an
autonomous natural or positive law. Law is what States think is law. This
view is constantly assumed in discussion about custom. Thus, Brierly writes:

> ... in order to establish the existence of an international custom what is
> sought for is a general recognition among States of a certain practice as
> obligatory.[135]

---

[133] In particular, it undermines statements such as those by the ICJ in the *Fisheries Jurisdiction* Cases, Reports 1974 p. 23 (§ 53) and *Tunisia–Libya Continental Shelf* Case, Reports 1982 p. 37 (§ 23) according to which a clear distinction was to be made with what States had willed at the III UNCLOS and what was present law on the matter.

[134] *D'Amato* (Custom) p. 34. For an early formulation, see *Hall* (International Law) p. 5. See also *Lachs* 113 RCADI 1964/III p. 98. For an elaboration, see *Kratochwil* (International Order) pp. 49–51.

[135] *Brierly* (Law of Nations) p. 61. See also American Law Institute: *Restatement* (Second) Foreign Relations Law of the U.S. p. 3.

Or, as Brownlie points out:

> ... there is the principle that the general consent of States creates rules of general application. The definition of custom is essentially a statement of this principle.[136]

In other words, you may discuss as much as you wish about the duration, generality, consistency or moral appropriateness of a practice but the fact remains that if States recognize something as custom then, for all practical purposes, it is custom. And conversely, however much converging practice you might be able to come up with as evidence for a rule, it still would not amount to custom if States do not accept it as such.

Lawyers have had little difficulty to interpret case-law in this sense. In the *Wimbledon* Case (1925) the PCIJ seemed to ascribe to a pure psychologism by concluding that the rule according to which artificial waterways connected to open seas and permanently used could be assimilated to natural straits in respect of warship passage was valid as custom because of a "general opinion" among States to that effect.[137] In the *Lotus* Case (1927) it rejected the French view that the practice of abstaining from the exercise of jurisdiction over foreign vessels in the High Seas had become a customary rule as the abstentions had not been based on States' "being conscious of having a duty to abstain".[138]

The *Asylum* Case (1950) supports psychologism in two ways. First, the Court refrained from accepting as custom a practice which had not been motivated by a subjective sense of obligation.[139] Second, it held that even if such practice had been established it still would not have been applicable to Peru which had not accepted it.[140] In several other cases, too, what has seemed important has not been the presence of a material practice but whether the States have accepted the rule.[141]

---

[136] *Brownlie* (Principles) p. 2. See also *Villiger* (Custom) (arguing that the two approaches "converge" in this way) p. 21; *Cheng* (Macdonald-Johnston: Structure and Process) p. 531.

[137] PCIJ: *Wimbledon* Case, Ser A 1 p. 28.

[138] PCIJ: *Lotus* Case, Ser. A 10 p. 28. *Sørensen* (Sources) thinks this to be the sole express reference by the PCIJ to the psychological element, pp. 109–110. But see also PCIJ: *European Commission of the Danube* Case, Ser. B 14 pp. 36–37.

[139] ICJ: *Asylum* Case, Reports 1950 p. 286. The Peruvian case had rested precisely on the absence of a "conviction juridique" or "identité des motifs", see *Scelle* (oral argument), *ibid.* Pleadings I pp. 119–120.

[140] *Ibid.* Reports 1950 pp. 277–278.

[141] See ICJ: *Nottebohm* Case, Reports 1955 p. 22; *Right of Passage* Case, Reports 1960 p. 40; *North Sea Continental Shelf* Cases, Reports 1969 pp. 44–45 (§ 78); *US Military and Paramilitary Activities* Case, Reports 1986 pp. 97–98 (§§ 184, 185).

If these cases are read together with the Court's view that a practice need not be universal nor followed for a long period – indeed, in the *Fisheries Jurisdiction* Cases (1974) it was sufficient that a "general consensus" had emerged[142] – then the consequence is clear: custom emerges with the sole emergence of the psychological element. Whatever States regard to be binding is binding – and only in respect of the States which so regard. If material criteria of generality, consistency or duration are relevant, they are only so as evidence of the presence or absence of psychological acceptance.

But if the psychological condition (be it "will" or "belief") is necessary and sufficient for something to be custom, then we lose the basis for holding a custom binding on a State which has not accepted it and will not accept it at the moment of application. This is so because, as we have seen, nobody can justifiably claim to know better what it is that a State has willed or believed.[143] Were this otherwise, liberal-democratic politics would lack foundation. To base custom on the argument of "knowing better" makes it indistinguishable from naturalism and vulnerable to the objections against it. To base it on what *other* States have accepted violates sovereign equality.[144]

By making custom co-existent with what States will or believe – psychological consensus – the phenomenological claim will destroy its normative character. It engenders the Austinian conclusion that international law is simply an aggregate of State opinions. If these opinions differ, we lack a standpoint from which justifiable preference can be made. It is not only that we are unable to apply a custom against objecting States. Such custom, even if we could identify it, would be completely apologist as it would change with changing attitudes among States – attitudes, moreover, which we can know only *post facto* and by asking the States themselves.[145]

---

[142] ICJ: *Fisheries Jurisdiction* Cases, Reports 1974 p. 24 (§§ 53).

[143] *Shapiro* (Evolution) points out that the Cartesian view of the "privileged access" was accepted by Locke as a matter of course, pp. 144–145.

[144] *Haggenmacher* 90 RGDIP 1986 is, I think, correct in arguing that the "psychological element" works as a strategy to make decisions seem acceptable because consensually based pp. 109–110, 115–116. It cannot be controlling because we have no "privileged access" to others' psychological reality and because we are unable to infer it from a theory of justice. Similarly *Stein* 26 Harv.ILJ 1985 holds the subjective element simply a fictional juristic construction, p. 476.

[145] "An obligation whose scope is left to the free appreciation of the obliged, so that his will constitutes a legally recognized condition of the existence of the duty, does not constitute a legal bond," *Lauterpacht* (Function) p. 189.

To avoid this conclusion, we should leave the phenomenological view and hold that some non-psychological criteria are needed in order for custom to emerge and be identified. We must go back to materialism.

6.3.3   The re-emergence of materialism

Because of the apologist conclusions engendered by pure psychologism, doctrine tends towards reconciliation by a tacit consent argument – materializing the psychological element. Subjective acceptance is inferred from material behaviour. Behaviour is understood to manifest or "articulate" acceptance.[146] Attention is directed away from a search of the "real" *opinio juris* to the material practice, assumed to be relevant as "proof" thereof. Law is still *justified subjectively* but, it seems, now capable of *objective ascertainment*.

It is easy to interpret jurisprudence in this way. In the *Lotus* Case, one would have expected that the Court's rejection of the rule invoked by France due to the assumed lack of the *opinio juris* would have been accompanied with an examination of what States had willed or believed when refraining from exercising High Seas jurisdiction. But no such examination was carried out. All that the Court looked at was the material practice of abstention.[147] Likewise, in the *Asylum* Case, the Court rejected the existence of custom by merely examining what States had done, not their motivations.[148] Other cases manifest this lack of a specific method for ascertaining the *opinio juris*, too.

The Court's apparent reliance on the "general consensus" at the 1960 Conference on the Law of the Sea regarding the 12-mile fishery zone in

---

[146] See generally *D'Amato* (Custom) pp. 74–88. His argument is a good example of the effort to base law on pure psychology and then to move away from it into pure materialism. As we have seen, he argues, first, that all law is "phenomenological". But this will lead into the difficulty of knowing its content in an objective way. Therefore, he makes the point that: "a rule of law is not something that exists in the abstract ... Rules of law and states of mind appear *only* as manifestations of conduct. They are generalizations we make when we find recurring patterns of conduct", *ibid.* pp. 34, 268. Now the law exists in external behaviour, in "recurring patterns of conduct". Subjective views can be safely neglected while only their external manifestations count. This variation of the tacit consent theme is ultimately vulnerable to the criticisms in *supra* ch. 5.1.2. For similar strategy, see *Akehurst* XLVII BYIL 1974–75 pp. 36–37; *Bernhardt* 36 ZaöRV 1976 pp. 63–64; *Bleckmann* (Grundprobleme) pp. 122–123.

[147] See comments by *Lauterpacht* (Development) pp. 385–386; *Günther* (Völkergewohnheitsrecht) p. 66; *Haggenmacher* 90 RGDIP 1986 pp. 69–71.

[148] ICJ: *Asylum* Case, Reports 1950 pp. 277, 286. See also *Haggenmacher* 90 RGDIP 1986 pp. 50–51 and further pp. 57–61.

the *Fisheries Jurisdiction* Cases did not imply an unequivocal view in favour of the custom-forming effect of "pure" consensus. For, as the Court itself noted, this matter was not in dispute. In respect of the coastal State's preferential rights within the 50-miles zone – the real object of the dispute – the Court made a survey of post-1960 practice in the North West and North East Atlantic Fisheries commissions in which all three of the disputants were members. The rule on preferential rights was based on this practice.[149]

In the *North Sea Continental Shelf* Cases, too, the Court started by observing that the "essential point" was whether or not the practice it surveyed testified to the presence of an *opinio juris*.[150] But its conclusion that equidistance had not become "positive custom" followed after a standard survey of State practice, including its consistency and generality as well as a direct enumeration ("some fifteen cases") of equidistance delimitations. No additional survey of the *opinio juris* was concluded. The lack of it – and the absence of custom – was inferred from the lack of relevant practice.[151]

Similarly, in the constructive part of that judgement, the Court first stressed that the relevant principle (delimitation by agreement in conformity with equity) had become law in an apparently psychological process. It had "from the beginning reflected the *opinio juris* in the matter of delimitation".[152] But there was no study of State wills or beliefs which would have been separate from a study of what they had actually done.[153]

There seem to exist no means for the ascertainment of the presence of the psychological element which would be independent of an ascertainment

---

[149] ICJ: *Fisheries Jurisdiction* Cases, Reports 1974 pp. 24–27 (§§ 55–60). See also joint sep. op. *ibid.* pp. 47–52.

[150] ICJ: *North Sea Continental Shelf* Cases, Reports 1969 p. 44 (§ 77).

[151] *Ibid.* pp. 35, 42–43 (§§ 53, 73, 75).   [152] *Ibid.* p. 46 (§ 85).

[153] *Ibid.* pp. 48–50 (§§ 88–92, 97). Many have noted the apparent imbalance between the survey of the Parties' claimed rules and the Court's construction of its own rule. The standard of material practice required of the former seems much stricter than in the Court's almost impressionistic argument about its own agreement-equity rule. See *Lang* (Plateau) pp. 129–132; *Reynaud* (Jugement) pp. 156–157, 167; *Cheng* (Macdonald-Johnston: Structure and Process) pp. 541–542. For analysis, see also *Haggenmacher* 90 RGDIP 1986 pp. 541–542. In many cases the Court has made no mention of the "psychological element" at all. See e.g. PCIJ: *Chorzów Factory* Case, Ser. A 17 (basing its conclusion on arbitral practice) p. 47; ICJ: *Anglo-Norwegian Fisheries* Case, Reports 1951 (absence of material practice sufficed) p. 131; *Reservations* Case, Reports 1951 (reservation-making practice decisive) p. 25.

of the generality, consistency and duration of practice.[154] In this sense, the material element is primary and the *opinio* merely a hypothesis based on it. Sørensen summarizes his study of the practice of the PCIJ in the following words:

> ... ni la Cour ni les juges dissidents ne se sont jamais interessés a l'élement psychologique pour affirmer l'existence ou non-existence d'une coutume. La pratique générale et constante leur a suffi pour conclure qu'une coutume avait été née ... On a recouru à l'élement psychologique seulement dans le sens négatif que son absence empêche l'affirmation d'une règle coutumière.[155]

But even this seems to exaggerate the role of the psychological element. Also in cases where the Court's finding has been in the negative, there seems to have existed no specific method for ascertaining its absence. Lack of material practice has been sufficient. Virally observes:

> ... the Court, though it pays lip-service to the concept of *opinio juris* and though it has had occasions to speak of the "consciousness of a legal duty", is concerned less with analysis of mental states than with the examination and assessment of the facts proved.[156]

Among students of ICJ jurisprudence this conclusion is near-unanimous.[157] The Court examines material practice and makes a presumption about

---

[154] Thus, in the *US Military and Paramilitary Activities* Case, Reports 1986, the Court concluded that: "... existence in the *opinio juris* of States of the principle of non-intervention is backed by established and substantial practice", pp. 106–107 (§ 202).

[155] *Sørensen* (Sources) pp. 108–111, Similarly *idem* 101 RCADI 1960 pp. 47–51; *Virally* (Sørensen: Manual) pp. 134–135; *Müller* (Vertrauensschutz) pp. 83–85. See also *Suy* (Actes) p. 234; *Raestad* (Philosophie) p. 68. *O'Connell* (International Law I) notes: "The jurist observes actual practice, notes its generality, and then judges that it is due to a conception that the practice is a necessary part of the legal order. He is then justified in postulating the existence of a customary rule." p. 16. The problem here concerns the criteria for his judgement. If the psychological element has no reality, then the needed distinction between custom/usage can only be made by reference to a naturalistic theory of what is a "necessary part of the legal order" and what is not. See also *Lauterpacht* (International Law I) (stability and good faith make a conduct binding providing there is no clear *opinio* to the opposite effect) pp. 63–64. He notes further, that "the element of consent is satisfactorily met by the circumstance that a rule has been generally followed ..." p. 66.

[156] *Virally* (Sørensen: Manual) p. 134.

[157] See *supra* n. 155 and *Günther* (Völkergewohnheitsrecht) p. 70 (the *opinio* an "empty formula"); *Bernhardt* 36 ZaöRV 1976 p. 63; *Wolfke* (Custom) pp. 54, 121–129; *Bos* 25 GYIL 1982 pp. 32–37; *Unger* (Völkergewohnheitsrecht) p. 52; *Skubiszewski* 31 ZaöRV 1971 pp. 843, 853–854; *Séfériades* 43 RGDIP 1936 p. 144; *De Visscher* (Problèmes) p. 227. See also *Lachs*, diss. op. ICJ: *North Sea Continental Shelf* Cases, Reports 1969

State will or belief on the basis of it. In other words, the ascertainment of a normative custom is made by a study of material acts. In order to avoid the implication that States are bound irrespective of consent (and the objection of utopianism), the justification for this is received from the assumption that material practice reflects what States will or believe.[158] Even a tacit agreement theorist such as Strupp is forced into this position. Having first declared that the *only* element in custom is the psychological one, he goes on to argue that the content of the custom-argreement is to be ascertained from material practice. And he proposes no other way to determine it.[159]

But to say that material practice creates a presumption about consent does not, by itself, go far enough to make that practice normative. The point is whether such presumption can be rebutted or not. If it can be rebutted, then we are back in full psychologism.[160] For the only kind of evidence which can rebut a presumption created on perception of material acts is the State's *own knowledge* about its will or belief. As we cannot claim to "know better" we have nothing to argue against a State which says that a behaviour is not binding on it because it did not manifest its subjective consent.

Therefore, if we wish to achieve the original aim of having a custom which binds non-accepting States, too, we must regard the presumption as *non-rebuttable*.[161] But this is just another way of taking a fully materialistic position. A practice now binds regardless of whether it manifests real, psychological consent. And this position is vulnerable to the now familiar criticism; it will either 1) fail to distinguish between binding and non-binding usages, or 2) assume the existence of a non-consensual (naturalistic) criterion for making the distinction. We have

---

    p. 231; *Meijers* IX Neth.YBIL 1978 pp. 18–20; *Akehurst* XLVII BYIL 1974–75 p. 38; *Cahier* (Mélanges Guggenheim) p. 245; *Stein* 26 Harv.ILJ 1985 p. 476.

[158] See further *Jacqué* (Eléments), pp. 112–120, 220–223; *Gounelle* (Motivation) pp. 75–80.

[159] *Strupp* 47 RCADI 1933/I pp. 302, 304, 309 *et seq.*

[160] *Waldock* 106 RCADI 1962/II p. 51. See also *Stern*'s (Mélanges Reuter) discussion of the consequences of Tunkin's extreme psychologism pp. 489–490.

[161] Though lawyers do not often expressly discuss this question (and thereby avoid the *real* difficulty) they sometimes imply that the "presumption" is non-rebuttable – in particular if they stress the fictitious character of State will or hold custom binding on a good faith basis. See e.g. *D'Amato* (Custom) pp. 252–254, 258–262; *Kelsen* (Principles) pp. 450–451. *Müller* (Vertrauensschutz) points out: "Die Übung hat nicht lediglich Beweiswert für die hinterlegende Verhaltensnorm, sondern sie ist selbst rechtsbegründend durch die ... Erwartungen, die sie ... zu erzeugen geeignet ist." pp. 86 and generally 82–88.

seen that the psychological element was included precisely in order to achieve the former distinction without having to assume the correctness of the latter. If the psychological element loses its reality, its independently normative force, then we fall back into pure naturalism and the criticisms directed at it.

6.3.4 The re-emergence of psychologism: the circle closes

To avoid apologism, the theory of custom privileged the material element over the psychological one. But this led into the difficulty of distinguishing between custom-forming and other material practice. Standard argument makes this distinction by assuming that the criterion is whether or not the practice "reflects" State will or belief to be bound. But this is circular. For it assumes that the "wills and beliefs" can be known *independently* of the practice whose normativity we study – a position which was excluded by our argument about the need to look at material practice in the first place. Circularity could be avoided if there existed a general rule (whatever its status) as to which practices are custom-forming and which not. But no such rule exists. Indeed, inasmuch as we take seriously the view that law is matter of wills and beliefs, then we must realize that anything can reflect State will or belief about the law – any act may be creative of custom.

Thus, attempts to restrict the scope of practices qualifying as custom-formative by some general rule have been unsuccesful.[162] At least the following have been held relevant: 1) positive acts by States; 2) statements and claims by States such as, for example: a) official statements to the press or the public at large,[163] b) views by State representatives

---

[162] Lawyers have sometimes tried to exclude acts by State authorities not having the capacity to bind their Governments or mere statements or "statements in abstracto" from admissible categories of practice. Others have, however, held such acts or statements as typical ways of custom-formation. See *Strupp* 47 RCADI 1934/I pp. 313–315 and criticism by *Kopelmanas* XVIII BYIL 1937 pp. 130 *et seq*, 147–149: *Read*, diss. op. ICJ: *Anglo-Norwegian Fisheries* Case, Reports 1951 p. 191 and discussion in *D'Amato* (Custom) pp. 50–51; *van Hoof* (Rethinking) pp. 107–108; *Skubiszewski* 31 ZaöRV 1971 pp. 812–813; *Thirlway* (Customary Law) p. 58; *Akehurst* XLVII BYIL 1974–75 p. 3; *Parry* (Sources) p. 65. For cases recognizing the custom-forming effect of "statements", see ICJ: *Asylum* Case, Reports 1950 p. 277; *North Sea Continental Shelf* Cases, Reports 1969 (on the Truman Proclamation) pp. 32–33 (§ 47) and especially *US Military and Paramilitary Activities Case*, Reports 1986 pp. 100–101, 108–109 (§§ 190, 207).

[163] ICJ: *Nuclear Tests* Cases, Reports 1974 pp. 265–267 (§§ 34–41); *North Sea Continental Shelf* Cases, Reports 1969 pp. 25–26 (§§ 27–31).

at international conferences;[164] 3) acts and statements by municipal organs, such as heads of State, foreign offices, municipal courts etc;[165] 4) municipal laws and statutes;[166] 5) acts by international organizations and conferences;[167] 6) bilateral and multilateral treaties;[168] 7) abstentions

---

[164] ICJ: *US Military and Paramilitary Activities* Case, Reports 1986 pp. 100–101 (§ 190). See also generally *Ferrari-Bravo* 192 RCADI 1985/III pp. 262–274, 288 *et seq*. This is well manifested in the way in which "consensus" has been deemed to have custom-forming effect. See ICJ: *Fisheries Jurisdiction* Cases, Reports 1974 pp. 24–26 (§§ 55–58); *Tunisia–Libya Continental Shelf* Case, Reports 1982 p. 38 (§ 24); *Gulf of Maine* Case, Reports 1984 p. 294 (§ 34).

[165] For the abundance of material on this point, see *Parry* (Sources) pp. 10–13; *Akehurst* XLVII BYIL 1974–75 pp. 8–10; *Rousseau* (Droit international public I) pp. 331–333; *Skubiszewski* 31 ZaöRV 1971 pp. 814–818; *Wolfke* (Custom) pp. 145–147; *Bleckmann* (Festschrift Mosler) p. 109; *idem* (Grundprobleme) pp. 110–112; *Sørensen* (Sources) pp. 90–94; *Kopelmanas* XVIII BYIL 1937 pp. 147–149; *Ferrari-Bravo* 192 RCADI 1985/III pp. 259–261, 277–280. See also *Philippine Embassy Bank Account* Case (Federal Constitutional Court, FRG, 13 December 1977) 65 ILR 1984 pp. 166–167.

[166] In particular, in matters of jurisdictional delimitation, immunities, nationality etc. See *Finch* (Sources) pp. 54–56. See also ICJ: *Anglo-Norwegian Fisheries* Case, Reports 1951 pp. 134–136; *Ammoun*, sep. op. *North Sea Continental Shelf* Cases, Reports 1969 pp. 104–106; *Nottebohm* Case, Reports 1955 p. 22.

[167] On the recognition of the custom-forming character of UNGA resolutions, see ICJ: *US Military and Paramilitary Activities* Case, Reports 1986 pp. 99–106 (§§ 188, 191–192, 195, 202); *Dispute between Texaco Overseas Petroleum Company/California Asiatic Oil Company and the Government of the Libyan Arab Republic*, XVII ILM 1978 p. 30 (§ 87); *Dispute between the Government of Kuwait and the American Independent Oil Company (AMINOIL)*, XXI ILM 1982 pp. 1032–1033; Iran-US Claims Tribunal: *Sedco Inc. v. National Iranian Oil Company and Iran*, XXV ILM 1986 pp. 633–634. The literature on this point is extensive. See e.g. *Brownlie* (Principles) p. 14 and notes therein. For the recognition of ILC drafts as relevant "practice", see ICJ: *US Military and Paramilitary Activities* Case, Reports 1986 pp. 100–101 (§ 190); *North Sea Continental Shelf* Cases, Reports 1969 pp. 33–36 (§§ 48–56). See on this point also *Parry* (Sources) pp. 23–24. On the recognition of other non-binding instruments as evidence of custom, see also ICJ: *US Military and Paramilitary Activities* Case Reports 1986 (discussing the Final Act of the CSCE and a resolution of OAS General Assembly) pp. 102, 107 (§§ 192, 204).

[168] ICJ: *North Sea Continental Shelf* Cases, Reports 1969 pp. 41 (§ 71) and 43–44 (§§ 75–76). See also the dissenting opinions of *Tanaka*, ibid. pp. 174–177; *Sørensen* p. 244 *et seq*. See also *Asylum* Case, Reports 1950 p. 277; *Nottebohm* Case, Reports 1955 pp. 22–23; *Libya–Malta Continental Shelf* Case, Reports 1985 pp. 29–30 and 34–35 (§§ 35–39). See also Vienna Convention on the Law of Treaties, Art. 38 and comments in *Villiger* (Custom) pp. 183–187. Literature on this point, too, is extensive. See e.g. *Baxter* 129 RCADI 1970/I p. 25 *et seq*; *idem* XLI BYIL 1965–66 p. 275 *et seq*; *Thirlway* (Customary Law) pp. 80–94; *Villiger* (Custom) pp. 183–198 and *passim*; *D'Amato* (Custom) pp. 103–165.

by States from doing something[169] and 8) acts of private persons which the State has accepted.[170]

A flexible concept of custom-forming practice has developed. As it was suggested in 1950 by the ILC, in addition to positive acts by States, at least the following may be cited as "evidence of customary international law": "treaties, decisions of national and international courts, national legislation, diplomatic correspondence, opinions of national legal advisers, practice of international organizations . . ."[171] The list is not exhaustive. Indeed, there is no reason to exclude any category of acts or statements because *anything*, including silence and abstention, may manifest what a State wills or believes to be customary law. Schwarzenberger observes:

> For a rule of customary international law to emerge, no particular form is required . . . All that matters is that the generality of subjects of international law accept the rule as law.[172]

The matter is put even more clearly by Akehurst:

> . . . any act or statement by a State from which views can be inferred from international law . . .[173]

is custom-formative. Or, as Wolfke argues: "Everything depends on concrete circumstances".[174] The same conclusion is arrived at in the recent studies by Villiger, Ferrari-Bravo and others.[175] Anything can count as custom-formative practice provided that it only reflects State views about what is law in the matter.

Lawyers have observed problems in such construction. Jennings, for example, points out that:

---

[169] See e.g. ICJ: *Anglo-Norwegian Fisheries* Case, Reports 1951 p. 139 and further *Akehurst* XLVII BYIL 1974–75 pp. 8–10; *MacGibbon* XXXIII BYIL 1957 pp. 115–125, 141–149; *Bleckmann* (Grundprobleme) pp. 112–113; *Blum* (Historic Titles) pp. 38 *et seq*, 59–98.

[170] This is a natural consequence of custom's subjective basis. If the State accepts something as law, what basis is there to hold that the act was still *ultra vires*? See e.g. ICJ: *Hostages* Case, Reports 1980 pp. 33–35 (§§ 70–74); *Bleckmann* (Grundprobleme) pp. 110–111.

[171] Report of the ILC to the General Assembly. YILC vol. II pp. 368–372.

[172] *Schwarzenberger* (Dynamics) p. 6.   [173] *Akehurst* XLVII BYIL 1974–75 pp. 43–44.

[174] *Wolfke* (Custom) pp. 68, 51.

[175] *Villiger* (Custom) p. 7; *Ferrari-Bravo* 192 RCADI 1985/III p. 261. Similarly, *Ross* (Textbook) pp. 88–89; *Bos* 25 GYIL 1982 pp. 22–23; *Bernhardt* 36 ZaöRV 1976 p. 65; *Meijers* IX Neth.YBIL 1978 p. 19; *Reuter* (Droit international public) pp. 96–97; *Barile* 161 RCADI 1978/III p. 51; *Tanaka*, diss. op. ICJ: *North Sea Continental* Shelf Cases, Reports 1969 p. 176; *Martin* (L'Estoppel) p. 243; *Detter-Delupis* (Concept) p. 112.

> ... the difficulty today is in the now embarrassingly rich and varied range of
> evidences of *opinio juris*, not only in the digests of so-called state practice, but
> also in the daily spate of material, more or less with legal content, emerging
> from one more or less authoritative body or another ...[176]

The difficulty lies in the abundance of materials. If the sole criterion for something to count as custom-forming practice is whether it "reflects" the *opinio juris*, then we in fact lack the criterion altogether. For in order to be able to make use of such criterion, we should already know the *opinio juris*. In such case, however, the reference to any material practice would be superfluous – for it was relevant only as a "presumption" about the *opinio* which, it was assumed, can be really known only to the State itself. The construction is hopelessly circular.

It might be objected that certain forms of practice by their nature (automatically) imply certain views by the States adopting them. Under this view, it would not be necessary to decide in each case separately whether an act manifests the *opinio* or not. For example, it might be held self-evident that a State's extension of its maritime jurisdiction up to 200 miles reflects its view that such extension is permitted under customary law. To say that we should know the State's view in order to appreciate the relevance of such action would, in this view, be – although correct in principle – inapplicable in practice.

But State actions do not immediately reveal the meaning which they carry to the acting State. They need to be interpreted. Take, for example, the view which holds UN General Assembly resolutions as custom-forming "practice". Do we have the right to assume that a positive vote reflects the State's views about the law? This is quite uncertain. The vote may have been given as a political gesture, a confirmation of an alliance, for example, and wholly unrelated to what the State regards as custom. It may also have been given due to pressure exerted by a powerful State or in order to embarrass one's adversary. In neither case does it "reflect" any *opinio juris* in the State concerned. Moreover, it is possible to interpret the constant voting at the UN in the light of a widespread conviction within States that the resolutions will only exceptionally survive in the minds of other States. States vote freely because they have virtual certainty that no-one will cite the resolutions against them as binding law. In other words, it is possible (and frequent) to interpret UN decision-making in the light of the assumption – evidenced

---

[176] *Jennings* XXXVII Schw.JB 1981 p. 69.

by the lack of full powers of State representatives – that it is non-binding.[177] If this is so, then we cannot infer anything "automatically" from their voting-practice. On the contrary, we can interpret or evaluate the significance of a resolution only *after* we know what the States in fact willed or believed when voting.

Similar problems arise in interpreting State behaviour at codifying conferences. Inasmuch as the package-deal method is used, it seems clearly implausible to infer anything automatically from the positions taken by the States in such conferences or even from the provisions of particular treaties.[178]

The interpretation of municipal acts presents similar difficulties. Should these reflect the opinions of the heads of State, foreign ministers, Parliaments or what? What if these views conflict? Is it permissible to infer an international *opinio juris* from court judgements, without consulting the views of the foreign office, for example? Whose view will prevail in case of conflict?[179]

Take a further example. State A lets State B's warships enter its ports without permit or notification. Is this relevant evidence of a customary rule allowing such entry? State A's action may be interpreted at least in the following three ways: 1) it wishes to allow *all* military ships into its ports without permit or notification but holds this merely a matter of political convenience, not one of duty; 2) it allows only B's ships to do this because of a special relationship between them; 3) it does not think that any warships should enter any State's ports without previous notification or permit but lets B's ships do this because of fear of pressure by it. We do not know whether A's action can be interpreted as custom-forming practice nor, if it can, which rule it supports.

The problem of interpreting State action in respect of treaties is well-known. Is the fact that States conclude bilateral investment treaties evidence of custom which is in conformity or in conflict with the effective compensation clauses in such treaties? What about the evidentiary value of lump sum agreements whereby less than full compensation

---

[177] On these points generally, see *MacGibbon* (Cheng: Teaching) pp. 12–15; *Virally* (Mélanges Reuter) pp. 527–530; *Schachter* 178 RCADI 1982/V pp. 115–116; *Pomerance* (Self-Determination) pp. 65–66; *Arangio-Ruiz* (Friendly Relations) pp. 43–56, 59–61.

[178] See e.g. *Jennings* (Mélanges Reuter) p. 349 *et seq*; *de Lacharrière* (Bardonnet-Virally: Nouveau) p. 32. See also *Dispute between the Government of Kuwait and the American Independent Oil Company (AMINOIL)* XXI ILM 1982 (dismissing the evidentiary character of resolutions because of the "political" bargaining involved in adopting them) p. 1036.

[179] See *Parry* (Sources) p. 100.

has been awarded? How should one interpret delimitation agreements which use the equidistance principle? Do these support the customary nature of the equidistance rule or have such treaties been concluded precisely because custom has not seemed to include an unequivocal rule in favour of equidistance? All such agreements may be understood both ways:[180] as confirmations of a pre-existing custom (in which case we remain puzzled about the point in concluding them) or as conscious departures from custom (in which case custom's generally binding nature is lost). Neither interpretation is automatic or natural. It would be tempting to say that their value is what the States intended their customary value to be. But this is *petitio principii*: we have referred to treaties as evidence of custom in order to escape from referring to subjective views of States. We are left with nothing apart from a general reference to contextual evaluation. Or as De Visscher points out, the matter cannot be decided by any rule at all. It must be left:

> ... à la discrétion du juge qui se décide en fonction des particularités d'espèce.[181]

Just as friendship and hostility may be expressed in the same acts (e.g. intervention), so too any act may be cited to express the most varied kinds of wills or beliefs.[182] A State may pay damages caused by its industrial or military activities not because it would accept a rule of law conferring liability on it but in order to remove the political tension between it and the injured State.[183] A State may extend its fishery

---

[180] In the *Dispute between Libyan-American Oil Co. (LIAMCO) and the Government of the Libyan Arab Republic* XX ILM 1981, the Arbitrator regarded lump sum agreements as evidence of a custom which did not provide for full compensation, pp. 72–73. However, lump sum agreements were regarded as *deviations* from a customary standard by the Iran-US Claims Tribunal: *Sedco Inc. v. National Iranian Oil Company and Iran* XXV ILM 1986 p. 633. See also *supra* n. 178. On the relevance of equidistance agreements, see the conflicting positions by Libya and Malta in ICJ: *Libya–Malta Continental Shelf* Case, Reports 1985 p. 38 (§ 44). See also the *Equalization of Burdens Taxation* Case (Federal Constitutional Court, FRG, 4 May 1968) 61 ILR 1981 (the question of the custom-creative character of bilateral tax exemption agreement: such character was recognized in the Report by M. Seidl-Hohenveldern but rejected by the Court which treated them as exceptions) pp. 173–178.

[181] *De Visscher* (Problèmes) p. 233.

[182] See *Kennedy* 23 GYIL 1980 pp. 362–364 and *passim*. See also *infra* ch. 7.

[183] It is clearly doubtful whether such "ex gratia" payments as those made by the US to injured Japanese fishermen during the nuclear tests in the Pacific may be cited as evidence of custom (as it is sometimes done to support a rule for liability for environmental harm). See *Whiteman* (Digest 4.) p. 565. From one aspect, they do seem to testify to an *opinio necessitatis*. But as they incorporate an express denial of a

jurisdiction zone hoping or believing that this will not trigger off similar claims by other States and thinking its claim justified only by virtue of its special circumstance. A State may resort to violence for peaceful motives and refrain from force only because it has not yet developed the capacity for victory. Even open statements frequently rather hide than express State wills and beliefs. And so on.

The absurdity of believing that State practice would somehow be capable of an automatic interpretation is well-reflected in doctrines about the custom-forming significance of abstention from positive acts.[184] Consider, for example, absence of positive acts in the fields of disarmament, commercial space travel or deep seabed mining. Surely it cannot plausibly be held that because States have not engaged in such activities, a customary rule now prohibits them. Besides consent in a binding rule, silence or non-action may denote indifference, conscious non-participation in something considered illegal, lack of technical capacity, political manoeuvre or whatever.[185] It is impossible to make any presumptions about the *opinio juris* on the basis of such silence as a matter of *general rule*. It may be seen as relevant or irrelevant only *after* we know the will or belief which prompted the silence in the first place.

The same applies more generally: we cannot automatically infer anything about State wills or beliefs – the presence or absence of custom – by looking at the State's external behaviour. The normative sense of behaviour can be determined only once we first know the "internal aspect" – that is, how the State itself understands its conduct. But if, in custom-ascertainment, we have to rely on the internal aspect, then we lose custom's normativity.

To sum up: doctrine about customary law is indeterminate because circular. It assumes behaviour to be evidence of the *opinio juris* and the latter to be evidence of which behaviour is relevant as custom.[186] To avoid

---

duty, they cannot easily be fitted under a system which is based on the ascending principle that law emerges from a legislative will.

[184] It is regularly stated that such abstentions may be just as custom-forming as positive acts, see e.g. *Sørensen* (Sources) pp. 98–101; *Lauterpacht* XXVII BYIL 1950 p. 395; *Tunkin* 95 RCADI 1958/III p. 12; *MacGibbon* XXXIII BYIL 1957 pp. 120–123; *Blum* (Historic Titles) pp. 44–46 *et seq*; *Akehurst* XLVII BYIL 1974–75 pp. 8–10; *Rousseau* (Droit international public I) p. 317; *Bleckmann* (Grundprobleme) pp. 112–113.

[185] See also *Brownlie* (Principles) p. 7; *D'Amato* (Custom) pp. 81–82; *Vamvoukos* (Termination) pp. 252–253.

[186] Take for example *Barile*'s 161 RCADI 1978/III argument. According to him: "Faits probatoires qui permittent à l'interprète de relever l'existence d'une coutume

apologism, doctrine looks at the psychological element from the perspective of the material; to avoid utopianism, it looks at the material element from the perspective of the psychological. But it can permanently occupy neither perspective without becoming vulnerable to criticisms from the other. The movement between perspectives continues interminably.

This proves fatal to the practice of problem-solution. Because indeterminate, customary law doctrine can only produce solutions which remain vulnerable to the criticisms compelled by itself. Any proposed solution – that is, any attempt to cease the shifting of perspectives at some point – will have to appear as either apologist (because it prefers psychology to behaviour) or utopian (as it privileges behaviour over psychology). Though we can justify anything that States will or believe as custom we must also constantly remain vulnerable to the objection that our justification is "subjective" – inadmissible as a legal solution.

6.4   Resulting dilemmas: general/particular, stability/change

To illustrate how the doctrine of custom fails to provide material resolution to normative problems, I shall take a look at how it lends equal support to contradicting arguments about the generality and particularity of custom and about the significance of its early and late origin. Being unable to establish priority between such arguments, doctrine defers substantive resolution into contextual evaluation under a principle of equitableness – evaluation which is, by the doctrine's *own assumptions*, undetermined by law.

6.4.1   *General v. particular*

Alongside the idea of custom as general law there exists an interpretation of custom as an aggregate of reciprocal inter-State relationships.[187] The former view stresses custom's normativity, the latter its concreteness. Both are illustrated in standard arguments about the generality of

---

juridique ... ne sont contemplés, quand au nombre et à la qualité, par aucune norme superieure, mais sont toujours et exclusivement ceux qui ... ont eu une influence concernant l'existence de cette conscience." p. 51. In other words, to determine the "conscience" on which the rule of law is based you must have regard to any evidence that might have had influence on the existence of that conscience. The problem is that unless one bases the evidentiary value of some items on a theory of justice (and disposes with any effort to make the law correspond to somebody's real conscience), one should already know that conscience – in which case no interpretation is needed.
[187] See e.g. *Simma* (Reziprozität) p. 48 *et seq.* See also *supra* n. 6.

custom v. the principle of persistent objector, general v. particular custom and the relations between custom and treaty. The problems encountered result from doctrine's inability to prefer either normativity or concreteness and its attempt to explain both opposing argument equally valid.

In the *North Sea Continental Shelf* Cases (1969) Denmark and the Netherlands claimed that the "equidistance-special circumstances rule" in Article 6 of the 1958 Continental Shelf Convention had become binding on the Federal Republic of Germany despite the fact that the latter had not ratified the Convention. The Court first observed that "the most convenient way" of dealing with this was on the basis of the following question:

> ... does the equidistance-special circumstances principle constitute a mandatory rule, either on a conventional or a customary international law basis ... Another and a shorter way of formulating the question would be to ask whether ... the (Federal Republic, MK) is under a legal obligation to accept the application of the equidistance-special circumstances principle.[188]

Though the Court considered these only two ways of asking the same question, they imply differing approaches as to how one should argue about custom. The former question lays emphasis on custom's *erga omnes* validity, the latter on its binding force against the Federal Republic. The Court did construct its answer so as to assume this difference but by holding both approaches equally valid. First, the Court enquired whether the equidistance-special circumstances rule was opposable to the Federal Republic on the basis of its acceptance thereof. Denmark and the Netherlands argued that Article 6 of the 1958 Convention had become binding on the Federal Republic because:

> ... by conduct, by public statements and proclamations, and in other ways, the Republic had unilaterally assumed the obligations of the Convention.[189]

The claim was that the Federal Republic was bound regardless of the generally normative character of the Convention, because of its subjective consent. The Court answered in the negative. The various acts invoked did not evidence German consent.[190]

---

[188] ICJ: *North Sea Continental Shelf* Cases, Reports 1969 p. 23 (§ 12). For the following analysis, see also *Kennedy* (Structures) pp. 90–99.
[189] *Ibid.* p. 25 (§ 27).   [190] *Ibid.* p. 27 (§ 32).

Therefore the Court went on to enquire, second, whether the equidistance:

> ... must be regarded as involving a rule that is part of the *corpus* of general international law; – and like the other rules of general customary international law, is binding on the Federal Republic automatically and independently of any specific assent, direct or indirect, given by the latter.[191]

The claim now was that the Federal Republic could be bound regardless of its specific assent. Again, the Court denied this. Equidistance had not become a rule of general custom, neither as an *a priori* fundamental rule on the continental shelf, nor through general practice and the *opinio juris*.[192]

Behind the Court's approach lies the assumption that customary obligations may arise in an ascending process, as a result of consent as well as in a descending way, irrespective of consent. Neither is given preference and the Court does not discuss the question of possible conflict. This was unnecessary as Germany's consent and general custom pointed in the same direction.

The same approach is visible also in more recent delimitations. In the *Tunisia–Libya Continental Shelf* Case (1982), the ascending argument was expressed in terms of the parties' historic rights and a *modus vivendi* between them,[193] while the descending argument constructed generally binding law in terms of the "natural prolongation", special circumstances and equity.[194] In the *Gulf of Maine* Case (1984), the distinction between "special" and "general" law was made explicitly[195] and in the *Libya–Malta Continental Shelf* Case (1985) it appeared in the distinction between arguments about acquiescence and those about the general law on the shelf.[196] The approach is not restricted to delimitation. In the *U.S. Military and Paramilitary Activities* Case (1986), the Court took pains to distinguish the ascending point about agreement between the parties from points about the objectively binding nature of the rules invoked as general custom.[197]

---

[191] *Ibid.* p. 28 (§ 37).
[192] *Ibid.* pp. 29–32 (§§ 39–42) (on the "fundamentalist thesis") and 32–46 (§§ 47–82) (on the "positive law" argument).
[193] ICJ: *Tunisia–Libya Continental Shelf* Case, Reports 1982 pp. 68 (§ 90), 69 (§ 92), 70 (§ 95) and 71–77 (§§ 97–105).
[194] *Ibid.* pp. 43–49 (§§ 36–50).
[195] ICJ: *Gulf of Maine* Case, Reports 1984 p. 300 (§ 114).
[196] ICJ: *Libya–Malta Continental Shelf* Case, Reports 1985 p. 28 (§ 24) *et seq.*
[197] ICJ: *US Military and Paramilitary Activities* Case, Reports 1986 pp. 97–100, 107 (§§ 184, 185, 187, 189, 203).

The curious fact emerging from these cases is that the two approaches are devoid of relative superiority. This issue has not been expressly discussed by the Court but is implicitly assumed by the Court's very silence and the order of treating the arguments. In the *Tunisia–Libya* Case acquiescence and historic rights were treated as a "special circumstance" to which the general customary rule referred. The ascending argument worked, as it were, *within* the descending one. In the *Gulf of Maine* Case, the Court treated the categories of "special" and "general" law as simply separate. In the *North Sea* and the *Libya–Malta* cases it undertook *first* an enquiry into whether the Parties had subjectively accepted some law between them and only then, since the conclusion on that point had been negative, it turned to general law.[198] This sequence was reversed in the *Tunisia–Libya* and the *Gulf of Maine* Cases in which the Court started out with a discussion of general law and only having observed its inconclusiveness turned to the consensualist argument.

All this can only reflect the absence of a hierarchy between the ascending and descending arguments. But it creates a puzzle: had the Court considered that the Federal Republic had accepted equidistance in the North Sea cases, would it still have enquired on the general law which, as the Court pointed out, allowed no derogation? What if this would have provided for another rule? Had the Chamber in the *Gulf of Maine* case found that general law did contain a rule about a single maritime boundary, would it still have gone into an analysis of "special law" to see if it provided for another rule. Which would then have been given preference?

Lack of hierarchy renders discourse indeterminate. The two approaches cannot be equally valid as they are based on conflicting premises. The sense of the ascending, psychological argument is that State assent – and assent only – is creative of obligations. To be effective, such assent must be capable of overriding any general law. The argument about the binding nature of general custom is premised on the descending, materialistic assumption that such custom binds even against conflicting will. The indeterminacy of the Court's approach is hidden by its

---

[198] In the *Libya–Malta Continental Shelf* Case, Reports 1985, the Court observed that it was "unable to discern any pattern of conduct on either side sufficiently unequivocal to constitute either acquiescence or any helpful indication of any view of either Party ... Its decision must be accordingly based on the application of the submissions made before of principles and rules of international law," p. 29 (§ 25). See also ICJ: *Burkina Faso–Mali Frontier* Case, Reports 1986 pp. 570 *et seq*, 575–576 (§§ 34 *et seq*, 43).

conclusion that both point in the same direction. General practice is in harmony with individual will. This allows it to by-pass the question of hierarchy. But it is quite uncertain whether such an assumption of harmony between consent and general law can be consistently maintained.

In what follows I shall discuss, first, the hidden materialism in discourse about the "requirement of generality" and how this is betrayed by an unleashed psychologism behind the persistent objector doctrine. Thereafter, I shall discuss attempts to distinguish "particular custom" from mere illegal deviation and the inability of doctrine to create a hierarchy between particular and general custom and treaties and general custom.

The ambiguous relationship between the two approaches is manifested in the curiously inconclusive discussion about the generality of a practice to have eligibility for custom. The question "how many States are needed" cannot even be meaningfully discussed unless we have first decided to prefer either psychologism or materialism.

For a purely psychological theory of custom, a "requirement of generality" has no normative status at all. Custom binds only States which have consented to it. "Generality" becomes a description of the custom's scope of application, not a condition for its validity.[199] Even as a presumption of consent, "generality" cannot have normative force. For if the presumption is rebuttable (as it must be, under the psychological theory), the only way to rebut it is that the State denies its consent. In which case it is that consent (or lack of it) which settles the question of normativity and no need for a presumption arises.

A normative *requirement* of generality can exist only in a materialistic theory of custom which assumes that a practice may be binding even on non-consenting States. For clearly, to argue that the requirement of generality means that *all* States must have participated in it is merely a restatement of the psychological position. But as the ICJ noted in the *North Sea* Cases, equidistance could be binding on the Federal Republic without its assent if other States had accepted it in a manner "both extensive and virtually uniform".[200] The whole discussion about how extensive must a practice be to be valid as custom is meaningful only on

---

[199] This is explicitly admitted by such tacit agreement lawyers as *van Hoof* (Rethinking) pp. 111–112; *Skubiszewski* 31 ZaöRV 1971 p. 830 and *Suy* (Actes) pp. 220–221.

[200] ICJ: *North Sea Continental Shelf* Cases, Reports 1969 p. 43 (§ 74); *Asylum* Case, Reports 1950 ("constant and uniform usage") p. 276. Similarly, *US Military and Paramilitary Activities* Case, Reports 1986 p. 98 (§ 186). For the view that full uniformity is not needed, see further *Claim against the Empire of Iran* Case (Supreme Federal Court,

the assumption that once that degree has been attained, the rule binds *all* States.[201] But this conclusion can be objected with the standard argument against majority legislation. The persistent objector doctrine is needed to safeguard non-consenting States' sovereign equality.

Although case-law on the persistent objector is thin, doctrine has overwhelmingly assumed it.[202] This is understandable. It is not merely an annex in the general theory of custom. It makes the views of other States something less than *jus cogens vis-à-vis* the non-consenting State.[203] Sovereign equality requires a State to have the right to protest against a norm or refrain from recognizing a situation which it finds non-acceptable.[204] But this doctrine has an uneasy relationship with the requirement of generality. If *all* States which have not accepted a custom may classify themselves as persistent objectors, then the normativity of general custom is lost. Can we establish the category of persistent objectors in a way which is opposable to non-accepting States and allows regarding at least some of them bound?

FRG, 30 April 1963) 45 ILR 1972 pp. 61–62; *National Iranian Oil Co. Pipeline Contracts* Case (Oberlandsgericht, 4 May 1982) 65 ILR 1984 p. 214.

[201] The fluidity and contextual nature of this criterion is generally stressed. It is understood to be something less than unanimity but more than simple majority. Many lawyers also stress the need to include "interested States" in it. For different formulations see e.g. *Kunz* 47 AJIL 1953 p. 666; *Skubiszewski* 31 ZaöRV 1971 pp. 827, 829; *Rousseau* (Droit international public I) pp. 319–320; *van Hoof* (Rethinking) pp. 110–111; *Cavaré* (Droit international I) p. 221; *Brierly* (Law of Nations) pp. 61–62; *Stein* 26 Harv.ILJ 1985 p. 458; *Verdross-Simma* (Völkerrecht) pp. 279–280; *Wolfke* (Custom) pp. 29–30; *Bleckmann* 36 ZaöRV 1976 (making the point that custom may arise even in face of conflicting State practice) pp. 374 *et seq*, 379–383.

[202] For standard cases, see ICJ: *Asylum* Case, Reports 1950 pp. 277–278; *Anglo-Norwegian Fisheries* Case, Reports 1951 p. 131. For doctrine, see *Brownlie* (Principles) pp. 10–11; *Merrills* (Anatomy) pp. 2–3; *Akehurst* XLVII BYIL 1974–75 pp. 24–25; *Fitzmaurice* XXX BYIL 1953 p. 26; *Waldock* 106 RCADI 1968/II pp. 49–50; *Blum* (Historic Titles) p. 48. For recent discussion, see *Charney* LVI BYIL 1985 pp. 1–24; *Stein* 26 Harv.ILJ 1985 pp. 457–482.

[203] *Weil* 77 AJIL 1983 pp. 433–438; *Vamvoukos* (Termination) p. 260; *Stein* 26 Harv.ILJ 1985 p. 463 *et seq*. *Charney* LVI BYIL 1985 notes the tension in that many of those who have rejected a purely consensual view on custom still adhere to the persistent objector rule, pp. 5–6, 16. He argues that the rule is *not* necessary because consensualism is incorrect, pp. 16–21. However, his arguments are problematic. Though consensualism is much criticized, nothing has come to replace it. Neither of the two alternatives – naturalism and majority legislation – has been generally accepted. Indeed, powerful arguments from sovereign equality contradict them. It is not enough, then, to show that the persistent objector rule cannot be held because consensualism is no longer in fashion. Most lawyers (and States) still adhere to it in one way or another and Charney provides no convincing argument as to why they should not.

[204] See e.g. *Suy* (Actes) pp. 47–80.

The persistent objector doctrine has not been regarded as a threat to custom's normativity because it is assumed that the objector cannot prevent the *emergence* of a customary norm but only its *application* to itself.[205] But in many cases this does not correspond to what is objected against. The objection may concern the norm's *erga omnes* validity, not merely its application. Arguably, this is the case with United States opposition to the customary nature of prohibition of unilateral seabed mining and Soviet Union's opposition towards the rule of restricted immunity. These States deny that *any* such custom has emerged.[206] It is because the objection can *always* be formulated in such a manner that we remain incapable of delimiting the category of persistent objectors.

In principle, as persistent objectors only States qualify which have voiced their objection *before* the rule's emergence. If this temporal criterion were absent, then no rules would be applicable to non-accepting States. But it may be circumvented by directing objection to the rule's emergence instead of its application. Let us take a hypothetical argument. State A objects to the application of rule X against it. It argues that X is not valid as custom. To this, B might answer that in order to invoke the persistent objector rule A should have protested already when X emerged. But this is not at all what A is disputing. It accepts the orthodox interpretation of the persistent objector doctrine but points out that "how could I have protested before because I never realized that there was a rule-creation process going on?" This is crucial. If B wishes to remain consistent with the assumptions about sovereign equality behind the persistent objector doctrine, then it is not open for it to say "but you should have known" and press upon that point. To insist that A "should have known" by reference to what other States know, for example, or some standard of reasonableness, is to imply that A might be bound even if it really did not know[207] – and thus impose other States' will and knowledge or a naturalistic standard on A. Both implications seem unacceptable. By first challenging the very existence of a custom or at least one's knowledge thereof it remains possible for a State to oppose the application of the custom in respect of it. Even if the State is hard pressed so as not to be able to to deny the *inter alios* existence of the

---

[205] *Akehurst* XLVII BYIL 1974–75 p. 24; *Charney* LVI BYIL 1985 pp. 2–3.

[206] *Stein* 26 Harv.ILJ 1985 pp. 460–463.

[207] Therefore, the presumption against objection, argued by *Brownlie* (Principles) pp. 10–11, merely avoids the question. The point is whether or not it may be rebutted. A decision on this point will inevitably entail taking either a fully psychological or a fully materialistic stand. See *supra* at nn. 160–161.

norm, it will still have the possibility of qualifying itself as a persistent objector as it may argue that it learned about the norm (or that the norm was intended to apply in respect of it, too) only now and thus voice its "objection" at the moment of application.

Let me now turn to the question of particular custom. Since the decision by the ICJ in the *Asylum* Case (1950), if not before, it has been accepted that alongside general custom, there may exist regional[208] or even bilateral customs.[209] This is indistiguishable from affirming that obligations created by recognition, acquiescence or tacit agreement qualify as custom.[210] The difficulties with this view relate, first, to the normative character of particular custom and, second, to the possibility of distinguishing between illegal deviation and particular custom.

In the first place, it seems difficult to hold non-general custom as other than fully psychological (consensual).[211] To hold otherwise would assume the existence of a non-consensual manner of selecting the group of States assumed to be bound by it.[212] This seems a difficult proposition to accept because particular custom is based on a particular, or

---

[208] ICJ: *Asylum* Case, Reports 1950 pp. 276–278. See also PCIJ: *Free City of Danzig* Case, Ser. B 18 p. 13; *European Commission on the Danube* Case, Ser. B 14 p. 17.

[209] ICJ: *US Nationals in Morocco* Case, Reports 1952 pp. 199–200; *Right of Passage* Case, Reports 1960 pp. 39–40.

[210] See *Blum* (Historic Right) p. 38 *et seq*; *Fitzmaurice* XXI BYIL 1953 p. 31 n. 3. On the different kinds of non-general custom, see *Reuter* (Droit international public) p. 96; *Rousseau* (Droit international public I) pp. 320–323; *Butler* (Cheng: Teaching) pp. 45–52; *Guggenheim* 11 ÖZöRV 1961 p. 327 *et seq*; *D'Amato* (Custom) p. 233; *Bleckmann* 36 ZaöRV 1976 pp. 399–405.

[211] Most lawyers stress the contractual (tacit agreement) character of non-general customs. See e.g. *Sørensen* (Sources) (noting that what justifies speaking of "custom" here at all is that the agreement has been inferred by courts from the duration and continuation of practice) p. 104; *idem* 101 RCADI 1960/III p. 43; *Reuter* 103 RCADI 1961/II p. 465; *De Visscher* (Problèmes) pp. 244–245; *Rousseau* (Droit international public I) p. 322; *Menzel-Ipsen* (Völkerrecht) p. 83; *Unger* (Völkergewohnheitsrecht) pp. 78–82. *D'Amato* (Custom), too, stresses the significance of consent in "special custom" (though he does not exclude the possibility that this consent be tacit) pp. 246 *et seq*, 263. *Cohen-Jonathan* VII AFDI 1961 tries to keep local custom distinct from tacit agreement by reference to the slow and fragmentary way in which the *opinio* emerges in the former) pp. 122–125, 133, 137–139. *Thirlway* (Customary Law) argues that a local custom might be binding in a "geographical region or a community" even against States which have not specifically accepted it and have not actively opposed it, pp. 135–137. See also *Haggenmacher* 90 RGDIP 1986 (noting the tendency of non-general custom to lose its "customary" character) pp. 33–35.

[212] The criterion then being e.g. membership in a community "either a geographical region or a community of interest", *Thirlway* (Customary Law) pp. 137–141. Similarly, *Akehurst* XLVII BYIL 1974–75 pp. 29–30; *Bos* 25 GYIL 1982 p. 44.

significant element which enjoins a group of States together. What this element is and whether it is present in a State cannot be determined without regard to the State's self-understanding. Can the Calvo and Drago doctrines, often classed as regional South-American custom,[213] be applied in respect of all South American States? Believing so would interpret geography as the significant element in them. But this surely is an implausible interpretation. Are they not rather expressions of a specific economical relationship between capital-importing and capital-exporting countries? If this is what is significant in them, they should rather be applicable as special custom between industrialized and developing States. But there is hardly enough practice or *opinio juris* to support such an extension of those doctrines. But even if there were, could we still define the two groups in a manner unrelated to the acceptance by States of their belonging to them? It seems impossible to impose a classification of a State as either "developing" or "industrialized" against its own classification.[214]

We are easily led to think of the special case where the significant element in a particular custom is its regional character or some common interest. Fitzmaurice distinguishes also the following two cases: 1) a customary rule deviating from general custom but is recognized generally as a matter of historic right; 2) a customary practice whereby States grant some privileges to each other but not to the community at large.[215] Other variables, for example expectations of reciprocity, cultural, ethnic or political ties or differences, might, in the opinion of the relevant States, count as significant. As "significance" involves evaluative judgement, it does not seem justifiable to include a non-consenting State within the ambit of a particular custom.

A difficult problem is posed by the *non-existence of hierarchy* between general and particular customs. Associated with the consensual nature of particular custom, this threatens the normativity of general law. For example, even if we held that there existed a general rule on non-intervention, we seem unable, within the confines of our assumptions, to overrule thereby an argument about a particular custom

[213] *Green* 74 RGDIP 1970 p. 85; *Rousseau* (Droit international public I) p. 322. See also *Cohen-Jonathan* VII AFDI 1961 pp. 133–134.
[214] *Butler* (Cheng: Teaching) p. 48; *Bleckmann* 36 ZaöRV 1976 p. 400, 403; *idem* (Grundprobleme) pp. 129–130.
[215] *Fitzmaurice* XXX BYIL 1953 pp. 68–69. See also *MacGibbon* XXXIII BYIL 1957 pp. 122–123; *Blum* (Historic Titles) pp. 52–55 *et seq.*

allowing a right of intervention within some politically defined group of States.[216]

It may be objected that the question about hierarchy is set in a false way, that there in fact exists no particular custom independently of a determination of whether it is in conformity with (or at least not against) a general custom. But this argument assumes the *jus cogens* character of general custom. It assumes that general rules limit the possibilities of particular "legislation". But general custom does not seem to act in this way. The need to provide for law's concreteness – *lex specialis derogat lege generali* – makes it necessary to allow derogations from general law – the Scandinavian 4-mile limit of the territorial sea being the standard example.

Some lawyers have even claimed that particular customs must prevail because they better reflect concrete circumstances.[217] Leaving aside the difficult problem of what "particular" and "general" in this context mean,[218] this would leave unclear the status of the *lex posterior* rule. It can hardly be maintained that subsequent general law is unable to overrule antecedent special law. Nor does it seem possible to argue that subsequent particular (and, as we have seen, consensual) law always overrules antecedent general law (whether or not this is consensual).

The impossibility of making general preference in favour of general or particular customs is evident once we realize that such preference will immediately destroy the point of the other. If general custom prevails, then there can be no particular custom at all because even the non-existence of a rule can, under the doctrine of sovereignty, be conceptualized as a general custom allowing the State full freedom. If particular (and consensual) customs were overriding, then no general law would have normative force. The former suggestion leads into utopianism, the latter into apologism. A general preference leads into assuming, either,

---

[216] See *Fitzmaurice* (IIL 1973) pp. 219–221. *Tunkin* (Theory) distinguishes between the "general" non-intervention standard applicable in respect of US actions in the Dominican Republic and Chile while distinguishing a set of "particular" rules of socialist internationalism applicable in respect of USSR action in Hungary and Czechoslovakia, pp. 46–47, 431 *et seq.* See also *Cohen-Jonathan* VII AFDI 1961 pp. 123–124.

[217] *Dupuy* (Mélanges Rousseau) p. 82. To the same effect, *Akehurst* XLVII BYIL 1974–75 p. 29; *Cohen-Jonathan* VII AFDI 1961 pp. 132–134, 136–137. *Thirlway* (Customary Law) also suggests that the *lex specialis* rule should be given precedence, p. 95. The same is suggested, in a tentative way, in *Sørensen* (Sources) pp. 249–250. *Wolfke* (Custom) denies its applicability, pp. 94–95. The matter is discussed but left unresolved by *Villiger* (Custom) p. 36.

[218] See *Akehurst* XLVII BYIL 1974–75 p. 273.

that there is only one kind of custom and that it exists as *jus cogens* or that all custom is simply subjective agreement.

This lack of principled hierarchy between general and particular custom was visible in the maritime delimitations, considered above. The disturbing question about possible conflict was neither raised nor answered. A similar strategy appears in the few cases dealing expressly with particular custom. Neither in the *Asylum* (1950) nor the *Right of Passage* Cases (1960) the Court bothered going into what general law said on the issues involved.[219] The particular customs were simply assumed coherent with general law. Bleckmann observes here an interpretative strategy to explain away possible conflicts.[220] But it destroys the determinate character of both kinds of custom. We cannot be sure, on the basis of the cases cited, whether law allows deviation from general custom through a particular one or prohibits it. And if we cannot be sure of this, we really have no rule on custom at all. All we have is a general appeal for the *contextual evaluation* of the normative significance of the two forms of custom applicable.[221]

Similar considerations apply to the question whether treaties prevail over custom or *vice-versa*. Though some lawyers have suggested a general priority of the treaty,[222] most writers recognize that no *prima facie* hierarchy exists.[223] This is a natural consequence of the view which sees custom only as a kind of unwritten treaty.[224] But it follows also from the inability to consistently prefer *jus cogens* over consent. Accent is put on

[219] In the *Right of Passage* Case, Reports 1960, the Court simply held it "unnecessary" to go into the question of the general customary status of transit rights, p. 43.

[220] See *Bleckmann* 36 ZaöRV 1976 pp. 376–383.

[221] Such evaluation being typically concerned with the significance of the "generality element", the scope of interested States, the intensity and justifiability of the interests involved in the general and the particular custom and so on. See e.g. *Bleckmann* 36 ZaöRV 1976 pp. 394–399. For a discussion of the absence of hierarchy between general and "special" customs with particular reference to ICJ practice, see *D'Amato* (Custom) (noting that special customs tend to become applicable when general custom is unclear and observing that this is likely to be an unsatisfactory solution as special customs are based on mutual acceptance – an acceptance usually denied in case of dispute) pp. 257–263.

[222] See e.g. *Schwarzenberger* (International Law I) p. 16; *Lauterpacht* (International Law I) (noting the need to make exceptions to this rule) pp. 86–89; *Kelsen* (Principles) p. 438.

[223] See *Heilborn* 11 RCADI 1926/I p. 29; *Scelle* 46 RCADI 1933/IV p. 435; *Reuter* 103 RCADI 1961/II pp. 484–486; *Rousseau* (Droit international public I) pp. 342–343; *Virally* 183 RCADI 1983/V pp. 170–171; *Akehurst* XLVII BYIL 1974–75 pp. 275–278; *Sur* (L'interprétation) pp. 163–166; *Sørensen* (Sources) pp. 237–251; *Monaco* (Festschrift Mosler) pp. 609–610.

[224] *Anzilotti* (Cours) p. 94.

eliminating conflicts by interpretation, i.e. by manipulating the sense of the treaty process or the custom so as to make *prima facie* conflicts disappear.[225]

In the *North Sea Continental Shelf* Cases (1969), the Court seemed to adhere to a *lex specialis* rule in its consideration of the relations between the 1958 Convention and custom. It observed that:

> ... the provisions of the Convention will prevail in the relations between the Parties, and would take precedence of any rule having a more general character, or deriving from another source.[226]

But this is contradicted by the Court's distinction, considered above, concerning the consensual character of treaty and the non-consensually binding nature of general custom. Clearly, if this distinction was correct, or if at least some customs have *jus cogens* character – as commonly assumed – then such generalized preference is simply illegitimate. Moreover, it is generally accepted that subsequent custom may abrogate earlier treaties by *desuetude* or modify them.[227] This is obviously true also *vice-versa* – indeed the point of many treaties has been to avoid applying an earlier custom *inter partes*, that is, to create an exception to old custom while some multilateral treaties have intended to replace old custom altogether.

Whatever character a treaty or a custom might have seems determinable only through a *contextual evaluation*, not by general rule.[228] But can

---

[225] Common methods being either reading the treaty "against the background" of custom or, in a reverse way, holding treaty as "evidence" of custom. For the former, see e.g. ICJ: *Gulf of Maine* Case, Reports 1984 p. 291 (§ 83). For the latter, see *supra* n.168.

[226] ICJ: *North Sea Continental Shelf* Cases, Reports 1969 p. 24 (§ 25).

[227] Obviously, this may be explained either subjectively, as a result of further agreement, or objectively, as a result of change of circumstances, see e.g. *Air Services Agreement* Arbitration, 69 RGDIP 1965 pp. 249–255; *Vamvoukos* (Termination) pp. 220, 225–227, 266–303. See also *Thirlway* (Customary Law) pp. 130–132; *Villiger* (Custom) p. 215 *et seq*; *Schwarzenberger* (International Law I) p. 199.

[228] Relevant factors being then, for example, the possible *jus cogens* character of the custom or the treaty, the treaty's character as "codifying" or its purpose of creating a special regime among the parties, the objective of the treaty and the social importance of the custom and so on. It is in fact difficult to think of any principled limits to the criteria involved in such assessment. On treaties creating "special regimes" or "special law", see e.g. ICJ: *US Nationals in Morocco* Case, Reports 1952 pp. 199–201; *Gulf of Maine* Case, Reports 1984 p. 300 (§ 114). For comments, see *Doehring* 36 ZaöRV 1976 p. 77 *et seq*; *Bleckmann* 29 ÖZöRV 1978 p. 184; *Baxter* 129 RCADI 1971/I pp. 81–91. See also *Monaco* (Festschrift Mosler) p. 615. That there is no general rule by which the evaluation could be made will ultimately make it impossible to decide in a specifically legal way whether a specific regime is legitimate exception to or illegal deviation from a

such evaluation be imposed on a State which does not share the evaluer's view of contextual significance? If it can, then we seem to be arguing on a utopian basis, if it cannot, then we have nothing to solve the conflict with.

6.4.2   Time and customary law: the antinomy of stability and change

The problem of time in relation to customary law has two aspects. First, the duration of a practice for a determined period may be suggested as a criterion for distinguishing custom-formative practice from mere usage. Second, the duration of practice may also be a criterion for distinguishing conduct which is in conformity with the law from behaviour which is not. Although these are aspects of the same concern, namely the concern to relate law closely to concrete State behaviour while still maintaining critical distance from it, they are here discussed separately in order to show the doubly unsuccessful result of doctrine's attempt to achieve a reconciliation. Once more, doctrine is led from general statements about the need to "balance" stability and change into contextual studies about the equitableness of alternative solutions.

The duration of a practice is often presented as a criterion for its status as customary law. For:

> ... clearly the necessity of requiring the repetition of acts as an element in the formation of a customary rule results from the very notion of custom.[229]

The requirement of repetition, including both the duration of a practice and its consistency,[230] seems an intuitively natural element in custom. But

---

general custom. See further *D'Amato* 77 AJIL 1983 (discussing the difficulties which would ensue if non-parties to the 1982 UNCLOS would establish a treaty regime amongst themselves: a tribunal would either need to recognize both regimes or engage in a very controversial evaluation of the merits of each) pp. 281–285.

[229] *Kopelmanas* XVIII BYIL 1937 p. 129. For a discussion of the impact of the German historical school conception of custom in international law, see *Carty* (Decay) pp. 31–33.

[230] ICJ: *Asylum* Case, Reports 1950 p. 276; *US Nationals in Morocco* Case, Reports 1952 p. 200; *Right of Passage* Case, Reports 1960 p. 40; *North Sea Continental Shelf* Cases, Reports 1969 ("virtual uniformity") p. 43 (§ 74). See also *Interpretation of the Treaty between USA and Italy* Arbitration, 72 RGDIP 1968 p. 484. Common to these cases, however, is that the requirement of time rather more acted as evidence of one State's tacit consent or acquiescence in a *bilateral* context than any independently normative requirement. See also *MacGibbon* XXXIII BYIL 1957 pp. 119–121.

it is unclear whether that requirement has any normative force at all. To uphold it against conflicting State consent seems utopian. If States agree in holding something as "custom", what basis is there to deny it as such, even if it were not accompanied by long-standing and consistent practice?

In respect of general custom, we can witness a marked de-emphasis on the requirement of duration. In the *Abu Dhabi* Arbitration (1951), Lord Asquith of Bishopstone held that a nine-year period was too short for a general customary regime of the continental shelf to emerge.[231] Later, however, the ICJ has noted that:

> ... the passage of only a short period of time is not necessarily or of itself, a bar to the formation of a new rule of customary law.[232]

In the *Fisheries Jurisdiction* Cases (1974), the Court held a 12-year practice quite sufficient in this respect.[233] But no *general rule* on the required length of time has emerged. Doctrine has been unable to develop "standards or criteria for determining how much time is necessary to create a usage that can qualify as custom".[234] Bos states the orthodox position. The required duration:

> ... necessarily depends on the circumstances of each particular case.[235]

Lately, however, this discussion has been devoured by the doctrine of instant custom. If one act may create custom, then to speak of any requirement of duration is superfluous. The element of time – like that of generality – loses its normative nature and becomes a description of one class of customary norms.[236] It is true, of course, that the doctrine

---

[231] *Petroleum Development (Trucial Coast) Ltd. v. the Sheikh of Abu Dhabi.* 1 ICLQ 1952 p. 251.

[232] ICJ: *North Sea Continental Shelf* Cases, Reports 1969 p. 43 (§ 74).

[233] ICJ: *Fisheries Jurisdiction* Cases, Reports 1974 p. 23 (§ 52).

[234] *Vamvoukos* (Termination) p. 250.

[235] *Bos* 25 GYIL 1982 p. 28. See also *Tanaka,* diss. op. ICJ: *North Sea Continental Shelf* Cases, Reports 1969 p. 178; *Rousseau* (Droit international public I) p. 317; *Skubiszewski* 31 ZaöRV 1971 p. 837; *Sørensen* 101 RCADI 1960/III p. 39. For *Lauterpacht* XXVII BYIL 1950, the required duration "must be proportionate to the degree and the intensity of the change that it purports, or is asserted, to effect", p. 393. Similarly *Waldock* 106 RCADI 1962/II p. 44.

[236] Hence many argue that time is not at all a necessary element in custom. See e.g. *Fitzmaurice* XXX BYIL 1953 p. 31; *MacGibbon* XXXIII BYIL 1957 pp. 120–121; *Chaumont* 129 RCADI 1970/I pp. 435–436; *Akehurst* XLVII BYIL 1974–75 pp. 15–16; *Bernhardt* 36 ZaöRV 1976 pp. 67, 72; *Ferrari-Bravo* 192 RCADI 1985/III pp. 247–250; *Wolfke* (Custom) pp. 67–68; *Schwarzenberger* (Dynamics) pp. 6–7; *Blum* (Historic Titles) pp. 52–53; *Bleckmann* (Grundprobleme) pp. 118–119.

of instant custom has not secured full acceptance. But the objections relate more to its classification as "custom" than to its character as law. It seems difficult to deny the status of law from a consensus, even if not accompanied by positive acts, which States agree to hold binding.

Time as a criterion distinguishing between custom and usage has direct connection with the materialistic and psychological arguments about custom. The former perspective emphasizes law's autonomy and normative character. It may be associated with a claim for stability. Law cannot be infinitely flexible and custom's social role is precisely to resist unwarranted, hasty change. Under this view, the requirement of duration possesses independent normative value. The more ancient the custom, the more normative it is.[237] The psychological perspective emphasizes law's concreteness, its role as an instrument of politics, of will. In order to fulfil its social function, custom must be responsive to social change. But it cannot only accommodate change, it must speed it up, help in the creation of a better society. From this perspective, custom's point is precisely in its flexibility, its non-formal nature and its capacity to create law through instant consensus.The more ancient the custom, the more obsolete it is.[238]

Both approaches alone lead into absurd results. A purely materialistic position freezes custom into a general command for States to do what they have always done. It seems utopian, conservative and devoid of relation to present will and interest. A purely psychological position cannot provide the security and stability for which law is enacted in the first place. It accepts any new will or act as a potential change in law. It seems apologist and non-normative. Neither position can be preferred as a matter of general rule. Somehow, the demands of stability and change need to be "balanced".[239] But this simply restates the problem. If there is no rule on how such balancing should be undertaken, then we have no criteria by which to overrule the initially opposing arguments

---

[237] This is the historic school's conception of custom.

[238] This view of custom is, not unnaturally, taken by Third-World lawyers. It was manifested in the *Dispute between the Libyan American Independent Oil Company (LIAMCO) and the Government of the Libyan Arab Republic*, XX ILM 1981 in which the Arbitrator studied the customary law status of the rule of full compensation in nationalizations of foreign property. He dismissed the claimant's precedents which had allowed such compensation on the grounds that these cases were "already old and given before the recent evolution of the concept of nationalization", p. 70. See also Iran–US Claims Tribunal: *Flexi-van Leasing Inc. v. Iran*, diss. op. *Kashani* (arguing that the Tribunal neglected to take account of newer precedents) 70 ILR 1986 p. 519.

[239] *Lauterpacht* (Function) pp. 248–250 *et seq*; *Fitzmaurice* (IIL 1973) pp. 207–209, *van Hoof* (Rethinking) pp. 103–104.

from stability or change. To do this, we should argue from an external criterion of justice which can be used to weigh these *prima facie* plausible arguments *vis-à-vis* each other.

One consequence of this dilemma is doctrine's inability to explain change in customary law while preserving its normative force. From a purely psychological perspective, explaining change in custom is no problem. Some States have merely started behaving in another manner and that, for them, settles all there is to settle. But this is simple apologism. To preserve (old) custom's normative character, we must assume that the only manner in which customary rules can change is by States first breaking the law until this law-breaking becomes so general that it becomes the rule. But how can it be that "each deviation contains the seeds of new rule"?[240] Does this not run counter to the *ex injuria non jus oritur* and the *pacta sunt servanda* principles as well as assume the non-existence of *jus cogens?*[241] Efforts to deal with this problem counter similar dilemmas as efforts to explain custom-formation in terms of different stages. It is suggested that not all deviation need be *contra legem* but that it may fit within the general and abstract formulation of the old rule. A new custom may start "alongside the law" and only gradually encroach on the old law's domain.[242]

But such explanations merely avoid answering the question. If there is change in law (and not just some "re-interpretation" or "concretization"), then something which has been binding has ceased being so and something which has been a violation has become general law. To speak of a process of consolidation, or a change of the old *opinio juris* into an *opinio non-necessitatis* and thereafter into an *opinio juris* for the new rule are like attempts to divide one by two in order to arrive at zero. Unless we accept a completely psychological approach, then we must assume that some practice has gone against an old rule and gradually overridden whatever support the old rule had. Before that took place, however, that practice must necessarily have been illegal deviation. The only way to avoid denying the normative character of the *ex injuria* or *pacta sunt servanda* principles – without taking a fully psychological view – is to assume that a fundamental change of circumstances has

---

[240] *D'Amato* (Custom) p. 98. This is the standard suggestion. See also *Merrills* (Anatomy) pp. 8–9.

[241] *Akehurst* XLVII BYIL 1974–75 p. 8.

[242] *Verdross-Simma* (Völkerrecht) pp. 286–287; *Bleckmann* 36 ZaöRV 1976 p. 383; *van Hoof* (Rethinking) p. 103; *Gould-Barkun* (Social Sciences) p. 182; *Suy* (Actes) p. 263; *Thirlway* (Customary Law) p. 131.

taken place outside the law which has made old custom obsolete and justified the new one. And this leads, once more, to evaluative considerations of the context.

The fundamental change doctrine might allow us to envisage action which otherwise would seem like deviation as not deviation, after all. This resembles the *rebus sic stantibus* doctrine, held generally valid in respect of treaties.[243] If we think of custom as tacit agreement, then there exists no difficulty to apply the *rebus* doctrine in respect of custom, too. However, care should be taken not to include into "fundamental change" a change in State practice or the *opinio juris*. This is, of course, a change in customary law, pure and simple. If the "fundamental change" doctrine is to have meaning in respect of custom, it must denote a change, not in the law but in the conditions, for a particular State, of its carrying out its customary duties.[244]

Stated in such manner, the *rebus* doctrine becomes indistinguishable from applying *equity* in order to release a State from obligations which have become too burdensome. This brings out the fact that at issue in the "balancing" of stability and change are not so much views about the significance of time as different conceptions of what is equitable in certain circumstances and what is not.[245] In other words, we cannot

---

[243] See *supra* ch. 5 n. 113.

[244] See also *Tavernier* (Recherches) p. 11. The standard example of a change in customary law is the movement from "absolute" to "restricted" conception of sovereign immunity. Though the scope of the change remains somewhat disputed, those favouring the latter conception argue it usually from some fundamental change in the manner sovereigns have started to engage themselves in commercial activities. See e.g. *Trendtex v. Central Bank of Nigeria* (CT. of Appeal), 64 ILR 1983 pp. 128, 129, 150 and *Philippine Admiral* Case (Privy Council) 64 ILR 1983 pp. 97–108. For a review of this development, see *Badr* (Immunity) *passim*.

[245] See also *McWhinney* (Essays Lachs) p. 198; *idem* (UN Lawmaking) pp. 29–37; *Tavernier* (Recherches) pp. 43–44. It is precisely this "political" aspect of the *rebus* doctrine which is the object of criticism by many lawyers. See *Lauterpacht* (Function) pp. 270–272; *Carty* (Decay) pp. 65–66, 78–81. Similarly *Bourquin* 64 RCADI 1938/II (regarding the *rebus* doctrine non-juridical because of its lack of precision) pp. 394–406. In the *Fisheries Jurisdiction* Cases, Reports 1973 Iceland disputed the validity of the compromissory clause in the 1961 Exchange of Notes between it and, respectively, the United Kingdom and the Federal Republic of Germany, as well as the applicability of the customary 12-mile fishery zone in respect of it on the basis of "changed circumstances" – that is the "ever-increasing exploitation of fishery resources in the waters surrounding Iceland" which were said to affect its "vital interests", p. 18 (§ 35). That the Court held these arguments as relevant (though not decisive) and saw the matter as one of "balancing" is manifested in the way it constructed applicable law on the basis of an equitable appraisal of the Parties' "historic" and "preferential" rights, *ibid*. Reports 1974 pp. 30, 33 (§§ 69, 78).

reach "justice" through the use of some legally formulated temporal metaphor. We must know justice before we can give conflicting formal-temporal criteria definite priority.

Let me illustrate these difficulties by reference to the *intertemporal law* doctrine. The question is whether the legal effects of a fact or a situation in the past should be evaluated on the basis of the law contemporary with it or on the basis of law valid at the time of application. A precise statement of the doctrine has proved difficult. The classical formulation by Max Huber contains two elements. First:

> ... a juridical fact must be appreciated in the light of the law contemporary with it, and not the law in force at the time when a dispute in regard to it arises.[246]

But there is more:

> The same principle which subjects the act creative of a right to the law in force at the time the right arises, demands that the existence of the right, in other words its continued manifestations, shall follow the conditions required by the evolution of law.[247]

The first statement expresses the principle of the law's non-retroactivity. Support for it may be sought from two directions. It can be argued in an ascending way, by reference to the need to honour original State will and in a descending fashion, referring to the need for legal security.[248] But the second statement points in the opposite direction. It provides that the validity of a right at each period of time should be evaluated by reference to the law in force at that time. It may also be argued from two

---

[246] *Island of Palmas* Case, II UNRIAA p. 845.

[247] *Ibid.* p. 839. For the intertemporal law doctrine generally, see *Sørensen*, Rapport provisoire 55 IIL Yearbook 1973 p. 1 *et seq.* Resolution by the Institute of International Law, 58 IIL Yearbook 1975 p. 537 *et seq.* See also *Tavernier* (Recherches) *passim*; *Baade* 7 JIR 1957 (with a review of this doctrine in private and public international law) pp. 229–256; *Schwarzenberger* (International Law I) pp. 6–7; *Lauterpacht* (Function) pp. 283–285.

[248] On the non-retroactivity principle generally, see *Tavernier* (Recherches) pp. 128–134, 171–174; *Bindschedler-Robert* (Mélanges Guggenheim) p. 185; *Kelsen* (Principles) p. 197; *Schwarzenberger* (International Law I) p. 7; *Fitzmaurice* XXXIII BYIL 1957 pp. 225–226. The non-retroactivity principle has secured wide acceptance in the law of territorial sovereignty. See e.g. *Clipperton Island* Case, II UNRIAA p. 1110; *Grisbadarna* Case, XI UNRIAA pp. 159–160; *Delagoa Bay* Case (Lapradelle-Politis III) p. 618; *Baade* 7 JIR 1957 pp. 239–245. See also ICJ: *US Nationals in Morocco* Case, Reports 1952 pp. 184, 189.

perspectives, by reference to present State will and the need to make law responsive to social change.[249]

Both legs of the intertemporal law doctrine have been criticized in a predictable fashion. The principle of non-retroactivity has seemed excessively conservative and non-responsive to changing conceptions of justice.[250] The principle of retroactivity has seemed to create insecurity and destability and violate original intent.[251]

The opposition between the two parts of the doctrine covers much of the dispute between "old" and "new" States. The continuing validity of colonial titles based on discovery or occupation of *terra nullius* reaches the nucleus of the law on decolonization. Although third world argument often claims the invalidity of those titles *ab initio*, the view that even if they had been valid once, they can no longer be hold so is not far behind.[252]

In the *Western Sahara* opinion (1975) the ICJ was requested to answer the question "Was Western Sahara, at the time of colonization by Spain a territory belonging to no-one (*terra nullius*)".[253] The Court did not share the view of Ambassador Bedjaoui, referring expressly to the second part of the intertemporal law doctrine, that it would be "shocking" if the Court applied 19th century law and not the new UN law on self-determination.[254] The Court observed that the question had "to be

---

[249] Retroactive application, too, has secured acceptance. *Tavernier* (Recherches), for instance, having studied 1802 treaties from the period 1942–1951 finds 165 (9.1%) with a provision for retroactive application, pp. 27–59. The doctrine of domestic jurisdiction being a "relative" matter, dependent on the state of international law, is essentially a restatement of this principle. See PCIJ: *Nationality Decrees* Case, Ser. B 4 p. 24. For other cases on retroactivity, see *Tavernier* (Recherches) pp. 103–113; *Baade* 7 JIR 1957 p. 247. The judgements of the Nürnberg and Tokio War Tribunals are generally considered an example. Retroactivity has seemed possible if the norm is argued on a *jus cogens* basis. See *Tavernier* (Recherches) pp. 157–162; *Bindschedler-Robert* (Mélanges Guggenheim) p. 186; oral argument by *Bedjaoui*, ICJ: *Western Sahara* Case, Pleadings IV pp. 492–493, 498–500. The Institute of International Law has generalized the retroactivity principle so as to apply whenever a rule relates to a class of facts and a further fact of the same class appears after the rule has come to existence, Yearbook 1975 p. 539 (it may, however, be doubted whether this is retroactivity at all, "rules" having the capacity, by definition, to apply to subsequent facts referred to in them).

[250] McWhinney (Essays Lachs) pp. 180–181.

[251] *Jessup* 22 AJIL 1928 pp. 739–740; *Tavernier* (Recherches) pp. 271–276.

[252] For a discussion of this point in the Indian arguments regarding the Goa crisis and Spanish arguments in relation to Gibraltar, see *Tavernier* (Recherches) pp. 65–68. See also oral argument by *Bedjaoui*, ICJ: *Western Sahara* Case, Pleadings IV p. 450 *et seq.*

[253] ICJ: *Western Sahara* Case, Reports 1975 p. 14 (§ 1).

[254] *Ibid.* oral argument, *Bedjaoui*, Pleadings IV pp. 489, 492.

interpreted by reference to the law in force at that period", that is in 1884.[255] This seems open for criticism as a "conservative" choice. To avoid this criticism, however, we can turn to Judge Dillard's explanation according to which the first part of the intertemporal law doctrine was used because this was suggested by the wording of the question, that is by the will of present UN community itself.[256] The Court took pains to explain its function here as that of a UN organ and went into an extensive discussion of the present law of decolonization.[257] It aimed at reconciliation: Old law was preferred but this was because the present community (and law) required it. But such reconciliation achieves no determinate priority between stability and change. Once again, these are assumed to point in the *same direction*. As a result of reading the case, we still do not know the rule – how to act in *future* case if past and present law would seem to conflict.

The dichotomy past/present law expresses the tension between original and present soverignty – for example, original and present occupation. By establishing the "critical date" at a point in time relatively close to that of its judgement in the *Eastern Greenland* (1933) and *Minquiers and Ecrehos* (1953) Cases, the Court seemed to prefer the present over the past. This solution was possible because in both cases the Court's decision was constructed on the consent, in the form of recognition or acquiescence, of *both sovereigns*. The Court expressly refrained from preferring either part of the intertemporal law doctrine.[258] Considerations relating to acquired and historic rights have been balanced as against prescription without neither having *a priori* preference. Such preference – if it needs to be made – can only be contextually constructed by reference to criteria about equity which, in one way or another, are traced back to subjective consent.[259]

These problems may be illustrated also by reference to the *South West Africa* (1966) and *Namibia* (1971) Cases. Though the cases concern

---

[255] *Ibid*. Reports 1975 pp. 38–39 (§ 79).

[256] *Dillard*, sep. op. *ibid*. pp. 123–124. The Court's "conservative" choice was criticized by Judges *Ammoun, Forster* and Judge *ad hoc Boni, ibid*. pp. 85–87, 103, 173–174.

[257] *Ibid*. pp. 29–37 (§§ 48–72).

[258] PCIJ: *Eastern Greenland* Case, Ser. A 53 p. 45. In the *Minquiers and Ecrehos* Case, Reports 1953, both Parties had made extensive reference to events dating back to the Middle Ages and agreed on the validity of the intertemporal law doctrine. The Court, however, observed that it could not draw from such ancient events any inference as to the present rights of the Parties, pp. 55, 56. The Court based British sovereignty ultimately on both British possession and French recognition thereof, pp. 59–60, 66–67. See also comment by *Baade* 7 JIR 1957 p. 244.

[259] *Brownlie* (Principles) pp. 132–133, 156–164.

treaty interpretation, they provide a good illustration of how the law can be used so as to generate opposite but equally valid outcomes in the stability/change conflict.

In the former case, the Court asked itself whether the claimants had a legal interest in the subject-matter of their claim and answered this in the negative after an extensive analysis of the mandates system as it existed under the League of Nations' period.[260] To determine the claimants' rights:

> ... the Court must place itself at the point in time when the mandates system was being instituted ... the Court must have regard to the situation as it was at that time ...[261]

In other words, the Court held that rights flowing from an international convention had to be interpreted by reference to the law in force at the time of its conclusion. By contrast, in the Namibia opinion it construed the South African mandate in view of ideas which had gained international acceptance only after the League's dismissal. The Court observed that the relevant parts of the Covenant were "evolutionary". Therefore:

> The Court must take into consideration the changes which have occurred in the supervening half-century, and its interpretation cannot remain unaffected by the subsequent development of law.[262]

The Court now held that the mandate was to be interpreted in light of present law.

This contrast is further highlighted by the manner in which the Court dealt with the "sacred trust of civilization" concept. In the *South West Africa* Case this was considered a "moral ideal" which was divested of such "specifically legal character" that it could have been creative of rights and obligations in the League.[263] In the Namibia opinion, the sacred trust was used as an "evolutionary" concept which was capable of

[260] ICJ: *South West Africa* Case, Reports 1966 p. 18 (§ 6) *et seq.*
[261] *Ibid.* p. 23 (§ 16). This is, of course, simply a restatement of the non-retroactivity principle.
[262] ICJ: *Namibia* Case, Reports 1971 p. 31 (§ 53). This principle is particularly often applied in respect of human rights instruments. See e.g. ECHR: *Tyrer* Case, Ser. A 26 pp. 15–16 (§ 31); *Marckx* Case, Ser. A 31 p. 19 (§ 41). See also joint diss. op. ECHR: *Deumeland* Case, Ser. A 100 (arguing that the principle is enshrined in the Vienna Convention of the Law of Treaties) pp. 35–36 (§ 12).
[263] ICJ: *South West Africa* Case, Reports 1966 pp. 34–35 (§§ 49–54).

association with the present law's objectives of "self-determination and independence".[264]

These conflicting outcomes are usually interpreted so that in the former case the Court preferred stability (that is, past over present), in the latter, change (that is, present over past). Depending on the critic's perspective, the Namibia Case is either seen as a healthy move away from a mistaken precedent or a political decision ignoring established law. Either one or the other contained an incorrect application of law. But these interpretations fail to understand that it is possible to argue both cases on the basis of established law because *it is that law itself which is contradictory*, both outcomes are equally correct within the system.

Many have argued that while the *South West Africa* Case was decided on the basis of original *intent* (of the drafters of the Covenant) the Namibia opinion used teleological and equitable considerations.[265] In other words, the contrast is explained by the former case manifesting a consensualist, the latter a justice-based approach. The question of the possible non-conformity of the cases with the law would then seem to depend on whether the law in fact prefers consent or justice.

But if the law really preferred consent or justice, it would seem vulnerable to the objections of being apologist or utopian. The same applies to the two cases. To be acceptable, neither can make such preference. And in fact, both avoid making it. It is thus possible to produce a contrary explanation of the contrast between them. For while the *South West Africa* Case did make express reference to original intent, such intent was construed by reference to the text of Article 22 of the Covenant. There is no study whatsoever of State intentions which would have been independent of a study of this text. Quite the contrary, the Mandates system was interpreted "having regard to the structure of the League" in what seemed like a thoroughly systemic and not a will-based argument at all.[266]

On the other hand, the Namibia opinion may be understood in thoroughly consensual light. First, the Court was careful to read its "teleological" interpretations in light of the intent of League members. The parties to the Covenant "must . . . be deemed to have accepted" the

---

[264] ICJ: *Namibia* Case, Reports 1971 p. 31 (§§ 52–53).
[265] See e.g. *Schwarzenberger* (International Law III) pp. 149 *et seq*, 176; *Bollecker* XVII AFDI 1971 pp. 287–298.
[266] ICJ: *South West Africa* Case, Reports 1966 pp. 28–29 (§ 33).

"evolutionary" character of the "sacred trust" concept.[267] Second, the Namibia opinion seems consensualist also in its effort to accommodate the views ("philosophy", writes Judge Fitzmaurice) of the present UN majority.[268]

In other words, *both cases* assume the correctness of a consensualist and a justice-based (teleological, "systemic") way of looking at the opposition past law/present law. The consensualist strand manifests itself in the way both cases seem to base themselves on the consent of original drafters and the present UN community. The justice-related strand manifests itself in the way both cases argue about texts, teleology and system.

This argumentative structure – the way both cases assume that the law makes no priority between consent and justice – renders both cases coherent and simultaneously makes them vulnerable to contrasting criticisms about which (or whose) consent is relevant and what justice says. These are the points at which the cases – and their critics – diverge. Scholars have criticized the 1966 case as it failed to give effect to the consent of present UN community and worked with a conservative theory of justice. And Judge Fitzmaurice's criticism of the 1971 case is based on the overruling of original consent in favour of an anarchic theory of justice.

But neither outcome – and neither criticism – can be preferred within the system. For this would imply that we can *know* consent or justice in an objective way – a position inadmissible under the Rule of Law. It is not the law's or the Court's preference for past or present which explains the contrast between the two cases. No such general preference exists. Which is to be preferred depends on what can be proved consensually or by recourse to justice. The contrast between the two cases is a *contrast in the interpretations of the Court of what is required by consent or justice.*

In order to make a definite preference between these interpretations ("what did the drafters really intend?", "what was the system of the

---

[267] ICJ: *Namibia* Case, Reports 1971 p. 31 (§ 53). Particular attention was given to the rejection of the idea of annexation in the negotiations which preceded the adoption of Article 22 of the Covenant, pp. 28 (§ 45), 30 (§ 50). Thus, *Bollecker* XVII AFDI 1971 argues that the "teleological" interpretation was linked with an anlysis of the subjective wills and interests of South Africa and other League members at the time, pp. 291, 296. See also *Simma* (Macdonald-Johnston: Structure and Process) p. 496.

[268] Thus Judge *Fitzmaurice*, diss. op. ICJ: *Namibia* Case, Reports 1971 criticized the opinion for interpreting the mandate in a subjective, political way by giving effect to the "philosophy" or intentions of "different organs fifty years later", p. 223.

League really like?", "what does present the UN Community really wish?", "what does 'evolution' require?" etc.) we should be able to know real consent or justice in an objective way. But such knowledge is not open to us. Ultimately, it is for this reason that the Court could prefer past as well as present and still remain within a formally coherent argument. But because both cases turn on contestable interpretations about consent and justice, both are open to challenge by somebody whose interpretations differ. The contrast between the two cases is a contrast between different interpretations of *what kind of* and *whose* consent it is that counts and *which kind* of teleology it is that is working. But these are questions to which no *legal answers* can be given. The making of a decision between claims of stability and change is always both contextual and indeterminate. It is contextual because we are able to make a preference only by looking at contextual will and justice. It is indeterminate because there exist no *legal* criteria whereby differing views about will and justice could be resolved.

6.5 Strategy of closure: custom as bilateral equity

It does not seem at all possible to establish a general custom, opposable to a State, by means of looking at general State practice and the *opinio juris*. This is so because the argument is circular. We have recourse to material practice only because there is no way to find out what the *opinio juris* is without asking the States themselves and thereby lapsing into apologism. But we cannot hold *all* material practice as binding. In order to distinguish between normative and non-normative practice we need either to have a theory of the intrinsically normative character of some actions – and become vulnerable to the objection of utopianism – or focus on the subjective meaning of the practice to the States themselves – a possibility excluded by our previous denial of it being possible to know the *opinio* independently of its manifestations in practice.

Judicial practice does not – indeed cannot – support any of these approaches in a permanent way. Sometimes it seems as if the material character of practice were preferred, sometimes the presence or absence of the *opinio juris*. Sometimes justice seems preferred, sometimes consent. But both positions will seem unjustified. Under the assumptions of the liberal doctrine of politics, neither consent nor justice can be known in an objective way.

Hence, to achieve argumentative closure, the doctrine of custom looks beyond its general theory. This takes place by two moves. First, there is the move to thinking about custom as a series of "opposabilities",[269] a set of *bilateral* relations which can be appreciated without having to take a stand on general law. Second, there is the tendency to construe the normative sense of bilateral relations in terms of equity.

6.5.1 Bilateralization

We have seen that one understanding regards custom as a "process of reciprocal interaction" in which States constantly present claims *vis-à-vis* each other and acquiesce in them. The emergence of custom is, from such perspective, "a process by which the better of two conflicting claims prevails".[270] The merit of this view seems to lie in its concreteness. The law need not be ascertained in an abstract, *erga omnes* manner. Obligation is based on a particular legal relationship which is interpreted so as to reflect an individual norm.[271] Merrills notes:

> ... opposability of particular claims is a far more significant issue than their conformity with an uncertain customary rule.[272]

Analytical mind is immediately tempted by this reduction of abstract categories into specific legal relationships.[273] Even a rapid glance at the jurisprudence of the ICJ shows that it has tended to base obligations rather on the specific relation between the disputing States than general

---

[269] The term "opposability" is derived from ICJ: *Anglo-Norwegian Fisheries* Case, Reports 1951 in which the Court (in the French text) observed that the Norwegian system of straight baselines had, on the basis of consolidation, become "opposable à tous les Etats", p. 138. Later, in the *Fisheries Jurisdiction* Cases, Reports 1974, the Court discussed the Icelandic extension of its fishery zone on the basis of whether it was "opposable" to the claimant States, p. 29 (§ 68). See further generally *Charpentier* (Reconnaissance) *passim*.

[270] *D'Amato* (Custom) p. 18. For this perspective in general, see *Strupp* 47 RCADI 1934/I pp. 317–322; *McDougal* 49 AJIL 1955 pp. 356–358; *MacGibbon* XXXIII BYIL 1957 pp. 115–117; *Wolfke* (Custom) pp. 63–65, 121–129; *Akehurst* XLVII BYIL 1974–75 p. 38; *Skubiszewski* 31 ZaöRV 1971 p. 824; *Simma* (Reziprozität) pp. 40–43. See also *Suy* (Actes) pp. 261–262; *Müller* (Vertrauensschutz) pp. 100–103. See also *Venkata Raman* (Reisman-Weston: Toward) pp. 368–371 *et seq.*

[271] *Müller* (Vertrauensschutz) points out: "Was als Recht gilt, wird infolge des Mangels an zentralen Organen der Rechtsetzung in einem weiteren Bereich von den Rechtssubjekten selbst in einem ständigen Prozess als Vereinbarung, Anerkennung, Duldung, Betätigung oder Bestreitung konkretisiert." p. 35.

[272] *Merrills* (Anatomy) p. 5.

[273] Compare *Hohfeld* (Concepts) p. 35 *et seq.* See generally *Achterberg* Rechtstheorie 1978 pp. 385 *et seq*, 398–402. See also *Akehurst* XLVII BYIL 1974–75; *Simma* (Reziprozität) p. 48 *et seq*; *Decaux* (Réciprocité) pp. 110–125.

rules. In the *Anglo-Norwegian Fisheries* Case (1951), the Court established British obligations on the basis of its "prolonged abstention" from protesting against Norway's system of delimitation.[274] In the *Right of Passage* Case (1960) the applicable norm was inferred from the Parties' past behaviour *vis-à-vis* each other.[275] And in the *South West Africa* Case (1966) the very rationale of dismissing the claims of Ethiopia and Liberia was based on interpreting the issue in terms of bilateral relations instead of being concerned with an application of rules valid *erga omnes*.[276] The question of the Applicants' *locus standi* could seem relevant only if the norms invoked were understood so as to govern bilateral instead of general relationships.[277]

---

[274] ICJ: *Anglo-Norwegian Fisheries Case*, Reports 1951 pp. 118, 138–139. The character of the Norwegian system as a historic right, as pointed out by some of the judges, did not signify any general rule to that effect, merely the opposability of the Norwegian system to the United Kingdom. See *Hackworth*, declaration, *ibid*, p. 144; *Hsu Mo*, sep. op. *ibid*, p. 154. Even Judge *Read*, dissenting, did not dispute the Court's approach, merely that the system had become opposable, *ibid*. p. 191.

[275] ICJ: *Right of Passage* Case, Reports 1960 p. 39.

[276] ICJ: *South West Africa* Case, Reports 1966 p. 54 (§ 100).

[277] A further strategy of bilateralization has occurred in connection with the way the Court has turned down applications to intervene in the proceedings to protect one's legal interest in the case in pursuance of Article 62 of the ICJ Statute. The Court has said that Article 59 of the Statute which restricts the effects of a judgement to the parties in the case already provides sufficient protection. See e.g. ICJ: *Tunisia–Libya Continental Shelf (Application of Malta for Permission to Intervene)* Case, Reports 1981 pp. 16 (§ 28) *et seq*, 20 (§ 35). *Libya–Malta Continental Shelf (Application of Italy for Permission to Intervene)* Case, Reports 1984 p. 18 (§ 28) *et seq*, 26 (§ 42). The effect of this view is, of course, that the Court defines itself unable to pronounce anything on matters of general law. For a criticism of this strategy, see e.g. *Jennings*, diss. op. *ibid*. pp. 148 *et seq*, 157–160.

That the doctrine of third party intervention immediately emerges basic issues about sovereignty, equality and consent is evident. Initially, of course, the point of Article 62 is to protect the interests and sovereignty of third States. Their rights should not be determined in a process to which they are outsiders. However, as the Court pointed out in both of the above-mentioned cases, to pronounce on the interests of the third States is tantamount to recognizing them. But if a third State can have its rights recognized in a process in which it either itself is not a party or becomes a party irrespective of the consent of the original parties, this will violate the consent of the latter and, at the same time, the "principles of reciprocity and equality of States", ICJ: *Libya–Malta Continental Shelf Case (Application of Italy for Permission to Intervene)* Reports 1984 p. 22 (§ 35). This point is stressed by *Jiménez de Aréchaga* (Festschrift Mosler) pp. 453–465. Thus, in order to protect the *original* parties, the Court has excluded intervention. To protect *third* States, it has had to refer to Article 59 of the Statute which restricts the effects of the judgement to the parties thereto. The cost has been, as dissenting judges have observed, that Article 62 and the institution of intervention have been rendered practically pointless. See *Ago*, diss. op. ICJ: *Libya–Malta*

In the *Fisheries Jurisdiction* Cases (1974) the Court's tendency to think about custom in terms of bilateral opposability was even more evident. It refrained from answering the Applicants' submission according to which Iceland's extension of its fishery zone had "no foundation in international law".[278] The matter, as the Court saw it, concerned the delimitation of the Applicants' historic rights *vis-à-vis* Iceland's preferential right. Instead of general law, the case was decided on the basis of what norms had become "opposable" between the States involved.[279]

Similarly, in the *Nuclear Tests* Cases (1974), the Applications of Australia and New Zealand seemed originally to concern the application of general law to the French nuclear weapon tests.[280] But the Court interpreted the submissions so as to aim simply at the cessation of the particular French tests, conducted in the vicinity of the Applicants' territories in the Pacific.[281] In its effort to "isolate the real issue in the case",[282] the Court construed the applicable law on the basis of the Parties' bilateral relations. Specific attention was paid to the exchanges of diplomatic correspondance between them. The final solution – that France had taken a unilateral obligation to terminate testing – was not

---

Continental Shelf Case *(Application of Italy for Permission to Intervene)* Reports 1984 pp. 115 *et seq*, 129–130; *Schwebel*, diss. op. *ibid.* p. 147: *Sette-Camara*, diss. op. *ibid.* pp. 71 *et seq*, 83–89. See also *Chinkin* 80 AJIL 1986 p. 495 *et seq*. (noting the tendency towards bilateralization and concluding that the Court's practice has made intervention "no more than a remote possibility") pp. 529–531.

[278] ICJ: *Fisheries Jurisdiction* Cases, Reports 1974 p. 6 (§ 11).

[279] *Ibid.* p. 34 (dispositif). The Court felt itself capable of discussing the issue on a bilateral basis after it had rejected the "narrow interpretation" of the applications according to which its jurisdiction would have been restricted to determining the general law on the issue. As the Court saw it, the task entrusted to it related to the "respective rights in the fishery resources" of the parties and that deciding this would require to "take into consideration all relevant elements in administering justice between the parties", *ibid.* pp. 20–22 (§§ 42–48).

[280] See especially Application instituting proceedings by the Government of Australia, 9 May 1973, ICJ: *Nuclear Tests* Cases, Pleadings I pp. 3 *et seq*, 14–15 (arguing that the tests are "not consistent with applicable rules of international law"). For the New Zealand formulation, see Application by the Government of New Zealand, *ibid.* Pleadings II pp. 3 *et seq*, 8–9 (arguing that the tests violated "New Zealand's rights under international law"). Moreover, both States also argued about the tests violating rights of all States, Australia specifically claiming that they infringed the freedom of the High Seas.

[281] ICJ: *Nuclear Tests* Cases, Reports 1974 pp. 260–263 (§ 25–30). The Court observed: "the original and ultimate objective of the Applicant (Australia) was and has remained to obtain the termination of these tests; thus its claim cannot be regarded as being a claim for a declaratory judgement", p. 263 (§ 30).

[282] *Ibid.* p. 262 (§ 29).

based on a general rule but on a certain interpretation of the bilateral relationship between France and the two Applicants.

The Court's strategy of bilateralization – its apparent neglect of the formulations of the submissions – has been the object of severe criticism. Declining to give normative effect to general human rights standards in the South West Africa judgement was controversial. In the Fisheries cases, Judge Ignacio-Pinto noted that failing to answer the Applicants' main submission, the Court:

> ... failed to perform the act of justice requested of it.[283]

In the Nuclear Tests cases, too, a strong minority held that the Court's re-interpretation of the Applications was an illegitimate way of avoiding to address the issue of whether the carrying out of the tests was in conformity with general international law or not.[284] But despite the Court's recognition of its capacity to make declaratory judgements,[285] making them is hazardous business. Giving effect to standards of non-discrimination in the *South West Africa* Case would, as the Court noted, have involved it in the midst of political controversy.[286] The same is true of the Fisheries and

---

[283] *Ignacio-Pinto*, diss. op. ICJ: *Fisheries Jurisdiction* Cases, Reports 1974 p. 36. Many other judges, too, deplored the manner in which the Court seemed to overrule the Applicants' main contention. See *ibid, Gros* diss. op, p. 148 *et seq*; *Singh*, declaration, p. 39; *Petrén*, diss. op. pp. 150–153; *Onyeama*, diss. op. p. 171. For a more sympathetic view, see *Dillard*, sep. op. pp. 55–57; *Waldock*, sep. op. p. 119. See also *Gross* (Gross: Future) pp. 756–762. He points out that the Court departed from its judicial role and acted as an *amiable compositeur* in what amounts to a political settlement, p. 757.

[284] Joint diss. op. (*Onyeama, Dillard, Jiménez de Aréchaga, Waldoc*) ICJ: *Nuclear Tests* Cases, Reports 1974 pp. 312–317; *ibid. Barwick*, diss. op. pp. 443–444. To the same effect, see *Schachter* 178 RCADI 1982/V p. 192.

[285] See e.g. ICJ: *Northern Cameroons* Case, Reports 1963 p. 37; *Nuclear Tests* Cases, Reports 1974 p. 263 (§ 30).

[286] On the submissions of Ethiopia and Liberia, see ICJ: *South West Africa* Case, Reports 1966 pp. 10–14. The Court held that the Parties' argument concerned the *erga omnes* application of the League of Nations' mandates system. It regarded that no such *erga omnes* norms had been involved in the enforcement provisions of Article 22 of the Covenant. Third States could plead only if the matter concerned some of the "special interest provisions" in the mandates – such were not in issue here, *ibid.* pp. 20–34 (§§ 10–48) and 44 (§ 80) *et seq.* The Court specifically denied the existence of *actio popul
aris* in international law, *ibid.* p. 47 (§ 88). In addition, as pointed out above, it held that the "humanitarian considerations" which had been invoked throughout the case, did not involve legal obligations which Ethiopia and Liberia could have success-fully relied upon, *ibid.* pp. 34–35 (§§ 49–54). For a contrary view, see *ibid. Jessup*, diss. op. pp. 429 *et seq*, 432–433, 441. Whether or not the case is interpreted so as to involve a denial of *actio populäris* or of the existence of general law in the matter, the point is

Nuclear Tests judgements. As the joint separate opinion in the former observed, the position of general law on fishery jurisdiction was very uncertain. No specific limit was "generally accepted".[287] Moreover, the matter was under political deliberation within the III UN Conference on the Law of the Sea.[288] Pronouncing on it would either have involved the Court in an on-going political debate or required using a rule so wide as to be virtually meaningless.[289]

In the *Nuclear Tests* Cases, the Court faced a similar dilemma. On the one hand, it would have been very difficult to hold atmospheric testing prohibited by a customary rule. All nuclear powers had conducted such tests and had never implied, nor had third States implied (by protesting, for example) that they were illegal.[290] Arguing by reference to some non-practice related principle would have involved the Court in what would have seemed like a political argument in a matter of controversy. On the other hand, holding such tests permitted would not only have impaired the Applicants' sovereign rights but would also have gone against a strong current of popular opinion in favour of prohibiting such tests and seriously affected the Court's image.[291]

Bilateralization of the law serves as a strategy to avoid the difficulties in arguing by general custom. Applying a general rule may seem like an abstract, inflexible way of dealing with international controversies,

that its argument made it possible for the Court to avoid taking a stand on an issue which – had it decided either way – would have involved it in political controversy.

[287] Joint sep. op. (*Forster, Bergson, Jiménez de Aréchaga, Singh, Ruda*) ICJ: *Fisheries Jurisdiction* Cases, Reports 1974 p. 47 and generally pp. 46–52. Similarly, *ibid. De Castro*, sep. op. pp. 89–96.

[288] *Ibid. Dillard*, sep. op. p. 56.

[289] It is relevant to note, however, that the structure of the Court's argument, despite the apparent lack of reference to "general law", still remains "ascending-descending" and that it is concerned with justifying the solution so that neither general views about the law nor the views of the parties are violated while considerations of equity, or justice, are also given effect to. Thus, Iceland's "preferential right" was based on *both* "the contemporary practice of states" generally as well as on the Applicants' explicit recognition thereof. ICJ: *Fisheries Jurisdiction* Cases, Reports 1974 pp. 25, 24–26 (§§ 55–58) and pp. 26–27 (§ 59). On the other hand, the Applicants' "historic rights" were based on their previous behaviour as well as Icelandic recognition, *ibid.* pp. 28–29 (§§ 63, 65). Thus, the solution followed the strategy of wiping material conflict away: everybody had agreed. Moreover, what everybody had agreed also corresponded to what justice seemed to require: the Court considered the solution also to reflect equitably both Icelandic and British–German fishing interests, *ibid.* pp. 26–29 (§ 59, 62, 66).

[290] *Petrén*, sep. op. ICJ: *Nuclear Tests* Cases, Reports 1974 pp. 303–306. In the same sense, see also *Franck* 69 AJIL 1975 p. 612 *et seq*; *Rasmussen* 29 GYIL 1986 pp. 264–266.

[291] *Ibid. Petrén*, sep. op. p. 306.

invariably invested with particularized issues. As the law needs anyway to be linked to the consent or interest of the disputants, it seems only natural to focus attention on what they have said or done in their relations *inter se*. The problem is, now, how to achieve distance from particular State positions.[292] After this movement towards concreteness, a movement towards normativity is needed.

6.5.2 Recourse to equity

It seemed difficult to appreciate the significance of custom's different elements – practice v. *opinio juris*, generality, duration – without a contextual evaluation. The strategy of bilateralization helps to delimit the relevant context. We have already seen that a part of sources doctrine aimed to construct the law of bilateral relations on the basis of the parties *past behaviour*. This created the problem of how past behaviour should be interpreted and surfaced the opposition between consent- and justice-based interpretations neither of which could be consistently preferred.[293]

Therefore, doctrine on custom includes past behaviour into its ascertainment of bilateral norms only as an element in the overall character of those relations. The attempt has been to construe the normative sense of bilateral relations in an overall equity. As the ICJ has pointed out, in such construction, there is no limit to the considerations which might be held as relevant.[294]

What counts, simply, is that the solution comes about as the most equitable one. The law applicable arises from a process of "balancing".[295] In the *Fisheries Jurisdiction* Cases (1974), the ICJ refrained from pronouncing on general law and explained the conflict in terms of the opposition between the Applicants' "historic" and Iceland's "preferential" rights.[296]

---

[292] Of course, such a procedure looks, from a contrasting perspective, like an attempt to depart from the judicial function into making political compromises. See e.g. the comments on the Nuclear tests judgement by *Thierry* XX AFDI 1974 pp. 291–295; *Bollecker-Stern, ibid,* p. 333.

[293] See *supra* ch. 5.

[294] ICJ: *North Sea Continental Shelf* Cases, Reports 1969 p. 50 (§ 93). In other words, the choice and evaluation of the criteria are all dictated by the overall goal of equitableness. *Tunisia–Libya Continental Shelf* Cases, Reports 1982 pp. 49 (§ 50), 59 (§ 70); *Gulf of Maine* Case, Reports 1984 pp. 312–313 (§§ 155–158).

[295] See *supra* ch. 4.5. For further review of the tendency in legal practice to integrate equity – particularized justice – in the assessment of State rights and obligations, see *Villiger* 25 Arch.VR 1987 pp. 174–201. See also the argument in *Herman* 33 ICLQ 1984 pp. 853–858.

[296] See *supra* ch. 1 n. 113, ch. 4 nn. 151–152.

What was needed, the Court noted, was the balancing of these rights *vis-à-vis* each other.[297] Neither could be used as a determining rule in itself. Though the Parties' past behaviour was not irrelevant in such balancing, it was not only past behaviour (the reciprocal recognition by the Parties of their respective claims) which determined what was equitable. The Court laid weight also on the needs of the Icelandic fishing community and the fishing interests of the Applicants. The balance between the *prima facie* rights was achieved by what was a purposive strategy to attain maximal cost-benefit effectiveness.[298]

Similarly, the *Nuclear Tests* Cases (1974) involved an attempt by the Court to reach a compromise which would safeguard all Parties' important interests. The strategy of inferring French obligation from France's own will and from a re-interpretation of the Applicants' submissions seemed to preserve the sovereign equality of all while also making the decision correspond to what seemed like the most just solution.[299]

But there are obvious difficulties in thinking about custom as bilateral equity. If there is "no limit to the considerations" that a Court might need to take into account in determining equity, then, by definition, legal rules are absent and the choice will seem dependent on the law-applier's theory of justice, that is, according to orthodox assumptions, on his subjective preference.

To avoid this, it might be argued that the construction of equity means simply the giving of effect, not to somebody's theory of justice but to the *intrinsically equitable (or just) character of the criteria used.* This is an argument which transgresses the bilateralization of custom. Many lawyers, frustrated with the indeterminacy of general custom, have suggested that the very construction of general customary law is dependent on the equitable (just) character of the practice involved or the putative norm.

Oscar Schachter, among others, has argued that whether a rule needs confirmation from State practice or *opinio juris* depends on the *value* of that rule. A norm considered essential to peace and expressing "a basic universally held moral principle" would retain its validity also against inconsistent State practice while a jurisdictionary rule, for example, "should not be maintained in the face of substantial or inconsistent

---

[297] ICJ: *Fisheries Jurisdiction* Cases, Reports 1974 pp. 30–33 (§§ 69–79).
[298] *Ibid.*   [299] See *supra* ch. 5.3. and ch. 6 at nn. 280–282.

State conduct".[300] Many practices – violations of human rights, nuclear weapon testing, space spies, wars of aggression etc. – have not been understood as permitted though many States regularly engage in them.[301] The brevity with which the ICJ justified its customary rules of non-use of force, self-defence and territorial sovereignty as custom in the *U.S. Military and Paramilitary Activities* Case (1986) points in the same direction. These were considered binding custom less because there was evidence of concurring pratice or *opinio juris* than for their intrinsically just character.

But such suggestion will, at the end of the day, point beyond the liberal doctrine of politics. For it assumes that we can *know* the just or equitable character of some forms of behaviour regardless of what States themselves think about them. It involves assuming the objectivity of a material theory of justice.

It may be argued that one need not assume a material theory of justice in order to regard many non-practice-based rules as binding. Such rules may have emerged "spontaneously", through the development of a conviction that they should be so.[302] But basing norms on some psychological consensus seems both difficult – because such consensus seems capable of objective ascertainment only through its manifestation in State practice – and also outright apologist. Accepting that the prohibition of mass-destruction weapons, or, for example, massive violations of human rights, is based on some consensus among States implies the acceptance that in a world of Nazi regimes they would not be so. There seems no way out from assuming that if such weapons or acts are illegal, their illegality results from their immoral character and not from a psychological conviction. Of course, whether these norms should be held "legal" or "moral" hinges on certain empirical assumptions about the motives which people have when acting under a conflict between "legal" and "moral" demands.[303] Without going into this

---

[300] *Schachter* 178 RCADI 1982/V p. 118. *Jenks* (Prospects) concludes his study of the practice of the ICJ in respect of custom-ascertainment as follows: "Custom as a basis of legal obligation neither can nor should be rigidly separated from general principles of law, equity, public policy and practical convenience. In judging whether the available proof of custom is sufficient it is legitimate for the Court to take into account the reasonableness and expediency of the alleged custom in the light of these other considerations." p. 264. See also *Parry* (Sources) p. 86; *Detter-Delupis* (Concept) p. 115.

[301] *Hoffmann* (Deutsch-Hoffmann: Relevance) pp. 51–52.

[302] *Bernhardt* 36 ZaöRV 1976 pp. 72–73.

[303] *Soper* (Coleman-Paul: Philosophy and Law) p. 31 *et seq.*

debate, it may be noted that presenting the available choice as one between thinking of such norms in consensual terms or leaving them "beyond" the law, then, on doctrine's own assumptions, their validity becomes a matter of subjective opinion.

But often doctrine does attempt to base custom on the justness or equitableness of certain acts. This leads it into stressing the "creative" aspects of custom-ascertainment. Bleckmann, for example, observes that there are no hard and fast rules on what counts as relevant "practice". This is a "Problem der juristischen Wertung"[304] – ascertaining and preferring general interest to particular interests.[305] But this makes "general interest", as understood by a judge, simply *jus cogens*. Clearly, such suggestion cannot be accepted because it both overrides individual States' rights and does this by reference to evaluative calculations which cannot be pressed into the Rule of Law at all.

Thus many lawyers have come to despair. They point out that custom-ascertainment is not a process in which pre-existing rules are ascertained at all. The meaning of State behaviour – whether it discloses a norm or not – cannot be established in an objective fashion. What is involved is legislative *construction* by the judge.[306] Haggenmacher observes:

> Le juge ne se trouve jamais devant les phénomenes saisissables à l'état pur et qu'il se bornerait à enregistrer. La régularité d'un comportement, bien qu'elle pose en général pour la donnée primordiale et la base d'une coutume, n'existe pas en elle-même. Elle est le produit d'un découpage artificiel, d'un arrangement plus ou moins arbitraire fait en retrospective dans un tissu de faits de tous ordres. Il y a toujours choix et mis en perspective de données plus ou moins disparates, entre lesquelles on établit une certaine logique . . .[307]

That *lex lata* and *lex ferenda* are indistinguishable in this way has often been conceded. Discussing codification and progressive development, the ILC concluded that it is impossible to maintain a strict distinction

---

[304] *Bleckmann* (Grundprobleme) p. 113; *idem* (Festschrift Mosler) pp. 89 *et seq*, 99–100.

[305] *Idem* (Grundprobleme) pp. 113–115. Likewise, *Unger* (Völkergewohnheitsrecht) points out that the process of ascertaining the *opinio juris* involves a definite weighing of the different State views against each other in order to arrive at a normative (non-subjective) *communis opinio*, pp. 40–41, *passim*.

[306] See e.g. *Kopelmanas* XVIII BYIL 1937 pp. 141–143; *Jenks* (Prospects) p. 263; *Sørensen* (Sources) p. 110; *idem* 101 RCADI 1960/III p. 51; *Sur* (L'interprétation) pp. 188–191. See also *Carty* (Decay) pp. 3–4.

[307] *Haggenmacher* 90 RGDIP 1986 p. 115.

between the two.[308] This is accepted wisdom among doctrine as well.[309] Custom-identification is often understood to be indissociable from custom-creation. This is not a simple matter of technique, an unfortunate inability to keep separate the legislative and judicial tasks. Each restatement is also a reformulation, it solves old problems, gives rise to new ones.[310] The very act of codifying customs creates normative consequences which go further than the anterior, uncodified custom.

Similarly, the ascertainment of custom in legal disputes involves giving normative meaning to separate and fragmentary State actions. This involves not only simple description of how States have behaved or what they have "thought". It contains assessments and evaluations which sometimes give binding character to actions which have not been supported by widespread or lengthy practice and which simply overrule some international actors' self-understandings about which rules are normative and which are not.[311] This is why States and scholars are able to argue for contradictory rules by the same facts. Facts or beliefs

[308] Report to the General Assembly, YILC 1956 vol. II p. 256.

[309] See e.g. *Thirlway* (Customary Law) p. 18; *Villiger* (Custom) p. 123; *Virally* (Mélanges Reuter) pp. 522–523; *Jennings* (Progress) pp. 30–31; *Onuf* (Falk-Kratochwil-Mendlowitz) pp. 265–276.

[310] See further *Koskenniemi* XVIII Oikeustiede-Jurisprudentia 1985 pp. 152–156.

[311] *Haggenmacher* 90 RGDIP 1986 pp. 115–116. That State behaviour is inevitably looked at from the point of view of an anterior conceptual system is, of course, what I discussed in chapter 4 under "constructivism". A further example of how State practice is appreciated (custom/not custom) only after an evaluation of the character of that practice is provided by the law of sovereign immunity. Thus, in *Trendtex v. Central Bank of Nigeria* Case (Ct. of Appeal) 64 ILR 1983, Lord Denning first noted the traditional rule according to which international law rests on a consensus between States. But he went on to note that in many matters – and specifically in matters of State immunity – there is no consensus at all. But this does not mean that there would be no rule on the subject. It just shows States have different views about its content. What a Court dealing with such a problem must do is to seek "guidance from the decisions of other countries, from the jurists who have studied the problem, from treaties and conventions and, above all, define (MK) the rule in terms which are consonant with justice rather than adverse to it", pp. 126–127. In other words, it is possible to decide hard cases on the basis of non-written (customary) rules only when we first know what standards allow the isolation of certain practice as "normative" and permit the exclusion of deviating ones. We have seen that such constructivism in fact dominates the field on non-written law. In addition to examples given earlier, we may note that in respect of the arbitral practice concerning remedies for the breach of international obligations, for example, it has been pointed out that there has been no noticeable difference between cases in which the tribunals have been authorized to decide *ex aequo et bono* and cases where no such authorization has been given. The customary law of remedies coalesces with what seems equitable, *Gray* (Judicial Remedies) pp. 10–11.

do not determine what is normative about them. This is done by the conceptual apparatus from which they are perceived.

Custom-ascertainment does involve the identification and balancing of evaluative criteria. These may be the liberty of the High Seas and the territoriality of jurisdiction, as in the *Lotus* Case, or the freedom of navigation and the security of the coastal State as in the *Corfu Channel* Case, or the exclusivity of territorial jurisdiction and the right to exercise protection as in the *Right of Passage* Case, and so on.[312] For Haggenmacher, such elements work in the manner of "principles" which a Court has to evaluate against each other.[313] De Visscher, too, argues that custom-identification has necessarily to do with an evaluation of the interests at stake:

> Il s'agit donc ici non pas seulement de considérer les régularités obser-
> vées, mais de les évaluer en fonction des impératifs moraux et sociaux qui
> guident l'effort humain dans sa poursuite d'une organisation meilleure
> du droit.[314]

But such instrumentalism is not really reconcilable with the Rule of Law. As long as "impératifs moraux" or the character of ideal social organization remain matters of political dispute, and we possess no metatheory by which to balance conflicting principles, deciding cases on such basis will appear like illegitimate subjectivism.

To sum up, conventional doctrine of custom seems either circular or empty. The two-element theory refers constantly from one element to the other without being able to remain in either. The theory of custom as equity contains no criteria for the evaluation of legal relationships. This consequence remains hidden as long as custom is thought in terms of "opposabilities" in which the States' conduct is interpreted so as to

---

[312] A further instructive case is the *Barcelona Traction* Case, Reports 1970 in which the ICJ was concerned with finding out whether, *inter alia*, customary law provided for a remedy to the shareholders of a company whose national State had not taken diplomatic action against legislative measures in the host State. The Court first observed the indeterminacy of State practice on this point, p. 40 (§ 63). It then went on to discuss the case as one opposing shareholder interests with the interest of "security and stability" in international commercial contracts and ended up favouring the latter. The applicant (Belgium, representing the shareholders) did not have *jus standi* because granting it "would be contrary to the stability which is the object of international law to establish in international relations", p. 50 (§ 97).

[313] *Haggenmacher* 90 RGDIP 1986 pp. 118–124.

[314] *De Visscher* (Problèmes) pp. 221, 237–242 (emphasizing the judge's "creative" role in custom construction).

render the same norm. But this strategy will remain vulnerable to the criticism against purely consensual or non-consensual interpretations. An ultimate strategy of hiding indeterminacy consists in thinking of customary norms as procedural ones, that is, as only indicating certain procedures whereby States should reach agreement among themselves.[315] However, this strategy downplays the reality of conflict and fails to indicate to the States themselves how their conflict should be settled – and surely settling conflicts is what we understand law to exist for.

---

[315] Thus, the ICJ has frequently constructed the applicable norm so as to refer only to further negotiations between the Parties ("with a view to reach an agreement"). See ICJ: *North Sea Continental Shelf Cases*, Reports 1969 p. 46 (§ 85); *Gulf of Maine Case*, Reports 1984 pp. 292, 299 (§§ 87–90, 112.1.) In the *Fisheries Jurisdiction Cases*, Reports 1974, the Court observed that the duty to negotiate on the extent of the parties' fishery limits was the "most appropriate method" for drawing such limits and followed "from the very nature of the respective rights of the Parties", pp. 31, 33 (§§ 73, 75). In the *Interpretation of the Agreement between Egypt and the WHO*, Reports 1980, the Court founded the obligation to negotiate the conditions of the transfer of the WHO regional office in Alexandria on the "contractual" nature of the relationship between Egypt and the WHO, pp. 93, 95–96 (§§ 43, 49). In each case, the Court thought the rule to refer simply to further negotiations while the conditions or "criteria" to be taken account of were left to the determination of the parties (who were directed to seek an equitable result, a political balance).

A similar turn to procedure has been evidenced in the ILC project on "liability for injurious consequences of acts not prohibited by international law". As the topic has been defined, it concerns all that vast area of inter-State conduct which is *not* governed by prohibitory rules (i.e. the State's "private realm" under the *Lotus* Principle, see *supra* ch. 4.4.). The Special Rapporteurs have suggested that even in such areas States might be held under an obligation to "cooperate" and to establish "regimes" for the prevention and settlement of conflicts. For "The first aim of the present topic is to induce States that foresee a problem of transboundary harm to establish a régime ... The second aim ... is to provide a method of settlement ..." *Quentin-Baxter*, Fourth Report, YILC 1983 vol. II/I p. 221 (§ 69). The suggested rule (bordering somewhere between *lex lata* and *lex ferenda*) 1) suggests further to States that they establish regimes of information-cooperation-negotiation-reparation; 2) in the absence of agreed regimes, refers to negotiation with a list of guidelines on how to achieve a "balance of interests". See *Quentin-Baxter*, Third Report (Schematic Outline) YILC 1982 vol. II/I pp. 62–64 and *Barboza* Second Report, A/CN.4/402, 13 May 1986, (on point 1) pp. 8–10, 16–21 (§§ 14–20, 34–41); (on point 2) pp. 21–25 (§§ 42–47).

Variations of world order: the structure of international legal argument

According to the social conception, law is a social phenomenon, not a set of abstract, unhistorical maxims of natural justice. It is linked to concrete conditions of social life – indeed, it reflects an underlying social reality.[1] But legal concepts and categories are not given by society in any automatic way. "Society" is not simply a lot of people (or States) behaving but includes the ideas through which people (and States) look at what they are doing. Therefore the law, too, must bear a connection to those ideas. So, even as it reflects the social context, it also reflects normative views about that context. In other words, law implies an interpretation of what society is like now and what should be done in order to make it better. To enact consumer protection legislation, for example, implies a social theory, an interpretation according to which, unless legislation were enacted, society's natural condition would overrule consumer interests in some unacceptable fashion.

So, it should be possible to read the law "backwards" in order to reveal the interpretation which it carries of the world in which we live. In this chapter I propose to do just that. I shall look at international law in order to see what kind of an understanding it mediates of present international society and what type of world order it aims to achieve. As Roberto Unger has pointed out, the idea that law embodies a set of authoritative concepts and categories which can be used to settle social conflict

---

[1] Common to modern criticisms of early and professional naturalism is that these are portrayed to work with a fixed, unchanging law, unresponsive to variations in social context. Naturalism, it is argued, defined law "in terms of trans-empirical entities rather than features of social process". It is "contrasted with modern methods of scientific inquiry". *Lasswell-McDougal* (Essays Rao) pp. 72–76. But naturalists quickly retort that this completely miscasts traditional jusnaturalism. It was not only that many of its maxims could be derived only by attempting to fully grasp the (objective) character of the present but its whole system of practical reason was directed towards producing right action having regard to time and place. See e.g. *Finnis* (Natural Law) pp. 23–55; *Strauss* (Natural Right) (for a conception of changing, history-related natural law) pp. 120–164; *Tolonen* (Luonto) pp. 10–14, 73 *et seq*, 246–266.

without having to refer to political ideals implies that law itself sustains some defensible and coherent scheme of human association.[2] The experience which we have countered in central realms of doctrine, however, tends to suggest otherwise. For if it is the case that conflict-solution cannot coherently be undertaken without going beyond the available legal concepts and categories then the legal project seems in some relevant sense faulted or at least incomplete.

I shall begin the chapter by outlining two perspectives on world order – two competing understandings of the character of present international society and what should be done to make it more acceptable. I shall argue that the law lacks a principle for choosing either one and therefore contains both within itself. The accommodation of the two understandings is made possible by the *formal* character of legal concepts and categories. But this formality makes the law fail as a normative project (7.1). I shall illustrate this by reference to examples from four doctrinal fields (7.2). Finally, I shall analyse the logic of international legal argument as it moves so as to accommodate the two projects in itself and becomes manipulable so as to support conflicting solutions to normative problems.

7.1 The sense of the legal project: towards community or independence?

We have seen that the liberal doctrine of politics examined society by assuming a tension between individual freedom and communal order and took for itself the task of reconciling the two. It could not fully prefer community because that would have overruled individual rights and freedoms in an unacceptable way. It could not fully prefer individual freedom because that would have made social life impossible. It reconciled the two by thinking of one in terms of the other. A legitimate community was one which could be referred back to uncoerced individual choice. Enforcible freedoms were those which the community chose to regard as legal rights.[3] This argumentative structure allowed the liberal to defend liberal society in both individualistic and communitarian terms.

---

[2] *Unger* (Critical) pp. 2, 5–8.
[3] That the unresolved tension between community/individuality lies at the heart of liberal political theory is a critics' pet theme. See e.g. the seminal article by *Kennedy* 28 Buffalo L. R. 1979 pp. 205 *et seq*, 211–221. He argues that the contradiction between altruism and individualism is insoluble. Altruism cannot be preferred because there are no objective

A similar strategy characterizes the international legal project. It describes social life among States alternatively in terms of community and autonomy. These descriptions support conflicting demands for freedom and order. In the one case, community is interpreted as negative collectivism and autonomy (independence, self-determination) is presented as the normative goal. In the other, autonomy is interpreted as negative egoism and community (integration, solidarity) as what the law should aim at. Neither community nor autonomy can be exclusive goals. To think of community as the ultimate goal seems utopian: as there is no agreement on the character of a desirable community, attempts to impose it seem like imperialism in disguise. To think of autonomy as the normative aim seems apologist: it strengthens the absolutist claims of national power-elites and supports their pursuits at international dominance.

These two dangers are transformed into controlling conditions for international legal argument. They can be avoided only if arguments become such as to contain the ideals of community and autonomy *both* within themselves so that they can exclude the appearance of Mr Hyde in each other.[4] An acceptable world order seems to be one which can construct community without falling into totalitarianism and which provides for autonomy without degenerating into furthering egoism.

The communitarian project reflects an understanding of the present as an intolerable anarchy of egoistic sovereignties. Without law, communal order among States would be impossible. So, the law is needed to

values. A would-be altruist needs to fall back on individualism as the totalitarianism of assuming there to be objective values seems more unacceptable than it. But individualism cannot, either, be preferred because it is incapable of generating social order or any generally applicable project for a just society. An individualist with a social project needs to build on altruistic premises. Yet, not even a balance seems possible because this would require a metatheory of values which does not, and indeed cannot, exist in a system exhaustively dictated by the individualism/altruism opposition. *Idem* Harvard L. R. 1976 pp. 1775–1776. See also generally *ibid.* pp. 1713–1725. On the use of this "fundamental contradiction" as a critical theme, see further *Michelmas* Nomos XXVIII pp. 73–82; *Hunt* 6 Oxford JLS 1986 pp. 20–24; *Kelman* (Guide) pp. 15–113.

[4] It is easy to see this strategy at work within the UN Charter. On the one hand, the Organization is portrayed as the communitarian effort *par excellence*; the Preamble affirms that it has been set up to "establish conditions under which justice and respect for ... obligations" would reign. Peace, security and common interests are iterated. On the other hand, the Organization is based on the principle of sovereign equality and "nothing in the Charter shall authorize the UN to intervene in matters which are essentially within the domestic jurisdction of the State" (Art. 2(2), 2(7)). Throughout, the Charter seeks to affirm communitarian justice as well as sovereignty and self-determination.

impose community. This project emerges in at least three standard forms. First, there is what Lauterpacht would call the "Grotian tradition in international law"[5] although it goes back to the writings of the Spanish theologists[6] and even further to Stoic philosophy.[7] This approach sees the pre-legal world already vested with a normative project (a higher law, natural reason etc.) which it is the task of the law to express and enforce. If one believes there to be such a thing as moral truth then that truth must be universally valid and in this sense offer a point of view from which the law's project can only be a communitarian one.[8]

Being sceptical about objective values, however, most modern lawyers pursue another communitarian approach. They aim to combat national egoism by referring to the factual – political, economic, cultural or ecological – interdependence between States.[9] This is taken to admit a normative conclusion:

> Humanity today, taking into consideration the whole world, knows that 'one world' has become the imperative of survival.[10]

Much of what I have called "idealism" – Judge Alvarez' work being the prime example – encapsulates such an approach.[11] It, too, starts from a negative experience of autonomy as egoism and proceeds so as to compel normative order by referring to norms "naturally" given by the needs of interdependence.

---

[5] *Lauterpacht* XXIII BYIL 1946 pp. 19–21, *passim*. See also *Schiffer* (Legal Community) pp. 30–48.

[6] See e.g. *Suarez* (Tractatus) Bk II, ch. 19 (pp. 341–350). But see also *Brierly* (Basis of Obligation) pp. 358–365; *Hinsley* (Sovereignty) pp. 187–194.

[7] For a brief discussion, see *Parkinson* (Philosophy) pp. 10–14.

[8] This, of course, is *Verdross's* perspective on international law, see e.g. (Einheit) p. 119 *et seq* and *passim*. See further *Sauer* (Souveränität) p. 93 *et seq*. For recent constructions, see e.g. *Mayall* (Donelan: Reason) pp. 122–141; *Frost* (Normative) p. 120 *et seq*.

[9] In fact, the interdependence argument has a longer history than it is usually realized. It is found in *Suarez* (Selections) Bk II, ch. XIX.9 (p. 349). It is one of the constitutive assumptions behind 19th century professionalism. See *supra* ch. 2.3. For a good example, see also *Reeves* 3 RCADI 1924/II pp. 72 *et seq*, 78–82. As this argument has it, problems of change implicit in industrialization are solvable only by joint rule. See e.g. *Fitzmaurice* (IIL 1973) p. 260; *Lauterpacht* (International Law I) pp. 29–30. For a review, see *Brewin* (Mayall: Community) p. 46. The argument is common in socialist as well as Third-World legal rhetoric. See e.g. *Tunkin* (Mélanges Chaumont) p. 543; *Bedjaoui* (New International Economic Order) p. 245 *et seq*.

[10] *Röling* (Expanded World) p. 6. See also e.g. *Anand* 197 RCADI 1986/II pp. 17–20.

[11] See *supra* ch. 3.3.4.

A third communitarian strategy attacks chauvinism by some, often implicit, argument concerning the universality of human nature, culture, socio-economic deep-structure or interests.[12] Writers refer to a unifying "conscience universelle",[13] or a legal logic which compels a harmonious perspective from which all States appear as legal subjects, vested with equal rights and duties.[14] The Friendly Relations Declaration, passed by the UN General Assembly in 1970 is explicit:

> All States enjoy sovereign equality. They have equal rights and duties and are equal members of the international community.[15]

The three views speak about *value, interest* and *nature*. Each occupies a descending perspective: they look at international social life from the

---

[12] See further *Bull* (Anarchical) pp. 65–74; *Mayall* (Donelan: Reason) pp. 133–135.

[13] A good example is provided by *Duguit*'s critical individualism. For him, the idea of the State as a juristic person is metaphysical and therefore lacks objective foundation. (Traité I) p. 393 *et seq.* An objective, legal conception of international law is not something existing between such fictions but between individuals. The collective consciousness of individuals is the source of law, municipal as well as international. At the constitutive (pre-legal) level this consciousness manifests itself as a sentiment of social and moral solidarity, *ibid.* pp. 41, 45, 47–56. This is then transformed into a collective consciousness about the existence of sanction – in international law an "intersocial reaction", manifested, for example, in the acts of the victorious powers at the end of the First World War, in particular the establishment of the League of Nations, *ibid.* pp. 102, 99–110, 559–564. See also *Krabbe* 13 RCADI 1926/III pp. 576–581; *Stammler* (Lehrbuch) pp. 281–285.

[14] Though often criticized as lacking a communitarian perspective, positivism by no means always tends towards individualism, See, in particular, *Kelsen* (Souveränität) p. 102 *et seq; idem* (Principles) pp. 569–580. See also *idem* 18 ZaöRV 1958 in which he points out that both monistic constructions imply a communitarian outlook – the primacy of international law implying pacific and the primacy of municipal law implying imperialistic communitarianism, pp. 244–246. His strong preference for the former has a natural consequence in his doctrine of reprisals and war as community sanction (even when carried out by a single State). See e.g. *idem* (Law and Peace) p. 57; (Principles) pp. 19–39. Another consequence is his view that international law's "essential function" is to *delimit* national jurisdiction. See *idem* (Principles) p. 307 *et seq.* For a recent universalist conception, resembling Kelsen's, see *Carreau* (Droit international) pp. 41–61. For many, the very idea of international law implies the existence of a community. See e.g. *Oppenheim* (International Law I) pp. 8–13; *Verdross* (Verfassung) pp. 3–9; *Suontausta* (Souveraineté) p. 22; *Brierly* (Law of Nations) p. 41; *Mosler* 36 ZaöRV 1976 pp. 11–14.

[15] UNGA Res. 2625 (XXV) 24 October 1970, sect. 6. Proponents of the New International Economic Order, in particular, usually regard that there is, behind that project: "une autre conception de la société internationale reposant sur d'autres principes: la société internationale est une communauté des peuples unie par un objectif commun: la lutte pour le développement contre la misère et les inégalités", *Borella* (Mélanges Chaumont) p. 81.

conceptual matrix provided by the community/autonomy opposition and appear to prefer the former: common values override individual policies, common interests override individual wants, human nature is social, not individualistic.[16] But each argument seems difficult to sustain. Firstly, of course, values appear subjective.[17] Secondly, no such common interests seem to exist which could be distinguished from the interests of individual States.[18] Thirdly, there is no immediate perception of what human nature is. Views on this are matters of convention. To think otherwise would be to engage in nostalgic utopias.[19]

Moreover, each descending argument is threatening. As values are subjective, arguments from a natural justice, common interests or nature seem like imperialism in disguise. To speak of the world as a

---

[16] Many international lawyers have stressed the law's role in establishing conditions for a positive world community. For a concise view, see *Schiffer* (Legal Community) p. 99 *et seq.* For an influential work, see *Jenks* (Common Law) *passim*, and esp. pp. 174–176. (For criticism, see *Stone* (Visions) pp. 15–19.) For other communitarian projects, emphasizing the role of law and international institutions, *Friedmann* (Changing) esp. pp. 297–381; *Henkin* (How) pp. 314–319. International blueprint movements, such as the "World Peace Through Law" and the Princeton-based "World Order Models Project" have had remarkably little success. The former's attempt to reform the UN into world government has seemed utopian while the latter's liberal-progressive orientation has remained without a credible, consistent programme. See generally *Clark-Sohn* (World Peace); *Falk-Kim-Mendlowitz* (Toward) pp. 1–9 and 147 *et seq*; *Folk* (Reisman-Weston: Toward) pp. 150–151, 152–161. See also *Ferencz* (Common Sense), esp. p. 43 *et seq.*

[17] See e.g. *Verzijl* (I) pp. 348–359. See also *Nardin* (Law, Morality) arguing against a "purposive" conception of international society. For him, international society can only be based on a "practical" conception which provides the formal-procedural (and in that sense objective) framework within which (essentially subjective) purposes (i.e. politics) can be pursued, pp. 3–24 and *passim*.

[18] Thus *Bentham* (Introduction to the Principles of Morals and Legislation, Works I): "The community is a fictitious *body*, composed of individual persons who are considered as constituting as it were its *members*. The interest of the community then is what? – the sum of the interests of the several members who compose it", p. 2. This is readily recognized by *Bleckmann* (Grundprobleme) pp. 81–82, 285. For the impossibility to argue consistently from common (public) interests, dissociable from individual ones, under liberalism, see *Levine* (Liberal Democracy) pp. 62–70, 117–118; *Unger* (Knowledge) pp. 81–83.

[19] The problem is that an "internal aspect" is needed and this may not provide a very communitarian outlook. See e.g. *Pleydell* (Mayall: Community) pp. 167–181; *Vincent* (Non-intervention) makes this point by stressing the natural separation of national communities through the overriding loyalty these receive from their citizens, p. 375. For the impossiblity to argue normatively about natural essences under liberalism, see *Unger* (Knowledge) pp. 31–33, 79–80.

community seems, at best, a moralist fiction. Because subjective, it tends to degenerate into an outright harmful totalitarianism: Who would prevent the communitarian myth from turning into a negative utopia?[20] Reference to a natural solidarity is question-begging. For "il y a la solidarité du lion et l'antilope, ou encore celle du maître et l'esclave".[21] Certainly, developing or socialist States view with suspicion Western-liberal internationalism which aims to tear down the same national barriers which those States have only recently succeeded to establish against Western influence.[22] From this perspective, the law's purpose is not to express controversial ideas about morality, common interests or the nature of international law or relations but to protect self-determination, national identity and the pursuance of domestic policies.[23]

Individualistic approaches to world order describe the present by emphasizing the absence of common values or interests in international life.[24] They stress the importance of differences between States and see community simply as the totalitarianism of the powerful. For this

---

[20] *Hayek* (Road to Serfdom) argues that attempts to introduce centralized planning in international economy "cannot be anything but a naked rule of force", pp. 165, 164–172. See also the criticism in *Vincent* (Non-intervention) pp. 294–303, 362–375 and *Weil* 77 AJIL 1983 (against the idea of the UN General Assembly "representing" mankind) p. 441.

[21] *Le Fur* 54 RCADI 1935/IV p. 83.

[22] Tunkin (Theory) pp. 255–256, 366–377. For criticisms of internationalism as a new form of Western imperialism, see *Bedjaoui* (New International Economic Order) pp. 228–230; idem (Festschrift Abendroth) pp. 67–76; *Ghozali* (Mélanges Chaumont) pp. 300–301. See also *Tieya* (Macdonald-Johnston: Structure and Process) pp. 968–969; *Bull* (Anarchical Society) pp. 257–281.

[23] See especially *Corbett* (Law and Society) attributing lack of community among States on the lack of social solidarity, manifested in the absence of international coercive organization, pp. 3–15, 36–52, 259 et seq. To the same effect, see *Landheer* (Sociology) pp. 22–25, 72–73, 82–83; *Fitzmaurice* (IIL1973) pp. 305–307. This view does not abstract itself from making moral claims. Its insistence on national self-reliance and freedom to decide national questions by the State itself implies a moral view which values independence over the (negative) utopia of community (totalitarianism). *Vincent* (Non-intervention) notes: ". . . those who first expounded the doctrine of non-intervention thought it primarily as a principle of justice either arising from or being part of the doctrine of fundamental rights of states", p. 344. See also *Kaufmann* 54 RCADI 1935/IV pp. 325–327, 335–336, 338–341, 348 et seq.

[24] *Strupp* 47 RCADI 1934/I ("international community" simply a metaphorical way to refer to what States will) p. 301 and passim. See further *De Visscher* (Theory) arguing that international order lacks the character of "true" community as the common good is indistinguishable from the good of States, pp. 88–100. To the same effect, see *Fawcett* (Law and Power) pp. 21–22. See also *Bozeman*'s pessimistic conclusions (Multicultural) pp. 180–186 and passim, and *Stone*'s argument about the illusory character of interdependence (Visions) pp. 4–9, 10 and passim.

approach, the communitarian project – however well-meaning – will fail as it is based on a mistaken characterization of the conditions of world order.

According to the individualist approach, totalitarianism can be avoided only by laying stress on the ultimate freedom of the State to decide whether to participate in communal activity or not. It stresses that a beneficial international order must be based on freely concluded cooperative arrangements in which States can realize their enlightened self-interests. The law should not impose community on States but enable them to create one. International organizations, for example, should not be seen as organs of some fictitious community but as cooperative arrangements whereby power policy is directed into peaceful channels.[25]

The strength of this argument lies in the inability of the communitarian vision to prove its assumed values, interests or nature. For if no-one can know these in an objective way, there is no justification to claim that the law should impose them on States. True enough, the individualist will say, there is need for order – but such order can avoid becoming a threat to State autonomy only if it is based on coordinative action between States themselves.

The latter – ascending – approach, however, tends likewise to be threatening. In its insistence on the absence of common values it fails to explain why States should make these cooperative arrangements in the first place or remain bound by the arrangements they have made if calculations of self-interest do not support this. If States are essentially individualistic and have the right to be so will they not undertake cooperation only in order to increase domination? To argue – as a

---

[25] There are two opposing perceptions about the character of international organizations. On one ("legalistic") interpretation, these constitute the rudiments of international social organization and the move towards institutions is a movement from natural (anarchical) liberty into society. Thus *Mosler* (International Society) argues that: "... the increasing number of international organizations have come to play such an important and permanent part in international relations that they now form a kind of superstructure over and above the society of States", p. 175. See also *supra* n. 16 and ch. 3.3.4. For a contrasting interpretation, these organizations only reproduce national antagonisms (and in particular the East-West rift) in another context. See e.g. *Schwarzenberger* (Frontiers) pp. 148–163; *Robinson* 94 RCADI 1958/II pp. 514–530, 560–581, *passim*; *Franck* (Nation against Nation) *passim*; *Arangio-Ruiz* (Friendly Relations) pp. 228–233 and passim; *Tunkin* (Theory) pp. 305 *et seq*, 344–357; *Touret* 77 RGDIP 1973 pp. 160–161; *Hoffmann* (Deutsch-Hoffmann: Relevance) pp. 49–51. See also *de Lacharrière* (Mélanges Chaumont) p. 372.

"realist" must, unless he has become a sceptic – that cooperative action will in the end best enhance international order is to move away from this position into assuming that there *do* exist extralegal forces of inter-dependence or history which bind States together and explain why a *bellum omnium* does not necessarily have to prevail between them.[26] To avoid the conclusion that anarchy is inevitable – that is, to construct a meaningful legal project in the first place – the individualist needs to assume that the protection of self-determination and independence also best enhances the general interest – a position which will reveal itself to be a descending, communitarian one.

This conclusion is parallelled by the communitarian lawyer's ultimate inability to explain why his postulated community would avoid becom-ing a negative utopia otherwise than by referring back to freely concluded agreements between States.[27] By basing community on agree-ment, however, he will occupy the same place as his initial opponent. He will need to assume that the existence of free and individualistic States with a given right to make a social order of their liking is prior to any community between them.

Standard discourse about world order constantly projects an opposi-tion between the two views I have outlined. It is expressed in the tendency to group international lawyers into utopians and deniers, for example.[28] It is present in the distinction between a law of subordination and a law of coordination, or a law of common ends and a law of procedure.[29] It is transformed into the metaphors of international law as a "vertical" or a "horizontal" system and in the distinctions between

[26] This is *Tunkin*'s (Theory) strategy. The contractual basis of international law does not threaten the system as "sovereignty" is interpreted as a healthy moral principle which corresponds to the constraining "laws of societal development", pp. 305 *et seq*, 319–321. Similarly *Bedjaoui* (New International Economic Order) p. 245 *et seq*. Others, too have pointed out that one cannot really start the system from the existence of individual States without assuming the existence of prior rules which define "statehood" and give it normative significance. See e.g. *Kelsen* (Souveränität) pp. 314–319; *Huber* (Grundlagen) pp. 48–49 and *supra* ch. 4.

[27] *Jessup*'s (Modern) dilemma is illustrative. Throughout his constructive work he stresses that "the acceptance of the hypothesis of community interest" is necessary. Yet, he must concede that whatever this is can only be decided by the States themselves, pp. 135, 2, 12, 17, 154–156. Ultimately, all depends on their good will (and it is doubtful whether he is entitled to assume the presence of such good will, in view of the justifications for his criticisms of sovereignty).

[28] See e.g. *Lachs* (Teacher) pp. 13–28.

[29] The idea of international law as a law of coordination was a perfectly logical con-sequence of the breakthrough of the liberal doctrine of politics. On the one hand, it

international/transnational; world law/inter-State law; Charter system/ Westphalia system etc.[30]

As the persistence of these dichotomies – and the corresponding arguments – suggests, neither of the polar opposites occupies a definite superiority *vis-à-vis* the other. Each seems defensible only if it receives support from its opposite: How can competences be allocated or boundaries established in a "horizontal system" without the existence of "vertical" criteria to which States would have to be bound? Or, conversely, how could such values exist or at least become known in any other way than through "horizontal" or "coordinated" State action? And so on.[31]

The inability to establish definite priority between the projects for community and autonomy is reflected in the paradoxical characterization of the international world as an "anarchical society".[32] The international theorist moves happily from the corner in which he argues about the inevitability of the division of the world into separate States into the corner in which he argues about world community, world economics or the need of interdependence.[33]

seemed impossible to imagine authorities or standards superior to the individual State and its consent. On the other hand, the Rule of Law could not be simply rejected. The idea of law as procedural "coordination" seemed to provide for the latter while still not violating the former. See e.g. *Jellinek* (rechtliche Natur) *passim*; *Kaufmann* (Wesen) p. 130 *et seq*. For the immensely popular metaphorical opposition between coordination/ subordination, see e.g. *Friedmann* 127 RCADI 1969/II pp. 58–50; *Merrills* (Anatomy) pp. 41–42; *Reuter* (Droit international public) p. 13–29; *Bull* (Anarchical Society) pp. 69–71; *Cassese* (Divided) pp. 30–32, 396–407 and *passim*; *Menzel-Ipsen* (Völkerrecht) pp. 40–41; *Schwarzenberger* (Frontiers) pp. 13–16, 29–36; *Castberg* 138 RCADI 1973/I pp. 11–12; *Suontausta* (Souveraineté) pp. 24–34; *Brierly* (Law of Nations) p. 46; *Bleckmann* (Grundprobleme) pp. 270–278. For critical views over the distinction, see *Lauterpacht* (Function) pp. 412–438; *de Lacharrière* (Mélanges Chaumont) pp. 368–381. See also the discussion in *Dupuy* (Communauté) pp. 17–28.

30 For an influential discussion of the opposition between "Westphalia" and "Charter" systems, see *Falk* (Falk-Black: Future) p. 43 *et seq*.

31 See e.g. *Lauterpacht* (Function) pp. 407–420; *Trelles* 43 RCADI 1933/I pp. 403–405; *Nardin* (Law, Morality) pp. 36–37.

32 *Bull* (Anarchical Society). See also *Nardin* (Law, Morality) (explaining anarchism – "absence of Government", not "absence of rule" – as compatible with society) pp. 37–42.

33 For discussion, see *Donelan* (Donelan: Reason) pp. 18–19, 90–91; *Wight* (Butterfield-Wight: Diplomatic Investigations) pp. 92–102; *Manning* (Nature) pp. 7–8. For an early account of this dichotomous manner of conceptualizing international relations, see *Lorimer* (Droit) pp. 11–12. For a review, see *Verdross-Simma* (Völkerrecht) pp. 30–38. See also *Coplin* (Functions) pp. 171–176; *Schwarzenberger* 10 CLP 1957 pp. 264–266; *Schiffer* (Legal Community) pp. 200–201 (pointing out the two perceptions within the

But the result is fatal. To understand why this is so we must remember that the social conception excluded the possibility that law existed to enhance material principles of justice. In its quest for social order, the law has only the pre-legal freedom and autonomy of the State to rely upon. To explain the legal order as something else than coercion, it must explain how the conditions of community can be developed out of association between free and autonomous States. This requires that "community" – like its counter-part, "autonomy" – be defined *in a purely formal way* – without regard to anybody's ideals about the desirable limits of autonomy or kinds of community. Any other solution would involve arguing from a material theory of justice. It would – so the argument goes – make an arbitrary preference between the values of free and autonomous States. But it is precisely because "autonomy" and "community" are defined in a formal way that they become vulnerable to valid criticisms from alternative and equally legitimate *substantive* perspectives. Any attempt to enhance community will, from some State's autonomous perspective, look like increasing totalitarianism. Any view which aims to give substance to autonomy will appear from another point of view, like giving effect to unbridled egoism. It is only as long as the ideal social order remains formal that it can accommodate autonomy and community and be acceptable. Immediately as it is given concrete content – as soon as it becomes a programme of *what to do* – it will appear to overrule somebody's preferred substantive view and seem illegitimate as such. Because lawyers have defined themselves incapable of arguing from alternative material views about desirable forms of social order they have nothing to argue against somebody's interpretation of the proposed order as substantially unacceptable.

7.2   The failure of legal formality: examples

To seem legitimate, a legal project for world order must appear formal. It must appear to give effect to communal solidarity between States and safeguard their rights of independence and self-determination. And indeed, this is the way modern legislative projects present themselves.

League of Nations). *Bull* (Anarchical Society) distinguishes between three perceptions: the Hobbesian (state of war), Kantian (procedural cooperation) and Grotian (moral community), pp. 24–27. For a similar "anatomy of international thought", see *Wight* 13 Rev.Int.Stud. 1987 pp. 221–227.

To see why they still fail to produce acceptable conditions for world order I shall look at four examples: the New International Economic Order, sovereign immunity, the 1982 UN Convention on the Law of the Sea and the idea of peace. Each is initially constituted in a formal-procedural fashion and seems acceptable as long as it stays such. Once they are applied to the solution of normative problems – that is, once there is dispute – they either fail to indicate any solution or refer to some contested notion of material justice.

The New International Economic Order (NIEO), as expressed in countless UN General Assembly resolutions seems like – and is interpreted from a Third-World perspective as – a communitarian effort *par excellence*.[34] And yet, its core appears to lie in the enhancement of national independence and self-determination in economic matters.[35] This is what makes it initially acceptable. It is opposed to the structures of economic domination of the present international system (totalitarianism) and it aims to combat the egoism of a group of (developed) States. But this not only makes it possible to support the NIEO from a communitarian and individualist perspective but likewise to criticize it from both. For a developed State, the NIEO may seem like a harmful form of economic collectivism (blocking private investment, creation of production cartels etc.)[36] or simple national egoism (discrimination,

---

[34] See in particular, *Caldera* 196 RCADI 1986/I (the NIEO as a means to safeguard the good of the international community itself) pp. 391–400. See also e.g. *Benchikh* (Benchikh-Charvin-Demichel: Introduction) pp. 116–119; *Bedjaoui* (New International Economic Order) pp. 236–240. The communitarian strand of the NIEO rhetoric is best exemplified in the idea of the "common heritage of mankind". See e.g. UN Convention on the Law of the Sea, Art. 136.

[35] Thus, the Charter of Economic Rights and Duties of States, UNGA Res. 3281 (XXIX), 12 December 1974, is mindful of "the strengthening of the economic independence of developing nations" and proclaims that every State "has and shall freely exercise full permanent sovereignty ... over all its wealth, natural resources and economic activities" (Art. 2(1)). Throughout, emphasis is on sovereignty, independence, territorial integrity. That the point of the NIEO is to strengthen Third-World autonomy needs hardly be stressed. For standard discussion, see e.g. *Buirette-Maurau* (Tiers-monde) p. 87 *et seq*; *Pellet* (Développement) pp. 10–17, 86–96. For a useful review of the state of the NIEO as a *legal* project, see Progressive Development of the Principles and Norms of International Law relating to the NIEO, Report by the UN Secretary General, 24 October 1984, UN Doc. A/39/504. Add.1. *Ide* (Festschrift Abendroth) summarizes the liberal project buried within the 1974 Charter. It "tente de faire coexister la souveraineté avec la solidarité dans la cadre de la communauté internationale", p. 127.

[36] On the economically inequitable effect of the nationalization standard of the 1974 Charter, see e.g. *Weston* (Lillich: Injuries) pp. 107 *et seq*, 113–117; *McWhinney* (Conflict) (on the harmful effect of production cartels) p. 134.

nationalization, neglect of contractual obligations, etc.).[37] The opposing characterizations – and the respective criticisms – seem equally justified because the NIEO cannot decide between them without taking a stand in political conflict. This would involve either overruling one group of sovereigns in favour of another one or deciding between the competing communal values of, for example, economic efficiency and just distribution. Both choices are eminently political and seem incapable of being resolved by any distinctly legal technique. The irony is that economic disputes constantly demand resolution by legal rules. And when we look at the content of those rules – particularly the rules about "permanent sovereignty", the focal legal issue in the NIEO – we find that they immediately refer *beyond* themselves, beyond the law – into standards of appropriate (just) compensation or good faith.[38] As the law in this way only repeats the political problem and declines to solve it (what is "appropriate" or "just"?), it is little wonder that many have become sceptical as to the possibilities of a *legal* realization of the NIEO.[39]

Sovereign immunity provides another example. Initially, the *rationale* of exempting foreign States from the territorial State's jurisdiction seems to stem from the need to respect the former's autonomy (sovereignty, dignity, independence).[40] Such an interpretation of the rule would, however, fail to safeguard the territorial State's equal autonomy. The rule's content cannot be constructed so as to protect the autonomy of only one of the disputing States – this would look like a totalitarian way of violating sovereign equality. The problem appears to lie rather in delimiting or balancing the conflicting sovereignties.[41] The *Sabbatino*

---

[37] See e.g. *Fitzmaurice* (IIL 1973) pp. 228–230. The "absoluteness" of Third-World claims on sovereignty is noted by many. See *Seidl-Hohenveldern* 186 RCADI 1986/III pp. 51–52; *Lillich* (Lillich: Injuries) p. 16.

[38] See *supra* ch. 4. and e.g. *Jiménez de Aréchaga* (Hossain: Legal Aspects) pp. 231–232.

[39] For recent critical analyses of development law, see e.g. *Bennouna* (Mélanges Chaumont) pp. 61–67; *Borella* (*ibid.*) pp. 78–80. See also *Cassese* (Divided) pp. 372–375; *Virally* 183 RCADI 1983/V pp. 328–332.

[40] This standard justification is usually attributed to *Marshall*, C. J. in the *Schooner Exchange* Case, Scott (Cases) p. 302. See further *Lauterpacht* (International Law 3) (critical view) pp. 317, 328–333; *Akehurst* (Modern Introduction) p. 109; *Wallace* (International Law) p. 108; *Brownlie* (Principles) pp. 323, 325–326; *Carreau* (Droit international) pp. 341–343. In its basic form, it tends to suggest what has been called "absolute" immunity. Thus, in the Soviet (socialist) view, this rule is implied in the very notion of sovereignty. See *Boguslavsky* X Neth.YBIL 1979 pp. 167–177; *Enderlein* (*ibid.*) pp. 113–114 *et seq.*

[41] The *Schooner Exchange* case may also be interpreted in this light. It is now taken to emphasize the territorial sovereign's sovereignty by basing the rule on immunity on its (tacit) consent. See *Badr* (Immunity) pp. 9–14. But as *Brownlie* (Principles)

Case (1964) is instructive. The United States Supreme Court applied the Act of State doctrine here not because – as that doctrine had commonly been explained – it needed to protect Cuban sovereignty and independence but because the matter related to the political competence of the executive (the need to protect US independence and sovereignty) and, in particular, because "progress towards the goal of establishing the rule of law among nations" required this (the communitarian argument).[42] For the Court, sovereign immunity protected autonomy as well as community. The problem is that this tends to make the rule very uncertain as it may be argued from any of the exclusive points about initial autonomy or from contested visions of what is needed to protect communal order.

The standard way to establish the needed balance between the conflicting sovereignties is to make use of the distinction between the foreign sovereign's "public" and "private" acts. But this has tended to be unhelpful and has given rise to very varying jurisprudence.[43] The problem is, once again, that the distinction and the way it is applied rests on "political assumptions as to the proper sphere of State activity and of priorities in State policies"[44] which cannot easily be contained in formal

observes: the question cannot be decided by stressing "sovereignty" as "two sovereignties are in issue and it is the manner of their relation which is the debated question of law", p. 333. Similarly *Lauterpacht* (International Law 3) pp. 325–326; *Crawford* LIV BYIL 1983 p. 87.

[42] *Banco Nacional de Cuba v. Sabbatino et al.* 35 ILR 1967 pp. 43, 34–42. Yet, as many have noted, the practical effect of the Sabbatino argument is to establish arbitrary preference for the foreign sovereign over the domestic one and over international standards. Consequently, the US Congress reacted against the decision and virtually repealed it by subsequent legislation. For recent criticisms, see e.g. *Garcia-Amador* (Claims I) pp. 440–443; *Halberstam* 79 AJIL 1985 pp. 74–91.

[43] This is noted by many. See e.g. *Lauterpacht* (International Law 3) pp. 318–321; *Brownlie* (Principles) p. 321; *Carreau* (Droit international) pp. 344–345. And, of course, it is noted that the very distinction "does not take into account the character of the socialist State", *Enderlein* X Neth.YBIL 1979 p. 113. Similarly, *Boguslavsky* (*ibid*). pp. 169–170.

[44] *Brownlie* (Principles) pp. 331–332. The most extended recent treatment of the problem argues that an "objective test" (*jure imperil* acts being "acts which private persons are basically incapable of carrying out") is possible and in effect coalesces with the test of jurisdiction. Local courts would simply ascertain whether they possess jurisdiction and the issue of immunity would become resolved accordingly. *Badr* (Sovereign Immunity) pp. 63–70, 86–97. But what private persons have been able to do is a matter which has varied both historically and geographically and the problem is that a sovereign can hardly be confronted effectively with a claim that whatever its view on the matter is, there is some intrinsically natural standard for what private persons are/are not capable of doing. Thus *Crawford* LIV BYIL 1983 notes that recent instruments on the matter have taken a pragmatic approach ("balance of principles and considerations") which leaves the matter to be decided on contextual considerations, pp. 114–118.

rules. As Crawford notes, though there may be consensus on restrictive immunity, we still:

> ... lack a rationale, a connected explanation, for this state of affairs ... which would enable us to draw the distinction between cases in which States ... are entitled to immunity ... and cases in which they are not.[45]

It is quite characteristic that while the NIEO originally appeared in a communitarian light and sovereign immunity seemed connected with the need to protect State autonomy, both are capable of being interpreted equally well from the reverse perspective. The NIEO seemed to prefer some States' independence and self-determination while sovereign immunity was capable of decision only from the perspective of a community policy in regard to drawing the *jure imperil/jure gestionis* distinction. Had the communitarian perspective been lacking, then the projects would have preferred sovereigns against each other in an illegitimate way. Had the independence aspect been absent, the principles of distributive justice or economic efficiency or the manner of making the private/public distinction would have appeared too political.

The 1982 UN Convention on the Law of the Sea repeats the tension between communal and individualistic demands. This is easy to see in the two standard explanations of what the Convention aims to achieve.

According to one interpretation, States act as separate, egoistic entities which only look after their own needs and interests at the expense of those of others. The natural state of the oceans is a harmful *laissez-faire*

---

[45] *Crawford* LIV BYIL 1983 p. 75. A similar problem-structure is contained in extraterritorial jurisdiction. Here, there is a conflict between the autonomy of the territorial State and the State exercising jurisdiction. The conflict emerges from both States' defining their autonomy on a *substantive view* of the limits of that autonomy. The former may refer to a principle of economic sovereignty or non-intervention, the latter to the "effects doctrine". As the issue cannot be decided by reliance on formal autonomy (because the limits of autonomy were defined by substantive views), doctrine and practice have moved to consider these issues under a "balancing of interests" test and stressing good faith. See e.g. *Meng* 44 ZaöRV 1984 pp. 675–783; *Lowe* 34 ICLQ 1985 pp. 730–731 *et seq*; *Gerber* 77 AJIL 1983 (a review of US and German practice with the argument that the latter provides more refined criteria for undertaking the balance) pp. 758 *et seq*, 777–783. This move, however, has prompted the predictable criticism that it "involves judicial discretion to solve a problem of international politics, not legal analysis to resolve an issue of transnational law" and that "directing a general search for reason and fairness is in no meaningful sense a rule of law", *Maier* 76 AJIL 1981 pp. 295, 318. He suggests that the decision should be based on "systemic values", pp. 303–320. But, as we have seen, this can hardly make the assessment seem more objective than a balancing test – the values themselves being object of controversy.

in which communal interests and needs are constantly overridden. In that case, the order of the oceans is constantly in a precarious state and therefore needs rules – such as the Convention – to prevent individualism from leading into anarchy. From such perspective, the Convention may be interpreted as a step from egoism to community.[46]

But the Convention also allows depicting the oceans as dominated by the collectivism of the technologically advanced States, the prevailing economic and power structures. In this case, rules are needed to strengthen autonomy and self-determination. Did not this common effort result in the closing of 40% of the oceans' surface into areas of exclusive resource use? From such perspective, the Convention appears as a step from totalitarianism to autonomy.[47]

These conflicting understandings of the character of the social environment of the oceans and the point of the Convention reveal the way the Convention aims to safeguard both communal and individualistic values.[48] It aims to solve the tension between such values by creating a formal-procedural framework for the conduct of inter-sovereign relations. The assumption is that if only the system is such as not to preclude any sovereign's policy but to provide the channels – the "architecture" – through which policies may be conducted, it will have contributed to world order without infringing upon sovereign freedom.[49] Like modern law in general, this strategy either ignores conflict or creates a rhetoric for unending referral of conflict away

[46] *Allott* 77 AJIL 1983 reads the Convention as a part of the general post-war trend away from "unfettered freedom" to power being legally shared and that in the Convention States act as "representatives of the international community", pp. 25–27. Similarly *Dupuy* (Mélanges Reuter) p. 241. The view that the Convention marks a step away from "unfettered freedom" is particularly stressed by Third-World lawyers. See e.g. *Sarin* (Festschift Abendroth) pp. 280–287; *Anand* (*ibid.*) pp. 215–233.

[47] See e.g. *de Lacharrière* (Bardonnet-Virally: Nouveau) (pointing out the superiority of sovereignty over organization in the Convention) pp. 15–16. *McDougal-Burke* (Public Order) note: "It is ironic that despite initial recognition of mutual dependence, the outcome of the Third Law of the Sea Conference placed much of its emphasis on exclusive use of authority", pp. xiiv, lviii–lix. The reliance on sovereignty in the Convention is likewise stressed by *Fitzmaurice* (IIL 1973) pp. 217–219; *McWhinney* (Conflict) pp. 131–132. Thus *Chimni* 22 IJIL 1982 argues that the Convention only perpetuates the free enterprise regime and the egoism of the powerful, pp. 69–82.

[48] Many have discussed the tension between the Convention's communitarian and individualist aspects. See e.g. *Dupuy* (Mélanges Reuter) pp. 221–241; *Cassese* (Divided) p. 392; *Cahin* (Mélanges Chaumont) p. 112.

[49] For a useful analysis of the Convention as procedural "architecture" – a system of deferral of material solution beyond the Convention-text, see *Kennedy* (Structures) pp. 201–245.

from the centres of law to the periphery, to become ultimately resolved beyond law by agreement or by political standards of equity.

The Convention contains at least three separate but interrelated topics: space, activities and compensation. To reach the Convention's structure and meaning and to reveal its strategy of referral, we need to look at why such topics are put together and how they are dealt with.

The Convention speaks at length of geographical *spaces*: territorial sea, contiguous zone, exclusive economic zone (EEZ), the High Seas, continental shelf, deep seabed. The Convention does two things in respect of each. First it defines them by setting them into conceptual opposition: territorial sea is defined by its opposition, on the one hand, to the High Seas, on the other to internal waters, the contiguous zone and EEZ; the contiguous zone is defined by its opposition to the territorial sea and the High Seas etc.; the continental shelf is defined by distinguishing it from land territory and the deep seabed and *vice-versa*. And so on. The question is: what makes these oppositions important (and not for instance fresh/salt waters, navigation/preservation waters etc.)? The answer is evident. In each opposition is at issue the primacy (power) of the coastal State against the primacy (power) of States at large. The spatio-conceptual distinctions aim to establish boundaries between the individual (coastal State) and the community.[50] Second, these boundaries are so constructed as to mark off limits of jurisdiction. They are not about what is permitted or prohibited but what is permitted/prohibited *to whom*. The Convention treats the oceans from the perspective of jurisdictional competences, *not* from the point of view of, for example, economic or ecological goals. The sea is, as it were, a bundle of competences and the problem is not what one should or should not do with the sea but who has the competence, who can decide.[51]

[50] This is a traditional way of understanding rules abut maritime spaces. In the *Anglo-Norwegian Fisheries* Case, Reports 1951 the ICJ refused a coastal State's right to define its maritime space unilaterally, as such definition inevitably involved an "international aspect", p. 132. The most extensive treatment of the balancing aspect in maritime spaces law is in *McDougal-Burke* (Public Order) pp. 1 *et seq*, 51–56, *passim*.

[51] The Convention's treatment of territorial sea is illustrative. First, overall jurisdiction (sovereignty) is allocated to the coastal State (Art. 2). This is followed by the geographical delimitation (Arts. 3–16). Finally, a set of provisions are introduced to limit the overall jurisdiction (innocent passage, conditions of costal regulation, Arts. 17–32). In the absence of rules on what States should/should not do in the territorial sea, the Convention creates competences and delimits them. Pollution, for example, is treated by allocating the coastal State the right to "adopt laws and regulations" which will contain the material law on the matter (Arts. 194(2), 207, 208, 210, 211(44), 212) – the sole restriction being that these laws conform to what has been internationally (elsewehere) agreed.

In principle, it would be possible to imagine a Convention which would speak only of geographically delimited spaces. It would allocate jurisdiction either to the coastal State or to States at large depending on the distance of the particular space from, for example, the baseline of the coastal State's territorial sea. However, it is well-known that the history of the law of the sea is not really put up from a conflict between the coastal State and the community but between the former and maritime States, the latter favouring the freedom of the sea.[52] To use geographical distance as the sole criterion for jurisdiction would put maritime States in a disadvantageous position. It would overrule their sovereign interests in an unacceptable way.

Hence, the Convention picks up another subject-matter, *activities*, and creates a specific discourse concerning navigation, use of living resources, seabed activities and scientific research which cuts through the previous topic. In respect of each, the Convention refers material rules away from itself by allocating the right to decide on the manner of conducting them further, either to the coastal State or to States "in cooperation" or to "competent international organizations". The provisions are, again, about jurisdiction, not about what is permitted or prohibited. Each activity is covered by an initial provision on general competence which is followed by a series of exceptions which aim to safeguard the interests of other States. Thus, the coastal State has the competence to decide on the allowable catch within the EEZ.[53] Yet, once it has made this determination, it should agree with other States on the use of the surplus catch.[54] The coastal State has the exclusive right to regulate marine scientific research on its continental shelf and EEZ.[55] Others may conduct research only on its consent.[56] Yet, it should ("in normal circumstances") not withhold its consent.[57] The uses of the deep seabed (the Area) are to be regulated by the International Seabed Authority. But if a mineral deposit exists partly within the jurisdiction of the coastal State, the former should pay "due regard" to its interests.[58] Again, the provisions are about jurisdiction and competence. How activities are to be carried out is referred to further decision by another body which should make the decision always with due regard to others' interests. The Convention is constantly aiming to secure a balance and provide each State with what it needs.

---

[52] See e.g. *O'Connell* (Law of the Sea 1) pp. 1–2, *passim*.   [53] Art. 61(1).
[54] Art. 62(2).   [55] Art. 245.   [56] Art. 246(2).   [57] Art. 246(3–6).
[58] Art. 142(1–2).

But it is still not sufficient to speak simply of spaces with the qualification that certain activities are singled out for special treatment – left
as a privilege for those who can afford to engage in them. First, this
creates the danger that these activities will have adverse effects – e.g.
pollution – which extend to States which have no say in how the
activities are conducted. Second, such an approach would leave States
which are both geographically and economically worse off in an exceedingly disadvantageous positon. To create a comprehensive legal order,
the Convention needs to single out regulatory frameworks which allow
these States' views to be taken account of as well.

Consequently, the Convention addresses itself to a third topic which
reaches beyond the previous two and concerns itself with *compensating*
the disadvantages which would follow from allocating jurisdiction to an
individual State with the reservation that certain activities may be
undertaken by others, too. This is treated in a similar fashion as the
previous two, by discussing decision-making procedures and not by
creating compulsory compensation regimes. Thus, the establishment
of pollution control measures, whenever third States' interests might
be involved, is referred to "competent international organizations".[59]
The provisions on transfer of technology refer to future cooperation by
"States directly or through competent international organizations".[60] In
the absence of material provisions on such transfer, States merely agree
to "promote" ("where feasible and appropriate") such transfer or to
"endeavour to foster favourable economic and legal conditions for it"[61] –
with due regard for all legitimate interests.[62] Most remarkably, the
provisions on the deep seabed, instead of creating material compensatory duties, establish a massive procedure (the International Seabed
Authority) within which, under a complicated decision-making system,
compensatory measures would be adopted in the future.[63]

These three topics – space, activities, compensation – are put together
so as to provide for the concerns of all sovereigns. Each is treated in a
formal-procedural way so as not to preclude any sovereign policy or any
agreement which might be achieved when States sit down to discuss

---

[59] Arts. 197, 200, 209, 210(4), 211(1), 212. *Boyle* 79 AJIL 1985 notes that here, too, the
Convention provides "only a general framework of powers and duties, not a code of
specific standards", p. 350. It attributes competences of regulation and – perhaps – an
obligation to regulate but remains silent on the content of regulation. See also generally
Hakapää (Marine Pollution) *passim*.
[60] Arts. 266(1), 271, 272, 273.   [61] Arts. 266(1–3), 270.   [62] Arts. 267, 274.
[63] Arts. 150–187.

their potential conflicts. The implicit assumption is that conflict is not inevitable but that when States are forced into cooperation they will realize that everybody's interests are best served if agreements are achieved. This assumption is what made the Convention possible in the first place.

But oceans' resources are scarce. Everybody cannot have everything. The Convention seemed needed because what were lacking were rules to solve conflicts over resource use. The Convention itself does acknowledge the possibility of conflict by including an elaborate conflict-settlement mechanism. In conflict, we need to make specific the rules of the Convention – we need to see what the Convention allows or prohibits and how it proposes to deal with jurisdictional problems in case States disagree. At this point, however, the Convention remains silent. In its concern to safeguard all States' interests it begs the question of what to do when disagreements arise within the formal framework it sets up.

The way the Convention refers material solution away from itself has been exhaustively treated by David Kennedy.[64] Here I shall only illustrate the Convention's "strategy of referral" in view of a limited number of conceivable conflicts to which the Convention offers no solution.

A first strategy repeats the general structure of the Convention. In case of dispute, the States should reach agreement. The difficult issue of liability and compensation for marine pollution is an example. Having affirmed that States are "responsible for the fulfilment of their international obligations regarding the protection and preservation of the marine environment"[65] (which obligations? – another referral to standards outside the Convention), the Convention goes on to address the issue of liability. But all it has to say about this is that:

> States shall further cooperate in the implementation of existing international law and the further development of international law relating to responsibility and liability for the assesment and compensation for damage.[66]

No material rule emerges from the Convention. Resolution is referred away, either into general law or into a later agreement. We have seen that the conflictual topic of transfer of technology was treated in a similar fashion – resolution is referred to further decision by the States concerned ("directly or through competent international organizations").[67]

---

[64] *Supra* n. 49. [65] Art. 235(1). [66] Art. 235(3). [67] *Supra* nn. 60–62.

Conflicts over resource use are also referred into further agreement. The use of the surplus catch within the EEZ is to be decided by agreement.[68] Conflicts over the uses of specific species of fish are to be dealt with by agreement.[69] So are the rights of landlocked[70] and geographically disadvantaged States.[71] The production policies of the International Seabed Authority are to be decided by agreement between "all interested parties".[72] The ways to promote marine scientific research are to be decided by agreement.[73] And so on.[74]

The Convention might have combined its strategy of referral with material norms about what should be taken account of when agreements are made (though it is unclear whether we could in such case speak about "agreement" – decision by binding standards resembling rather some kind of local administration). But it does not. The apparently material provisions are loaded with terms such as "on an equitable basis", "when appropriate", "feasible", "objectives", "endeavour", "promote", "paying due regard" etc. which make sure that any non-procedural standard refrains from setting up a general *rule* on whatever matter it deals with. Everything is made dependent on a contextual assessment. It is hardly doubtful that this strategy will look unhelpful as disputes crystallize on the question of what it is that is "feasible", "appropriate" etc. in the particular context.

The second, already familiar, strategy refers to equity in cases of jurisdictional conflict. Take the EEZ, for example. The rights of the coastal State and of other States in that area should be exercised "with due regard to" each other.[75] Article 59 takes up the issue of possible conflict: in case the Convention has not attributed specific rights (and in cases where a party can claim that the matter is not covered by the rights established previously) and a conflict "of interests" emerges:

> ... the conflict should be resolved on the basis of equity and in the light of all relevant circumstances taking into account the respective importance of the interests involved to the parties as well as to the international community as a whole.

---

[68] Art. 62(2).   [69] Arts. 66(3)a, d, 67(3).   [70] Arts. 69(2), 125(2).
[71] Art. 70(3).   [72] Art. 151(1)a.   [73] Art. 243.
[74] For the references to further agreement in the Convention, see the index in the publication: The Law of The Sea; UN Convention on the Law of the Sea with Index and Final Act, UNP E.83. V.5, New York 1983 pp. 193–194.
[75] Arts. 56(2), 58(3).

Once again, the Convention treats conflict – by refusing to treat it. It starts out by assuming that States are capable of taking "due regard" of each other's interests. If there is conflict, it is to be settled by equity and by taking all possible considerations into account. The Convention refrains from setting down a rule and refers to further procedure – without indicating how that procedure should be conducted.[76] As we have seen, such solution is either empty as guidance or inadvertently based on the assumption that "equity" can be treated in a legal manner.

The same approach is used to deal with all jurisdictional conflicts. Material rules are assumed to exist beyond the Convention, in some natural equity or in general international law. Article 15 tells States that if they have problems in delimiting their territorial sea they should reach agreement. If no agreement is made, then no State should proceed beyond the median line, apart from the case of special circumstances – a roundabout way of referring to equity.[77] Articles 77 and 83 repeat this strategy in respect of the EEZ and the continental shelf. In conflict, there should be agreement. Such agreement shall be made:

> ... on the basis of international law, as referred to in Article 38 of the Statute of the International Court of Justice, in order to achieve an equitable solution.

One seeks in vain for a material rule. Resolution is to be found in agreement or in standards external to the Convention. Needless to say, this begs the issue of the disputing States' inability to reach agreement and their differing views about what general international law or equity might say about how they should proceed.[78] Surely the Convention was needed precisely because problems had emerged in these respects.

[76] This procedural strategy is usefully discussed by *Allott* 77 AJIL 1983, noting that Articles 74 and 83 on delimitation – "and countless other provisions in the Law of the Sea Convention – are not simply contractual terms; nor do they lay down rules of law in the classical sense. They *delegate decision-making powers*", p. 24.

[77] The Court of Arbitration in the *Anglo-French Continental Shelf* Case (1977) XVIII UNRIAA applied Article 6 of the Continental Shelf Convention of 1958 by constructing an "equidistance-special circumstances rule" which gave "particular expression to the general norm that, failing agreement, the boundary between States ... is to be determined on equitable principles", p. 45 (§ 70).

[78] Many have criticized this strategy of referring material solution into contextual equity. *Attard* (Exclusive Economic Zone) speaks of the "failure of UNCLOS III to produce a viable EEZ delimitation formula", p. 237 and generally on the "balancing" involved, pp. 221–276. For a criticism of Articles 74 and 83, see also *Caflisch* (Bardonnet-Virally: Nouveau) noting that the Convention not only lacks a rule about dispute-solution, it also lacks a constraining procedure as Article 298(1) allows the State to opt out from

In case there is no agreement, the disputing States are referred into further procedure – third party settlement. Here we might expect that the Convention should become controlling. But it does not. This is so because it fails to indicate which rules the dispute-settlement body might use – apart from the general reference to equity and general international law. And it leaves the recourse to binding settlement in most serious issues at the discretion of the disputing States themselves.[79]

It is well known that the frequent references to equity or general law were included in the Convention so as to avoid taking a stand on rival views about the proper principles to be used. The reference to good faith and abuse of rights in Article 300 fulfils the same function. It tempers down whatever unacceptable constraint a State might feel that the Convention provides. This strategy combines nicely with the main technique of the Convention – avoiding addressing material conflict and proceeding so as to assume that States have good reason to follow the Convention's formal channels and to reach agreement by any standards they might deem appropriate. But here the Convention betrays its own project. To assume that States will agree or that external standards remain controlling is equivalent to assuming that the conditions which the Convention aims to create were already present. By referring to agreement, general law and equity, the Convention assumes that States will agree on how to delimit their jurisdictional competences,

---

compulsory procedures for boundary disputes, pp. 107–114. *Charney* 78 AJIL 1984 notes that these articles were drafted "in relatively empty diplomatic language", p. 583. See also *Hossain* (Hossain: Legal Aspects), noting the lack of specifically *legal* means to construct equity in a maritime context, pp. 193–207. The Chairman of the negotiating group on delimitation, Judge *Manner* (Essays Lachs), points out that the Articles followed from a compromise in which the participants could maintain their conflicting positions, p. 640. Similarly, *Rosenne* (Festschrift Bindschedler) pp. 415–417, 424.

[79] First, the Parties' preferred methods always override those of the Convention (Art. 280). This applies to the "compulsory" methods as well (Art. 287(1)). If none is chosen, the matter will be referred to arbitration (Art. 287(3)). Yet, the controlling nature of this provision is mitigated by the ingenious formulation which links its applicability only to specific types of disputes (Art. 297(1)). Moreover, even here provision is made for automatic and optional exceptions which leave the most important jurisdictional issues (disputes over fishing in the EEZ, marine scientific research, maritime boundaries, military activities and activities in respect of which the Security Council exercises its functions) outside compulsory settlement (Arts. 297, 298). For general discussion on the dispute-settlement system of the Convention, see *Hakapää* 5 Essays in International Law, Finnish Branch of ILA, pp. 57–66; *Churchill-Lowe* (Law of the Sea) pp. 295–299; *Sarin* (Festschrift Abendroth) pp. 299–306. For legislative history and analysis, see *Adede* (Settlement of Disputes).

that there is no important disagreement on what the appropriate (external) rules say and that States are capable of knowing and applying the relevant principles of distributive justice (equity). Were this so, the Convention would, of course, have been pointless.

Finally, I shall illustrate the failure of the procedural strategy by reference to the idea of peace by law.

Initially, of course, peace appears like the ultimate communitarian project. Simultaneously, it seems the best guarantee for individual States' autonomy and inviolability. But this is so only if peace is conceived in a formal fashion, as absence of inter-State violence.[80] If it were not formal, it would imply a doctrine of just war to cope with situations which do not correspond to the postulated material criteria. But, as the modern criticism of the just war has it, such criteria would be inevitably manipulable and involve a threat to international order as well as State autonomy.[81] Being formal-procedural, this conception of peace has a natural connection with the Rule of Law.[82]

But it is not at all evident that the formal conception of peace can claim overriding normative force. Stated in the abstract it seems beyond reproach. But problems emerge when we attempt to apply it into practice. Is peace under *any* conditions really preferable to violence? Would a *pax Hitleriana* have been sanctioned by international law? Or, in less hypothetical terms, were the armed intervention by India in Bangladesh in 1971 or by Tanzania in Uganda in 1976 really such gross violations of international law? What about Biafra? Should somebody have intervened by armed forces even if that had meant war?[83]

---

[80] Due to the apparent manipulability of the concept of "war", the contrary to peace is now simply defined as "threat or use of force", see United Nations Charter, Art. 2(4).

[81] The impossibility of achieving an objective definition of just war, notes *Corbett* (Law and Society), achieved that the doctrine "ended in bankruptcy", p. 211.

[82] *Lauterpacht* (Function) observes: "In a sense, peace is morally indifferent, inasmuch as it may involve the sacrifice of justice on the altar of stability and security. Peace is eminently a legal postulate." p. 438. Similarly *Ferencz* (Common Sense) p. 43 *et seq.*

[83] For further hard cases and a strong preference for non-intervention, see *Akehurst* (Bull: Intervention) pp. 95–104; *Higgins* (82 *ibid.*) p. 37; *Fawcett* (Law and Power) pp. 114–115. See also ICJ: *Corfu Channel* Case, Reports 1949 p. 35; UNGA Res. 2131 (XX) 21 December 1965 (Inadmissibility of Intervention in the Domestic Affairs of States); UNGA Res. 42/22, Annex 18 November 1987 (Declaration on the Enhancement of the Effectiveness of the Principle of Refraining from the Threat or Use of Force in International Relations), Preamble, para. 17, operative part, para. 7. The difficulty with an absolute non-intervention principle (aside from its sometimes politically obverse consequences) is that it makes no nonsense to say that sometimes it is necessary to intervene to preserve peace. Historically, this may even have been its principal

The problem is analogous to later liberals' dissatisfaction with the Hobbesian premise that social peace under a Leviathan is always preferable to the natural state. Locke (like Marx, for instance) found this assumption unwarranted – a perfectly logical inference from his theological perspective.[84] If one looks at the world through a system of material value then the assumption that factual authority is legitimate simply because it is there is clearly unwarranted. It may, of course, be but its being factually authoritative is no guarantee of its being legitimate and by itself contains no presumption that any forcible action to overthrow it would be even less acceptable.

But the Hobbesian argument tends also to be vulnerable to a criticism which does not assume the existence of a set of transcendent values. It leads into a denial of freedom and self-determination – the sole normative premises left when transcendent values have been denied. A Leviathan may seem like the best alternative only if one thinks that people have no good reason to comply with *any* ethical demands (because these are matters of private superstition) or that in any case people are inherently incapable of acting in a morally responsible way.[85] But if ethical standards do not matter, then there is no reason for the Leviathan, either, to treat his subjects in an ethical way. Hence, the Hobbesian order tends *automatically* to reduce people into a state of passive obedience and legitimize whatever acts those in power would wish to undertake.

But if ethics and politics are possible, then no Leviathan – no social peace – can claim legitimacy merely because it exists and there might sometimes be compelling reasons for morally responsible people to seek to overthrow it – even by forcible means. That international law recognizes this is manifest in the two orthodox exceptions it allows for its near-categorical prohibition of force: self-defence and collective action

justification. In other words, peace may be associated with intervention as well as non-intervention and even absolute preference for peace cannot tell us whether intervention should be admitted or not. Little wonder that when Talleyrand was asked to explain the notion of non-intervention in 1832, he observed that "C'est un mot métaphysique et politique qui signifie à peu près la même chose qu'intervention", quoted by *Wight* (Butterfield-Wight: Diplomatic Investigations) p. 115.

[84] On Locke's theological background, his insistence on value being other than what people evaluate and his reliance on a naturalist conception of "trust", see *Dunn* (Rethinking) pp. 21 *et seq*, 32–33, 41–54.

[85] This is the core of the "realist" view which holds that ethics has no place in international relations. For discussion and criticism, see *Beitz* (Political Theory) pp. 11–66; *Frost* (Normative) pp. 13–36; *Walzer* (Just Wars) pp. 4–20.

through the UN Security Council.[86] The *rationale* of those exceptions
lies in a denial that *de facto* power converts into *de jure* authority and the
admission that States may react by force when they feel their freedom –
as defined by their *substantive* view on the limits of that freedom – is
threatened. It is precisely because these views are substantive – and
hence disputed – that mere reliance on a formal non-intervention
principle tends to seem both unhelpful and sometimes outright
apologist.[87]

The idea that law – social order – must legitimize itself by reference to
what people (States) regard as good norms is premised on the assumption
that politics is possible and that people have good reasons to formulate and
comply with ethical demands. If this is so, then it is unclear if self-defence
and collective action can be regarded as the sole justifications for the use of
force. Indeed, many would extend the list of permissible exceptions to wars
of national liberation and self-determination.[88] Still others would include
massive violations of human rights.[89]

These justifications are, of course, disputed, and the disputes reflect
alternative theories about just principles of international behaviour.
This is why Hobbesian realists retort that opening the door for exceptions will open Pandora's box. In the absence of objective criteria, they
fear, utopian ideals will lead into apologist practice.[90] Though this
argument is important, it is doubtful whether it can remain the final

[86] On the standard consensus, see e.g. *Bishop* 115 RCADI 1965/II pp. 437–438; *Brownlie*
(Use of Force) p. 251 *et seq*; *Akehurst* (Bull: Intervention) pp. 95 *et seq*, 104–108; *Wallace*
(International Law) pp. 221–223.
[87] *Vincent* (Non-intervention) pp. 301, 314–315.
[88] See UNGA Res. 2625 (XXV) 24 October 1970 (under principle e.) and 42/22, Annex
18 November 1987 (in fine). For wars of liberation as just wars under the Charter, see
Abi-Saab (Falk-Kratochwil-Mendlowitz: International Law) p. 416; *Tieya* (Macdonald-
Johnston: Structure and Process) p. 972; *Hingorani* (Modern) p. 337. See also the
discussion in *Vincent* (Non-intervention) pp. 261–277.
[89] See e.g. *D'Amato* 79 AJIL 1985 p. 403. Similarly *Carreau* (Droit international) (reserving the right to "flagrant violations of international law", including the right of
protection of nationals) pp. 502–505. See also *Brierly* (Law of Nations) pp. 427–428;
Verzijl (I) p. 242.
[90] See e.g. *Vincent* (Non-intervention) pp. 342–349; *Henkin* (How) pp. 144–145. Typical
discussion will oppose points such as these: *Reisman* 78 AJIL 1984 construes Article 2(4)
of the UN Charter so as to allow intervention to overthrow tyrannical Governments as
these cannot give expression to the principle of self-determination – a principle of
overriding character in the Charter system, pp. 642–645. This is opposed by *Schachter*
(*ibid.*), arguing that this allows the strong to manipulate the law so as to subjugate
the weak by intervention, pp. 645–650. The difficulty, of course, is that *both* the *status
quo* as well as intervention may be used to further justice as well as injustice,

word on the issue. Many would insist that if the law sanctioned just any kind of Leviathan it would not itself be worthwhile.

Clearly, the case of armed humanitarian intervention is a difficult one. Though non-intervention seems like a natural consequence of the rejection of material natural law, it still does not seem difficult to imagine cases (actual or hypothetical) in which such a prohibition would be outright harmful and should not merit respect.

It is necessary to see that the intuition which sometimes supports military intervention is itself supported – just like the non-intervention principle – by the liberal principles of freedom and self-determination.[91] For if it is the case that only such Government is legitimate which can be justified by further reference to the the people (consent, interests, ethnic background or whatever) and a domestic government grossly violates principles of domestic legitimacy, it is difficult to see why it should be internationally treated as if its representativity were a matter of course. Obviously, difficult calculations about, e.g. utility, human rights and political tradition will be included in a deliberation of whether to hold an intervention legitimate or not. But it is not only because these considerations are difficult, or that on balance intervention should be restricted to very serious cases and limited by its object and duration, that we are entitled to assume the absolute illegality of intervention. For the non-intervention principle as a rule of law is only a restatement of the State's initial, formal freedom. Just as there is no guarantee against the State using that freedom in a way which violates other States' or its citizens' freedoms, there can be no *inherent* preference on one State's self-definition of where the limits of its freedom lie against other States' substantive views on the same matter. It is symptomatic that although the law seems to possess a fairly categorical (and hence, formal) non-intervention principle, any serious juristic discussion on intervention

---

self-determination and tyranny, and that no formal, general rule seems able to provide a satisfactory solution. Even an attempt to "balance" the risks – including the common proposal to refer the issue to a contextual standard of proportionality and harm – will entail calculations of the justice of alternative solutions.

[91] See e.g. *Graham* 13 Rev.Int.Stud. 1987 pp. 137–139. I have already pointed out the connection between the domestic analogy and non-intervention in *supra* ch. 2. See also *Carty* (Decay) pp. 87–93 *et seq* and the discussion of the positions of J. S. Mill and Kant by *Vincent* (Non-intervention) pp. 54–58. The liberal's dilemma – that non-intervention seems compelled by sovereign freedom while the very idea of freedom sometimes requires penetrating the veil of sovereignty – is usefully discussed by *Hoffmann* (Bull: Intervention) pp. 23–24 and *Beitz* (Political Theory) pp. 71 *et seq*, 90–92, 121–123.

always points towards the weighing of material factors such as proportionality, importance of the interests to be protected and the like.

The difficulty is that if we take liberal justice seriously, then we must concede that it is sometimes possible – even necessary – to overrule formal peace by developing criteria which, by their links to competing theories of justice, point beyond the Rule of Law but which – as Carty observes – "provide the only useful terms in which one may reflect on the normative dimensions of intervention".[92] If we try this, we shall end up in a discussion which threatens to allow any State's preferred criterion as a permissible *causa belli*.[93] Choosing only some among many competing criteria means having to overrule sovereign equality or assuming that justice can be discussed in an objective way. If we hold on to the formal notion of non-intervention then we shall both prefer some States' values (those supporting the *status quo*) over the values of others and undermine the neutrality on which the Rule of Law was legitimized. Today's pragmatic solution seems to be to retain the formal principle but to concede that it may sometimes be morally necessary to breach it – without saying this out loud. And we do not say it out loud because we really have no clue about how to cope with our strong moral intuitions or what to do with the freedom we are supposed to have.

Let me summarize the lesson of these four examples in a somewhat more abstract way. The idea that law can provide objective guidance in legal problem-solution is, under the social conception of law, premised on the view that legal concepts and categories faithfully translate the actual into a programme for the ideal. But what is "actual" might be conceived in different ways. We have seen that a pre-enlightenment view saw the actual in terms of its intrinsic nature, its participation in a natural *telos*. Social life was looked at from the perspective of theological

---

[92] *Carty* (Decay) p. 112. The problem of a legal institution of (non-)intervention is, as *Wight* (Butterfield-Wight: Diplomatic Investigations) observes, that "international law can only make a system out of it by losing touch with diplomatic facts", p. 111. He notes that a doctrine which is based on "Western values" directs one constantly to seek for a contextual *via media* between the extremes of interventionism and non-interventionism, pp. 111–120.

[93] One diplomatic effort to engage in such discussion was the drafting of the Definition of Aggression. See UNGA Res. 3314 (XXIX) 14 December 1974. For a perceptive criticism, see *Stone* (Aggression), arguing that the final formulation was an empty compromise which added nothing to Article 2(4) of the Charter. The participating States, he contends, were less interested in deciding the issue than in maximizing the political gain and stigmatizing as much as possible of their adversaries' actions, pp. 146–151, *passim*.

purpose or man's natural sociability and the law was needed to give expression to these. Classical lawyers discarded this view. The character of the actual depended on what human beings thought about it. It followed that the law, too, was to be related, not to some natural ends but to the human experiences of what actuality was like and what was needed to make it more acceptable.

But human experience of the actual is varying. What some envisage as justice others think of as injustice. Because there appear to exist no external standards to prefer these experiences, the law cannot do this, either. Instead of expressing principles of justice, the law must only transform, or mediate, extralegal consensus about social norms. The problem is not only – although it is so in an important way – that this makes law powerless when no consensus exists or against States not participating in it. The problem is also that to seem acceptable, law must appear through concepts which remain neutral by reference to ongoing political disagreement. They must appear such as to be capable of supporting formal demands for autonomy as well as for community.

But curiously, whenever disputes arise, these concepts seem capable of being invoked as justifications for decision only *after* a meaning has been projected to them from some of the rival visions of justice whose conflict the law pretended to transgress. There is no automatic, objective sense to the available legal concepts or categories at all. The strategy of legal formality fails because the content of positive autonomy/community can only be decided through a principle of justice which allows one to characterize some present social arrangement either as intolerable totalitarianism or unfettered egoism.[94] The meaning of legal concepts and categories becomes dependent on their user's previous commitments about substantive justice:

ideal: community   autonomy

concept:

actual: totalitarianism   egoism

---

[94] Naturalistically oriented lawyers sometimes notice this clearly. *D'Amato* 79 AJIL 1985 observes the way both the United States and Nicaragua, during the *US Military and Paramilitary Activities* Case, used "spurious" legal arguments which were so designed as to be compatible with the academic tradition – dressing the issue in terms of the general principles of aggression and self-defence – which seem wholly irrelevant to what "unbiased, reasonable observers" would understand as the core issues of the events (human rights, regional stability etc.), pp. 657–664.

In other words, the social conception of law fails because social actuality can be described in different ways. Sometimes we attain the description of present conditions as intolerable totalitarianism (subordination to militarily or economically advanced powers, everybody's submission to the good will of the nuclear powers, cultural imperialism etc.). At other times the present looks like anarchical egoism (pollution, over-use of natural resources, arms race etc.). Consequently, we sometimes legislate in order to enhance independence, sometimes to attain community. But whichever reason we give, we remain vulnerable to having others interpret our legislative project as either egoism or totalitarianism. This is possible because "autonomy" and "community" are purely formal notions and because we have excluded from ourselves the possibility of giving them material sense. We have felt that discussion about the acceptability of different types of community or autonomy and choosing between them will involve us in a political argument.

In the following section I shall describe how this ambiguity about the sense of the legislative project of international law has given us a set of formal concepts which can be used so as to support any material practices and thus renders problem-solving practice incapable of attaining material resolution without going beyond its constitutive assumptions.

7.3 Reversibility and the structure of international legal argument

The idea that law can provide objective resolutions to actual disputes is premised on the assumption that legal concepts have a meaning which is present in them in some intrinsic way, that at least their core meanings can be verified in an objective fashion. But modern linguistics has taught us that concepts do not have such natural meanings. In one way or other, meanings are determined by the conceptual scheme in which the concept appears.

Now the problem of indeterminacy which we have surveyed throughout this book results precisely from the fact that there is no one conceptual scheme in the way we use our legal language. I have discussed this phenomenon by reference to the emergence of the descending and ascending patterns of argument in crucial doctrinal spheres. They provide two conceptual schemes which define themselves by their mutual exclusion. The problem is that each concept (argument, doctrine) may be included in both patterns. If we relate these patterns to the twin projects surveyed in the preceding section, we see that each concept used in argument may given an interpretation which links it to autonomy or community. Because neither seems able to be consistently preferred, these concepts *must* be capable of including both meanings. And this leads to what could be called the phenomenon of *reversibility*.

By reversibility I mean the capacity of each legal concept (argument, doctrine) to be projected with a meaning which links it both to the ascending and the descending conceptual scheme. Take, for example, the non-intervention principle. It seems descending and communitarian as it may be understood to aim towards a world based on equality, mutual respect, peace and toleration. Simultaneously, as it strengthens States' claims to self-determination, freedom and independence, it may be understood from an ascending, individualistic perspective. Again, self-determination may be interpreted as a claim for justice, solidarity and equality (descending interpretation) as well as a claim for freedom and independence (ascending interpretation). Correspondingly, it may be criticized as a totalitarian principle (as it denies self-determination from smaller units) or as a separatist, egoistic policy. Neither of these interpretations has any intrinsic priority *vis-à-vis* the other. Whichever we choose is not dependent on their natural essence but on our (interpreter's) position in regard to some principle of justice.

We have seen that in standard disputes disputants were capable of putting forward views between which no definite priority could be made. In disputes about sovereignty "facts" were opposed to "law", in sources "justice" was opposed to "consent" and in custom a "psychological element" was opposed to a "material" one. *All* standard disputes in these fields seemed to involve precisely these oppositions. Moreover, the relevant legal concepts seemed capable of being invoked by both disputants because they were able to confer those concepts' reverse interpretations. And the problem-solver seemed unable to decide between the disputants' interpretations without moving beyond the concepts themselves into a theory of justice which it was not open for the legal problem-solver to do.

Let me state the phenomenon of reversibility in a somewhat similar way as David Kennedy has done.[95] Imagine five familiar pairs of concepts which might be used in actual legal argument:

1. independence/equality
2. consent/justice
3. domestic jurisdiction/international concern

---

[95] See *Kennedy* 23 GYIL 1980 pp. 361–366; *Floum* 24 Harv. ILJ 1983 pp. 279–283.

4. *de facto* possession/*de jure* recognition
5. jurisdiction/immunity.

Initially, it seems that many disputes involve just such oppositions. Somebody asserting full independence might be opposed with an argument about this violating another's equality. Somebody invoking consent might be opposed with another's argument about justice. A State invoking its domestic jurisdiction might be opposed by an argument about the matter being of international concern. A State claiming a piece of territory by reference to actual possession could be opposed with the argument that such possession has never been recognized. A State invoking jurisdiction might be opposed by an argument about the other State's immunity from such jurisdiction. The identity, or point, of each of the opposing terms seems to lie in the way it claims priority over the other. To be independent seems to require that one is not bound while equality seems to require restricting independence. Domestic jurisdiction has sense only as a negation of international concern and *vice versa*. And so on. Which term does the law prefer?

Each concept, or argument, on the *left* side may first be taken to express the ascending conceptual scheme while those on the *right* side appear, in such case, as descending ones. At issue in each dispute would then seem to be preferring either autonomy or community. Of course, we have seen that such preference cannot consistently be made. But imagine that it *could* be made. Take the case of a well-meaning dispute-solver who might believe that the law in fact required that he prefer the concept which gives the States more "freedom" or which best enhances "community". Imagine, in other words, that somebody would come to decide these disputes who would lack commitment to juristic rationality and who would simply think that the law preferred one or the other of the conceptual opposites. You might think that at least that person could consistently solve the opposition.

And yet, he could not because the *available concepts themselves contain both principles within them*. This is so because we may *reverse* these initial associations and think that the concepts on the left in fact prefer community while those on the right prefer individualism. A State claiming equality may, for example, claim it in order to achieve greater economic independence – conversely, a State claiming independence is also making a claim about its equality *vis-à-vis* other (independent) States. A State invoking justice can only demonstrate the content of its norm by reference to what States have accepted – a State invoking consent can only do this by assuming that the relevance of its consent can be derived from justice. A State making the point of domestic jurisdiction must make this by reference to international rules. The content of international rules is dependent on what States domestically decide. *De facto* possession may be a criterion of territorial acquisition only if generally recognized as such – general recognition of possession as lawful must (if recourse to the justice of possession is excluded) explain itself by the *de facto* effectiveness of possession. Invoking jurisdiction entails invoking immunity from another State's power – appealing to immunity is to make a point about one's own jurisdiction. Even if our imagined dispute-solver preferred autonomy or community he could still not make a consistent decision because he would not know which position to prefer. He would first need to know *what kind of autonomy, what type of community is needed* – he would have to have a substantive vision of the kind of order the law is meant to enforce before he could give either of the opposing terms a determinate meaning and before making a decision would be possible. But if he possessed such knowledge, he would have no need to apply the formal-legal concepts at all. He could directly appreciate the justness of the parties' positions.

Reversibility results from the way our legal concepts need to conserve both projects, both conceptual schemes within themselves. For if it were the case that concepts which preferred either community or autonomy would always be preferred, then legal argument would be pointless. Merely to state the dispute would be to state its correct solution. The opposing arguments (arguments which preferred the concept which law would not prefer) would not simply be valid legal arguments at all. Clearly, this is not the case. In some way all arguments used in above examples are valid legal arguments and the issue seems to be only to decide a relative preference between them. But such preference becomes impossible because the *initially opposing arguments come to look indistinguishable.* Because each legal concept can and must be argued from an ascending as well a descending perpective the sole criterion for making a preference is lost.

To participate in international legal argument is essentially to be able to use concepts so that they can be fitted into both patterns, so that they can be seen to avoid the dangers of apologism or utopianism and support both community and autonomy. The dilemma is that this makes contradictory solutions to normative problems seem equally valid. Both parties argue in terms of independence *and* equality, consent *and* justice, domestic jurisdiction *and* international concern, *de facto* possession *and de jure* recognition, jurisdiction *and* immunity. To over-rule the disputants' interpretations would be possible only through a theory of the essential meaning of the concepts used. But this would be equivalent to arguing on the basis of a theory of natural justice.

Take the case of transfrontier pollution.[96] Noxious fumes flow from State A into the territory of State B. State A refers to its "sovereign right to use its natural resources in accordance with its national policies". State B argues that A has to put a stop to the pollution. It interprets A's position to be an individualistic, ascending one while it makes its own argument seem a communitarian, descending one.[97] It might refer to a norm of "non-harmful use of territory", for example, and justify this by reference to analogies from rules concerning international rivers and natural resources as well as precedents and General Assembly resolutions.[98]

State A can now retort by saying that norms cannot be opposed to it in such a descending fashion. A is bound only by norms which it has accepted. It has never accepted the analogies drawn by B. This would force B either to argue that its preferred norm binds irrespective of acceptance – in which case it stands to lose as its argument would seem utopian – or to change ground so as to make its position seem ascending as well. State B might now argue that the pollution violates its own freedom and constitutes an interference in its internal affairs – as Australia did in the *Nuclear Tests* Cases (1974).[99] B's position would now seem both descending (in respect to A) and ascending (in respect to B itself).

---

[96] See also *Michelmas* Nomos XXVIII p. 77.

[97] So stated, both States can refer to the formulation in Principle 21 of the 1972 Stockholm Declaration – widely held to be expressive of the customary law on international pollution. According to the Principle: "States have, in accordance with the Charter of the United Nations and the principles of international law, the sovereign right to exploit their own resources pursuant to their own environmental policies, and the responsibility to ensure that activities within their jurisdiction or control do not cause damage to the environment of other States …" Report of the UN Conference on the Human Environment, Stockholm 5–16 June 1972, UN Doc. A/CONF.48/14. On the customary status of the two sides of the principle, see *Koskenniemi* XVII Oikeustiede-Jurisprudentia 1984 pp. 100–103.

[98] See *ibid.* 1984 pp. 118–181; *idem* 3 Suomen Ympäristöoikeustieteen julkaisuja 1982 p. 52 *et seq.*

[99] ICJ: *Nuclear Tests* Cases, Pleadings I p. 14. See also *Handl* 69 AJIL 1975 p. 50 *et seq.*

To counter this last argument by B, A needs to make a descending, communitarian point. It may argue that there is a norm about friendly neighbourliness, for example, such as that observed in the *Lake Lanoux* Case (1957), which requires that States tolerate minor inconveniences which result from legitimate uses of neighbouring States' territories.[100] B cannot demand complete territorial integrity. A's position is now both ascending (in respect of A itself) and descending (in respect of B).

The argument could be continued. Both parties could support the descending, communitarian strand in their positions by referring to equity, general principles and the like to deny the autonomy (egoism) of the other. And they could support their ascending arguments by further emphasis on their independence, consent, territorial integrity, self-determination etc. to counter their adversary's communitarian (totalitarian) arguments. Moreover, they could support their descending arguments about non-harmful use of territory (B) and good neighbourliness (A) by further ascending points concerning State practice or the other's tacit consent or acquiescence. And they might suppport the ascending emphasis on their sovereignty (A) and territorial integrity (B) by further descending points about systemic values, general principles, equity and so on.

As a result, the case cannot be decided by simply preferring the ascending arguments (autonomy) to the descending ones (community) or *vice-versa*. Both arguments support both positions. The case cannot be solved by reference to any of the available concepts (sovereignty, non-harmful use of territory, territorial integrity, independence, good neighbourliness, equity, etc.) as each of the concepts may be so construed as to support either one of the claims. And the constructions have no inherent preference. They are justifiable only within conceptual schemes. And the conceptual schemes cannot be preferred because they rely on each other. A decision could be made only by going beyond the concepts altogether. In which case we would have left the Rule of Law. A court could say that one of the positions is better as a matter of equity, for example. Or it might attempt to "balance" the claims.[101] But in justifying its

---

[100] *Lake Lanoux* Case, XII UNRIAA p. 316. Likewise, in the *Trail Smelter* Case, III UNRIAA, the Tribunal noted that only such pollution was unlawful "when the case is of serious consequence", p. 1965. For the rejection of the principle of complete territorial integrity, see further *Koskenniemi* XVII Oikeustiede-Jurisprudentia 1984 pp. 121–127, 152–164.

[101] Thus, writers on international environmental law regularly end up in conceptualizing the conflict in terms of balancing the equities. See *Koskenniemi* XVII

conception of what is equitable in a way which deviates from the equity the parties have put forward, the court will simply have to assume a theory of justice – a theory, however, which it cannot justify by further reference to the legal concepts themselves.

Reversibility occurs in all normative problems. Take, for example, the relations between a foreign investor and the host State. The view which emphasizes individualism, separation and consent (the ascending point) may be put forward to support the host State's sovereignty – its right to nationalize the corporation without "full, prompt and adequate" compensation.[102] But the same position can equally well be derived from descending points about justice, equality or solidarity or the binding character of the new international economic order, for example. The home State's case may be argued in a similar way, by laying emphasis on *that* State's freedom, individuality and consent – as expressed in the acquired rights doctrine[103] – or the non-consensually binding character of the *pacta sunt servanda* norm, good faith or other convenient conceptions of justice. To make a choice, the problem-solver should simply have to prefer one of the sovereignties *vis-à-vis* the other – in which case sovereign equality is overruled – or it should use another theory of justice (or equity) – which it cannot, however, justify by reference to the Rule of Law.[104]

Oikeustiede-Jurisprudentia 1984 pp. 128–164 and the notes therein. See also *supra* ch. 4 n. 149. As we have seen, the turn to balancing seems to be the only way to escape from *any* situation in which what is prohibited or permitted to States may seem uncertain. Thus, having situated the topic "international liability for injurious consequences arising out of acts not prohibited by international law" in precisely that area (i.e. the field in which States' responsibility does not apply), the Special Rapporteur for the ILC noted that here it was not a matter of applying existing rules on lawfulness/non-lawfulness but of determining what the (primary) rules themselves should be and that "This always entails a true weighing of opposing interests, putting a little more into one scale and taking a little from the other, until ... the scales are evenly balanced", *Quentin-Baxter* Third Report, YILC 1982 vol. II/I p. 54 (§ 14). See also the comments in *Magraw* 80 AJIL 1986 pp. 311–313, 327; *Pinto* XVI Neth.YBIL 1985 pp. 38–42; *Handl* (*ibid.*) pp. 66, 76–77; *Goldie* (*ibid.*) p. 204 *et seq*.

[102] This, of course, is the standard reading of Article 2(2) of the Charter on Economic Rights and Duties of States. That the right to nationalize was an "expression of the State's territorial sovereignty" was also stressed in the otherwise fairly conservative Award in the *Dispute between Texaco Overseas Petroleum Co./California Asiatic Oil Co. v. the Government of the Libyan Arab Republic*, XVII ILM 1978 p. 21 (§ 59).

[103] See *Saudi Arabia v. Arabian American Oil Co. (ARAMCO)* (1958) 27 ILR pp. 117 *et seq*, 168 and e.g. *White* (Lillich: Injuries) pp. 188–192.

[104] The conflict of sovereignties and the need to take both into account was stressed e.g. ICJ: *Barcelona Traction* Case, Reports 1970 p. 33 (§ 37). *Seidl-Hohenveldern* 198 RCADI 1986/III ends his discussion of the matter by stressing the importance of the

A further example is provided by the puzzlement of lawyers as to how they should understand the relationship between the principles of self-determination and territorial integrity, both having been enshrined in countless UN General Assembly Resolutions.[105] The problem, as we now can understand it, is that neither of the conflicting principles can be preferred because they are ultimately the same. When a group of people call for territorial integrity they call for respect for their identity as a self-determining entity and *vice-versa*. In order to solve the conflict, one should need an external principle about which types of human association entail this respect and which do not. And this seems to involve arguing on the basis of contested, political views about the type of organization the law should materially aim at.[106]

These examples are, of course, simplified. In judicial or arbitral practice the positions and changes do not appear in such clear-cut fashion. Doctrine is burdened with complex mechanisms for hiding the tensions within it. But legal argument may always be analysed so as to reflect this structure: the disputants interpret each other's claims as manifesting either the ascending or the descending position. Thereafter they develop the appropriate counter-position. Discourse follows this stucture:

$$Ax(-y) \ / \ By(-x);$$
$$A-x(y) \ / \ B-y(x).$$

principle of good faith and noting that: "A solution therefore should recognize the home State's and the Host State's sovereign right to the investment concerned and should endeavour to find an equitable balance between them", p. 54. See also *supra* ch. 4 n.153.

[105] See in particular UNGA Res. 1514 (XV) 14 December 1960; 2625 (XXV) 24 October 1970. On this much-belaboured conflict, see e.g. *Pomerance* (Self-Determination) pp. 43–47 and *passim*; *Koskenniemi* 82 LM 1984 pp. 449–452; *Carty* (Decay) pp. 57–60.

[106] For the different criteria to go in a definition of the "self" which is entitled to self-determination, see e.g. *Pomerance* (Self-Determination) pp. 14–23. He notes correctly that the formal and absolute character of the right of self-determination makes it a "logically meaningless proposition, because the grant of self-determination to one entails its denial from another", p. 71. *Guilhaudis* (Droit des peuples) notes the silent (political) preference UN practice makes to apply the principle exclusively to colonial situations, pp. 32–36 *et seq*, 44–66, 87. UN law which both affirms the right of integrity of the State and a right of secession remains, he argues, "donc fondamentalement contradictoire et sa construction demeure très inachevée", pp. 137–138. See also *Beitz* (Political Theory) pp. 105–115, 121–123. *Jackson* 41 Int'l Org. 1987 makes the useful point that as statehood has been dissociated from the criterion of effectiveness, it has tended to become the consequence of a doctrine of just war (of self-determination) and the law has been opened up to "neoclassical" theorizing about the political appropriateness of particular types of territorial regimes, pp. 519 *et seq*, 526–533.

Arguments proceed by arranging themselves first into contradiction which is then negated into its contrary. The initial positions of A and B ((x) and (y)) are first presented as contradicting (x = −y; y = −x). Because both remain vulnerable to the criticism from their opposite, they must move into another level to accommodate each other there. Here A comes to espouse B's initial point (y) and B comes to adopt A's first view (x). The arguments are both internally inconsistent and indeterminate. Neither set of arguments can be given preference as *they are ultimately the same.* The fact that they are presented by different States remains their only difference.

It is vital to see that the ascending and descending character of the arguments does not result from the arguments' intrinsic meanings. A position, concept or argument is recognized as descending or ascending only in its opposition to a deviating one. Whether it manifests either pattern is the result of *projection* from a contrasting view. The problem is that this projection will make the position, concept or argument immediately vulnerable to the threats of apologism/utopianism. Therefore, it has to be defended by projecting it in the opposite light as well. But if that opposition is lost, then also their sense is lost. Contrasting views seem to emerge from the same premises. The arguments, concepts or positions become mere empty words.

The formal coherence of international legal argument is received from the possibility of using the descending/ascending opposition so as to *create* argumentative conflict. This makes it "feel" natural and recognizably "legal". The mechanism of association-projection whereby argumentative differences are created is what legal argument is about. This gives it the aura of being formally patterned, neutral and determinate. It also explains why familiar oppositions keep re-emerging and why we seem unable to do away with them.

But the coherence thereby received is simply formal. It is not a coherence which can produce, or justify, material solutions. True, solutions are accepted or not but this is no effect of the legal argument. They result either from the factors legal realists have been at pains to point out – from the problem-solver's more or less (usually less) articulate theory of justice or his wish to prefer one sovereign over another. But in each case, the solution will remain controversial and vulnerable for valid criticism which is compelled by the legal argument itself.

That there is no real discourse going on within legal argument at all but only a patterned exchange of argument relates to the way the Rule of

Law leads lawyers to deal with concrete social disputes in a *formal and neutral* way. Discourse points constantly away from the material choice which the problem for any non-lawyer would immediately be about. International pollution, for example, opposes the economic interests of State A with the environmental values in State B. By not addressing those issues directly (because they are "subjective politics") legal argument is left oscillating between justifications which relate the applicable norm to both States' sovereignty and consent and justifications which say that neither State's sovereignty or consent needs to be given effect.

In order to justify a material solution we should have a theory which says, either, that some States' sovereignty or consent can override other States' sovereignty or consent or that nobody's sovereign consent is relevant. In the foregoing chapters I have repeatedly observed that the problem-solver would need to possess a theory of material justice in order to justify material solutions. This seemed unacceptable because the Rule of Law is premised on the idea that theories of justice are neither objective nor neutral and that this is good reason for excluding them from any specifically legal argument. But, I have argued, the Rule of Law itself leads to disappointing conclusions as it remains indeterminate in its core, incapable of giving any solutions to material disputes while being subject to manipulation so as to render any solution acceptable.

Beyond objectivism

8.1 The unfoundedness of objectivism

8.1.1 The structure of legal argument revisited

I started this book by the observation that international lawyers are like lawyers in general in believing that they can produce statements relating to the social world which are "objective" in some sense that political, ideological, religious or other such statements are not. I hastened to add that this did not signify any committal to naïve views about the automatic character of law-application. I tried to define objectivity as loosely as possible without detracting from the way in which international lawyers themselves think about the law and about the character of their statements about it. I did this by the twin criteria of concreteness and normativity and left these on purpose ambiguous so as to allow maximal coverage. By "concreteness" I meant that the law was to be verifiable, or justifiable, independently of what anyone might think that the law *should be*. By "normativity" I wanted to say that the law was to be applicable even against a State (or other legal subject) which *opposed* its application to itself.

Stated in such a fashion, I believe that the minimal conditions for objectivity are met. The identity of law *vis-à-vis* political opinions can be upheld only if both concreteness and normativity can be provided for. For if the law could be verified, or justified, only by reference to somebody's views about what the law should be like, it would have no distance from that person's political opinions. Similarly, if we could apply the law only against those legal subjects which accept it, we could not distinguish it from those legal subjects' political views. Concreteness and normativity are, in this sense, necessary and sufficient conditions for the law's objectivity.

Now, the bulk of this work has gone to demonstrate that these conditions cannot simultaneously be met. First, concreteness seemed to require that we exclude not only explicit political opinions from the process of verifying, or justifying, the law's content but that we also exclude theories of justice. For, it is held, theories of justice are "subjective", they cannot be verified or justified regardless of the political opinions held by some people. Therefore, modern lawyers adopted what I called a "social conception of law". Law arises as a concrete social process. If only we examine those processes carefully enough we shall be able to delineate what emerges as "law" from them.

This surfaced the problem that the meaning of "social processes" did not impose itself on an observer in any automatic way but only through interpretation. There were two ways in which they could be interpreted. One may believe that some processes encapsulate law regardless of what the State(s) involved in them have thought about them or how they experienced what was going on. Some behaviour might be understood to reflect law because that seems just. But this conflicts with our original assumptions. For it entails assuming that something may be law although nobody thinks it so. An internal aspect was needed to avoid the potentiality of illegitimate constraint. Therefore, the moderns have conceptualized social processes in terms of States consenting to or dissenting from norms. But this strategy lost the law's normativity unless it was accompanied with an argument about "knowing better" – an argument which seemed indistinguishable from an argument about abstract justice.

So, the social conception of law does not lead us away from the dilemma of having to prefer either a theory of justice or some State's will. We can decide on the meaning of a social process only *after* we have decided whether to interpret it in terms of justice or consent. If we insist that the law be normative, then we must rely on some non-consensual standard – if we persist in demanding that it be concrete, then we have nothing but the State's own view on which to rely.

The contradiction between the demands for concreteness and normativity accounted, as we have seen, for the way in which legal argument arranged itself in crucial doctrinal areas. There was always a "descending" argument which attempted to ensure the law's normativity and this was always countered by an "ascending" one which provided for the law's concreteness. The former led beyond State will in a manner which seemed vulnerable because non-concrete (utopian); the latter led into particular State will and seemed unacceptable because non-normative (apologist). To seem acceptable, doctrines tended constantly towards a reconciliation. They looked at normativity from the perspective of concreteness and concreteness from the point of view of normativity.

To make an ascending point you had to give a descending justification; and to verify or justify your descending argument, you had to produce an ascending point.

This was easiest to see in the contrast between naturalism and positivism but extended to all other areas of standard doctrine – sovereignty, sources, custom, world order – as well. Each doctrinal topic was constituted by an initial opposition between two concepts (theories, approaches, perspectives, understandings) which seemed to explain that topic in mutually exclusive ways. But neither concept could be fully preferred – neither was able to provide a coherent doctrine alone. As they needed support from each other, doctrine was moved to deny the initial opposition in a way which begged the problems which the doctrines were made to solve in the first place. Juristic discussion appeared to remain in a constant flux. It could find no position in which to remain permanently. Each conclusion seemed vulnerable to valid criticisms from a contrasting perspective.

In other words, the structure of international legal discourse on *all* doctrinal spheres undermined the objectivity on which it constructed itself. In all spheres, lawyers are left with uncertainty and seemingly valid argument to challenge whatever conclusion they have come to. Moreover, they constantly make assumptions and enter into arguments which conflict with the way in which they initially defined "law" as something separate from politics, ideologies, moral or religious theories and so on. This was particularly visible in the constant recourse to equity, good faith and the like. As rules were incapable of providing adequate justifications for legal decision, they were understood from the point of view of an undefined justice. But, as Unger has noted:

> The greater the commitment to equity and solidarity as sources or ideals of law, the less it is possible to distinguish ... law from ideas of moral obligation or propriety that are entrained in the different social settings within which disputes may arise. And the less importance do positive rules have in law.[1]

This may be less a cause for despair than for hope. But to explain why it is that lawyers need to take seriously their unconscious shift into arguing from moral obligation, it is first necessary to outline why the objectivist dream was faulted from the outset.

---

[1] *Unger* (Modern Society) p. 214.

8.1.2   A fundamental dilemma: ideas/facts

With a degree of simplification, it can be argued that Western metaphysics has always been about whether what really exist are ideas or facts.
A group of philosophers who for our purposes may be called "idealists"
have, since Plato, suggested that deep down the world is constituted of
ideas. What appear to us as physical, biological, historical or other facts
are only surface appearances, or aspects, of the more general ideas on
which they are dependent. Another group of equally respectable philosophers have shared what is now (but has not necessarily always been) a
commonsense view that the world is put together from separate facts.
Discussions which have not referred to such facts have been either
without any object at all or an around-the-corner way of speaking
about facts without explicitly referring to them. In order to make
sense of such discussions, they must be translated so as to show their
connection with the reality-creating facts. We may call these philosophers "realists".

It is easy to see that idealism and realism entail radically different
epistemologies. For an idealist, to know something in an objective way is
to have penetrated through the veil of everyday facts into the essence of the
object, into its "idea". Remaining at the level of perception, or facts as they
appear to senses is to remain bound by subjective illusion. The realist, on
the other hand, sees things in quite the opposite light. For him, to know
something is to perceive it as it manifests itself to the senses. For him,
objective knowledge is attained by perceiving facts in their purity, without
the distorting effect of ultimately subjective ideas.

Both epistemologies remain problematic. Idealism has not made a
convincing argument about how ideas can be grasped objectively, without reference to facts, at least to the fact of the subject's own existence
(Descartes). An objective idealism (Hegel) explains that the ideas manifest themselves in some process external to the observer. But how can the
observer *know* that he has grasped that objective, external idea in its
authenticity? Thus, a subjective idealism (Kant) retorts that the ideas are
in truth the subject's own projections. This will, however, lead ultimately into the impossibility of knowing anything objectively on an
inter-individual level. Realism, on the other hand, has been unable to
exclude the influence of ideas from its project of grasping facts. An
objective realism (Marx) explains that facts are "out there" and determining what we can see in them but cannot explain how the amorphous
mass of information which our senses have about those facts can become

organized into "knowledge". A subjective realism (Hume) which constructs the world from the impressions or data which have appeared on
our senses has been unable to show that these "data" really have a
connection with something beyond our phenomenological world. To
ground the possibility of inter-individual knowledge, idealism needs
reference to "facts" which are external to individual subjects. To explain
the organization of sense-data into useful "knowledge" in our minds,
realism needs reference to "ideas".[2]

While idealism and realism seem opposite they still need to rely on
each other. Philosophy is in a dilemma: though it explains knowledge as
a relation between the knowing subject and the object (whether an idea
or a fact) it seems incapable of keeping the two separate. In some way,
we seem trapped in a circle in which the subject's subjectivity is constructive of the objects perceived while that subjectivity seems to possess
existence only in relation to a pre-existing framework of ideas and facts.
Hence, a part of modern philosophy has rejected the epistemological
enterprise and the idea of objectivity associated with it altogether. These
philosophers have held that there just is no such ultimate ground for the
testing of propositions which we feel could be plausible candidates for
"truth" that they could be fitted within any of the suggested models of
knowledge. They have either wanted to do away with the object/subject
distinction altogether or have reformulated objectivity so as to relate to
the ways whereby agreement is reached on certain matters or to the
frame of mind of persons engaged in knowledge-production.[3] These

---

[2] For the way in which philosophical problems arrange themselves through an opposition
between an external (objective) and internal (subjective) point of view, see also *Nagel*
(Rajchman-West: Post-Analytic Philosophy) pp. 31 *et seq*, 38–46. For a "deconstructi-
vist" outlook, see also *Harland* (Superstructuralism) pp. 70–76.

[3] *Newell* (Objectivity) has noted that "objectivity" presents itself with two faces. On the
one hand, it refers to knowing something which "is really out there", external and
independent of the knowing subject. This, however, adds nothing to whatever concern
we might have to engage in a dispute about the modes of having knowledge about
objects. On the other hand, it may also refer to the character of methods (absence of bias)
in the process of knowledge-production. A dispute about what one would have reason to
believe tends to turn on this latter question. Here there is no question of the acceptance
as "knowledge" only something that is "external". Objectivity now concerns the character of the common practices of knowledge-production, pp. 16–38. See also *Rorty*
(Mirror) (making the distinction between objectivity as "correspondence with external
reality" and as "reasoned agreement"), pp. 333–334, *et seq*. *Unger* (Social Theory)
expresses the turn towards the latter conception as a move from the search of absolutely
incorrigible truths to an attempt to secure maximal corrigibility, pp. 80–81.

philosophers have stressed the conventional character of truth[4] – even of
scientific truth.[5]

---

[4] Among modern philosophers an influential view which rejects the conventional ("external") idea of objectivity is that presented by *Wittgenstein* (On Certainty). For him, any of
our justified beliefs can be ultimately taken back to propositions which are no longer
supported by evidence but are simply accepted within a system ("structure") of convictions grounded in a shared (empirical) "form of life". Ultimately, such propositions and
their embeddedness in the forms of life are "the elements in which arguments have their
life", p. 16 (§ 105). See also pp. 15–16, 21, 28, 35–36 (§§ 102, 144, 204, 274, 298). The case
against "foundationalist" epistemology, the attempt to provide an ultimate, objective
basis for our beliefs has been made most forcefully by *Rorty* (Mirror). Having shown how
attempts to provide such basis in philosophy have failed, he suggests a hermeneutic
vision (though, he claims, not as a successor discipline to epistemology) in which there is
no "hope for the discovery of antecedently existing common ground, but *simply* hope for
agreement, or, at least, exciting and fruitful disagreement", p. 318. The notion of objectivity as correspondence with something external is rejected as a "self-deceptive effort to
eternalize the normal discourse of the day", p. 11. For him, the justification of beliefs is a
"social phenomenon rather than a transaction between 'the knowing subject' and
'reality'", p. 9. "The only usable notion of 'objectivity' is 'agreement'", p. 337. In reaching
agreement, all that controls the process is whatever criteria for good argument prevail in
the community. He contrasts "systematic" with "edifying" philosophy and, noting the
failure of the former, opts for the latter, the point of which is simply "to keep conversation going rather than to find objective truth", pp. 377, 365 *et seq*. Ultimately, he notes,
only this kind of attitude will avoid thinking of other people in terms of their relations
with external objectivities rather than *pour-soi vis-à-vis* each other, pp. 375–377. See
also *idem* (Rajchman-West: Post-Analytic Philosophy) pp. 3–16. For a review and
discussion of this movement into pragmatic relativism in philosphy, see also and
generally *Newell* (Objectivity); *Bernstein* (Beyond Objectivism) (discussing the apparent
convergence in recent theory of natural and human sciences away from positivism and
from the "Cartesian anxiety" with objective truth into hermeneutics. He argues that the
latter, in turn, contains an implicit – but insufficient – critical trend and discusses how
philosophers such as Arendt, Rorty and Habermas have been led into a philosophy of
critical praxis) pp. 150–164, 171–231.

[5] In the philosophy of science, the same view has been argued by *Kuhn* (Structure). He
points out that scientific truths are always paradigm-dependent. A paradigm, loosely
defined as "an accepted model or pattern" or "disciplinary matrix" (pp. 24, 182) is not
something external to scientific results but determines what can count as such and hence
as "truths" for the paradigm in question. An upshot of this argument is that paradigms
cannot be validated by the methods they use to validate their results – in particular, they
cannot be validated by the perception of facts, as "something like a paradigm is
prerequisite to perception itself", p. 113. In other words, "there can be no scientifically
or empirically neutral system of language or concepts", (p. 146) which could arbitrate
between differing paradigms. These remain incommensurable as, literally, "the proponents of competing paradigms practice their trade in different worlds", p. 150. The
scientific "revolutions" which occasion paradigm-changes involve, in this sense "changes
of world view" (pp. 94–102, 111 *et seq*) which cannot be dictated by laws of logic or
scientific proof but which work through techniques of argumentative persuasion, not

This dialectic goes to the heart of social theory. Neither rationalism nor empiricism seems acceptable as such.[6] On the one hand, as Peter Winch writes, arguing against naïve but popular empiricism, "the concepts we have settle for us the form of experience we have of the world".[7] On the other hand, these concepts are internalized in a process of socialization and do not come about as autonomous constructions of the individual. As Max Horkheimer puts it, the consciousness we possess of the society is "a product of the human society as a whole".[8] A social theory which aims to avoid reductionism needs to explore the embeddedness of facts and ideas in each other; the way in which social behaviour is induced by normative conceptions which, again, are constructed by reference to specific social environments. This involves not only the description of the understandings and concepts which social agents may have but requires going deeper, to decide which of the rival understandings better reflects the character of our social practices. This will entail speaking of norms and practices independently of participant understandings in a way which will inevitably cast the social theorist himself as a participant in political debate.

8.1.3   Ideas and facts in international law: the problem of method

It should not be difficult to notice how international legal discourse repeats the indeterminacy of Western philosophy by opposing legal

---

excluding, for example "idiosyncrasies of autobiography or personality", pp. 152–159. The Kuhnian view is applied into an analysis of the structure of international legal scholarship by *Ginther* (Festschrift Lipstein) (isolating three "incommensurable" paradims – Western, socialist and Third World) pp. 31–56.

[6] See, in particular, *Taylor* (Philosophy) (arguing for a "hermeneutic" approach – an approach which links phenomena through common meanings instead of causal or logical relations) pp. 15 *et seq*, 52–57, *passim*. See also *Unger* (Modern Society) pp. 8–23, 245–262.

[7] *Winch* (Idea) especially pp. 14–15, 83–91. More recently, this view has been adopted by studies of law as a semiotic system. See e.g. *Carrión-Wam* (Carzo-Jackson: Semiotics) pp. 53–54.

[8] *Horkheimer* (Critical) p. 200. The point is that Winchian relativism (understanding society through the rules which its members have internalized) cannot distinguish between rule- and constraint-governed behaviour, ideology and physical power. It fails to see how people are constrained by rules they are unaware of. Though hermeneutics is needed to overcome positivism, Critical Theory is needed to overcome the relativism implied by the latter. Though language may be a kind of meta-structure on which social processes depend, language as tradition is itself dependent on power and reproduces relations of domination. See e.g. *Giddens* (Central Problems) pp. 244–245. See also *MacIntyre* (Self-images) pp. 213–229 and further *Bernstein supra* n. 4.

"idealism" with a legal "realism" and being unable to make consistent preference for either.[9]

According to one view, international law is a set of ideas, manifested in the form of rules. This is followed by an epistemology according to which to know international law objectively is to grasp those rules in their authenticity. State behaviour, will or interest are sociological facts which may have had an effect on the law but which are external to its present content. To concentrate on facts is both an epistemological error (as it fails to notice that facts appear through conceptual apparatuses) and loses the law's normativity, its capacity of being opposed to naked power.[10]

According to another view, international law is fact. This is accompanied by an epistemology according to which rules are only "transcendental nonsense". To make sense of them, they must be referred back to the (social, biological, economic, power-based etc.) facts (needs, interests) to which they give more or less adequate expression. To stare at the abstract formulations of rules is doctrinal subjectivism. A concrete study of law needs to relate rules to their social context.[11]

These positions seem both exhaustive and mutually exclusive. Yet, both produce convincing criticisms of each other and must constantly lean towards each other. To escape from endless interpretative controversies, the law-as-idea approach must posit itself on the plane of the law-as-fact view. It must look at the assumedly impartial arbiter of facts. To become normative, the law-as-fact view must assume that there exist ideas which tell which facts are relevant and in which sense (i.e. which

---

[9] See e.g. *MacCormick-Weinberger* (Institutional) pp. 1–6, 33–41.

[10] *Kaufmann* 54 RCADI 1935/IV notes: "Toute analyse approfondie des réalités conduit à des éléments idéaux qui, bien que non palpables par les sens exterieures et loin de n'avoir qu'une existence subjective et psychologique, sont d'ordres objectifs et constitutifs des phénomènes réels: il s'agit de catégories réelles d'ordre général et éternel, de formes substantielles inhérents aux substances particulières et individuelles", p. 319. The same idea is contained – though in less sophisticated form – in the postulation by *Bos* (Macdonald-Johnston: Structure and Process) of a "general concept of law", working as a kind of Platonic Idea, the "essence" of the term "law" (containing the ideas of the law's normativity, its non-voluntary character, *pacta sunt servanda* and that nobody can transfer a right he does not have), pp. 52–53, 59, 67–68, 73.

[11] See e.g. *Giraud* 110 RCADI 1963/III, noting that what is needed is "non pas de démontrer et d'analyser des textes et fixer leur portée, mais de constater des faits et d'établir entre eux des rapports de causalité ou de circonstance, pp. 462–463. Law is a "jeu des forces" – ultimately of physical force, p. 482 *et seq.* Only the methods of political science can grasp such forces in an "objective and neutral" way, pp. 462–465 *et seq.* See also *supra*, ch. 3.3.3.

facts are law-creative, which deviation). But this will make both positions vulnerable to the criticisms they originally voiced against each
other.

The two perspectives involve persisting disputes about the correct
way to pursue international legal doctrine, about method. For one
group of lawyers, doctrine's proper function is the exposition of valid
norms. Sociological analysis may have a function, too, but it is separate
from and secondary to the main function of interpretation and systematization of rules. Unless the legal method were so distinguished, it
would coalesce with that of the historian or political scientist. Another
group of lawyers criticize such an understanding as idealistic and too
far removed from the facts of power and politics in international
relations. These lawyers point out the indeterminacy of doctrinal interpretation and the irrelevance of academic discussion which omits
considerations of fact.

Method, as pursued by doctrine, is constant movement away from
doctrine itself to something beyond it – a solid epistemological foundation. Why should doctrine feel justified in producing the kinds of
conclusions it produces? The answer, it is assumed, can only be found
by referring to method which provides an external, objective guarantee
of the conclusions reached.[12]

It is difficult to imagine what other a juristic method could aim at
apart from vindicating doctrine's conclusions by reference to normative ideas or social practices. Even a lawyer who avoids taking a side
on the methodological controversy seems compelled to adopt one or
the other or try a reconciliation. The problem is that however much
doctrine shifts position (from ideas to facts, facts to ideas), the
impartial guarantor, the secure epistemological foundation seems
beyond reach. There is no such resting-ground where it could be
concluded that this idea, this fact, is the ultimate objectivity. For
facts and ideas are always in need of interpretation in which the
interpreting subject's subjectivity – his conceptual matrix – plays a
prominent role.

---

[12] See generally *Bleckmann* (Grundprobleme) pp. 9–36. *Kunz* 56 AJIL 1962 observes that
the "crisis" of international law and method is caused by subjectivism, "wishful thinking . . . presenting one's own wishes, mere proposals *de lege ferenda*, as law actually in
force", pp. 488–499. See also *Falk* 61 AJIL 1967, arguing for a move "away from
impression to scientific inquiry", pp. 477 *et seq*, 487–495.

8.1.3.1 The interpretation of facts: the relations of law and society reconsidered

I have argued that the modern international lawyer writes from within a social conception of law. This position is grounded in modern criticisms of natural law and legal formalism. In its instrumentalist (Pound, McDougal, Bedjaoui), social solidarity (Scelle, Falk) and economist (Marxism) versions, this view criticizes the attempt to base law on natural justice or legal logic. To be objective, these lawyers assume, the legal method must aim at social context. These lawyers ridicule the indeterminacy of interpretation and the attempt to think of international law a complete system. They point out the subjectivism in adopting *a priori* definitions of international law.[13]

However, the very proliferation of realist doctrines shows that mere reference to society does not provide the impartial epistemological foundation sought after. Which facts are relevant? These might be facts of human biology, of social solidarity, interdependence, relations of power or hegemony, for instance. But such facts are overlapping. It is possible to look at any State behaviour from any of such perspectives – and a host of others. Take the case where the troops of Apologia cross the frontiers of Utopia. This "fact" might be described from different perspectives. One account might see there naked use of power by the rulers of Apologia to subvert Utopian sovereignty and self-determination. Another might see there a natural expression of human solidarity in which Apologia fulfils its political obligation against Utopia's population. A third account might see there an intricate attempt to re-establish the balance of power, distorted by a third State's actions elsewhere on the globe. A fourth description might point to some economic or historical law which expresses itself in such action. And so on. The meaning of the facts under scrutiny does not appear in a pure form. To understand Apologia's action – whether it should be called intervention, self-defence or humanitarian assistance, for example – one needs to lay an interpretative matrix on the events. And the choice of the matrix

---

[13] The standard argument against law-as-ideas lawyers' inability to cope with "normative-ambiguity" of legal words is contained in *McDougal* 82 RCADI 1953/I pp. 143–157. See also *Morison* (Macdonald-Johnston: Structure and Process) (as legal rules always appear through interpretation, their binding force is illusory) pp. 150–151, 157; *idem* (Reisman-Weston: Toward) (the objectivity of the law-as-process view residing in its externality to the legal process and its concern with predicting instead of making decisions) pp. 5–13.

not only involves controversial choices over what is significant in social phenomena but is also anterior to the facts to be described and really determines what count as relevant "facts" in the first place.[14]

There is a common-sensical view which tells us that facts can be grasped in their purity by observation. This view appears frequently as a "functionalist" doctrine which aims to study international law as a set of responses to social needs or interests. It is premised on the idea that needs and interests are primary, "real" and determining while the law is secondary and determined and that, consequently, a legal method must be constructed as empirical observation of those needs and interests.[15] Morton Kaplan, for example, suggests that instead of fruitless conceptual exercises, international lawyers should start focusing attention to the "constitutional structures and processes in the international arena", meaning thereby that legal study should concentrate on the "real world" struggles for power and wealth and the logic of any institutional arrangements which may have been established.[16] In particular, legal

[14] For a cogent defence of the "indispensability of political theory" in studying conceptual matrices which give currency to competing descriptions of social events, see *MacIntyre* (Seidentop-Miller: Nature) pp. 19–33.

[15] In social theory, "functionalism" is usually associated with the work of Durkheim and Parsons. For accounts of functionalism in international theory, see *Bull* (Anarchical) pp. 75–76 and in international law, see *Falk* 61 AJIL 1967 pp. 487–495. Most of what I have labelled "policy-approach" and "idealism" (see *supra* ch. 3.3.4.) moves in a functionalist atmosphere – law is seen as an expression of "interdependence" or "needs" of the community. For a clear statement of the functionalist position in international law, see e.g. *Giraud* 110 RCADI 1963/III. For him, law is caused by politics – political force, sometimes expressed in "solidarities", sometimes in factual power. These account for its "effectiveness", pp. 427–437, 447–450, 465 *et seq*, 482–487, 690–705. Similarly, *Sahović* 199 RCADI 1986/IV (An adequate method needs to be based on "les facteurs qui influencent généralement et ont influencé tout spécialement aux cours des dernières décennies le développement de droit international", p. 184. Consequently, he aims to construct a theory of such "factors" – most important of these being the objective-material forces of power and politics. These must be studied to arrive at better predictive hypotheses, pp. 193–194, 208–211). For a critical discussion of the "positivist bias" entailed by the analogy made by functionalists between social and natural sciences, see *Frost* (Normative) pp. 13–17.

[16] *Kaplan* (Falk-Black: Future I) sees the societal sphere to be on the move from a "balance of power" system to a "loose bipolar" one and predicts future change into the direction of "détente", "unstable blocks" and "development" models, pp. 155–182. For an elaboration, see *Kegley* (Onuf: Lawmaking) p. 176 *et seq*. In this spirit, *Fatouros* (Falk-Black: Future) notes that the question whether or not new States are bound by classical law is "irrelevant" and that what "is important . . . is whether and how far the rules of classical inernational law do correspond to present-day conditions and needs", pp. 318, 319.

change should be deduced from "system change", within the determining, societal sphere.[17] The lawyer's task would become the construction of "models", reminiscent of Weberian ideal-types to be used in predicting normative outcomes.[18]

Recent studies have used quantitative methods to elucidate international legal change by reference to systems change and the incidence of arbitration by reference to socio-historic context.[19] I do not deny the heuristic value of such studies.[20] No doubt they have been encouraged by the assumed advances in empirical sociology, focusing on hard "facts". But my point is that such functionalism is severely misguided as it ignores the determining power of the law as a conceptual scheme which controls our perception of the facts of international society.

However, many recent theories about the relationship of concepts and the world they are directed at do not support such functionalism. According to these theories, our perception of facts is always conditioned by conceptual schemes which have already organized the world in some intelligible fashion. These theories point out that *all* knowledge about facts is interpreting knowledge, that the "real world" cannot be grasped in its purity but only in its reflection in a conceptual scheme. These conceptual schemes – social theories, scientific paradigms,

[17] *Gould-Barkun* (Social Sciences) pp. 24 *et seq*, 209–214.
[18] See e.g. *Johnston* (Macdonald-Johnston: Structure and Process) pp. 200–203; *Gould-Barkun* (Social Sciences) pp. 4 *et seq*, 65–93, *passim*. For the "prediction" aspect in the policy-approach, see *Morison* (Reisman-Weston: Toward) pp. 13, 61–64. Compare *Boyle* (World Politics) (employing a five-function model to measure international law's role in conflict-solution) pp. 67–70, 81–84. *Falk's* (Future) distinction between the "Westphalia" and "Charter" systems to describe and explain "the structures and processes by which international law is created, applied and transformed", like his projected future systems, likewise rests on this view of the lawyer's (and the law's) task, pp. 32–33, 37–38, 43–69. The attempt to "predict" international legal change by reference to determining "models" is also the core of the methodological discussion in *Sheikh* (Behavior) pp. 321–327. See also the essays by *Slouka, Gottlieb* and *Kegley* (Onuf: Lawmaking) pp. 109–209. Many conventional lawyers, too, have assumed a functionalistic approach when discussing the relations of law and society. For them, the law is seen unproblematically as a set of responses to impulses from the societal sphere. See e.g. *Friedmann* (Changing) *passim*, *Schwarzenberger* (Frontiers) pp. 9–64; *Jenks* 138 RCADI 1973/I pp. 463–468.
[19] See *Kegley* (Onuf: Lawmaking) pp. 173–209 and especially pp. 177–181; *Raymond* (Conflict Resolution) pp. 2–6 and *passim*.
[20] See, however, the *caveat* concerning objectivity in such matters by *Gordon* 36 Stanford L. R. 1984 pp. 69–71. Some international lawyers, likewise, have expressed (methodological, not principled) doubts about the reliability of sociological generalizations regarding international behaviour. See *Stone* (Visions) pp. 1–9; *Fawcett* (Law and Power) pp. 9–10.

assumptions, psychological predispositions etc. – "fabricate" what we feel as neutral facts.[21]

The most obvious conceptual scheme which controls our perception is language. As Roland Barthes points out, reality is divided by language, not by itself.[22] Contrary to the common-sensical view, language does not reflect the world but interprets it, carves it up, makes sense of the amorphous mass of things and events in it. In this sense, facts are constructed as they are perceived though language. Just as language is conventional, so is the world it mediates. There is no necessary, "objective" reason why some aspects of the world are categorized while some are not. The feeling of sense and relevance which we relate to the world is not the reason but the effect of language.[23]

These theories suggest that there is no such pure observation of international reality as law-as-fact lawyers assume. In some way or other, our conventional ways of speaking about international relations and international law seem to determine what we can believe to take place in international life. The concept of the "State" is a banal example.

---

[21] See *Goodman* (Ways of Worldmaking), p. 91, *passim*; *Giddens* (Central Problems) pp. 243–245 and e.g. *Quine* (Ontological Relativity) pp. 1–68.

[22] *Barthes* (Elements) pp. 126–127.

[23] The primacy of language to thought is a common theme in much recent social theory. In structuralism, this conclusion is derived from the insight by *Saussure* (Cours) that the meanings of linguistic expressions are not determined through their reference to the world but "from the inside", from the momentary set of relations into which linguistic units have organized themselves, p. 65 *et seq*. *Lévi-Strauss* (Structural) applies this view into anthropological study, noting that "language continues to mold discourse beyond the consciousness of the individual, imposing on our thought conceptual schemes which are taken as objective categories", p. 19. See also *ibid.* pp. 68–69 (language as a *condition* of culture). From a Wittgensteinian perspective, *Winch* (Idea) notes that "our idea of what belongs to the realm of reality is given for us in the language we use", p. 15. A hermeneutical standpoint stresses the significance of the non-reflective "prejudice" or preunderstanding which is incorporated into the language with which we address social life. *Gadamer* (Philosophical) notes that by learning a language we learn a certain interpretation of the world. Thus, "(w)e are always biased in our thinking and knowing by our linguistic interpretation of the world", pp. 59–68. To think otherwise would engender an "illusion of reification" which conceals the fundamentally linguistic – and hence social – character of our experience, pp. 77–78. Much of the idea of such "prejudice" is incorporated in Habermas' conception of the "interest of knowledge". See *Habermas* (Knowledge); *idem* (Theory) pp. 8–9, 15–25. For a discussion of such preunderstanding in law, see e.g. *Esser* (Vorverständnis) *passim*, *Aarnio* (Denkweisen) pp. 123–133; *idem* (Philosophical) p. 133; *Lenoble-Ost* (Droit, Mythe) pp. 3–4, 134–137. Applying Merleau-Ponty's corresponding view to law, the latter regard the common-sensical view an "epistemological obstacle" on the way to study legal consciousness, pp. 317–319.

While the term originally translated a certain combination of population, territory and government, it has come to work independently as a
naturalized scheme which allows us to interpret, for instance, the social
process of people showing papers to uniformed men in well-guarded
places as the socially meaningful activity of crossing interstate boundaries. The concept is so deeply rooted in out conceptual apparatus that,
as C.A.W. Manning notes, if it were suddenly dropped, our perception
of international behaviour would be:

> ... like thinking of a fleet at sea as simply a lot of sailors behaving –
> without reference to the performance of ships.[24]

Similarly, legal terms such as "owner", "contract", "corporation" or "intervention", "treaty", "Government" appear not to mirror social reality but
constitute what can be seen in it.[25] It is simply impossible to think of a
political balance of power, for example, without having internalized a
legal-formal concept of the State and some idea of binding contract
whereby alliances can be formed. Though it would be incorrect to say
that the 19th century system of Great Power primacy was a legal construction, its functioning presupposed legally formulated agreement on
European matters and the principal method of maintaining the system –
collective intervention – was a legal construction. Similarly, when
American and Soviet leaders meet today, the context of their discussion
is structured and the choices delimited by the goal of reaching legally
formulated agreement.

The same point can be made in different ways. There are many
examples of how doctrinal (conceptual) developments have affected
the way we think about international behaviour. The scholarly effort
which in the 1950s and 1960s separated human rights law from the laws
of diplomatic protection, jurisdiction and international responsibility

---

[24] *Manning* (Nature) p. 7.
[25] See e.g. *Gordon* 36 Stanford L. R. 1984 pp. 102–113; *Kelman* (Guide) pp. 253–257. For a
similar criticism of the Marxist view which holds law a passive, super-structural
element, see *Collins* (Marxism) pp. 81–85. See further generally *Plamenatz* (Man and
Society 2) pp. 277–292 and a defence of Plamenatz' view against the attack by
G. A. Cohen, by *Lukes* (Miller-Seidentop: Nature) pp. 111–119. See also *Frost*
(Normative) (noting the impossibility, in international theory, of characterizing the
"structure" of world society in abstraction from international norms or a power-
relation without reference to the normative ideas whereby such power justifies itself)
pp. 54–72. *Brownlie* (Essays Schwarzenberger) notes specifically that "legal concepts
have an indelibility and effect, the reality of which is not sufficiently mirrored by the
language of power and power politics", p. 23.

resulted in a new way of looking at existing practices. Where the individual had formerly been treated in the context of inter-State rights and duties, the new classification of a set of human rights norms made it possible to focus attention on forms of behaviour formerly excluded from discourse as matters of domestic jurisdiction.[26]

It does not seem possible to distinguish between a determining, societal sphere and a determined legal sphere in the way that the law-as-fact approach assumed. In some relevant sense, legal concepts and categories – MacCormick's and Weinberger's "institutional facts" – come to determine what we perceive as social reality.[27] Moreover, it is useful to notice that if facts had such objective essences as assumed by the law-as-fact view and those facts were normative in their own right, this would contradict with the liberal theory of politics as it would do away with human choice. The premise of individual freedom requires that people be free to determine the normative sense of social events.

Ultimately, the law-as-fact view must rely on an anterior, conceptual criterion of significance which tells which facts should be singled out from the mass of actions and events in international life and what they should be taken to mean. In order to prove the significance of the chosen criterion, however, one cannot make further reference to facts. One must move beyond one's original position and start to discuss "significance" in its own right – and this takes one to what seems like a law-as-ideas view, a theory about the justice of alternative conceptual matrices.

8.1.3.2 The interpretation of ideas: the problem of language

Le Fur and Kelsen, a naturalist and a positivist, rejected the law-as-fact view precisely for the reasons outlined above.[28] The latter makes the further point that norms do not merely permit or prohibit behaviour. They also work as interpretative matrices whereby we organize the social world and project meaning to individual events and actions. Like language, international norms interpret for us what we can see in

---

[26] For discussion of the normative effects of international doctrine, see e.g. *Bleckmann* (Funktionen) pp. 21 *et seq*, 277–282, *passim*; *Lachs* (Teaching) pp. 202–209, *passim*.

[27] *MacCormick-Weinberger* (Institutional) pp. 13–16, 49–67. On the world-constitutive character of legal language, see also *Peller* 73 Calif.L. R. 1985 pp. 1181–1191; *Lenoble-Ost* (Droit, Mythe) pp. 108–112; *Carrion-Wam* (Carzo-Jackson: Semiotics) p. 52 *and passim*. See also the discussion of legal "fictions" by *Salmon* 175 RCADI 1982/II pp. 287–294 and of the constructive character of the fact description of the norm, pp. 297–303.

[28] *Le Fur* 54 RCADI 1935/IV pp. 72–106; *Kelsen* (Rechtslehre) pp. 4–5; *idem* 14 RCADI 1926/IV pp. 240–241. See also *Tucker* (Lipsky: Law and Politics) pp. 40–41.

international reality. The fact that people have moved in an embassy can be understood as the social fact of seeking asylum only once we share the concepts, ideas, of asylum, extradition and jurisdiction and so on.

Many lawyers persist in starting their doctrinal work from a definition of international law. They believe that whatever phenomena we might wish to single out as "law" can only be determined by a prior conceptual choice. Some modern reformists seem to think that the problems of law and order are predominantly conceptual ones.[29] But curiously, though these lawyers start from a conventionalist view about language, when pursued to defend their choices, they start to move within objectivist assumptions. They start to argue that their definition is better because it better reflects the "natural" character of international life, the will of States or some idea of natural justice.[30]

Detter-Delupis, for example, notes that the present conceptual system of international law, dominated by "normativist" tendencies, has become inadequate. Therefore, she suggests a new system, an improved (highly elaborate) classification of legal rules. Initially, she seems to be arguing in terms of utilitarian justice. For she proposes that the lawyer's conceptual system should be reconstructed by reference to a "hypothetical goal of international society" – increasing the welfare of mankind.[31] But obviously, "welfare" is a contested subject. Detter-Delupis does not discuss its character nor on what basis scarce resources should be distributed. The hypothetical goal is simply stated, not argued. Moreover, she makes no attempt to demonstrate how her classification fulfils this goal. Nor does she compare her system with other systems in this respect. In the end, she argues that her system is better as it better takes account of a "principle of legal relevance" – a principle which says that a concept should be preferred if it better reflects the changes in international society.[32] Thus, defending her system, she moves into a

---

[29] See, in particular, *Bos* (Macdonald-Johnston: Structure and Process) pp. 51 *et seq*, 68–73.

[30] See also the criticism by *Boyle* 26 Harv.ILJ 1985 (pointing out that any definition of "international law" will contain a "practical point of view" (a conception of purpose or justice) which, however, is regularly left undiscussed in order to present the definition in a credible, essentialist way – a fact which renders disagreement about definitions incapable of ending up in rational resolution) pp. 328–329, 330 *et seq*, 339–340.

[31] *Detter-Delupis* (Concept) pp. 46–47.

[32] *Ibid.* pp. 42–43, 88–90. For example, she believes that a theory of legal subjects should reflect the changes in the actual number of relevant international actors, pp. 18–34. The same movement characterizes the construction by *Bos* (Macdonald-Johnston: Structure and Process) in that defending his conceptual choice against that of the naturalist Krabbe he notes that his concepts are not "contradicted by reality", pp. 63–64, 69–71.

law-as-fact view and becomes vulnerable to the criticisms presented in the previous section. Why should one prefer what exists (as a fact) simply because it exists?

The construction by Detter-Delupis is an extreme example of an attempt to deal with the problem of the ambiguity of meaning in law. Because she believes it to be not a lawyer's task to elaborate on the political principles which would go to defend one or other conception of "welfare" (because she wishes to be objective) she shrinks from even attempting this. And this forces her to leave her initial law-as-idea approach. In this way, she may appear to argue in a realistic way but becomes vulnerable to the criticism that as facts are theory-dependent her choice and interpretation of facts – in particular her claim that those facts support *her* system – is left unargued and has no convincing force whatever towards someone who does not already share a belief in an identical conceptual system.

Of course, law is a particularly linguistic affair. Even an initial analysis of a definition which holds law as an aggregate of "rules" reveals that rules are both linguistic units as well as ideas, or meaning-contents. The problem of the objectivity of a juristic method which concentrates on rules is how we can reach the normative ideas which are assumed to stand behind the linguistic formulations of rules in a reliable manner.[33]

According to an intuitive view about language, linguistic expressions stand as "representatives" of meanings. Meanings are external to the linguistic expressions. But some representative part of them is normally present in the expressions themselves. This "representative part" refers to the extralinguistic world in a way which makes it possible to pin down the expression's meaning. The task of interpretation is to make present that representative part which is momentarily absent and thus to restore the truth of the pure meaning. Though the linguistic expressions in which rules appear may have a penumbra of uncertainty, it is possible through legal interpretation to arrive at the correct meaning by referring the ambiguous expression to something beyond it, for example a drafter intent, textual or social context or some idea of justice.[34]

But it is difficult to sustain this view. Critics have pointed out that the canons of legal interpretation fail to reach that pure meaning in its authenticity. Interpretations rest controversial. The doctrine which

---

[33] This is precisely where the Kelsenian system fails to live up to its own ideal of objectivity. If, as Kelsen admits, interpretation is a political act, then there is no distinct legal process at all. See *Goodrich* 3 Legal Studies 1983 pp. 253, 256, 261–266.

[34] For this traditional view of legal interpretation, see e.g. *Degan* (L'interprétation) *passim*.

studies law as rules begins to seem weak and subjective in its failure to create the kind of certainty about the meanings of rules on the existence of which it bases its claim to superiority over the law-as-fact approach.

The problem is that the external, extraconceptual referent of the rule seems always unattainable. For that referent cannot very well be a fact as we have already seen that facts were constructed by the concepts – rules – which were available and whose ambiguity was the issue. Neither, as many have noted, is authorial intent (State will) attainable in its purity. "Normal meaning", "context" and "purpose", likewise, seemed to emerge as constructive justifications for an interpretation rather than something which existed "by themselves" and could be looked at when concepts proved ambiguous.[35]

Linguistics has long since left the view that expressions have a natural referent in the world of facts. Somehow, the sense of expressions is determined from within language itself, from the relations into which the expressions of language have organized themselves. For structural linguistics, for example, the meaning of an expression is determined by its relation to all other expressions in that language. For it, language appears like a net full of holes – its expressions have no meaning which would be present in them. Such meaning is determined by the strings which differentiate the holes from each other. We know a house from a mansion only through the difference which has been established between them at a conceptual level. There is no such "house-ness" or "mansion-ness" which we could point at so as to grasp the "real" sense of those expressions.[36]

The difficulty is, as Jacques Derrida puts it, in an oft-quoted passage, that "il n'y a pas de hors-texte":

---

[35] Consequently, though stressing the political aspects of interpretation, many lawyers still assume that politics does not govern *all* legal concepts and that the interpretive community of lawyers can (by tradition) arrive at coherent interpretations. See e.g. *De Visscher* (Problèmes) pp. 13–48, 69 *et seq*; *Sur* (L'interprétation) (interpretation as balancing law and politics) p. 65 *et seq*. See also *McDougal-Lasswell-Miller* (Interpretation) (interpretation neither "easy" nor arbitrary) pp. 6–11. Other critics have argued that absent an objective meaning, interpretation can only bring forth the Parties' subjective meanings, *McDougal* 61 AJIL 1976 pp. 995–1000. Yet, if the text has no intrinsic sense, then it is useless as a means for attaining original intent as well.

[36] For a useful criticism, see *Williams* XXII BYIL 1945 (words do not have essential meanings – as this is so, any controversy about sense must look beyond abstract definitions, into the material context) pp. 146 *et seq*, 158–163. See also *supra* Introduction, n. 4.

> ... if reading must not be content with doubling the text, it cannot
> legitimately transgress itself to be something other than it, toward a
> referent (a reality that is metaphysical, historical, psycho-biographical
> etc.) or toward a signified outside the text whose content could take place,
> could have taken place outside language ...[37]

By interpretation we can only attain new expressions and texts which are
just as indeterminate as the original texts were. There remains no
extralinguistic, non-textual method of checking the objective correctness of the interpretation arrived at. The "idea" or the "rule" seems
unattainable in its objective, true sense.[38] Defining "aggression", for
example, by a list of further expressions ("invasion", "attack", "armed
force by a State") does not relieve us from the burden of having
to interpret *those* expressions.[39] The problem is that in case somebody
disagrees with our interpretation, we are left with very little means
to convince him and, unless we are both ready to enter into an
open-minded discussion about the justice of adopting particular interpretations (in which case, of course, there is no certainty that we shall
agree in the end) the danger of endless conceptual referral can hardly be
avoided.

We cannot convince someone who disagrees with our interpretation
by referring to the correspondence between our interpretation and the
expression's "real" extraconceptual meaning. That would assume
that we are already in possession of the correct meaning – in which
case the whole interpretative effort would be unnecessary. But the
world of "pure ideas" recedes always to the backgound and remains
incapable of being grasped without the mediation of the prison-house of
language.

There is, then, no "objective" meaning to the linguistic expressions of
rules. To be sure, many legal theorists have stressed the openness of
language and the constructive role of interpretation. Interpretation
creates meaning rather than discovers it. But conventional theories
have regarded this as a marginal problem, existing in law's penumbral areas. The analysis here suggests, however, that it affects every

[37] *Derrida* (Of Grammatology) p. 158. For useful commentary on the consequences of this
view to interpretation in general, see *Mitchell* (Mitchell-Rosen: Interpretation)
pp. 56–89. See also *Culler* (Structuralist Poetics) pp. 241–252.
[38] See also *Salmon* 175 RCADI 1982/II pp. 285–287.
[39] See UNGA Res. 3314 (XXIX) 14 December 1974 and the criticism by *Stone* (Aggression)
pp. 4–13 and *passim*.

disagreement within international law, from the definition of *that* expression to the finding of the sense of contested rules. Far from being marginal, it is the very core of law – the generator of there being a possibility to disagree. In this sense, the finding that there is no objective meaning to legal concepts, no extratextual referent which could be pointed at when disagreements arise provides the most serious threat we have hereto encountered to the possibility of delimiting law from arguments within "essentially contested" political concepts.[40]

Some lawyers have suggested that even if interpretations cannot be validated by reference to an objective meaning of texts or practices, they might still be validated by reference to a consensus within some reference-group (of international lawyers, for example). This seems a curious position. It fails to explain why someone who does not participate in that consensus should accept what for him is only a majority's interpretation. For surely an interpretation cannot be authoritative simply because some people espouse it and *regardless of the grounds* on which they have done so. So, theories about consensual validation must provide criteria for what count as good reasons for adopting particular interpretations. And the dispute turns then on the appropriateness of some over other reasons. In the end, consensus theorists are forced to present a list of principles which contain the criteria for the appropriateness of interpretations – and these seem vulnerable to the criticisms which have been directed against naturalistic criteria of "good" interpretations.[41]

This is not to say that the consensualist approach is useless. In the next section I shall argue that there is nothing else apart from authentic consensus on which normative problems can justifiably be solved. The point here is that what counts as "authentic" – in contrast to unfounded – consensus cannot be decided on a consensual basis without circularity. The sorts of arguments which go to demonstrate the authentic character of opinions cannot pretend to the kind of objectivity which would escape the criticism of being political.

---

[40] The difficulty is, as critics have noted, that the absence of objective meaning tends to make nonsense of the liberal jusification for the Rule of Law. See *Brest* 90 Yale L. J. 1981 p. 1063; *Tushnet* 96 Harvard L. R. 1983 pp. 781 *et seq*, 804–824; *Unger* (Knowledge) pp. 109–111; *Balkin* 96 Yale L. J. 1987 pp. 772 *et seq*, 781–785.

[41] See e.g. *Aarnio* (Oikeussäännösten) p. 163 *et seq*.

8.2   Nihilism, critical theory and international law

The discussion – or, it may now be fair to say, criticism – in the preceding chapters suggests that the terms of discourse offered to us by the conceptual system of international law are unhelpful for the solution of the kinds of problems they attempt to deal with. Whether lawyers believe the law to be a set of ideas or of facts, they remain incapable of discussing it in a way which would guarantee the secure epistemological basis of their conclusions. They are constantly referred away from that conceptual system into contestable considerations of the justice, or equity, of particular situations. Lawyers seem compelled to assume either that justice is, after all, capable of discussion in an objective way or forced to renounce their legal identity altogether.

But it seems hardly plausible to assume that politics (justice and equity), when properly conceived, would ultimately be capable of discussion in such a way as to relieve us from uncertainty.[42] Though it seems clear that dispute-solution cannot avoid going into what it is just or equitable to do, the discussion has in no way shown that the way back's to Vitoria's unquestioned faith would be open for the modern lawyer.[43] The Enlightenment project is still with us.

That project builds upon the assumption that politics is subjective. From this, liberal doctrine drew the conclusion that left on its own, politics will degenerate into anarchy. Therefore, it needs to be constrained by non-political rules.[44] This is another way of expressing the need for the law to carry within itself an objective and neutral representation of society and to provide a uniquely rational basis for ordering

---

[42] *Sur* (L'interprétation) concludes his review of naturalist and sociological theories by noting that these may be good guides for political action but they fail to establish a "fondement objectif du droit", p. 32. Now some modern liberals have wanted to discard this view and tend towards one or another type of moral objectivism (Dworkin, Lauterpacht, for instance). But as *Dunn* (Rethinking) notes, the problem with this "Utopian liberalism" is that it has until now failed to grasp adequately the metaethical issue of what is involved in (and how to defend) moral objectivism, pp. 161–163. The same applies, of course, to the move to arguing in terms of justice or equity within the legal process.

[43] Though some still believe it is. See *Verdross-Koeck* (Macdonald-Johnston: Structure and Process) pp. 42, 23 *et seq.* But, as *Gomez Robledo* 172 RCADI 1981/III remarks ("avec honnêteté et tristesse") we seem bound to work with a formal notion of binding law (*jus cogens*) which cannot be given definition (cannot be said) as this would involve the inclusion of values – and values are contested, p. 207.

[44] "... the health of the political realm is only maintained by conscientious objection to the political", *Wight* (Butterfield-Wight: Diplomatic Investigations) p. 122.

social life. The law's legitimacy seems to rest on how it fulfils these demands. For they secure that the values which individuals have expressed in the marketplace of politics are correctly transformed into patterns of social constraint.

Similarly, international law is thought to contain a rational vision for the ordering of international life which contrasts with the self-interested, anarchy-oriented policies of individual States. Unless international law contained such an autonomous rationality, it would seem difficult to justify why States which feel that their values have not been adequately reflected in it should still comply with its demands.[45]

Such a vision of autonomous legal rationality is, of course, firmly embedded in international legal education and the professional self-understanding of international lawyers. It establishes the identity of the legal field as something separate from the political (and therefore inherently suspect) fields of diplomacy and statesmanship. The very existence of a separate legal doctrine and curriculum and the presence of the legal adviser's office in foreign ministries transform this quest for an external, impartial standpoint towards international society, a standpoint which allows one to understand and participate in international affairs without having to involve oneself in an argument about political preference.

This vision of the law is severely threatened by the discussion in the previous two sections. For whether we think of law as a set of rules or some constellation of behaviour we seem unable to grasp it through a specifically legal method which would not involve a discussion of about contested ideas about the political good. The lawyer could only record that whatever differences of view about the correct law there existed, these disagreements were not capable of being dealt with by a legal method which would have secured the objectivity and impartiality of the result. Any suggested method only seemed to involve the lawyer in further discussion about principles, purposes and systemic justice which were themselves subject of political dispute.

This experience was clearest in the different substantive fields of international doctrine which constantly pointed away from hard-and-fast rules into contextual appreciation of the circumstances of each case. But recourse to equity (in its different forms) was, it seemed, in contradiction with the ideal of the Rule of Law. What was equitable seemed to depend on evaluative choices which were defined as subjective and arbitrary by the law's very self-constitutive assumptions. Equity

---

[45] See further *Boyle* 26 Harv.ILJ 1985 pp. 347–349.

challenged the formality, generality and neutrality of the legal process. Recourse to it re-emerged the problem of uncertainty and the fear of political abuse which it was the purpose of the Rule of Law to dispose of.

Charles Taylor, among many modern philosophers and social theorists, has noted that "uncertainty is an uneradicable part of our epistemological predicament".[46] This is no place to enquire any deeper into what some have called the post-modern condition, the feeling that "all that is solid melts into air". Suffice it to note that the international lawyer's uncertainty is not unrelated to a more general turn to relativism and/or scepticism in contemporary thought and experience.[47]

These reflections may appear to give a hopeless picture of the possibilities of international law as doctrinal argument and social practice. If "all" is interpretation and interpretation has no solid epistemological foundation, what basis is there to embark on any specifically legal enterprise at all? If the solution of international normative problems by reference to legal concepts was possible only by manipulating those concepts so as to make it seem that no problem existed at all (recourse to tacit consent), by refusing to make substantive solution (recourse to procedure) or by leaving the ground of those concepts altogether (recourse to equity), why should one bother with those concepts in the first place? In other words, it may appear that critical reflection leads necessarily into a kind of legal nihilism. Therefore, it might be objected that these criticisms – borrowed from fields alien to the law – should not be taken too seriously because they are anyway only "theoretical" and distract the lawyer from his more pragmatic tasks of trying to establish *ad hoc* consensus on norms in those areas of State conduct in which that is possible.

It is unclear what force such defence may have. To renounce critical reflection simply as one feels that it will lead into nihilism is not in itself a rational counter-argument. It simply betrays another, and possibly aggravated, version of nihilism as it argues, in effect, that it is better to continue living in an illusion, whatever the consequences, rather than to analyse what part of the illusion might be worth preserving and what simply obstructs constructive effort.[48]

---

[46] *Taylor* (Philosophy) p. 18.

[47] For the link between the loss of legal certainty and the postmodern condition, see *Goodrich* (Reading) pp. 210–214.

[48] *Singer* 94 Yale L. J. 1984 notes that "(t)he unstated premise behind this fear is the idea that we are entitled to have an opinion only if we can back it up by a method for

The counter-argument might, however, be taken to suggest that the problem is not one of intellectual nihilism but of social practice. It might be argued that excessive criticism and stressing the conflictual character of notions of justice will only leave the field of international relations a devil's playground. If there is only subjectivity and uncertainty, will this not leave States free to act in any way they please with ultimately destructive consequences to international order? Nihilism, on this view, will end up letting each State freely impose its will on others as it refuses to recognize the constraints of an external rationality over subjective will.

Leaving aside the plausibility of the causal assumptions involved in such argument, I think it important to show that such consequence does not follow from adopting a critical position towards the illusion of objectivity in legal argument. The point is that one is not committed to irrationality or to an "anything goes" morality even if one rejects the view that law contains an external, privileged vision of society. It simply gives effect to the intuition that the lawyers' expectations of certainty should be downgraded and that they – as well as States and statesmen – must take seriously the moral-political choices they are faced with even when arguing "within the law" and accept the consequence that in some relevent sense the choices are theirs and that they therefore should be responsible for them.[49]

To show that the inevitable movement to politics in legal argument does not compel apologism requires taking a position against the view that politics (justice, morals) is *simply* subjective and arbitrary as such. This requires showing that political views can be held without having to believe in their objectivity and that they can be discussed without having to assume that in the end everybody should agree. There is all the more reason to take up this question as the kind of deconstruction operated in the foregoing chapters may be taken to

deciding legal and moral questions that can compel agreement by its inherent rationality", p. 48. See also *Goodrich* (Reading) p. 216; *Unger* (Critical) pp. 95–97. Reflection, observes *Williams* (Ethics) "can destroy knowledge", pp. 148, 156–173. Taking a critical look towards what we think we know will frequently – perhaps always – raise doubts about whether we are justified in thinking we "know" it. Yet, this is hardly an argument *against* reflection but rather its principal justification.

[49] The argument that moral views can be held without having to believe that they are "objective" is made e.g. by *Rorty* (Mirror) pp. 333–334. For useful discussion, see also *Fishkin* Nomos XXVIII (arguing that continuing to rely on an unfulfilled dream of objectivity will lead liberalism into legitimation crisis) pp. 207–231; *Gaus* (*ibid.*) (for a constructive argument maintaining that subjective value makes no nonsense of moral discourse) pp. 241–269. See also e.g. *Putnam* (Meaning) pp. 83–94 and generally the essays in *Honderich* (ed: Morality and Objectivity).

imply that ultimately all discourse will disperse into an unending play of conceptual oppositions in which there is ultimately no basis to prefer conflicting ideas *vis-à-vis* each other.[50] One way to argue this is to see politics less in terms of ready-made principles clashing against each other than a human practice of continuous criticism of and conversation about present conditions of society and the ways to make them more acceptable.

Downgrading the expectations of certainty will involve a revision of the concept of legal knowledge which the international lawyer can hope to attain. It is useful to note a difference between what some have called "objectifying" (reifying) and "critical" (edifying, reflective) knowledge.[51] The former is something which is produced by what Raymond Geuss has called "objectification mistake" – a mistake in the epistemic properties of one's knowledge.[52] An objectification mistake can be seen to take place when a social agent (lawyer) takes something which results from human construction as external to such construction, standing on its own, autonomous power. An international lawyer, for instance, might believe that a norm is valid because of its logical properties or because it is embedded in an external code of values or pattern of

---

[50] A deconstructive outlook is often taken to imply a relativist (if not indeed nihilist) philosophy of politics. See e.g. *Merquior* (Prague to Paris) (deconstruction marking an "unholy alliance of Nietzsche and formalism") pp. 189 *et seq*, 199. *Dews* (Logics) has, however, usefully pointed out that when pressed against the wall, deconstructivists have been led to abandon their Nietzschean grounds in order to defend their political views, pp. 33–44, 200–219 and *passim*.

[51] The distinction critical/objectifying knowledge is central to the criticism of the enlightenment project carried out by the Frankfurt School social theorists. They have argued that the dogmatic ("scientist") separation of the subject and object of political thought and scientific work has produced a reified consciousness which extends from social practice to social theory. See, in particular *Horkheimer* (Critical) *passim* and pp. 188–243. Within the latter this occasioned in the 1960s the famous "Positivismusstreit" between critical theorists such as Adorno and Habermas and "critical rationalists" such as Popper and Albert. See generally *Adorno* (ed: Positivist Dispute), in particular the essays by *Habermas* and *Adorno*, pp. 131–162 and 68–86. See further *Habermas* (Theory) pp. 253–282 and comments in *Geuss* (Idea) pp. 27–31. See also *Held* (Introduction) pp. 175 *et seq*, 183–187; *Larrain* (Concept) (reviewing the critical-Marxist notion of scientific objectivity as ideology) p. 172 *et seq*. For a programmatic work by Frankfurt School theorists, see *Adorno-Horkheimer* (Dialectic). For secondary literature (apart from the very useful works by *Geuss* and *Held*, quoted above), see also *Jay* (Dialectical) (a history and survey of the different trends in the School). The connection between the scientist principle of analysis and liberal individualism has also been usefully discussed outside the tradition. See *Unger* (Knowledge) pp. 46–49, 81–83, 121–124.

[52] *Geuss* (Idea) p. 71 *et seq*.

behaviour. Both the law-as-idea and law-as-fact lawyers regularly make just such a mistake.

Social theorists have discussed at length the possibilities and character of knowledge which would not be objectifying in the above sense.[53] This has seemed important because objectifying knowledge has seemed to work as an ideology, or a "false consciousness" – that is, it has not only given social agents a mistaken picture of the epistemic standing of their beliefs but also of the possibilities for transformative action.[54] They have been induced to think as natural and inevitable something which is merely contingent and contestable and therefore to regard as utopian illusion any effort to think out alternative ways in which the actual could be transformed towards the ideal. Therefore, these theorists have suggested the development of ways of thinking which would reveal the context-bound, projected character of forms of experience which have been taken as natural.[55]

---

[53] For the application of Rorty's argument (*supra* n. 4) in the development of "edifying" legal outlooks, see *Singer* 94 Yale L. J. 1984 pp. 57–59.

[54] For a review of the notion of ideology as false consciousness in Habermas and the Frankfurt School, see *Geuss* (Idea) pp. 12–22. This is one of the several Marxist notions of ideology. For more extended reviews, see *Larrain* (Concept) pp. 35–83, 172 *et seq*; *McLellan* (Ideology) pp. 10–34. For a (Marxist) reading of law as ideology, see e.g. *Sumner* (Reading) pp. 10–25 and *passim*. For a deconstructive outlook, the notion is problematic as it tends to imply the existence of a privileged ("objective", non-ideological) standpoint towards social relations. See *Foucault* (Power/Knowledge) p. 118. But see also *idem* (Archaeology) pp. 184–186 and the comment on his position in *Dews* (Logics) pp. 313–316 and *Lement-Gillan* (Foucault) pp. 112–114. Likewise, *Lévi-Strauss* (Structural) replaces it with the notion of the "myth", pp. 206–231. See also *Barthes* (Mythologies) pp. 148–149 *et seq*; *Lenoble-Ost* (Droit, Mythe) pp. 280–294 and 9–11, 17 *et seq*, 219–251 (arguing that the idea of the law's completeness and the rationality of the legislator work as mythical projections of man's insecurity and lust for power); *Carrion-Wam* (Semiotics) (stressing the ideological character of *all* natural language) pp. 54–57.

[55] The importance of revealing false consciousness lies, for critical theorists, in the anaesthetic socio-psychological consequences of living under an objectification mistake; "ideology" will involve the human being's alienation from power and politics and his loss of self as an active participant in social relations. See, in particular, *Adorno-Horkheimer* (Dialectic) pp. 3–80, 120–167; *Marcuse* (One-Dimensional) pp. 1–199. See also *Unger* (Knowledge) pp. 29–62. The notion of "legitimacy" is crucial. For the function of ideology is to legitimize – that is, stabilize and justify – domination and hegemony. See *Geuss* (Idea) pp. 15–19. Once ideology is threatened, also those stabilization and justification mechanisms become threatened. For a classical analysis of the crisis tendencies in Western-capitalist society, resulting from the inability of liberal ideology to legitimize consistently the crisis-abatement practices of liberal society, see *Habermas* (Legitimation) pp. 33–94 and for an application of this argument to the crisis of

But this is no answer to the charge of nihilism. If everything is relative to a point of projection, what basis is there to make preference between different projections? In order to escape the problem of incommensurability a critical lawyer needs to provide grounds for justifying why one projection (norm, interpretation, theory) is better than another. Moreover, he needs to do this without involving himself in an objectification mistake, that is, arguing that his view is better because it better reflects what is external to questions of political preference. In other words, the downgrading of expectations of legal certainty must be accompanied by the demonstration that there might be good reason to have some instead of other preferences though there is no external guarantee for the objective correctness of those preferences. This is really the crux of the matter and if it is impossible to provide a knockdown argument to show that nihilism is not inevitable, this is only a consequence of the argument so far and gives effect to the modern insecurity about how one should think of the ends of social organization and human life.

I noted earlier that to avoid the reductionism in thinking of social life either in terms of normative ideas or behavioural regularities we needed to conceive these as embedded in each other. Each normative view was relative to a set of social conditions and each behaviour embodied a conception of its ideal purpose. A critical understanding of present world order, for instance, needs to include an explication of its institutions and of the normative commitments which these institutions entail – commitments which may or may not coincide with the commitments which participants in those institutions may feel they entail.

The embeddedness of norms in institutions and behaviour, the ideal in the actual, provides a basis for critical politics which does not need to rely on utopian justice nor become an apology of actual power.

international legitimation, see *Gordon* (Gross: Future) pp. 336–357; *Navari* (Donelan: Reason) pp. 118–121. Applied in law generally this criticism attempts to show that the appearance of neutrality and determinacy of norms is an ideologically loaded way of disguising the fact that they privilege some views or positions. See the essays in 36 Stanford L. R. 1984 and therein, in particular, *Gordon* pp. 181–182 n. 92; *Hutchinson-Monihan* pp. 206–213 and *Tushnet* pp. 597–598. See also *Peller* 73 Calif.L. R. 1985 pp. 1156–1158; *Gordon* (Kairys: Politics) pp. 287–290; *Kelman* (Guide) pp. 262–268 *et seq.* The classical example of a study of an objectification mistake is the Marxist analysis of the concept of "value" as a fetish, an ideological representation of human relations as natural relations between things. See *Marx* (Capital) I.I.IV. Such an analysis of the law will regard the idea of norms being "objective" as an ideological representation of the overriding character of the power which they legitimize. See e.g. *Miaille* (Introduction) pp. 107–108.

It necessitates a two-dimensional (or dialectical, if you prefer) pro-gramme in which falling into utopianism is checked by the acknowl-edged need to understand the present constantly better while the lapse into apologism is countered by a viewpoint which looks at the present from a conception of its ideal purpose.

It follows that there must be two kinds of criteria for critical knowledge, one negative, the other positive. Criticism must provide us knowledge both of the social actuality and its alternative (or alternatives).[56] This dualism bears a relation to the modern programme of reconciling what we know of the actual with what we know of the ideal. But the reconcilia-tion is not sought from an eclecticism which simply adds prescription to description. The point is to conceive these as not separate from each other but essentially aspects of the same human consciousness – a consciousness which both supports a set of social practices and provides the centre from which those practices may be evaluated and, ultimately, transformed.

The first, negative aspect of this programme directs itself towards existing social consciousness as it is expressed in conventional descrip-tive and normative characterizations of present social arrangements. Applied in international law, the critical programme takes under scru-tiny existing consciousness about international law and reality as this is expressed in conventional legal concepts and categories. This approach refuses to take norms or behaviour at face value as it aims to attain non-objectifying knowledge of both. Therefore, it tries to penetrate the naturalness or givenness (objectivity) of those concepts and reveal their context-bound character.[57] Once conventional consciousness will thus appear as contingent and contestable, the actual will manifest itself in a new light. We get a novel description of social conditions which may or may not trigger off the need for transformative action because it will reveal the political ideals embedded in our original description.

Applied in legal analysis, this aspect of critical knowledge seeks actively to do away with the belief that some norms are there and that

---

[56] The problem, as *Habermas* (Theory) summarizes it, is how to construct a theory which would provide knowledge of what is right and good without relinquishing scientific rigour (utopianism) and about actual social relations without legitimizing them (apology), p. 44.

[57] For an application of this idea in international law, see *Boyle* 26 Harv.ILJ 1985 (objec-tivism – "fetishism of essences" – "subverts enlightened rationality and replaces it with reified ideas, thus ruling out the possibility of real discourse") pp. 358, 328–329, 339–340, 352–353; *Cahin* (Mélanges Chaumont) (discussing the "myths" of the "peace in the Middle East", "durable organization of Poland" and "common heritage") pp. 89–115.

we have knowledge of them because they are the ultimate objectivity. It seeks to undo the naturalness of conventional ways of thinking about the law and proceeds to show that the way we conceptualize it binds us to certain, more fundamental commitments – commitments which may or may not be ones that we like to make. And we may not like to make them for the reason that, for example, they 1) conflict with our other, even more fundamental views; 2) do not reflect what we have understood to be in our interests or 3) are internally inconsistent.[58]

The kind of deconstruction of international legal concepts which I have operated in the preceding chapters is an example of such an enterprise.[59] It has shown that the Rule of Law does not live up to its own ideal of objectivity and fails to provide protection for values which we have considered important. We have seen that it thinly hides from sight political choices which are inevitable in the solution of practical disputes but provides no criteria on which such choices can be made. And we have seen (if only in passing) what kinds of political value go to justify these choices. The positive aspect of the critical programme is considerably more difficult to outline. Like liberalism, critical thought is committed to the idea that there is no external hierarchy for political values. Any attempt to enforce norms on people, free to make authentic choices, can only appear as unfounded domination. The critical theorist seems trapped in this dilemma: although he may produce a convincing criticism of the objectifying character of present social (or legal) consciousness, he seems incapable of explaining why, or how, his own preferred standpoint, his substantive conception of the ideal social arrangement, would not involve just another "false consciousness" and legitimize oppression under some suspect argument about "positive freedom" or "knowing better".[60] The problem is that:

---

[58] See further *Geuss* (Idea) pp. 31–44, 79–88. For the argument that the revelation of a belief as "false consciousness" will, for rational agents, make action towards the dissolution of the conditions which had produced it *mandatory*, see *Bhaskar* (Scientific Realism) pp. 165–166, 175–180.

[59] As *Dews* (Logics) notes, deconstruction implies a *perspectival* approach to social dispute. It brings out those value-options, interests and desires which make the dispute subjectively real to the participants in it, pp. 205–216. On the critical character of deconstruction, see *Balkin* 96 Yale L. J. 1987 pp. 764–767; *Goodrich* (Reading) ("open the law to debate") pp. 21–24, 218, *passim*. See also generally *Kelman* 36 Stanford L. R. 1984 p. 293 *et seq*.

[60] This is the standard (and powerful) counter-argument by orthodox liberals. It is well expressed in *Berlin* (Four Essays) in which he distinguishes between the classical (negative) concept of liberty as absence of constraint and the originally beneficial

> There cannot be a criterion for non self-delusion which would itself be
> proof against self-delusion.[61]

The critical lawyer's critical commitment, his negative programme,
tends to turn against whatever constructive vision he may have in
mind.[62]

Addressing this difficulty may be started by noting that though
critical lawyers often assume that the criticism of indeterminacy "dele-
gitimizes" standard discourse, it is uncertain whether it really does this.
The assumption that it does is premised on the belief that there is
somewhere a more determinate, and in that sense more objective way
of grasping the issues lawyers are faced with. But this cannot be accepted
consistently with the criticisms in the preceding chapters. The criticism
has only shown that standard discourse is very vulnerable to well-known
criticisms, compelled by itself, and that its vulnerability results from its
arbitrarily restricting the argumentative possibilities open for lawyers.[63]
The critical argument's critical potential lies in showing that it is possible to escape from the frustratingly weak character of legal discourse by
extending the range of permissible argumentative styles beyond the
points in which it is usually held that legal argument must stop in
order to remain "legal". The criticism has not shown that the issue of
consent *versus* justice, for example, would be a non-problem or that
it could be overcome by some magic formula. But it has shown that
unless lawyers start to discuss justice, or the reality and importance of

addition thereto of (positive) liberty as capacity for self-fulfilment and the tendency of
the latter to become used as an apology for totalitarianism, pp. 118 *et seq*, 122–134, 141
et seq. This has been countered by the view that a meaningful conception of the former
must provide for some conception of the latter and that the latter's degradation into
apologism can be avoided by institutional safeguards. See *Macpherson* (Democratic)
pp. 95 *et seq*, 110–119; *Taylor* (Philosophy) pp. 211–229.

[61] *Taylor* (Lloyd: Social Theory) p. 80.

[62] This is particularly applicable to a criticism such as *Falk*'s (Reisman-Weston: Toward).
To the extent that he puts forward general values for "world order transformation",
these seem unobjectionable (minimization of violence, maximization of welfare etc.),
p. 150. Stated so, however, they seem utopian and when analysed, contain conflicting
ideas (when will violence remain justified? How to distribute welfare?). In the end, Falk
is forced into a totalitarian position. There must be a "central guidance system" to
overrule conflicting values (though he does not discuss the values he privileges), p. 151.
The problem is that as long as he hopes to design one, coherent system for world order,
he will have to do this either by meaningless generalization or by overriding somebody's
values.

[63] In this way, it opens a wider range of alternatives to conceptualize the social world and
to grasp power within them. See also *Singer* 94 Yale L. J. 1984 pp. 58–59; *Kennedy* 26
Harv.ILJ 1985 pp. 378–384.

consent, on their merits, the law will remain weak and manipulable and deprived of justifying power.

The issues of consent and justice, permissibility of intervention, the types of groups which should possess self-determination, ways to prevent environmental degradation and to promote economic well-being, among a host of others, are real and difficult. The fact that they are dealt with by a specific style and method which attempts to contain these issues in a uniform style of specifically legal discourse is where the lawyer's problems lie. Having excluded sociological enquiries into causal relationships and political enquiry into acceptable forms of containing power, the lawyer has been left with a particularly idiosyncratic and limited arsenal of argumentative possibilities. The problem is not to do away with these issues but to extend the range of permissible arguments so as to grasp those issues closer to what is significant in them.[64]

The criticism up to now has not flouted the lawyer's arguments on their merits. It has only shown the way in which addressing the normative issues of international politics through a formal Rule of Law approach will very rapidly show itself as an unsatisfactory argumentative strategy. Arguments from legal principles are countered with arguments from equally legal counter-principles. Rules are countered with exceptions, sovereignty with sovereignty. Refusing to engage in sociological enquiries about causes and effects and to assess political weights to be given to particular arguments, the lawyer can only find himself in an argumentative deadlock.

All along this book we have witnessed how, every now and then, lawyers have already extended the range of argumentative options open to them. They have argued about economic interests, social progress, the need of political stability and so on. Yet, they have done this in secret, perhaps more by intuition than by reasoned choice. Sometimes these extensions have been vigorously objected against. But more often everything has passed in silence. This "internal development" is something which grounds the critical lawyer's positive programme. He must show that these deviations from the Rule of Law are inevitable and that if

---

[64] This is the point in *Carty's* (Decay) imaginative book in which he argues, for example, that dressing issues of self-determination in the legal garb of intervention and customary law excludes from discussion issues of significance: "... to test official argument against the traditional criteria of general customary law is the surest way to reach no understanding of the issues involved", p. 115.

one hopes to establish a legal practice with more than a marginal role in international affairs one needs to take them seriously.

This takes us back to the inherently *conflictual* character of those intellectual structures within which international lawyers have sought to contain power. We have seen that disputed ideas about political justice and the character of international society are in some way or other present in the "deep-structure" of all international legal argument – sometimes even quite on the surface of it. Coping with normative problems has seemed to give us immediate access to conflictual notions about possible and desirable forms of social organization. In order to avoid the accusation that he is merely another objectivist in disguise – and thus himself vulnerable to the objections about apologism/utopianism – the critical lawyer must accept the reality of conflict. He must renounce the presumption of the existence of an external rationality in which all possible conflicts would have already been solved and the professional image of the lawyer as the one possessed with a unique technique for seizing these solutions.[65]

Once the lawyer understands that the conflictual character of legal concepts and categories is merely a visible side of the conflictual character of social life he can construct a realistic programme of transformation without engaging in totalitarian utopias. Only then he can appreciate the character of normative problem-solution for what it is; a *practice* of attempting to reach the most acceptable solution in the particular circumstances of the case. It is not the application of ready-made, general rules or principles but a conversation about what to do, here and now. We have difficulty to conceive the matter thus only because the Enlightenment project has led us so far from the ideal of normative practice and has provided us with such a distorted picture of what is involved in it.[66]

Sovereignty, freedom, consent, self-determination, equality, solidarity, justice, equity etc. are, as we have seen, general maxims which seem both unobjectionable and irrelevant. Behind them work conflicting views about what to do here and now, incompatible suggestions for how to solve particular normative problems. Critical practice attempts to reach those conflictual views, bring them out in the open and suggest practical

---

[65] Lawyers "have tended to be forgetful both of the irrationality and chance embedded in social life as well as of the instability and change intrinsic to human purpose and human personality", *Goodrich* (Reading) p. 209.

[66] See generally *MacIntyre* (After Virtue). See also *Spragens* Nomos XXVIII pp. 336–355.

arrangement for dealing with conflict without denying its reality. Some of the conflictual views have to be overridden. Others are provided with only partial satisfaction. But this is legitimate under two conditions: first, the solution must be arrived at through an open (uncoerced) discussion of the alternative material justifications; two, the critical process must continue and put that rival justification – as it will now have become part of dominant consciousness – to future criticism. The legitimacy of critical solutions does not lie in the intrinsic character of the solution but in the openness of the process of conversation and evaluation through which it has been chosen and in the way it accepts the possibility or revision – in the authenticity of the participants' will to agree.[67]

Critical-normative practice does not justify solutions by their "objectivity". It does not claim that its solutions would correctly transform some general rule or principle. It avoids the charge of apologism as a result of the openness of the process and as it implies that in another context a different solution might be arrived at. It avoids utopianism because it does not rely on general principles and directs itself to what is best of the available alternatives here and now.

It is now possible to see that a criticism of objectivism neither entails anarchy nor cynical nihilism as a necessary consequence. The critical project implies both an institutional and a normative ideal. Rorty writes:

> ... the desire for (critical, MK) objectivity is not the desire to escape the limitations of one's community, but simply the desire for as much inter-subjective agreement as possible ... (thus it is also a, MK) desire to extend the reference to "us" as far as we can.[68]

---

[67] It is difficult to deny the point that behind all communication – including discussion about norms – lies the presupposition that rational agreement is possible: "expectation of discursive redemption of normative validity claims is already contained in the structure of intersubjectivity", *Habermas* (Legitimation Crisis) p. 110. Would we not make such claims, normative discourse would seem pointless. See also *MacIntyre* (After Virtue) pp. 8–10 and *Williams* (Ethics) pp. 171–173. Relying upon Habermas, *Carty* (Decay) proposes that international lawyers should seek to identify the "real" arguments – arguments of subjective significance – in conflict and to construct an "ideal discourse" within which these issues can be discussed with the aim of reaching "mature" solutions, pp. 111–128 (using the examples of Falklands crisis and the Israeli invasion in Lebanon). See also *Kratochwil* (Falk-Kratochwil-Mendlowitz: International Law) pp. 639–651 (arguing for a type of practical reasoning which "makes the definition of 'legalness' no longer dependent upon disembodied normative structures", p. 640).

[68] *Rorty* (Rajchman-West: Post-Analytic Philosophy) p. 5. For the idea of legal argument as "conversation", not deduction – drawing expressly upon Rorty – see *Singer* 94 Yale L. J. 1984 p. 51 *et seq.*

The institutional ideal of a "conversant culture" implies a community in which people view each other – precisely because their choices are "subjective" – as equals, equally human, equally facing a conflictual reality, and equally uncertain in their humanity about how to live. It imposes both openness and a search for agreement to our institutional practices.[69]

Behind this institutional ideal, however, there is an even deeper normative ideal. This is the ideal of *authentic commitment*. What is involved in authentic commitment ("ethic of responsibility") has been usefully summarized by Moorhead Wright in three terms. It involves 1) the accountability of each for the choices one makes; 2) the exercise of discretionary power so as take account and fairly assess the widest range of consequences of one's acts, and 3) responsiveness to the claims of others. The ideal of authentic commitment directs normative conversation away from abstract principles of natural law, away from formal rules and the liberal ethic of consent and the market-place.[70] It recognizes that normative commitment may follow not only from whatever people might have consented to (although it does regard consent important) but also by virtue of the context in which they live. Authentic commitment means, in other words, respecting the conflictual character of social life. It tries to make life possible in conflict – indeed, it sees life in terms of constant coping with conflict, not in terms of assimilation into nostalgic utopia.

The normative ideal of authentic commitment may further be characterized from two perspectives. On the one hand, it respects the insight that nobody can legitimately impose his values on others and that each person's choices should be respected. On the other hand, it recognizes that no person is fully autonomous but that each person's choices are constrained by the conditions which surround him and by the choices which others make and have previously made. This establishes two kinds of rational constraints for the critical lawyer's positive progamme. First, it compels to present social ideals in other terms than as attempts to realize a given background unity, a nostalgic vision of religion, of biological, social or historical necessity. For such programmes

---

[69] *Rorty* (Mirror) sees the point of "edifying" knowledge in that it will make human beings appear as responsible subjects rather than objects. To "freeze over" culture in a belief that one has found the objective essence will result in a "dehumanization of human beings", pp. 337, 375–379. See also *Unger* (Critical) pp. 23, 25–31, *passim*.

[70] *Wright* (Mayall: Community) pp. 158–166.

ultimately fail to give effect to authentic commitment. They impose an external, deterministic idea of community which is constantly in danger of transforming into an apology of effective power.[71] Second, it compels a movement towards the construction of social institutions which are not only open and revisable but which positively encourage revision and the imagining of alternative institutional frameworks and thus give currency to what is probably most human in us: our capacity to transgress the boundaries of any existing consciousness, any framework of ideas or institutions which are usually taken as given and immutable.[72]

Hence, we see that the negative and positive aspects of the critical programme are *indissociable*. Criticism without an ideal of community is without direction and degenerates into cynicism. Reliance on acceptance by social agents alone remains blind to the conditions in which society allows its members to consent to or dissent from norms.[73] The twin method of criticism and a normative practice oriented towards openness and revision respects the insights produced during the criticism of objectivity. Conflict will remain but it is by recognizing it and declining to solve it by reference to objective rules that the critical programme can slowly proceed towards (instead of promising to realize at once) decreasing domination and increasing the sense of an authentic community between disagreeing social agents.

To make this discussion more concrete and relate it to the situation and tasks of international law a radical revision of what can be put forward as a constructive project for international lawyers seems called for. In this book I can do no more than to give a brief and very tentative outline of what a constructive project would be like which builds upon the criticisms I have undertaken and which still makes it possible for the lawyer to engage in construction, both at the level of the practice of dispute-solution and at the level of legal theory. In so doing I shall rely

---

[71] *Unger* (Critical) pp. 103–108.

[72] Unger (Critical) pp. 25–42, 91–117; *idem* (Social Theory) pp. 20–25, 180–185, 200–215. See also more generally *idem* (False Necessity).

[73] A decisive weakness in theories which base legitimacy on simple consent is that they fail to grasp the effect of the social context upon the choices which people make. For this criticism and an alternative "three-dimensional" analysis of social power, see *Lukes* (Power) pp. 11 *et seq*, 21–25. See further *Unger* (Knowledge) (on the metaphor of critical thought as a spiral of decreasing domination through criticism and thus enhancing authentic community and the possibility of rational consensus and *vice-versa*) pp. 242–244; *idem* (Modern Society) pp. 239–242. For the ideological character of a social science which looks at its object through subjective experiences thereof, see also *Adorno* (Adorao: Positivist Dispute) pp. 70–77, 84–86.

strongly on Roberto Unger's radical project and, in particular, the distinction he makes between "routines" and "formative contexts".[74] The construction I have in mind attempts to explain how it is possible for a critical lawyer to maintain his identity as a lawyer without giving up the (political) commitment to the criticism of objectification mistakes as illegitimate – and hence, illegal – domination.

8.3   Routines and contexts: a tentative reconstruction

It was Max Weber who pointed out that the legal order is always a projection of the legal staff's knowledge of it.[75] This is merely another way of noting the indissociability of the social world and the concepts and categories through which it appears to us. But it highlights the fact that in a relevant sense law is what lawyers do and think and that the problem of the law cannot be dissociated from that of the identity of the lawyer. In this final section I shall enquire into the possibilities of re-establishing the identity of international law by re-establishing that of the international lawyer as a social agent. The problem is what the lawyer should do in an inherently conflictual reality of international life.

The experiences of apology and utopia reproduce a familiar dilemma which social agents confront when trying to locate themselves in the social world. To have identity as conscious agents they must fight constantly against alienation and assimilation. They must participate in social routine and yet, do this from a distance. To be a conscious actor requires relatedness to the social world in a way which makes it possible to live in the present without losing the sense of beyond. Looked at from this perspective, the problem of international law is not whether the law adequately reflects some ideas or some facts but whether and how one can *live* in and through it, whether one be a practitioner or a theorist, a diplomat or a professor.[76]

---

[74] *Unger* (Social Theory) pp. 18–25, 62, 88–89 and generally *idem* (False Necessity).
[75] *Weber* (On Law) pp. 6–7, 198 *et seq.*
[76] In psychoanalytic terms, the assumption of a unified, authoritative normative order may be understood as a flight from – or repression of – the painful experiences of conflict and uncertainty. *Lenoble-Ost* (Droit, Mythe) explain this as follows: Belief in a coherent normative order is taken as a positive solution of the Oedipal conflict and equalled with the human being's entry into the symbolic universe (of law). The ambivalence between desire (for mother) and fear (of castration) is solved by the introjection of the father, that is, the all-powerful normative order: "Cette production culturelle ... se produit comme discours cloturé; cloturé, fixité à la mesure des fascinations

The beginnings of an answer can be traced by making a distinction between two facets of social life, routine and formative context. The former denotes the visible, regular practices of social life. The latter consists of the institutional and imaginative constraints within which routine works and which routine helps to reproduce. The feeling of apologism arose when it seemed that we took routines too much for granted while ignoring the imaginative and institutional constraints. The experience of utopia, again, was that we concentrated on imaginative and institutional structures in abstraction from their expression (actual or possible) in routine. To cope with these two experiences, it is necessary to outline for the lawyer an existence in routine which constantly aims at transforming the contexts which shape it and an intellectual directedness towards context-transformation without losing touch of its embeddedness in routine.[77] This is what the ideal of authentic commitment demands from the lawyer himself.

8.3.1   Routines: from legal technique to normative practice

For the international lawyer, social existence means participation in legal routine and yet doing this so as not to be wholly submerged in it. True, the lawyer is constrained. But inasmuch as he experiences the conflicting pull of the criticisms of apology and utopia, he is not fully so. Nor is he then completely alienated into a world of private phantasy. To feel this conflict involves living in uncertainty. But to lose uncertainty is to lose one's sense of the reality and the personal character

identificatoires par lesquelles les désirs narcissistiques, qui n'ont pas désarmé, survivent à se fonder dans la figure du garant: l'auteur du Texte", pp. 348 and generally 331–340. The law makes conflict go away. It takes on the appearance of the external third, the solver of conflict, a father in possession of "truth". See further *ibid.* pp. 347–350 and e.g. *Frank* (Modern Mind) pp. 11, 17, 89, *passim*. For reviews of the use of the theory of repression in critical social thought, see also *Jay* (Dialectical) pp. 86–112; *Geuss* (Idea) pp. 19–20, 39–42. A beneficial trait in realist criticisms of "normative-ambiguity" has been its consequent stress on personal responsibility (though this has sometimes been set aside for belief in some postulated – and contestable – general moral-political principles). See e.g. *Weston* (Reisman-Weston: Toward) pp. 124–130.

[77] Such perspective aims to grasp what *Giddens* (Central Problems) has termed the duality of structure; we have just as little reason to think of human agents as fully constrained by the structures which surround them as we have to think of them as autonomous builders of those structures, pp. 5, 69–73. On a dualistic, or "transformative" model of social action as a condition for the possibility of emancipation, see also *Bhaskar* (Scientific Realism) pp. 122–129, 160 *et seq*; *Outhwaite* (Philosophies) (against both individualist and holist reductionisms) pp. 108–119.

of one's choices. It would mean complete assimilation into routine or phantasy.

Routine, I have said, is the visible facet of social life which expresses itself in the everyday practices of international law. It consists of foreign office lawyering, dispute-solution, writing and applying legal texts and concepts. In short, it expresses itself in our engaging in the sort of debates and arguments which this book has been about. In routine, the international lawyer, diplomat, adviser, leads his life in international law. In routine, a crucial place is occupied by *roles*. The role is what, for the most part, shapes routine. In occupying and fulfilling the roles which are open to us we reproduce those imaginative and institutional constraints through which any particular society establishes its identity.[78] There is a powerful image of the international lawyer which is the intellectual projection of a set of corresponding roles. Legal adviser, judge, arbitrator, professor, diplomat connote some of those roles which international law seems to offer. Each exists in and is reinforced by the different legal practices of international lawyering. The routine of international law is most immediately shaped by these roles.

To reproduce itself, society ideally needs no more than the roles which inhabit it. Simultaneously, roles are a constant threat to consciousness and identity. There is this dilemma: to participate in routine, one needs to do this through a role. But the more one immerses oneself in one's role, the less one is actually participating as a conscious agent at all.

It is hardly an exaggeration to say that there is uncertainty about the particular role, the particular contribution of the international lawyer in international affairs. Traditionally, this has been a role of the impartial technician – the "judge" – whose identity lies in his objectivity. The judge stays aside from social conflict and comes in only at determined points to perform the task of ascertaining the law's content in a neutral way. The lawyer is needed because only he possesses this particular technique. We often associate with the judge a special kind of "integrity" – a full devotion to the role, humility in face of political conflict, moderation and impartiality. This sense of a peculiar integrity and a belief in the crucial social significance of the judge fully executing his role is well expressed by Fitzmaurice – himself one of the most consistent incarnations of the role of the judge:

---

[78] For one critical discussion of the roles which help to reproduce liberal society, see *MacIntyre* (After Virtue) pp. 73–87.

The social function which law has to perform is precisely that of supplying the legal element so necessary in international, as in human affairs, and so indispensable to a full and satisfactory consideration and settlement of the problems that arise. But the value of the legal element depends on its being free of other elements, or it ceases to be legal. This can only be achieved if politics and similar matters are left to those whose primary function they are, and if the lawyer applies himself with single-minded devotion to his legal task ... By practising this discipline and these restraints, the lawyer may have to renounce, if he has ever pretended to it, the dominance of the rule of *lawyers* in international law, but he will establish something of a far greater importance to himself and to the world – the Rule of Law.[79]

In his memorial article on Fitzmaurice, Jennings further explains that it was the former's pre-occupation:

... to defend the juridical integrity of international law, as a complete and consistent system impartially applied ... (for the, MK) authority of the entire system ultimately depends on the maintenance of that integrity.[80]

Yet, all along this book we have seen that the international judge's arguments, his specifically legal tools, constantly take him away from the privileged terrain of objective law, into discretion which seemed just another name for subjective politics. Even when he did not overtly use discretion, he used rules and principles and interpreted them in ways which seemed to involve contested political assumptions. It was not that there would not have been consistent and self-conscious lawyers who tried their best to fulfil the role of the judge and keep in check their subjectivity. The very operations which they used to carry out this task were premised on politics and conflictual as such. For the judge, it must ultimately remain an incomprehensible dilemma and source of professional frustration and personal disappointment why it is that equally competent lawyers, with equal amounts of professional integrity constantly come up with conflicting solutions to the same problems.

---

[79] *Fitzmaurice* Transactions of the Grotius Society 1953 p. 149. Quite consistently, he chooses as the topic for his general course the "standpoint of the Rule of Law", *idem* 92 RCADI 1957/II pp. 1–227.

[80] *Jennings* LV BYIL 1984 p. 22. He notes further: "Fitzmaurice would not care whether his suggestions were dubbed radical or conservative. What mattered to him was (a) whether they were genuinely juridical arguments and (b) whether they would stand up to juridical reason and scrutiny", p. 33.

So, the ideal of integrity has seemed to involve a self-justifying illusion. The role of the modern lawyer can no longer be conceived in terms of being a "judge". He is much more thought of as the "adviser". But the tension within the role of the "adviser" is obvious and often recalled. On the one hand, he is thought of as the Grotian cosmopolite, the academically trained jurist who goes from court to court to advise sovereigns on the secrets of the law. On the other hand, there is the image of the bureaucrat, the adviser to his Government on how best to fulfil national interest without breaking the law.[81] Both images may be associated with positive as well as negative characterizations and professional posts within international organizations, governments and business. The role of the adviser, torn between a commitment to the community and his national State (corporation, organization) is what constitutes the modern lawyer's realistic professional option. And yet, it is an option which seems to demand the lawyer to lead a schizophrenic existence; he must be a believer and a non-believer, a judge and a politician at the same time.

Many people believe that international law offers a promise of a more just society. Yet, once they enter it, they will realize that there is no coherent and objective project for a better world embedded in the concepts which they are taught. They do not become impartial judges who pass sentences on petty politicians and diplomats in the interests of a world community. They will find out that the system of international legal concepts refers justice away from itself and that the professional use of those concepts requires an ambiguous commitment either to an uncertain internationalism which is threatened by degeneration into

---

[81] Thus, for *Macdonald* 156 RCADI 1977/III, the legal adviser is "... an employee of his government. His duty is to his government", p. 385. Yet, he must also "remain sensitive to the needs and interests of the international community and to the integrity of the international legal system itself", p. 387. He is neither a "watchdog" of international law nor of national interest but must constantly balance both aspects of his work, pp. 389–391. Likewise, the organization of the legal adviser's office reflects this. He may be a "lawyer-diplomat" – in which case, however, there is threat of national bias – or he may be an "in-house lawyer" – in which case he is threatened by separation from political reality, pp. 414–458. *Brownlie* LIV BYIL 1983, too, notes that the adviser needs a "good balance of optimism and scepticism" – to find the balance is a juristic task and is opposed to "any special brand of idealism or (to, MK) fashionable ideas borrowed from that most vacuous of spheres, political science", p. 63. It is simply a matter of "common sense", p. 66. Not unsurprisingly, *Fitzmaurice* 59 AJIL 1965 makes an unmitigated preference for separate organization for the legal adviser's bureau, distinct from policy-making tasks, pp. 77–84. This (objectivist) perspective is shared by *Jennings* LV BYIL 1983, pp. 17–18; *Sinclair* (Cheng: Teaching) pp. 123 *et seq*, 133–134.

elitism or it makes them national bureaucrats of the kind they wished to avoid by choosing international law from their available options of specialization.[82]

This is but another transformation of the movement from law to equity. Absence of objectivity forces the lawyer (as the adviser, no longer the judge) to choose between a commitment to international or national values. Yet, the system gives him no idea on what basis this choice could be made nor on how to reconcile, even *ad hoc*, the conflicting demands. The dangers of cynicism or uncritical adoption of some value-system loom constantly large. Whatever the lawyer does, there seems to exist no specifically *legal* commitment for him to make. He may become a manipulator of one or another system but he must then remain in constant doubt about whether somebody else would really do his job better.[83]

The question for the lawyer is whether it is possible to re-establish a special identity for him. How to fulfil the ideal of integrity in the absence of an objective law? For nothing said so far has diminished the value of integrity. Impartiality, maturity, openness, compassion, commitment, etc. still seem important qualities. It is only the conventional stress on the subjective – and as such, arbitrary – character of value which seems to make talk about such qualities an idle exercise in self-admiration.

But there you are. The routine of international law can be entered only through the roles. And yet, I believe that the tension within the role of the adviser – the tension between commitment to communal and national values – and the internal development of legal argument which we have surveyed provide a possibility for reformed routine; a routine which allows the lawyer to escape from the limitations of the role and help to create a better society while enabling him to live a conscious and meaningful life as a lawyer in the midst of the actuality of social and political conflict. This involves looking further into the need to move from legal technique to normative practice.

Originally, there was the idea of a World Rule of Law – the belief that international law had developed into a "universal formal order" which allowed the lawyer to take a "world order perspective".[84] This was

---

[82] See also *Kennedy* 26 Harv.ILJ 1985 pp. 361–384.

[83] He is forced to attempt to "balance the claims" – a task which makes him vulnerable to conservative criticism about his neglect of impartial general principles: "A balancing court will always appear as an uncertain usurper of the veins of power", *Kahn* 97 Yale L.J. 1987 p. 59.

[84] *Jenks* (Common Law) pp. 77, 62 *et seq*, 74–89. See also the works cited *supra* ch. 7 n. 6.

expressed not only in self-conscious "blueprint movements" but also, and more significantly, in the doctrines which held the law a "complete system" which either provided ready answers to all normative problems (by recourse to presumptions, general principles, systemic values or the like) or at least significantly reduced the discretion within which politics was to function. From this coherent body of law the lawyer was to draw consequences in the solution of normative problems which lay at hand. The lawyer's identity lay in his skill as the managing technician of this invisible international "system".

But we have seen that international law is constantly open to conflict. Rules are few and ambiguous and loaded with exceptions. To maintain the idea of a complete system – and a specifically legal identity of their task – lawyers have recourse to "deep-structural" purposes or principles, economic laws, the needs of interdependence, moral necessities etc. But these are unable to sew the legal fabric together because they are themselves subject of political controversy. They do not seem to represent World Law but give currency to views only partially represented in the world. If they seem unobjectionable in their conventional formulation, then they can be interpreted so as to accommodate the most varied positions to the same issues. The idea of the "complete system" cannot be salvaged because the constructive operations whereby internal coherence is produced are both in themselves controversial and produce systems which fail to reflect collective experience. From this it resulted that when legal arguments were formulated, they seemed utopian, when applied, apologist. Legal technique is powerless to explain them in any other way.[85]

What happened, as we have seen, is that the lawyer sometimes used his technique to make a hazardous leap into *ad hoc* equity or justice. But this was stepping out of the lawyer's role, as perceptive critics immediately noted. He was now arguing about what it was good to do, here and now, instead of applying neutral rules or principles. It is this internal

---

[85] See further *Carty* (Decay) pp. 108–111. See also *Ginther* (Festschrift Lipsky) (discussing the incommensurability of Western, Soviet and Third World "paradigms" of international law) pp. 31 *et seq*, 47–56. The idea of law as a complete system is a main target of critical attacks. *Tushnet* 96 Harvard L. R. 1983 notes that the postulation of a set of coherent principles will ultimately conflict with liberalism's abstract individualism. In the absence of social consensus, any principle must incorporate conflicting substantive views and its application one way or the other will override somebody's individual choice, pp. 804–824. To the same effect, see *Fishkin* (Tyranny), *passim*. See also *Dorsey*'s 82 AJIL 1988 criticism of the policy-approach postulation of universal values, pp. 40–51.

movement in professional routine which provides hope. Renouncing general principles and the technique which draws consequences from them, the lawyer can re-establish his threatened identity in the reality of conflict. The integrity demanded of him may be seen, not as a devotion to "rigorous" legal-technical analysis, but as commitment to reaching the most just solution in the particular disputes which he is faced with.[86]

The international lawyer should take seriously the partial character of his experience. He possesses no more objective information about what solutions to offer than the parties in the conflict he deals with. There is no one, coherent explanation of international society, no indivisible legal system which he could rely upon. Uncertainty and choice are an ineradicable part of his practice. Denying this, he will retreat into assimilation or phantasy. Accepting it, he can re-establish an identity for himself as a social actor. This involves a refusal to engage in discussions about general principles or lawlike explanations of international conduct. Rather than be normative in the whole (and be vulnerable to the objections of apologism-utopianism) he should be normative in the small. He can attempt, to the best of his capability, to isolate the issues which are significant in conflict, assess them with an impartial mind and offer a solution which seems best to fulfil the demands of the critical programme, as outlined in the previous section. In this way, he can fulfil his authentic commitment, his integrity as a lawyer.

But is this not merely another way of saying that the modern development towards pragmatism was really beneficial? Yes and no. This kind of pragmatism is beneficial but it has nothing to do with unreflective technique. For issues of *ad hoc* justice are both difficult to solve and can

---

[86] Having discussed the political character of law-application, *Salmon* 175 RCADI 1982/II argues that this does not lead into arbitrariness. It compels open discussion aimed at bringing out the conflicting values and a search of the widest possible agreement in the community in which the decision is to be carried out, pp. 391–393.

Yet, it is doubtful whether such discussion – as Salmon assumes – is at all possible within existing institutional frameworks. Many have seen the move into practical reason as the only way for liberal theory to rescue what there still is to be rescued. *Dunn* (Rethinking) observes that liberalism's future lies in its becoming concrete – moving from abstract meditations about justice into proposing what one should do, here and now, pp. 163, 167–170. See also *Unger* (Knowledge) p. 254. For a corresponding appeal regarding legal practice, see *Singer* 94 Yale L. J. 1984 pp. 61–66 and regarding international law, see *Boyle* 26 Harv.ILJ 1985 pp. 353, 358–359. *Carty* (Decay) concludes: "The potential task for legal doctrine is to reconstruct conflict situations in accordance with basic principles of possible understanding, a theory of knowledge based on the development of argument, rather than the search for objectivity or experience as such", p. 114.

never be solved with the kind of certainty lawyers once hoped to attain. Their solution in a justifiable way requires entering intellectual realms formerly held prohibited from the lawyer. Answers to the questions about what to do cannot be meaningfully given without taking a stand on what is possible and good to do in the particular circumstances in which the problem arose. And this involves venturing into history, economics and sociology on the one hand, and politics on the other. It involves the isolation and appreciation of what is significant in the particular case – in other words, realizing whatever authentic commitment there might exist for the parties in conflict. This is a task of practical reason. If my formulation of it seems question-begging and leaves open the "method" whereby it should be conducted, this is only because no such given "method" can be outlined in the abstract which would fulfil what is reasonable in some particular circumstance.

Does this imply losing a commitment to the whole, to peace and world order? No, but it does force into seeing that commitment in a new light. It is not a commitment which seeks to realize given principles or ready-made social arrangements. It aims to construct the whole as a structure of open political conflict and constant institutional revision. The whole will be seen as a system which enables, as far as possible, particularized solutions, aimed at realizing authentic commitment. But it gives no intrinsic weight to solutions, once adopted, and it is ready to make constant adjustments once this seems called for. It positively *excludes imperialism and totalitarianism*. Beyond that, however, it makes no pretention to offer principles of the good life which would be valid in a global way.

This kind of self-image of international law and the role of the lawyer respects the conflictual character of both. It acknowledges the absence of consensus on political values between international actors while still not declining to propose solutions to conflicts which have become threatening. It offers the lawyer a renewed sense of his particular task in the constant struggle for the procuring and distribution of spiritual and economic values. Engaging in practical reasoning the lawyer engages himself in what is a transforming routine *par excellence*. It involves appreciating the particularity of each problem and declining to accept as inevitable routine institutional solutions applied elsewhere, in other contexts.

The intellectual and institutional structures of modern society which bind the lawyer to his conventional role are unable to answer questions of practical rationality as they are premised on the idea that the only justifiable arguments are those which are "objective". Engaging in practical reasoning, the lawyer shall have to recognize that solving normative problems in a justifiable way requires, besides impartiality and commitment, also wide knowledge of social causality and of political value and, above all, capacity to imagine alternative forms of social organization to cope with conflict. It shall lead him to overstep the boundaries between practice and doctrine, doctrine and theory. The construction of contextual justice will demand an imaginative effort to rethink the contexts in which traditional roles have been formulated and in which their social effects have remained so unsatisfactory. The rethinking of contexts, again, makes it possible to imagine alternative social routines both for the lawyer and his "clients" while the very dynamism of the process excludes claims of objectivity and universal normative truth.

8.3.2 Contexts: from interpretation to imagination

Once the idea of objective principles and natural social laws is discarded, then normative problem-solution cannot proceed by simply interpreting what *is already* there. It will have to involve an attempt to *imagine* new and alternative ways to cope with social conflict. This is another consequence of the refusal to see law as something external to consciousness. True, the routines in which we participate do restrict the power of imagination. They also provide us with ways to cope with conflict which have been tried out earlier and whose consequences we are familiar with. But routines do not fully determine what we can imagine. To believe otherwise, we should have to assume a fully deterministic image of human existence.[87] But this would be an image which we could not support by what we know. For social contexts have varied and we still lack a theory which would be able to explain these variations in terms of natural laws.[88]

Imagining contextual equity fundamentally undermines the way in which we see the social world divided into given "international" and "national" realms. The criteria which make one solution seem more equitable than another have no significant relation to the fact that the

---

[87] *Putnam* (Meaning) is surely correct in doubting whether we really should *regret* that we are unable to resemble physical science in studying human behaviour. Is this not rather a consequence of our specific humanity? pp. 66–77.

[88] For the rejection of the idea of a "context of all contexts", see *Unger* (Social Theory) pp. 84–87, 90–93, 135 *et seq.*

disputing entities present themselves as "States". Our capacity to solve normative problems has not depended on our technical capability to "infer" rights or obligations from the nature of statehood or that of the international community but on our power to imagine an alternative social world in which to locate the conflict. This might have required privileging the livelihood of fishing communities (*Anglo-Norwegian Fisheries* Case), the security of international business (*Barcelona Traction* Case) or simply "social progress" (*Guardianship of Infants* Case) to alternative ways of seeing what is significant in a conflict.[89]

The conceptual framework which sees the world as naturally divided into States neither explains conflict nor justifies its solution. Competing descriptions refer us constantly to voices crying out for the realization of economic and spiritual values. Statehood was merely a way to silence those voices. Moving into equity, the lawyer finally let some of them become heard. Rethinking of contexts will involve imagining social institutions which will no longer permanently privilege some voices under a category of statehood which has no particular value by itself.

Clearly, the concepts and categories of international law seem much less "natural" than those of municipal law. International law is "an exceptionally flexible and supple fabric".[90] From Grotius to Mancini, Scelle to Kelsen and Falk, international lawyers have been able to practise their trade by virtually doing away with statehood. It has become a conventional commonplace to stress its "fictitious" character. That this has not been accompanied with transforming routine results from their having still been confined within the ideal of a World Rule of Law and an alternative "natural" organization of humankind. They failed to grasp the way in which the conceptual matrices themselves are an arena of actual and potential political struggle.

Lawyers who have been critical of statehood have merely replaced one naturalistic idea with another. Usually, they have succumbed to the temptation of analysis and assumed that reality exists at the level of individual particles, single human beings. This way of describing global social life fails to respect the multiform ways in which human beings are linked together through communal ties whose reality is grounded in their attaching such importance to them. To conceptualize social life in terms of individuals freely entering into relations with each other in the

[89] ICJ: *Anglo-Norwegian Fisheries* Case, Reports 1951 p. 133; *Barcelona Traction* Case, Reports 1970 pp. 48–50; *Guardianship of Infants* Case, Reports 1958 p. 71.
[90] *Butler* (Cheng: Teaching) p. 49. See further *Kennedy* 26 Harv.ILJ 1985 pp. 378–379.

great market-place of the world is merely a way to impose another grand-scale Western-liberal framework on a conflicting reality. The interminable discussion of whether the "true" subjects of international law are States or individuals fails to recognize the differences in our communal ties. Any attempt to overrule those ties will immediately seem like irrelevant utopianism or harmful totalitarianism. Indeed, it may be that the State/individual opposition contains no alternatives at all but that we think of individuals as autonomous and equal entities only because we have internalized a formal conception of statehood from the perspective of which individuals do appear in such a way.[91]

Alternatives to these two ways of looking at global life share in this error of trying to persuade us that they have finally understood its true essence, residing in some religious, economic, cultural, or other such "deep-structure". They tell us that conflict has to do with an opposition between "believers" and "non-believers", "rich north" and "poor south", "communist regimes" and "capitalist regimes", and so on. Yet, when these explanations are formulated and used in political pro-grammes, they will fail to respect the infinitely more varied character of collective and individual experience.

The idea of one coherent explanation of the character of global social life and a coherent programme for world order needs to be rejected. People act under varying contextual constraints and their ideal social arrangements are dissimilar – indeed conflicting. There is no "deep-structural" logic or meta-narrative (of history, economics, etc.) to which we could refer to wipe existing conflict away. Recourse to such narratives can only appear as power disguised as knowledge. The problem takes the form of classical tragedy: mutually incommensurable goods claim our allegiance and we can satisfy any of them only at the cost of others.[92]

It follows that normative justifications should not seek to realize any one, coherent scheme of global organization. Normative solutions need to be justified by respecting the existence of conflicting ideals of social organization and by seeking to secure the revisability of each agreed arrangement. The argument will remain indeterminate and political. And yet, only its remaining so will prevent it from being just another totalitarian apology.

---

[91] *Siedentop* (Miller-Siedentop: Nature) pp. 57–72.
[92] The tragic character of human life, torn between equally valid but mutually exclusive goods, is interestingly discussed in *MacIntyre* (After Virtue) pp. 204 *et seq*, 223–225. See also *Finnis* (Natural Law) pp. 92–95; *idem* (Fundamentals) pp. 66–67.

Let me take an example. Many will concede that reliance on statehood sometimes fails to give currency to a deeply felt notion of justice. They would probably agree that it should be replaced by a form of organization which better guarantees the self-determination of national or ethnic groups. In such case, there would good reason to seek to realize such self-determination for groups which feel they have been unjustly denied it. Yet, this should not be done under the assumption that national or ethnic solidarities are a "natural" form of human organization. It should not be argued from an overriding "principle" of self-determination nor be given *prima facie* preference against other, conflicting ideals. If we have reason to prefer a self-determination paradigm in some circumstance, it is only for the reason that most people, when they think about the matter, will probably see it as a good idea. If they did not, there would be no reason to apply it.

Similarly, we might seem puzzled by the way a conflict about the distribution of resources seems incapable of being solved by referring to some *ab initio* rights in the statehood of the entities who present conflicting claims. In such case, it seems tempting to postulate a notion of "just and equitable shares". But this, too, remains more like restating the conflict than offering a solution. To make reasoned decision, we need to renounce arguing from statehood or some general principles of natural justice. We need to look at the conflicting values which the claims embody. These might be the value of respecting the life-pattern of fishing communities or the preservation of natural resources. The solution should be reasoned on the grounds of causal knowledge about the consequences of alternative choices and the significance of communal forms of organization which are affected by our choice. To be sure, we remain uncertain. The aspect we have underprivileged will continue to have a claim on us. But it is less in the once-adopted solution that our justice lies. It lies in the character of the process which brings forth the solution.

Renouncing the idea of a "natural" human organization means renouncing the search for a World Rule of Law which could be abstracted in one "deep-structural" explanation and appear as a set of coherent principles which the lawyer would only have to "interpret" in order to make justifiable solutions to normative conflicts. Normative imagination – reasoned folly – must take over where the technique of legal interpretation left off. Its point lies in persuading people that experiments in living are worth a try and that in the absence of a natural social order every actual institution, too, remains only an experiment.

As international lawyers, we have failed to use the imaginative possibilities open to us. We became suspicious of theory because it made claims of comprehensiveness and normativity which it could not sustain. Our practice was marginalized because it denied the reality of conflict and failed to address issues which were significant. We have felt that extending upon imagination we must renounce the security which our legal roles offered us. Yet, remaining within the roles seemed to require unreflective assimilation or engaging in phantasy. We were not relieved from the painful task of living and choosing in the midst of political conflict. Instead of impartial umpires or spectators, we were cast as players in a game, members in somebody's team. It is not that we need to play the game better, or more self-consciously. We need to re-imagine the game, reconstruct its rules, redistribute the prizes.

Epilogue

1 A retrospective

I have always found writing a messy affair. It has never proceeded according to plan. Starting on a text, I seldom possess more than the roughest skeleton of an outline for the argument I wish to make or the sections through which it might enfold. Reconstruction of what I now think *From Apology to Utopia* is about, cannot, therefore, hope to bring to light any very sharply defined programme I had when I wrote it in 1989. That programme developed in twists and turns during the work and my own view of it has not been unaffected by the passage of time. But it now seems right to say – although I would probably not have put it in this way at the time – that the book was conceived in order to articulate and examine two types of unease I had about the state of international law as a professional practice and an academic discipline. First, existing reflection on the field had failed to capture the experience I had gained from it through practice within Finland's Ministry for Foreign Affairs, especially in various United Nations contexts. In particular, I felt that none of the standard academic treatments really captured or transmitted the simultaneous sense of rigorous formalism and substantive or political open-endedness of argument about international law that seemed so striking to me. Second, there seemed to me no good reason why the "field" of international law or the ambition of the international lawyer (matters which are of course not unconnected) should be limited intellectually or politically in the way they were. After all, the profession had historically developed as a cosmopolitan project that had dealt with enormously important questions of international justice, peace and war, the fate of nations and the lives of individuals and human groups. Transmitted to its practitioners in the 1980s when this book was conceived, it had become a bureaucratic language that made largely invisible the political commitment from which it had once arisen or which animated its best representatives. I wanted to resuscitate the sense, or even the unavoidability, of that commitment for a meaningful international legal practice.

There was, in other words, both a descriptive and a normative concern somewhere behind this book. As I now recapitulate them in this retrospective, my interest is not autobiographical. Instead, I wish to provide an intellectual framework within which *From Apology to Utopia* situates itself and within which, I think now as I did then, any assessment and critique of its achievement should take place. Although the book was conceived and written some time ago, the two concerns have not gone away. It is true, of course, that much about the world has changed since then. In the early 1990s international law experienced an enthusiastic revival, and after 2001 a period of sober disillusionment. The hopes and disappointments have been reflected not only in professional publications but also increasingly in the public media and debates within civil society. Institutional activities within human rights and the environment, international criminal law, and the economic field have significantly increased. While the scope of international law has widened, a deeper-seeming functional specialization has set in. But the basic doctrines, approaches and – above all – tensions and contradictions that have structured the field since the late 19th century have not changed markedly. In the language of what follows, although it has become possible to say new things in the law, the *grammar* which one uses to say those things has remained largely unchanged. This suggests to me that the descriptive and the normative concerns of *From Apology to Utopia* remain as important as they were at the end of the 1980s. The ascendancy of a new "imperial" rhetoric in world politics – sometimes in a moral tone, sometimes through classical *realpolitik* – may even have highlighted the need to think about international law's role anew. In the following sections I will reformulate those projects in a language that might hopefully respond to some of the criticisms that have been made about this book and provide an initiation as well as a research agenda for new readers who, like I did when I first wrote the book, feel trapped in a professional language that always somehow fails to deliver its seductive promise.

2   The descriptive project: towards a grammar of international law

My descriptive concern was to try to articulate the rigorous formalism of international law while simultaneously accounting for its political open-endedness – the sense that competent argument in the field needed to follow strictly defined formal patterns that, nevertheless, allowed (indeed enabled) the taking of any conceivable position in regard to a dispute or a problem. Existing academic works seemed to me too focused on either the formal or the substantive without suggesting a plausible account of the relations between the two. On the one hand, they discussed rules and principles, legal subjects and legal sources – in short, the various textbook topics – as if these were unconnected with the ways of using them in argument in the institutional contexts in which international lawyers worked. I was unhappy with the way much of the relevant literature portrayed international law as a solid formal structure whose parts (rules, principles, institutions) had stable relations with each other; and also, where this did not seem to be the case, with the view that it was the task of doctrine to (re-)create such relations. I was particularly frustrated by attempts to fix the meaning of individual rules, principles or institutions in some abstract and permanent way, irrespective of the changing situations in which legal interpretations were produced.

On the other hand, if these writings fell on the side of excessive formalism, I was equally disappointed by "political" treatments according to which international law was best seen as an instrument for more or less shared "values" or "interests" or its significance lay in whether it made nations "behave" towards some postulated end-state. Little seemed to be gained by thinking about international legal argument as being "in fact" about something other than law. Had I responded to my superiors at the Ministry when they wished to hear what the law was by telling them that this was a stupid question and instead given them my view of where the Finnish interests lay, or what type of State behaviour was desirable, they would have been both baffled and disappointed, and would certainly not have consulted me again. Reducing international law to its objectives or likely consequences would have given no sense whatsoever of what it was to produce a legal opinion, or of the significance of the legal service for people who continued to think of it as not only a distinct, but also an apparently valuable, service.

In other words, fulfilment of my first ambition – to describe international law in a way that would resonate with practitioner experience – necessitated that I resist the pull of either excessive "formalism" or excessive policy-oriented "realism". In the course of writing, however, I began to realize that this way of stating the problem also contained the seeds of its resolution. The objective could not be to find some ingenious "third way" – a novel vocabulary or technique – to impose on the practice or theory of international law. Instead, I needed to think about my own experience as far from idiosyncratic and to examine the contrast between "formalism" and "realism" as an incident of the *standard experience of any international lawyer* in the normal contexts of academy or practice. It was not to be done away with, but exploited as a key insight in a reconstruction of what international law was about, in particular when examined from the *inside* of the profession – instead of from the outside as political theorists, international relations scholars, philosophers or sociologists did. For the latter, international law's hesitant and dichotomous nature was always a "problem" in need of resolution before it could assist them in making whatever political or academic point they wished to make. It was *they* who needed to think of international law as a solid system of preferences, and to them that its complex fluidity remained so frustrating: "What do you mean 'on the one hand/on the other hand'? Can't you just tell me what the law *is*!"[1]

For international lawyers, however, the contrast between "formalism" and "realism" was, I realized, merely another case of the oscillation between normativity and concreteness, utopia and apology that defined the very problem-setting of their discipline. It was that dichotomy that explained the fluidity and open-endedness of the discipline while also accounting for its formal rigour – the sense that arguments had to be presented strictly in accordance with the conventions of professional culture and tradition in order to be heard. What I needed to do was not to do away with this opposition but to make it my central theme, to think of it as the very basis or – to put it philosophically – the *condition of possibility* of there being something like a distinct experience of international law in the first place. To do that, I began to think of international law as a language and of the opposition as a key part of its (generative) grammar.

---

[1] This is today seen most strikingly in the enthusiasm of political scientists for compliance studies. Attempts to find out whether or not States comply with their commitments presume, of course, firm knowledge of what there is to comply with. For a lawyer, however, a "compliance problem" turns regularly into a puzzle about the relevant obligations – perhaps this type of "compliance" was never foreseen, perhaps alternative forms of compliance were also provided, or perhaps compliance was conditioned by some fact that has failed to materialize, maybe circumstances have changed, etc. – speculation that is bound to make the non-lawyer despair.

2.1   *What a grammar is*

Imagine that you wanted to learn a new language and that you were told that this consisted of learning all the words in that language. You would be surprised, no doubt, and the task would seem truly monumental. Yet, of course, that is not how languages are taught, or learned. A language is not merely a large (indeed truly enormous) mass of words, and the competence of the native language-speaker does not reside in the kind of word-mastery that this image presumes. Nevertheless, this is how the professional competence of an international lawyer is often (implicitly) understood. In thousands upon thousands of pages, textbooks offer a huge number of rules for the student to learn. These rules are grouped by subject-areas (territory, use of force, law of the sea, etc.) which organize the field often by reference to larger "principles". But surely the competence of the international lawyer is just as little about knowing all those rules or principles as the competence of the native language-speaker is about mastery of a large vocabulary. Words are only raw material that the language-speaker uses in order to formulate sentences and grasp meanings transmitted as part of the social life of native language-speakers.

In the same way, "competence" in international law is not an ability to reproduce out of memory some number of rules, but a complex argumentative practice in which rules are connected with other rules at different levels of abstraction and communicated from one person or group of persons to another so as to carry out the law jobs in which international lawyers are engaged. To be able to do this well, such connecting has to take place in formally determined ways. As we go through law school, we gradually receive an intuitive grasp of how this takes place. We develop an ability to distinguish between competent arguments and points put forward by lay persons using the same vocabulary but doing that in ways that – whatever one may think of the substance of these points – somehow fail as *legal* arguments.[2] Public debates during great crises such as the Kosovo intervention in 1999 or the Iraq war in 2003 often manifest this. Whatever their political position, lawyers often feel uneasy when bits of legal discourse are thrown about in journalist or partisan discourses; and even when they do not

---

[2] See also my Letter to the Editors of the Symposium, in Steven R. Ratner and Anne-Marie Slaughter, *The Methods of International Law* (Washington, American Society of International Law, 2004), pp. 109–125.

mind this, they are still able to recognize – and hold important – the distinction between professional and non-professional uses of legal words.[3]

The descriptive thesis in *From Apology to Utopia* is about such intuitions. It seeks to articulate the *competence* of native language-speakers of international law. It starts from the uncontroversial assumption that international law is not just some haphazard collection of rules and principles.[4] Instead, it is about their use in the context of legal work. The standard view that international law is a "common language" transcending political and cultural differences grasps something of this intuition. So do accounts of the experience that even in the midst of political conflict, international lawyers are able to engage in professional conversation in which none of the participants' competence is put to question by the fact that they support opposite positions.[5] On the contrary, lawyers may even recognize that their ability to use rules in contrasting ways is a key aspect of their competence – reflected in popular caricatures of lawyers as professional cynics.[6] Whatever our

---

[3] This is why we instruct students or younger colleagues to learn by following up closely what legal institutions – courts in particular – and respected members of the profession do or have done in particular cases, how they have connected rules to each other so as to produce complex arguments that we recognize as exemplary in their power, their ability to create or contest some suggested meaning. We tell students to read cases and pleadings so as to be able to reproduce the kinds of argumentative patterns that the profession has learned to recognize as aspects of its specific character instead of, say, parts of a political or moral discourse or manifestations of some other competence, for example that of a sociologist or geographer.

[4] The sense that international law forms a "system" is so deeply embedded in legal thinking that H. L. A. Hart's famous description of it as a set of primary (treaty) rules unconnected with each other has never been accepted by international lawyers. Cf. *The Concept of Law* (Oxford, Clarendon, 1961), ch. 10. The fact that there has been no general agreement about what the "systemic" nature of international law means gives expression to the fact that systemic theories, too, are an aspect of international legal discourse, amenable to the play of utopia and apology. To view international law as *language* is, of course, another attempt to account for its systemic character.

[5] Thus Sir Robert Jennings, for instance, wrote: "in this culturally, ideologically, and economically divided world, it is international law itself which provides a common language, the language in which these very differences are described and defined, explained, and the different aspirations propagated", "International Courts and International Politics", Joseph Onoh Lecture 1986, David Freestone et al., *Contemporary Issues in International Law* (The Hague, Kluwer, 2002), p. 26.

[6] I have discussed this tension in my "Between Commitment and Cynicism: Outline for a Theory of International Law as Practice" in: *Collection of Essays by Legal Advisers of States, Legal Advisers of International Organizations and Practitioners in the Field of International Law* (United Nations, 1999), pp. 495–523.

view about the moral status of the profession, however, that status is not an aspect of a person's quality as a "native language-speaker of international law". Or to put this in another vocabulary, international law is not necessarily representative of what is "good" in this world.

This is why the linguistic analogy seems so tempting. Native language-speakers of, say, Finnish, are also able to support contrasting political agendas without the question of the genuineness of their *linguistic* competence ever arising. *From Apology to Utopia* seeks, however, to go beyond metaphor. Instead of examining international law *like* a language it treats it *as* a language.[7] This is not as exotic as it may seem.[8] No more is involved than taking seriously the views that, whatever else international law might be, at least it is how international lawyers argue, that how they argue can be explained in terms of their specific "competence" and that this can be articulated in a limited number of rules that constitute the "grammar" – the system of production of good legal arguments.[9]

But why concentrate "only" on the competence of a small and marginal group of legal professionals? Why not speak directly to the legal rules and principles, the behaviour of States, the stuff of law as a part of the international social or political order? *From Apology to Utopia* assumes that there is no access to legal rules or the legal meaning of international behaviour that is independent from the way competent

---

[7] In this, as perceptive commentators have noticed, it resembles the systems-theoretical perspective on sociology of Niklas Luhmann. For Luhmann, society *is* communication. This enables him to deal with the paradoxes and aporias of social systems not as functional mistakes that should be "corrected" but as necessary aspects of communicative systems that are self-referentially validated. See especially Niklas Luhmann, *Die Wissenschaft der Gesellschaft* (Frankfurt, Suhrkamp, 1992), and, Luhmann, *Law as a Social System* (Transl. by Klaus A. Ziegert, ed. by Fatima Kastner, Richard Nobles, David Schiff and Rosamund Ziegert, Oxford University Press, 2004). For an introductory application of Luhmannian systems-theory in international law, see Gunther Teubner, "Globale Zivilverfassungen: Alternatives zur staatszentrierten Verfassungtheorie", 63 ZaöRV (2003), pp. 1–28 and Andreas Fischer-Lescano, "Die Emergenz der Globalverfassung", 63 ZaöRV (2003), pp. 716–760.

[8] For example, Martin Loughlin has recently defined public law as a "vernacular language", thereby highlighting its nature as a complex practice that resists reduction to general principles or procedures. Instead Loughlin sees it as "an assemblance of rules, principles, canons, maxims, customs, usages, and manners that condition and sustain the activity of government". *The Idea of Public Law* (Oxford University Press, 2003), p. 30.

[9] The "goodness" of those arguments, it must be stressed, is not a function of one's view of the moral or political merits of the position being defended. Colleagues may well admire the skill of a lawyer arguing for a case they know he or she is bound to lose.

lawyers see those things. Imagine someone suggested setting aside the language which physicists use to describe the physical world, or that we should begin to talk of human health independently of how medicine views it. The suggestion would seem strange, and surely unacceptable. No doubt there exists a physical or a physiological reality that in some sense is independent of the way competent professionals see it. But there is no more reliable *access* to those worlds than what is provided by the languages of physics and medicine, as spoken by the competent language-speakers of *those* disciplines. In this sense, law is what lawyers think about it and how they go about using it in their work.

This insight may be defended by various philosophical arguments, and I made some of them in the introduction. But philosophy does not set the book's horizon. Instead, *From Apology to Utopia* seeks to articulate practitioner experience as against doctrinal accounts of the field. One of these was the experience that competent lawyers were always able to support opposite sides with good legal arguments. To describe such argumentative oppositions in terms of one side being right and the other wrong seemed hopelessly naive – after all, that seemed to put to question the competence of the side that was "wrong" or "lost" the case. "Winning" or "losing" seemed always less connected to the intrinsic worth of the arguments than the preferences of the institution before which they were made.[10] It was not "winning" or "losing" but ability to take on opposite sides in *any* international controversy that was the key to professional competence. Mainstream doctrine described the field in terms of rules and principles with a stable meaning that would always privilege some policies or institutions over others. This suggestion seemed to me astonishingly blind to the way professionally rigorous argumentation could be invoked to support whatever one needed to support. Were the lawyers defending the lawfulness of the Iraq war of 2003 simply incompetent lawyers? Surely the problem was elsewhere. Of course, the intuitions and preferences of international lawyers are often quite predictable. Arguments are grouped in typical ways, reflecting mainstream positions as familiar as the minority positions routinely invoked to challenge them.[11] Majority and minority positions develop

---

[10] I discuss the question of institutional or structural bias in section 3.3 below.

[11] The way the disciplinary vocabulary of international law has developed between the end of the nineteenth century and today by grouping into a "mainstream" and a "counter-point", moving through periods of "consensus and renewal" on the one hand, and "anxiety and disputation" on the other, is usefully depicted in David Kennedy, "When Renewal Repeats: Thinking against the Box", 32 *New York University Journal of*

slowly, like literary styles. We can sometimes survey their being engaged in a spiral-like movement in which yesterday's challengers ("decolonization", for instance, or "human rights") become today's mainstream and are in turn challenged by new vocabularies ("failed States" or "free trade") without a clear prospect of *Aufhebung* or even a "reasonable balance" providing closure. Nothing about those positions is produced by law – though they are all equally amenable to being dressed in it.

This experience captures, as I explained in chapter 1, the famous distinction between discovery and justification, or the sense in which legal arguments do not *produce* substantive outcomes but seek to *justify* them. As a language of justification, international law is a means to articulate particular preferences or positions in a formal fashion, accessible to professional analysis: the movement of armed personnel across boundaries becomes "aggression" or "self-defence", an official act a matter of "sovereignty" (or "immunity") or a "human rights violation".[12] The law constructs its own field of application as it goes along, through a normative language that highlights some aspects of the world while leaving other aspects in the dark.[13] Whether a particular justification then seems plausible and the position defended is accepted depends on how it fits with the structural bias in the relevant institutional context. Two patterns emerge: one is the formal style in which arguments must be made in order to seem professionally plausible; the other is the substantive outcome that appears to satisfy the structural bias.[14]

The legal justifiability of a decision is not the same as a causal account of why it was taken. The latter has to do with things legal realists have always referred to: ambition, inertia, tradition, ideology and contingency. The UN Charter did not cause the Security Council to enact a sanctions regime against Iraq in 1990 or the launch of "Operation Desert Storm" the following January. But the question of the legal justifiability of those activities could only be answered in terms of the law of the UN

International Law and Politics (2000), especially pp. 340–397. Kennedy has told a similar story concentrating on the development of international law in the United States in "Tom Franck and the Manhattan School", 35 *New York University Journal of International Law and Politics* (2003), pp. 397–435.

[12] See further my "Theory: Implications for the Practitioner", in Philip Allott et al., *Theory and International Law: An Introduction* (London 1991), especially pp. 35–45.

[13] This is the basis of the recent "constructivist" interest in the law as an instrument for structuring the field of political contestation. But it is equally reflected in the "realist" complaints against judicial settlement: law reduces a conflict to sometimes irrelevant particularities, failing to account for the historical context.

[14] For the latter, see in more detail section 3.3 below.

Charter and the use of force. Whether, again, it seems at all useful to pose the question of legal justifiability depends on the institutional context. How is a culture of formalism viewed there? If the predominant concerns are those of instrumental effectiveness, or "governmentality", then formalism may seem beside the point or even counterproductive.[15] But if what seems important is institutional contestability, then the absence of aspects of that culture – predictability, transparency, accountability – will always appear a scandal. The relative value of these two cultures cannot be decided in an absolute way – each has a beneficial as well as a dark aspect – and it is not difficult to see them as political adversaries in particular situations.[16] International lawyers' professional bias has not unnaturally been to a culture of formalism. The grammar that *From Apology to Utopia* sketches may thus also be read as an analysis of the possibilities and limits of political contestation through the adoption of a culture of formalism in a particular institutional environment.[17]

Standard studies link international law's political role to the way in which its rules and principles can be associated with, and advance, normative ideas taken from some more or less fixed extralegal world. Here, however, the meaning of legal language is derived from what point is being made by it in a particular context, in regard to what claim, towards which audience. What interests are being supported, what opposed by it?[18] This is the politics of law for which the existence of a grammar is absolutely crucial but which is not exhausted by mere grammar-use. The politics of international law is what competent international lawyers do. And *competence is the ability to use grammar in order to generate meaning by doing things in argument.* Thus, for instance,

---

[15] The understanding of "governmentality" as a purely instrumental attitude to the activity of "governing" in which rules have (at best) a tactical role derives from Michel Foucault and is often articulated as a critique of recent American unilateralism. See, for instance, Judith Butler, *Precarious Life. The Powers of Mourning and Violence* (London, Verson, 2004), especially pp. 93–100. For the original statement of the position, see Michel Foucault, *Naissance de la biopolitique. Cours au Collège de France 1978–1979* (Paris, Gallimard, 2004). I have used this in e.g. "Global Governance and Public International Law", 37 *Kritische Justiz* (2004), pp. 241–254.

[16] This is the theme of chapter 6 ("Out of Europe") of my *The Gentle Civilizer of Nations. The Rise and Fall of International Law 1870–1960* (Cambridge University Press, 2001).

[17] For a discussion, see my "The Place of Law in Collective Security", 17 *Michigan Journal of International Law* (1996) pp. 455–490.

[18] This point has been powerfully made by Quentin Skinner. See e.g. the essays in his *Visions of Politics I* (Cambridge University Press, 2003). Similarly, Reinhard Koselleck, "Begriffsgechichte and Social History", in *Futures Past. On the Semantics of Historical Time* (Columbia University Press, 2004), pp. 75–92.

"sovereignty" cannot be grasped by examining the "idea of sovereignty" somehow floating autonomously in conceptual space but by studying how that word is invoked in institutional contexts so as to make or oppose particular claims. An account of "sovereignty" in international law must show the ways it is being used in the relevant professional contexts and how some uses have stabilized and then again been challenged by alternative uses. Such shifts of meaning take place in a conceptual universe that is always in principle open for contestation and polemics.

This is what I mean in chapters 4 to 6 as I point out that there is always a "pure fact" argument to counter a "legal" argument when the vocabulary of "sovereignty" is invoked; a point about "consent" to be made to challenge the adversary's point about "justice" when "sources" are debated; or a notion of the "*opinio juris*" to make doubtful the inference one's opponent has made of the meaning of State practice as "custom". As I further illustrate in those chapters, what "sovereignty", "treaty" or "customary law" mean is not determined by philosophical reflection about the way facts turn to norms or justice links to consent but how those expressions are used by lawyers in particular situations. It may be a part of professional training that one learns to theorize about "sovereignty", "sources" or "custom" and that training may add direction and complexity to one's arguments. Indeed, it would be strange if legal training would not do precisely that. But it does not lead practitioners any closer to the *ideas* of "sovereignty", "legal source" or "custom", firmly fixed in some conceptual or historical bedrock. It makes them more effective language-users and the fact that it does so is the only unchanging criterion through which its success may be measured – after all, it would be a bad excuse for medicine to stop curing people in order to concentrate on creating a philosophically sophisticated theory of human health.

By sketching the rules that underlie the production of arguments in international law, *From Apology to Utopia* seeks to liberate the profession from its false necessities. Although international law is highly structured as a language, it is quite fluid and open-ended as to what can be said in it. For example, each of the four types of doctrine discussed in chapter 3 accommodates aspects of its adversary. "Realism", as political scientists have often pointed out, is based on an "idealism"[19] and

---

[19] On the "idealism" of a political realist such as Hans Morgenthau, see my *Gentle Civilizer*, *supra*, note 16, pp. 468–471. See likewise, Richard Ned Lebow, *The Tragic Vision in Politics. Ethics, Interests, Orders* (Cambridge University Press, 2003), pp. 275–284 and *passim*.

vice-versa,[20] while "rules" and "processes" are ultimately indistinguishable and, pressed upon by argument, turn into each other: a rule is created by and interpreted in process, a process is defined as rule-observance. As the subtle distinctions between doctrinal positions are lost in argument, it becomes evident that they do not embody fundamentally contradicting theories or approaches, but are better understood as aspects of a general system – a language – whose parts are interdependent not by way of logic or causality but through what – for want of a better word – could be called "style".[21] As arguments about consent turn out to be (or rely upon) arguments about justice, points about State sovereignty turn into arguments about national self-determination, facts transform themselves into rules, and each such opposition turns around once again, the language of international law forms stylistic paths in which we can recognize fragments of liberal political theory, sociology, and philosophy. By focusing on those moves, *From Apology to Utopia* instructs international lawyers in the nature of what they intuitively recognize as their shared competence. In particular, it shows them that nothing of this competence requires commitment to particular political ideas or institutional forms. Future horizons need not be limited by past ambitions.

2.2 The grammar articulated: sovereignty and sources

The grammar that emerges from the analyses in *From Apology to Utopia* takes its starting-point from the tension between concreteness and normativity that structures all (competent) international legal speech. Any doctrine or position must show itself as concrete – that is, based not on abstract theories about the good or the just but on what it is that States do or will, have done or have willed. A professionally competent argument is rooted in a *social concept of law* – it claims to emerge from the way international society is, and not from some wishful construction of it.[22] On the other hand, any such doctrine or position must also show

---

[20] As Hersch Lauterpacht noted in his polemic against E. H. Carr. Lauterpacht, "Professor Carr on International Morality", in *International Law. Being the Collected Works of Hersch Lauterpacht* (Elihu Lauterpacht ed., vol. II, Cambridge University Press, 1978), pp. 67–69.

[21] See my "Letter to the Editors", *supra*, note 2.

[22] For an overview (and critique) of the variations of the "social concept" in modern law, see Brian Z. Tamanaha, *A General Jurisprudence of Law and Society* (Oxford University Press, 2001).

that it is not just a reflection of power – that it does not only tell what States do or will but what they *should* do or will. It must enable making a distinction between power and authority and, in other words, be normative. The more concrete an argument is, the less normative it appears, and *vice-versa*. This tension structures international law at various levels of abstraction.

It is expressed, for example, in the way it is possible to give a full description of international law from the perspective of what I call *doctrines of sovereignty* and *doctrines of sources*.[23] The former start from the assumption that international law is based on sovereign statehood, the latter derive the law's substance from the operation of legal sources. Thus, after an initial section that seeks to historicize the subject (and to underwrite the social concept of law), textbooks or general courses at the Hague Academy and elsewhere always begin discussion of the law's substance with a chapter either on "sovereignty" (a discussion of "subjects") or on "sources" (often by reference to Article 38(1) of the Statute of the International Court of Justice).[24] These become the foundation for the rest of the law in the subsequent chapters, explained from a particular perspective, sometimes a bias or a style. The story about international law's basis in statehood is a "hard", historically inclined narrative that assures the reader of the law's suave realism, its being not just a compilation of the author's cosmopolitan prejudices. Thinking of international law being generated by "sources" opens the door for a "softer", cosmopolitan vision focusing on the present "system"

---

[23] In philosophical language, it is possible to proceed from either statehood or rules about statehood as the law's transcendental condition.

[24] For texts that open up the law's substance by "sources", see e.g. Peter Malanczuk, *Akehurst's Modern Introduction to International Law* (7th edn, London, Routledge, 1997), pp. 35–62. At the outset of his *Principles of Public International Law* (6th edn, Oxford University Press, 2003), Brownlie observes that "the sources of international law and the law of treaties ... must be regarded as fundamental: between them they provide the basic particulars of the legal regime", p. 3. To the same effect, see Patrick Daillier and Alain Pellet, *Droit international public* (7th edn, Paris, LDGJ, 2002), who start the substance of the law from "La formation du droit international", p. 110. For a few examples that start from statehood, see e.g. Antonio Cassese, *International Law* (Oxford University Press, 2001), pp. 3, 46, Pierre-Marie Dupuy, *Droit international public* (4th edn, Paris, Dalloz, 1998), p. 25 and especially his "L'Unité de l'ordre juridique international. Cours général de droit international public", 297 RCADI (2002), p. 95. Brierly is straightforward: "as a definite branch of jurisprudence the system which we now know as international law ... for its special character has been determined by that of the modern European states-system", *The Law of Nations* (6th edn by C. H. M. Waldock, Oxford University Press, 1963), p. 1.

constituted by treaty texts, UN resolutions, peremptory norms or general principles. Where diplomacy provides the professional horizon for the former, the latter's focus is often on a formal "system" or notions of "community": where the former appears "ascending", the latter seems "descending" in the image of this book.

Both approaches are correct; each has resources to ground and explain the law. Yet each is vulnerable to criticisms from its opposite: sovereignty seems too servile to power to become a reliable basis for a normative system, while sources fail to give a good account of where the law emerges if not from concrete State power and policy. Much of 20th-century international jurisprudence may be described as tidal fluctuations of emphasis between sovereignty and sources, sociological approaches and formalism: the mainstream may have been grounded in a humanitarian ("sources") critique of sovereignty – but that critique has been always followed by a sobering rejoinder about the continued centrality of state power ("sovereignty"). For every Hans Kelsen, a Carl Schmitt has been waiting around the corner, for every Lauterpacht, a Brierly. Each Georges Scelle has had his Charles de Visscher and every Manley Hudson his Myres McDougal. As the century grew old, a pragmatic eclecticism set in.[25] The two merged into each other: what "sovereignty" means and when what it creates amounts to "law" can only be determined through an external criterion – sources; what "sources" are and how they operate must depend on what is produced by "sovereignty". A reservation, after all, cannot be incompatible with the object and purpose of a treaty – but what that object and purpose is, must remain for each State to decide.[26] And so finally, in the new millennium everyone is both "idealist" and "realist", in favour of "rules" and "facts" simultaneously, learning with every position also the critique of that position.[27] As "sovereignty" and "sources" merge into and yet remain in tension with each other, their relationship will ensure the endless generation of international legal speech – and with it, the continuity of a profession no longer seeking a transcendental foundation from philosophical or sociological theories.

[25] See the epilogue of my *Gentle Civilizer, supra,* note 16, pp. 510–517.
[26] See chapter 5.5.2 above.
[27] Because of the way in which "realism" and "idealism" have each learned the lesson they receive from each other, it has begun to seem impossible to distinguish the two from each other: as lawyers and human rights activists today embrace the language of military power, nobody is more serious about law and humanitarianism than military officials. See further David Kennedy, *The Dark Sides of Virtue. Reassessing International Humanitarianism* (Princeton University Press, 2004), pp. 266–272.

As sovereignty and sources remain the two grand trajectories through which lawyers come to legal problems, each is internally split so as to allow the articulation of any adversity as opposing legal claims.

2.2.1 Sovereignty

The grammar of sovereignty is constituted by the oscillation between fact-oriented and law-oriented points as explained in chapter 4. Sovereignty must reflect some actual authority over territory. State failure is at least in part caused by the "sudden swing from effectiveness to legality" that decolonization meant – moral concerns trumping actual (imperial) power.[28] And yet, the eventual general acceptance of the Baltic "continuity thesis" in 1991–1992, for example, testifies to the sense that even where power is firmly established, it may still not turn into law if it seems egregiously unjustified.[29] *Ex facti non jus oritur.* None of the successor States in the former Yugoslavia could expect to be recognized by seizing as much territory as possible. But as international recognition conditioned Balkan sovereignty upon normative criteria it also reproduced the danger of imperialism against which the "pure fact" view was once created. The contrast between the strict declarativism of Opinion 1 of the Arbitration Commission of the Yugoslavian Peace Conference and the refusal by the members of the European Communities (as they then were) to treat new Balkan entities as States unless they complied with humanitarian demands testifies to the vitality of sovereignty doctrines as discussed in chapter 4.[30] Abstract standards (such as self-determination) justify recognition policies that create the reality they purport to reflect – with the result that effective power sometimes fails to bring about statehood (not only in Southern Rhodesia or Taiwan but also in Abkhasia and Serbian Krajina) whereas

---

[28] Gerard Kreijen, *State Failure, Sovereignty, and Effectiveness. Legal Lessons from the Decolonization of Sub-Saharan Africa* (The Hague, Nijhoff, 2004).

[29] See Lauri Mälksoo, *Illegal Annexation and State Continuity: The Case of the Incorporation of the Baltic States by the USSR* (The Hague, Nijhoff, 2003). I have discussed the continuity problem in Martti Koskenniemi, "The Present State of Research", in Pierre Michel Eisemann and Martti Koskenniemi, *La succession d'Etats: La codification à l'épreuve des faits/State Succession: Codification Tested against the Facts* (The Hague Academy of International Law, Nijhoff, 2000), pp. 119–125.

[30] See Opinion 1 of the Arbitration Commission, 31 ILM (1991), pp. 1494–1497 and the EU Declaration on the Recognition of New States in Eastern Europe and the Soviet Union, 16 December 1991, *ibid.* pp. 1485–1487. See further the discussion in Martti Koskenniemi, "National Self-Determination Today: Problems of Legal Theory and Practice", 43 ICLQ (1994), pp. 241–269.

non-effective power does so (not only in Burma or Lebanon in the 1970s but also in Georgia and Moldova in the 1990s).[31]

As before, it is possible to attack established power with the argument that it is unjustified and defend it with the argument that at least it is there to prevent "fratricidal struggles" (*uti possidetis*).[32] The law here defers to views about justified power which are, *on the law's own premises*, matters of political choice. Hence the move into context, deformalization: any problem seems amenable to decision only on the basis of the circumstances. It is possible to see a structural pattern in any series, over a period, of such choices. If that pattern is towards letting sleeping dogs lie (i.e. in favour of the *uti possidetis*), then we can perhaps attribute it to the policy of prudence on the part of a profession that has learned to think of territorial change as inherently dangerous.

Some of this may be illustrated by the increasingly fact-focused territorial jurisprudence of the ICJ in the 1990s. That the Court has been able to hold a party in *contra legem* occupation may reflect the fact that the disputes have been between Third World States or dealt with claims by an international pariah (such as Israel).[33] Many of the cases have been about the interpretation of colonial treaties and the determination of the weight of colonial or post-colonial *effectivités*. No determining criteria have emerged to assess the parties' actions on the ground and any such activities by one party should be paired with acquiescence on the other party's side.[34] The basic position is the "legal" view: *effectivités* cannot replace pre-existing title. This, however, does not apply where "the *effectivité* does not co-exist with any legal title", in which case "it must invariably be taken into consideration".[35] But the initial position may be made even weaker by first contesting the self-evidence of the

---

[31] Davic Raic, *Statehood and the Law of Self-Determination* (The Hague, Kluwer, 2002), pp. 372–393, 402–438.

[32] ICJ: *Burkina Faso–Mali Boundary* Case, Reports 1986, p. 565 (para. 20). For a useful discussion of the twin images of boundary drawing as giving effect to geographical "facts" and as an instrumentality in the context of self-determination claims, see Vasuki Nesiah, "Placing International Law: White Spaces on a Map", 16 LJIL (2003), especially pp. 22–34.

[33] E.g. ICJ: *Chad–Libya Territorial Dispute*, Reports 1994, p. 6; *Legal Consequences of the Construction of a Wall in the Occupied Palestinian Territory*, Reports 2004, especially paras. 70–78.

[34] ICJ: *Case Concerning the Land, Island and Maritime Frontier*, Reports 1992, p. 565 (para. 347). See further Malcolm Shaw, "International Court of Justice. Recent Cases", 42 ICLQ (1993), pp. 931–933.

[35] ICJ: *Burkina Faso–Mali Boundary* Case, Reports 1986, p. 587 (para. 63) referred to in the *Bakassi Peninsula* Case, Reports 2002, p. 353, para. 68.

meaning of the relevant treaty and then invoking *effectivités* as *evidence* for the correct meaning. This leaves the argumentative positions open and the grammar of sovereignty may start its work so as to produce the contextual jurisprudence we have today.

For example, in the *Case Concerning Sovereignty over Pulau Ligitan and Pulau Sipadan* (2002), Indonesia based its claims on a British–Dutch Treaty of 1891, Malaysia on a series of agreements through which the Sultan of Sulu, the alleged original ruler of the islands, had transferred them to successor States and finally to Malaysia. None of these old instruments was decisive. Instead, the Court repeated the "pure fact" justification (see section 4.7 above), according to which title required both "intention and will to act as sovereign" and "some actual exercise or display of such authority". There was, however, no single rule on how to measure this. As in *Eastern Greenland*, it needed to weigh the *effectivités* invoked by the two sides *vis-à-vis* each other and held that very little – namely "measures taken to regulate and control the collecting of turtle eggs and the establishment of a bird reserve" by Malaysia – sufficed as relevant facts.[36] As these were unaccompanied by protest on Indonesia's side, the resulting judgment could be received from Malaysia's action ("concrete") without violating Indonesia's will ("normative").[37] By contrast, in the *Kasikili/Sedudu Island* Case (1999), also having to do with the silence of an original colonial treaty, the undisputed presence of the members of the Masubia population in what is now Namibia as well as military patrolling by South Africa in the disputed area were dismissed as evidence of title owing (unlike the collection of turtle eggs) to what the Court saw as absence of *animus occupandi*: indigenous agriculture was not exercised *à titre de souverain* and lacked the "necessary degree of precision and certainty".[38]

Finally, in the *Cameroon–Nigeria Land and Maritime Boundary* (*Bakassi Peninsula*) Case (2002), the Court did find a series of applicable colonial treaties that left the disputed territories in the Lake Chad and Bakassi Peninsula region to the Cameroons. The approximately 20-year

---

[36] ICJ: *Case Concerning Sovereignty over Pulau Ligitan and Pulau Sipadan*, Reports 2002, pp. 682 and 684 (paras. 134 and 145).

[37] *Ibid.* p. 685 (para. 148).

[38] ICJ: *Kasikili/Sedudu Island* Case, Reports 1999, pp. 1105–1106 (paras. 98–99). It is striking to what extent this argumentation resembles the points made by late-19th century lawyers characterizing the forms of "native" authority in Africa so as to divest it of legal force. See further my *Gentle Civilizer*, pp. 136–155 and Jörg Fisch, *Die europäische Expansion und das Völkerrecht* (Stuttgart, Steiner, 1984), pp. 297–314.

presence of Nigerians in those regions, including regular acts by health and education authorities, were in the Court's view such as "could normally be considered to be *à titre de souverain*".[39] But such acts could not override treaty-based title. Nor did the Court find any acquiescence by Cameroon in giving up title in favour of Nigeria. However, here as well as in the, in some respects similar, *Libya–Chad Territorial Dispute* (1994), the Court made clear that this result could be received from the consent of the occupying State, too. When consulted at its independence and in its contacts with neighbours, Nigeria had never claimed that its frontier remained undelimited. Because in 1961–1962 "Nigeria [had] clearly and publicly recognized Cameroon title to Bakassi", its activities therein could not have been *à titre de souverain*.[40]

And yet, it was impossible to uphold such a clear-cut opposition between "title" (law) and "*effectivités*" (fact): "the established modes of acquisition of title under international law ... take into account many other variables of fact and law".[41] Though consolidation (i.e. the "facts" invoked by Nigeria) was ruled out as an independent basis of title, it was presumed to be *included* in title, there being little else other than acts of "consolidation" parties may invoke to support their claims for the accepted reading of the treaty. This is why Nigeria could hold Cameroon's argument "question-begging and circular".[42] As the Court itself has put it: "In fact, the concept of title may also, and more generally, comprehend any evidence which may establish the existence of a right, and the actual source of that right."[43]

The relationship between "title" and "*effectivités*" is a transformation of the basic opposition between "law" and "fact" in the grammar of sovereignty. Though the two are not identical (but are in some sense antithetical), they also depend on each other: law can only be accessed through fact: a behaviour receives meaning when it is understood as (for example) "subsequent practice". Although *effectivités* cannot overrule "title", the latter cannot show itself reliably without some reference to

---

[39] ICJ: *Cameroon–Nigeria Land and Maritime Boundary (Bakassi Peninsula)* Case, Reports 2002, p. 353 (para. 67).

[40] *Ibid.* p. 416 (para. 223). See also *ibid.* pp. 341–342, 343–344 (paras. 52, 54–55). Likewise, in the *Qatar–Bahrain Maritime and Territorial Dispute*, the Court was able to rely on a colonial act (a British decision of 1939) in view of its being satisfied that the parties had consented to it, Reports 2001, pp. 83 (para. 137) and 85 (para. 148).

[41] *Ibid.* p. 352 (para. 65).   [42] *Ibid.* p. 351 (para. 64).

[43] ICJ: *Burkina Faso–Mali Boundary* Case, Reports 1986, p. 564 (para. 18).

what has taken place on the ground. Whether one relies on "*effectivités*" (*Pulau Ligitan and Pulau Sipadan*) or "title" (*Bakassi Peninsula*) is a matter of pure choice: if the latter seemed crucial in *Bakassi Peninsula* and *Aouzou Strip*, we may surmise that this might have been because the Court did not wish to reward aggression by a regional hegemon. When that concern is not there – as it was not in the decision by the *Ethiopia–Eritrea Boundary Commission* (2002), *effectivités* could even override existing title: "eventually, but not necessarily so, the legal result may be to vary a boundary established by a treaty".[44]

These examples illustrate the grammar at work under sovereignty doctrines: when one party says "law" (e.g. a treaty-based "title") the other says "fact" (e.g. possession, *effectivités*). At this stage, both have a good critique of their adversary's position but neither is secure in its own. Hence each will occupy its adversary's original ground: *effectivités* are invoked to defend "title"; previous case-law and doctrine (i.e. "law") are invoked to defend a particular reading of *effectivités*. The debate can continue interminably. The more stress is on "facts", the easier it is for the other party to invoke the "Baltic defence" – those facts are illegal! And whatever "legal" arguments a party may bring, it must at some point ground them on something actually going on "in fact". As neither of the avenues can be followed as a matter of *general preference*, any closure will always be based on an ad hoc decision whose rightness resides in the fact that it *feels so*.

This is what we have witnessed in maritime delimitation. In the *Jan Mayen* Case (1993), for instance, the Court pointed out that in drawing a single maritime boundary it could rely both on Article 6 of the 1958 Continental Shelf Convention and on customary law on the delimitation of the fishery zones. Each provided for drawing an equidistance (median) line, followed by an assessment of whether "special" or "relevant" circumstances justified a deviation.[45] This led to a balancing

---

[44] *Ethiopia–Eritrea Boundary Commission* (2002), para. 3.29, reported in 106 RGDIP (2002), p. 702. The Commission defined *effectivités* precisely in the above way, as "activity on the ground tending to show the exercise of sovereign authority by the Party engaging in that activity", *ibid.* But there is no reason why *effectivités* would only be reduced to evidence of title. For "[i]t is quite possible that practice or conduct may affect the legal relations of the Parties even though it cannot be said to be practice in application of the Treaty or to constitute an agreement between them", *ibid.* para. 3.6,

[45] ICJ: *Jan Mayen* Case, Reports 1993, pp. 61 and 62 (paras. 51 and 53). As the Court pointed out, rules over the continental shelf and fishery zones were "closely inter-related". ICJ: *Qatar–Bahrain Maritime and Territorial Dispute*, Reports 2001, para. 231. Thus, "[f]rom a delimitation of the maritime zones beyond the 12-mile line it will first

standard – "to determine 'the relative weight accorded to different considerations' in each case"[46] – that has left the Court free to *modify* the median line by "geographical equity" (for example, by taking account of the difference in the length of the coastlines), or by the need to ensure access to fishery resources,[47] as well as to *follow* the median line and to dismiss all suggested deviations from it.[48] The well-known problems with "equity" are only in part obscured by routine references to previous jurisprudence.[49] "One has to conclude that the application of the law pertaining to maritime delimitation remains as mysterious as ever."[50]

Though this type of "*justice transactionnelle*" has also come under criticism, it is hard to see what could – or should – be done about it.[51] It would be wrong to interpret it as somehow more arbitrary than recourse to straightforward "rules". For the mystique is only relative, as competent lawyers who usually have a fair idea about the structural bias know. In the *Great Belt* Case (1991), for instance, Finland withdrew its case in large part because of the expectation that the Court would follow its "sovereignty" jurisprudence and juxtapose Finland's right of passage with the Danish (sovereign) right to conclude what had been the largest single industrial project in Danish economic history. This might have led the Court to hold that Denmark was obliged to modify the bridge plan while Finland would be called upon to participate in the resulting costs. In the Finnish assessment, any such payments would, however, have exceeded the economic interest in continuing passage by oil rigs unchanged. Therefore, it decided to agree to a settlement.[52]

The deformalization of sovereignty doctrines extends beyond territorial jurisprudence to the law concerning shared natural resources,

---

provisionally draw an equidistance line and then consider whether there are circumstances which must lead to an adjustment of that line", *ibid.* para. 230.

[46] ICJ: *Jan Mayen* Case, Reports 1993, p. 63 (para. 58).

[47] See especially *ibid.* pp. 67, 72 (paras. 65 and 76).

[48] ICJ: *Qatar–Bahrain* Case, Reports 2001, pp. 111–115 (paras. 232–249).

[49] It is noteworthy, for instance, that the Court could now dismiss the socio-economic factors invoked by the parties by a rather brief reference to its having done so in the *Tunisia–Libya* Case (thus conspicuously omitting reference to the *Anglo-Norwegian Fisheries* Case of 1951), *Jan Mayen* Case, Reports 1993, p. 74 (para. 80).

[50] Malcolm Evans, "The Law of the Sea", in: Malcolm Evans (ed.), *International Law* (Oxford, 2003), p. 649.

[51] See Georges Abi-Saab, "Cours général de droit international public", 207 RCADI (1987), pp. 267, 269.

[52] See generally Martti Koskenniemi, "Case Concerning Passage Through the Great Belt", 27 *Ocean Development and International Law* (1996), pp. 278–279.

uses of international watercourses, environmental protection, as well as prevention and liability for transboundary damage.[53] In each field, the relevant law is framed in contextual terms, such as expressed in arbitral jurisprudence, for example, that holds nationalization of natural resources sometimes lawful, sometimes not, sometimes allowing full, sometimes less than full ("equitable") compensation,[54] as well as in framework treaties that define the applicable standard as an equitable balance of interests, perhaps supplemented by a set of non-exhaustive "criteria" plus a procedure for notification, negotiation and "soft" dispute settlement.[55] Even where there are apparently "hard" rules – such as the provisions for emission reduction under Article 2 of the 1987 Montreal Protocol on the Protection of the Ozone Layer – their effect is moderated by thinking of failure to carry out the required reductions in terms of "non-compliance" rather than breach of treaty.[56] This turn from (hard) rules to (soft) standards is perfectly understandable. It would be as unrealistic to lay down a rule of "sovereign freedom" as it would be to enact a rule on "no pollution" to govern transboundary harm. Where an entitlement to pollute (e.g. in the form of the so-called "Harmon principle") may seem reasonable in view of the benefits that industrial activities bring to local populations (especially in developing States), any such generalized entitlement would also be a recipe for environmental disaster. But a general prohibition against causing transboundary harm would be equally unacceptable as it would hurt the most vulnerable economies in a disproportionate way. For each State, full prohibition is both desirable as it relates to the activities of its neighbours and threatening as it curtails its own activities.

The law of State succession is another example of the way in which the grammar of sovereignty produces a fully contextualized normativity. The Vienna Conventions of 1978 and 1983 contain a large number of

---

[53] See further my "The Limits of International Law: Are There Such?", *Might and Right in International Relations*, XXVIII *Thesaurus Acroasiarum* (1999), pp. 19–50.

[54] See chapters 4.5 and 7.2 above. See also Tuomas Kuokkanen, "International Law and the Expropriation of Natural Resources", XI FYBIL (2000), p. 348.

[55] A typical example is the ill-fated Convention on the Non-Navigational Uses of International Watercourses, A/RES/51/229 (8 July 1997). For a theorization of this whole branch of law in terms of a search for contextual equity, see Eyeal Benvenisti, *Sharing Transboundary Resources. International Law and Optimal Resource Use* (Cambridge University Press, 2002).

[56] See further, Martti Koskenniemi, "Breach of Treaty or Non-Compliance? Reflexions on the Enforcement of the Montreal Protocol", 3 *Yearbook of International Environmental Law* (1992), pp. 123–162.

detailed provisions on State succession in regard to treaties (1978) and State property, archives and debts (1983). According to the main rule in the former, treaty rights and obligations continue for the successor State unless otherwise is agreed or appears from the context. The latter is based on the principle of territoriality, again modified in regard to what seems reasonable. A study carried out by the Hague Academy of International Law on the various cases of State succession in the 1990s concluded that it was not possible to determine what their effect had been as all the variations could be explained as "observance" of the deformalized provisions of the treaties.[57]

In conclusion, the grammar of sovereignty shifts between assuming the full rights of States (concrete) and their complete submission to a binding law (normative). Closure is attained by balancing formulas such as "reasonable" or "optimal" use, "equitable utilization", or, simply, by agreeing to seek agreement in a local or otherwise situation-specific context.[58] Deformalization is a product of a legal grammar that insists that the law must reflect the society that it is expected to regulate while remaining autonomous from a society it is supposed to transform.

2.2.2 Sources

Whereas "sovereignty" explains the law by reference to its basis in the world of State behaviour, "sources" start from the opposite end. They enable us to assess the normative meaning of State behaviour (legal/illegal) using autonomous criteria.[59] However, just like "sovereignty", sources, too, are internally split by contrasting ways to explain their origin and significance. This was discussed in chapters 5 and 6 through the opposition between will-based and justice-based understandings that reflect the liberal theory of political obligation.[60] On the one

---

[57] Pierre Michel Eisemann and Martti Koskenniemi (eds.), *La succession d'États: La codification à l'épreuve des faits/State Succession: Codification Tested against the Facts*, (The Hague, Nijhoff, 2000).

[58] For a recent example, see the Draft Principles on the Allocation of Loss in the case of Transboundary Harm Arising out of Hazardous Activities, adopted by the International Law Commission in first reading in 2004, in Draft report of the ILC on the Work of its Fifty-Fifth Session, A/CN.4/L.656 (22 July 2004).

[59] On the various understandings of the notion of "source" of international law, and the argumentative trajectories produced by them, see my "Introduction", in Martti Koskenniemi (ed.), *Sources of International Law* (Aldershot, Ashgate, 2000), pp. xi–xxvii.

[60] One of the incidents of the abandonment of theoretical ambition by international law is the fate of the debates on the "basis of obligation" that flourished from Georg Jellinek's

hand, any obligation must derive its force and meaning from beyond the State will. As Hersch Lauterpacht put it,

> an obligation whose scope is left to the free appreciation of the obligee, so that his will constitutes a legally recognized condition for the existence of the duty, does not constitute a legal bond.[61]

On the other hand, any obligation must also be referred back to such will – for otherwise it would appear as an objective morality, existing outside consent and thus indefensible in liberal-democratic terms.[62] The grammar of sources is received from the fashion in which it leads us to understand formal sources (treaty-texts, consistent behaviour) by reference to a substantive "intent" underlying them while simultaneously interpreting that "intent" by what it is that those formal sources say on their surface, suggesting that what they say should accord with that which is "reasonable", in accordance with "good faith", "effet utile" or some other such context-sensitive standard.

Chapters 5 and 6 contained many examples of this double oscillation (consent/justice, form/substance). The fact that little can be added to it results from the way the grammar reflects a familiar understanding of politics and society: social meaning is generated through individual psychologies, while what those psychologies produce is conditioned by the material conditions in which they are formed. Understanding will depend on what it might seem good to think people *should* will in view of everything we know about their material situatedness. In the *Tadić* Case (2003), the International Criminal Tribunal for the Former Yugoslavia (ICTY) interpreted its statute by reference to "the humanitarian goals of the framers of the Statute" that endowed it with a wide notion of "crimes against humanity" – one that did not contain the criterion of

---

work in the 1880s to the writings of James Brierly in the 1930s. As noted in chapter 5.1 above, this ended with the doctrine's inability to break through the positivism/naturalism fix and its integration of both "consent" and "justice" strands within itself. Since then, the theoretical debate has reappeared on the agenda of International Relations where it is often treated in terms of questions about the "legitimacy" of international law, almost unexceptionally conceived in an instrumentalist way. My view of this can be gleaned in "Legitimacy, Rights, and Ideology. Notes towards a Critique of the New Moral Internationalism", 7 ASSOCIATIONS (2003), pp. 349–373.

[61] Hersch Lauterpacht, *The Function of Law in the International Community* (Oxford, Clarendon, 1933), p. 189.

[62] The double-sidedness of liberal legal theory is famously articulated in Jürgen Habermas, *Faktizität und Geltung. Beiträge zur Diskurstheorie des Rechts und den demokratischen Rechtsstaats* (Suhrkamp, 1992), especially pp. 166–237.

"discriminatory intent".[63] Yet, why would *that* be the correct interpretation? Would not regular principles of criminal law rather have spoken in favour of a more limited standard – *in dubio pro reo*? Surely the Tribunal framed its interpretation not by wishing to follow standard techniques of criminal law – after all, very little about the ICTY was "standard" – but in view of the bias to guarantee as wide a scope for international prosecutions as possible. Again, the point is not that this was "wrong" or "political" – the opposite interpretation would have been no less so – but that the interpretative choices remain just that – choices – that refer back to formal sources and techniques of interpretation that seek to canvass a plausible notion of what people (such as the framers) may "intend" but which remain undetermined by them.

A similar pattern was visible in the *Qatar–Bahrain* Case in the 1990s in which Bahrain had denied that the "agreed minutes" of a 1990 meeting between the Qatari and Bahraini ministers constituted an international agreement. The Bahraini foreign minister insisted: "at no time did I consider that when agreeing to the Minutes I was committing Bahrain to a legally binding agreement".[64] The Court compared the 1990 Minutes with an agreement of 1987 whose validity was not in doubt and overruled this by the (objective) "nature of the texts". The minutes not only were written as a record of the meeting but enumerated a set of commitments and "thus create rights and obligations under international law for the Parties". Read together with that earlier agreement, the 1990 Minutes only constituted a "reaffirmation of commitments previously referred to".[65] The decision was based both on intent on the side of Bahrain, in particular the non-problematic intent of 1987, and on the non-intent-based point about the way the Minutes had been written and the "nature of the texts". Each strand in the argument could be challenged by pressing it further: how did the Court arrive at its interpretation of the 1987 agreement? How does one assess the "nature" of a text irrespective of what the parties "intend" to say? But there is no more closure to the critiques than there was for the Court's decision. The only test of the decision is the pragmatic one: did the parties settle? Did the problem "go away"?

The *Chad–Libya Territorial Dispute* (1994) falls into the same group in the Court's territorial jurisprudence as *Temple* and *Bakassi Peninsula*,

---

[63] *Prosecutor v. Tadić (Appeal against Conviction*, Case IT-94-1-A), 124 ILR (2003), p. 176 (paras. 284, 285).

[64] ICJ: *Qatar–Bahrain* Case, Reports 1994, p. 121 (para. 26).   [65] *Ibid.* (para. 25).

with treaty interpretation central and no attempt to strike a balance.[66] Libya lost its case, and it can only be speculated to what extent this was influenced by its status as diplomacy's *enfant terrible*. Here, however, the case is instructive of the way (objective) form and (subjective) consent interact so as to enable the Court to bring about the appearance of argumentative closure. The Court declined to follow Libya to the history of that contested territory. The issue of sovereignty was conclusively resolved by the 1955 Treaty of Friendship and Good Neighbourliness that referred to earlier delimitation instruments concluded between the colonial powers – in particular a 1919 Agreement between France and Italy. The Court found the place of the boundary from those agreements practically where Chad suggested it should lie. That this did not violate Libya's sovereignty was guaranteed by showing how Libya itself had consented to that boundary by its behaviour and statements during the negotiations to the 1955 treaty: "the Libyan Prime Minister expressly accepted the agreement of 1919", while just what had been left open had been the demarcation of the boundary in implementation of that agreement.[67]

Libyan consent here was (with express reference to the *Temple* Case) drawn from a number of inferences, including from the (non-consensually binding) principles of ordinary meaning of the treaty text, its object and purpose, as well as the non-treaty principle of the stability and finality of frontiers. In other words, it was held that Libya had consented. In the pleadings, Libya attacked this understanding of "justice" by drawing attention to the unequal relationship between Libya and France in the negotiations that led to the 1955 Treaty. As a developing State that had only recently gained its independence, it was at a disadvantage, lacking the technical knowledge needed to carry out a complex boundary negotiation.[68] It never pursued this line, however – possibly in view of what it might have encountered from Chad's side had the pleadings seriously turned to a relative weighing of the injustices the two may have suffered.

---

[66] For an extended analysis, see my, "L'affaire du différend territorial (*Jamahiriya arabe libyenne c. Tchad*). Arrêt de la Cour internationale de justice du 3 février 1994", XL AFDI (1994), pp. 442–464.

[67] The Court expressly noted that it need not have examined the *travaux préparatoires* to confirm its interpretation. Technically, this is quite true. It did this only to protect Libya's consent, to show that it had, in fact, agreed to Chad's position. ICJ: *Chad–Libya Territorial Dispute*, Reports 1994, p. 28 (para. 56) and generally pp. 26–28 (paras. 53–56).

[68] *Ibid.* p. 20 (para. 36).

The *Kasikili/Sedudu* Case (1999), too, was largely based on sources, in particular on the interpretation of an 1890 spheres of interest agreement in East Africa between Britain and Germany. This produced no embarrassment, however, as the will of the parties was not conceived in terms of their colonialist plans but from "objective" points about normal meaning and functional arguments about needs of navigation as important then as today.[69] It is not necessary to base Botswana's victory on the Court's undoubted reluctance to use South African military acts as justifications of Namibian sovereignty. The circumstances were taken account of by the Court's careful emphasis on a communiqué from 1992 between the presidents of Namibia and Botswana in which they promised that existing economic and navigational activities could continue unhampered.[70] The Court construed this as an agreement binding on both parties, and constituted a regime of boundary activity that was derived from the consent of the parties and within which formal delimitation in favour of Botswana was acceptable.[71]

But the most striking example of *justice transactionnelle* is surely the *Gabčíkovo–Nagymaros* Case (1997). The Court found both Slovakia and Hungary in breach of the original 1977 Treaty that provided for the construction of a series of locks in the Danube frontier region. Hungary, which had repudiated the Treaty in 1992, claimed that the Treaty had lapsed owing to a fundamental change of circumstances, ecological necessity and Slovakia's prior breach. For the Court, none of this undermined the binding force of the original treaty, however. Hungary had violated the Treaty, which continued to remain in force.[72]

But Hungary's arguments did pile up in an informal fashion so that they – in particular the environmental arguments – then became key parts of the "territorial regime" or the "joint regime" that the Court understood the Treaty to have created and which now needed to be "restored".[73] The Court even used the language of sustainable development, pointing out that "vigilance and prevention are required on

---

[69] ICJ: *Kasikili/Sedudu Island* Case, Reports 1999, p. 1074 (para. 45).

[70] *Ibid.* pp. 1106–1107 (para. 102).

[71] See especially the way the Court constructed subsequent practice as independent confirmation (objective) of the binding force of its construction of the 1992 agreement (subjective) – an indication that "the Parties have undertaken to one another" to uphold free navigation on the basis of equality and non-discrimination, *ibid.* pp. 1107–1108 (para. 103).

[72] ICJ: *Gabčíkovo–Nagymaros* Case, Reports 1997, pp. 57–68 (paras. 89–115).

[73] See especially *ibid.* pp. 71–72, 79 (paras. 123, 144).

account of the often irreparable character of damage to the environment".[74] And, in a manner that resembled the *Nuclear Tests* Cases discussed in chapter 5.3 above, it reconciled party "consent" with what seemed to be required by "justice":

> the intentions of the parties ... should prevail over its literal application. The principle of good faith obliges the parties to apply it in a reasonable way and in such a manner that its purposes can be realized.[75]

The Court first rejected the *rebus sic stantibus* – but then also held that it was impossible to overlook the fact that parts of the Treaty had been "overtaken by events".[76] It read the Treaty functionally and concluded that the objectives of the treaty relationship "must be attained in an integrated and consolidated programme" that the parties were to develop on the basis of the indications in the judgment. They were to make sure that the "use, development and protection of the watercourse is implemented in an equitable and reasonable manner".[77]

Gabčíkovo illustrates how sources arguments rotate around the poles of "consent" (the 1977 Treaty) and "justice" (environmental concerns) and then find a resolution in a pragmatic accommodation of *de facto* considerations. An attempt to canvass a law binding on sovereigns succeeds only on condition it is based on the consent of sovereigns. But a consensual law is not really binding unless what "consent" means is interpreted from the perspective of what it might be *just* to mean – thus giving rise to the problem of how the Court might justify its notion of "justice" (or good faith) and impose it on a non-consenting party. The points about consent and justice, form and content reappear in competent legal argument as a kind of preparation for the final anti-formal choice. That choice is, of course, always risky. Do colleagues understand the practical wisdom of deciding in this way? Might the parties feel the decision biased? Are outsiders satisfied by the care with which it has been made clear that nothing of this individual case will prejudice their positions in the future?

2.2.3   Conclusions on grammar: from rules and processes to decisions

From its initial division into "sovereignty" (concreteness) and "sources" (normativity), the grammar of international law splits each of these

---

[74] *Ibid.* p. 78 (para. 140).   [75] *Ibid.* p. 79 (para. 142).   [76] *Ibid.* p. 77 (para. 136).
[77] *Ibid.* p. 80 (para. 150).

argumentative trajectories into further contrasting strands – fact/law; consent/justice – in which each polar opposite is read by reference to the other. The relevant "fact" is that which "law" identifies as such; the applicable "law" is what emerges from the appropriate "fact". The only "just" base to hold States bound is the degree to which they have "consented", while what "consent" means is determined by what seems (contextually) "just". The process of institutional decision-making consists of a competent making of these moves. Failure to make them will immediately invoke a critical response from the professional audience. But though the moves build up a defensible argument, they do not "produce" the decision. The argumentative architecture allows *any* decision, and thus also the critique of any decision without the question of the professional competence of the decision-maker ever arising. Participants and observers will continue to disagree on the particular interpretations of the facts and the law, but the disagreements will remain internal to the profession and invoke the same argumentative moves the Court itself made. They are matters of "feel" and choice; they are the politics of international law. This does not mean that decisions would be random or difficult to predict (as shown by *Great Belt*, among other cases). Competent lawyers are aware of patterns and tendencies. In any language, some expressions are used more than other expressions. This is not a function of the grammar, however, but of the social and cultural context in which native speakers act.

The descriptive project of *From Apology to Utopia* was to reconstruct the argumentative architecture of international law in its many varia-tions so as to produce an account of it as a language and a professional competence. But though this is a complex architecture, and novel variations of the basic moves are constantly invented, it is not an account of how legal decisions are made – it is about how they are *justified* in argument. A grammar is not a description of what native language-speakers say in fact – it is an account of *what it is possible to say* in that language. In order to proceed beyond language as a structure of possible speech acts, and into the social pragmatics of performative speech, a change of focus was needed.

3   The normative project: from grammar to critique

The other ambition in *From Apology to Utopia* looked beyond descrip-tion. It was to provide resources for the use of international law's professional vocabulary for critical or emancipatory causes. That this was the more difficult task was reflected in three types of distinct, though related, responses the book has received from its critics. One of them focuses on the semantics of the linguistic analysis contained herein, another on its pragmatics. According to these two responses, whatever critical virtue the book may have is only due to its claims being wildly exaggerated. Although it may have some bite in marginal or extreme situations, it has no such effect in the routine administration of the law. A third criticism is a more fundamental attack on the normative pretensions of this book.

3.1   The nature of indeterminacy

The articulation of the experience of fluidity in *From Apology to Utopia* has sometimes been misunderstood as a point about the semantic open-endedness or ambiguity of international legal words. This has occasioned the criticism that the book overstates its case, that in fact the meanings of legal words are more stable and create more predictable behavioural patterns than the argument would allow. Legal hermeneutics, it has been pointed out, routinely distinguishes between "core meanings" on which professional lawyers agree and peripheral meanings that may be subject to political controversy, and the former suffice to give rise to a solid legal practice.[78] But the claim of indeterminacy here is not at all that international legal words are semantically ambivalent.[79] It is much stronger (and in a philosophical sense, more "fundamental") and states that even where there is no semantic ambivalence whatsoever, international law remains indeterminate because it is based on contradictory premises and seeks to regulate a future in regard to which even single actors' preferences remain unsettled. To say this is not to say much more than that international law emerges from a political process whose participants have contradictory priorities and rarely know with clarity how such priorities should be turned into directives to deal with an uncertain future. Hence they agree to supplement rules with exceptions, have recourse to broadly defined standards and apply rules in the context of other rules and larger principles. Even where there is little or

---

[78] See e.g. Andreas Paulus, *Die internationale Gemeinschaft im Völkerrecht. Eine Untersuchung zur Entwicklung des Völkerrechts im Zeitalter der Globalisierung* (Munich, Beck, 2001), pp. 211–217, and Jason A. Beckett, "Behind Relative Normativity: Rules and Process as Prerequisites of Law", 12 EJIL (2001), pp. 643–647.

[79] I tried to make this point originally in chapter 1.2.2 where I stated that the theory of "relative indeterminacy" was in fact parasitical upon the acceptance of "determinacy".

no semantic ambiguity about an expression in a rule – say, about "armed attack" in Article 51 of the UN Charter – that expression cannot quite have the normative force we would like it to have. It cannot because it is also threatening – what about an imminent attack? The same reason that justifies the rule about self-defence also justifies setting aside its wording if this is needed by the very rationale of the rule – the need to protect the State. And because no rule is more important than the reason for which it is enacted, even the most unambiguous rule is infected by the disagreements that concern how that reason should be understood and how it ranks with competing ones: what is it, in fact, that is necessary to "protect the State" and how does that reason link with competing ones such as those of "peaceful settlement"?[80]

It follows that it is possible to defend *any* course of action – including deviation from a clear rule – by professionally impeccable legal arguments that look from rules to their underlying reasons, make choices between several rules as well as rules and exceptions, and interpret rules in the context of evaluative standards. The important point I wish to make in *From Apology to Utopia* is not that all of this should be thought of as a scandal or (even less) a structural "deficiency" but that indeterminacy is an absolutely central aspect of international law's acceptability.[81] It does not emerge out of the carelessness or bad faith of legal actors (States, diplomats, lawyers) but from their deliberate and justified wish to ensure that legal rules will fulfil the purposes for which they were adopted. Because those purposes, however, are both conflicting as between different legal actors and unstable in time even in regard to single actors, there is always the risk that rules – above all "absolute rules" – will turn out to be over-inclusive and under-inclusive. The rules will include future cases we would not like to include and exclude cases

---

[80] I have discussed the need to set aside clear formulations of rules by reference to the (contested, political) reasons behind those rules, e.g. in "The Lady Doth Protest too Much: Kosovo, and the Turn to Ethics in International Law", 65 *Modern Law Review* (2002), especially pp. 163–168, and (by reference to human rights) in "The Effect of Rights on Political Culture", in Philip Alston (ed.) *The European Union and Human Rights* (Oxford University Press, 1999), pp. 99–116. For the "paradox of good law producing a bad result", and a reference to contextual jurisprudence, see Thomas M. Franck, *Recourse to Force* (Cambridge University Press, 2002), pp. 174–178.

[81] I would say "legitimacy", were it not that the vocabulary of "legitimacy" itself tends to turn into a politically suspect claim about the existence of a meta-discourse capable of adjudicating the claims unresolved in its object-discourses and, thus, inaugurating legitimacy experts as a kind of world-tribunal. See my "Legitimacy, Rights and Ideology", *supra*, note 60, pp. 349–373.

that we would have wanted to include had we known of them when the rules were drafted. This fundamentally – and not just marginally – undermines their force.[82] It compels the move to "discretion" which it was the very purpose to avoid by adopting the rule-format in the first place.

This is easiest to illustrate by reference to the rules concerning the use of force. For example, Article 16 of the Covenant of the League of Nations committed the members to take immediate economic and, if necessary, military action against a member that had gone to "war" in breach of its obligations under the Covenant. This provision failed to include "police action" (and thus allowed Japan to consolidate its occupation of Manchuria in 1931–1932 before effective League action could be undertaken) but would have included a duty on all members to retaliate against Italy after its attack on Abyssinia in 1936 – and thus would have forced a consolidation of the Hitler–Mussolini axis at a moment when the most important task of European diplomacy was to prevent just that. Article 16 did not fail because it was open-ended. It failed because it was not open-ended enough. Hence, of course, the flexible formulation of "threat or use of force" in Article 2(4) of the Charter and the wide discretion of the Security Council under chapter VII. But now it is precisely that discretion that seems responsible for the scandals of selectivity and partiality that have appeared to undermine the UN's collective security system. In order to end that scandal, debates on humanitarian use of force since the 1990s have always commenced with a search for "clear (formal) criteria" so as to check possible misuse by Great Powers. But the more clear-cut and "absolute" such criteria would be, the more daunting the problems of over-inclusiveness and under-inclusiveness. From the perspective of preventing discretion and political misuse the best criterion would be a numeric one – say, intervention is allowed if "500" are killed. And yet, this would be unacceptable because it would allow intervention against the practice of abortion

---

[82] Although this language may sound awkward in an international law context, the demonstration of the simultaneous over-inclusiveness and under-inclusiveness of (formal) rules is a key part of the American legal realist critique of rule-formalism. For a (very didactic) contemporary discussion, see Cass R. Sunstein, *Legal Reasoning and Political Conflict* (Oxford University Press, 1996), pp. 130–135. It has also been widely used in Critical Legal Studies. See especially Mark Kelman, *A Guide to Critical Legal Studies* (Harvard University Press, 1987), pp. 40–63. The problems with clear-cut "idiot rules" have also been usefully outlined in Thomas M. Franck, *The Power of Legitimacy Among Nations* (Oxford University Press, 1990), pp. 67–83 and *passim*.

in the secular West (over-inclusive) but prevent military action when "only" 499 are tortured to death (under-inclusive). In order to avoid such problems, any criterion will necessarily have to include a contextual assessment of the seriousness of the situation – that is, to open the door of discretion that it was the point of the exercise to close.[83] It is for this same reason that the definition of "aggression" will always either fail or end up as a long list of examples, with the proviso for analogous situations and reasonable use of discretion.[84] Although everyone would wish there to be a binding definition to constrain future adversaries, nobody would wish to be hampered in their own action by such definition when action appears necessary.

"Trap for the innocent and signpost for the guilty" – this famous quote from Anthony Eden is one way to point to the dangers of over-inclusiveness and under-inclusiveness.[85] The ICJ did not give a direct answer to the question about the *Legality of the Threat or Use of Nuclear Weapons* in 1996 precisely because it could not exclude the possibility of an extreme danger for the very existence of a State where the limited use of tactical weapons – if they were the only means available – might be not only reasonable but even fully in accord with the purpose of the Charter as a system for protecting States.[86] Any prohibition is always also a permission (of what is precisely not prohibited) and the clearer the prohibition, the more unexceptionable the permission. To believe in the absoluteness of the words "if an armed attack occurs" in Article 51 of

[83] For two carefully formulated (and thus necessarily open-ended) sets of criteria, see e.g. Danish Institute of International Affairs, *Humanitarian Intervention. Legal and Political Aspects* (Copenhagen, 1999), pp. 103–111; Report of the International Commission on Intervention and State Sovereignty, *The Responsibility to Protect* (Ottawa, 2001), pp. 32–37. See also the "five criteria of legitimacy" in the Report of the UN High-Level Panel on Threats, Challenges and Change, UN Doc. A/59/565 (2 December 2004), pp. 57–58 (para. 208). For one of the more useful discussions of this problem – shunning domestic analogies – see Simon Chesterman, *Just War or Just Peace? Humanitarian Intervention and International Law* (Oxford University Press, 2001), pp. 226–232.
[84] See UNGA Res 3314 (XXIX), 14 December 1974.
[85] For a critique of the exercise, see Julius Stone, *Conflict Through Consensus. UN Approaches to Aggression* (Sydney, Maitland, 1977). See also Ian Brownlie, *International Law and the Use of Force* (Oxford University Press, 1963), pp. 355–358. Brownlie thinks it possible and desirable to have such definitions. And maybe it is – not least owing to the *Bildung* effects of any negotiating process. Yet the point is that any definition *must* remain open-ended or else it might strike at the wrong States at the wrong moment – but that the open-endedness maintains all the problems associated with the use of discretion by those in powerful positions.
[86] ICJ: *Threat or Use of Nuclear Weapons*, Reports 1996, p. 263 (paras. 96–97).

the Charter would be to authorize States to destroy each other by economic boycotts or by triggering natural catastrophes where the only way to prevent this would be first use of armed force. If – as it is conventional to argue – international law is not a suicide pact, then provisions on the use of force must be read by reference to their reasonable purpose. If that purpose is to protect the State then surely we cannot interpret the provisions so as to bring about just that result. The ICJ's treatment of the right to life, environmental protection and humanitarian law in the *Legality of the Threat or Use of Nuclear Weapons* is an exemplary case of the Court trying to avoid being caught in absolutism: every rule invoked before the Court was subjected to a contextual assessment of "arbitrariness", "proportionality" and "relative effect". Nothing depended on semantic ambivalence – it was the ambivalence of the facts (namely what *are* the actual effects of nuclear weapons? When might their use be the last alternative available?) and not the law that necessitated the indeterminacy of the Court's response.[87]

This same logic affects all the debates about the need to "define" legal notions such as "terrorism", "self-defence", "freedom of speech", etc. It is not that such definitions would be impossible – they are *undesirable* in view of the complexity of the international social world.[88] And that complexity is not only about our ignorance about the facts of the future – it reflects our contrasting assessments of those facts: How should we understand the difference between "terrorist" and "freedom fighter"? Where is the line between dangerous "pre-emption" and understandable "prevention"? When might it be right to ban a publication because its content violates the right of privacy of a public figure? Such questions are matters of changing political assessment. They cannot be resolved by legislation *in abstracto*. Or better, they cannot be resolved by legislation *in abstracto* when the need to regard

---

[87] *Ibid.* p. 240 (para. 25), "arbitrariness"; p. 241 (para. 26), the need to take into account "the circumstances specific to each case"; p. 245 (para. 42), "proportionality". I have analysed both the deformalization at work in the Court's opinion and its dangers in "Faith, Identity and the Killing of the Innocent. International Lawyers and Nuclear Weapons", 10 LJIL (1997), pp. 137–162 and "The Silence of Law/The Voice of Justice", in Laurence Boisson de Chazournes and Philippe Sands (eds.), *International Law, the International Court of Justice, and Nuclear Weapons* (Cambridge University Press, 1999), pp. 488–510.

[88] On this problem, particularly in regard to the definition of "terrorism", see further Franck, *The Power of Legitimacy, supra*, note 82, pp. 69–71, 86–89; Jarna Petman, "The Problem of Evil and International Law", in Jarna Petman and Jan Klabbers (eds.), *Nordic Cosmopolitanism* (The Hague, Nijhoff, 2003), pp. 128–133.

some group as terrorists, the need to take self-defence action *now*, or to prohibit the damage to a person's private life outweighs the benefit that abstract law-obedience would bring. In domestic societies we can usually live with the inevitable over-inclusiveness and under-inclusiveness of rules because the benefits of generalized obedience weigh so much more heavily than the occasional injustices brought about by such obedience. When rules regulate matters of routine – thousands upon thousands of cases – then the resulting stability removes the insecurity and fear of misuse of authority that would accompany the absence of clear-cut rules. This, we normally think, seems much more valuable than the occasional injustice produced by the rule's blindness to individual situations.[89] But when a rule seeks to regulate a rare case of some importance we are automatically thrown back to assess the compliance pull of the rule in its empty form against the need to act decisively *now*, whatever the rule might say. Whichever way our decision would go, everything would depend on that *decision* – and not the rule.

The indeterminacy treated in *From Apology to Utopia* is then not about semantic openness of legal speech. There is nothing necessarily unclear about "if an armed attack occurs" or "territorial inviolability" or "right to life". The indeterminacy is about the relationship of those expressions to their underlying reasons and to other rules and principles that makes it sometimes seem necessary to deviate from a formally unambiguous provision in view of new information or a new circumstance, to sacrifice a smaller good (abstract legality) in view of realizing a larger one.[90] The deformalization of international law that we have surveyed in the preceding pages points to the apparent necessity of applying the *reason* for the rule over the empty form of the rule (e.g. allowing self-defence even where no prior armed attack has occurred) or finding a pragmatic balance between the various rules and principles and other normative materials (most frequently "rights") and choosing between rules and exceptions. It points to the apparent paradox that

---

[89] This presumes, of course, that social stability itself is not seen as the problem. If that is the case, then we are in what can only be called a revolutionary situation. I have restated these points in many places and in regard to many types of legal substance. See, in regard to the use of force, "The Lady Doth Protest too Much", *supra*, note 80, pp. 159–175 and, in regard to human rights law, "The Effect of Rights on Political Culture", *supra*, note 80, pp. 99–116. See also my "The Turn to Ethics in International Law", IX *Romanian Journal of International Relations* (2003), pp. 15–29, and "Solidarity Measures. State Responsibility as a New International Order?", 72 BYIL (2001), pp. 337–356.

[90] A useful discussion of the unavoidability of "decisionism" in this sense is in Duncan Kennedy, "A Semiotics of Critique", 22 Cardozo L. R. (2001), pp. 1165–1167.

even a "literal" application is always a choice that is undetermined by
literality itself. There is no space in international law that would be
"free" from decisionism, no aspect of the legal craft that would not
involve a "choice" – that would not be, in this sense, *a politics of
international law*.

3.2   Grammar and the social world: the role
of antagonism

The other challenge to *From Apology to Utopia* focused on the social
pragmatics of the legal profession. The point has been made that owing
to its concentration on adversarial procedures, the book has come to
exaggerate the role of conflict in international law. Had the focus been
on legislation instead of adjudication, what would have emerged would
have been a "movement towards consensus as the governing principle
of international law".[91] In this regard, the book is too "abstract" or
"theoretical" and "rel[ies] on derivational logic to construct these
seemingly awesome problems".[92] Modern international law, so this
argument goes, no longer relies on absolutes but always seeks to balance
between extremes. No plausible theory about international law's binding force is today either naturalist or positivist or relies simply on "rules"
or "facts". No treaty is defended either in terms of the consent of
the parties or the justice of its outcome. In all spheres, the plausible
positions are situated in the middle-ground where the world of legal
rhetoric is immensely richer than the straw-man portrayed in *From
Apology to Utopia*. It is only because the standard of determinacy is set
so high – exorbitantly high – that indeterminacy may seem to constitute
a problem. But if legal argument is understood as a pragmatic rhetoric,
then indeterminacy would be nothing but the normal condition of all
argumentative activity. Instead of a mindless "relativism", there would
be healthy "pluralism".[93]

However, nothing in the foregoing chapters seeks to deny the existence of what Vaughan Lowe has called "a constant move to reconciliation" or his point that, "after all, the system works for most of the

---

[91] David J. Bederman, book review of *From Apology to Utopia* in 23 *New York Journal of
International Law and Politics* (1990), p. 225.

[92] Rosalyn Higgins, *Problems and Process. International Law and How We Use It* (Oxford,
Clarendon, 1994), p. 15.

[93] Friedrich V. Kratochwil, "How do Norms Matter?", in Michael Byers (ed.), *The Role of
Law in International Politics. Essays in International Relations and International Law*
(Oxford University Press, 2000), pp. 43–51.

time".[94] Of course many judgments rendered by international courts remain unchallenged. Many settlements reached through the language of the law lay the basis for peaceful relations. Many doctrinal constructions attain a solid professional consensus. Precisely because the extreme positions are vulnerable to obvious and well-known objections, convergence towards the centre must indeed become a key aspect of legal practice. The claim of *From Apology to Utopia* is not that no middle-ground is ever found but that *the process of seeking and maintaining the middle-ground is a terrain of irreducible adversity*. Consensus is, after all, the end-point of a hegemonic process in which some agent or institution has succeeded in making its position seem the universal or "neutral" position. There is no "centre", no pragmatic meeting-point existing independently of arguments that seek to make a position seem "central" or "pragmatic" while casting the contesting positions as "marginal" or "extreme". All law is about lifting idiosyncratic ("subjective") interests and preferences from the realm of the special to that of the general ("objective") in which they lose their particular, political colouring and come to seem natural, necessary or even pragmatic. This is why law-making and consensus-building are so hugely important. They enable political victory without having to fight to the death.[95]

When Kratochwil writes that rule-scepticism dissolves "as soon as we leave the atomistic world of the single speaker and take more seriously the notion that language is an intersubjective practice",[96] I can only agree. Hermeneutics is right in that intersubjectivity is important. But it is wrong to reduce the professional context to one that "operates on the basis of common understandings and shared beliefs".[97] In fact we know virtually nothing of "understandings" or "beliefs": the insides of social agents remain irreducibly opaque. The interpretative techniques lawyers use to proceed from a text or a behaviour to its "meaning" *create* (and do not "reflect") those meanings. Perhaps consensus was produced by

---

[94] Vaughan Lowe, book review of *From Apology to Utopia* in 17 *Journal of Law and Society* (1990), p. 386.

[95] This is of course true of all universalizing languages, pragmatic or non-pragmatic, and my discussion has not been unaffected by points such as made in E. H. Carr, *The Twenty-Years' Crisis 1919–1939* (2nd edn, London, Macmillan, 1946). The idea of law (that is, legal ideology) as a universalizing project is also usefully discussed in Duncan Kennedy, *A Critique of Adjudication (fin de siècle)* (Harvard University Press, 1997), pp. 39–70.

[96] Kratochwil, "How do Norms Matter?", *supra*, note 93, p. 52.

[97] Ian Johnstone, "Treaty Interpretation: The Authority of Interpretive Communities," 12 *Michigan Journal of International Law* (1991), p. 449.

coercion, perhaps the other party acted out of ignorance or in order to deceive. We cannot know. In its innocent search for a "moment" of "meeting of horizons" hermeneutics remains blind to the way it forces the unity of meaning on an otherwise unknowable world. Hermeneutics, too, is a universalization project, a set of hegemonic moves that make particular arguments or preferences seem something other than particular because they seem, for example "coherent" with the "principles" of the legal system. Of course, making such arguments is an intrinsic part of legal practice. But they offer no more of an authentic translation of the "raw" preferences of social actors into (universal) law than do alternative techniques such as legal positivism or natural law, for instance. In fact, consensus-seeking (like appeals to love) may often hide a subtle authoritarianism. It does not have the same meaning to the one who can live without consensus as it has to the one who must purchase it by giving up everything else. Describing this as romance instead of struggle only adds insult to injury.

The fact that people (and States) sometimes agree is as much a sociological fact as that they often disagree, and political scientists spend much energy in explaining why they do. A number of factors are relevant here: time, interest, money, ambition, power.[98] But such factors are irrelevant as responses to the *normative* question about the justifiability of a particular consensus. In the search for justifiability, again, every argument is vulnerable to the logic of apology and utopia. Of course, no argument can continue interminably. At some point, it is better to agree than to fight, and the competent lawyer is constantly keeping an eye on that point. But there is no *legal* criterion that will say when it has been reached. And even when it has been reached, the law will always possess resources for re-opening the debate, undoing the settlement, attacking the ("unjust") hegemony of the mainstream.

The binarism of *From Apology to Utopia* presumes that the lawyer comes to a normative problem always from some perspective, to defend a client, an interest, a theory. This is why the field of legal argument is

---

[98] Liberal legal theory resorts to devices such as the "reflective equilibrium" or "incompletely theorized agreements" to describe the pragmatic middle-ground between abstract theories (on which people disagree) and brute facts within which most people are able to accept a common course of action. See e.g. Sunstein, *Legal Reasoning, supra,* note 82, pp. 35–61. To this, decisionist critique only adds the gloss that this is so not owing to the constraining force of the decision process but out of a maxim of strategic action that suggests that it is almost always useful to compromise. See Kennedy, "A Semiotics of Critique", *supra,* note 90, p. 1166.

constructed in an adversarial way: a defence is meaningful only as a defence *against* something, perhaps against a formal adversary in court or a political development that might go against one's interest or undermine something one holds "right". The adversarial nature of (international) law is not, however, an anthropological or sociological datum about it – even less an essentialist claim about its "nature". It is an internal, constitutive presupposition of legal argument itself. For under the liberal theory of politics, as we have seen, the point of law is to lead society away from politics, understood as an effort to move from a state of contestation and conflict into one governed by rational rules, principles and institutions. Antagonism is embedded in the *raison d'être* of the law itself and carried within it as the endlessly repeated rejection of its "other" ("discretion", "politics", "power", "violence", "corruption", etc.). In a world of angels, tyrants and technocrats, no law would be needed.

This is why most international lawyers share the intuition that the paradigm of their profession lies in arguing in front of a court, in favour of a client and against an adversary. To describe this as an unacceptably antagonistic image of the profession is to have little understanding not only of how the profession "feels" about itself but also of the dynamics of the legal grammar. This is not to say that lawyers should be understood as aggressive manipulators, constantly poised to "find a problem for every solution". Nor is it to say that different aspects of the legal craft would not be differently affected by the presence of adversity: the contrast between hard and soft law and the development of informal, non-adversarial dispute-settlement mechanisms illustrate aspects of the law that claim to rely on shared meanings and consensus. As law increasingly meshes with social processes, so the description of society moves from a stark Hobbesian nightmare to a more "communitarian" image. The background idea is something like this: as society becomes more integrated, the (artificial) egoism of individual actors cedes more room to their (natural) altruism so that the need of law diminishes until at some imaginary point ethics and natural love allow the (now fully integrated) community to govern itself without formalism. Until that point, however, it is useful to remember what E. H. Carr wrote about moments of international history that imagined themselves as particularly "ethical" but in which "the whole ethical system was built on the sacrifice of the weaker brother".[99]

---

[99] Carr, *Twenty-Years' Crisis*, p. 49. The sense that one person's "authentic, informal dialogue" is another's "exercise of brute power" – and a critique of the (old) CLS critique of the

3.3   Structural bias

But the articulation of the experiences of indeterminacy and hegemonic conflict amounts only to a weak critical thesis.[100] For it states only that no decision is "compelled" by the legal structure and that the judge or the lawyer could always decide otherwise. This links to the most-often quoted sentence in the book, namely that "international law is singularly useless as a means for justifying or criticizing international behaviour" (p. 67 above). Taken out of its context, this is wrong – for international law *is* constantly used to justify or criticize international behaviour. In the context where it appears, however, its point remains valid: although international law has justifying or critical force, that force is inexplicable by the liberal political theory that is invoked as its foundation. If we take liberalism seriously, then international law can only seem an abysmal fraud.

The weak thesis bears two corollaries. First, it goes some way towards undermining the liberal doctrine of politics by suggesting that it cannot have the kind of justifying or legitimating power it claims to have. That critique is only "weak", however, because little seems to depend on it. For, as I have later realized, international law is not a theoretical discipline. Its "basis" or core does not lie in theory but in practice – it works – and, notwithstanding a few exceptions, seeking an abstract grounding has never been its strength, or even a characteristic part of it. This is the inherent weakness of internal or "immanent" critique – a demonstration that a practice does not live up to its justifying explanations has no force when the practitioners themselves do not take those explanations seriously.[101] Though it is possible to describe this in terms

---

pernicious effects of formal rights – is well articulated in Patricia Williams, *The Alchemy of Race and Rights. Diary of a Law Professor* (Harvard University Press, 1991). The paradoxes of "leftist legalism" are discussed in Kennedy, *Critique of Adjudication, supra*, note 95, pp. 327–376. For a useful discussion and criticism of association of law with informal social practices see also Simon Roberts, "After Government? On Representing Law without the State", 68 *Modern Law Review* (2005), *supra*, note 95, pp. 1–24.

[100] Many academic lawyers have made this point in different ways. One of them is Vaughan Lowe, for whom legal concepts come in "particular pairs or groups of norms appropriate for application to particular kinds of factual situation" and represent "competing approaches to the analyses of those situations": "The Politics of Law-Making", in Michael Byers (ed.), *The Role of Law in International Politics* (Oxford University Press, 2000), p. 214. For a discussion of the (legal realist) view of legal rules and principles always coming in contradictory pairs, see also Kennedy, *Critique of Adjudication, supra*, note 95, pp. 83–85.

[101] This is the point made with great force in Peter Sloterdijk, *Critique of Cynical Reason* (Minnesota University Press, 1987).

of the profession acting in bad faith, this would presume an excessively ambitious view of theory. The critique of pragmatism is not that practice is not "based on" a well-articulated set of abstract statements about the world – perhaps no such foundation can be constructed. Pragmatism is vulnerable to critique as it offers no vocabulary that would distance the practitioner from daily work in order to enable its critical evaluation, including by reference to alternative (but imagined) practices. In such situations, practice becomes ideology, its continuing pursuit the sole criterion for its success.[102]

The other corollary of the indeterminacy critique is that it highlights the "gap" between the available legal materials (rules, principles, precedents, doctrines) and the legal decision. By drawing attention to that "gap", *From Apology to Utopia* draws attention to international law's political nature, or, as I put it above, describes the practice of law as a "politics".[103] This is a rather classical form of ideology critique whose point is to undermine the feeling of naturalness we associate with our institutional practices.[104] This critique, too, is only "weak", however, as it merely points to the "political" nature of law but says nothing about why this would be a problem. "All right, so all this involves a choice; but what is wrong with that?" In particular, nothing in this book suggests that there should be a turn towards a "more political" jurisprudence. It is not only that "political jurisprudence" (by which we usually mean deformalized styles of legal argument) may serve many different types of interest and, though it is today often linked with the Left, this has not always been the case.[105] If the law is already, in its core, irreducibly

---

[102] This is how Herbert Marcuse assessed the legitimating force of American "democracy studies" in the 1950s: "the criteria for judging a given state of affairs are those offered by (or, since they are those of a well-functioning and firmly established social system, imposed by) the given state of affairs. The analysis is 'locked'; the range of judgment is confined within a context of facts which excludes judging the context in which the facts are made, man-made, and in which their meaning, function, and development are determined": *One-Dimensional Man. Studies in the Ideology of Advanced Industrial Society* (with a new introduction by D. Kellner, London, Routledge, 1994 [1964]), pp. 115–116.

[103] I have summarized this in "The Politics of International Law", 1 EJIL (1990), pp. 4–32.

[104] The various ways in which critique works are usefully outlined in Susan Marks, *The Riddle of All Constitutions. International Law, Democracy, and the Critique of Ideology* (Oxford University Press, 2000), especially pp. 18–29.

[105] Deformalized and political jurisprudence is associated with the politics of the Right (even extreme right) in Christian Joerges and Navraj Ghaleigh, *Darker Legacies of*

"political", then the call for political jurisprudence simply fails to make sense. The critique is only "weak" as it is not about the political perversion or moral corruption of legal decision-making. It only shows the inevitability of political choice, thus seeking to induce a sense that there are more alternatives than practitioners usually realize, that impeccable arguments may be made to support preferences that are not normally heard; that if this seems difficult through the more formal techniques, then less formal techniques are always available – and the other way around: in a thoroughly policy-oriented legal environment, formalism may sometimes be used as a counter-hegemonic strategy.[106]

So it is perhaps no wonder that, to some readers, *From Apology to Utopia* appeared "fundamentally acritical", especially if compared to the writings of proponents of institutional transformation, presenters of grand blueprints.[107] In their view, the book was "rather vague in its normative visions of the international community" or outright failed "to commit to an affirmative image of international law's role in the world order".[108] From a Marxian perspective, its linguistic orientation appeared as an "idealism", lacking an explanation for why its categories remained indeterminate and why indeterminacy would be such a problem.[109] Although there has been little serious criticism of the analysis and exposition of the "grammar", the last chapter of the book – "Beyond objectivism" – has been seen to offer "pretty weak medicine for what it

European Law. The Shadow of National Socialism and Fascism over Europe and its Legal Traditions (Oxford, Hart, 2003).

[106] This is how the political aspect of Hans Kelsen's formalism is depicted in Jochen von Bernstorff, *Der Glaube an das Universale Recht. Zur Völkerrechtstheorie Hans Kelsens und seiner Schüler* (Baden-Baden, Nomos, 2001).

[107] Ian Scobbie, "Towards the Elimination of International Law: Some Radical Scepticism about Sceptical Radicalism in International Law", LXI BYIL (1990), p. 352. The contrast Scobbie has later made is in particular to the writings of Philip Allott. My own view of Allott's important work can be gleaned in "International Law as Therapy. Reading the Health of Nations", 16 EJIL (2005), pp. 329–341.

[108] Hilary Charlesworth and Christine Chinkin, *The Boundaries of International Law. A Feminist Analysis* (Manchester University Press, 2000), p. 35; similarly Hilary Charlesworth, "Subversive Trends in the Jurisprudence of International Law", ASIL Proceedings 1992, p. 127. For the latter quote and a lengthy analysis, see Nigel Purvis, "Critical Legal Studies in Public International Law", 32 Harv.ILJ (1991), pp. 116 *et seq.* and (with special reference to the nihilism charge) pp. 121–127.

[109] China Miéville, "The Commodity-Form Theory of International Law: An Introduction", 17 LJIL (2004), pp. 272–275 *et seq.* My own thoughts about the relationship of Marxism and "deconstruction" are now recorded in "What Should International Lawyers Learn from Karl Marx?", *ibid.* pp. 236–242.

advertized as such a dread disease".[110] Critics made typically two points. Some claimed that the utopian sketch of a "foundationless" conversation in chapter 8 was undermined by everything in the foregoing seven chapters.[111] Others suggested that the proposal fell on the side of the apologetic: to advocate only incremental change ("normative in the small") was to capitulate to the enemy.[112] Privately and publicly, colleagues have suspected that the last chapter remained internal to the liberalism indicted by the book and could escape from the criticisms in the foregoing chapters only by assuming an aesthetic posture of tragic conflict and incommensurability or by taking (postmodern) delight in an endless repetition of paradoxical formulations.[113]

The fact that there is no alternative institutional blueprint in this book is not an incidental oversight. Readers have been right to suggest that the first seven chapters made it impossible to engage in institution-building. Indeed, it made institution-building seem, as David Kennedy would say, "part of the problem".[114] Since its inception towards the end of the 19th century, modern international law has understood itself as above all an institution-building project. The more suspicious the profession has become of its theories or its abstract doctrines, the more important it has seemed to it to rescue respectability by proposing institutional schemes for the international "governance" of this or that problem. Today, it often seems that academic work in the field is justifiable only if it ends up in a proposal for institutional reform. From the perspective of *From Apology to Utopia*, however, the offer of policy-relevance by engaging in institution-building was a poisoned chalice. As soon as one engaged in *those* debates, two consequences would follow.

---

[110] Bederman, book review of *From Apology to Utopia, supra,* note 91, p. 228.

[111] See e.g. Ulrich Fastenrath, book review of *From Apology to Utopia* in 31 Arch.VR (1993), p. 184.

[112] Anthony Carty, "Liberalism's 'Dangerous Supplements': Medieval Ghosts of International Law", 13 *Michigan Journal of International Law* (1991), p. 171. This is also the sense of the criticism by Scobbie, "Towards the Elimination of International Law", *supra,* note 107.

[113] See Outi Korhonen, "Silence, Defence or Deliverance?", 7 EJIL (1996), pp. 1–29. The paradoxical effort to be "the last objective writer" involved in this is pointed at by David Kennedy in his book review in 31 Harv.ILJ (1990), pp. 387–389. However, Purvis, delightfully, includes Kennedy among those "New Stream purists" who have "produced what can be understood as the last modernist text of international law", in "Critical Legal Studies in Public International Law", *supra,* note 108, p. 127.

[114] See especially Kennedy, *Dark Sides, supra,* note 27.

First, all the rest of what one had to say would then be simply written
off as a prologue to the institutional proposal and relevant only to the
extent that the proposal seemed pragmatically realizable or otherwise
appropriate. Even if one did not wish to enter the terrain of the pragmatic adversary, this is how everyone would read the text henceforth:
"Oh yes, of course, those analyses are pretty clever – but see how banal
his politics are, how vulnerable his contribution to the betterment of the
human condition to all those problems we know so well from our own
practices." If it is true that the main target of *From Apology to Utopia* is
a culture of pragmatic instrumentalism as transmitted through the
language of international law, then far from being an oversight, avoiding
that type of conversation was a matter of intellectual and political life
and death.

But second, it also followed from the indeterminacy analysis itself that
matters of institutional design were far less relevant for the distribution
of material and spiritual values in the world than was commonly
assumed. An institution is a set of rules and procedures. If it was true
that rules and procedures did not have essential meanings, but that what
they meant was dependent on the decision-making practices that took
place within them, then the possibilities of political transformation were
much more widely open than was usually assumed – but no institution,
whatever its past or its ideology, could claim to be "naturally" working
towards the political good. Institutions, much recent critical writing
suggested, were in themselves indeterminate. On the one hand, societies
did not possess homogenous or well-defined functional needs or interests
that could be met by legal institutions. In fact, different groups reacted
differently to their situation and formulated different and often contradictory institutional projects to affect their situation. On the other hand,
the same institutional structure might have opposite effects in different
social and cultural environments.[115] Free markets, just like socialism,
produce wealth *and* poverty, and it was a complex and indeterminate
set of causalities that intervened to distribute these between different
social groups.[116]

---

[115] In addition to the sources in the Introduction and chapter 8, see especially
Guyora Binder, "Beyond Criticism", 55 *University of Chicago Law Review* (1988),
pp. 888–915 and Kelman, *Guide to Critical Legal Studies, supra*, note 82, pp. 242–268.
[116] See e.g. Kerry Rittich, *Recharacterizing Restructuring. Law, Distribution and Gender in
Market Reform* (The Hague, Nijhoff, 2002), pp. 132–143.

When chapter 8 of *From Apology to Utopia* refrained from proposing new institutional structures, instead calling upon the imagination of new institutional practices, this gave voice to the insight that progressive legal work was available in a number of different professional environments. It was possible, as generations of international lawyers had done, to imagine the United Nations as the constitution of the world and thereby to try to push for increased decision-making powers for *those* institutions. But how might that affect the distribution of spiritual or material values in the world? The Security Council as a "Temple of Justice"?[117] The Commission on Sustainable Development or the review of the activities under the UN's Millennium Declaration were hardly adequate as platforms for advocating beneficial political change. It seemed often much more important to describe the UN in terms of the unending bureaucratic wrangling between member States and different parts of the organization itself, a bastion for privilege and an obstacle for change. Progress towards just distribution might be much more efficiently reached through work in a national administration, a transnational economic organization or even a multinational company. This, however, few colleagues were ready to hear. International law came with a firmly entrenched prejudice in favour of public-law-governed institutions with diplomatic representations, nationalist rhetoric and scarce resources. That prejudice, it seemed to me, constituted a wholly arbitrary and counterproductive limitation of the profession's horizon.[118]

In fact, the principal object of the criticisms of *From Apology to Utopia* is not international law as a form of argument or a professional competence – after all there is no other professional grammar (of "international relations", say, or "political theory") in which the world's problems would have been resolved in a more satisfactory way. The main concern is the a priori commitment by the profession to certain institutional models – especially the reading of multilateral diplomacy as an incipient form of a public-law-governed world federation.[119]

[117] Martti Koskenniemi, "The Police in the Temple. Order, Justice and the UN; A Dialectical View", 5 EJIL (1995), pp. 325–348.

[118] This accounts for the move to private international law, comparative law and "general jurisprudence" in much recent critical writing.

[119] This is the view – or better, strategy – I associate with the reconstructivist scholarship of the inter-war, and especially with the work of Hersch Lauterpacht. The latest version of the argument is in "Hersch Lauterpacht 1897–1960", in Jack Beatson and Reinhard Zimmermann (eds.), *Jurists Uprooted. German-Speaking Emigré Lawyers in Twentieth-Century Britain* (Oxford University Press, 2004), pp. 601–662.

My intuition was – and remains – that the most serious problems of the international world are related to its sharp division into a relatively prosperous and peaceful North and an impoverished and conflict-ridden South[120] (it is not necessary to take these descriptions in their original geographical sense[121]) and that our practices, institutions and conceptual frameworks somehow help to sustain it. Undoubtedly international law may be used for valuable purposes – for challenging aspects of the international political or economic system, for instance. In practice, however, it is constantly directing attention away from important problems by defining them as "political" or "economic" or "technical" and thus allegedly beyond the law's grasp. The profession's obsessive focus is on great crises, war and civil war, terrorism and political collapse, the actions of the UN Security Council, the doings of international public-law institutions.[122] This focus is accompanied by an astonishing insensitivity to the permissive role of legal rules – the way they liberate powerful actors and reproduce day by day key aspects of the world that, although they are contingent and contestable, have begun to seem natural or unavoidable. Why is it that concepts and structures that are themselves indeterminate nonetheless still end up always on the side of the status quo?[123]

These intuitions lead me to what I now think is the main political point of *From Apology to Utopia*. For the "weak" indeterminacy thesis to turn into a "strong" one, it needs to be supplemented by an empirical argument, namely that irrespective of indeterminacy, *the system still de*

[120] For useful sociological descriptions of the structuring effect of the centre/periphery divide on the globalized world, see Boaventura de Sousa Santos, *Towards a New Common Sense. Law, Science and Politics in the Paradigmatic Transition* (London, Routledge, 1995). The importance and intensity of that divide is perhaps best described within Luhmannian sociology. See Luhmann, *Law as a Social System, supra,* note 7, pp. 292–304. See also Hauke Brunkhorst, *Solidarität. Von der Bürgerfreundschaft zur globalen Rechtsgenossenschaft* (Berlin, Suhrkamp, 2002), pp. 153–217.

[121] The internalization of boundaries – including that between the "developed" and the "developing" States within nations, even individuals – is a theme in Etienne Balibar, *Politics and the Other Scene* (London, Verso 2002).

[122] See Hilary Charlesworth, "International Law: A Discipline of Crisis", 65 *Modern Law Review* (2002), pp. 377–392. For a sustained argument about the implication of the international system (and thus its non-neutrality) in the injustice of global wealth-distribution, see also Thomas Pogge, *World Poverty and Human Rights* (Cambridge, Polity, 2002) and *idem,* "The Influence of the Global Order on the Prospect of Genuine Democracy in the Developing Countries", 14 *Ratio Juris* (2001), pp. 326–343.

[123] This question is of course at the heart of Kennedy, *Dark Sides, supra,* note 27.

facto prefers some outcomes or distributive choices to other outcomes or choices. That is to say, even if it is possible to justify many kinds of practices through the use of impeccable professional argument, there is a *structural bias* in the relevant legal institutions that makes them serve typical, deeply embedded preferences, and that something we feel that is politically wrong in the world is produced or supported by that bias.[124] This is not difficult. As pointed out above, the fluidity of international law does not deny the fact that there exists at any one time a professional consensus or a mainstream answer to any particular problem. Although, logically speaking, all positions remain open and contrasting arguments may be reproduced at will, in practice it is easy to identify areas of relative stability, moments where a mainstream has consolidated or is only marginally threatened by critique. Professional competence in international law is precisely about being able to identify the moment's hegemonic and counter-hegemonic narratives and to list one's services in favour of one or the other.

Thus it may be observed, for example, that though both free trade and social regulatory objectives are written into the WTO treaties, the former are always taken as the starting-point while the latter have to struggle for limited realization, or that though every exercise of sovereign privilege affects peoples' lives, only the exercises of sovereignty by Third World governments call for intervention by the "international community", or that while the self-limitation to "public" or "sovereign" activities that marks international law's field of application does treat all the world equally, it creates an "empire of civil society" within which private power can be used to create and maintain a system of (especially economic) constraints.[125] It might even be suggested that since its inception in the sixteenth century, international law has been used to facilitate European expansion and to discipline and subordinate

---

[124] See Kennedy, *Critique of Adjudication, supra,* note 95, pp. 59–60.

[125] The general form of the argument is available e.g. in Justin Rosenberg, *The Empire of Civil Society. A Critique of the Realist Theory of International Relations* (London, Verso, 1994). That public law regulation makes invisible the way it authorises private constraint can be gleaned e.g. in Claire Cutler, *Private Power and Global Authority: Transnational Merchant Law in the Global Political Economy* (Cambridge University Press, 2003). The argument that focus on military interventions by the West describes the interveners as "knights in white armour" while leaving invisible the constant, overwhelming intervention by Western economic and financial institutions is made in Anne Orford, *Reading Humanitarian Intervention. Human Rights and the Use of Force in International Law* (Cambridge University Press, 2003).

non-European peoples.[126] But discussions of structural bias need not
move at such abstract levels of international law's sociology or its
history. Useful work may be done by a close analysis of the application
of particular doctrines. A typical demonstration of structural bias would
describe extraterritorial jurisdiction, for example, so as to show that
while domestic courts in the West sometimes extend the jurisdiction of
domestic anti-trust law, they rarely do this with domestic labour or
human rights standards, though nothing in the standards themselves
mandates such distinction.[127] A similar demonstration in the context of
the "terrorism" debate might show how bias depends on "Orientalist"
images of violence and perceptions of "threat" current in the Western
imagination.[128] A discussion of a human rights or a good governance
regime might show how those, in principle open-ended, standards end
up in supporting different policies depending on the hierarchy of institutional priorities.[129] In any institutional context, there is always such a
structural bias, a particular constellation of forces that relies on some
shared understanding of how the rules and institutions should be
applied. That itself is not a scandal. The recent discussion of the conditions of "self-defence" by the International Court of Justice, for instance,
tends to strengthen the position of militarily less active powers.[130] But
when the bias works in favour of those who are privileged, against the

[126] See especially Antony Anghie, *Imperialism, Sovereignty and the Making of International Law* (Cambridge University Press, 2005). This is supported by the reading of "huma-nistic" international jurisprudence from the early seventeenth century in Richard Tuck, *The Rights of War and Peace. Political Thought and the International Order from Grotius to Kant* (Oxford University Press, 2000). See also my *Gentle Civilizer*, ch. 2.

[127] Robert Malley, Jean Manas, Crystal Nix, "Note. Constructing the State Extra-Territorially: Jurisdictional Discourse, the National Interest, and Transnational Norms", 103 Harv. LR (1990), pp. 1273–1305.

[128] Ileana Porras, "On Terrorism. Reflections on Violence and the Outlaw", in Dan Danielsen and Karen Engle (eds.), *After Identity. A Reader in Law and Culture* (Routledge, 1995), pp. 294–311. In this regard, the perspectivist approach to the definition of "threats" taken by the UN High-Level Panel on Threats, Challenges and Change quite usefully points to the political biases involved in the contrast between different threat-perceptions and, as a consequence, the determination of priorities of institutional policy. UN Doc A/59/565, especially pp. 15–50.

[129] For the latter, see Samuli Seppänen, *Good Governance in International Law* (Helsinki, Erik Castrén Institute Research Reports, 2003).

[130] See e.g. ICJ: *Oil Platforms* case, Reports 2003, pp. 25–35 (paras. 45–72) and *Legal Consequences of the Construction of a Wall*, Reports 2004, paras. 138–139. On the other hand, repeated uses of force may take place in the law's shadow as long as their aim appears to be not to violate anybody's "sovereignty". See Christine Gray and Simon Olleson, "The Limits of the Law on the Use of Force: Turkey, Iraq and the Kurds", 12 FYBIL (2000), p. 387 and further references there.

disenfranchised, at that point the bias itself becomes "part of the problem". That is when the demonstration of the contingency of the mainstream position can be used as a prologue to a political critique of its being an apology of the dominant forces.[131]

This gives sharper focus also to the debates concerning the proliferation of international institutions – a process that will now appear as being precisely about challenging embedded biases. The emergence of a special "human rights law" with its own institutions will then appear as an effort to challenge the positions taken by traditional law-applying organs. Human rights would never have risen to a "constitutional" status in the European legal system had not the European Court of Human Rights in Strasbourg and the European Court of Justice in Luxembourg started to think of them in "constitutional" terms, thus reversing priorities in regard to the law on legal subjects as well as the manner of interpreting reservations and the competence of law-applying organs.[132] The same considerations apply to the creation of special and a fortiori "self-contained" regimes in trade law and environmental law, international criminal law or indeed in regional legal systems. Through "fragmentation", new institutions take upon themselves new tasks, sometimes in order to collapse old preferences (e.g. the replacement of the standard of "effective control" in foreign involvement in civil wars by the stricter "overall control"), sometimes to create firm exceptions to those preferences (e.g. reservations regimes to human rights treaties) or then just to articulate confrontation between differing preferences (e.g. trade and environment).[133] One should not think of this as a new phenomenon of a particularly confused moment. When Hersch Lauterpacht wrote that there are no intrinsic limits to the jurisdiction of international tribunals and suggested that they should routinely pronounce on as many incidental questions as possible, he was undertaking a subtle ("hegemonic") manoeuvre to embolden those (judicial) institutions whose biases he shared to declare them as universal preferences.[134]

---

[131] For one overview of relevant literatures, see Deborah C. Cass, "Navigating the Newstream", 65 *Nordic Journal of International Law* (1996), pp. 341–383.

[132] See Martti Koskenniemi and Päivi Leino, "Fragmentation of International Law? Postmodern Anxieties", 15 LJIL (2002), pp. 553–579.

[133] For this frame of analysis, see my "Function and Scope of the *Lex specialis* Rule and the Question of 'Self-Contained Regimes'", Preliminary Report 2004, UN Doc. ILC(LVI)SG/FIL/CRD 1 and Add 1. See also *Report of the ILC on the Work of its Fifty-fifth Session* (2003), A/58/10, pp. 270–271 (para. 419).

[134] See Hersch Lauterpacht, *The Development of International Law by the International Court* (2nd edn, London, Stevens, 1958).

If the politics of international law is largely a debate about the jurisdiction of particular institutions, this reflects the realization that once one knows which institutions will deal with a matter, one already knows how it will be disposed of.

Now most of *From Apology to Utopia* is devoted to the demonstration of the indeterminacy thesis. As immanent critique, it shows that the justifying principles of international law – the liberal doctrine of politics – in fact fail as justifying principles. In contrast to the demonstration of the indeterminacy thesis which is made at a *general* level, structural bias must be shown by reference to *particular* institutions or practices. How are values or benefits distributed by existing legal institutions? Some of my later writings have sought to show how biases emerge and operate in the law of force,[135] the law of the sea,[136] human rights law[137] and through "fragmentation".[138] These studies complement the indeterminacy thesis by drawing attention to the politics of international law in action – the way the generality of legal language is used to buttress particular policies or preferences.[139] They seek to show that out of any number of equally "possible" choices, some choices – typically conservative or *status quo* oriented choices – are *methodologically privileged* in the relevant institutions. Their power, however, depends wholly on the expectation that once structural bias has been revealed, many people will link it to what they feel are unacceptable features in the international system. In case one does not feel the system unjust, or fails to perceive the connection between the bias and the injustice, then the critique will seem either pointless or wrong.

In principle, international lawyers should be particularly responsive to this technique. After all, international law emerged as a professional

---

[135] "Police in the Temple", *supra*, note 117, pp. 325–348.

[136] "The Privilege of Universality. International Law, Economic Ideology and Seabed Resources" (together with Marja Lehto), 65 *Nordic Journal of International Law* (1996), pp. 533–555.

[137] "Effect of Rights on Political Culture", *supra*, note 80, pp. 99–116, and "Human Rights, Politics, and Love", *Mennesker & rettigheter* (*Nordic Journal of Human Rights*, 4/2001), pp. 33–45.

[138] "Fragmentation. Postmodern Anxieties", *supra*, note 132, pp. 553–579.

[139] I have articulated this process in terms of a theory of "hegemony" in "International Law and Hegemony: A Reconfiguration", 17 *Cambridge Review of International Affairs* (2004), pp. 197–218, as well as in "Legal Universalism: Between Morality and Power in a World of States", in Sinkwan Cheng (ed.), *Law, Justice and Power: Between Reason and Will* (Stanford University Press, 2004), pp. 46–69.

practice in the late 19th century not out of enthusiasm for, but from a *critique of, the political world of Great Power primacy,* as part of a social project to spread domestic liberal reform and internationally to support peace, disarmament, human rights, the civilization of "Eastern" nations, as well as economic and social progress.[140] From the outset, international institutions were conceived less in terms of routine administration than progressive transformation of the international system.[141] One of the discipline's great names, Alejandro Alvarez, for example, was able to preach the turn to a "new international law" in virtually unchanging terms from the first decade of the twentieth century until the late 1950s.[142] He was not alone. All the discipline's great names, from Walther Schücking to Hermann Mosler in Germany, Georges Scelle to René-Jean Dupuy in France, Hersch Lauterpacht to Philip Allott in Britain, as well as contemporary non-European jurists such as P. S. Anand, Mohammed Bedjaoui or Yasuaki Onuma, have preached the message of global solidarity and fundamental change. A typical international law work is still animated by the idea of the great transformation (perhaps understood as "constitutionalization" of the international system, even federalism) in favour of human rights and environmentalism, indigenous causes, self-determination, economic redistribution and solidarity – often against Great Powers.[143] But something happened to international law during those long years. The effort to streamline it with the utopias of political, economic and technological modernity failed to advance in the expected way. Periods of enthusiasm and reform were followed by periods of disillusionment and retreat.[144] The ebb and flow between optimism and pessimism has now made it exceedingly hard to take in full seriousness Kant's liberal projection of "universal history with a cosmopolitan purpose".[145] If the language of beneficent transformation remains an

---

[140] See my *Gentle Civilizer, supra,* note 16, ch. 1.

[141] I discuss this in connection with Hersch Lauterpacht in chapter 5 of *Gentle Civilizer, supra,* note 16, pp. 357 *et seq.*

[142] See Alejandro Alvarez, *La codification du droit international – ses tendencies, ses bases* (Paris, Pedone, 1912); *idem, Le droit international nouveau dans ses rapports avec la vie actuelle des peuples* (Paris, Pedone, 1959).

[143] Martti Koskenniemi, "Repetition as Reform. Georges Abi-Saab's Cour Général", 9 EJIL (1998), pp. 405–411. See also Anne Orford, "The Destiny of International Law", 17 LJIL (2004), pp. 441–476.

[144] See Kennedy, "When Renewal Repeats", *supra,* note 11, pp. 340–397.

[145] Immanuel Kant, "Idea for a Universal History with a Cosmopolitan Purpose", in Hans Reiss (ed.), *Political Writings* (Cambridge University Press, 1991), pp. 41–53.

intrinsic part of international legal rhetoric, it is rarely articulated with a
great deal of confidence.

To understand the depth of this experience it should be noted
that being an international lawyer has not just involved taking a
"critical" attitude towards the international system but doing so
from the perspective of the idea of law as the expression of the
"social".[146] Most 20th-century international lawyers were advocates of
an anti-formalist, sociological jurisprudence, calling for the adaptation of
the law to history's evolutionary scheme.[147] Clichés about international-
ization, harmony of interests, interdependence and globalism were
thrown against "Realists" who persisted in stressing the importance of
the unchanging laws of *Realpolitik*. But just like in domestic legal systems,
the turn to sociology as an *Ersatz* moral foundation to political life failed
as it transpired that the "social" was not a uniform datum out of which
one could extract normative consequences.[148] It turned out repeatedly
to be impossible to read a single direction or purpose into social change,
and different States and groups of people have continued to be
differently poised in regard to the changes they see around themselves.
It was this experience, above all, that marked the turn towards
pragmatism in the discipline in the 1950s and split it in two. On the
one side were European lawyers directing their attention to regional
construction and taking an extremely formal view of international law
and especially of the UN Charter – an attitude they could never have
taken in regard to their domestic institutions. On the other side were
lawyers from the United States, suspicious of institutional formality and
claims of sovereign equality and reconceiving international law – including
the UN – from the perspective of its instrumental usefulness. In the
novel political constellation of the 1990s and the new millennium, the
promise of progress often moved from international law to amorphous
systems of functionally specialized "governance" of international
problems.

---

[146] See especially Duncan Kennedy, "Two Globalizations", 36 *Suffolk University Law
Review* (2003), pp. 648–674.

[147] For examples of this type of approach, see also Kelman, *Guide to Critical Legal Studies*,
supra, note 82, pp. 244–253.

[148] Apart from the article cited above ("Two Globalizations"), see also Duncan Kennedy,
"The Disenchantment of Logically Formal Rationality, or Max Weber's Sociology in
the Genealogy of the Contemporary Mode of Western Legal Thought", 55 *Hastings Law
Journal* (2004), pp. 1031–1076. See further my *Gentle Civilizer*, *supra*, note 16, ch. 4.

Indeed it does not seem possible to believe that international law is automatically or necessarily an instrument of progress. It provides resources for defending good and bad causes, enlightened and regressive policies. Some have found this suggestion insupportable. They have wished to see international law as always *already containing their ideal of the good society* so that it would suffice, outside political choice, to commit oneself to international law so as to ensure oneself of the rightness of what one does.[149] But if the view of legal indeterminacy is right, then such a "heroic" image cannot be sustained. Political choices cannot be grounded on law. It may of course be sometimes right to share the bias of one's institution. But it is certainly always necessary to be aware of that bias and its character as such – a choice – as well as its consequences. How does it affect the distribution of material and spiritual values? What does it *do* to its practitioners?

The traditional way to respond to this has been to insist on international law's marginality from international life and the hardness of the struggle for a "Rule of Law". This prefaces the old project of bringing law to bear on the darkness of politics. But, as German inter-war jurisprudence from Kelsen to Lauterpacht and even Carl Schmitt and Hans Morgenthau suggested, there is no such opposition between "law" and "politics". It is in fact possible (and follows from indeterminacy) to describe all of the international world as *already regulated by the rules of law* – perhaps by the technique of the "exclusion of the third" (Kelsen) or by accepting the postulate of material completeness (Lauterpacht). Both Schmitt and Morgenthau held it impossible to distinguish law from politics by any general rule – whether something was dealt with as a "legal" or a "political" problem was a matter of strategy: which institution would be best placed to deal with it?[150] In a somewhat similar vein, David Kennedy has suggested that lawyers and human rights activists should conceive themselves as men and women of power, managing a system of rules and concepts and institutions that has no intrinsic limits and that is always already "there" permitting or authorizing aspects of the world that otherwise seem as if they were areas of free, political choice. Very few people, including diplomats, or political and military leaders, ever think of

---

[149] Martti Koskenniemi, "Between Commitment and Cynicism: Outline for a Theory of International Law as Practice". In: *Collection of Essays by Legal Advisers of States, Legal Advisers of International Organizations and Practitioners in the Field of International Law* (United Nations, 1999), pp. 495–523.

[150] See my *Gentle Civilizer, supra,* note 16, ch. 6.

themselves as "free" in any substantive, existentialist sense. There is always a professional vocabulary or a technical adviser that will dictate this or that solution outside "politics" for the politician to grasp.[151]

From this perspective, international law might be altogether central in structuring the way in which the political and economic world appears, constructing the field of opportunities open for participants and determining their relative bargaining power in a formally egalitarian system of concepts and institutions. It is international law that tells us who qualifies as a "member" of the international community and what such membership entails. It is international law that defines the basic forms of interaction between the members (diplomacy, treaties, intergovernmental and non-governmental organizations, transnational private activities, contracts, etc.), defines the objectives towards which they may hope to be acting ("ownership", "jurisdiction", "authority") and thus also, what it is that may emerge as objects of desire in the first place ("right", "self-determination", "territorial possession", etc.). Here the law would show itself not as a limiting but an *enabling* device. One need not be Talleyrand or a student of the League debates on the Spanish Civil War in order to realise that even non-intervention is intervention – namely intervention on the side of the *status quo*. And there is no essential limit for such a reading of international law as a set of wide-ranging authorizations for the use of power and privilege – in fact, this is the most traditional (though of course contested) reading of the law as it emerges from the case of the SS *Lotus*.[152]

Thinking about international law in this way not only throws light on aspects of international law's involvement in the construction and maintenance of an international political and economic system (for instance, on its responsibility in the creation of international economic and political crises and not just in their mitigation)[153] but also follows logically from the combination of the critique of indeterminacy and structural bias. If international law is indeterminate, then there is no limit to the extent it can be used to justify (and of course, to criticize)

---

[151] Kennedy, *Dark Sides, supra*, note 27, pp. 327–357. This view of a transformation of Western modes of governance ("governmentality") from the use of the "jurisdiction" of law to "veridiction" by expert systems managing "truth regimes" is powerfully articulated e.g. in Foucault, *Naissance*.

[152] See chapter 4 *supra*.

[153] This is shown in Anne Orford's argument about the "international community's" pervasive involvement in East Timor and Bosnia from a point in time much earlier than its highly publicized military "interventions". See her *Reading Humanitarian Intervention, supra*, note 125.

existing practices. If there is a structural bias, then international law is always already complicit in the actual system of distribution of material and spiritual values in the world.[154] From this perspective, the task for lawyers would no longer be to seek to expand the scope of the law so as to grasp the dangers of politics but to widen the opportunity of political contestation of an always already legalized world.

And yet, such contestation may also be carried out through the grammar of international law. Sometimes internalizing the language of international law may mean also internalizing a structural bias. Biographically, what starts out as commitment may turn to indifference, even cynicism, as the institutional practice becomes an end in itself, a brick in the wall of a structure of preferences. At that point, transformative action becomes necessary, a new bias needs to be set up, a new interpretation adopted, an unorthodox choice made. It is an important moment of enlightenment when it becomes evident that this can be done in a professionally plausible manner. But again, nothing of our ability to challenge the bias is grounded in the law itself. The choice will be just that – a "choice" that is "grounded" in nothing grander than a history of how we came to have the preferences that we have and what we know of the world and our relationship to it. "Theory" may be needed to create awareness of the origin and conse- quences of our choices – perhaps a theory of "justice" or of economic efficiency – but those theories do not fully justify our choices. A "gap" will remain between all such languages and what it is that we choose, whether the bias, or its contrary. The existence of this "gap" is not insignificant for professional practice. If the practice is not determined by an anterior structure or vocabulary, then it cannot be reduced to an automatic produc- tion of such a structure or vocabulary either. The decision is made, and its consequences are thus attributable not to some impersonal logic or structure but *to ourselves*.

4 Conclusion

International law is what international lawyers make of it. To commit oneself to international law is to allow its grammar to enter as one's

---

[154] The international legal system's complicity in poverty through its allocation of borrowing rights and natural resource privileges to formal elites in the Third World is discussed in Pogge, *World Poverty and Human Rights*, *supra*, note 122, pp. 91–117. See also Paul D. Ocheje, "Refocusing International Law on the Quest for Accountability in Africa – The Case against the 'Other Impunity'", 15 LJIL (2002), pp. 749–777.

second nature but still to maintain the position of choice – at a minimum a choice to work with colleagues with certain preferences in institutions with a certain bias. Those may be the right preferences, of course, but they are not produced or even strongly supported by legal argument – that is, any more strongly than opposite preferences. Legal work will require choice. None of the available alternatives can pretend to be controlling. Formalism and anti-formalism, positivism and natural law, as well as any alternative legal vocabularies, may be associated with cosmopolitan liberalism as well as conservative nationalism. Nor do particular legal–institutional choices have pre-determined legal consequences. Whatever effects one's formalism or one's anti-formalism will have for one's legal practice, just like whatever effects the legal institution one imports will have on one's target society, can only be contextually determined. Situationality, as Outi Korhonen has put it, is a key aspect of legal practice.[155]

The virtues and vices of international law cannot be discussed in the abstract. What might its significance be today, for the choices that men and women of law now have to make? Recently, I have argued in favour of a "culture of formalism" as a progressive choice. This assumes that although international law remains substantively open-ended, the choice to refer to "law" in the administration of international matters – instead of, for example, "morality" or "rational choice" – is not politically innocent. Whatever historical baggage, including bad faith, such culture entails, its ideals include those of accountability, equality, reciprocity and transparency, and it comes to us with an embedded vocabulary of (formal) rights. Although these notions and vocabularies are again indeterminate so that we might see conservatives and liberals, market theorists and socialist agitators all have recourse to them, as parts of a distinct professional tradition they are biased both against moral vocabularies of imperial privilege and economic techniques underwriting privatized *de facto* relationships. Whatever virtue a culture of formalism might have must be seen in historical terms. The call for "constitutionalization" we hear in Europe today may give direction to an anti-imperial Left political programme – but it may equally well consolidate types of authority that seek to perpetuate Europe's comparative advantage.

---

[155] Outi Korhonen, *International Law Situated. An Analysis of the Lawyer's Stance Towards Culture, History and Community* (The Hague, Kluwer, 2000).

From Apology to Utopia should be read with both its descriptive and its critical ambition in mind. I still find myself constantly using its central theses to analyse recent developments in international law. I continue to read international cases by reference to the framework provided by the tension between normativity and concreteness as elaborated in *From Apology to Utopia*. I have used that framework to argue both for the need of law to remain silent so that what needs to be articulated outside law can be so articulated, as well as for the use of law to give voice to claims or to indict violations that otherwise would seem matters of political strategy or preference.[156]

Perhaps there is a certain repetitive, even reductionist tone in these arguments – though I have tried to play it down by choices of substance and style. In lectures and private conversation I find myself often speaking of the "machine" that this book sketches for the production of competent arguments in the field. It was precisely in order to take distance from the cool structuralism of *From Apology to Utopia* that a few years ago I published an intellectual history of the profession in the years of its prime.[157] The purpose of that book was not to repudiate anything written in the foregoing pages but to show how individual lawyers, both as academics and practitioners (this is a contentious distinction – after all, academics, too, practise the law, and it is only the context in which they do so that makes them special), have worked in and sometimes challenged the structure sketched there, how they have acted in a conceptual and professional world where every move they make is both law and politics simultaneously and demands both coolness and passion – a full mastery of the grammar and a sensitivity to the uses to which it is put.

---

[156] "Faith, Identity and the Killing of the Innocent", *supra*, note 87, pp. 137–162 (silence), and "What Should International Lawyers Learn from Karl Marx?", *supra*, note 109, pp. 244–246 (voice).

[157] *Gentle Civilizer*, *supra*, note 16.

BIBLIOGRAPHY

A Books and monographs

A.1 Philosophy, social and legal theory and method

Aarnio, Aulis: Denkweisen der Rechtswissenschaft. Wien–New York 1979.
  Legal Point of View. Six Essays on Legal Philosophy. Yleisen oikeustieteen laitoksen julkaisuja 3. Helsinki 1978.
  Oikeussäännösten tulkinnasta: tutkimus lainopillisen perustelun rationalisuudesta ja hyväksyttävyydestä. Vantaa 1982.
  On Legal Reasoning. Turun yliopiston julkaisuja B 144. Turku 1977.
  The Rational as Reasonable: a Treatise on Legal Justification. Dordrecht 1986.
Adorno, Theodor (ed): The Positivist Dispute in German Sociology. (Translated by Glyn Adey and David Frisby) London 1977.
Adorno, Theodor – Horkheimer, Max: Dialectic of Enlightenment. (Translated by John Cumming) London 1979.
D'Amato, Anthony: Jurisprudence: A Descriptive and Normative Analysis of Law. Dordrecht–Boston–London 1984.
Arnaud, André-Jean: Essai d'analyse structural du Code Civil français. Le règle du jeu dans la paix bourgeoise. Paris 1973.
Atiyah, P. S.: An Introduction to the Law of Contract. 3rd ed. Oxford 1982.
  Promises, Morals, and Law. Oxford 1981.
Austin, John: Lectures on Jurisprudence and on the Philosophy of Positive Law. (12th impression) London 1913.
  The Province of Jurisprudence Determined. (Introduction by H. L. A. Hart) London 1954.
Balibar, Etienne: Politics and the Other Scene. London 2002.
Barry, Brian: The Liberal Theory of Justice. A Critical Examination of the Principal Doctrines in 'A Theory of Justice' by John Rawls. Oxford 1975.
Barthes, Roland: Elements of Semiology. In: Writing Degree Zero/Elements of Semiology. London 1984.
  Mythologies. (Selected and Translated from the French by Annette Lavers) London 1985.
Beitz, Charles R.: Political Theory and International Relations. Princeton, N.J. 1979.

Bentham, Jeremy: Bentham's Handbook of Political Fallacies. Rev.ed. Baltimore 1952.

A Fragment on Government. Edited with an introduction by F. C. Montague. London 1931.

The Works. Published under the Superintendence of John Bowering, Vols. I–XI. Edinburgh 1843.

Berger, Peter L. – Luckmann, Thomas: The Social Construction of Reality. A Treatise in the Sociology of Knowledge. Repr. New York 1980.

Berlin, Isaiah: Four Essays on Liberty. Oxford 1969.

Bernstein, Richard J.: Beyond Objectivism and Relativism; Science, Hermeneutics and Practice. Oxford 1983.

Bernstorff, Jochen von: Der Glaube an das Universale Recht. Zur Völkerrechtstheorie Hans Kelsens und seiner Schüler. Baden-Baden 2001.

Bhaskar, Roy: Scientific Realism & Human Emancipation. London 1986.

Bleckmann, Albert: Die Aufgabe einen Methodenlehre des Völkerrechts. Probleme der Rechtsquellenlehre im Völkerrecht. Heidelberg 1978.

Die Funktionen der Lehre im Völkerrecht. Köln–Berlin–Bonn–München 1981.

Grundprobleme und Methoden des Völkerrechts. Freiburg 1982.

Bodin, Jean: Les six livres de la république. Paris 1583.

Bos, Maarten: A Methodology of International Law. Amsterdam 1984.

Bozeman, Adda B.: The Future of Law in a Multicultural World. Princeton 1971.

Brunkhorst, Hauke: Solidarität. Von der Bürgerfreundschaft zur globalen Rechtsgenossenschaft. Berlin 2002.

Bull, Medley: The Anarchical Society. A Study of Order in World Politics. New York 1977.

Butler, Judith: Precarious Life. The Powers of Mourning and Violence. London 2004.

Carlyle, R. W. and A. J.: A History of Mediaeval Political Theory in the West, Vols. I–IV. Edinburgh–London, Vol. I (2nd ed.) 1927. Vols. II–IV 1909–1922.

Carr, E. H.: The Twenty-Years' Crisis 1919–1939. 2nd ed. London 1946.

Carzo, Domenico – Jackson, Bernard (eds.): Semiotics, Law and Social Science. Roma 1985.

Cassirer, Ernst: The Myth of the State. Oxford 1946.

Chomsky, N: Selected Readings. (Ed. by Allen, J. P. B. – van Buven, Paul) Oxford–London 1971.

Coleman, Jules – Frankel Paul, Ellen (eds.): Philosophy and Law. Oxford–New York 1987.

Collingwood, R. G.: The New Leviathan or Man, Society, Civilization and Barbarism. Oxford 1947.

Collins, Hugh: Marxism and Law. Oxford 1982.

Cox, Richard H: Locke on Peace and War. Washington DC 1982.

Culler, Jonathan: On Deconstruction. Theory and Criticism after Structuralism. London 1985.

Ferdinand de Saussure. London 1978.

The Pursuit of Signs; Semiotics, Literature, Deconstruction. Melbourne–London–Henley 1983.

Structuralist Poetics. Structuralism, Linguistics and the Study of Literature. London–Henley 1975.

Derrida, Jacques: Of Grammatology. (Translated and with translator's preface by Gayatri Chakavorty Spivak) Baltimore–London 1976.

Positions. (Translated by Alan Bass) Chicago 1981.

Writing and Difference. (Translated by Alan Bass) Chicago 1978.

Dews, Peter: Logics of Disintregation. Post-Structuralist Thought and the Claims of Critical Theory. London 1987.

Donelan, Michael (ed.): The Reason of States. London–Boston–Sydney 1978.

Duguit, Leon: Traité de droit constitutional. Paris 1927.

Dunn, John: Rethinking Modern Political Theory. Essays 1979–1983. Cambridge 1986.

Western Political Theory in Face of the Future. Cambridge 1979.

Dworkin, Ronald: Law's Empire. Cambridge, Mass. 1986.

Taking Rights Seriously. Cambridge, Mass. 1980.

Esser, Josef: Vorverständnis und Methodenwahl in der Rechtsfindung. Rationalitätsgarantien der richterlichen Entscheidungspraxis. Frankfurt am Main 1970.

Feinberg, Joel: Harm to Others. The Moral Limits of the Criminal Law; 1. New York 1984.

Finnis, John: Fundamentals of Ethics. Oxford 1983.

Natural Law and Natural Rights. Oxford 1980.

Fishkin, James S: Tyranny and Legitimacy. A Critique of Political Theories. Baltimore–London 1979.

Foucault, Michel: Naissance de la biopolitique. Cours au Collège de France 1978–1979. Paris 2004.

The Archaeology of Knowledge. (Translated by A. M. Sheridan Smith) London 1985.

The Order of Things; an Archaeology of the Human Sciences. London, Tavistock 1970.

Power/Knowledge. Selected Interviews and other Writings 1972–1977. ed. by Colin Gordon. (Translated by Colin Gordon, Leo Marshall, John Mepham, Kate Soper) Brighton 1986.

Frank, Jerome: Law and the Modern Mind. London 1949.

Franklin, H. Julian: Jean Bodin and the Rise of Absolutist Theory. Cambridge 1973.

Friedmann, Wolfgang: Legal Theory. (2nd ed.) London 1949.

Friedrich, Carl Joachim: The Philosophy of Law in Historical Perspective. (2nd ed.) Chicago 1963.

Frost, Mervyn: Towards a Normative Theory of International Relations. A Critical analysis of the philosophical and methodological assumptions in the discipline with proposals towards a substantive normative theory. Cambridge 1986.

Gadamer, Hans-Georg: Philosophical Hermeneutics. (Translated by David E. Linge) Berkeley–Los Angeles–London 1977.

Gardies, Jean-Louis: Essai sur les fondements a priori de la rationnalité morale et juridique. Paris 1972.

Gény, F.: Méthode d'interprétation et sources en droit privé positif. Essai critique. Précéde d'une préface de Raymond Salailles (2ème éd.) I–II. Paris 1919.

Geuss, Raymond: The Idea of a Critical Theory; Habermas & the Frankfurt School. Cambridge 1981.

Giddens, Anthony: Central Problems in Social Theory. Action, Structure and Contradiction in Social Analysis. London–Basingstoke 1983.

Gierke, Otto von: Die Grundbegriffe des Staatsrechts und die neuesten Staatsrechtstheorien. Tübingen 1915.

Glucksmann, Miriam: Structuralist Analysis in Contemporary Social Thought. A Comparison of the Theories of Claude Lévi-Strauss and Louis Althusser. London 1974.

Goldsmith, M. M.: Hobbes' Science of Politics. New York–London 1966.

Goodman, Nelson: Ways of Worldmaking. Indianapolis 1984.

Goodrich, Peter: Reading the Law. A Critical Introduction to Legal Method and Techniques. Oxford–New York 1986.

Gould, Wesley L. – Barkun, Michael: International Law and the Social Sciences. Princeton 1970.

Graham, Keith (ed.): Contemporary Political Philosophy. Cambridge 1982.

Habermas, Jürgen: Faktizität und Geltung. Beiträge zur Diskurstheorie des Rechts und den demokratischen Rechtsstaats. Berlin 1992.

Legitimation Crisis. (Translated by Thomas McCarthy) Boston 1975.

Theory and Practice. (Translated by John Viertel) London 1977.

Haggenmacher, Peter: Grotius et la doctrine de la guerre juste. Paris 1983.

Harland, Richard: Superstructuralism. The Philosophy of Structuralism and Post-Structuralism. London–New York 1987.

Hart, H. L. A.: The Concept of Law. Oxford 1961.

Essays in Jurisprudence and Philosophy. Oxford 1983.

Hayek, F. A.: The Road to Serfdom. London 1946.

Hegel, G. W. F.: Grundlinien der Philosophie des Rechts. (Vierte Aufl.) Herausgegeben von Johannes Hoffmeister, Hamburg 1955.

Held, David: Introduction to Critical Theory. Horkheimer to Habermas. London 1980.

Hinsley, F. H.: Sovereignty. New York 1966.

Hobbes, Thomas: Leviathan. Edited with an Introduction by C. B. Macpherson, Harmondsworth 1982.

Hoffmann, Stanley: Duties Beyond Borders; On the Limits and Possibilities of Ethical International Politics. Syracuse 1981.

Hohfeld, Wesley Newcomb: Fundamental Legal Conceptions as Applied in Judicial Reasoning. New Haven 1978.

Honderich, Ted (ed): Morality and Objectivity. A Tribute to J. L. Mackie. London–Boston–Henley 1985.

Horkheimer, Max: Critical Theory. Selected Essays. Translated by Matthew O'Connell et al. New York 1972.

Hume, David: Essays. Moral, Political and Literary. (The World's Classics 33.) London 1904.

A Treatise of Human Nature, Being an Attempt to Introduce the Experimental Method of Reasoning into Moral Subjects and Dialogue Concerning Natural Religion. Edited, with an Introduction by Ernest C. Mossner. Harmondsworth 1987.

Jackson, Bernard S.: Semiotics and Legal Theory. London–Boston–Henley 1985.

Jacobini, H. B.: A Study of the Philosophy of International Law as Seen in Works of Latin American Writers. The Hague 1954.

Jay, Martin: Dialectical Imagination. A History of the Frankfurt School and the Institute of Social Research 1923–1950. Boston–Toronto 1973.

Jellinek, Georg: Allgemeine Staatslehre. (3. Aufl.) Berlin 1914.

Joerges, Christian – Ghaleigh, Navraj: Darker Legacies of European Law. The Shadow of National Socialism and Fascism over Europe and its Legal Traditions. Oxford 2003.

Jørgensen, Stig: Values in Law: Ideas, Principles and Rules. Köbenhavn 1978.

Jouvenel, Bertrand de: Sovereignty: An enquiry into the political good. Cambridge 1957.

Kairys, David (ed.): The Politics of Law: A Progressive Critique. New York 1982.

Kant, Immanuel: Zum ewigen Frieden und ausgewählte Stücke. (Dokumänte der Menschlichkeit, Band 7) München–Wien–Berlin 1919.

Kaltenborn von Stachau, F.: Kritik des Völkerrechts. Leipzig 1847.

Kaplan, Morton A. – Katzenbach, Nicholas: The Political Foundations of International Law. New York–London 1961.

Kelman, Mark: A Guide to Critical Legal Studies. Cambridge, Mass. 1987.

Kelsen, Hans: Allgemeine Staatslehre. Berlin 1925.

General Theory of Law and State. (Translated by Anders Wedberg) Cambridge, Mass. 1946.

Das Problem der Souveränität und die Theorie des Völkerrechts. Tübingen 1920.

Reine Rechtslehre. Einleitung in die rechtswissenschaftliche Problematik. Leipzig–Wien 1934.

Der soziologische und der juristische Staatsbegriff. Kritische Untersuchung der Verhältnisses von Staat und Recht. Tübingen 1922.

Kennedy, Duncan: A Critique of Adjudication (fin de siècle). Harvard 1997.

Kielmansegg, Peter Graf: Volkssouveränität; eine Untersuchung der Bedingungen demokratischen Legitimität. Stuttgart 1977.

Kratochwil, Frederick V.: International Order and Foreign Policy. A Theoretical Sketch of Post-War International Politics. Boulder, Colorado 1978.

Kuhn, Thomas S.: The Structure of Scientific Revolutions. (2nd ed.) Chicago 1970.

Kurzweil, Edith: The Age of Structuralism. Lévi-Strauss to Foucault. New York 1980.

Landheer, Bart: On the Sociology of International Law and International Society. The Hague 1966.

Larrain, Jorge: The Concept of Ideology. London 1979.

Lebow, Richard Ned: The Tragic Vision in Politics. Ethics, Interests, Orders. Cambridge 2003.

Lement, Charles – Gillan, Garth: Michel Foucault: Social Theory and Transgression. New York 1982.

Lenoble, J. – Ost, F.: Droit, mythe et raison: essai sur la dérive mythologique de la rationalité juridique. Bruxelles 1980.

Lessnoff, Michael: Social Contract. London 1986.

Lévi-Strauss, Claude: The Savage Mind. London 1981.

Structural Anthropology. (Translated by Clare Jacobson and Brooke Guilford Schoepf) Harmondsworth 1979.

Levine, Andrew: Liberal Democracy: A critique of its theory. New York 1981.

Lipsky, George A. (Comp. and ed.): Law and Politics in the World Community. Berkeley and Los Angeles 1953.

Lloyd, Christopher (ed.): Social Theory and Political Practice. Wolfson College Lectures 1981. Oxford 1983.

Locke, John: Two Treatises of Government. (Introduction by W. S. Carpenter) London–Melbourne 1984.

Loughlin, Martin: The Idea of Public Law. Oxford 2003.

Luhmann, Niklas: Die Wissenschaft der Gesellschaft. Frankfurt 1992.

Law as a Social System. (Translated by Klaus A. Ziegert, ed. by Fatima Kastner, Richard Nobles, David Schiff and Rosamund Ziegert) Oxford 2004.

Lukes, Steven: Power. A Radical View. London 1980.

Lyons, David: Ethics and the Rule of Law. Cambridge 1985.

MacCormick, Neil: Legal Reasoning and Legal Theory. Oxford 1978.

Legal Right and Social Democracy: Essays in legal and political philosophy. Oxford 1982.

MacCormick, Neil – Weinberger, Ota: An Institutional Theory of Law. Dordrecht–Boston–Lancaster–Tokyo 1986.

MacIntyre, Alasdair: After Virtue. A Study in Moral Theory. (2nd ed.) London 1985.

Against the Self-images of the Age. Essays in Ideology and Philosophy. London 1983.

Whose Justice? Which Rationality? London 1988.

Macpherson, C. B.: Democratic Theory; Essays in Retrieval. Oxford 1973.
The Political Theory of Possessive Individualism; Hobbes to Locke. Oxford 1962.

Maine, Sir Henry: Ancient Law. (With Introduction by J. H. Morgan) London 1954.

Manning, C. A. W.: The Nature of International Society. London 1962.

Manning, D. J.: Liberalism. London 1976.

Marcuse, Herbert: One-Dimensional Man. Studies in the Ideology of Advanced Industrial Society. Boston 1968.
One-Dimensional Man. Studies in the Ideology of Advanced Industrial Society (with a new introduction by Douglas Kellner). London 1994.

Marx, Karl: Capital. A Critical Analysis of Capitalist Production. London 1909.

Mayall, James (ed): The Community of States. A Study in International Political Theory. London–Boston–Sydney 1982.

McLellan, David: Ideology. Milton Keynes 1986.

Merquior, J. G.: From Prague to Paris. A Critique of Structuralist and Post-Structuralist Thought. London 1986.

Miaille, Michel: Une introduction critique au droit. Paris 1976.

Midgley, E. B. F.: The Natural Law Tradition and the Theory of International Relations. 1975.

Mill, John Stuart: On Liberty. (Edited with an Introduction by Gertrude Himmelfarber) Harmondsworth 1987.

Miller, David – Siedentop, Larry (eds.): The Nature of Political Theory. Oxford 1983.

Mitchell, Sollace – Rosen, Michael (eds.): The Need for Interpretation. Contemporary Conceptions of the Philosopher's Task. London–New Jersey 1983.

Morgenthau, Hans J: Politics Among Nations: The struggle for power and peace. (3rd ed.) New York 1961.

Murphy, Cornelius F.: The Search for World Order: A study of thought and action. Dordrecht 1985.

Nardin, Terry: Law, Morality and the Relations of States. Princeton, N. J. 1983.

Newell, R. W.: Objectivity, Empiricism and Truth. London–New York 1986.

Norris, Christopher: Deconstruction. Theory and Practice. London 1972.

Nozick, Robert: Anarchy, State and Utopia. New York 1974.

O'Hagan, Timothy: The End of Law? Oxford 1984.

Olivecrona, Karl: Rättsordningen. Idéer och fakta. Lund 1966.

Outhwaite, William: New Philosophies of Social Science. Realism, Hermeneutics and Critical Theory. Basingstoke–London 1987.

Parkinson, F.: The Philosophy of International Relations. A Study in the History of Thought. Beverly Hills 1977.

Pateman, Carole: The Problem of Political Obligation; A Critical Analysis of Liberal Theory. New York–Brisbane–Toronto 1979.

Peczenik, Alexander: Juridikens metodproblem. Rättskällelära och lagtolkning. (2. upplaga) Stockholm 1980.

Perelman, Chaim (ed.): Le problème des lacunes en droit. Bruxelles 1968.

Perelman, Ch. – Olbrechts – Tyteca L.: Traité de l'argumentation, I–II. Paris 1958.

Piaget, Jean: Structuralism. (Translated and edited by Channinah Maschler) London 1973.

Plamenatz, John: Man and Society, Vol. 2. (5th Impression) London 1969.

Pogge, Thomas: World Poverty and Human Rights. Cambridge 2002.

Prott, Lyndel V.: The Latent Power of Culture and the International Judge. Abingdon 1979.

Pufendorf, Samuel: De Jure Naturae et Gentium Libri Octo, transl. by Oldfather-Oldfather. Carnegie Endowment for International Peace, Classics of International Law No. 17. Oxford–London 1934.

   De Officio Hominis et Civis Juxta Legem Naturalem Libri Duo, transl. by Frank Gardner Moore. Carnegie Endowment for International Peace. New York 1927.

Putnam, Hilary: Meaning and the Moral Sciences. London 1978.

Quine, W. V.: Ontological Relativity and Other Essays. New York–London 1969.

Raphael, D. D.: Problems of Political Philosophy. Rev.ed. London 1982.

Rawls, John: A Theory of Justice. Oxford 1973.

Raestad, Arnold: La philosophie du droit international public. Oslo 1949.

Remec, Peter Pavel: The Position of the Individual in International Law according to Grotius and Vattel. The Hague 1960.

Robey, David (ed.): Structuralism. An Introduction. Oxford 1982.

Rorty, Richard: Philosophy and the Mirror of Nature. Oxford 1986.

Rose, Gillian: Dialectic of Nihilism. Post-Structuralism and Law. Oxford 1984.

Rosenberg, Justin: The Empire of Civil Society. A Critique of the Realist Theory of International Relations. London 1994.

Rosenthal, Bent: Etude de l'oeuvre de Myres Smith McDougal en matière du droit international public. Paris 1970.

Ross, Alf: On Law and Justice. London 1958.

Rousseau, Jean Jacques: The Social Contract. (Translated and introduced by Maurice Cranston) Harmondsworth 1986.

Salvador, Massimo: The Liberal Heresy; Origins and Historical Development. London 1977.

Sandel, Michael: Liberalism and the Limits of Justice. Cambridge 1982.

Saussure, Ferdinand de: Course in General Linguistics. Bungay, Suffolk 1981.

Savigny, Friedrich Karl von: System des heutigen Römischen Rechts. Erster Band, Berlin 1840.

Schapiro, J. Salwyn: Liberalism. Its meaning and history. Princeton 1958.

Schmitt, Carl: Political Theology: Four chapters on the concept of sovereignty. (Translated by George Schwab) Cambridge, Mass. 1985.

Schwarzenberger, Georg: Power Politics. A Study of World Society. (3rd ed.) London 1964.

Seung, T. K.: Structuralism & Hermeneutics. New York 1982.

Shapiro, Ian: The Evolution of Rights in Liberal Theory. Cambridge 1986.

Sheikh, Ahmed: International Law and National Behavior. A Behavioral Interpretation of Contemporary International Law and Politics. New York–London–Sydney–Toronto 1974.

Sheridan, Alan: Michel Foucault. The Will to Truth. London–New York 1980.

Simmonds, N. E.: The Decline of Juridical Reason. Doctrine and Theory on the Legal Order. Manchester 1984.

Simmons, Alan John: Moral Principles and Political Obligations. Princeton 1979.

Simson, Werner von: Die Souveränität im rechtlichen Verständnis der Gegenwart. Berlin 1965.

Skinner, Quentin: Visions of Politics I. Cambridge 2003.

Sloterdijk, Peter: Critique of Cynical Reason. Minnesota 1987.

Somló, Felix: Juristische Grundlehre. Leipzig 1917.

Sousa Santos, Boaventura de: Towards a New Common Sense. Law, Science and Politics in the Paradigmatic Transition. London 1995.

Spiropoulos, Jean: Théorie générale du droit international. Paris 1930.

Spragens, Thomas A. Jr. The Irony of Liberal Reason. Chicago 1981.

Stammler, Rudolf: Lehrbuch der Rechtsphilosophie. (2. Ausgabe) Berlin–Leipzig 1923.

Stein, Peter: Legal Evolution. The Story of an Idea. Cambridge 1980.

Stephen, J. K.: International Law and International Relations. An attempt to ascertain the best method of discussing the topics of international law. London 1884.

Stone, Julius: Visions World Order. Between State Power and Human Justice. Baltimore–London 1984.

Strauss, Leo: Natural Right and History. Chicago 1953.

Suarez, Francisco S. J.: Selections from three works. Vol II. The Translation – De legibus, ac deo legislatore, 1612 – Defensio fidei Catholicae, et apostolicae adversus anglicanae sectae errores, 1613: – De triplici virtute theologica, fide, spe et charitate, 1621: Carnegie Endowment for International Peace; The Classics of International Law No. 20 Oxford–London 1944.

Sumner, Colin: Reading Ideologies. An Investigation into the Marxist Theory of Ideology and Law. London–New York 1979.

Sunstein, Cass R.: Legal Reasoning and Political Conflict. Oxford 1996.

Tamanaha, Brian Z.: A General Jurisprudence of Law and Society. Oxford 2001.

Taylor, Charles: Philosophy and the Human Sciences. Philosophical Papers 2. Cambridge 1985.

Tolonen, Hannu: Luonto ja Legitimaatio. Normatiivisten asiantilojen johtaminen aristotelisen luonnonoikeustradition valossa. Vammala 1984.

Tuck, Richard: Natural Rights Theories: Their origin and development. Cambridge 1981.

Tuori, Kaarlo: Valtionhallinnon sivuelinorganisaatiosta. Julkisoikeudellinen tutkimus komiteatyyppisten elinten asemasta Suomen valtio-organisaatiossa. 1. Teoreettinen ja historiallinen tausta. Vammala 1983.

Twining, William (ed.): Legal Theory and Common Law. Oxford 1986.

Tönnies, Ferdinand: Community and Association. (Translated by Charles P. Loomis) London 1955.

Ullmann, Walter: Law and Politics in the Middle Ages; an introduction into the sources of medieval political ideas. London–Bristol 1975.

Unger, Roberto Mangabeira: The Critical Legal Studies Movement. Harvard 1986.

False Necessity. Anti-Necessitarian Social Theory in the Service of Radical Democracy. Part I of Politics, a Work in Constructive Social Theory. Cambrdige 1987.

Knowledge and Politics. New York 1975.

Law in Modern Society. Toward a Criticism of Social Theory. New York 1976.

Social Theory: Its Situation and its Task. A Critical Introduction to Politics, a Work in Constructive Social Theory. Cambridge 1987.

Vattel, Emmerich de: Le droit des gens ou principes de la Loi Naturelle, appliqués à la conduite et aux affairs des Nations et des Souverains I–II. Londres 1758.

Vecchio, Giorgio del: Humanité et unité du droit. Essais de philosophie juridique. Paris 1963

Viehweg, Theodor: Topik und Jurisprudens. Habilitationsschrift. München 1953.

Villey, Michel: Le droit et les droits de l'homme. Paris 1983.

Wahl, Francois: Qu'est ce qu'est le structuralisme? 5. Philosophie. La philosophie entre l'avant et l'après du structuralisme. Paris 1968.

Walker, T. A.: The Science of International Law. London 1893.

Walzer, Michael: Just and Unjust Wars. A Moral Argument with Historical Illustrations. Harmondsworth 1980.

Wasserstrom, Richard A.: The Judicial Decision. Toward a theory of legal justification. Stanford 1961.

Watson, Alan: The Evolution of Law. Oxford 1985.

Weber, Max: Max Weber on Law in Economy and Society. Edited with an introduction by Max Rheinstein. Translated by Edward Shils and Max Rheinstein. Cambridge, Mass. 1954.

West, Ranyard: International Law and Psychology. Two Studies: The intrusion of order in conscience and society. Dobbs Ferry 1974.

Williams, Bernard: Ethics and the Limits of Philosophy. London 1985.

Williams, Patricia: The Alchemy of Race and Rights. Diary of a Law Professor. Harvard 1991.

Winch, Peter: The Idea of a Social Science and Its Relation to Philosophy. London–Henley 1977.

Wittgenstein, Ludwig: On Certainty. (Edited by G. E. M. Anscombe and G. H. von Wright. Translated by Denis Paul and G. E. M. Anscombe) Oxford 1969.

A.2 International law and international relations: general works

(Abendroth, Wolfgang): New Directions in International Law. Essays in Honour of Wolfgang Abendroth. Rafael Gutiérrez Girardot-Helmut Ridder-Manihar Lal Sarin-Theo Schiller (eds.). Frankfurt–New York 1982.

Akehurst, Michael: A Modern Introduction to International Law. (4th ed.) London 1982.

Alvarez, Alejandro: La codification du droit international – ses tendencies, ses bases. Paris 1912.

Le droit international nouveau dans ses rapports avec la vie actuelle des peuples. Paris 1959.

Anghie, Antony: Imperialism, Sovereignty and the Making of International Law. Cambridge 2005.

Anzilotti, Dionisio: Cours de droit international. Premier volume: Introduction – Théories générales. Paris 1929.

Aron, Raymond: Paix et guerre entre les nations. Paris 1962.

Ayala, B.: De jure et officiis bellicis et disciplina militari libri III, 1582, Carnegie Endowment for International peace; The Classics of International Law, Vol. II. The Translation, 1912.

Barkun, Michael: Law Without Sanctions. New Haven–London 1968.

Baty, Thomas: International Law. London 1909.

International Law in Twilight. Tokyo 1954.

Benchikh, M. – Charvin, R. – Demichel, F.: Introduction critique au droit international. Lyon 1986.

Benedik, W. – Ginther, K. (eds.): New Perspectives and Conceptions of International Law: An Afro-European Dialogue. Wien 1983.

Bernhardt, R. (Ed.): Encyclopedia of Public International Law – Max-Planck-Institute for comparative public law and international law. Volume 7. History of International Law. Foundations and principles of international law. Sources of international law. Law of treaties. North Holland. Amsterdam/New York/Oxford 1984.

(Bindschedler, Rudolf): Festschrift für Rudolf Bindschedler. Herausgegeben von Emanuel Diez, Jean Monnier, Jörg P. Müller, Heinrich Reimann und Luzius Wildhaber. Bern 1980.

Blix, Hans: Sovereignty, Aggression, Neutrality. Stockholm 1970.

Bluntschli, J. C.: Das moderne Völkerrecht des civilisierten Staaten als Rechtsbuch dargestellt. (2. Auflage) Nördlingen 1872.

Boyle, Francis Anthony: World Politics and International Law. Durham 1985.

Brierly, James Leslie: The Basis of Obligation in International Law and other Papers. Selected and edited by Sir Hersch Lauterpacht and C. H. M. Waldock. Oxford 1958.
The Law of Nations. (6th ed.) Oxford 1963.

Briggs, Herbert: The Law of Nations. Cases, Documents and Notes. (2nd ed.) New York 1952, London 1953.

Brownlie, Ian: Principles of Public International Law. (3rd ed.) Oxford 1979.

Bull Hedley (ed.): Intervention in World Politics. Oxford 1985.

Bulmerincq, A. von: Praxis, Theorié und Codification des Völkerrechts. Leipzig 1874.
Die Systematik des Völkerrechts von Hugo Grotius bis auf die Gegenwart. Karow, Dorpat 1858.

Butterfield, H. – Wight M. (eds.): Diplomatic Investigations. Essays in the Theory of International Politics. London 1966.

Bynkershoek, Cornelis van: Questionum juris publici libri duo, Vol. II, a translation. Carnegie Endowment for International Peace; The Classics of International Law No 14. Oxford 1930.

Carreau, Dominique: Droit International. Paris 1986.

Carty, Anthony: The Decay of International Law? A reappraisal of the limits of legal imagination in international affairs. Manchester 1986.

Cassese, Antonio: International Law in a Divided World. Oxford 1986.
International Law. Oxford 2001.

Cavaré, Louis: Le droit international public positif, tôme I. (3ème éd. mis à jour par Jean-Pierre Quéneudec) Paris 1967.

Charlesworth, Hilary – Chinkin, Christine: The Boundaries of International Law. A Feminist Analysis. Manchester 2000.

(Chaumont, Charles): Le droit des peuples à disposer d'eux-mêmes; méthodes d'analyse du droit international. Mélanges offerts à Charles Chaumont. Paris 1984.

Cheng, Bin (eds.): International Law. Teaching and Practice. London 1982.

Clark, Grenville – Sohn, Louis B.: World Peace through World Law. Cambridge, Mass. 1958.

Cobbett, Pitt: Leading Cases and Opinions on International Law. London 1937–1947.

Coplin, William D.: The Functions of International Law. An Introduction to the Role of International Law in the Contemporary World. Chicago 1966.

Corbett, Percy Elwood: Law and Society in the Relations of States. New York 1951.

Creasy, E. S.: First Platform of International Law. Voorst–London 1876.

Cutler, Claire: Private Power and Global Authority. Transnational Merchant Law in the Global Political Economy. Cambridge 2003.

Davis, G. B.: Outlines of International Law with an Account of its Origin and Sources and of its Historical Development. London 1888.

Detter-Delupis, Ingrid: The Concept of International Law. Uppsala 1987.

Deutsch, Karl – Hoffmann, Stanley (eds.): The Relevance of International Law. Garden City, New York 1971.

Dhokalia, R. P.: The Codification of Public International Law. Manchester 1970.

Dickinson, Ewin Dewitt: The Equality of States in International Law. Cambridge 1920.

Dore, Isaak I.: International Law and the Super Powers: Normative Order in a Divided World. New Brunswick, N. J. 1984.

Dupuy, René-Jean: La communauté internationale entre le mythe et l'histoire. Paris 1986.

Elias, Taslim O.: Africa and the Development of International Law. London–New York 1972.

New Horizons in International Law. Alphen aan den Rijn 1979.

Falk, Richard: The Status of Law in International Society. Princeton 1970.

Falk, Richard A. – Black, Cyril E. (eds.): The Future of the International Legal Order, Vol. I, Trends and Patterns. Princeton 1969.

Falk, R. – Kim, S. – Mendlowitz, S.: Toward a Just World Order. Vol. 1 of Studies on a Just World Order. Boulder, Colorado 1982.

Falk, R. – Kratochwil, F. – Mendlovitz, S.: International Law – A Contemporary Perspective. Boulder–London 1985.

Fauchille, Paul: Traité de droit international public. (8ème éd., entièrement refondue, completée et mise au courant, du Manuel de droit international public de Henry Bonfils I, 1) Paris 1921.

Fawcett, James: Law and Power in International Relations. London 1982.

Fenwick, Charles G.: International Law. (4th ed.) New York 1965.

Ferencz, Benjamin: A Common Sense Guide to World Peace. London–Rome–New York 1985.

Fisch, Jörg: Die europäische Expansion und das Völkerrecht. Stuttgart 1984.

Franck, Thomas M.: The Power of Legitimacy Among Nations. Oxford 1990.

Recourse to Force. Cambridge 2002.

Friedmann, Wolfgang: The Changing Structure of International Law. London 1964.

Gentili, Alberico: De Iure Belli Libri Tres, 1612, Carnegie Endowment for International Peace; The Classics of International Law, No. 16. Oxford–London 1933.

Gounelle, Max: La motivation des actes juridiques en droit international public. Paris 1979.

Griffith, W.: International Law: History, Principles, Rules and Treaties. London 1892.

Gross, Leo: Essays on International Law. The Hague 1982.

Grotius, Hugo: De jure belli ac pacis, libri tres, Carnegie Endowment for International Peace; The Classics of international law, No 3, Vols. I–III The Translation, Oxford–London 1925.

Guggenheim, Paul: Lehrbuch des Völkerrechts. Zürich 1948.

Traité de droit international public. Avec mention de la pratique internationale de la Suisse, Vols. I–II. Genève 1953–54.

Recueil d'études de droit international en hommage à Paul Guggenheim. Genève 1968.

Hackworth, Green Haywood: Digest of International Law, 1–8. Washington 1940–44.

Hall, W. E.: A Treatise on International Law. (8th ed. by A. Pearce Higgins) Oxford 1924.

Halleck, H. W.: International Law; or Rules Regulating the Intercourse of States on Peace and War. San Francisco 1861.

Hatschek, Julius: Völkerrecht als System rechtlich bedeutsamer Staatsakte. Leipzig 1923.

Heffter, August Wilhelm: Das Europäische Völkerrecht der Gegenwart. (Siebente Ausgabe) Berlin 1882.

Henkin, Louis: How Nations Behave. Law and Foreign Policy. (2nd ed.) New York 1979.

Herczegh, Géza: General Principles of Law and the International Order. Budapest 1969.

Higgins, Rosalyn: Problems and Process. International Law and How We Use It. Oxford 1994.

Hingorani, R. C.: Modern International Law. New York–London–Rome 1984.

Holland, T. E.: Studies in International Law. Oxford 1898.

Hosack, J.: On the Rise and Growth of the Law of Nations, as Established by General Usage and by Treaties. London 1882.

Huber, Max: Die soziologischen Grundlagen des Völkerrechts. Berlin 1928.

Hudson, Manley: La Cour Permanente de Justice Internationale. Paris 1936.

Hussain, Ijaz: Dissenting and Separate Opinions at the World Court. Dordrecht–Boston–Lancaster 1984.

Institut de droit international: Livre du centenaire 1873–1973. Evolution et perspectives du droit international. Bâle 1973.

Jacqué, Jean-Paul: Eléments pour une théorie de l'acte juridique en droit international public. Paris 1972.

Jellinek, Georg: Die rechtliche Natur der Staatenverträge. Berlin–Wien 1880.

Jenks, C. Wilfred: The Common Law of Mankind. London 1958.

The Prospects of International Adjudication. London–New York 1964.

Jessup, Philip C.: A Modern Law of Nations – An Introduction. New York 1952.

The Price of International Justice. New York–London 1971.

Transnational Law. New Haven 1966.

Kaufmann, Erich: Das Wesen des Völkerrechts und die Clausula Rebus Sic Stantibus. Tübingen 1911.

Kelsen, Hans: Law and Peace in International Relations. Cambridge, Mass. 1948.
  Principles of International Law. (Edited and Revised by Robert M. Tucker)
  New York–Chicago–San Francisco–Toronto–London 1966.
Kennedy, C. M.: The Influence of Christianity upon International Law.
  Cambridge 1856.
Kennedy, David: International Legal Structures. Baden-Baden 1987.
  The Dark Sides of Virtue. Reassessing International Humanitarianism.
  Princeton 2004.
Klüber, J.-L.: Droit des Gens Moderne de l'Europe. Avec un supplement con-
  tenant une bibliographic choisie du droit des gens. (Nouvelle éd. annotée et
  completée par M.A.Ott.) Paris 1861.
Korhonen, Outi: International Law Situated. An Analysis of the Lawyer's Stance
  Towards Culture, History and Community. The Hague 2000.
Koskenniemi, Martti: The Gentle Civilizer of Nations. The Rise and Fall of
  International Law 1870–1960. Cambridge 2001.
Kosters, J.: Les fondements du droit des gens. IX Bibliotheca Visseriana 1925.
Krakau, Knud: Missionsbewusstsein und Völkerrechtsdoktrin in den vereinigten
  Staaten von Amerika. Frankfurt am Main 1967.
Lacharrière, Guy de: La politique juridique extérieure. Paris 1983.
Lachs, Manfred: The Teacher in International Law (Teachings and Teaching). The
  Hague–Boston–London 1982.
  Essays in International Law in Honour of Judge Manfred Lachs. Edited by
  Jerzy Makarczyk. The Hague 1984.
Lapradelle, A. de: Maîtres et doctrines du droit des gens. (2ème éd.) Paris 1950.
Lapradelle, A. de – Politis, J. – Salomon, A.: Recueil des arbitrages internationaux,
  tôme III, Paris 1954.
Laurent, F.: Histoire du droit des gens et des relations internationales. Vols. 1–18
  Gand 1850–70.
Lauterpacht, Hersch: The Development of International Law by the International
  Court. London 1958.
  The Function of Law in the International Community. Oxford 1933.
  International Law, Volume I: The General Works, Vols. II–III, The law of
  peace 1–6. Cambridge 1970–1977.
  Private Law Sources and Analogies of International Law. London 1927.
Lawrence, T. J.: A Handbook of Public International Law. (10th ed.) London 1925.
Levi, Werner: Contemporary International Law. A Concise Introduction.
  Boulder, Colorado 1979.
Lissitzyn, Oliver: International Law in a Divided World. Carnegie Endowment for
  International Peace (542 International Conciliation) 1963.
Lipsky, George A. (comp. and ed.): Law and Politics in the World Community.
  Essays on Hans Kelsen's Pure Theory and Related Problems in International
  Law. Berkeley–Los Angeles 1953.

(Lipstein, Kurt): Multitum non Multa. Festschrift für Kurt Lipstein. Herausgegeben von Peter Fenerstein und Clive Parry. Heidelberg 1980.

Lorimer, James: Principes de droit international. (Trad. Ernst Nys) Bruxelles–Paris 1885.

Mann, F. A.: Studies in International Law. Oxford 1973.

Marks, Susan: The Riddle of All Constitutions. International Law, Democracy, and the Critique of Ideology. Oxford 2000.

Martens, G.-F. de: Précis du droit des gens moderne de l'Europe. (2ème éd.) Vol. 1–2. Paris 1864.

Martens, F. de: Traité de droit international, tômes I–III. (Trad. Alfred Léo) Paris 1883–1884, 1887.

Macdonald, R. St. J. – Johnston, Douglas M. (eds.): The Structure and Process of International Law: Essays in Legal Philosophy, Doctrine and Theory. The Hague 1983.

McDougal, Myres S. – Feliciano, Florentino P.: Law and Minimum World Public Order. The Legal Regulation of International Coercion. New Haven 1961.

Toward World Order and Human Dignity. Essays in honor of Myres S. McDougal. Ed. by W. Michael Reisman & Burns H. Weston. New York 1976.

(McNair, Lord): Cambridge Essays in International Law. Essays in Honour of Lord McNair. Cambridge 1965.

McWhinney, Edward: Conflict and Compromise: International Law and World Order in a Revolutionary Age. Alphen aan den Rijn 1981.

Menzel, Eberhard – Ipsen, Knud: Völkerrecht. München 1979.

Merignhac, A.: Traité de droit public international. Vols. 1–3. Paris 1905–1912.

Merillat, H. C. L. (ed.): Legal Advisers and Foreign Affairs. Dobbs Ferry 1966.

Merrills, J. G.: Anatomy of International Law. London 1976.

Moser, J. J.: Versuch des neuesten europäischen Völkerrechts in Friedens- und Kriegszeiten. Frankfurt am Mayn 1777–1780.

Mosler, Hermann: The International Society as a Legal Community. Alphen aan den Rijn 1980

Völkerrecht als Rechtsordnung, internationale Gerichtsbarkeit, Menschenrechte: Festschrift für Hermann Mosler. Herausgegeben von Rudolf Bernhardt, Philip Geck, Günther Jaenicke, Walter Steinberger. Berlin 1983.

Nussbaum, Arthur: A Concise History of the Law of Nations. (Rev. ed.) New York 1954.

Nys, E.: Le droit international. Les principes, les théories, les faits. Vols. 1–3. Bruxelles 1912.

O'Connell, D. P.: International Law I–II. (2nd ed.) London 1970.

Ompteda, D. H. L.: Litteratur des gesammten sowohl natürlichen als positiven Völkerrechts. Regensburg 1785.

Onuf, Nicholas G. (ed.): Law-Making in the Global Community. Durham, N. C. 1982.

Oppenheim, L: International Law. A Treatise, Vol. I Peace. (2nd ed.) London 1912.
International Law. A Treatise, Vol. I Peace. (Edited by H. Lauterpacht, 8th ed.) London 1955.

Orford, Anne: Reading Humanitarian Intervention. Human Rights and the Use of Force in International Law. Cambridge 2003.

Parry, Clive: The Sources and Evidences of International Law. Manchester 1965.

Phillimore, Sir Robert: Commentaries upon International Law. (3rd ed.) Vols. I–IV London 1879.

Pinto, Roger: Le droit des relations internationales. Paris 1972.

Politis, Nicolas: Les nouvelles tendences du droit international. Paris 1927.

(Rao Khrisna): Essays in International Law. In Honour of H. Krishna Rao. Ed. by M. H. Nawaz. Leyden 1976.

Rayneval, Gérard J. M. de: Institutions du droit de la nature et des gens. (2ème éd.) Paris 1803.

Reuter, Paul: Droit international public. (5ème éd.) Paris 1976.
Le droit international: unité et diversité. Mélanges offerts à Paul Reuter. Paris 1981.

Rittich, Kerry: Recharacterising Restructuring. Law, Distribution and Gender in Market Reform. The Hague 2002.

Rosenne, Shabtai: Practice and Methods of International Law. London–Rome–New York 1984.

Ross, Alf: A Text-book of International Law. General Part. London 1947.

Rousseau, Charles: Droit international public, tôme I: introduction et sources. Paris 1970.
La communauté internationale. Mélanges offerts à Charles Rousseau. Paris 1974.

Röling, B. V. A.: International Law in an Expanded World. Amsterdam 1960.

Sauer, Ernst: Souveränität und Solidarität. Göttingen 1954.

Scelle, Georges: Précis de droit des gens. Principes et systématique. I Partie. Introduction. Le milieu intersocial. Paris 1932.
Précis de droit des gens. Principes et systematique. II Partie. Droit constitutionnel international. Paris 1936.

Schiffer, Walter: The Legal Community of Mankind. New York 1954.

Schwarzenberger, Georg: The Dynamics of International Law. Milton 1976.
The Frontiers of International Law. London 1962.
The Inductive Approach to International Law. London–New York 1965.
International Law, Volume I. London 1949.
International Law, Volume III: International Constitutional Law. London 1976.
International Law and Order. London 1971.

Schwarzenberger, Georg – Brown, E. D.: A Manual of International Law. (6th ed.) London 1976.

(Schwarzenberger, Georg): Contemporary Problems of International Law. Essays in Honour of George Schwarzenberger on his Eightieth Birthday, edited by Bin Cheng and E. D. Brown. London 1988.

Schwebel, Stephen (ed.): The Effectiveness of International Decisions. Leyden 1971.

Scott, James Brown: Cases on International Law. Washington 1902.

Law, the State and the International Community. Vols. 1–2. New York 1939.

The Spanish Origin of International Law. Lectures on Francisco de Vitoria (1480–1546) and Francisco Suarez (1548–1617). Washington 1932.

Scott, J. B. – Jaeger, W. H. E.: Cases on International Law. Washington 1937.

Seppänen, Samuli: Good Governance in International Law. Helsinki 2003.

Starke, J. G.: An Introduction to International Law. (8th ed.) London 1977.

Stowell, E. C.: International Law: A Restatement of Principles in Conformity with Actual Practice. London 1931.

Sørensen, Max: Les sources du droit international. Etude sur la jurisprudence de la Cour Permanente de Justice Internationale. Copenhagen 1946.

Manual of Public International Law. Glasgow 1968.

Triepel, Heinrich: Völkerrecht und Landesrecht. Leipzig 1899.

Truyol y Serra, A.: Doctrines contemporaines du droit des gens. Paris 1951.

Tuck, Richard: The Rights of War and Peace. Political Thought and the International Order from Grotius to Kant. Oxford 2000.

Tunkin, G. I.: Theory of International Law, London 1974.

Twiss, Travers: Le Droit des Gens ou des Nations, considerées comme communautés politiques independantes. Tôme I, nouvelle éd. Paris 1887.

Vallat, Francis: International Law and the Practioner. Manchester 1966.

van Vollenhoven, C.: Scope and Content of International Law. XXVI Bibliotheca Visseriana, X, 1932.

Verdross, Alfred: Die Einheit des rechtlichen Weltbildes auf Grundlage der Völkerrechtsverfassung. Tübingen 1923.

Die Verfassung der Völkerrechtsgemeinschaft. Wien–Berlin 1926.

Verdross, Alfred – Simma, Bruno: Universelles Völkerrecht. Theorie und Praxis. Berlin 1976.

Verzijl, J. H. W.: International Law in Historical Perspective. Vols. 1–10. Leiden, Alphen aan den Rijn 1968–79.

Symbolae Verzijl (van Aschbach, ed.) The Hague 1958.

Vinogradoff, Sir Paul: Historical Types of International Law. I Bibliotheca Visseriana I pp. 1–70, 1923.

Visscher, Charles de: Les effectivités du droit international public. Paris 1967.

Theory and Reality in Public International Law. Princeton 1957.

Vitoria, Francisco: De indis et de iure belli relectiones, 1696. Carnegie Endowment for International Peace; The Classics of International Law. Washington 1917.

Walker, T. A.: History of the Law of Nations. Cambridge 1899.

Wallace, Rebecca M.: International Law. London 1986.

(Wehberg, Hans): Rechtsfragen der internationalen Organisation. Festschrift für Hans Wehberg. Herausgegeben von Walter Schätzel und Hans-Jürgen Schlochauer. Frankfurt am Main 1956.

Westlake, John: Chapters on the Principles of International Law. Cambridge 1894. International Law I. (2nd ed.) Cambridge 1910.

Wheaton, Henry: Elements of International Law. Text of 1866 with notes. Carnegie Endowment for International Peace; The Classics of International Law, No. 19. Oxford–London 1936.

Whiteman, Marjorie M. (ed.): Digest of International Law, Vol. 5. Department of State Publication 7873 Released June 1965.

Wolff, Christian: Jus Gentium Methodo Scientifica Pertractatum. Carnegie Endowment for International Peace; The Classics of International Law, No. 13 Oxford – London 1934.

Woolsey, T. D.: Introduction to the Study of International Law. Designed as an aid in teaching, and in historical studies. (5th ed.) London 1879.

Zorn, A.: Grundzüge des Völkerrechts. (2. Aufl.) Leipzig 1903.

Zouche, Richard: Iuris et iudicii Fecialis, sive Iuris Inter Gentes, et Questionum de Eodem Explicatio. Translated by J. L. Brierly. Carnegie Endowment for International Peace; The Classics of International Law. Washington 1911.

A.3   *International law: particular subjects*

Adede, A. O.: The System for Settlement of Disputes under the United Nations Convention on the Law of the Sea. Dordrecht–Boston–Lancaster 1987.

d'Amato, Anthony: The Concept of Custom in International Law. Cornell, Ithaca 1971.

Anand, R. P.: New States and International Law. Delhi–Bombay 1972.

Alibert, Christiane: Du droit de se faire justice dans la société internationale depuis 1945. Paris 1983.

Arangio-Ruiz, Gaetano: The UN Declaration on Friendly Relations and the System of Sources of International Law. Alphen aan den Rijn 1979.

Attard, David: The Exclusive Economic Zone in International Law. Oxford 1987.

Badr, Gamal Moursi: State Immunity: An analytical and prognostic view. The Hague–Boston–Lancaster 1984.

Bardonnet, Daniel – Virally, Michel (eds.): Le Noveau droit de la mer. Paris 1983.

Bedjaoui, Mohammed: Towards a New International Economic Order. Paris–New York–London 1979.

Bell, Coral: The Conventions of Crisis: A study in diplomatic management. Oxford 1971.

Benvenisti, Eyeal: Sharing Transboundary Resources. International Law and Optimal Resource Use. Cambridge 2002.

Bergbohm, C.: Staatsverträge und Gesetze als Quellen des Völkerrechts. Dorpat 1876.

Blum, Yehuda Z.: Historic Titles in International Law. The Hague 1965.

Bowett, D. W.: Self-Defence in International Law. Manchester 1958.

Brownlie, Ian: International Law and the Use of Force by States. Oxford 1981 (reprint of the 1963 ed.).
     Principles of Public International Law. 6th ed. Oxford 2003.

Buirette-Maurau, Patricia: La Participation du tiers-monde dans l'élaboration du droit international. Paris 1983.

Bull, Hedley (ed.): Intervention in World Politics. Oxford 1984.

Bynkershoek, Cornelis van: De foro legatorum liber singularis 1744. Carnegie Endowment for International Peace; The Classics of International Law, No. 21, The Translation, 1946.

Canaris, Claus-Wilhelm: Die Feststellung von Lücken im Gesetz, Berlin 1964.

Castañeda, Jorge: Legal Effects of UN Resolutions. New York–London 1969.

Charpentier, Jean: La reconnaissance international et l'évolution du droit des gens. Paris 1956.

Chen, Ti-Chiang: The International Law of Recognition. London 1951.

Cheng, Bin: General Principles of Law as Applied by International Courts and Tribunals. London 1953.

Chesterman, Simon: Just War or Just Peace? Humanitarian Intervention and International Law. Oxford 2001.

Churchill, R. R. – Lowe, A. V.: The Law of the Sea. Manchester 1983.

Crawford, James: The Creation of States in International Law. Oxford 1979.

Cukwurah, A. O.: The Settlement of Boundary Disputes in International Law. Manchester 1967.

Daillier, Patrick – Pellet, Alain: Droit international public. 7ème éd. Paris 2002.

Danish Institute of International Affairs: Humanitarian Intervention. Legal and Political Aspects. Copenhagen 1999.

Decaux, Emmanuel: La reciprocité en droit international. Paris 1980.

Degan, V. D.: L'équité et le droit international. La Haye 1970.
     L'interprétation des accords en doit international. La Haye 1963.

Dennert, Jürgen: Ursprung und Begriff der Souveränität. Stuttgart 1964.

Dugard, John: Recognition and the United Nations. Cambridge 1987.

Dupuy, Pierre-Marie: Droit international public. 4ème éd. Paris 1998.

Elagab, Omer Yousif: The Legality of Non-Forcible Counter-Measures in International Law. Oxford 1988.

Elias, Taslim O.: The International Court of Justice and Some Contemporary Problems. The Hague 1983.

Elkind, Jerome B.: Non-appearance before the International Court of Justice. Functional and Comparative Analysis. Dordrecht 1984.

Eisemann, Pierre Michel – Koskenniemi, Martti (eds.): La succession d'Etats: La codification à l'épreuve des faits/State Succession: Codification Tested against the Facts. The Hague 2000.

Finch, George A.: The Sources of Modern International Law. Carnegie Endowment for International Peace. Division of International Law Monograph Series 1, 1937.

Fisher, Roger: Improving Compliance with International Law. Charlottesville, VA 1981.

Franck, Thomas A.: Nation Against Nation: What Happened to the U.N. Dream and what the U.S. can do about it? New York–Oxford 1985.

Gamble, John King jr. & Fischer, Dana D.: The International Court of Justice. An analysis of a failure. Lexington 1976.

Garcia Amador, F. V.: The Changing Law of International Claims, Vol. I. New York–London–Rome 1984.

Gianni, G.: La coutume en droit international. Paris 1931.

Gilson, Bernard: The Conceptual System of Sovereign Equality. Leuven 1984.

Gray, Christine: Judicial Remedies in International Law. Oxford 1986.

Gross, Leo: The Future of the International Court of Justice 1–2. New York 1976.

Guilhaudis, Jean-François: Le droit des peuples à disposer d'eux-mêmes. Grenoble 1976.

Günther, Herbert: Zur Entstehung von Völkergewohnheitsrecht. Berlin 1970.

Hakapää, Kari: Marine Pollution in International Law. Material Obligations and Jurisdiction with Special Reference to the Third United Nations Conference on the Law of the Sea. Helsinki 1981.

Heydte, August Freiherr von der: Die Geburtstunde des Souveränen Staates, Regensburg 1952.

Higgins, Rosalyn: The Development of International Law through the Political Organs of the United Nations, London 1963.

International Law and the Reasonable Need of Governments to Govern. An Inaugural Lecture. London 1982.

Hoof, G. J. H. van: Rethinking the Sources of International Law. Deventer 1983.

Hossain, Kamal (ed.): Legal Aspects of the New International Economic Order. London–New York 1980.

Howard-Ellis C.: The Origin, Structure, Works of the League of Nations. London 1928.

International Commission on Intervention and State Sovereignty Report: The Responsibility to Protect. Ottawa 2001.

James, Alan: Sovereign Statehood. The Basis of International Society. Boston–Sydney 1986.

Jennings, R. Y.: The Acquisition of Territory in International Law. Manchester 1963.

Keith, Kenneth James: The Extent of the Advisory Jurisdiction of the International Court of Justice. Leyden 1971.

Kelsen, Hans: The Law of The United Nations. New York 1964.

Kim, Jung-Gun – Howell, John M.: Conflict of International Obligations and State Interests. The Hague 1972.

Kooijmans, P. H.: The Doctrine of the Legal Equality of States: An inquiry into the foundations of international law. Leyden 1964.

Kreijen, Gerard: State Failure, Sovereignty, and Effectiveness. Legal Lessons form the Decolonization of Sub-Saharan Africa. The Hague 2004.

Lang, Jack: Le plateau continental de la mer du nord; Arrêt de la CIJ 20.2.1969. Paris 1970.

Lansing, Robert: Notes on Sovereignty. From the Standpoint of the State and of the World. Washington 1921.

Lauterpacht, Hersch: Recognition in International Law. Cambridge 1948.

Lillich, Richard (ed.): International Law of State Responsibility for Injuries to Aliens. University of Virginia 1983.

Malanczuk, Peter: Akehurst's Modern Introduction to International Law. 7th ed. London 1997.

Mälksoo, Lauri: Illegal Annexation and State Continuity: The Case of the Incorporation of the Baltic States by the USSR. The Hague 2003.

Martin, Antoine: L'estoppel en droit international public. Précedé d'un aperçu de la théorie de l'estoppel en droit anglais. Paris 1979.

McDougal, Myres S. – Lasswell, Harold – Chen, Lung-Chu: Human Rights and World Public Order. The Basic Policies of an International Law of Human Dignity. New Haven 1980.

McDougal, Myres S. – Lasswell, Harold – Miller, James C.: The Interpretation of Agreements and World Public Order. Principles of Content and Procedure. New Haven 1967.

McDougal, Myres S. – Lasswell, Harold Burke William: The Public Order of the Oceans. A Contemporary International Law of the Sea. (2nd ed.) New Haven 1985.

Müller, Jörg P.: Vertrauensschutz im Völkerrecht. Köln–Berlin 1971.

McNair, Lord: The Law of Treaties. Oxford 1986 (reissue of the 1961 edition).

McWhinney, Edward: The World Court and the Contemporary International Law-Making Process. Alphen aan den Rijn 1979.

UN Lawmaking: Cultural and Ideological Relativism and International Lawmaking in an Era of Transition. Paris–New York 1984.

Ninčić, Djura: The Problem of Sovereignty in the Charter and in the Practice of the United Nations. The Hague 1970.

O'Connell, D. P.: The International Law of the Sea (edited by I. A. Shearer) I–II. Oxford 1982–84.

Okeke, Chris N.: Controversial Subjects of Contemporary International Law. Rotterdam 1974.

Oppenheim, L.: The League of Nations and its Problems. London 1919.

Paulus, Andreas: Die internationale Gemeinschaft im Völkerrecht. Eine Untersuchung zur Entwicklung des Völkerrechts im Zeitalter der Globalisierung. Munich 2001.

Pellet, Alain: Le droit international du développement. Paris 1978.

Pomerance, Michla: Self-Determination in Law and Practice: The new doctrine in the United Nations. The Hague 1982.

Raic, David: Statehood and the Law of Self-Determination. The Hague 2002.

Rajan, M. S.: United Nations and Domestic Jurisdiction. Bombay–Calcutta–Madras 1958.

The Expanding Jurisdiction of the United Nations. Bombay–Dobbs Ferry 1982.

Raymond, Gregory A.: Conflict Resolution and the Structure of the State System. An Analysis of Arbitrative Settlements. Alphen aan den Rijn 1980.

Reuter, Paul: Introduction au doit des traités. (2ème éd.) Paris 1985.

Reynaud, André: Les différends du plateau continental de la Mer du Nord. Devant la Cour Internationale de Justice. Paris 1975.

Roche, Alexander George: The Minquiers & Ecrehos Case. Genève 1959.

Rosenne, Shabtai: The Law and Practice of the International Court. (2nd rev. ed.) Dordrecht–Boston–Lancaster 1985.

Schmitt, Carl: Nationalsozialismus und Völkerrecht. Vortrag. Berlin 1934.

Shaw, Malcolm M.: Title to Territory in Africa. International Legal Issues. Oxford 1986.

Simma, Bruno: Das Reziprozitätselement in der Entstehung des Völkergewohnheitsrechts. München–Saltzburg 1970.

Siorat, Lucien: Le Problème des lacunes en droit international. Paris 1959.

Stone, Julius: Conflict Through Consensus: UN Approaches to Aggression. Baltimore–London 1977.

Suontausta, Tauno: La souveraineté des Etats. Helsinki 1955.

Sur, Serge: L'Interprétation en droit international public. Paris 1974.

Suy, Eric: Les actes juridiques unilateraux en droit international public. Paris 1962.

Sztucki, Jerzy: Jus Cogens and the Vienna Convention on the Law of Treaties; a Critical Appraisal. Wien–New York 1974.

Tavernier, Paul: Recherches sur l'application dans le temps des actes et des règles en droit international public. Paris 1970.

Thirlway, H. W. A.: International Customary Law and Codification. Leiden 1972.

Tucker, Robert W.: The Inequality of Nations. New York 1977.

Unger, R.-Fidelio: Völkergewohnheitsrecht – objektives Recht oder Geflicht bilateraler Beziehungen. Seine Bedeutung für einen "persistent objector". München 1978.

Vamvoukos, Athanassios: Termination of Treaties in International Law. The Doctrines of Rebus Sic Stantibus and Desuetude. Oxford 1985.

Villiger, Mark, E.: Customary International Law and Treaties. Dordrecht–Boston–Lancaster 1985.

Vincent, R. J.: Nonintervention and International Order. Princeton 1974.

Visscher, Charles de: De l'équité dans le reglement arbitral ou judiciaire des litiges de droit international public. Paris 1972.

Problèmes d'interprétation judiciaire en droit international public. Paris 1963.

Wolfke, Karol: Custom in Present International Law. Wroclaw 1964.

Zoller, Elisabeth: La bonne foi en droit international public. Paris 1977.

Örvik, Nils: The Decline of Neutrality 1914–1941. Oslo 1953.

B Articles

Abi-Saab, Georges: Cours général de droit international public. 207 RCADI 1987 p. 267.

Wars of National Liberation and the Laws of War. In: Falk-Kratochwil-Mendlowitz (eds.): International Law. A Contemporary Perspective. Boulder–London 1985 pp. 410–437.

Abu-Sahliel, Sami A. Aldeeb: La définition internationale des droits de l'homme et l'Islam. 89 RGDIP 1985 pp. 625–718.

Achterberg, Norbert: Rechtsverhältnisse als Strukturelementen des Rechtsordnung/ Prolegomena zu einem Rechtsverhältnistheorie. 9 Rechtstheorie 1978 pp. 385–410.

Adorno, Theodor W.: Sociology and Empirical Research. In: Adorno (ed.): The Positivist Dispute in German Sociology. London 1977 pp. 68–86.

Ago, Roberto: Positive Law and International Law. 51 AJIL (1957) pp. 691–753.

Science juridique et droit international. 90 RCADI 1956/II pp. 849–895.

Akehurst, Michael: Custom as a Source of International Law. XLVII BYIL 1974–75 pp. 1–53.

Equity and General Principles of Law. 25 ICLQ 1976 pp. 801–825.

Humanitarian Intervention. In: Bull (ed.): Intervention in World Politics. Oxford 1984 pp. 95–118.

Alexidze, L. A.: Legal Nature of *Jus Cogens* in Contemporary International Law. 172 RCADI 1981/III pp. 219–316.

Allott, Philip: Language, Method and the Nature of International Law. XLV BYIL 1971 pp. 79–135.

Power Sharing in the Law of the Sea. 77 AJIL 1983 pp. 1–30.

D'Amato, Anthony: An Alternative to the Law of the Sea Convention. 77 AJIL 1983 pp. 281–285.

Modifying the US Acceptance of the Compulsory Jurisdiction of the World Court. 79 AJIL 1985 pp. 385–405.

Nicaragua and International Law: the "Academic" and the "Real". 79 AJIL 1985 pp. 657–664.

The Neo-Positivist Conception of International Law. 59 AJIL 1965 pp. 321–324.

What "Counts" as Law? In: Onuf (ed.): Lawmaking in the Global Community, Durham N. C. 1982 pp. 83–107.

Amselek, Paul: Quelques réflexions sur la notion de "sources du droit". XXVII Arch. de philo. du droit 1982 pp. 251–258.

Anand, R. P.: Freedom of the Sea: Past, Present and Future. In: Girardot-Ridder-Sarin-Schiller (eds.): New Directions in International Law. Essays in Honour of Wolfgang Abendroth, Frankfurt–New York 1982 pp. 215–233.

Role of International Adjudication. In: Gross (ed.): The Future of the International Court of Justice, Vol. 1 New York 1976 pp. 1–21.

Sovereign Equality of States in International Law. 197 RCADI 1986/II pp. 9–228.

Arnaud, André-Jean: Structuralisme et droit (notes de lecture ou directions de recherche). XIII Arch. de philo. du droit 1968 pp. 283–301.

Une méthode d'analyse structurale en histoire du droit. Vorstudien zur Rechtshistorie, Sonderheft – Ius Commune 6. Frankfurt 1977 pp. 263–343.

Baade, Hans W.: Intertemporales Völkerrecht. 7 JIR 1957 pp. 229–256.

Baldwin, Simon E.: The International Congresses and Conferences of the Last Century as Forces Working Towards the Solidarity of the World. 1 AJIL 1907 pp. 565–578.

Balkin, J. M.: Deconstructive Practice and Legal Theory. 96 Yale L.J. 1987 pp. 743–785.

Ballreich, Hans: Wesen und Wirkung des "Konsens" im Völkerrecht. In: Bernhardt-Geck-Jaenicke-Steinberger (eds.): Völkerrecht als Rechtsordnung, Internationale Gerichtsbarkeit, Menschenrechte. Festschrift für Hermann Mosler. Berlin–Heidelberg–New York 1983 pp. 1–24.

Barberis, J. A.: L'élement materiel de la coutume international d'après la Cour de la Haye (1922–67). XIV NTIR 1967 pp. 367–381.

La prescroption adquisitiva y la costumbre en el Derecho Internacional. 45 RDI 1967 pp. 233–243.

Bardonnet, Daniel: Equité et les frontières terrestres. In: Le droit international: unité et diversité. Mélanges offerts à Paul Reuter, Paris 1981 pp. 35–74.

Barile, Giuseppe: La structure de l'ordre juridique international; règles générales et règles conventionelles. 161 RCADI 1978 III pp. 9–126.

Basdevant, Jules: Règles générales du droit de la paix. 58 RCADI 1936 IV pp. 475–690.

Baxter, R. R.: Treaties and Custom. 129 RCADI 1970/I pp. 27–105.

Multilateral Treaties as Evidence of Customary International Law. XLI BYIL 1965–66 pp. 275–300.

Beckett, Jason A.: Behind Relative Normativity: Rules and Process as Prerequisites of Law. 12 EJIL 2001 pp. 643–647.

Bederman, David J.: Book review of *From Apology to Utopia*. 23 New York Journal of International Law and Politics 1990 pp. 217–229.

The 1871 London Declaration and a Primitivist View of the Law of Nations. 82 AJIL 1988 pp. 1–40.

Bedjaoui, Mohammed: Remanances de 'théories sur la souveraineté limitée' sur les ressources naturelles. In: Girardot-Ridder-Sarin-Schiller (eds.): New Directions in International Law. Essays in Honour of Wolfgang Abendroth. Frankfurt–New York 1982 pp. 63–77.

Benchikh, Madjid: Vers un nouveau droit international? Le droit du développement. In: Benchikh-Charvin-Demichel (eds.): Introduction Critique au droit international. Lyon 1986 pp. 89–119.

Bennouna, Mohamed: Réalité et imaginaire en droit international du développement. In: Le droit des peuples à disposer d'eux-mêmes: méthodes d'analyse du droit international. Mélanges offerts à Charles Chaumont, Paris 1984 pp. 59–72.

Bentham, Jeremy: Principles of International Law. In: Bentham, Jeremy, The Works, published under the superintendence of John Bowring, Vol. II Edinburgh–London 1843 pp. 535–571.

Benton, Ted: Realism, Power and Objective Interests. In: Graham (ed.): Contemporary Political Philosophy, Cambridge 1982 pp. 7–33.

Bernhardt, Rudolf: Customary International Law. In: Encyclopedia of International Law, Vol. 7 1984 pp. 61–66.

Ungeschriebenes Völkerrecht. 36 ZaöRV 1976 pp. 50–76.

Bierzanek, Remiagiz: La non-reconnaissance et le droit international contemporaine. VIII AFDI 1962 pp. 117–137.

Binder, Guyora: Beyond Criticism. 55 University of Chicago Law Review 1988 pp. 888–915.

Bindschedler, Rudolf L.: Die Anerkennung im Völkerrecht. 9 Arch.VR 1961–62 pp. 377–397.

Bindschedler-Robert, Denise: De la rétroactivité en droit international public. In: Recueil des Etudes de droit international en hommage à Paul Guggenheim, Geneve 1968 pp. 184–200.

Bishop, W. W.: General Course on Public International law, 1965. 115 RCADI 1965/III pp. 151–470.

Bleckmann, Albert: Die Handlungsfähigkeit der Staaten; System und Struktur der Völkerrechtsordnung. 29 ÖZöRV 1978 pp. 173–196.

Die Praxis des Völkergewohnheitsrechts als Konsekutive Rechtsetzung. In: Bernhardt-Geck-Jaenicke-Steinberger (eds.): Völkerrecht als Rechtsordnung, Internationale Gerichtsbarkeit, Menschenrechte. Festschrift für Hermann Mosler, Berlin–Heidelberg–New York 1983 pp. 89–110.

The Subjective Right in Public International Law. 28 GYIL 1985 pp. 144–162.

Völkergewohnheitsrecht trotz wiedersprüchlicher Praxis? 36 ZaöRV 1976 pp. 374–406.

Zur Strukturanalyse im Völkerrecht. 9 Rechtstheorie 1979 pp. 143–176.

Blix, Hans: Contemporary Aspects of Recognition. 130 RCADI 1970/II pp. 587–704.

Blondel, André: Les principes généraux de droit devant la Cour Permanente de Justice Internationale et la Cour Internationale de Justice. In: Recueil d'Etudes de droit international en hommage à Paul Guggenheim pp. 201–236, 1968 Genève.

Boegner, M.: L'Influence de la Réforme sur le développement de droit international. 6 RCADI 1925/I pp. 245–323.

Bogdan, Michael: General Principles of Law and the Problem of Lacunae in the Law of Nations. 46 NTIR 1977 pp. 37–53.

Boguslavsky, Mark M.: Foreign State Immunity: Soviet Doctrine and Practice. X Neth.YBIL 1979 pp. 167–177.

Bollecker-Stern, Brigitte: L'affaire des essais nucléaires français devant la Cour Internationale de Justice. XX AFDI 1974 pp. 295–333.

L'avis consultatif du 21 juin 1971 dans l'affaire de la Namibie (Sud-Est Africain). XVII AFDI 1971 pp. 281–333.

Borella, François: Le nouvel ordre économique international et le formalisme juridique. In: Le droit des peuples à disposer d'eux-mêmes: méthodes d'analyse du droit international. Mélanges offerts à Charles Chaumont, Paris 1984 pp. 73–88.

Bos, Maarten: The Identification of Custom in International Law. 25 GYIL 1982 pp. 9–53.

Will and Order in the Nation-State System: Observations on Positivism and International Law. In: Macdonald-Johnston (eds.): The Structure and Process of International Law. The Hague 1983 pp. 51–78.

Bothe, Michael: Legal and Non-Legal Norms – a Meaningful Distinction in International Relations. XI Neth.YBIL 1980 pp. 65–95.

Bourquin, Maurice: Règles générales du droit de la paix. 35 RCADI 1931/I pp. 5–227.

Stabilité et mouvement dans l'ordre juridique international. 64 RCADI 1938/II pp. 351–475.

Bowett, D. W.: The Arbitration Between the United Kingdom and France Concerning the Continental Shelf Boundary in the English Channel and South-Western Approaches. XLIX BYIL 1978 pp. 1–29.

Estoppel Before International Tribunals and Its Relation to Acquiescence. XXXIII BYIL 1957 pp. 176–202.

Boyle, Alan E.: Marine Pollution under the Law of the Sea Convention. 79 AJIL 1985 pp. 347–372.

Boyle, James: Ideals and Things: International Legal Scholarship and the Prison-House of Language. 26 Harv. ILJ 1985 pp. 327–359.

Bozeman, Adda B.: On the Relevance of Hugo Grotius and De Jure Belli ac Pacis for our Times. 1 Grotiana 1980 pp. 65–124.

Brest, Paul: The Fundamental Rights Controversy: the Essential Contradictions of Normative Constitutional Scholarship. 90 Yale L.J. 1981 pp. 1063–1109.

Brewin, Christopher: Sovereignty. In: Mayall (ed.): The Community of States, London 1982 pp. 34–48.

Brierly, J. L.: Le fondement du caractère obligatoire du droit international. 23 RCADI 1928/III pp. 467–549.

Matters of Domestic Jurisdiction. VI BYIL 1925 pp. 8–19.

Règles générales de droit de la paix. 58 RCADI 1936/IV pp. 5–237.

Briggs, Herbert W.: Recognition of States: Some Reflexions on Doctrine and Practice. 43 AJIL 1949 pp. 113–121.

Reservations to the Acceptance of Compulsory Jurisdiction of the International Court of Justice. 93 RCADI 1958/I pp. 223–367.

Brown, Philip: The Legal Effects of Recognition. 44 AJIL 1950 pp. 617–640.

Brownlie, Ian: The Calling of an International Lawyer. Sir Humphrey Waldock and His Work. LIV BYIL 1983 pp. 7–47.

Recognition in Theory and Practice. In: Macdonald-Johnston (eds.): The Structure and Process of International Law. The Hague 1983 pp. 627–641.

The Relation of Law and Power. In: Cheng-Brown (eds.): Contemporary Problems of International Law; Essays in Honour of Georg Schwarzenberger on his Eightieth Birthday. London 1988 pp. 19–24.

Bruns, Viktor: Das Völkerrecht als Rechtsordnung. 1 ZaöRV 1929 pp. 1–56.

Bull, Hedley: The State's Positive Role in World Affairs. In: Falk-Kim-Mendlowitz (eds.): Toward a Just World Order, Vol. 1 of Studies on a Just World Order. Boulder, Colorado 1982 pp. 60–73.

Butler, Peter F.: Legitimacy in a States-System: Vattel's Law of Nations. In: Donelan (ed): The Reason of States, London 1978 pp. 45–63.

Butler, William E.: Regional and Sectional Diversities in International Law. In: Cheng (ed.): International Law: Teaching and Practice, London 1982 pp. 45–52.

Caflisch, Lucius: Les zones maritimes sous juridiction nationale, leurs limites et leur delimitation. In: Bardonnet-Virally (eds.): Le nouveau droit de la mer. Paris 1983 pp. 35–116.

Cahier, Philippe: Le comportement des états comme source de droits et obligations. In: Recueil d'Etudes de droit international en hommage à Paul Guggenheim. Genève 1968 pp. 237–265.

Cahin, Gérard: Apport du concept de mythification aux méthodes d'analyse du droit international. In: Le droit des peuples à disposer d'eux-mêmes; méthodes d'analyse de droit international. Mélanges offerts à Charles Chaumont. Paris 1984 pp. 89–116

Caldera, Rafael: The Juridical Basis of a New International Order. 196 RCADI 1986/I pp. 391–201.

Caminos, Hugo – Molitor, Michael R.: Progressive Development of International Law and the Package Deal. 79 AJIL 1985 pp. 871–890.

Campbell, A.: International Law and Primitive Law. 8 Oxford JLS 1988 pp. 169–197.

Carrión-Wam, Roque: Semiotica Juridica. In: Carzo-Jackson (eds.): Semiotics, Law and Social Sciences, Roma 1985 pp. 11–68.

Carty, Anthony: Liberalism's "Dangerous Supplements": Medieval Ghosts of International Law. 13 Michigan Journal of International Law 1991 pp. 161–171.

Cass, Deborah C.: Navigating the Newstream. 65 Nordic Journal of International Law 1996 pp. 341–383.

Castberg, Frede: International Law in Our Time. 138 RCADI 1973/I pp. 1–26.

La méthodologie du droit international public. 43 RCADI 1933/I pp. 313–383.

Catellani, Enrico: Les Maîtres de l'école italienne du droit international au XIXe siècle. 46 RCADI 1933/IV pp. 709–823.

Cavaglieri, Arrigo: Règles générales du droit de la paix. 26 RCADI 1929/I pp. 315–583.

Chakste, Mintants: Soviet Concepts of the State, International Law and Sovereignty. 43 AJIL 1949 pp. 21–36.

Charlesworth, Hilary: International Law: A Discipline of Crisis. 65 Modern Law Review 2002 pp. 377–392.

Subversive Trends in the Jurisprudence of International Law. ASIL Proceedings 1992 p. 127.

Charney, Jonathan: Ocean Boundaries between Nations: A Theory for Progress. 78 AJIL 1984 pp. 582–606.

The Persistent Objection Rule and the Development of Customary International Law. LVI BYIL 1985 pp. 1–24.

Charvin, Robert: Le discours sur le droit international. In: Benchikh-Charvin-Demichel: Introduction critique au droit international. Lyon 1986 pp. 29–51.

Chaumont, Charles: L'ambivalence des concepts essentiels du droit international. In: Makarczyk (ed.): Essays in International law in Honour of Judge Manfred Lachs. The Hague 1984 pp. 55–64.

Cours général de droit international public. 129 RCADI 1970–1 pp. 333–528.

Chemillier-Gendreau, M.: A propos de l'effectivité en droit international. XI RBDI 1975 pp. 38–46.

Cheng, Bin: Custom: The Future of General State Practice in a Divided World. In: Macdonald-Johnston (eds.): The Structure and Process of International Law. The Hague 1983 pp. 513–554.

Justice and Equity in International Law. 8 CLP 1955 p. 185.

United Nations' Resolutions on Outer Space: "Instant" International Customary Law? 5 IJIL 1965 pp. 23–48.

Chimni, B. S.: The New Regime of the Oceans: Illusion or Reality? 22 IJIL 1982 pp. 69–89.

Chinkin, C. M.: Third-Party Intervention before the ICJ. 80 AJIL 1986 pp. 495–531.

Christie, George: Objectivity in the Law. 78 Yale L. J. 1969 pp. 1311–1350.

Cohen-Jonathan, Gérard: La coutume locale. VII AFDI 1961 pp. 119–140.

Colin, Jean-Pierre: L'Esperiance en question ou la crise du Système Juridique International. XVIII RBDI 1984–85 pp. 776–793.

Colliard, Claude-Albert: Spécificité des Etats, théorie des statuts juridiques particuliers et l'inégalité compensatrice. In: Le droit international: unité et diversité. Mélanges offerts à Paul Reuter. Paris 1981 pp. 153–180.

Collins, Hugh: Contract and Legal Theory. In: Twining (ed.): Legal Theory and Common Law. Oxford 1986 pp. 136–154.

Corbett, Percy Elwood: The Consent of States and the Sources of the Law of Nations. VI BYIL 1925 pp. 20–30.

Cranston, Maurice: Introduction. In: Rousseau, Jean Jacques: The Social Contract, Harmondsworth 1986 pp. 9–43.

Crawford, James: The Criteria for Statehood in International Law. XLVIII BYIL 1976–77 pp. 93–182.

International Law and Foreign Sovereigns: Distinguishing Immune Transactions. LIV BYIL 1983 pp. 75–118.

Culler, Jonathan: The Linguistic Basis of Structuralism. In: Robey (ed.): Structuralism. Oxford 1973 pp. 20–36.

Dalton, Clare: An Essay in the Deconstruction of Contract Doctrine. 94 Yale L.J. 1985 pp. 997–1114.

Delaume, Georges R.: Economic Development and Sovereign Immunity. 79 AJIL 1985 pp. 319–346.

Demichel, Francine: Le droit international contemporain, un droit hétérogene de transition. In: Benchikh-Charvin-Demichel: Introduction critique au droit international. Lyon 1986 pp. 53–88.

Deutsch, Karl W.: The Probability of International Law. In: Deutsch-Hoffman (eds.): The Relevance of International Law. New York 1971 pp. 80–114.

Djuvara, Mircea: Le Fondement de l'ordre juridique positif en droit international. 64 RCADI 1938/II pp. 485–616.

Doehring, Karl: Gewohnheitsrecht aus Vorträgen. 36 ZaöRV 1976 pp. 77–95.

Dominicé, Christian: A propos du principe de l'estoppel en droit des gens. In: Recueil d'études de droit international en hommage à Paul Guggenheim. Genève 1968 pp. 327–365.

Donelan, Michael: Introduction. The Political Theorists and International Theory. In: Donelan (ed.): The Reason of States. London 1978 pp. 11–24, 75–91.

Dorsey, Gray L.: The McDougal-Lasswell Proposal to Build a World Public Order. 82 AJIL 1988 pp. 41–51.

Duisberg, Claus-Jürgen: Das Subjektive Element in Völkergewohnheitsrecht unter besonderer Berücksichtung der Rechtsprechung des Internationalen Gerichtshofes. 12 JIR 1965 pp. 140–157.

Duncanson, Ian: Hermeneutics and Persistent Questions in Hart's Jurisprudence. Juridical Review 1987 pp. 113–130.

Dupuy, Pierre-Marie: L'Unité de l'ordre juridique international. Cours général de droit international public. 297 RCADI 2002.

Dupuy, R.-J.: Coutume sage et coutume sauvage. In: La communauté internationale. Mélanges offerts à Charles Rousseau. Paris 1974 pp. 75–87.

Eagleton, Clyde: Organization of the Community of Nations. 36 AJIL 1942 pp. 229–241.

Ehrlich, Ludwik: The Development of International Law as a Science. 105 RCADI 1962/I pp. 177–265.

Elias, Taslim O.: Modern Sources of International Law. In: Friedmann-Henkin-Lissitzyn (eds.): Transnational Law in a Changing Society. Essays in Honor of Philip C. Jessup. New York 1972 pp. 34–69.

El-Erian, Abdullah: International Law and the Developing Countries. In: Friedmann-Henkin-Lissitzyn (eds.): Transnational Law in a Changing Society. Essays in Honor of Philip C. Jessup. New York 1972 pp. 84–98.

Enderlein, Fritz: The Immunity of State Property from Foreign Jurisdiction and Execution: Doctrine and Practice of the German Democratic Republic. X Neth.YBIL 1979 pp. 111–124.

Erich, Rafael: La naissance et la reconnaissance des Etats. 13 RCADI 1926/III pp. 431–507.

Evans, Malcolm: The Law of the Sea. In: Evans (ed.): International Law. Oxford 2003 pp. 623–656.

Falk, Richard: The Interplay of Westphalia and Charter Conceptions of the International Legal Order In: Falk-Black (eds.): The Future of the International Legal Order, Vol. I Trends and Patterns. Princeton 1969 pp. 32–70.

New approaches to the Study of International Law. 61 AJIL 1967 pp. 477–495.

The New States and the International Order. 118 RCADI 1966/II pp. 7–102.

The Role of Law in World Society: Present crisis and future prospects. In: Reisman-Weston(eds.): Toward World Order and Human Dignity. Essays in Honor of Myres S. McDougal. New York-London 1976 pp. 132–166.

Farer, Tom: Political and Economic Coercion in Contemporary International Law. 79 AJIL 1985 pp. 405–413.

Fastenrath, Ulrich: Book review of *From Apology to Utopia*. 31 Archiv des Völkerrechts 1993 pp. 182–184.

Fatouros, A.: The Participation of the "New" States in the International Legal Order. In: Falk-Black (eds.): The Future of the International Legal Order. Vol. I Trends and Patterns. Princeton 1969 pp. 317–371.

Fawcett, J. E. S.: General Course on Public International Law. 132 RCADI 1971/I pp. 363–558.

Favre, Antoine: Les principes généraux du droit, fonds commun du droit des gens. Recueil d'études de droit international en hommage à Paul Guggenheim. Paris 1968 pp. 366–390.

La source première du droit des gens: les principes généraux du droit. 27 Annuaire de l'Association du Auditeurs et Anciens Auditeurs de l'Academie de Droit International de la Haye 1957 pp. 15–27.

Fenwick, Charles G: The Progress of International Law during the Past Forty Years. 79 RCADI 1951/II pp. 1–70.

Ferrari Bravo, Luigi: La coutume international dans la pratique des Etats. 192 RCADI 1985/III pp. 243–316.

Fiedler, Wilfried: Unilateral Acts in International Law. In: Bernhardt (ed.): Encyclopedia of Public International Law, Volume 7, Amsterdam 1984 pp. 517–522.

Fischer-Lescano, Andreas: Die Emergenz der Globalverfassung. 63 ZaöRV 2003 pp. 716–760.

Fishkin, James S.: Liberal Theory and the Problem of Justification. Nomos XXVIII pp. 207–231.

Fitzmaurice, Gerald: Enlargement of the Contentious Jurisdiction of the Court. In: Gross (ed.): The Future of the International Court of Justice, Vol. 2. New York 1976 pp. 461–498.

The Future of Public International Law and of the International Legal System in the Circumstances of Today, Institut de Droit International, Livre du Centenaire 1873–1973 Evolution et perspectives du droit international. Bâle 1973 pp. 196–328.

The General Principles of International Law: Considered from the Standpoint of the Rule of Law. 92 RCADI 1957/II pp. 1–227.

Hersch Lauterpacht – the Scholar as Judge I. XXXVII BYIL 1961 pp. 1–71.

Judicial Innovation – Its Uses and Its Perils – As Exemplified in Some of the Work of the ICJ During Lord McNair's Period of Office. Cambridge Essays in International Law, Essays in Honour of Lord McNair. 1965 pp. 24–47.

The Law and Procedure of the International Court of Justice 1951–54: General principles and sources of law. XXX BYIL 1953 pp. 1–70.

The Law and Procedure of the International Court of Justice, 1951–54: Points of substantive law, Part I. XXXI BYIL 1954 pp. 371–429.

The Law and Procedure of the International Court of Justice 1951–54: Points of substantive law, Part II. XXXII BYIL 1955–6 pp. 20–96.

The Law and Procedure of the International Court of Justice 1951–54: Treaty interpretation and other treaty points. XXXIII BYIL 1957 pp. 203–293.

Legal Advisers and Foreign Affairs. 59 AJIL 1965 pp. 72–86.

The Problem of Non-Liquet: Prolegomena to a Restatement. In: La communauté internationale. Mélanges offerts à Charles Rousseau. Paris 1974 pp. 84–112.

Some Problems Regarding the Formal Sources of International Law. In: Symbolae Verzijl. The Hague 1958 pp. 153–176.

The United Nations and the Rule of Law. XXXVIII Transactions of the Grotius Society 1953 pp. 135–150.

Vae Victis or Woe to the Negotiators! 65 AJIL 1971 pp. 358–373.

Floum, Joshua: Book Review: Law Making in the Global Community. Ed. by Nicholas G. Onuf, Durham, N. C. 1982. 24 Harv.ILJ 1983 pp. 256–293.

Franck, Thomas M.: Of Gnats and Camels: Is there a Double Standard at the United Nations? 78 AJIL 1984 pp. 811–833.

Word Made Law: The Decision of the ICJ in the Nuclear Test Cases, Editorial comment. 69 AJIL 1975 pp. 612–620.

François, J.-P. A.: Règles générales du droit de la paix. 66 RCADI 1938/IV pp. 5–289.

Fried, John H. E.: International Law – Neither Orphan nor Harlot neither Jailor nor Never-Never Land. In: Deutsch-Hoffmann (ed.): The Relevance of International Law. New York 1971 pp. 124–176.

Friedmann, Wolfgang: General Course in Public International Law. 127 RCADI 1969/II p. 39.

The Growth of State Control over the Individual and its effect upon the Rules of State Responsibility. XIX BYIL 1938 pp. 118–150.

Human Welfare and International Law: A Reordering of Priorities. In: Friedmann-Henkin-Lissitzyn (eds.): Transnational Law in a Changing Society. Essays in Honor of Philip C. Jessupp. New York 1972 pp. 113–136.

The Jurisprudential Implications of the South West Africa Case. 6 Columbia J of Transnat'l Law 1967 pp. 1–16.

Selden *redivivus* – Towards a Partition of the Seas? 65 AJIL 1971 pp. 757–770.

The Uses of 'General Principles' in the Development of International Law. 57 AJIL 1963 pp. 279–299.

Fur, Louis le: Règles générales du droit de la paix. 54 RCADI 1935/IV pp. 5–307.

La Théorie du droit naturel depuis le XVIIIe siècle et la doctrine moderne. 18 RCADI 1927/III pp. 263–439.

Gardot, André: Jean Bodin; sa place parmi les fondateurs du droit international. 50 RCADI 1934/IV pp. 545–747.

Gaus, Gerald F.: Subjective Value and Justificatory Political Theory. Nomos XXVIII pp. 241–269.

Geck, Philip: Völkerrechtliche Verträge und Kodifikation. 36 ZaöRV 1976 pp. 96–144.

Gerber, David J.: The Extraterritorial Application of the German Antitrust laws. 77 AJIL 1983 pp. 751–783.

George, Stephen: Schools of Thought in International Relations. In: Donelan (ed.): The Reason of States. London 1978 pp. 206–213.

Ghozali, N. E.: Les fondements du droit international public. Approche critique du formalisme classique. In: Le droit des peuples à disposer d'eux-mêmes: Méthodes d'analyse du droit international. Mélanges offerts à Charles Chaumont, Paris 1984 pp. 297–314.

Gidel, Gilbert: Droits et devoirs des Nations. La Théorie classique du droits fondamentaux des Etats. 10 RCADI 1925/V pp. 541–597.

Gihl, Torsten: The Legal Character and Sources of international Law. 1 Scandinavian Studies in Law 1957 pp. 53–92.

Ginther, Konrad: Systemwandel und Theoriedynamik im Völkerrecht. In: Multitum non Multa. Festschrift für Kurt Lipstein. Heidelberg 1980 pp. 31–56.

Giraud, Emile: Le Droit international public et la politique. 110 RCADI 1963/III pp. 423–801.

Goldie, L. F. E.: Concepts of Strict and Absolute Liability and the Ranking of Liability in Terms of Relative Exposure to Risk. XVI Neth.YBIL 1985 pp. 175–248.

Golding, Martin: A Note on Discovery and Justification in Science and Law. Nomos XXVIII pp. 124–140.

Gómez Robledo, Antonio: Le ius cogens international: sa genèse, sa nature, ses fonctions. 172 RCADI 1981/III pp. 9–217.

Goodrich, Peter: The Rise of Legal Formalism; or the defenses of legal faith. 3 Legal Studies 1983 pp. 248–266.

Gordon, Edward: Changing Attitudes Towards Courts and Their Possession of Social Decision Prerogatives. In: Gross (ed.): The Future of the International Court of Justice, Vol I. New York 1976 pp. 336–364.

Gordon, Robert W.: Critical Legal Histories. 36 Stanford L. R. 1984 pp. 59–125.
New Developments in Legal Theory. In: Kairys (ed.): The Politics of Law. New York 1982 pp. 281–313.

Gottlieb, Gideon: Global Bargaining: The legal and diplomatic framework. In Onuf (ed.): Lawmaking in the Global Community. Durham, N. C. 1982 pp. 109–130.

Graham, Gordon: The Justice of Intervention. 13 Rev.Int.Stud. 1987 pp. 133–146.

Gray, Christine: International Law: 1908–1983. 3 Legal Studies 1983 pp. 267–282.

Gray, Christine – Olleson, Simon: The Limits of the Law on the Use of Force: Turkey, Iraq and the Kurds. 12 FYBIL 2000 p. 387.

Green, L. C.: Is There a Universal International Law Today? XXIII CanYIL 1985 pp. 3–33.
Les nouveaux états et le droit international. 74 RGDIP 1970 pp. 78–106.

Gros, André: La recherche des consensus dans les discussions de la Cour Internationale de Justice. In: Bernhardt-Geck-Jaenicke-Steinberger (eds.): Völkerrecht als Rechtsordnung, internationale Gerichtsbarkeit, Menschenrechte. Festschrift für Hermann Mosler. 1983 pp. 351–9.

Gross, Leo: Conclusions. In: Gross (ed.): The Future of the International Court of Justice, Vol. 2. New York 1976 pp. 727–786.

The International Court of Justice: consideration of requirements for enhancing its role in the international legal order. In: Gross (ed.): The Future of the International Court of Justice, Vol. 1. New York 1976 pp. 22–104.

The Peace of Westphalia. 42 AJIL 1948 pp. 20–41.

States as Organs of International Law and the Problem of Autointerpretation. In: Lipsky (ed.): Law and Politics in the World Community. Berkeley-Los Angeles 1953 pp. 59–88.

Guggenheim, Paul: Contribution à l'histoire des sources du droit des gens. 94 RCADI 1958/II pp. 5–81.

Lokales Gewohnheitsrecht. 2 ÖZöRV 1961 pp. 327–334.

Les principes de droit international public. 80 RCAD I 1952/I pp. 1–187.

What is Positive International Law? In: Lipsky (ed.): Law and Politics in the World Community. Berkeley-Los Angeles 1953 pp. 15–30.

Habermas, Jürgen: The Analytical Theory of Science and Dialectics. In: Adorno (ed.): The Positivist Dispute in German Sociology. London 1977 pp. 131–162.

Haggenmacher, Peter: La doctrine des deux elements du droit coutumier dans la pratique de la cour internationale. 90 RGDIP 1986 pp. 5–125.

Hakapää, Kari: Some Observations on the Settlement of Disputes in the New Law of the Sea. In: Essays on International Law. Finnish Branch of the International Law Association 1946–1986, Helsinki 1986 pp. 57–66.

Halberstam, Malvina: Sabbatino Resurrected: the Act of State Doctrine in the Revised Restatement of U.S. Foreign Relations Law. 79 AJIL 1985 pp. 67–91.

Handl, Günther: Liability as an Obligation Established by a Primary Rule of International Law. Some Basic Reflections on the ILC's Work. XVI Neth.YBIL 1985 pp. 49–79.

Territorial Sovereignty and the Problem of Transnational Pollution. 69 AJIL 1975 pp. 50–76.

Hart, H. L. A.: Introduction. In: Austin, John: The Province of Jurisprudence Determined and the Uses of the Study of Jurisprudence. London 1954.

Heilborn, Paul: Les sources du droit international. 11 RCADI 1926/I pp. 1–62.

Heller, Thomas C.: Structuralism and Critique. 36 Stanford L. R. 1984 pp. 127–198.

Herman, Lawrence: The Court Giveth and the Court Taketh Away: An Analysis of the *Tunisia–Libya Continental Shelf* Case. 33 ICLQ 1984 pp. 823–858.

Higgins, Rosalyn: The Identity of International Law. In: Cheng (ed.): International Law, Teaching and Practice. London 1982 pp. 27–44.

Integrations of Authority and Control: Trends in the literature of international law and international relations. In: Reisman-Weston (eds.): Toward World Order and Human Dignity, Essays in Honor of Myres S. McDougal. New York 1976 pp. 79–94.

Intervention and International Law. In: Bull (ed.): Intervention in World Politics. Oxford 1984 pp. 29–44.

Hobza, Antoine: Questions de droit international concernant les religions. 5 RCADI 1924/IV pp. 371–423.

Hoffmann, Stanley: International Law and the Control of Force. In: Deutsch-Hoffmann (eds.): The Relevance of International Law. New York 1971 pp. 34–66.

The Problem of Intervention. In: Bull, Hedley (ed.): Intervention in World Politics. Oxford 1984 pp. 7–28.

Hoffmann, Kenneth B.: State Responsibility in International Law and Transboundary Pollution Injuries. 25 ICLQ 1976 pp. 509–542.

Hossain, Kamal: General Principles, the Charter of Economic Rights and Duties of States and the NIEO. In: Hossain (ed.): Legal Aspects of the New International Economic Order. London-New York 1980 pp. 1–9.

Hudson, Manley O.: The Law Applicable by the Permanent Court of International Justice. Harvard Legal Essays; in honor of and presented to Joseph Beale and Samuel Williston. Harvard 1934 pp. 133–157.

Hunt, Alan: The Theory of Critical Legal Studies. 6 Oxford JLS 1986 pp. 1–45.

Hutchinson, Allan C. – Monihan, Patrick: Law, Politics and the Critical Scholars: The Continuing Drama of American Legal Thought. 36 Stanford L. R. 1984 pp. 199–246.

Ida, Ryuichi: La structure juridique de la charte des droits et devoirs économiques des Etats. In: Girardot-Ridder-Sarin-Schiller (eds.): New Directions in International Law. Essays in Honour of Wolfgang Abendroth. Frankfurt–New York 1982 pp. 118–137.

Jackson, B. S.: Structuralisme et "sources du droit". 27 Arch. de philo. du droit. Paris 1982 pp. 147–160.

Jackson, Robert H.: Quasi-States, Dual Regimes and Neoclassical Theory: international jurisprudence and the Third World. 41 Int'l Org. 1987 pp. 519–549.

Jacqué, Jean-Paul: A propos de la promesse unilateral. In: Le Droit International: unité et diversité; Mélanges offerts à Paul Reuter. Paris 1981 pp. 327–346.

Janis, M. W.: Jeremy Bentham and the Fashioning of "International Law". 78 AJIL 1984 pp. 405–418.

Jenks, C. Wilfred: Economic and Social Change and the Law of Nations. 138 RCADI 1973/I pp. 455–502.

The Scope of International Law. XXIII BYIL 1946 pp. 1–53.

Jennings, Robert: General Course on Principles of International Law. 121 RCADI 1967/II pp. 323–606.

Government in Commission. XXIII BYIL 1946 pp. 112–141.

International Courts and International Politics, Joseph Onoh Lecture 1986. In: Freestone et al: Contemporary Issues in International Law. The Hague 2002.

Law-Making and Package Deal. In: Le droit international; unité et diversité, Mélanges offerts à Paul Reuter, Paris 1981 pp. 347–355.

Sir Gerald Gray Fitzmaurice. LV BYIL 1984 pp. 1–64.

Teachings and Teaching in International Law. In: Makarczyk (ed.): Essays in International Law in Honour of Judge Manfred Lachs. The Hague 1984 pp. 121–131.

The Identification of International Law. In: Cheng (ed.): International Law; Teaching and Practice. London 1982 pp. 3–9.

The Progressive Development of International Law and Its Codification. XXIV BYIL 1947 pp. 301–329.

What is International Law and How Do We Tell It When We See It? XXXVII Schw. JB 1981 pp. 59–88.

Jessup, Philip C.: The Palmas Island Arbitration. 22 AJIL 1928 pp. 735–752.

Jiménez de Aréchaga, Eduardo: Application of the Rules of State Responsibility for the Nationalisation of Foreign-Owned Property. In: Hossain (ed.): Legal Aspects of the New International Economic Order. London-New York 1980 pp. 220–233.

Customary International Law and the Conference on the Law of the Sea. In: Makarczyk (ed.): Essays in International Law in Honour of Judge Manfred Lachs. The Hague 1984 pp. 575–585.

International Law in the Past Third of a Century. 159 RCADI 1978/I pp. 1–344.

Intervention under Article 62 of the Statute of the International Court of Justice. In: Bernhardt-Geck-Jaenicke-Steinberger (eds.): Völkerrecht als Rechtsordnung, internationale Gerichtsbarkeit, Menschenrechte. Festschrift für Hermann Mosler. Berlin–Heidelberg–New York 1983 pp. 453–465.

Johnstone, Ian: Treaty Interpretation: The Authority of Interpretive Communities. 12 Michigan Journal of International Law 1991 pp. 371–450.

Johnson, D. H. N.: Acquisitive Prescription in International Law. XXVII BYIL 1950 pp. 332–354.

International Court of Justice, Judgements of May 26, 1961 and June 15, 1962. The Case Concerning the Temple of Preach Vihear – a Note. 11 ICLQ 1962 pp. 1183–1204.

Johnson, Phillip E.: Do You Sincerely Want to Be Radical? 36 Stanford L. R. 1984 pp. 247–292.

Johnston, Douglas M.: The Heritage of Political Thought in International Law. In: Macdonald-Johnston (eds.): The Structure and Process of International Law. The Hague 1983 pp. 179–226.

Kahn, Paul W.: The Court, the Community and the Judicial Balance: The Jurisprudence of Justice Powell. 97 Yale L. J. 1987 pp. 1–60.

Kant, Immanuel: Idea for a Universal History with a Cosmopolitan Purpose. In: Reiss (ed.): Political Writings. Cambridge 1991 pp. 41–53.

Kaplan, Morton A.: Constitutional Structures and Processes in the International Arena. In: Falk-Black (eds.): The Future of the International Legal Order, Vol. I Trends and Patterns, Princeton 1969 pp. 155–182.

Kartashkin, V.: The Marxist-Leninist Approach: The theory of class struggle and contemporary international law. In: Macdonald-Johnston (eds.): The Structure and Process of International Law. The Hague 1983 pp. 79–102.

Kato, L. L.: Recognition in International Law: some thoughts on traditional theory, attitudes of and practice by African states. 10 IJIL 1970 pp. 299–323.

Kaufmann, Erich: Règles générales du droit de la paix. 54 RCADI 1935/IV pp. 313–615.

Kearney, Richard D.: Sources of Law and the International Court of Justice. In Gross (ed.): The Future of the International Court of Justice, Vol. I. New York 1976 pp. 610–723.

Keens-Soper, Maurice: The Practice of a States-System. In: Donelan (ed.): The Reason of States. London 1978 pp. 25–44.

Kegley, Charles W. Jr: Measuring Transformation in the Global Legal System. In: Onuf (ed.): Lawmaking in the Global Community. Durham, N. C. 1982 pp. 173–209.

Kelman, Mark: Trashing. 36 Stanford L. R. 1984 pp. 293–348.

Kelsen, Hans: Contiguity as a Title to Territorial Sovereignty, in: Festschrift für Hans Wehberg, hrsg. von Schätzel und Schlochauer, Frankfurt am Main 1956 pp. 200–210.

Die Einheit von Völkerrecht und staatlichem Recht. 19 ZaöRV 1958 pp. 234–248.

The Essence of International Law. In: Deutsch-Hoffmann (eds.): The Relevance of International Law. New York 1971 pp. 115–123.

Les Rapports de système entre le droit interne et le droit international public. 14 RCADI 1926/IV pp. 231–331.

Théorie du droit international coutumier. I RITD 1939 pp. 253–274.

Théorie du droit international public. 84 RCADI 1953/III pp. 1–203.

Théorie générale du droit international public: problèmes choisis. 42 RCADI 1932/IV pp. 121–351.

Kennedy, David: Book Review – How Nations Behave (2nd ed.) By Louis Henkin. 21 Harv. ILJ 1980 pp. 301–321.

Book Review. 31 Harv.ILJ 1990 pp. 387–389.

International Legal Education. 26 Harv.ILJ 1985 pp. 361–384.

Primitive Legal Scholarship. 27 Harv.ILJ 1986 pp. 1–98.

The Move to Institutions. 8 Cardozo L. R. 1987 pp. 841–988.

The Sources of International Law. 2 Am.U.J.Int'l L. & Pol'y 1987 pp. 1–96.

Theses About International Law Discourse. 23 GYIL 1980 pp. 353–391.

Tom Franck and the Manhattan School. 35 New York University Journal of International Law and Politics 2003 pp. 397–435.

When Renewal Repeats: Thinking against the Box. 32 New York University Journal of International Law and Politics 2000 pp. 335–500.

Kennedy, Duncan: A Semiotics of Critique. 22 Cardozo LR 2001 pp. 1147–1189.

Form and Substance in Private Law Adjudication. 89 Harvard L.R. 1976 pp. 1685–1778.

The Disenchantment of Logically Formal Rationality, or Max Weber's Sociology in the Genealogy of the Contemporary Mode of Western Legal Thought. 55 Hastings Law Journal 2004 pp. 1031–1076.

The Structure of Blackstone's Commentaries. 28 Buffalo L.R. 1979 pp. 205–382.

Two Globalizations of Law. Legal Thought: 1850–1968. 36 Suffolk University Law Review 2003 pp. 631–679.

Kleffens, E. N. van: Sovereignty in International Law. 82 RCADI 1953/I pp. 1–131.

Koh, Jean Kyongun: Reservations to Multilateral Treaties: How International Legal Doctrine Reflects World Vision. 23 Harv.ILJ 1982–3 pp. 70–116.

Kopelmanas, Lazare: Custom as a Means of the Creation of International Law. XVIII BYIL 1937 pp. 127–151.

Korhonen, Outi: Silence, Defence or Deliverance? 7 EJIL 1996 pp. 1–29.

Korowicz, M. S.: Some Present Problems of Sovereignty. 112 RCADI/I 1961 pp. 1–120.

Korovin, Eugene A.: The Second World War and International Law. 40 AJIL 1946 pp. 742–755.

Koselleck, Reinhard: Begriffsgechichte and Social History. In: Futures Past. On the Semantics of Historical Time. Columbia 2004 pp. 75–92.

Koskenniemi, Martti: Between Commitment and Cynicism: Outline for a Theory of International Law as Practice. In: Collection of Essays by Legal Advisers of States, Legal Advisers of International Organizations and Practitioners in the Field of International Law. United Nations 1999 pp. 495–523.

Breach of Treaty or Non-Compliance? Reflexions on the Enforcement of the Montreal Protocol. 3 Yearbook of International Environmental Law 1992 pp. 123–162.

Case Concerning Passage Through the Great Belt. 27 Ocean Development and International Law 1996 pp. 255–289.

Faith, Identity and the Killing of the Innocent. International Lawyers and Nuclear Weapons. 10 LJIL 1997 pp. 137–162.

General Principles: Reflections on constructivist thinking in international law. XVIII Oikeustiede-Jurisprudentia 1985 pp. 117–163.

Global Governance and Public International Law. 37 Kritische Justiz 2004 pp. 241–254.

Hersch Lauterpacht 1897–1960. In: Beatson-Zimmermann (eds.): Jurists Uprooted. German-Speaking Emigré Lawyers in Twentieth-Century Britain. Oxford 2004.

Human Rights, Politics, and Love. Mennesker & rettigheter 2001 pp. 33–45.

International Law and Hegemony: A Reconfiguration. 17 Cambridge Review of International Affairs 2004 pp. 197–218.

International Law as Therapy. Reading the Health of Nations. 16 EJIL 2005 pp. 329–341.

International Pollution in the System of International Law. XVII Oikeustiede-Jurisprudentia 1984 pp. 91–181.

Introduction. In: Koskenniemi (ed.): Sources of International Law. Aldershot 2000 pp. xi–xxvii.

Jackson, Bernard S. Semiotics and Legal Theory. RKP, London–Boston–Henley 1985, Book Review. 84 LM 1986 pp. 1142–1147.

L'affaire du différend territorial (Jamahiriya arabe libyenne c. Tchad). Arrêt de la Cour internationale de justice du 3 février 1994. XL AFDI 1994 pp. 442–464.

Legal Universalism: Between Morality and Power in a World of States. In: Cheng (ed.): Law, Justice and Power: Between Reason and Will. Stanford 2004 pp. 46–69.

Legitimacy, Rights, and Ideology. Notes towards a Critique of the New Moral Internationalism. 7 ASSOCIATIONS 2003 pp. 349–373.

Letter to the Editors of the Symposium. In: Ratner-Slaughter (eds.): The Methods of International Law. Washington 2004 pp. 109–126.

Maantietellinen yhteenkuuluvuus oikeusperusteena kansainvälisissä alueriidoissa. 82 LM 1984 pp. 429–452.

National Self-Determination Today: Problems of Legal Theory and Practice. 43 ICLQ 1994 pp. 241–269.

The Effect of Rights on Political Culture. In: Alston (ed.): The European Union and Human Rights. Oxford 1999 pp. 99–116.

The Lady Doth Protest too Much: Kosovo, and the Turn to Ethics in International Law. 65 Modern Law Review 2002 pp. 159–175.

The Limits of International Law: Are There Such? Might and Right in International Relations. XXVIII Thesaurus Acroasiarum 1999 pp. 19–50.

The Place of Law in Collective Security. 17 Michigan Journal of International Law 1996 pp. 455–490.

The Police in the Temple. Order, Justice and the UN; A Dialectical View. 5 EJIL 1995 pp. 325–348.

The Politics of International Law. 1 EJIL 1990 pp. 4–32.

The Present State of Research. In: Eisemann-Koskenniemi: La succession d'Etats: La codification à l'épreuve des faits/State Succession: Codification Tested against the Facts. The Hague 2000 pp. 65–132.

Repetition as Reform. Georges Abi-Saab's Cours Général. 9 EJIL 1998 pp. 405–411.

Solidarity Measures. State Responsibility as a New International Order? 72 BYIL 2001 pp. 337–356.

The Silence of Law/The Voice of Justice. In: Boisson de Chazournes-Sands (eds.): International Law, the International Court of Justice, and Nuclear Weapons. Cambridge 1999 pp. 488–510.

Theory: Implications for the Practitioner. In: Allott et al: Theory and International Law: An Introduction. London 1991 pp. 3–45.

The Turn to Ethics in International Law. IX Romanian Journal of International Relations 2003 pp. 15–29.

Valtion kansainvälinen vastuu yksityisen toiminnan aiheuttamasta kansainvälisestä ympäristövahingosta. 3 Suomen ympäristöoikeustieteen julkaisuja 1982 pp. 1–168.

What Should International lawyers Learn from Karl Marx? 17 Leiden Journal of International Law 2004 pp. 229–246.

Koskenniemi, Martti – Lehto, Marja: The Privilege of Universality. International Law, Economic Ideology and Seabed Resources. 65 Nordic Journal of International Law 1996 pp. 533–555.

Koskenniemi, Martti – Leino, Päivi: Fragmentation of International law? Postmodern Anxieties. 15 LJIL 2002 pp. 553–579.

Krabbe, H.: L'idée moderne de l' Etat. 13 RCADI 1926/III pp. 513–581.

Kratochwil, Friedrich: Is International Law "Proper" Law? 69 ARSP 1983 pp. 13–46.

Of Law and Human Action: A jurisprudential plea for a world order perspective in international legal studies. In: Falk-Kratochwil-Mendlovitz (eds.): International law – A Contemporary Perspective. Boulder–London 1985 pp. 639–651.

How do Norms Matter? In: Byers (ed.): The Role of Law in International Politics. Essays in International Relations and International Law. Oxford 2000 pp. 35–68.

Kraus, Herbert: Système et fonctions des traités internationaux. 50 RCADI 1934/IV pp. 311–400.

Kunz, Josef L.: Die Anerkennung von Staaten und Regierungen im Völkerrecht. In: Handbuch des Völkerrechts I. 3. Hrsg. von Fritz Stier-Somlo, Stuttgart 1928.

The Changing Science of International Law. 56 AJIL 1962 pp. 488–499.

The Changing Law of Nations. 51 AJIL 1957 pp. 77–83.

Critical Comments on Lauterpacht's Recognition in International Law. 44 AJIL 1950 pp. 713–719.

The Nature of Customary International Law. 47 AJIL 1953 pp. 662–669.

Kuokkanen, Thomas: International Law and the Expropriation of Natural Resources. XI FYBIL 2000 pp. 325–357.

Lacharrière, Guy de: La réforme du droit de la mer et le rôle de la conférence des nations unies. In: Bardonnet-Virally (eds.): Le nouveau droit de la mer. Paris 1983 pp. 1–33.

Lacharrière, René de: Notes sur les orientations de la doctrine. Le droit des peuples à disposer d'eux-mêmes: méthodes d'analyse du droit international. Mélanges offerts à Charles Chaumont. Paris 1984 pp. 363–381.

Lachs, Manfred: The Development and General Trends of International Law in Our Time. 169 RCADI 1980/V.

The International Law of Outer Space. 113 RCADI 1964/III pp. 7–103.

The Threshold in Law-Making. In: Bernhardt-Geck-Jaenicke-Steinberger (eds.): Völkerrecht als Rechtsordnung, internationale Gerichtsbarkeit, Menschen- rechte. Festschrift für Hermann Mosler. Berlin–Heidelberg–New York 1983 pp. 493–501.

Lammers, J. G.: "Balancing the Equities" in International Environmental Law. RCADI Coll. 1984 pp. 153–165.

Lapradelle, A. de: Progrés ou déclin du droit international? In: La communauté internationale. Mélanges offerts à Charles Rousseau. Paris 1974 pp. 139–152.

Lasswell, Harold D. – McDougal, Myres S.: Trends and Theories about Law: Clarity in Conceptions of Authority and Control. In: Nawaz (ed.): Essays in International law in Honour of Krishna Rao. Leyden 1976 pp. 68–91.

Lauterpacht, Hersch: Codification and Development of International Law. 49 AJIL 1955 pp. 16–43.

Decisions of Municipal Courts as a Source of International Law. BYIL 1929 pp. 65–95.

Professor Carr on International Morality. In: Elihu Lauterpacht (ed.): International Law. Being the Collected Works of Hersch Lauterpacht. Vol. II. Cambridge 1978.

The Grotian Tradition in International Law. XXIII BYIL 1946 pp. 1–53.

Règles générales du droit de la paix. 62 RCADI 193 7/IV pp. 99–422.

Some Observations on the Prohibition of "non Liquet" and the Completeness of the Law. Symbolae Verzijl. La Haye 1958 pp. 196–221.

Sovereignty Over Submarine Areas. XXVII BYIL 1950 pp. 376–433.

Spinoza and International Law. VIII BYIL 1927 pp. 89–107.

Lavalle, Robert: About the Alleged Customary Law Nature of the Rule Pacta Sunt Servanda. 33 ÖZöRV 1982 pp. 9–28.

Lee, Luke T.: The Law of the Sea Convention and Third States. 77 AJIL 1983 pp. 541–568.

Lillich, Michael B.: The Current Status of the Law of State Responsibility for Injuries to Aliens. In: Lillich (ed.): International Law of State Responsibility for Injuries to Aliens. Virginia 1983 pp. 1–59.

Lissitzyn, Oliver J.: Treaties and Changed Circumstances (rebus sic stantibus). 61 AJIL 1967 pp. 895–922.

Lowe, A. V.: The Problems of Extraterritorial Jurisdiction: Economic Sovereignty and the Search for a Solution. 34 ICLQ 1985 pp. 724–746.

Lowe, Vaughan: Book review of *From Apology to Utopia*. 17 Journal of Law and Society 1990 pp. 384–389.

    The Politics of Law-Making. In: Byers (ed.): The Role of Law in International Politics. Oxford 2000 pp. 207–226.

Lukes, Steven: Can the Base be Distinguished from the Superstructure? In: Miller-Seidentop (eds.): Nature of Political Theory. Oxford 1983 pp. 103–119.

Macdonald, R. St J.: The Role of the Legal Adviser of Ministries of Foreign Affairs. 156 RCADI 1977/III pp. 385–482.

McDougal, Myres S.: The Hydrogen Bomb Tests and the International Law of the Sea. 49 AJIL 1955 pp. 356–361.

    International Law, Power and Policy: A Contemporary Conception. 82 RCADI 1953 pp. 133–259.

    The ILC Draft Articles upon Interpretation: Textuality Redivivus. 61 AJIL 1967 pp. 992–1000.

McDougal, Myres S. – Reisman, W. Michael: International Law in Policy-Oriented Perspective. In: Macdonald-Johnston (eds.): The Structure and Process of International Law. The Hague 1983 pp. 103–129.

McDougal, Myres S. – Lasswell, Harold D. – Reisman, W. Michael: The World Constitutive Process of Authoritative Decision. In: Falk-Black (eds.): The Future of the International Legal Order. Volume I: Trends and Patterns. Princeton 1969 pp. 73–154.

MacGibbon, I. L.: Customary International Law and Acquiescence. XXXIII BYIL 1957 pp. 115–145.

    Estoppel in International Law. 7 ICLQ 1958 pp. 468–513.

    Means for the Identification Law. In: Cheng (ed.): International Law, Teaching and Practice. London 1982 pp. 10–26.

    The Scope of Acquiescence in International Law. XXXI BYIL 1954 pp. 143–186.

MacIntyre, Alasdair: The Indispensability of Political Theory. In: Miller-Seidentop (eds.): The Nature of Political Theory. Oxford 1983 pp. 17–33.

McNair, Arnold Duncan: Treaties and Sovereignty. In: Symbolae Verzijl. La Haye 1958 pp. 222–237.

McWhinney, Edward: Time Dimension in International Law. In: Makarczyk (ed.): Essays in International Law in Honour of Judge Manfred Lachs. The Hague 1984 pp. 179–199.

    The Legislative Rôle of the World Court in an Era of Transition. In: Bernhardt-Geck-Jaenicke-Steinberger (ed.): Völkerrecht als Rechtsordnung, international Gerichtsbarkeit, Menschenrechte. Festschrift für Hermann Mosler. Berlin–Heidelberg–New York 1983 pp. 567–579.

Magraw, Daniel Barstow: Transboundary Harm: the ILC's Study of 'International Liability'. 80 AJIL 1986 pp. 305–330.

Maier, Harold: Extraterritorial Jurisdiction at a Crossroads: An Intersection between Public and Private International Law. 76 AJIL 1982 pp. 280–320.

Malley, Robert – Manas, Jean – Nix, Crystal: Note. Constructing the State Extra-Territorially: Jurisdictional Discourse, the National Interest, and Transnational Norms. 103 Harv.L.R. 1990 pp. 1273–1305.

Manner, Eero J.: Settlement of Sea-Boundary Delimitations According to the Provisions of the 1982 Law of the Sea Convention. In: Makarczyk (ed.): Essays in International Law in Honour of Judge Manfred Lachs. The Hague 1984 pp. 625–643.

Marek, Krystyna: Le problème des sources du droit international dans l'arrêt sur le plateau continental de la Mer du Nord. VI RBDI 1970 pp. 44–78.

Marshall, Geoffrey: The Roles of Rules. In: Miller-Seidentop (eds.): The Nature of Political Theory. Oxford 1983 pp. 183–195.

Mayall, James: International Society and International Theory. In: Donelan (ed.): The Reason of States. London 1978 pp. 122–141.

Mbaye, Keba: Le droit au dévéloppement en droit international. In: Makarczyk (ed.): Essays in International Law in Honour of Judge Manfred Lachs. The Hague 1984 pp. 163–178.

Meessen, Karl M.: Antitrust Legislation Under Customary International Law. 78 AJIL 1984 pp. 783–810.

Meijers, H.: How Is International Law Made? – The Stages of Growth of International Law and the Use of its Customary Rules. IX Neth.YBIL 1978 pp. 3–26.

Meng, Werner: Völkerrechtliche Zulässigkeit und Grenzen Wirtschaftsverwaltungsrechtlichen Hoheitsakte mit Auslandswirkung. 44 ZaöRV 1984 pp. 675–782.

Mensch, Elizabeth: The History of Mainstream Legal Thought. In: Kairys (ed.): The Politics of Law. New York 1982 pp. 18–37.

Mepham, John: The Structuralist Sciences and Philosophy. In: Robey (ed.): Structuralism; an introduction. Oxford 1973 pp. 104–137.

Michelman, Frank: Justification (and Justifiability) of Law in a Contradictory World. NOMOS XXVIII pp. 71–99.

Miéville, China: The Commodity-Form Theory of International Law: An Introduction. 17 LJIL 2004 pp. 272–275.

Mitchell, Sollace: Post-Structuralism, Empiricism and Interpretation. In: Mitchell-Rosen (eds.): The Need for Interpretation. London–New Jersey 1984 pp. 54–89.

Monaco, Riccardo: Cours général sur les principes de droit international public. 125 RCADI 1968/III pp. 93–335.

Observations sur la hiérarchic des sources du droit international. In: Bernhardt-Geck-Jaenicke-Steinberger (eds.): Völkerrecht als Rechtsordnung, international Gerichtsbarkeit, Menschenrechte. Festschrift für Hermann Mosler. Berlin–Heidelberg–New York 1983 pp. 599–615.

Moore, John Norton: Law and National Security. In: Falk-Kratochwil-Mendlovitz (eds.): International Law: A contemporary perspective. Boulder–London 1985 pp. 47–58.

Morellet, Jean: Le principe de la souveraineté de l'Etat et le droit international public. XXXIII RGDIP 1926 pp. 104–119.

Morgenthau, Hans J.: Positivism, Functionalism and International Law. 34 AJIL 1940 pp. 260–284.

Morison, William L.: Myres S. McDougal and XX Century Jurisprudence: A comparative essay. In: Reisman-Weston (eds.): Toward World Order and Human Dignity, Essays in Honor of Myres S. McDougal. New York 1976 pp. 3–78.

The Schools Revisited. In: Macdonald-Johnston (eds.): The Structure and Process of International Law. The Hague 1983 pp. 131–176.

Mosler, Hermann: The International Society as a Legal Community. 140 RCADI 1974/IV pp. 1–320.

Völkerrecht als Rechtsordnung. 36 ZaöRV 1976 pp. 6–49.

Mouton, Jean-Denis: Les arrêts de la cour européenne des droits de l'homme comme actes de discours. Contribution à la méthodologie de la fonction jurisdictionelle. In: Le droit des peuples à disposer d'eux-mêmes: méthodes d'analyse du droit international. Mélanges offerts à Charles Chaumont. Paris 1984 pp. 407–431.

Müller, Jörg-Paul – Cottier, Thomas: Acquiescence. In: Bernhardt (ed.): Encyclopedia of Public International Law. Volume 7, Amsterdam 1984 pp. 5–7.

Estoppel. In: Bernhardt (ed.), Encyclopedia of Public International Law. Volume 7, Amsterdam 1984 pp. 78–81.

Munkman, A. L. W.: Adjudication and Adjustment – International Judical Decision and the Settlement of Territorial and Boundary Disputes. XLVI BYIL 1972–73 pp. 1–116.

Münch, Fritz: Bemerkungen zum ius cogens. In: Bernhardt-Geck-Jaenicke-Steinberger (eds.): Völkerrecht als Rechtsordung, internationale Gerichtsbarkeit, Menschenrechte. Festschrift für Hermann Mosler. Berlin–Heidelberg–New York 1983 pp. 617–628.

Das Wesen der Rechtsprechung als Leitbegriff für die Tätigkeit Internationalen Gerichtshofs. 31 ZaöRV 1971 pp. 712–729.

Münch, Ingo von: Zur Objektivität in der Völkerrechtswissenschaft. 9 Arch.VR 1961–2 pp. 1–26.

Nagel, Thomas: Subjective and Objective. In: Rajchman-West (eds.): Post-Analytic Philosophy. New York 1985 pp. 31–47.

Navari, Cornelia: Knowledge, the State and the State of Nature. In: Donelan (ed.): The Reason of States. London 1978 pp. 102–121.

Nawaz, Tawfique: Equity and the New International Economic Order. In: Hossain (ed.): Legal Aspects of the New International Economic Order. London–New York 1980 pp. 113–122.

Nesiah, Vasuki: Placing International Law: White Spaces on a Map. 16 LJIL 2003 pp. 1–36.

Nippold, O.: Le développement historique du droit international depuis le Congrés de Vienne. 2 RCADI 1924/I pp. 1–121.

Nippold, Otfried: Introduction. To: Wolff, Christian: Jus Gentium Methodo Scientifica Pertractatum. Carnegie Endowment for International Peace, the Classics of International Law No. 13, Vol II. Oxford–London 1934.

Nisot, Joseph: Art. 2, Par. 7 of the UN Charter as Compared with Art. 15, Par. 8 of the League of Nations Covenant (a note). 43 AJIL 1949 pp. 776–779.

Le "jus cogens" et la Convention de Vienne. 76 RGDIP 1972 pp. 692–697.

Nys, Ernest: Introduction. To: Vitoria, Francisco: De Indes et de Iure Belli Relectiones. Carnegie Endowement for International Peace, the Classics of International Law, Washington 1917.

Ocheje, Paul D.: Refocusing International Law on the Quest for Accountability in Africa – The Case against the "Other Impunity". 15 LJIL 2002 pp. 749–777.

Olney, Richard: The Development of International Law. 1 AJIL 1907 pp. 418–430.

Onuf, Nicholas G.: Global Law-Making and Legal Thought. In: Onuf (ed.): Lawmaking in the Global Community. Durham, N.C. 1982 pp. 1–81.

International Codification: Interpreting the last half-century. In: Falk-Kratochwil-Mendlowitz (eds.): International Law. A contemporary perspective. Boulder–London 1985 pp. 264–278.

International Legal Order as an Idea. 73 AJIL 1979 pp. 244–266.

Oppenheim, L.: The Science of International Law: Its Task and Method. 2 AJIL 1908 pp. 313–356.

Orford, Anne: The Destiny of International Law. 17 LJIL 2004 pp. 441–476.

Ouchakov, N. A.: Le développement des principes fondamentaux du droit international dans l'Acte Final sur la sécurité et la coopération en Europe. In: Makarczyk (ed.): Essays in International Law in Honour of Judge Manfred Lachs. The Hague 1984 pp. 217–233.

Paskins, Barrie: Obligation and the Understanding of International Relations. In: Donelan (ed.): The Reason of States. London 1978 pp. 153–170.

Peller, Gary: Metaphysics and American Law. 73 Calif.L.R. 1985 pp. 1151–1290.

Pellonpää, Matti: International law and Compensation for Taking of Alien Owned Property: Recent Trends in Arbitral Practice. 3 KOIG 1986 pp. 334–370.

Petman, Jarna: The Problem of Evil and International Law. In: Petman-Klabbers (eds.): Nordic Cosmopolitanism. The Hague 2003 pp. 111–140.

Pirotte, Olivier: La Notion d'équité dans la jurisprudence récente de la Cour Internationale de Justice. 77 RGDIP 1973 pp. 92–135.

Pleydell, Alan: Language, Culture and the Concept of International Political Community. In: Mayall (ed.): The Community of States. London 1982 pp. 167–181.

Pogge, Thomas: The Influence of the Global Order on the Prospect of Genuine Democracy in the Developing Countries. 14 Ratio Juris 2001 pp. 326–343.

Politis, Nicolas: Le Problème des limitations de la souveraineté et de la théorie de l'abus des droits dans les rapports internationaux. 6 RCADI 1925/I pp. 5–116.

Pollux: The Interpretation of the Charter. XXIII BYIL 1946 pp. 54–82.

Porras, Ileana: On Terrorism. Reflections on Violence and the Outlaw. In Danielsen-Engle (eds.): After Identity. A Reader in Law and Culture. 1995 pp. 294–313.

Potter, Pitman B.: Développement de l'organization internationale (1815–1914). 64 RCADI 1938/II pp. 71–155.

Pound, Roscoe: Philosophical Theory and International Law. 1 Bibliotheca Visseriana 1923 pp. 71–90.

Preuss, Lawrence: Art. 2, par. 7, of the Charter of the United Nations and Matters of Domestic Jurisdiction. 74 RCADI 1949/I pp. 553–651.

Purvis, Nigel: Critical Legal Studies in Public International Law. 32 Harv. ILJ 1991 pp. 81–127.

Quadri, Rolando: Cours général de droit international public. 113 RCADI 1964/III pp. 237–483.

    Le fondement du caractère obligatoire du droit international public. 80 RCADI 1952/I pp. 579–633.

Rasmussen, Pär Hjalte: Le juge international, en évitant de statuer obéit-il à un devoir juridique fondamental? 29 GYIL 1986 pp. 252–276.

Redslob, Robert: Le principe de nationalités. 37 RCADI 1935/III pp. 5–78.

Reeves, Jesse S.: La Communauté internationale. 3 RCADI 1924/II pp. 5–90.

Reinsch, Paul S.: International Administrative Law and National Sovereignty. 3 AJIL 1909 pp. 1–45.

Reisman, W. Michael: Coercion and Self-Determination: Construing Charter Article 2(4). 78 AJIL 1984 pp. 642–645.

Reuter, Paul: Principes de droit international public. 102 RCADI 1961/II pp. 425–655. Quelques réflexions sur l'équité en droit international. XV RBDI 1980–81 pp. 165–186.

Roberts, Simon: After Government. On Representing Law without the State. 68 Modern Law Review 2005 pp. 1–24.

Robinson, Jacob: Metamorphosis of the UN. 94 RCADI 1958/II pp. 497–584.

Rolin, Henri: Les principes de droit international public. 77 RCADI 1950/II pp. 309–475.

Root, Elihu: The Sanction of International Law. 2 AJIL 1908 pp. 451–457.

Rorty, Richard: Solidarity or Objectivity? In: Rajchman-West (eds.): Post-Analytic Philosophy. New York 1985 pp. 3–19.

Rosas, Allan: Om den internationella domstolens opartiskhet. 108 JFT 1972 pp. 237–271.

Rosenne, Shabtai: Equitable Principles and the Compulsory Jurisdiction by International Tribunals. Festschrift für Rudolf Bindschedler. Bern 1980 pp. 407–425.

Ross, Alf: Tû-tû. 70 Harvard L. R. 1957 pp. 812–825.

Rousseau, Charles: Principes de droit international public. 93 RCADI 1958/I pp. 373–548.

Rovine, Arthur W.: The National Interest and the World Court. In: Gross (ed.): The Future of the International Court of Justice, Vol I. New York 1976 pp. 313–335.

Rubin, Alfred P.: The International Legal Effects of Unilateral Declarations. 71 AJIL 1977 pp. 1–30.

Ruddy, F. S.: The Acceptance of Vattel. Grotian Society Papers 1972 pp. 177–196.

Sahović, Milan: Rapports entre facteurs matériels et facteurs formels dans la formation de droit international. 199 RCADI 1986/IV pp. 179–231.

Salmon, Jean: Le fait dans l'application du droit international. 175 RCADI 1982/II pp. 257–414.

Quelques observations sur les lacunes en droit international public. In: Perelman (ed.): Le Problème des lacunes en droit. Bruxelles 1968 pp. 313–337.

Salvioli, Gabriele: Les règles générales de la paix. 46 RCADI 1933/IV pp. 5–163.

Sarin, Manihar Lal: Reflexions on the Progress made by the Third UNCLOS. In: Girardot-Ridder-Sarin-Schiller (eds.): New Directions in International Law. Essays in Honour of Wolfgang Abendroth. Frankfurt am Main 1982 pp. 278–315.

Scelle, Georges: Règles générales du droit de la paix. 46 RCADI 1933/IV pp. 331–697.

Le phénomène juridique de dédoublement fonctionnel. In: Schätzel-Schlochauer (eds.): Rechtsfragen internationalen Organisation. Festschrift für Hans Wehberg. Frankfurt am Main 1956 pp. 324–342.

Schachter, Oscar: Creativity and Objectivity in International Tribunals. In: Bernhardt-Geck-Jaenicke-Steinberger (eds.): Völkerrecht als Rechtsordnung, internationale Gerichtsbarkeit, Menschenrechte. Festschrift für Hermann Mosler. Berlin–Heidelberg–New York 1983 pp. 813–822.

International Law in Theory and Practice: General Course in Public International Law. 178 RCADI 1982/V pp. 9–396.

The Invisible College of International Lawyers. 72 North-Western University Law Review 1977 pp. 217–226.

The Legality of Pro-Democratic Intervention. 78 AJIL 1984 pp. 645–650.

Towards a Theory of International Obligation. In: Schwebel (ed.): The Effectiveness of International Decisions. Leyden 1971 pp. 9–31.

Schindler, Dietrich: Contribution à l'état des facteurs sociologiques et psychologiques du droit international. 46 RCADI 1933/IV pp. 233–324.

Schreuer, C. H.: The Interpretation of Treaties by Domestic Courts. XLV BYIL 1971 pp. 255–301.

Schroeder, Christopher: Liberalism and the Objective Point of View: a Comment on Fishkin. Nomos XXVIII pp. 100–123.

Schwarzenberger, Georg: The Forms of Sovereignty. 10 CLP 1957 pp. 264–295.

International Law and the Problem of Political World Order. In: Cheng (ed.): International Law: Teaching and Practice. London 1982 pp. 55–66.

Schücking, Walter: Preface. In: Pufendorf: De Officio Hominiis et Civis Juxta Legem Naturalem Libri Duo. Carnegie Endowment for International Peace. Classics of International Law, New York 1927.

Scobbie, Ian: Towards the Elimination of International Law: Some Radical Scepticism about Sceptical Radicalism in International Law. LXI BYIL 1990 pp. 339–362.

Scott, James Brown: The Legal Nature of International Law. 1 AJIL 1907 pp. 831–866.

The Work of the Second Hague Peace Conference. 2 AJIL 1908 pp. 1–28.

Séfériadès, S.: Aperçus sur la coutume juridique international et notamment sur son fondement. 43 RGDIP 1936 pp. 129–196.

Principes généraux du droit international de la paix. 34 RCADI 1930/IV pp. 181–489.

Seidentop, Larry: Political Theory and Ideology: the Case of the State. In: Miller-Seidentop (eds.): The Nature of Political Theory. Oxford 1983 pp. 53–73.

Seidl-Hohenveldern, Ignaz: International Economic Law. General Course on Public International Law. 198 RCADI 1986/III pp. 9–264.

Shaw, Malcolm: International Court of Justice. Recent Cases. 42 ICLQ 1993 pp. 931–933.

The Western Sahara Case. XLIX BYIL 1978 pp. 118–154.

Sicault, Jean-Didier: Du caractère obligatoire des engagements unilateraux en droit international public. 83 RGDIP 1979 pp. 633–688.

Simma, Bruno: Consent: Strains in the Treaty System. In: Macdonald-Johnston (eds.): The Structure and Process of International Law. The Hague 1983 pp. 485–511.

Sinclair, Ian: The Practice of International Law: The foreign and commonwealth office. In: Cheng (ed.): International Law. Teaching and Practice. London 1982 pp. 123–134.

Singer, Joseph William: The Player and the Cards: Nihilism and Legal Theory. 94 Yale L.J. 1984 pp. 1–78.

Skubiszewski, Krzysztof: Elements of Custom and the Hague Court. 31 ZaöRV 1971 pp. 810–854.

Remarks on the Interpretation of the United Nations Char-ter. In: Bernhardt-Geck-Jaenicke-Steinberger (eds.): Völkerrecht als Rechtsordnung, Internationale Gerichtsbarkeit, Menschenrechte. Festschrift für Hermann Mosler. Berlin–Heidelberg–New York 1983 pp. 891–902.

Slouka, Zdenek J.: International Law-Making: A view from technology. In: Onuf (ed.): Lawmaking in the Global Community. Durham, N. C. 1982 pp. 131–171.

Soper, Philip: Choosing a Legal Theory on Moral Grounds. In: Coleman-Paul (eds.): Philosophy of Law. Oxford–New York 1987 pp. 33–48.

Spivak, Gayatri Chakavorty: Translator's Preface. In Derrida: Of Grammatology. Baltimore–London 1976.

Spragens, Thomas A.: Justification, Practical Reason and Political Theory. Nomos XXVIII pp. 335–357.

Stein, Ted L.: The Approach of a Different Drummer: The principle of the persistent objector in international law. 26 Harv. ILJ 1985 pp. 457–482.

Stern, Brigitte: La coutume au coeur du droit international: Quelques réflexions. In: Le droit international: unité et diversité. Mélanges offerts à Paul Reuter. Paris 1981 pp. 479–499.

Stone, Julius: Approaches to the Notion of International Justice. In: Falk-Black (eds.): The Future of the International Legal Order, Vol. I Trends and Patterns. Princeton 1969 pp. 372–460.

   Non Liquet and the Function of Law in the International Community. XXXV BYIL 1959 pp. 124–161.

   Non Liquet and the International Judicial Function. In: Perelman (ed.): Le problème des lacunes en droit. Bruxelles 1968 pp. 305–311.

   Problems Confronting Sociological Enquiries Concerning International Law. 89 RCADI 1956/I pp. 61–180.

Strebel, Helmut: Quellen des Völkerrechts als Rechtsordnung. 36 ZaöRV 1976 pp. 301–346.

Strupp, Karl: Les règles générales du droit de la paix. 47 RCADI 1934/I pp. 257–595.

Stuart Klooz, Marie: The Rôle of the General Assembly of the United Nations in the Admission of Members. 43 AJIL 1949 pp. 246–261.

Suh, Il Ro: Voting Behavior of National Judges in International Courts. 63 AJIL 1969 pp. 224–236.

Sørensen, Max: Principes de droit international public; cours général. 101 RCADI 1960/III pp. 1–254.

Tammes, A. J. P.: The Status of Consent in International Law. II Neth.YBIL 1971 pp. 1–28.

Taylor, Charles: Political Theory and Practice. In: Lloyd (ed.): Social Theory and Political Practice. Oxford 1983 pp. 61–85.

Teubner, Gunther: Globale Zivilverfassungen: Alternativen zur staatszentrierten Verfassungstheorie. 63 ZaöRV 2003 pp. 1–28.

Thierry, Hubert: Les arrêts du 20 décembre 1974 et les relations de la France avec la Cour Internationale de Justice. XX AFDI 1974 pp. 286–298.

Tieya, Wang: The Third World and International law. In Macdonald-Johnston (eds.): The Structure and Process of International Law. The Hague 1983 pp. 955–976.

Touret, Denis: Le Principe de l'égalité souveraine des Etats. Fondement du droit international. 77 RGDIP 1973 pp. 136–199.

(Barcia) Trelles, Camilo: Francisco Suarez (1548–1617); Les théologiens espagnoles du XVIe siècle et l'école moderne du droit international. 43 RCADI 1933/I pp. 385–553.

Triepel, H.: Les rapports entre le droit interne et le droit international. 1 RCADI 1923 pp. 77–121.

Trindade, A. A. C.: The Domestic Jurisdiction of States in the Practice the United Nations and Regional Organizations. 25 ICLQ 1976 pp. 715–765.

Tucker, Robert W.: The Principle of Effectiveness in International Law. In: Lipsky (ed.): Law and Politics in the World Community. Berkeley–Los Angeles 1953 pp. 31–48.

Tunkin, G.: Coexistence in International Law. 95 RCADI 1958/III pp. 1–81.

    Droit international et modèle généralement reconnu du système international. In: Le droit des peuples à disposer d'eux-mêmes. Méthodes d'analyse du droit international. Mélanges offerts à Charles Chaumont. Paris 1984 pp. 541–554.

Tushnet, Mark: Critical Legal Studies and Constitutional Law: An Essay in Deconstruction. 36 Stanford L.R. 1984 pp. 623–648.

    Following the Rules Laid Down: A Critique of Interpretativism and Neutral Principles. 96 Harvard L.R. 1983 pp. 781–827.

Vallée, Charles: Quelques observations sur l'estoppel en droit des gens. 77 RGDIP 1973 pp. 949–999.

Venkata Raman, K.: Toward a General Theory of International Customary Law. In: Reisman-Weston (eds.): Toward World Order and Human Dignity. Essays in Honor of Myres S. McDougal. New York–London 1976 pp. 365–402.

Venturini, Gian Carlo: La portée et les effets juridiques des attitudes et des actes unilateraux des états. 112 RCADI 1964/II pp. 363–468.

Verdross, Alfred: Entstehungsweisen und Geltungsgrund des universellen Völkerrechtlichen Gewohnheitsrechts. 29 ZaöRV 1969 pp. 635–653.

    Le fondement du droit international. 16 RCADI 1927/I pp. 251–321.

    Règles générales du droit international de la paix. 30 RCADI 1929/V pp. 275–507.

    Les principes généraux du droit dans la jurisprudence internationale. 52 RCADI 1935/II pp. 195–251.

    Les principes généraux de droit dans le système des sources du droit international public. In: Recueil d'études de droit international en hommage à Paul Guggenheim. Genève 1968 pp. 521–530.

    Zum Problem der Völkerrechtlichen Grundnorm. In: Schätzel-Schlochauer (eds.): Rechtsfragen der internationalen Organisation. Festschrift für Hans Wehberg. Frankfurt am Main 1956 pp. 385–394.

Verdross, Alfred – Koeck, Heribert Franz: Natural Law: The tradition of universal reason and authority. In: Macdonald-Johnston (eds.): The Structure and Process of International Law. The Hague 1983 pp. 17–50.

Vergé, Ch.: Introduction. In: Martens, G.-F., Précis du droit des gens moderne de l'Europe, 2ème éd. Vols. 1–2. Paris 1864 pp. I–LV.

Villey, Michel: Le droit de l'individu chez Hobbes. XIII Arch. de philo. du droit 1968 pp. 209–231.

Villiger, Mark: Die Billigkeit im Völkerrecht. 25 Arch.VR 1987 pp. 174–201.

Vinogradoff, Paul: Historical Types of International Law. I Bibliotheca Visseriana 1923 pp. 3–70.

Virally, Michel: Panorama du droit international contemporain; cours général de droit international public. 183 RCADI 1983/V pp. 9–382.

A propos de la "lex ferenda". In: Le droit international: unité et diversité; Mélanges offerts à Paul Reuter. Paris 1981 pp. 519–533.

Réflexions sur le "jus cogens". XII AFDI 1966 pp. 5–29.

Le rôle des "principes" dans le développement du droit international. Recueil d'études de droit international en hommage à Paul Guggenheim, Genève 1968 pp. 531–554.

The Sources of International Law. In: Sørensen (ed.): Manual of Public International Law. Glasgow 1968 pp. 116–174.

Visscher, Charles de: Cours général de principes de droit international public. 86 RCADI 1954/II pp. 449–552.

Positivisme et le "jus cogens". 75 RGDIP 1971 pp. 5–11.

Waldock; C. H. M.: The Anglo-Norwegian Fisheries Case. XXVIII BYIL 1951 pp. 114–171.

The Control of the Use of Force by States in International Law. 81 RCADI 1952/II pp. 455–517.

Disputed Sovereignty in the Falkland Islands Dependencies. XXV BYIL 1948 pp. 311–353.

General Course on Public International Law. 106 RCADI 1962/II pp. 1–250.

The Legal Basis of Claims to the Continental Shelf. XXXVI Transactions of the Grotius Society 1950. London 1951 pp. 115–148.

The Plea of Domestic Jurisdiction Before International Law. XXXI BYIL 1954 pp. 143–186.

Wassilikowski, A.: International Law: How Far is it Changing? In Makarczyk (ed.): Essays in International Law in honour of judge Manfred Lachs. The Hague 1984 pp. 307–311.

Watson, J. S.: Autointerpretation, Competence and the Continuing Force of Article 2(7) of the UN Charter. 71 AJIL 1977 pp. 60–83.

Weil, Prosper: Towards Relative Normativity in International Law. 77 AJIL 1983 pp. 413–442.

Weiler, Rudolf: Ein aktuelles Vergleich; Das Völkerrecht zur Zeit den spanischen Spätscholastik und sein Wiederkehr heute nach der Periode des nachgrotianischen Völkerrechts. Rechtstheorie Beiheft 6, 1984 "Recht als Sinn und Institution" pp. 71–78.

Weissberg, Guenter: The Role of the International Court of Justice in the United Nations System: The First Quarter Century. In Gross (ed.): The Future of the International Court of Justice, vol. I. New York 1976 pp. 131–208.

Wengler, Wilhelm: La crise de l'unité de l'ordre juridique international. In: La Communauté internationale. Mélanges offerts à Charles Rousseau. Paris 1974 pp. 329–340.

Weston, Burns H.: The New International Economic Order and the Deprivation of Foreign Property; Reflections upon the Contemporary Debate. In: Lillich (ed.): International Law of State Responsibility for Injuries to Aliens. Virginia 1983 pp. 89–148.

Widdows, Kelvin: What is an Agreement in International Law? L BYIL 1979 pp. 117–149.

Wight, Martin: An Anatomy of International Thought. 13 Rev.Int.Stud. 1987 pp. 221–227.

Western Values in International Relations. In: Butterfield-Wight (eds.): Diplomatic Investigations. Essays in the Theory of International Politics. London 1966 pp. 89–131.

Wildhaber, Luzius: Sovereignty and International Law. In: Macdonald-Johnston (eds.): The Structure and Process of International Law. The Hague 1983 pp. 425–452.

Williams, Glanville L.: International Law and the Controversy Concerning the Word "Law". XXII BYIL 1945 pp. 146–163.

Wright, Moorhead: An Ethic of Responsibility. In: Mayall (ed.): The Community of States. London 1982 pp. 158–166.

Wright, Quincy: Custom as a Basis for International Law in the Post-War Period. 7 IJIL 1967 pp. 1–14.

Legal Positivism and the Nuremberg Judgement. 42 AJIL 1948 pp. 405–414.

Some Thoughts about Recognition. 44 AJIL 1950 pp. 548–559.

Yablon, Charles M.: Law and Metaphysics. Book Review. Kripke, Saul: Wittgenstein on Rules and Private Language. Cambridge, Mass. 1982. 92 Yale L.J. 1987 pp. 613–636.

Zemanek, Karl: Majority Rule and Consensus Technique in Law-Making Diplomacy. In: Macdonald-Johnston (eds.): The Structure and Process of International Law. The Hague 1983 pp. 857–888.

Ziccardi, Piero: Les caractères de l'ordre juridique international. 95 RCADI 1958/ III pp. 267–405.

C Table of cases

C.1 *Permanent Court of International Justice (Series A & B)*

C.2   *International Court of Justice*

Anglo-Norwegian Fisheries, Reports 1951 p. 116
Anglo-Iranian Oil Company, Reports 1951 p. 89
Haya de la Torre, Reports 1951 p. 71
Reservations to the Convention on Genocide, Reports 1951 p. 15 (Reservations Case)
Ambatielos, Reports 1952 p. 28
United States Nationals in Morocco, Reports 1952 p. 176
Minquiers and Ecrehos, Reports 1953 p. 47
Nottebohm (Preliminary Objection), Reports 1953 p. 111
Effect of Awards of Compensation, Reports 1954 p. 47
Nottebohm, Reports 1955 p. 4
Administrative Tribunal of the ILO, Reports 1956 p. 77
Norwegian Loans, Reports 1957 p. 9
Right of Passage, Reports 1957 p. 125
Guardianship of Infants, Reports 1958 p. 55
Frontier Land, Reports 1959 p. 209
Interhandel (Preliminary Objection), Reports 1959 p. 6
Case Concerning the Arbitral Award of 1906, Reports 1960 p. 192
    (Arbitral Award Case)
IMCO Maritime Safety Committee, Reports 1960 p. 150
Right of Passage (Merits), Reports 1960 p. 6
Certain Expenses of the United Nations, Reports 1962 p. 151
South West Africa (Preliminary Objections), Reports 1962 p. 319
Temple of Preah Vihear, Reports 1962 p. 6 (Temple Case)
Northern Cameroons, Reports 1963 p. 15
Barcelona Traction (Preliminary Objections), Reports 1964 p. 6
South West Africa (Second Phase), Reports 1966 p. 4
North Sea Continental Shelf, Reports 1969 p. 3
Barcelona Traction (Second Phase), Reports 1970 p. 3
Namibia (South West Africa), Reports 1971 p. 16
Fisheries Jurisdiction (Jurisdiction), Reports 1973 pp. 4, 49
Nuclear Tests (Interim Measures), Reports 1973 pp. 99, 135
Fisheries Jurisdiction (Merits), Reports 1974 pp. 3, 175
Nuclear Tests (Merits), Reports 1974 pp. 253, 457
Western Sahara, Reports 1975 p. 12
Aegean Sea Continental Shelf, Reports 1978 p. 3
Interpretation of the Agreement of 25 March 1951 between the WHO and Egypt,
    Reports 1980 p. 73
US Diplomatic and Consular Staff in Tehran, Reports 1980 p. 3
    (Hostages Case)
Tunisia–Libya Continental Shelf (Application of Malta for Permission to
    Intervene), Reports 1981 p. 3
Tunisia–Libya Continental Shelf, Reports 1982 p. 18

C.3   Other cases (in alphabetical order)

B. P. Exploration Co. v. Government of the Libyan Arab Republic (Award, 1 August 1974) 53 ILR 1979 p. 297

Brandt v. Attorney-General of Guayana (Court of Appeal, Guayana, 8 March 1971) 71 ILR 1986 p. 450

Clipperton Island Case (Award, 28 January 1931) II UNRIAA p. 1105

Case A/1 (Iran-US CT, 14 May 1982, 3 August 1982) 68 ILR 1985 p. 523

Case No. 2321 (1974), International Chamber of Commerce, 65 ILR 1984 p. 450

Claim against the Empire of Iran Case (Supreme Federal Court, FRG, 30 April 1963) 45 ILR 1972 p. 57

Delagoa Bay Case (Award, 24 July 1875) Lapradelle-Politis III p. 596

Deumeland Case (ECHR: Ser.A.100/1986)

Dispute between the Government of Kuwait and the American Independent Oil Co. (AMINOIL) 66 ILR 1984 pp. 519–627

Decision of the ICSID ad hoc Committee Setting aside the Award Rendered on the Merits in the Arbitration between AMCO Asia Corp. et Al. and Indonesia, (20 November 1984) XXV ILM 1986 p. 1441

Dispute between Texaco Overseas Petroleum Company / California Asiatic Oil Company v. the Government of the Libyan Arab Republic (Award, 19 January 1977) XVII ILM 1978 p. 3

Equalization of Burdens Taxation Case (Federal Constitutional Court, FRG, 4 May 1968) 61 ILR 1981 p. 162

Ethiopia – Eritrea Boundary Commission (2002) 106 RGDIP 2002 p. 702

Flexi-van Leasing Inc. v. Iran (Iran-US CT: Case No. 36, 15 December 1982) 70 ILR 1986 p. 496

Frigerio v. Federal Department of Transport (Federal Tribunal, Switzerland, 22 November 1968) 72 ILR 1987 p. 679

Golder Case (ECHR: Ser.A.18/1975)

Golpira v. Iran (Iran-US CT: Case No. 211, 29 March 1983) 72 ILR 1987 p. 493

Grisbadarna Case (Award, 23 October 1909) XI UNRIAA p. 147

Guatemala-Honduras Boundary Case (Award, 23 January 1933) II UNRIAA p. 1307

Hurtige Hane Case (Scott–Jaeger: Cases) p. 61

International Military Tribunal: Trial of Major War Criminals. Nuremberg 14.11.1945–1.10.1946. Vol. I. Nürnberg 1947 December 1981) 62 ILR 1982 p. 595

Interpretation of the Treaty between USA and Italy (Award, 17 July 1965) 72 RGDIP 1968 p. 461

Ireland v. the United Kingdom (ECHR: Ser.A.25/1978)

Island of Palmas Case (Award, 4 April 1928) II UNRIAA p. 829

Kronprins Adolf Case (Award, 18 July 1932) II UNRIAA p. 1239

König Case (ECHR: Ser.A.27/1978)

INDEX

à titre de souverain 579
absolute rights 133–135, 143, 225, 252
Abu Dhabi Case 451
abuse of rights 257–258, 496
accretion 283
acquiescence 286–289, 295, 296,
  355–364, 379–381, 440, 445,
  578–579
Admission of a State to the UN Case
  371–379
adversarial procedures 596, 599
aggression 405, 531, 570, 580, 593
Air Services Agreement Case 360
Akehurst, M. 433
Allot, P. 66, 268, 611
Alvarez, A. 209, 212–215, 477, 611
Anand, P. S. 611
Anglo-French Continental Shelf Case
  261
Anglo-Norwegian Fisheries Case 49, 61,
  256–257, 259, 267, 293–296, 392,
  463, 558, 581n. 49
Anzilotti, D. 232
Aquinas, T. 97
Arbitral Award Case 379–381
Aron, R. 60, 198, 200
"ascending" pattern (in contrast to
  "descending") 59–60, 71, 82,
  83–84, 107, 124 *et seq*, 139,
  143 *et seq*, 161, 167, 168–171,
  224–228, 286, 287, 295, 303–304,
  309, 326, 332, 370, 384–385,
  397, 409, 417, 438, 440, 441,
  477–483, 503–512, 514, 575
Asylum Case 247, 257, 267, 425, 427,
  445, 448
Austin, J. 125–126, 128, 325

authentic commitment 546, 555
autonomy (v. community) 474–512
Ayala, B. 104

Bakassi Peninsula Case 580, 585
balance of power 111, 120, 149, 151,
  179, 199, 522, 526
Balkan sovereignty 576
Baltic "continuity thesis" 576
"Baltic defence" 580
Barcelona Traction Case 46, 404–405,
  558
Barthes, R. 525
baselines 293
basis of obligation 307 *et seq*, 583n. 60
Bedjaoui, M. 215, 611
Bentham, J. 92
bilateralization (of custom) 461–467
binding force 16 *et seq*, 27, 184 *et seq*,
  201–202, 210, 258, 311, 378, 393,
  394, 587, 596
Bleckmann, A. 396, 448
Bluntschli, J. 274, 415
Bodin, J. 78–79, 90, 229
Bos, M. 451
Boyle, F. 207–209
Brierly, J. 168–169, 248, 424, 575
Brownlie, I. 425
Burkina Faso–Mali Frontier
  Case 263, 577nn. 32–35,
  579n. 43

*Cameroon–Nigeria Land and Maritime
  Boundary (Bakassi Peninsula)*
  Case 578, 580
Carr, E. H. 599
cession 283, 286

Lightning Source UK Ltd.
Milton Keynes UK
UKHW01n1314130918
328741UK00011B/151/P